The Plantagenet Roll of the Blood Royal, Being a Complete Table of All the Descendants Now Living of Edward III., King of England

THE PLANTAGENET ROLL

OF THE

𝔅𝔩𝔬𝔬𝔡 ℜ𝔬𝔶𝔞𝔩

TABLE

SHOWING THE DESCENT OF

ARTHUR WILLIAM VAISEY, Esq.

FROM

EDWARD III., KING OF ENGLAND

KING EDWARD III., $\overset{1328}{=}$ Philippa of Hainault,
1312 + 1377. c. 1309 + 1369.

Lionel, Duke of Clarence, K.G., = Lady Elizabeth de Burgh,
1338 + 1368. + 1363.

Philippa of Clarence, = Edmund, 3rd Earl of March,
1355 + 1382. 1352 + 1381.

Roger, Lady Elizabeth Mortimer, = (1) Henry, Lord Percy, K.G., called
4th Earl of March, 1371 + after 1417. "Hotspur," 1364 + 1403.
1374 + 1398.
=
a quo Henry, 2nd Earl of Northumber- $\overset{1414}{=}$ Lady Eleanor Nevill.
King George V. land, 1393 + 1455.

Henry, 3rd Earl of Northum- $\overset{c. 1446}{=}$ Eleanor, Lady Poynings,
berland, 1421 + 1461. c. 1420 + 1473.

Henry, 4th Earl of Northumberland, K.G., $\overset{1476}{=}$ Lady Maud Herbert.
c. 1449 + 1489.

Henry, 5th Earl of Northumberland, K.G., $\overset{a. 1502}{=}$ Catherine Spencer,
1478 + 1527. + 1542.

Lady Margaret Percy, (2) $\overset{c. 1516}{=}$ Henry, 1st Earl of Cumberland. K.B.,
+ 1544. 1493 + 1542.

Henry, 2nd Earl of Cumberland, K.B., $\overset{1552}{=}$ (2) Hon. Anne Dacre,
1517 + 1570. + 1581.

Francis, 4th Earl of Cumberland, K.B., $\overset{1589}{=}$ Grizel, Lady Abergavenny, née Hughes,
1559 + 1641. + 1613.

Lady Frances Clifford, (2) $\overset{1614}{=}$ Sir Gervase Clifton, 1st Bt.,
c. 1594 + 1627. 1587 + 1660.

Margaret Clifton, + 1698. = (2) William Whichcot of Fotherby,
co. Linc.

George Whichcot of Harpswell, = (3) Frances Katharine Meres,
co. Linc., M.P., 1653 + . 1669 + 1731.

Katherine Whichcot, $\overset{1723}{=}$ John Maddison of Stainton Vale,
1701 + 1787. co. Linc., 1691 + 1746.

George Maddison of Stainton Vale, &c., $\overset{1757}{=}$ Mary Baugh, + 1791.
Lt.-Col. 4th Foot, 1729 + 1807.

John Thomas Maddison of Norton, $\overset{1781}{=}$ Matilda MacNeill.
Col. 4th Foot, 1759 + 1837.

Jane Maddison, da. and co-h., $\overset{1821}{=}$ John Dent of Thirsk, co. York,
1795 + 1829. + 1839.

Special Table for
Ruvigny's
"Plantagenet Roll of
the Blood Royal,"
Mortimer-Percy
Volume, Part I.

Emma Dent, da. and co-h. $\overset{1851}{=}$ Thomas Vaisey of Stratton, co. Glouc.,
1825 + 1903.

Arthur William Vaisey, 1852, 10th in $\overset{1876}{=}$ Esther Bevir.
descent from King Edward III.
See p. 160

Harry $\overset{1903}{=}$ Eleonora	Roland	Margaret.	Violet. $\overset{1907}{=}$ John	Lilian.	Veronica.	May.	Olive.	Iris.
Bevir Mary Maddison			Brooke					
Vaisey, Quennell. Vaisey,			Scrivenor.					
1877. 1886.								

Arthur William	Juliana	Thomas Vaisey	Phebe,
Vaisey, 1905.	Margaret, 1904.	Scrivenor, 1908.	1910.

= Gillian, Brown d. 1958

Elizabeth Helen   Roger Allen   Clare Margaret.

Lady Elizabeth Mortimer, widow of Henry Lord Percy, K. G.
called Hotspur, and her second husband Thomas Lord
Camoys, K. G. from a rubbing of the brass in Trotton
Church, Sussex. 1419. by F. R. Fairbank. M. D., F. S. A.

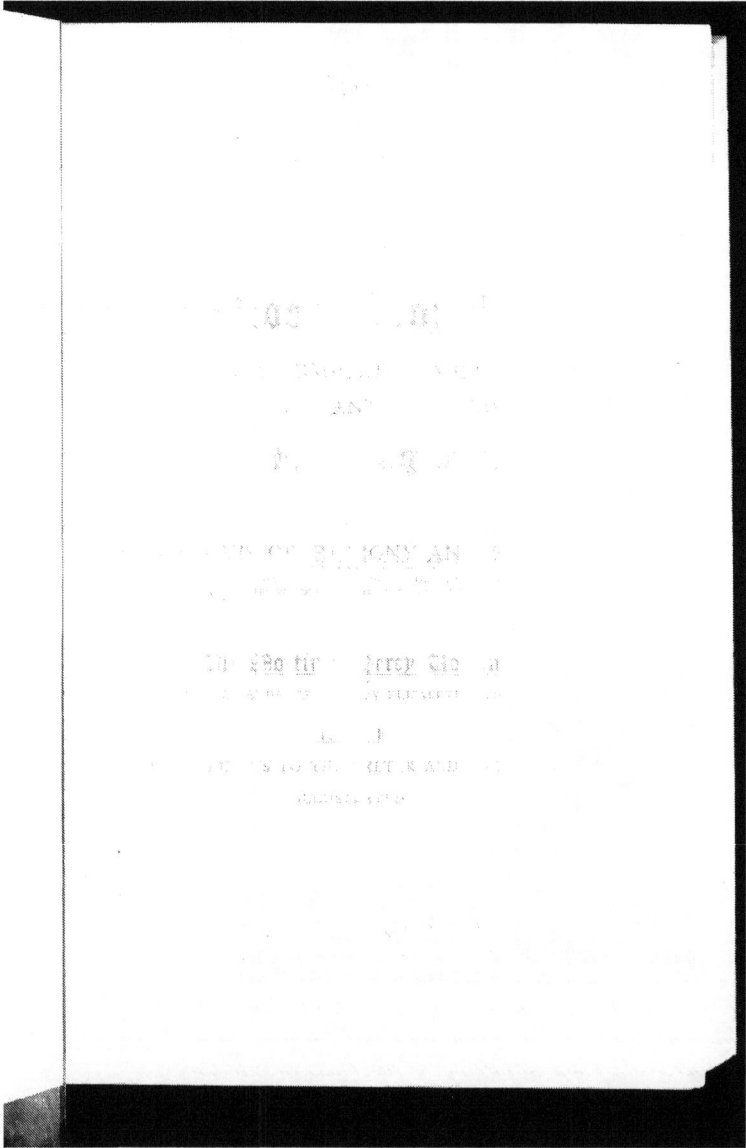

THE

PLANTAGENET
ROLL

OF THE

Blood Royal

BEING A COMPLETE TABLE OF
ALL THE DESCENDANTS NOW LIVING OF

Edward III., King of England

BY

THE MARQUIS OF RUVIGNY AND RAINEVAL

AUTHOR OF "THE BLOOD ROYAL OF BRITAIN, "THE JACOBITE PEERAGE, BARONETAGE, AND
KNIGHTAGE, "THE MOODIE BOOK,' "THE NOBILITIES OF EUROPE." ETC

The Mortimer-Percy Volume

CONTAINING THE DESCENDANTS OF LADY ELIZABETH PERCY, née MORTIMER

PART I

WITH SUPPLEMENTS TO THE EXETER AND ESSEX VOLUMES

ILLUSTRATED

LONDON
MELVILLE & COMPANY
12 BUCKINGHAM STREET, W.C

1911

Printed by BALLANTYNE, HANSON & Co
At the Ballantyne Press, Edinburgh

PREFACE

THE Descendants of King Edward IV and of his brother and sister, George, Duke of Clarence, and Anne, Duchess of Exeter, and of their aunt Isabel, Countess of Essex and Eu, having been given in the preceding volumes, the present volume of the PLANTAGENET ROLL OF THE BLOOD ROYAL treats of those of Lady Elizabeth Mortimer, wife first of Henry, Lord Percy, K G, called "Hotspur," and, secondly, of Thomas, Lord Camoys, K G

The plan followed is identical with that adopted in the Clarence and Exeter Volumes. The lines from the Lady Elizabeth are traced out in a series of Tables until about the beginning of the last century, then in the body of the book the descendants of the various persons last named in the Tables are set out in the order of primogeniture. The full dates of birth, marriage, and death are given, and in the cases of married persons the names of the husband and wife, &c

In the Tables the dates of birth, marriage, and death are given whenever possible, but as the object of the writer has been merely to trace out the living descendants of Edward III, and in order to keep the work within bounds, he has been obliged to omit (except in some few cases, where it has been thought desirable to show the descent of a title) the names of persons who died without issue, or whose issue subsequently failed, and also the parentage of the wives

In the case of a person having been married more than once, only the name of the wife or wives (or husband or husbands) by whom he (or she) had issue are given, the figure in round brackets immediately following the marriage mark (=) signifying whether she (or he) is first, second, or third wife (or husband). Similarly, if the figure precedes the marriage mark, it signifies that he (or she) married as first or second wife (or husband), as the case may be. Wherever the compiler has been able to give the dates of birth and marriage, he has considered this sufficient indication of whether the children are by the first or second marriage, but where the dates have not been obtainable, the figure before the names shows of which marriage they are the issue

When a name in the Tables is in italics, it signifies that they have a previous descent which has been already shown

In the Roll itself considerations of space have again rendered it necessary to adopt the briefest possible description, and the words "and had issue" must be held to refer only (with the exceptions mentioned above) to those children who are now living, or whose issue now survives, or those concerning whose issue, or possible issue, the author has been unable to obtain particulars

Each Section is headed by the name of the person last named in the Tables, and their children are 1a, 2a, &c. The issue of the a's, grandchildren of the head of the line, are b's, and the children of these last, great-grandchildren of the head of the line, are similarly c's, and so on, the d's being children of the c's, and great-great-grandchildren of the head of the line, &c

Preface

The dates of birth and death immediately follow the names of the persons to whom they refer   In the cases of births, marriages, and deaths outside the United Kingdom, the author has endeavoured to give the place as well as the date

The surnames of noblemen are given in round brackets after their Christian names, and the nationality of their title is indicated by the initials and names within square brackets immediately following them [1]

The Lady Elizabeth Mortimer, whose descendants are here set out, was the elder daughter [2] of Edmund (Mortimer). 3rd Earl of March, by his wife the Lady Philippa, only child and heir of Lionel (of Antwerp), Duke of Clarence, the eldest of the four sons of King Edward III of whom issue now survives   Her brother Roger, 4th Earl of March, was declared heir to the crown of England by King Richard II, and was the father of the Lady Anne Mortimer, who by her marriage with Richard (Plantagenet), Earl of Cambridge, transmitted the hereditary right to the throne to the House of York, and was the ancestress of King Edward IV and of all the successive sovereigns of England (with the exception of Henry VII) from that day to this, and equally so of all those whose names are recorded in the Tudor Roll and in the Clarence, Exeter, and Essex Volumes of the present series

Lady Elizabeth was born at Usk, 12 February 1371, and married the famous Henry, Lord Percy, K G, called "Hotspur," son and heir of Henry, 1st Earl of Northumberland   He was descended in the male line from Josceline of Louvain, brother of Queen Adeliza, second wife of King Henry I, and younger son of Godfrey, sovereign Duke of Lorraine and Count of Brabant, who, marrying Maud, daughter and eventual heiress of William, 3rd feudal Lord Percy, assumed her name but retained his own paternal arms, and was himself of the Royal Blood, Henry, 3rd Lord Percy of Alnwick (father of the 1st Earl of Northumberland), having married the Lady Mary Plantagenet, daughter of Henry, Earl of Lancaster, and granddaughter of Edmund, Earl of Lancaster, the second son of King Henry III

Lord Percy was born 20 May 1364, was knighted by King Edward III in April 1377 along with the future Kings, Richard II and Henry IV, who were almost exactly of his own age, was made a K G at the age of 24 in 1388, and won his sobriquet of "Hotspur" owing to the restless activity he displayed as Warden of the Marches in repressing the inroads of the Scottish Borderers [3]   He was the English commander at the famous

---

[1] The initials E S I G B, U K, F, H R E, and P S, standing for England, Scotland, Ireland, Great Britain, the United Kingdom France, the Holy Roman Empire, and the Papal States   With regard to foreign titles of nobility, it was the original intention of the author to give these in the language of their nationality, but it would have appeared absurd to have written *Herzog von Teck*, or to have referred to the *Freiherr Heinrich von Worms, M P*, after much consideration therefore, he decided to give them in English, adding the foreign equivalent in brackets immediately following, so '3rd Baron of Hugel (Freiherr von Hugel)'— '7th Count of Salis (Graf von Salis),' after the plan recently adopted in the *Almanach de Gotha*   It is to be wished that some settled rule might be adopted by the Press   To take one case, which might be multiplied without end, *Duc d'Orléans* or *Duke of Orleans* are both equally correct but the *Duke d'Orleans*, which one constantly sees, is certainly a misnomer   The Spanish Minister is nearly always described as "Marquis of Villalobar," while the Italian Ambassador figures as "Marquis di San Giuliano"   Surely it should be "Marquis of" or "Marchese di"   All the older writers used to translate the names and titles into English, and thus appears to be the only way if any uniform plan is to be attempted, and is moreover the plan adopted to-day by such high authorities as the compilers of the British Museum Catalogue

[2] Her younger sister, Lady Philippa, born at Ludlow, 21 November 1375, married 1st, John (Hastings), Earl of Pembroke   2ndly, 15 August 1390, Richard (Fitzalan), 11th Earl of Arundel, and 3rdly after April 1398, John (Poynings) Lord St John, but *d s p s* at Halnaker, co Sussex, 24 September 1401

[3] Walsingham, ii p 114

VI

preface

Battle of Otterburn (Chevy Chase), 10 August 1388—"the best-fought and severest of all the battles I have related in my history," says Froissart— where, though Douglas, the Scottish commander, was slain, Percy himself was made prisoner, and of Homildon Hill, 14 September 1402, where he defeated the Scots and captured the Earl of Douglas He joined his father in supporting Henry of Lancaster's usurpation of the crown, it being the subsequent boast of the Percies that they had placed Henry IV on the throne, but afterwards taking mortal offence at the King's refusal to allow him to ransom his brother-in-law Sir Edmund Mortimer whilst claiming the prisoners whom he (Percy) had taken at Homildon Hill, he rose in rebellion and was defeated and slain at the Battle of Shrewsbury, 23 July 1403, by an unknown hand, either by a spear or by an arrow which had pierced his brain After that "sory bataill," the fore-runner of the Wars of the Roses, was finished, his body, over which the King is said to have shed tears, was delivered to his kinsman Thomas (Nevill), Lord Furnival, who buried it in his family chapel at Whitchurch, sixteen miles from the battlefield. But a day or two later, in order to prevent any rumour that he was still alive, it was taken up and placed for public exhibition between two millstones near the pillory in Shrewsbury, somewhere near the present site of the Post Office, guarded by armed men, and then beheaded and quartered His head was placed over the gate of York, " there to remain so long as it can last," and his four quarters were salted and sent in sacks to the Mayors of London, Bristol, Newcastle-on-Tyne, and Chester, the cost of their carriage being £13, 15s [1] On 3 November following, however, the King ordered that his head and quarters should be delivered to his widow, who buried them in the Northumberland tomb in York Minster. She was put under arrest after Hotspur's death,[2] but was subsequently released, and married, secondly, as his second wife, Thomas (de Camoys), 1st Lord Camoys, K G , who commanded the left wing of the army at the Battle of Agincourt She was living 1417/8, and may have been the " Isabel Camoyse, wife of Thomas Camoys, Knt ," who died 1444, and was buried in the Friars Minors

Lord Camoys died 28 March 1419, and was buried at Trotton, co Sussex, where there is a beautiful brass, with the effigies of himself and Lady Elizabeth, a photogravure of which, taken from a rubbing by Dr Fairbank, is given as a frontispiece to this volume

She had issue by her first husband a son, Henry, who was restored as 2nd Earl of Northumberland by Henry V., 11 November 1414, and a daughter, Lady Elizabeth, wife first of John, 7th Lord Clifford, K G , and 2ndly, of Ralph (Nevill), 2nd Earl of Westmorland, and by her second another daughter, the Hon. Alice Camoys, wife of Sir Leonard Hastings, who all three had issue (see Table II) The statement sometimes made that she was the mother of Sir Richard de Camoys is incorrect

On the death of the 7th Earl of Northumberland in 1572 the repre-sentation of Hotspur and Lady Elizabeth devolved upon his daughters and co-heirs The elder Lady Elizabeth married Richard Woodruffe of Wolley, co York, and had issue, but none of her descendants have been traced to the present day (see p 567) The younger Lady Lucy married Sir Edward

---

[1] ' Battlefield Church, Salop, and the Battle of Shrewsbury,' by the Rev W G D Fletcher, M A , F S A , 1903, p 13   [2] *Fœdera,* viii p 334

ᴘreface

Stanley, K B , and her heir of line is Viscount Gage, who is thus the senior known representative of Lady Elizabeth Mortimer and Lord Percy

The descendants of Lady Elizabeth are very much more numerous than those of her brother the Earl of March   The present part of the Mortimer-Percy Volume deals with those of Henry, 4th Earl of Northumberland, K G (d 1486) and of his sister, Lady Elizabeth Gascoigne, and contains between nine and ten thousand new names   The actual number of their living descendants who are traceable, however, amounts to some thirty or forty thousand, and they have between them 135,520 descents   Owing, however, to the many inter-marriages with descendants of the Earl of March, the great majority of these have already appeared in one or other of the volumes previously published, in right of a senior descent from him , and owing to the ever-increasing number of descendants and descents which naturally occur as the lines are carried further back, the compiler has in the present index been reluctantly compelled to abandon the plan he had hitherto followed of setting out in the index the name of every descendant whether or not they have already appeared in former volumes, and to confine the index to the present part to the names which actually appear in the body of the work   It will be easily understood how this course has been forced upon him when it is pointed out that all the Clarence,[1] and that 14,478 Tudor,[2] 31,752 Exeter, and 12,176 Essex descents repeat in the present part   To prevent any inconvenience, however, a new plan has been adopted of adding an index of the numbers instead of the names which repeat, so that any one can at once see whether he or she is descended from Edward III through the Mortimer-Percy marriage   This plan will be found fully explained on page 607, and is the plan which will be followed with duplicate descents in all future volumes

With this part is included a Supplement, containing some further descendants of the Duchess of Exeter and the Countess of Essex, which the compiler has since succeeded in tracing

Summarising the five volumes already published, it will be found that some fifty thousand descendants[3] of King Edward III have been traced, and that they have between them over 300,000 descents, all clearly shown by the numbers attached to each name   Included in the Roll are the names of all the crowned heads of Europe, with the exception of the King of Servia and the Prince of Montenegro, of the majority of our hereditary legislators, of the members of all the royal and princely houses of Europe, of many of the higher nobility of France, Germany, Austria, Hungary, Poland, Bohemia, Italy, Spain, Portugal, Russia, Belgium, and of

---

[1] By the marriages respectively of the Hon Jane Nevill and Henry, Lord Stafford (both descendants through the Mortimer-Percy marriage , see the present Part, Tables XXVI and XXI) with Henry (Pole) Lord Montagu and the Lady Ursula Pole, grandchildren of George, Duke of Clarence (see Clarence Vol , Table II)

[2] Largely in consequence of the marriage of Henry (Clifford), 2nd Earl of Cumberland (a Mortimer-Percy descendant , see Table VIII), with the Lady Eleanor Brandon a granddaughter of King Henry VII (see Tudor Roll, Table XIV)

[3] As far as the compiler has been able to trace them, the living descendants of King Edward IV appear to amount to some 12 000 , and those of the Duke of Clarence, of the Duchess of Exeter, and the Countess of Essex to some 18,000, 25,500 and 18,000 respectively , while the present instalment of Lady Elizabeth Mortimer's descendants number some 30,000   In consequence of inter-marriages, however, a considerable number, is already mentioned, are descended from all five, while others again are descended from four, or three, or two of them   He has not had time to work out the exact number of these inter marriages, but a rough estimate fixes the net number of the descendants of Edward III already traced at the above number

the old aristocracy of the Southern States of America, together with many of those of our baronets and county families with their cadets, who so largely go to make up the professional classes, but with some few exceptions, none have descended to or are at least traceable among the trading or labouring classes

While tracing hundreds of entirely new lines of descent, it has been the duty of the author to discard others which will not stand in the light of modern investigation. This has been especially so in the case of the Mortimer-Percy lines. For instance, the oft-repeated statement that Lady Eleanor Percy, a daughter of the 3rd Earl of Northumberland, married Reginald (West), 6th Lord De La Warr, is demonstratively incorrect, and this would have been at once seen had the old Peerage writers been more careful in comparing their dates. The will of Henry, 3rd Earl of Northumberland, is dated 1 November 1458, and in it he mentions his three daughters, Eleanor, Margaret, and Elizabeth, *all then unmarried*[1] Lord De La Warr died on the 27 August 1450, not 1451, as stated by Collins and others. The writs issued on his death are dated 1 September, 29 Hen VI, which is clearly 1450, and the inquisitions in pursuance were taken in various counties within the next few weeks.[2] From these we learn that Richard West, Esq, was his son and heir and over 19 years of age. Richard West was consequently born not later than 1431, in which year his supposed grandfather, the Earl of Northumberland, *was six years of age!* The Lord De La Warr who died in 1450 was, moreover, at least 30 years older than his alleged father-in-law.[3] This of course cuts out the many lines traced through the Wests, several of which have been printed. Equally incorrect are the lines traced through the marriage of Thomas Frewen, M.P., in 1671, with Bridget Laton,[4] and through the alleged marriage of Thomas ap John Vaughan of Plas Thomas, co Salop, with Joan, said to have been a daughter of Philip Jennings of Dudleston, by Diana, da of Sir William Bowyer, Bt[5]

[1] Collins ("Peerage of England," vol. ii, p. 373) quotes this will, and yet both at this reference and at vol. v, p. 382, proceeds to marry Eleanor to Lord De La Warr

[2] *Ex informn* Sir Henry Maxwell Lyte. The author has also to thank Sir George Armytage, Bt and Mr. Erskine F. West for assistance in running this statement to earth

[3] The Editor has not been able to trace the genesis of the statement of the alleged marriage, but Mr. Erskine F. West suggests that possibly Lady Eleanor Percy married Lord De La Warr's grandson, Reginald West, whose name, and nothing more, appears in several MSS in the British Museum

[4] See Burke's "Landed Gentry," 1906, p. 657. The statement there is that Bridget was the sister and heir of Charles and the daughter of Sir Thomas Laton by his wife, Bridget Sandford, which Sir Thomas was the son and heir of another Sir Thomas Laton of Laton and Sexhow, by his wife, the Hon. Mary Fairfax, the said Mary Fairfax being a descendant of Edward III, through Mortimer-Percy (see Table XV). Bridget Sandford was, however, the *second wife of the first named Sir Thomas Laton*. Sir Thomas married twice, first Mary Fairfax (who died 1636), by whom he had, with others (see Table XV), a son, Thomas, incorrectly styled *Sir Thomas* in the above pedigree. This Thomas died s.p. ("Harl MS," p. 2118) having married Anne, daughter of Ambrose Pudsey, who survived him, and married, secondly, Walter Strickland (Whitaker's "Craven," p. 126). Admon of Thomas Laton, Esquire of East Laton, Yorks, was granted to Anne Laton, his widow, 20 April 1679. Sir Thomas married 2ndly, 1637, the said Bridget, widow of Ambrose Pudsey of Bolton, and daughter of Sir Richard Sandford, by whom he had issue Charles, who d s.p. and Bridget who married, 1671, Thomas Frewen, M.P., and had issue. The M.I. to the Rev. John Frewen at Sapcote, Leics, recites that his mother, Bridget Frewen, was the only (so) daughter of Sir Thomas Laton of East Laton and Sexhow by Dame Bridget, his second wife, relict of Ambrose Pudsey and daughter of Sir Richard Sandford, and the minutes of the Committee for the advancing money, 1649-50, have a reference to Bridget, wife of Sir Thomas Layton, to the effect that she had a jointure, and that she applied for one fifth and was refused. The pedigree at the Herald's College gives Sir Thomas's marriages correctly, but seems itself to need verifying in other particulars

[5] See Burke's "Royal Descents," n xix, and "Landed Gentry" (1906, p. 1718). According to this pedigree, Philip Vaughan, the *great grandson* of Thomas ap John Vaughan, was bapt 10 October 1690, while Diana Bowyer was bapt 7 October 1680, only ten years and three days *before her great grandson!*

preface

The author has, of course, also ignored all the descents traced from Sir William St Leger, Lord President of Munster, it having been clearly established now for some years that it was not Sir William's father, Sir Warham St Leger, but his great-uncle, another Sir Warham, who married the Ursula Nevil [1] The author hopes that those who find themselves omitted in consequence of the above will not consider him personally responsible, and he will hope in some future volume to have the pleasure of restoring their names in right of some other and more correct descent

The author must himself plead guilty to an unfortunate slip in the Clarence volume Following Berry and others, he has in Table LXII. made Elizabeth Meux, the third wife (married at St Dunstan's West, London, 2 May 1710) of Sir John Miller, 3rd Bt, the mother of all his children, whereas she appears to have had only one child to survive, viz Elizabeth, wife of Sir Edward Worsley of Gatcombe. The other children appear to have all been by the first wife, Margaret, daughter of John Peachy, who died 23, and was buried in Chichester Cathedral, 25 September 1710 Sir Thomas, 4th Bt, was baptized 4 April 1689, and matriculated at Oxford 1706 7, aged 18 This cuts out sections 548 and 549 (pp 506–515) and 556, 557, and 558 (p 518), Nos 21953–22365, a total of 413, but as Nos 21987–22002 (Chichesters), 22003–22012 (Hortons), 22015–22020 (Carpenter-Garniers), 22041–22095 (Garniers), 22103–22135 (Delmes), and 22136–22365 (Keppels) reappear in right of their descents in the Essex (p 632), Mortimer-Percy (pt i p 306), Tudor (p 171), and Exeter (pp 243, 385, 243) vols respectively, the actual number of names which come out is only 63 The author is indebted to Arthur E Garnier, Esq, for calling his attention to this error

In the next part it is hoped to complete the other descendants of Lady Elizabeth Mortimer, and as this will at the same time finish all the lines from Lionel, Duke of Clarence, a further Supplement will be added, and the Editor will be very glad to hear of any omissions which may have been noticed in order that he may include them in this Supplement

Future volumes will deal with the descendants of John (Plantagenet, called of Gaunt), Duke of Lancaster of Edmund (Plantagenet, called of Langley), Duke of York, of Thomas (Plantagenet, called of Woodstock), Duke of Gloucester, and of the Lady Isabel Plantagenet wife of Ingelram (de Coucy), Earl of Bedford

There are of course, many who affect to laugh at any work treating of Royal descents, and a volume which is devoted to setting forth the individual descent of various more or less obscure personages is naturally of purely personal interest to those whose descent it sets forth, but the present series approaches the subject from a totally different point—from the historical, not from the personal, and aims at treating in a fairly exhaustive manner of all the descendants of, and descents from, the greatest of our Plantagenet kings While preparing this work the author has received some hundreds of letters from persons in every quarter of the globe, descended not only from Edward III, but in many cases our early Norman and Saxon sovereigns, requesting that their descents may be included, and surprise has in some cases been expressed because the writer,

[1] See Table XXVII The compiler refers to this because descents through this alleged marriage figure so often in previously printed works on Royal descents and he is being constantly referred to them.

x

Preface

while casting no doubt on the genuineness of the particular descent, has been obliged to explain, either that it did not come within the scope of his work, or else that a descent from, say, John of Gaunt, could not be included in the volume dealing with those from George of Clarence

The author is always glad to receive copies of all Royal descents They are all carefully arranged, and those coming from Edward III will, if found correct, be duly included in their proper order It is, however, impossible for him to say off-hand whether such and such a descent is correct The work is not an easy one to prepare, and it is absolutely necessary for him to confine himself to the particular line of descent upon which he may for the moment be engaged.

Others say that a Royal descent is of no interest, since so many enjoy it, but allowing that there are some 80,000 or even 100,000 descendants of Edward III now living, what is that out of a total of, say, 100,000 000 persons of British descent, and even if Edward I may be justly termed the father of the British people, it is quite a different thing to be able to trace the line Let it be remembered that while a word from the King can put one in ' the Peerage," or a successful financial speculation in the Landed Gentry," birth alone entitles one to a place in the Plantagenet Roll, for on one side at least there must be a strain of gentle blood, through which it is possible to trace ancestry [1] to the feudal and crusading days

As the Rev W. G D Fletcher, a well-known authority on the subject, so truly remarks [2] "The tracing and working out the descent of living persons from kings and princes of England is often of vastly greater interest than tracing their pedigrees back in the direct male line A family pedigree is too often a string of the names of almost unknown persons, with their place of abode, the dates of baptism and marriage and death, and the date and proof of their will Useful men, no doubt these ancestors were in their day, but they were for the most part 'unknown to history' It is given to but few to have in the male line a Marlborough, a Nelson, a Clive a Wellington, a Fox, a Burke a Pitt, a Cromwell a Lely, or a Reynolds for an ancestor Whereas every Royal descent necessarily implies the possession of distinguished historical personages as ancestors—men and women who meet us in the pages of history, kings, warriors, statesmen, Knights of the Garter, canonised saints, and so forth And if it be sometimes urged that, after all, the quantity of Royal blood that flows in any person's veins must be infinitesimally small, the same holds true of the blood of our paternal ancestors, we only have one-half of our fathers' blood, one-quarter of our grandfathers', one-eighth of our great-grandfathers', and so on"

Embracing, as this work does, all classes, from the sovereign to the peasant, it serves to unite all in a common interest in the traditions of the past Who studying history, or visiting the tombs of the Edwards in Westminster Abbey, or reading Lytton's Last of the Barons," could fail to feel a better citizen knowing that step by step, and link by link, he is descended in a clear unbroken line from those who built up the foundations of our mighty Empire, and is united by blood to our common sovereign

But putting on one side the question of the interest or value of a

[1] It should be remembered that any one whose name occurs in this Roll can trace an ancestry back in an unbroken line to William the Conqueror and Alfred the Great, to St Louis and to the Emperor Charlemagne

[2] See "Notes on some Shropshire Royal Descents, by the Rev W G D Fletcher, M A F S A

preface

Royal descent, this series forms a valuable means of recording the genealogies of many important families which do not come within the scope
of any of the other genealogical works, and of the cadet and colonial
branches of those that do   The Peerages, &c are naturally more concerned
with the fortunes of the titled or landed lines, but the Plantagenet Roll
aims at making the pedigrees of such families as come within its scope
exhaustive, and the Editor ventures to think that the pedigree here given
will be found of use to future generations quite apart from Royal descent,
and that the recording those branches settled beyond the seas equally
with those at home will help to cement the feeling of kinship between
the different parts of the Empire, and so help towards that closer union
of the British-speaking States which it is the duty of all to promote

Every effort has been made to make the Roll as complete as possible,
and to thoroughly revise and bring the particulars up to date, and for
this purpose proofs have been submitted to all those named therein whose
addresses the writer was able to ascertain, and he desires to return his
most grateful thanks for the courtesy and assistance which have been
extended to him on all hands   It is sometimes invidious to particularise,
but he must especially acknowledge his indebtedness to the Rev E. H.
Fellowes, the Rev W G D Fletcher, F S A, Sir George Armytage, Bt,
Sir Henry Maxwell Lyte, M Bylveld, Editor of the *Nederlands Adelsboek*,
the Rev C Moor, D D, Sir Robert A Morris, Bt, Major Raymond Smythies,
Erskine E West, Esq, Charles E Lamb, Esq, Mrs Seton, the Baroness
Deichmann, Mrs Lomas, Col R V Riddell, Arthur G Garnier, Esq,
R E Elliott-Chambers, Esq, Miss Oswald (formerly Williamson), Miss
Marcon, and some scores of others, far too numerous to enumerate, who
have not only assisted with particulars concerning their own families,
but have gone to considerable trouble in assisting him to trace out other
lines of descent, in searching parish registers, and in obtaining dates   Nor
must he omit to accord his grateful thanks to Sir James Balfour Paul, the
Lord Lyon King of Arms, for his always prompt and ready replies to
inquiries addressed to him, to the Editor of *Notes and Queries* for inserting
numerous questions, or his indebtedness to works like Burke's " Peerage "
and " Landed Gentry," Debrett's " Peerage " &c

In compiling this work, the author can truthfully say that he has
made every effort to make it as complete as possible, each descent is
treated on its own merits, and no distinction is made, whether it be that
of the peer or the yeoman, *and absolutely no charge or condition has been
made for the insertion of any name or descent in this book*

There are, of course, many lines which the writer has been unable
to trace, the very magnitude of the task making all the conclusions
arrived at of a more or less tentative nature, and he is only too fully
aware of the number of other errors and imperfections which must, almost
of necessity, occur in a first attempt of this kind, but he asks for the
kind indulgence of his readers, and he will be most grateful to all those
who will point out to him omissions or other errors which may come
under their notice   They will all be included in a supplementary volume
with which the series will close

31 *January* 1911

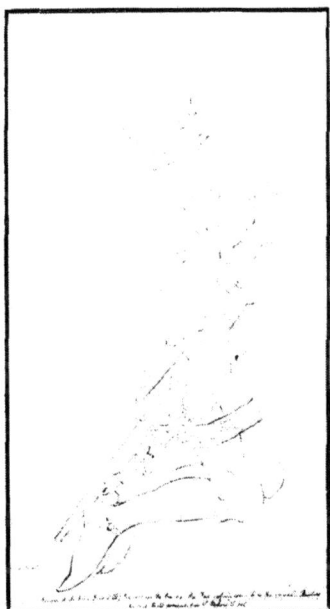

KING EDWARD THE THIRD, 1312-1377.
AT THE AGE OF 44.

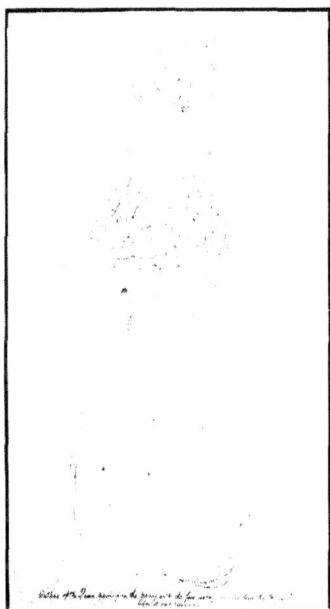

QUEEN PHILIPPA OF HAINAULT.
DIED 1369.

*From tracings of the original figures painted about 1356 on the East Wall of
St. Stephen's Chapel, Westminster (the old House of Commons).*

Edward III, King of England, ¹³¹² = **Philippa of Hainault,**
1312-1377. c. 1309-1369.

Edward, (1) Prince of Wales, "the Black Prince," 1330-1376. = ¹³⁶¹ Lady Joan Plantagenet, "of Kent," 1328-1385.

Lionel of Antwerp, Duke of Clarence, K.G., 1338-1368. = (1) Lady Elizabeth de Burgh, 1363.

John of Gaunt, Duke of Lancaster, K.G., 1340-1399. = ¹³⁵⁹ (1) Lady Blanche Plantagenet, "of Lancaster," 1341-1369. = ¹³⁷¹ (2) Constance of Castile, c. 1354-1394. = ¹³⁹⁷ (3) Katherine Swynford, née Roet, c. 1350-1403.

Edmund of Langley, Duke of York, K.G., 1341-1402. = ¹³⁷¹ (1) Isabel of Castile, 1355-1394.

Thomas of Woodstock, Duke of Gloucester, 1354-1397. = c. 1375 Lady Eleanor de Bohun, 1399.

Lady (1) Isabel Plantagenet, 1332-1379. = ¹³⁶⁵ Ingleram, Lord of Coucy, Earl of Bedford, K.G., 1339-1397.

Richard II, King of England, 1367-1400, s.p.

Philippa of Clarence, c. 1355-1382. = ¹³⁶⁸ Edmund de Mortimer, 3rd Earl of March, 1352-1381.

Lady Mary de Bohun, 1369-1394. = (1) Henry IV, King of England, 1366-1413.

Henry, Lord Percy, called Hotspur, 1403. (1) = Lady Elizabeth Mortimer, 1371-1444. = (2) Thomas, Lord Camoys, K.G., 1419.

For Descendants see The Mortimer-Percy volume.

Edmund, 5th Earl of March, declared heir to throne of England, 1424, s.p.

Richard, 3rd Duke of York, K.G., declared heir to throne of England, 1411-1460.

Lady Anne (1) = Richard, Earl of Cambridge, c. 1375-1415. Mortimer.

Edward IV, King of England, 1441-1483.

Elizabeth Wydeville, c. 1437-1492. =

Lady Cecily Nevill, 1415-1495. =

George, Duke of Clarence, K.G., 1449-1478. = Lady Isabel Nevill, 1451-1476.

Richard III, King of England, 1450-1485, s.p.

Lady Anne Plantagenet, 1439-1476. = (1) Henry Holland, Duke of Exeter, 1430-1473, s.p. = (2) Sir Thomas St. Leger.

Lady Isabel Plantagenet, 1484. = Henry, Count of Eu, 1st Earl of Essex, 1406-1483.

Edmund Tudor, Earl of Richmond, c. 1430-1456. = (1) Lady Margaret Plantagenet, alias Beaufort, b. 1441-1509.

Henry VII, King of England, 1455-1509. = ¹⁴⁸⁶ Elizabeth, da., and in her issue (1556) sole h. of King Edward IV, 1466-1503.

Edmund, 3rd Duke of Somerset, 1471-f., s.p.

Henry, 2nd Duke of Somerset, 1483-f., s.p.

Lady Eleanor Plantagenet, alias Beaufort, 1436-1501. = James Butler, Earl of Ormonde and Wiltshire, K.G., 1420-1461.

John, Duke of Somerset, K.G., 1404-1444. = Margaret, Lady St. John, née Beauchamp.

Edmund, Duke of Somerset, K.G., c. 1406-1455. = ¹⁴³⁵ Lady Eleanor Beauchamp, 1407-1468.

Thomas of Beaufort.

Lady Joan Plantagenet, alias Beaufort, 1445. = (1) James I., King of Scotland, 1394-1437. = (2) Sir James Stewart, the Black Knight of Lorn.

Sir Henry Fitz Lewis, of Horden, co. Essex.

For Descendants see The Tudor Roll of "The Blood Royal of Britain."

Lady Katherine Plantagenet. = Henry III., King of Castile and Leon, 1379-1406.

Lady Elizabeth Plantagenet, c. 1366-1426. = (1) John Holland, Duke of Exeter, 1400.

Richard, Earl of Cambridge, c. 1375-1415. = Lady Anne Mortimer.

Edward, 2nd Duke of York, K.G., 1373-1415.

Lady Constance Plantagenet, 1416. = Thomas le Despencer, Earl of Gloucester, K.G., 1373-1400.

Humphrey, 2nd Duke of Gloucester, 1399.

Lady Anne Plantagenet, 1383-1438. = (1) Edmund, 5th Earl of Stafford, 1378-1403. = (2) William Bourchier, Earl of Eu, c. 1374-1420.

Robert de Ferrers, (2) Ralph Nevill, 1st Earl of Westmorland, K.G., 1364-1425. = ¹³⁷⁹ ³Lady Joan Plantagenet, alias Beaufort, 1440.

Henry V., King of England, &c., 1387-1422. = ¹⁴²⁰ Catherine of France, 1401-1437.

Lady Philippa Plantagenet, 1415. = ¹³⁸⁷ John I., King of Portugal, 1433.

Lady Margaret Holland, 1429. = ¹³⁹⁹ (1) John of Beaufort, Marquis of Dorset, c. 1372-1410.

Henry VI., King of England, 1421-1471, s.p.s.

William Paston of London, c. 1465. = Lady Anne Plantagenet, alias Beaufort, 1443-a. 1496. = (1) Robert, Lord Howth, 1486. = (2) Sir Richard Fry, 1494. = (3) John Fry, 1516.

Lady Joan Plantagenet, alias Beaufort, 1518.

Lady Margaret Plantagenet, alias Beaufort, 1434-1490. = ¹⁴³⁹ Sir James Stewart, the Black Knight of Lorn.

Humphrey, Earl of Stafford, (1) = Lady Margaret Plantagenet, alias Beaufort. = (2) Sir Richard Darrell, 1455.

Lady Elizabeth Plantagenet, alias Beaufort.

Sir Robert Spencer, of Chilton Foliot, Wilts, 1509. = (2) Lady Eleanor Plantagenet, alias Beaufort.

Line merged into that of Edward IV. See The Tudor Roll of "The Blood Royal of Britain."

For Descendants see The Plantagenet Roll of "The Blood Royal of Britain" (Exeter volume).

For Descendants see The Plantagenet Roll of "The Blood Royal of Britain" (Clarence volume).

For Descendants see The Tudor Roll of "The Blood Royal of Britain."

I

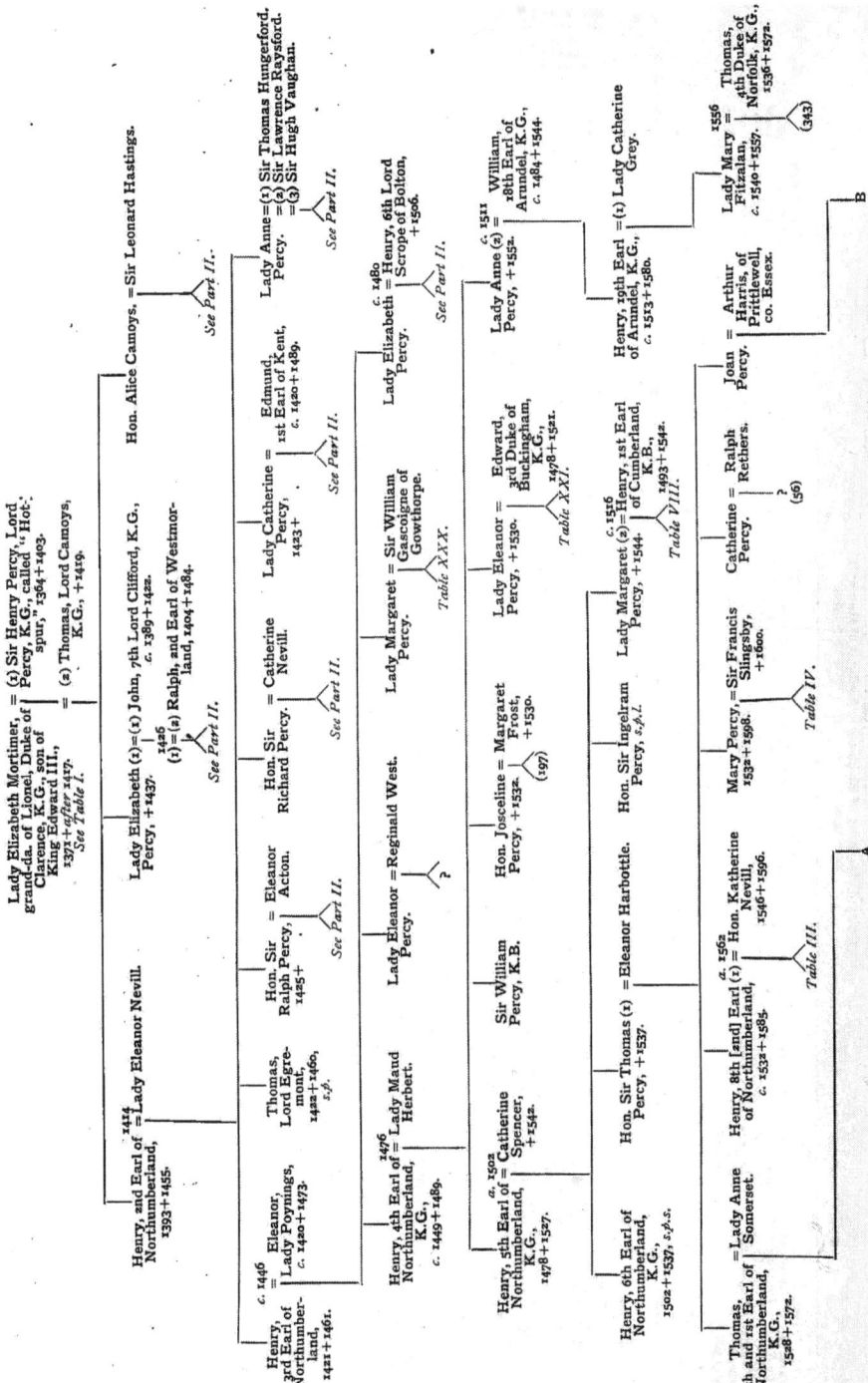

TABLE II

Lady Elizabeth Mortimer, = (1) Sir Henry Percy, Lord
grand-da. of Lionel, Duke of | Percy, K.G., called "Hot-
Clarence, K.G., son of | spur," 1364+1403.
King Edward III., | = (2) Thomas, Lord Camoys,
1371+after 1417. | K.G., +1419.
See Table I.

Hon. Alice Camoys, = Sir Leonard Hastings.
See Part II.

Lady Anne = (1) Sir Thomas Hungerford.
Percy. = (2) Sir Lawrence Raysford.
= (3) Sir Hugh Vaughan.
See Part II.

Lady Catherine = Edmund,
Percy, 1st Earl of Kent,
1423+ c. 1420+1489.
See Part II.

Lady Elizabeth = Henry, 6th Lord
Percy. Scrope of Bolton,
c. 1480 +1506.
See Part II.

Lady Anne (2) = William,
Percy, +1552. 8th Earl of
c. 1511 Arundel, K.G.,
c. 1484+1544.

Henry, 19th Earl = Lady Catherine
of Arundel, K.G., Grey.
c. 1513+1580. = (1)

Lady Mary = Thomas,
Fitzalan, 4th Duke of
c. 1540+1557. Norfolk, K.G.,
1556 1536+1572.

(343)

B

Henry, 2nd Earl of = Lady Eleanor Nevill
Northumberland, 1444
1393+1455.

Lady Elizabeth (1)=(1) John, 7th Lord Clifford, K.G.,
Percy, +1437. c. 1389+1422.
(1)=(2) Ralph, and Earl of Westmorland, 1404+1484.
1425
See Part II.

Henry, 3rd Earl of = Eleanor,
Northumberland, Lady Poynings,
1421+1461. c. 1420+1473.
c. 1446

Thomas,
Lord Egre-
mont,
1422+1460,
s.p.

Hon. Sir = Eleanor
Ralph Percy, Acton.
1425+
See Part II.

Hon. Sir = Catherine
Richard Percy. Nevill.
See Part II.

Lady Catherine = Percy,
1443+

Henry, 4th Earl of = Lady Maud
Northumberland, Herbert.
K.G., c. 1449+1489. 1476

Lady Eleanor = Reginald West.
Percy.

Lady Margaret = Sir William
Percy. Gascoigne of
Gowthorpe.
Table XXX.

Henry, 5th Earl of = Catherine
Northumberland, Spencer,
K.G., +1542.
1478+1527. a. 1502

Sir William
Percy, K.B.

Hon. Joscelline = Margaret
Percy, +1532. Frost,
+1530.
(197)

Lady Eleanor = Edward,
Percy, +1530. 3rd Duke of
Buckingham,
K.G.,
1478+1521.
Table XXI.

Henry, 6th Earl of = Eleanor Harbottle.
Northumberland,
K.G.,
1502+1537, s.p.s.

Hon. Sir Thomas (1) = Eleanor Harbottle
Percy, +1537.

Lady Margaret (2)=Henry, 1st Earl
Percy, +1544. of Cumberland,
c. 1516 K.B.,
1493+1544.
Table VIII.

Hon. Sir Ingelram
Percy, s.p.l.

Thomas, = Lady Anne
7th and 1st Earl of Somerset.
Northumberland,
K.G.,
1528+1572.

Henry, 8th [and] Earl (1) = Hon. Katherine
of Northumberland, Nevill,
c. 1532+1585. 1546+1596.
d. 1562
Table III.

Mary Percy, = Sir Francis
1532+1598. Slingsby,
+1600.
Table IV.

Catherine = Ralph
Percy. Rethers.
2
(56)

Joan = Arthur
Percy. Harris, of
Prittlewell,
co. Essex.

A

2

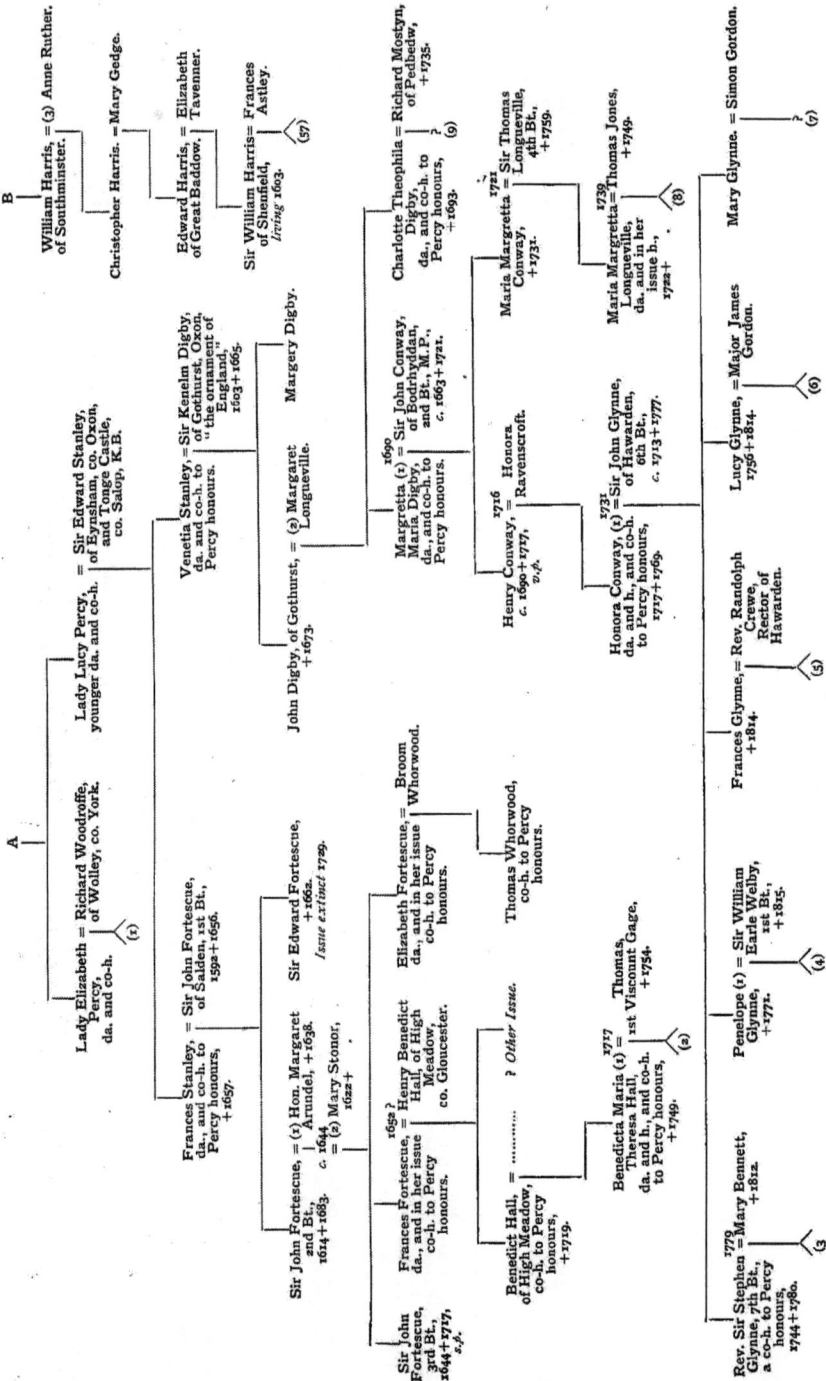

A

B

William Harris, = (3) Anne Ruther, of Southminster.

Christopher Harris. = Mary Gedge.

Edward Harris, = Elizabeth of Great Baddow. | Tavenner.

Sir William Harris = Frances of Shenfield, | Astley. *living* 1603.

(57)

Lady Elizabeth = Richard Woodroffe, Percy, | of Wolley, co. York. da. and co-h.

(1)

Lady Lucy Percy, = Sir Edward Stanley, younger da. and co-h. | of Eynsham, co. Oxon, and Tonge Castle, co. Salop, K.B.

Charlotte Theophila = Richard Mostyn, Digby, | of Pedbedw, da., and co-h. to | +1735. Percy honours, | +1693. | (9)

Venetia Stanley, = Sir Kenelm Digby, da. and co-h. to | of Gothurst, Oxon, Percy honours. | "the ornament of | England," | 1603+1665.

Margery Digby.

Maria Margretta = Sir Thomas Conway, | Longueville, +1731. | 4th Bt., | +1759.

John Digby, of Gothurst, = (2) Margaret +1673. | Longueville.

Maria Margretta = Thomas Jones, Longueville, | +1749. da., and in her issue b., 17az+

(8)

Frances Stanley, = Sir John Fortescue, da. and co-h. to | of Salden, 1st Bt, Percy honours, | 1592+1656. +1657.

Sir Edward Fortescue, +1662. *issue extinct* 1729.

Elizabeth Fortescue, = Broom da., and in her issue | Whorwood. co-h. to Percy | honours.

Margretta (1), = Sir John Conway, Maria Digby, | of Bodrhyddan, da., and co-h. to | and Bt., M.P., Percy honours. | c. 1663+1721.

Sir John Fortescue, = (1) Hon. Margaret 2nd Bt, | Arundel, +1638. | c. 1644 1614+1663. | = (2) Mary Stonor, | 16a2+

Frances Fortescue, = Henry Benedict da., and in her issue | Hall, of High co-h. to Percy | Meadow, honours. | co. Gloucester. 165a?

Thomas Whorwood, co-h. to Percy honours.

Henry Conway, = Honora c. 1690+1717, | Ravenscroft. s.p. 1716

Honora Conway, (1), = Sir John Glynne, da. and h., and co-h. | of Hawarden, to Percy honours, | 6th Bt, 1727+1769. | c. 1713+1777. 1731

Sir John Fortescue, 3rd Bt, 1644+1717, s.p.

Benedict Hall, = ... of High Meadow, co-h. to Percy honours, +1719.

? *Other Issue.*

Benedicta Maria (1) = Thomas, Theresa Hall, | 1st Viscount Gage, da. and h., and co-h. | +1754. to Percy honours, | 1717 +1749.

(a)

Mary Glynne, = Simon Gordon.

(7)

Lucy Glynne, = Major James 1756+1814. | Gordon.

(6)

Frances Glynne, = Rev. Randolph +1814. | Crewe, Rector of | Hawarden.

(5)

Penelope (1) = Sir William Glynne, | Earle Welby, +1771. | 1st Bt, | +1815.

(4)

Rev. Sir Stephen = Mary Bennett, Glynne, 7th Bt, | +1812. a co-h. to Percy | honours, | 1744+1780. 1779

(3)

3

Henry, 8th Earl of (1) *a.* 1562 = Hon. Katherine Nevill,
Northumberland, 1546 + 1596.
c. 1532 + 1585.
See Table II.

Hon. George
Percy, of
Virginia.

Henry, 9th Earl of = Dorothy, Lady Perrot, 1594
Northumberland, *née* Lady Dorothy
1564 + 1632. Devereux,
+ 1619.

Lady Eleanor = Sir William Herbert,
Percy, 1st Lord Powis,
1582 + 1651. *c.* 1572 + 1655.

Hon. = (1) Sir Robert
Katherine | Vaughan.
Herbert. = (2) Sir James
Palmer, of
Dorney Court,
co. Bucks.
(16)

Percy, = Elizabeth
2nd Lord Powis, Craven.
+ 1667.

William, = Lady
1st Marquis Elizabeth
[and Duke] Somerset,
of Powis, K.G., + 1692.
1617 + 1696. 1654
(15)

Algernon, = (1) Lady
10th Earl of Anne Cecil,
Northumberland, + 1637.
K.G., 1642
1602 + 1668. = (2) Lady
Elizabeth
Howard,
c. 1608 + 1705.
a. 1630

Henry,
Lord
Percy,
+ 1659.
unm.

Lady
Dorothy
Percy,
1598 + 1650.
c. 1615 = Robert,
2nd Earl of
Leicester,
K.B.,
1595 + 1677.
(14)

Joceline, (1)
11th Earl of
Northumberland,
1644 + 1670.
= Lady
Elizabeth
Wriothesley,
c. 1646 + 1690.
1662

Lady
Elizabeth
Percy,
1636 + 1717.
= Arthur,
1st Earl of
Essex,
+ 1683.
1653
(13)

Lady Elizabeth (1) = Charles, 6th Duke
Percy, da. and h., of Somerset,
c. 1667 + 1722. 1682 1662 + 1748.

Lady Katherine = Sir William Wyndham
Seymour, 3rd Bt.,
+ 1791. *c.* 1687 + 1740.
1708
(12)

Algernon, 7th Duke of = Frances Thynne,
Somerset, Earl of 1699 + 1754.
Northumberland,
1684 + 1750.
1713

Lady Elizabeth Seymour, = Sir Hugh Smithson, 1st Duke
da. and h., of Northumberland,
1716 + 1776. 1714 + 1786.
1740

Algernon, 1st Earl = Isabella Susanna
of Beverley, Burrell,
1750 + 1830. 1750 + 1812.
1775
(11)

Hugh, 2nd Duke of = (2) Frances Julia
Northumberland, K.G., Burrell,
1742 + 1817. 1752 + 1820.
1779
(10)

TABLE IV

Mary Percy, = Sir Francis Slingsby,
1532 † 1598.   † 1600.
See Table II.

Sir Henry = Elizabeth
Slingsby.   Vavasour,
             † 1609.

Rev. Charles = Elizabeth
Slingsby,   Ellis.
D.D., R. of
Rothbury,
1561 +

Sir William = Elizabeth
Slingsby, of   Board.
Kippax,
c. 1562 † 1624.

1600
Sir Guildford = Margaret
Slingsby,   Watter.
1565 + 1631.

Sir Francis = Elizabeth
Slingsby.   Cuff.

1631
Sir Henry = Hon.
Slingsby,   Barbara
1st Bt.,   Belasyse,
1601 † 1658. 1609 † 1641.

⟨17⟩

Elizabeth = Sir Thomas
Slingsby.   Metcalfe, of
             Nappa,
             c. 1579 † 1650.

⟨52⟩

Maria = Sir Walter
Slingsby, Bethell, of
† 1662.   Alne,
           † 1622.

Table V.

⟨53⟩

Katherine = Sir John
Slingsby,   Fenwick,
1584 + c. 1621. 1st Bt.,
             † 1658.

1603
Alice (1) = Thomas
Slingsby.   Waterton,
            of Walton,
            1585 + 1641.

⟨40⟩   ⟨41⟩

Anne
Slingsby.

⟨54⟩

Frances = Bryan
Slingsby, Stapylton,
† 1656.   of Myton,
           † 1658.

Table VII.

Eleanor (1) = Sir Arthur
Slingsby,   Ingram, of
† 1647.   Temple
              Newsham,
              † 1655.

⟨55⟩   ⟨51⟩

James
Metcalfe,
of Nappa,
c. 1604 +

Margaret
Hicks.

Scrope
Metcalfe,
Major,
Royal
Army,
† 1665.

Henry
Metcalfe,
living
1665.

Thomas
Metcalfe,
of Nappa,
1665.

1645
(2) Grace
Armytage,
née
Rockley,
1614 +

Frances (2) = Sir William
Metcalfe.   Robinson,
               of Newby,
               1601 † 1658

Thomas
Metcalfe,
last of
Nappa,
c. 1687 + 1756,
marr.

James
Metcalfe.

Thomas
Robinson,
of York,
† 1678.

Elizabeth = Elizabeth
Metcalfe,   Tancred,
da. and h., † 1664.
1647 +

⟨18⟩   ⟨19⟩

John
Lodge,
of Leeds.

1654

Sir Metcalfe
Robinson,
1st Bart.,
c. 1629 † 1688.

Elizabeth = Philip
Robinson.   Rycot.

⟨20⟩

Margaret
Robinson.

1653
William = Weddell, of
Earswick,
1634 † 1676.

⟨21⟩

Frances =
Robinson.

Robert
Belt, of
Overton,
1637 † 1667.

⟨22⟩

5

TABLE V

Maria Slingsby, +1622, See Table IV. = Sir Walter Bethell of Alne, co. York, +1622.

Sir Hugh Bethell, of Ellerton, 1605+. = Frances Frankland, +1673.

Slingsby Bethell, Sheriff of London, 1617+. = Mary Burrell. (28)

Rev. William Bethell, D.D., +1685. = Bridget Bourchier, +1652.

Francis Bethell, 1603.

Frances Bethell, +1684, = Sir George Marwood, 1st Bart., M.P., 1601+1680. 1625. Table VI.

Mary (1) Bethell. = Thomas Hesketh, of Heslington, co. York. 1637

Matilda Bethell = Rev. Robert Goodwin. (39)

Anne Hesketh, da. and co-h., 1676+1718. = James Yarburgh, of Snaith, co. York, +1730. 1692 (38)

? Other das.

Bourchier Bethell, 1652+. Walter Bethell, 1653+. Slingsby Bethell, 1657+. Nicholas Bethell, 1658+. Hugh Bethell, 1659+. Mary Bethell, 1654+. Bridget Bethell, 1656+. Frances Bethell, 1664+.

William Bethell, of Swindon and Ellerton, 1647+1699. = Elizabeth Brooke. (1) 1688

Elizabeth Bethell, da. and event. sole h., 1693+1765. = Sir William Codrington, 1st Bt., +1738.

Sir William Codrington, and Bt., P.C., M.P., 1719+1792. = Anne Acton, +1778. 1736 (29)

Edward Codrington, of London, 1732+1775. = Rebecca Le Sturgeon, +1770. 1759 (30)

Bridget Codrington. = William Dowdeswell, of Pull Court, P.C., M.P., +1775. 1747 (31)

Walter Bethell, of Ellerton, +1629. = (1) Anne Savile, n'e Palmes, +1653. (2) Mary Vavasour, +1659. 1650 / 1656 (23)

Henry Bethell. Hugh Bethell. Mary Bethell = Arthur Robinson, of Buckton, +1703.

Lucy Bethell = John Mottram, of Bishops Dyke, co. York. (25)

Ursula Bethell, 1634+ = John Palliser, of Newby Wiske, +1639. (26)

Frances Bethell = Henry Bellingham, 1694 (27)

Elizabeth Bethell. (27)

Bethell Robinson, of Buckton, 1684+1718. = Mary Heseltine. (24)

6

9

TABLE VI

Frances Bethell, $\overset{1625}{=}$ Sir George Marwood,
+1684.   1st Bart., M.P.,
See Table V.   1601+1680.

Sir Henry $\overset{1663}{=}$ (2.) Dorothy
Marwood, | Bellingham.
2nd Bt.,
c. 1635+1725.

George $=$ Mary
Marwood, | Swennock.
of Hamburg,
living 1665.

Walter
Marwood,
living 1665.

Barbara $=$ (1.) Sir Thomas
Marwood, | Hebblethwaite,
living 1679. | of Norton, M.P.,
1628+1668.

Anne $\overset{1657}{=}$ William
Marwood, | Metcalfe, of
living 1679. | North Allerton,
1635+1698.

Frances $=$ (1.) Sir
Marwood, | Richard
living 1679. | Weston,
living 1679.

George $=$(1) Constance
Marwood, | Spencer.
1665+1700,
s.p.

Elizabeth $=$ John
Marwood, | Pierce,
1666+1726. | of Lazenby
Hall,
+1694.

Sir
Samuel
Marwood,
3rd Bt.,
1672+1739,
s.p.

Sir
William
Marwood,
4th Bt.,
c. 1681+1740,
s.p.

Thomas (2) $=$ (2) Anne
Metcalfe, | Greene,
of the | *née* Green,
Porch House, | 1670+
North Allerton,
1661+1717.

Henry
Metcalfe,
1668+

Hannah
Metcalfe,
1667+

Margaret (1) $\overset{1692}{=}$ Daniel
Metcalfe, | Lascelles,
1665+1690. | of Stank
Hall, M.P.,
1655+1734.

Jane
Marwood,
1688+1764.
$\overset{1709}{=}$ Cholmley
Turner,
of Kirk
Leatham,
M.P.,
1685+1757.

Rev. Thomas $\overset{1742}{=}$ Anne Smelt,
Metcalfe, | +1804.
of the
Porch House,
1706+1774.

Jane
Turner,
da. and h.
$\overset{1745}{=}$ Philip
William
Casimir van
Straubenzee,
+1765.

⟨32⟩   ⟨33⟩   ⟨34⟩   ⟨35⟩   ⟨36⟩   ⟨37⟩

7

TABLE VII

Frances Slingsby, = Bryan Stapylton,
+ 1656.   of Myton,
See Table IV.   + 1658.

Ursula = Thomas
Stapylton,   Pepys, of
+ 1693.   Hatcham
             Barnes,
             co. Surrey,
             1640+

(50)

Frances Stapylton, + 1684. = John Hutton, of Marske, 1625 + 1664.

(49)

c. 1654
Olive (2) = (1) Sir William
Stapylton,   Vavasour, of
1620 + 1714. Copmanthorpe,
              1st Bt.,
              + 1658.
              = (2) Richard
              Topham,
              of Weston.

1670
Frances = (1) Sir
Vavasour,   Thomas
da. and h., Norcliffe,
1654 + 1731. of Langton,
             1641 + 1684.

1697
Fairfax = Mary
Norcliffe, of   Hesketh, of
Langton,   Heslington,
1674 + 1721.   + 1739.

1728
Frances = Sir John
Norcliffe, da. and   Wray,
event. h.,   12th Bt.,
1700 + 1770.   1689 + 1752.

(48)

Robert
Stapylton,
Capt. R.N.,
living 1665.

Jane = (—)
Stapylton,
living 1743.

Rev. Henry = Mary
Stapylton,   Orchard,
R. of Thornton   + 1755.
Watlass,
+ 1748.

(47)

Olivia
Stapylton,

Miles
Stapylton, Adm. R.N.,
issue ext.

1739
Grace = Very Rev.
Robinson,   William
da. and   Freind, D.D.,
co-h.,   Dean of
1718 + 1766. Canterbury.

(44)

Miles = Elizabeth
Stapylton, J.P. Hynde.

1655

Elizabeth = John
Stapylton.   Dodsworth,
              of Thornton
              Watlass,
              1659+

(46)

Frances = Elizabeth
Lowe, of   (or Frances)
Brightwell, Corrance.
+ 1754.

(45)

Anne = (1) Robert
Robinson,   Knight.
da. and   (2) James
co-h.   Cresset.

?

Richard,
1st Lord Rokeby,
Archbishop of
Armagh, + 1794, unm.

Sir William
Robinson, 2nd Bt.,
+ 1785, unm.

Sir Thomas
Robinson, 1st Bt.,
+ 1777, s.p.

Frances
Stapylton.

Margaret
Stapylton.

Grace
Stapylton.

Anne
Stapylton.

Elizabeth
Stapylton.

= John
Lowe.

Thomas
Robinson,
of Rokeby,
+ 1719.

1680
Sir Bryan = Ann Kaye,
Stapylton,   1664 + 1730.
2nd Bt.,
1657 + 1727.

Sir Henry = Lady
Stapylton,   Elizabeth
of Myton,   Darcy,
1st Bt.,   1644+
c. 1617 + 1679.

1650

William = Anne
Robinson,   Walters.
of Rokeby,
only son,
+ 1719.

Henry Waller,
M.P.,
Wycombe,
Bucks.

= Elizabeth
Stapylton.

(43)

Penelope Stapylton.

Diana Stapylton.

Mary Stapylton.

Anne Stapylton.

Christopher
Stapylton.

Robert Stapylton.

Henry Stapylton.

Francis Stapylton.

1706
Sir John = Mary
Stapylton,   Sandys.
3rd Bt.,
1684 + 1733.

1742
Rev. Sir = Leckie
Martin   Love,
Stapylton,   + c. 1797.
7th Bt.,
1723 + 1801.

Sir John Stapylton,
6th Bt., 1718 + 1785.

Sir Bryan Stapylton,
5th Bt.,
c. 1714 + 1772.

4th Bt.,
c. 1708 + 1752.

Rev. John
Bree,
.. 1734 + 1796.

= Anne
Stapylton, da. and
(1817) h.

(42)

Sir Martin
Stapylton,
8th Bt.,
1751 + 1817.

8

Lady Margaret Percy, (2)= Henry, 1st Earl of Cumberland, K.B.,
c. 1516 +1544.
+1542.
See Table II.

Lady Elizabeth Clifford. — 1533 Sir Christopher Metcalfe, of Nappa, c. 1513 +1574. (196)

Lady Maud Clifford. = John, 3rd Lord Conyers, +1557.
Table X.X.

Lady Catherine Clifford, +1598. (1)= John, 8th Lord Scrope, of Bolton, +1549. (2)= Sir Richard Cholmley, of Roxby, c. 1514 +1579.
c. 1530.
Table XIII.

Henry, 2nd Earl of Cumberland, K.B., 1517+1570. — 1537 (1)= Lady Eleanor Brandon, +1547. (2)= Hon. Anne Dacre, +1581. 1554.

George, 3rd Earl of Cumberland, K.G., 1558+1605. — 1577 = Lady Margaret Russell, 1560+1616.

Francis, 4th Earl of Cumberland, K.B., 1559+1641. — 1580 = Grizel, Lady Abergavenny, née Hughes, +1613.

Lady Margaret Clifford, c. 1540+1596. = Henry, 4th Earl of Derby, K.G., +1593. (84)

= Lady Frances Clifford, +1592. — 1577 Philip, 3rd Lord Wharton, 1555+1625.
Table X.

Lady Frances Clifford, c. 1594+1647. — 1614 = Sir Gervase Clifton, 1st Bt., 1587+1660.
Table IX.

Henry, 5th Earl of Cumberland, K.B., 1591+1643. — 1610 = Lady Frances Cecil, c. 1594+1644.

Lady Anne Clifford, suo jure 14th Lady Clifford, 1590+1676. — 1609 (1)= Richard, 3rd Earl of Dorset, 1589+1624. (2)= John, 2nd Earl of Thanet, c. 1607+1664. 1629

Elizabeth, suo jure = Richard, 2nd Earl of Cork, Lady Clifford, 1st Earl of Burlington, 1618+1691. 1612+1698. 1635 (67)

Nicholas, 3rd Earl of Thanet, 1631+1679.

John, 4th Earl of Thanet, 1638+1680.

Richard, 5th Earl of Thanet, +1684.

Thomas, 6th Earl of Thanet, 1644+1729. — 1684 = Lady Catherine Cavendish, +1712. (58)

Lady Mary Savile, +1751. — 1722 = Sackville, 7th Earl of Thanet, 1688+1753. (59)

Elizabeth Wilbraham, +1714.

Hon. Sackville Tufton, 1646+1721.

Christopher, 1st Viscount Hatton, 1632+1706. — 1668 = Lady Cecilia Tufton, 1648+1672.

Hon. Anne Hatton, da. and h., c. 1665+1743. (2)= Daniel, 2nd Earl of Nottingham, 6th Earl of Winchilsea, 1647+1730. 1685

Lady Mary Tufton, +1674. c. 1671 (1)= Sir William Walter, 2nd Bt., +1694. (66)

Daniel, 8th Earl of Winchilsea, 1689+1769. — 1738 (2)= Lady Mary Palmer, +1757. (60)

Hon. William Finch, P.C., M.P., +1766. — 1746 (2)= Lady Charlotte Fermor, 1725+1813. (61)

Hon. John Finch, +1763.

Hon. Edward Finch-Hatton, M.P., +1771. — 1746 = Elizabeth Palmer.

Lady Essex Finch, 1688+1721. — 1793 = Sir Roger Mostyn, 3rd Bt., c. 1675+1739. (63)

Lady Charlotte Finch, +1773. — 1726 = Charles, 6th Duke of Somerset, K.G., 1662+1748. (64)

Thomas, 1st Marquis of Rockingham, 1690+1750. — 1716 = Lady Mary Finch, +1761. (65)

George Finch-Hatton, of Eastwell, 1747+1823. — 1785 = Lady Elizabeth Mary Murray, 1760+1825. (62)

= Elizabeth Younger, +1762.

Lady Essex Finch.

9

B

TABLE IX

Lady Frances Clifford, (2) = Sir Gervase Clifton of Clifton, 1st Bt., K.B., M.P., 1587 + 1666.
c. 1594 + 1627. *See Table VIII.*

Margaret Clifford, + 1668.
= (1) Sir John South, of Kelstern, 1609 + 1648.
= (2) William Whichcot, of Fotherby, co. Linc. 1618 +
= (3) Robert, 6th Lord Hunsden. + 1692, *s.p.*

Frances Clifford.

Anne Clifford.
= (1) Robert Tempest (2) = Sir Francis Rodes, 2nd Bt., of Bracewell. + 1651.
= (2) Anthony Eyre.

Sir Clifford Clifton, + 1670. = Frances Finch.

Arabella Clifton, da. and (1686) co-h. = Adm. Sir Francis Wheler.

Catharine Clifton, da. and (1686) co-h. = Sir John Parsons, 2nd Bt., *c.* 1656 + 1704.

Francis South, 1639+ (73)

John South, of Kelstern, co. Linc. Knt. of the Royal Oak, 1660. = Elizabeth Tempest.

George Whichcot, of Harpswell, co. Linc., M.P., 1653+

Elizabeth = John South, of Kelstern, *ltn.* 1660.

Alice Whichcot, 1659+

Frances Whichcot, 1651+ = James Nelthorpe, of Little Grimsby, 1670 + 1756.

(1) Frances Katharine Meres, 1669 + 1731 =
George Whichcot = (2) Jane Trigate.

Elizabeth Whichcot, 1706 + 1774 = Ven. William Bassett, Archdeacon of Stow, 1703 + 1765.

Katherine Whichcot, 1701 + 1787.
= John Maddison, of Stainton Vale, 1691 + 1746.

Frances Whichcot, + 1720.

Sarah Tomlinson, 1710 + 1804. = Rev. John Whichcot, 1704 + 1750.

Thomas Whichcot, of Harpswell, M.P., *c.* 1700 + 1776.

Sir William Clifton, 3rd Bt., 1663 + 1686, *unm.*

Francis Wheler. = ——— Crofts.

Rev. William Wheler.

Jane Smith.

Sarah Wheler, + 1807. = Rev. John Mills, 1714 + 1791.

Frances Whichcot, da. and h., 1733 + 1811. = William Hildyard, of Grimsby, + 1781.

George Maddison, of Stainton Vale, 1729 + 1807.

Mary Baugh, + 1791.

Katherine Maddison, + 1724.

John Lawrence, of Putney, 1695+

Theodosia Maddison, 1725 + 1821.

John, 2nd Lord Monson, 1727 + 1774.

Anne Maddison, *c.* 1728 + 1783. = Rev. Sir William Anderson, 6th Bt., + 1785.

Sir Christopher Whichcot, 4th Bt., 1738 + 1786. (74)

Jane Whichcot, da. and in her issue h., + 1812.

Jane Wheler, = Henry, 2nd Viscount Hood, 1753 + 1836. (71)

Jane Lambarde, 1764 + 1836. = John Randolph, Bishop of London, + 1813. (70)

Mary Lambarde, 1758+ = Rev. John Hallward, + 1866. (69)

Multon Lambarde, of Sevenoaks, 1757 + 1836. = Aurea Otway, + 1828. (68)

Thomas Lambarde, of Sevenoaks.

(1) Frances Dutton, + 1735. = Sir William Parsons, 3rd Bt., 1686 + 1760.

Grace Parsons, da. and in her issue h., + 1812.

Sir Mark Parsons, 4th Bt., *c.* 1741 + 1811, *s.p.*

William Parsons, 1718 + 1751.

Mary Frampton.

Jane South, 1671+ (73)

Margery Maria South, + 1665.

Leonard Pinkney.

Elizabeth South, + 1664.

Tempest South, + 1669.

IO

TABLE X

Lady Frances Clifford, = Philip, 3rd Lord Wharton, 1555 + 1625.
1577 *See Table VIII.*

Hon. Sir George Wharton, + 1609, v.p.

Hon. Sir Thomas Wharton, + 1622, v.p. = Lady Philadelphia, Carey, liv. 1635. (1611)

Hon. Eleanor Wharton. = William Thwaytes, of Long Marston.

Hon. Frances Wharton. = c. 1599 Sir Richard Musgrave, of Edenhall, 1st Bt., K.B., M.P., c. 1585 + 1615. *See Table XII.*

Philip, 4th Lord Wharton, 1613 + 1695. = (1) Elizabeth Wandesford, + c. 1635 = (2) Jane Goodwin, 1618 + 1658. (1632)

Sir Thomas Wharton, K.B., 1615 + 1684. = (2) Jane Robinson, née Dand, + 1714. (1677)

Elizabeth Wharton, da. and in her issue, if any, co-h. = —— Bennet. (100)

Jane Wharton, da. and in her issue co-h. = John Digby, of Mansfield Woodhouse. (99)

Hon. Lucy Loftus, 1669 + 1716. (1692)

Thomas, 1st Marquis of Wharton, 1648 + 1715. = (2)

Hon. Goodwin Wharton, M.P., + 1704, f.s.p.

1 (2) Hon. Elizabeth Wharton, da. and in her issue (1731) co-h. = Robert, 3rd Earl of Lindsay, + 1701.

Robert, 1st Duke of Ancaster, 1660 + 1723. = Anne Casey.

2 Hon. Anne Wharton, da. and (?) in her issue (1731) co-h. = William Carr.

3 Hon. Margaret Wharton, da. and in her issue (1731) co-h. = (1) Major Dunch, of Pusey, c. 1651 + 1679, *issue extinct*; (2) Sir Thomas Seyliard, 2nd Bt., 1648 + 1692; (3) William Ross. (1690)

Philip, 1st Duke of Wharton, 1698 + 1731, s.p.

(1) Mary Wynne, + 1689. 1698; (2) Albinia Fassingdon, + 1745. 1705 (91)

2 Hon. Mary Wharton, da. and in her issue (1731) co-h. = (1) William Thomas, of Wenvoe, *issue extinct*; (2) Sir Charles Kemeys, 3rd Bt., M.P., 1651 + 1702. 1658

3 Hon. Philadelphia Wharton, da. and in her issue (1731) co-h. = (1) Sir George Lockhart, of Carnwath; (2) Capt. John Ramsay. *See Table XI.*

Sir Charles Kemeys, 4th Bt., M.P., 1688 + 1735.

Jane Kemeys, da. and h., + 1747. = Sir John Tynte, 2nd Bt., M.P., 1683 + 1710. 1704

Peregrine, 2nd Duke of Ancaster, 1686 + 1742. = Jane Brownlow, + 1736. 1711

Lord Vere Bertie, + 1768. = Anne Casey. 1726

Lord Montagu Bertie, + 1753. = Elizabeth Piers. (89)

Lady Louisa Bertie. = Thomas Bludworth. 1736 (90)

Sir John Tynte, 4th Bt., 1707 + 1740, *nnm.*

Sir Charles Kemeys-Tynte, 5th Bt., 1710 + 1785, s.p.

Rev. Sir Charles Tynte, *afterwards* Kemeys-Tynte. 1704

Sir Halsewell Tynte, 3rd Bt., 1705 + 1730, s.p.

Jane (1) Tynte, da. and in her issue 1785 h., + 1741. = Major Ruisshe Hassell, R.H.G. (92)

Peregrine, 3rd Duke of Ancaster, 1714 + 1778. = (2) Mary Panton, + 1793. 1750 (85)

Brownlow, 5th Duke of Ancaster, 1727 + 1809, s.p.s.

Lady Mary Bertie, + 1774. = Samuel Greatheed, of Guy's Hill, co. Warwick. 1747 (86)

Lady Jane Bertie, + 1793. = Gen. Edward Matthews. 1743 (87)

Lady Caroline Bertie, + 1774. = George Dewar, of Hartsbourne, Tarrant, Hants, 1707 + 1785. 1753 s.p.

(88) (86) (85)

II

TABLE XI

Hon. Philadelphia Wharton. = (1) Sir George Lockhart, of Carnwath, Lord President of the Court of Session, c. 1630 + 1689.
See Table XV.

= (2) Capt. John Ramsay.

George Lockhart, of Carnwath, author of the "Lockhart Papers," 1673 + 1731. = Lady Euphemia Montgomerie.

Philip Lockhart, c. 1690 + 1715.

Barbara Lockhart, 1677 + = 1(1) James Lockhart, yr. of Castlehill.
= (2) Hon. Daniel Carmichael + 1708.

(98)

George Lockhart, of Carnwath, 1700 + 1764. = 1727 Fergusia Wishart.

(93)

Alexander Lockhart, of Craighouse, Lord Covington of Session. = 1725 Margaret Pringle.

(94)

Thomas Lockhart.

James Lockhart.

Philip Lockhart.

Margaret (3) Lockhart, + 1762. = (1) John, 6th Earl of Wigtown, c. 1673 + 1744.
= (2) Peter MacElligot, Major-Gen. Austrian Service.

(95)

Grace Lockhart, + 1738. = 1724 (1) John, 3rd Earl of Aboyne, + 1732.
(1) = 1734 (2) James, 8th Earl of Moray, K.T., c. 1708 + 1767.

(96)

Kate.
Susan.
Joan.

Mary (2) Lockhart. = John Rattray, of Edinburgh, M.D.

(97)

I 2

TABLE XII

Hon. Frances Wharton. *See Table X.* = c. 1599 Sir Richard Musgrave, of Edenhall, 1st Bt., K.B., c. 1585 + 1615.

Sir Philip Musgrave, 2nd Bt., 1608 + 1678. = Juliana Hutton, + 1659.

William Musgrave.

Frances Musgrave = Edward Hutchinson, of Wickham Abbey, co. Yorks. (115)

Rev. Thomas Musgrave, D.D., Dean of Carlisle, c. 1639 + 1686. = (1) Mary Harrison.

Margaret Musgrave, da. and h. = Ralph Shipperdson, of Murton and Pidding Hall, + 1709. (114)

Elizabeth Musgrave. = John Wyneve, of Brettenham, co. Suffolk. (113)

Dorothy Musgrave. = ? James Hawley, of Brentford, co. Middlesex. (113)

Sir Christopher Musgrave, 4th Bt., c. 1631 + 1704. = (1) Mary Cogan, c. 1636 + 1664. = (2) Elizabeth Franklin.

George Musgrave, Keeper of the Ordnance. = Sarah Young, née Rosell. (112)

Philip Musgrave, + 1689, s.p. = 1685 Hon. Mary Legge.

Barbara (2) = 1720 Thomas Howard, of Corby Castle, + 1740. (111)

Sir Richard Musgrave, 3rd Bt., + c. 1687. = Margaret Harrison.

Mary Musgrave, da. and h. = Thomas Davison, of Blackiston, co. Durham.

Sir Christopher Musgrave, 5th Bt., M.P., 1688 + 1735. = 1711 Julia Chardin, + c. 1763.

Sir Philip Musgrave, 6th Bt., M.P., 1711 + 1795. = 1742 Jane Turton, + 1802. (102)

Rev. Christopher Musgrave. = 1757 Perfect, née ,—. (101)

Hans Musgrave, Lt.-Col. (103)

Rev. Chardin Musgrave, D.D., Provost of Oriel Coll., Oxon. c. 1724 + 1768. = Catherine Tipping, c. 1730 + 1795. (104)

Mary Musgrave. = (1) Hugh Lumley. = (2) John Pigott. (105)

Julia Musgrave, + 1778. = Edward Hasell, of Dalemain, Cumberland, 1716 + 1778. (106)

Barbara Musgrave. = (1) John Hogg, of Scotland. = (2) Chief Baron Idle. (107)

Anne Musgrave, + 1750. = Henry Aglionby, of Nunnery, 1715 + 1770. (108)

Elizabeth Musgrave. = (1) Edward Spragge, of Greenwich. = (2) John Johnstone, of London. (109)

Dorothy Musgrave, 1727 + 1799. = Rev. William Wroughton, 1716 + 1776. (110)

13

TABLE XIII

Lady Catherine Clifford, = (1) John, 8th Lord Scrope, of Bolton,
+1598.
= (2) Sir Richard Cholmley, of Roxby,
c. 1514 + 1579.
See Table VIII.

Henry, 9th Lord Scrope, K.G., K.B., c. 1534 + 1591. = (1) Hon. Mary North, +1558. = (2) Lady Margaret Howard, 1543 + 1590.

Hon. Margaret (1) = Sir John Constable, of Kirkby Knowle, 1547 + 1579.

Hon. Elizabeth Scrope. = Thomas Pudsey, of Barforth.
Table XIV.

Catherine Cholmley = Richard Dutton, of Whitby. (181)

Thomas, 10th Lord Scrope, K.G., c. 1567 + 1609. = c. 1584 Hon. Philadelphia Carey, +1627.

Sir Henry Cholmley, of Whitby and Roxby, +1616. = Margaret Babthorpe, +1628. (117)

Hon. Mary Scrope (1) = Sir William Bowes, of Bradley Hall, co. Durham, +1611. (1630) h., +1589.

Sir Henry Constable, of Burton Constable, c. 1557 + 1607. = c. 1575 Margaret Dormer, +1637.

Joseph Constable, of Upsall, co. York. = Mary Crathorne. (170)

Margaret Constable, +1663. = Sir Edward Stanhope, of Edlington Grimston, co. York. (168)

Mary Constable, +1669. = c. 1610 Sir Thomas Blakiston, 1st Bt., 1582 + 1630. (169)

Emmanuel, 11th Lord Scrope, Earl of Sunderland, 1584 + 1630, s.p.l.

Henry, 1st Viscount Dunbar, c. 1588 + 1645. = c. 1614 Mary Tufton, +1659.

Catherine Constable, 1579 + 1626. = c. 1594 Thomas, 1st Viscount Fairfax of Emley, 1574 + 1636. Table XVI.

Dorothy Constable, +1632. = Roger Lawson, of Burgh, +1623, v.p. Table XVIII.

Hon. Catherine Constable, liv. 1653. = William Middleton, of Stockeld, +1658. (119)

Hon. Margaret Constable, liv. unm. 1659.

Catherine Eure, of Bradley, suo jure de jure 12th Lady Scrope, liv. 1631. = Hon. Sir William Bowes, of Bradley, 1566 + 1639.

Mary Forcer, +1669. = Sir William Eure, of Elvet, de jure 14th Lord Scrope, 1608 + liv. 1666.

John, 2nd Viscount Dunbar, 1615 + c. 1667. = c. 1606 Hon. Mary Brudenell. (118)

Thomas Eure, de jure 13th Lord Scrope, +1643.

Peter Eure, de jure 15th Lord Scrope, 1654 + 1669.

Mary Eure, de jure 16th Lady Scrope, c. 1661 +. = Michael Johnson, of Twyzell House, co. Durham, +1714. (116)

14

TABLE XIV

Catherine Constable, (1) = Thomas, 1st Viscount = (2) Elizabeth Gerard.
1579 + 1645.   Fairfax, of Emley,
See Table XVIII.   1574 + 1636.

Thomas, and Viscount Fairfax, c. 1604 + 1641. = Alathea Howard, + 1677.

Hon. Henry Fairfax, + 1650. = Frances Barker.

Hon. William Fairfax, of Lythe, co. York. = Mary Cholmley.

Hon. Nicholas Fairfax, + 1657. = Isabel Bickwith.

Hon. Jordan Fairfax, + 1668.

Hon. John Fairfax, + 1634.

Hon. Mary Fairfax, + 1635. = Sir Thomas Laton, of Saxehowe, 1597 + 1651. See Table XV.

Hon. Catherine Fairfax, + 1666. = (1) Robert Stapylton, of Wighill, + 1634. (2) Sir Matthew Boynton, 1st Bt., + 1647. (3) Sir Arthur Ingram, of Temple Newsham, + 1655. (4) William Wickham.

Hon. Jane Fairfax. = Cuthbert Morley.

Hon. Dorothy Fairfax. = (1) John Ingram. (2) Sir Thomas Norcliffe. See Table XVIII.

William, (1) = Elizabeth Smith, + 1692.
3rd Viscount Fairfax, 1630 + 1648.

Thomas, 4th Viscount Fairfax, + 1651, unm.

Hon. Alathea Fairfax, da. and h. = William, 3rd Lord Widdrington, + 1695. c. 1677 (120)

Charles, 5th Viscount Fairfax, + 1711. = Abigail Yates.

Hon. Nicholas Fairfax. = Elizabeth Chaytor, née Davison.

Hon. Philip Fairfax.

Hon. Mary Fairfax.

Hon. Catherine Fairfax, + 1715. = George Methuin, of Methuin. (122)

Frances Fairfax. = Henry Fairfax, of Hurst, co. Berks. (1) = Browne. 1697

John Fairfax.

Charles Gregory, 9th Viscount Fairfax, + 1772.

William, 8th Viscount Fairfax, + 1738.

Alathea Fairfax, da. and in her issue (1793) h. = Ralph Pigott, of Whitton. (127)

Charles 6th Viscount Fairfax, + 1715.

Nicholas Fairfax, + 1702. = Mary Weld.

Charles 7th Viscount Fairfax, + 1719, unm.

Alathea Fairfax. = John Forster. (121)

David, 9th Earl of Buchan, 1672 + 1745. = Frances Fairfax, da. and h. + 1719. (1) 1697

Henry David, 10th Earl of Buchan, 1710 + 1767. = Agnes Steuart, + 1778. 1739

Lady Frances Erskine, 1700 + 1774. = Col. James Gardiner, + 1745. 1726 (126)

Lady Katherine Erskine, 1697 + 1733. = Hon. William Fraser, of Fraserfield, M.P., 1691 + 1727. 1724

William Fraser, of Fraserfield, 1725 + 1788. = Rachel Kennedy, + 1800. 1752 (125)

David Steuart, 11th Earl of Buchan, 1742 + 1829, s.p.

Hon. Henry Erskine, M.P., 1746 + 1817. = (1) Christian Fullerton, c. 1754 + 1804. 1772 (123)

Thomas, 1st Lord Erskine, 1750 + 1823, 1818. = (1) Frances Moore + 1805. (2) Sarah Buck, + 1825. 1770 (124)

15

TABLE XV

Hon. Mary Fairfax, *c.* 1615 = Sir Thomas Layton or Laton, (1)
+1656. of Laton and Sexhow, co. York,
See Table XVII. 1597 + 1651.

- David Laton, +1632.
- Charles Laton, 1635 + 1636.
- Thomas Laton, of Sexhow, 1621 + 1659. *s.p.* = Anne Pudsey.
- Sir Robert Laton, of East Laton and Sexhow. + = Anne [——], (821)
- Bryan Laton, of East Laton in 1671. = [——], (829)
- Mary Laton. = Sir Henry Foulis, 1st Bt., +1643.
- Elizabeth Laton, 1618 + 1616.
- Catharine Laton, 1618 + . = John Eden, of Windleston, co. Durham. *Table XVI.*
- E—— Laton, +1633.
- Margaret Laton. = William Layton, of Delamayne, 1624 + *circ.* 1664. (151) *n*
- Anne Laton, *s.p.*

Sir David Foulis, 3rd Bt., 1665 + 1694. = Katherine Watkins, 1631 + 1717.

Mary Foulis, (2) +1694. 1660 = Robert Shafto, of Benwell, Northumberland, 1626 + 1668. (139)

Catherine Foulis, (2) 1637 + 1704. = Sir Ralph Cole, of Brancepeth, 2nd Bt., M.P., +1704. *Issue aft. ext.* 1720.

Sir William Foulis, 4th Bt., 1659 + 1741. 1688 = Anne Laurence, +1690.

Honor Foulis, 1663 + 1755.

William Chaloner, of Guisboro, 1655 + 1715. 1682 = Mary Foulis.

Mary Foulis = William Turner, of Stainsby. (138)

Catherine Foulis, +1745. = John Rudd, of Durham, +1733.

Apr. s.p.

Sir William Foulis, 5th Bt., c. 16.0 + 1756. 1721 = Hon. Mildred Dawnay, +1780. (130)

Edward Chaloner of Guisboro', +1717. = Anne Bowes.

John Chaloner, *liv.* 1743.

Rev. William Chaloner, 1687 + = Anne Hodgson. 1724 (132)

Catherine Chaloner. = G—— Melthorp, of York. (133)

Honor Chaloner, c. 1696 + 1778. = Rev Thomas Lamplugh, Canon Resid. of York, +1747.

Cordelia Chaloner. = Richard Graham, of Whitewell, co. York. 1732 (137)

William Chaloner, of Guisboro, +1756. = Mary Finny. (131)

Katherine Lamplugh, da. and co-h. +1804. 1754 = Rev. Godfrey Wolley, 1722 + 1788. (134)

Anne Lamplugh, da. and co-h. 1759 = John Raper, of Lotherton. (135)

Jane Lamplugh. = Samuel Pawson, of York. (136)

TABLE XVI

Catherine Laton,[1] = John Eden, of Windleston and West Auckland, co. Durham, +1675.
1618+c. 1686. *See Table XV*.

Sir Robert Eden, 1st Bt, 1672, M.P., +1720. = Margaret Lambton, +1730.

John Eden, of Newcastle, Merchant. = Elizabeth Hendmarsh. (149)

Rev. Laton Eden, Rector of Hartbourne, Northumberland. = —— Johnson. (150)

Sir John Eden, 2nd Bt, +1728. = Catherine Shafto. (1715)

Catherine Eden.

Elizabeth Eden. = Matthew Whitfield, of Whitfield, co. Northumberland. (147)

Anne Eden.

Hannah Eden. = James Mickleton, co. Durham. (148)

Sir Robert Eden, 3rd Bt, +1755. = Mary Davison, +1794. (1739)

Sir John Eden, 4th Bt, 1740+1812. = (2) Dorothea Johnson, +1792. (1767) (140)

Sir Robert Eden, 1st Bt, Gov. of Maryland, 1741+1784. = Hon. Caroline Calvert, +a. 1803. (1763) (141)

William, 1st Lord Auckland, +1814. = Eleanor Elliott, 1758+1818. (1776) (142)

Thomas Eden, +1805. = Mariana Jones. (1783) (143)

Morton, 1st Lord Henley, 1758+1830. = Lady Elizabeth Henley, +1821. (1783) (144)

Dulcibella Eden. = Matthew Bell, of Woolsington, +1811. (1767) (145)

Catherine (2) Eden. = Most Rev. John Moore, Archbishop of Canterbury, 1730+1805. (1770) (146)

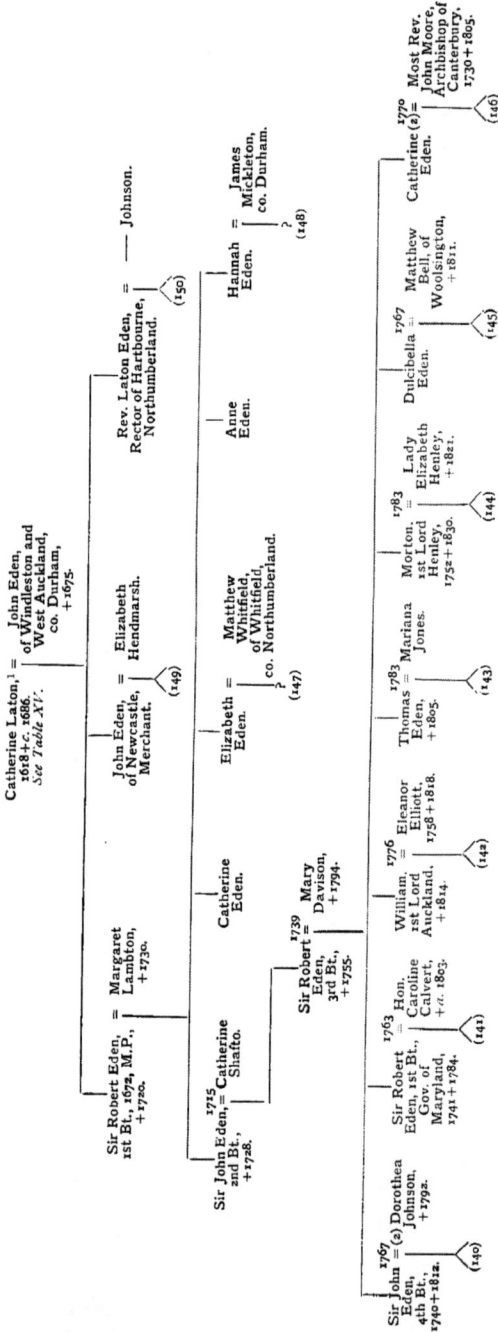

[1] Pedigree in "Herald's College." The Harl. MS. 2118, however, makes Catherine m. Thomas ——, ar., and gives her sister Margaret as wife of John Eden

TABLE XVII

Hon. Dorothy Fairfax, (2) = (1) John Ingram,
+1686.   +s.p.
See Table XIV.   =(2) Sir Thomas Norcliffe,
        of Langton,
        +1670.

Sir Thomas Norcliffe, = 1670 Frances *Vanbuear*,
of Langton,   1654 + 1731.
1641 + c. 1684.
(154)

Dorothy Norcliffe, = 1660 William Grimston,
1643 + 1673.   of Grimston Garth,
        1640 + 1711.

Frances = Nicholas Richards,
Norcliffe.   of Westminster.
(160)

Antonia = 1675 John Hatfeild,
Norcliffe,   of Laughton,
+ 1707.   co. York,
       1635 + 1710.

Elizabeth = 1714 Henry
Hatfeild,   Marshall, of
1681 + 1744.   Newton Kyme,
        co. Yorks,
        c. 1683 + 1760.

Dorothy = William
Hatfeild.   Woodhouse,
      of Reresby,
      co. Leicester.
(158)

Thomas = [——].
Hatfeild,
of
London.

William = 1760 Susanna Hatfeild,
Marshall, of   *née* Hatfeild,
Newton Kyme,   + 1793.
1718 + 1775.
(159)

Mary = 1698 John
Riche,   Hatfeild,
1681 + 1742.   of
      Laughton,
      1676 + 1751.
(157)

Antonia = E. Wilmot,
Hatfeild,   of Duffield.
da. and h.
(158)

Alathea = 1695 Benjamin
Grimston,   Laughton,
1672 +   of New Hill,
      co. Yorks,
      1663 +
      Appendicits s.p.

Anne = Thomas
Grimston,   Ryder.
1669 +
(156)

Dorothy = 1684 Nathaniel
Grimston,   Gooch, of
1663 + 1700.   Hull,
      + 1705.
(156)

Thomas = Dorothy
Grimston,   Legard,
of Grimston Garth,   + 1729.
1665 + 1737.

Thomas = 1722 Jane Close.
Grimston,
of Grimston
Garth,
1702 + 1751.

John = 1753 *Jane Legard*,
Grimston,   1734 + 1758.
of Grimston
Garth,
1725 + 1780.
(155)

18

TABLE XVIII

Dorothy Constable, = Roger Lawson,   Anne Lawson = Henry Widdrington,
+ 1632   of Hilton,   of Bentland
Se. Table XIII   + 1623,   co Northumberland
                     r. f.   (1672)

James Lawson = [—]   Dorothy = William Blakiston,
              (1666)   Lawson,   of Sheldrow,
                          + 1712   co Durham,
Frances Lawson   1616+

Henry Lawson, = Anne Hodgson
of Brough,
+ c. 1696

Sir John Lawson, = Katherine   Nicholas Blakiston   Ralph Blakiston, = Mary   William Blakiston,   Henry Blakiston,   Anne Blakiston,   Jane Blakiston,
of Brough,   Howard   of Sheldrow,   of   Sampson   of Sheldrow,   + 1673   1646 + 1662   + c. 1704
1st Bt,   + 1668   1648 + 1733   Chester-le-Street,   + 1737
1665 + 1698   + 1704   (1651)

Henry Lawson, = Catherine
of Brough,   Fenwick
+ 1644

Sir Henry = Elizabeth   Anne Swinburne, = Nicholas Thornton,
Lawson,   Knightley   *living* 1708   of Witton,
2nd Bt,   + 1735   co Northumberland,
c. 1663 + 1726 (1641)   + 1700
                                                   (1653)

Isabel = Sir John
Lawson   Swinburne
da and h 1st Bt
        + 1706

Sir William Swinburne, = Mary Englefield   Thomas Swinburne, = Mary Thornton,
2nd Bt,   (1697)   1705+   *née* Meaburne,
+ 1716   + 1772
                                                                     (1662)

Sir John Swinburne, = Mary Bedingfeld,
3rd Bt,   + 1761
1698 + 1745 (1721) (1611)

19

TABLE XIX

Hon. Elizabeth Scrope, = Thomas Pudsey, of Bolton,
+ 1620.   in Craven and Barforth,
See Table XVIII.   1531 + 1576.

Thomas Meynell, = Winifred Pudsey, 1570 + 1604.

Anne Meynell. = Thomas Grange, of Harlsey, co. York. (180)

Margaret Pudsey, 1560 + . = Robert Trotter, of Skelton Castle, *liv.* 1623.

Mary Meynell. = George Pole, of Spinkhill. (180)

Mary Twaites, + 1669. = Anthony Meynell, of Kilvington, 1594 + 1669.

George Nevill. = Elizabeth Pudsey. ~ (178)

Thomas Pudsey, = [——], of Hackforth, York, 1567 + 1620. (175)

George Trotter, of Skelton, + 1647. = (2) Mary Boyce.

Hugh Trotter. | George Trotter. | Mary Trotter. = John Fulthorpe, of Tunstall, co. Durham. (178)

Margaret Trotter. ~ = George Lawson. (178)

Hannah Trotter. ~ = Charles Penott. (178)

Ambrose Pudsey, of High Close, Stanwich, and Picton, York, 1565 + 1623.
= (1) Anne Dent, *who* + 1612.
= (2) Jane Wilkinson.

²Catherine Pudsey (174) = Robert Place, of Picton, co. York.

Sir Henry Trotter, of Skelton Castle, + 1625. = Catherine Witham.

Anne Pudsey, 1655 + . = Thomas Pudsey, of Blackwell and Picton, 1654 + 1723. = Lucy [——], + 1724.

Henry Pudsey, 1561 + .

¹Elizabeth Pudsey, *liv.* 1623. | Mary Salvin, 1619 + 1706. = ² Michael Pudsey, of Lawfield, 1619 + 1698.

Edward Trotter, of Skelton, c. 1637 + 1708. = (1) Mary Lowther.
= (2) William Bowen, of Bridlington, 1654 + . Catherine Trotter.

Mary Trotter, da. and co-h.

William Pudsey, of Bolton, 1556 + 1669. = (1) Elizabeth Roxby, + 1601. = (2) [——].

Anne Pudsey. = (1) Walter Strickland. = (2) Thomas Layton. *s.p.*

Anne Pudsey, 1690 + . | William Hullock, of Barnard Castle, Merchant.

Mary Pudsey, 1690 + . = William Hullock, 1708 +

Michael Pudsey, of Staindrop, Merchant, 1680 + 1749. = [——], + 1729. *Issue extinct* 1710.

John Trotter, c. 1659 + 1701, *v.p.* = Elizabeth Lawson.

Catherine Trotter, da. and co-h. = Joseph Hall, of Durham, + 1733. (176)

¹Stephen, 1610 + . | William, 1615 + . | Ralph, 1616 + | Valentine, 1618 + | ¹Mary, *liv.* 1620. | Isabel, 1592 + 16—. | Trothe, 1594 + 16—. | Elizabeth, *liv.* 1620. | ²Anne, 1610 + . | Jane, 1612 + .
= (1) Rosamund Ramsden, + 1619. = (2) Bridget Pennington, *a "virtuous" Lady Laton,* + 1664.

Ambrose Pudsey, of Bolton, 1594 + *liv.* 1620. (172)

Roger Talbot. = Elizabeth Pudsey. (172)

Sir Hoverden Walker, Rear-Adm., R.N., + 1728. = Jane Pudsey, + *s.p. or s.p.s.*

Ambrose Pudsey, of Bolton, + 1680. = Jane Davison, + 1720.

Elizabeth Pudsey. = John Webb (? Weld). ~ (172)

Jane Pudsey, 1683 + 1708. = (1) William Dawson, of Langcliffe, 1675 + 1762. (171)

Thomas Pudsey, 1691 + .

Ambrose Pudsey, of Leeds, in 1714. = Elizabeth Marsden, + 1699.

TABLE XX

Lady Maud Clifford. = John, 3rd Lord Conyers, +1557.
See Table VIII.

¹ Hon. Elizabeth Conyers, 2nd da., and in her issue (1644) h. = Thomas Darcy, +1605.

Conyers, 4th Lord Conyers, &c., c. 1571 + 1654. = Dorothy Belasyse +1663.

Conyers, 1st Earl of Holderness, 1599 + 1689. *a.* 1619 = Grace Rokeby, + 1654. (182)

Hon. Sir William Darcy. = Dorothy Selby. (183)

Hon. Henry Darcy, of Newpark, co. York. = Mary Scrope.

Hon. Thomas Darcy, of Winkborne.

Hon. James Darcy, of Sedbury Park, M.P., +1621. = Isabel Wyvill. (185)

Hon. Barbara Darcy, 1600 + 1696. 1617 = Matthew Hutton, of Marske, 1597 + 16.. (186)

Hon. Ursula Darcy. = John Stillington, of Kelfield, co. York, + 1658. (187)

Hon. Margaret Darcy. = Sir Thomas Harrison. (188)

Hon. Dorothy Darcy. = John Dalton, of Hawkswell, co. York, 1603 + 1644. (189)

Hon. Grace Darcy, 1616 + 1680. (1) 1639 = George Best, of Middleton, Quernhow. (2) = Sir Francis Molineux, 1613 + 1639, of Mansfield, co. Notts, + 1666.

Hon. Mary Darcy. = Acton Burnell, of Winkburn Hall, co. Notts. (195)

Henry Darcy, of Colborn and Sedbury. 1705 = Katherine Goddard.

Henry Best, of Middleton Quernhow, +1674. = Katherine Danby, 1637 + 1688.

Darcy Molineux, H.S. co. Notts, 1652 + 1716. 1675 = Elizabeth Bassett.

Francis Molineux, of St. Gregory, by St. Paul, London. = Mary Tancred.

Dorothy Molineux. = Lucius Henry, 6th Viscount Falkland, 1687 + 1730. (194)

Maria Catherine Darcy, da. and h., + 1747. 1738 = Sir Robert Hildyard, 3rd Bt., + 1781. (184)

Katherine Best, da. and event. h., 1683. *a.* 1683 = Edward Goddard, of Leatherhead, co. Surrey, 1683. (190)

William Molineux, Mayor of Doncaster, 1681 + 1756. = Katherine Squire, *née* Shepherd. (191)

John Molineux, of Mansfield, + 1754. = Mary Birch, + 1735. (192)

Dorothy (1) Molineux, da. and co-h., + 1722. 1704 =

Lucy. Elizabeth. Mary. Dorothy. Grace. Theodosia. Isabel.

Lucius Charles, 7th Viscount Falkland, + 1785. 1734 (1) Jane, Lady Villiers, *née* Butler, + 1751. (193)

= Tobet Hodgson. (195)

21

TABLE XXI

Lady Eleanor Percy, = Edward, 3rd Duke of Buckingham, K.G., +1590. 1478 +1521. *See Table II.*

Henry, 1518 = Ursula Pole (grandda. of George, Duke of Clarence, K.G.), +1570. Lord Stafford, 1501 +1563. (198)

Lady Elizabeth (2) = Thomas, 3rd Duke of Norfolk, K.G., 1473 +1554. Stafford. c. 1513 *Table XVI.*

Lady Katherine = Ralph, 4th Earl of Westmorland, 1495 +1549. Stafford, c. 1543 1555. *Table XVI.*

Lady Mary (3) = George, 3rd Lord Abergavenny, K.G., +1535. Stafford. *Table XXVI.*

Thomas, 1st Viscount = (1) Hon. Elizabeth Marney, c. 1565. Bindon, c. 1520 +1582. = (2) Gertrude Lyte. *Table XXII.*

Lady Mary Howard, c. 1533 = Henry, Duke of Richmond +1557. (nat. son of Henry VIII.), c. 1519 +1536, *s.p.*

Henry, Earl of 1532 = Lady Frances Surrey, K.G., Vere, 1517 +1547. +1577.

Henry, 1st Earl of Northampton, K.G., +1614, *s.p.*

Thomas, 4th Duke 1556 (1) Lady Mary Fitzalan, +1557. of Norfolk, K.G., 1536 +1572. 1557 (2) Hon. Margaret Audley, +1564.

Lady Jane n. 1564 Charles, Howard, 6th Earl of +1593. Westmorland, +1601. (256)

1577 Hon. Elizabeth Dacre. = 2 Lord William Howard, +1640. *Table XXVII.*

2 Lady Margaret Howard, +1591. 1580 (1) Robert, Earl of Dorset, +1609. (255)

Catherine Rich, *née* Knevet. c. 1583 2 Thomas, 1st Earl of Suffolk, K.G., 1561 +1626. 1614 Lady Elizabeth Cecil, 1590 +1672. (254)

Hon. Anne Dacre. 1571 1 Philip, Earl of Arundel, def. 1557 +1595.

(A) 1591 Lady Elizabeth Home, +1633. Theophilus, 2nd Earl of Suffolk, K.G., 1584 +1640.

(66) 1606 Lady Alathea Talbot, *suo jure* Lady Furnival, &c., +1654. Thomas, 21st (14th) Earl of Arundel, K.G., 1585 +1646.

Lady (2) = Henry, 9th Lord Margaret Scrope, of Bolton, Howard, K.G., +1591. 1543 +1590. (260)

Lady Mary Howard.

Henry, 11th Lord = Lady (1) Berkeley, Catherine 1534 +1613. Howard, +1596.

Hon. Catherine Berkeley.

Hon. Joan Berkeley.

Hon. Frances Berkeley, c. 1564 +1595. 1587 Sir George Shirley, 1st Bt., +1622. (259)

Lady (1) Catherine Howard, +1596. = John Zouch, of Codnore, co. Derby. (258)

Hon. Mary Berkeley. = Hon. Sir Thomas Berkeley, K.B. = Hon. Elizabeth Carey.

Elizabeth Stanhope. = George, 12th or 8th Lord Berkeley, K.B., +1658. (B)

Bottom row

Hon. Henry Howard. = Elizabeth Bassett. *Issue extinct.*

Hon. Sir Charles Howard. = Mary Darcy, *née* Fitz. (252)

Hon. Sir Robert Howard, K.B.

Hon. Sir William Howard, K.B.

Edward, 1st Lord Howard, of Escrick, K.B., +1675. = Hon. Mary Butler, +1634. (226)

Lady Elizabeth Howard, 1586 +1658. 1605 William, 1st Earl of Banbury, K.G., 1547 +1632. 1632 Edward, 4th Lord Vaux, 1587 +1661. (227)

Lady Frances Howard, 1589 +1632. 1606 (1) Robert, Earl of Essex, +1646. 1613 (2) Robert Howard, Earl of Somerset, +1645. (228B)

Lady Catherine Howard. 1608 William, 2nd Earl of Salisbury, K.G., c. 1590 +1668. *Table XXV.*

(Genealogical pedigree chart — text oriented in various directions)

Elizabeth Mas-singberd, + 1708. (257) — 1691

George, 1st Earl of Berkeley, c. 1627 + 1698.

~ Richard Brett, of co. Som. (221)

Lady Catherine Boyle, 1653 + 1681.

William, 2nd Earl of Inchiquin, c. 1640 + 1692. (1)

William, 3rd Earl of Inchiquin, c. 1662 + 1719. — 1691

(2) Mary Villiers, + 1753.

Lady Margaret Boyle, + 1683. (1)

Sir Edward Villiers, = (1) (223)

Lady Frances Howard, + 1677. — 1689

1709 — Robert, 19th Earl of Kildare, 1675 + 1744.

Lady Mary O'Brien, 1692 + 1780. (220)

Hon. Henry Boyle, + 1693.

Lady Mary O'Brien.

Thomas Wal-singham, of Scad-bury, co. Kent, + 1691. (222)

Lady Anne Howard. — 1665

Lady Mary Sack-ville, + 1710. (211)

1717 — Robert Sandford of Castlerea. (219)

1760 — Joseph Deane, 3rd Earl of Mayo, + 1794.

Elizabeth Meade, + 1807. (214)

Roger, 2nd Earl of Orrery, 1646 + 1684. (211)

Lady Henrietta O'Brien, 1694 + 1730. (219) — 1730

Mary Jephson. (218)

Hon. James O'Brien, M.P. + 1756. (218)

John, 2nd Earl of Mayo, s.p.

Lady Margaret Howard, 1623 + 1689.

Roger, 1st Earl of Orrery, 1621 + 1679. — 1640

Margaret = Rt. Hon. Joseph Deane, Baron of the Exchequer, + 1715.

Margaret Boyle, + 1717.

William, 4th Earl of Inchiquin, + 1777. (217)

Anne, suo jure Countess of Orkney, s.s. (217) — 1720 (1)

George FitzGerald, of Turlough, + 1782. (202)

Hon. Mary Hervey, 1726 + 1815.

Algernon, 10th Earl of Northumberland, K.G. 1602 + 1668. (212) — 1642 (2)

Lady Elizabeth Howard, + 1705. (209)

George, 8th Lord Aubigny, + 1650. (209)

James, 1st Earl of Newburgh, + 1642. (1) (1) (2) — 1670

Col. John Pitt. (208)

Lady Diana Howard, + 1710.

Henrietta Hobart, c. 1681 + 1767. (208) — 1706

Charles, 9th Earl of Suffolk, 1675 + 1733.

William :: = (1) Harriet Boyle, + 1746. (213) — 1711 — 1726

Martha Beaufoy Garth. (213)

William = Martha Beaufoy Garth.

Henry, 1st Earl of Shannon, 1706 + 1764. (212) — 1726 (2)

Lady Harriet Boyle, + 1746.

John FitzGerald, M.P. + 1741. (216)

Margaret Deane, da. and co-h. (216)

Constantine, 1st Lord Mulgrave, 1744 + 1775. (201) — 1743

Hon. Lepell Hervey, 1723 + 1780. (201)

John, 1st Lord Lisle, + 1781. (215) — 1735 (1)

Catherine Deane, da. and co-h. (215)

John, 1st Earl of Mayo, c. 1705 + 1790. — 1725

Mary Deane, da. and co-h. + 1774.

Edward, 8th Earl of Suffolk, c. 1671 + 1731, unm.

Henry, 10th Earl of Suffolk, 1706 + 1745, s.p.

Charles William, 7th Earl of Suffolk, 1693 + 1722, s.p.

Lady Auberie Anne Penelope O'Brien, c. 1670 + ?. (1) — 1691

Henry, 6th Earl of Suffolk, c. 1670 + ?.

Sir Robert Smyth, 2nd Bt. c. 1709 + 1783. (206)

Lady Louisa Caroline Isabella Hervey, 1715 + 1770. (206) — 1731

Frederick Augustus, 4th Earl of Bristol, B. of Derry, 1730 + 1803.

Elizabeth Davers, + 1800. (200) — 1752

Dorothy Pitfield, née Ashley, + 1761. (205)

Hon. Felton Hervey, M.P. 1712 + 1773. (205)

Catherine Aston, of Aston. — 1730

Rev. the Hon. Henry Hervey, afterwards Aston, 1700 + 17—. (203)

Anne Coghlan, + 1761. — 1744

Hon. Thomas Hervey, M.P. 1699 + 1775. (203)

Augustus John, 3rd Earl of Bristol, 1724 + 1779, unm.

Mary Lepell, + 1768. — 1720

John, Lord Hervey, 1696 + 1743, v.p.

George William, 2nd Earl of Bristol, 1721 + 1775, unm.

Elizabeth Felton, co-h. + 1741.

John, 1st Earl of Bristol, 1665 + 1751. — 1695

James, 3rd Earl of Suffolk, 1620 + 1689. (207)

George, 4th Earl of Suffolk, c. 1625 + 1691. (207)

Catherine Alleyne. = (1) — 1683

Henry, 5th Earl of Suffolk, 1627 + 1709. — 1691

Hon. Mary Stuart, + a. 1691.

Lady Susan Rich. (1) — 1640

Barbara, Lady Wentworth, previously Wenman, née Villiers. (2) — 1649

Lady Elizabeth Howard, co-h. to B. of Howard de Walden, 1656 + 1681. — 1681

Sir Thomas Felton, 4th Bt., M.P. + 1709.

Edward, Lord Griffin, of Braybrooke, c. 1630 + 1710. — 1692

1 Lady Essex Howard, co-h. to B. of Howard de Walden, + 1721. *Issue ext.* — 1691

George William, 2nd Earl of Bristol, 1721 + 1775, unm.

23

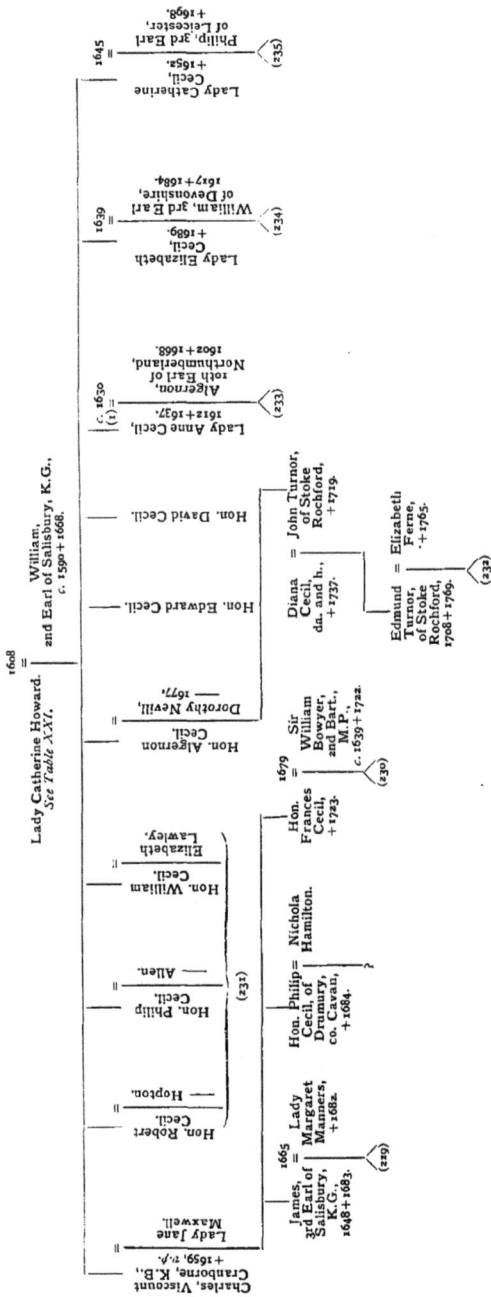

TABLE XXII

William, 2nd Earl of Salisbury, K.G., c. 1590 † 1668. = Lady Catherine Howard. See Table XXI. (1608)

Charles, Viscount Cranborne, K.B., † 1659, v.p. = Lady Jane Maxwell.

James, 3rd Earl of Salisbury, K.G., 1648 † 1683. (229) = Lady Margaret Manners, † 1682. (1665)

Hon. Robert Cecil. = — Hopton.

Hon. Philip Cecil. = — Allen. (231)

Hon. Philip Cecil, of Drumury, co. Cavan, † 1684. = Nichola Hamilton.

Hon. William Cecil. = Elizabeth Lawley.

Hon. Frances Cecil, † 1723. = Sir William Bowyer, 2nd Bart., M.P., c. 1639 † 1722. (230) (1679)

Hon. Algernon Cecil. = Dorothy Nevill, 1677.

Hon. Edward Cecil.

Hon. David Cecil.

Diana Cecil, da. and h., † 1737. = John Turnor, of Stoke Rochford, † 1719.

Edmund Turnor, of Stoke Rochford, 1708 † 1769. = Elizabeth Ferne, † 1765. (232)

Lady Anne Cecil, 1612 † 1637. = (1) Algernon, 10th Earl of Northumberland, 1602 † 1668. (c. 1629) (233)

Lady Elizabeth Cecil, † 1689. = William, 3rd Earl of Devonshire, 1617 † 1684. (1639) (234)

Lady Catherine Cecil, † 1652. = Philip, 3rd Earl of Leicester, † 1698. (1645) (235)

24

Lord William Howard [1577] = Hon. Elizabeth Dacre.
(Belted Will Howard) +1640.
See Table XXVI.

Margaret (1) Howard, + a. 1640. [1620] = Sir Thomas Cotton, 2nd Bt., M.P., 1594 + 1662.

Frances Cotton.

Elizabeth = Sir Henry Bedingfeld, of Oxburgh, co. Norfolk. Howard.
One son d.s.p. 2 das.

Mary = Sir John Wintour, of Lydney, co. Glouc. Howard. (445)

Elizabeth Eure. (244)

Thomas Howard.

Dorothy Widdrington.

Sir Charles Howard. (243)

Alathea = Thomas, 2nd Viscount Fairfax, Howard. c. 1604 + 1641. (241)

Sir Francis Howard, of Corby, co. Cumberland = (1) Margaret Preston, + 1625. (2) Mary Widdrington, +1672. 1588 + 1660. (242)

[Elizabeth = Bartholomew Fromond, of Cheam, co. Surrey.] Howard.

Margaret Caryl. = Sir Philip Howard, + s.p.

Sir William Howard = Hon. Mary Eure.

Lucy Cotton, + 1684. = Sir Philip Wodehouse, 1st Bt., M.P., 1608 + 1681.

Sir John Cotton, 3rd Bt., M.P., 1621 + 1703. = (1) Dorothy Anderson, 1668 (2) Elizabeth Honywood, 1697 + 1702. (246)

Margaret Wodehouse. = Thomas Savage, of Elmley Castle. (254)

Anne Wodehouse, + 1727. [1686] = Sir Nicholas l'Estrange, 4th Bt., M.P., 1661 + 1724.

Lucy l'Estrange, da. and in her issue co-h., 1699 + 1739. [1721] = Sir Jacob Astley, 3rd Bt., 1692 + 1760. (450)

Blanch Wodehouse. [1661] = Sir Jacob Astley, 3rd Bt., M.P., c. 1639 + 1729. (253)

Armine l'Estrange, da. and co-h., + 1768. = Nicholas Styleman, of Snettisham, + 1746. (249)

Anne Samwell, née Strutt. = John Wodehouse, of Feltwell. (252)

(1) Hon. Mary Fermour, + 1729. = Sir John Wodehouse, 4th Bt., M.P., 1669 + 1754.

Sir Henry l'Estrange, 6th Bt., + 1760. s.p.

(1) Mercy Gaybon, née Parker. = Edmond Wodehouse, of E. Lexham, co. Norfolk. (251)

Anne Downing.

Sir Thomas l'Estrange, 5th Bt., 1689 + 1751. s.p.

Anne Armine. = Sir Thomas Wodehouse, + 1671, s.p.

Mary [1705] Thomas Downing. Barnardiston, da. and in her issue co-h. of Bury. (240)

Sir Charles Mordaunt, 6th Bt., + 1778. (248)

c. 1656 = Sir George Downing, 1st Bt., M.P., c. 1623 + 1684. Frances Howard, + 1683.

Sophia (2) [1739] Wodehouse, + 1738.

John Cotton, 1650 + 1681. = Frances Downing, da. and in her issue co-h. (239)

c. 1660 = Sir John Lawson, 1st Bt., + 1698. Catherine Howard, + 1668. (238)

Letitia Bacon, + 1758. (247)

Sir Jonathan Atkins, Governor of Jersey, + 1702. = Mary Howard, + 1703. (237)

Sarah Garrard. = Charles Downing, c. 1660 + 1740.

1738 = Sir Armine Wodehouse, 5th Bt., M.P., 14 + 1777.

Charles, c. 1696. Downing.

Hon. Anne Howard, + 1703. = Charles, 1st Earl of Carlisle, 1629 + 1685. (236)

1683 = Lady Catherine Cecil, + 1688. Sir George Downing, 2nd Bt., 1656 + 1711.

Sir Jacob Garrard Downing, 4th Bt., c. 1700 + 1764, s.p.

Sir George Downing, 3rd Bt., K.B., M.P., c. 1685 + 1749, s.p.

25

D

TABLE XXIV

Thomas, 1st Viscount Bindon, = (1) Hon. Elizabeth Marney,
 c. 1542;
 c. 1530 + 1582. = *c.* 1510 + *a.* 1565.
 See Table XXV. = (2) Gertrude Lyte.

1 Henry, = Frances
2nd Viscount Meautys.
Bindon,
c. 1542 + 1591.

1 Thomas,
3rd Viscount
Bindon, K.G.,
+ 1610/1, *s.p.*

1 Hon. Francis
Howard.

† *Certainly s.p.m. and apparently s.p.*

1 Hon. Giles
Howard.

" Hon. Charles =
Howard,
alias Lyte.

[——].

Hon. Grace = John Horsey,
Howard. of Clifton,
 co. Dorset.
 (269)

Hon. Douglas (1) = Sir Arthur Gorges,
Howard, da. and of Chelsea,
co-h., + 1572. + 1625.
 (261)

Catherine Howard, (2) = Sir Thomas
eld. da. and co-h., Thynne,
+ 1650. of Longleat.

Hon. Anne = Sir William Thornhurst,
Howard, of Agline Court, co. Kent,
da. and co-h. 1575 + 1606.
 (260)

Sir Henry Frederick = Hon. Mary
Thynne, 1st Bt., Coventry.
1615 + 1680.

Elizabeth = Sir Thomas Nott,
Thynne. of Richmond,
 co. Surrey.
 (268)

Thomas, = Lady
1st Viscount Frances
Weymouth, Finch,
1640 + 1714. + 1712.
 (262)

Henry Frederick = Dorothy
Thynne, Clerk to Philips.
Privy Council,
+ 1705.

Catherine = John,
Thynne, 1st Viscount
+ *a.* 1713. Lonsdale,
 1628 + 1700.

Thomas (1) = *Lady Mary Villiers*,
Thynne, 1709
+ 1710. + 1735.
 (263)

John,
Thynne.

Dorothy = John,
Thynne, 1st Lord Chedworth,
1692 + 1717. + 1742.

Mary
Thynne.
 (264)

Richard,
2nd Viscount
Lonsdale,
+ 1713,
s.p.

Henry,
3rd Viscount
Lonsdale,
+ 1751,
s.p.

Hon. Mary = Sir John
Lowther, Wentworth.
da. and co-h.
 (265)

Hon.
Elizabeth
Lowther,
da. and co-h.,
+ 1764.

Sir William = 1696
Ramsden,
2nd Bt.,
1672 + 1736.
 (266)

Hon. = Sir Joseph
Margaret Pennington,
Lowther, 2nd Bt.,
da. and + 1744.
co-h.,
+ 1738. 1706
 (267)

26

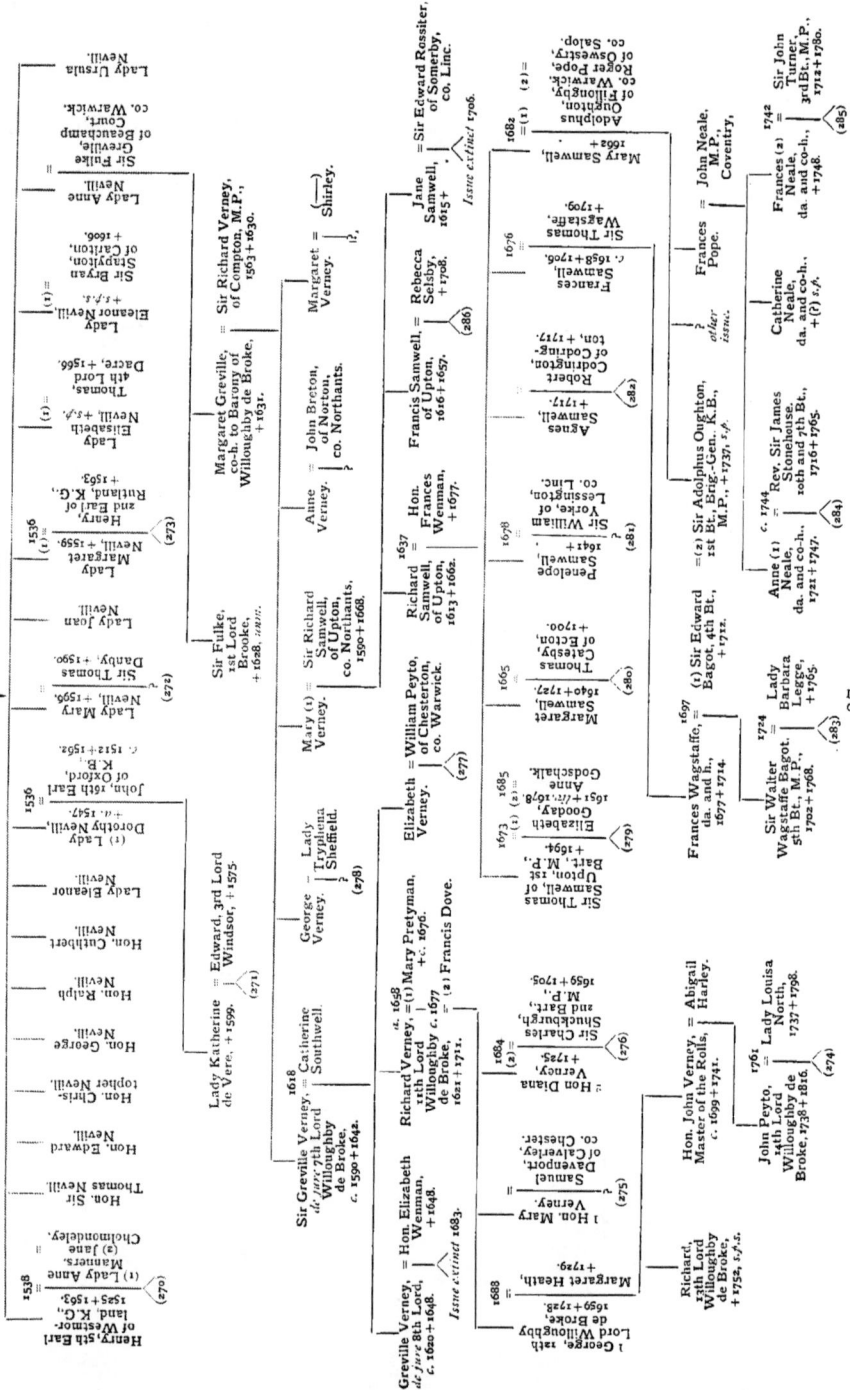

Ralph, 4th Earl of Westmorland, c. 1495 + 1549. = Lady Katherine Stafford, + 1555. *See Table XXXI.*

- Lady Ursula Nevill.
- Lady Anne Nevill. = Sir Fulke Greville, of Beauchamp Court, co. Warwick.
- Lady Eleanor Nevill, (1) + s.p.s. = Sir Bryan Stapylton, of Carlton, + 1606.
- Lady Elisabeth Nevill, + s.p. (1) = Thomas, 4th Lord Dacre, + 1566. (1)
- Lady Margaret Nevill, + 1559. = Henry, 2nd Earl of Rutland, K.G., + 1563. (1) 1536
- Lady Joan Nevill = Sir Thomas Danby, + 1590.
- Lady Mary Nevill, + 1596. (1) = John, 16th Earl of Oxford, K.B., c. 1512 + 1562. 1536
- Lady Dorothy Nevill (1) + d. 1547.
- Lady Eleanor Nevill.
- Hon. Cuthbert Nevill.
- Hon. Ralph Nevill.
- Hon. George Nevill.
- Hon. Christopher Nevill.
- Hon. Edward Nevill.
- Sir Thomas Nevill.
- Henry, 5th Earl of Westmorland, K.G., c. 1602 + 1648. = (1) Lady Anne Manners, 1525 + 1563. 1538 = (2) Jane Cholmondeley. (270)

Margaret Greville, co-h. to Barony of Willoughby de Broke, + 1631. = Sir Richard Verney, of Compton, M.P., 1563 + 1630. (273)

- Sir Fulke, 1st Lord Brooke, + 1628. *unm.*
- Margaret Verney. = ?, 2. ... Shirley. (272)
- Lady Katherine de Vere, + 1599. = Edward, 3rd Lord Windsor, + 1575. (271)
- Sir Greville Verney, *de jure* 7th Lord Willoughby de Broke, c. 1590 + 1642. = Catherine Southwell. 1618
- George Verney. = Lady Tryphena Sheffield. 2. (278)
- Mary (1) = Sir Richard Samwell, of Upton, co. Northants. 1590 + 1668. = Mary Verney.
- Anne Verney. = John Breton, of Norton, co. Northants. ?
- Elizabeth Verney. = William Peyto, of Chesterton, co. Warwick. (277)
- Richard Samwell, of Upton, 1613 + 1662. 1637 = Hon. Frances Wenman, + 1677.
- Jane Samwell, 1615 + ... = Sir Edward Rossiter, of Somerby, co. Linc. (2) *Issue extinct 1706.*
- Rebecca Selsby, + 1708. = Francis Samwell, 1664 + 1657. (286)
- Mary Samwell, 1682 + ... = (1) Adolphus Oughton, of Filongley, co. Warwick. = (2) Roger Pope, of Oswestry, co. Salop.

Greville Verney, *de jure* 8th Lord, c. 1602 + 1648. = Hon. Elizabeth Wenman, + 1648. *Issue extinct 1683.* (270)

- Richard Verney, 11th Lord Willoughby de Broke, 1621 + 1711. = (1) Mary Pretyman, d. 1658 + c. 1676. = (2) Francis Dove.
- Anne Godschalk (1) 1673 + ... Elizabeth, 1685 + 1694. (1) = Sir Thomas Samwell, of Upton, 1st Bart., M.P., (279)
- Margaret Samwell, 1640 + 1727. = Thomas Catesby, of Ecton, + 1700. (280)
- Penelope Samwell, + 1641. = Sir William Yorke, of Lessington, co. Linc. (281)
- Agnes Samwell, + 1717.
- Robert Samwell, of Codrington, + 1717. (282)
- Frances Samwell, c. 1658 + 1706. = Sir Thomas Wagstaffe, + 1709. 1676
- Frances Pope.
- Catherine Neale, da. and co-h., + (?) s.p.
- Frances Neale, da. and co-h., + 1748. = John Neale, M.P., Coventry. 1742
- Sir John Turner, 3rd Bt., M.P., 1714 + 1780. (285)

- George, 12th Lord Willoughby de Broke, 1659 + 1728. 1 = Margaret Heath, + 1729. 1688
- 1 Hon. Mary Verney. = Samuel Davenport, of Calverley. (275)
- Sir Charles Shuckburgh, 2nd Bart., M.P., 1659 + 1705. (2) = Hon. Diana Verney, + 1735. 1684 (276)
- Richard, 13th Lord Willoughby de Broke, + 1752, s.p.s.
- John Peyto, 14th Lord Willoughby de Broke, 1738 + 1816. = Lady Louisa North, 1737 + 1798. 1761 (274)
- Hon. John Verney, Master of the Rolls, c. 1699 + 1741. = Abigail Harley.
- Frances Wagstaffe, da. and ..., 1677 + 1714. 1697 = (1) Sir Edward Bagot, 4th Bt., + 1712.
- Sir Walter Wagstaffe Bagot, 5th Bt., 1702 + 1768. = Lady Barbara Legge, + 1765. 1724 (283)
- Anne (1) Neale, da. and co-h., 1721 + 1747. = (2) Sir Adolphus Oughton, 1st Bt., Brig.-Gen. K.B., M.P., + 1737, s.p. = Rev. Sir James Stonehouse, 10th and 7th Bt., 1716 + 1765. 1744 (284)
- Catherine Neale, da. and co-h., + (?) s.p.

TABLE XXVI

Lady Mary (3) = George, 3rd Lord
Stafford.   Abergavenny,
See Table XXVI.   K.G., K.B.,
     +1535.

Hon. Mary Nevill. = Thomas, 9th Lord Dacre, +1541.

Table XXVIII.

Hon. (1) = Sir Warham
Ursula St. Leger,
Nevill. of Ulcomb,
co. Kent,
+1599.

Table XXVII.

Hon. Jane Nevill. = Henry, 1st Lord Montagu. K.G., c. 1492 +1539.
(312)

Hon. William Brooke, ? 10th Lord Cobham, 1527 +1597.

Hon. (1) = Dorothy Nevill, +1559.

Sir John St. Leger, of Annery, co. Devon.

Hon. Catherine Nevill.

Henry, 4th Lord Abergavenny, +1587. = (1) Lady Frances Manners, +1576.
(287)

Frances Brooke, ? da. and h. = (1) Thomas Coppinger, | (2) Edmund Beecher.

Eulalia St. Leger, da. and co-h. = (1) Edmund Tremayne, of Collacombe, s.p.s. +1582. (2) Tristram Arscott, of Annery, +1621. 1576 1583
(306)

Sir Francis Coppinger, 1579 +1626. = Hon. Frances de Burgh.
(311)

William Coode, of Morval, M.P., 1573 +1655. (2) = (2)

John Langford, of Coxworthy, co. Devon. (1) =

Anne Stukeley, *living* 1656.   *Issue extinct.*

Gertrude Stukeley, *living* 1632. = Humphrey Bury, of Colyton, co. Devon, +1631.
(309)

Mary Stukeley, +1632. = Simon Weekes, of Brodhurst, co. Devon, +1626.
(308)

John Stukeley, of Affeton, co. Devon, c. 1551 +1611. = Frances (1) St. Leger, da. and co-h.

Sir Lewis Stukeley or Stucley, of Affeton, Vice-Admiral of Devon and Cornwall, c. 1580 +1620. = (1) Frances Monk.
(305)   B

Mary Granville, +1608. = Arthur Tremayne, of Collacombe. 1586
(299)

Sir Richard Granville, of Stow, +1588. = Mary St. Leger, da. and co-h., +1623.

Bridget Granville, +1647. = (2) Sir Christopher Harris, of Radford, co. Devon, M.P., +1625. (1) Rev. John Weekes, Preb. of Bristol. (2) = (1) 1625
(292)

Sir Bernard Gran-ville, of Stow, 1559 +1636. = Elizabeth Bevill.
A

28

Genealogical chart (rotated). Principal entries:

Robert Dillon = Frances Stucley. (307)

John Courtenay, of Molland = 2 Mary Stucley. (304)

Anna Stucley, + 1623.

Arthur Stucley, living 1611.

Philip Mayow, of Bray, + 1697 = Frances Stucley, 1653. (303)

Scipio Stucley, living 1611.

[——] Luttrell, + 1687 = Honor Stucley, + 1687. (302)

Margery Coode = Lewis Stucley, living 1611. 1627. (306)

Susanna Dennis, + 1692 = Lewis Stucley, + 1687, 1673. (301)

Araminta Weeks = Hugh Stucley, living 1611. 1691. (305)

Elizabeth Sydenham = Sir Thomas Stucley, of Affeton, 1620 + 1663. (300)

Honor Halse, (1)=(2) Elizabeth Coode = John Stucley, of Affeton, + 1638. 1691. (299)

Nicholas Glynn, of Glynn, M.P., c. 1627 + 1697 = Gertrude Denys, da. and event. h., + 1675. (297)

Sir Halswell Tynte, 1st Bt., M.P., + 1702. (294)

Grace c. 1671 = Grace Fortescue, da. and co-h., + 1694.

Mary (2) = Sir William Drake, 4th Bt. M.P., 1659 + 1716. 1705. Mary Prideaux, 4th da., 1658 + 1729, s.p.

Several das.

Roger Prideaux, + s.p.

Colonel Richard Thornhill, + 1656. (2) 1653.

Joan Granville, 1635 + 1708.

Sir Simon Leach. (1) 1691.

Sir Thomas Higgons, M.P., 1624 + 1691. (2)

Bridget Granville, 1699 + 1692. (295)

Anne Prideaux = John Prideaux.

Colonel Robert Fortescue, of Filleigh, 1617 + 1677. (2)

Grace Granville, + 1624. (1)

Sir Peter Prideaux, 3rd Bt, M.P., 1626 + 1705. 1645.

Peter Prideaux, Fellow All Souls, Oxon.

Susanna Prideaux = Phineas Cheek. (293)

Sir John Prideaux, 6th Bt, 1695 + 1766. 1719 = Hon. Anne Vaughan, + 1767. (292)

Christopher Harris, of Lanrest, M.P., + 1623, s.p. (1); Anthony Denys, of Orleigh, + 1641 (2). 1624. = Gertrude Granville, 1597 + 1682.

John Granville, of Lincoln's Inn, 1601 + living 1641.

Sir Richard Granville, "the King's General in the West," + 1659 = Mary, Lady Howard, née Fitz, + 1671. (296)

Elizabeth Granville, 1621 + 1692.

Anne Morley. (289)

Bernard Granville, M.P., + 1701.

Peter Prideaux = (1) Susanna Coffin, née Lellond. (2) (291)

Sir Bevil Granville, of Stow, 1596 + 1643 = Grace Smythe.

Jane Wyche, 1648 + 1701. (288)

John, 1st Earl of Bath. 1652.

Sir Edmund Prideaux, 4th Bt., 1647 + 1729. 1672 = (1) Susanna Austin, née Winstanley, + 1687. (2) Elizabeth Saunderson, + 1702. c. 1695.

Sir Edmund Prideaux, 5th Bt., 1675 + 1729. 1710 = (1) Mary Reynardson, + 1712. (2) Anne Hawkins, + 1741. 1714. (290)

29

1 Hasted's "Kent," iii. 170. Berry's "Kent Genealogies," p. 466.
2 One m. the Rev. — Harwood.

TABLE XXVII

Hon. Ursula Nevill. (1) = Sir Warham St. Leger, of
See Table XXVI. | Ulcomb, co. Kent, +1599.

Anthony (1) 1578 Mary
St. Leger, Scott.
of Ulcomb,
+1603

Nicholas Henry George = Margaret Margaret William Anne = Thomas Mary Jane Jane William
St. Leger, St. Leger. St. Leger, [—] St. Leger, St. Leger, Diggres, of St. Leger, St. Leger, St. Leger, Kingsmill,
+1589 +1620. 1564+1574 1555+1636 Barham, co. +1578 +1562. 1562+ of Ireland,
Kent, M.P. +1650
+1595.

(310)

Thomas Anthony Francis Ursula Mary
St. Leger, St. Leger, of St. Leger. St. Leger, St. Leger,
+1587. Hollingbourne 1598+ +1603. ? only child,
1591+1626. 1584+1602.

Sir Warham = Mary
St. Leger, Heyward.
of Ulcomb, +1602.
+1631.

Sir Anthony St. Leger, Thomas John St. Leger, Rebecca Warham Rowland Dudley St. Leger, of Anne [—], + Francis George Heyward St. Leger, Alexander Ursula St. Leger.
of Ulcomb, which he St. Leger, (br. 1640, +a. 1673. [—] St. Leger, St. Leger, St. John's, Thanet, 1646. St. Leger, St. Leger, of Heywards Hill, St. Leger. +1624.
sold c. 1648, c. 1680. +1608. lic. 1691. +1672. +1622. Gen. of Bandon, 1644. +1642. 1617+1634. 1619+1620. co. Cork, 1621+1684. 1623+1646.
+1614.

Barbara Lady 1692 (313) 1677 (315) Richard (314) John (316) Barbara Lady Barrett, (317)
Thornhurst, w. Mary (3) = Robert, Warham = Mary St. Leger. St. Leger, née St. Leger.
Shirley, +1639. St. Leger, 1st Baron St. Leger, of Hey- Gregory. of Cork, Jane [—] Sir Robert
da. and h., Lexinton, wards Hill, +1730. St. Leger, Douglas [not
+1663. +1668. lic. 1691. +1735. Dudley], of
Glenbervie,
3rd Bt.,
+1692.

Heyward Mary 1679 John Ursula Rev. Daniel Katherine Mary
St. Leger, St. Leger, Gillman, of St. Leger, Horsmanden, Rector of St. Leger. St. Leger.
of Cork, +1718. Curraheen, +1624. Ulcombe, +1655.
+1688. co. Cork,
1645+1725

(318)

Thomas Culpepper. William Codd, of
Pelicans, Watering-
bury.

Gertrude 1631 1632
St. Leger, lic. 1672.

Certainly s.p.m. and apparently s.p.

30

Hon. Mary Nevill. = Thomas, 9th Lord Dacre,
See Table XLVI. +1541.

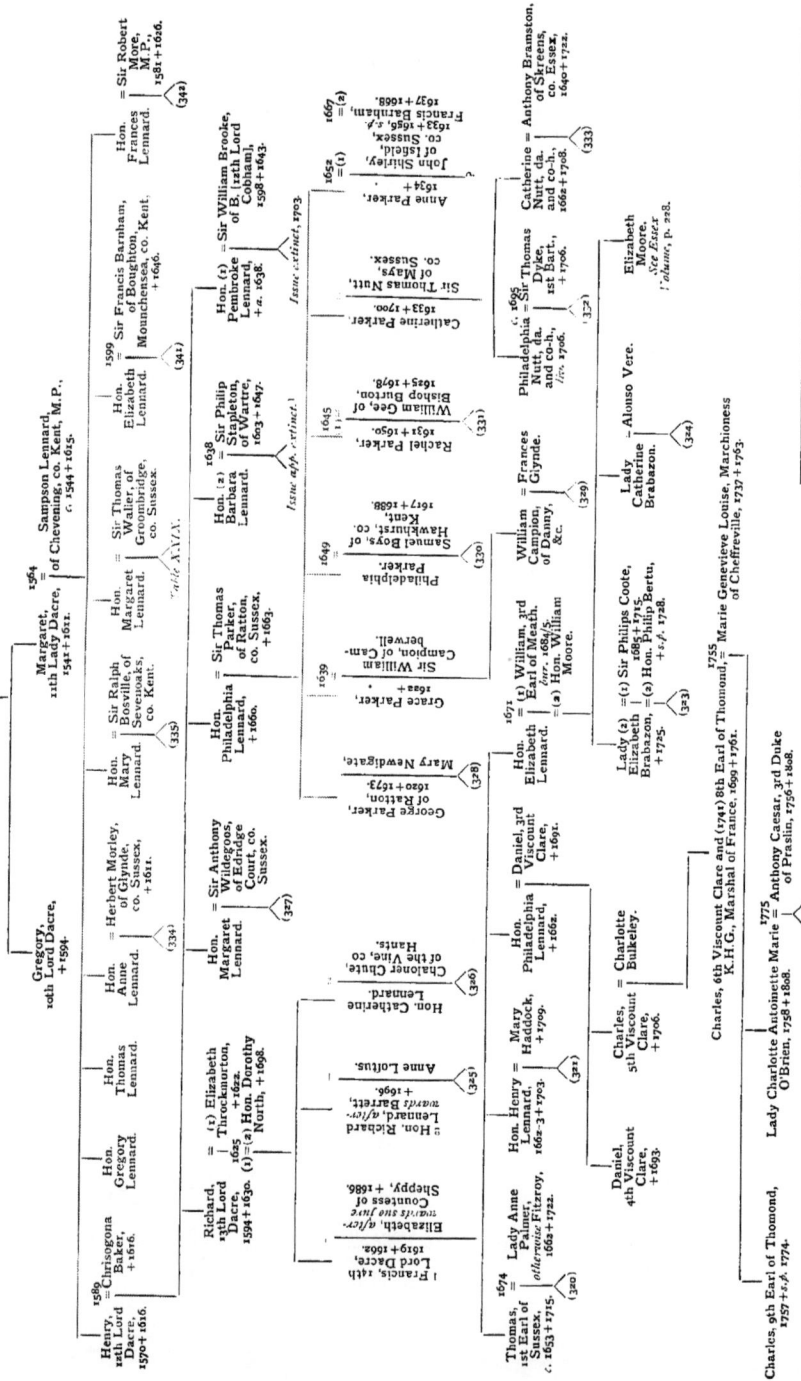

Margaret, | Sampson Lennard,
11th Lord Dacre, = of Chevening, co. Kent, M.P.,
1544 +1611. | c. 1544 +1615.

Gregory,
10th Lord Dacre,
+1594.

Henry, = Chrisogona 1580 Hon. Gregory Hon. Thomas Richard, = (1) Elizabeth 1645 Hon. Catherine Anne Loftus. ᵢ Hon. Richard Elizabeth, *after-* ₁ Francis, 12th 1674 Lady Anne
12th Lord Dacre, Baker, Lennard. Lennard. 13th Lord Throckmorton, Lennard. +1696. Lennard, *after-* Countess of Lord Dacre, Palmer, *other-*
1590 +1616. +1616. Dacre, +1622. *wards* Barrett. Sheppy, +1686. 1619 +1662. *wise* Fitzroy,
1594 +1630. (i) =(2) Hon. Dorothy 1662 +1722.
North, +1698.

Thomas,
1st Earl of
Sussex,
c. 1653 +1715.

See the Exeter Volume, Table XLIX.

¹ *Issue extinct.* *Issue extinct, 1703.*

31

TABLE XXIX

Hon **Margaret** = Sir Thomas **Waller**,
Lennard of Groomsbridge,
See Table XXXIII co Surrey

Elizabeth = Sir Francis
Waller Barham
?

Bridget = Sir Thomas
Waller More
?

Sir **William** = (1) Jane Reynell,
Waller, the +1733
Parliamentary =(2) Lady Anne Finch
General
1597-1668 =(3) Hon Anne Paget

Walter = ?
Waller, ? , ?
+?

Thomas = **Mary**
Waller, of **Waller**
Westminster

¹**Margaret** = Sir William
Waller, Courtenay,
+1694 *c* 1643 1st Bt., +1702

Ann (1) = Sir Philip **Harcourt**,
Waller of Stanton Harcourt
M P , +1688

²Sir **William** = **Catherine**
Waller, **Stradling**
+1700

Katherine = **Richard**
Waller **Courtenay**,
da and co-h +1694

Richard **Waller** = **Lucy**
of Rockbourne, **Waller**,
co Hants , &c
+1715

(336)

(340)

(338)

Simon 1st Viscount = (1) **Rebecca**
Harcourt, Lord High **Clark**,
Chancellor, +1687
1661-+1727
1680

(339)

Thomas Waller, = **Anne**
of South Lambeth **Smyth**,
1 +1731 +1781

(337)

32

TABLE XXX

Lady Margaret Percy. = Sir William Gascoigne,
of Gowthorpe.
See Table II.

Sir William = (1) Alicia
Gascoigne, | Frognall.
of Gowthorpe, | Hon. Margaret
1467† 1551. = (2) Latimer.

Thomas
Gascoigne.

Elizabeth = Sir
Gascoigne, | George
† 1553. | Talbuys,
| 1467† 1517.
See Table XXXII.

Margaret = Ralph,
Gascoigne. | 3rd Lord
| Ogle,
| † 1512.
See Part II.

Agnes = Sir
(or Anne) | Thomas
Gascoigne. | Fairfax.
See Part II.

Dorothy = Sir Ninian
Gascoigne. | Markenfeld.
See Part II.

¹ Sir William = (1) Margaret Wright.
Gascoigne, = (2) Margaret Fitzwilliam.
of Gowthorpe.

¹ Sir = Elizabeth
Henry | Boynton.
Gascoigne.

Marmaduke = Joan
Gascoigne. | Redmayne,
| 1520†

² John = Barbara
Gascoigne, | [——].
of Wheldale.

¹ Margaret = Sir Thomas
(? Bridget) | Middleton,
Gascoigne. | of Stockeld.

¹ William = Beatrice
Gascoigne, | Tempest.
of Gowthorpe,
† 1569.

¹ Francis = (1) Anne
Gascoigne, | Vavasour.
1537† 1578. = (2) Elizabeth
| Anne.

¹ Bridget = (1) Sir Matthew
Gascoigne. | Redman.
= (2) William
Gascoigne, of Caley.

¹ Dorothy = Richard
Gascoigne. | Thimelby,
| of
| Horncastle.
See Part II.

¹ Alice = (1) Edward Hazlewood,
Gascoigne. | of Maydeswell.
= (2) Thomas Gascoigne.
A.p.h. s.p.

² Barbara = Hon.
Gascoigne. | Leonard
| West.

Margaret Gascoigne, = Thomas Wentworth, of
da. and h., | Wentworth Woodhouse,
1537† 1592. | † 1587.

Sir William = Anne
Wentworth, 1st Bt., | Atkinson,
1562† 1614. | † 1611.

Elizabeth = Thomas
Wentworth. | Danby.
See Part II.

Hon. = Michael
Margaret | Darcy.
Wentworth.
See Part II.

Catherine = Thomas Gargrave,
Wentworth, | of Nostel,
† 1631. | † 1595.
A da. d.s.p.

Mary = Sir
Wentworth. | Richard
| Hutton.
See Part II.

Thomas, 1st Earl of = (2) Lady
Strafford, "the patriot," | Arabella Holles,
1593† 1641. | † 1631.

Sir William = Elizabeth
Wentworth. | Savile.
(345)

Sir George = Frances
Wentworth. | Ruishe.
See Table XXXI.

Anne = Sir George Savile,
Wentworth, | of Thornhill,
| 1593† 1614, *v.p.*
See Part II.

William, 2nd Earl
of Strafford, K.G.,
1626† 1695. *s.p.*

Lady Anne Wentworth, = Edward, 2nd Earl
da. and event. h., | of Rockingham,
1629† 1696. | 1650† 1689
(344)

33

E

TABLE XXXI

Sir George Wentworth. = Frances Ruishe.
See *Table XXX.*

Ruishe Wentworth, of Sarre, = Susan Adye.
in the Isle of Thanet.

Mary Wentworth, (1) = Thomas, 7th Lord Howard of
da. and h., +1718. [1707] Effingham, 1682 +1725.

Hon. Anne Howard, (2) = Sir William Yonge,
da. and co-h. [1729] 4th Bt., P.C., K.B.,
+1725. c. 1693 +1755.

⟨346⟩

Hon. Mary Howard, (1) = George, 1st Baron
da. and co-h., [1733] Vernon,
+1740. 1708 +1780.

George, 2nd Baron = (2) Georgiana
Vernon, [1786] Fauquier,
1735 +1813. +1823.

Hon. Mary = George Adams,
Vernon. [1763] afterwards Anson,
of Orgrave.

⟨347⟩

Thomas, = Lady Anne
1st Viscount [1774] Margaret
Anson, Coke,
1767 +1818. +1843.

Sir George = Frances
Anson, [1800] Hamilton,
G.C.B., +1834.
1769 +1849.

⟨348⟩

⟨349⟩

Sir William = Louisa
Anson, [1815] Frances
1st Bt., Mary
1772 +1847. Dickenson.
+1831.

⟨350⟩

Edward = Harriet
Anson, [1808] Rams-
1775 +1857. bottom,
+1858.

⟨351⟩

Sambroke = Elizabeth
Anson, Hawkins,
Lieut.-Col., +1866.
1778 +1846.

⟨352⟩

Rev. = Mary Anne
Frederick [1807] Lovett.
Anson,
1779 +1867.

⟨353⟩

Mary = Sir Francis
Anson, [1785] Ford,
1763 + 1st Bt,
M.P.,
1758 +1801.

⟨354⟩

Anne = Bell
Anson, [1792] Lloyd,
1768 +1822. +1845.

⟨355⟩

34

TABLE XXXII

Elizabeth = Sir George
Gascoigne. | Talboys.
+1553. | +1467 +1517.
See Table XXX.

George, 1st
Baron Talboys,
+1539.
Issue extinct.

Elizabeth = Sir
Talboys, | Christopher
da. and event. | Willoughby.
co-h.

Cecilia = (1) William
Talboys, | Ingilby, of
da. and event. | Ripley, co. York.
co-h. | =(2) John Torney,
| of Kaineby.

Anne Talboys, = (1) Sir Edward
da. and event. | Dymoke,
co-h. | of Scrivelsby.
| =(2) Sir Robert
| Carr.

See Part II.

Sir William = Anne
Ingilby, | Mallory,
of Ripley, | +1588.
1518 +1578.

See Part II.

John Ingilby, = (1) Anne Gale,
of Lawkland, | *nec* Clapham.
+1608.

Frances,(1) = James Pulleyne,
Ingilby. | of Killinghall,
| co. York.

See Part II.

Elizabeth = (1) ? Sir Francis
Ingilby. | Slingsby,
| = | (2) Richard
| ? | Maltus.

See Part II.

Thomas = Anne
Ingilby, of | Lawson.
Lawkland,
1564 +1622.

Charles
Ingilby,
living 1608.

John Ingilby,
Bar.-at-Law,
+1608.
=?

Anne Ingilby, = Sir William Gascoigne,
+1637. | 1st Bt., +1637.

Margaret
Ingilby.

See Part II.

Elizabeth = Ralph
Ingilby. | Creswell.

Joan
Ingilby.

John Ingilby, = (1) Margaret
of Lawkland, | Townley.
+1648. | =(2) Mary Lake,
| +1667.

William = [---]
Ingilby, of
Pallethorp.

Francis
Ingilby.

Anne = (1) Robert Kellingbeck,
Ingilby. | of Allerton, co. York,
| +1644.
| =(2) William Charnock,
| of Leyland, co. Lanc.

See Part II.

Catherine = (----)
Ingilby. | Kay, of
| Cleveland,
| co. York.
| ?

Mary
Ingilby.

William =
Watson, of
Austwick,
co. York.
?

² Columbus = Anne
Ingilby, of | Proctor,
Clapdale Hall, | +1737.
1642 +1716.

² Sir Charles = Alathea
Ingilby, of | Eyston,
Austwick, | +1745.
Baron of the
Exchequer,
1644 +1719.

² John
Ingilby.

1 Isabel
Ingilby.

= Richard
Sherburn, of
Stonyhurst,
co. Lanc.

² Mary
Elizabeth
Ingilby.

(356)

(357)

See Part II.

(358)

35

THE PLANTAGENET ROLL

OF THE

BLOOD ROYAL OF BRITAIN

Descendants of Lady Elizabeth Mortimer (grandda. of Lionel (of Antwerp) Duke of Clarence, K.G.), wife 1st of Henry, Lord Percy, called Hotspur, *d c p* (being killed at the Battle of Shrewsbury) 23 July 1403, 2ndly of Thomas, 1st Lord Camoys, K G.

1 Descendants of Lady ELIZABETH PERCY [1] (Table II), apparently living and then a widow 19 June 1604,[2] *m* RICHARD WOOD-ROFFE of Wolley, co York ; and had issue 1*a* to 3*a*

   1*a Maximilian Woodroffe, son and h*[2][3]

   2*a Joseph or Joshua Woodroffe,*[3][4][5] d (–) , m *Magdalene, da and h of Roger Billings of Marthagure, co Denbigh, and had issue 1b to 5b*
   1*b Charles Woodroffe,*[3][4][5] d *unm*[3]
   2*b Joseph Woodroffe*[3]'
   3*b Francis Woodroffe*[3]'
   1*b Foljambe Woodroffe of Wakefield, tradesman,*[3][5][9] *m and had issue*[3] 1*c to 2c*

   1*c Francis Woodroffe of Wakefield,*[3] m *and had issue (with a da who d young)* 1*d to 4d*
   1*d William Woodroffe*[2]
   2*d Francis Woodroffe*[3]
   3*d Charles Woodroffe*[3]
   4*d Mary Woodroffe,* m (—) *Wilson of Bedal*[3]

   2*c William Woodroffe of Wakefield,*[3] m *and had issue* 1*d*
   1*d Elizabeth Woodroffe of Wakefield, living there 1773*[3]
   5*b Mary Woodroffe*[3][5]

   3*a Lucy Woodroffe*[5]

---

[1] See Appendix
[2] *Mis Gen et Her* , ii 379
[3] " Pedigree and Memorials of the Woodroffe Family," by Miss M S Wood-roffe, 1878
[4] Harl MS , 6070, f 123 [144]
[5] Hunter's " Deanery of Doncaster," ii 387

The Plantagenet Roll

2 Descendants of BENEDICTA MARIA THERESA HALL, a co-h to the Baronies of Percy, Poynings, and Fitzpayne [E] (Table II), d 25 July 1749, m as 1st wife, c 1717, THOMAS (GAGE), 1st VISCOUNT GAGE [I], d 21 Dec 1754; and had issue 1a to 2a

1a *William Hall* (Gage), 2nd *Viscount Gage* [I], 1st *Baron Gage* [G B], b 1 Jan 1718, d s p 11 Oct 1791

2a Hon *Thomas Gage, Governor and Comm -in-Chief of H M's Forces in North America*, d 2 Ap 1788, m 8 Dec 1758, Margaret, da of Peter Kemble, President of the New Jersey Council, d 9 Feb 1824, and had issue 1b to 6b

1b *Henry* (Gage), 3rd *Viscount Gage* [I], 2nd *Baron Gage* [G B], b 4 Mar 1761, d 29 Jan 1808, m 11 Jan 1789, Susannah Maria, da and h of Gen William Skinner, d 29 Ap 1821, and had issue 1c to 2c

1c *Henry Hall* (Gage), 4th *Viscount Gage* [I], 3rd *Baron Gage* [G B], b 14 Dec 1791, d 20 Jan 1877, m 8 Mar 1813, Elizabeth Maria [*descended from the Lady Isabel Plantagenet* (see Essex Volume, p 134)], da of the Hon Edward Foley of Stoke Edith, d 13 June 1857, and had issue 1d to 4d

1d Hon *Henry Edward Hall Gage, Lieut -Col Royal Sussex Militia*, b 9 Jan 1814, d 8 Sept 1875, m 31 Aug 1840, Sophia Selina [*descended paternally from George, Duke of Clarence, K G* (see Clarence Volume, p 638), *and maternally from his aunt, the Lady Isabel Plantagenet* (see Essex Volume, p 59)], da of Sir Charles Knightley, 2nd B rt [G B], d 4 May 1866, and had issue 1e to 2e

1e *Henry Charles* (Gage), 5th Viscount Gage [I] and 4th Baron Gage [G B], senior known representative and heir-general of Henry "Hotspur," Lord Percy, and his wife, Lady Elizabeth, da of Edmund (Mortimer), 3rd Earl of March, and the Princess Philippa, only child of Lionel (of Antwerp), Duke of Clarence, K G, the eldest of the sons of king Edward III of whom issue now survives, and co-h to the Earldom of Northumberland (1377) and Baronies of Percy (1299) and Poynings (1337) [E] (*Firle Place, Lewes, Carlton, Bachelors'*), b 2 Ap 1854, m 23 July 1894, Leila Georgiana [descended from George, Duke of Clarence, K G (see Clarence Volume, p 605)], da of the Rev Frederick Peel, and has issue 1f to 4f

1f Hon Henry Rainald Gage, b 30 Dec 1895

2f Hon Irene Adelaide Gage

3f Hon Vera Benedicta Gage

4f Hon Yvonne Rosamond Gage

2e Selina Elizabeth Gage, m 1st, 22 July 1862, Henry Cavendish Cavendish (1852), *formerly* Taylor of Chyknell, co Salop, J P, D L (div Jan 1872), 2ndly, 1873, J White, and has issue 1f to 3f

1f Edith Selina Cavendish, m 24 May 1893, Major Hubert Cornwall Legh, King's Royal Rifle Corps

2f Ethel Julia Cavendish

3f Elfrida Geraldine Cavendish

2d Hon *Edward Thomas Gage, Lieut -Gen and Col Comdg R H A, C B*, b 28 Dec 1825, d 21 May 1889, m 1st, 17 Jan 1856, Arabella Elizabeth (see p 40), da of the Hon Thomas William Gage, d 8 Nov 1860, 2ndly, 17 Nov 1862, Ella Henrietta (29 Clifton Crescent, Folkestone), da of James Marse [by his wife, Lady Caroline, nee Berkeley], and had issue 1e to 8c

1e [1] William Henry St Quintin Gage, b 12 Feb 1858

2e [1] Francis Edward Gage, b 13 Oct 1860

3e [2] Ella Molyneux Berkeley Gage, Major and Hon Lieut -Col 3rd County of London Imp Yeo, *late* 14th Hussars (*Marlborough, Cavalry*), b 29 Sept 1863, m 30 Oct 1888, Ethel Marion, da of John Lysaght of Springfort, co Gloucester, and has issue 1f

1f John Fitzhardinge Berkeley Gage, b 3 June 1901   [Nos 1 to 13]

38

HENRY CHARLES, 5TH VISCOUNT GAGE.

THE SENIOR KNOWN REPRESENTATIVE OF THE LADY ELIZABETH PERCY, *née* MORTIMER

# of The Blood Royal

4e [2] James Seton Drummond Gage, *late* Lieut 5th Dragoons, b 28 June 1870

5e [2] Moreton Foley Gage, Major 7th Dragoons, served in Uganda 1898-9 and South Africa 1900-2 (*Army and Navy, Marlborough*), b 12 Jan 1873, m 1902, Annie Massie, da of William Everard Strong of New York City, U S A , and has issue 1/ to 2/

    1/ Berkeley Everard Foley Gage, b 27 Feb 1904

    2/ Edward FitzHardinge Peyton Gage, b 3 July 1906

6c [1] Mary Cecil Elizabeth Wilhelmina Gage, m 28 Dec 1882, the Rev Henry Stewart Gladstone, *formerly* Vicar of Honingham (*Hazelwood, King's Langley, Herts*), and has issue 1/ to 2/

    1/ Thomas Henry Gladstone, b 21 Mar 1889

    2/ Kathleen Mary Gladstone, b 15 Mar 1887

7e [1] Georgiana Elizabeth Gage (5 *Eaton Terrace, S W*)

8e [2] *Mabel Maria Gage*, b 10 *June* 1866, d 12 *May* 1901, m 27 *Ap* 1899, *Lieut -Col William Eliot Peyton, D S O , 15th Hussars, and had issue*

3d Hon *Caroline Harriet Gage*, b 23 *July* 1823, d 8 *May* 1888, m 4 *May* 1847, Standish Prendergast (*Vereker*), 4th Viscount Gort [I], b 6 *July* 1819, d 9 *Jan* 1900, *and had issue* 1e to 8e

    1e John Gage Prendergast (*Vereker*), 5th Viscount Gort [I], b 28 *Jan* 1849, d 15 *Aug* 1902, m 28 *Jan* 1885, Eleanor (*East Cowes Castle, I W , Hamsterley Hall, co Durham*, 13 *Grosvenor Gardens, S W*), *da and co-h of Robert Smith Surtees of Hamsterley Hall* (re-m 2ndly, 27 *June* 1908, *Col Staching Meux Benson), and had issue* 1/ to 2/

    1/ John Standish Surtees Prendergast (Vereker), 6th Viscount Gort [I] (*East Cowes Castle, I W*), b 10 July 1886

    2/ Hon Standish Robert Gage Prendergast Vereker, b 12 Feb 1888

    2e Hon *Foley Charles Prendergast Vereker, Capt R N* , b 21 *June* 1850, d 24 *Oct* 1900, m 25 *Mar* 1876, Ellen Amelia (*Hawkridge, Hayward s Heath), da of the Rev Henry Michael Myddelton Wilshere, Rector of Simon's Town, Cape Colony, and had issue* 1/ to 8/

    1/ Standish Henry Prendergast Vereker, Assist Resident N Nigeria, *formerly* Vice-Consul at Cherbourg, served in South Africa with Imp Yeo , two medals, b 12 Nov 1878, m 25 Mar 1908, Eleanor Elizabeth, da of Henry Bott of Brentford, M R C S

    2/ Leopold George Prendergast Vereker, Lieut R N R , b 26 Jan 1881 (H R H. the *late* Duke of Albany sponsor)

    3/ Maurice Charles Prendergast Vereker, b 21 Aug 1884

    4/ Foley Gerard Prendergast Vereker, Naval Cadet, b 12 Ap 1893

    5/ Violet Eva Vereker, b 23 Mar 1882

    6/ Lilian Isolda Vereker, b 1 May 1883

    7/ Muriel Agnes Vereker, b 19 Oct 1886

    8/ Ivy Mary Vereker, b 21 Feb 1888

    3e Hon Jeffrey Edward Prendergast Vereker, *formerly* Major R A (*Naval and Military*), b 27 Mar 1858, m 1902, Deno, da of Capt (—) Head

    4e Hon Isolda Caroline Vereker, m 23 Nov 1870, Sir Charles William Frederick Craufurd, 4th Bart [G B] (*see p* 41) (*Annbank House, co Ayr, United Service*), and has issue 1/ to 9/

    1/ George Standish Gage Craufurd, D S O , Capt 1st Batt Gordon Highlanders and Staff Officer W African Frontier Force, has Chitral medal with clasps, and Queen's medal with five clasps and King's medal with two clasps for South African War, where he comm Batt Mounted Inf with rank of Major, b 19 Nov 1872

    2/ Quentin Charles Alexander Craufurd, Lieut R N , b 11 Feb 1875, m 1 Oct 1899, Ann, da of Thomas Blackwell

    3/ Alexander John Fortescue Craufurd, b 22 Mar 1876   [Nos 14 to 36

The Plantagenet Roll

4/ Charles Edward Vereker Craufurd, Lieut R N , *b* 17 July 1885

5/ Hester Jane Laline Craufurd

6/ Laline Isolda Craufurd

7/ Isolda Mabel Cecil Craufurd, *m* 9 Nov 1909, Hugh Walter Wilson [only surviving son of John Walter Wilson of Shotley Hall]

8/ Eleanor Mary Dorothea Craufurd

9/ Margaret Elizabeth Maria Craufurd

5e Hon Mabel Elizabeth Vereker (10 *Wilton Street, S W*)

6e Hon Laline Maria Vereker

7e Hon Elizabeth Maria Vereker, *m* 1st, 7 Dec 1886, William Harvey Astell of Woodbury Hall, co Beds, J P , D L , *b* 26 Nov 1860, *d* 20 Ap 1896, *m* 2ndly, 12 June 1902, Philip (Sydney), 3rd Baron de L'Isle and Dudley [U K], representative and heir general of the Lady Anne, sister of Kings Edward IV and Richard III (*Penshurst Place, Tonbridge, Ingleby Manor, Middlesbrough*), and has issue 1/ to 3/

1/ Richard John Vereker Astell (*Woodbury Hall, Sandy, co Beds, 16 Sloane Gardens, S W*), *b* 7 Sept 1890

2/ Laline Annette Astell, *b* 1 Oct 1888

3/ Cynthia Elizabeth Violet Astell, *b* 10 Aug 1893

8e Hon Corinna Julia Vereker

4d Hon Fanny Charlotte Gage, *b* 8 Nov 1830, *d* 23 Jan 1883, m 15 Feb 1853, Capt William Tomline, late 10th Hussars

2c Hon Thomas William Gage of Westbury, co Hants, *b* 4 Aug 1796, *d* 25 Jan 1855, m 12 June 1821, Arabella Cecil, da of Thomas William St Quintin of Scampston Hall, co York, *d* 25 Feb 1840, and had issue 1d

1d Arabella Elizabeth Gage, *d* 8 Nov 1860, m as 1st wife, 17 Jan 1856, Gen the Hon Edward Thomas Gage C B , *d* 21 May 1889, and had issue

See pp 38-39, Nos 10-11 and 18-21

2b John Gage of Rogate, co Hants, *b* 23 Dec 1767, *d* 24 Dec 1816, m 20 May 1793, Mary, da and h of John Milbanke, *d* 9 Nov 1846, and had issue 1c to 3c

1c Rev Thomas Wentworth Gage, *d* 19 Mar 1837, m 17 Feb 1831, Lady Mary Elizabeth, da and co-h of Charles (Douglas), 5th Marquis of Queensberry [S], *b* 4 Nov 1807, *d* 16 May 1888, and had issue 1d to 2d

1d Charles Wentworth Gage, *b* 28 Feb 1832, *d* 17 May 1868, m June 1862, Georgina (*Woodlands, Peterborough, Canada West*), da of C Toker of Montreal, and had issue 1e

1e Charles Wentworth Gage, *b* 1 June 1868

2d Fanny Gage (2 *Downe Terrace, Richmond Hill*)

2c Charlotte Margaret Gage, *d* 9 Sept 1855, m 20 Oct 1825, John Hodgetts Foley, afterwards Hodgetts-Foley of Prestwood, M P , J P , D L [descended from the Lady Isabel Plantagenet (see Essex Volume, p 134)], *b* 17 July 1797, *d* 13 Nov 1861, and had issue 1d

1d Henry John Wentworth Hodgetts-Foley of Prestwood, M P , J P , D L , *b* 9 Dec 1828, *d* 24 Ap 1894, m 12 Dec 1854, the Hon Jane Frances Anne, da of Richard (Vivian), 1st Baron Vivian [U K], *b* 20 May 1824, *d* 2 Dec 1860, and had issue 1e

1e Paul Henry Hodgetts Foley, now Foley, J P , D L , F S A (*Prestwood, Stourbridge, Stoke Edith, Hereford*), *b* 19 Mar 1857, *m* 9 Feb 1904, Dora, da and h of Hamilton W Langley

3c Louisa Henrietta Gage, *b* 21 Dec 1809, *d* (-), m 16 Nov 1847, Ernst Rodolph (de Bertouch), 1st Baron de Bertouch [Denmark, 23 Jan 1839], Councillor of the Danish Legation in London, *b* 20 Feb 1808, *d* 8 July 1869, and had issue 1d

[Nos 37 to 58

40

# of The Blood Royal

1d Montagu William Ferdinand (de Bertouch), 2nd Baron de Bertouch [Denmark], Master of the Hunt to the King of Denmark (*Las Palmas*), *b* 24 Aug 1851, *m* 31 July 1882, Beatrice Caroline, da of James Elmslie, and has issue 1e

1e Baron Ernst Rudolph Ferdinand Julian de Bertouch (27 *Scarsdale Villas, London, W*), *b* 1 July 1884, *m* 8 Jan 1907, Gladys Zara Mary, da of Thomas Barns of Tilworth, Axminster, Capt King's Own Scottish Borderers, and has issue 1f

1f Baron Ernst Rudolph Anton Gauthier de Bertouch, *b* 17 Jan 1908

3b *Maria Theresa Gage*, d 21 Ap 1832, m 2 Mar 1792, *Sir James Craufurd, afterwards (R L 25 June 1812) Creg in-Craufurd, 2nd Bart* [G B], *b* 11 Oct 1861, d 9 July 1839, *and had issue 1c to 2c*

1c *Rev Sir George William Craufurd, 3rd Bart* [G B], [*descended from King Henry VII (see* Tudor Roll, p 283)], *b* 10 Ap 1797, d 24 Feb 1881, m 1st, 15 Feb 1843, *the Hon Hester, sister to William, 1st Earl of Lovelace* [U K], *da of Peter (King), 7th Baron King* [G B], *b* 2 May 1806, d (*at Pisa*) 18 May 1848, *and had issue 1d*

1d Sir Charles William Frederick Craufurd, 4th Bart [G B], Lieut (ret) R N (*Annbank House, co Ayr, United Service*), *b* 28 Mar 1847, *m* 23 Nov 1870, the Hon Isolda Caroline (see p 39), da of Standish Prendergast (Vereker), 4th Viscount Gort [I], and has issue

See pp 39–40, Nos 34–42

2c *Jane Craufurd*, d 25 May 1884, m 1st, 12 Oct 1823, *Gen Christopher Chowne (R L 3 Dec 1811), formerly Tilson*, d 15 July 1834, *2ndly*, 29 Aug 1836, *the Rev Sir Henry Richard Dukenfield, 7th Bart* [E], *d s p* 24 Jan 1858

4b *Louisa Elizabeth Gage*, d 21 Jan 1832, m 13 Feb 1794, *Sir James Henry Blake, 3rd Bart* [G B], d 21 Feb 1832, *and had issue 1c to 6c*

1c *Sir Henry Charles Blake, 4th Bart* [G B], *b* 23 May 1794, d 20 Ap 1841, m 1st, 2 Aug 1819, *Mary Anne, da of William Whitter of Midhurst*, d 20 Ap 1841, *and had issue 1d to 2d*

1d *Rev Henry Bunbury Blake, Rector of Hessett*, *b* 14 May 1820, d s p 20 Ap 1873, m 1 July 1847, *Frances Marion, da of Henry James Oakes of Nowton Court, and had issue 1e to 5e*

1e Sir Patrick James Graham Blake, 5th Bart [G B] (*Bardwell Manor, Bury St Edmunds*), *b* 23 Oct 1861, *m* 18 Oct 1883, Emma Gertrude, da of Thomas Pilkington Dawson of Groton House, co Suffolk, and has issue 1f to 2f

1f Cuthbert Patrick Blake, Lieut R N, *b* 2 Jan 1885

2f Veronica Blake

2e Marion Louisa Blake

3e Emma Gage Blake, *m* 24 Aug 1892, George Henry Fillingham (*Syerston Hall, Newark*), and has issue 1f

1f George Augustus Fillingham, *b* 23 Oct 1893

4e Julia Porteus Blake

5e Mary Anne Thellusson Blake

2d *William Gage Blake of Nowton Hall*, b 14 Nov 1821, d 1889, m 16 June 1859, *Mary, da of the Rev James I Bennet of Cheveley, and had issue 1e to 3e*

1e Constance Gage Blake, *m* 1883, Edward Charles Harrison Bennet, *formerly of Copdock, Ipswich*, and has issue 1f to 2f

1f Judith Harrison Bennet

2f Bridget Mary Bennet

2e Evelyn Gage Blake

3e Henrietta Lillie Gage Blake

2c *Rev William Robert Blake, Vicar of Great Barton, co Suffolk*, b 1800, d (²s p) 6 Dec 1868.   [Nos 59 to 84

The Plantagenet Roll

3c James Bunbury Blake of Thurston House, co Suffolk, b 1802, d July 1874, m 1 Nov 1831, Catherine, da and co-h of Sir Thomas Pilkington, 7th Bart [S], d July 1899, and had issue 1d

1d George Pilkington Blake, J P, Col Comdg Suffolk Imp Yeo, formerly 84th Regt, served in Indian Mutiny 1857-58 (Willesboro', Ashford, Kent), b 23 Ap 1835, m 1st, 15 May 1860, Adeline, da of James King King of Staunton Park, M P, d Ap 1890, 2ndly, July 1893, Adela Mary, widow of Thomas Duffield, da of Theobald Theobald of Sutton Courtney Abbey, J P, and has issue 1e to 4e

1e Eustace James Pilkington Blake (St Leonards, East Sheen), b 26 Mar 1865, m 1889, Ethel Minna, da of Col P B Schrieber, Royal Scots, and has issue 1f to 2f

1f Norman Pilkington Blake, ⎱ b (twins) 1890
2f Violet Hilda Blake, ⎰

2e Adeline Annie Blake, m 1884, Hardinge Hay Cameron, Ceylon C S

3e Kathleen Mary Blake, m 1888, Francis Millett Rickards (Ashtead, near Epsom), and has issue 1f

1f Thomas Millett Rickards, b 1889

4e Geraldine Blake, m 1907, Edward Thomas of Ceylon

4c. Thomas Gage Blake, b 1805, d (? unm)

5c Louisa Annabella Blake, d (-), m May 1827, Francis King Eagle, Bencher M T, County Court Judge, d 8 June 1856, and had issue 1d

1d Francis Blake Eagle, 11th Light Dragoons, b 6 Dec 1833, d 3 Feb 1879, m 1 Nov 1865, Emma Ellen, da of Lieut Henry Bond, and had issue 1e to 8e

1e Francis Elwyn Burbury Eagle, Major R M L I, r.t, b 29 Aug 1866

2e Maude Campbell Eagle

3e Rose Eagle

4e Violet Eagle

5e Lilian Dundas Eagle

6e Kathleen Emma Louisa Eagle

7e Cecil Mary Eagle

8e Evelyn Gage Wing Eagle

6c Emily Eliza Blake, d 26 Jan 1859, m Michael Edwards Rogers, d 21 Ap 1832, and had issue 1d

1d Emily Louisa Merilena Rogers, m 1863, the Rev J H Marshall of New Zealand, and has issue (5 children)

5b Charles Margaret Gage, d Sept 1844, m as 1st wife, 22 Ap 1802, Adm Sir Charles Ogle, 2nd Bart [U K], b 24 May 1775, d 16 June 1858, and had issue 1c to 3c

1c Sir Chaloner Ogle, 3rd Bart [U K], b 18 July 1803, d (at Brussels) 3 Feb 1859, m 5 Ap 1842, Eliza Sophia Frances, d r and h of William Thomas Roe of Withdean Court, co Sussex, d 12 May 1886, and had issue 1d to 2d

1d Sir Chaloner Roe Majendie Ogle, 4th Bart [U K], b 2 June 1843, d unm 29 Nov 1861

2d Hebe Emily Maritana Ogle, d 28 May 1889, m 19 July 1865, Eldred Vincent Morris Curwen, J P (Withdean Court, co Sussex), and had issue 1e to 2e

1e Chaloner Frederick Hastings Curwen, b 20 July 1866, d 3 Mar 1897, m Elizabeth, da of Sir William Gordon Cameron, K C B, and had issue (2 children)

2e Edith Margaret Spence Curwen

2c Charlotte Arabella Ogle, d 22 July 1840, m (at Paris) 15 Ap 1836, Jules, Baron de Briedenbach, of Darmstadt

3c Sophia Ogle, d 23 Ap 1896, m 17 Aug 1830, the Rev Edward Chaloner

[Nos 85 to 102

42

# of The Blood Royal

Ogle of Kirkley Hall, Preb of Salisbury, b 7 Aug 1798, d 7 Nov 1869, *and had issue* 1d *to* 5d

1d. Newton Charles Ogle, J P, D L (*Kirkley Hall, near Newcastle-on-Tyne*), b 19 Feb 1850, m 26 Nov 1895, Lady Lilian Katharine Selina [descended from King Henry VII (see the Tudor Roll, p 303)], da of William (Denison), 1st Earl of Londesborough [U K], d 31 July 1899, 2ndly, 12 Oct 1903, Beatrice Anne [descended from George, Duke of Clarence, K G (see Clarence Volume, p 426)], da of Sir John William Cradock-Hartopp, 4th Bart [G B], and has issue 1e to 3e

　　1e John Francis Chaloner Ogle, b 1 Dec 1898

　　2e Hester Mary Ogle, b 31 July 1904

　　3e Bridget Catherine Ogle, b 1908

　　2d Annie Charlotte Ogle

3d Sophia Henrietta Ogle, m as 2nd wife, 24 June 1879, the Most Rev Hugh Willoughby Jermyn, D D, Lord Bishop of Brechin 1875-1903, and Primus of Scotland 1886-1901, d 1903

4d Isabel Ogle (*Chesters, Humshaugh, co Northumberland*), m 12 Dec 1860, Nathaniel George Clayton of Chesters and Chilwood Park, J P, D L, b 20 Sept 1833, d 5 Sept 1895, and has issue 1e to 6e

　　1e *John Bertram Clayton of Chesters and Charlwood Park*, b 9 Oct 1861, d 8 Ap 1900, m 26 Jan 1886, Florence Octavia (*Chesters, Humshaugh, co Northumberland, Charlwood Park, Surrey*), da of Cadogan Hodgson Cadogan of Brinkburn Priory, and had issue 1f to 2f

　　　　1f Eleanor Clayton

　　　　2f Diana Pauline Clayton

　　2e Edward Francis Clayton, Major Scots Guards (78 *Portland Place, W*), b 21 Aug 1864, m 24 Feb 1900, Jeanne Marie Renée, da of Alexandre Leon Raymond Crublier de Fougères, Councillor General of the Canton of Ardentes

　　3e George Savile Clayton, b 20 Oct 1869

　　4e Mary Sophia Clayton, m 18 Jan 1883, Mark Fenwick (*Abbotswood, Stow-on-the-Wold*)

　　5e Isabel Evelyn Clayton, m 14 July 1891, Robert Lancelot Allgood (*Nunwick, co Northumberland*)

　　6e Alice Pauline Clayton, m 20 Sept 1905, Hubert Swinburne, LL B Camb [son and heir of Sir John Swinburne, 7th Bart [E] (see p 294)] (*Wellington, Brooks'*), and has issue 1f

　　　　1f Joan Swinburne

5d Alice Katherine Ogle, m 21 Feb 1874, George A Fenwick, and has issue

6b *Emily Gage*, b 25 Ap 1776, d 28 Aug 1838, m *as 1st wife*, 27 Aug 1807, Montagu (*Bertie*), *5th Earl of Abingdon* [E], b 30 Ap 1784, d 16 Oct 1854, *and had issue*

See the Exeter Volume, pp 78-79, Nos 146-177　　　　　　　[Nos 103 to 150

3 Descendants of the Rev Sir STEPHEN GLYNNE, 7th Bart [E], Rector of Hawarden, and a co-h to the Earldom of Northumberland (1377), Baronies of Percy (1299) and Poynings (1337) [E] (Table II), b c 1744, d 1 Ap 1780, m Aug 1779, MARY, da of Richard BENNETT of Farncot, co Salop, d 1 June 1812, and had issue 1a

1a *Sir Stephen Richard Glynne, 8th Bt, and a co-h to the Earldom of Northumberland (1377), Baronies of Percy (1299) and Poynings (1337)* [E], b posthumous May 1780, d. (*at Nice*) 5 Mar 1815, m 11 Ap 1806, *the Hon Mary, da of Richard (Aldworth-Neville-Griffin), 2nd Baron Braybrooke* [G B], b 5 Aug 1786, d 13 May 1851, *and had issue* 1b *to* 4b

43

The Plantagenet Roll

1b Sir Stephen Richard Glynne, 9th and last Bt, a co-h to the Earldom of Northumberland (1377) and Baronies of Percy (1299) and Poynings (1337) [E], b 22 Sept 1807, d unm 17 June 1874

2b Rev Henry Glynne, M A , Rector of Hawarden, b 9 Sept 1810, d 30 July 1872, m 13 Oct 1843, the Hon Lavinia, da of William Henry (Lyttelton), 3rd Baron Lyttelton [G B], d 3 Oct 1850, and had issue 1c to 2c

1c Mary Glynne, a co-h to the Earldom of Northumberland (1377) and Baronies of Percy (1299) and Poynings (1337) [E], unm

2c Gertrude Jessy Glynne, a co-h to the Earldom of Northumberland (1377) and Baronies of Percy (1299) and Poynings (1337) [E] (37 Lennox Gardens, S W), m as 2nd wife, 21 Oct 1875, George Sholto (Douglas-Pennant), 2nd Baron Penrhyn [U K], b 30 Sept 1836, d 10 Mar 1907, and has issue 1d to 8d

1d Hon George Henry Douglas-Pennant Capt Reserve of Officers, late Grenadier Guards, b 26 Aug 1876

2d Hon Charles Douglas-Pennant, late Coldstream Guards (Soham House, Newmarket), b 7 Oct 1877 m 28 Jan 1905, Lady Edith Anne, da of Vesey (Dawson), 2nd Earl of Dartrey [U K]

3d Hon Gwynedd Douglas-Pennant, m 18 Nov 1899, William Eley Cuthbert Quilter, J P [son and h of Sir Cuthbert Quilter, 1st Bart [U K], M P] (Methersgate Hall, Woodbridge), and has issue 1e to 3e

1e George Eley Cuthbert Quilter, b 23 Nov 1900

2e John Raymond Quilter, b 25 Feb 1902

3e Inez Quilter, b 22 Jan 1904

4d Hon Lilian Douglas-Pennant

5d Hon Winifred Douglas-Pennant

6d Hon Margaret Douglas-Pennant, m 29 July 1909, Andrew Francis Augustus Nicol Thorne

7d Hon Nesta Douglas-Pennant

8d Hon Elin Douglas-Pennant.

3b Catherine Glynne, b 6 Jan 1813, d 14 June 1900, m 25 July 1839, the Right Hon William Ewart Gladstone, P C , M P , D C L , four times (1868-74, 1880-85, 1886, and 1892-94) Prime Minister, b 29 Dec 1809, d 19 May 1898, and had issue 1c to 7c

1c William Henry Gladstone, M P , D L , b 3 June 1840, d 4 July 1891, m 30 Sept 1875, the Hon Gertrude (41 Berkeley Square, W), da and co-h of Charles (Stuart), 12th and last Lord Blantyre [S], and had issue 1d to 3d

1d William Glynne Charles Gladstone of Hawarden Castle (Hawarden Castle, co Flint), b 14 July 1885

2d Evelyn Catherine Gladstone

3d Constance Gertrude Gladstone

2c Rev Stephen Edward Gladstone, M A (Oxford), Rector of Barrowby, formerly of Hawarden (Barrowby Rectory, Grantham), b 4 Ap 1844, m 29 Jan 1885, Annie Crosthwaite, da of Charles Bowman Wilson of Liverpool, M D , and has issue 1d to 6d

1d Albert Charles Gladstone, b 28 Oct 1886

2d Charles Andrew Gladstone, b 28 Oct 1888

3d Stephen Deiniol Gladstone, b 9 Dec 1891

4d William Herbert Gladstone, b 8 Aug 1898

5d Catherine Gladstone

6d Edith Gladstone

3c Henry Neville Gladstone, J P (78 Eaton Square, S W , Burton Manor, Cheshire), b 2 Ap 1852, m 30 Jan 1890, the Hon Maud Ernestine, da and co-h of Stuart (Rendel), 1st Baron Rendel [U K]

1c Herbert John (Gladstone), 1st Viscount Gladstone of Lanark, P C , M P ,

[Nos 151 to 175

44

# of The Blood Royal

M A, Oxford, 1st Governor-General of South Africa (9 *Buckingham Gat., S W*, *Sandycroft, Littlestone, Kent*), b 7 Jan 1854, m 2 Nov 1901, Dorothy Mary, da of the Right Hon Sir Richard Horner Paget, 1st Bart [U K], P C

5c Agnes Gladstone, m 27 Dec 1873 the Very Rev Edward Charles Wickham, D D, Dean of Lincoln, *formerly* Head Master of Wellington College (*The Deanery, Lincoln*), d 18 Aug 1910, and has issue 1d to 5d

1d William Gladstone Wickham, B A, b 3 Jan 1877

2d Rev Edward Stephen Gladstone Wickham M A, Curate of St Simon Zelotes, Bethnal Green, E, b 2 Mar 1882

3d Catherine Mary Lavinia Wickham, Head of Bishop Creighton House, Lillie Road, Fulham, S W

4d Lucy Christian Wickham

5d Margaret Agnes Wickham

6c Mary Gladstone, m 2 Feb 1886, the Rev Henry Drew, Rector of Hawarden and Canon of St Asaph (*Hawarden Rectory, Flints*), d 1910, and has issue 1d

1d Dorothy Mary Catherine Drew

7c Helen Gladstone, *late* Warden of the Women's University Settlement, Blackfriars, and *formerly* Vice Principal Newnham College, Cambridge (*Sundial, Hawarden*)

4b *Mary Glynne* b 1813, d 17 Aug 1857 m *as 1st wife*, 25 *July* 1839, George William (Lyttelton), 4th Baron Lyttelton [G B] *and Baron Westcote* [I], *and a Baronet* [E], P C, K C M G, b 31 *Mar* 1817 d 19 *Ap* 1876, *and had issue* 1c to 11c

1c Charles George (Lyttelton), 8th Viscount Cobham and 5th Baron Lyttelton, &c [G B], 5th Baron Westcote [I] and 11th Baronet [E] &c, &c (*Hagley Hall, Stourbridge*), b 27 Oct 1842, m 19 Oct 1878, the Hon Mary Susan Caroline [descended from King Henry VII through five different lines, from George, Duke of Clarence, through five from Anne (Plantagenet), Duchess of Exeter, through nine, and from Isabel (Plantagenet), Countess of Essex, through nineteen], da of William George (Cavendish), 2nd Lord Chesham [U K] and has issue 1d to 7d

1d Hon John Cavendish Lyttelton, Assist Private Secretary to High Commr for South Africa (Earl Selborne) since 1905, *formerly* Lieut Rifle Brigade, b 23 Oct 1881, m 30 June 1908, Violet Yolande, da of Charles Leonard of 18 Kensington Palace Gardens, W, and Gloria, Cape Colony, and has issue 1e

1e Charles John Lyttelton, b 8 Aug 1909

2d Hon George William Lyttelton, b 6 Jan 1883

3d Hon Charles Frederick Lyttelton, b 25 Jan 1887

4d Hon Richard Glynne Lyttelton, b 16 Oct 1893

5d Hon Maud Mary Lyttelton, m 25 Feb 1908, the Hon Hugh Archibald Wyndham (*Kroomdraai, Standerton, S Africa*)

6d Hon Frances Henrietta Lyttelton

7d Hon Rachel Beatrice Lyttelton

2c Rev the Hon Albert Victor Lyttelton, M A, Curate in Charge of St John's, Hawarden, *formerly* Priest Vicar of Bloemfontein Cathedral (*St John's Parsonage, near Mold*), b 29 June 1844

3c Hon Sir Neville Gerald Lyttelton, K C B, Gen and Gen Officer Comdg-in-Chief in Ireland, *formerly* Comm-in-Chief in Transvaal, &c (*Royal Hospital, Dublin*), b 28 Oct 1845, m 1 Oct 1883, Katharine Sarah da of the Right Hon James Archibald Stuart Wortley, and has issue 1d to 3d

1d. Lucy Blanche Lyttelton, m 2 June 1908, Charles Frederick Gurney Masterman, M P, Parl Under Sec of State for Home Affairs (46 *Gillingham Street, Eccleston Square, S W*)

2d Hilda Margaret Lyttelton, m as 2nd wife, 23 Feb 1909, Arthur Morton Grenfell (23 *Great Cumberland Place, S W*)

3d Mary Hermione Lyttelton

[Nos 176 to 198

The Plantagenet Roll

4c Hon George William Spencer Lyttelton, C B , M A , F R G S , &c , Private Sec to the Premier (Rt Hon W E Gladstone) 1892-4 (49 *Hill Street, Berkeley Square, W*), *b* 12 June 1847

5c *Right Rev the Hon Arthur Temple Lyttelton, D D , Lord Bishop of South-ampton,* b 7 *Jan* 1852 , d 19 *Feb* 1903 , m 3 *Aug* 1880, *Kathleen Mary, da of George Clive of Perrystone, co Hereford,* d 13 *Jan* 1907 , *and had issue* 1d *to* 3d

   1d Archer Geoffrey Lyttelton, Lieut 2nd Batt Welsh Regt , *b* 7 May 1884

   2d Stephen Clive Lyttelton, Sub-Lieut R N , *b* 17 June 1887

   3d Margaret Lucy Lyttelton (21 *Carlton House Terrace, S W*)

6c Hon Robert Henry Lyttelton, M A , a Solicitor and member of the firm of Stow, Preston, & Lyttelton, of Lincoln's Inn Fields (85 *Vincent Square, S W*), *b* 18 Jan 1854 , *m* 14 July 1884, Edith, da of Sir Charles Santley

7c Rev the Hon Edward Lyttelton, M A , Headmaster of Eton since 1905, *formerly* of Haileybury College and Hon Canon of St Albans, &c (*Eton College, Windsor*), *b* 23 July 1855 , *m* 21 Dec 1888, Caroline Amy, da of the Very Rev John West, D D , Dean of St Patrick's, Dublin , and has issue 1d to 2d

   1d Nora Joan Lyttelton

   2d Delia Lyttelton

8c Right Hon the Hon Alfred Lyttelton, Bar-at-Law, P C , K C , M P , Member Gen Council of the Bar, Dep High Steward Cambridge University, &c , *formerly* Secretary of State for the Colonies (16 *Great College Street, Westminster, S W*), *b* 7 Feb 1857 , *m* 1st, 21 May 1885, Octavia Laura, da of Sir Charles Tennant, 1st Bart [U K], d 21 Ap 1886 , 2ndly, 18 Ap 1892, Edith Sophy, da of Archibald Balfour , and has issue 1d to 2d

   1d Oliver Lyttelton, *b* 15 Mar 1893

   2d Mary Frances Lyttelton

9c Hon Meriel Sarah Lyttelton, *m* 19 July 1860, the Right Hon John Gilbert Talbot, P C , M P , J P , D L [E of Shrewsbury Coll , a descendant of Anne (Plantagenet) Duchess of Exeter] (*Falconhurst, Eden Bridge, Kent, 10 Great George Street, S W*), and has issue 1d to 9d

   1d George John Talbot, K C , M A , Bar-at-Law, Chancellor of the Dioceses of Lincoln, Ely, Lichfield, and Southwark (36 *Wilton Crescent, S W* , 4 *Paper Buildings, Temple, E C*), *b* 19 June 1861 , *m* 3 June 1897, Gertrude Harriot, da of Albemarle Cator of Woodbastwick Hall, co Norfolk , and has issue 1e to 3e

      1e John Bertram Talbot, *b* 10 June 1900

      2e Thomas George Talbot, *b* 21 Dec 1901

      3e Mary Meriel Gertrude Talbot

   2d Bertram Talbot, *formerly* Clerk to House of Commons (*Monteviot, Ancrum, co Roxburgh*), *b* 27 Ap 1865 , *m* 21 Feb 1903, Victoria Alexandrina, Dowager Marchioness of Lothian [S] [a descendant of King Henry VII , &c], da of Walter Francis (Scott), 5th Duke of Buccleuch, &c [S], K G

   3d John Edward Talbot, B A (Oxon), Senior Examiner in Board of Education (12 *Stanhope Gardens, S W*), *b* 14 May 1870 , *m* 27 Ap 1898, Mabel, da of Archibald Balfour , and has issue 1e to 4e

      1e Evan Arthur Christopher Talbot, *b* 31 May 1903

      2e Richard Eustace Talbot, *b* 11 Feb 1907

      3e Anne Meriel Talbot

      4e Joan Ankaret Talbot

   4d Mary Talbot, *b* 14 July 1862 , d 25 May 1897, m 14 Ap 1896, *the Ven Winfrid Oldfield Burrows, Archdeacon of Birmingham,* and had issue 1e

      1e Hilda Mary Burrows

   5d Caroline Agnes Talbot, *m* 13 Oct 1891, Talbot Baines (*Weetwood Lodge, Leeds*), and has issue 1e to 4e

46
                   [Nos 199 to 222

# of The Blood Royal

1e Frederick John Talbot Baines, *b* 25 July 1892

2e Edward Russell Baines, *b* 28 Oct 1899

3e Henry Wolfe Baines, *b* Feb 1905

4e Susan Meriel Talbot Baines

6d Meriel Lucy Talbot

7d Evelyn Talbot, twin

8d Gwendolen Talbot, *m* 6 Dec 1905, Guy Stephenson, Barrister-Law, Assist Director of Public Prosecutions [a descendant both paternally and maternally from George (Plantagenet), Duke of Clarence, K G] (41 *Egerton Gardens S W*) and has issue 1e

1e Augustus William Stephenson, *b* 1 Mar 1909

9d Margaret Isabel Talbot, *m* 2 July 1904, Randall Mark Kerr McDonnell, Viscount Dunluce [son and h of the 6th Earl of Antrim [I], and a descendant of George (Plantagenet), Duke of Clarence, K G] (*Walney Old Vicarage., Barrow-in-Furness*), and has issue 1e

1e Hon Rose Gwendolen Louisa McDonnell, *b* 23 May 1909

10c Hon Lucy Caroline Lyttelton, Hon LL D (Leeds), *formerly* Maid of Honour to Queen Victoria (21 *Carlton House Terrace, S W*), *m* 7 June 1864, Lord Frederick Charles Cavendish, M P, *d s p*, being murdered 6 May 1882

11c Hon Lavinia Lyttelton, *m* 29 June 1870, the Right Rev Edward Stuart Talbot, D D, 1st Lord Bishop of Southwark, *formerly* (1895-1905) 100th Lord Bishop of Rochester &c [E of Shrewsbury Coll, a descendant of Anne (Plantagenet}, Duchess of Exeter] (*Bishop's House, Kensington, S W*), and has issue 1d to 5d

1d Rev Edward Keble Talbot, a Member of the Community of the Resurrection, Mirfield, *b* 31 Dec 1877

2d Rev Neville Stuart Talbot, Curate of Armley, Leeds, *formerly* Lieut 1st Batt Rifle Brigade, *b* 21 Aug 1879

3d Gilbert Walter Lyttelton Talbot, *b* 1 Sept 1891

4d Mary Catherine Talbot, *m* 6 Ap 1901, the Rev Lionel George Bridges Justice Ford, Headmaster of Repton (*Repton Hall, Derbyshire*), and his issue 1e to 3e

1e Arthur Edward Ford, *b* 23 Mar 1905

2e Neville Montague Ford, *b* 18 Nov 1906

3e Richard Lionel Ford, *b* 30 Aug 1908

5d Lavinia Caroline Talbot   [Nos 223 to 242

4 Descendants of PENELOPE GLYNNE (Table II), *d* Feb 1771, *m* as 1st wife, Sir WILLIAM EARLE WELBY of Denton, 1st Bt [U.K], *d* 6 Nov 1815, and had issue 1a to 2a

1a Sir William Earle Welby, 2nd Bt [U K], M P, *b* 14 Nov 1768, d 3 Nov 1852, m 30 Aug 1792, Wilhelmina, da and h of William Spry, Governor of Barbadoes, *d* 4 Feb 1847, and had issue 1b to 7b

1b Sir Glynne Earle Welby, afterwards (R L 5 July 1861) Welby-Gregory, 3rd Bt [U K], *b* 26 June 1806, d 23 Aug 1875, m 6 Mar 1828, Frances, da of Sir Montague Cholmeley, 1st Bt [U K], d 9 Oct 1881, and had issue 1c to 6c

1c Sir William Earle-Welby, afterwards (R L 27 D c 1875) Welby Gregory, 4th Bt [U K], M P, *b* 4 Jan 1829, d 26 Nov 1898, m 4 July 1863, the Hon Victoria Alexandrina Maria Louisa, *formerly* Maid of Honour to Queen Victoria, da of the Hon Charles Stuart-Wortley, and had issue 1d to 2d

1d Sir Charles Glynne Earle Welby, 5th Bt [U K], C B, J P, D L, *formerly* (1900-6) M P for Newark and (1900-2) Assist Under Secretary of State for   [No 243

The Plantagenet Roll

War (*Denton Manor, Grantham, Carlton, &c*), b 11 Aug 1865, m 24 Nov 1887, Lady Maria Louisa Helena, da. of Lord Augustus Hervey, and has issue 1e to 5e

    1e Richard William Gregory Welby, b 6 Oct 1888

    2e Oliver Charles Earle Welby, b 26 Jan 1902

    3e Dorothy Geraldine Welby

    4e Katherine Amothe Welby

    5e Joan Margaret Welby

    2d Emmeline Mary Elizabeth Welby, m 11 Oct 1893, Henry John Cockayne-Cust, J P , D L , *formerly* M P and Editor *Pall Mall Gazet.*, heir-presumptive to the Barony of Brownlow [G B] (*St James Lodge, Delahay Street, S W , Carlton, &c*)

    2c Rev Walter Hugh Earle Welby, J P , M A (Oxon), *late* Rector of Harston (*St George's Lodge, Ryde, I W*), b 19 Aug 1833 , m 1st, 1 Oct 1861, Frances, da. of the Right Rev Alfred Ollivant, Lord Bishop of Llandaff, d 3 Jan 1875 , 2ndly, 8 Oct 1878, Florence Laura, da. of the Rev George Sloane Stanley, Rector of Branstone, and has issue 1d

    1d¹ Frances Alice Welby

    3c Edward Montagne Earle Welby, J P , M A (Oxon), Bar -at-Law, now Police Magistrate for Sheffield (*Norton House near Sheffield*) b 12 Nov 1836 , m 3 Feb 1870 Sarah Elizabeth, da. and h of Robert Everard of Fulney House, co Lincoln, d 25 Feb 1909 , and has issue 1d to 5d

    1d Edward Everard Earle Welby now (R L 6 Ap 1894) Welby-Everard, J P , B A (Oxon), Bar -at-Law (*9 Eccleston Square, S W , Gosberton House, near Spalding*), b 22 Dec 1870 , m 27 June 1899, Gwladys Muriel Petra, da. of the Rev George Herbert, and has issue 1e to 3e

        1e Philip Herbert Earle Welby-Everard b 7 May 1902

        2e Christopher Earle Welby-Everard, b 9 Aug 1909

        3e Clemence Penelope Olga Welby Everard

    2d Glynne Everard Earle Welby, Capt 1st Batt South Wales Borderers, b 24 Nov 1872

    3d Hugh Robert Everard Earle Welby, b 27 July 1885

    4d Cicely Elizabeth Welby

    5d Margaret Sarah Welby

    4c Alfred Cholmeley Earle Welby, Lieut -Col (ret) 2nd Dragoons, J P , C C for East Finsbury, *formerly* M P for Taunton (*26 Sloane Court, S W , Carlton*) b 22 Aug 1849 , m 11 Feb 1898, Alice Désirée, da. of A E Copland Griffiths, and has issue 1d to 3d

    1d Ranulf Alfred Earle Welby, b 23 Nov 1902

    2d Amyse Mary Welby

    3d Eda Désirée Welby

    5c May Elizabeth Welby, m 1st, 22 Mar 1860 John Richards Homfray of Penllyn Castle, co Glamorgan, d 8 Aug 1882 , 2ndly, 13 Nov 1893, Col George Shirley Maxwell (*Penllyn Castl , Cowbridge*), and has issue 1d to 2d

    1d John Glynne Richards Homfray of Penllyn Castle, J P , *late* Capt 1st Life Guards (*8 Grand Avenue Mansions, Hove*), b 13 June 1861 , m 1893, Rose Ellen, da. of Charles Henry Simmons

    2d Herbert Richards Homfray, J P , *late* Lieut -Col Comdg and Hon Col 2nd Vol Batt Welsh Regt, *formerly* 1st Life Guards, b 23 Sept 1864 , m 13 June 1889, Blanche Jessie da. of Charles Henry Williams of Roath Court, Cardiff, and has issue 1e to 4e

        1e Herbert Charles Richards Homfray, b 22 Sept 1890

        2e John Richards Homfray, b 18 Oct 1893

        3e Francis Richards Homfray, b 23 Dec 1897.

        4e Gwenllian Mary Homfray

[Nos 244 to 271

# of The Blood Royal

6c Alice Welby, m as 2nd wife, 19 Sept 1860, George Troyte Bullock, *sometime* (R L 31 Dec 1852) Troyte Bullock, and now (R L 5 May 1892) Troyte Chafyn-Grove, of Zeals and North Coker House, F S A, J P, D L, High Sheriff co Dorset 1888 (*Zeals House, near Mere, Wilts. North Coker House, Yeovil*), and his issue 1d to 6d

    1d Edward George Troyte-Bullock, J P, Lieut-Col Dorset Yeo Cav, *late* Capt Royal Dragoons (*Silton Lodge, Dorset*), b 17 Sept 1862, m 6 Jan 1898, Grace Amy Margaret, da of Col John Mount Batten of Upcerne Manor, C B, and his issue 1e to 4e

        1e George Victor Troyte-Bullock, b 1900
        2e Elizabeth Grace Troyte-Bullock
        3e Mary Winifred Troyte-Bullock
        4e Cicely Violet Troyte-Bullock

    2d Hugh Ambrose Troyte Bullock (*Wolfville, Nova Scotia*), b 27 July 1867, m 16 Sept 1891, Rosa Margaret, da of John Caulfield, and has issue 1e

        1e Margaret Troyte-Bullock

    3d Cecil John Troyte-Bullock, Capt Somerset L I, b 17 May 1869, m 1904, Joan Acland, da of Leonard Harper of Jersey

        4d Mabel Cicely Troyte-Bullock
        5d Evelyn Mary Troyte Bullock
        6d Alice Christine Troyte-Bullock

  2b Right Rev Thomas Earle Welby, D D, *Bishop of St Helena*, b 11 *July* 1810, d 6 *Jan* 1899, m 1837, *Mary Ann*, da of A Browne, d 1896, and had issue 1c to 10c

    1c *Henry Earle Welby*, b 1838, d 16 *June* 1869, m 1866, *Cecilia*, da of T Bland of Georgetown, Cape Colony, and had issue 1d

        1d Hugh Earle Welby, b 1867

    2c Charles Earle Welby, Hon Fellow Allahabad Univ, and Capt Agra Vol Rifles, *formerly* Inspector of Schools in Indian Educational Service (Allahabad), b 26 Dec 1850, m 21 June 1880, Annie Williams, widow of Walter Conroy, C E, da of (———), and has issue 1d

        1d Thomas Earle Welby, *Sub-Editor Madras Mail*, b 18 July 1881

    3c *Arthur Thomas Earle Welby*, *Gen Manager Rio Denver Rai'road, U S A*, b 15 *Feb* 1855, d 8 *Aug* 1909, m 1st, 1874, *Phœbe*, da of Capt de Cew, d 1895, 2ndly, 1898, *Maria* (*Denver, U S A*), da of J F Mitchell, and had issue 1d to 5d

        1d² Alfred Earle Welby, b 1899
        2d² Charles Earle Welby, b 1901
        3d¹ Wilhelmina Cecilia Welby
        4d¹ Helena Beatrice Welby
        5d² Muriel Welby

    4c *Frederick Earle Welby*, F R C S E, b 1858, d 21 Oct 1900, m 1883, *Janet Anne*, da of F Henderson of Wick, and had issue 1d to 4d

        1d Francis Thomas Glynne Earle Welby, b 1888
        2d Mary Caroline Welby
        3d Edith Jessie Welby
        4d Gladys Welby

    5c Penelope Welby (*Haughton, Falmouth*), m 2 July 1863, Major-Gen John Haughton, R A, d 26 Aug 1889, and has issue 1d to 2d

    1d John Welby Haughton, L R C P (*Falmouth*), b 16 Ap 1866, m 9 June 1896, Florence Maud Audrey, da of Lieut-Col Shonbridge, and has issue 1e to 4e

        1e Wilfrid John Haughton
        2e Florence Penelope Audrey Haughton.
        3e Joan Astor Haughton
        4e Mary Patricia Haughton

[Nos 272 to 301

49

The Plantagenet Roll

2d Hugh Latimer Haughton, Capt 92nd Punjaubis, b 18 Sept 1870, m 29 Dec 1903, Kathleen Elizabeth, da of T Paterson of Dublin

6c Wilhelmina Welby (155 Colcherne Court, South Kensington, S W), m 14 Jan 1864, Major-Gen Robert Burton, R E, d s p 11 Aug 1894

7c Elizabeth Welby (Bradford Peverill, Dorchester)

8c Caroline Welby (6 Bishop Wards College, The Close, Salisbury), m 1st, 17 Aug 1867, Charles Henry Fowler, M D, d 7 Ap 1877, 2ndly, 25 June 1884, the Rev Francis William Curré, Vicar of St Katherines, Marlborough, d 2 July 1901, and has issue 1d to 3d

1d Charles William Henry Fowler, D S O, late Capt S A Constabulary, formerly Imp L H, served through Boer War 1899-1902, mentioned in despatches, medal and six clasps, b 13 July 1869, m July 1903, Florence, da of John Becker of Cape Town, and has issue 1e

1e Florence Beatrice Fowler

2d Cecil Welby Fowler, b Nov 1870, m 1896, Isobel Mounsey, da of Capt Gilfillan of Cape Town, s p

3d Frances Beatrice Caroline Curré

9c Katherine Welby (Mentone, Petworth, Sussex), m at St Paul's Cathedral, St Helena, 7 Aug 1873, Saul Solomon of St Helena, d 10 Ap 1896, and has issue 1d to 4d

1d Arthur Francis Welby Solomon, Bar-at-Law, b 30 Ap 1874

2d Cyril Welby Solomon, b 29 Oct 1875, m and has issue a son and 3 das

3d Homfray Welby Solomon, Merchant, b 3 Ap 1877, m and has issue a da

4d Mary Jessica Solomon, Actress and Novelist

10c Edith Frances Welby (Bradford Peverill, Dorchester), m 19 Feb 1884, Surgeon Lieut-Col Robert Mark Bradford

3b Rev Arthur Earle Welby, Rector of Holy Trinity, Hulme, Manchester, b 22 Aug 1815, d 1884, m 13 May 1813, Julia, da of Capt George Macdonald, 68th Regt, d 18 Oct 1892, and had issue 1c to 7c

1c William Macdonald Earle Welby, b 22 Nov 1815, d 4 Oct 1885, m 2ndly, 3 Feb 1878, Jessie (391 Commissioner Street, Johannesburg), da of Frederick Lucas of Grahamstown, Cape Colony, and had issue 1d to 4d

1d Spencer Earle Welby, b 8 Mar 1879

2d Glynne Earle Welby, b 11 Nov 1881

3d Isabel Florence Welby

4d May Welby

2c George Henry Francis Earle Welby, b 31 Dec 1846

3c Charles Earle Welby, b 12 May 1848

4c Richard Earle Welby, late Capt 5th Batt Rifle Brigade, &c (Naish Priory, North Coker, Yeovil), b 3 Jan 1854, m 1st, 1886, Mary Isabella, da of Thomas Paget of Forton, near Lancaster, d s p s 1892, 2ndly, 1899, Alice Frances, widow of Vice-Adm Frederick Charles Bryan Robinson, da of Lieut-Col Cyril Blackburne Tew

5c Julia Gertrude Welby, m 21 June 1894, Richard John Linton (12 Augusta Gardens, Folkestone)

6c Caroline Charlotte Welby, d (-), m 12 Aug 1871, Richard Evans, and had issue

7c Sarah Wilhelmina Mary Welby (Barrowby, Lincolnshire)

4b Wilhelmina Welby, d 1874, m 17 May 1825, the Rev Frederick Browning, Preb of Salisbury, d 3 Dec 1858

5b Penelope Welby d 5 June 1834, m 8 May 1825, Clinton James Fiennes-Clinton, M P [Duke of Newcastle Coll], b 13 May 1792, d 11 Ap 1833, and had issue 1c to 2c   [Nos 302 to 324

# of The Blood Royal

1c Rev Henry Fiennes-Clinton, M A (Durham), Rector of Cromwell (*Cromwell Rectory Nottingham*), b 5 Feb 1826, m 9 July 1850, Sarah Katherine, da of the Rev John B Smith, D D, d 23 Mar 1898, and has issue 1d to 8d

1d Rev Henry Glynne Fiennes-Clinton B A (Oxford), Rector of St James', Vancouver, British Columbia, b 31 Jan 1854

2d *Charles Edward Fiennes-Clinton*, b 24 *July* 1855, d 11 *Jan* 1888, m 3 Ap 1885, *Alice Gertrude, da of William Waring, M D , and had issue 1e*

1e Edward Henry Fiennes-Clinton, b 4 Ap 1886

3d Clement Walter Fiennes-Clinton, a Solicitor, b 3 Dec 1856, m 1885, Lucy Eleanor, da of Henry J Hassell, and has issue 1e to 2e

1e Henry Fiennes-Clinton, b 1885

2e Eleanor Clement Fiennes-Clinton

4d Eleanor Katherine Fiennes-Clinton, m 15 Oct 1872, the Rev Seymour Bentley, *late* Vicar of Markham Clinton, Tuxford (*Bute, Whitby*), and has issue 1e to 3e

1e Seymour Rothwell Bentley, b 27 Sept 1873

2e Frank Middleton Bentley, b 23 Oct 1876

3e Agnes Mary Bentley

5d Ida Mary Fiennes-Clinton, m 31 Dec 1878, A Swainson Allen of Bromyard, co Hereford

6d Susan Charlotte Catherine Fiennes-Clinton, m 7 Aug 1884, Alfred Temple Roberts, and has issue 1e to 2e

1e Katherine Helen Temple Roberts

2e Gwendoline Roberts

7d Madeline Isabella Fiennes-Clinton, m 20 Aug 1889, the Rev Cecil Warburton Knox (see below), and has issue 1e

1e Madeline Fiennes-Clinton Knox

8d Adela Rachel Fiennes-Clinton, m 23 July 1891, Henry Mitchell Hull, C M G (*Cromwell, Shortheath, Farnham*)

2c *Mary Katherine Fiennes-Clinton*, b 26 *Dec* 1830, d 1 *Feb* 1873, m 12 *Dec* 1855, *Gen Thomas Knox, R A , d 29 Oct* 1878, *and had issue 1d to 4d*

1d Welby Francis Knox, b 15 Dec 1859

2d Henry Fiennes-Clinton Knox, b 15 Mar 1861

3d Arthur Rice Knox, D S O, Major R A, b 8 Mar 1863

4d Rev Cecil Warburton Knox, Curate of St Margaret's, Westminster, *formerly* Rector of Harston, b 2 Nov 1865, m 20 Aug 1889, Madeline Isabella, da of the Rev Henry Fiennes-Clinton (see above), and has issue

See above, No 310

6b *Katherine Welby*, d 11 *May* 1869, m 13 *May* 1822, *the Rev Thomas Welby Northmore (see p* 52), d v p 16 *July* 1829, *and had issue 1c to 2c*

1c *Rev Thomas Welby Northmore of Cleve (which he resigned to his younger brother), Vicar of Kirk Hammerton and Weston, b 20 Aug 1823, d 12 Sept 1908,* m 3 *June* 1865, *Elizabeth, da of William Moore, and had issue 1d to 3d*

1d Thomas Welby Northmore, b 22 June 1866, m 5 Sept 1903, Margaret Ainsworth, da of Lieut -Col Gritton, R M , and has issue 1e

1e Thomas William Welby Northmore, b 18 Sept 1906

2d Geoffrey Northmore, b 28 Ap 1868

3d Evelyn Lydia Margaret Northmore, m 29 Aug 1901 Arthur Cecil Allanson Bailey (*Hornapark, Lifton, Devon*), and has issue 1e to 2e

1e Thomas Noel Allanson Bailey, b 5 Jan 1909

2e Cicely Evelyn Bailey

2c John Northmore of Cleve, co Devon, J P (*4 Abbey Mead, Tavistock*), b 1 June 1826, m 1st, 25 Aug 1863, Jemima Hayter, da of the Rev William

[Nos 325 to 353

51

The Plantagenet Roll

Hames, d s p 7 Ap 1869, 2ndly, 20 Feb 1873, Harriet Olympia Morshead, da of Northmore Herle Pierce Lawrence of Launceston, d 1 Sept 1875, 3rdly, 16 Feb 1899, Sarah Selina Persse, widow of the Rev Richard Henry Donovan, R N, da of Stephen William Creaghe of Castle Park, Golden, co Tipperary, and has issue 1d to 2d

1d John Northmore of Cullompton, b 3 Sept 1874, m 5 Sept 1903, Marion Colquhoun da of Hay Macdowell Grant, and has issue 1c to 2c

 1c John Grant Lawrence Northmore, b 18 June 1904

 2c Judith Marion Northmore

2d Olympia Northmore, m 21 Dec 1899, the Rev Richard Henry O'Donovan, Chaplain R N, and has issue 1e to 3e

 1e Terence O'Donovan, b 5 Mar 1907

 2e Norah Katherine O'Donovan

 3e Mary O'Donovan

7b *Elizabeth Welby* b 1804, d 18 Nov 1888, m 17 Feb 1829, *Thomas James Ireland of Ousden Hall,* co *Suffolk,* d 2 July 1863 *and had issue* 1c to 5c

1c Elizabeth Mary Ireland, m as 3rd wife, 29 Aug 1856, Welby Brown Jackson, Judge of the Sudder Court, Calcutta [Bt (1815) Coll], d 17 Nov 1890, and has issue 1d

 1d Cecil Welby Jackson, M F, *late* Major 3rd Bengal Cav, b 2 June 1861, m 24 July 1894, Violet Emily Caroline, da of Col Richard George Bolton, R H G (see below), and has issue (2 children)

2c Agnes Ireland, m 8 June 1852, the Rev Henry Warburton, Rector of Sible Hedingham, Essex, d (–), and has issue (3 sons living, 1 a clergyman)

3c Beatrice Ireland, m 1st, Lieut-Col Richard George Bolton, 2nd Lancashire Mil, *previously* R H G [son of Richard Bolton of Silliott Hill and Ballyshoonock, co Waterford], d 1889, 2ndly, 1896, Lieut-Col Frowd Walker (81 *Queen's Gate, S W*), and has issue 1d to 5d

 1d Richard George Ireland Bolton, Major Scots Guards, b 15 Jan 1865

 2d Alice Bolton, m Capt Dudley Loftus *late* Gren Guards, and has issue (1 child)

 3d Violet Emily Caroline Bolton, m 24 July 1894, Major Cecil Welby Jackson, M F, and has issue

 See above

 4d Maud Bolton, m 1st, A Bradshaw, d (–), 2ndly, Henry Harris, and has issue (2 children)

 5d Amy Bolton, m 5 Aug 1896, Lionel Beresford Bethell [B Westbury Coll] (*Charwelton Lodge, Byfield, Northants*) and has issue 1e to 2e

  1e Vivian Lionel Slingsby Bethell, b 5 June 1897

  2e Rupert Patrick Bethell, b 9 Sept 1902

4c Emily Ireland, m 9 Nov 1869, Sir William Algernon Kay, 5th Bt [U K], Lieut-Col (ret) 68th Regt (*St Lawrence House, Canterbury, Naval and Military*), and has issue 1d to 2d

 1d William Algernon Ireland Kay, Capt King's Royal Rifle Corps, b 21 May 1876

 2d Annie Evelyn Ireland Kay

5c Caroline Charlotte Ireland (*Owsden House, Lewes*), m as 2nd wife, 10 Aug 1880, Sir Alexander Entwisle Ramsay, 4th Bart [U K], d 1 Oct 1902, s p s

2a *Penelope Welby,* d 7 Nov 1792, m as 1st *wife, Thomas Northmore of Cleve,* co *Devon, M A, F R S* (see p 269), b 1766, d *May* 1851, *and had issue* 1b

1b *Thomas Welby Northmore, M I, Capt Scots Fusilier Guards, afterwards in Holy Orders and Rector of Winterton,* b 10 *July* 1791, d s p 16 *July* 1829, m 13 *May* 1822, *Katherine,* da *of Sir William Earle Welby, 2nd Bart* [U K], *M P,* d 11 *May* 1869, *and had issue*

See pp 51-52, Nos 347-360   [Nos 354 to 389

52

# of The Blood Royal

5 Descendants of FRANCES GLYNNE (Table II), d 25 Nov 1814, m
the Rev. RANDOLPH CREWE, LL B, Rector of Hawarden,
d (-), and had issue 1a to 2a [1]

1a Anne Crewe
2a Mary Crewe, d. (-), m (—) Chorley

6 Descendants of LUCY GLYNNE (Table II), b 26 Jan 1756, d
24 May 1814, m at Bath, Major JAMES GORDON, — Regt,
d (-), and had issue (with a son d young) 1a to 2a

   1a Lucy Wheler Gordon, da and co-h, b 30 Nov 1781, d 14 Aug 1866, m
11 Sept 1806, Richard Bateson of Newlands, Wallasey, co Chester, b 25 Dec 1770,
d 24 Feb 1863, and had issue (with 4 sons and 4 das d s p) 1b to 3b
   1b James Glynne Bateson of Wallasey, co Chester, b 20 June 1808, d 2 July
1866, m 21 Jan 1840, Anna, da of the Rev R Phillips of Bettws yn-Rhos, d
1908, and had issue (with 5 children d young) 1c to 5c
   1c Arthur William Bateson, b 28 Nov 1852
   2c Herbert Glynne Bateson, b 23 Feb 1855
   3c Constance Anne Bateson, m 15 Ap 1873, Capt Thomas Sidney St Clair
Smith, now (1874) St Clair, 49th Royal Berkshire Regt, d 14 Ap 1899, and has
issue (with a son d young) 1d to 6d
   1d James Sidney St Clair, on Staff of Egyptian State Railway, b in India
17 Oct 1874
   2d Percy Raymond St Clair, on Staff of Daily Journal, Chicago, b 15 July
1880, m 26 July 1909, Virginia, da of (—) Corse-Hunt, U S Army
   3d Constance St Clair
   4d Adah Johnes St Clair
   5d Lilian St Clair
   6d Norah Gladys St Clair
   4c Amy Charlotte Bateson
   5c. Ethel Bateson

   2b Rev William Henry Bateson, D D, Master of St John's College, Cambridge, b 3 June 1812, d 27 Mar 1881, m 11 June 1857, Anna, da of James
Aikin of Liverpool, and had issue (with a da d young) 1c to 6c
   1c William Bateson, M A, F R S, Professor of Biology, Cambridge University
(Merton House, Grantchester, Cambridge), b 8 Aug 1861, m 16 June 1896, Beatrice,
da of Arthur Durham, Senior Surgeon Guy's Hospital, and has issue 1d to 3d
   1d John Bateson, b 22 Ap 1898
   2d Martin Bateson, b 1 Sept 1899
   3d Gregory Bateson, b. 9 May 1904
   2c Edward Bateson, a Judge in Egyptian Native Tribunal (Zagazig, Egypt),
b 29 Sept 1868, unm
   3c Margaret Bateson, Editor Public Work and Women's Employment Dept
Queen Newspaper, and writer on various subjects connected with women, m
1901, William Emerton Heitland, M A, Fellow of St John's College, Cambridge
(Carmefield, Newnham, Cambridge)   [Nos 390 to 406

---

[1] Burke's " Landed Gentry," 1906, p 1407 Mr G C Chambers says there
were also four sons, and adds " In a subscription list of 1818 in a neighbouring
parish I find the Rev Offley Crewe for £20; and among the subscribers to a History of Hawarden, published in 1822, occur the Rev Charles Crewe of Longdon,
Worc, and Richard Glynne Crewe of Tamworth, Staff, Esq I think these may
without error be taken as three of the four sons, who, however, are all supposed to
have died s p "

The Plantagenet Roll

4c Anna Bateson, Market Gardener (*New Milton, Hants*), *unm*

5c *Mary Bateson, Fellow of Newnham College, Cambridge, and Historical Writer,* b 12 *Sept* 1865, d *unm* 30 *Nov* 1906

6c. Edith Bateson, Artist, R A Exhibitor, &c, *unm*

3b *Frederick Septimus Bateson,* b 24 *Mar* 1820, d 21 *May* 1900, m *at St Petersburg,* 3 *Sept* 1849, *Eliza, da of Thomas Frost,* d 23 *Ap* 1909, *and had issue (with a son d unm)* 1c *to* 4c

1c Gordon Bateson (*Church Stretton, Salop*), b 8 *Ap* 1853, m. 15 *Sept* 1888, Ellen Tindal, da of John Stevens, Bar at-Law

2c Frederick Bateson (*Sandhurst, near Gloucester*), b 22 *Aug* 1858, m 4 *Mar* 1885, Agnes, da of Frederick William Ormerod, and has issue 1d *to* 2d

1d Glynne Bateson, b 5 Feb 1886

2d Dorothy Bateson

3c Alfred Bateson (*Pheasants Hill, Hambledon, Henley, Engstuen, Drøbak, Norway*), b 20 *Nov* 1860, m 6 Feb 1901, Helga, da of Capt Lauritz Marius Wilse, Christiansand Brigade, Norwegian Army, and has issue 1d *to* 2d

1d Frederick Noel Wilse Bateson, b 25 Dec 1901

2d Richard Gordon Bateson, b 16 Nov 1903

4c *Emily Bateson,* m 8 June 1882, Robert Wood Williamson [eldest son of Professor William Crawford Williamson, D C L , F R S] (*The Croft, Didsbury*), s p

2a *Mary Anne Gordon, da and co-h,* d 1859, m 2 *Dec* 1817, *William Chambres Chambres of Plas Chambres,* d 27 *Sept* 1861, *and had issue (with a da, Mrs Hughes,* d s p *)* 1b *to* 8b

1b *William Chambres of Wallasey Grange, co Chester, J P , D L , High Sheriff co Denbigh and an Alderman of Liverpool,* b 9 *Mar* 1820, d 26 *Aug* 1893, m 2 *Oct* 1849, *Louisa Mellis, da of Lieut -Col Maddock, 10th Bengal N I ,* d 23 *Mar* 1905, *and had issue* 1c *to* 7c

1c Reginald Gordon Chambres of Pentre, *formerly* Hon Major 3rd Batt Loyal North Lancashire Regt (*Pentre, Kempsford, near Fairford, Gloucester*), b 8 Aug 1854, m 27 July 1881, May, da and h of Markland Barnard of Galley Dean, co Essex, *formerly* of the Hon Body Guard, and has issue 1d

1d Gwendolen May Gordon Chambres

2c Algernon Dennel Chambres, Stockbroker (*Wold House, Hawarden, Chester*), b 16 Mar 1856, m 3 Jan 1889, Annie, da of Thomas Burton Hassall, and has issue 1d

1d Madeline Chambres

3c Louisa Chambres (*Wern Cottage, Mochdre, near Colwyn Bay*), *unm*

4c Florence Chambres, m 16 May 1896, as 2nd wife, John Wood (see p 55) (*Bramerton Lodge, Carlisle*), s p

5c Ethel Chambres (*Wern Cottage, Mochdre, near Colwyn Bay*), *unm*

6c Blanche Chambres (*The Mount, Boughton, Chester*), m 14 June 1883, Alfred Shaw of Hoole, Cheshire, d (–), and has issue 1d

1d Phyllis Shaw

7c Gwendolen Chambres, m 16 Oct 1885, Edward Cazenove, Stockbroker, Major Northamptonshire Imp Yeo (*Cottesbrooke Cottage, Northampton*), and has issue 1d *to* 2d

1d Ralph de L'Hérisson Cazenove, b 11 July 1892

2d Philip Henry de L'Hérisson Cazenove, b 21 Dec 1901

2b *Philip Henry Chambres of Llysmeirchion, J P , D L , High Sheriff co Denbigh* 1867, b 29 *Sept* 1822, d 31 *Aug* 1909, m 1st, 7 *Sept* 1848, *Mary, da of the Rev Robert Chambres Chambres,* d 21 *Mar* 1860, 2ndly, 2 Oct 1862, *Louisa, da of Richard Lloyd Williams of Denbigh, M D , and had issue (with others* d s p *)* 1c *to* 7c

1c Henry Chambres Chambres (*Carlett Cottage, Eastham, Cheshire*), b 24 Nov

[Nos 407 to 429

1849, *m* 2 Sept 1876, Maria Josephine, da of Thomas Langton Birley of Carr Hill, co Lanc, and has issue (with a son *d* young) 1*d* to 2*d*

    1*d* Josephine Chambres

    2*d* Maria Chambres

    2*c* *Robert Chambres Chambres*, b 10 *Jan* 1851, d 17 *July* 1897, m 11 *Dec* 1879, *Martha Ann (Huntington Court, Kington, co Hereford), da of George Hamerton Crump of Chorlton Hall, co Chester, J P*, and had issue 1*d* to 5*d*

        1*d* Robert Noel Chambres, *b* 11 Mar 1882

        2*d* Philip Chambres, *b* 15 Dec 1885

        3*d* John Hamilton Chambres, *b* 21 May 1887

        4*d* Winifred Chambres

        5*d* Harriet Gladys Chambres

    3*c* Edward Lloyd Chambres (*Canada*), b 10 May 1868, m 24 Feb 1897, Winifred Ellen, da of George Banner, and has issue 1*d* to 2*d*

        1*d* Eileen Chambres, *b* 26 May 1903

        2*d* Dorothea Grace Chambres, *b* 6 May 1907

    4*c* Caryl Lloyd Chambres (*176 Warwick Road, Carlisle*), *b* 20 Dec 1871, m 15 July 1896, Madge, da of Francis Reading of Rugby, co Warwick, and has issue 1*d* to 3*d*

        1*d* Mona Chambres, *b* 24 May 1896

        2*d* Betty Glynne Chambres, *b* 6 Jan 1905

        3*d* Gwendoline Maud Lloyd Chambres, *b* 17 Aug 1907

    5*c* Hugh Lloyd Chambres, *b* 24 Aug 1874, m 3 Ap 1907, Susanna Langford, da of Hercules E Brown of Burton Hall, Kingskerswell, co Devon, and has issue 1*d*

        1*d* Cora Langford Chambres, *b* 17 Dec 1909

    6*c* Mary Chambres, *unm*

    7*c* Maud Chambres (*Great Saughall, near Chester*), m 12 Jan 1886, Thomas Edward Hassell, *d* (being drowned off Port Erin, Isle of Man) 21 Oct 1899, and has issue (with an elder son, Lionel, drowned with his father) 1*d*

        1*d* Alexander Burton Hassell, *b* 22 July 1896

    3*b* *Charles Crewe Chambres of the Eyrie, Wallasey, co Chester*, b 4 Ap 1828, d 26 Feb 1866, m 6 *June* 1860, *Lucy, da of John Bewley of the Slopes, Wallasey, and had issue* (with a son, Austin, d *unm*) 1*c* to 2*c*

    1*c* Rev Gordon Crewe Chambres, M A (Oxon), Headmaster, Wigan Grammar School, *b* 26 Ap 1861, *unm*

    2*c* Huldah Crewe Chambres

    4*b* *Lucy Chambres*, b 3 Sept 1818, d at Mold 7 Oct 1871, m at Liverpool 30 May 1839, *Charles Hughes Ingleby, Bar-at-Law*, d 9 May 1849, and had issue (with a son, Charles, d *unm*) 1*c*

    1*c* *Fanny Ingleby*, b 19 Nov 1842, d 3 Jan 1893, m as 1st wife, 18 May 1870, *John Wood, C E* (see *p* 54) (*Bramerton Lodge, Botcherby, Carlisle*), and had issue (with 2 sons d s p) 1*d* to 2*d*

        1*d* John Crewe Wood (*53 Bath Road, Swindon, Wilts*), *b* 31 Aug 1873

        2*d* Florence Margaret Wood, *unm*

    5*b* Penelope Chambres (*Tycroes, Llandulas, Abergele*)

    6*b* Emma Chambres (*Lystonville, Porthill, Shrewsbury*), m 23 Jan 1849, the Rev Hugh George Robinson, Canon of York, *d* 16 June 1882, and has issue 1*c* to 9*c*

    1*c* Hugh Malcolm Robinson, Dep Chief Inspector of Factories (*Home Office, S W*), *b* 13 Feb 1857, *m* 2 Ap 1884, Annie Elizabeth Helen, da of Major Hugh Henry Christian, and has issue 1*d* to 3*d*

        1*d* Hugh George Robinson, *b* 11 May 1886

        2*d* Helen Gertrude Robinson

        3*d* Annie Cloberry Robinson

[Nos 430 to 458

The Plantagenet Roll

2c William Christian Robinson (*New Zealand*), b c 1859, m and has issue 3 das

3c. Frederick Hampden Robinson (*Fall Hill, Fredericksburg, Virginia*), b 14 Jan 1864, m 1897, Elizabeth, da of Capt Murray Lee Taylor, and has issue 1d to 2d

1d Frederick Robinson, b 1903.

2d Butler Braine Thornton Robinson, b Feb 1899

4c Alfred Falkland Robinson (*Johannesburg*), b 6 Aug 1865, m 1895, Helena, da of (—) van Eysen, and has issue 1d

1d Hugh Falkland Robinson, b 23 Jan. 1896

5c Emma Chambres Robinson (*London and Church Stretton*), m 19 Sept 1882, Henry David Boyle, and has issue 1d

1d David Hugh Montgomerie Boyle, b 1 Sept 1883.

6c Gertrude Robinson, m 27 Oct 1882, Augustus Walter Francis Warde (*Ouray, Colorado, U S A*), and has issue 1d

1d Doris Warde

7c Mary Jane Robinson, } *unm.*
8c Edith Robinson }

9c Charlotte Emily Robinson, m 1894, Hugh Bovill (*Bovill, Idaho, U S A*), and has issue 1d to 2d

1d Dorothy Bovill

2d Gwendoline Bovill

7b Mary Anne Chambres } (*Tycroes, Llandulas, Abergele*)
8b Grace Chambres }   [Nos 459 to 475

7. Descendants, if any, of MARY GLYNNE (see Table II.), d (–), m. SIMON GORDON, *living* 1802.[1]

8. Descendants of MARIA MARGRETTA LONGUEVILLE [eldest da and in her issue sole h of Sir Thomas Longueville, 4th Bart [E.]] (Table II.), b 1722, d (–); m. 1st, 1739, THOMAS (sometimes called JOHN) JONES, d. 29 Sept. 1749, and had with other issue 1a

1a *Thomas Jones of The Court, Wrexham, Lieut 104th Regt and afterwards Capt Denbigh and Merioneth Militia,* b 1740, d (*being shot in a duel by his Guardian, R S Manning*) 26 Oct 1799, m 1st, at Wrexham, 4 May 1767, *Jane, da of John Jones of Aberkin, co Carnarvon,* d 1 Oct 1768, 2ndly, Anne, da of (—) Lloyd, d 27 June 1796, and had issue 1b to 6b

1b. *Thomas Longueville Jones, afterwards Longueville of Prestatyn,* b 18 Sept 1768, d 21 Dec 1831, m 30 Nov 1796, Anne, da of John Gibbons of Oswestry, d 13 June 1861, and had issue 1c to 2c

1c *Thomas Longueville Longueville of Penyllan, co. Salop,* b 7 July 1803, d 27 Oct 1888, m 9 Oct 1838, Anne, da of Charles Thomas Jones of Oswestry (see p 63), d 8 Feb 1884, and had issue 1d to 2d

1d *Thomas Longueville of Penyllan, J P (Llanforda Hall, Oswestry),* b 29 Ap 1841, m 29 June 1868, Mary Frances, da and h of Alexander Robertson of Balgownie Lodge, co Aberdeen, and has issue 1e to 4e   [No 476

---

[1] Betham's "Baronetage," 1802, ii 264 They apparently had no issue in 1822 and presumably d s p.

56

# of The Blood Royal

1e Reginald Longueville, Major Coldstream Guards, b 26 Mar 1869
2e Edward Longueville, Lieut Coldstream Guards, b 22 Dec 1877
3e Francis Longueville, b 23 Dec 1892
4e Mary Margaret Anne Isabel Longueville

2d Anna Maria Longueville (*Penyllan, Oswestry*)

2c *Rev John Gibbons Longueville*, b 18 *Sept* 1810, d 14 *July* 1882, m
29 Mar 1836, *Agnes Frewin, da of John Timothy Swainson of Elm Grove, co
Lanc., Comptroller of H M's Customs for the Port of Liverpool*, d 11 *Jan* 1904,
and had issue 1d *to* 2d
   1d Edith Longueville (2 *Park Place, Torquay*)
   2d Cecile Longueville, m Frank Parker of Chester

2b² *Edward Jones*, b 17 *Ap* 1774, d (-), m *Charlotte, da of* (—) *Stevens*,
and had issue 1c *to* 3c
   1c Rev Harry Longueville Jones, *M A , Fellow Magdalen Coll , Oxon , living*
28 *Jan* 1858
   2c Charlotte Jones, *unm*
   3c (—) Jones, m (—) Naylor, living in Italy

3b *Hugh Jones of Larkhill, co Lancaster*, b 20 *Sept* 1776, d 1842, m
24 *Mar* 1806, *Elizabeth, of Larkhill, da of Benjamin Heywood of Stanley Hall,
Wakefield, co York*, d 1848, *and had issue* 1c *to* 6c
   1c *Richard Heywood Jones of Babsworth Hall, co York, J P*, b 20 *Oct* 1810,
d 6 *Jan* 1874, m 11 *Oct* 1836, *Margaret, da of John Harrison of Ambleside*, d
9 *Sept* 1877, *and had issue* 1d *to* 4d
      1d *Richard Heywood Jones, afterwards* (*R L* 22 *Jan* 1891) *Heywood-Jones
of Babsworth Hall, J P, Major and Hon Lieut -Col Yorkshire Dragoons Yeo
Cavalry*, b 28 *July* 1853, d 11 *June* 1900, m 17 *July* 1888, *Caroline Margaret
(Babsworth Hall, near Pontefract), da of Francis John Johnston of Dunsdale,
Westerham [by his wife Caroline, da of Sir Hardman Earle, 1st Bart [U.K]], and
had issue* 1e *to* 4e
         1e Margaret Heywood Heywood-Jones
         2e Violet Mary Heywood-Jones
         3e Caroline Earle Heywood-Jones
         4e Cicely Longueville Heywood-Jones
      2d Katherine Jones
      3d Mary Venetia Jones, m 18 June 1868, the Rev Clarke Watkins Burton,
M A , Rural Dean and Hon Canon of Carlisle, Rector of Cliburne (*Templesowerby,
near Penrith*), and has issue 1e to 4e
         1c Katherine Venetia Burton
         2e Florence Burton, m 20 Jan 1898, Charles Willding Willding-Jones, *late*
Rifle Brigade (see p 61) (*Hampton Hall, Malpas*), and has issue 1f to 4f
            1f Conway Willding-Jones, b 28 Oct 1901
            2f. Charles Longueville Willding-Jones, b 28 Jan 1905
            3f Rona Mary Willding-Jones
            4f Diana Anne Willding-Jones
         3e Mary Burton
         4e. Angela Margaret Burton
      4d Elizabeth Jones

   2c *Benjamin Heywood Jones of Larkhill, J P , D L , High Sheriff co Lancaster* 1869, b 1812, d. 1872, m 1848, *Louisa Elizabeth, da of Hugh Hornby of
Sandown, Liverpool , and had issue* 1d *to* 5d
      1d Arthur Heywood Jones of Larkhill (*Larkhill, West Derby, Lancashire*), b
1851
      2d Oliver Heywood Jones   [Nos 477 to 502

57

The Plantagenet Roll

3d Llewellyn Heywood Jones

4d Benjamin Noel Heywood Jones

5d Annie Louisa Heywood Jones (*Frampton Hall, Boston, Lincolnshire*), m 14 July 1874, Francis Foljambe Anderson, J P [2nd son of Sir Charles Henry John Anderson, 9th Bart [E], and a descendant of George (Plantagenet), Duke of Clarence, K G (see Clarence Volume, p 608)], d v p 15 Sept 1881, and has issue 1e to 3e

1e Margaret Louise Anderson, m 7 June 1905, Wilfred Arthur Duncombe, now (R L 6 June 1905) Duncombe-Anderson, Lieut Reserve of Officers, *formerly* 6th Dragoon Guards [E of Feversham Coll and a descendant of the Lady Anne, sister of King Edward IV, &c (see Exeter Volume, pp 205, 647) (*Lea Hall, Gainsborough*), and has issue 1f to 2f

1f Antony John Duncombe-Anderson, b 4 Feb 1907

2f Roland Frederick Duncombe-Anderson, b 18 Ap 1908

2e Katharine Helen Anderson, m 9 Mar 1904, Richard Coningsby Sutton [Bt of Norwood (1772) Coll], d 12 Sept 1905, and has issue 1f to 3f

1f Francis Richard Heywood Sutton, b 9 Feb 1905

2f Olinda Margaret Sutton, } b (twins) posthumous 4 Mar 1906
3f Olivia Katharine Sutton, }

3e Frances Olive Anderson

3c *Elizabeth Anne Jones*, d 16 *Jan* 1880, m 10 *Sept* 1828, *Samuel Bright of Sandheys, Liverpool, and Ashfield, co Lancaster, J P*, b 25 Sept 1799, d 28 *Jan* 1870, *and had issue* 1d *to* 7d

1d *Henry Arthur Bright of Ashfield, J P*, b 9 Feb 1830, d 5 *May* 1884, m 26 *June* 1861, *Mary Elizabeth (26 Gloucester Square, London), da of Samuel Henry Thompson of Thingwall Hall, Liverpool, D L, and had issue* 1e *to* 5e

1e Allan Heywood Bright, J P, M P for Oswestry 1904-6 (*Ashfield, Knotty Ash, Liverpool, Gorse Hey, Moss Lane, West Derby, Liverpool, Brookside, Weston Rhyn, Salop*), b 24 May 1862, m 10 June 1885, Edith, da of Alfred Turner, J P, and has issue 1f

1f Edith Honora Bright

2e Henry Yates Bright (*Lima, Peru, 26 Gloucester Square, W*), b 21 Aug 1865, m 14 Sept 1904, Elena, da of Capt Manuel Ferreyros, Peruvian Navy, and has issue 1f

1f Henry Edward Yates Bright, b 19 Feb 1906

3e Rev Hugh Bright, M A (Camb), Vicar of King Cross, Halifax, b 4 May 1867

4e Elizabeth Phœbe Bright, m 18 Dec 1889, Charles Merivale [son of Dean Merivale] (18 *Norfolk Crescent, London, W*), and has issue 1f to 2f

1f Alexander Merivale, b 2 Dec 1901

2f Phœbe Merivale, b 2 Jan 1891

5e Mary Honora Bright

2d *Heywood Bright of Sandheys, J P*, b 20 *Oct* 1836, d *Mar* 1897, m 4 *Nov* 1884, *Dorothea Anne (The Danes, Little Berkhamsted, Herts), da of Col John Ireland Blackburne of Hale Hall, and had issue* 1e

1e Ursula Dorothea Elizabeth Bright

3d Samuel Bright (5 *Huskisson Street, Liverpool*), b 15 Jan 1843

4d Sarah Elizabeth Mesnard Bright (90 *Chatham Street, Liverpool*), m 20 Nov 1852, George Melly, J P, D L, M P for Stoke-on-Trent 1868-75, d 1894, and has issue 1e to 7e

1e George Henry Melly, Shipowner (90 *Chatham Street, Liverpool*), b 5 Mar 1860

2e Hugh Mesnard Melly, Wool Broker (*The Quinta, Greenhayes Road, Liverpool*), b 23 July 1863, m 1st, 11 Aug 1886, Cicely Anne, da of William Durning

[Nos 503 to 527

# of The Blood Royal

Holt of Liverpool, *d* 23 Mar 1890, 2ndly, 4 Dec 1895, Eleanor Lawrence, da of Peter Owen of Capenhurst, co Chester, and has issue 1*f* to 5*f*

1*f* Hugh Peter Egerton Mesnard Melly, *b* 6 Oct 1896
2*f* André John Mesnard Melly, *b* 9 Oct 1898
3*f* ¹ Margaret Mesnard Melly
4*f* ¹ Joan Mesnard Melly
5*f* ² Eleanor Mesnard Melly

3*e* William Rathbone Melly, Merchant (*Liverpool*), *b* 30 Mar 1867
4*e* Samuel Heywood Melly (15 *Parkfield Road, Liverpool, S*), *b* 31 May 1871, *m* 7 July 1898, Edith Matilda, da of John Roylance Court of Birkdale, and has issue 1*f* to 2*f*

1*f* Francis Heywood Melly, *b* 27 Dec 1899
2*f* Dorothy Heywood Melly

5*e* Mary Eveline Melly
6*e* Florence Elizabeth Melly
7*e* Ellen Beatrice Melly, *m* 13 July 1881, F Rawdon Smith, J P, Encaustic Tile Manufacturer, and has issue 1*f* to 4*f*

1*f* George Francis Rawdon Smith, M B, *b* 8 May 1882
2*f* William Herbert Rawdon Smith, *b* 24 Oct 1887
3*f* Edward Rawdon Smith, *b* 2 July 1890
4*f* Beatrice Emma Rawdon Smith

5*d* Elizabeth Bright (*Sudley, Mossley Hill, Liverpool*), *m* 1 Dec 1853, George Holt, *d.* 3 Ap 1896, and has issue 1*e*

1*e* Emma Georgina Holt

6*d* Harriette Bright
7*d* *Anna Maria Bright*, d 22 *May* 1904, m 15 *Sept* 1874, *Archibald Weir of St Munghos, Malvern, M D*, d 17 *May* 1894, *and had issue* 1*e* to 3*e*

1*e* Hugh Heywood Weir, M A, M B (Camb), M R C S (Eng), L R C P (Lond) (*St Luke's Hospital, Chemulpo, Korea*), *b* 29 Aug 1875, *m* 13 Feb 1904, Margaret, da of the Rev Frederic Charles Skey of Weare
2*e* George Alexander Weir, Capt 3rd Dragoon Guards, B A (Camb), *b* 31 Dec 1876
3*e* Henry Bright Weir, M A (Camb), M R C S, L R C P (Lond) (*St Thomas' Hospital, London*), *b* 23 June 1880

4*c* *Mary Ellen Jones*, d 23 *Sept* 1865, m 28 *Jan* 1836, *Robertson Gladstone of Court Hey, Liverpool, J P* [*Bt of Fasque Coll and brother of the Right Hon W E Gladstone*], b 15 *Nov* 1805, d 23 *Sept* 1875, *and had issue* 1*d* to 3*d*

1*d* Walter Longueville Gladstone, heir-presumptive to Baronetcy [U K] (*Court Hey, Broad Green, Liverpool*), *b* 30 Sept 1846
2*d* *Mary Ellen Gladstone*, d 17 *Sept* 1895, m 16 *Feb* 1860, *Robert Gladstone, J P. (Woolton Vale, near Liverpool)*, *and had issue* 1*e* to 11*e*

1*e* Arthur Steuart Gladstone, *b* 27 Nov 1860
2*e.* John Steuart Gladstone, *b* 13 Aug 1862
3*e* Robert Gladstone, *b* 6 May 1866
4*e* Ernest Steuart Gladstone, *b.* 6 July 1867
5*e* Mary Ellen Gladstone
6*e* Katherine Steuart Gladstone
7*e* Flora Steuart Gladstone
8*e* Edith Steuart Gladstone
9*e* Margaret Steuart Gladstone
10*e* Helen Steuart Gladstone
11*e* Lilian Steuart Gladstone

[Nos 528 to 561

59

The Plantagenet Roll

3d *Anna Maria Heywood Gladstone*, d 14 May 1901, m 14 *Dec* 1870, *Edward John Thornewill of Dove Cliff, Burton-on-Trent*, d 22 *Mar* 1901, *and had issue* 1e *to* 4e

 1e Edward Noel Thornewill, *b* 25 Dec 1874

 2e Hugh Pearson Thornewill, *b* 25 Feb 1876

 3e Arthur Basil Thornewill, *b* 2 Dec 1877.

 4e Hilda Mary Thornewill

5c *Harriette Jones*, d 1855, m *Daniel Neilson of Hundhill, Pontefract*

6c *Emma Jones*, d 2 *Jan* 1904, m 28 *Oct* 1840, *the Hon Richard Denman* (*see p* 166) [*B Denman Coll*], d 19 *Mar* 1887, *and had issue* 1d *to* 6d

1d *Richard Denman*, b 3 *Jan* 1842, d v p 5 *Ap* 1883, m 31 *May* 1871, *Helen Mary, da. of Gilbert M'Micking of Miltonise, co Wigtown, and had issue* 1e *to* 3e

 1e Thomas (Denman), 3rd Baron Denman [U K], P C, K C V O, a Lord in Waiting to King Edward VII 1905-1907, and Capt Comdg 35th Squadron Imp Yeo in South Africa 1900-1901 (*Balcombe Place, Sussex, Stony Middleton, Derby*), *b* 16 Nov 1874, *m* 26 Nov 1903, Gertrude Mary, da of Sir Weetman Dickinson Pearson, 1st Bt [U K], M P, and has issue 1*f* to 2*f*

  1*f* Hon Thomas Denman, *b* 2 Aug 1905

  2*f* Hon Anne Judith Denman

 2e Hon Richard Douglas Denman, Private Sec to Postmaster-Gen (9 *Swan Walk, Chelsea, S W*), *b* 24 Aug 1876, *m* 11 Feb 1904, Helen Christian, da of Sir Thomas Sutherland, G C M G, LL D

 3e Hon Anna Maria Heywood Denman, *m* 13 July 1895, Sir John Emmott Barlow, 1st Bart [U K], M P, J P (*Torkington Lodge, Hazelgrove, near Stockport, Bryn Eirias, Colwyn Bay, &c*), and has issue 1*f* to 4*f*

  1*f* John Denman Barlow, *b* 15 June 1898

  2*f* Thomas Bradwall Barlow, *b* 7 Mar 1900

  3*f* Nancy Mary Emmott Barlow.

  4*f* Anna Elizabeth Barlow

2d Thomas Hugh Anderson Denman, Barrister, Lincoln's Inn (*Lavant, Chichester*), *b*. 16 Jan 1855, *m* 28 Jan 1890, Margaret Evelyn [descended from King Henry VII (see Tudor Roll, p 313)], da of Charles Watson Townley of Fulbourn Manor, Cambridge, and has issue 1e *to* 3e

 1e Richard Charles Denman, *b* 16 Aug 1896

 2e John Evelyn Thomas Denman, *b* 21 Dec 1901.

 3e Margaret Cecil Denman

3d *Emma Sophia Georgiana Denman*, *m* 1st, 31 Oct 1872, Capt Oswin Cumming Baker-Cresswell of Cresswell, J P, d 26 Feb 1886, 2ndly as 2nd wife, 7 Sept 1892, Henry George (Liddell), 2nd Earl of Ravensworth [U K], *d s p m* 22 July 1903, 3rdly, 30 Ap 1904, James William Wadsworth, and has issue 1e *to* 4e

 1e Addison Francis Baker-Cresswell of Cresswell and Harehope, Capt. Northumberland Imp Yeo, *late* Scots Guards (*Cresswell, Morpeth, Harehope, Alnwick*), *b* 8 Nov 1874, *m* 2 Feb 1899, Idonea, da of S F Widdrington of Newton Hall, co Northumberland, and had issue 1*f* to 3*f*

  1*f* John Baker-Cresswell, *b* 7 Dec 1899

  2*f* Addison Joe Baker-Cresswell, *b* 2 Feb 1901

  3*f* Cynthia Mary Baker-Cresswell

 2e Henry Baker-Cresswell, Capt *late* 15th Hussars, *b* 17 Mar 1876

 3e Susan Elizabeth Baker-Cresswell, *m* 13 July 1896, Frederick P Barnett; and has issue

 4e Mary Emma Baker-Cresswell, *m* 16 Oct 1897, Col Frederick Charlton Meyrick [s and h of Sir Thomas Meyrick, 1st Brt [U K], C B], and a descendant

[Nos 562 to 586

of King Henry VII , &c (see the Essex Volume, Tudor Supplement, p 486)]
(*Bush, Pembroke*) , and has issue 1f to 3f

 1f Thomas Frederick Meyrick, *b* 29 Nov 1899

 2f Mary Cicely Meyrick

 3f Rachel Eva Meyrick

 4d Elizabeth Margaret Denman (14 *St George's Road, S W*), *m* 20 Jan 1870,
Sir Peniston Milbanke 9th Bart [E], J P , D L , *b* 14 Feb 1847, *d* 30 Nov 1899,
and has issue 1e to 2e

 1e Sir John Peniston Milbanke, 10th Bart [E] V C , Major 10th Hussars
(19 *Eaton Terrace, S W*), *b* 9 Oct 1872 *m* 6 Dec 1900, Amelia (Leila) dr of the
Hon Charles Frederick Crichton , and has issue 1f to 2f

  1f John Peniston Charles Milbanke, *b* 9 Jan 1902

  2f Ralph Mark Milbanke, *b* 11 Ap 1907

 2e Mark Richard Milbanke (*Bath*), *b* 17 Mar 1875

 5d Anna Maria Denman, *m* 16 July 1867, Reginald Garton Wilberforce, J P ,
D L [a son of the Lord Bishop of Winchester, and a descendant of the Lady Anne,
sister of Kings Edward IV and Richard III] (*Bramlands, Hensfield, Sussex*), and
has issue

 See the Essex Volume, Exeter Supplement, p 660, Nos 56226 216-229

 6d Eleanora Denman, *m* 11 Feb 1907, Richard Patrick Boyle Davey (200
Ashley Gardens, S W)

 4b *Charles Thomas Jones of Oswestry*, b (*twin*) (*at Wrexham*) 28 Aug 1777
d 16 Oct 1857, m (*at St Thomas', Liverpool*) 27 Dec 1802, *Maria, da of (—)
Welsh*, d (-), *and had issue (with 3 sons who d ~ p)* 1c to 3c

 1c *Charles Wildding Jones of the Dingle, Liverpool*, b 2 Feb 1805 , d 11 *Jan*
1849, m 1st, 27 *Ap* 1831, *Mary, da of William Preston of Birchfield*, d 1 *Jan*
1833 , 2ndly (*in Chester Cathedral*) 21 *Aug* 1843, *Elizabeth, da of John Hassall of
Chester*, d 27 *May* 1902, *and had issue* 1d *to* 3d

 1d Wildding Jones, now (R L 28 July 1891) Wildding Jones of Hampton Hall,
M A (Oxon) (*Hampton Hall, Malpas, Cheshire*), b 27 May 1832, m 17 June
1863, Catherine Anne, da of James Thomas Murray of Edinburgh, W S , and has
issue 1e to 3e

 1e Charles Wildding Wildding-Jones, *late* Rifle Brigade, b 14 Ap 1864, m
20 Jan 1898, Florence, da of the Rev Canon Clarke Watkins Burton , and has
issue

 See p 57, Nos 494-497

 2e Murray Wildding Wildding-Jones b 11 June 1867

 3e Venetia Marie Wildding Wildding-Jones

 2d Charles Digby Jones (12 *Chester Street, Edinburgh*), b 4 Nov 1844, m
3 Sept 1872, Aimee Susanna, da of Surgeon Major Robert Christie, 3rd Bengal
Cav , and has issue 1e to 3e.

 1e Charles Kenelm Digby Jones, F G S , Mining Engineer (*Maroa, Rhodesia*),
b 28 June 1873, *m* 18 Mar 1896, Lily Christine, da of Col Joseph Beauchamp
Leggett, 10th Madras Inf , and has issue 1f to 2f

  1f Philip Kenelm Digby Jones, *b* 10 Mar 1897

  2f Mary Elizabeth Digby Jones, *b* 1 June 1901

 2e *Robert James Thomas Digby Jones V C , Lieut R E ,* b 27 Sept 1876 , d
unm (being killed in defence of Wagon Hill, Ladysmith) 6 *Jan* 1900

 3e Owen Glyndwr Digby Jones, Capt R E , b 8 Jan 1880 m 2 July 1907,
Gwenllian Cecil, da of the Rev George Philipps

 3d Richard Everard Jones (*Fassfern, Kinloch il, R S O Inverness-shire*), b
12 Dec 1848, *m* 25 June 1872, Louisa Mary Anne, da of Major Hector Macneil,
one of H M Corps of Gentlemen-at-Arms to Queen Victoria, and has issue
1e to 3e

[Nos 587 to 624

The Plantagenet Roll

1e Willding Everard Jones, Capt Lovat Scouts, Imp Yeo, b 13 Sept 1884

2e Lilly Everard Jones, unm

3e Eva Conway Everard Jones, m 4 Feb 1903, Capt Edward Sinclair Gooch, Berkshire Yeo formerly 7th Hussars [nephew of Sir Daniel Gooch, 1st Bart [U K], M P] and has issue 1f

    1f Bridget Mary Gooch, b 3 Mar 1904

2c Maria Diana Jones, b 25 Oct 1809, d 20 Oct 1894 m 6 Ap 1831, the Rev Thomas Griffith Roberts, Rector of Llanrwst, d 28 Aug 1852, and had issue 1d to 6d

    1d Thomas Vaughan Roberts, b 31 Jan 1832 d 29 June 1903, m 13 Dec 1865, Julia, da of Capt William Way Baker, 32nd Madras N I , and had issue 1e to 3e

    1e Hugh Alexander Roberts, Solicitor, b 13 Sept 1866 m 10 Sept 1908, Eleanor (see p 90) da of John Henville Hulbert of Stakes Hill, co Hants

    2e Ada Charlotte Roberts, m 29 July 1899, Francis Adolphus Jones, and has issue 1f to 3f

        1f Humphrey Charles Vaughan Jones, b 27 July 1900

        2f Philip Sydney Jones, b 4 July 1902

        3f Barbara Winifred Jones b 24 Jan 1907

    3e Winifred Roberts, unm

    2d Susan Ellen Roberts (1 Great Bedford Street, Bath), m 6 Aug 1867, the Rev Abraham Matchett, Rector of Timmingham, co Norfolk, d 17 Sept 1883, and has issue 1e to 4e

    1e Anwyl Charles Matchett, M B (Edin), Surgeon (Nether Stowey, Bridgwater), b 25 July 1868, m (at Marseilles) 3 Aug 1903, Céline Celestine Raphael, da of Paul A d'Ondits of Hellette, Basse Pyrenees

    2e Rev James Trevor Matchett, M A (Camb), Vicar of St Michael-at-Thorn (2 Wood Street, Norwich), b 15 Jan 1871, m 9 July 1907, Cicely Mary, da of Albert Ketteringham of Norwich, and has issue 1f

        1f Charles Paul Trevor Matchett, b 24 Jan 1909

    3e Ethel Susan Matchett

    4e Mabel Katharine Matchett, m 10 Ap 1901, Sidney Herbert Hayes, Tea Planter (Lethenty Hatton, Ceylon) and has issue 1f to 3f

        1f Trevor Sidney Hayes, b (in Ceylon) 21 May 1903

        2f Herbert Leonard Hayes, b (in Ceylon) 5 Sept 1905

        3f John Douglas Hayes, b 22 May 1909

    3d Maria Roberts (9 West Cromwell Road, S W), m 15 Aug 1861, Henry Vallings, d 30 Sept 1901 and has issue 1e to 3e

    1e Henry Alan Vallings, Major 29th Punjabis, b 24 Ap 1866, m 25 Nov 1899, Gertrude, da of (—) Whitchurch, and has issue 1f to 2f

        1f Doris Gwendolen Vallings, b (in India) 18 Jan 1902

        2f Gertrude Colleen Vallings, b (in India) 7 Mar 1907

    2e Gertrude Maria Vallings

    3e Gwynedd Maud Vallings, m 7 June 1894, Walter French Dunsterville (Lushill, Stock, Essex), and has issue 1f

        1f Marie Iseult Dunsterville

    4d Margaret Anne Roberts, unm

    5d Louisa Roberts, m 23 June 1863, Alexander Brooke (Handford, Cheshire), and has issue 1e to 8e

    1e Alexander Trafford Brooke, Merchant (34 Craven Hill Gardens, W), b 14 May 1864, unm

    2e Richard Hadden Brooke, J P , Merchant (Bombay), b 30 Mar 1878, unm

    3e Eleanor Mary Brooke, unm   [Nos 625 to 655

4e Louisa Beatrice Helen Brooke, *m* 31 July 1890, Harcourt Augustine Francis Chambers, Accountant Merchant Taylors Company (*Herongate, Brentwood*), s *p*

5e Florence Brooke, *m* 14 Oct 1890, John Anderson (*Ceylon*), and has issue 1*f* to 5*f*

    1*f* Alexander Bruce Anderson, *b* in Ceylon 25 Sept 1899

    2*f* Elsie Florence Anderson, *b* in Ceylon

    3*f* Hilda Eleanor Anderson, *b* in Ceylon

    4*f* Margaret Doris Anderson, *b* in Ceylon

    5*f* Janet Beatrice Anderson

6e Elsie Frances Brooke, *m* (at Bombay) 7 Ap 1903, Major Joseph George Hulbert, I M S (see pp 89-90), and has issue 1*f*

    1*f* Richard Carson Hulbert, *b* (in India) 10 July 1907

7e Constance Brooke, *m* 18 Ap 1900, Thomas Todd (*Elmhall, Hartford, Cheshire*), and has issue 1*f*

    1*f* Dorothy Annie Todd, *b* 24 Jan 1907

    8e Margaret Brooke, *unm*

    6*d* Elizabeth Roberts, *unm*

3c *Anne Jones*, d 8 Feb 1884, m 9 Oct 1838, *her cousin, Thomas Longueville Longueville, formerly Jones of Penyllan*, d 27 Oct 1888 *and had issue*

See p 56, Nos 476-481

5b *Harriette Jones* b 4 Dec 1780 d 17 Feb 1846, m 26 Feb 1802 *Francis Edge Barker of Llyndir, co Denbigh*, d 10 June 1827, *and had issue* (*with 2 other sons and 2 das who died unm*) 1c to 4c

    1c *Richard Barker of Chester and Llyndir, co Denbigh*, b 2 Sept 1808, d 20 Dec 1877, m 27 June 1833, Sarah, da of *Henry Potts of Chester and Glinyrafon, co Flint*, d 12 Nov 1881, *and had issue* (*with 2 other sons who died young*) 1d to 4d

    1d *Francis Henry Barker of Llyndir*, b 8 June 1834 d 11 Mar 1903, m 14 Jan 1858, Elizabeth Anne, da of *John Henry Yates of Preston Brook, co Chester*, d 20 Dec 1901, *and had issue* (*with an eldest son who d unm*) 1e *to* 8e

    1e Harry Yates Barker (*Chester, Llyndir, co Denbigh*), b 1 Ap 1861, m 17 Ap 1888, Amelia da of *Benjamin Dodsworth of York*, and has issue 1*f* to 2*f*

    1*f* Francis Brock Barker, *b* 30 Mar 1893

    2*f* Winefride Mary Barker, *b* 5 July 1895

    2e Ernest Longueville Barker, Bank Manager (*Dulverton, Somerset*), *b* 17 July 1862, m Oct 1901, Grace Alice, da of (—) McOstrich, of London

    3e Walter Hugh Barker, Architect (*Plymouth*), b 19 June 1865, m 1 Aug 1903, Lilian, da of (—) Turner, and has issue 1*f*

    1*f* Edward Yates Barker, *b* 18 Ap 1905

    4e Geoffrey Lionel Barker, Land Agent (*Newton Abbot, Devon*), b 6 Nov 1869, m 20 Feb 1908, Mabel Annie, da of *Thomas Rees*, and has issue 1*f*

    1*f* Lionel Rees Barker *b* 28 June 1909

    5e Francis Guy Barker (*Lower Whitcroft, Hereford*), b 25 Aug 1875 m 16 Oct 1907 Ethel, da of Col Carie Fulton, *late* Durham L I

    6e Ethel Barker, *unm*

    7e Mabel Barker, *m* 4 June 1903, George Henry Rogerson, Solicitor (*Chester*), and has issue 1*f*

    1*f* Elizabeth Mabel Rogerson *b* 16 July 1905

    8e Maud Elizabeth Barker (*Southsea*), *m* 8 Jan 1895, Capt Augustus Frederick Cooper, Royal Welsh Fusiliers, d (—) and has issue 1*f* to 2*f*

    1*f* Frederick Augustus Cooper, *b* 14 Jan 1899

    2*f* Jane Cooper

[Nos 656 to 689

The Plantagenet Roll

2d Richard Longueville Barker, Land Agent (10 *Eaton Road, Chester. St Werburgh Chambers, Chester*), b 14 Mar 1837, m 1 Nov 1860, Rosabel Charlotte, da of the Rev George Heywood, Rector of Ideford, Devon, d s p 29 Jan 1886

3d *Frederick Barker*, b 28 *July* 1840, d 4 *Dec* 1908, m 18 June 1872, *Phœbe Susannah, da of Col Vincent Williams, Royal Welsh Fusiliers, and had issue (with a da who died young)* 1c t) 4c

1c Philip Longueville Barker, I C S (*Amritsar, Punjab*), b 19 Dec 1874, m 24 Dec 1900, Edith Agnes Frances Marn, da of the Rev Henry Atkinson Gibson, M A , and his issue 1f to 3f

1f Phœbe Sybil Barker
2f Gwynedd Mary Barker
3f Ursula Gladwyn Barker

2c Richard Vincent Barker, Royal Welsh Fusiliers, b 13 June 1880, *unm*

3c Sybil Margaret Barker, m 1st, Charles Frederick Balfour, I C S , d 1907, 2ndly, 2 Sept 1908, Major James Crark, Indian Cavalry , and has issue (with a da who died young) 1f to 2f

1f Philip Maxwell Balfour, b 10 Mar 1898
2f Ronald Hugh Balfour, b 6 Nov 1901

4c Winifred Mary Barker, m 1908, Nigel Fosberry

1d Henrietta Barker, m 17 Ap 1873, Hugo Rice-Wiggin, one of H M 's Inspectors of Schools (*Bourton-in-the Water, Glos*), and has issue 1e

1e Cecil Frances Sarah Rice Wiggin

2c *Thomas Francis Barker*, b 29 *Oct* 1810 d 25 *Ap* 1878, m 13 *Sept* 1836, *Eliza Anne, da of (—) Booth , and had issue (with 3 other sons and a da who d s p)* 1d to 5d

1d Henry Barker (*Chester*), b 17 Nov 1843 , m 12 Ap 1887, Emily, widow of Col Brownrigg, da of (—) Tottenham, s p

2d *Francis Barker*, b 1 *June* 1844 , d 2 *Nov* 1878, m 14 *Oct* 1874, *Eliza beth, da of (—) Lord of Rawtenstall, co Lanc , and had issue* 1c

1e Ethel Barker, m 19 Feb 1903, John Howarth Massey (*Clitheroe*)

3d Eliza Harriette Barker, *unm*

4d Annie Barker, m 17 July 1867, Charles Edward Ashburner, *late* Indian Army , and has issue 1e to 4e

1e Charles Edward Ashburner
2e Lionel Ashburner
3e Arthur Ashburner
4e Violet Ashburner

5d Mary Barker, m 8 Aug 1877, James Henry Ewart, *late* Seaforth High- landers (*The Lodge, Weston Underwood, Olney, Bucks*) , and has issue 1e to 3c

1e John Murray Ewart, b 23 Sept 1884
2e James Alan Ewart b 16 Nov 1887
3e Monica Mary Ewart, b 4 Dec 1889

3c *Harriette Barker*, b 9 *Ap* 1805, d 27 *May* 1861, m the Rev *Francis Bryans*, d 5 *May* 1877, *and had issue* 1d to 3d

1d *Rev Francis Richard Bryans, formerly Rector of Greatham*, b 2 Feb 1835 , d 7 *Jan* 1909 m 18 *Oct* 1864, *Anna Maria [descended from King Henry I II , &c (see Tudor Roll, p 513,] (Clevelands, Babbacombe , Torquay), da of Gibbs Crawford Antrobus of Eaton Hall, co Chester, J P , D L [Br Coll], and had issue* 1e to 2e

1e Edith Anne Bryans
2e Bessie Bryans m 1901 S Wood

2d Edward de Villus Bryans, b 17 Sept 1846, *unm*

3d Harriette Bryans, b 4 Nov 1836, d 19 May 1906, m 31 Mar 1869, Patrick Robertson Buchanan , and had issue 1e

1e Nora Harriette Buchanan, b 26 Nov 1874

[Nos 690 to 717

# of The Blood Royal

4c *Mary Anne Barker*, **b** 12 *June* 1812, d 1 *Oct* 1882 m 21 *Jan* 1831, *Charles Townshend* [7th *son of John Stanislaus Townshend of Trevallyn co Denbigh, J P*], d 24 *July* 1893, *and had issue* 1d *to* 2d

1d *Harriette Dorothea Townshend*, b 29 *Nov* 1836, d 27 *May* 1878 m 5 *July* 1859, *the Rev Latham Wickham* [*son of Archdeacon Wickham*], d 3 *Sept* 1901, *and had issue* 1e *to* 6e

1e Robert Townshend Wickham (*Chester*), b 28 Ap 1860 m 22 Feb 1898, Elinor [a descendant of the Lady Anne, sister of King Edward IV (see the Exeter Volume, p 378)], da of James George Edwards of Broughton, co Hants, and has issue 1f to 3f

1f Lance Townshend Wickham, b 15 July 1902

2f Robert George Wickham, b 14 June 1905

3f Hugh Charles Wickham, b 23 Ap 1908

2e Charles Townshend Wickham (*Twyford School, Winchester*) b 11 June 1862, m 8 Ap 1891, Flora Millicent, da of Col William Parker of Hanthorpe Hall, Bourne, co Linc

3e Harry Townshend Wickham (*The Close, Newport-Pagnell, Bucks*), b 5 Jan 1866, m 20 Ap 1893, Elizabeth Caroline, da of W Soutar of Dundee

4e John Herbert Townshend Wickham (*Westwood, Wanganui, New Zealand*), b 10 Oct 1868, m 14 Ap 1898 Jessica Clarice, da of George Buckland Worgan of Wanganui, and has issue 1f

1f Philip Latham Wickham, b at Wanganui 1 June 1904

5e Dorothea Gladwyn Wickham, m 2 July 1885, George William Palmer, *formerly of Greenwood, co Hants* (*Wanganui, New Zealand*), and has issue 1f to 4f

1f George Palmer, b 21 June 1888

2f Harry Mark Palmer, b 21 Oct 1889

3f Frederick Ralph Palmer, b 7 Jan 1891

4f Richard Hugh Palmer, b 13 Ap 1893

6e Susan Harriette Latham Wickham, m Sept 1906, the Rev Ernest Henry St Aubyn Trenow, Curate of All Saints, Leamington Spa

2d *Susan Marian Townshend*, m 10 Nov 1864, Hugh Robert Hughes of Ystrad, co Denbigh, d 8 Feb 1895, *and has issue* (with a da who died young) 1e *to* 5e

1e Marian Margaret Hughes, m 30 Ap 1900, the Rev Edward James Davies, B A, Rector of Nantglyn (*Nantglyn Rectory, Denbigh*), and has issue 1f to 3f

1f Hugh Edward Townshend Davies, b 9 Ap 1907

2f Marian Margaret Davies, b 22 July 1901

3f Katharine Mildred Davies, b 7 Dec 1903

2e Susan Gladwyn Hughes, m 30 Ap 1895, Guy Francis, Solicitor (*Denbigh*)

3e Katherina Christina Hughes, *unm*

4e Muriel Hester Hughes, *unm*

5e Vera Hughes, m M Guy Thompson (*The Old Bank, Oxford*)

6b *Maria Jones*, b 17 Ap 1782, d (*at Hamburg*) 7 Dec 1816, m as 1st *wife* (*at Llanrwdr*) 23 Aug 1802, *Thomas Lowndes*, d 4 May 1836, *and had issue* (*with 2 sons and a da who d s p*) 1c

1c *Maria Lowndes*, b 20 Jan 1811, d 1 Dec 1877 m 1812, *her cousin, Thomas John Lowndes*, d 2 Dec 1855 *and had issue* 1d *to* 1d

1d *Hugh Lowndes*, b 12 Jan 1813, d 8 Ap 1907, m 1st (*at West Derby Parish Church*), 2 June 1870, Lydia Jane, da of William Kenney Tyrer, d (-) 2ndly (*at Chester*), 22 Oct 1901, Amy, widow of Frederick Eaton, da of G S Chapman *of Manchester and Monte Video*, *and had issue* (*with 2 das who d in infancy*) 1e *to* 2e

1e *Amy Frances Lowndes*, m (*at West Kirby*) 8 Oct 1902, Walter Maclver, *and has issue* 1f *to* 2f

1f Peter Graeme MacIver

2f Eleanor Audrey Graeme MacIver

[Nos 718 to 743

65

The Plantagenet Roll

2c Ella Constance Lowndes, m (at Gresford) 21 Ap 1896, James Allan Macfie, and has issue 1f

1f Ellaline Lydia Joan Macfie

2d Thomas Lowndes, b (—) m 1900, C M E, da of (—) Devey

3d Jane, called Lilly, Lowndes, b in New Zealand

4d Mary Lowndes   [Nos 744 to 748

9 Descendants if any, of CHARLOTTE THEOPHILA DIGBY (Table II), d 17 Mar 1693, m the Rev RICHARD MOSTYN of Pedbedw, d 1735 [1]

10 Descendants of HUGH (PERCY), 2nd DUKE OF NORTHUMBERLAND [G B], K G (Table III), b 14 Aug 1742, d 10 July 1817, m. 2ndly, 23 May 1779, FRANCES JULIA, da of Peter BURRELL of Beckenham, co Kent, d 28 Ap 1820, and had issue 1a to 3a

1a Hugh (Percy), 3rd Duke of Northumberland [G B], K G, b 20 Ap 1785, d s p 11 Feb 1847

2a Algernon (Percy), 4th Duke of Northumberland [G B], K G, P C, b 15 Dec 1792, d s p 12 Feb 1865

3a Lady Emily Percy b 7 Jan 1789, d 20 June 1844, m 19 May 1810, James (Murray), 1st Baron Glenlyon [U K], K H [2nd son but in his issue (14 Sept 1846) heir of the 4th Duke of Atholl [S], K T], d 12 Oct 1837, and had issue 1b to 2b

1b George Augustus Frederick John (Murray), 6th Duke of Atholl [S], 3rd Earl of Strange [G B], 10th Baron Strange [E], 2nd Baron Glenlyon [U K], &c, &c, K T, b 20 Sept 1814, d 16 Jan 1864, m 29 Oct 1839, Anne, V A, da of Henry Home Drummond of Blair Drummond, co Perth, d 18 May 1897, and had issue 1c

1c John James Hugh Henry (Stewart-Murray), 7th Duke of Atholl [S], 4th Earl Strange [G B], 11th Baron Strange [E] and 3rd Baron Glenlyon [U K], &c, also 6th Baron Percy [G B], K T (Blair Castle, Blair Atholl, Perthshire, Dunkeld House, Dunkeld, 84 Eaton Place, S W), b 6 Aug 1840, m 29 Oct 1863, Louisa, da of Sir Thomas Moncreiffe, 7th Bt [S] d 8 July 1902, and has issue 1d to 6d

1d John George Stewart Murray, Marquis of Tullibardine, M V O, D S O, Capt and Brevet-Major Royal Horse Guards and Col Comdt Scottish Horse Yeo (Marlborough, &c), b 15 Dec 1871, m 20 July 1899, Katharine Marjory, da of Sir James Henry Ramsay, 10th Bt [S]

2d Lord George Stewart-Murray, Capt 1st Batt Black Watch, b 17 Feb 1873

3d Lord James Thomas Stewart-Murray, Lieut Queen's Own Cameron Highlanders, b 18 Aug 1879

4d Lady Dorothea Louisa Stewart-Murray, m 5 Feb 1895, Lieut -Col Harold Goodeve Ruggles-Brise, Grenadier Guards

5d Lady Helen Stewart-Murray

6d Lady Evelyn Stewart-Murray

2b Lord James Charles Plantagenet Murray, b 8 Dec 1819, d 3 June 1874, m 6 Nov 1851, Elizabeth Marjory, da of George Fairholme of Greenknowe, co Berwick [by his wife the Hon Caroline Elizabeth, née Forbes], d 11 Oct 1888, and had issue 1c

1c Caroline Frances Murray (8 Royal Crescent, Bath)   [Nos 749 to 756

---

[1] The Topographer, London, 1790, ii 212

66

# of The Blood Royal

11. Descendants of ALGERNON (PERCY), 1st EARL OF BEVERLEY [G B]
(Table III), *b.* 21 Jan 1750, *d* 21 Oct 1830, *m* 8 June
1775, ISABELLA SUSANNAH, da of Peter BURRELL of Beckenham, co Kent, *d* 24 Jan. 1812, and had issue 1*a* to 5*a*.

1*a George* (Percy) *2nd Earl of Beverley and* (1865) *5th Duke of Northumberland* [G B], b 22 June 1778, d 22 Aug 1867, m 22 June 1801, *Louisa Harcourt, da of the Hon James Archibald Stuart-Wortley, d 30 June 1848, and had issue* 1*b to* 3*b*

1*b Algernon George* (Percy), *6th Duke of Northumberland* [G B] *&c*, K G, P C, b 2 May 1810, d 2 Jan 1899, m 26 May 1845, *Louisa, da and h of Henry Drummond, M P [E of Perth Coll], d 18 Dec 1890, and had issue* 1*c to* 2*c*

1*c* Henry George (Percy), 7th Duke of Northumberland, &c [G B] and 11th Bt [E], K G, P C, D C L, LL D, *formerly Treasurer of H M Queen Victoria's* Household (*Alnwick Castle, Northumberland, Albury Park, Guildford,* 2 *Grosvenor Place, W, Carlton, &c*), b 29 May 1846, m 23 Dec 1868, Lady Edith, da of George Douglas (Campbell), 8th Duke of Argyll [S], K G, K T, and has issue 1*d* to 9*d*

1*d* Henry Algernon George, Earl Percy, M P, *formerly* Under-Sec of State for Foreign Affairs, &c (64 *Curzon Street, W, Carlton*), b 21 Jan 1871

2*d* Lord Alan Ian Percy, Capt Grenadier Guards, b 17 Ap 1880

3*d* Lord William Richard Percy, Barrister I T, b 17 May 1882

4*d* Lord Eustace Sutherland Campbell Percy, b 21 Mar 1887

5*d* Lady Edith Eleanor Percy

6*d* Lady Margaret Percy

7*d* Lady Victoria Alexandrina Percy

8*d* Lady Mary Percy

9*d* Lady Muriel Evelyn Nora Percy

2*c* Lord Algernon Malcolm Arthur Percy, J P, D L, a Mil A D C to H M the King and Col Comdg 3rd Batt Northumberland Fusiliers (*Guy s Cliffe, Warwick*), b 2 Oct 1851, m 3 Aug 1880, Lady Victoria Frederica Caroline, da of William Henry (Edgcumbe), 4th Earl of Mount Edgcumbe [G B], P C, G C V O, and has issue 1*d* to 2*d*

1*d* Algernon William Percy, J P, Lieut 3rd Batt Northumberland Fusiliers (*Travellers', Bath, &c*), b 29 Nov 1881

2*d* Katharine Louisa Victoria Percy, *m* 15 Sept 1904, Josceline Reginald Heber-Percy (see p 68) (*Chesford Grange, Kenilworth*), and has issue 1*e to* 2*e*

1*e* David Josceline Algernon Heber-Percy, b 10 June 1909

2*e* Mary Katharine Victoria Heber-Percy

2*b* Lord Josceline William Percy, b 17 July 1811, d 25 July 1881, m 8 Aug 1818, *Margaret, widow of the Right Hon Sir Robert Grant, P C, M P, da of Sir David Davidson of Cantry, and had issue* 1*c*

1*c* George Algernon Percy, *formerly* Lieut Col Grenadier Guards, b 17 May 1849

3*b Lady Margaret Percy,* b 16 May 1813, d 15 Oct 1897, m 23 Sept 1841, *Edward Richard* (Littleton), *2nd Baron Hatherton [U K], d 3 Ap 1888, and had issue*

See the Tudor Roll, pp 187-188, Nos 20969-20990, also the Essex Volume, pp 241-242, Nos 30328-30364

2*a Right Rev the Lord Hugh Percy,* D D, *Lord Bishop of Carlisle,* b 29 Jan 1784, d 5 Feb 1856, m 1st, 19 May 1806, *Mary, da of the Most Rev Charles Manners-Sutton, Archbishop of Canterbury [D of Rutland Coll and a descendant of Anne (Plantagenet), Duchess of Exeter], d 4 Sept 1831, and had issue* 1*b to* 7*b*
[Nos 757 to 809

The Plantagenet Roll

1b Algernon Charles Percy, afterwards (R L 4 Feb 1847) Heber-Percy of Hodnet Hall, co Salop, and Airmyn Hall, co York, J P, b 29 June 1812, d 24 Jan 1901, m 29 July 1839, Emily [descended paternally from Isabel (Plantagenet), Countess of Essex, and maternally from George (Plantagenet), Duke of Clarence, K G, and his sister Anne, Duchess of Exeter], da and h of the Right Rev Reginald Heber, Lord Bishop of Calcutta, d 8 Nov 1902, and had issue 1c to 11c

1c Algernon Heber-Percy of Hodnet and Airmyn, J P, D L, C A, and High Sheriff (1908) co Salop, Capt and Hon Major Shropshire Yeo Cav and 2nd Vol Batt Shropshire L I, formerly Lieut. R N (Hodnet Hall, Salop Airmyn Hall, Goole, Yorks, Carlton, &c), b 23 Feb 1845, m 25 Jan 1867, Alice Charlotte Mary, da and h of the Rev Frederick Vernon Lockwood [by his wife Mary Isabella, née Percy, descended also from King Henry VII, Anne (Plantagenet), Duchess of Exeter, &c], and has issue 1d to 2d

1d Algernon Hugh Heber-Percy, formerly Lieut Shropshire Yeo Cav, b 13 July 1869, m 15 July 1903, Gladys May, da of William Edward Montagu Hulton Harrop of Lythwood Hall, Shrewsbury, and has issue 1e to 3e

    1e Algernon George William Heber-Percy, b 27 Ap 1904

    2e Cyril Hugh Reginald Heber Percy, b 18 Dec 1905

    3e Alan Charles Heber-Percy, b 4 May 1907

2d Josceline Reginald Heber-Percy (Chesford Grange, Kenilworth, Warwick), b 2 Sept 1880, m 15 Sept 1904, Katharine Louisa Victoria, da of Lord Algernon Percy (see above), and has issue

See p 67, Nos 770-771

2c Reginald Josceline Heber-Percy, Lieut -Col Life 4th Batt Rifle Brigade (Chineham, Basingstoke), b 2 May 1849, m 28 Nov 1894, Gundreda, da of Hardy Eustace of Castlemore, co Carlow

3c Hugh Louis Heber-Percy, F R G S (Ferney Hall, Onibury, Salop), b 7 Jan 1853, m 10 June 1899, Harriet, da of Henry S Earp of Dunstall, Wolverhampton

4c Rev Henry Vernon Heber-Percy, M A (Camb). Rector of Leasingham (Leasingham Rectory, Sleaford), b 16 Ap 1858, m 5 Oct 1886, Judith Elizabeth, da of Sir Vincent Rowland Corbet 3rd Bt [U K], and has issue 1d to 5d

    1d Neville Henry Heber-Percy, b 6 Feb 1890

    2d Hermione Constance Heber-Percy

    3d Aleen Judith Heber-Percy

    4d Rachel Joan Heber-Percy

    5d Hilda Bridget Heber-Percy

5c Alan William Heber-Percy, J P (Durweston, Blandford), b 27 Mar 1865, m 8 Aug 1893, the Hon Susan Alice, da of William Henry Berkeley (Portman), 2nd Viscount Portman [U K], and has issue 1d to 6d

    1d Hugh Alan Heber-Percy, b 5 Dec 1897

    2d Bryan Heber Percy, b 29 Nov 1903

    3d Peter Heber-Percy, b 3 Nov 1908

    4d Margaret Eleanor Heber-Percy

    5d Ida Mary Heber-Percy

    6d Constance Emily Heber-Percy

6c Ethel Cecilia Heber-Percy, m 7 June 1870, the Hon Alexander Frederic Hood (see p 143) [V Hood Coll] (Airmyn Hall, Goole, Yorks), and has issue

See the Tudor Roll, p 188, Nos 21015-21019

7c Agnes Katherine Heber Percy

8c Maude Ellen Heber-Percy, m 12 Aug 1880, Col Sir Edward Law Durand, 1st Bart [U K], C B (35 Ennismore Gardens, S W), and has issue

See the Tudor Roll, p 188 Nos 21022-21028   [Nos 810 to 847

# of The Blood Royal

9c Gertrude Amelia Heber-Percy, m 5 Sept 1895, John James Hardy Rowland Eustace (*Castlemore, co Carlow*), and has issue

See the Tudor Roll, p 189, Nos 21030-21033

10c Evelyn Mary Heber-Percy, m 16 July 1889, Francis Monckton (*Stretton Hall, Stafford, Somerford Hall, Brewood*), and has issue

See the Tudor Roll, p 189, Nos 21035-21040

11c Isabel Harriet Heber-Percy, m 2 Sept 1891, Andrew Greville Rouse-Boughton-Knight, J P [Bt of Lawford (E 1641) and of Downton (G B 1791) Coll] (38 *Norfolk Square, Hyde Park, W , Wormesley Grange, Hereford*), and has issue

See the Tudor Roll, p 189, Nos 21042-21044

2b *Rev Henry Percy, Rector of Greystoke, Canon of Carlisle, b 5 June 1813*, d 6 Sept 1870, m 1 Feb 1841, *Emma Barbara, da of Capt Benjamin Baker Galbraith of Olderigg, Queen's Co*, d Nov 1877, and had issue 1c to 5c

1c *Alfred Percy, b 5 May 1850, d 20 Aug 1907, m 2ndly 14 Feb 1899, Mary (Burlington Street, North Walkerville, South Australia), da of James Hyland*, and had issue 1d to 2d

   1d Henry Percy, b 13 Ap 1901

   2d Mary Percy

2c. Edward Galbraith Henry Percy, b 1854

3c Josceline Hugh Percy, *formerly* Capt 1st Vol Brig. W Div R A (49 *Talbot Road, Highgate, N*), b July 1856, m 12 Oct 1892, Grace Anne, da of Edward Percy Thompson (see p 70), and has issue 1d to 4d

   1d Henry Edward Percy, b 6 Aug 1893

   2d Josceline Richard Percy, b 1894

   3d Margaret Percy

   4d Constance Percy

4c Elizabeth Mary Percy, m 25 May 1871, the Rev John Adams, *formerly* Vicar of Offchurch (3 *Reddington Road, Hampstead*), and has issue 1d to 6d

   1d Rev Henry Theophilus Adams, Vicar of Newbold Pacey (*Newbold Pacey Vicarage, Warwick*), b 1872, m 1900, May, da of Charles Chapman of Carlecotes Hall, York, and has issue 1e to 3e

      1e John Simon Leslie Adams, b 1901

      2e Hugh Adams, b 1906

      3e Isabel Adams

   2d John Cadwallader Adams, *formerly* Lieut R M L I (*Junior Naval and Military*), b 1873

   3d Hugh Geoffrey Coker Adams, b 1880, m and has issue a da

   4d. Edward Josceline Percy Adams, b 1888

   5d Elsie Emma Mary Adams, m 1898, Thomas Owen Lloyd (*The Priory, Warwick*), and has issue

   6d Kathleen Alice Georgina Adams, m 1905, Fulwar Estoteville Skipwith, Lieut Bombay, Baroda, and Central India Railway Vol [Bt of Prestwould (1622) Coll], and has issue 1e to 2e

      1e Grey Henry Skipwith, b 1908

      2e Elizabeth Kathleen Skipwith

5c Emma Annie Isabel Percy, m 16 Ap 1884, Herbert Cranstoun Adams, *formerly* Lieut.-Col 1st Devonshire R G A (Vol), V D (*Exmouth*), and has issue 1d to 6d

   1d Henry Launcelot Elford Adams, b 4 Mar 1885

   2d John Percy Fitzherbert Adams, b 16 Ap 1891

[Nos 848 to 886

The Plantagenet Roll

3d Alan St George Adams, b 23 Ap 1894

4d Alice Barbara Adams

5d Margaret Hyale Adams

6d Norah Roberta Adams

3b *Hugh Josceline Percy of Eskrigg, co Cumberland, J P , D L , b 9 Dec 1817 , d 9 Feb 1882 , m 24 Oct 1859, Anne, da of Joseph Story, d 25 Mar 1901, and had issue 1c to 2c*

1c Edward Josceline Percy (*Eskrigg, Wigton, Cumberland*), b 30 Nov 1864 , m 23 Jan 1907, Nellie, da of John Jarvie

2c Agnes Ellen Josceline Percy, m 6 Sept 1888, Frederic George Mather, and has issue 1d to 2d

1d Marjorie Helen Mather

2d Phyllis Mather

4b *Mary Isabella Percy, b 18 Feb 1808, d Mar 1878 , m 21 July 1840, the Rev Frederick Vernon Lockwood, Preb of Canterbury, d 1 July 1851 , and has issue*

See the Tudor Roll, p 190, Nos 21073-21075

5b *Lucy Percy, b 28 Ap 1811 , d Jan 1887 , m 13 Feb 1832, Henry William Askew of Glenridding and Comshead Priory, d 1890 , and had issue*

See the Tudor Roll, p 190, Nos 21076-21093

6b *Gertrude Percy, b 30 Aug 1814 d 27 Ap 1890, m 12 July 1834, William Pitt (Amherst), 2nd Earl [U K] and 3rd Baron [G B] Amherst, d 26 Mar 1886 , and had issue*

See the Tudor Roll pp 190-191, Nos 21094-21113

7b *Ellen Percy, b 7 Nov 1815 , d 1899 , m 5 Ap 1836, the Rev Edward Thompson, d 3 Ap 1838 , and had issue*

See the Tudor Roll, p 191, Nos 21114-21121

3a *Lord Josceline Percy, C B , Vice-Admiral R N , b (twin) 29 Jan 1784 , d 19 Oct 1856 , m 9 Dec 1820 Sophia Elizabeth, da of Moreton Walhouse of Hatherton, co Stafford, d 13 Dec 1875 , and had issue 1b to 3b*

1b *Sophia Louisa Percy, b 21 Dec 1821, d 7 Nov 1908, m 7 July 1846, Col Charles Bagot [B Bagot Coll], d 20 Feb 1881 , and had issue*

See the Tudor Roll, pp 191-192, Nos 21123-21129

2b Emily Percy, m 17 July 1852, Gen Sir Charles Lawrence D'Aguilar, G C B (4 *Clifton Crescent, Folkestone*) , and has issue 1c

1c Emily Gertrude D'Aguilar

3b Charlotte Alice Percy, m 13 Ap 1858, Edward Percy Thompson (16 *St Andrew's Road, Southsea*) , and has issue 1c to 5c

1c Henry Thompson, Lieut R N , b 1864

2c Alexander Maurice Thompson, b 1869

3c Grace Anne Thompson, m 12 Oct 1892, Capt Josceline Hugh Percy (49 *Talbot Road, Highbury, N*) , and has issue

See p 69, Nos 896-899

4c Gertrude Thompson

5c Constance Thompson

4a *Lady Charlotte Percy, b 3 June 1776 , d 26 Nov 1862, m as 2nd wife, 25 July 1795, George (Ashburnham), 3rd Earl of Ashburnham [G B], K G , d 27 Oct 1830 , and had issue*

See the Tudor Roll, pp 192-94, Nos 21141-21184

5a *Lady Emily Charlotte Percy, b 9 Nov 1786 , d 22 May 1877 ; m 25 July 1808, Andrew Mortimer Drummond [E of Perth Coll], d 1 June 1864 , and had issue*

See the Tudor Roll, pp 194-195, Nos 21185-21229   [Nos 887 to 1051

70

# of The Blood Royal

12 Descendants of Lady KATHERINE SEYMOUR (Table III), d 9 Ap
1791 , m as 1st wife, 15(21) July 1708, Sir WILLIAM
WYNDHAM of Orchard Wyndham, 3rd Bart [E]. b c 1687 .
d. 17 July 1740 , and had issue

See the Tudor Roll, Table L , &c , and pp 263-292, Nos 24402-25349
[Nos 1052 to 1999

13 Descendants of Lady ELIZABETH PERCY (Table III), b 1 Dec
1636 , d 5 Feb 1717 , m 19 May 1653, ARTHUR (CAPEL),
1st EARL OF ESSEX [E], d 13 July 1683 , and had issue

See the Exeter Volume, Table XXVII , and pp 374-386, Nos 26747-28169
[Nos 2000 to 3122

14 Descendants of Lady DOROTHY PERCY (Table III), bapt 20 Aug
1598 , d. 19 Aug 1650 , m c Jan 1615, ROBERT (SYDNEY),
2nd EARL OF LEICESTER [E], K B , b 1 Dec 1595 ; d 2 Nov
1677 ; and had issue

See the Essex Volume, Table VI , and pp 88-102, Nos 9363-13712
[Nos 3423 to 7772

15 Descendants of WILLIAM (HERBERT), 1st [DUKE and] MARQUIS
OF POWIS [E], K G (Table III), b c 1617 , d 2 June 1696 ,
m. 2 Aug 1654, Lady ELIZABETH, da of Edward (SOMERSET),
2nd Marquis of Worcester [E], d. Mar 1692 , and had issue

See the Clarence Volume, Table XXXV , and pp 382-392, Nos 14421-15000
[Nos 7773 to 8352

16 Descendants, if any, of the Hon KATHERINE HERBERT (Table
III.), d. (–) , m 1st, Sir ROBERT VAUGHAN of Llwydiarth and
Llangedwyn, co Montgomery , 2ndly, Sir JAMES PALMER of
Dorney Court, co Bucks , and had (with possibly other issue
by 2nd husband) 1a [1]

1a Eleanor Vaughan, da and eventual h , d (–) , m John Purcell of Nant-
cribba, co Montgomery, M P , J P , living 1662 , and had issue 1b to 2b
1b. Mary Purcell, da and co-h ,'d (–) , m 1672, Edward Vaughan of Glanllyn ,
and had issue 1c
1c Anne Vaughan of Llydiarth and Llangedwyn, d s p s 14 Mar 1748, m
as 1st wife, Sir Watkin Williams-Wyn, 3rd Bart [E], M P , d 23 Sept 1749
2b Catherine Purcell, d (–) , m Sir John Copley

17. Descendants of Sir HENRY SLINGSBY, 1st Bart [E] (Table IV), b
14 Jan 1602 , d., being judicially murdered on Tower Hill,
8 June 1658 , m 7 July 1631, the Hon. BARBARA, da. of
Thomas (BELASYE), 1st Viscount Fauconberg [1] [E], bapt
11 Oct 1609 ; d 31 Dec 1641 , and had issue

See the Exeter Volume, Table LXII , and pp 645-657, Nos 55517-56278
[Nos 8353 to 9114

---

[1] Lloyd's " Sheriffs of Montgomeryshire," pp 225, 489

The Plantagenet Roll

18 Descendants, if any surviving, of ELIZABETH METCALFE (Table IV), *b.* 16 47, being aged 18 in 1665, and then *unm.*, *d* (-), *m* JOHN LODGE, and had issue 1*a* to 2*a*

1*a John Lodge of Ripon*, d 1789, m 1755, *Elizabeth, da of Matthew Ellerton of London, and had issue 1b to 3b*

1*b John Lodge*, d (²s p) 1801, m *Margaret, da of the Rev Richard Owen of Bodsilin, co Carmarthen*

2*b Francis Lodge*, d (²s p) 1826

3*b Adam Lodge*, d 5 *Ap* 1837, m *Mary, da of the Rev Richard Owen of Bodsilin afsd , and had issue (with a son, Richard Owen, d young) 1c to 3c*

1*c John Lodge, afterwards Ellerton, of Bodsilin,* d (²s p), m 24 *Aug* 1837, *Lady Henrietta Barbara [descended from the Lady Anne Plantagenet (see the Exeter Volume, p 633), widow of the Rev Frederick Manners Sutton, da of John (Lumley-Savile), 7th Earl of Scarborough [E],* d 27 *July* 1864

2*c Adam Lodge, Bar -at-Law, M T ,* d (²s p)

3*c Mary Catherine Lodge,* d (²s p), m *T G Hindle of Woodfold Park, co Lanc*

2*a Francis Lodge,* m (——)

19 Descendants of THOMAS ROBINSON of York, Turkey Merchant (Table VI), *bur* 16 July 1678 ; *m* 31 Dec 1654, ELIZABETH, da of Charles TANCRED of Arden, co York, *bur* 15 May 1664 , and had issue 1*a* to 3*a*

1*a Sir William Robinson of Newby, 1st Bt [G B], M P ,* b *c* 1656, d 22 Dec 1736, m 8 *Sept* 1679, *Mary, da of George Aislabie of Studley Royal, co York , and had issue 1b to 4b*

1*b Sir Metcalfe Robinson, 2nd Bt [G B],* b *c* 1683 d *unm* ²6 Dec 1736

2*b Sir Tancred Robinson, 3rd Bt [G B], Rear-Admiral R N ,* b *c* 1685, d 3 *Sept* 1754, m *again* 1713, *Mary (see p 73), da of Rowland Norton of Dishforth, bur* 26 *July* 1748, *and had issue 1c to 4c*

1*c Sir William Robinson, 4th Bt [G B],* b 1713, d s p 4 *Mar* 1770

2*c Sir Norton Robinson, 5th Bt [G B],* b 1715, d *unm Feb* 1792

3*c Mary Robinson,* b *c* 1716, d 4 *Ap* 1790, m *Thomas Peirse (or Pierce) of Pierseborough, co York*

4*c Margaret Robinson*

3*b Thomas (Robinson), 1st Baron Grantham [G B], P C , K B , one of the Regents of the Realm, 1755, &c* b *c* 1693, d 30 *Sept* 1770, m 13 *July* 1737, *Frances [a descendant of the Lady Anne, sister of King Edward IV , &c], da of Thomas Worsley of Hovingham, co York, bur* 6 *Nov* 1750, *and had issue*

See the Exeter Volume, pp 642-643, Nos 54166-51395

4*b Anne Robinson,* d 15 *Jan* 1768, m *as 2nd wife, Thomas Worsley of Hovingham, co York,* b 16 *Nov* 1686, bur 2 *Mar* 1750, *and had issue 1c*

1*c Anne Worsley,* d 1765, m *in or before* 1756, *William Bastard of Kitley, co Devon, who was gazetted a Baronet [G B],* 4 or 24 *Sept* 1779, *but took no steps to obtain the Patent,*² b 1 *Sept* 1727, d 1782, *and had issue 1d to 2d*

1*d John Pollexfen Bastard of Kitley, M P , Col Devon Militia,* d s p *(at Leghorn)* 4 *Ap* 1816   [Nos 9115 to 9344

---

¹ Burke's "Royal Descents and Pedigrees of Founder's Kin," p 75, and Foster's "Yorkshire Pedigrees," under Metcalfe

² See G E C 's "Complete Baronetage"

# of The Blood Royal

2d Edmund Bastard of Kitley, M P Lieut-Col Devon Militia, b 7 Feb 1758, d (at Sharpham) June 1816, m Jane, da and h of Capt Philemon Pownall of Sharpham, co Devon, d (at Exmouth) 7 Mar 1822, and had issue 1e to 3

1e Edmund Pollexfen Bastard of Kitley, M P, b 12 July 1784, d 8 June 1838, m 22 Jan 1824, the Hon Anne Jane, da of George (Rodney), 2nd Baron Rodney [G B], d 25 Ap 1833, and had issue

See the Clarence Volume, pp 202-203, Nos 3998-4019

2e John Bastard of Sharpham, M P, Capt R N, b 1787, d 11 Jan 1835, m 7 Oct 1817, Frances, da and co-h of Benjamin Wade of the Grange, co York, d 23 May 1870 and had issue (with 2 sons who d s p) 1f to 2f

1f John Pownall Bastard of Sharpham, a Capt in the Army, b June 1818, d 14 Nov 1886, m. 10 Nov 1841, Anne Esther, da of Jacob L Ricardo, d 14 June 1889, and had issue (with an elder son who died young) 1g to 2g

1g John Algernon Bastard, b Oct 1844, d 20 Nov 1908, m 2 Sept 1879, Olivia Gertrude Louisa, da of Gen E S Claremont, C B, and had issue 1h to 2h

2h Reginald Bastard, Lincolnshire Regt, b 2 Oct 1880

2h Violet Lilian Bastard, b 13 Mar 1884

2g Emmeline Laura Bastard, m 1st, as 2nd wife, 26 June 1873, Horace (Pitt), 6th Baron Rivers [U K], d s p 31 Mar 1880, 2ndly, 2 July 1881, Montague George Thorold, late R N [second son of Sir John Charles Thorold, 11th Bt (see p 310)] (Honington Hall, Grantham, 1 Abbot's Court, Kensington Square, W)

2f Frances Bastard, V A, Bedchamber-Woman to Queen Victoria, d 11 Ap 1902, m 2 July 1850, William Frederick Waldegrave, Viscount Chewton [s and h of 8th Earl Waldegrave [G B], C B], d of wounds received at the Alma, 7 Oct 1854, and had issue

See the Exeter Volume, p 179, Nos 6402-6413

3e Rev Philemon Pownall Bastard, d (?s p), m Mary, da of Mr Justice Park

2a Tancred Robinson, M D, second son in 1665, d (-), m Alathea, da of (——) Morley, and had issue 1b

1b William Robinson, d (-), m Dorothy, da of Dr Cook of Derby [1]

3a Margaret Robinson, d (-), m Rowland Norton of Dishforth, co York, d (-), and had issue 1b

1b Mary Norton, bur 26 July 1748, m c 1713, Sir Tancred Robinson, 3rd Bt [G B], Rear-Admiral R N, d 3 Sept 1754, and had issue

See p 72   [Nos 9345 to 9381]

20 Descendants of ELIZABETH ROBINSON (Table IV), d (-), m PHILIP RYCOT, East India Merchant

21 Descendants, if any surviving, of MARGARET ROBINSON (Table IV), living a widow 1698, m (settlements dated 15 Aug) 1653, WILLIAM WEDDELL of Earswick, co York, Lord of the Manor of Wigginton, b c 1634, will dated 28 May 1676, and had issue 1a to 3a [2]

1a Margaret Weddell, da and in her issue co-h, d (-), m Alexus Elcock of York, Merchant, bur 22 Ap 1700, and had issue, who took the name of Weddell and became extinct sometime after Ap 1792

---

[1] Foster's "Yorkshire Pedigrees"
[2] Whitaker's "Richmond," ii 122

The Plantagenet Roll

2a Dorothy Weddell, da and in her issue co-h, d (-), m 3 May 1688, Joseph Tomlinson of York, living 1712, and had issue 1b

1b Frances Tomlinson, da and whose issue, if surviving after 1792, became h, b c 1699, d 12 June 1751, m Major Charles Weddell, b c 1691, d 1768, and had issue 1c

1c Thomas Weddell of York, d (-), m 1777, Jane, da of Henry Briggs of Pendleton, co Lancaster

3a Joan Weddell, d (-), m (—) James, and had issue

22 Descendants, if any surviving, of FRANCES ROBINSON (Table IV), d (-), m ROBERT BELT of Overton, co York, bapt 2 May 1637, bur 26 Mar 1667; and had issue 1a to 3a [1]

1a Frances Belt, } both b before 13 Sept 1665, named in father's will
2a Margaret Belt, } 22 Mar 1667
3a. Mary Belt, bapt 5 Aug 1667

23 Descendants, if any surviving, of WALTER BETHELL of Ellerton, co York (Table V.), bapt 28 July 1629, living, aged 37, 9 Sept. 1665, m. 1st, 10 Mar. 1650, ANN, widow of (—) Savile of Copley, da of Sir George PALMES of Naburn, bur 22 Mar 1653, 2ndly, 29 Jan 1656, MARY (? ANNE), da of Peter VAVASOUR of Spalding Moor, bur. 23 Dec. 1659; and had issue 1a to 2a [2]

1a [1] Hugh Bethell, b 1658, living, aged 7, 1665
2a. Mary Bethell (? bur 21 Ap 1687)

24 Descendants of BETHELL ROBINSON of Buckton, co York, Solicitor (Table V.), bapt 24 Jan. 1684, bur 1718, m MARY, da of Thomas HESELTINE; and had issue surviving in 1874 [3]

25 Descendants of LUCY BETHELL (Table V), d (-), m JOHN MOTTRAM of Bishop Dyke Hall, Kirk Fenton, co York, who was living and aged 36, 21 Mar. 1665, and had then issue 1a [4]

1a. Bethell Mottram, son and h, living and aged 6, 21 Mar 1665

26 Descendants of URSULA BETHELL (see Table V), bapt 13 Jan 1634; d (-), m. JOHN PALLISER of Newby Wiske, b 1639, and had issue 1a to 4a

1a Thomas Palliser of Portobello and the Great Island, co Wexford, High Sheriff 1700, b 1661, d 1756, m Katherine, da of (—) Wogan, and ha dissue 1b to 2b

---

[1] Dugdale's "Visitation of Yorkshire," 1665, with additions by J W Clay, F S A *The Genealogist*, N S, xvi 171

[2] Foster's "Yorkshire Pedigrees"   [3] *Ibid*

[4] Dugdale's "Visitation of Yorkshire"

# of The Blood Royal

1b *William Palliser*, b 24 *June* 1699, d v p *before Nov* 1756, m *Mary, da of Philip Savage of Kilgibbon, and had issue* 1c [1]

1c *Katherine Palliser of the Great Island, co Wexford, da and event h,* d (-), m *John Wilson of Scarr,* d (-), *and had issue* 1d *to* 2d

1d *Christian Wilson of Scarr,* d (-), m *Elizabeth, da of Matthew Redmond of Kilgowan, co Wexford, and had issue* 1e *to* 2e

1e *John Wilson of Scarr,* d s p m

2e *Matthew Wilson, afterwards Palliser of the Great Island,* d (-), m 12 *Aug* 1812, *Jane, da of Christian Wilson of Sledagh,* d (-), *and had issue* 1f *to* 2f

1f *Christian Palliser of Begerin, J P,* d (-), m *Mary, da of Rudolphus William Ryan, Crown Prosecutor for co Wexford, and had issue* 1g

1g [da] *Palliser,* b 27 *June* 1877

2f *Rev Matthew Palliser,* Rector of White Church, m 1855, Sophia, da of the Rev Thomas Ottiwell Moore, Rector of Leskinfere, d 18 Ap 1856, and had issue 1g

1g Frederick Palliser, b Ap 1856

2d *Anne Wilson,* d (-), m *as 1st wife,* 1 Feb 1785, *Richard Waddy of Cloughheast Castle, co Wexford, M D,* b 13 *Ap* 1758, d 21 *July* 1819, *and had issue* 1e [2]

1e *Frances Waddy,* b 1789

2b *Juliana Hyde Palliser,* d (-), m 12 *Ap* 1732, *Capt John Orfeur,* d (-), *and had issue* 1c *to* 3c

1c *Dorothea Orfeur,* d (-), m (—) *Weston*

2c *Mary Orfeur,* d (-), m *George Robinson Walters* (see below), *Capt R N,* d 9 *Dec* 1789, *and had issue* 1d *to* 3d

1d *Sir Hugh Palliser Walters, afterwards* (R L 13 Dec 1798) *Palliser, 2nd Bart* [G B], b 27 Oct 1768, d (at Troyes) 17 Nov 1813, m 18 *Jan* 1790, Mary, da and co-h of *John Yates of Oldham, co Essex,* d 5 Aug 1823, *and had issue* 1e *to* 2e.

1e *Sir Hugh Palliser, 3rd and last Bart* [G B], b 8 *Mar* 1796, d (*unm*) 3 *Aug* 1868

2e *Mary Jane Palliser,* d Oct 1881, m 1st, 16 *Ap* 1822, *William Lockhart of Gormiston, co Lanark,* d (-), 2ndly, 11 *May* 1848, *John Manley Arbuthnot, Lord Keane,* d s p

2d *Alice Walters,* d (-), m *John Clough of York*

3d *Ursula Walters,* d (-), m *John Fletcher*

3c *Catherine Hyde Orfeur,* d 1814, m *Matthew Cavendish of Graigue,* d 1819, *and had (with other) issue* 1d

1d *James Gordon Cavendish,* m *Ann, da of Odiarne Coates of Green Court, co Herts, and had issue*

2a *Hugh Palliser of North Deighton, co York,* a *Capt in the Army,* b 1663, d (-), m *Mary, da of Humphrey Robinson of Thicket Priory, co York, and had issue* 1b *to* 2b

1b *Sir Hugh Palliser, 1st Bart* [G B], so cr. 6 *Aug* 1773 *with a spec rem, M P,* b 26 *Feb* 1723, d *unm* 18 *Mar* 1796

2b *Rebecca Palliser,* d (-), m *Major William Walters,* d 28 Feb 1789, *and had issue* 1c

1c *George Robinson Walters, Capt R N,* d 9 *Dec* 1789, m *Mary* (see above), *da and co-h. of Capt John Orfeur, and had issue*

[Nos 3982 to 3984

---

1 Burke's "Landed Gentry of Ireland," 1904
2 Burke's "Landed Gentry," 7th ed 1886, ii 1901

3a *Walter Palliser of North Deighton,* d (-), m *Elizabeth, da of* (—) *Sterne, and had issue* 1b *to* 2b

1b *Rev Walter Palliser, Rector of Stokenham, and Vicar of Great Drayton and Askham, co Notts,* d 1778

2b *Alice Palliser,* d (-), m *Robert Cooper.*

4a *Frances Palliser, living* 1665 [1]

27 Descendants, if any, of FRANCES BETHELL (Table V), d (-), m 8 Feb 1674, HENRY BELLINGHAM, and of her sister ELIZABETH.

28 Descendants, if any, of SLINGSBY BETHELL, Merchant and Sheriff of London (Table V.), *bapt* 27 Feb 1617, d (-); m MARY, da of (———) BURRELL of co Hunts

29 Descendants of Sir WILLIAM CODRINGTON, 2nd Baronet [G B], P C , M P (Table V), b 26 Oct 1719, d 11 Mar 1792; m 22 Feb 1736, ANNE, da of (—) ACTON of Fulham, d Sept or Nov 1778, and had issue 1a to 2a.

1a *Sir William Codrington, 3rd Bt [G B],* b c 1737, d *(at Rennes)* 5 *Sept* 1816, m *2ndly or 3rdly,*[2] 1804, *Eleanor, da of Godfrey Kirke of London,* d *(at Rennes)* 13 *Feb* 1816, *and had issue* 1b *to* 2b

1b *Sir William Raymond Codrington, 4th Bart [G B],* b *(at Rennes)* 25 *Jan* 1805, d *(at the Château de la Boullaye, Brittany)* 17 *Dec* 1873, m *(at St Servan Bosc, Ille et Vilaine)* 20 *May* 1828, *Anne Mary, da of Joseph Raphael Agrippin Le Fer de Bonaban of Bonaban, near St Malo,* d 27 *Oct* 1876, *and had issue* 1c *to* 4c

1c *Sir William Mary Joseph Codrington, 5th Bt [G B],* b *(at St Malo)* 13 *Mar* 1829, d *(at Rennes)* 1 *Mar* 1904, m 12 *Ap* 1856, *Mary (Château de la Boullaye, near Montfort, Brittany), da of Robert Roskell of Park House, Fulham, and had issue* 1d *to* 3d

1d Sir William Robert Codrington of Dodington, 6th Bt [G B], Capt and Brevet-Major, *late* 11th Hussars *(Standerton, Transvaal).* b 18 Ap 1867, m 25 Ap 1903, Joan, da of Henry Adams Rogers of Johannesburg, and has issue 1e to 2e

1e William Richard Codrington, b 22 Ap 1904

2e Frank Christopher Codrington, b 8 May 1908

2d George Raimond Codrington, b 14 Aug 1868

3d Alexander Joseph Codrington, b 9 Aug 1870, m 24 July 1905, Mary, da of Nicholas Roskell of 2 Warwick Gardens, Kensington

2c *Nancy Mary Codrington,* d (-), m 29 *Jan* 1856, *Alexandre Amaury de La Moussaye, —th* (17—) *and 3rd* (1819) *Marquis of La Moussaye* [F], b *(at La Poterie)* 16 *Sept* 1820 d s p

3c *Emilia Mary Caroline Codrington,* d (-), m 29 *July* 1861, *Lieut -Col James Pollock Gore, late* 1st *Royals*

4c *Sophia Mary Codrington,* d (-), m 2 *June* 1857, *Gustave Bernard de La Gatinais of Valle, near Lamballe*

2b *Mary Anne Eleanor Codrington,* d 1834, m 1826, *Charles Magon, an Officer* 6th *Hussars, in the French Army*

2a *Mary Codrington,* d (-), m *George Bernard*　　　　　[Nos 9385 to 9389

---

[1] Dugdale's " Visitation of Yorkshire," 1665　Surtees Soc Pub , xxxvi 94
[2] See G E C 's "Complete Baronetage " v 55 note b

# of The Blood Royal

30 Descendants of EDWARD CODRINGTON of London, Merchant (Table V.), *b* 22 June 1732; *d* (at Dijon) Feb 1775, *m* 4 May 1759, REBECCA, da of (—) LE STURGEON, *d* 1770, and had issue 1*a* to 3*a*

1*a* *Sir Christopher Codrington, afterwards* (*R L* 17 *Nov* 1795) *Bethell-Codrington, styled 4th Bt* [*G B*],[1] *M P*, b *Oct* 1764, d 4 *Feb* 1843, m 16 *Aug* 1796, *the Hon Caroline Georgiana Harriet, da of Thomas* (*Foley*), 2*nd Baron Foley* [*G B*], d 1 *Jan* 1843, *and had issue*
See the Clarence Volume, pp 354–355, Nos 11571–11594

2*a* *Sir Edward Codrington, G C B, M P, Admiral of the Red*, d 28 *Ap* 1851, m 27 *Dec* 1802, *Jane, da of Jaspar Hall of Otterburn, Hexham*, d 21 *Jan* 1837, *and had issue* 1*b to* 3*b*

1*b* *Sir William John Codrington, G C B, M P, G n and Com-in-Chief of the British Forces in the Crimea*, 1855, &c, b 26 *Nov* 1804, d 6 *Aug* 1884 m 7 *May* 1836, *Mary, V A, Bedchamber Woman to Queen Victoria, da of Levi Ames of the Hyde, Herts*, d 28 *June* 1898, *and had issue* 1*c to* 3*c*

1*c* Alfred Edward Codrington, C V O, C B, Major-Gen Comdg 1st London Div Territorial Force, *formerly* Comdg Coldstream Guards (*Preston Hall, Uppingham*, 110 *Eaton Square, S W*), b 4 May 1854, m 20 May 1885, Adela Harriet, da of Melville Portal of Laverstoke, co Hants, and has issue 1*d* to 4*d*

1*d* Geoffrey Ronald Codrington, Lieut Leicestershire Imp Yeo, b 13 May 1888
2*d* William Melville Codrington, b 16 Dec 1892
3*d* John Alfred Codrington, b 28 Oct 1898
4*d* Mary Adela Codrington

2*c* Jane Emily Codrington, m 13 Sept 1867, Sir Robert Uniacke Penrose-FitzGerald, 1st Bt [U K], J P, D L, *formerly* M P (*Corkbeg Island, Whitegate, co Cork*, 35 *Grosvenor Road, S W*)

3*c* Mary Codrington (2 *Lowndes Square, S W*), m 21 July 1864, Major-Gen William Earle, C B, C S I [Bt of Allerton (1869) Coll], b 18 May 1833, d (being killed at Kirbekan, Soudan) 10 Feb 1885, and had issue 1*d* to 2*d*

1*d* Rachel Mary Earle
2*d* Grace Elizabeth Earle, m 19 Ap 1893, John Russell Villiers [E of Clarendon Coll] (49 *Hans Place, S W*), and his issue 1*e* to 4*e*

1*e* Arthur Henry Villiers, b 27 Mar 1894
2*e* William Earle Villiers, b 6 Jan 1897
3*e* John Michael Villiers, b 22 Oct 1899
4*e* Richard Montague Villiers, b 10 Sept 1905

2*b* *Sir Henry John Codrington, K C B, Adm of the Fleet*, b 17 Oct 1808, d 4 *Aug* 1877, m 1st, 9 *Ap* 1849, *Helen Jane, da of C Webb Smith of Florence*, d 1876, *and had issue* 1*c to* 2*c*

1*c* Anne Jane Codrington, m 12 Jan 1882, Henry Stormont (Finch-Hatton), 13th Earl of Winchilsea and 8th Earl of Nottingham [E], &c [also a descendant of King Edward III through Mortimer-Percy (see p 129)] (*Harlech, co Merioneth*), and has issue 1*d* to 3*d*

1*d* Guy Montagu George Finch-Hatton, Viscount Maidstone, Lieut Royal East Kent Yeo, b 28 May 1885
2*d* Hon Denys George Finch-Hatton, b 24 Ap 1887
3*d* Lady Gladys Margaret Finch-Hatton

2*c* Ellen Codrington, m 27 July 1878, Sir John Roche Dasent, C B (26 *Elvaston Place, S W, Montrose House, St Vincent, W I*), and has issue 1*d* to 2*d*
[Nos 9390 to 9431

---

[1] He and his son assumed the baronetcy under the assumption that the 3rd Bart had *d s p l* See G E C's "Complete Baronetage," v 56

The Plantagenet Roll

1d Manuel Dasent, Lieut R N , *b* 13 May 1879

2d. Walter Dasent, Lieut R N , *b* 15 Nov 1880

3b *Jane Barbara Codrington*, d 3 Ap 1884 , m *Capt Sir Thomas Bourchier, R N , K C B*

3a *Caroline Codrington*, d (–) , m 28 Dec 1797, *Joseph Lyons (Walrond), 6th Marquis of Vallado [Spain], &c , of Antigua and Dulford House, co Devon,* b 1752 , d 13 Jan 1815 , *and had issue* 1b *to* 2b

1b *Lyons (Walrond), 7th Marquis of Vallado [Spain],* b 21 Ap 1800 , d (*unm*) 21 May 1819

2b *Bethell (Walrond), 8th Marquis of Vallado [Spain] and a co-h to the Barony of Welles [E], M P , J P , D L ,* b 10 Aug 1802 , d 1876 , m 10 Nov 1829, *Lady Janet, da of James (St Clair), 2nd Earl of Rosslyn [U K], G C B,* d Nov 1880, *and had issue* 1c

1c Henry (Walrond), 9th Marquis of Vallado and a Grandee of the 1st Class [Spain] and a co-h to the Barony of Welles [E], J P , *late* Lieut -Col and Hon Col 4th Batt Devon Regt (21 *Bloomfield Street, W*), *b* 9 Nov 1841 , m 1861, Caroline Maud, da of William John Clarke of Buckland Tous-saints, co Devon, J P , D L , and has issue 1d to 10d

1d Henry Humphrey Walrond, B A (Oxon) (28 *Pennsylvania Road, Exeter*), *b* 14 July 1862 , m 31 July 1901, Gertrude Gordon, da of Col Sir Stephen Hill, G C M G , C B , *s p*

2d Ernest Adolphus Walrond, *b* 22 Oct 1863 , m Oct 1891, Fannie Jane Helen, da of William Helm of Fresno, California and has issue 1e to 3e

1e Ernest Henry Walrond, *b* 31 July 1896

2e George Osmund Walrond, *b* 25 Aug 1898

3e Frank Helm Walrond, *b* 25 Oct 1895

3d Francis Arthur Walrond (50 *Addison Gardens, W*), *b* 8 Feb 1866 , m 24 Ap 1895, Muriel Gwendoline, da of Frederick J Methwold of Thorne Court, Bury St Edmunds, J P , F S A , and has issue 1e to 4e

1e Henry Humphrey Richard Methwold Walrond, *b* Oct 1904

2e Beryl Methwold Walrond, *b* 13 Feb 1896

3e Irene Fay Methwold Walrond, *b* 4 July 1897

4e Muriel Joan Methwold Walrond, *b* 11 Nov 1898

4d Herbert William James Walrond, *b* 9 Aug 1868 , *unm*

5d Conrad Montague Walrond, *b* 16 Aug 1869 , m 3 Aug 1908, Kate Dalrymple, da of F Woollven of Glasgow

6d George Stewart Basil Walrond, *b* 15 May 1876 , m 23 Dec 1903, Mabel, da of the Rev W H Bloxame, M A

7d Edith Maud Walrond, m 6 July 1887, the Rev Charles Francis Long Sweet, M A , Vicar of Stourpine (*Stourpane Vicarage, Dorset*), and has issue 1e to 3e

1e George Charles Walrond Sweet, *b* 4 Dec 1889

2e Leonard Herbert Walrond Sweet, *b* 15 June 1893

3e Dorothy Maud Walrond Sweet, *b* 7 Oct 1891

8d Beatrice Paulina Mabel Walrond, m 28 Nov 1900, Charles Christopher Davie (see Supplement) (21 *Selborne Road, Hove*) , and has issue 1e to 2e

1e Paul Christopher Davie, *b* (?) 31 Sept 1901

2e Ethel Margery Davie, *b* July 1901

9d Kate Gwendoline Walrond, m 7 Oct 1903, William Hatton Stansfeld (*The Larches, Iver Heath, Bucks*), s p

10d Sybil Mary Walrond, m 16 June 1903, Edward Frank Lumley Hopkins, and has issue 1e to 3e

1e Wirth Sybil Annette Hopkins, *b* 4 Dec 1904

2e Sylvia Gwendoline Alice Hopkins, *b* 6 July 1906

3e Janet Muriel Ada Hopkins, *b* 3 Jan 1909   [Nos 9132 to 9459

# of The Blood Royal

31 Descendants of BRIDGET CODRINGTON (Table V) *d* (-), *m* 1747, the Right Hon WILLIAM DOWDESWELL (see p 503) of Pull Court, co Worcester, P C, M P, Chancellor of the Exchequer 1765–66, *d* (at Nice) 6 Feb 1775, and had issue (with 9 others who *d.s p*) 1*a* to 2*a*

1*a* *John Edmund Dowdeswell of Pull Court, M P, Recorder of Tewkesbury 1798–1833, and a Master in Chancery 1820–50*, b *3 Mar* 1772, d 11 *Nov* 1851, m 4 *Sept* 1800, *Carolina, da of Charles Bretzcke*, d 6 *May* 1845, *and had issue* 1*b* to 2*b*

1*b* *William Dowdeswell of Pull Court, M P, J P, D L, High Sheriff co Worcester* 1855, b 18 *Oct* 1804, d 6 *Feb* 1887, m 19 *Mar* 1839, *Amelia Letitia, da of Robert Graham of Cossington House co Somerset*, d 24 *Jan* 1900, *and had issue* 1*c* to 2*c*

1*c* *William Edward Dowdeswell of Pull Court, M P*, b 13 *June* 1841, d s p 12 *July* 1893

2*c* Rev *Edmund Richard Dowdeswell of Pull Court, M A* (Oxon), *formerly* (1881–95) *Vicar of Bushley* (*Pull Court, Tewkesbury*), b 14 Jan 1815, *unm*

2*b* *Catharine Dowdeswell*, b 8 *Sept* 1801, d 5 *Aug* 1878, m 10 *Jan* 1833, *Richard Beauvoir Berens of Kevington, co Kent*, d 25 *Feb* 1859, *and had issue* 1*c* to 2*c*

1*c* Richard Berens of Kevington, J P, D L, High Sheriff co Kent 1893 (*Kevington, St Mary Cray, Kent*), b 15 *Mar* 1834, m 13 *June* 1860, *Fanny Georgina, da of Alexander Atherton Park, Master of the Court of Common Pleas*

2*c* *Catharine Frances Carolina Berens*, d 4 *Oct* 1892, m *Aug* 1880, *Lieut-Col Grant, late Rifle Brigade*

2*a* *Elizabeth Dowdeswell*, d 21 *Oct* 1830, m 21 *June* 1777 *Sir William Weller Pepys, 1st Bart* [U K], *a Master in Chancery*, b 1 *Jan* 1741, d 2 *June* 1825, *and had issue* 1*b* to 3*b*

1*b* *Charles Christopher (Pepys), 1st Earl of Cottenham* [U K], *Lord High Chancellor of Great Britain*, b 29 *Ap* 1781, d 29 *Ap* 1851, m 30 *June* 1821, *Caroline Elizabeth, da of William Wingfield Baker* [*by his wife, Lady Charlotte Maria, née Digby*], b 6 *Ap* 1868, *and had issue*
See the Essex Volume, pp 163–164, Nos 20495–20541

2*b* *Right Rev Henry Pepys, D D, Lord Bishop of Worcester* (1841–60), b 18 *Ap* 1783, d 13 *Nov* 1860, m 27 *Jan* 1821, *Maria, da of the Right Hon John Sullivan* [*by his wife, Lady Harriet née Hobart*], d 17 *June* 1885, *and had issue*
See the Clarence Volume, p 595, Nos 26139–26185

3*b* *Isabella Sophia Pepys*, d 21 *Ap* 1870 m 12 *Jan* 1813, *the Rev Thomas Whateley, Rector of Chetwynd, Salop*, d 10 *May* 1864, *and had* (*with possibly other*) *issue* 1*c*
1*c* Arthur Whateley (4 *Southwick Crescent, Hyde Park, W*)

[Nos 9460 to 9556

32 Descendants of JANE TURNER of Kirk Leatham, co York (Table VI), *d* (-), *m* 1745, PHILIP WILLIAM CASIMIR VAN STRAUBENZEL, Capt Dutch Guards, *d* 1765, and had issue

See the Essex Volume, Exeter Supplement, pp 640–642, Nos 52020 1–58

[Nos 9557 to 9614.

79

The Plantagenet Roll

33. Descendants, if any surviving, of ELIZABETH MARWOOD (Table VI), *bapt* 7 Mar 1666, *d* 26 Mar 1726, *m* 7 May 1685, JOHN PIERCE of Lazenby Hall [son and h of Richard Pierce of Hutton Bonville]. co York, *d.* 5 Oct 1694, and had issue [1]

34 Descendants of BARBARA MARWOOD (Table VI), living 1679, *m.* 1st, Sir THOMAS HEBBLETHWAITE of Norton, co York, M P, *bapt* 19 June 1628, *bur* 21 June 1668, [2] 2ndly, as 2nd wife, Sir FRANCIS COBB of Ottringham, [3] and had issue 1a to 8a

1a *James Hebblethwaite*, b c 1652, bur 10 Dec 1729, m *Bridget, da of Sir William Cobb of Ottringham*, d 13 June 1720, and had issue 1b to 3b

1b *Frances Hebblethwaite, da and co-h*, b c 1677, d 1 Ap 1720, m 8 Ap 1703, *Sir Francis Boynton of Burton Agnes, 4th Bt [E], M P*, bapt 17 Nov 1677, d 16 Sept 1739, and had issue 1c to 3c

1c *Sir Griffith Boynton, 5th Bt [E]*, b 24 May 1712, d 18 Oct 1761, m 5 Ap 1742, *Anne or Amy, da of Thomas White of Walling Wells, co Notts, M P*, d. 27 Feb 1745, and had issue 1d

1d *Sir Griffith Boynton, 6th Bt [E], M P, F S A*, b 22 Feb 1745, d 6·12 Jan 1778, m 1 Aug 1768, *Mary da of James Hebblethwaite of Norton and Bridlington* [2ndly, 21 July 1798, *George John Parkhurst of Hutton Ambro, co York, and Catesby Abbey, co Northants, by whom, who d June 1823, she had also issue and*], d 13 May 1815, and had issue

See the Exeter Volume, pp 547–549, Nos 49541–49587

2c *Francis Boynton of Otteringham*, b 10 Jan 1718, d (–), m 26 July 1762, *Charlotte, da of Sir Warton Pennyman-Warton, 5th Bt [E]*, and had issue 1d

1d *Francis Boynton*, b 27 Ap 1764, bur 9 Oct 1816, m *at York before 1785*, and had issue a son and a da [4]

3c *Constance Boynton*, b 15 Feb 1704, bur 9 Dec 1785, m 28 Ap 1741, *Ralph Lutton of Knapton, co York*

2b *Bridget Hebblethwaite, da and co-h*, bapt 6 Jan 1686, bur 26 Aug 1720, m (——) *Bushell*

3b *Barbara Hebblethwaite, da and co-h*, bapt 11 May 1695, d (–), m (——) *Cartwright of Malton*

2a *Thomas Hebblethwaite*, bapt 2 Oct 1657

3a *Charles Hebblethwaite*, bapt 20 Aug 1660, bur 11 Feb 1727, m *Margaret, da of William St Quintin of Muston* [son and h -app of 2nd Bt [L]], bur 19 June 1723 and had issue

See the Exeter Volume, pp 547–549, Nos 49541–49587

4a *Mountayne Hebblethwaite*, bapt (at Norton) 11 Aug 1662

5a *Frances Hebblethwaite*

6a *Barbara Hebblethwaite*, d 15 July 1735, *will as of Swanbourne, co Bucks, widow, prov by son-in-law, the Rev Benjamin Reynolds*, m *the Rev Thomas Gataker, Rector of Hoggerston, co Bucks*, bapt 8 Oct 1650, d 10 Nov 1701, and has issue 1b to 7b   [Nos 9615 to 9708

---

[1] Foster's " Yorkshire Pedigrees "

[2] Dugdale's " Visitation of Yorkshire," 1666, ed by J W Clay, F.S A *The Genealogist*, N S, xiv 48

[3] Presumably the Sir Francis Cobb of Ottringham, aged 60, 15 Sept 1666 See Dugdale's " Visitation of Yorkshire," 1666, Surtees Soc Pub, xxxvi 332, but this marriage is not noted there

[4] Foster's " Yorkshire Pedigrees "

# of The Blood Royal

1b Rev Edward Gataker, Rector of Mursley-cum-Salden, co Bucks, b 24 Jan 1684, d. 16 Sept 1729, m Elizabeth, da of (—), d 24 Oct 1781, in 87th year, bur in St Andrews, Hertford, and had issue (with 5 others) 1c to 2c

1c Thomas Gataker, Surgeon Extraordinary to George III, d 17 Nov 1768, m Anne, da of Thomas Hill of Court of Hill co Salop, d 22 July 1797, and had issue 1d to 2d

1d Thomas Gataker of Mildenhall, co Suffolk, b 1749, d 16 Nov 1841, m Mary, da of John Swale of Mildenhall, d at Worlington 4 Nov 1839, aged 92, and had issue (with a son d s p) 1e

1e George Gataker of Mildenhall, co Suffolk, and White Knights Park, co Berks, J P, D L, b 30 Mar 1792, d 30 Ap 1872, m 1st, 5 Nov 1825, Elizabeth Harrison, da of Thomas Wilkinson of Nether Hall, co Suffolk, d 1 Jan 1827, 2ndly, 29 Aug 1829, Sophia Sarah, da of Henry Samuel Partridge of Hockham Hall, d 28 July 1861, and had issue (with a son and 2 das d unm) 1f to 5f

1f Melmoth William Gataker, late of Mildenhall, formerly I S C (5 Marlborough Street, Bath), b 23 Jan 1841, m 30 Jan 1873, Jemima, da of Benjamin Wood of Long Newnton, co Wilts, and has issue 1g to 2g

1g Melmoth Leicester Swale Gataker (Branksome Manor, Bournemouth), b 4 Jan 1874, m 14 Feb 1899, Annie Madeline, da of George W Young of Branksome Manor, and has issue 1h to 2h

1h Violet Louisa de Morel Gataker, b 30 Ap 1900

2h Muriel Elaine Georgina Gataker, b 19 Oct 1904

2g Reginald Henry Winchcombe Gataker (Boisdale, Wooroolin, Queensland), b 8 June 1875, m 26 Nov 1901, Christian Esson, da of George Gordon of Ellangowan, Banchory, co Kincardine, and has issue 1h to 2h

1h Reginald Melmoth Gordon Gataker, b 14 Sept 1903

2h Godfrey George Ormond Gataker, b (—)

2f Charles Frederick Gataker (Milden, Maryborough, Queensland), b 22 Ap 1843, m 20 Sept 1869, Fanny Gulliver, da of William Barns of Maryborough, afsd, and has issue 1g to 5g

1g Melmoth Leofric Gataker, b 31 Mar 1872, m 5 Nov 1896, Clara, da of Josiah Mason Illidge of Gympie, Queensland, and has issue 1h to 3h

1h Melmoth Leofric Gataker, b 2 Nov 1903

2h Minnie Lucy Gataker, b 22 Ap 1899

3h Amy Maud Gataker, b 27 Feb 1901

2g George William Frank Gataker, b 13 Sept 1873

3g Charles James Gataker, b 9 Oct 1876

4g Walter Reynardson Gataker, b 26 Oct 1878, m 21 Feb 1901, Sarah Kathleen, da of James Milles of Nanango, Queensland, and has issue 1h to 2h

1h Doris Marian Gataker, b 13 Sept 1904

2h Kathleen Elsey Gataker, b Sept 1905

5g Minnie Georgina Elizabeth Gataker, m 22 Ap 1905, Reginald Julius (Brisbane, Queensland)

3f Frank Anthony Gataker, late Lieut R N, b 24 Dec 1844, m 30 Oct 1873, Margaret, da of Benjamin Harding, of Wadhurst Castle, co Sussex

4f[1] Elizabeth Mary Gataker, m as 2nd wife, 2 Feb 1858, the Rev Walter John Partridge, M A, Rector of Caston, d 28 Dec 1891 s p

5f[2] Louisa Sophia Gataker

2d Annie Gataker, d (—), m 19 Dec 1771, Stamp Brooksbank, of Chesterfield St, Mayfair [2nd son of Stamp Brooksbank of Healaugh Manor, co Yorks, and Hacknay House, co Midx], d 1802, and had issue (with 2 sons d s p) 1e

1e Annie Brooksbank, d (—), m 10 Dec 1795, the Rev William Lilliers Robinson [2nd son of Sir George Robinson, 5th Bt [E], M P] d 14 Jan 1829, and had issue 1f to 3f   [Nos 9709 to 9729.

81

The Plantagenet Roll

1f Rev Sir George Stamp Robinson, 7th Bt [E], Rector of Cranford and Hon Canon of Peterborough, b 29 Aug 1797, d 9 Oct 1873, m 24 May 1827, Emma, da of Robert Willis Blencowe, of Hayes, co Midx, d 20 Jan 1874, and had issue (with 3 sons and 3 das who d s p) 1g to 2g

    1g Sir John Blencowe Robinson, 8th Bt [E] b 20 May 1830, d s p 10 Aug 1877

    2g Rev Sir Frederick Laura Robinson 9th Bt [E], J P, Rector of Cranford, b 28 June 1843, d 6 Feb 1893, m 14 Dec 1870, Madeline Caroline, da of Frederick Sartoris of Rushden Hall co Northants, and has issue 1h to 4h

        1h Sir Frederick Villiers David Robinson, 10th Bt [E], Lt 2nd Batt Northamptonshire Regt (Cranford Hall, near Kettering), b 1 Dec 1880, unm

        2h Evelyn Dorothy Robinson, m 31 Jan 1900, Lindsay Ralph Bagnall

        3h Margery Sybil Robinson

        4h Sylvia Joan Robinson, m 27 Ap 1903, Major Charles Edward Bagnall, a collector in Uganda

    2f Caroline Penelope Robinson, d ( ), m 29 Oct 1834, Herman Merivale, C B Bar-at-Law, I T, permanent Under Sec of State for India, d (-), and had issue (with a da who d s p) 1g to 2g

    1g Herman Charles Merivale, b 27 Jan 1839, m 13 May 1878, Elizabeth, da of John Pitman

    2g Isabel Frances Merivale, m 16 Ap 1863, William Peere Williams-Freeman, of Clapton, co Northants, Sec H M Diplo Ser, d 18 Sept 1884, and had issue (with 2 sons and a da d s p) 1h to 3h

        1h Rev Lionel Peere Williams-Freeman of Clapton, M A (Camb), Vicar of Exwick (Exwick Vicarage, Exeter), b 18 May 1867, m 23 Ap 1896, Louisa, da of Charles Hope, of Gorleston Priory, and has issue 1i to 5i

            1i William Peere Williams-Freeman, b 8 Oct 1909

            2i Mary Leonora Williams-Freeman, b 17 Nov 1898

            3i Dorothy Francis Williams-Freeman, b 29 Dec 1899

            4i Cecilia Williams-Freeman, b 25 Oct 1901

            5i Violet Williams-Freeman, b 19 Mar, 1906

        2h Agnes Caroline Williams-Freeman

        3h Violet Mary Williams-Freeman, m as 2nd wife, 15 Ap 1902, Arthur Charles Hammersley, Banker (see p 281) (56 Princes Gate, S W), and has issue 1i to 3i

            1i Christopher Ralph Hammersley, b 4 Jan 1903

            2i David Frederick Hammersley, b 15 July 1904

            3i Monica Violet Hammersley

    3f Emma Robinson, d 9 June 1902, m 12 Nov 1834, the Rev William Duthy, Rector of Sudborough, co Northants, J P, b 18 Aug 1796, d 29 Sept 1889, and had issue 1g to 6g

    1g Archibald Edward Duthy Col R H A, b 4 Jan 1818, d 10 Nov 1906, m 4 Nov 1891, Madeline Alice, da of James Price, and had issue 1h to 3h

        1h Archibald Elder Desmond Campbell Duthy

        2h Reginald Edward Athelstan Duthy

        3h Humphrey William Gilbert Duthy.

    2g John Walter Brand Duthy, formerly Indian Telegraph Dept (Islip Grange, Thrapston), b 31 Jan 1848, m 6 June 1883, Georgina Penelope, da of George Rooper, and has issue 1h

        1h George Duthy, b 24 May 1885

    3g Rev Reginald Henry Duthy, B A (Oxon) (All Hallows Presbytery, Orange St, Borough), b 10 Nov 1850, unm

    4g Georgina Caroline Duthy, m 26 Mar 1856, the Rev Charles William

[Nos 9730 to 9753

82

# of The Blood Royal

Sillifant, Rector of Weare Gifford and Rural Dean (*Hughenden, Parkstone*), and has issue 1*h* to 7*h*

    1*h* Charles Herbert Sillifant, *b* 12 Dec 1866

    2*h* Gertrude Caroline Emma Sillifant

    3*h* Emily Harriet Sillifant.

    4*h* Georgina Francis Sillifant

    5*h* Mabel Sillifant

    6*h* Edith Sillifant

    7*h* Beatrice Charlotte Sillifant

    5*g* Caroline Anna Duthy

    6*g* Edith Mary Duthy, *m* 21 Aug 1867, Major John William Barn Hawkesworth, J P (*Wallington, Oxon , Stokeford, Wareham*), and has issue 1*h* to 2*h*

    1*h* Charles Edward Mackenzie Hawkesworth, *b* 25 June 1868

    2*h* Thomas Ayscough Fitzwilliam Hawkesworth, *b* 8 Sept 1870

    2*c* *Elizabeth Gataker,* b 1725, d *at St Albans* 4 *July* 1790, m *the Rev Edward Bourchier, M A , J P , Rector of Bramfield 1740–75, and Vicar of All Saints and St John's, Hertford.* 1740–71 [*descended from King Edward I. through Harrison, Villiers, St John, Scrope, Welles, and Segrave*], b 7 *Aug* 1707 , d 17 *Nov* 1775, *and had issue* 1*d to* 9*d*

    1*d* *Rev Edward Bourchier, M A , Vicar of All Saints and St John's, Hertford,* 1771–85, *Rector of Bramfield* 1775 ⋅5, b 6 *Sept* 1738 , d 14 *Dec* 1785, m *Catherine, da of William Wollaston of Finborough, co Suffolk, M P,* d 4 *Feb* 1801 , *and had issue (with 3 das d young)* 1*e* to 2*e*

    1*e* *Rev Edward Bourchier, M A , Rector of Bramfield,* b 13 *July* 1776 , d 21 *Ap* 1810, m 7 *Feb* 1804, *Harriet, da of Robert Jenner of Lincoln's Inn Fields,* d 18 *Jan* 1864 , *and had issue* 1*f* to 9*f*

    1*f* *Edward Bourchier,* b 6 *July* 1810

    2*f* *Francis Bourchier,* b 10 *Aug* 1812

    3*f* *Robert Jenner Bourchier,* b 2 *Oct* 1818 , d (*s p*) 1 *Oct* 1883

    4*f* *Sir George Bourchier, K C B , Major-Gen R A ,* b 23 *Aug* 1821, d (–), m 1st, 16 *July* 1851, *Georgiana Clemenson da of John Graham Lough of London,* d 2 *Mar* 1868 . 2ndly, 23 *May* 1872, *Margaret Murchison, da of Col Bartleman,* d 13 *July* 1881 , *and had issue* 1*g* to 5*g*

    1*g* George Lough Bourchier, *b* 29 July 1855 , *m* 11 Oct 1879, Mary Catherine, da of the Rev Barcroft Boake, Principal of Colombo Academy

    2*g* Edward Herbert Bourchier, *b* 24 Nov 1856

    3*g* Arthur Charles Francis Bourchier, M A (Oxon), Actor Manager (*The Albany, Piccadilly, W , Otway Cottage, Bushy Heath*), *b* 15 Aug 1864 , *m* 9 Dec 1894, Violet Augusta Mary, commonly called ' Violet Vanbrugh,' the well-known actress [descended from the Lady Anne, sister of Kings Edward IV and Richard III (see Exeter Volume, p 118)], da of the Rev Reginald Henry Barnes, Prebendary of Exeter, *s p*

    4*g* Herbert Eustace Bourchier, *b* 13 Jan 1874

    5*g* Ina Maude Mary Bourchier

    5*f* *Harriet Jenner Bourchier,* b 29 *Nov* 1804, d 11 *Ap* 1883, m *the Rev W Harris*

    6*f* *Catherine Anne Jenner Bourchier,* d 7 *Aug* 1819

    7*f* *Elizabeth Jenner Bourchier,* d 7 *June* 1860, m *the Rev G North*

    8*f* *Louisa Jenner Bourchier,* b 26 *Jan* 1809 , d (–)

    9*f* *Emma Jenner Bourchier,* b 9 *Ap* 1814, d (–)

    2*e* *Blanch Maria Bourchier,* d (–)

    2*d* *Charles Bourchier, a Member of Council of Bombay,* b 13 *May* 1739,

83

The Plantagenet Roll

d 28 *Nov* 1818, m 1*st*, 7 *Oct* 1773, *Barbara, da of James Richardson of Knock-shinnock, co Dumfries,* d 18 *Nov* 1781, 2ndly, 25 *Jan* 1787, *da of the Rev Benjamin Preedy, D D ,* d 27 *Ap* 1822, *and had issue (with 3 sons d. young)* 1e *to* 6e

1e *Samuel Bourchier, H E I C S ,* b *Oct* 1781, d *in Bombay* 1813, m. *Harriet, da of Major-Gen Robert Lewis, H E I C S ,* d 1850, *and had issue (with 4 sons d young)* 1f *to* 3f

1f *Robert Francis Bourchier, Capt 4th Bombay N I ,* d 1837, m 21 *July* 1832 *Antoinette Anna Louisa, da of Capt the Hon John Rodney [B Rodney Coll],* d (-), *and had issue* 1g *to* 2g

1g *Robert Lennox Bourchier, Lt -Col R M A ,* b 1838, d 12 *May* 1882, m 14 *Oct* 1859, *Mary, da of Philips Hast, Lieut R N ,* d (-), *and had issue* 1h *to* 5h

    1h Philip Lennox Walter Bourchier, b 13 *Aug* 1870

    2h Rodney Lewis Bourchier, b 21 *Jan* 1875

    3h Raymond Walter Harry Bourchier b 26 *Feb* 1880

    4h Mary Bourchier

    5h Amabel Bourchier

2g Harriet E Lennox Bourchier (26 *Taswell Road, Southsea*)

2f *Harriet Bourchier,* d (-), m 1827, *John Burnett, Bombay C S , and had issue* 1g

1g Marianne Burnett

3f *Jane Bourchier,* d (-), m 1829, *Capt William Chambers Bombay N I , and had issue* 1g

1g Jane Chambers, m 1853, *Capt George Geach, and had issue* 1h

1h George Chambers Geach

2e *Rev Charles Spencer Bourchier, M A , Rector of Great Hallingbury, co Essex,* b 22 *Feb* 1791, d 22 *July* 1872, m 13 *Ap* 1814, *Eliza, da of Samuel Harman, of Hadley, Barnet,* d 22 *Jan* 1880, *and had issue (with a son d young)* 1f *to* 4f

1f *Legendre Charles Bourchier, Col 98th Regt and Comdt of Kurrachee during the Mutiny,* b 13 *Mar* 1815, d 27 *Ap* 1866, m 22 *Aug* 1850, *Margaret, da of the Rev Thomas Beane Johnstone Rector of Chilton, and had issue (with a da d young)* 1g *to* 3g

1g Charles Legendre Johnstone Bourchier, *Capt Cape Colonial Forces, formerly* 35th *and* 65th *Regts,* b *Aug* 1851, m 18 *Ap* 1873, Annie Werge, widow of A Kaye da of E H Howey of Tynemouth, d 25 *May* 1874, *and had issue* 1h

1h Charlie Heumphrey Johnstone Bourchier, b 25 *Mar* 1874

2g Helen Johnstone Bourchier

3g Margaret Georgiana Johnstone Bourchier, m 31 *May* 1881, Peter Purves of Brampson, *and had issue* 1h *to* 2h

1h Douglas Bourchier Johnstone Purves, b 21 *May* 1883

2h Helen Georgiana Johnstone Purves

2f *Georgiana Anne Bourchier,* d (-), m *Richard Weller Chadwick, and had (with other) issue* 1g

1g Edward Frederick Chadwick, *late* 33rd *Regt,* b (—), m 20 *Sept* 1882, Anna Louisa (? Amy) (see p 85), da of the Rev Charles Torkington

3f Marianne Frances Bourchier, twin

4f Emily Dorothy Bourchier

3e *Richard James Bourchier of Malta and* 67 *Victoria Street, Westminster,* b 16 *June* 1793, d (-); m 1*st*, (—), da of (—) *Lander, and had issue (a son and 3 das)*

4e *Elizabeth Bourchier,* d *Nov* 1856, m 22 *Oct* 1779, *James Torkington (see p* 91) *of Great Stukeley, co Hunts, Bar -at-Law,* d 7 *May* 1828[1] *or* 6 *Feb* 1852[2], *and had issue (with 12 others who d unm)* 1f *to* 2f   [Nos 9772 to 9789

---

[1] Foster's " Noble and Gentle Families," n 609   [2] Ibid , n 606

# of The Blood Royal

1f Laurence John Torkington of Great Stukeley, Lieut 4th Light Dragoons,
b 27 Sept 1809, d 7 May 1874, m 26 Sept 1839, Mary Anne, da of Lieut-Col
Walker, R A, d 1874, and had issue (with a son d unm) 1g to 5g

1g Charles Torkington of Great Stukeley, co Hunts, and Stukeley, The Leven,
Tasmania, Capt 41st Regt (Roslyn, Salisbury Road, Seaford, Sussex), b 20 July
1847, m 3 Aug 1875, Florence Elizabeth Caroline [descended from George, Duke
of Clarence, K G (see Clarence Volume, p 185)], da of Richard George Coke of
Brimington Hall, co Derby, and has issue 1h to 4h

    1h Gerard Stukeley Torkington, I S C, 69th Punjabis, b 23 Sept 1878

    2h Charles Coke Torkington, Welsh Regt, b 7 Mar 1881

    3h. John Elmsley Bourchier Torkington, Manchester Regt, b 19 Nov 1884

    4h Dorothy Mary Torkington.

2g Mary Dorothy Torkington

3g Alice Torkington

4g Isabella Torkington

5g Gertrude Torkington, m 1 Oct 1868, the Rev John Allen, M A, D D
(Oxon), Vicar of St Mary's, Lancaster, and Hon Canon of Manchester, d (-)

2f Rev Charles Torkington, Rector of Almer, co Dorset, b 13 Dec 1817,
d (-), m 1st, 1842, Anna, da of James Powell, of Clapton, co Midx, d 8 Nov
1847, 2ndly, Nov 1848, Ellen Eliza, da of the Rev H Cookson, and had issue
(with a son and 2 das d young) 1g to 6g

1g Henry Torkington, Lieut-Col and Hon Col late R A, b 26 May 1843, m
Oct 1875, Annie Ibbetson, da of William G Browne, and has issue 1h to 3h

    1h Richard Humphrey Torkington, b 1 May 1878

    2h Oliver Miles Torkington, Capt Scottish Rifles, b 29 Aug 1880

    3h Mary Catherine Torkington

2g Edward Torkington, b 15 Jan 1856

3g Charles Richard Torkington, b 26 Mar 1860

4g¹ Catherine Torkington

5g² Georgina Torkington

6g² Amy (? Anna Louisa) Torkington, m 30 Sept 1882, Col Edward
Frederick Chadwick of Chetnole, Sherborne, Dorset (see p 84)

5c² Georgiana Bourchier, b 1787, d 8 Mar 1862, m James Garden Seton,
of the Hanaper Office, in the Court of Chancery, and had issue

6c² Caroline Bourchier, b 16 Feb 1792, d 1820, m as 1st wife, 31 Mar
1814, the Rev Theodore Dury, Rector of Westmill, co Herts, d 2 Oct 1850, and
had issue (who all d s p)

3d George Bourchier, b 11 May 1741

4d John Bourchier, Capt R N, Lieut Gov of Greenwich Hospital, b 26 Sept
1747, d 30 Dec 1808, m 1st, Mary, da of the Rev Richard Walter, Chaplain
R N, d 26 Nov 1789, 2ndly, Dec 1790, Charlotte, da of Thomas Corbett of
Darnhall, co Chester, Bar-at-Law [who m 2ndly, 27 July 1810, Capt Piatt, S Line
Mil, 3rdly, F J Sandars Lang of Keston, co Devon, and], d 5 Jan 1839, and
had issue (with 2 sons and 3 das d s p) 1e to 9e

1e Henry Bourchier, Rear-Adm of the Blue, b Oct 1787 at Lille, d 14 Oct
1852, m Mary, da of Lieut-Col John Macdonald, d at Ostend 9 Feb 1852, and
had issue 1f to 2f

1f Macdonald Bourchier, Comm R N, b 6 Aug 1814, d (-) m 1st, 5 Dec
1843, Mary Eliza, da of Rear-Adm John Hancock, C B, d 19 June 1872 2ndly,
12 May 1874, Charlotte Brumby, da of John Holland, Lieut R N, and had issue
(with a son d young) 1g to 3g

1g Seton Longuet Bourchier, b (twin) 19 Oct 1844, m 25 July 1877,
Georgiana Martin, da of James N Merriman, M D, Apothecary Extraordinary to
Queen Victoria, and has issue (with a da d young) 1h to 2h

[Nos 9790 to 9808

85

M

1*h* Olive Longuet Bourchier

2*h* Emily Marion Bourchier, twin

2*g* Mary Eliza Sophia Bourchier

3*g* Alice Gertrude Bourchier

2*f* *Henry Prescott Pellew Bourchier, Capt P & O Service*, b 9 Nov 1816, d 1 Aug 1856 , m .1*p* 1851, *Mary Jane, da of the Rev Edward Ince, Vicar of Wigtoft,* d 13 Mar 1856 , *and had issue* 1g *to* 4g

1*g* Henry Edward Bourchier, Comm R N (*Highfield House, Steep, Petersfield*), b 5 Mar 1852, m 16 Oct 1878, Jane Burnett, da of J Williamson, and has issue 1*h*

2*h* Lily McDonald Bourchier

2*g* Mary Jane Bourchier (*Grove Villa, High Street, Feltham, Midx*)

3*g* Henrietta Catherine Bourchier, m 21 Sept 1881, William Booth Williamson (*Grove Villa. High Street, Feltham, Midx*), and has issue 1*h* to 6*h*

1*h* Owen McDonald Williamson, b 11 Ap 1886

2*h* Jack Cecil Bourchier Williamson, b 15 May 1891

3*h* Kenneth Bourchier Williamson, b 27 Aug 1898

4*h* Mary Sophia Williamson, m 8 Ap 1908, the Hon John Morgan-Owen

5*h* Charlotte Dorothy Williamson

6*h* Alice Marguerite Williamson

4*g* Alice Bourchier (*Grove Villa, High Street, Feltham, Midx*)

2*e* *William Bourchier, Comm R N*, b 1791, d *in Canada* 22 Jan 1844 , m 1st, *in Canada,* 8 Ap 1821. *Amelia, da of John Mills Jackson of Downton, co Wilts* , 2ndly, c 1834/5, *Laura, previously wife of Lieut Robert Wrangham Lukin. da of Robert Preston of London,* d 29 Ap 1898 , *and had issue* 1*f* to 4*f*

1*f* [1] *Eustace Fane Bourchier, Lieut -Gen R E , C B , K L H* , b 25 Aug 1822 , d 16 Jan 1902, m 1st, *Anne Jane, da of Charles Stuart Pillans of Rosebank, Rondebosch,* d 6 Ap 1868 , 2ndly, 25 Aug 1869, *Maria, widow of Wilmot Seton of the Treasury, da of* (—), d s p *by him* 6 1 eb 1882 , *and had issue (with 5 das)* 1g *to* 2g

1*g* *Charles Edward Stewart Bourchier,* d (*in Pietermaritzburg*) May 1904

2*g* Alfred Heseltine Bourchier

2*f* [2] *Henry Seton Bourchier, Lieut -Col R M L I* , sometime British Resident at Lukoja on the Niger (*Wayside, South Brent, S D.von*), b 17 Feb 1842 , m 28 May 1868, Jessie Caroline, da of Col Robert Hawkes, 80th Regt , and has issue 1*g* to 2*g*

1*g* Charles Bourchier, Tea Planter, Ceylon, b 8 Dec 1886

2*g* Mabel Jessie Bourchier

3*f* [2] *Georgina Fanny Bourchier*, b 2 Oct 1836 , d (*at Brisbane*) 12 Aug 1893 , m *at St Mary's, The Boltons. South Kensington,* 23 May 1865, *Edward Raven Priest of Cromer, Chemist,* d (*at Brisbane*) 9 Nov 1885 , *and had issue* (see Appendix)

4*f* [2] Laura Ellen Bourchier (7 *Huggen's College, North Fleet, Kent*), unm

3*e* *Thomas Bourchier, twin with* 4e, d (—) , m *Anne, da of Morris Graham, of Deal* , *and had issue (with a son d young)* 1*f* to 2*f*

1*f* *William Sutherland Bourchier, Staff Comm R N* , b 15 Nov 1823 , d June 1904 , m 1st, 8 Sept 1850, *Mina Glover, da of John Aldrich, Master R N* , d 1852 , 2ndly 1 May 1856, *Mary, da of Isaac Halse of Sloane Street, Chelsea,* d 1893 , *and had issue* 1g *to* 4g

1*g* [1] *Mina Mary Bourchier,* m 1874, Frederick D'Iffanger (85 *Gloucester Terrace, Hyde Park, W*), s *p*

2*g* [1] *Florence Anne Bourchier,* m 1878, William Cooper Keates, L R C P , M R C S (20 *East Dulwich Road, S E*), and has issue 1*h* to 3*h*

1*h* Courtnay Cooper Keates

2*h* Bransby Cooper Keates

3*h* Florence Mina Mary Keates, m (—) Wild   [Nos 9809 to 9833

3g² *Emily Halse Bourchier*, d 1907, m 1886, F *Thomas*, *and had issue* 1h
to 2h

    1h Leeson Thomas

    2h Donald Thomas

    4g² Ethel Annie Bourchier, *unm*

2f. *Thomas Bourchier, Lieut R N*, *took part in the searches for Sir John
Franklin,* b 10 *Sept* 1827, d 9 *July* 1866, m 22 *Jan* 1853, *Anne Bourchier, da
of John Allrich Master R N*, d 1 *Mar* 1909 *and had issue (with* 2 *sons and a
da d unm)* 1g *to* 4g

    1g William Thomas Bourchier, New South Wales C S, b 9 Oct 1857, *unm*

    2g Alfred Eustace Bourchier, Fleet Paymaster, R N (1et), b 1 June 1859, *unm*

    3g Annie Undine Bourchier ⎫
    4g Mary Bedford Bourchier ⎭ (97 *Victoria Road, Southsea*)

4e *James O'Brien Bourchier, J P, settled in Canada,* b (*twin with* 3c) c 1797,
d 28 *Aug* 1872, m *Jeanne, da of James Lyall of Canada, West, and had issue
(with* 6 *das)* 1f *to* 2f

    1f William Bourchier, *m* and has issue [1]

    2f John Raines Bourchier, *m* and has issue [1]

5e *John Bourchier, M D*, b 4 *Mar* 1802, d 11 *Feb* 1842, m 23 *Ap* 1836,
Sophia, da of Edward Phillips of Winchester, M D, d 18 *Ap* 1859, *and had
issue* 1f

    1f Rev Walter Bourchier, M A and Fellow of New College (Oxon), Vicar of
St Olave's, E, *formerly* of Steeple Morden (*St Olave's Vicarage Hanbury St, E*),
b. 20 Dec 1837, *m* 20 Ap 1876, Harriet Louisa Eliza, da of John Peach
MacWhirter, Bengal C S, and has issue 1g to 5g

        1g Walter John Majendie Bourchier, b 26 Feb 1877

        2g Rev Basil Graham Bourchier M A (Camb), *formerly* Curate of St Ann's,
Soho (*The Vicarage, Garden Suburb, Hampstead, N W*), b 13 Feb 1881

        3g Philip Claud Walter Bourchier, b 28 Oct 1891

        4g Constance Corbett Bourchier, *m* 26 Dec 1907, Horace R Brown, M D

        5g Sybil Audrey Bourchier, *m* 23 June 1908, Capt Maurice Capel Miers,
Somerset Light Infantry

6e [1] *Mary Sophia Bourchier*, b 11 *Aug* 1786, d 9 *May* 1884, m 21 *Aug*
1822, *the Rev Edward Ince, M A, Vicar of Wigtoft-with-Quadring, co Linc*, d
6 *Aug* 1840, *and had issue* 1f *to* 2f

    1f *Rev Edward Cumming Ince, of Sunbury House, Watford, and Mairick
Abbey, co York, M A (Camb), Vicar of Christ Church, Battersea,* 1867–77, b
17 *May* 1825, d 7 *Dec* 1899, m 14 *Aug* 1850, *Elizabeth Margaret Caroline, da
of John Gason, of co Wicklow, M D*, d 10 *June* 1902, *and had issue (with* 2 *sons
and a da d young)* 1g *to* 4g

        1g Rev Edward John Cumming Ince, now (R L 11 Aug 1893) Whittington-
Ince, M A (Camb), Rector of Wormington (*Wormington Rectory, Broadway R S O,
Worcestershire*), b 4 Feb 1852, *m* 23 Jan 1884, Annie Nora, da of Joscelline
Frederic Watkins, of Watford, J P, and has issue 1h to 9h

            1h Edward Watkins Whittington-Ince, b 3 Oct 1886

            2h William Berkeley Whittington-Ince, b 22 Feb 1889

            3h Charles Henry Whittington-Ince, b 27 Mar 1892

            4h Ralph Piggott Whittington-Ince, b 19 May 1898

            5h Nora Marjorie Whittington-Ince

            6h Elinor Gladys Whittington-Ince

            7h Anna Louisa Whittington-Ince

            8h Mary Elizabeth Whittington-Ince

            9h Annie Caroline Whittington-Ince

[Nos 9831 to 9858

---

[1] Foster's "Noble and Gentle Families"

The Plantagenet Roll

2g Rev Henry Gason Ince, M A (Oxon), Vicar of Stanley 1888–1902 (*Maesbury, Cavendish Road, Bournemouth*), b 24 Sept 1857, m 20 July 1887, Margaret, da of William Fellows Sedgwick of Cashio Bridge, Watford, and has issue 1h to 4h

  1h Cecil William Gason Ince, b 1 Aug 1888
  2h Henry Montague Ince, b 26 Sept 1889
  3h Douglas Edward Ince, b 10 Nov 1890
  4h Norman Sedgwick Ince, b 9 Feb 1892

3g Rev James Berkeley Cumming Ince, M A (Camb) (*31 Laurence Road, Hove, Sussex*), b 26 Nov 1862, m 1st, 19 Ap 1893, Emma Augusta, da of William Edward Parry Hooper of the Admiralty, 2ndly, 4 May 1905, Ethel, da of Russell Oates of Knaresborough, and has issue 1h to 5h

  1h Gordon Bourchier Ince, b 5 Feb 1896
  2h Berkeley Russell Ince, b 5 Feb 1906
  3h Margaret Cumming Ince, b 5 Feb 1894
  4h Violet Berkeley Ince, b 21 Mar 1901
  5h Ethel Grace Gason Ince, b 23 Jan 1908

4g Anna Elizabeth Ince, m 29 June 1904, Frederick Du Drury [youngest son of Henry Du Drury of Blackheath] (*Woolsery, Portchester Road, Bournemouth*), s p

2f *Mary Jane Ince*, d 13 Mar 1856, m Ap 1851, Capt Henry Prescott Pellew Bourchier, d 1 Aug 1856, and had issue

See p 86, Nos 9813–9823

7e *Charlotte Margaret Bourchier*, d 21 July 1852, m 1819, Capt Edward Parke, R M, d 14 Nov 1835, and had issue (with 2 das who d unm) 1f to 3f

  1f Richard Parke, C B, Col R M, b 21 Mar 1821; d 2 Mar 1892, m 8 May 1862, Louisa, da of Right Rev the Hon Edward Grey, Lord Bishop of Hereford [E Grey Coll], d 16 May 1904, and had issue 1g to 2g

    1g Edward Parke, B A (Oxon), of the Dept of the Official Receiver in Bankruptcy, b (—), unm
    2g Annie Louisa Parke, unm

  2f Frederick Parke, Capt R N b 18 May 1828, d 22 Nov 1900, m 27 Mar 1856, Lucy Anne, da of William John Wickham of Winchester, d 7 Jan 1906, and had issue 1g to 6g

    1g Charles Parke, b 7 July 1857, m Evelyn, da of (—) Lewis, and has issue 1h to 4h

      1h Frederick Parke, b 1886, m 8 Feb 1910, Clara, da of (—) Barber
      2h Ethel Parke, m 1905, J van Norman, and has issue (2 das)
      3h Louise Parke, unm
      4h Gertrude Parke, unm

    2g William Parke, b 1859, unm
    3g Ernest Richard Parke, b 1861, m July 1890, Maude, da of (——) Brown.
    4g Arthur Fiennes Wickham Parke, b 1865, m 1901, J——, da of (—) McCormac, and has issue 1h to 2h

      1h Richard Philip Wickham Parke, b 28 July 1906
      2h Gwendolin Maude Parke, b 28 Aug 1902

    5g Gertrude Mary Parke, unm
    6g Mabel Lucy Parke m 25 Feb 1891, William Henry Christopher Macartney, M D (*Riverhead House, Sevenoaks*), s p

  3f *Caroline Mary Parke*, d 8 May 1901, m 6 Jan 1842, the Rev Isaac Philip Prescott, M A (Oxon), Rector of Kelly, co Devon [son of Admiral Sir Henry Prescott, G C B], d 10 Aug 1898, and had issue (with a son and da d unm) 1g to 1g   [Nos 9859 to 9895

88

# of The Blood Royal

1g *Arthur Edward Prescott*, b 8 *Mar* 1852, d 6 *May* 1888, m 20 *Nov* 1877, *Kathleen* (18 *College Court Mansions, Hammersmith, W*), *da of the Rev Henry Clarke, Rector of Guisborough , and has issue* 1h *to* 4h

   1h Henry Cecil Prescott, b 1 Mar 1882

   2h Arthur Robert Prescott, b 23 June 1886, m 1906, E Cynthia, da of George Betts , and has issue 1i

      1i Constance Cynthia Prescott, b 19 Jan 1908

   3h Kathleen Mary Prescott, m 28 Dec 1904, Eng -Lieut George Henry Starr, R N , and has issue 1i

      1i Mary Cecilia Starr

   1h Constance Alice Prescott

2g *Charlotte Alice Prescott*, d 20 *Aug* 1865 , m 25 *July* 1861, *Joseph Kaye a Master of the Supreme Court of Judicature , and had issue* 1h

   1h Alice Mary Kaye

3g Mary Prescott, m 25 July 1877, Capt Hardy McHardy, R N , Chief Constable of Ayrshire (*Ayr*), and his issue (with a son d young) 1h to 5h

   1h Robert Prescott McHardy, b 18 Aug 1882

   2h Graham Goodenough McHardy, b 31 Oct 1889

   3h Mary Alice McHardy

   4h Emily Lees McHardy

   5h Edith Margaret McHardy

4g Beatrice Jane Prescott

8e *Anne Bourchier*, d 29 *Ap* 1877 , m 5 *July* 1826, *John Spice Hulbert of Stakes Hill Lodge, co Hants, J P* , d 21 *Feb* 1844 , *and had issue (with 2 sons and a da d unm)* 1f *to* 4f

   1f *John Henville Hulbert*, b 2 *June* 1831, d 8 *May* 1908, m 1st, 20 *June* 1854 *Anna Maria, da of David John Day of Rochester*, d 22 *Sept* 1864, 2ndly, 26 *Oct* 1865, *Harriet, da of the Rev Joseph Carson, D D* , *Vice Provost of Trinity College, Dublin*, d 14 *Dec* 1884, *and had issue (with a da d young)* 1g *to* 15g

      1g Walter Hulbert, B A (Camb) (*Stakes Hill Lodge, Waterlooville, Hants*), b 4 June 1856, m 1 Oct 1891, Ella Millicent, da of John Crawford Dodgson, Bengal C S , and has issue 1h to 2h

         1h George Dodgson Hulbert, b 13 May 1898

         2h Winifred Beatrice Agnes Hulbert, b 18 Feb 1896

      2g Henry Hulbert, Hop Planter (*Sardis, British Columbia*) b 5 June 1858, m in Vancouver, B C , 11 Oct 1899, Alice Margaret Victoria, da of Thomas George Askew, of Victoria, B C , and has issue 1h to 5h

         1h *Walter Andrew Bourchier Hulbert*, b 28 *Aug* 1902, d 10 *Jan* 1903

         2h John Eric Bourchier Hulbert, b 21 Oct 1906

         3h Audrey Margaret Ella Hulbert, b 4 Jan 1904

         4h Anna Imogen Hulbert,⎫ twins, b at Sardis, 3 Oct 1909
         5h Ethel Muriel Hulbert, ⎭

      3g Charles Hulbert a Master in Chancery (*Hillfield, Harrow, Midx*), b 5 Feb 1860 , m 22 June 1887, Frances Mary, da of William Richardson Jolly , and has issue 1h to 4h

         1h Charles Geoffrey Keith Hulbert, b 22 Mar 1888

         2h Henry Bourchier Hulbert, b 16 May 1892

         3h Frances Sarah Nancy Hulbert, b 29 Aug 1893

         4h Margaret Joan Hulbert, b 27 Nov 1894

      4g John Hulbert, of Messrs Metcalfe, Hussey & Hulbert of Lincoln's Inn, Solicitors (3 *Campden House Road, London, W*), b 12 Sept 1866 , unm

      5g Joseph George Hulbert, M B (Camb), M R C S , L R C P (Lond), Major
                                                                [Nos 9896 to 9924

89

The Plantagenet Roll

Indrin M S, *b* 14 Sept 1867, *m* at Bombay 7 Ap 1903, Elsie Frances [also descended from King Edward III through Mortimer Percy (see p 63)], da of Alexander Brooke of Handford, co Chester, and has issue (with an elder son, Alexander Joseph, *d* in infancy) 1*h*

    1*h* Richard Carson Hulbert, *b* in India 10 July 1907

6*g* William Henville Hulbert (3 *Campden House Road, London, W*), *b* 29 Aug 1869

7*g* Thomas Ernest Hulbert, Capt Skinner's Horse, Indian Army, *b* 13 July 1879, *m* 2 Ap 1907, Kathleen Beatrice, da of Thomas H Harvey, of Blackbrook Grove, Fareham

8*g*[1] Agnes Hulbert, *unm*

9*g*[1] Ethel Hulbert, *m* 9 May 1887, Duncan Bell-Irving [2nd son of Henry Bell-Irving of Millbanke, Lockerbie] (*Vancouver, British Columbia*), and has issue 1*h* to 4*h*

    1*h* Duncan Peter Bell-Irving, *b* 3 Jan 1888

    2*h* Robert Bell-Irving, *b* 30 July 1893

    3*h* Agnes Bell-Irving, *b* 26 Jan 1889

    4*h* Dorothy Ethel Bell-Irving, *b* 13 May 1890

10*g* Anna Hulbert, *m* 27 June 1891, Andrew McCreight Creery [3rd son of the Rev (—) Creery, Rector of Kilmore, co Down]'(*Vancouver, British Columbia*) and has issue 1*h* to 6*h*

    1*h* Kenneth Andrew Creery, *b* 11 Feb 1894

    2*h* Cuthbert John Creery, *b* 11 Ap 1895

    3*h* Ronald Hulbert Creery, *b* 12 Feb 1897

    4*h* Leslie Charles Creery, *b* 9 Dec 1898

    5*h* Wallace Bourchier Creery, *b* 22 Feb 1900

    6*h* Irene Anna Creery, *b* 10 Mar 1892

11*g*[1] Ella Hulbert, *unm*

12*g*[2] Fanny Hulbert, *unm*

13*g*[2] Eleanor Hulbert, *m* 10 Sept 1908, Hugh Alexander Roberts, Solicitor, [also descended from King Edward III through Mortimer-Percy (see p 62)] (35 *Brunswick Gardens, Kensington, W*)

14*g*[2] Caroline Edith Hulbert (*Geneva*), *unm*

15*g*[2] Olivia Mary Hulbert (3 *Campden Hill Gardens, London, W*), *unm*

2*f* Mary Hulbert (*The Elms, Ringwood, Hants*), *b* 12 May 1829, *m* 22 Aug 1850, Henry Geldart Metcalfe, of Ringwood, co Hants, M A (Oxon), *b* 22 May 1824, *d* 29 Oct 1899, and had issue (with 2 sons *d* young) 1*g* to 7*g*

1*g* Henry Hulbert Metcalfe, M I C E (47 *Queen Street, Auckland, Bridgwater Road, Parnell, New Zealand*), *b* 30 Oct 1851, *m* 25 Mar 1878, Jessie Alexandra, da of M Hamilton, of Cheltenham, and has issue 1*h* to 6*h*

    1*h* Henry Ernest Metcalfe, A M I C E, *b* 29 Dec 1879

    2*h* George Hamilton Metcalfe, *b* 23 Ap 1887

    3*h* Ellen Mary Metcalfe, *b* 29 Mar 1881

    4*h* Marion Sarah Metcalfe, *b* 13 July 1882

    5*h* Dorothy Caroline Metcalfe, *b* 2 Nov 1884

    6*h* Phyllis Metcalfe, *b* 17 Mar 1889

2*g* John Greetham Metcalfe, Senior Partner in the firm of Metcalfe, Hussey & Hulbert, of 10 New Square, Lincoln's Inn, Solicitors (*Bramleigh, Richmond, Surrey*), *b* 8 Jan 1855, *m* 21 June 1890, Elizabeth Rose, da of Edward Walter Williamson, See to the Law Society, and has issue 1*h* to 3*h*

    1*h* Percy Hulbert Metcalfe, *b* 26 Jan 1892

    2*h* Isabella Brenda Metcalfe, *b* 5 Mar 1894

    3*h* Eileen Mary Metcalfe, *b* 6 Aug 1902   [Nos 9925 to 9957

# of The Blood Royal

3g Arthur Henry Metcalfe, *b* 31 Mar 1859, *m* 6 Oct 1896, Agnese, da of (—) Doyle, and has issue 1h to 3h.

    1h Rolland Metcalfe, *b* 15 Sept 1897

    2h Fanny Metcalfe, *b* 28 Dec 1898

    3h Vera Metcalfe, *b* 18 Nov 1900

4g Mary Georgina Metcalfe, *m* 18 Sept 1890, Jeffrey Gott

5g Clara Warren Metcalfe, *unm*

6g Constance Alice Metcalfe, *m* 4 Mar 1890, Alfred Mason Hayes, P W D, Madras, *d* Feb 1897, and has issue (with an elder da, Constance Mary, *d* 24 May 1894) 1h

    1h Amy Evelyn Hayes, *b* 27 Mar 1892

7g Florence Charlotte Metcalfe, *unm*

3f *Annie Caroline Hulbert*, d 6 Aug 1857, m *as 1st wife*, 21 Mar 1855, *Major Henry Leslie Hunt, 67th Regt*, d 17 Dec 1880, *and had issue* 1g

1g Rev Henry de Vere Hunt, B A (Camb), Rector of Ahascragh (*Ahascragh Rectory, Ballinasloe*), *b* 12 Mar 1856, *m* 20 July 1882, Mary Catherine Caroline, da of the Rev Peter William Browne of Blackrock, co Lane, and has issue 1h to 4h

    1h Henry Leslie Hunt, *b* 21 Ap 1890

    2h Alice Kathleen Hunt, *b* 15 Sept 1883

    3h Eleanor Caroline Hunt, *b* 21 July 1885

    4h Vera Mary Hunt, *b* 11 Dec 1886

4f Fanny Hulbert

9e *Susanna Bourchier*, b 13 Ap 1800 d 9 Nov 1875, m 21 Mar 1827, *John Cole of Easthorpe Court, co Linc, who became,* 27 July 1854, *de jure 4th Duke of Polignano (Duca di Polignano)* [Naples], d 12 Ap 1855, *and had issue (with a da d s p)* 1f to 2f

1f *John Charles (Cole), 5th Duke of Polignano* [Naples], *of Easthorpe Court,* d s p 14 Ap 1897

2f James (Cole, now Edwin-Cole), 6th Duke of Polignano (Duca di Polignano) [Naples, 26 Aug 1730], &c, J P, Bar-at-Law (*Swineshead Hall, via Boston, co Linc*), *b* 27 Ap 1835, *m* 7 Dec 1880, Mary Barbara, da of Gent Huddleston, s p

5d *Richard Bourchier*, b 11 May 1749

6d *Mary Bourchier*, b 1 Oct 1737, d 1813, m *the Rev James Torkington, of Stukeley Hall and Rector of Little Stukeley, co Hunts [descended from the Lady Anne, sister of Edward IV (see the Exeter Volume, p 662)],* d (–), *and had issue* 1e to 4e

1e *James Torkington, of Great Stukeley,* d 7 June 1828, m 22 Oct 1799, *Elizabeth, da of Charles Bourchier, and had issue*

See pp 84-85, Nos 9790-9807

2e *Edward Torkington*

3e *Mary Torkington*

4e *Dorothy Torkington*

7d *Elizabeth Bourchier,* b 6 June 1745, d 18 Feb 1791, m *the Rev William Lloyd, Preacher of the Charter House, and of Much Hadham, and had issue*

8d *Frances Bourchier,* b 6 Sept 1746, d (–), m *John Howell (?) of Ross*

9d *Julia Charlotte Bourchier,* b 11 Feb 1752, d (–), m (—) *Ionge of London*

    2b *Charles Gataker*

    3b *Thomas Gataker*

    4b *George Gataker,* d (–), m (—), da of (—) *Nash and had issue*

    5b *William Gataker,* b 1691, d (–), m *Ann, da of James Willett*

    6b *Barbara Gataker,* b (–), m *1st, John Pitcairn of London, Merchant,* 2ndly (—) *Withers of co Kent, and had issue* 1c

    1c *Barbara Pitcairn,* d (–), m *Thomas Carter of Dunton, co Bucks*

[Nos 9974 to 9991

The Plantagenet Roll

7b *Frances Gataker*, b c 1678, d 1715, m *the Rev Benjamin Reynolds, Rector of Hoggeston*, d 18 Dec 1758, in his 82nd year, and had issue 1c

 1c *Rev Benjamin Reynolds, Rector of Hoggeston*, b c 1703, d 1 Nov 1781

 7a *Theodosia Hebblethwaite*, bapt 4 Dec 1658

 8a *Margaret Hebblethwaite*, bapt 10 June 1665

35 Descendants, if any, of FRANCES MARWOOD (Table VI.), b. c 1642, living 1679, m 1st, Sir RICHARD WESTON of Gray's Inn, Bar -at-Law, living 1679, 2ndly, as 2nd wife (lic. 4 May), 1682, Sir EDWARD SMITH, 1st Bart [E], K.B, d (s p by her) 1707.

36. Descendants of the Rev THOMAS METCALFE of Northallerton and Sand Hutton co York, M A (Table VI), bapt. 28 Mar 1706, d 10 Feb. 1774, m Ascension Day, 1742, ANNE, da of William SMELT of Kirkby Fleetham, co York, M D., d 10 Feb 1804, and had issue 1a to 3a.

1a *Rev George Metcalfe, afterwards Marwood, of Northallerton and Little Busby Hall, Canon Residentiary of Chichester*, b 28 Nov 1746, d 1 Dec 1827, m 1st, 1780, *Margaret, da of Francis Peirson of Mowthorpe Grange, co York*, 2ndly, *Lucy widow of Capt Charles Dodgson, da of James Hume*, and had issue 1b to 3b

 1b *George Metcalfe Marwood of Busby Hall*, b 29 June 1781, d 9 Jan 1842, m 1 Aug 1804, *Mary, da of Capt John Quantock of Norton House, co Somerset*, d 23 May 1838, and had issue 1c to 3c

 1c *George Metcalfe Marwood of Busby Hall, J P, D L*, b 31 Dec 1808, d 8 Ap 1882, m 28 Oct 1854, *Frances Anne, da of the Rev Frederick Peel, Preb of Lincoln*, d 19 Oct 1886, and had issue 1d to 11d

 1d *George Frederick Marwood of Busby Hall, &c, J P*, b 8 Ap 1858, d s p 23 May 1898

 2d William Francis Marwood of Busby Hall, J P, Hereditary Lord and Chief Bailiff of Langburgh Wapentake (*Busby Hall, Carlton in Cleveland, York*), b 1 Feb 1863

 3d Henry Marwood, Lieut -Col Comdg 2nd Batt North Staffordshire Regt (*Multan, India*), b 6 July 1864, m 14 May 1898, Ethel Mary J, da and h of Henry G Piggott of Sheffield Gardens, Kensington, and has issue 1e to 2e

  1e George Henry Marwood, b 31 Aug 1901

  2e Ethel Mary Marwood, b 4 Mar 1899

 1d Arthur Pierson Marwood (*Winchelsea*), b 21 Aug 1868, m 4 Feb 1903, Caroline da of Matthew Cranswick of Hunmanby, co York, s p

 5d Frances Mary Marwood (3D *The Mansions, Earl's Court Road, S W*)

 6d Emily Caroline Marwood, m as 2nd wife, 21 Feb 1876, Edward Heneage Wynne-Finch, J P, Bar -at-Law (*Stokesley Manor, York*), and has issue 1e to 3e

  1e Arthur Wynne-Finch, b 15 Oct 1878

  2e Griffith Wynne-Finch, Lieut King's Royal Rifle Corps, b 16 Oct 1880

  3e Helen Wynne-Finch

 7d Lucy Susanna Marwood, m 21 Feb 1881, Charles Napier Kennedy (*Bigfrith End, Cookham Dean*), and has issue 1e to 3e

  1e George Lawrence Kennedy, b 24 Nov 1881

  2e John Pitt Kennedy, Lieut Scottish Rifles, b 12 Aug 1883

  3e Horace Tristram Kennedy, b 25 Nov 1887   [Nos 9992 to 10005

# of The Blood Royal

8d Elinor Edith Marwood, *m* 4 June 1891, Charles Moore Kennedy, B L [son of John Pitt Kennedy, Judge Advocate, Calcutta High Court] (*Leaves Green, Keston, Hayes, Kent*), and has issue 1e to 4e

1e Tristram Gervais Kennedy, *b* 11 June 1897
2e David Kennedy, *b* (twin) 20 Oct 1901
3e Margaret Kennedy, *b* 23 Ap 1896
4e Virginia Kennedy, *b* (twin) 20 Oct 1901

9d Clara Charlotte Marwood
10d Lilian Marwood
11d Rose Marwood

2c *Margaret Marwood*, *b* 12 Mar 1809, *d* 2 Nov 1877, *m* 13 Dec 1842, Rear Adm Colson Festing, R N, *b* 12 Sept 1795, *d* 12 Oct 1870, *and had issue* (with a son d unm) 1d to 3d

1d Henry Marwood Colson Festing, Comm R N (ret) (*Glencree, Paignton, Devon*), *b* (—), *m* (—)

2d Michael Morton Metcalfe Festing, Capt (ret) 20th Foot (21 *Park Crescent, Oxford*), *b* 28 Jan 1851, *m* 27 Ap 1881, Mary Elizabeth, da of Thomas Hicks of Stanghow, Cleveland, and has issue 1e to 2e

1e Michael Colson Festing, *b* 15 Sept 1885
2e Margaret Vera Festing, *b* 18 July 1882

3d Mary Georgina Festing, *unm*

3c *Anne Frederica Marwood*, *b* 1823, *d* 12 Sept 1884, *m* (at Stokesley, co York), 1845, *the Rev Henry Boyick Scougall, Vicar of Rudgeley, co Stafford*, *b* (at Tawstock, co Devon) 1822, *d* (at Ilfracombe) 8 Oct 1865, *and had* (with another son and da who d unm) *issue* 1d to 5d

1d Henry Scougall
2d John Hearnage Scougall
3d Charles Scougall
4d Hugh Boyick Watkin Scougall

5d Frederica Elizabeth Scougall, *m* 6 July 1875, the Rev Alfred Henry Malan [grandson of Dr César Malan of Geneva] (*Allarnon Sanctuary, Launceston, Cornwall*), and has issue (with a da who died in infancy) 1e to 2e

1e Francis Malan, *b* 30 May 1877
2e Lionel de Mérindol Malan, *b* 16 Mar 1884

2b¹ *Margaret Metcalfe*, *b* 1795, *d* (-), *m* 1822, the Rev Charles Hutchinson of Firle, co Sussex, Canon of Chichester, *d* (-), *and had issue*

3b² *Mary Anne Marwood*, *b* 1813, *d* 22 Mar 1870, *m* William Wilcox, Collector of H M Customs, Sunderland, *d* (-), *and had issue*

2a *Cornelius Metcalfe of Manchester and London, Merchant*, *b* 6 Oct 1749, *d* after 1795, *m* Dec 1773, Sarah, da of Samuel Bayley of Manchester, and had issue 1b to 3b

1b *Thomas Metcalfe of Lincoln's Inn and Portland Place, London, and Regency Square, Brighton*, *b* 16 Oct 1781, *d* (-), *m* Christiana Bristane, da and h of Henry Kerr Cranstoun [eldest son of the Hon George Cranstoun, 4th son of William, 5th Lord Cranstoun [S]], *d* (-), *and had issue* 1c to 6c

1c *Thomas Metcalfe*, *b* 31 Aug 1809, *d* 1843, *m* Grace, da of William Shepperd, London, Banker, *d* (-), *and had issue* 1d

1d William Marwood Metcalfe, Capt Royal Elthorne L I, *b* 1839

2c *Henry Cranstoun Metcalfe, Civil and Sessions Judge at Tipperah, Bengal*, *b* 20 Sept 1810, *d* (-), *m* (—), da of (—), and had issue 1d

1d Henry Howe Metcalfe, late B C S, *b* (—), *m* and has issue

3c *Ernest Metcalfe, Major 48th Madras Native Infantry, Assist Resident Counsellor, Prince of Wales Island*, *b* 5 Jan 1823, *d* 1866, *m* 1861, Julia Catherine, da of John Shaw of London and Crayford co Kent, *d* (-), *and had issue* 1d to 2d

[Nos 10006 to 10027

93

N

The Plantagenet Roll

1d Hope Cranstoun Metcalfe (*Dearbrook, Hersham Road, Walton-on-Thames*), *b* (at Penang, Strait Settlements) 22 Feb 1866, *m* 1894, Edith, da of (—) Kirkpatrick, and has issue (with one other) 1e to 2e

    1e Frances Hope Metcalfe

    2e Sylvia Metcalfe

    2d Katharine Mary Metcalfe, *b* at Harylun, Mysore, *m* (—)

    4c *Christiana Metcalfe* d (—), m *George Clutterbuck Tugwell of Bath, Banker* d (—), and had issue 1d to 2d

    1d Rev George Tugwell, M A (Oxon), Rector of Bathwick, Bath 1871–1894, author of various well-known works (*Southcliffe, Lee, Ilfracombe*), *b* (—), s *p*

    2d Henry William Tugwell (*Crowe Hall, Bath*), *b* (—), *m* and has issue (2 das)

    5c *Julia Henrietta Metcalfe*, d (—), m *Francis Ommanney of Platt House, Putney*, and had issue

    6c *Emily Metcalfe*, d (—), m *Francis Orme*, and had issue

    2b *Anne Metcalfe*, d (—), m *James Currie of London*, and had issue

    3b *Dorothy Metcalfe*, d (—) m *George William Babington, Surgeon 3rd Dragoons* d (—), and had (with possibly other) issue 1c

    1c *Cornelius Metcalfe Stuart Babington of Hertford Street, Mayfair, Physician*

    3a *Rev Francis Metcalfe*, M A (Camb), *Rector of Kirkbride, &c*, b 30 Ap 1752, d 11 Nov 1822 m 12 Nov 1785, Harriett, da of John Clough of York, d 9 June 1803, and had issue 1b

    1b *Henry Metcalfe, Lieut 32nd Regt*, b 10 Feb 1791, bur 7 Oct 1828, m Mary, da of (——) Gibson of Guernsey, and had issue 1c to 2c

    1c Anne Metcalfe, living unm 1873

    2c Harriet Metcalfe, living a widow s *p* 1873, m (—)

    2b *John Metcalfe, Capt H E I C S*, b 9 Mar 1791, d (at Madras) 18 June 1833, m 2ndly, 30 Sept 1828, Keturah, widow of the Rev John Jeffreys, da of George Yarnold of Worcester, d 5 Jan 1858, and had issue 1c

    1c *John Henry Metcalfe of Crayke Castle, co York, a well-known Antiquary*, d unm

    3b *Thomas Metcalfe*, b 28 Dec 1796, d s p m 1879, m and had issue

                               [Nos 10028 to 10035

37 Descendants of MARGARET METCALFE (Table VI), *b*. 1665, *bur* 20 Dec 1690, *m* as 1st wife, 1672, DANIEL LASCELLES of Stank and North Allerton, M P, High Sheriff co York 1719, *b* 6 Nov 1655, *d* 5 Sept. 1734, and had issue 1a to 2a

    1a *Mary Lascelles*, bapt 13 Sept 1683, d 25 Ap 1727, m 27 Aug 1706, *Cuthbert Mitford of North Allerton*

    2a *Elizabeth Lascelles*, d (—), m 10 Sept 1713, *George Ord of Longridge, co Northumberland*, d 25 Feb 1745

38 Descendants of ANNE HESKETH of Heslington, co York (see Table V), *b* 2 Ap 1676, *d* 19 Ap. 1718, *m* (lic dated 31 Oct) 1692, Lieut.-Col JAMES YARBURGH of Snaith Hall, co York, a godson of King James II., *bur* 9 Mar. 1730, and had issue 1a

    1a *Charles Yarburgh of Heslington and Snaith Hall, event sole h*, b 10 May 1716, d 6 Aug 1789, m 2ndly, Sarah, da of Sylvanus Griffin of Wirksworth, and had issue 1b

94

# of The Blood Royal

1c Sarah Yarburgh, da and in her issue (1852) sole h, bapt 18 Mar 1761, d 21 Oct 1785, m as 1st wife, 1 Aug 1782, John Græme of Sowerby House, co York, J P, D L, b 7 Aug 1759 d 24 Feb 1841, and had issue 1c

1c Alicia Maria Græme, da and event h, b 1784, d 3 Jan 1867, m 17 May 1810, George Lloyd of Stockton Hall, near York, b 21 May 1787, d 12 Mar 1863, and had issue 1d to 4d

1d George John Lloyd, afterwards (R L 15 Ap 1875) Yarburgh, of Heslington Hall, J P, b 28 July 1811, d 16 May 1875, m 23 July 1840, Mary Antonia, da of Samuel Chetham Hilton of Pennington Hall, co Lancaster, d Jan 1868, and had issue 1e to 2e

1e Mary Elizabeth Yarburgh d 22 Oct 1884, m 8 May 1862 George William (Bateson, sometime (R L 15 Ap 1876) Bateson de Yarburgh, and finally de Yarburgh-Bateson), 2nd Baron Deramore [U K], d 29 Ap 1893, and had issue 1f to 5f

1f Robert Wilfred (de Yarburgh-Bateson), 3rd Baron Deramore and a Bart [U K], J P, D L, C C, Major Yorkshire Hussars, &c (Heslington Hall, Yorkshire, Belvoir Park, Belfast), b 5 Aug 1865, m 1st, 15 July 1897, Lucy Caroline, da of William Henry Fife of Lee Hall, Northumberland, d 26 Oct 1901, 2ndly, 26 June 1907, Blanche Violet, da of Col Philip Saltmarshe of Daresbury, J P, and has issue 1g

1g Hon Moira Faith Lilian de Yarburgh-Bateson

2f Hon George Nicholas de Yarburgh-Bateson, J P (North Cliff, Filey Carlton) b 25 Nov 1870, m 12 Dec 1900, Muriel Katharine, da of Arthur Grey (formerly Duncombe) of Sutton Hall, Easingwold, and has issue 1g to 2g

1g Stephen Nicholas de Yarburgh-Bateson, b 18 May 1903

2g Judith Katharine de Yarburgh-Bateson, b 22 Mar 1909

3f Hon Eustace de Yarburgh-Bateson, b 13 Oct 1884

4f Hon Mary Lilla de Yarburgh-Bateson

5f Hon Katherine Hylda de Yarburgh-Bateson

2e Susan Anne Yarburgh, d 21 May 1908, m 25 Jan 1865, Charles Lethbridge, J P, High Sheriff co Hants 1895 [Bt [U K] 1804 Coll] (Heytesbury, Wilts, Carlton), and had issue 1f to 6f

1f Ambrose Yarburgh Lethbridge, late Lieut Grenadier Guards, b 2 Nov 1874, d 11 Sept 1909, m 4 Feb 1898, Violet (Trevissome, Flushing, Falmouth), da of Charles Townsend Murdoch, M P, and has issue 1g to 3g

1g Thomas Charles Lethbridge, b 23 Mar 1901

2g Ambrose William Speke Lethbridge, b 6 Ap 1907

3g Jacintha Lethbridge, b 7 June 1904

2f Mary Lethbridge, m 19 Ap 1888, the Rev Herbert Barnett, Vicar of Bracknell (Bracknell Vicarage, Berks), and has issue 1g to 3g

1g John Canning Lethbridge Barnett, b 27 May 1891

2g Alice Mary Barnett

3g Bridget Susan Barnett

3f Dorothea Lethbridge, m 17 Nov 1892, Arthur Finch Charrington (East Hill, Oxted, Surrey, Oxford and Cambridge), and has issue 1g to 4g

1g Peter Ronald Lethbridge Charrington, b 27 June 1897

2g John Arthur Pepys Charrington, b 17 Feb 1903

3g Lettice Mary Charrington, b 28 June 1906

4g Susan Auriol Charrington, b 26 Sept 1908

4f Ellinor Lethbridge

5f Ruth Lethbridge, m 14 Jan 1904, Willoughby Arthur Pemberton (11 Lower Belgrave Street, S W, White's, St James'), and has issue 1g to 2g

1g Mordaunt Ashington Sigerist Pemberton, b 15 Mar 1907

2g Camilla Lethbridge Pemberton, b 5 Oct 1905

6f Rachel Lethbridge

[Nos 10036 to 10060

The Plantagenet Roll

2d Rev. *Yarburgh Gamaliel Lloyd, afterwards Lloyd-Greame of Sewerby House, co York, J P* b 18 *July* 1813, d 30 *May* 1890, m 7 *May* 1839, *Editha Christian, da of William Augustus Le Hunte of Astramount, co Wexford, d* 1900, *and had issue* 1e

1e Yarburgh George Lloyd-Greame of Sewerby House, M A (Camb), J P, Lieut.-Col (*ret*) Yorkshire Artillery Militia (*Sewerby House, Bridlington*), b 15 June 1840, m 6 Aug 1867, Dora Letitia, da of the Right Rev James Thomas O'Brien, Lord Bishop of Ossory, and has issue 1f to 4f

1f Yarburgh Lloyd-Greame, *late* Lieut Yorkshire Artillery, b 19 May 1872, m 11 Jan 1898, Alice Mary, da of Major George Mark Leycester Egerton of The Mount, York, and has issue 1g to 2g

1g Yarburgh Derek Lloyd-Greame, b 1902

2g Nancy Lloyd-Greame

2f Philip Lloyd-Greame

3f Editha Lloyd-Greame

4f Dora Lloyd-Greame, m 1904, Capt George Martin Hannay, *formerly* King's Own Scottish Borderers

3d Rev. *Henry Lloyd, M A (Camb), Rector of Yarburgh,* b 31 *Dec* 1815, d 17 *Nov* 1862, m 30 *Sept* 1857, *Anne Eliza, da of the Rev William Roy, D D,* d 27 *May* 1903, *and had issue* 1e *to* 3e

1e George William Lloyd of Stockton Hall, J P, M A (Camb) (*Stockton Hall, near York*), b 4 Mar 1861, *unm*

2e Henry John Greame Lloyd, Major Cornwall Militia, *late* Duke of Cornwall's L I (*Byams, Marchwood, Hants*), b 6 June 1862, m 9 Dec 1886, Caroline Emily, da of John Harris Peter-Hoblyn of Colquite, co Cornwall, and has issue 1f to 5f

1f Cyril Gascoigne Lloyd, b 11 Sept 1887

2f John Rodney Lloyd, b 21 June 1890

3f Henry Greame Lloyd, b 2 Dec 1892

4f Caroline Doris Lloyd

5f Kathleen Anne Lloyd

3e Alicia Margaret Lloyd

4d *Edward Lloyd of Lingcroft, near York,* b 27 *May* 1823, d 4 *Feb* 1869, m 21 *Sept* 1854, *Rosabella Susan, da of George Lloyd of Cowsby Hall, co York,* d 20 *July* 1909, *and had issue* 1e *to* 3e

1e Georgina Rosabella Lloyd, m 15 July 1879, George St Maur Palmes, *late* 11th Hussars [himself a descendant of King Edward III] (*Lingcroft, near York*), and has issue 1f to 5f

1f Geoffrey St Maur Palmes, b 26 Dec 1881

2f Edward William Eustace Palmes, b 23 Aug 1884

3f Bryan Wilfrid Palmes, b 3 June 1891

4f Cecil Muriel Palmes, m 1908, Alick May Cunard, Lieut 5th Royal Irish Rifles, and has issue 1g

1g [son] Cunard

5f Joan Mary Georgina Palmes

2e Edith Maria Greame Lloyd, m 22 Ap 1879, Frederick Reynard of Sunderlandwick and Hobgreen, J P, D L (*Sunderlandwick, Driffield, Hobgreen, Ripley*), and has issue 1f to 2f

1f Claude Edward Reynard, b 9 Feb 1880

2f Charles Frederick Reynard, b 14 Jan 1889

3e Cecil May Lloyd, m 9 Nov 1887, Henry Charles Talbot Rice, *late* Capt 4th Batt Gloucester Regt [B Dynevor Coll] (*North Cerney House, Cirencester*), and has issue 1f to 3f

1f Harry Talbot Rice, b 27 July 1889

2f John Arthur Talbot Rice, b 3 Jan 1892

3f David Talbot Rice, b 11 July 1903

[Nos 10061 to 10089

96

# of The Blood Royal

39 Descendants, if any, of MATILDA BETHELL (Table V), d (-),
m the Rev ROBERT GOODWIN

40 Descendants, if any surviving, of KATHERINE SLINGSBY (Table
IV), bapt. 31 July 1584, d a 1621, m as 1st wife (he
dated) 1603, SIR JOHN FENWICK of Fenwick, 1st Bart [E], d
1658, and had issue (with a son who d s p e p) 1a to 2a

   1a *Catherine Fenwick*
   2a *Elizabeth Fenwick*

41 Descendants of ALICE SLINGSBY (Table IV), d (-), m as 1st
wife, THOMAS WATERTON of Walton Hall, co York, b c. 1585,
d 1641, and had issue 1a to 7a

   1a *Thomas Waterton of Walton Hall*, d (-) m *Alice, widow of Edward
Clarke of Wintersct, da of (—) Wetherby and had issue 1b to 4b*
   1b *Thomas Waterton of Walton Hall*, d (-), m *Catherine, da of Nicholas
Fairfax of Gilling, and had issue 1c*
   1c *Charles Waterton of Walton Hall*, bun 25 Jan 1726, m 1st, *Anne, da of
Sir William Gerard 4th Bart [E], 3rdly Anne, da of William Poole [Bt of Poole
Coll], living 1726, and had issue 1d to 1d*
   1d *Charles Waterton of Walton Hall, imprisoned at York, 1716, as a Jacobite*
d (-), m 1733, *Mary da of Cresacre More of Bamborough [6th in descent from
Sir Thomas More], and had issue 1e to 4e*
   1e *Thomas Waterton of Walton Hall*, bun 19 Mar 1805, m *Anne, da and h
of Edward Bedingfield [Bt Coll], and had issue 1f to 2f*
   1f *Charles Waterton of Walton Hall, Author of "Wanderings in South
America" &c, b 3 12 June 1782, d 27 May 1865, m (at Bruges) 11 May 1829,
Anne, da of Charles Edmonstone of Cardiess Park, co Dumbarton, d 27 1p 1830,
and had issue 1g*
   1g *Edmund Waterton of Walton Hall and afterwards of Deeping Waterton,
Knight of the Order of Christ, Private Chamberlain to H H Pop Pius IX, J P,
D L, F S A, &c, b 7 Ap 1830, d 1887, m 1st, 20 Aug 1862, Margaret Alicia
Josephine, da and co-h of Sir John Ennis, 1st Bt [U K], d (at Cannes) 26 Dec
1879, 2ndly, 15 Nov 1881, Helen, da and h of John Mercer of Alston Hall, co
Lancaster, J P, and had issue 1h to 7h*
   1h *Charles Edmund Maria Joseph Aloysius Waterton of Deeping Waterton,
co Lincoln, b 10 June 1863, d 23 Feb 1897, m 1890, Josephine, da of John Rock
of Northbank, Shepton Mallet, and had issue 1i to 4i*
   1i Joseph Waterton (*Deeping Waterton Hall, Market Deeping*), b 18 Nov
1893
      2i Charles Waterton
      3i Edmond Waterton
      4i John Waterton

   2h *Thomas More Mary Joseph Pius Waterton (Johnstone, Enfield, Martinstown, co Meath), b 8 July 1876*
   3h¹ Mary Paula Pia Waterton, a Canoness Regular of St Augustine s, Bruges
   4h¹ Agnes Mary Pia Waterton
   5h¹ Josephine Mary Everilda Pia Waterton
   6h² Monica Mary Colette Paula Waterton
   7h² Ethelburga Mary Magdalen Pega Waterton   [Nos 10090 to 10099

The Plantagenet Roll

2*f Isabel Waterton*, d (–), m *John Philips Steel of Wakefield* [1]

2*c Christopher Waterton of Woodlands, co York, and Demerara*, d 10 Oct 1809, m *Anne, widow of Edward Bermingham, da of John Waddell, M D* , d 29 Aug 1821, *and had issue 1f to 3f*

1*f George Waterton of Woodlands, and afterwards (1851) of Hunslett and of Dublin in 1865*,[2] *an Officer in the Austrian Service*, d (–), m 185–, *the Baroness Matilda, widow of Maurice, Baron Mack von Leiberich* (d 28 Feb 1831), *da of Joseph Felix William Domini (von Barco), Baron Barco [H R E 1745], b* 27 Dec 1803, d (–)

2*f Henry Waterton of Winsford Lodge, co Chester, in* 1843, d (–), m *Isabella, da of William Wallace Ogle of Cawsey Park, Northumberland*, d 1889, *and had issue 1g to 4g*

  1*g* Charles Waterton, *b* (—),   ⎫ settled in New Zealand
  2*g* Bertram Robert Waterton, *b* (—), ⎬
  3*g* Rev Canon George Webb Waterton (*Durran-hill, Carlisle*), *b* (—)
  4*g Frances Waterton*, d 12 Feb 1890, m 1st, 4 June 1860, *Edward Seymour-Ball Hughes*, d 1866 ?, 2ndly, 24 June 1872, *Sir Maurice Duff-Gordon, 4th Bt [U K]*, d 5 May 1896, *and had issue 1h to 3h*

    1*h Charles Ball-Hughes*, b Dec 1862, d Mar 1897

    2*h* Marie Louise Ball Hughes (22 *Royal Avenue, Sloane Square, S W*), m 12 Aug 1885, Henry Arthur Tennent, d 6 Nov 1905, *and has issue 1i to 5i*

      1*i* Marguerite Lucy Tennent, *b* 1 July 1886
      2*i* Violet Frances Tennent, *b* 24 Sept 1887
      3*i* Myrtle Marie Ida Tennent, *b* 10 Oct 1888
      4*i* Olive Cecili Tennent, *b* 21 Nov 1889
      5*i* Iris Veronica Tennent, *b* 18 Nov 1890

    3*h* Caroline Lucie Duff-Gordon, m 1 July 1902, Aubrey William Waterfield (*Northbourne Abbey, Eastry, R S O*) *and has issue 1i*

      1*i* Henry Gordon Ottiwell Waterfield, *b* 24 May 1903

3*f Matilda Waterton*, d 14 July 1865, m 25 July 1829, *Edmund William Jerningham [B Stafford Coll]*, d 2 Nov 1860, *and had issue*
See the Clarence Volume, pp 448–449, Nos 19067–19104

3*e Mary Waterton*, b 1733, d (*unm*)[3]
4*e Anne Waterton*, d (–), m [——] *Daly*[3]

2*d Robert Waterton*[3]
3*d Joseph Waterton*[3]
4*d Catherine Waterton*[3]
2*b John Waterton*[3]
3*b Alice Waterton* [1]
4*b Anne Waterton* [1]

2*a* Priscilla Waterton, bur 10 Sept 1638 ~ p s, m *as 1st wife, Thomas Beckwith of Aickton*

3*a Elizabeth Waterton*, d (–), m *as 2nd wife, Francis Malham of Elslack in Craven*, b 22 May 1660, d (–), *and had issue 1b* [1]

  1*b Francis Malham, aged* 16, May 1666

4*a* Mary Waterton, d (–), m 1st, *William Ramsden of Lascelles Hall, co York*, d shortly before 30 Sept 1639, 2ndly, *Sir Thomas Smith of Broxton* [brother to 1st Lord Carrington [5]], *and had (with possibly others by 2nd husband) issue 1b.*

[Nos 10100 to 10148

---

[1] Foster's "Yorkshire Pedigrees"   [2] *Freih Taschenbuch*, 1865, p 22
[3] Foster's "Yorkshire Pedigrees"   [4] Whitaker's "Craven," p 91

[5] She was possibly his second wife In Nichol's "Leicester" (iii 29) he is said to have married the daughter and heiress of Sir Thomas Blackston [Blakiston, 1st Bart, see p 299], and no issue is mentioned

# of The Blood Royal

1b John Ramsden, h to father, and aged 51 years and 2 months 30 Sept 1639

5a Rosamund Waterton
6a Anne Waterton, m Francis Middelton
7a Frances Waterton

42 Descendants of ANNE STAPYLTON [sister and h of Sir Martin Stapylton of Myton, 8th and last Bart [E]] (Table VII), *d* (-), *m* 1770, the Rev. JOHN BREE, M A, and Fellow of Balliol College, Oxford, and Rector of Marks Tey, co Essex, *d* 1796, and had issue 1*a* to 3*a*.

1a Martin Bree, afterwards (R L 13 July 1811) Stapylton of Myton b Sept 1771, d 7 Mar 1842, m 1st, Sophia, da of William Parsons of Plymouth 2ndly, Anne, da of William Curtis of Chiswick, and had issue 1b to 4b
1b Stapylton Stapylton of Myton, b 22 Jan 1798, d 8 July 1864, m 2ndly, 5 Aug 1830, Margaret, da of Thomas Tomlinson of York, d 29 Nov 1885, and had issue 1c to 2c
1c Henry Miles Stapylton of Myton, J P, D L, b 8 July 1831, d s p 25 Mar 1896
2c Martin Bryan Stapylton, M A (Oxon), J P, Bar-at-Law b 23 Nov 1832, d 2 Jan 1894, m 11 Dec 1860, Mary Jane, da of John Brymer of Islington House, Dorset, d 1 Jan 1885, and had issue 1d to 4d
1d Miles John Stapylton of Myton, Lord of the Manor of Eston, co York, J P, D L, Major late Yorkshire Hussars and 21st Lancers (Myton Hall Helperby), b 28 Mar 1869, m 14 Feb 1900, Norah Evelyn, da of J H Love of Hawkhills, Easingwold, and has issue 1e to 3e
1e Miles Henry Stapylton, b 29 Jan 1901
2e Ursula Evelyn Mary Stapylton
3e Norah Cecilia Stapylton
2d Martin Frederick Stapylton, late R N, b 1 Oct 1873, m 3 Sept 1901, Ethel Horatia, da of J H Love of Hawkhills, Easingwold, and has issue 1e
1e Olive Love Stapylton
3d Laura Mary Stapylton, m 1st 19 Dec 1882, Col Huntly Bacon of Apton Hall, co Essex, d 9 June 1897. 2ndly, Aug 1898, James Leslie Wanklyn, formerly M P Central Bradford (75 Chester Square, S W, Jasleagh House, Leenane Galway) and has issue 1e
1e Vera Marguerite Bacon, m Arthur T Hodgson of Smallwood, co Staff, late 60th Rifles
4d Violet Louise Stapylton, m 11 Ap 1894, Edmund Clarke Schomberg of Seend House, J P, D L, High Sheriff co Wilts 1902 (Seend House, Melksham)

2b Rev Martin Stapylton, Rector of Barlborough, d 1869, m 17 July 1828, Elizabeth Henrietta Stote, da of the Rev James Watson Stote Donnison of Feliskirk, co York, d 1887, and had issue 1c to 8c
1c Rev Martyn Stapylton, M A (Durham), Rector of Barlborough b 12 June 1830, d (-), m June 1866, Esther, da of the Rev Robert Cock, d 30 Dec 1869, and had issue 1d to 2d
1d John Stapylton, b 21 Ap 1867, m 1891, Annie Mathilde, da of Henry Carter Moore, and has issue 1e to 2e
1e Henry Bryan Stapylton, b 8 Ap 1892
2e Elizabeth Olive Stapylton
2d Hilda Stapylton
2c Harriet Elizabeth Stapylton

[Nos 10149 to 10161]

99

The Plantagenet Roll

3c *Jane Emma Stapylton,* d 7 Dec 1865, m *as 1st wife,* 16 Nov 1854, *Richard Laurence Pemberton of The Barnes and Bainbridge Holme, co Durham, J P, D L,* b 12 Oct 1831, d 21 June 1901, *and had issue* 1d *to* 6d

1d John Stapylton Grey Pemberton of The Barnes and Bainbridge Holme, *formerly* (1900-1906) M P for Sunderland *(The Barnes, Sunderland, Bainbridge House, near Sunderland, Belmont Hall, near Durham, &c),* b 23 Dec 1860, m 1st, 11 June 1890, Janet Maud (see p 102), da of Lieut-Col Sir Thomas Horatio Marshall, C B, d 20 Oct 1892, 2ndly, 22 Ap 1895, Nina, da of Hercules Grey Ross, B C S, *and has issue* 1e *to* 3e

1e Richard Laurence Stapylton Pemberton, b 10 Ap 1891

2e² Nina Penelope Pemberton

3e² Eleanor Mary Pemberton

2d Ralph Hylton Pemberton, b 17 July 1864

3d Ellen Pemberton m 14 June 1885, Col Emilius Clayton, R A, and has issue (3 sons and 2 das)

4d Mary Laurence Pemberton

5d Laura Penelope Pemberton

6d Jane Emma Stapylton Pemberton, m 12 Sept 1894, Edmund Robert Durnford *(Fagoo, Bengal),* and has issue (a da)

4c *Laura Anne Stapylton,* d 13 Dec 1858, m *as 1st wife,* 16 Dec 1857, *Lieut-Col Sir Thomas Horatio Marshall, C B, J P (Bryn-y-Coed, Bangor),* and had issue 1d

1d Henry Stapylton Marshall, b 4 Nov 1858

5c Susan Mary Roper Stapylton

6c Margaret Monica Stapylton, m 14 Ap 1863, George Thomas John Bucknall (Sotheron-Estcourt), 1st Lord Estcourt [U K], J P, D L *(Estcourt, near Tetbury, Darrington, W R Yorks)*

7c *Frances Blanche Stapylton,* d 2 June 1861, m 9 Ap 1860, *Rudolph Zwilchenbart of Liverpool,* and had issue 1d

1d Blanche Zwilchenbart, m Col de Courcy Daniell, *late* R A, and has issue (3 das)

8c *Octavia Constance Stapylton,* d (-), m *the Cavaliere F F Figulelli (Rome),* and had issue 1d

1d Francesca M S Figulelli, now living in Italy

3b *Bryan Stapylton,* d (-), m *Lucy, da of the Rev A Johnson, Rector of South Stoke, near Bath,* and had issue

4b *Laura Anne Stapylton,* b 1809, d 23 Oct 1894, aged 86, bur *at Brompton,* m 1829, *Thomas Vardon of Esher formerly Librarian to the House of Commons,* b 1799 d 12 Ap 1867, *and had (with a son, Capt Noel Hasenden Bryan Vardon, who d s p Dec 1883) issue* 1c *to* 2c

1c *Eva Dora Anne Vardon,* b 20 Dec 1831, d 8 Dec 1881, m 1852, *Charles James Durant,* b June 1829, d *(at Sidmouth)* 14 Jan 1903, *and had (with 2 younger sons who d s p) issue* 1d

1d Charles Richard Durant, educ at Eton (13 *Egerton Gardens, S W, The Manor House, White Waltham),* b 20 Sept 1853, m 27 Sept 1887, the Hon Nora Augusta Maud [descended from the Lady Anne, sister to King Edward IV, &c (see Exeter Volume, p 239)] widow of Alexander Kirkman Finlay, da of Hercules George Robert (Robinson), 1st Baron Rosmead [U K], P C, G C M G, and has issue 1e

1e Noel Henry Colin Finlax Durant, b July 1888

2c *Laura Emily Bethune Vardon,* d (-), m *Capt F Walker, 7th Dragoon Guards* [Nos 10162 to 10177

# of The Blood Royal

2a *John Bree of Emerald, Keswick,* d (—), m *Eliza, da of (—) Bearcroft,* and had issue 1b to 6b

  1b *John Bree,* d in India

  2b Henry Bree, d 1837

  3b *Charles Robert Bree of Colchester,* M D, F Z S, J P, *Author of "Birds of Europe not observed in the British Isles,"* d s p Oct 1886, m 19 Dec 1845, *Frances Elizabeth, da of Sir Augustus Brydges Henniker, 3rd Bart* [U K], d 19 Nov 1906

  4b. *Stapylton Bree,* d at sea

  5b *Right Rev Herbert Bree, Lord Bishop of Barbados 1882–1899, formerly Vicar of Brampton,* d (—), m 1st, July 1860, *Jane Sarah, da of Edgar Rust d'Eye, Rector of Drinkstone,* d 18 June 1863, 2ndly, Nov 1865, *Mary Harriet, da of W Newland of Bramley, co Surrey,* d (—), and had issue 1c to 7c

    1c Charles Herbert Bree, b 20 May 1851

    2c Edward Henry Bree, b Oct 1852

    3c Arthur Stapylton Bree, b 1854

    4c John Bree, b 1858

    5c¹ Janet Bree, m 22 June 1887, Robert Michael Nowell-Usticke of Polsue Philleigh, J P (*Polsue Philleigh, near Grampound Road, Cornwall*), and his issue

    See below, Nos 10190–10191

    6c² Mabel Eleanor Bree

    7c² Evelyn Mary Bree

  6b *Emily Bree,* d (—), m *the Rev George Thomas Hall,* M A (Camb), *Vicar of Ilbrighton 1899–1908* (*Kingsland, Shrewsbury*)

  3a *Rev Robert Francis Bree of Sydenham,* M A, d (—), m 2ndly, (—), *da of (—) Richards of Ireland,* and had issue 1b to 4b

  1b *Rev Robert Stapylton Bree,* M A, *Rector of Tintagel, co Cornwall,* d 1851, m 1st, *Fanny, da of the Rev J Bindlass of York,* d (—), 2ndly, 5 Nov 1838, *Philippa Allen, da and co-h of Sir Edwin Bayntun Sandys, 1st Bart* [U K], d (—), and had issue 1c to 5c

    1c² Robert Bree

    2c² Miles Bree, b 1845

    3c *Emma Charlotte Sophia Bree,* d (—), m 10 Ap 1844, *the Rev Edwin Montfort Stephen Sandys,* d 14 Dec 1854, and had issue

    4c *Lucy E Marianne Bree,* d (—), m 20 Ap 1858, *Stephen Usticke Nowell-Usticke* (R L 23 Feb 1852), *previously Beauchamp, of Falmouth,* J P b May 1818, d Mar 1875, and had issue 1d to 6d

    1d *Robert Michael Nowell-Usticke of Polsue Philleigh,* J P, Capt Cornwall and Devon Miners Art., &c (*Polsue Philleigh, near Grampound Road, Cornwall*), b 20 Oct 1859, m 22 June 1887, Janet (see above), da of the Right Rev Herbert Bree, D D, Lord Bishop of Barbados, and has issue 1e to 2e

      1e Robert Stapylton Nowell-Usticke, b 2 Mar 1892

      2e Phyllis Evelyn Nowell-Usticke

    2d Michael Stanley Nowell-Usticke, b 1864

    3d William G Nowell-Usticke, b 1866, m 1889, Elizabeth, da of Charles Wright of Wirksworth, and has issue 1e to 3e

      1e Gordon Wright Nowell Usticke, b 9 Sept 1894

      2e Claude Stapylton Nowell-Usticke, b 20 July 1898

      3e Robert Stanley Nowell-Usticke, b 25 Ap 1901

    4d Charles Michael Nowell-Usticke b 1869, m 14 June 1900, Margaret de Visme, da of Charles Wright of Wirksworth, and has issue 1e

      1e Charles de Visme Nowell-Usticke, b 30 May 1902

[Nos 10178 to 10198

The Plantagenet Roll

5d Lucy Elizabeth Nowell-Usticke, d 5 June 1888, m 2 June 1881, Capt. George Hewat, King's Own Scottish Borderers, and had issue 1e to 2e

  1e Dora Lucy Hewat

  2e Frances Hewat

6d Minna Georgiana Nowell-Usticke, m 11 Jan 1905, David Pearson (Edinburgh)

5c Laura Bree, d (-), m T Watson Chapman, Lieut R N

2b. Rev Edward Nugent Bree of Auckland, New Zealand, M A, d (-), m 1st, Hanna, da of (—) Fox of St Bees, co Cumberland, d (-), 2ndly, E, da of (—) King of Hereford, d (-), and had issue 1c to 4c

  1c Miles Reginald Bree, b 2 Oct 1849, d 30 Ap 1899, m 1st, at Auckland, N Z, 5 Nov 1873, Louisa, da of Col Balneavis, 58th Regt, d (-), 2ndly, at Gore, 7 July 188-, Sarah Eliza (Gore, New Zealand), adopted da of Judge Mansford of Port Chalmers, N Z, and had issue 1d to 6d (with 2 sons and a da, d s p)

  1d² Brian Stapylton Bree, b 21 June 1883

  2d² Reginald Nugent Stapylton Bree, b 30 Nov 1890

  3d² Edward Nugent Stapylton Bree, b 16 Oct 1893

  4d¹ Ethel Balneavis Bree, b 1 Oct 1876, m A Jordan (Dunedin, New Zealand)

  5d² Monica Louisa Stapylton Bree, b 10 June 1884, d 20 Jan 1907

  6d² Adela Lucy Stapylton Bree, b 4 Aug 1887, m at Wellington, N Z, 17 June 1908, Guy Hardy Scholefield [son of John Hoick Scholefield] (88 Glencldon Road, Streatham, S W), and has issue 1e

  1e Jack Hardy Bree Scholefield, b 10 Oct 1909

  2c Eleanor Annie Bree, m George Burnett (Wanganui, New Zealand)

  3c Lucy Martina Bree, m as 2nd wife, 28 Nov 1862, Col Sir Thomas Horatio Marshall, C B, J P, late 3rd Mil Batt Cheshire Regt (Bryn-y-Coed, Bangor, Hartford Beach, Cheshire), and has issue 1d to 7d

  1d Thomas Edward Marshall, Major R A (Malta), b 28 July 1865

  2d John Marshall, Lieut R N (Brynhild, Festing Grove, Southsea), b 12 Nov 1868, m 21 Aug 1897, Hilda Renée, da of Capt Herbert Lempriere, late Hants Regt, and has issue 1e to 2e

    1e George Herbert Lempriere Marshall, b 23 Feb 1901

    2e Renee Marshall

  3d Reginald Marshall, b Dec 1870

  4d Rev Charles Cecil Marshall, Vicar of St Chad's (St Chad's Vicarage, Far Headingley, Leeds), b 26 May 1872, m 2 Aug 1905, Ethelred Hope, da of Charles Havelock, and has issue 1e

    1e Mary Havelock Marshall

  5d Agnes Bertha Marshall, m 24 Sept 1884, Sydney Platt [youngest son of John Platt of Werneth Park, Oldham, M P, J P, D L] (24 Lowndes Square, S W), and has issue 1e to 2e

    1e Lionel Sydney Platt, 17th Lancers, b 1 Oct 1885

    2e Ena Guendolen Platt

  6d Janet Maud Marshall, d 20 Oct 1892, m as 1st wife, 11 June 1890, John Stapylton Grey Pemberton of The Barnes and Bainbridge House, late M P (The Barnes, near Sunderland, &c), and had issue

See p 100, No 10163

  7d Everilda Lucy Marshall, m 21 Ap 1906, Major Robert Warren Hastings Anderson, Highland Light Infantry [2nd son of Col J W Anderson of Bourhouse, Dunbar]

  1c Alice Bree, b c 1852, d at Napier, N Z, 21 Ap 1895, m at All Saints Church, Ponsonby, Auckland, N Z, Horace William Baker of Napier, and had issue 1d to 3d

102   [Nos 10199 to 10221

# of The Blood Royal

1d Tudor Nugent Baker, b 9 Aug 1881, m Dec 1906, Elsie, da of (—) Bayley of Taranake, N Z , and has issue 1e

1e Horace Holland Baker, b 3 Jan 1909

2d Horace Mathias Baker, b 23 Feb 1887 unm

3d Adèle Gwendoline Baker, m at St John's Cathedral, Napier, N Z , 21 Nov 1896, Walter Menzies Fulton (see p 212) (Box 5465, Johannesburg), s p s

3b Mary Anne Bice d (—), m N Smith

4b Julia Bice, d (—), m Charles Douglas, Capt in the Guards

[Nos 10222 to 10225

43 Descendants, if any, of ELIZABETH STAPYLTON (Table VII), d (—), m HENRY WALLER, M P for Wycombe, co Bucks

44 Descendants of GRACE ROBINSON (Table VII.), b 5 Jan 1718 , d 26 Nov 1766, m Ap 1739, the Very Rev WILLIAM FREIND, D D., Dean of Canterbury, d (—) ; and had issue 1a to 4a

1a Robert Freind, b 1740, d (?s p) 20 Jan 1789

2a Rev William Maximilian Freind, Rector of Chinnor, co Oxon, d 11 June 1804, m 25 Feb 1778, Deborah, da and h of Thomas Walker of Woodstock, co Oxon, d 13 June 1781, and had issue 1b

1b Deborah Susannah Freind, da and coent (1795) h, d 24 May 1810, m as 1st wife, 26 May 1802, Henry Jeffrey (Flower) 4th Viscount Ashbrook [I], b 6 Nov 1776, d 4 May 1847, and had issue 1c to 3c

1c Henry (Flower), 5th Viscount Ashbrook [I], b 17 June 1806, d 3 Aug 1871, m 7 June 1828, Frances (see p 108), da of the Ven Sir John Robinson, previously Freind, 1st Bt [U K], d 15 June 1886, and had issue 1d to 6d

1d Henry Jeffrey (Flower), 6th Viscount Ashbrook [I], b 26 Mar 1829, d s p 14 Dec 1882

2d William Spencer (Flower), 7th Viscount Ashbrook [I], b 23 Mar 1830, d s p s 25 Nov 1906

3d Robert Thomas (Flower), 8th Viscount Ashbrook [I], formerly Lieut -Col Royal Canadian Regt (Castle Durrow, Durrow, Queen's Co , Knockatrina House, Durrow, Queen's Co , Carlton), b 1 Ap 1836, m 18 July 1866, Gertrude Sophia (see p 108), da of the Rev Sewell Hamilton of Bath, and had issue 1e to 5e

1e Hon Llowarch Robert Flower (Knockatrina House, Durrow, Queen s Co), b 9 July 1870, m 11 Feb 1899, Gladys Lucille Beatrice [descended from the Lady Isabel Plantagenet (see the Essex Volume, p 289)], da of Gen Sir George Wentworth Alexander Higginson, K C B

2e Hon Reginald Henry Flower, b 15 June 1871, m 10 May 1901, Kate, da of Col Cuming of Crovar, co Cavan

3e Hon Frances Mary Flower, m 2 Sept 1893, Harry Ernest White [2nd son of Gen Sir Robert White of Aghavoe, K C B] (Aghavoc, Queen's Co), and has issue 1f

1f Robert Llowarch White, b 19 Jan 1896

4e Hon Eva Constance Gertrude Flower

5e Hon Gertrude Flower

1d Hon Mary Sophia Flower, b 17 June 1832, d 17 Ap 1886, m 2 Oct 1860, Major Robert Blakeney, 48th Regt , d 20 June 1902, and had issue (with a younger da d unm) 1e to 4e

1e Henry Ross Blakeney, b 2 Ap 1862

2e Frederick Robert Blakeney, b 16 May 1863

3e Ernest Charles Cecil Blakeney, b 27 Jan 1869

4e Frances Alice Blakeney

[Nos 10226 to 10236

The Plantagenet Roll

5d *Hon Frances Esther Flower*, b 17 Mar 1834, d 21 May 1881, m 14 *July* 1857, *John Capel Philips of the Heath House, co Staffs, and Newlands, co Glouc, J P, D L*, d (-), *and had issue (with a son d young)* 1c to 4e

1e Burton Henry Philips (see below), C M G, Lieut-Col Reserve of Officers, *formerly Royal Welsh Fusiliers (The Heath House, Teane, co Stafford)*, b 1 Oct 1858, m 10 Feb 1904, Lucy Madeline, da of Col George Blucher Heneage Marton of Capernwray, *and his issue* 1f

　1f Audrey Adelaide Philips

　2c John Augustus Philips, b 1 Jan 1861, *unm*

　3c Frances Margaret Philips, m 1885, Ernest Capel Cure [youngest son of Robert Capel Cure of Blake Hall, co Essex and a descendant maternally of King Henry VII] (see Tudor Roll p 451)]

　4c Bertha Mary Philips

6d Hon Caroline Gertrude Flower (*Capernwray Hall, Burton, Westmorland*), m 1 May 1866, George Blucher Heneage Marton of Capernwray, J P, D L, and High Sheriff co Lancaster 1877, M P Lancaster 1885-86, Hon Col 3rd and 4th Batt R Lancaster Regt, d 18 Aug 1905, *and his issue* 1e to 10.

1c George Henry Powys Marton of Capernwray (*Capernwray, co Lancaster, White's*), b 11 Ap 1869

2c Richard Oliver Marton, D S O, Capt R A, is 1st Assist Sup of Experiments at School of Gunnery, b 24 Aug 1872, m 4 Ap 1899, Margaret Elizabeth [descended from King Henry VII (see Tudor Roll, p 101)], da of Egerton Leigh of Jodrell Hall [by his wife, Lady Elizabeth, *née* White], *and has issue* 1f to 2f

　1f Oliver Egerton Christopher Marton, b 25 May 1903

　2f Guy Burton Heneage Marton, b 5 Nov 1904

　3c Rev Lancelot Edward Marton, b 27 July 1878

　4c Lionel Marton, Lieut Royal Berks Regt, b 7 Aug 1879

　5c Augusta Adelaide Cecily Marton, m 20 Oct 1896, Stanley Hughes Le Fleming, J P, D L, High Sheriff co Westmorland, Hon Major Westmorland and Cumberland Yeo, Lord of the Manors of Backermet, Skeriwith, Kirkland, and Brathmuire, co Cumberland, Coniston, co Lancaster, and Rydal, co Westmorland (*Rydal Hall, Ambleside, Carlton*) *and has issue* 1f to 3f

　　1f Michael George Le Fleming, b 17 July 1900

　　2f Richard Cumberland Le Fleming, b 22 July 1901

　　3f [da] Le Fleming, b 27 May 1905

　6c Lucy Madeline Marton, m 10 Feb 1904, Lieut-Col Burton Henry Philips, C M G (*The Heath House, Teane*), *and has issue*

　　See above, No 10238

　7e Florence Augusta Marton, m 16 Feb 1901, John Ralph Aspinall [son and h of Ralph John Aspinall of Standen Hall, co Lanc, J P, D L] (*30 Queen's Gate Terrace, S W*)

　8c Alice Caroline Marton

　9e Adelaide Esther Marton

　10c Georgina Mary Marton

2c *Hon Susannah Sophia Flower*, b 5 July 1803, d 6 Nov 1864, m 1st, 21 May 1824, *the Rev William Robinson* [2nd son of the Ven Sir John Robinson, 1st Bt [U K] (see p 107)], d Dec 1834, 2ndly, 29 Dec 1836, *William Wilson Campbell of Dublin, M D*, d 1856, *and had issue (with possibly others by 2nd husband)* 1d to 2d

1d Caroline Susannah Robinson, d (-), m Aug 1851, *Major-Gen Arthur J Macan Rainey of Trowscoed Lodge, Leckhampton Road, Cheltenham*, *and had issue*

2d Helena Robinson, d June 1899, m 21 Sept 1880, *Sewell Hamilton* (see p 108)

3c *Hon Caroline Flower*, b 30 July 1807, d 17 Ap 1840, m *as 1st wife,*
[Nos 10237 to 10258.

# of The Blood Royal

26 *Mar* 1829, *Henry Every* (see p 107), 1st *Life Guards* [*son and h app of Sir Henry Every, 9th Bt* [*E*]], d v p 27 *Feb* 1853 *and had issue* 1d *to* 5l

    1d *Sir Henry Flower Every*, 10th Bt [*E*], D L , b 23 *Dec* 1830, d 26 *Feb* 1893 , m 2ndly 12 *Oct* 1859, *Mary Isabella* (18 *Montagu Street*, W), da *of the Rev Edmund Hollond of Benhall Lodge, Saxmundham* (see p 108) , *and had issue* 1e *to* 8e

    1e *Henry Edmund Every, Capt South Wales Borderers*, b 9 *Oct* 1860 , d v p 1 *Dec* 1892 , m 18 *Nov* 1884, *Leila Frances Harford*, da *of the Rev Henry Adderley Box*, M A , d 4 *Feb* 1890, *and had issue* 1f

    1f *Sir Edward Oswald Every*, 11th Bt [*E*] (*Egginton Hall, Burton-upon Trent*), b 14 *Jan* 1886 , m 17 *Aug* 1909, *Ivy Linton*, da of Major *Alfred Meller* of Rushmere, co Suffolk

    2e *Right Rev Edward Francis Every*, D D , M A (Camb), Lord Bishop of the Falkland Islands (*Calle Industria, Buenos Aires*), b 3 Ap 1862

    3e *Ernest Hollond Every* (*Colorado Springs, U S A*), b 10 *July* 1870 , m. 20 *Dec* 1902, *Beatrice May*, da of *Harvey Young* of Colorado Springs , and has issue 1f *to* 2f

        1f *Ernest Henry Every*, b 14 *Feb* 1906

        2f *Patricia Every*, b 26 *May* 1904

    4e *Alice Vere Every*

    5e *Eleanor Maude Every* (18 *Montague Street*, W)

    6e *Constance Margaret Every*

    7e *Clara Helen Every*, m as 2nd wife, 11 *Oct* 1899 the Rev *Edward Digby Stopford Ram* of Clonattin, co Wexford, Rector of Oxted [descended from King Henry VII (see the Tudor Roll, p 161)] (*Oxted Rectory, Surrey*) , and has issue 1f to 2f

        1f *Abel James Ram*, b 3 *Nov* 1902

        2f *Andrew Ram*, b 26 *May* 1908

    8e *Agnes Mabel Every*

    2d *Oswald Every, Capt 75th Foot*, b 26 *June* 1835 d 26 *Jan* 1892 , m 1st, 3 *June* 1862, *Cecilia Charlotte*, da *of Henry Charles Burney*, LL D , d 1882 , 2ndly, 1885. *Florence Amy* (4 *Westerfield Terrace, Westens Lane, Liscard*), da *of William Sheridan of Fawsley, co Devon*, *and had issue* 1e *to* 9e

    1e *Edward Every*, b 1865

    2e *Oswald Every*, J P , Lieut *late West India Regt*, *formerly Sergeant* 21st Lancers, has West Africa Medal and Clasp 1898-1899 (*Hampton Hill Worthen, Salop*), b 25 *May* 1872 m 11 *Feb* 1902, *Edith*, da of James *Whitaker* of Hampton Hall, co Salop, J P

    3e *Victor George Every*, b 1886

    4e *John Every*, b 1888

    5e *Francis Flower Every*, b 1890

    6e¹ *Florence Every*, b 29 *May* 1863 , d 14 *May* 1908 , m 23 *Sept*, 1886, *the Rev Alexander Frederick de Gex*, J P Rector of *Meshaw and Creacombe* (*Meshaw Rectory, South Molton, Devon*), *and had issue* 1f

        1f *Ruthven Gore de Gex*, b 4 *July* 1887

    7e¹ *Beatrice Every*, b 29 *May* 1865 , d 5 *Dec* 1893 , m 13 *Dec* 1887, *Thomas Husband Gill, Solicitor* (3 *St Aubyn Street, Devonport*) , and had issue 1f to 3f

        1f *Eric Every Gill*, b 16 *Sept* 1888

        2f *Oswald Tom Every Gill*, b 15 *Aug* 1891

        3f *Basil Every Gill*, b 24 *Nov* 1893

    8e¹ *Cissy Vere Every*.

    9e¹ *Mabel Every*

    3d *Caroline Penelope Every* (*Avenue Lodge, Eastbourne*), m 29 Ap 1872, Sir George Ebenezer Wilson Couper, 2nd Bt [U K], K C S I , C B , C I E , d 5 *Mar* 1908, and has issue 1e to 7e   [Nos 10259 to 10282

The Plantagenet Roll

1e Sir Ramsay George Henry Couper, 3rd Bt [U K], *formerly* Lieut King's Royal Rifle Corps, Afghan Medal with two clasps and Bronze Star, *b* 1 Nov 1855, *m* 1884, Nora Emma S, da of Horatio Willson Scott of Hampstead, and has issue 1f to 3f

1f Guy Couper, *b* 12 Mar 1889

2f Sybil Couper

3f Evelyn Couper

2e Victor Arthur Couper, Lieut-Col 4th Batt the Rifle Brigade, has Burmese and Punjab Medals (*Naval and Military*), *b* 4 Ap 1859

3e Edward Edmonston Couper, Lieut-Col Comdg 9th Gurkha Regt, has Indian Frontier Medal (*East India United Service*), *b* 15 Dec 1860 *m* 28 June 1899, Daisy Ethel Aylmer, da of Henry E Rose of Whiteshools, Bourton-on-the-Water, and has issue 1f

1f John Victor Hay Couper, *b* 1902

4e James Robert Couper (*Mansfield House, Moffat*), *b* 24 June 1863, *m* 27 Oct 1897, Jessie, da of John Kissock of Drummore, co Kirkcudbright, and has issue 1f to 4f

1f George Robert Cecil Couper, *b* 15 Oct 1898

2f John Every Couper, *b* 15 Nov 1900

3f Jem Ramsay Couper, *b* 13 Mar 1904

4f Doris Helen Couper, *b* 14 Mar 1907

5e Caroline Georgiana Jane Elizabeth Couper, *m* 6 Sept 1881, Major-Gen Frederick William Benson, C B, is in charge of Administration, Southern Command, has South African Medal with 3 clasps, &c (*Salisbury. Army and Navy*)

6e Ada Lucy Couper

7e Maude Madeline Couper

4d *Jane Charlotte Rose Every*, d 5 *July* 1874, *m* 23 *Nov* 1858, *the Rev Rowland Mosley, Rector of Egginton* [Bt Coll], d 24 *July* 1888 *and had issue* 1e *to* 8e

1e Arthur Rowland Mosley, J P, Major *formerly* 6th Dragoons, has Queen's Medal with 3 clasps and King's with 2 clasps for South African War (*The Hollies, Linslade, Leighton Buzzard, Cavalry, &c*), *b* 8 May 1862, *m* 16 Oct 1899, Henrietta, da of Henry Bolden

2e Godfrey Mosley, of Messrs Taylor, Simpson & Mosley, 35 St Mary's Gate, Derby, Solicitors, B A (Oxon), Major 5th Batt Sherwood Foresters (*35 St Mary's Gate, Derby*), *b* 15 June 1863

3e Ashton Edward Mosley (*Peterborough, Ontario*), *b* 24 Oct 1868

4e Wilfred Rowland Mosley, Architect (*Windsor Road, Slough*), *b* 25 Ap 1872

5e Theresa Jane Mosley ⎫
6e Mildred Isabel Mosley ⎬ (*Glenbrook, Duffield Road, Derby*)
7e Sybil Georgiana Rose Mosley ⎪
8e Jane Agnes Muriel Mosley ⎭

5d Mary Georgiana Every (104 *Beaufort Street, S W*), *m* 21 Oct 1863, the Rev William Mills Parry Pym, Vicar of Corsham, d 19 July 1872, and has issue 1e to 3e

1e Paul John Every Pym, *b* 28 Ap 1870 *unm*

2e Guy William Every Pym (*Malahtri Geraldine, New Zealand*) *b* 9 July 1871, *m* 2 Mar 1905, Elsie, da of Robert George Alcorn of West Maitland, Australia, M D, and has issue 1f to 3f

1f Guy Pym, *b* 2 May 1906

2f Jack Pym, *b* 7 Nov 1907

3f Vere Pym, *b* 19 Aug 1909

3e Caroline Vere Pym, *m* 4 Oct 1883, Alfred Edward Flood (*Roxborough, Cookham, Berks*), s p   [Nos 10283 to 10312

# of The Blood Royal

3a Ven Sir John Robinson (R L 29 Nov 1793), previously Freind, 1st Bt [U K], so cr 14 Dec 1819, Archdeacon of Armagh, b 15 Feb 1751, d 16 1f 1832, m 1786, Mary Anne, da of James Spencer of Rathangan, co Kildare, d 19 Jan 1834, and had issue 1b to 9b

1b Sir Richard Robinson 2nd Bt [U K] b 4 Mar 1787, d 2 Oct 1847, m 25 Feb 1813, Lady Helena Eleanor, da of Stephen (Moore), 2nd Earl of Mount Cashell [I], d at Paris 23 Sept 1859, and had issue 1c to 4c

1c Sir John Stephen Robinson, 3rd Bt [U K], C B, Hon Col 6th Batt Royal Irish Rifles, b 27 Sept 1816, d 21 May 1895, m 2 Sept 1841, Sarah Blackett, da of Anthony Denny of Barham Wood, co Herts [Bt of Tralee Coll], by his wife the Hon Mary Patience, née Collingwood d 26 Oct 1875, and had issue 1d to 2d

1d Sir Gerald William Collingwood Robinson, 4th Bt [U K], b 11 Feb 1857, d unm 31 May 1903

2d Maud Helena Collingwood Robinson of Rokeby, m 26 Mar 1890, Richard Johnston Montgomery of Beaulieu (Beaulieu, co Louth, Killineer House, co Louth Rokeby Hall, co Louth), s p

2c Sir Richard Harcourt Robinson, 5th Bt [U K], formerly Lieut-Col 60th Rifles (3 Harley Gardens, S W, Army and Navy), b at Pisa, 4 Feb 1828, unm

3c Helena Esther Florence Robinson, b at Florence 1817, d 22 Dec 1900, m as 2nd wife, 10 Jan 1849, Lieut Col Baron Knut Philip Bonde, K N S (R N O), K C N (R N Ekk), K L H (R F H L) [B Bonde [Sweden, No 20, 1802] Coll] b 1815, d Oct 1871, and had issue 1d to 3d

1d Baron Carl Bonde, Lord of the Manors of Fituna, &c, b 1853, d (apparently s p) a 1890

2d Baroness Ingeborg Helena Bonde, b 1849, d (? unm) a 1880

3d Baroness Florence Charlotte Lucie Bonde, b 1851, d (-), m 1870, Kammarherren John Henning von Horn, K D D (R D D O)

4c Elizabeth Selina Robinson, b at Paris, d 16 June 1891, m 26 Oct 1843, Adolphe, Viscount de St Geniez, and had issue (a son and da)

2b Rev William Robinson, Rector of Boveagh, co Derry, b 20 Dec 1793, d Dec 1834, m 21 May 1824, the Hon Susannah Sophia, da of Henry Jeffrey (Flower), 4th Viscount Ashbrook [I], and had issue

See p 104

3b Sir Robert Spencer Robinson, K C B, F R S, Admiral R N, Comptroller of the Navy 1861-1871, b 6 Jan 1809, d s p 27 July 1889

4b Jane Robinson, d 31 Aug 1860, m 1st, 2 Aug 1825, George Powney, d (2 s p) 1827, 2ndly, as 2nd wife, 20 Feb 1814, Henry Every [son and h app of the 9th Bt, see p 104], d (? s p by her) 27 Feb 1853

5b Louisa Robinson, d 24 Dec 1849, m as 2nd wife, 20 Dec 1821, the Rev William Knox [E of Ranfurly [I] Coll], d 26 Feb 1860, and had issue 1c to 2c

1c Anne Eliza Knox, d (-), m 25 Sept 1856, the Ven James Gaspard le Marchant Carey, Archdeacon of Essex, d 1885, and had issue 1d

1d Gaspard William Carey, b 9 Aug 1861

2c Frances Emily Knox, d 26 May 1863, m as 1st wife, 7 Nov 1858, Robert Vesey Truell of Ballyhenny, co Wicklow, d 27 Feb 1867, and had issue 1d to 2d

1d Louisa Anne Truell

2d Phoebe Editha Truell, m as 2nd wife, Feb or July 1896, Robert Vesey Stoney of Rosturk Castle, &c, J P, D L, High Sheriff co Mayo 1884 (Rosturk Castle, co Mayo, Inaskerkin, co Mayo, Knockadoo, co Roscommon), and has issue 1e to 2e

1e Thomas Samuel Vesey Stoney, b 23 Aug 1898

2e Robert Vesey Stoney, b 24 Sept 1903   [Nos 10313 to 10319

The Plantagenet Roll

6b *Caroline Robinson*, b 1801 , d 4 *May* 1886, m 2 *Nov* 1822, *John James (Pomeroy)*, *5th Viscount Harberton* [*I*], b 29 *Sept* 1790, d 5 *Oct* 1862 , *and had issue* 1c

1c James Spencer (Pomeroy), 6th Viscount Harberton [I], J P (3 *Ashburn Place*, *S W* , 19 *Albert Road*, *Great Malvern*), b 23 Nov 1836 , m 2 Ap 1861, Florence Wallace, da of William Wallace Legge of Malone House, co Antrim, D L , and has issue 1d to 3d

1d Hon Ernest Arthur George Pomeroy, *formerly* Capt 3rd Batt Royal Dublin Fusiliers, has S African Medal (6 *Camden House Chambers*, *Kensington*, *W*), b 1 Dec 1867

2d Hon Ralph Legge Pomeroy, *formerly* Capt 5th Dragoon Guards, served in S Africa 1899-1902 (*Hexford Manor*, *Weedon*, *Isthmian Cavalry*), b 31 Dec 1869 , m 25 June 1907, Mary Katherine, da of Arthur William Leatham of Miserden Park, co Glos, J P , and has issue 1e

1e Henry Ralph Mostyn Pomeroy, b 12 Oct 1908

3d Hon Hilda Evelyn Pomeroy (*Juniper Hill*, *Rickmansworth, Herts*), m 5 Oct 1892, Thomas Arthur Carless Attwood of Sion Hill, Wolverley, F S A , from whom she obtained a decree of nullity of marriage 1902

7b *Frances Robinson*, b 1803 , d 15 *June* 1886 , m 7 *June* 1828, *Henry (Flower)*, *5th Viscount Ashbrook* [*I*], d 3 *Aug* 1871 , *and had issue*

See p 103, Nos 10226-10258

8b *Selina Robinson*, d 30 *Aug* 1873 , m *Nov* 1833, *the Rev Sewell Hamilton of Bath*, d (–) , *and had issue* 1c *to* 2c

1c Sewell Hamilton, b (—), m 21 Sept 1880, Helena, da of the Rev William Robinson (see p 104), d June 1899

2c Gertrude Sophia Hamilton, m 18 July 1866, Robert Thomas (Flower), 8th Viscount Ashbrook [I], &c (*Castle Durrow*, *Durrow*, *Queen's Co*), and has issue

See p 103, Nos 10227-10232

9b *Isabella Robinson*, d 23 *Jan* 1818 , m *as 1st wife*, 6 Feb 1839, *the Rev Edmund Hollond of Benhall Lodge, co Suffolk*, d 19 *May* 1884 , *and had issue* 1c *to* 5c

1c Edmund William Hollond of Benhall Lodge, M A , Bar -at-Law, b 18 Ap 1841 , d 2 Jan 1900 , m 20 Jan 1876, Ada (*Benhall Lodge, Saxmundham*), da of Robert Rygate of Wellington, N S W , and had issue 1d

1d Edmund Robert Hollond of Benhall, B A , J P (*Benhall Lodge, Saxmundham, Suffolk*), b 24 Nov 1876

2c John Robert Hollond, J P , D L , M A , Bar -at-Law, *formerly* (1883-1885) M P for Brighton (*Wonham, Devon*), b 2 Nov 1843 m 17 Aug 1870, Fanny Eliza, da of Frederick Keats of Braziers, co Oxon , and has issue 1d to 6d

1d Robert Edward Hollond, b 21 July 1871

2d Spencer Edmund Hollond, Capt Rifle Brigade (41 *Princes Gate, S W*), b 19 Mar 1874 , m 5 Oct 1905, Lula, da of Charles Pfizer of New York , and has issue 1e

1e Christopher Arthur Spencer Hollond

3d Ellen Fanny Hollond, m 13 Sept 1899, Edward Cornwall Nicholetts (*The Manor House, Brent Knoll, Somerset*), and has issue 1e to 2e

1e Gilbert Edward Nicholetts, b 9 Nov 1902

2e Nina Joyce Nicholetts

4d May Beatrice Hollond

5d Florence Nina Hollond, m 10 Oct 1905, Capt Edward Lisle Strutt [B Belper Coll] (*Travellers'*, *White's*, *Alpine*)

6d Monica Hollond

3c Mary Isabella Hollond (18 *Montagu Street*, *W*), m 12 Oct 1859, Sir Henry Flower Every, 10th Bt [E], d 26 Feb 1893 , and has issue

See p 103, Nos 10259-10270   [Nos 10320 to 10389

# of The Blood Royal

4c Esther Harriett Hollond, m 24 Ap 1867, the Rev Basil Kilvington Woodd, L L M [son and h -app of Basil Thomas Woodd of Conyngham Hall, M P], d v p 16 Ap 1886, and has issue 1d to 4d

1d Basil Aubrey Woodd of Conyngham Hall, J P, B A (Cumb), Bar -at -Law, Lieut Yorks Hussars Imp Yeo (*Conyngham Hall, Knaresborough, 35 Tite Street, Chelsea*), b 1869, m 12 Dec 1895, Rosalie, da of John Dyson of Moorlands, near Crewkerne, and has issue 1e to 2e

2e *Iris Rosalie Woodd*, b 10 May 1897, d 9 Ap 1906

2e Elaine Jane Woodd, b 24 Jan 1899

2d Evelyn Anthony Woodd, b 13 Dec 1870

3d Dorothy Eugenia Woodd, m 10 Jan 1900, Hugh Roubiliac Roger-Smith, M.D, M R C S (Eng), L R C P (Lond) (1 *College Terrace, Fitzjohn's Avenue. N.W*), and has issue 1e to 3e

1e Raymond Roger-Smith, b 21 Nov 1902

2e Basil Hugh Roger Smith, b 5 May 1909

3e Barbara Roger-Smith, b 6 Ap 1904

4d Gertrude Frances Woodd, m 7 Sept 1907, Thomas Walter Breed (*Tellham Hill, Battle, Sussex*), and has issue 1e

1e Nancy Gertrude Breed, b 13 Aug 1908

5c Fanny Louisa Hollond, m Oct 1884, John Dyson, *formerly* Judge at Feyzabad, Oude

4a Grace Freind, d 1809, m 1765, Lieut -Gen Campbell, R M , d 1812, and had issue   [Nos 10390 to 10400

45 Descendants of FRANCIS LOWE of Baldwyn Brightwell, co Oxon (Table VII.), d June 1754, m ELIZABETH or FRANCES, da of John CORRANCE of Parham, d (–), and had issue 1a

1a *Catherine Lowe, da and event sole h*, d 1789, m 1717, *William Lowndes of Astwood Bury, co Bucks*, b 1712, d v p 1773, and had issue 1b to 2b

1b *William Lowndes, afterwards* (1780) *Lowndes-Stone of Astwood Bury, co Bucks, and Baldwyn Brightwell, co Oxon*, b 1750, d May 1830 m 15 July 1775, *Elizabeth, da and co h of Richard Garth of Morden, co Surrey* d Feb 1837, and had issue 1c to 7c

1c *William Francis Lowndes-Stone of Brightwell Park, J P, D L, D C L, High Sheriff co Oxon* 1834, b 27 Oct 1783, d 1858, m 3 Oct 1811, *Caroline, da of Sir William Strickland of Boynton, 6th Bart* [E], d 11 Ap 1867, and had issue

See the Clarence Volume, pp 233-235, Nos 4817-4865

2c *Rev Richard Lowndes, afterwards* (R I. 20 Mar 1837) *Garth, of Morden*, b 1790, d 1862 m *Mary, da of the Rev Robert Douglas of Salwarpe*, d 1819, and had issue 1d to 3d

1d *Hon Sir Richard Garth of Morden, Q C, M P, Chief Justice of Bengal* 1875, b 11 Mar 1820, d 23 Mar 1903, m 27 June 1847, *Clara, da of William Loftus Lowndes, Q C*, d 15 Jan 1903, and had issue 1e to 7e

1e Richard Garth (*Birse, Rugby Road, Brighton*), b 2 June 1848, unm

2e *George Douglas Garth*, b 15 May 1852, d 6 Jan 1900, m 12 Oct 1878, *Mildred (Morden, Iffley Road, Oxford), da of Arthur Noverre of London*, and had issue 1f to 5f

1f George Douglas Garth, Brewer,   ⎫
2f Arthur Douglas Garth, Jute and Gunny Broker ⎬ b (twins) 26 Jan 1880
Calcutta),   ⎭

3f Humphrey Garth, B A, Chartered Accountant, b 8 Oct 1881

4f Margaret Garth

5f Primrose Garth   [Nos 10401 to 10455

The Plantagenet Roll

3e William Garth, Bar-at-Law (*Russell Street, Calcutta*), b 26 Aug 1854

4e Charles Garth, b 10 July 1870, m Mabel, da of George Day Harrison, has a da

5e May Eliza Guth (6 *Alfred Place West, S W*), m 20 Ap 1869, Henry Leigh Pemberton [youngest son of Edward Leigh Pemberton of Torry Hill, Sittingbourne], b 1835, d 29 Mar 1895, and has issue (with 2 sons and a da d unm) 1f to 5f

1f Cyril Leigh Pemberton, b 6 May 1873, m 15 June 1909, Mary Evelyn, da of Matthew Megaw of Pont Street, S W

2f Norman Leigh Pemberton, b 31 July 1874

3f Harry Leigh Pemberton, b 3 Feb 1878

4f Guy Leigh Pemberton, b 23 June 1883

5f Dorothy Leigh Pemberton

6e Helen Frances Garth, m 5 May 1881, Capt Alexander Evans-Gordon, B S C , and has issue 1f to 5f

1f Kenmure Alick Garth Evans-Gordon, b 20 Aug 1885

2f Marjorie Evans-Gordon, m (—)

3f Madeline Evans-Gordon, m (—)

4f Jean Evans-Gordon, } twins
5f Joan Evans-Gordon, }

7e Evelyn Selina May Garth, m 3 July 1887, Herbert Tyrrell Griffiths of 5 Kensington Square, W M D, d 1905, and has issue (with a son, Leslie Valentine, d young) 1f to 3f

1f Richard Evelyn Griffiths, b 8 Ap 1888

2f Ivon Herbert Griffiths, b 11 Ap 1891

3f Joyce May Griffiths, b 16 Dec 1901

2d Elizabeth Garth, b 1827, m George Cecil Henry, Col R A , and has issue 1e to 2e

1e Charles Cecil Henry, b 1865, m 24 Sept 1901, Mary, eldest da of the Rev Frank Kewley, and has issue 1f to 2f

1f John Charles Henry, b 1907

2f Barbara Henry

2e Mabel Mary Henry

3d Frances Garth (*Brightwell, Farnham, Surrey*), b 12 July 1833, m 23 Oct 1855, Patrick Lewis Cole Paget, Col Scots Guards, d 17 July 1879, and has issue 1e to 4e

1e Gertrude Frances Paget, m 1884, Phelips Brooke Hanham, Col *late* R A , and has issue 1f to 2f

1f Esmond Henry Paget Hanham, b 12 Mar 1887

2f Patrick John Hanham, b 15 Oct 1893

2e Florence Mary Emily Paget

3e Violet Evelyn Paget, m 27 Nov 1906, the Rev George Harvey Ranking (135 *Lambeth Road, S E*)

4e Mildred Eileen May Paget, m 12 Oct 1889, Henry Lloyd Powell, Major R H A (*Burton Hall, Christchurch, Hants*), and has issue 1f to 3f

1f Ivon Powell, b 1893

2f Gladys Powell

3f Dorothy Mary Powell

3c *Henry Owen Lowndes*, b 1795, d (—), m 1827, *Sarah Anne, da of Augustus Turnbull of (—), America, and had issue 1d to 2d

1d Kate Lowndes, d s p , m (—)

2d Mary Lowndes, m (—) Stevens of Boston, U S A , and has issue

[Nos 10456 to 10489

110

# of The Blood Royal

4c *Elizabeth Lowndes*, d 20 Nov 1865, m 6 June 1802, *John Fane of Wormsley* [E of Westmorland Coll], d 4 Oct 1850, *and had issue*

See the Exeter Volume, pp 356-358, Nos 25861-25927

5c *Catherine Lowndes*, d (-), m 1812, *the Rev John Holland, Vicar of Aston Rowant, co Oxon* d 13 Nov 1844, *and had issue (dau only child)* 1d

1d *Catherine Holland*, d unm 23 May 1843

6c *Anne Lowndes*, d 21 Aug 1864, m 13 July 1822, *William Henry Sharp*, b 27 May 1782, d 13 Oct 1844, *and had issue* 1d

1d Anne Sharp (*Balmore, Caversham Reading*), m 3 Sept 1861, Robert Parker Radcliffe, Major-Gen R A, d 29 Mar 1907, and has issue 1e to 5e

1e Robert Edmund Lowndes Radcliffe (*Egmont Binfield, Bracknell*), b 16 Ap 1865, m 7 June 1894, Gertrude, da of Charles Combe of Cobham Park, co Surrey, J P, D L, High Sheriff 1885, and has issue 1f

1f Joyce Naomi Aileen Radcliffe

2e William Scott Warley Radcliffe, Major Shropshire Light Infantry, b 3 July 1866, m 14 June 1906, Cecily Mary, youngest da of the Hon Cecil Parker of Eccleston Paddocks, co Chester, and has issue 1f to 2f

1f Cynthia Alice Radcliffe

2f Meriel Margaret Radcliffe

3e Annie Elsie Radcliffe

4e Mabel Maud Radcliffe, m 2 June 1897, the Rev Bertram Long, M A (Camb), Rector of Wokingham (*The Rectory, Wokingham*), and has issue 1f to 3f

1f Frederick Kenneth Radcliffe Long, b 20 May 1900

2f Monica Elsie Long

3f Doris Mary Long

5e Evelyn Mary Radcliffe, m 25 Ap 1900, the Rev Walter Alexander Thackeray (*Nidd Vicarage, Ripley, Yorks*), and has issue 1f to 4f

1f Guy St Vincent Radcliffe Thackeray, b 22 Jan 1902

2f Colin Michael Carnegie Thackeray, b 12 May 1903

3f Bernard John Martin Thackeray, b 6 Oct 1905

4f Una Madeline Agatha Thackeray

7c *Mary Lowndes*, b 4 Feb 1793, d 10 Nov 1863 m 8 Oct 1812, *Edward Jodrell*, b 19 Nov 1785, d 14 Sept 1852, *and had issue* 1d *to* 3d

1d *Edward Jodrell, Capt 18th(?) 10th Royal Irish*, b 9 Aug 1813, d 27 Jan 1868, m 4 July 1843, *Adela Monckton, da of the Rev Sir Edward Bowyer-Smijth of Hill Hall, co Essex, 10th Bt* [E], b 11 Oct 1823, d 23 Sept 1896, *and had issue* 1e *to* 3e

1e Sir Alfred Jodrell, 4th Bt [G B] (*Bayfield Hall, Holt, Norfolk*), b 13 Aug 1847, m 25 Feb 1897, Lady Jane, da of James Walter (Grimston), 2nd Earl of Verulam [U K]

2e Adela Jodrell, m as 2nd wife, 2 June 1885, Sir John Henry Seale, 3rd Bt [U K] (*Wonastow Court, Monmouth*), s p

3e Marianne Jodrell (*Glaven, Harvey Road, Guildford*), m 5 Nov 1868, Frederick John Nash Ind, Major *late 37th Regt*, b 2 Jan 1832, d s p 11 Mar 1906

2d *Rev Henry Jodrell, Rector of Gisleham, co Suffolk*, b 28 Jan 1817 d 16 Dec 1896, m 19 Oct 1843, *Eloisa Fanny Harriet, 2nd Countess of Cape St Vincent (Condessa de Cabo de San Vincent)* [*Portugal*], *da of Adm Sir Charles Napier, 1st Count of Cape St Vincent (Conde de Cabo de San Vincent)* [*Portugal*], *K C B, and had issue* 1e *to* 5e

1e Eloisa Napier Jodrell, m 15 Oct 1870, David John Dickson Safford Col Royal West Kent Regt, b 26 Aug 1837, d 7 Ap 1901, and has issue 1f to 4f

1f Charles John Napier Safford, Capt South Wales Borderers, b 22 June 1871, d 1910, unm   [Nos 10490 to 10577

III

2*f* Napier Edward Frederick Safford, Capt West India Regt, *b* 24 July 1872, *m* 5 June 1901, Louisa Annie Margaret, da of (—) Jewell, and has issue 1g to 2g

1*g* John Charles Safford, *b* 15 June 1905

2*g* Violet Heloise Dorothea Safford

3*f* Maude Heloise Safford, *m* Frank Cox, and has issue 1g to 2g

1*g* Eileen Marjorie Cox

2*g* Mavis Heloise Cox

4*f* Stella Fanny Safford

2*e* Fanny Jodrell (11 *St Andrews Road, W*), *m* 3 June 1879, Henry Hope of Mutland Place, co Hants, *d s p* 12 Ap 1900

3*e* Mary Campbell Jodrell, *m* 28 June 1881, the Rev Philip Sherlock Gooch, Rector of Benacre co Suffolk, *d s p* 29 Ap 1909

4*e* Celia Cator Jodrell, *m* 10 July 1872, the Rev Lewis Richard Charles Bagot, Vicar of Stanton Lacy [B Bagot Coll, and a descendant of King Henry VII (see the Tudor Roll, p 369)] (*Stanton Lacy Vicarage, Bromfield, Salop*), and has issue 1*f* to 4*f*

1*f* Carol Ernest Bagot, *b* 9 Mar 1877, *unm*

2*f* Ysolde Cicely Bagot *m* 1899, B Gordon Snell, *s p*

3*f* Gladys Mary Beatrice Bagot, *m* 18 Jan 1905, Frank Herbert Leake (*Lee Mills House, Cork*), and has issue 1g to 2g

1*g* Maureen Avice Leake

2*g* Merrell Gladys Leake

4*f* Enid Avice Bagot, *m* Sept 1905, Reuben James Charles Jewitt (*Exning, Newmarket*), and has issue 1g

1*g* Dermod James Boris Jewitt, *b* 13 Oct 1908

5*e* Madeleine Jane Jodrell, *m* 3 Sept 1879, Arthur Keane Tharp (112 *St James' Court, Buckingham Gate, S W*, *Eaglehurst, Southampton*)

3*d* Mary Jodrell, *b* 2 Aug 1828, d 29 Mar 1875, *m* 30 May 1854, *Charles Bishop of Marston Lodge, co Oxon,* b 9 Dec 1833, d 26 Oct 1866, *and had issue* 1c

1*e* Mary Louisa Jodrell Bishop, *m* 8 Sept 1880, Frederick Marcus Worsley, *s p*

2*b* Catherine Lowndes, d (? *unm*) [Nos 10578 to 10596

16 Descendants of ELIZABETH STAPYLTON (Table VII), *d.* (—), *m* JOHN DODSWORTH of Thornton Watlass, co York, D L, *b c* 1650, *d* (—), and had issue 1*a* to 2*a*

1*a* John Dodsworth of Thornton Watlass, d (—), *m* 8 Feb 1719, *Henrietta, sister of Matthew Hutton, Archbishop of Canterbury, da of John Hutton of Marske* [also a descendant of King Edward III (see p 120)], d 1797, *and had issue* 1b to 2b

1*b* Henrietta Maria Dodsworth, da and co-h, d (—), *m* 20 July 1761, *Sir Silvester Smith of Newland Park, co York, 1st Bt* [*G B*], so cr 22 Jan 1784, d 15 June 1789, *and had issue* 1c to 2c

1*c* Sir Edward Smith, afterwards (R L 21 May 1821) Dodsworth, 2nd Bt [*G B*], b 13 Aug 1768, d s p 31 Dec 1845

2*c* Sir Charles Smith, afterwards (R L 12 Mar 1846) Dodsworth, 3rd Bt [*G B*], b 22 Aug 1775, d 28 July 1857, *m* 8 June 1808, *Elizabeth, da and h of John Armstrong of Lisgoole, co Fermanagh, by his wife, the Hon Sophia, née Blayney,* d 12 June 1853, *and had issue*

See the Exeter Volume, p 286, Nos 11625-11646 [Nos 10597 to 10618

# of The Blood Royal

2b Elizabeth Dodsworth, da and co-h, b c 1723, d 5 Dec 1772 m c 1750, the Rev James Tunstall. D D , Canon Residentiary of St David's, d 28 Mar 1762, and had issue (of whom 7 das at least survived him,[1] only 3, however, were living in 1772, viz) 1c to 3c

1c Henrietta Maria Tunstall, d (–) , m 14 June 1775, John Croft of Oporto, Merchant, d (–) , and had issue 1d

1d Sir John Croft of Doddington Hall, co Kent, 1st Bt [U K], so c 3 Oct 1818, and 1st Baron da Serra da Estrella [Portugal], so c 11 Dec 1853, K T S D C L , F R S , &c , b (at Oporto) 21 May 1778 , d 5 Feb 1862, m 1st, 1 Aug 1816, Amelia Elizabeth, da of James Warre, d 20 Oct 1819 2ndly, 24 July 1827, Anne Knox, da of the Rev John Radcliffe, Rector of Limehouse, d 5 Mar 1887 and had issue 1e to 2e

1e Sir John Frederick Croft, 2nd Bt [U K], 2nd Baron da Serra da Estrella [Portugal], b 31 Aug 1828 , d 24 May 1904, m 4 June 1856, Emma, da of John. Graham of Skelmorlie Castle, co Ayr and had issue 1f to 12f

1f Sir Frederick Leigh Croft, 3rd Bt [U K], and Baron da Serra da Estrella [Portugal] (Doddington Place, Sittingbourne), b 14 Feb 1860

2f Francis Edgar Croft, b 19 Oct 1861 , m 1891, Zoe, da of (—) Bromley , and has issue 1g to 3g

1g Lilian Mary Croft

2g Cynthia Croft

3g Eleanor Croft

3f William Graham Croft, b 26 Dec 1862

4f Percy Hutton Croft, b 27 Oct 1872

5f Tom Radcliffe Croft, b 1878

6f Constance Margaret Graham Croft, m 14 July 1887 Gilbert Charles Bourne of Cowarne Court, D L (Cowarne Court, Ledbury, Savile House, Oxford), and has issue 1g to 2g

1g Robert Croft Bourne, b 15 July 1888

2g Cecily Radcliffe Bourne

7f Gertrude Mary Croft, m 31 Aug 1893, Arthur John Chitty, Bar at Law [eldest son of the Right Hon Sir Joseph Chitty, P C] (27 Hereford Square, S W , Huntingfield, Faversham, Kent), and has issue 1g to 3g

1g James Malcolm Chitty, b 1898

2g Margaret Hyacinth Chitty

3g Violet Ada Pamela Chitty

8f Elinor Violet Croft, m 13 Oct 1896, Walter Graham Crum (Dalmottar House, Old Kirkpatrick) and has issue 1g

1g Joscelyn Margaret Campbell Crum

9f Ethel Mary Croft, m 1st, 17 Ap 1890, Hubert Hedworth Grenville Wells, d 17 Ap 1904 , 2ndly, 1906, Alfred Benjamin (Holly Lodge, Cookham, Berks), and has issue 1g to 2g

1g Yvo Hedworth Fortescue Grenville Wells, b 6 Sept 1893

2g Rose Allada Grenville Wells

10f Editha Croft, m 6 Mar 1906, Bateman Lancaster Rose, a Member of the London Stock Exchange and Partner in the firm of Linton, Clarke, & Co [5th son of Sir Philip Rose, 1st Bt [U K]] (1 Cromwell Road, S W), and has issue 1g

1g Ronald Paul Lancaster Rose, b 1907

11f Lucy Croft, m 17 Oct 1905, Donald Hatt Noble Graham, Cadet of Anthrey , and has issue

12f Mildred Jessie Graham Croft   [Nos 10619 to 10642

---

[1] "Dict Nat Biog," lvii p 315 Foster (" Yorkshire Pedigrees, Dodsworth ") calls him Dean of St Paul's, and only mentions the 3 das, so presumably the others died unm)

The Plantagenet Roll

2e Elizabeth Anne Croft (*Holme Priory, Wareham*), m 26 Aug 1843, Sir Harry Stephen Meysey-Thompson of Kirkby, 1st Bt [U K], so cr 26 Mar 1874, M P, J P, D L, b 11 Aug 1809, d 17 May 1874, and has issue 1f to 9f

1f Henry Meysey (Meysey-Thompson), 1st Baron Knaresborough [U K], so cr 26 Dec 1905, 2nd Bt, J P, D L, *formerly* M P for Handsworth, &c (*Kirkby Hall, York*), b 30 Aug 1845, m 21 Ap 1885, Ethel Adeline (see p 218), da of Sir Henry Pottinger, 3rd Bt [U K], and has issue 1g to 5g

    1g Hon Claude Henry Meysey Meysey-Thompson, Lieut Rifle Brig, b 5 Ap 1887

    2g Hon Violet Ethel Meysey-Thompson

    3g Hon Helen Winifred Meysey-Thompson

    4g Hon Doris Mary Pottinger Meysey-Thompson

    5g Hon Gwendolen Carles Meysey-Thompson

2f Richard Frederick Meysey-Thompson, Lieut-Col Reserve of Officers, *formerly* Lieut-Col and Hon Col 4th Batt W Yorkshire Regt, &c (*Nunthorpe Court, York*), b 17 Ap 1847, m 14 July 1879, Charlotte, da of Sir James Walker of Sand Hutton, 1st Bt [U K], and has issue 1g to 2g

    1g Algar De Clifford Charles Meysey-Thompson, b 9 Nov 1885

    2g Violet Ileene Cassandra Meysey-Thompson, m 17 Oct 1905, Major Charles William Cuffe-Knox, 4th Batt Rifle Brigade (*Creagh, co Mayo*)

3f Albert Childers Meysey-Thompson, Q C, *Bar-at-Law*, b 13 July 1848, d 20 Mar 1894, m 19 Aug 1882, Mabel Louisa [*a descendant of King Henry VII*], da of Rev the Hon James Walter Lascelles [E. of Harewood Coll], and had issue 1g

    1g Hubert Charles Meysey-Thompson, B A (Camb), Bar-at-Law (*Broxholme, Ripley*), b 9 June 1883

4f Rev Charles Maude Meysey-Thompson, M A, *Rector of Claydon*, b 5 Dec 1849, d 12 Sept 1881, m 28 Ap 1874, Emily Mary (*Hillthorpe House, Scarborough*), da of Sir James Walker of Sand Hutton, 1st Bt [U K], and had issue 1g

    1g Harold James Meysey-Thompson, Capt 4th Batt Rifle Brig (*Army and Navy, Bachelors'*), b 24 Sept 1876

5f Arthur Herbert Meysey-Thompson, *late* Lieut Yorkshire Hussars (*Scarcroft, Yorks*), b 5 Oct 1852, m 1 June 1896, Horatia Dorothy, da of Sir Hedworth Williamson, 8th Bt [E] and has issue 1g to 3g

    1g Guy Herbert Meysey-Thompson, b 21 Sept 1901

    2g Sylvia Dorothy Meysey-Thompson

    3g Diana Elizabeth Meysey-Thompson

6f Ernest Claude Meysey-Thompson, M P, J P, Major Yorkshire Hussars (*Spellow Hill, Staveley, Knaresborough*), b 18 Feb 1859, m 1 Nov 1894, Alice Jane Blanche, da of Col John Joicey of Newton Hall, M P, and has issue 1g to 2g

    1g Onslow Victor Claud Meysey-Thompson, b 1 June 1897

    2g Alice Hildegarde Eva Meysey-Thompson

7f Elizabeth Lucy Meysey-Thompson, m 23 Sept 1868, Walter Stafford (Northcote), 2nd Earl of Iddesleigh [U K], 9th Bart [E], C B, &c (*Pynes, near Exeter*), and has issue 1g to 3g

    1g Stafford Henry Northcote, Viscount St Cyres (*Brooks', Athenaeum*), b 29 Aug 1869

    2g Lady Rosalind Lucy Northcote

    3g Lady Elizabeth Mabel Northcote

8f Mary Caroline Meysey-Thompson, m 2 July 1878, William Henry Bond, *late* Royal Scots (*Tyneham, Wareham*), and has issue 1g to 5g

    1g Algernon Arthur Garneys Bond, Capt and Adj 4th Batt Rifle Brig, b 21 July 1879

[Nos 10643 to 10667

# of The Blood Royal

2g William Ralph Garneys Bond, Sudan C S , b 12 Dec 1880

3g Edith Cicely Garneys Bond

4g Lilian Mary Garneys Bond

5g Margaret Helen Garneys Bond

9f Amelia Annie Meysey-Thompson

2c *Catherine Tunstall (6th da)* d 18 May 1807 , m 1st, *the Rev Edward Chamberlayne, Rector of Charlton* , 2ndly, *as 2nd wife*, 28 July 1806, *Horatio (Walpole), 2nd Earl of Orford [U K]* d (s p by her) 15 June 1822

3c *Jane Tunstall,* d 26 May 1841 , m 1st, *Stephen Thompson,* d (−) , 2ndly, 3 Nov 1792, *Sir Everard Home, 1st Bt [U K], F R S President R C S and Sergeant-Surgeon to King George III* , b 6 May 1716, d 31 Aug 1832 , **and had issue 1d to 3d**

1d *Sir James Everard Home, 2nd Bt [U K],* b 25 Oct 1798, d s p

2d *Mary Elizabeth Home,* b c 1795, d 9 Ap 1811 m 28 Oct 1815, *Charles Powlett Rushworth [son of Edward Rushworth of Farringford Hill, I W , by his wife, the Hon Catharine, da and co-h of Leonard (Troughear), 1st Lord Holmes of Kilmallock [I 1797], b c 1790, d 15 Oct 1854, and had (with 2 other sons and 4 das who d s p) issue 1e to 4e*

1e *Edward Everard Rushworth C M G , D C L , Colonial Secretary and Lieut - Governor of Jamaica,* b 23 Aug 1818, d of yellow fever in Jamaica 10 Aug 1877 , m 1st, 13 Jan 1855, *Amelia Adelaide, da of Horatio Nelson de les Derniers of Vaucheul, Lower Canada, d (−) , and had (with a son and 2 das who d unm) issue 1f to 4f*

1f Edward Henry Rushworth, b 2 Dec 1864, unm

2f William Arthur Rushworth (*United States*), b 3 Nov 1866 , m and has issue a son and da

3f Harriet Jane Rushworth, m 21 Jan 1875 Gilbert Robertson Sandbach [son of the Rev Gilbert Sandbach of Woodlands, co Lancaster] (*Stoneleigh, Rossett, Denbigh*) , and has issue 1g to 6g

1g Gilbert Robertson Sandbach, b 22 Aug 1892

2g Adelaide Mary Sandbach, b 1 July 1878

3g Doris Annette Sandbach, b 10 Jan 1883

4g Eleanor Katherine Sandbach, b 6 Jan 1884

5g Violet Marion Sandbach, b 10 Aug 1885

6g Margaret Elizabeth Sandbach, b 3 Aug 1895

4f Rosamond Linda Rushworth m 16 Ap 1884, the Rev Cecil Evan Smith, Rector of Titsey (*Titsey Rectory, Limpsfield, Surrey*) , and has issue 1g to 4g

1g Everard Cecil Smith, Lieut 3rd Batt Royal Fusiliers 1908, educ Winchester Coll 1897-1903, and Sandhurst 1904-1905, b 3 Feb 1885

2g Charles Home Cecil Smith, educ Winchester Coll 1902-1906 and Trinity Coll , Camb , 1907, b 8 May 1889

3g Rosamond Mary Cecil Smith, b 21 Dec 1885

4g Linda Katharine Cecil Smith, b 27 Jan 1891

2e *Horatia Ann Rushworth,* b 21 July 1823 , d 5 Mar 1859, m 12 July 1851, *Marcus Staunton Lynch-Staunton of Clydagh, co Galway, Bar -at-Law,* d 19 Oct 1896 , *and had issue 1f to 2f*

1f Charles Rushworth Lynch-Staunton of Clydagh, Inspector Local Government Board, Ireland, 1892 (*Clydagh, Headford, Tuam*), b 1851

2f Alice Lynch Staunton

3e *Rosamond Rushworth,* b 17 Oct 1830 , d 24 June 1904, m 3 Oct 1861, *Sir Arthur Townley Watson, 2nd Bt [U K 1866], K C,* d 15 Mar 1907, *and had issue 1f to 4f*

1f Sir Charles Rushworth Watson, 3rd Bt [U K] (*Reigate Lodge, Reigate K5 The Albany, Piccadilly, The Elms, Prior's Hardwick, &c , Travellers'*), b 21 Sept 1865.   [Nos 10668 to 10689

115

The Plantagenet Roll

2f Arthur Watson, now Cotton-Watson, Capt 4th Batt Royal Irish Rifles (*Isthmian*), b 3 Aug 1870

3f Mabel Frederica Watson, m 11 Aug 1887, the Rev Reginald Fitz-Hugh Bigg-Wither, Rector of Wonston (*Wonston Rectory, Micheldever, Hants*), and has issue 1g to 2g

　1g Olga Mary Bigg-Wither

　2g Joan Gertrude Bigg-Wither

4f Amy Catherine Rose Watson

4e Frederica Rushworth, b 13 Dec 1836, m 4 Oct 1855, the Rev William Birkett, d (-), and has issue 1f to 4f

　1f Trevor Birkett

　2f Mary Birkett,

　3f Leonora Birkett,　} all m to Germans and residing abroad

　4f Frederica Birkett,

3d *Charlotte Home*, b 26 Dec 1802, d 21 *Jan* 1878, m 1823, *Capt Bernard Yeoman, R N* [*also descended from King Edward III through the Mortimer-Percy marriage (see p 252)*], d 23 Ap 1836, *and had (with an elder son, Henry Lievrard, who d s p) issue 1e to 3e*

　1e Constantine Laurence Yeoman, Capt R H A and Lieut-Col Turkish Army (25 Orchard Street, Brentford, Middlesex), b 1828, unm

　2e Linda Constantia Yeoman, m 4 Aug 1857, Francis Rowden of the Inner Temple, Bar-at-Law (72 *Braybrooke Road, Hastings*), and has (with a son and a dr who d s p) issue 1f to 6f

　　1f Francis Constantine Bernard Rowden, b 22 Ap 1860, unm

　　2f Linda Everardina Rowden, unm

　　3f Rosa Charlotte Rowden, m 25 Mar 1901, John Richards Orpen, Bar at-Law (*Dublin*), and has issue 1g

　　　1g Dorothy Esther Penelope Orpen

　　4f Dora Rowden, unm

　　5f Eva Rowden, unm

　　6f Maud Octavia Rowden, m 14 Nov 1906, Frederick Oddin-Taylor, D L (*Norwich*), s p

　2e *Rosa Charlotte Yeoman*, b 12 *May* 1831, d 21 *May* 1908, m 18 *Feb* 1857, *the Rev Edward Woodyatt, M A (Oxon), Vicar of Over (St John's Vicarage, Over, Cheshire), and had issue 1f to 8f*

　　1f Nigel Gresley Woodyatt, Col Ghurka Rifles, b 30 Mar 1861, m 12 Nov 1887, Florence Emily Stewart, da of Arthur Blakeley Patterson, C S I , and has issue 1g

　　　1g Reginald Nigel Gresley Woodyatt, b 1890

　　2f Edward Woodyatt (*Trunch, North Walsham, Norfolk*), b 23 Dec 1867, m Oct 1903, Lillian, da of James Blanchflower of Norfolk, d 1907, and has issue 1g

　　　1g Gwendolen Yeoman Woodyatt

　　3f Bernard Hale Woodyatt, M R C S , Surg Albert Infirmary, Winsford (*Over, Winsford*), b 1 June 1869, unm

　　4f George Everard Staples Woodyatt, Capt 7th Batt Royal Fusiliers (86 *Eaton Terrace, S W*), b 27 Mar 1873, m 3 Oct 1894, Rosalie Frances Helen, da of Capt Luxmoore Brooke of Ashbrook Towers, co Chester, and has issue 1g

　　　1g Henry Luxmoore Brooke Woodyatt, b 19 Sept 1897

　　5f Henry Constantine Woodyatt, M R C S , Staff Surgeon R N , b 18 May 1875, unm

　　6f Florence Woodyatt, unm

　　7f Rosa Louisa Woodyatt, m 21 Ap 1895, James Henry Wakeman Best [son

[Nos 10690 to 10718

116

of James Best of Holt Castle, co Worcester] (*The Stocks, Suckley, Worcester*), and has issue 1g to 4g

    1g James Edward Best, *b* 1 Jan 1905

    2g Violet Rosalie Best, *b* 8 Ap 1896

    3g Florence Beatrice Best, *b* 5 July 1898

    4g Doris May Best, *b* 17 May 1902

    8f Edith Beatrice Woodyatt

    2a *Dorothy Dodsworth*, d (-), m (—) *Bartlet of Nutwitheral, in the parish of Masham*   [Nos 10719 to 10723]

47 Descendants of the Rev HENRY STAPYLTON, M A (Oxon), Rector of Thornton Watlass and Marske, co York (Table VII), *d* 9 Feb 1748, *m* MARY, da and h of the Rev. (—) ORCHARD, *bur* 22 Dec 1755, and had issue 1*a* to 5*a*

    1a *Rev John Stapylton, M A, Rector of Thornton Watlass*, bapt 19 *Sept* 1707, d 3 Oct 1767, m 2ndly, 4 Feb 1751, *Lucy, da of Thomas Wycliffe of Gailes, co York, and had issue* 1b

    1b *Henry Stapylton of Norton, co Durham, J P*, d Aug 1835, m 3 *Jan* 1786, *Mary Ann, da and h of Capt Robert Gregory, R N* [*by his wife, (—), da and event h of Rear-Adm Polycarpus Taylor of Norton*], d (—), *and had issue* 1c *to* 3c

    1c *Robert Martin Stapylton, Army Pay Office*, b 21 Sept 1793, d 17 *Jan* 1864, m 16 *Ap* 1818, *Martha Eliza, da of John Bockett of Southcote Lodge, co Berks*, d (—), *and had issue* 1d *to* 1d

    1d *Robert George Stapylton, Bar-at-Law*, b 13 Aug 1820, d 6 Jan 1873, m 24 May 1855, *Madalina Clementina, da of the Rev George Hull Bowers, D D, Dean of Manchester*, d (—), *and had issue* 1e *to* 3e

    1e Rev Robert Miles Stapylton, *b* 15 Ap 1864, *m* 1892, Margaret, da of the Rev T Sharpe, Rector of Little Downham and Canon of Ely, and has issue 1f

        1f John Miles Stapylton, *b* 18 Nov 1896

    2e Olive Harriet Stapylton, *unm*

    3e Mary Ursula Stapylton, *m* Walter H Thorley

    2d *Henry Stapylton, emigrated to Australia 1852*, b 15 Aug 1834, d 6 May 1902, m *at St Andrew's Church, Braidwood*, 6 Jan 1859, *Margaret, da of Edward O'Conor of Dublin and had issue* 1e *to* 3e

    1e Robert Miles Stapylton (*Norton, Wardell Road, Dulwich Hill, Sydney, N S W*), *b* 20 Oct 1859, *m* 24 Jan 1885, Elizabeth, da of William McCann of Sydney, N S W

    2e Edward Stapylton, Justice Dept, *b* 9 Nov 1862, *m* Jane, da of Henry Underhill, J P, and has issue 1f

        1f Edward Stapylton

    3e Henry Miles Stapylton, Postal Telegraph Dept, *b* 25 Oct 1865, *m* Caroline, da of C Womsen, and has issue 1f *to* 4f

        1f Alan Stapylton

        2f Miles Stapylton

        3f Robert Stapylton

        4f Margaret Stapylton

    3d Miles Stapylton (20 *Mortlake Road, Kew, Surrey*), *b* 9 Feb 1836, *m* 1 Feb 1868, Sarah Dorcas, da of the Rev Benjamin Bradney Bockett, M A, Vicar of Epsom, and has issue 1c *to* 5c   [Nos 10724 to 10736]

The Plantagenet Roll

1e *Bryan Stapylton, Vol Paget's Horse,* b 23 Nov 1870, d *of wounds in South Africa* 13 Mar 1901

2e *Alan Stapylton,* M I C E, b 16 May 1872, m 27 Oct 1904, Beatrice, da of the Rev S Goldney, M A , and has issue 1/

    1/ Mabel Grace Stapylton, b 26 July 1905

3e Ella Mary Stapylton, *unm*

4e Mabel Dorcas Stapylton, *unm*

5e Kathleen Eliza Stapylton, m 16 Sept 1905, Horatio John Nelson Hawkins, C E, s p

    4d Mary Jane Stapylton, *unm*

2c *Mary Frances Stapylton,* d 18 May 1878, m 2 Dec 1824, *Marshall Robinson, afterwards (R L* 19 Aug 1828) *Fowler, of Preston Hall, co Durham* [*Robinson of Herrington Coll*], d 28 Feb 1871, *and had issue (with 2 sons d s p)* 1d to 2d

1d *Robinson Fowler, Bar-at-Law, Stip Mag at Manchester,* b 15 Mar 1828, d 16 Jan 1895, m 1st, 18 June 1849 (*dissolved* 1 Feb 1859), *Olivia Stapylton* (see p 119), da *of George William Sutton of Elton Hall, co Durham* , 2ndly, 29 Aug 1859, *Anne Agnes Erskine, da of Very Rev the Hon Henry David Erskine, Dean of Ripon* (see p 227), *and had issue* 1e to 3e

1e *Marshall Robinson Fowler, afterwards (D P* 1878) *Stapylton,* b 2 May 1850, d 21 Ap 1894, m 28 Dec 1878, *Alice Edith, da of* (—) *Attwood,* d 17 Dec 1881, *and had issue* 1/

    1/. Algernon Marshall Stapylton, *formerly in the Army (Australia),* b 17 Sept 1881, *unm*

2e George Stapylton Fowler, b 30 Mar 1851, *unm*

3e Florence Mary Fowler, *unm*

2d *Marshall Fowler of Preston,* J P, *cos Durham and York (Otterington House, Northallerton),* b 3 May 1834, m 19 Dec 1893, *Emily Hindman, widow of Robert Walton, da of Capt James William Armstrong,* R N , s p

3c *Olivia Stapylton,* b 13 Ap 1793, d Feb 1883, m 21 Ap 1824, *George William Sutton (R L* 17 Oct 1822), *previously Hutchinson, of Elton Hall, co Durham,* d 1852, *and had issue (with a son and da d unm)* 1d to 3d

1d *John Stapylton Sutton (Faceby, Northallerton),* b 23 Nov 1832, m 1855, *Sarah Jefferson, da of John Charles Maynard of Hartsey Hall, Northallerton,* and has issue 1e to 3e

1e *George William Sutton, Land Agent (Eaglescliffe, Yarm),* b Dec 1857, m 1900, Laura, da of (—) Johnson, d 1902, and has issue 1/

    1/ Eric John Stapylton Sutton, b 28 Dec 1901

2e Catherine Olivia Sutton, *unm*

3e *Laura Eugenie Sutton (Faceby Manor, Northallerton),* m 19 Ap 1886, *Martin Morrison of Faceby Manor,* d Feb 1900, *and has issue* 1/ to 6/

    1/ Ronald John Martin Morrison, b 10 Aug 1884

    2/ Martin James Morrison, b 20 Aug 1893

    3/ James William Sutton Morrison, b 11 Dec 1897

    4/ Hilda Olive Eugenie Morrison

    5/ Riva Sarah Mary Morrison

    6/ Florence Beryl Morrison

2d *Grace Sutton,* b 12 Aug 1826, d 17 Dec 1891, m 4 June 1850, *the Rev Henry Master, Vicar of Skeffling, co Yorks,* b *at Winestead, Hull,* 20 June 1813, d 18 June 1898, *and had issue* 1e to 6c

1e Reginald Henry Master, b 19 June 1851, *unm*

2e *George Sutton Master (New Zealand),* b 11 July 1855, m Rose, da of (—) Andrewes of Hull, and has issue (4 sons and 3 das)

[Nos 10737 to 10759.

# of The Blood Royal

3e Rev Arthur Gerald Maister, Vicar of Mumby (*Mumby Vicarage, Alford*) *b* 20 Feb 1862, *m* 19 Sept 1899, Edith Jane, da of John Reed, *s p*

4e Henrietta Grace Maister, *unm*

5e Olivia Lucy Maister (*Ravenser, Easington, Hull*), *unm*

6e Edith Everild Maister, *m* May 1888, the Rev John Thomas, Vicar of Cutcombe (*Cutcombe Vicarage, Dunster, Somerset*), and has issue 1*f*

1*f* Henry Evan Eric Thomas, *b* 26 May 1900

3*d* Olivia Stapylton Sutton, b 2 May 1830, d 20 Oct 1872, m as 1st wife, 18 June 1849, Robinson Fowler of London, Bar-at-Law, d 16 Jan 1895, and had issue

See p 118, Nos 10743-10745

2a Elizabeth Stapylton, bapt 26 Aug 1698, d (–), m Richard Tennant

3a Sarah Stapylton, bapt 19 Feb 1703, d 29 Sept 1783, m 8 Aug 1733, *Thomas Raisbeck of Stockton and Durham, Solicitor, Mayor of Stockton 1737-1738, 1747-1757, d Feb 1765, and had issue 1b to 2b* [1]

1b Thomas Stapylton Raisbeck of Stockton, Solicitor, Mayor of that town 1769, 1770, and 1788, b c 1740, d 4 Dec 1794, m Sarah, da of Leonard Robinson of Stockton, d 5 Mar 1813, and had issue 1c

1c Leonard Raisbeck of Stockton, Solicitor, d s p 1845

2b William Raisbeck of Newcastle-on-Tyne, living 1768, m Mary, da of (—) Gunn, and had issue (a son who d s p and) 1c to 2c

1c Sarah Raisbeck, } d (? unm)
2c Mary Raisbeck, }

4a Olivia Stapylton, bapt 19 Sept 1707, d (–), m 13 Ap 1738, the Rev *Thomas Robinson, M A, Rector of Wycliffe, co York, and had issue 1b*

1b Mary Robinson, d 19 July 1815, m 1771, Joshua Greenwell of Kibblesworth, co Durham, d 26 Aug 1797, and had issue 1c

1c Robinson Robert Greenwell of Newcastle, b 3 Ap 1778 d Nov 1841, m 2 Feb 1819, Elizabeth, da of John Mellar of Whitby, d 7 Jan 1822, and had issue 1d

1d Rev William Greenwell of Carr Mount, co York, M A, b 5 Nov 1819, d 30 Mar 1899, m 15 May 1851, Jane, da of the Rev William Blow, M A., Rector of Goodmanham, d 22 Dec 1879, and had issue 1e to 5e

1e Leonard William Greenwell, b 26 June 1853

2e Harold Stapylton Greenwell, b 10 Jan 1857

3e Augusta Isabella Greenwell, m 22 Oct 1878, Alan Greenwell (34 *Old Elvet, Durham*), and has issue 1*f* to 2*f*

1*f* Alan Leonard Stapylton Greenwell, b 29 Jan 1880

2*f* William Basil Greenwell, Lieut Durham L I, b 29 Oct 1881

4e Olivia Greenwell

5e Ethel Edith Mary Greenwell

5a Henrietta Stapylton, bapt 3 Sept 1714, d (–), m 14 Feb 1740, John Soux of London 　　　　　　　　　　　　　　　　　　[Nos 10760 to 10774

48 Descendants of FRANCES NORCLIFFE of Heslington (Table VII), *b* 16 Sept 1700, *d* 15 July 1770, *m* 4 Mar 1728, SIR JOHN WRAY of Sleningford, 12th Bt [E], *b* 24 Oct 1689; *d* 26 Jan 1752, and had issue

See the Clarence Volume, pp 574-581, Nos 21241-24413
　　　　　　　　　　　　　　　　　　[Nos 10775 to 10977

---

[1] Nichol's "Topographer and Genealogist," ii 91

119

The Plantagenet Roll

49 Descendants of FRANCES STAPYLTON (Table VII), bur 5 May 1684, m (settlement dated 13 Sept) 1651, JOHN HUTTON (see p 310) of Marske, co York, b 6 Oct 1625, d 21 Mar 1664, and had issue 1a to 3a

1a John Hutton of Marske, b 14 July 1657, bur 2 Mar 1731, m (settlement dated 24 Nov) 1680, Dorothy, da and co-h of William Dyke of Frant, co Sussex, bur 7 Jan 1743, and had issue 1b to 4b

1b John Hutton of Marske, bapt 18 Nov 1691, d 16 Jan 1768, m 2ndly, 5 Mar 1726, the Hon Elizabeth, da and co-h of James (Darcy), 1st Lord Darcy of Navan [G B], bapt 13 Oct 1706 bur 10 June 1739, and had issue

See the Exeter Volume, pp 555-558, Nos 49684-49747

2b Most Rev Matthew Hutton, D D, Lord Bishop of York 1747-1757, and of Canterbury 1757-1758, b 3 Jan 1692, d 19 Mar 1758, leaving issue now extinct

3b Timothy Hutton, bapt 31 Mar 1696

4b Henrietta Hutton, bapt 23 Oct 1701, d 1797, m 8 Feb 1719, John Dodsworth of Thornton Watlass, co York, and had issue

See p 112, Nos 10597-10723

2a Frances Hutton, b 7 Mar 1653, d (-), m Andrew Wanley of Eyford, co Gloucester

3a Olive Hutton, b 30 Nov 1656, d (-), m Thomas Alcock of Chatham, bur (at Marske) 13 Dec 1698   [Nos 10978 to 11168

50 Descendants, if any surviving, of URSULA STAPYLTON (Table VII), d (admon. to da 21 Ap) 1693, m THOMAS PEPYS of Hatcham, Barnes, and Merton Abbey, co Surrey, Master of Jewel Office to Kings Charles II and James II and VII, bapt 16 Jan 1640, d. (-), and had (with possibly other) issue 1a

1a Olivia Pepys, m before 21 Ap 1693, Sir Edward Smith of Edmondthorp, co Leicester [1]

51 Descendants of ELEANOR SLINGSBY (Table IV), d 1647, m as 1st wife, Sir ARTHUR INGRAM of Temple Newsham (Table IV), d 1655, and had issue 1a to 2a

1a Henry (Ingram), 1st Viscount Irvine [S], bapt 8 Ap 1641, bur 13 Aug 1666, m (lic dated 7 June) 1661, Lady Essex, da of Edward (Montagu), 2nd Earl of Manchester [E], d (will dated 4, prov 13 Oct) 1677, and had issue

See the Essex Volume, Table X, and pp 149-152, Nos 17211-17285

2a Arthur Ingram of Barrowby, co York, d 13 Sept 1713, m Jane, da of Sir John Mallory of Studley, co York, bur 3 Aug 1693, and had issue 1b to 6b

1b Thomas Ingram, d 19 Feb 1703, m Frances, da and h of John Nicholson of York, M D [m 2ndly, John Wood of Copmanthorpe, Bar-at-Law, and] d 23 Mar 1740, and had issue (with 2 sons who d in infancy) 1c

1c Frances Ingram, presumably dead s p before 1708

2b Arthur Ingram, a Turkey Merchant, heir to his nephew Arthur, May 1708,
                                                  [Nos 11169 to 11243

[1] "Genealogy of the Pepys Family, 1273-1887," by W C Pepys   London, 1887   Pedigree V

# of The Blood Royal

d (-), m *Elizabeth, da of* (—) *Barns, and had issue which became extinct* 22 *May* 1830

 3b *Mallory Ingram*
 4b *Mary Ingram*
 5b *Katherine Ingram*
 6b *Elizabeth Ingram,* d *Ap* 1717 ,[1] m *as 1st wife,* 1709, *Anstrupus Danby of Swinton and Farnley, co York,* b 1680, d 12 *Mar* 1750, *and had issue which became extinct* 4 *Dec* 1833

52 Descendants, if any surviving, of the Rev CHARLES SLINGSBY, Rector of Rothbury (Table IV), *bapt* 22 Nov 1561, d (-), m ELIZABETH, da of John ELLIS of Bamborough, co York, and had issue 1a to 3a [2]

 1a *Thomas Slingsby, aged* 17 *and unm* 1617, bur 10 *Feb* 1670
 2a *Margaret Slingsby,* m *Thomas Barret of York*
 3a *Mary Slingsby, aged* 20, 1617

53 Descendants, if any surviving, of Sir WILLIAM SLINGSBY of Kippax, co Midx , D L, Carver to Queen Anne of Denmark (Table IV), d. Aug 1624 ; m. ELIZABETH, da of Sir Stephen BOARD of Boardshill, co Sussex , and had issue 1a to 2a [3]

 1a *Henry Slingsby, Master of the Mint to King Charles I , and as such author of the motto* " Decus et Tutamen " *which appears on the coinage,* b c 1620, d (-) m *according to some,* (—), *da of Sir* (—) *Cage, and to others, Catherine, da of Sir William Lowther of Great Preston , and who had issue* 1b
 1b *Elizabeth Slingsby, da and in* 1697 *sole h ,* d (-), m *Adlard Cage of Thavies Inn, Midx*

 2a *Elizabeth Slingsby, aged* 8 in 1627

54 Descendants, if any surviving, of Sir GUILDFORD SLINGSBY, Comptroller of the Navy (Table IV), *bapt* 7 Oct. 1565 , d at sea 1631 , m 1609, MARGARET, da of William WATTER of Cundall, Lord Mayor of York in 1620, and had issue 1a to 11a

 1a *Guildford Slingsby, Lieut of the Ordnance Office and Sec to the great Earl of Stafford,* bur 26 *Jan* 1642
 2a *Sir Robert Slingsby of Newcells,* 1st Bt [E], so cr 16 *Mar* 1661, b c 1611, d s p 26 Oct 1661
 3a *Percy Slingsby*
 4a *Walter Slingsby*
 5a *George Slingsby*
 6a *Francis Slingsby of St Martin's in the Fields, will proved* 1670
 7a *Sir Arthur Slingsby of Bifrons,* 1st Bt [E], so cr 19 *Oct* 1657, b c 1623, bur 12 *Feb* 1666, m (—), *a Flemish lady who was living* 26 *Ap* 1666, *and had issue* 1b *to* 4b

---

[1] J Fisher's "History of Masham," p 244
[2] Foster's " Yorkshire Pedigrees "   [3] Ibid

The Plantagenet Roll

1b *Sir Charles Slingsby of Bifrons, 2nd Bt [E], living abroad 1670, sold Bifrons 1677, after which nothing is known of him*

2b *Peter Slingsby, living abroad with brother 1670*

3b *Anna Charlotte Slingsby, bapt 4 Jan 1664, d (-), m Sir Edward Nightingale, de jure 5th Bt [E], bapt 27 Aug 1658, d 2 July 1723, and had issue* See the Exeter Volume, Table XXXIII and pp 428-433, Nos 34734-34997

4b *Mary Slingsby, b posthumous and bapt at Patrixbourne 26 Ap 1666*

8a *Dorothy Slingsby, d (-), m Jeffrey Nightingale of Kneesworth, co Camb*

9a *Margaret Slingsby*   10a *Mary Slingsby*   11a *Anne Slingsby*
[Nos 11244 to 11507

55 Descendants, if any surviving, of Sir FRANCIS SLINGSBY of Kilmore, co. Cork (Table IV), d. (-), m ELIZABETH, da of Hugh CUFF of Cuff Hall, co Somerset, and had issue 1a to 7a [1]

1a *Francis Slingsby*   4a *Catherine Slingsby*   6a *Elizabeth Slingsby*
2a *Henry Slingsby*   5a *Anne Slingsby*   7a *Jane Slingsby*
3a *Mary Slingsby*

56 Descendants, if any, of CATHERINE PERCY, sister to the 7th and 8th Earls of Northumberland [E] (Table II), d (-), m RALPH [RITHER] RETHERS

57. Descendants of Sir WILLIAM HARRIS of Shenfield Manor, in Margaretting, co Essex, Knighted at the Coronation of King James I, 23 July 1603 (Table II), d (-), m FRANCES, da of Thomas ASTLEY of Writtle, and had (with possibly other) issue 1a

1a *Frances Harris, bur at Walter Belchamp, 1678, m Oliver Raymond of Belchamp Hall, co Essex, M P for Essex in Cromwell's Parliaments, 1653 and 1656, d (-), and had issue 1b to 21b*

1b *St Clere Raymond, disinherited on account of marriage, became Steward to Duke of Rutland, d (-), bur at Grantham, m Anne, da of Lawrence Warkham, and had issue 1c to 9c*

1c *John Raymond, M A (Emmanuel College, Camb) and of Gray's Inn, bur in Walter Belchamp Church, 1690, m Anne, da of Sir Roger Burgoyne, 2nd Bt [E], and had issue a son, John, who d s p 1720*

2c *William Raymond of Belchamp Hall, after his nephew, d s p 1732, will dated 20 Oct 1727, proved P C C 9 July 1733*

3c *Samuel Raymond, d (-), being blown up in a ship, m and had issue 1d*

1d *William Raymond, living 20 Oct 1737, d (-), m and had issue 1e*

1e *Rev Samuel Raymond of Belchamp Hall, co Essex, inherited the family estates on the death of his great-uncle, 1732, d 5 Jan 1767, m Isabella, da of Richard Child of Lavenham, co Suffolk, M D, d (-), and had issue 1f to 2f*

1f *Rev Samuel Raymond of Belchamp Hall, Rector of Belchamp and Middleton and Vicar of Bulmer, co Essex, b 1744, d 18 Jan 1825, m 1780, Margaretta, da of the Rev Nathaniel Brook Bridges, Rector of Orlingbury [by his wife Ann, nee Smythies], d 29 Sept 1849, and had issue 1g to 3g*

1g *Samuel Milbank Raymond of Belchamp Hall, J P, b 6 Feb 1787, d 18 Jan 1863, m 7 Mar 1808, Sarah, da of the Rev William Cooke, Rector of Preston, and had issue 1h to 3h*

---

[1] Foster's " Yorkshire Pedigrees "

# of The Blood Royal

1h Rev John Mayne St Clere Raymond of Belchamp Hall, sometime Vicar of Dinnington, &c , b 23 July 1811, d 1 Dec 1893, m 12/13 May 1857, Louisa Anne, da of the Rev Charles Fisher, Rector of Ovington-cum-Tilbury, d 7 Feb 1895, and had issue 1i

1i Samuel John St Clere Raymond of Belchamp Hall, J P , b 11 July 1859, d 9 Ap 1900, m 22 Oct 1884, Margaret Charlotte Montague (The Rectory House, Great Yeldham, Essex), da of Francis Smithies of Headgate House, Colchester, and had issue 1j

1j Samuel Philip St Clere Raymond of Belchamp Hall, Lord of the Manor of Belchamp Walter and Patron of Belchamp-cum-Bulmer, &c (Belchamp Hall, near Sudbury, Suffolk), b 26 Ap 1886

2h. Isabella Raymond, b at Belchamp, 19 Mar 1810, d at Bury St Edmunds, 18 Ap 1848, m Rowland Dalton of Bury St Edmunds, Surgeon, b 10 Jan 1801, d at Bury St Edmunds, 21 Aug 1890, and had issue 1i to 7i

1i Henry Dalton, Naturalist (82 Boulevard du Port Royal, Paris), b 18 Mar 1836, m

2i Oliver Dalton, Clerk in the Custom House, London, b 8 May 1842, d 11 Oct 1881, m

3i Walter Dalton, emigrated to the United States, where he is still living, b 11 Feb 1844, m

4i Alfred Dalton, emigrated to the United States, where he is still living, b 11 Oct 1846, m

5i Isabella Dalton, m 20 Sept 1859, Francis Winter Clarke, Surgeon (Wrentham, Foxenden Road, Guildford)

6i Margaretta Dalton (Asngarth, Parkstone Avenue, Parkstone), m 31 Oct 1870, Francis Reginald Statham of Liverpool, Author, d 4 Mar 1908, and has issue (with a 3rd son, Gilbert, who d 19 Sept 1894) 1j to 4j

1j Paul Bernard Statham, Draughtsman and Surveyor, b 22 Aug 1871

2j Claude Oliver Statham, Electrical Engineer, b 5 Feb 1877

3j Margaret Lilian Statham

4j Violet Statham, m 7 June 1905, John Henry Crake Vaughan [eldest son of Prebendary Vaughan of Wraxall, near Bristol], and has issue 1k

1k Margaret Christine Vaughan, b 21 July 1908

7i Octavia Dalton, unm

3h Emma Brereton Raymond, m 16 Feb 1858, Frederick Perry, d 24 Dec 1885, and has issue 1i

1i Rev Clement Raymond Perry, D D (Oxford), Rector of Mickfield (Mickfield Rectory, Suffolk), b 8 Dec 1858, m 25 July 1888, Florence Kathleen, da of Henry John Thorp, M D , and has issue 1j to 3j

1j Arthur Stanley Raymond Perry, b 26 Sept 1892

2j Edward John St Clere Perry, b 21 June 1901

3j Winifred Eleanor Victoria Perry, b 21 Oct 1896

2g Rev Oliver Raymond, LL B , Rural Dean, Rector of Middleton and Vicar of Belchamp, b 9 Jan 1794, d 15 Sept 1869, m 4 Feb 1817, Anne, da of the Rev Charles Andrewes, Rector of Flempton, d 1 June 1863, and had issue 1h to 7h

1h Rev Oliver Edward Raymond, M A (Camb), Rector of Middleton (Middleton Rectory, Sudbury, Suffolk), b 22 Nov 1825, m 1st, 30 Jan 1851, Ellen Jane, da of William Foster, d 23 May 1876, 2ndly, 6 Ap 1880, Frances Elizabeth (see p 126), da of John Greene, and has issue 1i to 6i

1i Oliver John Raymond, b 23 Ap 1853, m 27 Nov 1880, Clara Catherine, da of (—) Robson, d 30 May 1900, and has issue 1j to 4j

1j John Raymond, b 5 Feb 1890

2j Katharine Margaret Raymond, b 9 Oct 1881

3j Ellen Gertrude Raymond, b 11 June 1883

4j Olive Mary Raymond, b 8 Mar 1886

[Nos 11508 to 11530

123

The Plantagenet Roll

2ı Rev Philip Foster Raymond, Senior Chaplain to the Forces (*Aldershot*), b 11 July 1855, m 19 Jan 1881, Christine Louisa, da of Thomas Ruggles Fisher, and has issue 1ı to 4ı

   1ı Hugh Philip Raymond, b 15 Feb 1889

   2ı Cicely Raymond, b 22 Nov 1881

   3ı Eva Christine Raymond, b 3 Ap 1884

   4ı Lois Raymond, b 8 Feb 1891

3ı Percy Algernon Raymond, b 22 Sept 1860, m 17 July 1886, Amy, da of (—) Turner, and has issue 1ı to 3ı

   1ı Harry Turner Raymond, b 11 Feb 1893

   2ı Ada Louisa Raymond, b 24 Ap 1887

   3ı Mildred May Raymond, b 23 Oct 1903

1ı Lionel Charles Raymond, Assist Manager Colonial Sugar Refining Coy (*Fiji*), b 20 Mar 1868 m 13 Feb 1895, Edith, da of (—) Dornwell, and has issue 1ı to 2ı

   1ı Oliver Claude Raymond, b 2 Dec 1895

   2ı Rowland Lionel Raymond, b 12 Jan 1899

5ı Ellen Margaret Isabella Raymond, m 10 Oct 1883, Robert George Hallowell-Carew, *formerly* a Tea Planter in Assam (*see* p 125) (8 *Raleigh Villas, Exmouth*), and has issue 1ı to 2ı

   1ı Robert Raymond Hallowell-Carew, Lieut R N, b 6 Sept 1884

   2ı Margaret Maude Hallowell-Carew, b 27 Aug 1886

6ı Mary Louisa Raymond, *unm*

2h Rev Charles Andrewes Raymond, M A, Vicar of Bray (*Bray Vicarage, Maidenhead*), b 16 Oct 1833, m 5 Ap 1864, Elizabeth, da of the Rev John Maynard, Rector of Sudbourne, and has issue 1ı to 3ı

1ı Rev William Maynard Raymond, Vicar of SS Peter and Paul, Upper Teddington (*Upper Teddington, Midx*), b 23 Feb 1868, m 27 Jan 1898, Julia May, da of the Rev Charles Cooke of Alverley Hall, Doncaster, and has issue 1ı to 5ı

   1ı Oswald William Edward Raymond, b 22 May 1902

   2ı Hugh Medlicott Raymond, b 17 Oct 1903

   3ı Monica Raymond

   4ı Nancy May Raymond

   5ı Audrey Mary Raymond

2ı Anne Maynard Raymond, m 3 Jan 1895, the Rev Thomas Henry Wrenford, Vicar of Littlewick (*Littlewick Vicarage, Maidenhead*), and has issue 1ı

   1ı Cecil Raymond Brookes Wrenford, b 23 May 1896

3ı Katharine Elizabeth Raymond, m 18 Nov 1896, the Rev Robert Perceval Newhouse, Vicar of St Laurence's, Reading (*St Laurence's Vicarage, Reading*), and has issue 1ı to 3ı

   1ı Katharine Raymond Newhouse

   2ı Clare Maynard Newhouse

   3ı Mary Perceval Newhouse

3h *Margaretta Lyon Raymond*, b 22 Nov 1817, d 23 *Jan* 1852, m 9 *Oct 1845, George Ure Skinner* [*son of Dean John Skinner of Forfar and grandson of John Skinner, Lord Bishop of Aberdeen*], d 9 *Jan* 1867, *and had issue (with a son and da d in infancy)* 1ı to 2ı

1ı Margaretta Raymond Skinner (30 *Gordon Road, Ealing*), m 30 Ap 1872, the Rev George Ruggle Fisher, Chaplain to H M Forces, *previously* 102nd Regt, Medal and Clasps for Pegu, 1852–1853, d 22 Oct 1894, and has issue 1ı to 2ı

   1ı Mary Agnes Fisher

   2ı Margaret Eleanor Fisher

[Nos 11531 to 11562

# of The Blood Royal

2*i* Mary Elizabeth Skinner (*Inchgarth, 31 Broad Park Avenue, Ilfracombe*), m 12 Jan 1875, Lieut.-Col Edward Staines Daniell, 102nd Regt, medal and clasps for Pegu 1852-1853 and Lucknow, *b* 20 July 1828, *d* 19 Nov 1906, and has issue 1*j* to 6*j*

1*j* George Edward Staines Daniell (*Omata Valley, Waitotara, New Zealand*), *b* 31 Dec 1875

2*j* William Raymond Daniell, Capt 123rd Outram's Rifles, *formerly* Devon Regt, South African medal and 4 clasps, *b* 15 Dec 1878

3*j* James Skinner Daniell (*New Zealand*), *b* 17 Nov 1883

4*j* Charles John Williamson Daniell, Electrical Engineer, *b* 1 Dec 1885

5*j* Agnes Katharine Raymond Daniell, m 17 Ap 1906, Charles Orpen Tuckey, Mathematical Master at Charterhouse School (*Godalming*), and has issue 1*k*

1*k* Richard Edward Orpen Tuckey, *b* 16 Feb 1907

6*j* Margaret Swayne Daniell

4*h* *Agnes Raymond*, *b* 14 *Oct* 1819 d s p s *July* 1904, m 18 *July* 1848, *the Rev James Skinner, M A , Vicar of Newland, co Worcester*, d s p

5*h* *Katharine Raymond*, *b* 19 *Mar* 1822, *d* 27 *Oct* 1874, m as 2nd *wife*, 14 *June* 1855, *John Greene of Bury St Edmunds* (see p 126), *d* 29 *Jan* 1867, and had issue (*with a son and da who d unm*) 1*i* to 3*i*

1*i* Edith Anne Greene (12 *Oakfield Road, Clifton, Bristol*)

2*i* Mary Beatrice Greene, m 6 Aug 1879, Reginald John Lake of Lincoln's Inn, Bar-at-Law (*Beodricesworth, Alexandra Road, Watford*), and has issue 1*j* to 8*j*

1*j* John Stephen Raymond Lake, Capt 3rd South Wales Borderers, served in South Africa Feb 1900-Ap 1902, *b* 3 Dec 1881

2*j* Reginald St George Lake, Lieut Bedfordshire Regt, *b* 4 Dec 1887

3*j* Michael Neville Lake, *b* 3 Oct 1890

4*j* Helen Mary Beatrice Lake

5*j* Edith Carleton Lake

6*j* Margaretta Eunice Lake

7*j* Beatrice Victoria Lake

8*j* Katherine Madeline Lake

3*i* Madeline Greene (15 *Alexandra Road, Clifton, Bristol*), m 19 Ap 1899, Wilfred Martin Barclay of Clifton, F R C S , L R C P , d s p 9 May 1903

6*h* Anne Ryecroft Raymond (1 *Carlton Hill, Exmouth*), m 1st, 24 Sept 1846, Walter Tyson Smythies, d s p 23 Oct 1848, 2ndly, 17 July 1851, Capt Robert Hallowell-Carew, 36th Regt, *d* 18 Ap 1903, and has issue 1*i* to 2*i*

1*i* Robert George Hallowell-Carew, *formerly* Tea Planter in Assam (8 *Raleigh Villas, Exmouth*), *b* 9 May 1852, m 10 Oct 1883, Ellen Margaret Isabella, da of the Rev Oliver Edward Raymond, and has issue

See p 124, Nos 11544-11545

2*i* *Walter Raymond Hallowell-Carew*, *b* 12 *Sept* 1853, *d* 22 *Oct* 1896, m 1 *May* 1889, *Edith May, da of A Porch, and had issue* 1*j*

1*j* Marjorie Hallowell-Carew, *b* 31 Mar 1891

7*h* *Juliana Raymond* (*Bray Vicarage, Berks*), *unm*

3*g* *Isabella Raymond*, *b* at Belchamp Hall 3 *Mar* 1784, *d* 8 *Sept* 1858, m 14 Nov 1809, *the Rev Henry Yeats Smythies, M A , B D , Fellow of Emmanuel Coll (Camb), Vicar of Stanground cum-Farcett, co Hunts, J P , b* at South Moreton, co Berks, 15 Feb 1765, *d at* Stanground 20 *June* 1842, and had issue (*with 6 other children who* d s p) 1*h* to 3*h*

1*h* *Rev Raymond Brewster Smythies, M A (Camb), &c , b* 18 June 1824 d *at Brighton* 19 *Jan* 1861 m *at Rugby* 27 *Dec* 1859 *Isabella Jane* [a descendant of *the Lady Isabel Plantagenet* (see Essex Volume, p 306)], *da of the Rev*

[Nos 11563 to 11587

The Plantagenet Roll

Charles Alleyne Anstey, M A [grandson of Christopher Anstey of Trumpington Hall, co Camb] [who re m 2ndly, 1868, Major-Gen Robert Yeld Chambers, and] d 28 July 1903, and had issu 1i

1i Raymond Henry Raymond Smythies, Major *late* 40th Regt, served in South African War 1900-1901, medal with three clasps, author of "Historical Records of 40th Regt" (20 *Addison Court Gardens, W, Army and Navy*), b at Rugby, 19 Nov 1860, *unm*

2h *Margaretta Smythies, b 26 Feb 1812, d 20 Ap 1853, m as 1st wife, 12 Ap 1836, John Greene of the Abbey Ruins, Bury St Edmunds (see p 125), b 15 Aug 1810, d 29 Jan 1867, and had issue (with 2 elder das who d unm)* 1i *to* 3i

1i *John Smythies Greene of the Panels, Bury St Edmunds, Solicitor, b 5 Aug 1842, d 17 Oct 1884, m 4 July 1867, Eleanor Annie, da of the Rev Charles Buchanan Wollaston, Preb of Chichester, d 6 Aug 1893, and had issue* 1j *to* 6j

1j John Wollaston Greene, Solicitor (*The Panels, Bury St Edmunds*), b 1 Sept 1869

2j *Cecil Wollaston Greene, b 13 Nov 1872, d 16 Feb 1909, m 31 Jan 1905, Lucy Gertrude, da of Surg-Major Isaac Newton, and had issue* 1k

1k John Cecil Wollaston Greene b 15 June 1908

3j Kenneth Wollaston Greene, Solicitor (*Bury St Edmunds*) b 10 Jan 1880, m 9 Sept 1909, Constance Agnes, da of Robert Jackson of Ormesby House, Huddersfield

4j Ella Wollaston Greene (*The Panels, Bury St Edmunds*)

5j Hilda Wollaston Greene, m 27 Aug 1907, R C F Maugham, H B M's Consul-Gen for Portuguese East Africa

6j Rhona Wollaston Greene (*The Panels, Bury St Edmunds*)

2i Rev Carleton Greene, Vicar of Great Barford (*Great Barford Vicarage, St Neots*), b 26 Jan 1844, m 4 Oct 1870, Jane Elizabeth, da of Col John Alexander Wilson, d 5 Mar 1903, and has issue 1j to 4j

1j Francis Carleton Greene, B A (Camb), b 18 May 1881

2j Marion Raymond Greene, m 31 Dec 1895 her cousin-german once removed, Charles Henry Greene (*St John's, Berkhamsted, Herts*), and has issue 1k to 4k

1k William Herbert Greene, b 25 Ap 1898

2k Charles Raymond Greene, M A (Oxon), b 17 Ap 1901

3k Henry Graham Greene, b 2 Oct 1904

4k Alice Marion Greene, b 30 Dec 1896

3j Maud Churchill Greene

4j Nora Carleton Greene

3i Frances Elizabeth Raymond Greene, m as 2nd wife, 6 Ap 1880, the Rev Oliver Edward Raymond, Rector of Middleton (see p 123)

3h *Emily Smythies, b 17 Sept 1820, d 3 Feb 1848, m as 1st wife, 4 Feb 1840, Edward Greene of Nether Hall, Bury St Edmunds, M P [younger brother of the above-named John Greene], b 17 Aug 1815, d 15 Ap 1891, and had issue* 1i *to* 4i

1i Sir (Edward) Walter Greene of Nether Hall, 1st Bt [U K], so cr 21 June 1900, J P, D L, High Sheriff co Suffolk 1897, Hon Col 3rd Batt Suffolk Regt and Major and Hon Lieut-Col Suffolk Imp Yeo, M P for Bury St Edmunds 1900-1906 (*Nether Hall, Thurston, Westgate House, Bury St Edmunds, Carlton, Royal Yacht Squadron*), b 11 Mar 1842, m 16 June 1864, Annie Elizabeth, da of the Rev Charles S Royds, Preb of Lichfield, and has issue 1j to 6j

1j Walter Raymond Greene, B A (Oxon), M P, J P, and *formerly* C C London, Hon Lieut in the Army, and Lieut-Col Comdg Royal Suffolk Hussars Yeo, and *formerly* (1895-1906) M P for Chesterton Div of co Camb (*Nether Hall, Thurston, 113 Mount Street, Carlton, &c*), b 4 Aug 1869

2j Edward Allan Greene, Lieut Royal Suffolk Hussars Yeo, b 12 Sept 1882

[Nos 11588 to 11607

# of The Blood Royal

3ƒ Agatha Royds Greene, m 17 Jan 1907, Major Harry Trevor Trevor, *late* Indian Army (*Larpool Hall, near Whitby, Yorks*), and has issue 1*k*

  1*k* Raymond Salusbury Rose Trevor, *b* 26 Dec 1907

4ƒ *Annie Mabel Greene*, d 5 *Ap* 1905, m 18 *Feb* 1890, *Arthur James Taylor of Strensham Court, J P , late 3rd Dragoon Guards* (*Strensham Court, near Tewkesbury*)*, and had issue* 1*k to* 5*k*

  1*k* John Walter Taylor, *b* 11 Aug 1891

  2*k* Charles Taylor, *b* 26 July 1892

  3*k* Arthur Taylor, *b* 2 Dec 1902

  4*k* Angelica Taylor, *b* 14 Oct 1895

  5*k* Philippa Mabel Taylor, *b* 21 Aug 1901

5ƒ Catharine Marion Greene, m 17 June 1897, Albert Julian Pell of Wilburton Manor, J P D L , Chairman Quarter Sessions, Capt and Hon Major 4th Batt Suffolk Regt (*Wilburton Manor, near Ely*), and has issue 1*k* to 2*k*

  1*k* Angela Lilian Adelaide Pell, *b* 29 Sept 1899

  2*k* Barbara Katharine Pell, *b* 16 Oct 1903

6ƒ Helen Lilian Royds Greene, m 6 June 1891, Basil Arthur Charlesworth, Bar-at-Law (*Gunton Hall, near Lowestoft*), and has issue 1*k* to 3*k*

  1*k* Frederick Raymond Charlesworth, *b* 1894

  2*k* Julian Basil Charlesworth, *b* 1899

  3*k* Kathleen Agatha Charlesworth, *b* 1892

2ɩ Emily Smythies Greene m 26 Sept 1864, Frederic Machell Smith (*Tichton Hall, Beverley, Yorks*), and has issue 1ƒ

1ƒ Kathleen Machell Smith, m 12 Mar 1903, Francis Edward Bradshaw-Isherwood, Capt York and Lancaster Regt [2nd son of John Henry Bradshaw-Isherwood of Marple Hall, co Chester, J P], and has issue 1*k*

  1*k* Christopher William Bradshaw-Isherwood, *b* 26 Aug 1904

3ɩ Julia Isabella Greene, m 27 July 1876, the Very Rev Thomas Charles Fry, D D , Dean of Lincoln, *formerly* Head Master, Berkhamsted School (*The Deanery, Lincoln*), and has issue 1ƒ to 2ƒ

  1ƒ Rev Charles Edward Middleton Fry, M A (Oxon), *b* 14 July 1882

  2ƒ Basil Homfray Fry, B A (Oxon), *b* 17 Mar 1884

4ɩ *Helen Emily Greene*, d 25 Oct 1880, m as 1st *wife*, 13 *Sept* 1870, *the Rev Thomas Holt Wilson, M A* (*Camb*), *Rector of Brayesworth, formerly Rector of Redgrave* (*Briarfield, Great Malvern*), *and had issue*

  See p 459, Nos 95383-95385 and 95388-95391

2ɩ *Isabella Raymond*, d s p *Dec* 1808, m 1st, *John Mayne of Telfont, co Wilts*, 2ndly, as 2nd *wife*, 12 *Ap* 1788, *Archibald* (*Cochrane*), *9th Earl of Dundonald* [S], d 1 *July* 1831

  4*c* *Edward Raymond* [1]

  5*c* *James Raymond* [1]

  6*c* *Joseph Raymond,*[1] d *before* 20 *Oct* 1727, *leaving issue, who had £50 each under the will of their uncle, William Raymond of Belchamp*

  7*c*-9*c* 1 *other son and* 2 *das* [1]

  2*b* *Oliver Raymond of London, Silk Merchant*

  3*b* *William Raymond*

  4*b* *Anne Raymond*, m 1st, *John Lawrence* 2ndly, *John Eden*

  5*b* *Frances Raymond*, m *John Darcy*

  6*b*-21*b* 16 *other children*   [Nos 11608 to 11637

---

[1] One of these was presumably the father or mother of the Mrs Anne Watkins who inherited £1500 under the will of her uncle, William Raymond of Belchamp, 9 July 1733

The Plantagenet Roll

58 Descendants of THOMAS (TUFTON), 6th EARL OF THANET [E]
(Table VIII.), b 30 Aug 1644, d 30 July 1729, m 14 Aug
1684, Lady CATHERINE, da and co-h of Henry (CAVENDISH),
2nd Duke of Newcastle [E], d. 20 Ap 1712, and had issue
1a to 3a

1a Lady Catherine Tufton, da and co-h, b 24 Ap 1691, d 13 Feb 1734,
m 23 Jan 1708, Edward Watson, Viscount Sondes, M P, d v p 20 Mar 1722,
and had issue
See the Exeter Volume, Table XIII, and pp 242-243, Nos 8843-9108

2a Lady Anne Tufton, da and co-h, b 9 Aug 1693, d 22 Mar. 1757, m
12 Feb 1709, James (Cecil), 5th Earl of Salisbury [E], d 9 Oct 1728, and had
issue
See the Exeter Volume, Table XI, and pp 216-219, Nos 7652-7738

3a Lady Mary Tufton, da and co-h, b 6 July 1701, d 12 Feb 1785, m 1st,
17 Feb 1718, Anthony (Grey) 3rd Lord Lucas [E], styled Earl of Harold, d s p v p
21 July 1723, 2ndly, as 3rd wife, 16 May 1736, John (Leveson-Gower), 1st Earl
Gower [G B], d 25 Dec 1754, and had issue
See the Exeter Volume, Table VIII, and pp 172-175, Nos 5149-5574
[Nos 11638 to 12116

59 Descendants of SACKVILLE (TUFTON), 7th EARL OF THANET [E]
(Table VIII), b 11 May 1688, d 4 Dec. 1753; m 11 June
1722, Lady MARY, da and co-h of William (SAVILE), 2nd
Marquis of Halifax [E], d 30 July 1751, and had issue

See the Exeter Volume, Table XXI, and p 321

60. Descendants of the Right Hon and Hon WILLIAM FINCH, P C,
M P (Table VIII), d 25 Dec 1766, m. 2ndly, 26 Aug 1746,
Lady CHARLOTTE, da of Thomas (FERMOR), 1st Earl of Pom-
fret [G B], b 16 Feb 1725, d. 11 July 1813, and had issue
1a to 2a

1a George (Finch), 9th Earl of Winchilsea and 3rd Earl of Nottingham [E],
K G, b 4 Nov 1752, d s p 2 Aug 1826

2a Sophia Finch, da and (herself or in her issue) co-h, d (–), m July
1772, Capt Charles Feilding, R N [E of Denbigh [E] and Desmond [I], Coll],
d (–) and had issue 1b to 3b

1b Charles Feilding, Rear-Adm R N, b 1780, d 2 Sept 1837, m 24 Ap
1804, Lady Elizabeth Theresa, widow of William Davenport Talbot of Lacock, da of
Henry Thomas (Fox-Strangways), 2nd Earl of Ilchester [G B.], d 12 Mar 1846,
and had issue
See the Exeter Volume, p 706, Nos 58365-58390

2b Sophia Charlotte Feilding, d 19 Sept 1834, m 22 July 1792, Lord Robert
Stephen FitzGerald, M P [D of Leinster Coll], d 2 Jan 1833, and had issue
See the Exeter Volume, pp 175-476, Nos 41754-41759, and Essex Volume,
Exeter Supplement, p 639, Nos 41759/1 to 41759/19

3b. Augusta Sophia Feilding, d (–), m 8 Mar 1813, George Hicks, d 1 Aug
1820
[Nos 12117 to 12168

# of The Blood Royal

61 Descendants of the Hon JOHN FINCH, M P., K.C., Solicitor-
General to George II when Prince of Wales (Table VIII),
d. 12 Feb 1763, *m* ELIZABETH, da of (—) YOUNGER, *d*
24 Nov 1762, and had issue 1*a.*

    1*a Elizabeth Finch, da and h*, d (–), m 2 *June* 1757, *John Mason of
Greenwich*

62 Descendants of GEORGE FINCH HATTON of Eastwell Park, co Kent
(Table VIII), *b* 1747, *d* 17 Feb 1823, *m* 10 Dec 1785,
Lady ELIZABETH MARY, da of David (MURRAY), 2nd Earl of
Mansfield [G B], *d.* 1 June 1825, and had issue 1*a* to 2*a*

    1*a George William (Finch Hatton), 10th Earl of Winchilsea and 5th Earl of
Nottingham [E],* b 19 *May* 1791, d 8 *Jan* 1858, m 1*st*, 26 *July* 1814, *Lady
Georgiana Charlotte, da of James (Graham), 3rd Duke of Montrose* [S], d 13 *Feb*
1835, 3*rdly*, 17 *Oct* 1849, *Fanny Margaretta (Halton, Sevenoaks), da of Edward
Royd Rice of Dane Court, co Kent, and had issue 1b to 5b*

    1*b George James (Finch-Hatton), 11th Earl of Winchilsea and 6th Earl of
Nottingham [E],* b 31 *May* 1815, d 9 *June* 1887, m 1*st*, 6 *Aug* 1846, *Lady
Constance Henrietta [a descendant of King Henry VII], da of Henry (Paget), 2nd
Marquis of Anglesey [U K],* d 5 *Mar* 1878, *and had issue 1c to 2c*

    1*c Lady Constance Eleanor Caroline Finch-Hatton (9 St George's Road, S W),*
m 3 June 1871, the Hon Frederick Charles Howard [E of Effingham, &c, Coll],
d 26 Oct 1893, and has issue 1*d* to 2*d*

    1*d* Gordon Frederick Henry Charles Howard, heir presumptive to the Earldom
of Effingham [U K], &c, *b* 18 May 1873, *m* 26 Jan 1904, Rosamond Margaret,
da of Edward H Hudson of Scarborough, and has issue 1*e* to 2*e*

    1*e* Mowbray Henry Gordon Howard, *b* 29 Nov 1905

    2*c* John Algernon Frederick Charles Howard, *b* 29 Dec 1907

    2*d* Algernon George Mowbray Frederick Howard, *late* Capt 3rd Batt King's
Own (*White's*), *b* 15 Sept 1874

    2*c Lady Hilda Jane Sophia Finch-Hatton* b 3 *Mar* 1856, d 8 *Feb* 1893,
m *as* 1*st wife, 23 Ap* 1877, *Henry Vincent Higgins, C V O, a Solicitor and member
of the firm of Treherne, Higgins & Co, formerly* 1*st Life Guards (1 Upper Berkeley
Street, S W), and had issue*

    2*b Murray Edward Gordon (Finch-Hatton), 12th Earl of Winchilsea and 7th
Earl of Nottingham [E],* b 28 *May* 1851, d 7 *Sept* 1898, m 27 *Oct* 1875, *Edith
[a descendant of Kings Henry VII and Edward IV, George, Duke of Clarence,
K G, Lady Anne Plantagenet, &c] (Haverholme Priory, Sleaford), da of Edward
William Harcourt of Stanton Harcourt, M P, and had issue 1c*

    1*c Lady Muriel Evelyn Vernon Finch-Hatton, m* 31 May 1897, Sir Richard
Arthur Surtees Paget, 2nd Bt [U K] (*Cranmore Hall, near Shepton Mallet, Clive
House, Roehampton, &c),* and has issue 1*d* to 3*d*

    1*d* Sylvia Mary Paget

    2*d* Pamela Winefred Paget

    3*d* Angela Sibell Paget

    3*b* Henry Stormont (Finch-Hatton), 13th Earl of Winchilsea and 8th Earl of
Nottingham [E], &c (*Harlech, co Merioneth, Carlton*), b 3 Nov 1852, m 12 Jan
1882, Anne Jane [also a descendant of King Edward III through Mortimer
Percy], da of Admiral of the Fleet Sir Henry John Codrington, K C B [Bt Coll]
and has issue

See p 77, Nos 9428-9430   [Nos 12169 to 12181

The Plantagenet Roll

4b *Lady Caroline Finch-Hatton*, b 6 *July* 1810, d 13 *Mar* 1888, m 2 *Feb* 1837, *Christopher Turnor* (see p 392) *of Stoke Rochford, M P , J P , D L , High Sheriff co Lincoln* 1823, b 4 *Ap* 1809, d 7 *Mar* 1886, *and had issue* 1c *to* 7c

1c *Edmund Turnor of Stoke Rochford, M P , J P , D L*, b 24 *Mar* 1838, d s p 15 Dec 1903

2c *Christopher Hatton Turnor*, b 16 *Dec* 1840, d (–), m *at Toronto, Alice, da of the Hon Hamilton H Killaly, and had issue* 1d

1d Christopher Hatton Turnor of Stoke Rochford (*Stoke Rochford, Grantham, Panton Hall, co Lincoln*), b 23 Nov 1873 m 7 Aug 1907, Sarah Marie Talbot [descended from George, Duke of Clarence. K G (see the Clarence Volume, p 81)], d and h of Admiral the Hon Walter Cecil Carpenter, *formerly* Talbot, R N

3c Algernon Turnor, C B , J P (*Goadby Hall, Melton Mowbray, 37 Pont Street, S W), b* 14 *Nov* 1845 *m* 3 *Aug* 1880, Lady Henrietta Caroline [a descendant both paternally and maternally of King Henry VII (see Tudor Roll, p 198)], da of Randolph (Stewart), 9th Earl of Galloway [S], and has issue 1d to 5d

1d Herbert Broke Turnor, b 22 Aug 1885

2d Christopher Randolph Turnor, b 16 Aug 1886

3d Marjorie Caroline Isabel Turnor

4d Algitha Blanche Turnor

5d Verena Henrietta Turnor

4c Graham Augustus Turnor, b 13 Sept 1853, m 1st, Annie, da of (—) Riddle, 2ndly, Beatrice, da of (—) Cranstone, and has issue 1d to 6d

1d Edmund Turnor

2d Effie Caroline Turnor

3d Constance Yolande Turnor

4d Charlotte Octavia Turnor

5d Bertha Kathleen Turnor

6d Edmunda Turnor

5c Edith Georgina Turnor, m 16 Sept 1868, Frederick Archibald Vaughan (Campbell), 3rd Earl [U K], and 4th Baron [G B] Cawdor, P C , a Member of the Council of H R H the Prince of Wales &c [descended from King Henry VII (see Tudor Roll)] (*Stackpole Court, Pembroke , Cawdor Castle, Nairn , 7 Princes Gardens, S W), and has issue*

See the Tudor Roll, pp 214–215, Nos 21735–21746

6c Bertha Kathleen Turnor

7c Dora Agnes Caroline Turnor, d 7 Ap 1899, m 27 July 1889, Benjamin Bloomfield Trench of Loughton Moneygall, King's Co (41 Onslow Square, S W), and had issue 1d to 2d

1d Sheelah Georgiana Bertha Trench

2d Theodora Caroline Trench

5b Lady Evelyn Georgiana Finch-Hatton, m 28 Feb 1883, Henry Edward Montagu Dorington Clotworthy (Upton), 4th Viscount Templetown [I], and a Rep Peer (*Castle Upton, Templepatrick, co Antrim, &c). and has issue* 1c to 3c

1c Hon Eric Edward Montagu John Upton, Lieut 2nd Batt King's Royal Rifle Corps, b 8 Mar 1885

2c Hon Henry Augustus George Mountjoy Heneage Upton, b 12 Aug 1894

3c Hon Margaret Evelyn Upton

2b Rev Daniel Heneage Finch-Hatton, Chaplain to Queen Victoria, b 1795 d 3 Jan 1866 m 15 Dec 1825, Lady Louisa, da of the Hon Robert Fulke Greville, by his wife Louisa, suo jure 2nd Countess of Mansfield [G B], d 11 Ap 1883 , and had issue

See the Tudor Roll, pp 199–200, Nos 21327–21341   [Nos 12182 to 12230

63 Descendants of Lady ESSEX FINCH (Table VIII), b c 1688, d 23 May 1721, m 20 July 1703, SIR ROGER MOSTYN of Mostyn, 3rd Bt [E], M P., d 5 May 1739, and had issue 1a

1a *Sir Thomas Mostyn of Mostyn, 4th Bt [E], M P*, b c 1704, d 24 May 1758, m c 1735, *Sarah, da and co-h of Robert Western of St Peter's, Cornhill, and of Rivenhall, co Essex*, d 28 May 1740, *and had issue 1b to 4b*

1b *Sir Roger Mostyn of Mostyn, 5th Bt [E], M P*, b c 1735, d 26 May 1796, m 19 May 1776, *Margaret, da and h of the Rev Hugh Wynne, LL D , Preb of Salisbury*, d 14 Oct 1792, *and had issue 1c to 2c*

1c *Sir Thomas Mostyn of Mostyn, 6th and last Bt [E], M P*, b c 1776, d (unm) 17 Ap 1831

2c *Elizabeth Mostyn, da and in her issue (29 Ap 1859) sole h*, d 26 Nov 1842, m 11 Feb 1794, *Sir Edward Pryce Lloyd, 2nd Bart [G B], afterwards (10 Sept 1831) 1st Baron Mostyn [U K]*, d 3 Ap 1854, *and had issue 1d*

1d *Edward (Lloyd, afterwards (R L 9 May 1831) Mostyn), 2nd Baron Mostyn [U K]*, b 13 Jan 1795, d 17 Mar 1884, m 20 June 1827, *Lady Harriet Margaret [a descendant of King Henry VII], da of Thomas (Scott), 2nd Earl of Clonmell [I]*, d 27 May (or 3 June) 1891, *and had issue*

See the Tudor Roll, pp 197–198, Nos 21271–21294

2b *Thomas Mostyn, certainly dead s p m before 17 Ap 1831*

3b *Anne Mostyn*, d 1802, m as 2nd wife, 1777, *Thomas Pennant of Downing, co Flint, D C L , the well-known Naturalist and Author*, d 16 Dec 1798, *leaving a son who d s p 1816* [1]

4b *Frances Mostyn*, d (? unm) .   [Nos 12231 to 12251]

64 Descendants of Lady CHARLOTTE FINCH (Table VIII), d 21 Jan 1773, m. as 2nd wife, 4 Feb 1726, CHARLES (SEYMOUR), 6th DUKE OF SOMERSET [E], K G, "the Proud Duke," d 2 Dec 1748, and had issue

See the Tudor Roll, Table L, &c, and pp 263, 292–311, Nos 24118–24401, 25350–26006   [Nos 12252 to 13192

65 Descendants of Lady MARY FINCH (Table VIII), d 30 May 1761, m 22 Sept 1716, THOMAS (WATSON), 1st MARQUIS [G B], and 6th BARON [E] OF ROCKINGHAM, K G, d 14 Dec 1750, and had issue.

See the Exeter Volume, Table XIII and pp 253–261, Nos 9608–9890
                                                [Nos 13193 to 13475

66 Descendants, if any surviving, of Lady MARY TUFTON (Table VIII), bur. 7 Feb 1674, m as 1st wife, c. 1671, SIR WILLIAM WALTER of Sarsden, 2nd Bt [E], d 5 Mar 1694, and had issue 1a to 2a

1a *Sir John Walter, 3rd Bt [E]*, b c 1673, d s p 11 June 1722
2a *Mary Walter, da and (either herself or in her issue) heir after the death s p 20 Nov 1731, of her half-brother Sir Robert, 4th and last Bt , living 1741* m 7 May 1698, *Sir Robert Rich of Sonning, 3rd Bt [E]*, d 9 Nov 1721, *and had issue 1b to 7b*

1 "Dict Nat Biog," xliv 322

131

The Plantagenet Roll

1b Sir William Rich, 4th Bt [E], d 17 July 1762, m Elizabeth, da of William Royal of Minstead, d 27 Ap 1771, and had issue 1c

  1c Sir Thomas Rich, 5th and last Bt [E], Adm R N, d s p 1 6 Ap 1803

2b Thomas Rich of Bombay, living 1741,

3b Charles Rich,

4b James Rich,

5b Daniel Rich, Matric St John's Coll, Oxon, aged 17, a Student of the Middle Temple 1734,

                  all presumably d s p m, and apparently also s p before 6 Ap 1803

6b [da] Rich, m Capt Wilson of the Guards

7b [da] Rich, m Walter Knight of Buscomb, co Berks

67 Descendants of Lady ELIZABETH CLIFFORD, suo jure de jure, 2nd BARONESS CLIFFORD [E] (Table VIII), b 18 Sept. 1618, d. 6 Jan 1691, m 8 July 1635, RICHARD (BOYLE), 2nd EARL OF CORK [I.] and 1st EARL OF BURLINGTON [E], d 15 Jan. 1698, and had issue 1a to 4a

1a Charles (Boyle), Lord Clifford of Lanesborough [E] and Viscount Dungarvan [I], bapt 12 Dec 1839, d v p 12 Oct 1694, m 1st, Lady Jane [a descendant of King Henry VII], da of William (Seymour), 2nd Duke of Somerset [E], d 23 Nov 1679, 2ndly, Lady Arethusa, da of George (Berkeley), 1st Earl of Berkeley [I], d 11 Feb 1743, and had issue 1b to 3b

  1b Charles (Boyle), 3rd Earl of Cork [I] and 2nd Earl of Burlington [E], b about 1671, d 9 Feb 1704, m 26 Jan 1688, Juliana, Mistress of the Robes to Queen Anne, da and h of the Hon Henry Noel, d 17 Oct 1750, and had issue
    See the Tudor Roll, Table XLI and pp 240-260, Nos 22551-23494

  2b Hon Mary Boyle, b c 1670, d 2 Oct 1709, m 1 Dec 1685, James (Douglas), 2nd Duke of Queensberry [E] and 1st Duke of Dover [E], K G, d 6 July 1711, and had issue
    See the Tudor Roll, Table XLIX and pp 263, Nos 23605-24117

  3b [2] Hon Arethusa Boyle, d (–), m James Vernon

2a Lady Frances Boyle, d about 1674, m 1st, Col Francis Courtenay, 2ndly, Ap 1662, Wentworth (Dillon), 4th Earl of Roscommon [I], d s p 18 Jan 1685

3a Lady Anne Boyle, d (–), m Jan 1668, Edward (Montagu), 2nd Earl of Sandwich [E], d in France shortly before 8 Dec 1688 and had issue 1b

  1b Edward (Montagu), 3rd Earl of Sandwich [E], b c Dec 1670, d 20 Oct 1729, m (a 11) July 1689 Lady Elizabeth, da and event co-h of John (Wilmot), 2nd Earl of Rochester [E], d in Paris 2 July 1757, and had issue 1c

    1c Edward Richard Montagu, Viscount Hinchinbroke, M P, b c 1690, d v p 3 Oct 1722, m 12 Ap 1707, Elizabeth [a descendant of Isabel (Plantagenet), Countess of Essex], da and h of Alexander Popham of Littlecote [m 2ndly, 30 July 1728, Francis Seymour of Sherborne, M P, and], d 20 Mar 1761, and had issue
    See the Essex Volume, Table XIV and pp 191, 192-193, Nos 26149-26468 and 26506-26809

4a Lady Henrietta Boyle, d 12 Ap 1687, m 1665, Lawrence (Hyde), 1st Earl of Rochester [E], K G, d 2 May 1711, and had issue 1b to 3b

  1b Henry (Hyde), 2nd Earl of Rochester and (12 Feb 1713) 4th Earl of Clarendon [L], b 1672, d s p m s 10 Dec 1753, m (lic 2 Mar 1692), Jane, da of Sir William Leveson Gower, 4th Bt [E], d 24 May 1725, and had issue 1c

    1c Lady Jane Hyde, da and eventual sole h, d 30 Jan 1724, m as 1st wife,
                  [Nos 13476 to 15256

# of The Blood Royal

27 Nov 1718, *William (Capel), 3rd Earl of Essex* [E], K G , K T , d 8 Jan 1743, *and had issue*

See the Exeter Volume, pp 379-384, Nos 26875-27087

2b *Lady Henrietta Hyde*, b c 1677 , d 30 May 1730, m 2 Jan 1694, *James (Scott), Earl of Doncaster and Dalkeith, K T* [son and h -app of the 1st Duke and Duchess of Monmouth [E] and Buccleuch [S], d v p 14 Mar 1705, *and had issue* 1c

1c *Francis (Scott), 2nd Duke of Buccleuch* [S] *and Earl of Doncaster* [E], *K T* , b 11 Jan 1695 , d 22 Ap 1751 , m 1st, 5 Ap 1720, *Lady Jane* [a descendant of King Henry VII], da of James (Douglas), 2nd Duke of Queensberry [S] and 1st Duke of Dover [E], d 31 Aug 1729, *and had issue*

See the Tudor Roll, Table XLIX and p 263, Nos 23605-24117

3b *Lady Mary Hyde*, d 25 Jan 1709, m *as 1st wife*, 17 Feb 1704, *Francis (Seymour, afterwards (1699) Seymour-Conway), 1st Baron Conway of Ragley* [E] *and Baron Conway and Killultagh* [I], d 3 Feb 1732, *and had issue* 1c

1c *Hon Mary Seymour Conway*, d (-), m *as 1st wife*, *Nicholas Price of Saintfield, co Down*, M P , d 1742, *and had issue* 1d

1d *Francis Price of Saintfield*, M P , d 1794, m *Charity, da of Matthew Forde of Seaforde, co Down* , *and had issue* 1e

1e *Nicholas Price of Saintfield*, J P , D L , High Sheriff co Down 1801, b 1 Oct 1754 , d (-), m Nov 1779, *Lady Sarah, da of Charles (Pratt), 1st Earl of Camden* [G B], d 7 Ap 1817 , *and had issue* 1f

1f *Elizabeth Anne Price of Saintfield, da and h* , d 6 Feb 1867 , m 17 June 1804, *James Blackwood, afterwards Price, of Strangford, co Down*, d 5 June 1855 , *and had issue* 1g to 7g

1g *James Charles Price of Saintfield*, J P , D L , High Sheriff co Down 1859, b 17 June 1807 , d 23 May 1894, m 18 May 1840, *Anne Margaret, da of Major Patrick Savage of Portaferry*, d 14 Mar 1877 , *and had issue* 1h to 3h

1h James Nugent Blackwood Price of Saintfield, J P , D L , High Sheriff co Down 1902, Brevet-Major *late* 60th Rifles, &c (*Saintfield House, Saintfield, co Down* , *Army and Navy*), b 13 Oct 1844 , m 5 Jan 1869, Alice Louisa [a descendant of George (Plantagenet) Duke of Clarence, K G (see Clarence Volume, p 279)], da of William Robert Ward, Diplo Service [V Bangor Coll], and has issue 1i to 3i

1i Conway William Blackwood Price (*United University*), b 28 July 1872

2i Rev Edward Hyde Blackwood Price, M A , Rector of St Nicholas' and Vicar of St Peter's, Droitwich, b 5 Feb 1875

3i Ethelwyn Mary Blackwood Price, m 27 Aug 1901, Richard Douglas Perceval, C E , J P (*Downpatrick, co Down*), and has issue 1j to 2j

1j Richard John Perceval, b 26 July 1902

2j Michael Charles Perceval, b 16 Feb 1907

2h Francis William Price, b 27 Dec 1847

3h Catherine Anne Price

2g *William Robert Arthur Price*, b 22 Jan 1813 , d (-), m 1st, May 1843, *Anna Eliza, da of the Rev William Jex-Blake of Swanton Abbots, co Norfolk*, d (-), 2ndly, *Henrietta, da of George Kenyon of Cefn, co Denbigh* , *and had issue* 1h

1h [1] Anna Maria Frances Price

3g *Rev Townley Blackwood Price*, b 5 Jan 1815 , d 1902, m 1st, Feb 1841, *Maria Catherine, da of the Rev William Jex-Blake of Swanton Abbots*, d (-), 2ndly, *Anne, da of the Rev the Hon Henry Ward* [V Bangor Coll], d 6 June 1852 , 3rdly, *Sarah Olivia, da of Henry Lyle of Knoctarna, co Derry* , *and had issue*

4g *Richard Blackwood Price, Lieut-Col R A* , b 12 May 1818 , d (-), m *Anne, da of Robert Wade of Clonebrancy* , *and had issue*

5g Mary Georgiana Price   [Nos 15257 to 15992

The Plantagenet Roll

6g Sarah Elizabeth Price, m 15 June 1848, the Rev Henry Montgomery Archdale of Thornhill, co Fermanagh, M A , b 28 Ap 1818 , d 14 Feb 1898 , and has issue 1h to 10h

1h Edward Archdale of Castle Archdale B A (Oxon), J P , D L , High Sheriff co Fermanagh 1902 (*Castle Archdale, Irvinestown, co Fermanagh , Trillick Lodge, co Tyrone*), b 22 Mar 1850

2h Henry Dawson Archdale, b 1851

3h James Blackwood Archdale, Major *late* R A and Army Ordnance Dept (*Lansdown, Camberley*), b 17 July 1853 , m Feb 1886, Elizabeth, da of George May of Cambridge , and has issue 1i

   1i. Henry Blackwood Archdale, b 15 Mar 1887

4h Audley Mervyn Archdale (*Parkside, Woodville Road, Bexhill-on-Sea*), b 1 Oct 1855 , m 17 Sept 1895, Mary Scott, da of George Elphinstone of Oakfield House, Streatham , and has issue 1i to 3i

   1i George Mervyn Archdale, b 14 Aug 1896

   2i Margaret Helen Archdale

   3i Beatrice Mary Archdale

5h Montgomery Archdale, b 1858

6h George Archdale, *late* Capt 5th Batt Royal Irish Rifles (*Dromord, Kesh, co Fermanagh*), b 27 Jan 1860 , m 28 Dec 1894, Mary, da of John Graham of Parade House, Cowes , and has issue 1i to 6i

   1i Mervyn Henry Dawson Archdale, b 11 Mar 1904

   2i George Montgomery Archdale, b 6 July 1907

   3i Helen Audley Archdale

   1i Mary Blackwood Archdale

   5i Sarah Matilda Archdale

   6i Joan Archdale

7h Elizabeth Price Archdale

8h Sarah Blackwood Archdale, m 10 Nov 1886, the Rev Edward Blanchard Ryan, Rector of Strangford (*Strangford Rectory, co Down*), and has issue

9h. Matilda Humphries Archdale

10h Richmal Magnell Archdale

7g *Elizabeth Catherine Price*, d (-) , m Oct 1841, *the Rev Alexander Orr*, d (-) , *and had issue*   [Nos 15993 to 16013

---

68 Descendants of MULTON LAMBARDE of Sevenoaks, co Kent (Table IX.), b. 29 July 1757 , d 19 Mar. 1836 , m 22 Sept. 1789, AUREA, da. and co-h of Francis OTWAY of Ashgrove, Sevenoaks, d 10 Mar. 1828 , and had issue 1a to 3a

1a *William Lambarde of Beechmont, co Kent*, b 18 Nov 1796, d 1 June 1866 , m 1 Oct 1818, *Harriet Elizabeth, da of Sir James Naesmyth, 3rd Bt* [S], d 25 Ap 1879 , *and had issue 1b to 9b*

1b *Multon Lambarde of Beechmont, co Kent*, b 31 Oct 1821, d 21 Dec 1896; m 27 Mar 1848, *Marianne Teresa Livesey, da of Edmund Turton of Brasted, co Kent, and of Larpool Hall, co Yorks , and had issue 1c to 7c*

1c William Gore Lambarde (*Bradbourne Hall, Riverhead, Kent , Beechmont, Sevenoaks*), b 22 May 1864 , m 10 Oct 1888, Florence Lucy, da of Howard Fetherstonhaugh of Bracklyn, co Westmeath , and has issue 1d to 2d

   1d Bridget Aurea Teresa Lambarde

   2d Deborah Silversten Fane Lambarde

2c Mary Teresa Louisa Lambarde, m 24 Ap 1890, Adam Young

3c Ellen Grace Lambarde, b 20 Feb 1887   [Nos 16014 to 16018

# of The Blood Royal

4c   Maude Eleanor Lambarde, b 1 Sept 1889

5c   Harriet Beatrice Aurea Lambarde, m 8 June 1886, Percy Francis Battiscombe of Shaw Well, J P (see below) (Shaw Well, Sevenoaks), and has issue 1d to 5d

    1d   Percival Ralph Battiscombe, b 18 Sept 1891

    2d   Gwendoline Aurea Battiscombe, b 15 May 1887

    3d   Ruby Cicely Teresa Battiscombe, b 3 May 1888

    4d   Violet Battiscombe, b 12 Ap 1889

    5d   Sylvia Battiscombe, b 1 June 1890

6c   Ethel Julia Lambarde, m 10 Jan 1893, Joseph William Underwood, 4th Hussars (Belle Vue, Sevenoaks), and has issue 1d to 2d

    1d   Gerald Joseph Underwood, b 3 June 1897

    2d   Keene Sybil Underwood, b 22 May 1894

7c   Edith Gwendoline Lambarde, b 12 Feb 1868

2b   John Lambarde, E I C S, b 28 Feb 1823, d 8 July 1848, m 16 Aug 1847, Mary Anne Priscilla, da of Thomas Haslam, Capt 25th Regt N I , and had issue 1c

    1c   Harriet Charlotte Lambarde, m 28 Oct 1879, William Henley Dodgson (Forest Lodge, Keston, Kent), and has issue 1d to 6d

        1d   William Lambarde Dodgson, Lieut R N , b 29 May 1880

        2d   John Henley Dodgson, b 16 Oct 1881

        3d   Raymond Charles Dodgson, b 11 Dec 1882

        4d   Arthur Douglas Dodgson, b 22 Aug 1884

        5d   Richard Heathfield Dodgson, b 4 July 1887

        6d   Cicely Charlotte Dodgson, b 17 Sept 1889

3b   Francis Lambarde, J P (Manor House Ash, Sevenoaks), b 24 Ap 1830, m 1 Nov 1866, Sophia Katharine Gambier, widow of John Barry Gurdon of Assington Hall, co Suff, da of Charles Douglas Halford of West Lodge, East Bergholt, co Suff, d 16 May 1903, and has issue 1c to 3c

    1c   Francis Fane Lambarde, Capt R A (Manor House, Ash, Sevenoaks), b 24 Dec 1868, m 18 Oct 1902, Marian Ethel, da of Joseph Hinks of Warwick

    2c   John Barrett Lambarde (Alix, Alberta, Canada), b 20 Dec 1874

    3c   Florence Edith Lambarde, b 11 Feb 1877

4b   Rev Charles James Lambarde (Ash Rectory, Sevenoaks), b 28 Aug 1833

5b   Eleanora Lambarde, b 20 Sept 1819, d 23 Ap 1884, m 5 Jan 1854, Percival Battiscombe of Shaw Well, Sevenoaks, d 30 July 1885, and had issue 1c to 4c

    1c   Percy Francis Battiscombe, J P (Shaw Well, Sevenoaks), b 15 Mar 1857, m 8 June 1886, Harriet Beatrice Aurea, da of Multon Lambarde of Beechmont, co Kent, and has issue

    See above, Nos 16021–16025

    2c   Christopher William Battiscombe (The Retreat, Canterbury), b 30 Mar 1858, m 24 Ap 1889, Beatrice Lucy, da of Capt Bird Smith, and has issue 1d to 2d

        1d   Christopher Francis Battiscombe, b 4 Ap 1890

        2d   Marjory Eleanor Battiscombe, b 2 May 1891

    3c   Eleanor Teresa Battiscombe (Arundel, West Byfleet, Surrey), b 30 July 1860, m 1 Sept 1885, the Rev Harold Brierley, Vicar of Bridstow, Ross, d s p 10 June 1906

    4c   Emily Harriet Battiscombe, b 7 July 1859

6b   Juliana Lambarde, b 20 Dec 1828, d 10 Nov 1906, m 1857, James Christie Traill of Hobbister, Orkney, and of Ratter, co Caithness, J P , D L , d 6 Feb 1899, and had issue 1c to 4c   [Nos 16019 to 16052

The Plantagenet Roll

1c James William Traill of Hobbister (*Castle Hill, co Caithness*), b July 1858, m 1887, Ethel, da of T J Sumner of Melbourne, South Australia, and has issue 1d to 2d

    1d Cecil James Traill, b Oct 1888

    2d Sinclair George Traill, b May 1890

2c Rev Randolph Richard William Traill (*Orcott College, Birmingham*), b. Sept 1863

    3c John Murray Traill, Bedfordshire Regt, b Oct 1865

    4c Minna Harriet Traill, b Ap 1862

7b Harriet Lambarde, b 27 Mar 1835

8b *Jane Aurea Lambarde*, b 10 Feb 1841, d 30 Dec 1882, m 17 Feb 1864, *Capt Henry Lumsden Battiscombe, and had issue 1c to 2c*

    1c Charles Battiscombe, Major R A, b 13 Aug 1865, m 13 Mar 1899, Maria Isabella, da of (—) Mills, and has issue 1d

        1d Christopher Robert Battiscombe, b 8 Nov 1902

    2c Maude Aurea Battiscombe, b 11 Jan 1871

9b *Alice Mary Lambarde*, b 28 Aug 1846, d 21 Ap 1900, m 29 Mar 1880, *Thomas Graham Jackson, R A, and had issue 1c to 2c*

    1c Hugh Nicholas Jackson, Royal Welsh Fusiliers (*Eagle House, Wimbledon*), b 21 Jan 1881

    2c Basil Hippisley Jackson, b 4 Feb 1887

2a *Bridget Aurea Lambarde*, b 16 Oct 1792, d 1 June 1826, m as 1st wife, 1 July 1823, *John Gurdon of Assington Hall, co Suff, J P, d 1869, and had issue 1b*

1b *John Barry Gurdon*, b 15 Ap 1825, d 28 Jan 1863, m 24 Feb 1857, *Sophia Katharine Gambier, da of Charles Douglas Halford of West Lodge, East Bergholt, co Suff* [re-m 2ndly, 1 Nov 1866, *Francis Lambarde, J P, of Manor House, Ash, co Kent* (see p 135)], *and had issue 1c to 3c*

    1c Philip Gurdon (*Con Int Road, Bedford*), b 2 Dec 1857, m 4 Nov 1885, Edith, da of the Rev Charles Holland, Rector of Petworth, co Sussex, and has issue 1d to 3d

        1d John Gurdon, b 21 Ap 1887

        2d William Nathaniel Gurdon, b 22 Oct 1890

        3d Eleanor Joyce Gurdon

    2c *Edward Barry Gurdon*, b 26 Ap 1860, d 18 Sept 1885, m 1882, *Julia, da of (—) Chandler of Sydney, N S W, and had issue 1d*

        1d Augustus Edward Philip Gurdon (*Sydney, New South Wales*), b 11 June 1883

    3c William Gurdon, Major R A, b 16 Ap 1862

3a *Mary Lambarde*, b 17 Nov 1801, b 2 Oct 1818, m 26 Nov 1835, *the Rev Richard Salwey, Rector of Ash, near Fawkham, co Kent [descended from the Lady Isabel Plantagenet* (see Essex Volume, p 318)], d 6 Feb 1895, and had issue 1b to 2b

    1b *Edward Richard Salwey, C E*, b 13 Ap 1843, d 5 May 1902, m 9 Ap 1874, *Ellen Isabel, da of Edward Burges of The Ridge, co Gloucester, and had issue 1c*

        1c Ellen Isold Salwey, m 17 Jan 1906, the Rev Edward Parry Liddon, Rector of Staverton (*Staverton Rectory, Northants*)

    2b Harriet Laura Salwey, m 28 Aug 1872, Matthew Edward Howard, and has issue 1c to 6c

        1c Arthur Edward Howard, b 6 Jan 1874, m 11 June 1896, Lucy, da of (—) MacSwiney of Dublin, M D, and has issue 1d

        1d Thelma Howard, b 24 Feb 1898   [Nos 16053 to 16074

# of The Blood Royal

2c Cecil William Howard, *b* 26 May 1875

3c Henry Bernard Howard, *b* 22 May 1877

4c Kenneth Salwey Howard, } *b* (twins) 14 Dec 1879
5c Kathleen Philippa Howard,

6c Clara Millicent Howard, *b* 13 Jan 1883 [Nos 16075 to 16079]

69 Descendants of MARY LAMBARDE (Table IX), *b* 17 Jan 1752, *d* (-), *m* 31 Aug. 1784, the Rev. JOHN HALLWARD, Vicar of Assington, co Suffolk *d* 24 Dec 1826; and had issue 1*a* to 2*a*

1*a* *Rev John Hallward, Rector of Easthorpe, co Essex, and later of Swepstone, co Leicester,* b 1791, d 6 June 1865, m *Emily Jane, da of Charles Powell Leslie of Glasslough, co Monaghan,* d (-), *and had issue* 1b to 4b

1*b* *Rev John Leslie Hallward, Rector of Gilston, co Herts,* b 29 Jan 1823, d 3 Oct 1896, m 22 Aug 1854, *Martha Clementina, da of the Rev Robert Govett, Vicar of Staines, co Middx,* d 22 Feb 1907, *and had issue* 1c to 5c

1*c* Norman Leslie Hallward of the Indian Educational Service (*United Service Club, Calcutta*), *b* 3 Mar 1859, *m* 14 Sept 1897, Evelyn Alice, da of Major-Gen Evelyn Pulteney Gurdon and has issue 1*d* to 2*d*

1*d* Bertrand Leslie Hallward, *b* 24 May 1901

2*d* Philip Norman Romaine Hallward, *b* 1 Feb 1903

2*c* Herbert Romaine Hallward, *b* 21 Oct 1860

3*c* Rev Lancelot William Hallward (*Cala Rectory, Tembuland, Kaffraria*), *b* 4 July 1867

4*c* Clement Govett Hallward, *b* 30 June 1870

5*c* Constance Maude Hallward (*21 Pembroke Gardens, S W*), *b* 15 Feb 1865.

2*b* *Charles Berners Hallward,* b 2 Aug 1825, d 6 Jan 1896, m 2 Oct 1850, *Elizabeth Anne, da of Peter Morgan of H M Dockyard, Woolwich,* d Nov 1874, *and had issue* 1c to 8c

1*c* Charles Morgan Leslie Hallward, b 8 Oct 1852, d July 1907, m *Kate, da of James Southerton,* and has issue 1*d* to 2*d*

1*d* Dorothy Hallward

2*d* Muriel Hallward

2*c* Cyril Randolph Hallward (*25 Hogarth Road, S W*), *b* 27 Jan 1857, *m* 1902, Mary, da of J Mugghston of Lytham, co Lanc

3*c* William Lambarde Hallward (*98 Lexham Gardens, Kensington*), *b* 9 Oct 1854, *m* 23 Aug 1888, Grace, da of William James Murray of Wolverton, co Norfolk, and has issue 1*d* to 3*d*

1*d* Basil Murray Hallward, *b* 17 Nov 1891

2*d* John Leslie Hallward, *b* 19 July 1889

3*d* Clare Joyce Hallward, *b* 9 June 1899

4*c* Reginald Francis Hallward (*Woodlands, Shorne, near Gravesend*), *b* 18 Oct 1859, *m* 2 June 1886, Adelaide Caroline, da of Robert William Bloxam of Ryde, I W, and has issue 1*d* to 5*d*

1*d* Reginald Michael Bloxam Hallward, *b* 2 Oct 1889

2*d* Christopher John Hallward, *b* 6 Jan 1898

3*d* Ruth Margaret Hallward

4*d* Patience Mary Hallward

5*d* Priscilla Evelyn Gabrielle Jeanette Hallward

5*c* Arthur Wellesley Hallward (*Milton House, Bedford Park, W*), *b* 4 Mar 1860, *m* 21 Sept 1887, Caroline Sarah, da of John Murley of Durlington, and has issue 1*d* to 2*d* [Nos 16080 to 16100]

137

1d Kenneth Leslie Hallward, b 1 Nov 1888

2d Marjorie Hallward, b 7 June 1890

6c Evelyn Elizabeth Hallward, m 9 Ap 1878, William Mackinlay (*Meppadi, South Wynaad, S India*), and has issue 1d

1d Maud Mackinlay, b 19 Oct 1882

7c Eleanor Frances Graeme Hallward, m 11 Mar 1902, Col James Ridgeway Dyas, Royal Warwickshire Regt (*Brook House, Woodbridge, co Suffolk*), and has issue 1d to 2d

1d John Hallward Dyas, b 26 Feb 1907

2d Eleanor Josephine Sprye Dyas, b 6 Oct 1909

8c Lilian Berkeley Hallward (112 *Cromwell Road, S W*)

3b *Rev Thomas William Onslow Hallward, Vicar of Frittenden, co Kent*, b 9 Aug 1827, d 24 June 1899, m 1 May 1863, Mary Sophia [a descendant of King Henry VII, &c] (*Maplehurst Farm, Staplehurst, Kent*), da of Henry Hoare of Iden Manor, Staplehurst, co Kent, and had issue

See the Tudor Roll, p 274, Nos 24735-24746, and the Exeter Volume, p 197, Nos 7100-7110

4b *Emily Jane Hallward*, b 31 Mar 1824, d 9 June 1906, m 22 June 1853, the Rev James Bradby Sweet, Vicar of Otterton, co. Devon, d 3 Jan 1897, and had issue 1c to 5c

1c James Leslie Sweet (2 *Bedford Row, London, W C*), b 25 Jan 1857, m 15 Oct 1885, Ellen Caroline, da of John Barclay, M D, and has issue 1d to 5d

1d John Laxon Leslie Sweet, b 21 July 1886

2d Gerald Herbert Leslie Sweet, b 13 May 1892

3d Cyril Vincent Leslie Sweet, b 19 July 1900

4d Margaret Leslie Sweet, b 24 June 1888

5d Winifred Mary Leslie Sweet, b 1 June 1897

2c William MacMurdo Sweet, I P W D, Superintending Engineer, Dacca (*Dacca, E. Bengal*), b 14 Feb 1860, m Feb 1895, May, da of John Francis Hunnard, and has issue 1d to 3d

1d Jack Sweet, b 20 Dec 1895

2d Richard MacMurdo Sweet, b 10 Nov 1899

3d Beryl Sweet, b 8 June 1898

3c Edward Hoare Sweet, M D (*Uckfield, Sussex*), b 6 Aug 1861, m 28 Jan 1904, Hilda Mary, da of the Rev Edward Sanderson, and has issue 1d

1d Enid Marjorie Sweet, b 15 Aug 1905

4c Florence Emily Caroline Sweet, m 12 Jan 1909, the Rev George Peregrine Barber Viner, Rector of Mottingham (*Mottingham Rectory, Kent*)

5c Mary Beatrice Sweet (*Church Lodge, Liss, Hants*)

2a *Rev Nathaniel William Hallward, Rector of Milden, co Suffolk*, d Oct 1884, m Harriet, da of Charles Powell Leslie of Glasslough, co Monaghan, M P, and had issue 1b to 2b

1b *Rev John William Hallward, Chaplain of Wandsworth Gaol*, d 5 May 1871, m 7 Dec 1859, Eliza (8 *Ashley Gardens, S W*), da of William Henning of Frome, co Dorset, and had issue 1c to 2c

1c Frederick Charles Leslie Hallward (4 *Ashley Gardens, S W*), b 16 Dec 1862, unm

2c Mary Augusta Leslie Hallward, m FitzPatrick Mackworth-Praed

2b Harriet Christina Hallward, m 1856, Arthur William Saunders of Tullig, co Kerry, and has issue 1c to 2c

1c Arthur Leslie Saunders, I C S (*Lucknow*), b 1862 m 1896, Edith Lilian, da of (—) Hughes-Hallett

2c William St Lawrence Saunders, Capt (ret) Suffolk Regt, b 13 June 1863

[Nos 16101 to 16138

# of The Blood Royal

70 Descendants of JANE LAMBARDE (Table IX). *b* 3 Oct 1764, *d* 14 Feb 1836, *m* 13 Sept 1785, the Right Rev. JOHN RANDOLPH, D D., Lord Bishop of London, *d* 28 July 1813, and had issue 1*a* to 3*a*

1*a* *Rev Thomas Randolph, Rector of Much Hadham, co Herts,* b 9 Nov 1788 d 2 *May* 1875, m 28 *May* 1813, *Caroline Diana, da of the Right Hon Sir Archibald Macdonald,* 1*st Bt* [*G B*] [*a descendant of King Henry III* (see Tudor Roll, Table LXXXIV)], *and had issue* 1*b to* 3*b*

1*b Rev Edward John Randolph, Rector of Dunnington and Chancellor and Prebendary of York,* b 17 *Ap* 1814, d 9 *Dec* 1898 m 5 *July* 1843, *Catharine, da of Sir George Rich,* d 24 *June* 1899, *and had issue* 1*c to* 11*c*

1*c* Rev Edward Seymour Loveson Randolph (17 *Trinity Gardens, Folkestone*), *b* 30 May 1849, *m* 23 Ap 1881, Agnes Katharine, widow of William Garforth of Wiganthorpe, co York, da of Major George Duff, 19th Lancers

2*c* Granville Walter Randolph (24 *Shaftesbury Avenue, Bradford*), *b* 10 Feb 1851, *m* 8 June 1881, Mildred Cassandra [a descendant of Anne of Exeter sister to Kings Edward IV and Richard III], da of Rev the Hon Charles James Willoughby , and has issue 1*g* to 4*g*

   1*g* Charles Edward Randolph, *b* 1 Jan 1883
   2*g* Thomas Granville Randolph, *b* 31 Oct 1886
   3*g* George Algernon Randolph, *b* 2 Ap 1890
   4*g* Hylda Mary Randolph

3*c* Charles James Randolph (*Saham Hall, Watton, Norfolk*), *b* 28 Dec 1858, *m* 16 July 1890, Richmond Emmeline Mary, da of F W H Scheuley, 60th Rifles

4*c* Rev William Frederick Herbert Randolph (*The Vicarage, Frome Selwood, Somerset*), *b* 8 Nov 1862, *m* 27 July 1898, Dorothy, da of the Rev Henry Montagu Villiers [E of Clarendon Coll , and a descendant of the Lady Anne, sister of King Edward IV (see the Exeter Volume, p 381)], Vicar of St Paul's, Knightsbridge, and Prebendary of St Paul's Cathedral, by his wife the Lady Victoria [a descendant of Kings Henry VII and Edward IV (see Tudor Roll, p 127)], da of John (Russell), 1st Earl Russell [U K], K G

5*c* Algernon Forbes Randolph, Col in the Army (ret) (*Army and Navy*), *b* 12 Ap 1865

6*c* Jane Caroline Randolph, *b* 5 May 1844

7*c* Agnes Catharine Randolph (*St John's Road, Newbury*), *m* 16 Oct 1879, Charles Howard, *d* 24 July 1907, s *p*

8*c* Caroline Flora Macdonald Randolph, *b* 30 Sept 1853

9*c* Mary Elizabeth Randolph, *m* 13 Oct 1881, James Frederick Digby Willoughby (*Southwell, Notts*) [B Middleton Coll , and a descendant of Anne of Exeter, sister to Kings Edward IV and Richard III], and has issue 1*d* to 4*d*

   1*d* Ronald James Edward Willoughby, Mid R N , *b* 7 May 1884
   2*d* Archibald Macdonald Willoughby, Mid R N , *b* 20 May 1887
   3*d* Bernard Digby Willoughby, *b* 8 Ap 1896
   4*d* Katherine Mary Seymour Willoughby

10*c.* Emily Ann Randolph (16 *Herbert Crescent, S W*), *m* 29 Jan 1885, Charles Edward Farmer , and has issue 1*d* to 5*d*

   1*d* Charles George Edgar Farmer, *b* 28 Nov 1885
   2*d* Harry Gamul Farmer, *b* 12 Mar 1887
   3*d* Hugh Robert Macdonald Farmer, *b* 3 Dec 1907
   4*d* Olive Agnes Emmeline Farmer, *b* 16 July 1895
   5*d* Ruth Alice Farmer, *b* 10 Aug 1896

11*c* Augusta Margaret Randolph, *b* 30 Dec 1860   [Nos 16159 to 16162

The Plantagenet Roll

2b Sir George Granville Randolph, K C B, Adm R N, b 26 Jan 1818, d
16 May 1907, m 4 Feb 1851, Eleanor Harriet, da of Joseph Arkwright of Mark
Hall, co Essex, d 5 Ap 1907, and had issue 1c to 3c

 1c Rev Rodney Granville Randolph (Moray Lodge, Duston, Northants), b
23 Nov 1851, m Oct 1884, Frances Charlotta, da of John Christopher Mansel
of Cosgrove, co Northants

 2c Rose Caroline Randolph, m 28 Ap 1885, the Rev Alfred George Lovelace
Bowling, formerly Vicar of St Barnabas, Hove (Moreton End House, Harpenden),
and has issue 1d to 6d

  1d Charles Randolph Bowling, b 18 Feb 1886

  2d Edwyn Randolph Bowling, b 27 Sept 1892

  3d Harold Randolph Bowling, b 4 Jan 1894

  4d Geoffrey Randolph Bowling, b 30 Aug 1898

  5d Rose Mary Bowling, b 2 Mar 1887

  6d Margaret Mary Bowling b 4 June 1896

 3c Violet Mary Randolph

 3b Rev Leveson Cyril Randolph, Vicar of St Luke's, Lower Norwood, b 1828,
d 1 Mar 1876, m 13 July 1854, Anne [a descendant of Anne of Exeter, sister to
King Edward IV, &c (see Exeter Volume, p 240)], da of Rev the Hon John
Evelyn Boscawen, Rector of Wootton, co Surrey, Canon of Canterbury, d 27 Feb
1899, and had issue 1c to 4c

 1c George Boscawen Randolph, J P (Steeple Aston, Oxon), b 28 Oct 1864

 2c Right Rev John Hugh Granville Randolph, D D, Lord Bishop of Guildford (Guildford), b 28 Jan 1866, m 31 Jan 1895, Beatrice Mary, da of the Rev
Samuel Back, Vicar of Maxstoke, and has issue 1d to 3d

  1d Joan Mary Randolph, b 14 Oct 1898

  2d Margaret Ann Randolph, b 22 Ap 1899

  3d Frances Edith Randolph, b 15 Oct 1901

 3c Margaret Catherine Randolph, b 30 Dec 1860

 4c Annie Eveline Randolph, b 28 Feb 1863

 2a Rev John Honywood Randolph, Rector of Saunderstead, co Surrey, b
8 Mar 1791, d June 1868, m 1814, Sarah, da of Richard Wilson of Bildeston,
and had issue 1b to 3b

 1b Rev John Randolph, Rector of Saunderstead, b 15 May 1821, d 11 July
1881, m 29 Ap 1851, Harriet, da of John Robert Bell, and had issue 1c to 3c

  1c Percy John Charles Randolph (Erdington, Worcestershire), b 11 Sept 1858,
m 16 Nov 1897, Constance, da of Richard Shaw

  2c Evelyn Sarah Frances Randolph } (7 Haldon Terrace Dawlish,

  3c Leila Frances Atwood Randolph }   S Devon)

 2b Hannah Georgiana Randolph, m 8 Jan 1857, the Rev Frederick John
Coleridge, M A, Rector of Cadbury 1855-1906 and R D 1873-97, b 4 Dec 1826,
d 20 Jan 1906, and has issue 1c to 5c

  1c Rev George Frederick Coleridge, Vicar of Crowthorne (Crowthorne Vicarage, Berks), b 10 Nov 1857, unm

  2c Hugh Fortescue Coleridge, D S O, Lieut-Col Loyal N Lancashire Regt,
served in S Africa 1899-1900 (Naval and Military, Gough Barracks, the Curragh,
co Dublin), b 11 Jan 1858, m 12 Sept 1906, Kathleen Grace Fane, da of Rear-
Adm John Hugh Bainbridge of Elfordleigh, Plympton

  3c James Duke Carmichael Coleridge, b 14 Jan 1860, unm

  4c Flora Augusta Townsend Coleridge, unm

  5c Constance Georgiana Randolph Coleridge, m 12 Ap 1894, John Henry
Cann (Gothelney Hall, Bridgewater), and has issue 1d to 2d

   1d Hugh John Cann, b 19 Sept. 1896

   2d Constance Nancy Coleridge Cann, b 7 Sept 1900   [Nos 16163 to 16189

140

# of The Blood Royal

3*b* Sarah Augusta Randolph, *m* 2 Nov 1848, Francis James Coleridge of the Manor House, Ottery St Mary, *b* 26 May 1825, *d* 5 June 1862, and has issue 1*c* to 7*c*

1*c* *Percy Duke Coleridge, Lieut R M L I* , *b* 1 Sept 1850, *d* 29 Mar 1881, *m* 27 *June* 1877, *Edith Laura Matilda* [*descended from King Henry VII* (see Tudor Roll, p 201)], *da of Capt Lovell Stanhope Richard Lovell* , *and had issue* 1*d to* 2*d*

    1*d* John Coleridge, *b* 25 Ap 1878, *m*

    2*d* Percy Coleridge, *b* 20 July 1880, *m*

2*c* Francis Randolph Cyril Coleridge, Chief Constable of Devon 1891–1907, *b* 27 Nov 1854, *m* 1 Aug 1903, Alice Gertrude, widow of Capt Hayhurst France, da of R N Hawks of Dolcorsllwyn, co Montgomery, *s p*

3*c* Frances Augusta Coleridge, *m* at Colombo, 20 Feb 1878, Robert Holme Sumner Scott

4*c* Harriet Georgiana Coleridge, *m* 26 Jan 1882, William Nicholas Connock Marshall, J P (*Treworgey, Liskeard, Cornwall*) , and has issue 1*d* to 2*d*

    1*d* Coleridge Connock Marshall, *b* 15 Mar 1883

    2*d* Monica A Connock Marshall

5*c* Emily Joanna Coleridge, *unm*

6*c* Dorothy Helen Coleridge, *m* 26 Jan 1882, Reginald Philip Sumner [3st son of Charles Sumner of Hempsted, co Glos , a County Court Judge]

7*c* Celia Elizabeth Coleridge, *unm*

3*a* *Rev George Randolph*, *b* 16 Feb 1797, *d* 1880, *m* 20 *Aug* 1822, *Catharine Elizabeth* [a descendant of *King Henry VII* (see Tudor Roll, p 536)], *da of the Rev Henry Roger Drummond, Rector of Fawsley, co Hants , and had issue* 1*b* [1]

1*b* Rev Cyril Randolph (*Chartham Rectory, Canterbury*), *b* 6 Feb 1826, *m* 30 Sept 1851, Frances Selina, da of Lionel Charles Hervey, and has issue 1*c* to 7*c*

1*c* *Felton George Randolph*, *b* 1 Ap 1854 , *d* 29 Dec 1906, *m* 14 *Jan* 1896, *Emily Margaret, da of Sir Evan Colville Nepean, C B* , *and had issue* 1*d to* 7*d*

    1*d* John Hervey Randolph, *b* 3 Mar 1897

    2*d* Cyril George Randolph, *b* 26 June 1898

    3*d* Thomas Berkeley Randolph, *b* 15 Mar 1904

    4*d* Mary Frances Elizabeth Randolph, *b* 24 Nov 1896

    5*d* Susan Emily Randolph, *b* 6 Aug 1900

    6*d* Margaret Isobel Randolph, *b* July 1902

    7*d* Barbara May Randolph, *b* 6 Mar 1906

2*c* Rev. Berkeley William Randolph, D D, Hon Canon of Ely (*Theological College, Ely*), *b* 10 Mar 1858

3*c* Hugh Lionel Randolph (110 *Reconquista, Buenos Ayres, Argentina*), *b* 20 July 1868, *m* 20 June 1899, Lily Constance, da of Charles Y Fell, of St John's, Nelson, N Z , and has issue 1*d* to 2*d*

    1*d* Bernard Nolan Randolph, *b* 1900

    2*d* Richard Seymour Randolph, *b* 1904

4*c* Gertrude Frances Randolph, *b* 25 Sept 1853

5*c* Selina Catharine Randolph, *b* 13 Ap 1859

6*c* Agnes Susan Randolph, *b* 2 Nov 1861

7*c* Florence Mary Randolph, *b* 23 Dec 1862   [Nos 16190 to 16216

---

[1] *N B* —These should be in Tudor Roll, p 536, between Nos 35767–35768

The Plantagenet Roll

71 Descendants of JANE WHELER (Table IX), d 6 Dec 1847, m 10 Sept 1774, HENRY (HOOD), 2nd VISCOUNT [G B] and BARON [G B and I] HOOD, b 25 Aug 1753, d 25 Jan 1836, and had issue 1a to 4a

1a *Hon Francis Wheler Hood, Lieut Col in the Army*, b 4 Oct 1781, d (*being killed in action on the heights of Aire*) 2 Mar 1814, m 11 Oct 1804, Caroline, da of Sir Andrew Snape Hamond, 1st Bt [G B], d 11 Mar 1858, and had issue 1b to 2b

1b *Samuel (Hood, afterwards (R L 12 Feb 1840) Hood-Tibbits), 3rd Viscount [G B] and Baron [G B and I] Hood*, b 10 Jan 1808, d 8 May 1846, m 27 June 1837, Mary Isabella, da and h of Richard John Tibbits of Barton Seagrove Hall, co Northants [*by his wife Horatia Charlotte, da of Thomas Lockwood and Charlotte, da of Lord George Manners-Sutton, a descendant of the Lady Anne, sister of King Edward IV (see Exeter Volume, p 165)*] [m 2ndly, 5 May 1849, George Hall of Brighton, M D, 3rdly, 17 June 1858, Capt John Boilase Maunsell], and d (–), and had issue 1c to 5c

1c *Francis Wheler (Hood), 4th Viscount [G B] and Baron [G B and I] Hood*, b 4 July 1838 d 27 Ap 1907, m 18 July 1865, Edith Lydia Drummond, da of Arthur H Ward of Calverley, Tunbridge Wells, and had issue 1d to 6d

1d Grosvenor Arthur Alexander (Hood), *5th Viscount [G B] and Baron [G B and I] Hood, late Major Grenadier Guards* (*Barton Seagrave, Kettering*, 17 Hertford Street, Mayfair, W) b 13 Nov 1868

2d Hon Horace Lambert Alexander Hood, M V O, D S O, Capt R N, b 4 Oct 1870

3d Hon Neville Albert Hood, Capt R A, b 4 Oct 1872, m 1908, Eveline Mary, da of Herman Usticke Broad of Trisilian, Falmouth, and has issue 1e

1e Edith Rosemary Hood

4d Hon Francis George Hood, b 28 Mar 1880, m 20 Oct 1901, Helen Kendell Mouncey, da of Lieut-Col the Hon Edward Gawler Prior of Victoria, B C, P C, Canada, and has issue 1e

1e Francis Basil Hood, b 5 Sept 1904

5d *Hon Mabel Edith Hood*, b 26 May 1866, d 18 Jan 1901, m 25 July 1889, Francis Denzil Edward (Baring), *5th Baron Ashburton* [U K] [*descended from King Henry VII*] (*The Grange, Alresford, Hants*), and had issue
See the Tudor Roll, p 454, Nos 31825–31829

6d Hon Dorothy Violet Hood

2c Hon Albert Hood, *late Rifle Brigade* (*Upham House, Bishop's Waltham, The Hook, Titchfield*), b 26 Aug 1841, m 2 June 1868, Julia Jane, da of Thomas Wynn Hornby of Upham House, co Hants, d 20 Aug 1906, and has issue 1d to 7d

1d Samuel Wynn Hornby Hood (*Cordridge, Bothy, Hants*), b 30 Mar 1869, m 29 Oct 1906, Ethel Norah, da of Lionel Smith

2d Albert Oscar Hood, *late Lieut 5th Batt Rifle Brigade*, b 2 Ap 1870

3d Edward Hood (*Dromore, co Kerry*), b 18 July 1872, m 27 Oct 1900, Nora Eveleen, da of Richard Mahony of Dromore Castle, co Kerry, D L

4d Alexander Frank Hood, *formerly Capt 3rd Vol Batt E Surrey Regt*, b 27 Jan 1874, m 21 June 1905, Gladys Ursula, da of Edward C Youell of Galatz, Roumania, and has issue 1e

1e Albert Edward Hood, b 23 Mar 1906

5d Robert Valentine Hood, b 5 Feb 1876

6d Emily Beryl Sissy Hood, m 19 Sept 1893, Edward (Digby), 10th Baron Digby [G B] [a descendant of King Henry VII (see the Tudor Roll, p 454)] (*Minterne House, Cerne Abbas, Dorset*, 16 Grosvenor Place, S W), and has issue 1e to 5e
[Nos 16217 to 16236

# of The Blood Royal

1e Hon Edward Kenelm Digby, b 1 Aug 1894
2e Hon Robert Henry Digby, b 24 Nov 1903
3e Hon Lettice Theresa Digby
4e Hon Geraldine Margot Digby
5e Hon. Venetia Jane Digby

7d Marguerite Jenny Hood, b 20 May 1881

3c Hon Alexander Frederick Hood (Airmyn Hall, Goole, Yorks), b 20 May 1843, m 7 June 1870, Ethel Cecilia [a descendant of King Henry VII, and also through Mortimer-Percy, &c], da of Algernon Charles Heber-Percy of Hodnet Hall, co Salop, and has issue
See p 68, Nos 834-838

2b Hon Caroline Hood, b 16 Oct 1807, d 9 May 1890, m 25 Feb 1834, Arthur Francis Gregory of Styvechale Hall, co Warwick, D L, d 27 Feb 1853, and had issue 1c

1c Francis Hood Gregory of Styvechale, J P, M A (Oxon), formerly Major 15th Hussars and A D C to Duke of Abercorn when Lord-Lieut of Ireland, to Lord Mayo when Viceroy of India, &c (Styvechale Hall, Coventry), b 29 Oct 1836

2a Samuel (Hood), 2nd Baron Bridport [I], b 7 Dec 1788, d 6 Jan 1868, m 3 July 1810, Charlotte Mary, suo jure 3rd Duchess of Bronté [Sicily], da and h of William (Nelson), 1st Earl Nelson [U K] and 2nd Duke of Bronté [Sicily] b 20 Sept 1787, d 29 Jan 1873, and had issue 1b to 5b

1b Alexander Nelson (Hood), 3rd Baron [I] and 1st Viscount [U K] Bridport and 4th Duke of Bronte [Sicily], b 23 Dec 1814, d 4 June 1904, m 2 Aug 1838, Mary [a descendant of Anne of Exeter, sister to King Edward IV, &c], da of Arthur Blundell Bandys Trumbull (Hill), 3rd Marquis of Downshire [I], d 15 July 1884, and had issue
See the Exeter Volume, pp 323-324, Nos 23985-24031

2b Hon Mary Sophia Hood, b 1 Dec 1811, d 29 Jan 1888, m as 2nd wife, 17 Aug 1841, John Lee Lee of Dillington, co Somerset, d 16 Aug 1874, and had issue 1c to 3c

1c Edward Hanning Lee (now D P 13 June 1876) Hanning Lee, J P, Col formerly Comdg 2nd Life Guards (Old Manor House, Bighton, Alresford), b 26 Aug 1845, m 1872, Georgiana Emma, da of Edward Marjoribanks of the Hall, Bushey, co Herts, and has issue 1d to 4d

1d Vaughan Alexander Hanning-Lee, Comm R N, b 1 Oct 1878
2d Francis Charles Hanning-Lee, Lieut R N, b 29 Sept 1880
3d Hazel Hanning-Lee, b 15 Aug 1877
4d Robina Marion Hanning-Lee, m as 2nd wife, 5 Feb 1902, Henry Edmund (Butler), 14th Viscount Mountgarret [I] [a descendant of King Henry VII, &c] (Ballyconra, co Kilkenny, &c), and has issue 1d

1d Hon Piers Henry Augustine Butler, b 28 Aug 1903

2c William Hanning Lee, late Col Comdg 2nd Dragoon Guards (Old Catton, Norwich), b 9 Dec 1846, m 31 Oct 1877, Emilie Georgiana, da of the Rev Alfred Bond, and has issue 1d

1d Seymour Hanning-Lee, b 25 Sept 1881

3c Emily Mary Lee, d Mar 1893, m 1st, Thomas Spragging Godfrey of Balderton Hall, co Notts, d (-), 2ndly, 28 Dec 1882, Major Gen Henry Lowther Balfour, R A, and had issue 1d to 4d

1d Edward Lee Godfrey, b 1868
2d Alice Sophia Godfrey, b 2 Jan 1865, d 12 May 1886, m as 1st wife, 21 Ap 1885, the Hon Francis Albert Rollo Russell (Steep, Petersfield), and had issue 1e

1e Arthur John Godfrey Russell, b 11 Mar 1886
3d Violet Lucy Godfrey
4d Edith Mary Adelaide Godfrey   [Nos 16237 to 16308

143

The Plantagenet Roll

3b *Hon Charlotte Hood*, b 8 *Aug* 1813, d 21 *Aug* 1906, m *as 2nd wife,* 4 *Sept* 1845, *Horace William Noel Rochfort of Clogrenane, co Carlow,* d 16 May 1891, *and had issue*

See the Exeter Volume, p 202, Nos 7263-7269

4b *Hon Catharine Louisa Hood*, b 25 *Mar* 1818, d 6 *Oct* 1893, m 18 *Ap* 1837, *Henry Hall of Barton Abbey, co Oxon,* d 17 *Nov* 1862, *and had issue* 1c *to 9c*

1c Alexander William Hall, M P, J P, D L, High Sheriff co Oxford 1867 (*Barton Abbey, Steeple Aston, Oxon*), b 20 June 1838, m 27 Aug 1863, Emma Gertrude, da of Edward Jowett of Eltofts, co York, and has issue 1d to 7d

1d Alexander Nelson Hall (*Cornwall Manor, Chipping Norton*), b 25 July 1865, m 4 Aug 1891, Susan Isabel, da of Col G C Porter of Fairford Park, co Gloucester, s p

2d Robin Henry Edward Hall (*The Priory, Prior's Marston, Byfield, R S O, Warwickshire*), b 29 Jan 1882, unm

3d Marion Alexandra Gertrude Hall, m 1889, Lieut-Col Malcolm Stewart Riach, 2nd Batt Cameron Highlanders (*Trentsin, North China*), and has issue 1e to 3e

1e Stewart Malcolm Alexander Riach, b Jan 1892

2e Ronald Riach

3e Nigel Riach

4d Muriel Hall, m 1890, the Rev Frank Langley Appleford, Rector of Castle Combe (*Castle Combe Rectory, near Chippenham*), and has issue 1e to 2e

1e Walter Alexander Nelson Appleford, b 5 Mar 1891

2e Doreen Langley Appleford, b 27 Nov 1901

5d Amabel Hall, m 15 Oct 1896, the Rev Spencer Henry Harrison, Rector of Aswarby (*Aswarby Rectory, Folkingham, Lincolnshire*), and has issue 1e

1e Rosaleen Verena Harrison b 23 June 1907

6d Mary Verena Hall, m 26 July 1899, Alfred Hewston Holmes, M D (*Down Hall, Rippingill, Lincolnshire*), and has issue

7d Monica Hall, m 2 July 1902, James Frederick Farquharson, and has issue 1e to 2e

1e William James Farquharson, b 26 Feb 1904

2e Ellen Constance Lorraine Farquharson, b 30 Dec 1906

2c Henry Samuel Hall, C B, V D (*25 Longridge Road, South Kensington, S W*), b 17 Oct 1839, m Jan 1874, Eleanor Elizabeth Mary, da of Gen Edward Boxer, R A, F R S, s p

3c Herbert Lee Hall, *late* 61st Regt, b 20 Nov 1841, unm

4c Hugh Hall, D C L, Bar-at-Law (*100 Holywell Street, Oxford*), b (—), m 9 Dec 1880, Elinor Mildred, da of the Rev John Wright Hopkins, Vicar of Aghern, co Cork, and has issue 1d

1d Hugh Frederick Gethin Hall, b 24 Oct 1881

5c Horatio Nelson Hall, b 11 Mar 1852, unm

6c Arthur Yonge Hall, b 23 Oct 1856, unm

7c Hilare Charlotte Hall, m 29 Dec 1863, John de Burgh Rochfort (*Clogrenane, co Carlow*), and has issue

See the Exeter Volume, p 202, Nos 7271-7277

8c Frances Caroline Hall

9c Catharine Hester Hall, m 1st, 16 May 1865, Stafford Majendie Brown, d 29 Ap 1892, 2ndly, 13 Aug 1892, George Ffrench (*Adderbury, near Banbury, Oxon*), and has issue 1d to 7d

1d. Stafford Brown, b 1 Nov 1866, m Emily Ella, da of (—), and has issue 1e

1e Stafford Meredith Brown, b 22 Ap 1898   [Nos 16309 to 16349

144

2d Majendie Brown, b 17 Jan 1871, m 8 June 1903, Geraldine May, da of Richard Berridge, and has issue 1e to 4e

1e Richard Majendie Brown, b 19 Aug 1907

2e Frances Helen May Brown, b 14 Oct 1903

3e Catharine Joan Brown, b 30 Dec 1904

4e Nora Ena Brown, b 9 Ap 1906

3d Horatio Nelson Brown, b 15 Oct 1876, m 18 Oct 1897, Annie Kate, da of Edward William May, and has issue 1e to 2e

1e Guy Nelson Brown, b 13 July 1901

2e Lorna Brown, b 14 Oct 1898

4d Nicholas George Ffrench, b 26 Oct 1893

5d Ethel Maud Brown, m 6 Feb 1895, Thomas Oates Halliwell, and has issue 1e to 2e

1e Eric Oates Halliwell, b 31 Dec 1903

2e Marjorie Halliwell, b 30 Oct 1895

6d Hilaire Katharine Esme Brown, m 19 Jan 1899, Edward Theodore Sandys, and has issue 1e to 3e

1e Edith Mary Sandys, b 17 Dec 1899

2e Sybil Esme Sandys, b 17 Nov 1900

3e Hilaire Mina Sandys, b 16 June 1903

7d Hester Sybil Alexandra Brown, m 30 July 1902, Edward Henry Hodge

5b *Hon Fanny Caroline Hood*, b 29 *Mar* 1821 d 2 *Oct* 1903, m 20 *May* 1845, *Sir John Walrond Walrond, 1st Bt* [U K], d 23 1p 1889, *and had issue*
See the Exeter Volume, pp 119-120, Nos 1455-1497

3a *Hon Susannah Hood*, b 17 *May* 1779, d 1 *Nov* 1823, m *the Rev Richard George Richards, Vicar of Hambleton, Hants*, bun 25 *June* 1841, *aged 68 and had (with possibly other) issue (a son, Major Hood Richards, who had a son and da who d unm)*

4a *Hon Selina Hood*, b 16 *Nov* 1782, d 17 *Jan* 1863, m 16 *Ap* 1805, *Vice-Admiral Sir Francis Mason, K C B*, d 27 *May* 1873, *and had issue* 1b *to* 4b

1b *Francis John Mills Mason*, b 4 *May* 1821, d 14 *July* 1899, m 7 *Aug* 1851, *Jane, da of William Morton of Kent's Green, co Worcester, d June* 1852, *and had issue* 1c *to* 2c

1c Rev Francis Wheler Randull Mason, M A (Oxon) Chaplain of Wroxall Abbey (*The Lers, Warwick*), b 11 *July* 1852, m 5 *Oct* 1887, Amy, da of the Rev Lester Lester of Swanage, and has issue 1d

1d Rachel Lois Mason

2c Rev Charles Arthur Mason, M A (Oxon), Vicar of Otterbourne, *formerly Canon of Allahabad* (*Otterbourne Vicarage, Winchester*), b 27 Nov 1858, m 15 Feb 1890, Laura Kate, da of Dr S Plumbe, and has issue 1d to 5d

1d Arthur Samuel Mason, b 27 May 1893

2d Gerald Francis Mason, b 30 Dec 1897

3d John Oscar Lawrence Mason, b 12 Sept 1899

4d Winifred Kate Mason

5d Ada Doris Hood Mason

2b *Charles Crawfurd Mason*, b 1826, d *in California* 1904, m 1854, *Lucy Ella* (Box 720, Post Office, Sherman, Los Angeles, California), *da of* (—) *Holmes, and had issue* 1c *to* 5c

1c William Robert Mason (*America*), b 186- m 1906, Violet, da of (—), d 1907

2c Hugh Francis Mason (*America*), b 1873

3c Edith Mary Mason, m Donald Grant, and has issue (3 children)

[Nos 16350 to 16420.

The Plantagenet Roll

4c Ethel Mason, m 1907, Ernest Cox

5c Sybil Mason, m Elliott Cox, and has issue (4 children)

3b Mary Sophia Mason (*Braunston, Rugby*), b 16 Mar 1816, m the Rev Charles Bucknill, d s p 1866

4b *Selina Ruth Ann Mason*, b 1 Dec 1818, d 29 May 1909, m *the Rev James William Knight*, d 28 Aug 1878, and had issue 1c to 2c

  1c Selina May Knight, unm

  2c Edith Mary Knight, m 17 Jan 1878, Alfred James Riley, Major 4th Batt Somerset L I (*Grove House, Kidlington, Oxon*), and has issue 1d to 5d

  1d Gerald Brook Riley, Lieut R N, b 5 Ap 1881

  2d Denys Linzee Brook Riley, b 5 Dec 1898

  3d Agnes Muriel Riley

  4d Elsie Mary Riley

  5d Edith Marjorie Riley, m 2 Aug 1906, the Rev George Duncan (*Shipton-on-Cherwell Rectory, Kidlington, Oxon*), and has issue 1e to 2e

    1e John Hugh Banchory Duncan, b 19 Oct 1907

    2e David Lionel Crawfurd Duncan, b 30 Ap 1909   [Nos 16421 to 16432

72 Descendants of SARAH WHELER (Table IX), d 25 Oct 1807; m 17 Nov 1749, the Rev JOHN MILLS, Rector of Barford and Oxhill, co Warwick, b 10 May 1712, d 21 Mar 1791, and had issue 1a to 4a

1a *William Mills of Bisterne, Southampton* M P, b 10 Nov 1750, d 20 Mar 1820, m 7 Ap 1786, *Elizabeth, da of the Hon Wriothesley Digby*, d 27 Dec 1828, and had issue

See the Essex Volume, pp 53-56, Nos 5513-5619

2a *Rev Francis Mills, Rector of Barford co Warwick*, b 29 June 1759, d 23 Ap 1851, m 26 Oct 1811, *Catharine* (see p 410), *da of Sir John Mordaunt, 7th Bt [E]*, d 7 May 1852, and had issue 1b to 2b

1b *Rev Henry Mills of Pillerton Manor, Kineton, co Warwick* b 1 Ap 1815, d 14 Nov 1906, m 9 Dec 1841, *Mary, da of the Rev Henry Hippisley of Lambourne Place, co Berks*, d 3 Sept 1892, and had issue 1c to 3c

1c Francis Mills (*Manor House Pillerton, near Warwick*), b 18 Jan 1844, m 27 Dec 1877, Selina Mary, da of the Rev Henry Charles Knightley [cadet of Fawsley, and a descendant of the Lady Anne Plantagenet, sister to King Edward IV, &c (see Exeter Volume, p 518)], and has issue 1d to 4d

  1d Henry Valentine Mills, b 23 Nov 1881

  2d Mabel Frances Mills

  3d Phœbe Mills

  4d Esther Mary Mills

2c Catharine Mills (*Carfax House, Barrow-on Humber, Clyde House, Ventnor, I W*), m 20 Ap 1882, the Rev Alfred Freeman, Vicar of Burgh-on-Bain, co Lincoln, d 31 July 1895, and has issue 1d to 3d

  1d Henry Alfred Freeman, C E, b 31 Jan 1883

  2d Katharine Mary Freeman

  3d Emma Sophia Freeman

3c Fanny Mills

2b *Arthur Mills of Budehaven, co Cornwall*, b 20 July 1816, d 12 Oct 1898, m 3 Aug 1848, *Agnes Lucy, da of Sir Thomas Dyke Acland, 10th Bt [E]*, d. 23 May 1895, and had issue 1c to 2c

1c Rev Barton Reginald Vaughan Mills (12 *Cranley Gardens, S W*), b 29 Oct 1857, m 1st, 10 July 1886, Lady Catharine Mary [a descendant of George
[Nos 16433 to 16550

146

(Plantagenet), Duke of Clarence, K G (see the Clarence Volume, p 591)], sister of Sydney (Hobart), 7th Earl of Buckinghamshire [G B], da of Frederick John Hobart, Lord Hobart, d 25 Sept 1889, 2ndly, 10 Jan 1894, Elizabeth Edith, da of Sir George Dalhousie Ramsay C B , and has issue 1d to 4d

 1d Arthur Frederick Hobart Mills, b 12 July 1887

 2d George Ramsay Acland Mills, b 1 Oct 1896

 3d Agnes Edith Mills

 4d Violet Eleanor Mills

 2c Dudley Acland Mills, Col R E (Broadlands, Jersey), b 24 Aug 1859, m Feb 1896, Ethel, da of Sir Henri Joly de Lotbinière, K C M G , and has issue (a son and 2 das)

 3a Selina Mills, d 1825, m 1780, James Molony of Kiltanon, co Clare, d 12 Oct 1823 , and had issue 1b to 2b

 1b James Molony of Kiltanon, b 18 Aug 1785, d 7 July 1871, m 1st, 17 Feb 1820, Harriet da of William Harding of Baraset, co Ware, d 8 Oct 1826 , 2ndly, 15 Ap 1828, Lucy, da of Sir Trevor Wheler, 8th Bt [E], d 14 May 1855 , and had issue 1c to 7c

 1c William Mills Molony of Kiltanon, Major 22nd and 83rd Regts , b 24 Ap 1825, d 7 Sept 1891, m 8 Nov 1865, Marianne Marsh, da and co-h of Robert Fannin of Leeson Street, Dublin, d 27 Jan 1880, and had issue 1d to 3d

  1d William Beresford Molony, late Capt King's Own Royal Lancashire Regt (Kiltanon, near Tulla, co Clare), b 25 Aug 1873, m 22 Feb 1905, Lena Annie Maria, da of George Wright of Heysham Lodge, co Lanc , s p

  2d Henrietta Mary Molony, m 28 July 1903, Marcus Thomas Francis Keane (Beech Park, Ennis, co Clare), and has issue 1e to 2:

   1e Marcus William Keane, b 2 Jan 1906

   2e Helen Louise Keane, b 17 Jan 1905

  3d Iva Kathleen Molony, m 10 June 1896, Capt John Raynsford Longley, East Surrey Regt (Devonport, Hidey Grange, Crownhill, South Devon) , and has issue 1e to 2e

   1e Charles Raynsford Longley, b 21 Dec 1897

   2e John Molony Longley, b 21 Sept 1906

 2c Rev Francis Wheler Molony, b 5 Ap 1829, d 27 Feb 1860, m 19 Oct 1853, Harriet, da of Capt G Baker, R N , d 11 Ap 1910, and had issue 1d

  1d James Arthur Molony (Enon Valley, Lawrence Co , Penn , U S A), b 29 Aug 1854 , m 14 Dec 1876, Annie, da of J W Hague of Enon Valley, Pennsylvania , and has issue (with a son and da d unm) 1e to 5e

   1e Harriet Eliza Molony, m 15 Mar 1900, Frank Chestney of New Castle, Pa , and has issue 1f to 3f

    1f Francis Edwin Chestney, b 21 Ap 1902

    2f James Chestney, b 29 July 1904

    3f Mabel Evelyn Chestney, b 18 Sept 1907

   2e Lucy Molony, m 25 Ap 1900, William J Buchanan of Grove City, Pa , and has issue 1f to 4f

    1f Arthur Vandeleur Buchanan, b 18 Jan 1901

    2f William Leo Buchanan, b 17 Sept 1903

    3f Grace Heyne Buchanan, b 27 May 1905

    4f Marion Louise Buchanan, b 30 Aug 1908

   3e Anna Kathleen Molony, m 6 Dec 1904, Allen Goodhart of Shippensburg, Pa , and has issue 1f to 2f

    1f Harry Allen Goodhart, b 8 June 1906

    2f Anna H Goodhart, b 28 Aug 1907

   4e Henrietta Charlotte Molony, m 13 Aug 1907, Albert Weaver of Tarentum, Pa , s p s

   5e Iva Molony   [Nos 16551 to 16577

The Plantagenet Roll

3c Edmund Weldon Molony, H E I C S , b 27 Mar 1830, d 30 Jan 1888, m 29 July 1863, Frances Selina (13 West Cliff Terrace, Ramsgate), da of (Conway) Arthur Edward Gayer, LL D , Q C (see p 149) , and had issue 1d to 6d

1d Edmund Alexander Molony, Assist Commissioner at Benares (Benares, India), b 17 Jan 1866 , m in India, 29 Nov 1898, Ethel Blanche, da of Herbert Smith of Bula, Aligarh, U P , India, s p

2d Frederick Arthur Molony, C E , b 11 Feb 1875

3d Eleanor Mary Molony, m 2 July 1901, George Whitty Gayer, Central Provinces Police, India, s p

1d Lucy Selina Molony

5d Alice Helen Molony

6d Lilian Edith Molony

1c Frederick Beresford Molony, H E I C S , b 15 June 1833 , d 13 Nov 1868, m 13 Oct 1858. Eleanor Jane (Clare Cottage, West Byfleet, Surrey), da of (Conway) Arthur Edward Gayer, LL D , Q C (see p 149), and had issue 1d to 5d

1d Francis Arthur Molony, Major R E , b 17 May 1863 , m 8 Nov 1888, Katharine Mary, da of John Williams Grigg of Tamerton Foliot, co Devon , and has issue 1e to 1e

1e Arthur Williams Molony, b 4 Oct 1892

2e Edward Frederick Molony, b 16 Mar 1899

3e Dorothy Katherine Molony

4e Margery Eileen Molony

2d Rev Herbert James Molony, D D , Bishop in Mid China 1908 (Ningpo, China), b 2 June 1865 , m 1st, 17 Sept 1895, Eva, da of the Rev Matthew Anderson, d at Mandla, C P , India, 12 Sept 1897 , 2ndly, 6 Aug 1908, Gertrude Elizabeth, da of the Rev Stewart Dixon Stubbs

3d Mary Selina Molony, unm

4d Eleanor Florence Molony, m 1st, 6 July 1892, Horatio Scott, M D , d s p 2 June 1893 , 2ndly, 25 Aug 1906, Francis Mackenzie Ogilvy (Blackthorns, West Byfleet, Surrey), s p

5d Agnes Freda Molony, m 1 Feb 1908, Edward Millington Synge (Clare Cottage, West Byfleet, Surrey)

5c Charles Mills Molony of St Catherine's Priory, Guildford, Col in the Army, C B., b 26 Jan 1836 , d 14 Aug 1901, m 2 Aug 1866, Eliza, da of Andrew Hamilton of Streatham , and had issue 1d to 3d

1d James Rowland Hamilton Molony, Solicitor (Shenfield, The Drive, Wimbledon , 28 Lincoln's Inn Fields, W C), b 28 Ap 1867 , m 12 Jan 1895, Emma Charlotte, da of Arthur Wienholt of Fassifern, Queensland , and has issue 1e to 4e

1e Trevor James Molony, b 7 July 1897

2e Marcus Vandeleur Molony, b 18 Dec 1898

3e Rowland Hutton Molony, b 10 Oct 1906

4e Clare Elizabeth Molony, b 7 Aug 1902

2d Trevor Charles Wheler Molony, D S O , Major R F A (Shalazan, Bergholt Road, Colchester), b 28 July 1868 , m 31 Oct 1899 Beatrice Annie, da of Major-Gen W H Beynon , and has issue 1c to 4e

1e Trevor St Patrick Molony, b 6 Sept 1900

2e Charles Beynon Molony, b 15 Jan 1906

3e Norman Molony, b 14 Ap 1907

1e. Pearl Molony, b 21 July 1903

3d Charles Vandeleur Molony, Capt late West Kent Regt , b 19 July 1870 , unm.

6c Mary Molony (Kiltanon), m 3 Jan 1856, Arthur Vandeleur, Major R A , of Rathblahine, co Clare, b 27 Ap 1829 , d 6 June 1860 , and has issue 1d to 2d

[Nos 16578 to 16604

148

# of The Blood Royal

1d Lucy Vandeleur, m 1881, Arbuthnot Butler Stoney, LL D , Bar-at-Law (*Rathlahine, Newmarket-on-Fergus, co Clare*), and has issue 1e to 3e

2e James Butler Stoney, b 30 Jan 1885

2e Arthur Vandeleur Stoney, b 8 Nov 1886

3e Mary Evelyn Stoney

2d *Emily Harriet Vandeleur*, d 27 Nov 1886, m *as 1st wife*, 29 Ap 1884, *Lord George Herbert Loftus, heir-presumptive to the Marquisate of Ely [I] and Barony of Loftus [U K], &c* (4 Alexandra Villas Brighton), and had issue 1e

1e Anna Mary Kathleen Loftus

7c Harriet Selina Molony (9 *Dartmouth Square, Dublin*), m 28 June 1859, the Ven Thomas Fitzgerald French, Rector of Castle Connell and Archdeacon of Killaloe, d 30 Dec 1884, and has issue 1d to 8d

1d Fitzgerald Charles French, b 1 May 1861, *unm*

2d Riversdale Sampson French, b 28 Dec 1862, m 6 Aug 1908, Lilian Elizabeth, da of Henry Morgan Lubery Crofton of Inchinappa, co Wicklow, J P [Bt of Mohill Coll]

3d Deane French (*Australia*), b 28 May 1864, m Sept 1903, Emily [da of (—) Crooke of Coonamble, Australia, and has issue 1e to 2e

1e Thomas FitzGerald French, b 16 Jan 1906

2e Isabel Harriet French, b 2 Aug 1904

4d Arthur James Piscoe French, b 3 Oct 1865, *unm*

5d Raymond William French, b 11 May 1867, m 11 Feb 1903, Sophia Rebecca MacMurrogh, widow (with issue) of Francis Richard Wolfe, da of Arthur MacMurrogh Murphy of Monmolin, ' The O'Morchoe of Oulartleigh'', and his issue 1e to 2e

1e Mary Dring French, b 3 Aug 1905

2e Sheela O'Morchoe French, b 3 Nov 1907

6d Harry O'Donovan French, b 12 Ap 1872, *unm*

7d Lucy Selina French, b 10 Ap 1860 *unm*

8d Agnes Mehan French, b 21 Oct 1868, *unm*

2b Edmund Molony, H E I C S , Secretary to Government of Bengal, b 27 July 1794, d in India 1830, m 27 Oct 1815, Frances Rosina, da of Henry Creighton of Goamally, East Indies, b 9 Aug 1795, d 7 Aug 1861, and had issue 1c to 2c

1c Rev Charles Arthur Molony, Vicar of St Lawrence, Ramsgate, b 22 Sept 1826, d 13 May 1894, m 4 Ap 1872, Mary Emily Jane (*Winton, Barton Fields, Canterbury*), da of Robert Deane Parker, H E I C S , and had issue (with a son, Francis Robert, b 14 Ap 1881, d 18 Mar 1882) 1d to 7d

1d Edmund Parker Molony (*Sault Ste Marie, Canada*), b 16 Feb 1873, m 19 Aug 1902, Charlena Jean, da of Charles Murray Gibson of Ontario and has issue 1e to 3e

1e Charles Edmund Gibson Molony, b 17 Nov 1903

2e James Robert Percy Molony

3e Mary Molony

2d Henry James Creighton Molony, Indian Police, b 2 July 1876

3d John Charles Molony, C E , b 23 June 1877

4d Arthur Deane Molony, Capt 7th Gurhka Rifles, b 7 Ap 1879

5d Percy William Molony, b 2 Jan 1883

6d Rosina Mary Molony, m 10 June 1908, Frank Mainwaring Furley

7d Katharine Grace Molony, *unm*

2c Frances Molony, b 10 Sept 1817, d 5 Jan 1908, m as 2nd wife, 9 Aug 1845, (Conway) Arthur Edward Gayer, LL D , Q C , b 6 July 1801, d 12 Jan. 1877, and had issue 1d to 4d

1d Rev Edmund Richard Gayer, M A , Vicar of Snitterfield (*Snitterfield* [Nos 16605 to 16633

149

The Plantagenet Roll

Vicarage, Stratford-on-Avon), b 23 Mar 1847, m 7 Aug 1873, Frances Sophia, da of the Rev Thomas D'Oyly Walters, and has issue 1c to 2c

1c Hugh Walters Gayer, late Capt Royal Garrison Artillery, b 13 May 1876, m 16 Nov 1899, Beatrice Ellen Mary, da of William Bull of 75 St Aubyns, Hove, and has issue 1f

  1f Eric Hugh Trelawny Gayer, b 10 Oct 1900

  2c Echlin Philip Gayer, b 11 Sept 1877

2d Rev Arthur Cecil Stopford Gayer, M A , Vicar of Chart Sutton (Chart Sutton Vicarage, near Maidstone), b 26 Aug 1856, m 21 Nov 1899, Ellen Marion, da of John Hart Sankey, J P , and has issue 1e to 2e

  1e Charles Murray Acworth Gayer, b 27 July 1904

  2e Dorothy Mabel Gayer, b 24 Ap 1902

  3d Lucy Harriette Gayer, unm

  4d Edith Mary Gayer, unm

  1a Frances Mills, d (?s p) 3 Mar 1795, m 13 Dec 1793, the Rev Thomas Cattell, Rector of Berkeswell, co Warwick   [Nos 16634 to 16641]

73 Descendants, if any, of FRANCIS SOUTH, bapt 3 Sept 1639, and of his nephew and nieces, TEMPEST SOUTH, bapt. 25 Nov. 1669, ELIZABETH SOUTH, Maid of Honour to Queen Mary of Modena, bapt 30 Aug 1664, wife of LEONARD PINKNEY, Verderer of Sherwood Forest, MARGERY MARIA SOUTH, bapt. 25 Ap 1665; and JANE SOUTH, bapt 12 Jan 1671 (Table IX)

74 Descendants of JANE WHICHCOT (Table IX), d 30 Jan 1812, m. 1762, Sir CHRISTOPHER WHICHCOTE of Aswarby Park, 4th Bt [E], bapt 15 Mar 1738, d 9 Mar 1786, and had issue 1a to 2a

1a Sir Thomas Whichcote, 5th Bt [E], b 5 Mar 1763, d 22 Sept 1828, m. 24 June 1785, Diana [also descended from Edward III through Mortimer-Percy (see p 397)], da of Edmund Turnor of Panton and Stoke Rochford, co Lincoln, d 4 Feb 1826, and had issue 1b to 6b

  1b Sir Thomas Whichcote, 6th Bt [L], b 10 Aug 1791, d 23 Aug 1829, m 9 Ap 1812, Lady Sophia [a descendant of the Lady Anne, sister to King Edward IV , &c (see the Exeter Volume, p 660)], da of Philip (Sherard), 5th Earl of Harborough [G B] [re-m 2ndly, 23 Ap 1840, the Hon William Charles Evans Freke and] d 23 Sept 1851, and had issue 1c to 3c

    1c Sir Thomas Whichcote, 7th Bt [L], b 23 May 1813, d 17 Jan 1892, m 2ndly, 25 Mar 1856, Isabella Elizabeth, da of Sir Henry Conyngham Montgomery, 1st Bt [U K], M P , d 29 Aug 1892, and had issue 1d

      1d Isabella Whichcote (Deeping St James' Manor, Market Deeping , 114 Ashley Gardens, S W), m 7 Sept 1875, Brownlow (Cecil), 4th Marquis [U K] and 13th Earl [E] of Exeter [descended from King Henry VII , &c], d 9 Ap 1898, and has issue 1e

        1e William Thomas Brownlow (Cecil), 5th Marquis [U K] and 14th Earl [E] of Exeter, Hereditary Grand Almoner, &c (Burghley House, near Stamford , 114 Ashley Gardens, S W), b 27 Oct 1876, m 16 Ap 1901, the Hon Myra Rowena Sibell [descended from King Henry VII , &c], da of William Thomas (Orde-Powlett), 4th Lord Bolton [G B], and has issue 1f to 2f

          1f David George Brownlow Cecil, Lord Burghley, b 9 Feb 1905

          2f Lady Letitia Sibell Winifred Cecil   [Nos 16642 to 16645]

# of The Blood Royal

2c Sir George Whichcote, 8th Bt [E], b 31 May 1817, d 14 Ap 1893, m 10 Ap 1866, Louisa Dav, da of Thomas William Clagett of Fetcham, and had issue 1d to 3d

1d Sir George Whichcote, 9th Bt [E], J P, D L (Aswarby Park, Folkingham, Lincoln), b 3 Sept 1870

2d Hugh Christopher Whichcote, b 18 Ap 1874

3d Louisa Mary Whichcote (Brooklyn House, Towcester)

3c Sophia Whichcote, d 1 Aug 1868, m 9 Jan 1810, the Rev Algernon Turnor (see p 392), d Aug 1842

2b Diana Whichcote, d 2 May 1853, m 1st, 11 Ap 1810, Herman Gerhard Hilbers, b at Colmar, Oldenburg, 9 May 1777, d 21 Dec 1822, 2ndly, as 1st wife, 24 Feb 1829, the Rev George Hambl ton of Wallingford (who m 2ndly and had 2 das), and had issue (with 3 elder sons and 2 das who d unm) 1c to 2c

1c George James Hilbers of Brighton, Consulting Physician, b 16 June 1818, d 30 Oct 1883, m 1842, Louisa Susannah, da of Robert Bates Mathews, R N, d 7 Ap 1906, aged 87, and had issue (with a son and 2 das who d in infancy) 1d to 10d

1d Rev George Christopher Hilbers, M A (Exeter Coll, Oxon), Rector of St Thomas', Haverfordwest, formerly Archdeacon of St David's (St Thomas' Rectory, Haverfordwest), b 24 Jan 1844, m 14 Oct 1875, Maria Frances Knowles, da of the Rev John Posthumous Parkinson, formerly Wilson, of Ravendale Hall, D C L, F S A

2d William Hilbers, Engineer (Karapot, Heene Road, West Worthing), b 16 July 1847, m 5 June 1883, Alice Maria da of Peter Stevens of Lympsham, co Somerset

3d Herman Gerhard Hilbers, M D, B A (St John's, Camb) (19 Montpelier Road, Brighton), b 30 Sept 1854, m 19 Aug 1886, Grace, da of H Mathias of Haverfordwest, J P

4d Diana Frances Turnor Hilbers

5d Louisa Hilbers

6d Frances Henrietta Hilbers, m 12 Oct 1891, the Rev Daniel Davies (Ystradyfodwg, Pentre, Rhondda, Glam)

7d Emily Hilbers, m as 2nd wife, 12 June 1888, James Balleny Elkington, J P, co Carmarthen (East Lodge, Leatherhead)

8d. Marian Hilbers, m 10 Aug 1880, Lindsay Stevenson Giesley Young (East Lodge, Leatherhead), and has issue 1e to 8e

1e Lindsay Loraine Young, b 12 Feb 1883 ⎫
2e Ronald Hilbers Young, b 11 Feb 1885, ⎪
3e Nigel Bellairs Young, b 4 Jan 1887, ⎪
4e Cranstoun Ridout Young, b 11 Mar 1890, ⎬ unm
5e Eric Herbert Young, b 2 Dec 1891, ⎪
6e Kathleen Marian Young, ⎪
7e Elsie Helen Young, ⎪
8e Eileen Violet Young, ⎭

9d. Edith Agnes Hilbers, m 23 June 1885, Herbert John Pulling, M R C S, L R C P [son of the Rev Prob Pulling of Eastnor, Ledbury] (11 Old Steine, Brighton), and has issue 1e to 2e

1e John Bernard Pulling, B A (Christ's Coll, Camb), entered St Bartholomew's Hospital Oct 1907, b 13 Sept 1887

2e Virginia Edith Pulling, B A, London

10d Alice Mary Hilbers

2c Margaret Sophia Hilbers, d 1896, m as 2nd wife, the Rev Frederick Tryon of Bulwick, d 1903, and had issue 1d to 3d

1d Manasseh Tryon, b (—), m and has issue several children

[Nos 16646 to 16669.

The Plantagenet Roll

2d Stephen Tryon (*Hallen Lodge, Henbury, near Bristol*), b (—), m and has 6 children

3d John Tryon (*Down Hall, Epsom*), b (—), m and has issue 3 children

3b *Henrietta Whichcote*, d 30 *May* 1810, m as 1st wife, 28 *Nov* 1807, *James Atty of Pinchbeck, co Lincoln*, d 17 *Oct* 1815, and had issue 1c

1c *James Atty of Rugby, co Warwick, and Pinchbeck, co Lincoln, J P, D L, Major Warwickshire Mil, previously 52nd Regt*, b 12 *Ap* 1810, d 11 *July* 1877, m 31 *May* 1831, *Catharine Adeline, da of Adlard Welby of North Rauceby, co Linc*, d 22 *Oct* 1889, and had issue (with others d s p) 1d to 5d

1d *Edward Arthur Atty of Pinchbeck*, b 16 *Mar* 1817, d 12 *Oct* 1882, m *Florence Laura, da of* (—) *Kelson* and had issue 1e to 4e

  1e James Edward Atty, b 27 *Jan* 1869
  2e Grace Catharine Atty
  3e Florence Atty
  4e Edith Marion Atty

2d *Robert Atty*, b 19 *May* 1819, m 21 *Ap* 1870, Gertrude, da of the Rev Ollivier Etough, and has issue 1e to 3e

  1e Welby Atty, b 1 *Ap* 1872, m *Aug* 1902, Freda, da of William Brown, and has issue 1f to 2f

    1f William James Welby Atty, b *May* 1905
    2f Daphne Freda Atty, b 8 Feb 1904

  2e *Gertrude Atty*, d 6 *Ap* 1909, m 22 *May* 1902, *Archibald Vaughan Campbell-Lambert* (*Foxearth Hall, and Lyston Hall, Essex*), and had issue 1f to 2f

    1f John Vaughan Campbell-Lambert, b *Nov* 1905
    2f Gertrude Eleanor Kathleen Campbell-Lambert, b 18 Sept 1903

  3e Eleanor Atty

3d *Adeline Atty* (*Cavendish Hall, Suffolk*), m 1st, as 2nd wife, 1 Feb 1860, James Malcolm of Freelands, co Oxford [Bt (1665) Coll], d 16 July 1878, 2ndly, as 2nd wife 19 Nov 1885, John Ramsey L'Amy of Dunkenny, d 26 *Mar* 1892, and has issue 1e to 2e

  1e Sir James William Malcolm of Innertiel, 9th Bt [S 1665], J P, *formerly Capt Royal Pembroke Artillery Mil* (*Tostock Place, Suffolk*), b 29 *May* 1862, m 14 Nov 1885, Evelyn Alberta, da of Albert George Sandeman of Presdales co Herts [by his wife, Donna Maria Carlota Perpetua, da of Pedro Jose (de Moraes-Sarmento), 2nd Viscount da Torre de Moncorvo [Portugal, 1835], Ambassador to the Court of St James'], and has issue 1f to 4f

    1f Michael Albert James Malcolm, b 9 *May* 1898
    2f Alexander Ernest William Malcolm, b 4 *Oct* 1900
    3f Elspeth Mary Isabel Malcolm, b 12 June 1899
    4f Griselda Helen Adeline Malcolm, b 10 July 1903

  2e Charles Edward Malcolm, *late Lieut Scots Guards* (*White's*), b 2 Dec 1865, m 28 Dec 1894, the Hon Beatrix Mary Leslie, previously wife of Charles Lindsay Orr Ewing, M P, da of William James (Hore-Ruthven), 8th Lord Ruthven [S], and has issue 1f to 3f

    1f Arthur William Alexander Malcolm, b 1 June 1903
    2f Honoria Adeline Malcolm
    3f Beltine Violet Malcolm

4d *Harriet Atty*, m 4 Jan 1860, Capt William Alexander Keir, V C, Mahratta Horse, s p

5d *Georgina Atty*

4b *Caroline Whichcote*, d 1844, m 4 *May* 1814, *Francis Willes of Row Green, co Herts*, and had issue (with a son, *Francis, who d s p*) 1c

1c Margaret Sophia Willes, m 27 Ap 1846, William Alexander Mackinnon of Acryse Park, and Belvedere, co. Kent, Chief of his Clan, F R S, J P, D L, High Sheriff for that co 1885, and M P Ryde 1852-3 and Lymington 1857-68, d 11 Sept 1903, and has issue 1d to 4d
                                  [Nos 16670 to 16695

152

# of The Blood Royal

1*d* Francis Alexander Mackinnon of Acryse Chief of his Clan, J P , D L , *late* Capt and Hon Major East Kent Yeo (*Acryse Park , near Folkestone , Belvedere, near Broadstairs*), *b* 9 Ap 1848 , *m* 19 Ap 1888, the Hon Emily Isabel, *dr* and co-*h* of Arthur William Acland (Hood), 1st and only Baron Hood of Avalon [U K], G C B , and has issue 1*e* to 3*e*

    1*e* Alexander Hood Mackinnon, Younger of Mackinnon, *b* 8 Jun 1892

    2*e* Arthur Avalon Mackinnon, *b* 8 Nov 1893

    3*e*. Aline Emily Hood Mackinnon

2*d* Sir William Henry Mackinnon K C B , C V O , Lieut -Gen and Director-Gen of Territorial Army at Headquarters, Vice-Chairman of Territorial Force Advisory Council, *formerly* Comdg Imp Yeo at Aldershot 1901-4, in South Africa 1899-1900, &c &c (15 *Ovington Square, S W , Guards', &c*) *b* 15 Dec 1852 , *m* 14 Dec 1881, Madeleine Frances, *dr* of Lt -Col Villiers La Touche Hatton of Clonard, *late* Grenadier Guards, and has issue 1*e*

    1*e* Nora Lynvola Mackinnon, *m* 9 Jan 1905, Capt Arthur George Edward Egerton, Coldstream Guards [descended from King Henry VII , &c], *s p*

    3*d* Caroline Emma Mackinnon

    4*d* Sophia Louisa Mackinnon

5*b* *Catherine Whichcote*, d 27 *June* 1860 , *m* 19 *Sept* 1816, *the Rev John* Hanmer [Baronet (1774) *Coll*], d 4 *Oct* 1850 , *and had issue* 1*c* to 5*c*

    1*c* *Francis Henry Hanmer, Col Indian Army b* 20 *Oct* 1825 , d 2 *Feb* 1876 , *m* 16 *Oct* 1860, *Mary Ann Catharine*, *dr* of *Charles Gordon of Edintore, co Banff, and Greshop, co Moray,* d 9 *June* 1879 , *and had issue* 1*d to* 2*d*

        1*d* *Norman Gordon Whichcote Hanmer (Fendalton, Christ Church, N Z),* *b* 3 *Aug* 1863 , *unm*

        2*d* *Flora Emmeline Mary Hanmer, m* 23 *Aug* 1887, Charles Thomas Gordon of Cairness (*Cairness, Aberdeen*), and has issue 1*e* to 4*e*

        1*e* John Charles Hanmer Gordon, *b* 28 Nov 1893

        2*e* Francis Walden Gordon, *b* 10 Oct 1895

        3*e* Stella Mary Gordon

        4*e* Marjorie Violet Gordon

    2*c* *Humphrey Hanmer,* *b* 20 *July* 1827 , *d* 24 *Dec* 1892 *m* 21 *Oct* 1856, *Harriet, dr of George Battarbee of Chorlton Hall, co Cheshire , and had issue* 1*d to* 2*d*

        1*d* George Hanmer (*Tilford Ferry Road, Christchurch, New Zealand*), *b* 11 Jan 1859 , *m* 12 May 1885, Ruth, *dr* of C Percy Cox , and has issue 1*e* to 6*e*

        1*e* Humphrey George Hanmer, *b* 6 Ap 1886

        2*e* John Percy Hanmer, *b* 7 July 1889

        3*e* Anthony Hugh Hanmer, *b* 18 Sept 1890

        4*e* Dorothy Harriet Hanmer, *b* 28 Jan 1888

        5*e* Madeline Ruth Hanmer, *b* 18 Sept 1890

        6*e* Municent Clara Hanmer, *b* 22 Dec 1891

        2*d* Catherine Hanmer (96 *Castle Road, Bedford*) *m* 19 Nov 1885, Edward Wingfield Hanmer, *d* 28 Feb 1901 , and has issue 1*e* to 4*e*

        1*e* Edward Henry John Hanmer, *b* 27 Nov 1888

        2*e* Humphrey Richard Hanmer, *b* 24 Nov 1890

        3*e* Evelyn Mary Harriet Hanmer, *b* 7 Feb 1887

        4*e* Florence Catherine Ahen Hanmer, *b* 9 Dec 1895

    3*c* *George Hanmer,* b 4 *Sept* 1833 , d 16 *Feb* 1906 , *m* 13 *July* 1871, *Margaret Eliza (Stone Cross House, Crowborough, Sussex), dr of the Rev William Spencer Edwards of Lewes , and had issue* 1*d*

        1*d* Thomas Anthony Hanmer, Resident Magistrate (*Mombasa*), *b* 17 Ap 1872

    4*c* *Sophia Hanmer,* d 1 Ap 1882 , *m* 1839, *John Lees Ainsworth of Barkside, co Lanc , and had issue (2 sons and 3 das , of whom only 2 das now survive)*

[Nos 16690 to 16722

5c *Catherine Hanmer*, d 1845, m *James Holmes*, and had issue (a son)

6b *Louisa Whichcote*, d 28 Aug 1889, m 30 Ap 1829, *the Rev C C Wheat*, and had issue

2a *Frances Whichcote*, d (–), m *William Manners*

75 Descendants of FRANCIS WHICHCOT (Table IX), *bapt* at Scotton 23 May 1733, d 25 Ap 1811, m at Harpswell 23 June 1761, WILLIAM HILDYARD of Grimsby, d 2 Dec 1781; and had issue 1a to 4a

1a *Rev William Hildyard, Rector of Winestead, co Yorks*, b 6 July 1762, d 25 Feb 1842, m 12 Dec 1793, *Catharine, da of Isle Grant of Ruckland, co Linc*, d 6 May 1855, and had issue 1b to 1b

1b *Rev Frederic Hildyard, Rector of Swanington, co Norfolk*, b 8 May 1803, d 1 Nov 1891, m 9 July 1840, *Letitia, da of John Shore of Guildford Street, London*, d 8 Oct 1896, and had issue 1c to 3c

1c *Rev William Hildyard, Rector of St Patrick Eleuthera, Bahamas*, b at Swanington, Norfolk, 19 Jan 1814 d at Nassau, Bahamas, 19 June 1873, m c 1870, *Harriet, da of (—) Wade*, d Oct 1896, and had issue 1d

1d Mary Hildyard, m 26 July 1905, *the Rev Aubrey Rothwell Hay Johnson, Rector of North Wootton* (*North Wootton Rectory, King's Lynn*), and has issue 1e to 3e

    1e Christopher Hildyard Johnson, b 10 July 1910
    2e Mary Hildyard Johnson, b 19 May 1907
    3e Elizabeth Dorothea Johnson, b 18 Jan 1909

2c Jessie Ellen Hildyard, m 27 Nov 1862, *the Hon Robert Henley Shaw Eden, J P* [B Auckland Coll] (*Tyddynllan, Llandrillo, Merioneth*), and has issue
See the Essex Volume, p 361, Nos 35503–35519

3c Kate Hildyard, m 5 Mar 1867, *Robert Arthur Barkley*, d 22 Ap 1910 (*Palgrave Priory, Diss*), and has issue 1d to 4d

    1d George Hildyard Barkley, b 29 Mar 1873
    2d Frederic Hildyard Barkley, b 30 Aug 1879
    3d Lettice Kate Barkley, *unm*
    4d Hilda Barkley, m 16 Oct 1899, *Ernest Barkley Raikes, Bar at Law* (*Bombay*), and has issue 1e to 4e

    1e Thomas Barkley Raikes, b 16 Dec 1902
    2e Robert Barkley Raikes, b 2 Mar 1904
    3e Ruth Martha Barkley Raikes, b 26 Aug 1906
    4e Elizabeth Barkley Raikes, b 17 Jan 1907

2b *Rev Horatio Samuel Hildyard, Rector of Lofthouse, in Cleveland*, b 17 Oct 1805, d 10 Ap 1886, m 12 June 1861, *Octavia* (*55 Upperton Gardens, Eastbourne*), *da of William Richardson of York*, and had issue 1c to 5c

1c *Horatio Nelson Hildyard*, b 11 May 1862, d 30 July 1900, m 21 Aug 1890, *Maud Lewis, da of Major Jackson*, and had issue 1d

1d Katharine Hildyard, b 16 July 1891

2c Henry Hildyard (*Hebron, Yarmouth, Nova Scotia*), b 27 Feb 1868, m 4 Oct 1889, *Maggie, da of (—) Davis*, and has issue 1d to 5d

    1d Robert Hildyard, b 16 July 1900
    2d Christopher George Hildyard, b 12 July 1902
    3d Frances Hildyard, b 15 Sept 1891
    4d Pearl Hildyard, b 25 Ap 1898
    5d Joan Hildyard, b 13 Dec 1904

3c Mary Louisa Hildyard, *unm*

4c Octavia Hildyard, *unm*

5c Elizabeth Frances Hildyard, *unm*   [Nos 16723 to 16763

154

# of The Blood Royal

3b Rev James Hildyard, B D , Rector of Ingoldsby, co Linc , b 11 Ap 1809 , d 27 Aug 1887 , m 19 Aug 1847, Elizabeth Matilda, da of George Kinderley, d 18 Ap 1894 , and had issue 1c to 2c

1c Nora Catherine Hildyard, m 11 Oct 1877, Col William Henry Vallack-Tom (Cawsand, Cornwall), s p

2c Evelyn Matilda Hildyard, unm

4b Rev. Alexander Grant Hildyard, Vicar of Madingley, co Camb , b 27 Aug 1812 , d 5 Ap 1885 , m 12 June 1851, Mary Ann (see p 156), da of George Hildyard of Hale End, co Essex, d 2 Dec 1903 , and had issue 1c to 3c

1c George Grant Hildyard (Market Deeping, Lincoln), b 4 Mar 1853 , unm

2c Robert Loxham Hildyard (27 Avenue Macmahon, Paris), b 26 May 1855 , m 1st, 30 Ap 1890, Mary Dalrymple, da of the Rev George Shand, Rector of Heydon, d 25 Sept 1891 , 2ndly, in Paris 17 Aug 1907, Marie Alexandrine, da of Eugene Loth of Reims , and has issue 1d to 2d

1d Peter Georges D'Eyncourt Hildyard, b 4 Mar 1910

2d Catharine Cecilia Hildyard, b 3 Ap 1891

3c Frederic William Hildyard (77 Lexham Gardens, South Kensington), b 6 Oct 1863 , m 5 July 1898, Elizabeth Cecilia, da of Hugh Wade-Gery, s p

2a Rev John Hildyard, Vicar of Bonby, co Lincoln, b 7 July 1763 , d 13 Nov 1827 , m 25 Sept 1787, Mary, da of Isle Grant of Ruckland, co Lincoln, d 17 Ap 1849 , and had issue 1b to 3b

1b Rev William Hildyard, Rector of Hameringham-cum-Scrayfield, co Linc , b 26 Dec 1790 , d 17 Mar 1872, m 8 Jan 1818, Mary, da of the Rev William Hett, Canon of Lincoln, d 28 Jan 1853 , and had issue 1c to 2c,

1c Rev Charles Frederic Hildyard of Bury, co Lancs, b 16 July 1823 , d 13 Jan 1906 , m 23 June 1857, Louisa Eliza, da of J W Hamilton, d 11 Dec 1886 , and had issue 1d to 7d

1d Rev William Hildyard (Wickmere Rectory, Norwich), b 9 May 1858 , m 17 Ap 1894, Ida Jane, da of Henry Lemon , and has issue 1e to 3e

1e Brian Rider Hildyard, b 17 Feb 1895

2e Denis Leslie Hildyard, b 24 Jan 1901

3e Jean Hyacinth Hildyard, b 17 Feb 1895

2d Francis Edward Hildyard (York Place, Ashton-under-Lyne), b 31 Aug 1859

3d Rev Lyonel D'Arcy Hildyard (Rowley Rectory, Little Weighton, Hull), b 5 Feb 1861 , m 8 Aug 1895, Dora Annie Florence Thoroton (see p 309), da of Capt Robert Charles Thoroton Hildyard, R E , and has issue 1e to 2e

1e Christopher Hildyard, b 28 Ap 1901

2e Noel Florence Dora Hildyard, b 22 Dec 1896

4d Cecil George Ormerod Hildyard, b 7 Ap 1865

5d Lucy Viola Margaret Hildyard (7 Hill House Road, Norwich), b 3 Ap 1867

6d Louisa Rosalind Hildyard, b 29 Mar 1869

7d Lilias Mary Hildyard, b 29 Mar 1869

2c Sophia Elizabeth Rose Hildyard, d 19 Mar 1910 , m as 2nd wife, 15 June 1865, the Rev Charles Richmond Tate, Vicar of Send and Ripley, co Surrey, afterwards Rector of Trent, co Som , Fellow of Corpus Christi Coll , Oxon , d 1 Aug 1895 , and had issue 1d to 4d

1d Harry Russell Tate (Kyambu, Nairobi, B East Africa), b 1 Sept 1870 , m 28 Dec 1907, Eveline Syndercombe, da of Henry Syndercombe Bower of Font mell Parva, co Dorset, J P

2d Joseph George Tate (West Marton, Skipton, Yorks), b 19 Ap 1875 unm

3d Sophia Hildyard Tate, m 30 Aug 1894, Evelyn Arthur Hellicar [son of the Rev Arthur Gresley Hellicar, Rector of Bromley, Kent] (Hildegarde, Bickley, Kent), and has issue 1e

1e Mary Gresley Hellicar, b 31 Dec 1896   [Nos 16764 to 16786

155

The Plantagenet Roll

1d Lucy Hett Tate (*Detroit, Michigan*), m 2 Aug 1889, James Talboys Barratt, d Sept 1901, and has issue 1e to 3e

  1e Charles Frederick Talboys Barratt, b 2 Nov 1892

  2e Nina Catharine Barratt, b 25 May 1890

  3e Lucy Barratt, b 7 July 1894

2b *George Hildyard of Hale End, co Essex*, b 1 June 1798, d 28 May 1872, m *at Walthamstow Parish Church*, 13 Sept 1823, *Jane, da and event sole h of Robert Loxham of Hale End*, d 10 Sept 1871, *and had issue* 1c

  1c *Mary Ann Hildyard*, b 29 Mar 1826, d 2 Dec 1893, m 12 June 1851, *the Rev Alexander Grant Hildyard, Curate of Laston, near Stamford*, d 5 Ap 1885, *and had issue*

  See p 155, Nos 16765–16769

3b *Mary Ann Hildyard*, b 30 Mar 1803, d June 1884, m 19 Oct 1832, *George Murray of Rosemount, co Ross*, and had issue 1c to 4c

  1c *William John Murray, afterwards* (R L 30 May 1882) *Bankes, of Rosemount*, b 19 May 1835, d 17 July 1884, m 19 Dec 1861, *Eleanor Slarkie Letterewe [descended from George, Duke of Clarence, K G* (see Clarence Volume, p 163)] (II instanley Hall Wigan), da of Meyrick Bankes of Winstanley, *and had issue*

  See the Clarence Volume, p 164, Nos 2600–2608

  2c *Hugh Hildyard Murray* b 24 June 1838, d 13 Sept 1896, m 16 Feb 1866, *Frances Jane, da of Herbert Park Marshall*, and had issue 1d to 3d

    1d Jessie Margaret Murray, M B, unm (14 Endsleigh Street, Tavistock Square, W C)

    2d Mary Ethel Murray, unm

    3d Edith May Murray, unm

  3c Caroline Georgina Murray, m 1st, Robert Blair of Blacksales, co Ayr, d (–), 2ndly, Frederick Torquito Portal Turner, d s p Jan 1910, and has issue 1d to 5d

    1d George Blair

    2d Frederick Blair

    3d Alice Maud Mary Blair (*Lismore, Letchworth, Hitchin*), unm

    4d Frances Blair, unm

    5d Hilda Caroline Hildyard Blair, m 26 Oct 1891, Frederick Thomas Verschoyle of Castle Troy, J P, Capt *late* 2nd Brig South Irish Div R A (*Castle Troy, co Limerick*), and has issue 1e to 3e

      1e Frederick Hildyard Hawkins Stuart Verschoyle, b 21 Nov 1894

      2e Hilda Caroline Gwendoline Verschoyle

      3e Mona Hamilton Verschoyle

  4c *Frances Isabella Murray*, b 1 Ap 1841, d *at Government House, Bermuda*, 14 May 1900, m *as 1st wife*, 11 June 1862, Gen Sir George Digby Barker, K C B, J P [*descended from George (Plantagenet), Duke of Clarence, K G*] (*Clare Priory, Clare, R S O, Suffolk*), and has issue

  See the Essex Volume, Clarence Supplement, p 553, Nos 21679/53–62

3a *Frances Hildyard*, b 8 Dec 1764, d (–), m *the Rev William Thorold of Weelsby House, co Lincoln*, d (–), *and had issue* 1b to 4b

  1b *Frances Charlotte Thorold*, d (–), m 29 May 1803, Robert Mansel, Adm R N , *and had (with other) issue* 1c

    1c *Maria Antonia Mansel*, d (–) m Henry Thorold of Cuxwold, co Linc , d 1871, *and had issue (with a son, Henry, killed in the Crimea)* 1d to 4d

      1d *William Thorold of Cuxwold Hall, Lord of the Manor and Patron of the Living*, d s p

      2d *Richard Thorold of Cuxwold Hall, Lord of the Manor and Patron of the Living, sometime 10th Hussars*, b 1843, d s p 1905, m 1885, *Alice Hamilton*

[Nos 16787 to 16826

156

# of The Blood Royal

(18 *John Street, Berkeley Square, W), widow of Edward S Potter of Fullwood co Glos , da of the Rev E Creek, Vicar of Stanmore, co Hants*

    3*d* Frederick Henry Thorold

    4*d* *Mary Sophia Thorold*, b May 1836 , d 2 Feb 1889 , m as 2 d wife, 6 Ap 1856, Richard Christopher Naylor of Hooton Hall, co Ch shire, d 30 Nov 1899 , *and had issue* 1*e* to 2*e*

    1*e* Mittie Naylor, *m* 14 June 1882, Derrick Warner William (Westenra) 5th [I] and 4th [U K] Baron Rossmore *(Rossmore Park, Casala Vale, co Monaghan)* and has issue 1*f* to 3*f*

        1*f* Hon William Westenra, *b* 12 July 1892

        2*f* Hon Richard Westenra, *b* 15 Oct 1893

        3*f* Hon Mary Westenra, *b* 1 Dec 1890

    2*e* Mary Naylor

    2*b* *Sophia Thorold*, d (-) , m *Edward Barker of Blacsook, co Monmouth*

    3*b* *Helen Thorold*, d 1865 , m *Alexander Grant, Solicitor for Scottish App als*, d 1852, *and had issue* 1*c* to 4*c*

    1*c* *Alexander William Thorold Grant, now* (R L 8 Nov 1861) *Grant-Thorold, of Weelsby House, co Lincoln, J P , D L High Sheriff co Lincoln* 1870, b 29 Feb 1820 , d 1 Feb 1908 , m 23 July 1863, *Anna Hamilton, da of Adm Sir James Stirling*, d 13 Oct 1899 , *and had issue* 1*d* to 3*d*

    1*d* Richard Stirling Grant-Thorold *(Craigalluchie, B C , 3 Grosvenor Gardens W)*, *b* 9 Aug 1868

    2*d* Hilda Grant-Thorold, *m* 12 Oct 1886, Lieut-Col Augustus Campbell Spencer, *late 5th Lancers and 1st Dragoon Guards* [D of Marlborough [E] and B Churchill [U K] Coll, and a descendant of King Henry VII (see the Tudor Roll, p 338)] *(Lascombe, Puttenham, Surrey)* , and has issue 1*e* to 2*e*

    1*e* Richard Augustus Spencer, Lieut R F A , *b* 14 Dec 1888

    2*e* Edward Almeric Spencer, *b* 26 Dec 1892

    3*d* Constance Mary Grant Thorold, *m* 17 Dec 1904, Richard Joshua Cooper, C V O , Lieut-Col Irish Guards *(3 Grosvenor Gardens, S W)*

    2*c* Frederick Augustus Grant, *b* (—) , *m* Katharine Arabella, da of (—) Clay , and has (with other) issue 1*d*

    1*d* James Erskine Grant

    3*c* Helen Grant, *m* Charles Ridley Hinds

    4*c* Katharine Grant, *m* Frederick Edward Hillersdon

    4*b* *Harriet Thorold*, d (-) , m *the Rev Joseph Gedge, Rector of Bilderton, co Suffolk*

    4*a* *Jane Hildyard*, b 27 Feb 1767 , d (-) , m *as 2nd wife at Louth*, 27 Feb 1792, *Thomas Marris of Barton-on-Humber, Banker*, d *at Leicester* 1843 , *and had issue (with 2 sons and a da d young)* 1*b* to 8*b*

    1*b* *Thomas Marris*, b. 3 Ap 1793, d *unm*

    2*b* *John Marris*, b 12 Sept 1795 , d *at Plymouth*

    3*b* *William Marris, Physician in London*, b 26 Aug 1797

    4*b* *Henry Marris*, b 5 Dec 1801 , d *in* 80s, m *and had issue* 1*c*

    1*c* *William Henry Marris of Leicester, Auctioneer*, d *after* 1890 , m *and had issue* 1*d*

    1*d* W H Marris, *formerly of Kibworth, co Leicester*, M D

    5*b*. *Robert Marris*, b 27 June 1803 , d c 1880 m *and had issue* 1*c* to 3*c*

    1*c* *Samuel Arthur Marris*, b 5 Sept 1812, d 10 Ap 1906 m 29 May 1865, *Emma, da of Charles Bream of Leicester*, d 30 Oct 1908 , *and had issue* 1*d* to 3*d*

    1*d* *Edward Hildyard Marris* (1 *Douglas House, Maida Hill, W*) b 10 Dec 1873 , m 18 Dec 1897, Ethel Mary, da of James Ward of Dublin , and has issue 1*e* to 2*e*

    1*e* Edward Hildyard Marris, *b* 24 Jan 1906

    2*e* Marjory Iris Marris, *b* 21 May 1899

[Nos 16827 to 16845

The Plantagenet Roll

2*d* Reginald Willows Marris (*Rangoon, Burmah*), *b* 12 June 1887, *unm*

3*d* Ethel Effie Marris, *m* 29 Aug 1908, Percy Alexander Shelley (63 *Magdalen Road, Wandsworth Common, S W*)

2*c* William Charles Marris, Accountant and Auditor (18 *New Street, Leicester*), *b* (—), *m* (—), da of (—), and his issue 1*d* to 7*d*

1*d* Robert William Marris, *b* 7 Jan 1876 *m* 17 Ap 1909, Hilda, da of John Cheater, and his issue 1*e*

1*e* Horace William Marris, *b* (—)

2*d* Lionel Percy Marris *b* 24 Dec 1877, *m* 11 Dec 1902, Edith Emily, da of John Loach, and his issue 1*e* to 3*e*

1*e* Nellie Loach Marris, *b* 28 July 1903

2*e* Dorothy Selina Marris, *b* 21 May 1906

3*e* Edith Loach Marris, *b* 26 May 1909

3*d* Henry Edward Marris, Grocer and Confectioner (27 *Jermyn Street, Leicester*), *b* 1 Dec 1879, *m* 25 Ap 1905, Jeanne Steven, da of James Agnew, and has issue 1*e* to 3*e*

1*e* William James Marris, *b* 6 Nov 1905

2*e* Henry Edward Marris, *b* 13 Nov 1906

3*e* Jenny Agnes Marris *b* 22 May 1908

4*d* Edith Wright Marris, *m* 29 Sept 1898, Percy Haslehurst Adams, and has issue (with a da *d* young) 1*e*

1*e* Francis William Adams, *b* 24 Mar 1901

5*d* Harriet Agnes Marris, *unm*

6*d* Fanny Helen Marris, *m* 4 June 1908, George Stonson Slater, *s p*

7*d* Dorothy Margaret Marris, *unm*

3*c* *Fanny Helen Marris*, d (? *unm*) 1898

6*b* *George Hildyard Marris, Farmer in Lincoln*, b 16 Mar 1808, d (—), *m and had large family*

7*b* *Jane Marris*, b 26 Nov 1799

8*b* *Helen Marris*, b 29 Sept 1806   [Nos 16846 to 16863

76 Descendants of FRANCES WHICHCOTE (Table IX), *d* 31 Mar 1720 , *m* JAMES NELTHORPE of Little Grimsby, co Lincoln, *bapt* 14 Mar 1670 , *d* (will dated 23 May 1755, proved 29 Ap) 1756 , and had issue 1*a* to 3*a*

1*a* *Rev Charles Nelthorpe, Rector of Broughton*, d (—), *m Eleanor, da of Nathaniel Maddison of Alvingham,* bapt 12 Feb 1691, bur 26 Oct 1770, *and had issue* 1*b*

1*b* *Eleanor Nelthorpe*, d (–), *m William Hollingworth*

2*a* *Richard Nelthorpe, living* 1740 [1]

3*a* *Griffith Nelthorpe of Little Grimsby*, d (will dated 10 Sept 1740, proved 10 Oct) 1755, *m Mary, da and co-h of John Nelthorpe of Bigby*, d (–), *and had issue* 1*b* to 2*b*

1*b* *John Nelthorpe of Little Grimsby Hall, co Linc*, d (–), *m Mary, da of Robert Cracroft of Hackthorn*, d (–), *and had issue* 1*c*

1*c* *Mary Jonetta Nelthorpe*, d 17 Jan 1822 *m as* 2nd *wife*, 4 Mar 1799, *William (Beauclerk), 8th Duke of St Albans* [E] [*a descendant of the Lady Isabel Plantagenet*], d 17 July 1825 , *and had issue*

See the Essex Volume, pp 175–179, Nos 23663–23795

[Nos 16864 to 16996

---

[1] Maddison's "Lincolnshire Pedigrees," ii 620, Harl Soc Pub

# of The Blood Royal

2b *Elizabeth Nelthorpe*, b c 1748, bur 23 *July* 1801 m 10 *May* 1768, *John Maddison of Alvingham, co Linc, and Gainsborough, High Sheriff co Linc* 1779, bapt 25 *Oct* 1718, bur 13 *July* 1785, *and had issue* [1] *1c to 3c*

1c *John Maddison of Gainsborough and Alvingham* bapt 4 *Feb* 1770, d 4 *Jan* 1838, m 25 *Mar* 1795, *Elizabeth, da of John Andrews of Alford*, d (-), *and had issue 1d to 3d*

1d *John Maddison*, bapt 25 *Mar* 1802, d *at Ackworth, co York*, m 25 *Aug* 1824, *Georgiana, da of Thomas Curtis of Bath*, d *Mar* 1871 *and had issue 1e*

1e *Katharine Mary Maddison*, b 14 *May* 1827, d 26 *Mar* 1902, m 19 *Ap* 1855, *the Rev Edmund Hall, Rector of Myland, co Essex*, d 7 *Feb* 1903, *and had issue 1f to 3f*

1f Rev George Clement Maddison Hall Rector of Southery (*Southery Rectory, Downham Market*), b 24 *Ap* 1856, m 7 *Aug* 1894, Katharine, da of the Rev Arthur Charles Copeman, and has issue (with a son, Henry Clement, who d young) 1g to 3g

    1g Basil Arthur Edmund Maddison Hall, b 9 *Ap* 1897

    2g Mary Doris Maddison Hall, b 31 May 1895

    3g Katharine Joyce Maddison Hall, b 28 Dec 1902

2f Mary Helen Constance Hall

3f Anna Mildred Elizabeth Hall, m 7 *Aug* 1888, the Rev James Henry Browne, Vicar of Roehampton (*The Vicarage, Roehampton, S W*), and has issue 1g to 3g

    1g Richard Maddison Browne, b 9 *Mar* 1891

    2g Maurice Edmund Browne, b 4 Sept 1892

    3g Margaret Dorothea Browne, b 23 Dec 1895

2d *Richard Thomas Maddison*, afterwards (*R L* 18 *Dec* 1849) *Combe, of Earnshill, co Som*, bapt 10 *Oct* 1813, d 1880, m 1850, *Elizabeth Delicia, da of Gen Sir John Mitchell, K C B*, *and had issue 1e to 2e*

1e Richard Thomas Combe, J P (*Earnshill, Curry Rivell, Somerset*), b 30 *Nov* 1854, m June 1903, Evelyn, da of Lieut-Col Francis Henry of Elmstree House, co Gloucester, and has issue 1f

    1f Evelyn Delicia Combe

2e Constance Delicia Combe

3d *Mary Combe Maddison*, b 1 *May* 1810, d 16 *Sept* 1879 m 18 *June* 1835, *Richard Hare, Comm R N*, d 27 *May* 1876, *and had issue 1c to 2e*

1e Richard Thomas Hare, Lieut-Col Indian Army, B C C (6 *Somerset Place, Bath*), b 6 June 1836 m Gertrude Adeline, da of the Rev John Joseph Spear, M A, and has issue 1f to 2f

    1f Ethel Gertrude Hare

    2f Mabel Maddison Hare

2e Robert Powell Hare, Lieut-Col *late* R H A, b 27 July 1842, m 27 July 1880, Christine Sarah, da of Donald Maclaine of Lochbuie, "The Maclaine," Chief of his Clan, J P, D L, and has issue 1f to 5f

    1f Richard Hare

    2f Stuart Hare

    3f-5f 3 das

2c *Rev George Maddison, Vicar of North Reston*, bapt 18 *Sept* 1775, d 26 *Oct* 1827, m *Elizabeth, da of the Rev Kingsman Baskett of Pocklington, co York*, d 1849, *and had issue 1d to 2d*

1d Ven George Maddison, *Vicar of Grantham, Archdeacon of Ludlow, &c*, b 9 *June* 1809, d 30 Jan 1895, m 12 *Oct* 1839, *Jane, da of Richard Philpott of Chichester*, d 5 *Mar* 1891, *and had issue 1e*   [Nos 16997 to 17014

---

[1] Maddison's "Lincolnshire Pedigrees," ii 620

The Plantagenet Roll

1c *Rev George Henry Maddison, Vicar of Tuckhill, co Salop,* b 9 *Mar* 1853, d 9 *Mar* 1898, m 16 *June* 1885, *Mary, da of the Rev John Temple, Rector of Bothenhampton, co Dorset, and had issue* 1f *to* 3f

   1f George Lionel Temple Maddison, b 26 Oct 1888.

   2f Elvira Mary Maddison, b 6 Mar 1886

   3f Gladys Mabel Maddison, b 15 May 1887

2d *Elizabeth Maddison* b 20 *Aug* 1804, d 27 *Jan* 1878, m 4 *Sept* 1832, *the Rev Charles Green Rector of Burgh Castle, co Suffolk,* d 9 *Aug* 1857, *and had issue* 1e

   1e Rev Charles Edward Maddison Green, *formerly Rector of Ledbury, Preb endary of Hereford, &c (St Katharine's, Ledbury),* b 24 July 1836, m 20 July 1869, Ella Doveton, dr of William Meybohm Rider Haggard of Bradenham Hall, co Norfolk, and has 1f to 3f

      1f Charles Arthur Maddison Green, b 17 June 1877, m 8 Ap 1907, Christian Margaret, da of the Rev George Lucas, Rector of Mulbarton, co Norfolk, and has issue 1g

         1g Hester Christian Maddison Green, b 8 Feb 1908

      2f Edward Roland Maddison Green, b 5 May 1887

      3f Ella Frances Maddison Green, m 15 Sept 1881, Harry Spencer Horsfal Bickham (*The Hilltop, near Ledbury*), and has issue 1g

         1g Richard Harry Spencer Bickham, b 28 July 1908

3c *Ann Maddison,* bapt *at Gainsborough* 25 Sept 1772

                              [Nos 17015 to 17023

77 Descendants of GEORGE MADDISON of Stainton Vale, co Linc, and *afterwards* (1799) of Dunstable Priory, co. Beds, Lieut-Col 4th Regt, &c ('Table IX'), *bapt* 20 Aug 1729; d 10 Jan 1807, m 11 Oct 1857, MARY, da and event h. of Capt Launcelot BAUGH, 41st Regt, *bur* 24 Jan 1791; and had issue 1a to 4a

1a *John Thomas Maddison of Norton, co Durham, Col 4th Regt of Foot,* b 9 *Ap* 1759, d *Jan* 1837, m 1781, *Matilda, da of* (—) *MacNeill of Gallichoilly, co Argyll,* d (-), *and had issue* 1b *to* 2b

   1b *Ann Theodosia Maddison,* d (-), m 1 *Ap* 1809, *Aubone Altham Surtees of Newcastle, and had issue* 1c

      1c *Matilda Sarah Surtees,* d (-), m (—) *Pyke, and had issue (with several das m with issue in New Zealand)* 1d

         1d Eldon Pyke

   2b *Jane Maddison,* b 11 Feb 1795, d 28 *Feb* 1829, m 30 *Oct* 1821, *John Dent of Thirsk, co Yorks* d 30 *July* 1859, *and had issue* 1c *to* 2c

      1c Matilda Mary Dent, b 3 Feb 1825, *living unm* 1910

      2c Emma Dent, b 28 Aug 1826, m 1 May 1851, Thomas Vaisey of Stratton, co Glouc, b 22 May 1825, d 10 May 1903, and has issue 1d to 4d

         1d Arthur William Vaisey (*Holly Field, Tring, Herts*), b 8 Feb 1852, m 7 Sept 1876, Esther, da of William Lawrence Bevir of Cirencester, and has issue 1e to 9e

            1e Harry Bevir Vaisey (*Lincoln's Inn*), b 22 June 1877, m 20 Aug 1903, Eleonora Mary, da of the Rev William Quennell, Rector of Shenfield, co Essex, and has issue 1f to 2f

               1f Arthur William Vaisey, b 20 Oct 1905

               2f Juliana Margaret Vaisey, b 7 Sept 1904

            2e Roland Maddison Vaisey, b 31 Dec 1886

            3e Margaret Vaisey, b 4 June 1878   [Nos 17024 to 17032

# of The Blood Royal

4c Violet Vaisey, m 7 Nov 1907, John Brooke Scrivenor (Batu Gajah, Malay States), and has issue 1f to 2f

    1f Thomas Vaisey Scrivenor, b at Batu Gajah 28 Aug 1908

    2f Phebe Scrivenor, b at Batu Gajah 9 Ap 1910

5e Lilian Vaisey, b 31 Aug 1881

6e Veronica Vaisey, b 24 June 1883

7e May Vaisey, b 27 May 1885

8e Olive Vaisey, b 13 Ap 1889

9e Iris Vaisey, b 5 June 1892

2d John Ernest Dent Vaisey (Loden, Whyteleafe, Surrey), b 28 Ap 1853, m 20 Ap 1880, Judith, da of William Lawrence Bevir of Cirencester and has issue 1e to 4e

    1e John Clerc Vaisey, b 24 Dec 1880

    2e Thomas Lionel Vaisey, b 11 Dec 1883

    3e Francis Dent Vaisey, b 3 Dec 1885

    4e Maud Vaisey, b 27 June 1882

3d Charles Thomas St Clere Vaisey, b 28 Jan 1857 d 5 June 1905, m 1 Sept 1888, Emily Jessie, da of John Guyse Sparke, Major Bengal S C, and had issue 1e to 2e

    1e Guy Maddison Vaisey, b 15 July 1889

    2e Monica Vaisey, b 3 May 1891

4d Edith Agnes Vaisey, unm

2a George Maddison, Lieut -Col 65th Regt b 24 Nov 1762, d 5 Aug 1816, m Sept 1793, Mary, da of the Rev Henry Alington of Swinhope, co Lincoln, d 14 June 1850, and had issue 1b

    1b George Wilson Maddison of Partney Hall, co Linc, J P, b 29 Ap 1797 d 10 June 1888 m 1 Mar 1825, Frances Elizabeth, da of Sir Alan Bellingham, 2nd Bt [G B], d 29 Ap 1886, and had issue 1c to 4c

        1c Henry Maddison of Partney Hall, b 16 Ap 1829, d 11 Feb 1906, m 28 Nov 1867, Clare, da of Francis Slater of Christchurch, New Zealand, and had issue 1d to 4d

            1d Henry George Maddison (Partney Hall, Spilsby, co Lincoln), b 23 Aug 1868

            2d Humphrey Maddison, Lieut 1st Batt Derbyshire Regt, b 23 Sept 1876

            3d Frances Emily Theodosia Maddison

            4d Clara Cornelia Maddison

        2c Sidney Maddison of Horncastle, co Lincoln b 27 Feb 1832, d 12 Feb 1909, m 3 Nov 1869, Elizabeth, da of Samuel Mann, and has issue 1d to 2d

            1d Edward Maddison (Orlando, Florida), b 2 Oct 1871

            2d Isabel Emilia Lucy Maddison, m 21 Ap 1896, Nicholas Caesar Corsellis Lawton of Wyvenhoe Hall, co Essex (2 Mount Pleasant Crescent, Hastings), and has issue 1e to 2e

                1e Sydney Corsellis Lawton, b 6 Dec 1896

                2e John Corsellis Lawton, b Aug 1868

        3c Rev Arthur Roland Maddison, F S A, Priest Vicar and Prebendary of Lincoln Cathedral (Vicar's Court, Lincoln), b 26 July 1843

        4c Frances Theodosia Maddison

3a Charles Maddison, Capt Bengal Cavalry b 5 Sept 1770, d 1845, m 1791, Mary, da of the Rev John Harrington, D D, Rector of Thruxton, and Prebendary of Salisbury, d (-), and had issue 1b

    1b Rev John George Maddison, d 1856, m 1815, Thomas Anne, da of Alexander Macrae of Jamaica, d 1864, and had issue 1c to 7c

        1c Rev Charles John Maddison of Douglas, Isle of Man b 1817, d (-), m

[Nos 17033 to 17057a

161

The Plantagenet Roll

1844 *Julia, da of the Rev Benjamin Cracknell of Bath,* d (-), *and had issue 1d to 5d*

   1d Julia Sophia Maddison

   2d Mary Thomasine Maddison

   3d Agnes Rowley Maddison

   4d Minna Isabel Maddison

   5d Theodosia Ellen Maddison

  2c *Alexander Macrae Maddison of Agivey, co Derry,* b 24 Dec 1820, d 1861, m 1856, *Eliza, da of Capt Stephen Sharp, R N,* d (-), *and had issue 1d to 4d*

   1d Roland John George Maddison

   2d Ida Agnes Maddison

   3d Maud Mary Maddison

   4d Hilda Frances Maddison

  3c *George Latham Maddison of Toronto,* b 2 Jan 1823, d 24 Dec 1881, m 11 Sept 1848, *Mary Catharine, da of the Rev Charles Winstanley, and had issue 1d to 3d*

   1d Alfred John George Maddison (*Richmond, Virginia, U S A*), b 24 June 1849

   2d *Charles Edmund Maddison,* b 25 Sept 1852, d 21 Jan 1895, m *Esther Ann, da of William Warwick of Toronto, and had issue 1e to 4e*

      1e William Warwick Maddison

      2e Muriel Maddison

      3e Grace Ina Maddison

      4e Alice Winstanley Maddison

   3d George Ernest Maddison, b 8 Feb 1854

  4c *Thomasine Maddison,* d 20 Jan 1893, m 1844, *Charles Sidney Hawkins of Over Norton House, co Oxon*

  5c *Sophia Maddison,* d (? s p), m 1847, *John Ettrick [4th son of William Ettrick of High Barnes, co Durham]*

  6c *Theodosia Maddison,* d (? s p), m *Col Conolly Dysart.*

  7c *Agnes Halford Maddison,* d (? s p), m *John Smythe [son of John Smythe of Ardmore, co Derry]*

  4a *Katharine Maddison,* b Dec 1769, d Aug 1823, m 21 May 1796, *Latham Blacker of Newent, co Glouc, Major 65th Regt, and had issue 1b to 3b*

  1b *Martha Blacker,* d 17 Feb. 1878, m 29 Dec 1823, *the Rev John Fendall of Meserdine co Glouc,* d 18 June 1862, *and had issue 1c to 2c*

   1c Catharine Jane Fendall (*Milbrooke, Albert Road, Malvern*)

   2c Harriet Fendall, b 28 July 1826, m 22 June 1848, John Fendall Newton [only son of the Rev John Farmer Newton, Vicar of Kirby in Cleveland, co York] (*Ardmillan, Oswestry*), and has issue 1d to 10d

   1d Benjamin Newton (*Yarm-on-Tees, York*), b 12 May 1860, m 19 May 1886, Selina, da of the Rev Alleyne FitzHerbert of Tissington, co Derby, and has issue 1e to 3e

      1e Robert Newton, b 23 Jan 1893

      2e May Gladys Newton, b 3 May 1887

      3e Daisy Frances Newton, b 5 June 1890

   2d William Latham Newton (*Holtby House, York*), b 12 Jan 1862, m 17 Feb 1886, Violet, da of (—) Harrison, and has issue 1e to 2e

      1e Giles Fendall Newton, b 27 May 1891

      2e Blanche Emily Newton, b 20 June 1887   [Nos 17058 to 17081

3d Mary Catharine Newton, m 27 Aug 1885, Leonard Apsley Smith (Nevent), and has issue 1e

1e John Leonard Apsley Smith, b 25 Oct 1886

4d Elizabeth Martha Newton, unm

5d Laura Harriet Newton, unm

6d Anne Eva Newton, unm

7d Frances Judith Newton, unm

8d Caroline Newton, m 21 Ap 1881, the Rev Arthur Gurmondsway Waldy, M A (Oxon), Rector of Yarm (Yarm Rectory, N R Yorks), and has issue 1e to 5e

1e John Newton Waldy, b 25 Feb 1884, m 2 Sept 1908, Mabel, da of John Robson of Newton Bellingham

2e Rowland Gray Waldy, b 20 June 1890

3e Cuthbert Temple Waldy, b 31 Aug 1891

4e Violet Mary Waldy, b 9 Dec 1887

5e Dorothy Elizabeth Waldy, b 6 Feb 1897

9d Rose Newton, unm

10d Mabel Theodosia Newton, unm

2b *Catharine Blacker* d 13 Aug 1865, m 5 July 1826, Richard Foley Onslow of Stardene, co Glouc, d 12 Mar 1879, and had issue

See the Essex Volume, pp 320-321, Nos 33255-33266

3b [da] Blacker [2]   [Nos 17082 to 17108

78 Descendants, if any, of KATHARINE MADDISON (Table IX.), *bapt* 26 May 1724, *d* (-), *m* JOHN LAWRENCE of Putney [grand-son of Sir John Lawrence, Lord Mayor of London during the Plague] [1]

79 Descendants of THEODOSIA MADDISON [Table IX), *b* at Ketton 15 June 1725, *d* 20 Feb 1821; *m* 23 June 1752, JOHN (MONSON), 2nd BARON MONSON [G B], *d* 23 July 1774, and had issue

See the Exeter Volume, Table XIII , pp 243-252, Nos 9109-9497
                                      [Nos 17109 to 17497

80 Descendants of ANNA MADDISON (Table IX), *b* c 1728, *d* at Lea 31 Aug 1783, *m* at Little Grimsby 7 Aug 1747, the Rev Sir WILLIAM ANDERSON of Broughton, 6th Baronet [E], *d*. 9 Mar 1785, and had issue 1a to 6a

1a *Sir Edmund Anderson, 7th Bt [E], b 11 Sept 1758, dsp 30 May 1799*

2a *Rev Sir Charles Anderson of Broughton and Lea Hall, 8th Bt [E]. Prebendary of Lincoln and Rector of Lea, b 5 Oct 1767, d 24 Mar 1846, m 13 Dec 1802, Frances Mary, da of Sir John Nelthorpe of Scawby, co Lincoln, 6th Bt [E], d 18 Aug 1836, and had issue 1b*

1b *Sir Charles Henry John Anderson, 9th and last Bt [E], b 25 Nov 1804, d 8 Oct 1891, m 11 Sept 1832, Emma, da of John Savile Foljambe of Osberton, co Notts, d 8 Aug 1870, and had issue*

See the Clarence Volume, p 608, Nos 26758-26762   [Nos 17498 to 17502

---

[1] See Crisp's " Visitation Notes," vi p 55

The Plantagenet Roll

3a *Anne Anderson*, b 28 May 1753, d 12 July 1830, m 1st, 30 Aug 1771, *Samuel Thorold of Harmston Hall, co Linc*, d 19 Jan 1820, 2ndly, (-) Rosser (or Roys), and had issue 1b to 2b

 1b *Louise Thorold*, d (-), m 28 Feb 1796, *Capt Simpson, 2nd Regt*

 2b *Theodosia Thorold*, d 1806, m Sept 1800 *Lieut Gibbons, 37th Regt*

4a *Catharine Maria Anderson*. b. 16 May 1756, d Nov 1788, m as 1st wife, 31 July 1777, *Arthur Lemuel Shuldham of Dunmanway, co Cork, and Pallas Green, co Limerick*, d Aug 1839 and had issue 1b to 4b

 1b *Edmund William Shuldham of Dunmanway, Lieut Gen H E I C S, Quartermaster-Gen at Bombay*, b 1 Dec 1778 d 17 Nov 1852, m 3 Dec 1817, *Harriet Eliza Bonar, da of Thomas Rundall, M D, of Bath*, d 31 July 1847, and had issue 1c

  1c *Harriet Maria Catharine Shuldham, da and (31 July 1904) in her issue h*, d 15 Aug 1884, m 5 Aug 1852, *George Patrick Perv (Evans-Freke), 7th Baron Carbery [I]*, d 25 Nov 1889, and had issue 1d

   1d *Hon Georgiana Dorothea Harriet Evans-Freke, m 22 June 1876, James Francis (Bernard), 4th Earl of Bandon [I]* (*Castle Bernard, Bandon, co Cork*)

 2b *Molyneux Shuldham, Comm R N*, b 27 Ap 1781, d 25 Feb 1866, m 3 Dec 1820, *Frances, da of th. Rev Thomas Naunton Orgil Leman* (see p 170) *of Brampton Hall, co Suffolk*, d 22 Jan 1866, and had issue 1c to 4c

  1c *Arthur James Shuldham, Col late 2nd Batt Inniskillen Fusiliers*, b 13 Sept 1823, d 17 Oct 1905, m 1st, 8 Jan 1857, *Katharine Dora, da and co-h of the Rev C E Dukinfield, Vicar of Edenhall, co Cumb*, d 19 Aug 1865, 2ndly, 11 Sept 1869 *Lucy Elizabeth, da of Sir William Sidney Thomas, 3rd Bt [G B]* and had issue 1d to 10d

   1d *Edmund Dukinfield Shuldham*, b 29 Nov 1857

   2d *Molyneux Charles Dukinfield Shuldham*, b 13 Aug 1861

   3d *Herbert Leman Dukinfield Shuldham*, b 13 Feb 1863

   4d *Sidney Arthur Naunton Shuldham*, b 27 June 1870, m 27 Oct 1900, *Florence Kate, da of A Perkins of Cape Town*

   5d *Victor Lemuel Shuldham*, b 23 Oct 1872, m 1 Jan 1906, *Violet, da of (—) Pedingham of East London, Cape Colony*, and has issue

   6d¹ *Margaret Evelyn Shuldham*, d 26 Aug 1893, m *the Rev A E Sewart*, and had issue

   7d¹ *Geraldine Maud Shuldham*, m 19 Jan 1901 *Henry Walker*, and has issue

   8d¹ *Eleanor Maria Shuldham*, m 9 Sept 1888, *the Rev Theodore Edward Fortescue Cole* (*Nagpur, Central Provinces, India*), and has issue 1e to 2e

    1e *Lancelot Arthur Shuldham Cole*, b 11 Ap 1891

    2e *Humfrey Theodore Shuldham Cole*, b 5 Dec 1896

   9d¹ *Dora Frances Mary Blanche Shuldham, unm*

   10d² *Violet Lucy Hester Shuldham*, m 11 June 1901, *Henry Manby Colegrave*, and has issue

  2c *Rev Naunton Lemuel Shuldham*, b 24 Sept 1831, d 24 July 1874, m 8 Aug 1866, *Sophia Frances, da of John Mathew Quantock of Norton Manor, co Som*, d 17 Ap 1874, and had issue 1d

   1d *Frank Naunton Quantock Shuldham* (*Norton Manor, Ilminster*), b 25 Mar 1868, m 9 Ap 1890, *Emily, da of William Macalpine Leny of Dalswinton and Glencoe*, and has issue 1e

    1e *Walter Frank Quantock Shuldham*, b 17 June 1892

  3c *Catharine Leman Shuldham*, m 5 July 1849, *the Rev William Wrighte Gilbert-Cooper, Vicar of Burwash Weald, co Sussex*, and has issue 1d to 6d

   1d *Arthur Edward Gilbert-Cooper*, b 4 Oct 1853

   2d *William Naunton Roger Gilbert Cooper*, b 14 Sept 1867, m *Mabel Evelyn, da of Surg-Gen H T Rose*

   3d *Mary Frances Gilbert-Cooper*   [Nos 17503 to 17520

4d Fanny Catharine Alice Gilbert-Cooper, m 27 Dec 1876, Ralph Sillery Benson, Madras Civil Service

5d Edith Shuldham Gilbert-Cooper, m 9 Ap 1885, Alfred Holland (see p 170)

6d Amy Dora Gilbert-Cooper

4c *Frances Molyneux Shuldham*, d 27 Aug 1854, m 1853, *Lieut -Col Henry Lye, 13th Bombay Native Infantry*, d 1872, and had issue 1d

1d Harry Shuldham Lye, now (21 Oct 1909) Shuldham-Lye, Capt Royal Irish Regt, b 15 July 1854

3b *Arthur Shuldham, Lieut -Col H E I C S*, b 1790, d 23 *Feb* 1835, m 1st, (—), da of (—) *Sibley*, d s p (-), 2ndly, 20 *Jan* 1823, *Charlotte, da of Innis Delamaine, Major H E I C S*, d 23 *Jan* 1867, and had issue 1c to 3c

1c Arthur Innis Shuldham, *late* Lieut -Col Indian Army, b 30 Ap 1830, m 5 Nov 1871, Julia, da of Thomas Barnes

2c Charlotte Katharine Shuldham, m 4 Ap 1843, Major-Gen Robert Unwin, and has issue 1d to 2d

1d Emily Constance Unwin, m 31 Dec 1874, Augustus Lawrence Francis Headmaster of Blundell's School, Tiverton (*Tiverton*), and has issue 1e to 4e

1e Augustus Claude Francis, b 22 Feb 1878

2e Harold Vansittart Francis, b 25 Sept 1883

3e Constance Amy Francis, m 4 Jan 1905, Richard John Baynton Hippisley of Ston Easton, J P, Major N Somerset Imp Yeo (*Ston Easton Park, near Bath, Junior Carlton*), and has issue 1f

1f John Preston Hippisley, b 1905

4e Hilda Francis

2d Mabel Unwin

3c Amelia Ward Shuldham, m 28 Feb 1854, Fitz-Edward Hall, C E, D C L, and has issue 1d to 2d

1d Richard Daniel Hall, b 18 Feb 1863

2d Katharine Frances Hall

4b *Maria Lucy Eliza Shuldham*, d 26 Oct 1817, m 3 *Sept* 1801, *the Rev Joseph Guerin, Rector of Bagborough and Norton Fitzwarren*, d 12 *Nov* 1863, and had issue 1c

1c Edmund Arthur Guerin, Col Indian Army, b 22 Ap 1804, d (-), m 20 *Sept* 1836, *Louisa, da of Joseph Gilbert*, and has issue 1d to 2d

1d Joseph Arthur Guerin, H E I C S, b 12 July 1837, m July 1871, Elizabeth Walker, da of the Rev Dudley Oland Crosse, Vicar of Pawlett, co Som, and has issue 1e to 2e

1e Joseph Guerin, b 25 Jan 1875

2e Emily Maud Guerin

2d *Emily Louisa Guerin*, d 9 *May* 1865, m 10 *Sept* 1856, *Charles Frederic Keays, Major-Gen Bombay Army*, and had issue 1e to 5e

1e Frederic Edmund Keays, b 25 Oct 1857

2e Henry Guerin Keays, b 9 Ap 1862, m 17 Aug 1884, Edith, da of George Jinman, M R C S

3e Arthur Maitland Keays, b 11 Ap. 1865

4e Evelyn Louisa Frances Keays, m 16 Feb 1878, Newton Plomer Fowell, Capt R H A

5e Maud Emily Keays

5a *Theodosia Dorothy Anderson*, b 4 *Ap* 1757, d 5 *May* 1831, m 1 *Jan* 1778, *the Rev Richard Vevers, Rector of Sarby, co Leicester, of Stoke Albany and of Kettering, co Northants*, d 17 *Jan* 1838, and had issue (*with 5 sons and 6 das d s p*) 1b [Nos 17521 to 17544

The Plantagenet Roll

1b *Theodosia Anne Levers, 1a and event h*, b 21 Nov 1779, d 28 June 1852, m 18 Oct 1804, *Thomas (Denman), 1st Baron Denman [U K], Lord Chief-Justice of England*, d 22 Sept 1854, *and had issue* 1c to 10c

1c *Thomas (Denman, afterwards (K L 29 Dec 1876) Aitchison), 2nd Baron Denman [U K]*, b 30 July 1805, d s p 9 Aug 1894

2c *Hon Richard Denman*, b 13 Jan 1814, d 19 Mar 1887, m 28 Oct 1840, *Emma [herself a descendant of Edward III through Mortimer-Percc], da of High Jones of Larkhill, co Lanc*, d 2 Jan 1904, *and had issue*

See pp 60-61, Nos 566-610

3c *Right Hon George Denman, P C, Q C, M P, a Judge of the High Court, &c*, b 23 Dec 1819, d 21 Sept 1896, m 19 Feb 1852, *Charlotte, da of Samuel Hope of Liverpool*, d 19 Dec 1905, *and had issue* 1d to 5d

1d George Lewis Denman, Metropolitan Police Magistrate (36 *Evelyn Gardens, S W*), b 5 May 1854

2d Arthur Denman, F S A, Clerk of Assize, S E Circuit 1887 (29 *Cranley Gardens, S Kensington*), b 1 May 1857, m 17 Dec 1884, Katharine Agnes [descended from George, Duke of Clarence, K G], da of Edward Nathaniel Conant of Lyndon Hall, co Rutland, and has issue

See the Clarence Volume, p 613, Nos 26863-26865

3d Lancelot Baillie Denman, *late Comm R N*, b 15 Jan 1861, m 27 Ap 1892, Blanche Isabella Pauline, da of William Ernest de Veulle of Jersey

4d *Charlotte Edith Denman*, b 15 May 1855, d 29 Dec 1884, m 19 June 1883, *the Rev William Henry Draper, Rector of Adel, formerly (1883-1889) Vicar of Alfreton and (1889-1899) of The Abbey, Shrewsbury (Adel Rectory, Leeds), and had issue* 1e

1e Mark Denman Draper, b 15 Dec 1884

5d *Grace Denman*, m 6 Nov 1890, *Sidney Gambier Parry (Downham House, near Billericay, Essex), and has issue* 1e to 3e

1e Michael Denman Gambier Parry, b 1891

2e Richard Gambier Parry, b 1894

3e Edith Joan Gambier Parry, b 1892

4c *Rev the Hon Lewis William Denman, Rector of Willian, co Herts*, b 23 Mar 1821, d 6 May 1907, m 1st, 18 June 1850, *Frances Marianne (see p 280), da of Thomas Eden of The Bryn, Swansea*, d 25 Ap 1862, 2ndly, 22 Aug 1865, *Frances Starkie Mary, da of Col Henry Armytage, Coldstream Guards*, d s p 24 Dec 1893, *and had issue* 1d to 4d

1d Lewis William Eden Denman (*Church Norton, Selsey, Chichester*), b 9 May 1857, m 5 Aug 1889, Emma, da of Charles Rainbow, and has issue 1e to 2e

1e Joseph Alban Denman, b 17 June 1890

2e Theodosia Victoria Denman

2d Frances Emily Denman }

3d Theodosia Louisa Denman } (*May Bank, Horsham Road, Sussex*)

4d Caroline Annie Denman }

5c *Hon Theodosia Denman*, b 16 Sept 1806, d 20 May 1895, m 21 Nov 1825, *Ichabod Charles Wright of Mapperley Hall, co Notts*, d 14 Oct 1871, *and had issue* 1d to 6d

1d *Charles Ichabod Wright of Stapleford Hall, co Notts, and Watcombe Park, co Devon, M P co Nottingham*, b 19 Sept 1828, d 9 May 1905, m 9 June 1852, *Blanche Louisa, da of Henry Coales Bingham of Wartnaby Hall, co Leic* and had issue 1e to 5e

1e Charles Bingham Wright of Mapperley, *late Capt S Notts Yeo Cav*, b 19 Nov 1854

2e Nevill Wright, b 20 Nov 1857

3e. Blanche Theodosia Wright   [Nos 17545 to 17609

166

# of The Blood Royal

4e Rosamond Frances Wright, m 15 Aug 1883, Elias John Webb of Tiddington, Major 4th Batt Worcester Regt (*Tiddington, Stratford-on-Avon, The Browns-end, co Glouc*)

5e Grace Henrietta Wright, m 7 Nov 1885 Richard Campbell Davys of Neuadd-fawr, co Carmarthen, and Askomel, co Argyll, J P, D L, d 15 Nov 1905 and has issue 1f to 4f

2f Ivor Elystan Campbell-Davys of Neuadd-fawr and Askomel (*Neuadd-fawr, Llandovery*), b 4 Aug 1890

2f Eva Gwladys Campbell-Davys

3f Grace Edith Campbell-Davys

4f Lilian Elan Campbell-Davys

2d Henry Smith Wright (*Oaklands Park, Chichester*), b 27 June 1839, m 1st, 17 Oct 1865, Mary Jane, da of William Cutledge of Woolthorpe, co Notts, d 4 Dec 1866, 2ndly 6 Feb 1869, Josephine Henrietta, da of the Rev John Adolphus Wright, Rector of Ickham, co Kent, and has issue 1e to 6e

1e Henry Adolphus Smith Wright, Capt *late* Royal Fusiliers (*Nutbourne Place, Pulborough, Sussex*), b 13 Dec 1869, m 8 June 1901, Dorothy Cécile Renton, da of Col E de Bury Barnett, and his issue (2 children)

2e George Lewis Smith Wright, b 30 Jan 1872, m 30 July 1902, Ismay, da of C C Hopkinson

3e Edward Henry Smith Wright, British South Africa Company (*3 Upton Park, Slough*), b 4 Sept 1875, m 23 July 1902, Isie Margaret, da of Gerald Young, and has issue 1f to 4f

1f Edward Gerald Smith Wright, b 7 Dec 1903

2f John Evelyn Smith Wright, b 19 July 1907

3f Henry Gordon Smith Wright, b 23 June 1908

4f Josephine Margaret Smith Wright

4e John Harold Smith Wright, Lieut R N, b 18 Aug 1882

5e[1] Edith Mary Wright, m Donald Campbell (*Templeton, Hungerford, Berks*)

6e[2] Alice Dorothea Smith Wright, m Richard Manders (*Stonehurst, Killiney, co Dublin*)

3d Frederick Wright (*Lenton Hall, co Notts*), b 12 Aug 1840, m 12 Feb 1863, Ada Joyce, da of the Rev John Bateman of East and West Leake, co Notts, and had issue 1e to 7e

1e Frederick Denman Wright, b 17 Dec 1872

2e Emily Theodosia Wright

3e Mary Neville Wright

4e Florence Ada Wright

5e Margaret Joyce Wright

6e Hilda Dorothy Wright

7e Maud Frances Bateman Wright

4d Rev George Howard Wright, Chaplain at Naples *formerly* Assist Chap at Rome (1902-1903) and San Remo (1903-1904), &c (*Whitehill House, near West Liss, Hants*), b 1 June 1845, m 12 July 1870, Anne Frances, da of the Rev Edmund Roberts Larken, and has issue 1e to 3e

1e George Denman Larken Wright, b 31 Aug 1872

2e Eric James Wright, b 12 Nov 1880

3e Theodosia Anne Emily Wright

5d Theodosia Harriet Wright, m 8 Sept 1863, William Houston Sinclair (*Morton Manor, Brading, I W*), and has issue 1e to 4e

1e Charles George Sinclair, b 5 Jan 1865

2e William Frederick Sinclair, b 26 Ap 1867

3e John Houston Sinclair, b 6 Dec 1869

4e Theodosia Agnes Sinclair

6d Frances Wright, m 30 May 1861 Edward William Cropper of Great Crosby, co Lanc, J P, b 7 July 1833 d 29 Jan 1906, and has issue 1e to 8e

[Nos 17610 to 17641

The Plantagenet Roll

1c Rev James Cropper, M A (Camb), Vicar of Penrith (*St Andrew's Vicarage, Penrith*), *b* 2 May 1862, *m* 8 Mar 1888, Ethel Frances, da of G Perceval Smith, and has issue 1*f* to 5*f*

  1*f* Paul Cropper, *b* 29 Jan 1889

  2*f* Edward Perceval Cropper, *b* 15 July 1896

  3*f* Richard Alfred Cropper, *b* 2 Dec 1899

  4*f* Frances Alice Cropper

  5*f* Martha Phyllis Cropper

2c John Cropper, *b* 17 Sept 1864, *m* 6 Feb 1895, Ann Ellen, da of T A Walker, and has issue 1*f* to 3*f*

  1*f* Thomas Andrew Cropper *b* 11 May 1898

  2*f* Dorothea Alice Denman Cropper

  3*f* Eleanor Grace Cropper

3c Charles Henry Edward Cropper, *b* 25 Jan 1866, *m* 30 Ap 1891, Ethel Mary, da of the Rev Conrad Green, and has issue 1*f* to 3*f*

  1*f* Charles Leonard Cropper, *b* 26 Jan 1894

  2*f* Alexander Cropper, *b* 8 Dec 1896

  3*f* Madge Ethel Cropper

4c Rev Frederick William Cropper, M A (Camb) (8 *Montpellier Terrace, Cheltenham*), *b* 1 Feb 1871, *m* 30 Dec 1897, Florence Barton, da of the Rev Thomas Davis Jones, Vicar of Caerwent, and has issue 1*f* to 2*f*

  1*f* Charles Frederick John Cropper, *b* 6 June 1901

  2*f* Violet Gwenllian Cropper

5c Frances Mildred Theodosia Cropper, *m* 17 Jan 1889, Conrad Theodore Green, and has issue

6c Anne Wakefield Cropper

7c Emily Mabel Cropper, *m* 28 Ap 1891, the Rev Hubert Edmund Hamilton Probyn (*Abbenhall Lodge, Mitcheldean, Glouc*) [descended from the Lady Anne, sister of King Edward IV (see Exeter Volume, p 198)], and has issue 1*f* to 3*f*

  1*f* Edward Hamilton Probyn, *b* 17 Sept 1908

  2*f* Emily Araminta Probyn

  3*f* Margaret Eleanor Probyn

8c Eveline Wright Cropper

6b *Hon Elizabeth Denman, b* 21 *Nov* 1807, *d* 5 *Aug* 1880, *m* 3 *May* 1838 *the Ven Francis Hodgson, Provost of Eton and Archdeacon of Derby, d* 29 *Dec* 1852, *and had issue* 1*d to* 4*d*

  1*d James Thornton Hodgson, b* 4 *May* 1845, *d* 1880, *m* 15 *June* 1872, *Maria Blanche, sister of Harry William Verelst of Aston Hall, co York, and had issue* 1*c to* 5*c*

    1c Francis Coke Denman Hodgson, *b* 10 Dec 1874

    2c James Vaughan Hodgson, *b* 3 July 1878

    3c Maud Vevers Hodgson

    4c Sybil Blanche Hodgson

    5c Lilian Verelst Hodgson

  2*d* Elizabeth Denman Hodgson, *m* 17 Ap 1882, Herbert Charles MacCarthy

  3*d* Matilda Frances Hodgson

  4*d* Jane Theodosia Hodgson

7b *Hon Frances Denman,* b 17 *Sept* 1812, *d* 29 *Ap* 1890, *m* 8 *July* 1846, *Admiral Sir Robert Lambert Baynes, K C B, d* 7 *Sept* 1869, *and had issue* 1*d*

  1*d* Henry Compton Anderson Baynes, *late* Capt R N, *b* 13 Oct 1852, *m* 21 Aug 1884, Isabel, da of Admiral Sir Joseph Nias, K C B

8b *Hon Margaret Denman,* b 8 *Aug* 1815, *d* 11 *June* 1899, *m* 1st, 23 *Nov* 1841, *Henry William Macaulay* [*brother of Lord Macaulay*] *d* 24 *Sept* 1846,

[Nos 17645 to 17677

# of The Blood Royal

2ndly, as 2nd wife, 10 Aug 1848, Edward Cropper of Swaylands, co Kent, J P, d 23 May 1877, 3rdly, 22 Ap 1879, Col John Owen, d s p 1890, and had issue 1d to 6d

1d Henry Denman Macaulay, late Lieut R N, b 10 Aug. 1843, m 18 Feb 1868, Selina, da of Sir Joseph Needham, Chief-Justice of Trinidad, and has issue 1e to 3e

    1e William Edward Babington Macaulay, b 2 Feb 1869

    2e Arthur James Denman Macaulay, R N, b 14 May 1870

    3e Thomas Cary Elwes Cropper Macaulay (Alexandria), b 15 Aug 1871

2d Joseph Babington Macaulay, b 17 Oct 1846, m 8 July 1869, Eleanor, da of Henry Studdy of Waddeton Court, co Devon, J P, D L, and had issue 1e to 5e

    1e Aulay Babington Macaulay, R M S, R N R, b Nov 1876, unm

    2e Edward Macaulay, b 3 Nov 1877, unm

    3e Eleanor Josephine Macaulay, unm

    4e Maud Olive Macaulay, m 19 Aug 1903, Robert Perry Bruce (Villa Arco, Via Soffiano, Florence), and has issue 1f to 4f

        1f Michael Macaulay Bruce, b 4 Sept 1904

        2f Robert Macaulay Bruce, } b (twins) 6 Feb 1906
        3f Nigel Macaulay Bruce, }

        4f Edward Macaulay Bruce, b 9 Feb 1908

    5e Lois Macaulay, unm

3d Edward Denman Cropper, now (R L 14 Nov 1874) Thornburgh-Cropper (Dingle Bank, Lancashire Swaylands, Kent), b 23 May 1854, m 4 July 1874, Minnie Virginia, da and h of William Butler Thornburgh of San Francisco

4d Amelia Margaret Elizabeth Cropper, m 1st, 4 June 1867, Henry Studdy of Waddeton Court, co Devon, Comm R N, d v p 13 Sept 1880, 2ndly, 1881, William Thomas Summers of Milton, co Pembroke (Esthlon, Newmarket Torcross, S Devon), and has issue 1e to 3e

    1e Henry Edward Macaulay Studdy, Capt (ret) late Rough Riders, served in S Africa (10 Souldern Road, West Kensington), b 19 Mar 1868, m 12 Jan 1893, Mary, da of John Grigg of Colebrook, Plympton, co Devon, and has issue 1f to 5f

        1f Henry Studdy, b 20 Ap 1894

        2f Edward Studdy, b 22 Sept 1895

        3f John Studdy, b 25 Oct 1901

        1f Arthur Redmond Studdy, b 11 Ap 1905

        5f Mary Studdy

    2e Eleanor Margaret Studdy, m as 2nd wife, 30 Jan 1892, Sir Harald George Hewett, 4th Bt [U K], Capt and Hon Major R G A (The Red House, Chilworth, Hants), and has issue 1f to 4f

        1f Harald Hewett, b 22 Oct 1892

        2f John George Hewett, b 23 Oct 1895

        3f George Nele Hewett, b 30 Aug 1901

        4f Margaret Hewett

    3e Anita Georgina Edith Studdy, m 1st, 9 Jan 1899, Capt David Longfield Beatty, late 4th Hussars, d 3 Ap 1904, 2ndly, 27 Ap 1909, Harold Lett (Kilgibbon, co Wexford), and has issue 1f

        1f Henry Longfield Beatty, b 4 Mar 1901

5d Florence Anne Cropper, m 1 July 1873, Arthur Frederick Holdsworth of Widdicombe, J P, late Capt South Devon and North Lincoln Militia, previously R N (Widdicombe House, Kingsbridge, Devon), and has issue 1e to 4e

    1e Arthur Mervyn Holdsworth, 1st Royal Berkshire Regt, b 5 Nov 1875

    2e Frederick John Cropper Holdsworth, 2nd Devonshire Regt, b 7 Nov 1886

    3e Florence Evelyn Holdsworth

    4e Joan Holdsworth

                                  [Nos 17678 to 17711.

The Plantagenet Roll

6d Marion Eliza Blanche Cropper, m 5 May 1878, Lieut.-Col Rowley Richard Conway Hill, *late* 31st Regt (*Hamble House, Hamble, Hants*), and has issue 1e to 9e

  1e Rowley Arthur Edward Hill, R H A, *b* 3 Jan 1879

  2e Hugh Rowley Hill, R F A, *b* 18 Feb 1880

  3e Conway Rowley Hill, R F A, *b* 16 Sept 1881

  4e Oliver Charles Rowley Hill R F A, *b* 22 Nov 1883

  5e Leslie Rowley Hill, R F A, *b* 28 Dec 1884

  6e Blanch Edith Hill

  7e Margaret Hill

  8e Janet Dorothy Hill

  9e Helen Irene Susan Hill

9c *Hon Anne Denman* b 26 June 1822 d (–), m 18 Aug 1846, *Frederick Holland Comm R N* d 21 July 1890, *and had issue 1d to 7d*

  1d Edward Holland, *b* 30 Aug 1850

  2d Frederick Arthur Holland, *b* 17 Oct 1853

  3d Richard Lancelot Holland, *b* 24 Ap 1858

  4d Alfred Holland, *b* 14 Aug 1859, *m* 9 Ap 1885, Edith Shuldham (see p 165), da of the Rev William Wrighte Gilbert-Cooper

  5d Annie Susan Holland

  6d Charlotte Holland   } (twins)

  7d Theodosia Caroline Holland }

10c *Hon Caroline Amelia Denman* b 26 Aug 1823 d (–), m 3 Feb 1846, *the Rev John George Beresford, Vicar of St Andrew's, Whittlesea, and Rector of Bedale,* d 17 July 1899, *and had issue*

See the Exeter Volume, p 215, Nos 9156–9207

6a *Henrietta Jane Anderson,* b 20 May 1761, d 9 Mar 1843, m 3 Dec 1783, *the Rev Naunton Thomas Orgill Leman of Brampton Hall,* co Suff, d 31 Jan 1837 *and had issue 1b to 2b*

  1b *Rev Robert Orgill Leman of Brampton Hall,* b 12 Ap 1799, d 24 Feb 1869, m 1st, 25 Mar 1824 *Isabella Camilla, da of Sir William Jervis Twysden, 7th Bt [E],* d 7 May 1850 2ndly, 29 May 1859, *Ellen Maria, da of the Rev John Alexander Ross Vicar of Westwell, co Kent, and had issue 1c to 5c*

  1c Naunton Robert Twysden Orgill Leman of Brampton Hall, *b* 12 Sept 1825, *m* 11 Aug 1869, Rose Elizabeth, da of the Rev John Alexander Ross, Vicar of Westwell, and has issue 1d

    1d Robert Naunton Orgill Leman, *b* 2 Oct 1870

  2c Anderson Thomas John Orgill Leman, *b* 31 Jan 1862

  3c[1] Frances Henrietta Eliza Flora Leman

  4c[2] Beatrice Amelia Ellen Leman

  5c[2] Ethel Helena Mary Leman

2b *Frances Leman,* d 22 Jan 1866, m 3 Dec 1820, *Molyneux Shuldham, Comm R N,* d 25 Feb 1866, *and had issue*

See pp 164–165, Nos 17501–17521   [Nos 17712 to 17807

---

81 Descendants of ELIZABETH WHICHCOT (Table IX), *bapt* at Harpswell 20 Mar 1706, *bur* at Glentworth 19 Feb 1774, *m* 19 Feb 1730, the Ven WILLIAM BASSETT, Archdeacon of Stow, *b* 7 June 1703, *bur* at Glentworth 13 July 1765, and had issue (with a son who *d s p* and 2 other das. known to have *d* in infancy) 1a to 10a

  1a *William Bassett,* d 18 Nov 1738

  2a *Richard Bassett of Glentworth,* b 15 Sept 1744, d 12 July 1805, m 1 July 1774, *Martha, da of Joseph Armitage of High Royd, Huddersfield,* d (–), and had issue 1b to 2b

# of The Blood Royal

1b *Rev Henry Bassett, Rector of North Thoresby* b 12 Ap 1778, d 1 May 1852, m 1 Oct 1811, *Catharine, da of John Fardell of Lincoln*, d 6 June 1859, and had issue 1c to 2c

1c *Henry Bassett of Ingham, co Linc*, b 18 Jan 1817, d 18 July 1888, m 3 Jan 1856, *Emily Mary, da of Henry Wood of London*, d 23 Feb 1897, and had issue 1d to 3d

1d *Rev Henry John Bassett B A (Oxon), Vicar of Hagnaby and East Kirkby (East Kirkby Vicarage, Spilsby)* b 17 Jan 1859, m 21 June 1894, Gertrude Mary, da of Perceta Brown of Glentworth Hall, co Linc, and has issue 1e

1e Ralph Perceta Henry Bassett, b 16 Feb 1896

2d Isabel Emily Bassett, *unm*

3d Katharine Phœbe Bassett, *unm*

2c *Catharine Mary Bassett*, b 5 Oct 1823, d 31 Jan 1902, m 4 June 1850, the Rev John Gilbert Day of Pitsford, co Northants, d 19 Nov 1903, and had issue 1d to 2d

1d Julia Catherine Day (*The Limes, Pleasbury Road Cheltenham*), m 25 Ap 1878, Frederick Charles Fardell, d 3 Aug 1899

2d Blanche Mary Day, *unm*

2b *Martha Bassett*, b 27 Sept 1776, d 18 Feb 1869, m 17 Oct 1798, John Wilson of Seacroft Hall and Cliffe Hall, co Yorks, d 12 Nov 1836, and had issue 1c to 2c

1c *Richard Bassett Wilson of Cliffe Hall, co Yorks*, b 3 Ap 1800, d 23 May 1867, m 5 Dec 1839, *Anne, da and co-h of William FitzGerald of Adelphi, co Clare*, d 11 July 1877, and had issue 1d to 7d

1d *John Gerald Wilson, C B*, b 29 Dec 1841, d 8 Mar 1902, m 4 June 1873, *Angelina Rosa Geraldine, da of Rev the Hon Henry O'Brien*, and had issue 1e to 6e

1e Murrough John Wilson (*Cliffe Hall, Darlington*), b 11 Sept 1875, m 16 Feb 1904, Sybil May, da of Sir Powlett Charles John Milbank, 2nd Bt [U K], and has issue 1f to 2f

1f Geraldine Edith Mary Wilson, b 19 Dec 1905

2f Kathleen May Wilson, b 16 Aug 1909

2e Denis Daly Wilson, Capt 17th Bengal Cavalry, b 22 Oct 1878

3e Frank O Brien Wilson, Lieut R N, b 30 Ap 1883

4e Harriet Anne Dorothy Wilson, m 12 July 1904, Frederick Richard Charles Milbank, J P [son and h app of Sir Powlett Charles John Milbank, 2nd Bt [U K], J P, D L] (*Abbey House, Ludlow*), and has issue 1f to 2f

1f Mark Vane Milbank, b 11 Jan 1907

2f John Gerald Frederick Milbank, b 17 Ap 1909

5e Gladys Mary Wilson, m 15 Aug 1905, John Beaumont Hotham, B A (Camb), a Clerk in the House of Lords [B Hotham Coll] (*70 Warwick Square, S W*), and has issue 1f to 2f

1f Dorothy Jean Hotham, b 12 Aug 1907

2f Margaret Hotham, b 14 Aug 1909

6e Geraldine Wilson

2d William Henry Wilson, *now* (R L 20 July 1872) FitzGerald-Wilson (*Adelphi, Corofin, co Clare*), b 22 Ap 1841, m 21 Nov 1885, Olave, da of Russell C Stanhope of Parsonstown Manor, co Meath, and has issue 1e to 2e

1e Francis William Wilson-FitzGerald, 1st Royal Dragoons, b 8 Dec 1886

2e Olave Clare Wilson-FitzGerald, b 11 Feb 1888

3d Maurice FitzGerald Wilson (*Ashburn Gardens, London, W*), b 4 Feb 1858, m 2 Aug 1884, Florence May, da of the Ven Hopkins Badnall, D D, Archdeacon of the Cape of Good Hope, and has issue 1e to 2e

1e Maurice Fiennes FitzGerald Wilson, b 22 June 1886

2e Bassett FitzGerald Wilson, b 1 Sept 1888   [Nos 17808 to 17831]

The Plantagenet Roll

4d *Juliana Cecilia Wilson*, d 15 Nov 1898, m 14 Sept 1865, *Thomas Charles Johnson Sowerby of Snow Hall, Darlington*, and had issue 1e to 8e

1e Charles Fitzgerald Sowerby, Capt R N, *b* 31 July 1866

2e William Bassett Sowerby (*Newcastle on Tyne*), *b* 13 Ap 1870, *m* 14 Sept 1900, Lena, da of William Hunter, and has issue 1f

1f Guy Spencer Sowerby, *b* 5 Aug 1905

3e Edward Chaytor Sowerby (*Sudborough, Northants*), *b* 2 Sept 1872, *m* 4 July 1907, Muriel, d of J Gardiner Mun of Farming Woods, co Northants, and has issue 1f

1f Thomas Mun Sowerby, *b* 6 Sept 1908

4e Maurice Eden Sowerby, Capt R E, *b* 5 Dec 1874

5e Gerald Sowerby, Lieut R N (*Myrtle, Newcastle, co Down*), *b* 31 July 1878 *m* 14 Jan 1904, Lady Mabel Marguerite, da of Hugh (Annesley), 5th Earl of Annesley [1], and has issue 1f

1f Gerald Francis Annesley Sowerby, *b* 5 Nov 1904

6e Mabel Frances Sowerby

7e Edith Mary Sowerby, *m* 12 Nov 1903, Sir Henry Spencer Moreton Havelock-Allan, 2nd Bt [U K] (*Blackwell Grange and Blackwell Hall, Darlington*)

8e Mary Gertrude Sowerby

5d Mary Lucia Wilson

6d Augusta Jane Wilson, *m* 30 June 1870, Thomas Robins Bolitho of Trengwainton (*Trengwainton, Hea Moor, R S O, Cornwall*), s p

7d Emily Gertrude Wilson, *m* 17 Dec 1878, James FitzGerald Bannatyne of Summerville, co Limerick (*Haldon, Exeter*), and has issue 1e to 3e

1e James FitzGerald Bannatyne, *b* 25 Nov 1883

2e Mary Stuart Bannatyne, *b* 1 May 1884

3e Victoria Vera Bannatyne, *b* 11 Sept 1887

2c *John Wilson of Seacroft Hall, co Yorks*, *b* 1 Jan 1808, *d* 29 Jan 1891, *m* 13 Ap 1846, *Anna Maria Isabella, da of Roderick Macleod of Cadbell, co Ross, M P*, d 26 Dec 1903, and had issue 1d to 4d

1d Darcy Bruce Wilson (*Seacroft Hall, near Leeds*), *b* 17 June 1851

2d Arthur Henry Wilson (*Sandridge Park, Totnes*), *b* 24 Ap 1853, *m* 12 Nov 1885, Alice Louisa, da of George Drake Wainwright, and has issue 1e

1e Gladys Sabine Fyers Wilson, *b* 6 Oct 1886

3d Constance Wilson, *m* 6 Jan 1887, the Rev Charles John Aylmer Eade, M A (Camb), Vicar of Aycliffe (*Aycliffe Vicarage, Darlington*), and has issue 1e to 3e

1e John Eade, *b* 18 Dec 1887

2e Charles Eade, *b* 19 July 1900

3e Aylmer Eade, *b* 29 Jan 1902

4d. Louisa Wilson

3a *Thomas Bassett*, *b* 22 Jan 1747

4a *John Bassett*, *b* 22 Feb 1748

5a *Charles Bassett*, *b* 21 July 1749, *was married and had a wife living at Glentworth in* 1811 [1]

6a *Frances Bassett*, b 22 Feb 1731

7a *Katherine Bassett*, b 14 Jan 1732

8a *Anne Bassett*

9a *Lydia Bassett*, b 17 Feb 1742

10a *Charlotte Bassett*, b 20 Sept 1743   [Nos 17832 to 17856

---

[1] Maddison's "Lincolnshire Pedigrees," i 107

# of The Blood Royal

82 Descendants of ELIZABETH TEMPEST (Table IX), *d* (–), *m* JOHN SOUTH of Kelstern, co Lincoln, who was nominated a Knight of the Royal Oak in 1660, and had issue

See p 150

83. Descendants, if any surviving, of ANNE CLIFTON (Table IX), *d* (–), *m* Sir FRANCIS RODES, 2nd Bt [E], *d* 1651, and had issue 1*a* to 2*a*

  1*a* *Sir Francis Rodes, 3rd Bt* [E], b *c* 1647, d 14 *Mar* 1675, m (*licence dated* 1 *May*) 1665, *Martha da of William Thornton of Grantham, co Linc*, d 25 *Oct.* 1719, *and had issue* 1*b* to 3*b*
  1*b* *Sir John Rodes, 4th Bt* [E], b 1670, d *unm Oct* 1743
  2*b* *Frances Rodes, da and co-h*, d (–), m *Gilbert Heathcote of Calthorp or Cuthorp, co Derby, M D*, *and had issue* 1*c* to 3*c*
  1*c* *Cornelius Heathcote, M D*, d (–), m *Elizabeth, da of* (—) *Middlebrooke*, *and had issue* 1*d* 1*e*
  1*d* *John Heathcote*, d (–), m *Millicent, da of* (—) *Satterthwaite*, *and had issue* (*with others whose issue is known to be extinct*) 1*e*
  1*e* *Mary Heathcote*, m 1st, (—) *Miers*, 2ndly, *Capt Massey*
  2*c* *Martha Heathcote*, d (–), m 1744, *Benjamin Bartlett of Bradford*
  3*c* *Elizabeth Heathcote*, d (–), m 1746, *Peter Acklom of Hornsey, co Yorks*
  3*b* *Anne Rodes, da and co-h*, d (–), m *William Thornton of Bloxham*
  2*a* *Jane Rodes*, d (–), m *Capt William Hossay of London*

84. Descendants of Lady MARGARET CLIFFORD (Table VIII), *b c* 1540, *d* 19 Sept. 1596, *m* 7 Feb. 1555, HENRY (STANLEY), 4th EARL OF DERBY [E], K G, *d.* 25 Sept 1593, and had issue

See the Tudor Roll, Table LXXXII, and pp 358–563, Nos 27543–36735
Nos 17857 to 27019

85 Descendants of PEREGRINE (BERTIE), 3rd DUKE OF ANCASTER AND KESTEVEN [G B] and MARQUIS OF LINDSEY, and 18th BARON WILLOUGHBY DE ERESBY [E], Hereditary Lord Great Chamberlain of England, P C (Table X), *b* 1714, *d* 12 Aug 1778, *m.* 2ndly, 27 Nov 1750, MARY, sometime Mistress of the Robes to Queen Charlotte, da of Thomas PANTON of Newmarket, co Cambridge, *d* at Naples Oct 1793, and had issue 1*a* to 3*a*

  1*a* *Robert (Bertie), 4th Duke of Ancaster and Kesteven* [G B], &c, b 17 Oct 1736, d *unm* 8 *July* 1779
  2*a* *Priscilla Barbara Elizabeth (née Bertie), 20th Baroness Willoughby de Eresby* [E], *Joint Hereditary Great Chamberlain of England*, b 16 *Feb* 1761, d 29 *Dec* 1828, m 23 *Feb* 1779, *Peter (Burrell), 1st Baron Gwydyr* [G B], b 16 *June* 1754, d 29 *June* 1820, *and had issue* 1*b* to 2*b*
  1*b* *Peter Robert (Burrell, sometime* (*R L* 5 *Nov* 1807) *Burrell-Drummond, and finally* (*R L* 26 *June* 1829) *Drummond-Willoughby), 21st Baron Willoughby de*

The Plantagenet Roll

Eresby [*E*] *and 2nd Baron Gwydyr* [*G B*]. *P C , &c , b* 19 *Mar* 1782 , *d* 22 *Feb* 1865 , *m* 19 *Oct* 1807, *Lady Clementina, da and h of James (Drummond),* 11*th Earl of Perth* [*S*] *and* 1*st Baron Perth* [*G B*], *d* 26 *Jan* 1865 , *and had issue* 1c *to* 3c

1c *Albéric (Burrell)* 22*nd Baron Willoughby de Eresby* [*E*], 3*rd Baron Gwydyr* [*G B*], *b* 23 *Dec* 1821 , *d unm* 26 *Aug* 1870

2c *Clementina Elizabeth,* suo jure 23*rd Baroness Willoughby de Eresby* [*E*], *&c , Joint Hereditary Great Chamberlain of England, da and* (1870) *co h , b* 2 *Sept* 1809 , *d* 13 *Nov* 1888 *m* 8 *Oct* 1827, *Sir Gilbert John Heathcote,* 5*th Bt* [*G B*], *afterwards* (26 *Feb* 1856) 1*st Baron Aveland* [*U K*] [*descended from King Henry VII*] *d* 6 *Sept* 1867 , *and had issue*

See the Tudor Roll, pp 206–207, Nos 21514–21530

3c *Hon Charlotte Augusta Annabella Drummond-Willoughby, Joint Hereditary Great Chamberlain of England, da and* (1870) *co-h , b* 3 *Nov* 1815 , *d* 26 *July* 1879 , *m as 2nd wife,* 10 *Aug* 1840, *Robert John (Smith, afterwards* (*R L* 26 *Aug* 1839) *Carrington),* 2*nd Baron Carrington* [*G B and I*], *b* 16 *June* 1796 , *d.* 17 *Mar* 1868 , *and had issue* 1d *to* 5d

1d *Charles Robert (Carrington, now* (*R L* 24 *Ap* 1896) *Wynn-Carrington),* 1*st Earl Carrington* [*U K*], 3*rd Baron Carrington* [*G B and I*], *Joint Hereditary Lord Great Chamberlain of England, K G , P C , G C M G , President of the Board of Agriculture, formerly Lord Chamberlain of the Household to Queen Victoria* 1892–1895, *Gov and Comm -in-Chief of New South Wales* 1885–1890, *&c &c (Gwydyr Castle, Llanrwst, Wales , Daws Hill, High Wycombe,* 53 *Prince's Gate, S W), b* 16 *May* 1843 , *m* 15 *July* 1878, *the Hon Cecilia Margaret* [a descendant of the Lady Isabel Plantagenet (see Essex Volume, p 16)], *da of Charles (Harbord),* 5*th Baron Suffield* [*G B*], *and has issue* 1e *to* 6e

1e *Albert Edward Samuel Charles Robert Wynn-Carrington, Viscount Wend-over, for whom* H M *the King stood Sponsor, b* 24 *Ap* 1895

2e *Lady Marjorie Cecilia Wynn-Carrington, m* 12 *Feb* 1901, *Charles Henry Wellesley (Wilson),* 2*nd Baron Nunburnholme* [*U K*], *D S O , &c (Fernby Hall, North Fernby, East Yorks) and has issue* 1f *to* 2f

1f *Hon Charles John Wilson, b* 25 *Ap* 1904

2f *Hon Cecilia Monica Wilson*

3e *Lady Alexandra Augusta Wynn-Carrington, for whom* H M *Queen Alexandra was Sponsor*

4e *Lady Ruperta Wynn-Carrington, m* 7 *Dec* 1905, *William Legge, Viscount Lewisham* [s and h of the 6th Earl of Dartmouth and a descendant of King Henry VII (see Tudor Roll, p 199)] *(Patshull House, Wolverhampton) , and has issue* 1f *to* 2f

1f *Hon Mary Cecilia Legge*

2f *Hon Elizabeth Legge*

5e. *Lady Judith Sydney Mee Wynn-Carrington*

6e *Lady Victoria Alexandrina Wynn-Carrington, for whom* H M *Queen Victoria was Sponsor*

2d *Hon Sir William Henry Peregrine Carington* (*R L* 21 *Aug* 1880), *previously Carrington, K C V O , C B , Extra Equerry to* H M *the King, formerly Equerry to* H M *the King and to Queen Victoria* 1882–1902, *Capt and Lieut -Col Grenadier Guards, M P for Wycombe* 1868–1883, *&c (Burfield, Old Windsor,* 6 *Cadogan Square, S W), b* 28 *July* 1845 , *m* 28 *Sept* 1871, *Juliet, da of Francis Warden*

3d *Hon Rupert Clement George Carington* (*R L* 21 *Aug* 1880), *previously Carrington, C V O , D S O , Lieut -Col Comdg* 68*th Australian Light Horse, formerly Col Comdg* 3*rd Regt. New South Wales Imperial Bushmen in South Africa* 1899–1902, *M P co Bucks* 1880–1885, *&c (Momalong, N S Wales), b* 17 *Dec* 1852 , *m Ap* 1891, *Edith, da of John Horsfall of Widgiewa, N S Wales, and has issue* 1e

1e Rupert Victor John Carington, *b* 1891   [Nos 27050 to 27080

# of The Blood Royal

4*d* Hon Augusta Clementina Carrington (11 *Hobart Place, S W , Dunalley Lodge, Halliford on-Thames*), m 7 July 1861, Archibald Campbell (Campbell), 1st Baron Blythswood [U K], *d s p* 8 July 1908

5*d* Hon Eva Elizabeth Carrington, m 5 July 1869, Charles Augustus (Stanhope), 8th Earl of Harrington [G B] [descended from George (Plantagenet) Duke of Clarence, K G (see Clarence Volume, p 348)] (*Elvaston Castle, near Derby, Harrington House, Craig's Court, Charing Cross, W C &c*), *s p*

2*b* Hon *Lindsey Merrik Peter Burrell*, b 20 June 1786, d 1 *Jan* 1848, m 13 *July* 1807, Frances, da of James Daniell, d 25 *Aug* 1846, *and had issue* 1*c to* 5*c*

1*c Peter Robert* (Burrell), *4th Baron Gwydyr and 5th Baronet* [G B], *&c,* b 27 *Ap* 1810, d 3 *Ap* 1909, m 1st, 10 *Dec* 1840, *Sophia, da and h of Frederick William Campbell of Barbreck,* d 14 *Mar* 1843, 2ndly, 8 *May* 1856, *Georgina, da of George Peter Holford of Westonbirt, co Glouc,* d 20 *Nov* 1892, *and had issue* 1*d to* 2*d*

1*d* Willoughby Merrik Campbell (Burrell), 5th Baron Gwydyr and 6th Baronet [G B], F R G S , J P , D L , Hon Col 4th Batt Suffolk Regt, *formerly* Capt Rifle Brig (*Stoke Park, Ipswich* 60 *Pont Street, S W , Carlton*), b 26 Oct 1841 , m 1st, 4 Sept 1873, Mary, da and h of Sir John Banks, K C B , M D , Physician-in-Ordinary to Queen Victoria, d 26 June 1898, 2ndly, 4 June 1901, Anne, da of John Ord of Overwhitton, co Roxburgh, and has issue 1*e*

1*e* Hon Catharine Mary Sermonda Burrell, m 16 July 1902, John Henniker Heaton (94 *Cromwell Road, S W*), and has issue 1*f* to 3*f*

1*f* John Victor Peregrine Henniker Heaton, b 10 Feb 1903

2*f* Peter Joseph Henniker Heaton, b 9 May 1907

3*f* Mary Araluen Henniker Heaton

2*d* [2] Hon Cicely Burrell

2*c Georgiana Charlotte Burrell*, b 1811, d 21 *Sept* 1843, m *as 1st wife*, 6 *Dec* 1838, *James Hamilton Lloyd Anstruther of Hintlesham Hall, co Suffolk, J P , D L* [*Baronet of Balcaskie Coll*], d 23 *Dec* 1882, *and had issue* 1*d*

1*d* Robert Hamilton Lloyd-Anstruther of Hintlesham, J P , D L , Major and Hon Lieut -Col *late* Rifle Brig , *formerly* M P for S E Suffolk 1886-1892 (*Hintlesham Hall, Ipswich*, 37 *Eccleston Square, S W*), b 21 Ap 1841, m 5 July 1871, Gertrude Louisa Georgina [descended from King Henry VII (see Tudor Roll, p 337)], da of Francis Horatio FitzRoy of Frogmore, co Hants [D of Grafton Coll], and has issue 1*e*

1*e* FitzRoy Hamilton Lloyd-Anstruther, Lieut Army Motor Reserve (12 *Chapel Street, Belgrave Square, S W*), b 5 July 1872, m 11 Oct 1898, the Hon Rachel [descended from King Henry VII (see Tudor Roll, p 216)], da of Augustus Cholmondeley (Gough Calthorpe), 6th Baron Calthorpe [G B], and has issue 1*f*

1*f* Richard Hamilton Lloyd-Anstruther, b 28 May 1908

3*c Susan Anne Burrell*, b 1816, d 16 *Aug* 1850, m 29 *July* 1839, *William Crosbie, afterwards* (R L 11 *Nov* 1880) *Talbot-Crosbie of Ardfert Abbey, co Kerry*, d 4 *Sept* 1899, *and had issue*

See the Exeter Volume, p 395, Nos 33269-33305

4*c* Hon *Marcia Sarah Elizabeth Burrell, had R H as da of a Baron* 17 *Dec* 1870, b 1821, d 22 *Oct* 1889, m 1st, 24 *Ap* 1851, *the Rev Charles Cameron,* d 1 *Dec* 1861 2ndly, 14 *Ap* 1868, *Walter Whittington, and had issue* 1*d to* 5*d*

1*d* Charles Hamilton Hone Cameron, L R C P,, M R C S , D P H (*Gildredge House,* 21 *The Goffs, Eastbourne*), b 30 Sept 1852, m 30 Ap 1878, Mary Louise Savile, da of Robert Walter Mexborough Shepherd, and has issue 1*e to* 4*e*

1*e* Charles Peter Gwydyr Cameron, Lieut R G A , b 18 Jan 1885

2*e* Ewen Paul Burrell Cameron, b 27 Sept 1897

3*e* Stella Willoughby Savile Cameron, m 1 Oct 1903, Clement Cobbold, Bar at Law (*Hyntle Place, Hintlesham, Suffolk, Belstead Lodge, Ipswich*), and has issue 1*f* to 2*f*   [Nos 27081 to 27130

The Plantagenet Roll

1f Cameron Fromanteel Cobbold, b 14 Sept 1901

2f Marcia Ruth Jean Cameron Cobbold

2d Marcia Frances Lyttleton Cameron, m 18 Ap 1888, the Rev Henry Kilburn Law, and has issue 1c to 4c

    1c Henry Merrik Burrell Law, b 11 Dec 1890

    2c Charles Lindsey Gwydyr Law, b 3 Aug 1893

    3c Marcia Georgina Cameron Law

    4c Margaret Frances Willoughby Law

3d Emma Georgina Cameron, m 22 Dec 1885, the Rev Thomas Kirkpatrick, d 30 May 1888, and has issue 1c

    1c Charles Edward Cameron Kirkpatrick, b 2 Dec 1886

4d Clare Charlotte Cameron, m 17 July 1883, the Rev William John Margetts, Vicar of Baildon (*Baildon Vicarage, near Shipley, Yorks*), and has issue 1c to 6c

    1c John Theodore Cameron Margetts, b 16 Feb 1892

    2c Grace Cameron Margetts

    3c Winifred Willoughby Margetts, m Jan 1910, Lucy Francis Taverner (*Kobe, Japan*)

    4c Dorothy Lucy Clare Margetts

    5c Marcia Georgina Lyttleton Margetts

    6c Mary Cicely Burrell Margetts

5d Lucy Amelia Cameron, m 24 July 1884, Edward Hill Dobson, and has issue 1c

    1c Stephanie Cicely Clare Dobson

5c Hon Charlotte Anne Burrell, had R W as da. of a Baron 17 Dec 1870, b 1822, d 8 Dec 1907, m 9 Oct 1851, Charles Wilmot Smith of Ballynanty House, co Liverpool, J P and had issue 1d to 5d

1d John Wilmot Crosbie Smith of Ballynanty (*Ballynanty House, Bruff, co Limerick, Killman Abbey, co Clare*), b 9 Feb 1853, m 1 Oct 1871, Jane Grant, da. of Andrew Sherlock Lawson of Aldborough, co York, and has issue 1e to 6e

    1e Charles Wilmot Smith, b 4 Sept 1880

    2e Andrew Wilmot Smith, Lieut. R N, b 21 May 1885

    3e Charlotte Isabella Smith

    4e [da] Smith

    5e [da] Smith

    6e [da] Smith

2d Willoughby Lloyd Smith, b 24 July 1859

3d George Charles Bertie Smith, b 4 Mar 1861

4d Emma Georgina Smith

5d Charlotte Mary Smith

3a Lady Georgiana Charlotte Bertie, b 7 Aug 1764, d 23 June 1838, m 25 Ap 1791, George James (Cholmondeley), 1st Marquis [U K], 4th Earl [E], and 6th Viscount [I] Cholmondeley, K G, d 10 Ap 1827 and had issue

See the Clarence Volume, pp 127-128, Nos 1503-1514 [Nos 27131 to 27201

86 Descendants of Lady MARY BERTIE (Table X.), d 23 May 1774, m 21 Feb. 1747, SAMUEL GREATHEED of Guy's Cliffe, co Warwick, and had (with possibly other) issue 1a.

1a Bertie Greatheed, afterwards (R L 20 May 1819) Bertie Greatheed of Guy's Cliffe, d (-), m (—), and had (with possibly other) issue 1b

    1b (--) Bertie-Greatheed of Guy's Cliffe, d (--), m (—), and had issue 1c

    1c Anne Caroline Bertie-Greatheed of Guy's Cliffe, b c 1805, d 8 June 1882, m 20 Mar 1822, the Hon Charles Percy, afterwards (R L 10 Ap 1826) Greatheed-Percy, d 11 Oct 1870, leaving issue a da who d unm 15 Feb 1891

# of The Blood Royal

87 Descendants of Lady JANE BERTIE (Table X), d 1793, m 1743, Gen EDWARD MATHEW, Equerry to King George III, Gen Comdg the Guards Brigade in North America, and *afterwards* Governor of Grenada 1784–1789, b c 1727, d 25 Dec 1805, and had issue 1a to 5a

    1a *Brownlow Mathew, afterwards* (R L 5 May 1819) *Bertie-Mathew*, b (–), d 29 Ap (?Sep) 1826, m 2 Ip 1807, *Harriet Ann* da of North Naylor, H E I C S [by his wife (—), sister of Sir Albemarle Bertie, Bt], d (–), and had issue (with 2 other sons and 3 das known to have d s p) 1b to 3b

      1b. *Edward Bertie-Mathew*

      2b *Jane Bertie-Mathew*, d (–), m *Alphonso (Ferrero) Marquis of La Marmora (Marchese della Marmora)* [Italy], K A I K C B , G C L H , Field Marshal, Premier and Minister of Foreign Affairs to King Victor Emmanuel II 1861–1866, &c , b 1804, d s p at Florence 5 Jan 1878

      3b *Elizabeth Bertie-Mathew*

    2a *Jane Mathew*, twin with 3a, d 5 June 1830, m 2 Sept 1766, *Thomas Maitland*, d 2 Dec 1797, and had issue (with 3 sons and a da , d s p) 1b to 4b

      1b *Sir Peregrine Maitland*, G C B General, commanded Guards at Waterloo, afterwards Governor and Com-in-Chief at the Cape of Good Hope 1843–1846, &c , b 6 July 1777, d 30 May 1854 m 1st, 8 June 1803, *the Hon Louisa, da of Sir Edward Crofton, 2nd Bt* [I], 2ndly, 9 Oct 1815, *Lady Sarah* [descended from King Henry VII (see Tudor Volume, p 408)], da of Charles (Lennox), 4th Duke of Richmond [E], Lennox [S], and Aubigny [F], K G , d 8 Sept 1873, and had issue (with a son by 1st wife, who d unm) 1c to 7c

        1c *Charles Lennox Brownlow Maitland*, C B , K L H , Col 1st Batt Duke of Edinburgh's Regt , Lieut-Gov Chelsea Hospital 1869–1870, b 27 Sept 1823 d (? unm)

        2c *Horatio Arthur Lennox Maitland*, Admiral R N , b 13 Mar 1834

        3c *Sarah Maitland*, d (–), m 14 Jan 1837, *Gen Thomas Bowes Forster* [son of Lieut-Col John Randall Forster], d 21 Mar 1870, and had issue (with a son d unm) 1d to 6d

          1d *Bowes-Lennox Forster*, Lieut-Gen , *formerly Col Comdg R A*, b 9 Oct 1837, m 18 Jan 1868, *Jessie Kate, da of William Mackenzie C B, C S I, Inspector-Gen of Hospitals, India, and Hon Physician to Queen Victoria*, and has issue 1e to 5e

            1e *William Anson Maitland Prendergast Forster*, b 21 Ap 1869

            2e *Stuart Boscawen Erode Desbrisay Forster*, b 5 Oct 1870

            3e *George Norman Bowes Forster*, b 26 Oct 1872

            4e *Lenox Weston Glendower Forster*, b 28 Sept 1874

            5e *Isabella Gertrude Forster*

          2d *Peregrine Henry Forster*, b 2 July 1848

          3d *Susan Charlotte Forster*, m 28 Ap 1874, *the Rev Charles Garbett*, M A (Oxon), Vicar of Tongham, d (–), and had issue 1e to 5e

            1e *Rev Cyril Forster Garbett*, M A (Oxon), Vicar of Portsea (*The Vicarage, Portsea*), b 6 Feb 1875

            2e *Basil Maitland Garbett*, b 13 July 1876

            3e *Clement Stewart Garbett*, b 21 July 1877

            4e *Leonard Gilhldin Garbett*, b 1 Mar 1879

            5e *Elsie Mary Katherine Garbett*

          4d *Sarah Caroline Forster*, m 20 Oct 1869, *Edward Howorth Greenly, Lord of the Manor of Titley*, M A (Oxon), J P , D L , High Sheriff co Hereford 1881, &c (*Titley Court, R S O , Hereford*), and has issue 1e to 5e

[Nos 27202 to 27216

177

The Plantagenet Roll

1e Walter Howorth Greenly, J P , D S O , Major 12th Lancers and Cavalry Staff Officer to the Inspector-Gen of the Forces (*Cavalry Club*), b 2 Jan 1875

2e John Henry Maitland Greenly, b 25 July 1885

3e Alice Maud Greenly, m 9 Jan 1907, Robert Napier Greathed, Capt R A , and has issue 1f

1f Elisabeth Sarah Greathed

4e Ethel Mary Greenly

5e Lucy Margaret Greenly, m 2 July 1902, the Hon Antony Schomberg Byng [3rd son of the 5th Earl of Strafford and a descendant of King Henry VII (see Tudor Roll, p 169)] (6 *Mansion Place, Queen s Gate, S W*), and has issue 1f to 2f

1f William Humphrey Schomberg Byng, b 31 May 1906

2f Gillian Sarah Byng

5d Emily Borlinga Forster

6d Louisa Margaret Jane Forster

1c *Caroline Charlotte Maitland, d 8 Jan 1897 . m 17 July 1837, John George Turnbull, Accountant Gen at Madras, d 2 Jan 1872, and had issue (with others d s p)* 1d *to* 3d

1d Charles Frederic Alexander Turnbull of Whiteways, co Surrey, Col (ret), *formerly Comdg Duke of Cornwall's L I , Extra A D C to the Com in-Chief at Aldershot 1881-1883,* b 26 June 1847 m 7 Jan 1890, Evelyn Selina, da of John Lambart Broughton of Tunstall, co Salop, and has issue 1e to 2e

1e Dudley Ralph Turnbull, b 15 Oct 1891

2e Sylvia Nora Evelyn Turnbull

2d *Caroline Maria Turnbull, d 1878, m 5 June 1860, Alexander William Adair of Heatherton Park, co Som , and Colhays, co Devon, J P , Lieut -Col Comdg 2nd Somerset L I , previously 52nd Foot,* b 28 Jan 1829 , d 1864, *and had issue (with a son and 2 das d young)* 1e *to* 2e

1e Gerald Adair, b 7 Nov 1865 , d (-)

2e Evelyn Adair, m 29 Ap 1883, Joseph E Wood [son of Joseph Carter Wood of Felcourt, co Surrey]

3d Georgina Sarah Turnbull (*Whiteways, Farnham, co Surrey*), m 5 Jan 1864, Allan Shafto Adair, J P , Major 13th L I , b 20 Dec 1836 d 26 Dec 1902, and has issue 1e

1e Desmond Adair, Lieut Gordon Highlanders, b 20 Dec 1865

5c *Georgina Louisa Maitland, d 5 Jan 1852 m as 1st wife, 2 Jan 1841, the Rev Sir Thomas Eardley Wilmot Blomefield, 3rd Bt [U K], d 21 Nov 1878 , and had issue*
See the Tudor Roll, pp 168-169, Nos 32924-32941

6c *Emily Sophia Maitland, d 16 Dec 1891, m 13 Jan 1846, Admiral Lord Frederic Herbert Kerr, R N [M of Lothian Coll], d 15 Jan 1896, and had issue*
See the Tudor Roll, p 469, Nos 32912-32963

7c *Eliza Mary Maitland, b 1832, d (-), m 14 July 1857 Major-Gen John Deshorough, R A , C B (Gross House, Northam, Bideford), and had issue*
See the Tudor Roll, p 469 Nos 32964-32973

2b *Rev Charles David Maitland, Incumbent of St James', Brighton formerly Capt R A ,* b 3 Sept 1785 , d 12 Oct 1865, m 15 Ap 1814, Elizabeth Adye, da *of John Miller, d 13 Aug 1874, and had issue* 1c *to* 5c

1c *Rev Charles Maitland, M A , M D , Author of " The Church in the Catacombs,"* b 6 Jan 1815 d 31 July 1866, m 5 Nov 1842, Julia Charlotte, *widow of James Thomas, da of Henry Barrett, d 29 Jan 1864, and had issue* 1d

1d *Julia Caroline Maitland, d 27 Feb 1890, m 18 July 1861, the Rev David Wauchope, M A (Oxon), formerly Rector of Church Lawford [Bt of Edmonstone (S 1667) Coll] (Bamster Gate, Southampton), and had issue* 1e *to* 3e

[Nos 27217 to 27282

178

# of The Blood Royal

1e Rev David Maitland Don Wauchope, M A (Oxon), *late Rector of Elstead* (*Elstead, Godalming*), b 4 Mar 1864, m 17 July 1888, Ethel Sarah, da of Lewis Maxey Stewart, and has issue 1f to 2f

    1f Andrew Maxey Wauchope, b 13 Dec 1890

    2f Oswald Stewart Wauchope, b 2 July 1897

    2e Anne Julia Wauchope

    3e Caroline Wauchope

2c Rev *Brownlow Maitland*, M A (*Camb*), *Minister of Brunswick Chapel Marylebone* 1819-1870, *and Second Chaplain to his uncle, Gen Sir Peregrine, Maitland, while Gov of the Cape of Good Hope*, b 12 June 1816 d 27 Oct 1902 m 1st, 19 July 1848, Josephine, da of *Alexander Erskine "of Dun,"* d 8 Dec 1870, 2ndly, 4 June 1872, Emily (41 *Montagu Square, W*), da of *Samuel Warren, Q C, D C L, F R S, M P, a Master in Lunacy and Author of "Ten Thousand a Year"*, and had issue (*with 3 sons and 2 das by 1st wife, who d s p*) 1d

    1d 2 Mary Eleanor Maitland

3c *Edward Maitland, Novelist and Essayist*, b 27 Oct 1824, d (-), m 3 May 1855, *Esther Charlotte, da of William Bradley of Sydney, N S W*, and had issue 1d

    1d Charles Bradley Maitland, Army Surgeon, Indian M S, b 5 Jan 1856

4c John Thomas Maitland, R N, b 4 Aug 1826, d 11 Mar 1855, m 1848, *Mary Jane, da of the Rev Francis Pym, Rector of Willian, co Bed* [*who m 2ndly, in Canada, c 1856 7, (—) Wainwright*], and had issue 1d

    1d Lionel Maitland, d (? s p) Sept 1873

5c Eardley Maitland, C B, Col R A, Superintendent Royal Gun Factory, Woolwich, served in Indian Mutiny, Relief of Lucknow, &c, has medal with 3 clasps (6 *Westbourne Mansions, Westbourne Terrace, W*), b 10 Nov 1833, m 1st, 29 May 1855, Elizabeth Odell, da of Thomas Baillie, d 6 Aug 1877, 2ndly, 15 Mar 1883, Caroline Helen, da of Thomas Metcalfe of Highgate, Hastings, and has issue (with 3 sons and a da who d s p) 1d to 4d

    1d 2 Eardly Thomas Maitland, b 1888

    2d 1 Ella Laura Katherine Maitland, m and has issue (3 das)

    3d 1 Emily Maitland, m and has issue (a son and da, the latter of whom is m with issue)

    4d 2 Helena Victoria Augusta Maitland, Novelist

3b Jane Maitland, d 18 May 1816, m *Lieut -Col Richard Warren, Scots Fusiliers*, d 1819, *and had issue* (*with 5 sons and 3 das who d s p*) 1c to 2c

1c Mary Jane Warren, d 28 Aug 1875, m 1st, 15 July 1825, *the Rev Cecil Smith of Lydeard House, co Som*, d 12 May 1861, 2ndly, 1867/8, *the Rev John Clare Pigot of Thrumpton Lodge, Weston-super-Mare*, d 2 Dec 1880, and had issue 1d

1d Cecil Smith of Lydeard House, J P, Bar -at-Law I T, b 31 May 1826, d 23 Sept 1891, m 28 Sept 1858, Amelia (see p 180), da of Sir Peter Stafford Carey, d 18 Dec 1880, and had issue 1e to 7e

1e Cecil Smith of the Croft, Botley, co Hants (6 *Ladbroke Square, W*), b 5 Jan 1860, m 7 Sept 1889, Elizabeth Emily, da of Philip John Hammond and has issue 1f to 2f

    1f Robert Philip Cecil Smith, b 16 Ap 1899

    2f Mary Cecil Smith

    2e Janet Charlotte Smith

    3e Caroline Ellen Smith

    4e Amy Smith

    5e Grace Smith.

    6e Mabel Smith

    7e Susan Constance Smith   [Nos 27283 to 27303

The Plantagenet Roll

2c *Emily Aubrey Warren*, d 2 Feb 1881, m 16 Feb 1835, *Sir Peter Stafford Carey, M A (Oxon), Bar-at-Law M T, Prof of English Law at Univ Coll, London*, 1838-1845, *Bailiff of Guernsey* 1845-1883, &c, d (-), and had issue (with a son and da who d s p) 1d to 6d

1d Frances Carey, m 7 Aug 1861, Col Ernest le Pelley, Seigneur of Sark, formerly 5th Foot, and has issue 1e to 5e

1e Ernest Brownlow le Pelley, b 1 June 1862

2e Edward Carey le Pelley, b 2 Nov 1870

3e Caroline Mary le Pelley

4e Fanny Ernestine le Pelley

5e Amelia Maitland le Pelley

2d *Amelia Carey*, d 18 Dec 1880, m 28 Sept 1858, *Cecil Smith of Lydeard House*, co Som, d 23 Sept 1891, and had issue

See p 179, Nos 27295-27303

3d *Caroline Carey*, d 6 Feb 1883, m 5 Dec 1860, Lieut -Col Julius Alphonso Carey, formerly Belgian Consul at Alicante, A D C to Lieut -Gov of Guernsey, and had issue (with a son who d young) 1e to 4e

1e Harold Stafford Carey, b 28 Sept 1861

2e Wilfred Sausmarez Carey, b 22 May 1863

3e Mervyn Dobree Carey

4e Elaine Biddulph Carey

1d *Beatrice Carey*, m 26 Dec 1867, Thomas Brooksbank, Bar-at-Law I T, and has issue 1e

1e Thomas Brooksbank, b 12 July 1878

5d *Emily Jane Carey*

6d *Sophia Stafford Carey*, d 19 Aug 1871, m 19 Aug 1863, *the Rev William John Mellish, M A (Camb), Rector of Winestead, Hull*, d (-), and had issue (with a son d young) 1e to 4e

1e John Stafford Mellish, b 5 Aug 1864

2e Peter Bertie Mellish, b 25 Nov 1866

3e Elizabeth Aubrey Mellish

4e Dorothea Katherine Mellish

4b *Caroline Maitland*, d 25 Nov 1830, m *Col William Roberts, R A*, d 9 July 1851, and had issue (with 4 sons d unm) 1c to 2c

1c *Henry Charles Roberts, Major Bengal Army*, b 29 Nov 1817 d 24 Feb 1880, m 12 May 1864, *Jane, da of John Beckley of Paignton*, co Devon, and had issue 1d to 3d

1d Henry Maitland Roberts, b 14 June 1868, unm

2d Laura Maria Roberts, m 8 Ap 1902, the Rev Lonsdale Ragg, Preb of Buckden, in Lincoln Cathedral, Author of "Dante and his Italy," "The Mohammedan Gospel of Barnabas," "The Church of the Apostles," and other works (Westminster Club, Whitehall Court, S W, Tickencote Rectory, Stamford), and has issue 1e

1e Beatrice Laura Victoria Ragg, b 6 Mar 1907

3d Edith Douglas Roberts (8 Ferndale, Tunbridge Wells)

2c *Bertie Mathew Roberts, Major 26th Cameronians, D L* co Lanc, b 11 Nov 1822, d 27 Oct 1894, m 1st 1 July 1852, *Frances Jane Lennard, da of Gen Sir William Cator K C B*, d 21 Sept 1867, 2ndly, 1872, *Laura, widow of Alexander Fortcall of Newton, N B, and da of Gen Henry Tufnell Roberts, Bengal Cav*, and had issue 1d to 2d

1d Rev Harry Bertie Roberts, M A (Oxon), Rector of West Wickham (West Wickham Rectory, Kent), b 28 Mar 1855, unm

2d William Bertie Roberts, Lieut Royal Welsh Fusiliers, b 29 June 1856, d 5 Dec 1899, m 12 Oct 1882, *Camille, da of John Corbett of Impney, Droit-*
[Nos 27304 to 27334.

wich, and Ynys-y-Maengwyn, co Merioneth, and had issue (with a da, Sylvia, who d young, 14 Jan 1907) 1e to 2e

1e Rev Roger Harry Bertie-Roberts, B A (Oxon), Assist Curate at Lillington, near Leamington, b 5 Oct 1883, unm

2e Cicely Bertie Roberts, unm

3a Mary Mathew,[1] d (-), m Lieut-Col Warren, Coldstream Guards

4a Anne Mathew, d (-), m as 1st wife, James Austen of Alton [elder brother of Adm Sir Francis William Austen, G C B, R N], d (-), and had issue 1b

1b Jane Anna Elizabeth Austen, d (-), m 1814, the Rev Benjamin Langlois Lefroy, Rector of Ashe [descended from King Henry VII, &c], d 1829, and had issue

See the Tudor Roll, pp 401-402, Nos 29804-29823

5a Penelope Susannah Mathew, b c 1764, d 27 Aug 1828, aged 64, m 1st, 1787, David Dewar of St Christopher's, W I, and of Enham House and Doles, co Hants, d 20 Nov 1794, 2ndly, 23 Oct 1799, Capt Charles Cumberland, Royal Horse Guards Blue [3rd son of Richard Cumberland "the dramatist"], b 21 May 1764, d 12 May 1835, and had issue 1b to 3b

1b David Albemarl. Bertie Dewar of Doles, co Hants, and Great Cumberland Place, London, d 25 Nov 1859, m 19 May 1821, Anne Louise, da of Col Richard Magenis [by his wife, Lady Elizabeth Anne, nee Cole, a descendant of the Lady Anne Plantagenet], d Nov 1855, and had issue

See the Exeter Volume, p 139, Nos 1975-1980

2b Richard Edward Cumberland of Middlecave House, co York, Comm R N, b 23 Sept 1800, d 2 Ap 1882, m 1st, 19 Jan 1828, Penelope Mary, da of (—) Bankhead, M D, d 15 Ap 1836, and had issue (with 2 other sons and a da who d unm) 1c to 4c

1c Charles Edward Cumberland, C B, J P, Major-Gen (ret) R E (Manor House, Maidstone), b 27 Jan 1830, m 1st, 12 June 1883, Elizabeth Anne, widow of the Right Rev Addington Venables Lord Bishop of Nassau, da of the Rev William Moss King, d 1891, 2ndly, 18 Ap 1907, Adelaide Annabella Mary McLeod [descended from George, Duke of Clarence, K G, brother of Kings Edward IV and Richard III (see Essex Volume, Clarence Supplement, p 561)], da of Philip Henry Crampton of Fassaro, co Wicklow

2c William Bentinck Cumberland, Hon Major-Gen and Col (ret) R A (21 Bramham Gardens South Kensington), b 21 July 1833, m 5 Sept 1865, Louisa Anna, da of Brig-Gen Manson, C B, R A, and has issue 1d to 3d

1d Louis Bertie Cumberland, Capt (ret) King's Royal Rifle Corps, b 1 July 1870

2d Adela Mary Cumberland

3d Norah Harriet Cumberland

3c Penelope Mary Elizabeth Cumberland, unm

4c Emma Anne Cumberland

3b Charles Brownlow Cumberland, Major-Gen and Col Comdg 96th Regt 1842-1856, b 21 Nov 1801, d 27 Nov 1882, m 2 Aug 1825, Russell, nat da of the Hon Archibald Gloucester of Mount Joshua, Antigua, d 28 June 1870, and had issue 1c to 7c

1c Richard Felix Wilson Cumberland, Capt 96th Regt, b 21 May 1826, d 28 June 1871, m 1855, Jessie, da of (—) Lavdale, and had issue (with a son who d young) 1d to 9d

1d Charles Thomas Cumberland, b 16 Dec 1850

2d George Landale Cumberland, b 4 June 1853

3d Richard Landale Cumberland, b 21 June 1855   [Nos 27335 to 27372

[1] Burke's "Landed Gentry," 1871, p 903   No such da is, however, mentioned in the pedigree in Foster's "Noble and Gentle Families"

The Plantagenet Roll

4d Bentinck Landale Cumberland, b 3 Jan 1864
5d Mary Gertrude Gordon Landale Cumberland
6d Jessie Landale Cumberland
7d Maud Landale Cumberland
8d Florence Landale Cumberland
9d Rose Landale Cumberland

2c *Charles Burrell Cumberland, General Surveyor, India*, b 21 Feb 1828, d at Bareilly, India, 17 Dec 1875, m 9 Oct 1865, Marianne, da of David Cowan of New Scone, co Perth, d 23 May 1869, and had issue 1d

1d Charles Russell Cumberland, b 12 Aug 1866

3c *George Bentinck Cumberland, Capt 96th Foot*, b 16 Ap 1829, d (-), m 1st, Georgina Anne, da of James Barlow, 2ndly, Mary, da of Walter Stocker, and had issue 1d to 6d

1d[1] James Bentinck Cumberland, b 1 June 1863
2d[1] Archibald Roland Cumberland, b 3 June 1867
3d[2] Walter Bertie Cumberland, b 15 Jan 1881
4d[1] Dora Russel Cumberland, b 7 July 1866
5d Adela Georgina Cumberland, b 22 Sept 1869
6d Marie Cumberland

4c Peregrine Bertie Cumberland of Melbourne, b 26 Jan 1834, m Lillie, da of (—), and has issue 1d to 5d

1d Charles Bertie Cumberland, b 1871 (? 19 *Darling Street, S Yarra, Melbourne*)
2d Reginald Gloucester Cumberland
3d Cecil George Cumberland
4d Vivian Bentinck Cumberland
5d Adela Muriel Cumberland

5c *Bentinck Laporte Cumberland, Lieut 82nd Foot*, b 3 Dec 1839, d (? unm)
6c *Georgiana Penelope Cumberland*, d 7 July 1877, m 29 Ap 1856, Capt William Archibald Eyton of Barford House, co Warwick, 96th Regt [3rd son of Thomas Eyton of Eyton, co Salop], d 11 Sept 1869, and had issue (with a da who d unm) 1d to 7d

1d William Charles Campbell Eyton (*Yeator House, Baschurch, near Shrewsbury*) b 2 Nov 1859
2d Archibald Cumberland Eyton, b 29 Aug 1866
3d Violet Elizabeth Eyton, m 9 Aug 1878, the Rev Francis Robert Dayrell, B A (Camb) [descended from King Henry VII, &c (see Tudor Roll, p 324, and Essex Volume Supplement, p 470)] (*Tyn Llan, Rhydyfelin, Aberystwyth, Lew Grange, Shrewsbury*), and has issue 1e to 2e

1e Francis William Dayrell, b 8 June 1882
2e Violet Elizabeth Mildred Dayrell, b 24 Dec 1879

4d Rose Adela Russel Eyton, b 10 June 1860
5d Lilias Agnes Charlotte Eyton, b 30 July 1861
6d Isabel Georgina Eyton, b 25 Aug 1862
7d Evelyn Margaret Eyton, b 6 Sept 1863

7c Adela Russell Cumberland

4b *George Burrell Cumberland, Lieut Col, formerly Major 42nd Highlanders*, b 10 Mar 1804, d 22 May 1865, m 9 Sept 1845, Margaret Delicia, da of Gen Sir John Macleod, K C B, C B, Col 77th Regt, d Dec 1902, and had issue (with a son who d young) 1c to 5c

1c George Bentinck Macleod Cumberland, *Lieut -Col, formerly Major the Black Watch*, served in Ashantee (1874) and Egyptian (1882) Campaigns (107 *Eaton Square, S W*), b 22 June 1846
2c Charles Sperling Cumberland, *Major formerly East Lancashire Regt* (10 *Duke Street, St James', S W*), b 5 Dec 1847   [Nos. 27373 to 27403

182

# of The Blood Royal

3c Elizabeth Penelope Cumberland, m 24 Nov 1875, Alexander Dick Cunyngham [2nd son of Sir William Hanmer Dick Cunyngham, 6th and 8th Bt [S]] (15 *Eccleston Square, S W , St James', Ranelagh, New, Edinburgh*), and his issue 1d to 4d

1d George Alistair Dick Cunyngham, Capt 2nd Batt Rifle Brig, served in South Africa 1900-1902, 2 medals and 5 clasps, b 11 May 1881, m Aug 1908, Sybil Vera Elise, da of Edward Stisted Mostyn Price of Gunley Hall, Clunbury, co Salop

2d Katharine Mary Delicia Dick-Cunyngham

3d Evelyn Dick-Cunyngham, m July 1907, Reginald Everitt Lambert [son of Edward Tiley Lambert of Tellham Court, Battle, co Sussex], and his issue 1e

1e Audrey Elizabeth Lambert

4d Mary Isabel Annie Dick-Cunyngham

4c Maud Fraser Cumberland

5c Amabel Mary Cumberland

5b *Georgina Cumberland, d (-). m at Broadwater, Sussex, 12 Sept 1831, the Rev Henry William Stuart, Chaplain H E I C S , d 5 Oct 1856 , and had issue* 1c to 6c

1c *Rev Henry Cumberland Stuart, M A (Camb), Incumbent of Wragby, b 31 Jan 1833, d (s p), m 7 Aug 1858, Eleanor Caroline, da of Lieut -Col Charles Bevan, d s p 18 May 1880*

2c Charles Bentinck George Stuart, b 9 July 1843

3c Arthur Edward Stuart, b 21 Dec 1850 , m June 1880, Mary Halton, da of William Jephson of Sutton, co Notts

4c Georgina Adela Anna Stuart

5c Mary Emily Eliza Stuart

6c Alice Rosalind Bertie Stuart   [Nos 27404 to 27416.

88 Descendants of Lord VERE BERTIE, M P (Table X), d 13 Sept 1768 , m 1736, ANNE, da of (—) CASEY of Braunston, near Lincoln, d (-), and had issue.

See the Clarence Volume, Table LXXIV , and pp 590-599, Nos 25396-26281
[Nos 27417 to 28302

89. Descendants of Lord MONTAGU BERTIE, Capt R N (Table X), d 12 Aug 1753 , m ELIZABETH, da of William PIERS, M P for Wells, d (-), and had issue

See the Clarence Volume, Table LXXIV , and pp 599-603, Nos 26282-26530
[Nos 28303 to 28551

90 Descendants, if any, of Lady LOUISA BERTIE (Table X), d (-), m 1736, THOMAS BLUDWORTH, Groom of the Bedchamber to the Prince of Orange

91 Descendants, if any, of the Hon ANNE WHARTON (Table X), d (-), m WILLIAM CARR, and of the Hon MARGARET WHARTON, d (-), m 1st, Major DUNCH of Pusey, d 1679 (by whom she had issue now extinct), 2ndly, c 1690, Sir THOMAS SEYLIARD or SULYARD, 2nd Bt [E], d s p 1692, 3rdly, WILLIAM ROSS

183

The Plantagenet Roll

92 Descendants of JANE TYNTE, da , and in her issue (25 Aug 1785)
h of Sir John Tynte, 2nd Bt [E], M P (Table X), d 1741 ,
m as 1st wife, at Gray's Inn Chapel, 23 Ap 1737, Major
RUISHE HASSELL, R H G , and had issue 1a

1a *Jane Hassell of Halswell co Somerset, and Cefn-Mably, co Glamorgan,
da and h, d 1825, m 1765 Col John Johnston afterwards (R L 29 Oct 1785)
Kemeys-Tynte, 1st Foot Guards, Groom of the Bedchamber and Comptroller to the
Household to H R H George Prince of Wales, afterwards King George IV , d 1807 ,
and had issue 1b*

1b *Charles Kemeys Kemeys-Tynte of Halswell and Cefn-Mably M P , Col
II Somerset Yeo , was declared by a Committee for Privileges of the House of Lords,
in 1845, senior co h to the Barony of Wharton [I], b 29 May 1778, d 23 Nov
1860, m 1798 Ann, widow of Thomas Lewis of St Pierre, dq of the Rev Thomas
Lawson of Bossaleg, d Ap 1835, and had issue 1c to 3c*

1c *Charles John Kemeys-Tynte of Halswell and Cefn-Mably, and of Burleigh
Hall, co Leic , M P , Col Royal Glamorgan Light Infantry Militia, senior co-h to
the Baronies of Wharton and Grey de Wilton [E], b 9 Ap 1800 d 16 Sept 1882 ,
m 1st, 1821, Elizabeth, da and co-h of Thomas Swinnerton of Butterton Hall,
co Stafford [by Mary, da of Charles Milborne of The Priory, Abergavenny, and his
wif Lady Martha nee Harley], d 10 May 1838, 2ndly, 15 Ap 1841, Vincentia,
da of Wallop Brabazon of Rath House, co Louth, d 14 Oct 1894, and had issue
1d to 10d*

1d *Charles Kemeys Kemeys-Tynte of Halswell, &c , J P , D L , Capt 11th
Hussars and Grenadier Guards, and Col 1st Somerset Militia, senior co-h to the
Baronies of Wharton and Grey de Wilton [E], b 16 Mar 1822 , d 10 Jan 1891,
m 1st 1848, Mary, da of the Rev George Frome of Punchnoll, co Dorset, d 14 May
1864 2ndly, 1873, Hannah, widow of Thomas Lewis, da of (—) d 17 Feb 1875 ,
and had issue 1e to 3e*

1e *Halswell Milborne Kemeys-Tynte of Halswell &c , J P , D L , Capt 1st
Somerset Militia, senior co-h to the Baronies of Wharton and Grey de Wilton [E],
b 5 June 1852, d 18 Feb 1899 , m 1875 Rosabella Clare, da of Theobald Walsh
of Tyrrelston, co Kildare [rem 2ndly, 2 June 1900, Lieut Col Henry de Courcy
Rawlins of Stoke Courcy], and had issue 1f to 3f*

1f *Charles Theodore Halswell Kemeys-Tynte of Halswell and Cefn-Mably,
J P , late Lieut Royal Monmouthshire Engineers (Mil) (Halswell Park, Goathurst,
Bridgwater Cefn-Mably, Cardiff), b 18 Sept 1876 , m 10 Aug 1899, Dorothy
(see p 393), da of Major Gen Sir Arthur Edward Augustus Ellis, G C V O , &c ,
and has issue 1g to 2g*

1g *Charles John Halswell Kemeys Tynte, b 12 Jan 1908*

2g *Elizabeth Dorothy Kemeys Tynte*

2f *Eustace Kemeys-Tynte of Burleigh Hall (Burleigh Hall, Loughborough, co
Leicester), b 10 Ap 1878 , m 13 Aug 1902, Annie, da of John Emerson , and has
issue 1g to 2g*

1g *Nicholas Halswell Kemeys-Tynte, b 4 Aug 1903*

2g *Eleanor Vanessa Rosabella Kemeys-Tynte*

3f *Mary Arabella Swinnerton Kemeys-Tynte, m 21 Ap 1909, Guy Colin
Campbell, Lieut King's Royal Rifle Corps [son and h app of Lieut Col Sir Guy
Theophilus Campbell, 3rd Bt [U K]]*

2e 1 *Rachel Elizabeth Henrietta Kemeys-Tynte*

3e 2 *Grace Kemeys-Tynte*

2d *John Brabazon Kemeys-Tynte, late Lieut 5th Fusiliers, previously R N ,
Baltic (1854) Medal, b 24 June 1842*

3d *St David Morgan Kemeys-Tynte, late Lieut West Somerset Yeo Cav
(10 Royal Crescent, Bath), b 1 Mar 1846, m 21 Ap 1897, Alice, widow of Anthony
Hammond, J P , da of the Rev Thomas J Lee* [Nos 28552 to 28562

# of The Blood Royal

4d Arthur Marcus Philipps Kemeys-Tynte, *late Capt. Royal Glamorgan Mil.*, Zulu (1879) and Canada (1885) Medals (*Ottawa, Canada*), b 22 Mar 1850 m Dec 1889, Ruby, da of R Clark of Ottawa

5d Fortescue Tracy Freke Kemeys-Tynte (*Lake Mills Wisconsin. U S A*), b 31 Jan 1856, m 17 Aug 1899, Gertrude, da of J D Waterbury of Oztalin, Wisconsin

6d Edward Plantagenet Kemeys-Tynte, *late Capt. 3rd Welsh Regt.*, Zulu (1879) Medal and Clasp (*Highleigh, Teignmouth*), b 13 Sept 1858, m 21 Feb 1889, Beatrice Mary, da of Lansdowne Daubeny of Norton Malreward, and his issue 1e to 2c

    1e Mary Vincentia Blanche Edwardina Kemeys-Tynte
    2c Beatrice Margaret Gwladys Clare Kemeys-Tynte

7d Vincentia Margaret Anne Kemeys-Tynte
8d Mabel Louisa Frances Kemeys-Tynte
9d Maud Maria Kemeys-Tynte, m 23 July 1885, Amherst Henry Gage Morris of Netherby (*Nunburnholme Rectory York*)
10d Blanche Elizabeth Plantagenet Kemeys-Tynte m 22 Oct 1909, the Hon Edgar Dawdney, *formerly* Lieut -Gov of British Columbia

2c *Louisa Kemeys-Tynte*, d 31 Aug 1872, m 1834, *Simon Fraser Campbell*, d 28 Mar 1872

3c *Henrietta Anne Kemeys-Tynte*, d 24 Mar 1880 m 14 Sept 1853, *Thomas Arthur Kemmis of Croham Hurst, Croydon, M P, J P, Capt Grenadier Guards*, b 16 Mar 1806, d 25 Dec 1858, *and had issue 1d*

1d Arthur Henry Nicholas Kemmis, J P, D L, *lat. Capt. 1st Somerset Militia*, High Sheriff King's Co 1862 (*Croham Hurst, Croydon*), b 13 July 1834, m 11 July 1862, Emma Jane, da of E Collins   [Nos 28563 to 28572

---

93 Descendants of GEORGE LOCKHART of Carnwath (Table XI), b 1700, d. Oct. 1764, m 15 Mar. 1727, FERGUSIA, da and co-h of Sir George WISHART of Clifton Hall, co. Edinburgh, d (-), and had issue 1a to 3a.

1a *James (Lockhart afterwards Lockhart-Wishart).* 1st Count of Lockhart (*Graf von Lockhart*) [H R E] *of Carnwath and Lee, K M T, a General in the Imperial Service and a Lord of the Bedchamber to the Emperor*, d 6 Feb 1790, m 1st, *Matilda, da of* (-) *Lockhart of Castle Hill*, d (-). 2ndly, 18 June 1770, *Marianne, da and h of Adam Murray of Belredding*, d (-), *and had issue 1b to 3b*

1b *Charles (Lockhart Wishart),* 2nd Count of Lockhart (*Graf von Lockhart*), [H R E], d s p 4 Aug 1802

2b[1] *Countess Matilda Theresa Lockhart-Wishart*, d 1 Feb 1791, m as 1st *wife*, 1788, *Lieut-Gen Sir Charles Lockhart-Ross of Balnagowan, 7th Bt* [S], *M P*, d 8 Feb 1814, *and had issue 1c*

1c *Matilda Lockhart-Ross of Oldliston*, d 4 Sept 1819, m 6 Jan 1812, *Adm Sir Thomas John Cochrane, G C B* [E Dundonald Coll], d 19 Oct 1872, *and had issue*

See the Exeter Volume, pp 625-626, Nos 53022-53062

3b[2] *Countess Matilda Lockhart Wishart*, d 11 Sept 1850, m 19 Feb 1791, *Anthony Aufrère of Hoveton and Foulsham Old Hall, co Norfolk, and had issue*

2a *Charles Lockhart, afterwards Macdonald of Largie, co Argyll*, b 28 Feb 1740, d (-), m 16 Aug 1762, *Elizabeth, da and h of John Macdonald of Largie, and had issue 1b to 6b*

1b *Sir Alexander Macdonald, afterwards* (1802) *Lockhart of Lee and Carnwath,* 1st Bt [U K], *so cr 24 May 1806, suc as head of the family on the death*   [Nos 28573 to 28613

185

The Plantagenet Roll

of his cousin, the 2nd Count of Lockhart, 1802, d 22 June 1816, m Jane, da of Daniel M'Neill of Gallichoilly co Argyll (who m 2ndly, John McNeill, Provost of Inveraray and) d 4 Sept 1857, and had issue 1c to 2c

1c Sir Charles Macdonald Lockhart of Lee and Carnwath, 2nd Bt [U K], b 8 Feb 1799, d 8 Dec 1832, m 29 Feb 1819, Emilia Olivia [descended from the Lady Ann sister of King Edward IV (see Exeter Volume p 469)], da of Lieut-Gen Sir Charles Lockhart-Ross, 7th Bt [S], d 24 June 1866, and had issue 1d

1d Mary Macdonald Lockhart, d 10 Dec 1851, m 15 Sept 1837, the Hon Augustus Henry Reynolds-Moreton, afterwards Moreton-Macdonald of Largie, M P [E Ducie Coll, and a descendant of King Henry VII, &c], d 11 Feb 1862, and had issue

See the Tudor Roll, pp 268-269, Nos 24520-24544

2c Sir Norman Macdonald Lockhart of Lee and Carnwath, 3rd Bt [U K], b 10 Dec 1802, d 9 May 1849 m 23 Feb 1836, Margaret, da of John M'Lean of Campbelltown, co Argyll, d 21 Jan 1895, and had issue 1d to 6d

1d Sir Norman Macdonald Lockhart of Lee and Carnwath, 4th Bt [U K], b 1845, d unm 20 May 1870

2d Sir Simon Macdonald Lockhart of Lee and Carnwath, 5th Bt [U K], M V O, Col late Comdg 1st Life Guards, formerly Brig-Gen Comdg Cavalry Brigade at the Curragh 1900-1901, and A D C to Com-in-Chief 1899-1900, &c (The Lee, Lanark, Carnwath House, Lanark, Carlton, &c), b 13 Mar 1849, m 14 Dec 1898, Hilda Maud, da of Col Augustus Henry Moreton-Macdonald [younger son of the Hon Augustus Henry Reynolds-Moreton and his wife Mary, née Macdonald Lockhart, named above]

3d Jane Margaret Maria Lockhart, d 16 May 1901, m 23 Sept 1862, Sir (William) Gerald Seymour Vesey FitzGerald, K C I E, C S I, J P, formerly Political A D C to Sec of State for India 1874-1901 (Carlton), and had issue 1e

1e Geraldine Tryphena Margaret FitzGerald

4d Maria Theresa Lockhart

5d Cordelia Euphemia Lockhart, d 20 June 1872, m 8 June 1867, John Stanley Mott of Barningham Hall, J P, late Major P W O Norfolk Art Mil [descended from King Henry VII] (Barningham Hall, Hanworth), and had issue 1e

1e Theresa Caroline Mott, m 20 July 1898, Major Charles Edward Radclyffe, D S O (Little Park, Wickham, Hants)

6d Esther Elizabeth Lockhart

2b John Macdonald, alias Lockhart, d (? s p)

3b James Macdonald, alias Lockhart, d (? s p)

4b Norman Macdonald, alias Lockhart of Tabrax, co Lanark, d (-), m Philadelphia, da of John M'Murdo of Dumfries, and had (with other) issue 1c

1c Elizabeth Macdonald, d 13 Oct 1888, m 1838, Eaglesfield Bradshaw Smith of Eyam, co Derby, and Blackwood House, co Dumfries

5b Elizabeth Macdonald, d (-), m 1st, Capt McNeill, d (-), 2ndly, 1801, William Putman McCabe

6b Matilda Macdonald, d (-), m John Campbell of Glensaddel

3a Clementina Lockhart, d 31 Mar 1803, m 1761, the Hon John Gordon (see p 188), Lieut Col 81st Regt [E of Aboyne Coll], d 30 Oct 1778, and had issue 1b to 2b

1b John Gordon, Major Gen and Col Comdt 2nd Brigade Bengal Cav, b 8 July 1765, d (? s p) 1832, m Nov 1810, Eliza, da of Robert Morris, M P for Gloucester

2b Grace Margaret Gordon, b 27 Sept 1766, d 1832, m 13 Ap 1794, William Graham of Mossknow, co Dumfries, d 1832, and had issue 1c to 3c

1c William Graham of Mossknow, J P, D L, Col 12th, 16th, and 17th Lancers, b 22 Jan 1797, d 2 May 1882, m 25 Feb 1830, Anne, da and h of Hugh Mair of Redhall and Wyseby, d 8 Jan 1887, and had issue 1d to 6d

[Nos 28614 to 28643

186

# of The Blood Royal

1d *William Mair Graham of Mossknow*, b 21 May 1832, d *unm* 27 *Feb* 1899

2d John Gordon Graham of Mossknow and Wyseby, J P , D L , Major-Gen *late* 1st Royal Dragoons (*Mossknow, near Ecclefechan*), b 11 July 1833 , m 11 Oct 1871, Susanna Elizabeth Touchet [descended from George (Plantagenet), Duke of Clarence, K G (see Clarence Volume, p 470)], da of Sir John Hay of Park, 7th Bt [S], and has issue 1e to 7e

   1e William Fergus Graham, *late* Lieut King's Own Scottish Borderers, b 13 Sept 1874

   2e Malcolm Hay Graham, twin, b 26 Sept 1877

   3e Claude Graham, Lieut Northants Regt , b 4 Sept 1881

   4e Cecil Erskin Graham, Lieut Border Regt , b 9 June 1883

   5e Violet Graham

   6e Alice Graham

   7e Mary Theresa Graham

3d *Charles Stewart Gordon of Gladstone, Queensland*, b 15 May 1835 d at *Gladstone*, 5 Dec 1883 , m 1862, Sarah, da *of G White*, and had issue (3 sons and 4 das)

4d Rosina Anne Graham

5d Grace Harriet Graham, m 6 Dec 1864, John Murray of Murraythwaite, co Dumfries, J P , Com R N , d 2 Aug 1872 , and has issue 1e to 5e

   1e William Murray of Murraythwaite, J P (*Murraythwaite, Ecclefechan*), b 31 Oct 1865 , m 12 Ap 1892, Evelyn, da of John Bruce , and has issue 1f to 3f

     1f Margaret Elizabeth Murray

     2f Vivian Murray

     3f Eleanor Justina Murray

   2e Marion Gertrude Murray

   3e Flora Murray

   4e Edith Murray

   5e Helen Murray

6d Clementina May Graham, m 6 Aug 1880, H Fowle Smith, Surgeon-Gen A M D (*Gretna Hall, Gretna Green*) , and has issue 1e

   1e Meliora Clementina Smith

2c *Clementina Graham*, d (?) *unm*

3c *Johanna Grace Graham*, d (-) , m 2 Ap 1829, *Erskine Douglas Sandford, Advocate, Sheriff of Galloway* [son *of the Lord Bishop of Edinburgh*], d (-) , and had issue 1d to 2d

1d William Graham Sandford, Diplo Service, one of the Royal Body Guard for Scotland, *formerly* Capt Royal Peeblesshire Rifles, b 30 Nov 1834

2d Frances Grace Margaret Sandford   [Nos 28644 to 28665

---

94 Descendants of ALEXANDER LOCKHART of Craighouse, a Lord of Session under the designation of Lord COVINGTON (Table XI) d (-), m 1725, MARGARET, da of Robert PRINGLE of Edgefield, a Lord of Session ,[1] and had (with possibly other) issue 1a

1a *William Lockhart, Capt R N , son and h served heir to father* 15 May 1783

---

[1] *Ex inform* Sir James Balfour Paul, Lord Lyon King

The Plantagenet Roll

95 Descendants, if any, of MARGARET LOCKHART (Table XI), d at Bath 24 Nov 1762, m 1st, as 3rd wife, JOHN (FLEMING), 6th EARL OF WIGTOUN [S], d (s p by her) 10 Feb 1744, 2ndly, PETER MACELLIGOT, a Major-Gen in the Austrian Service

96 Descendants of GRACE LOCKHART (Table XI), d 17 Nov 1738, m 1st, 20 June 1724, JOHN (GORDON), 3rd EARL OF ABOYNE [S], d 7 Ap 1732, 2ndly, as 1st wife, Dec 1734, JAMES (STUART) LORD DOUN, afterwards (1739), 8th EARL OF MORAY [S], K T, d 5 July 1767, and had issue 1a to 4a

1a Charles (Gordon), 4th Earl of Aboyne [S], b c 1728, d 28 Dec 1795, m 1st, 22 Ap 1759, Lady Margaret, da of Alexander (Stewart), 6th Earl of Galloway [S], d 12 Aug 1762, and had issue
See the Tudor Roll, Table CXXII, and pp 527-531, Nos 35196-35336

2a Hon John Gordon, Lieut-Col 81st Regt, b 19 June 1728 d 30 Oct 1778, m 1761, Clementina, da of George Lockhart of Carnwath, d 31 Mar 1803, and had issue
See p 187, Nos 28644-28665

3a Hon Lockhart Gordon, Judge-Advocat-Gen of Bengal, b 1732, d at Calcutta 24 May 1788 m 3 Oct 1770, the Hon Catherine (see Essex Volume, p 240), da of John Wallop, styled Viscount Lymington, d May 1813, and had issue 1b to 3b

  1b Rev Lockhart Gordon, b 28 July 1775, d (-), m
  2b Loudoun Harcourt Gordon, in the Army, b 9 May 1780
  3b Katherine Gordon

4a Francis (Stuart), 9th Earl of Moray [S], and 1st Baron Stuart of Castle-Stuart [G B], a Rep Peer, b 11 Jan 1737 d 28 Aug 1810, m 28 June 1763, the Hon Jean, da and in her issue (26 May 1878) h of John (Gray), 11th Lord Gray [S], d 19 Feb 1786, and had issue 1b to 3b

  1b Francis (Stuart), 10th Earl of Moray [S] and 2nd Baron Stuart [G B], K T, b (twin) 2 Feb 1771 d 12 Jan 1848, m 1st, 26 Feb 1795, Lucy, da of Gen John Scott of Balcomie, d 3 Aug 1798, 2ndly, 7 Jan, 1801, Margaret Jane, da of Sir Philip Ainslie of Pilton, d 3 Ap 1837, and had issue 1c to 5c

    1c Francis (Stuart), 11th Earl of Moray [S], and 3rd Baron Stuart [G B], b 7 Nov 1795, d unm 6 May 1859
    2c John (Stuart), 12th Earl of Moray [S], and 4th Baron Stuart [G B], b 25 Jan 1797, d unm 8 Nov 1867
    3c Archibald George (Stuart), 13th Earl of Moray [S], and 5th Baron Stuart [G B], b 3 May 1810, d unm 12 Feb 1872
    4c George Philip (Stuart), 14th Earl of Moray [S], and 6th Baron Stuart [G B] and (1878) 18th Lord Gray [S], b 14 Aug 1816, d unm 16 May 1895
    5c Lady Jane Stuart, b 30 Nov 1802, d 14 Mar 1880, m 1st, 25 Jan 1832, Sir John Archibald Drummond Stewart, 6th Bt [S], d s p 20 May 1838, 2ndly, 25 Aug 1838, Jeremiah Lonsdale Pounden of Brownswood, co Wexford, d 3 Mar 1887, and had issue 1d

      1d Eveleen (Pounden), 19th Lady Gray [S] (Brownswood, co Wexford, 14 The Boltons, S W), b 3 May 1841, m 9 Sept 1863, James Maclaren Smith, afterwards (R L 7 May 1897) Smith-Gray, d 26 Feb 1900, and had issue 1e to 4e

      1e James Maclaren Stuart Smith, now (R L 7 May 1897) Gray, Master of Gray, M A (Camb), late Capt Rifle Brigade (Cam-Difon, Llanwrtyd Wells, Brecon), b 4 June 1864   [Nos 28666 to 28830

2*e* Hon Ethel Eveleon Smith, *m* 23 July 1888, Henry Tufnell Campbell [son of John Thomas Campbell by his wife Lady Anne Katharine, *née* Bethune] (7 *Collingham Gardens, S W*)

3*e* Hon Thora Zelma Grace Gray

4*e* Hon Kathleen Eileen Moray Gray

2*b* Hon *Archibald Stuart*, b (*twin*) 2 Feb 1771, d 30 Oct 1832, m 17 Mar 1793, *Cornelia, da of Edmund Morton Pleydell of Milbourne St Andrew, Dorset*, d 1 Mar 1830, *and had issue* 1*c*

1*c Rev Edmund Luttrell Stuart, Rector of Winterborne Houghton Dorset*, b 21 Feb 1798, d 5 Nov 1869, m 2 Sept 1834, *Elizabeth, da of the Rev J L Jackson, Rector of Swanage*, d 28 Mar 1885, *and had issue* 1*d to* 4*d*

1*d Edmund Archibald (Stuart, sometime (1878-1895) Gray), 15th Earl of Moray [S], 7th Baron Stuart [G B]*, b 5 Nov 1840, d s p 11 June 1901, m 6 Sept 1877, *Anna Mary (Tarbat House, Kildary, Ross-shire, 7 Ainslie Place Edinburgh). da of the Rev George J Collinson*

2*d Francis James (Stuart, sometime (1895 1901) Stuart Gray) 16th Earl of Moray [S], 8th Baron Stuart of Castle Stuart [G B] J P formerly Major and Lieut -Col 1st Batt King's Liverpool Regt*, b 24 Nov 1842, d s p 20 Nov 1909, m 24 June 1879. *Gertrude Lloyer, da of the Rev Francis Smith Rector of Tarrant Rushton, Dorset*

3*d Morton Gray (Stuart sometime (1901-1909) Stuart-Gray), 17th Earl of Moray [S], 9th Baron Stuart of Castle Stuart [G B] (Darnaway Castle, Forres, Elgin, Castle Stuart, Inverness, Doune Lodge, Perth)*, b 16 Ap 1855, m 17 Dec 1890 Edith Douglas (see p 190), da of Rear-Adm George Palmer, *and has issue* 1*e to* 4*e*

1*e* Hon Francis Douglas Stuart-Gray, b 10 July 1892

2*e* Hon Archibald John Morton Stuart Gray, b 14 Nov 1894

3*e* Hon James Gray Stuart Gray, b 9 Feb 1897

1*e* Lady Hermione Moray Stuart-Gray

4*d* Lady *Cornelia Stuart, had Royal Warrant as da of an Earl 10 Ap 1897*, m 29 July 1873, the Rev William Henry Augustus Truell of Clonmannon, *formerly Vicar of Wall (Clonmannon, co Wicklow)*, *and has issue* 1*e to* 8*e*

1*e* Robert Holt Stuart Truell, b 6 Dec 1875

2*e* Edmund Gray Stuart Truell, b 14 Aug 1878

3*e* William Henry Stuart Truell, b 28 Feb 1890

4*e* Mary Louisa Truell, m 3 Sept 1903, John Milne, M B (68 *Manchester Old Road, Middleton, Manchester*), *and has issue* 1*f to* 2*f*

1*f* Richard Henry John Milne, b 1907

2*f* Elizabeth Marjorie Milne

5*e* Cornelia Isabel Truell, m 14 June 1900, Frank Mortimer Rowland, M D (26 *St John Street, Lichfield*), *and has issue* 1*f to* 5*f*

1*f* William George Stuart Rowland, b 22 Oct 1902

2*f* Ernest Mortimer Rowland, b 4 Mar 1904

3*f* Frank Edward Rowland, b 30 Sept 1905

4*f* Helen Isabel Rowland

5*f* Grace Elizabeth Rowland

6*e* Kathleen Augusta Truell

7*e* Gertrude Margaret Truell

8*e* Constance Elizabeth Truell

3*b Lady Grace Stuart*, d 23 Mar 1816, m 10 July 1789, *George Douglas of Cavers*, d 14 Nov 1811, *and had (with possibly other) issue* 1*c*

1*c James Douglas of Cavers*, b 9 Oct 1790, d 17 Aug 1861, m 7 Sept 1820, *Emma, da of Sir David Carnegie, 4th Bt [S] [E of Southesk Coll]*, b 29 May 1791, d 25 Sept 1882, *and had (with 1 other son and 2 das d s p) issue* 1*d to* 4*d*

[Nos 28831 to 28851

The Plantagenet Roll

1d *James Douglas of Cavers*, b 21 May 1822, d s p 29 *July* 1878

2d *Mary Douglas, da and in her issue* (1878) *co-h*, d 12 May 1859, m 15 *Ap* 1857, *William Elphinstone Malcolm of Burnfoot, co Dumfries*, d 30 Dec 1908, *and had issue* 1e

  1e May Malcolm of Cavers, m 12 Nov 1879, Edward Palmer, now Palmer-Douglas, J P, D L, Capt *late* Rifle Brigade (*Cavers, near Hawick*), and has issue (with a son, Malcolm, b 29 Mar 1882, d unm 12 Mar 1902) 1f

    1f Archibald Palmer-Douglas, B A (Camb), b 21 Aug 1880

3d *Emma Douglas, da and in her issue* (1878) *co-h*, b 10 *Jan* 1829, d 11 *Jan* 1870, m 3 *July* 1860 *Capt Robert Erskine Anderson, 107th Regt*, d 25 *Sept* 1903, *and had issue* 1e *to* 5e

  1e Robert Douglas Anderson, Major (ret) R A, b 11 Nov 1862, *unm*

  2e James Douglas Anderson, Major (ret) R A, b 27 Nov 1863

  3e John Hamilton Anderson, Major 2nd E Lancashire Regt, b 13 June 1865

  4e Emma Anderson

  5e Wilhelmina Christian Anderson, m 19 Dec 1906, Francis Edward Roberts, J P (*3 Sandown Terrace, Chester*)

4d Ellen Douglas, da and (1878) co-h, m 21 Oct 1859, Rear-Adm George Palmer, R N (*36 Eversley Road, Bexhill-on-Sea*), and has issue 1e to 4e

  1e George Douglas Palmer, b 1 June 1863

  2e Harry Douglas Palmer, Major R M L I, now attached to the Egyptian Army, Financial Sec Egyptian Army, *formerly* comdg 11th Soudanese, has 3rd Class Medjidie, b 22 Aug 1866, m 20 Jan 1909, Ethel Maud, da of J Borwick of 77 Prince's Gate, S W

  3e Ellen Douglas Palmer, m 12 Aug 1885, the Rev George Fossick Wilson (*Deronia, Heath Road, Weybridge*), and has issue 1f

    1f Stuart Douglas Wilson, R N, b 24 Mar 1890

  4e Edith Douglas Palmer, m 17 Dec 1890, Morton Gray (Stuart-Gray), 17th Earl of Moray [S], 9th Baron Stuart of Castle Stuart [G B], &c (*Kinfauns Castle, co Perth, Gray House, co Forfar*), and has issue

See p 189, Nos 28835-28838   [Nos 28855 to 28871

---

97. Descendants, if any surviving, of MARY LOCKHART (Table XI), d (-), m as 2nd wife, JOHN RATTRAY of Edinburgh, M D, cadet of Craighall, and had issue 1a [1]

  1a *Mary Rattray*

98 Descendants, if any surviving, of BARBARA LOCKHART (Table XI), b 16 Dec 1677, d (-), m 2ndly, the Hon DANIEL CARMICHAEL of Mauldsley, d Oct 1708, and had issue 1a

  1a *Daniel Carmichael of Mauldsley*, d 25 Oct 1765, m 24 *Jan* 1842, Emilia, da of the Rev John Hepburn, Minister of Old Greyfriars, Edinburgh, d 9 Jan 1769, and had issue 1b t) 3b

    1b *Thomas* (Carmichael), *5th Earl of Hyndford* [S], d *unm* 14 Feb 1811

    2b *Andrew* (Carmichael), *6th Earl of Hyndford* [S], b 1758, d *unm* 18 *Ap* 1817

    3b *Grizel Carmichael*, d (-), m *Archibald Nisbet of Carfin*, d 20 Oct 1807, *and had issue* 1c *to* 2c

      1c *Archibald Nisbet of Carfin, and, on the death of his uncle* (1817), *of Mauldsley*

      2c *Jean Nisbet*, d (-), m *Thomas Gordon of Harperfield*

---

[1] Douglas' "Baronetage of Scotland," i 278

# of The Blood Royal

99 Descendants of JANE WHARTON, da and in her issue co-h of the
Hon Sir THOMAS WHARTON, K B (Table X), d (—), m
JOHN DIGBY of Mansfield Woodhouse, and had issue (with 3
other das d s p) 1a to 4a

1a *Frances Digby*, bur 4 May 1736, m 1727, *Sir Thomas Legard 4th Bt* [E],
d 1735, *and had issue 1b to 2b*

1b *Sir Digby Legard, 5th Bt* [E], d 4 Feb 1773, m Aug 1755, Jane (see
p 196), da and event co h of George Cartwright, d 15 Sept 1811, and had issue
1c to 7c

1c *Sir John Legard, 6th Bt* [E], d s p 16 July 1807

2c *Sir Thomas Legard, 7th Bt* [E], bapt 3 Dec 1762, d 5 July 1830, m
26 Dec 1802, Sarah, da of (—) Bishop, d 26 Jan 1814, and had issue 1d to 3d

1d *Sir Thomas Digby Legard, 8th Bt* [E], b 30 May 1803 d 10 Dec 1860,
m 31 May 1832, *the Hon Frances* [a descendant of the Lady Anne, sister of King
Edward IV, &c], da of Charles (Duncombe), 1st Baron Feversham [U K], d
15 June 1881, and had issue

See the Exeter Volume, p 648, Nos 55763–55769

2d Henry Willoughby Legard, 9th Lancers, b 1805, d 21 Nov 1845, m
26 Oct 1839, Charlotte Henrietta [a descendant of the Lady Anne, sister of King
Edward IV, &c], da of Henry Willoughby of Birdsall, co York [B Middleton
Coll], d 25 Jan 1844, and had issue 1e to 2e

1e *Sir Algernon Willoughby Legard, 12th Bt* [E] (Ganton Hall, Yorks), b
14 Oct 1842, m 27 July 1872, Alicia Egerton, da of the Rev George Brooks, M A

2e Rev Cecil Henry Legard, M A (Camb), LL M, Rector of Cottesbrooke
(Cottesbrooke Rectory, Northampton), b 28 Nov 1843, m 29 Ap 1873, Emily
Mary, d of James Hall of Scorborough Hall, Beverley, and has issue 1f to 2f

1f Digby Algernon Hall Legard, B A (Camb) (Headon Lodge, Brompton
S O, Yorks), b 7 Dec 1876, m 2 June 1904, Georgiana Blanche Elaine, da of
William Joseph Starkey Barber-Starkey, and has issue 1g to 2g

1g Thomas Digby Legard, b 16 Oct 1905

2g John D'Arcy Legard, b May 1908

2f Gertrude Cassandra Legard, unm

3d Harriet Legard, d at Halifax 19 July 1851, m 14 Aug 1820, Edward
Nelson Alexander of Heathfield, Halifax [2nd son of Lewis Alexander of Hopwood
Hall, Halifax, Solicitor, by his wife Elizabeth, da of the Rev Edward Nelson of
Halifax, M A], b 16 May 1797, d at Windermere 20 Sept 1859, and had issue
1e to 4e

1e Rev Disney Legard Alexander, M A (Oxon), Vicar of Ganton, b 29 June
1821, d 25 Feb 1868, m 13 June 1849 Juana Maria, da of John Barrow of
Ringwood Hall, co Derby, d 6 Aug 1866, and had issue (with a son who d unm)
1f to 5f

1f Rev John Barrow Alexander, M A (Camb), formerly H B M's Vice-
Consul at Tacoma, Wash, U S A, 1884–1897, previously Rector of Port Townsend,
Wash (4 Warwick Gardens, Kensington, W), b 12 Mar 1850, unm

2f Edward Disney Alexander of Milton, co Northants, b 27 July 1857, d
30 Mar 1907, m 5 Aug 1886, Amy Frances Jane (see p 193), da of Francis
William Montgomery of Kettering, d 1902, and had issue (with a da, Amy Juana,
b Aug 1887, d young) 1g to 2g

1g Edward Montgomery Alexander of Milton House (Milton House, Northants, Borobridge, Yorks), b 22 Dec 1888

2g Noel Legard Alexander, b 24 Dec 1894

3f Henry Alexander (Bryn Mawr, Seattle, Wash, U S A), b 24 Nov 1860,
m at Raton, New Mexico, 2 June 1886, Katharine, da of William H Adams of
Raton afsd, and has issue 1g to 4g   [Nos 28872 to 28888

The Plantagenet Roll

1g Robert Disney Alexander, *b* 15 Aug 1887.

2g Winifred Alexander

3g Beatrice Alexander

4g Phyllis Alexander

4f Matilda Alexander (4 *Warwick Gardens, Kensington, W*), *m* 17 Sept 1868, Walter Hudson of York, Capt 100th Royal Canadian Regt, *afterwards in Holy Orders and Rector of Culton in Landrick, d* 24 Nov 1885 and has issue 1g to 9g

  1g Walter Alexander Hudson (*Riverside, California*), *b* 21 Feb 1872, *m* 24 July 1909, Anna Lent, widow of Joseph Gooding, da of (—) Viberg

  2g Francis Disney Hudson (*Riverside, California*), *b* 6 Aug 1873, *unm*

  3g Charles Louis Hudson (*Northallerton*), *b* 11 June 1875, *m* 20 Oct 1906, Ethel May, da of Marmaduke Proudlock, and has issue 1h

    1h Richard Disney Hudson, *b* 30 May 1909

  1g Emily Margarette Hudson, *m* 18 Aug 1906, Philip Karl Beisiegel (*Uppingham, Rutland*), and has issue 1h to 2h

    1h Walter Karl Beisiegel, *b* 13 July 1907

    2h Lilian Margarette Beisiegel, *b* 16 Ap 1909

  5g Grace Ellen Hudson

  6g Ethel Maud Hudson

  7g Mabel Juana Hudson

  8g Nora Blanche Hudson

  9g Nona Muriel Hudson

5f Ellen Alexander, *m* 19 Mar 1891, Robert Piper Loy (*Hunteville, Ontario, Canada*), and has issue 1g to 3g

  1g Walter Alexander Loy, *b* 9 Jan 1895

  2g Zoe Gwendolyn Alexander Loy, *b* 8 May 1893

  3g Mary Irene Alexander Loy, *b* 4 Feb 1896

2e Charlotte Matilda Alexander, b 3 Oct 1822, d 5 May 1876, *m at Halifax* 21 Oct 1847, *the Rev Thomas Andrew Walker, M A* (*Oxon*), *Rector of Kilham, d* 11 *Ap* 1905, *and had issue* 1f to 4f

  1f *Rev Onebye Robert Walker,* b 25 Sept 1849, d 4 *June* 1908, *m* 4 *June* 1878 *Fanny Hyniman, da of the Rev John Blair, Vicar of Brompton, and had issue (with 3 others d young)* 1g to 3g

    1g Robert Andrew Walker, *in* U S Navy, *b* 3 Nov 1883

    2g Fanny Walker, *b* 26 Ap 1879

    3g Hilda Blair Walker, *b* 29 Sept 1882

  2f Minnie Paula Walker, *m* at Ilford 3 Oct 1876, the Rev Arthur Ingleby, M A (*St Clement s, Heene, Worthing*), and has issue 1g to 3g

    1g Richard Arthur Oakes Ingleby, Solicitor (87 *Chester Terrace, Eaton Square, S W*), *b* 27 Jan 1879

    2g Charles Herbert Evelyn Ingleby (*Melbourne, Victoria*), *b* 2 May 1881

    3g Ethel Mary Rose Ingleby, *b* 6 July 1877

  3f Harriet Caroline Walker (*Worthing*), *unm*

  4f Nora Walker (*Hove*), *unm*

3e Eliza Alexander, b 1825, d 18 Dec 1867, *m Aug* 1848, *Richard Bowser, Bishop Auckland, Durham, Solicitor, d* 13 Feb 1882, *and had issue (with a son and da d young)* 1f to 2f

  1f Harry Moreland Bowser (*Bishop Auckland*), *b* 8 Dec 1863, *m* June 1895, Annie, da of (—) Lavender of Sydney, Australia

  2f Caroline Bowser, *m* 9 July 1879, Thomas Alexander McCullagh, M D (*Bishop Auckland, Durham*), and has issue 1g to 4g
         [Nos 28889 to 28920

# of The Blood Royal

1g Alexander McCullagh, Lieut R N, b 23 Ap 1880

2g Herbert Rochfort McCullagh, Durham L I, b 15 June 1881

3g Arthur Cecil Hays McCullagh, M B, b 20 Nov 1882

4g Florence Danvers McCullagh, b 1 June 1885

4e *Frances Catherine Alexander*, d 5 Mar 1892, m 1st, *Francis William Montgomery of Kettering*, d 28 Aug 1870, 2n lly, *John Brown Izon of Walsgrave Hall*, d (-), and had issue 1f to 2f

1f *Amy Frances Jane Montgomery*, b 3 Aug 1860 d 1902 m 5 Aug 1886, *Edward Disney Alexander of Milton, co Northants*, d 30 Mar 1907, and had issue

See p 191, Nos 28886-28887

2f Florence Montgomery, m 30 July 1890, the Rev Ernest Lembert Daniels, Rector of Holcott (*Holcott Rectory, Northants*), s p

3c *Rev William Legard*, Vicar of Ganton, d 19 Feb 1826 m 7 Feb 1803, *Cecilia Elizabeth, da of James Oldershaw of Stamford, M D*, d 31 Dec 1854, and had issue 1d to 3d

1d *James Anlaby Legard, Capt R N , K T S*, b 13 Oct 1805, d 25 June 1869, m 6 May 1845, *Catherine [a descendant of the Lady Anne, sister of King Edward IV], widow of Henry Ralph Beaumont, da of Sir George Cayley, 6th Bt [E]*, d 11 Mar 1887, and had issue

See the Exeter Volume, p 697, Nos 57863-57876 and Nos 57894-57897

2d *William Barnabas Legard Col Bengal Army*, b 27 Dec 1810, d 27 Jan 1890, m 11 Dec 1845, *Ann Maria, da of Richard Oneby Walker of London* d and had issue 1e

1e Evelyn Mary Legard, m 1886, William J Gillett (*Ashley House, Shalford, Surrey*)

3d *Rev Frederick Legard, settled in Australia*, d 26 June 1897, m and had issue [1]

4c *Digby Legard of Watton Abbey, co Yorks*, b 1766, d (-), m 11 Dec 1797, *Frances [a descendant of the Lady Anne, sister of King Edward IV , &c], da of Ralph Creyke of Marton, and had issue*

See the Exeter Volume, p 689, Nos 57567-57600

5c *Jane Legard*, bapt 8 July 1756, d (-), m 29 Oct 1785, (—) *Smith of Sunderlandwick, co York*

6c *Frances Legard*, b 3 July 1757, d 6 Ap 1827, m 19 Feb 1780, *Thomas Grimston* (see p 196) *of Grimston Garth and Kilnwick, co York*, b 29 Dec 1753, d 2 May 1821, and had issue 1d to 2d

1d *Charles Grimston of Grimston Garth and Kilnwick, J P , D L , Col East York Militia*, b 2 July 1791, d 21 Mar 1859, m 10 Nov 1823, *Jane, da of the Very Rev Thomas French, Dean of Killare [neice of 1st Baron Ashtown]*, d 26 Jan 1873, and had issue 1e to 13e

1e *Marmaduke Jerard Grimston of Grimston Garth and Kilnwick, J P , D L , Col East York Art Mil*, b 27 Nov 1826, d 14 Nov 1879, m 3 July 1856, *Florence Victoria, da of Col Hardress Robert Saunderson [by his wife Lady Maria, née Luttrell]* [m 2ndly, 2 Jan 1883, *Col Sir Edmund Frederick Du Cane, K C B , and*], d 7 June 1903, and had issue 1f to 2f

1f *Florence Maria Grimston, da and co-h , m as 2nd wife 10 Oct 1882, Edward Byrom of Culver and Kersall Cell, D L , High Sheriff co Devon 1888 (Culver, near Exeter, Kersall Cell, co Lancaster, Grimston Garth, co York)*, and has issue 1g to 2g

1g Edward Luttrell Grimston Byrom, b 25 June 1885.

2g Rose Effie Jerardine Byrom   [Nos 28921 to 28983

---

[1] Foster's " Baronetage,' 1880, p 355

The Plantagenet Roll

2f Rose Armatrude Frances Grimston, da and co h (*Grimston Garth, near Hull*), m 19 June 1889, Col George Bertie Benjamin Hobart, J P, D L, *late* R A [E of Buckinghamshire Coll and a descendant of George, Duke of Clarence, K G (see Clarence Volume, p 544)], d 27 Oct 1907, and has issue 1g

1g Armatrude Bertie Sophia Effie Hobart, b 20 May 1890

2e *Walter John Grimston of Bracken, co York*, Major R A, b 9 Feb 1828, d 18 Oct 1899, m 2ndly, 3 June 1865, Josephine, da of Thomas Green Wilkinson, and had issue 1f to 6f

1f Ernest Walter Grimston, heir male of the Grimstons of Grimston Garth, b 13 Sept 1876

2f Charlotte Josephine Grimston

3f Evelyn Maude Cecilia Grimston

4f Helena Winifred Grimston

5f Beatrice Letitia Grimston

6f Violet Adele Grimston

3e William Henry Grimston, J P, Hon Col 3rd Batt East Yorkshire Regt (*High Hall, Elton, Yorks*), b 1 Nov 1830, m 1st, 11 Ap 1860, Anna, da of George Harrison of Hailsham, co Sussex, d 1878, 2ndly, 27 July 1882, Catharine Sarah, da of John Charlesworth Dodgson-Charlesworth of Chapelthorpe Hall, co York

4e Daniel Thomas Grimston, LL B (*Camb*), b 8 July 1832, d 3 Mar 1872, m 1 Aug 1860, Jane Malvina Williamza [*a descendant of the Lady Isabel Plantagenet* (see Essex Volume, p 14)], da of George Morant, J P [re-m 2ndly, 3 Feb 1883, John Hugh Dillon, who d 30 Aug 1894], and had issue 1f to 5f

1f Sylvester George Grimston (*Montreal*), b 22 Oct 1863, m 21 Jan 1898, Mary Elizabeth, da of James Penfold, Manager of the Bank of British North America at Montreal

2f Charles Digby Grimston (*Montreal*), b 14 July 1867, m 14 Aug 1906, Olive, da of (—) Mills of Bracebridge, Ontario

3f Lydia Maude Grimston

4f Jane Malvina Williamza Grimston

5f Geraldine Mary Grimston

5e Rev Alexander Grimston, Canon of York and Vicar of Stillingfleet (*Stillingfleet Vicarage, Yorks*), b 27 Nov 1835, m 29 Oct 1863, Una Kate [descended from the Lady Isabel Plantagenet (see Essex Volume, p 255)], da of Capt Rowland William Taylor Money, and has issue (with a son, Charles Rowland, who d unm 9 Sept 1889) 1f to 6f

1f Edith Maud Grimston

2f Constance Eleanor Grimston

3f Alice Mabel Grimston

4f Hilda Grimston

5f Florence Brenda Grimston

6f Cicely Mildred Grimston

6e Maria Emma Grimston, b 23 Oct 1824, d 6 Mar /19 Ap 1907, m 8 July 1858, Major William Forbes, 77th Regt [youngest son of James Forbes of Kingairlock, co Ayr], d 29 Nov 1882, and had issue 1f to 5f

1f Katharine Annie Forbes (*Chelsea*), m 2 Oct 1893, Charles Blackwell Moneypenny, d 2 Aug 1894

2f Magdalena Gertrude Forbes, m 20 Oct 1890, Charles Irwin Clark Williams

3f Cecil Forbes

4f Alice Forbes

5f Marion Forbes.

7e Frances Dorothy Grimston (*Ardmore, Chislehurst*), m 24 Nov 1853, the Rev John Frewen Moor, M A, Vicar of Ampfield, near Romsey [descended from the Lady Anne, sister to Kings Edward IV and Richard III] (see Exeter Volume, p 424), d 5 Jan 1906, and has issue 1f to 2f   [Nos 28984 to 29010

# of The Blood Royal

1/ Rev Charles Moor, D D, *late* Vicar of Gainsborough and Canon of Lincoln (*Apley Rise, Westgate-on-Sea*), b 10 May 1857, m 10 July 1889, Constance Mary, da of Robert Moon M A, Bar-at-Law, and has issue 1g to 5g

1g Christopher Moor, b 2 Feb 1892.

2g Frewen Moor, b 28 Ap 1893

3g Oswald Moor b 26 July 1901.

4g Rosalie Moor

5g Veronica Moor

2/ Selina Mary Moor

8e Jane Grimston

9e Catherine Grimston, b 27 Jan 1829, d 8 Feb 1869, m 22 Sept 1856, the Rev Edward Gordon, Vicar of Kildale and afterwards of Atack, both co York (*Mundesley, Norfolk*), and had issue 1/ to 6/

1/ Rev Edward Cyril Gordon, Rector of Carrington (*Carrington Rectory, Wirksworth, Derby*), b 23 Oct 1858, m 12 Aug 1898, Ellen, da of R Y Bazett, H E I C C S, Bombay, s p

2/ Charles Grimston Gordon (*Southrepps, Norwich, Norfolk*), b 7 Mar 1860, m 4 Nov 1890, Florence, da of Harrison Hodgson, d 15 Sept 1892, and has issue 1g

1g Florence Gordon, b 25 Aug 1892

3/ Francis Gordon, b 2 Feb 1869, *unm*

4/ Helen Elizabeth Mary Gordon, *unm*

5/ Blanche Theodora Gordon, m Dec 1895, Edward Tisdall, Paymaster of the Forces, R N, s p.

6/ Lucy Beatrice Gordon, *unm*

10e Elizabeth Grimston (*Cheltenham*), m 4 May 1870, James King of Clara, co Fermanagh, and Langfield, co Tyrone, d c 1882, and has issue 1/ to 4/

1/ Rev Marmaduke James Gilbert King, Perpetual Curate of St. Gabriel's, Bishop Wearmouth (*Bishop Wearmouth*), b 3 Aug 1871, m 14 Nov 1906, Catherine Primrose, da of the Rev J C P Aldous, Vicar and Rural Dean of Dutfield, and has issue 1g

1g Elinor Catherine King

2/ Henry Charles King (*St Marnock's Farm, Salisbury, Rhodesia*), b 1 Ap 1873

3/ Alice Cicell King

4/ Florence Maude King

11e Maude Grimston (*The Ridgeway, Wimbledon*), m 24 June 1889, the Rev George Constantine, D D, d s p 6 Oct 1891

12e Cicell Grimston, m 29 Aug 1871, Capt Francis Loftus Tottenham (*The Garden House, Mildmay Park, N*), and has issue 1/ to 6/

1/ Percy Marmaduke Tottenham, Egyptian Irrigation Dept, b 17 Aug 1873, m 31 Aug 1909, Angel, da of Edward Mervyn Archdale of Riverside, co Fermanagh

2/ Francis Loftus Tottenham, R N, b 17 Aug 1880

3/ Anna Maude Tottenham, m 2 July 1907, Major Gen Henry Wylie (*Hill Top Cottage, Farnham Common*), s p

4/ Mabel Gertrude Tottenham, m 5 Oct 1907, Dudley Carmalt Jones, M D (*Eastcote*), and has issue 1g

1g Evelyn Carmalt Jones, b 20 July 1908

5/ Edith Leonora Tottenham, *unm*

6/ Grace Marguerite Tottenham, *unm*

13e Octavia Grimston (*Kingswood, Weybridge*), m 10 Jan 1867, Herbert Clifford Saunders, Q C, Bar-at-Law, d 25 Aug 1893, and has issue 1/ to 9/

[Nos 29011 to 29041

The Plantagenet Roll

1/ Herbert Stewart Saunders, M A , b 18 May 1872

2/ Una Mary Josephine Saunders, b 5 Sept 1869

3/ Maude Irene Saunders, b 23 Feb 1871

4/ Rose Pellipar Saunders, b 9 Aug 1873

5/ Grace Helena Saunders, b 30 Oct 1874

6/ Violet Constance Saunders, b 19 Feb 1876

7/ Florence Muriel Saunders, b 19 Nov 1878

8/ Cicell Ione Saunders, b 22 Ap 1881

9/ Octavia Elfrida Saunders, b 13 Oct 1885

2d Oswald Grimston of Mersham Bitterne, co Hants, b 22 Oct 1794 , d 31 July 1872, m 16 Sept 1830, Mary Ernle [descended from the Lady Isabel Plantagenet (see Essex Volume, p 255)], da of the Rev Kyrle Ernle Money M A , Preb of Hereford, d 8 Jan 1892 , and had issue 1e to 2e

1e Oswald James Augustus Grimston, J P , D L , late Col Comdg 3rd Batt Royal Warwickshire Regt (The Lodge, Itchen, co Hants), b 27 Aug 1831 , m 1st, 15 Ap 1856, Frances Eliza, da of Lieut-Col Henry Dundas Campbell, d 6 July 1869 , 2ndly, 21 Aug 1876, Louisa Mary, widow of John William Sanders, da of Capt Rowland Money, 41st Madras N I , and has issue (with a son who d s p) 1/ to 6/

1/ Rollo Estouteville Grimston, C I E , Lieut -Col Indian Army, b 26 Oct 1861

2/ Sylvester Bertram Grimston, Major Indian Army, b 27 Nov 1864 , m 16 May 1904, Nina, da of Lieut Col George William M caulay , and has issue 1g to 2g

1g George Sylvester Grimston, b 2 Ap 1905

2g Frances Nina Grimston, b 16 July 1907

3/ Lionel Augustus Grimston, b 18 Ap 1868

4/ Horace Legard Grimston, b 30 Jan 1880

5/[1] Brenda Grimston, m 4 July 1882, the Rev Owen Tudor, Vicar of Willingdon (Willingdon Vicarage, Sussex)

6/[2] Pauline Grimston, b 28 June 1877

2e Mary Adelaide Emma Grimston (Fir Bank, Ascot, Berks), m 19 Sept 1867, Gen James Michael, C S I , C F J , Knt of Grace of St John of Jerusalem, &c , J P , late Madras Staff Corps, d 17 Feb 1907 , and has issue 1/

1/ Mildred Douglas Michael

7c Henrietta Charlotte Legard, d (–); m (—) Smith of Yorkshire

2b Jane Legard, d 11 Nov 1758 , m 12 Mar 1753, John Grimston of Grimston Garth and Kilnwick, co York, b 17 Feb 1725 , d 21 June 1780 , and had issue 1c

1c Thomas Grimston of Grimston Garth and Kilnwick, b 29 Dec 1753 , d 2 May 1821 , m 19 Feb 1780, Frances, da of Sir Digby Legard, 5th Bt [E], d 1827 , and had issue

See p 193, Nos 28981–29061

2a Jane Digby, d (–), m Francis Fycher of Grantham Grange[1]

3a Mary Digby, d (–), m George Cartwright of Ossington, co Notts , and had issue (with a son and 3 other das all d s p) 1b to 4b

1b Mary Cartwright, da and event co-h , d s p 21 July 1764 , m 10 Ap. 1758, Sir Charles Louis Buck, 4th Bt [E], d s p 7 June 1782

2b Dorothy Cartwright,[2] da and event co-h

3b Jane Cartwright, da and event co-h , d 15 Sept 1811 , m Aug 1755, Sir Digby Legard, 5th Bt [E], d 4 Feb 1773 , and had issue

See p 191, Nos 28872–29061   [Nos 29042 to 29332

---

[1] Thoroton's ' Notts," i 317   [2] See note on p 197

# of The Blood Royal

4*b* *Anne Cartwright*,[1] *da and event co-h*

4*a* *Philadelphia Digby, da and co-h*, d 14 *Jan* 1765, m 17 30, *Sir George Cayley, 4th Bt [E], d Sept* 1791, *and had issue*
See the Exeter Volume, pp 696–698, Nos 57769–57955

[Nos 29333 to 29519

100 Descendants, if any, of ELIZABETH WHARTON (Table X), m (—) BENNETT, and of the Hon ELEANOR WHARTON, d (–), m WILLIAM THWAYTES of Long Marston

101 Descendants, if any, of MARY MUSGRAVE (Table XII), d (–), m THOMAS DAVISON of Blakiston, co Durham

102 Descendants of Sir PHILIP MUSGRAVE, 6th Bt [E], M P. (Table XII), b c 1711, d 5 or 25 July 1795, m 24 June 1742, JANE, da of John TURTON of Orgreave, co Stafford, d (will proved) 1802, and had issue 1*a* to 5*a*

1*a* *Sir John Chardin Musgrave, 7th Bt [E],* b 15 *Jan* 1757, d 24 *July* 1806, m 13 *July* 1791, *Mary, da of the Rev Sir Edmund Filmer, 6th Bt [E],* d 9 *Jan* 1838, *and had issue* 1*b* to 3*b*
1*b* *Sir Philip Christopher Musgrave, 8th Bt [E], M P,* b 12 *July* 1794, d s p s 16 *July* 1827
2*b* *Rev Sir Christopher John Musgrave, 9th Bt [E],* b 1798, d 11 *May* 1834 m *Sept* 1825, *Mary Anne, da* (see p 206) *of Edward Hasell of Dalemain,* d shortly before Oct 1895, *and had issue* 1*c* to 3*c*
1*c* *Georgiana Musgrave, da and co-h* d 11 *Ap* 1868, m 29 *July* 1847, *the Hon Frederick Petre [B Petre Coll],* d 18 *July* 1906, *and had issue*
See the Clarence Volume, p 372, Nos 12725–12739
2*c* *Augusta Musgrave* b 10 *Feb* 1830 d 11 *Oct* 1901, m 1*st*, 27 *Aug* 1850, *Col Henry Frederick Bonham,* 10th *Hussars* d 16 *Feb* 1856. 2*ndly,* 26 *May* 1857, *John Edward Cornwallis* (Rous), 2nd *Earl of Stradbroke [U K] and Baron Rous [G B], and* 7th *Bt [E],* d 27 *Jan* 1886, *and had issue* 1*d* to 8*d*
1*d* Henry Walter Musgrave Bonham, Col *formerly* Grenadier Guards (*Arthur's*), b 11 Nov 1852, m 26 Aug 1875, Georgiana, da of Thomas Sheriffe of Henstead Hall, Suffolk
2*d* George Edward John Mowbray (Rous), 3rd Earl of Stradbroke [U K], and Baron Rous [G B], 8th Bt [E], C V O, C B, Vice Adm of Suffolk, and Chairman Suffolk Territorial Force, &c (*Henham Hall, Wangford, Suffolk*) b 19 Nov 1862, m 23 July 1898, Helena Violet Alice, da of Lieut Gen James Keith Fraser, C M G [Bt Coll], and has issue 1*e* to 5*e*
1*e* John Anthony Alexander Rous, Viscount Dunwich, H M Queen Alexandra Sponsor, b 1 Ap 1903
2*e* Hon William Keith Rous, b 10 Mar 1907
3*e* Lady Pleasance Elizabeth Rous
4*e* Lady Catherine Charlotte Rous
5*e* Lady Betty Helena Joanna Rous

3*d* *Edith Charlotte Musgrave Bonham,* b 30 *May* 1851, d *at Johannesburg* 17 *Feb* 1903, m 21 *July* 1870 *the Rev William Belcher, formerly Vicar of Walberswick and Blythburgh, and Rector of Heveningham (Ipswich), and had issue* (*with a son who d young*) 1*e* to 4*e*

[Nos 29520 to 29541

---

[1] One of these is said to have m a Sir (—) Middleton

The Plantagenet Roll

1e Reginald George Holland Belcher, Lieut Lincolnshire Regt, twin, b 22 Ap 1878

2e Frederick Harry Bonham Belcher, twin, b 22 Ap 1878

3e Musgrave Vanneck Gordon Belcher, b 30 July 1881

4e Edith Augusta Anna Bonham Belcher m 25 Mar 1899, George Lipscombe, R N (Melrose, The Grange, Berks) and has issue 1f to 7f

 1f George Lipscombe, b 13 Dec 1899

 2f William Henry Lipscombe, b 30 May 1901

 3f Frederick Edmund Lipscombe, b 20 Nov 1904

 4f Edith Mary Lipscombe, b 5 Sept 1903

 5f Elizabeth Catherine Lipscombe, b 3 May 1906

 6f Margaret Mary Lipscombe b 28 July 1907

 7f Agnes Lipscombe, b 17 Ap 1909

4d Lady Augusta Fanny Rous, m 8 May 1880, Cecil Francis William Fane [E of Westmorland Coll], whom she divorced 1904, and has issue 1e to 2e

 1e Charles George Cecil Fane b 8 Ap 1881

 2e John Lionel Richards Fane, b 2 Jan 1884

5d Lady Sophia Evelyn Rous (Boscombe Cottage I W), m 20 Ap 1888, Capt George Hamilton Heaviside, 6th Dragoons, d 27 Nov 1906

6d Lady Adela Charlotte Rous, m 19 Feb 1887, Thomas Belhaven Henry Cochrane, M V O, J P, D L, Dept Gov, Steward and Sheriff of the Isle of Wight, and Capt of Carisbrooke Castle [E of Dundonald Coll, and a descendant of the Lady Anne, sister to King Edward IV, &c (see Exeter Volume, p 626)] (Carisbrooke Castle, I W Quarr Abbey, Ryde, I W)

7d Lady Hilda Maud Rous, b 3 Feb 1867, d 15 Aug 1901, m 31 Jan 1901 Charles Fitzroy Ponsonby M'Neill [descended from George (Plantagenet), Duke of Clarence, K G (see Clarence Volume, p 336)] (Carlton Curlieu Manor Hous near Leicester, Ki'sant House, Broadway, Worcester), and had issue 1e to 2e

 1e Ronald Frank Rous M'Neill, b 15 Jan 1894

 2e Brenda Mary Adela M'Neill, b 8 Nov 1897

8d Lady Gwendoline Audrey Adeline Brudenell Rous, m 26 June 1895, Lieut-Col Richard Beale Colvin, C B (Monkhams, Waltham Abbey), and has issue 1e to 2e

 1e Richard Beale Rous Colvin, b 12 Feb 1900

 2e Audrey Mary Maude Colvin

3c Harriet Musgrave, da and co-h, d 29 July 1863, m as 1st wife, 28 Ap 1851, the Right Hon Sir Walter Barttelot Barttelot of Stopham, 1st Bt [U K 9 June 1875], P C, M P C B, &c, (Col 2nd Sussex R I, b 10 Oct 1820, d 2 Feb 1893, and had issue 1d to 1d

1d Sir Walter George Barttelot of Stopham, 2nd Bt [U K], J P, D L, Major 2nd V B Royal Sussex Regt, previously 5th Dragoon Guards, b 11 Ap 1855, d (being killed in Boer War) 23 July 1900, m 3 June 1879, Georgiana Mary, da of George Edmond Balfour of Sidmouth Manor [re m 2ndly, 22 Oct 1902, Beville Molesworth St Aubyn], and had issue 1e to 3e

 1e Sir Walter Balfour Barttelot of Stopham, 3rd Bt [U K], Lieut 1st Batt Coldstream Guards, served in South Africa 1900-1902 (Stopham House Pulborough, 10 Berkeley Square, W), b 22 Mar 1880, m 17 Nov 1903, Gladys St Aubyn, da of William Collier Angove of 83 Onslow Gardens, S W, and has issue 1f to 2f

 1f Walter de Stopham Barttelot, b 27 Oct 1904

 2f William Frederick Geoffrey Nelson Barttelot, b 21 Oct 1905

 2e Nigel Kenneth Walter Barttelot, Lieut R N, and Com Instructor Royal

[Nos 29542 to 29566

198

# of The Blood Royal

Naval Vol Reserve, *b* 9 Ap 1883, *m* 10 Jan 1906, Dorothy Maud, da of Frederick Aldcroft Kay of Manchester

    3c Irene Margaret Mary Barttelot

    2d Edith Harriet Barttelot, *m* 12 June 1884, Major-Gen Henry Crichton Sclater, R A , C B, now Comdg 4th (Quetta) Div , *formerly* Q M G in India (*Flagstaff House, Quetta*)

    3d Evelyn Fanny Buttelot (13 *Egerton Place*, S W), *m* 29 Mar 1883, Charles Munro Sandham of Rowdell, co Sussex, *d* 1892, and has issue 1e to 3e

       1e Charles Barttelot Sandham, *b* 1887

       2e Edith Mary Georgina Sandham, *m* 1907, Hamilton Hugh Berners, Lieut Irish Guards

       3e Ada Margaret Sandham

    4d Ada Mary Barttelot, *m* 17 Oct 1882, Col William Frederick Cavaye, Comdg Middlesex Brig , E Command (40 *Egerton Crescent*, S W , *Birchenbridge, Horsham*)

    3b *Sir George Musgrave of Edenhall*, 10th Bt [*E*], *b* 14 *June* 1799, *d* 29 *Dec* 1872, *m* 26 *June* 1828, *Charlotte, da of Sir James Graham of Netherby*, 1st Bt [*G B*], *d* 26 *June* 1873, *and had issue* 1c *to* 4c

    1c *Sir Richard Courtenay Musgrave of Edenhall*, 11th Bt [*E*], M P , Lord-Lieut co Westmorland, *b* 21 *Aug* 1838, *d* 13 *Feb* 1881, *m* 17 *Jan* 1867, *Adora Frances Olga, da of Peter Wells* [re-m 2ndly, 18 *Ap* 1882, *Henry Charles* (*Brougham*), *3rd Lord Brougham and Vaux* [*U K*], *K C V O*], *and had issue* 1d *to* 5d

    1d *Sir Richard George Musgrave of Edenhall*, 12th Bt [*E*], D L , *late Argyll and Sutherland Highlanders* (*Edenhall, Langwathby, R S O , 17 Charles Street, Berkeley Square, W*), *b* 11 Oct 1872, *m* 9 Feb 1895, the Hon Eleanor [descended from the Lady Isabel Plantagenet (see the Essex Volume, p 46)], da of Charles (Harbord), 5th Baron Suffield [G B], and has issue 1e to 2e

       1e Nigel Courtenay Musgrave, *b* 11 Feb 1896

       2e Christopher Musgrave, *b* 4 May 1899

    2d Philip Richard Musgrave, *late* Lieut 3rd Batt Royal Sussex Regt (*Bachelors'*), *b* 26 Nov 1873 , *m* (—)

    3d Thomas Charles Musgrave (*Union*), *b* 28 Nov 1875

    4d Dorothy Anne Musgrave, *m* 12 June 1895, Henry Francis Compton (see p 467) of Minstead, J P , D L , *formerly* M P , &c (*Minstead Manor, Lyndhurst, Mapperton House, Beaminster, Dorset*), and has issue 1e to 3e

       1e Henry Richard Compton, *b* 12 Oct 1899

       2e Phyllis Dorothy Compton, *b* 17 Mar 1896

       3e Daphne Compton, *b* 24 Feb 1897

    5d Zoe Caroline Musgrave, *m* 16 Jan 1893, Alexander Farquharson of Invercauld, Lieut -Col Comdg 7th Batt Gordon Highlanders [descended from King Henry VII (see Tudor Roll, p 462)] (*Invercauld, Ballater, 40 Park Street, Grosvenor Square, W*), and has issue 1e to 2e

       1e Myrtle Farquharson

       2e Sylvia Farquharson

    2c Caroline Musgrave, *m* 8 Mar 1859, William Stanley of Dalegarth and Ponsonby, co Cumberland, J P , D L , *b* 14 Sept 1829, *d* 18 Dec 1881, and had issue 1d to 8d

    1d *Edward Stanley of Ponsonby Hall*, J P , D L , *b* 20 Nov 1859, *d unm* 26 *Feb* 1894

    2d William Stanley of Ponsonby Hall, J P , D L , *late* Capt Westmorland and Cumberland Yeo Cav (*Southwaite Hill, Carlisle*), *b* 10 Ap 1861

    3d Philip Stanley (21 *Palliser Road, West Kensington*), *b* 2 Mar 1870, *m* 3 Aug 1907, Norah, da of Edmund Stamp Mackrell of Craven House, Warminster, and has issue 1e to 2e

       1e Nicholas Austhwaite Stanley } (twins), *b* 28 Feb 1909
       2e Elizabeth Norah Stanley   }

[Nos 29567 to 29590

The Plantagenet Roll

4d *Charlotte Stanley*, d 18 *June* 1895 , m 10 *Dec* 1890, *John Henry Lowry*, and had issue 1e

  1e Caroline Lowry

5d Margaret Stanley, *m* 21 Ap 1897. the Rev Hildebrand Thomas Giles Alington, M A (Oxon), Rector of Newnham Courteney [Cadet of Alington of Swinhope] (*Newnham Courteney Rectory, Oxford*) and has issue 1e to 2e

  1e Noel Stanley Alington, *b* 4 Jan 1899

  2e Ursula Margaret Alington, *b* 9 Nov 1901

6d Lucy Mildred Stanley

7d Constance Madeline Stanley

8d Constance Augusta Stanley, *m* 17 July 1900 Alfred Russell Fordham of Melbourn Bury, J P , M A (Camb), Bar-at-Law (*Melbourn Bury, Royston*), and has issue 1e to 2c

  1e Alfred Stanley Fordham, *b* 2 Sept 1897

  2c Joyce Madeline Fordham

3c *Agnes Musgrave*, d 12 *Mar* 1901 , m 19 *June* 1862, *the Rev Malise Reginald Graham*, M A , Rector of Arthuret [Bt of Netherby Coll], b 15 *Feb* 1833 , d 18 *Nov* 1895 , *and had issue* 1d *to* 5d

  1d Arthur Malise Graham, *b* 1865

  2d *Reginald Graham*, *b* 22 *May* 1867 , d 15 *Feb* 1908 , m 21 *Jan* 1897, *Helen Dicia (2 Park Mansions, Albert Gate, S W), da of G S Herck of St Petersburg , and had issue* 1e

    1e Ernest Reginald Graham, *b* 7 Feb 1898

  3d Rev Ivor Charles Graham, Rector of Arthuret (*Arthuret Rectory, Long town, Cumberland*) *b* 1868

  4d Sophia Augusta Graham

  5d Maud Agnes Graham

4c *Sophia Musgrave m* 3 Aug 1869 Samuel Steuart Gladstone of Capenoch (*Capenoch, Dumfries* , 40 Lennox Gardens, S W), and has issue 1d to 2d

  1d Hugh Steuart Gladstone of Capenoch, J P , M A (Camb), F Z S , F R S E , *formerly* Lieut 3rd Batt K O S B , served in South Africa 1900-1902, has Queen's Medal with 3 Clasps and King's Medal with 2 Clasps (*Capenoch, Thornhill, Dumfries*), *b* 30 Ap 1877 , m 24 Jan 1906, Cecil Emily, da of Gustavus Arthur Talbot [E of Shrewsbury Coll], and has issue 1e

    1e John Gladstone, *b* 17 Jan 1907

  2d Winifred Steuart Gladstone, *m* 14 July 1896, Sydney Roden Fothergill of Lowbridge, J P , D L , Major Westmorland and Cumberland Hussars, served in S Africa as Capt 34th Imp Yeo 1902 (*Lowbridge House, Kendal, Westmorland*), and has issue 1e to 3e

    1e Richard Fothergill *b* 3 Jan 1901

    2e Christopher Francis Fothergill, *b* 21 Ap 1906

    3e Mildred Helen Sophia Fothergill

2a *Christopher Musgrave of Kempton Park, co Mttx*, d 11 *Aug* 1833 m *the Hon Elizabeth Anne [descended from the Lady Isabel Plantagenet] da of Andrew (Archer), 2nd Baron Archer [G B]*, d 8 *Aug* 1847 *and had issue*

See the Essex Volume, p 145, Nos 16461-16490

  3a *Jane Musgrave*, d (-) , m *Joseph Musgrave of Kypier* (see p 216)

  4a *Charlotte Musgrave*, d (-) , m 1774, *the Rev Charles Mordaunt* (see p 411), *Rector of Massingham* [2nt son of Sir Charles Mordaunt, 6th Bt [E]], d 22 *Jan* 1820, *and had issue* 1b

    1b *Rev Charles Mordaunt, Rector of Badgworth*, d (-) , m 1812, *Frances Harriet, da of James Spinow of Flax Bourton*, d 1866, *and had issue* 1c *to* 2c

      1c *John Mordaunt, 17th Lancers*, d 15 Nov 1881 , m 1st, 1843, *Harriet*
[Nos 29591 to 29641

# of The Blood Royal

Maria, da of Capt Cumberledge, R N , d 1849 , 2ndly, Isabel, da of Major Fletcher Norton Balmain, Madras Cavalry and had issue 1d to 9d

1d[1] James Spurow Mordaunt, Lieut-Col, *formerly Major Leinster Regt*, *b* 14 Nov 1843 , *m* (—), da of (—), and has issue 1e

   1e [son] Mordaunt, *b* 4 June 1886

2d[1] Francis Lionel Mordaunt

3d[1] John Mordaunt

4d[2] Harry Mordaunt

5d[2] Charles Mordaunt

6d[2] Philip Musgrave Mordaunt

7d[1] Mildred Mordaunt

8d[2] Harriet Isabel Mordaunt

9d[2] Katherine Mordaunt

2c *Charlotte Mordaunt*, d (-) , m *the Rev John Mathew, Rector of Chelvey, and had issue*

5a *Henrietta Musgrave*, d 16 June 1812 m 26 May 1774, Sir John Morris *of Clasemont, 1st Bt [U K], so cr 12 May 1806 b 15 July 1745, d 25 June 1819, and had issue* 1b to 3b

1b *Sir John Morris, 2nd Bt [U K], b* 14 July 1775 , d 21 Feb 1855, m 5 Oct 1809, *the Hon Lucy Juliana da of John (Byng), 5th Viscount Torrington [G B],* d 27 Nov 1881 *, and had issue* 1c to 7c

1c *Sir John Armine Morris 3rd Bt [U K], D L , b 13 July 1813 , d 8 Feb 1893, m 21 Dec 1847, Catherine, da of Ronald MacDonald, d 16 Mar 1890, and had issue* 1d to 7d

   1d Sir Robert Armine Morris of Clasemont, 4th Bt [U K], J P , D L , High Sheriff co Glamorgan 1900, *late Major Welsh Regt (Sketty Park, Swansea , West-cross, near Swansea), b* 27 July 1848 , m 12 Feb 1885, Lucy Augusta da of Thomas Cory of Nevill Court, Tunbridge Wells d 15 Nov 1902, and has issue 1e to 6e

      1e Tankerville Robert Armine Morris, *b* 9 June 1892

      2e John Torrington Morris, *b* 6 June 1896

      3e Lucy Gwladys Morris

      4e Valerie Ermyntrude Morris

      5e Dulcie Elaine Morris

      6e Sibyl Rowena Morris

   2d John Morris, *late Hon Lieut-Col Welsh Div R A (Castle House, Broad-stairs), b* 9 Sept 1850 *m* 25 July 1881, Jessie, da of William Fowler , and has issue (with a son, John Armine Robert, *b* 3 Oct 1882, d unm 16 May 1908, and a da d young) 1e

      1e Jessie Harriet Amy Blanch Morris

   3d George Cecil Morris, *b* 10 Ap 1852

   4d Arthur Ronald Morris, *b* 18 Nov 1855

   5d Herbert Morris, *b* 17 June 1858 , m 25 July 1880, Marjory Rachel, da of John Barton, and has issue 1e to 3e

      1e John Barton Morris, *b* 5 Mar 1882

      2e Herbert Morris

      3e Katherine Daisy Morris

   6d Henrietta Ellen Morris (*Harod, Sketty S O , Glamorganshire*), m as 2nd wife, 10 Oct 1876, Felix Hussey Webber, a Clerk in the House of Commons (see p 280), d 19 Ap 1905, and has issue 1e to 2e

      1e Horace Armine William Webber, Lieut R F A , *b* 28 Nov 1880

      2e Laura Gwendolen Webber, *m* 8 Sept 1899, Edmund Ussher David (*Yscal-log, Llandaff*), and has issue 1f to 2f

         1f Humphrey Edmund David, *b* 6 Sept 1900

         2f Rodney Felix Armine David, *b* 19 June 1907   [Nos 29642 to 29671

The Plantagenet Roll

7d *Amy Blanche Caroline Morris*, d 14 Aug 1907 m 1885, *Major Robert Bowen Robertson, 2nd Brig Welsh Div R A (Fairlawn, Chandlers, Hants)*, and had issue 1e to 6e

    1e Charles Airmine Bowen Robertson, b 1886

    2e Percy Robert Musgrave Robertson, b 1892

    3e Tudor Peregrine Morris Robertson, b 1896

    4e Amy Kate Alice Robertson

    5e Nellie Maude Robertson

    6e Rosamond Lucy Robertson

2c *George Byng Morris, J P , D L ,* b 25 Mar 1816, d 3 Dec 1899, m 23 Oct 1852, *Emily Matilda (Danygraig, Bridgend), da of Charles H Smith of Darwen Fawr, co Glamorgan ,* and had issue 1d to 10d

    1d Robert Townsend Morris, b 9 July 1853

    2d Charles Smith Morris, b 12 Dec 1854, m 1888, Maud Mary, da of the Rev George Alston, Rector of Studland, and has issue 1e to 4e

        1e Charles Alan Smith Morris, b 15 May 1895

        2e Mabel Travers Morris

        3e Daisy Emily Smith Morris

        4e Lucy Maud Morris

    3d George Lockwood Morris, *formerly Lieut Royal Monmouthshire Engineers Militia,* b 29 Jan 1859, m 1889, Wilhelmina, da of Thomas Cory , and has issue 1e to 3e

        1e Cedrick Lockwood Morris, b 1889

        2e Muriel Emily Morris

        3e Nancy Morris

    4d Musgrave Morris, b 18 Nov 1864, m 1892, Edith, da of K Lockhart of Minnedosa, Manitoba

    5d Thomas Byng Morris, b 24 July 1866, m 24 Aug 1898, Edith Amy, da of F S Bishop of Bennick, Dee Hills Park, Chester , and has issue 1e

        1e Rosamund Byng Morris

    6d Frank Hall Morris, b 16 July 1869

    7d Edith Charlotte Morris, m 1887, Francis Montagu Lloyd, J P , Bar -at-Law (*The Grange, Newnham-on-Severn*) and has issue 1e

        1e Leslie Skipp Lloyd, b 1891

    8d Fanny Matilda Morris, m 16 Sept 1882, Henry Bathurst Christie, C E , *formerly Ceylon P W D*

    9d Lucy Emily Morris, m 1887, Lieut -Col Henry Selwyn Goodlake, *late* 4th Batt Gloucestershire Regt , *formerly* Lancashire Fusiliers

    10d Rose Herbert Morris

3c *Frederick Morris, Comm R N ,* b 25 Jan 1819, d 23 Jan 1903, m 28 Jan 1854, *Agnes (Denmead, Cosham, Hants), da and h of Charles Brandford Lane of Castle Grant and Clermont, Barbados ,* and had issue 1d to 3d

    1d Frederick Morris, Major *late* Royal Welsh Fusiliers, Burmah (1885–1887), Hazara (1891), and China (1900) Medals and Clasps, is Sec Club of Western India, Poona (*Poona, Bombay*), b 20 Dec 1854 , m 1884, Sybil, da of John Rowland, B C S

    2d Charles Lane Morris, *formerly* Lieut 1st Warwickshire Mil , b 1857 , m 1903, Mabel Emily, da of the Rev Augustus Cooper of Upper Norwood, and Syleham Hall, co Suffolk

    3d Percy Byng Morris (*Denmead, Cosham, Hants*), b 1871

4c *Charles Henry Morris, C B , O L H , a Gen in the Army,* b 27 Feb 1824 , d 12 Oct 1887 , m 16 Sept 1869, *Lady Blanche [descended from George (Plantagenet), Duke of Clarence, K G (see Clarence Volume, p 628)] (Holly Mount, Lyndhurst, Hants), da of George Godolphin (Osborne), 8th Duke of Leeds [E], &c ,* and had issue 1d to 2d

[Nos 29672 to 29699

# of The Blood Royal

1d Ethel Harriet Morris, m 2 Dec 1905, Gerald Cloete, a Resident Magistrate, Orangia (*Frankfort, O R C*)

2d Lilla Guendolen Morris

5c *Henrietta Juliana Morris*, d 7 Oct 1871 m 2 Mar 1838, *Albert Lascelles Jenner*, 5th son of Robert Jenner of Wenvoe Castle, co Glamorgan, d Oct 1864, and had issue 1d to 2d

1d George Francis Butt Jenner, C M G, *formerly Minister Resident for Guatemala* 1897-1902, at Bogota 1892-1897, &c (*Villa les Alouettes, Cannes, St James'*), b 26 May 1840, m 1867, Stephanie, da of Alexis Emilianoff of Ragatova, Orel Govt, Russia

2d *Cecil Armine Jenner, Major Turkish Service*, d 1896, m and had issue 1e

1e Georgina Jenner

6c *Beatrice Charlotte Morris*, d (–) m *the Rev Thomas Charles Hyde Leaver*, M A, Rector of Rockhampton 1848-1859, d 1871 and had issue (a son and dr)

7c *Matilda Anne Cecilia Morris*, d 29 June 1906, m 26 May 1851, *Jesper Hall Livingstone of 12 The Strand, Ryde, I W*, d 1900, and had issue 1d to 3d

1d Hubert Armine Anson Livingstone C M G, R E, served in South Africa as Assist -Director of Railways, b 19 Aug 1863

2d Guy Livingstone, b 8 June 1868

3d Lucy Byng Livingstone, m 2 Oct 1875, Herman William Tinne, J P co Kent (*Union Club, S W*)

2b *Matilda Morris*, d (? s p) 5 July 1870, m 13 Nov 1807, *Edward Jesse of West Bromwich, co Stafford*

3b *Caroline Morris*, d (? s p) 26 Jan 1883, m 6 Sept 1824, *the Rev George Lillie Wodehouse Fauquier* [Nos 29700 to 29706]

103 Descendants if any, of the Rev CHRISTOPHER MUSGRAVE, Rector of Barking and Fellow of All Souls Coll, Oxon, d (–), m 1757, (—) widow of (—) PERFECT of Hatton Garden, and of Lieut -Col HANS MUSGRAVE (Table XII)

104 Descendants of the Rev CHARDIN MUSGRAVE, M A, D D, Provost of Oriel Coll, Oxon, 1757-1768 (Table XII), b c 1724, matric 3 Mar 1740 aged 16, d 8 Jan 1768, m CATHERINE, sister and h of Bartholomew Tipping of Woolley Park, co Berks (who d s p 13 Dec 1798), da of Bartholomew TIPPING, d 21 Feb 1795, and had issue 1a

1a *Mary Anne Musgrave of Woolley Park and Ibstone House, co Bucks, da and h*, b c 1767, d 28 Dec 1841, m 1788, her cousin, the Rev Philip Wroughton (see p 210), d 6 June 1812, and had issue 1b to 2b

1b *Bartholomew Wroughton of Woolley Park, co Berks, J P, D L*, b 18 Jan 1791, d s p 21 May 1858

2b *Philip Wroughton of Ibstone House and Woolley Park, J P, High Sheriff co Bucks* 1857, b 24 Dec 1805, d 28 Dec 1862, m 2ndly, 22 Ap 1841, *Blanche*, da of John Norris of Hughenden House, co Bucks, d 8 Jan 1903, and had issue 1c to 6c

1c *Philip Wroughton of Woolley Park, J P, D L, formerly M P for Berks* 1876-1885, and for the Abingdon Div 1885-1895, b 6 Ap 1846, d June 1910, m 4 Feb 1875, *Evelyn Mary*, da of Sir John Nedd, 1st Bt [U K] and had issue 1d to 7d

The Plantagenet Roll

1d Philip Musgrave Neeld Wroughton of Woolley Park, Lieut Berks Yeo (*Woolley Park, Wantage*), b 30 Aug 1887

2d Dorothy Florence Mary Wroughton, m 6 Aug 1908, the Rev Herbert Boyne Lavallin Puxley, Rector of Westonbirt (*Westonbirt Rectory, Glos*)

3d Muriel Evelyn Mary Wroughton

4d Florence Mary Wroughton, m 2 Feb 1904, Capt George Arthur Patrick Rennie, D S O, King's Royal Rifle Corps

5d Winifred Mary Wroughton, m 27 Ap 1901, Capt Sir Frederick Henry Walter Carden, 3rd Br [U K], 1st Life Guards (11 *Sloane Court, S W. Stargroves, Newbury*), and has issue 1e to 2e

   1e Henry Christopher Carden, b 16 Oct 1908

   2e Enid Evelyn Carden

6d Violet Blanche Mary Wroughton

7d Mary St Quintin Mary Wroughton

2c *Edward Norris Wroughton*, b 19 *July* 1847, d 11 *Oct* 1902, m 1872, *Florence, da of Henry Farren, d 29 Mar 1878, and had issue 1d to 3d*

1d John Bartholomew Wroughton, Capt Royal Sussex Regt, b 14 Feb 1874, m 7 Dec 1904, Alma May, da of Willoughby Oakes of Holmbrook, Farnborough

2d Edward Henry Wroughton (3 *Hare Court, Temple*), b 29 Oct 1875

3d Arthur Charles Wroughton, Lieut South Lancashire Regt, b 4 July 1877

3c William Musgrave Wroughton, Master of the Pytchley Hounds 1894–1902, and of the Woodland and Pytchley Hounds 1903–1908 (*Creation Lodge, Northampton, 77 Chester Square, S W*), b 24 Sept 1850 m 24 June 1880, Edith Constance, da of Henry Cazenove of Lilies, Aylesbury, and has issue 1d to 3d

1d Musgrave Cazenove Wroughton, b 1 Oct 1891

2d Cicely Musgrave Wroughton

3d Dulce Wroughton

4c Emma Louisa Wroughton, m 13 July 1861, Henry Joseph Toulmin of The Pré, *formerly* of Childwickbury, co Herts, J P, D L, Capt Herts Yeo Cav, *late* 13th Light Dragoons (*The Pré, near St Albans*), and has issue 1d to 10d

1d Henry Wroughton Toulmin, b 2 Mar 1871

2d Philip Musgrave Toulmin, b 1 Feb 1887

3d Mary Toulmin, m 1st, 26 Nov 1890, Algernon William George (Evans-Freke), 9th Baron Carbery [I] [descended from George (Plantagenet), Duke of Clarence, K G (see the Clarence Volume, p 262)], d 12 June 1898, 2ndly, 11 Feb 1902, Arthur Wellesley Sandford, M D (*Frankfield House, co Cork*), and has issue 1e to 4e

   1e John (Evans-Freke), 10th Baron Carbery [I] (*Castle Freke, co Cork*), b 10 May 1892

   2e Hon Ralfe Evans-Freke, b 23 July 1897

   3e Christopher Sandford, b 5 Dec 1902

   4e Anthony Sandford, b 14 Aug 1905

4d Evelyn Toulmin m 16 July 1901, Edward MacGregor Duncan (*Fernhill Cottage, Windsor Forest*)

5d Florence Josephine Toulmin, m 11 Feb 1897, Herbert Legard Fife, J P. (see p 191) [also a descendant of Edward III through Mortimer-Percy] (*Staindrop House, near Darlington*), and has issue 1e to 2e

   1e Dorothy Florence Fife

   2e Marjorie Agnes Fife

6d Edith Mabel Toulmin, m 19 June 1906, the Rev Alan Chaplin, M A (Camb), Rector of Chesterton [son of Clifford Chaplin of Broughton Astley Hall] (*Chesterton Rectory, Peterborough*), and has issue 1e to 2e

   1e Stephen Chaplin, b 30 Mar 1907

   2e Beryl Chaplin, b 28 Oct 1909

7d Lilian Toulmin, *unm*   [Nos 29707 to 29738

# of The Blood Royal

8d Constance Mary Toulmin, *unm*

9d Gladys May Toulmin, *unm*

10d Isobel Marguerite Toulmin, *unm*

5c *Mary Anne Wroughton*, d 14 *July* 1891, m 24 *May* 1870, *Col John Bonham of Ballintaggart, R H A , J P cos Kildare and Wicklow, and High Sheriff co Carlow* 1900 (*Ballintaggart, Colbinstown, co Kildare*), *and had issue 1d to 5d*

1d Francis Warren Bonham, *b* 1871

2d John Wroughton Bonham, *b* 1875

3d Georgina Maye Bonham

4d Mary Alice Bonham

5d Margaret Leslie Bonham

6c Blanche Caroline Wroughton.   [Nos 29739 to 29747

105 Descendants if any, of MARY MUSGRAVE, *m* 1st, HUGH LUMLEY, 2ndly, JOHN PIGOTT (Table XII)

106. Descendants of JULIA MUSGRAVE (Table XII), *d* 1778, *m* WILLIAM HASELL of Dalemain, co Cumberland, *b* 1716, *d* 1778; and had issue 1a to 4a

1a *Christopher Hasell*, 3rd *son, but in his issue* (6 *Ap* 1794) *h* , d (-), m (—), *da of* (—) *Goade*, d (-), *and had issue 1b to 2b*

1b *Edward Hasell of Dalemain*, b 1765, d 24 *Dec* 1825, m 1st, 1792, *Elizabeth, da of William Carus of Kirkby Lonsdale*, d 1810, 2ndly, 1812, *Jane, da of the Rev Robert Whitehead, Rector of Cronside*, d *Nov* 1816, *and had issue* 1c *to* 7c

1c *Edward Williams Hasell of Dalemain, J P , D L , Lieut -Col Comdg Westmorland and Cumberland Yeo Cav and Chairman of Quarter Sessions*, b 10 *July* 1796, d 7 *Ap* 1872, m 13 *July* 1826, *Dorothea, da of Edward King of Hungerhill, co York*, d 15 *June* 1885, *and had issue 1d to 8d*

1d John Edward Hasell of Dalemain, J P , D L , High Sheriff co Cumberland 1887, B A (Oxon), *late* Capt Westmorland and Cumberland Yeo Cav (*Dalemain, Penrith*), b 19 Sept 1839, m 4 July 1877, Frances Maud, da of Henry Flood of View Mount, co Kilkenny, and has issue 1e to 2e

1e Dorothy Julia Hasell

2e Eva Frances Hatton Hasell

2d Rev George Edmund Hasell, Rector of Aikton and Hon Canon of Carlisle (*Aikton Hall, Wigton, Cumberland*), b 26 Sept 1847, m 27 Oct 1880, Helen, da of the Rev William Sinclair [and grandda of Sir John Sinclair, 1st Bt [G B], P C , M P , F R S], and has issue 1e to 2e

1e Edward William Hasell, Thomas Exhibitioner, Queen's Coll , Oxon , 1906, b 16 Jan 1888

2e Godfrey Sinclair Hasell, b 2 Nov 1889

3d Dorothea Hasell

4d Elizabeth Julia Hasell

5d Alice Jane Hasell, m 5 Sept 1861, J M Formby

6d Mary Hasell, m 28 Sept 1854, W Parker

7d Henrietta Maria Hasell, m June 1876, H W Verey, Official Referee.

8d Frances Anne Hasell

2c *Christopher Hasell, Capt Bengal Army*, b 1814, d (? s p) *May* 1861

3c *William Lowther Hasell, Capt Bengal Army*, d (? s p) *June* 1849
                              [Nos 29748 to 29759.

The Plantagenet Roll

4c[1] *Mary Anne Hasell*, d *shortly before Oct* 1835, m *Sept* 1825, *the Rev Sir Christopher John Musgrave, 9th Bt* [*E*], d 11 *May* 1834, *and had issue*

See p 197, Nos 29520-29573

5c[1] *Julia Hasell*, d (? *unm*)

6c[1] *Jane Hasell*, d (? *unm*)

7c[2] *Maria Hasell*, d *Dec* 1855, m 11 *Ap* 1836 *Major George Graham, Registrar-Gen of Births Marriages, and Deaths* 1839-1879 [*Bt of Netherby Coll*], d 20 *May* 1888, *and had issue*

See the Tudor Roll, p 507, Nos 34307-34310, and Essex Volume, Tudor Supplement, pp 494-495, Nos 34307-34310 :

2b *Eliza Hasell*, d (-), m *Richard Haughton* (see below)

2a *John Hasell*, d (?)

3a *Julia Hasell*, d (-), m *Richard Haughton of Liverpool*, *and had* (*with possibly other*) *issue* 1b

1b *Richard Haughton*, d (-), m *Eliza* (see above), *da of Christopher Hasell*

1a *Jane Hasell*, b 22 *Ap* 1745, d 11 *Aug* 1820 m *as 2nd wife*, 3 *Oct* 1765, *William Salmond*, b 4 *Aug* 1737, d 4 *Aug* 1779, *and had issue* 1b *to* 2b

1b *James Hanson Salmond of Waterfoot, co Cumberland, Major General H E I C S, a distinguished Indian officer, was offered but declined a Baronetcy*, b 17 *Aug* 1766, d 1 *Nov* 1837, m 1st, 2 *July* 1798, *Louisa, da of David Scott of Dunninald, M P*, d *June* 1805, *and had issue* 1c

1c *James Salmond of Waterfoot, J P, Lieut-Col Westmorland and Cumberland Yeo Cav, previously 2nd Dragoon Guards, &c*, b 15 *June* 1805, d 24 *Nov* 1880, m 16 *Aug* 1832, *Emma Isabella* [*descended from George, Duke of Clarence, K G*], *da of D'Ewes Coke of Brookhill Hall, co Derby, J P, D L*, d 8 *Mar* 1886 *and had issue*

See the Clarence Volume, pp 186-187, Nos 3131-3176

2b *Francis Salmond, Capt H E I C S, and Master Attendant, Fort Marlbro, Sumatra*, b 28 *Nov* 1770, d 23 *Nov* 1823 m 21 *Dec* 1805, *Anne, da of Charles Salmond*, d 22 *Aug* 1812, *and had issue* 1c *to* 3c

1c *James William Salmond, Resident Councillor at Penang and Malacca*, b 16 *Aug* 1807, d 12 *Mar* 1818, m 3 *Oct* 1839, *Fenella Cullen, da of William Alexander Mackenzie of Seatwell and Strathgarve, co Ross*, d (-), *and had issue* 1d *to* 3d

1d *Francis Mackenzie Salmond, Lieut-Col Royal Scots Fusiliers*, b 11 *Mar* 1841, d 1 *Nov* 1900, m 22 *July* 1868, *Isabel Clara, sister of Sir R C Hart, V C, da of Lieut Gen Henry George Hart of Netherby, co Dorset, and had issue* 1e *to* 4e

1e Francis Mackenzie Salmond, b 15 Oct 1872

2e. Hubert Mackenzie Salmond, b 18 Dec 1874

3e Henry Bertram Salmond, b 8 Jan 1878

4e Isabel Frank Fenella Salmond

2d Fenella Salmond

3d *Julia Mary Salmond*, m 27 *Aug* 1879, the Rev. Theodore Crane Dupuis, Preb of Wells and Vicar of Burnham (*Burnham Vicarage, S O, Somerset*)

2c *Louisa Jane Salmond*, d (-), m 1843, *Andrew Grieve of Edinburgh, J P, and had issue*

3c *Emily Parker Salmond*, b 9 *June* 1812, d 9 *May* 1863, m 1850, *the Rev Charles Adam John Smith, Vicar of Macclesfield, and had issue*

[Nos 29760 to 29872

107 Descendants, if any, of BARBARA MUSGRAVE (Table XII), d (-), m 1st, JOHN HOGG of Scotland, 2ndly, CHIEF BARON IDLE

# of The Blood Royal

108 Descendants of ANNE MUSGRAVE (Table XII) *d* 1780, *m* HENRY AGLIONBY of Nunnery, co Cumberland, High Sheriff for that co 1763, &c, *b* 1715, *d* 1770, and had issue 1*a* to 4*a*

    1*a* *Christopher Aglionby of Nunnery,* d s p 1785, *last male of his family*
    2*a* *Elizabeth Aglionby, da and co-h* in 1785, d (? s p) 1822, m (—) *Bamber*

    3*a* *Anne Aglionby, da and co-h* in 1785, d (-), m *the Rev Samuel Bateman of Newbiggin Hall, co Cumberland, and had issue (apparently an only son)* 1*b*
    1*b* *Henry Aglionby Bateman, afterwards Aglionby of Newbiggin Hall and Nunnery, M P*, b 28 Dec 1790, d (? s p) 1854

    4*a* *Mary Aglionby, da and co h* in 1785, d 8 Sept 1816, m *John Orfeur Yates of Skirwith Abbey, co Cumberland, and had issue* 1*b to* 2*b*
    1*b* *Francis Yates, afterwards Aglionby of Nunnery, M P*, b 1780, d 1 July 1840, m 8 Feb 1814, *Mary, da of John Matthews of Wigton Hall, co Cumberland,* d 20 Aug 1854, *and had issue (with an elder da who d unm)* 1*c to* 2*c*
    1*c* *Mary Aglionby, da and co h,* d 7 Aug 1882, m *Ap 1845, the Rev Beilby Porteus, Canon of Carlisle,* d (-), *and had issue* 1*d to* 4*d*
    1*d* July Mary Porteus, da and co-h, m 27 Oct 1869, Capt James Mortimer Webster, 18th Royal Irish, s p
    2*d* Mary Aglionby Porteus da and co-h, m 28 Sept 1880, Comm the Hon Henry Noel Shore, R N [3rd son of Charles John, 2nd Baron Teignmouth [I]] (*Mount Elton, Clevedon*), and has issue 1*e to* 3*e*
    1*e* Hugh Aglionby Shore, in Public Works Dept, India, b 12 July 1881
    2*e* Lionel Henry Porteus Shore, Lieut R N b 18 Nov 1882
    3*e* Noel Beilby Porteus Shore, Indian Police, b 6 July 1887

    3*d* Emma Porteus, da and co-h, m 1st, 20 Jan 1880, Arthur Morres Hill, d (-), 2ndly, (—) Platt, s p
    4*d* Henrietta Porteus, da and co-h, m Major-Gen Robert Cole, Indian Army, and has issue 1*e to* 4*e*
    1*e* Alan Aglionby Cole, b 1886
    2*e* Humphrey Porteus Cole, b 1894
    3*e* Ursula Cole
    4*e* Doris Grace Cole

    2*c* *Jane Aglionby, da and co-h,* d 21 May 1874 m *Ap 1847, Charles Fetherstonhaugh of Staffield Hall, Penrith,* d (-), *and had issue* 1*d*
    1*d* *Elizabeth Aglionby Fetherstonhaugh, da and h,* d 1885 m 18 Oct 1871, Col *Arthur Cooper, now (R L 11 Aug 1885) Aglionby, of Staffield Hall and Drawdykes, C B, J P (Staffield Hall, Carlisle), and had issue* 1*e to* 2*e*
    1*e* Arthur Charles Aglionby, Bar-at-Law, Capt 3rd Batt Connaught Rangers, b 1872
    2*e* Constance Muriel Aglionby

    2*b* *John Yates of Virginia, U S,* b *at Skirwith Abbey, Cumberland,* 3 Ap 1779, d *at Nunnery 6 July* 1851, m 7 Ap 1803, *Julia, da of Robert W Lovell of Fredericksburg, Virginia,* d 8 June 1866, *and had issue (with 2 other sons and a da, Mrs Keyes, who* d s p) 1*c to* 5*c*
    1*c* *Charles Yates, afterwards (1851) Aglionby, of Nunnery,* b *at Germanna, Virginia,* 4 June 1807, d 30 Jan 1891, m 28 May 1844, *Fanny, da of Col James W Walker of Madison Co, Virginia,* d 29 Jan 1902, *and had issue* 1*d to* 3*d*
    1*d* Rev Francis Keyes Aglionby, M A, D D, Vicar of Christ Church, Westminster, *formerly Rector of Hampton Poyle, late of Nunnery, which he sold* 1892

[Nos 29873 to 29886

207

The Plantagenet Roll

(*Christ Church Vicarage, Victoria Street, Westminster, S W , Mount Pleasant, West Virginia, U S*), *b* 22 Nov 1848 , *m* 9 Aug 1876, Amy, da of the Right Rev Edward Henry Bickersteth, Lord Bishop of Exeter , and has issue 1e to 7e

    1e Francis Basil Aghonby, B C L , Solicitor, *b* 25 July 1878

    2e Charles Edward Aghonby, Lieut R N , *b* 26 June 1882

    3e John Orfeur Aghonby, *b* 16 Mar 1884

    4e Arthur Hugh Aghonby, B A (Oxon), *b* 4 Nov 1885

    5e Wilfred Henry Aghonby, *b* 16 Ap 1890

    6e Rosa Frances Aghonby

    7e Alice Mary Aghonby

    2d John Orfeur Aghonby, *b* 1 Mar 1851 , *unm*

    3d Jeanette Elizabeth Aghonby

    2c *Francis Yates of Flowing Springs, Jefferson Co , W Va , Col Virginia State Militia and a Member of the Virginian Senate,* b at *Walnut Grove, Jefferson Co , W Va ,* 24 *Sept* 1811, d at *Flowing Springs* 1 *Jan* 1892, m 1st, 1840, *Ann Elizabeth, da of Bacon Burwell of Jefferson Co , d at Flowing Springs* 28 *June* 1862, 2ndly, at *Charlestown,* 25 *June* 1863, Sydney *Virginia, da of Jabez Berry Rooker of co Stafford,* d 22 *Ap* 1899 , *and had issue* 1d *to* 5d

    1d *John Orfeur Yates, Confederate States Army,* b at *Flowing Springs* 22 *Ap* 1845 , d at *Gap View, in that co , Sept* 1899 , m at *Wytheville* 31 *Oct* 1878, *Emma (Roanoke, Virginia), da of Col Joseph Kent of Wythe Co , Va , and had issue* 1e *to* 6e

    1e Francis Yates, *b* at Wytheville

    2e Joseph Kent Yates, *b* at Wytheville

    3e Lewis Cochran Yates, *b* at Wytheville

    4e Frances Stuart Yates, *m* 2 Jan 1907, Wayte Bell Timberlake, Merchant (*Staunton, Va*), and has issue 1f

    1f Wayte Bell Timberlake, *b* 23 Nov 1908

    5e Mary Harrison Yates, *unm*

    6e Bettie Montgomery Yates, *unm*

    2d Arthur Bacon Yates (*Fredericksburg, Virginia*), *b* at Flowing Springs 28 July 1848 , *m* at Fredericksburg 23 Ap 1872, Susan, da of James Hord Bradley of Fredericksburg, Va , and has issue 1e to 4e

    1e Lucilla Bradley Yates, *unm*

    2e Ann Burwell Yates, *m* at Washington, D C , 2 June 1898, Alpheus Wilson Embrey of Fredericksburg, and has issue 1f to 4f

    1f Alpheus Wilson Embrey, *b* in Fredericksburg 13 Feb 1901

    2f Wilford Smith Embrey, *b* there 24 Aug 1907

    3f Anne Elizabeth Embrey

    4f Susan Julia Embrey

    3e Mary Louise Yates, *m* Louis Albert van Ericksen, and has issue 1f

    1f Mary Louisa van Ericksen, *b* in Birmingham, Alabama, 18 Jan 1900

    4e Susan Mallory Yates, *unm*

    3d[1] Janet Burwell Yates, *b* in Jefferson Co afsd , *m* at Flowing Springs 1 Nov 1870, Charles Valentine Wagner of Baltimore, Maryland, Cotton Broker, *formerly* Confederate States Army, served four years and six weeks under Generals Robert E Lee and Stonewall Jackson (1649 *Amsterdam Avenue,* 141st *Street, New York*), s p

    4d[1] Octavia Latane Yates (*Woodville Rappahannock Co , Virginia*), *b* at Flowing Springs afsd , *m* 29 Oct 1868, William Stephenson Mason of Charlestown, Jefferson Co , Stock Raiser, *formerly* Confederate States Army , and has issue 1e to 3e

    1e Anne Isabelle Mason, *b* in Charlestown afsd , *unm*

    2e Margaret Duncan Mason, *b* in Charlestown afsd , *unm*

    3e Virginia Stephenson Mason, *b* in Glen Ayre, Rapp Co , Va , *unm*

[Nos 29887 to 29917

208

# of The Blood Royal

5d² Mary Brooke Yates b at Flowing Springs afsd 8 Jan 1866, m there 14 Oct 1891, Adrian Garrett Wynkoop, Attorney-at-Law (306 South Samuel Street, Charlestown, W Va), and has issue 1e to 5e

    1e Adrian Garrett Wynkoop, b 20 Nov 1893

    2e Francis Yates Wynkoop, b 28 July 1899

    3e Brooke Lovell Wynkoop, b 3 Aug 1902

    4e Sydney Virginia Wynkoop

    5e Julia Yates Wynkoop

3c Janet Yates, b at Fox Neck, Culpepper Co, Va, 12 Jan 1804, d 25 Feb 1875, m in Jefferson Co, W Va, 19 Oct 1826, George Brooke Beall of Walnut Grove, Jefferson Co, W Va, b 1802, d 20 Aug 1855 and had issue (with 2 other sons and 2 das d unm) 1d to 5d

    1d Hezekiah Beall (Wortham, Texas), b 17 Aug 1830, m 1st, 4 May 1869, Nancy Jane, da of William O Alexander of Freestone Co, Texas, d s p s 1870, 2ndly, 9 Aug 1870, Arthurilla Wilmoth, da of Thomas Petigrew Groves of Freestone Co, afsd, and has issue (with a son and da d young) 1e to 7e

        1e George Brooke Beall (Armurillo, Texas), b 21 Feb 1872, unm

        2e William Willis Beall, b 15 June 1879, unm

        3e John Yates Beall, b 2 July 1882, m at Wortham, Texas, 20 July 1902, Eva Alice, da of (—) Evans of Wortham, and has issue 1f to 3f

            1f George William Beall, b 19 May 1908

            2f Ruth Elizabeth Beall, b 29 May 1903

            3f Lillian Adina Beall, b 15 Aug 1905

        4e Mary Yates Beall, unm

        5e Emma Webb Beall, m at Wortham afsd 16 Oct 1898, John Thomas Bounds (Wortham, Texas), and has issue 1f to 3f

            1f Kenneth Bounds, b 22 Aug 1902

            2f Thomas Allen Bounds b 27 July 1904

            3f Charles Hezekiah Bounds, b 29 Ap 1908

        6e Annie Elizabeth Beall, unm

        7e Julia Lovell Beall, unm

    2d John Yates Beall, Confederate States Navy, b 1 Jan 1835, d unm (being taken prisoner at Suspension Bridge, N Y, and shot in Governor's Island) 24 Feb 1865

    3d Mary Yates Keyes Beall (Charlestown, W Virginia), b 2 Jan 1829, unm

    4d Anne Orfeur Beall, b 24 June 1839, m 1 Dec 1870, David E Henderson, formerly Confederate States Army (Charlestown, W Virginia), and has issue

    5d Elizabeth Beall (Charlestown, W Virginia), b 6 May 1842, m 26 Ap 1881, Richard Henderson, Confederate States Army, d 22 June 1905

4c Anne Yates, b at Walnut Grove, Jefferson Co, Virginia, 15 July 1815, d at Sunny Sid., Madison Co, Virginia, 13 Ap 1857, m 18 Nov 1847, the Rev William Thomas Leavell, d at Hedgesville, Berkeley Co, W Va, 25 Aug 1899, and had issue 1d to 5d

    1d William Thomas Leavell, B L, M A, and Medalist of Washington and Lee University, Lexington, Va, d 4 Feb 1900, m 14 Ap 1898, Lucy Nelson, da of Robert Nelson Pendleton, and had issue 1e

        1e William Thomas Leavell (a da), b posthumous

    2d Rev Francis Keyes Leavell, in Holy Orders of the American Episcopal Church, M A, Medalist Washington and Lee University, d 19 Dec 1886, m Elizabeth Hunter, da of Charles Thurston, and had issue 1e

        1e Elizabeth Hunter Leavell

    3d Julia Yates Leavell (Charlestown, W Virginia), m at Media, Jefferson Co, W Virginia, 12 Oct 1869, Major Edward H McDonald, late 11th Virginia Cavalry, Confederate States Army, and has issue 1e to 10e [Nos 29918 to 29943

209

1c Edward Leavell McDonald, *b* 3 Sept 1870

2c William Thomas McDonald, *b* 6 Aug 1875

3c Angus William McDonald, *b* 2 May 1877

4c Peerce Naylor McDonald, *b* 5 July 1879

5c Marshall Woodrow McDonald (*Louisville, Kentucky*), *b* 24 Aug 1884

6c John Yates McDonald, *b* 10 Jan 1887

7c Francis Leavell McDonald, *b* 28 May 1891

8c Anne Yates McDonald

9c Julia Terrill McDonald

10c Mary Aghonby McDonald

4d Anne Elizabeth Leavell, *m* 30 Oct 1874, John Moncure Daniel, Clerk of Circuit Court, Jefferson Co , W Va , *formerly* Confederate States Army (*Charlestown, West Virginia*), and has issue 1e to 6e

1e William Aghonby Daniel, *b* in Jefferson Co 11 July 1878

2e John Moncure Daniel, *b* 26 May 1883, *m* 15 Dec 1908, Margaret, da of the Rev Richard Wilde Micou, D D , Professor at Episcopal Theological Seminary, Fairfax Co , W Va

3e Francis Warwick Daniel, *b* 4 July 1886

4e Anne Leavell Daniel

5e Elizabeth Julia Daniel

6e Mary Mildred Daniel

5d *Mary Aghonby Leavell*, d 10 May 1900, m *at Zion Church, Charlestown, W Virginia*, 31 Oct 1884 *Capt William R Johnson, formerly Confederate States Army (The Crescent, West Virginia) , and had issue* 1e to 4e

1e William Ransom Johnson

2e John Pegram Johnson

3e Francis Leavell Johnson

4e Mary Aghonby Johnson

5c *Julia Yates, b at Walnut Grove afsd 25 July 1819 , d there 3 June 1895 , m there 1 Oct 1839, William Lovell Terrill, b at Fredericksburg, Va , 9 Mar 1815 , d 15 Feb 1890, and had issue (with a son, John Uriel, d unm 15 Nov 1878, and a da , Anne Elizabeth, d unm 10 Feb 1900)* 1d

1d Julia Lovell Terrill (*Charles Town, West Virginia, U S A*)

[Nos 29944 to 29965

109 Descendants, if any, of ELIZABETH MUSGRAVE (Table XII), *d* (–), *m* 1st, EDWARD SPRAGGE of Greenwich , 2ndly, JOHN JOHNSTONE of London

110 Descendants of DOROTHY MUSGRAVE (Table XII), *b c* 1727 , *d* 31 Oct 1799, *bno* at St Thomas' Church, Salisbury, M I , *m* the Rev WILLIAM WROUGHTON, Rector of Welbourn, co Lincoln [son of the Rev Charles Wroughton, Rector of Codford St Peter, co Wilts, 1681–1729], *b* 1716, *d* 3 Aug 1770, and had issue 1a to 5a

1a *Rev Philip Wroughton, b* 1758 , d 6 June 1812 m 1788, *Mary Anne* (see p 203), *da of the Rev Chardin Musgrave, D D , d 28 Dec 1841, and had issue* See p 203, Nos 29707–29749

2a *George Wroughton of Adwick-le-Street, near Doncaster, Col 3rd West York Militia, b at West Wycombe c 1759 , d at Newington 24 Oct 1816 , m in India 17 Ap 1787, Diana Elizabeth, da of the Rev Thomas Denton, M A , Rector of Ashtead, Surrey, d 5 June 1849 , and had issue (with 4 sons and 2 das d s p)* 1b to 6b

[Nos 29966 to 30006

# of The Blood Royal

1b Robert Wroughton, Major 69th Bengal Infantry, and Dep Surveyor-Gen of India, b at Adwick 2 Aug. 1797, d at Futteghur, Bengal, 14 Feb 1850, m Sophia, da of Capt Wright, and had issue (with 2 sons who d s p) 1c to 6c

1c Frederic Turner Wroughton, C B, Col in the Army, b 20 Mar 1821, d 17 Sept 1878, m Sarah Cecilia Ann, da of (—) Fassell, d in Christchurch, N Z, 1908, and had issue 1d to 4d

1d Cecil Frederick Maurice Wroughton, Manager Union Bank, Ashburton (Ashburton, N Z), b 2 May 1859, m Ap 1891, Fanny Theresa, da of the Hon Alfred de Bathe Brandon of Wellington, N Z and has issue 1e to 2e

1e Frederick Brandon Wroughton, b 21 Nov 1897

2e Lucy Cecilia Wroughton, b 21 Mar 1892

2d Eva Hannah Wroughton, m George Callender of Christchurch, N Z

3d Mabel Fanny Wroughton, m James Callender of Invercargill, N Z, and has issue

4d Lilian Emma Wroughton, m (—) Addley of Christchurch, N Z

2c Robert Chardin Wroughton, Gen in the Army, b 3 Sept 1822 d Nov 1871, m Sarah, da of Col R L Stacy, C B, A D C, and had issue 1d to 4d

1d Robert Charles Wroughton, Indian Forest Service (16 Spencer Mansions, Queen's Club Gardens, W), m s p

2d Henry Bruce Wroughton, Capt R N (Ireland), m s p

3d Lewis Wroughton, Secretary to Basutoland Govt (Maseru, Basutoland), b (—), m 23 Ap 1902, Frances Charlotte, da of (—) Lloyd, and has issue 1e to 2e

1e Robert Lewis Wroughton

2e Henry Banastre Wroughton

4d Edith Isabella Wroughton, m Edward Turner (Hillbrook, Estcourt, Natal), and has issue (9 children)

3c Charles Nesbitt Wroughton, R N, b 4 Sept 1835, went to New Zealand, and has not since been heard of

4c Sophia Isabella Wroughton, b at Goruckpur, India, 26 July 1826, d 22 Dec 1879, m at Allyghur India, 15 Feb 1848, Capt George William Wright Fulton, Bengal Engineers, b 23 Nov 1825 d (being killed at the siege of Lucknow) 14 Sept 1857, and had issue 1d to 5d

1d Frederick Fulton (Napier, New Zealand), b 1 June 1850, unm

2d Robert Fulton, Col Indian Arms (Mitcham Lodge, Kimbolton Avenue, Bedford), b 12 July 1852, m 7 July 1894, Blanche Eleanor Moffatt, da of Col D W Martin, 75th Regt, and has issue 1e to 2e

1e John Oswald Fulton, b 16 July 1897

2e Gwendoline Fulton, b 19 Jan 1896

3d William Wright Fulton (Taihmu, Mangaweka, Rangitiki, New Zealand), b 30 May 1854, m 1879, Helen, da of R Bett of Marton, N Z and has issue 1e to 4e

1e Howard Fulton, b 9 June 1880

2e Norman Fulton, b 23 Mar 1883

3e Frederick Robert Fulton, b 2 June 1890

4e George William Wright Fulton, b 7 Mar 1901

4d George Sibley Fulton (Marton, Wanganui, New Zealand), b 27 Sept 1857, unm

5d Ellen Charlotte Fulton, m 1881, Charles William Wallace of Messrs R G Shaw & Co, of 88 Bishopsgate Street Within (6 Langford Place, St Johns Wood, N W), and has issue 1e to 5e

1e Charles William Wallace

2e Robert Wallace

3e Helen Charlotte Wallace

4e Tara Wallace

5e Jessie Helen Wallace

[Nos 30007 to 30034

211

The Plantagenet Roll

5c *Ellen Wroughton*, b 29 Oct 1837, d *at Dunedin, N Z*, 20 Nov 1887, m *at Mecan Meer, Punjaub*, 13 Jan 1858, *Lieut Gen John Fulton, B A*, b 4 Oct 1827, d *at Christchurch, N Z*, 14 July 1899, *and had issue (with a son and da d s p)* 1d to 8d

1d Sydney Wroughton Fulton, Stockbroker (369 *Collins Street, Melbourne, Victoria*), b 30 Jan 1859, m at St Columba's, Hawthorne, Victoria, 3 Jan 1894, Elizabeth Maude, da of John Simpson Armstrong, Q C, Bar -at-Law, and has issue 1c to 3c

    1c Sheelah Alice Wroughton Fulton, b at Brighton, Victoria, 20 Jan 1895

    2c Eileen Maude Wroughton Fulton, b at Heidelberg, Victoria, 16 Oct 1896

    3c Lorna Hope Wroughton Fulton, b at Melbourne 23 Nov 1899

2d Perceval James Fulton (*Warrnambool, Victoria*), b at Amritsur, India, 26 Mar 1860, unm

3d Walter Menzies Fulton (*Box 5465, Johannesburg*), b at Amritsur afsd 30 Oct 1866, m in St John's Cathedral, Napier, N Z, 21 Nov 1896, Adèle, Gwendoline (see p 105), da of Horace William Baker, s p

4d Onslow Henry Crofton Fulton (*Wallsend, New South Wales*), b at Amritsur afsd 21 Mar 1868, unm

5d Harry Townsend Fulton, D S O Major 2nd Batt 2nd Gurkhas, b at Dalhousie India 15 Mar 1869, m at St Thomas' Cathedral, Bombay, 1905, Ada Hermione, da of John Dixon of Auckland, N Z

6d Bertram Sproule Fulton, National Bank of South Africa (*Pretoria*), b at Lee, co Kent, 12 June 1871, m at Wellington, N Z, 1902, Lillian, da of (—) Loveday, and has issue 1e

    1e Hylmer Adèle Fulton, b 1906

7d Ethel Ann Fulton

8d Hilda Caroline Fulton, m 15 Sept 1908, Richard Bohm of the New Zealand and Union S S C Service (*Wellington, N Z*), and has issue 1e

    1e John Richard Fulton Bohm, b at Auckland, N Z, 24 June 1909

6c *Fanny Wroughton*, b 8 Jan 1844, d *at Ealing* 11 Nov 1897, m *at Amritsur, Punjaub*, 7 Nov 1863, *Col Oswald Menzies, Indian Army (32 Mount Park Road, Ealing)*, *and had issue* 1d to 3d

1d Georgina Fanny Menzies, m 7 Nov 1889, Robert Loraine Ker, and has issue 1e to 8e

    1e Thomas Menzies Ker, b 12 July 1890

    2e Margaret Ker, b 31 May 1891

    3e Joan Ker, b 19 Sept 1892

    4e Elsie Ker, b 28 Mar 1894

    5e Phyllis Ker, b 25 Mar 1897

    6e Helen Ker, b 7 Ap 1901

    7e Doris Ker, b 15 Oct 1903

    8e Ruth Ker, b 15 May 1905

2d Eliza Marion Menzies, m 4 Dec 1894, Capt Julian Stuart Dallas, Indian Army, and has issue 1e to 2e

    1e Juliet Dallas

    2e Eileen Dallas

3d Alice Norah Menzies, unm

2b *John Chardin Wroughton, H E I C S*, b at *Adwick* 19 May 1799, d *at Paris* 30 Nov 1854, m 2ndly, 1835, *Georgina Grace, da of the Hon Henry Chamier, Member of Council, Madras*, d at *Coimbatore* 6 Dec 1847, *and had issue (with 2 sons who d s p)* 1c to 1c

1c William Nesbitt Wroughton, Col Indian Army (1 *Lansdowne Road, Bedford*), b at Ootacamund 6 Feb 1840, m 1 Oct 1859, Morgiana C, da of Col J Bird, and has issue (with a son d s p) 1d to 7d.   [Nos 30035 to 30061

# of The Blood Royal

1*d* Henry William Frank Wroughton, in Salt Revenue Dept (*Bellary, India*), *b* 8 Aug 1860, *m* at Coonoor, Nilgiris, S India, 1 June 1887, Edith Amy, da of James Tavenor Nash, and has issue 1*e* to 3*e*

    1*e* Eric Nisbitt Macleod Wroughton, *b* 10 Mar 1888

    2*e* John Henry Theodore Wroughton, *b* 22 Aug 1892

    3*e* Edith Margaret Grace Wroughton.

2*d* Theodore Ambrose Wroughton, Canadian Rifles, *b* 1862, *m s p*

3*d* William Haultain Wroughton M D (*Witheral, Carlisle*), *b* 1871, *m* Edith, da of (—) Havers, and has issue 1*e* to 3*e*|

    1*e* John Wroughton

    2*e* William Edward Wroughton

    3*e* Dorothy Wroughton

4*d* Arthur Oliver Bird Wroughton, Capt R A M C (*Osborne*), *b* 29 Oct 1872, *m* 23 Aug 1905, Roberta, da of Major-Gen William Stenhouse, *s p*

5*d* Morgiana Lilian Wroughton, *b* 1864, *m* at Bangalore 25 July 1882, [Sir] Bannatyne Macleod, I C S, M A (Camb), Bar-at-Law, a District Magistrate, and by descent 6th Bt [S 1723][1] (*Madras*), and has issue 1*e* to 7*e*

    1*e* William Bannatyne Macleod, Lieut Indian Army, *b* at Bangalore 1883

    2*e* Roland Theodore Wroughton Macleod, *b* 1900

    3*e* Nesbitt Bannatyne Wroughton Macleod, *b* in India

    4*e* Alan James Macleod, *b* in England

    5*e* Alexander Macleod, *b* in England

    6*e* Marguerita Lilian Chimer Macleod

    7*e* Meriel Clare Wroughton Macleod

6*d* Grace Augusta Wroughton, *m* 1st, July 1891, Arthur Augustus Hewer, M D, d 1 July 1894, 2ndly, 5 May 1906, Ernest Leonard Mahon, Tea Planter (*Coorg, S India*), and has issue 1*c*

    1*c* John Arthur Langton Wroughton Hewer, *b* 21 Ap 1892

7*d* Frances Meriel Wroughton, *m* 1893/4, Major Leslie Warner Yale Campbell, Indian Army [son of Major-Gen Alexander Campbell], and has issue (with 2 das d young) 1*e* to 4*e*

    1*e* Kenneth Leslie Campbell

    2*e* Duncan Francis Lisle Campbell

    3*e* Joan Leslie Campbell, *b* in India

    4*e* Helen Patricia Campbell, *b* Aug 1909

2*c* *Francis John Wroughton, Col Comdg 9th Madras N I, b at Coimbatore 16 Aug 1841, d at Rangoon 12 June 1887, m at Tonghoo 28 Sept 1875, Margaret Georgina, da of John Algie of Lisduff, co Galway, and had issue 7 children, now dispersed in Cape Town, Basutoland, and the West Coast of Africa*

3*c* *Arthur Frederic Wroughton, b at Coimbatore 24 May 1844, d at South Norwood 12 Ap 1907.8, m 1st, Donata C S, da of N Armstrong, 30th Regt, 2ndly, Clara, da of (—) Wildgoose, and had issue 1d to 3d*

    1*d* [1] Stuart Abercrombie Wroughton, *b* in Canada 16 May 1875

    2*d* [1] Charles Wetherall Wroughton, *b* in Canada 17 May 1877

    3*d* [2] Chardin Wroughton, *b* 7 Dec 1899

4*c* *Grace Matilda Wroughton, b at Coimbatore 17 Aug 1845, d at Brighton 13 Oct 1893 4, m 1863, Capt Charles Maxtore Smith, d (–), and had issue (1 son and 4 das) 1d to 5d*

    1*d* Charles Wroughton Smith

    2*d* Alice Smith

    3*d* Minnie Smith

    4*d* Mabel Smith

    5*d* Rosalind Zeima Smith

[Nos 30062 to 30094

---

[1] Ruvigny's "Jacobite Peerage," p 110

2 E

3b *Nesbitt Wroughton, Capt 5th Madras Light Cavalry,* b *at Adwick* 11 *Feb* 1811, d *in London* 16 *Aug* 1855, m *at Sholapore, India,* 18 *Jan* 1814, *Jane, da of Edward Armstrong of the Hook, Applegirth, co Dumfries, Advocate, and Sheriff for that a/sd co,* d *at Jaulnah, India,* 23 *Nov* 1853, *and had issue (with* 2 *sons, Nevill Nesbitt Armstrong, Forest Ranger (1st Grade) in Punjaub,* b *at Sholapore* 10 *June* 1845, d s p *at Jhelum, N W P,* 12 *Aug* 1871, *and George Chardin Murray,* b 1848, d *at Jaulnah, Madras, Nov* 1853) 1c

1c Meriel Matilda Catherine Wroughton (*Adwick Villa, Harrow Road, Sudbury*), m *at the British Legation, Brussels,* 19 *July* 1888, Major Crommelin Henry Ricketts, Madras S C, d s p 11 Ap 1892

4b *Barbara Charlotte Wroughton,* b *ot Adwick* 8 *Ap.* 1796, d *at Guernsey* 16 *Ap* 1872, m 21 *July* 1823, *the Rev James Stewart Murray Anderson of Brighton, M A,* d *at Bonn* 22 *Sept* 1869, *and had issue (with* 2 *elder sons* d.s p) 1c *to* 3c

1c *Rev Fortescue Lennox Macdonald Anderson, Rector of St Baldred's, North Berwick,* b 15 *June* 1832, d 17 *June* 1899, m 1st, 23 *May* 1865, *Charlotte Frances, da of William Fisher,* d 31 *July* 1872, 2ndly, 6 *Oct* 1882, *Emma, da of John Sidley, and had issue (with a* 2nd da d *unm*) 1d *to* 8d

1d [1] Lennox Stuart Anderson, Sec Royal Portrush Golf Club (*Portrush, Ireland*), b 3 Sept 1870, m 1895, Mary Louisa, da of William Black Ferguson, and has issue 1e *to* 2e

1e Bernard Stuart Anderson, b 22 Mar 1896

2e James Fortescue Stuart Anderson, b 19 Sept 1906

2d [2] Fortescue Wroughton Anderson (76 *Pearl Street, Toronto, Canada*), b 3 Aug 1883, m 23 Oct 1909, Elizabeth Florence, da of John Cobourg McKendry of Ontario

3d [1] Helen Charlotte Maud Anderson, m 6 Jan 1891, George Gordon Robertson, Chartered Accountant (*St Baldred's, Mitcham, Surrey*), and has issue 1e *to* 2e

1e Lennox Gordon Robertson, b 15 Nov 1894

2e Maud Marian Schoedde Gordon Robertson, b 17 Dec 1891

4d [1] Meriel Anderson, m 6 Oct 1885, the Rev Cecil William Nash, Rector of Kincardine O'Neil (*Kincardine O'Neil Rectory, Aberdeenshire*), and has issue 1e *to* 3e

1e Thomas Stuart Nash, b 27 Mar 1889

2e George Cecil Nash, b 31 Dec 1897

3e Meriel Eileen Ella Vere Nash, b 5 Aug 1886

5d [1] Florence Wroughton Anderson, m Aug 1893, Major Charles Edward Sawyer (*Grancy Villa, Lausanne*), and has issue 1e *to* 3e

1e Edward Sawyer, b 1896

2e Dagmar Morwena Alice Sawyer, b Sept 1894

3e Brenda Hildegarde Sawyer, b 1899

6d [1] Blanch Anderson (*Salthorpe House, Wroughton, near Swindon*), unm

7d [2] Barbara Wroughton Anderson, m 5 Jan 1907, Allen Wynard Gardener (*Columbia, Isle of Pines, West Indies*), and has issue 1e *to* 2e

1e Violet Allen Gardener, b 7 Jan 1908

2e Barbara Allen Gardener, b 26 Aug 1909

8d [2] Diana Wroughton Anderson, unm

2c *Musgrave Wroughton Anderson of Studley Park, Melbourne,* b 1837, d 1870, m *in Australia* 1860, *Charlotte, da of the Hon Henry Miller of Melbourne* [*who m* 2ndly, 17 *Dec* 1872, *the Hon Sir Henry John Wrixon, K C M G, President Legislative Council of Victoria*], *and had issue (with a son* d *young)* 1d *to* 2d

1d Lilian Charlotte Anderson, m. 13 Feb 1889, Alan Sidney Wentworth

[Nos 30095 to 30116

# of The Blood Royal

Stanley, J P , Capt and Hon Major 4th Batt Suffolk Regt (*Chesterfield House, Great Chesterfield, Essex , Wellington*) , and has issue (with a son *d* young) 1*e*
  1*e* Alan Wroughton Wentworth Stanley, *b* 3 Jan 1891

  2*d* Helen Maud Anderson, *m* 18 Dec 1890, Charles Wentworth Stanley, *formerly* of Longstowe Hall, co Camb , J P , D L , M A (Camb), Capt and Hon Major 4th Batt Suffolk Regt (*Merton Grange, Gamlingay, co Camb , Wellington*) , and has issue 1*e* to 2*e*
    1*e* Charles Sidney Bowen Wentworth Stanley, *b* 20 Jan 1892
    2*e* Barbara Charlotte Wentworth Stanley, *b* 31 Jan 1901

  3*c* Diana Matilda Anderson, *m* 3 May 1854, Randolph Robinson (*Waldeck House, 19 South Parade, Southsea*) , and has issue 1*d*
    1*d* Maud Robinson, *m* 15 Nov 1881, John Ross Divett (*43 St Ronan's Road, Southsea*) , and has issue 1*e*
      1*e* Randolph Divett, R N , *b* 17 May 1883

  5*b* *Diana Denton Turner Wroughton*, b *at Doncaster* 5 Feb 1801 , d 27 May 1819 , m *as 1st wife*, 1818, *Lieut -Gen James Eckford, C B , d* 2 June 1867 , *and had issue* 1*c*
    1*c* *George Henry Eckford, Indian C S* , b 24 Aug 1818 , d 18 Oct 1877 , m *June* 1837, *Catherine, da of James Haldane, d* 31 May 1897 , *and had issue* 1*d*
      1*d* Emily Jane Eckford (*Rosario, 30 St Ronan's Road, Southsea*), *m* at Patna, Bengal, 24 Nov 1864, Col Andrew David Geddes, Col Commdg 83rd Regimental District, Belfast, *formerly* 27th Inniskillings, *d* at Belfast 23 Dec 1888 and has issue (with a son, Cosmo Gordon, and 2 das Marion Margaret and Caroline Gordon, *d unm*) 1*e* to 8*e*
        1*e* Ernest David Eckford Geddes, Capt and Brevet-Major R M A , *b* 15 Nov 1869
        2*e* Malcolm Henry Burdett Geddes, Capt 64th Pioneers, Indian Army, *b* 20 Feb 1874 , *m* 21 Oct 1905, Annie Vera Eleanor, da of Col James Christie, Indian Army , and has issue 1*f* to 2*f*
          1*f* Andrew James Wray Geddes, *b* 31 July 1906
          2*f* Eleanor Lilian Lorna Geddes
        3*e* Emily Ethel Geddes, *m* 8 Oct 1902, Capt Edward Augustus Alfred de Salis, D S O , 4th Batt Worcestershire Regt (*Imperial Service Club*), s p
        4*e* Diana Catherine Geddes *unm*
        5*e* Violet Alice Geddes, *m* 30 June 1903, Capt. Frederick Lewis Dibblee, R M A , and has issue 1*f* to 2*f*
          1*f* David Lewis Dibblee, *b* 10 Sept 1909
          2*f* Margaret Emily Dibblee
        6*e* *Lilian Maud Geddes*, d 4 July 1907 , m 20 Nov 1901, *Lieut Lionel Berkeley Holt Haworth, Indian Army, attached to Political Dept Indian Govt , and had issue* 1*f* to 2*f*
          1*f* Cyril Francis Rafe Haworth, *b* 3 Sept 1902
          2*f* Radclyffe Lionel Geddes Haworth, *b* 7 Aug 1904
        7*e* Mabel Ada Geddes, *m* 11 Ap 1908, Lieut Cyril Charles Johnson Barrett, Indian Army, attached to Political Dept Indian Govt (*Bombay*) and has issue 1*f*
          1*f* Edwin Cyril Geddes Barrett, *b* 15 Feb 1909
        8*e* Gwendoline Olivia Geddes, *unm*

  6*b* *Mary Frances Matilda Wroughton*, b *at Adwick* 15 Sept 1806 , d *at Brighton* 4 p 1872, m *her cousin, the Rev Robert Abercrombie Denton, d* 25 Feb 1857 , *and had issue* (with two sons *d* young) 1*c* to 2*c*
    1*c* Sir George Chardin Denton, K C M G , Governor of the Gambia, *formerly* Capt. 57th Regt (*Government House, Bathurst, Gambia*), *b* 22 June 1851 , *m* July
                                                                [Nos 30117 to 30139

215

The Plantagenet Roll

1879, Jean Margaret Alan, da of Alan Stevenson, d 19 July 1900, and had issue 1d to 2d

    1d George Clarke Denton, b 22 Ap 1881

    2d Julia Maud Mary Denton

  2c Julia Sibella Denton (*Hill'op, Headington Hill, Oxford*), m 1886, Fitzjames E. Watt, Commissary Gen, d s p Mar 1902

  3a *Francis Wroughton, H E I C S*, d (?–p) *in India*

  4a *Catherine Wroughton*, d (–), m as 1st wife, 1786, *the Rev Robert Price, LL D, Preb of Durham* [*descended from George, Duke of Clarence, K G*], d 7 Ap 1823, *and had issue*

  See the Clarence Volume, pp 361–362, Nos 12329–12372

  5a (—) *Wroughton*, d (–), m *Capt Mainwaring* [1]   [Nos 30140 to 30186

111 Descendants of BARBARA MUSGRAVE (Table XIII), d (–); m. as 2nd wife 1720, THOMAS HOWARD of Corby Castle, co Cumberland [D of Norfolk Coll] (see p 402), d 1740, and had issue 1a

  1a *Philip Howard of Corby Castle*, b 1730, d 8 *Jan* 1810, m 11 *Nov* 1754, *Anne* [*descended from the Lady Ann, sister of King Edward IV*, &c], da of *Henry Witham of Cliffe*, *and had issue*

  See the Exeter Volume, pp 558–559, Nos 49774–49891

                                        [Nos 30187 to 30304

112 Descendants of GEORGE MUSGRAVE, Storekeeper of the Ordnance at Chatham (Table XIII), d (–), m SARAH, widow of Lieut. Young, da of Benjamin ROSELL, and has issue 1a to 3a

  1a *Joseph Musgrave of Kypier*, d (–), m *Jane* (see p 200), da of *Sir Philip Musgrave, 6th Bt* [E]

  2a *Thomas Musgrave*

  3a *George Musgrave, M P for Carlisle* 23 *Mar* 1768 *to* 30 *Sept* 1774, d (–), m (—), da of (—), *and had issue* 1b

  1b *George Musgrave of Marylebone and Shillington Manor, co Bedford, J.P*, *and High Sheriff* 1828, b 8 *Sept* 1769, d 27 *June* 1861, m 19 *Aug* 1790, *Margaret*, da of *Edmund Kennedy of Grafton*, d 19 *Sept* 1859, *and had issue* 1c to 5c

  1c *Rev George Musgrave of Shillington Manor and Borden Hall, co Kent, M A* (*Oxon*), *Translator of Homer's* "*Oyyssey*," &c, b 1 *July* 1798, d 26 *Dec* 1883, m 1st, 4 *July* 1827, *Charlotte Emily*, da of *Thomas Oakes, Senior Member of Council and President of the Board of Revenue, Madras*, *and had issue* 1d

  1d *Edward Musgrave of Shillington Manor*, b 26 *Ap* 1835, d (–), m *July* 1860, *Henrietta Maria*, da of *John Teschemaker of Annsfert, British Guiana, D C L*, d (–), *and had issue* 1e to 3e

  1e *Horace Edgar Musgrave of Shillington Manor, co Beds, and Borden Hall, co Kent, Painter, New Brighton, Christchurch* (*Orari, South Canterbury, New*   [No 30305

---

[1] These particulars are taken from a MS pedigree lent by Philip Wroughton of Woolley and endorsed "This pedigree was drawn out by and is in the handwriting of my late brother, Charles Jackson, Esq, of Doncaster, from original information supplied by John White, Esq, of Doncaster, brother-in-law of Col George Wroughton of Adwicke le-Street Mr White's notes are in my possession —J E Jackson, Leigh Delamere, Wilts, October 28, 1883," and now amplified and brought down as far as possible

# of The Blood Royal

Zealand), *b* 3 Sept 1861, *m* 8 Ap 1891, Cecilia Elizabeth, da of George Arthur Emilius Ross of Stoney Croft, Riccarton, Christchurch, N Z and has issue 1*f* to 2*f*

    1*f* Christopher Musgrave, *b* 1 Feb 1893

    2*f* Ethel Marion Musgrave

    2*e* Philip Cranstoun Musgrave, Lieut R N, *b* 6 Aug 1863

    3*e* Ethel Henrietta Musgrave

    2*c Henry Musgrave J P , D L , Bar at-Law,* b 8 *July* 1800, d (-), m *Sarah Popplewell, da of Richard Pullan of Harewood, co York, d Sept* 1861, *and had issue* 1*d*

    1*d* George Arthur Musgrave of Horton, co Glouc, *b* 1843, *m* Aug 1867, Theresa, da and h of Jacques Jones of Hill House, co Glouc , and has issue 1*e* to 4*e*

    1*e* Henry Arthur Fitzherbert Musgrave, *b* 1869

    2*e* Richard Rosewell Musgrave, *b* 1872

    3*e* Arthur Franklyn Musgrave, *b* 1877

    4*e* Christopher Brooke Musgrave, *b* 1880

    3*c Thomas Musgrave,* d (*? s p*)

    4*c Georgiana Musgrave,* d (-), m 22 *Aug* 1822, *C Berners Plestow of Watlington Hall, co Norfolk, d May* 1849, *and had issue* 1*d to* 2*d*

    1*d* Charles John Berners Plestow, *late* 7th Dragoon Guards, *b* July 1823

    2*d Henry Berners Plestow,* b 1825 , d (*? s p*) *before* 1880

    5*c Emma Musgrave,* d (-), m *June* 1831, *James Higham* [*son of Samuel Higham, Comptroller of the National Debt Office*], d (-), *and had issue* 1*d to* 3*d*

    1*d* George Lascelles Higham, *b* 1834, *m* 1861, Eliza, da of (—) Gilbertson

    2*d* Henrietta Higham

    3*d* Emily Higham, *m* 1863, William Harrison Briscoe, and has issue

[Nos 30306 to 30318

113 Descendants, if any, of ELIZABETH MUSGRAVE, *d* (-), *m* JOHN WYNEVE of Brettenham, co Suffolk, and of DOROTHY MUSGRAVE, *d* (-), *m*. JAMES HAWLEY of Brentford, co Midx (Table XII)

114. Descendants of MARGARET MUSGRAVE (Table XII), *d* (-), *m*. RALPH SHIPPERDSON of Murton and Pidding Hall Garth, co Durham, Major Durham Militia 1712, *d* 16 June 1719 , and had issue [1] 1*a*

    1*a Edward Shipperdson of Pidding Hall Garth,* d (-), m *Margaret, da of George Baker of Elemore , and had issue* 1*b*

    1*b Ralph Shipperdson of Pidding Hall Garth,* d 8 *Nov* 1793 , m 1779, *Frances, da and event h of the Rev Samuel Kirkshaw, D D , Vicar of Leeds, and had issue* 1*c to* 3*c*

    1*c Edward Shipperdson of Pidding Hall Garth, J P , D L ,* b 20 *Sept* 1780, d *unm*

    2*c Frances Shipperdson,* d (-), m *William Appletree of Goldings, near Basingstoke,* d (-), *and had issue (at least)* 1*d*

    1*d* Francis Russell Appletree or Apletre of Goldings   [No 30319

---

[1] Burke's "Pedigrees of Founders' Kin," liv , "Commoners," i 108, and " Landed Gentry," 1–6

The Plantagenet Roll

3c *Margaret Shipperdson* d (-), m 9 Aug 1803, *Walter Charles Hopper of Belmont, co Durham*, b 25 July 1772, d 15 Jan 1853, and had issue 1d to 6d

1d *Rev Edmund Hector Hopper, afterwards (R L 25 Mar 1856) Shipperdson of Pittington Hall Garth, and Murton-in-the-Whins and The Hermitage, co Durham, J P, M A, and Fellow of Christ's College, Camb*, b 25 Sept 1806, d (-), m 1 Nov 1838, *Adeline, da of John Kerrich of Harleston, co Norfolk*, and had issue 1e to 3e

2e Thomas Henry Shipperdson, b 26 Aug 1839

2e *Mary Adeline Shipperdson* d 2 June 1866, m 10 Dec 1863, *Sir Henry Pottinger, 3rd Bt [U K], J P, D L &c (The Pines, Queen's Road, Richmond, Surrey)*, and had issue 1f

1f *Ethel Adeline Pottinger*, m 21 Ap 1885, *Henry Meysey(Meysey-Thompson), 1st Baron Knaresborough [U K], &c &c [also descended from Edward III through Mortimer-Percy] (Kirby Hall, near York)*, and has issue

See p 114, Nos 10645–10649

3e Isabella Henrietta Shipperdson

2d *Ven Augustus Macdonald Hopper, M A, J P, Archdeacon of Norwich*, b 11 Aug 1816 d (-), m 15 Ap 1847, *Charlotte, da of the Rev John Holmes of Gawdy Hall, co Norfolk*, and had issue 1e to 4e

1e Edmund Charles Hopper, b 23 June 1856

2e Anthony Shipperdson Hopper, b 17 June 1858

3e Anne Margaret Hopper

4e Constance Hopper

3d *Mary Anne Frances Hopper*, d 20 Jan 1868, m *John Smith of Burley House, Leeds*

4d *Caroline Elizabeth Hopper*, d (-), m *the Rev James Boucher [nephew ex sorore of Richard Pigott, 7th Viscount Molesworth [I]*

5d *Isabella Margaret Hopper*, d (-), m *Francis Russell Aplitre of Goldings, co Hants*

6d Frances Hopper   [Nos 30320 to 30331

115 Descendants of FRANCIS MUSGRAVE (Table XII), d (-), m EDWARD HUTCHINSON of Wickham, co York, aged 21, 1665; living 1690, and had issue 1a to 2a [1]

1a *Richard Hutchinson of Wickham, living 1706*

2a *William Hutchinson of York, Merchant*, living 1714, m *Elizabeth, da of Richard Washington of Ardwick, co York*, and had issue 1b

1b *Thomas Hutchinson of York, and afterwards of Newsham in that co, Merchant*, living 1738, m *Elizabeth, da of Jonathan Johnson of Earby Hall, in Newsham* and had issue 1c

1c *Francis Hutchinson of Newsham and Earby Hall*, d 1812 m *Anne, da of Thomas Newby of Barningham*, and had issue 1d to 5d

1d *William Hutchinson*, d 1830, m and had (with possibly other) issue 1e

1e *Anne Johnson Hutchinson*, d 19 Nov 1861, m *George Sowerby of Putteridge Park, co Herts, and Dalton Hall, co Yorks, J P, D L*, d 9 May 1868, and had (with other) issue 1f

1f *George Sowerby of Putteridge and Dalton afsd, and of Dalston Hall, co Cumberland, J P, Col Durham Militia*, b 17 Feb 1832, d 2 Aug 1888, m 29 Oct 1863, *Emily Isabella Jane, da of Robert Airey of Jesmond, Newcastle-on-Tyne* and had issue (with a son, Francis Hubert Airey, d unm in S Africa 21 Ap 1901) 1g to 5g

---

[1] Plantagenet-Harrison's "Yorkshire," p 183

218

# of The Blood Royal

1g Thomas George Sowerby of Putteridge, &c, J P, Lord of the Manor of Lilley, co Herts, Major and Hon Lieut-Col 3rd Batt Durham L I, served in S Africa 1900-1901 (*Putteridge Park, Luton, Herts, Dalston Hall, Carlisle, Dalton Hall Richmond, Yorks*), b 8 Ap 1866, m 8 July 1897, Ellen Catherine, da of Marlborough Robert Pryor of Weston Park, co Herts, and has issue 1h to 2h

2 1h Richard Thomas Reynolds Sowerby, b 5 May 1898

2 2h Hubert Dennison Sowerby, b 21 Jan 1902

2g Harry John Sowerby, J P, D S O, Lieut-Col and Hon Col Comdg 4th Batt Durham L I, served in S Africa 1900-1901 (*Dalton Hall, Richmond, Yorks*), b 28 Nov 1867

3g Emily Frances Annie Sowerby, m 12 June 1891, Frederick William Fellowes [descended from George, Duke of Clarence, K G, brother of Edward IV (see the Clarence Volume, p 87)] (*The Lane House, King's Walden, Hitchin*), and has issue 1h

2 1h Reginald William Lyon Fellowes, b 6 Aug 1895

4g Lilian Mary Sowerby

5g Violet Florence Sowerby

2d *Thomas Hutchinson*, b 1780, d (*s p*) 1873

3d *Elizabeth Hutchinson, m 1st, William Johnson of Early Hall, 2ndly, Joseph Glover of Dalton Fields, and had issue*

4d *Anne Hutchinson, m Michael Glover of Aldburgh, and had issue.*

5d *Margaret Hutchinson*, b 23 Ap 1787, d at *Newsham* 31 Dec 1861, m 13 Sept 1808, *Marley Harrison of Washton, co York [himself a descendant of the Plantagenets]*, b at *Stubb House, co Durham,* 22 Feb 1772, d 14 *July* 1822, and had issue (*with 6 other children, all of whom d ~ p ~, the last survivor, Penelope*, d 23 *Jan* 1902) 1e

1e *George Henry de Strabolgie Neville Plantagenet-Harrison, a Marshal-Gen in the Armies of various South American States, and afterwards a Gen in the Danish Service, and later in that of the German Confederation, Author of a "History of Yorkshire,"* &c, b 14 *July* 1817, d 2 *July* 1890, m *and had issue* 1f

1f Blanche Plantagenet Plantagenet-Harrison, m 27 Ap 1892, John Christopher Cam Routh (*Clints House, Gayle, near Hawes, Yorks, Baxterley, Rusthall, Tunbridge Wells*), s p   [Nos 30332 to 30340]

116 Descendants of MARY (*née* EURE), *suo jure de jure* 16th BARONESS SCROPE of Bolton [E][1] (Table XIII), b c 1651, being aged 15 in 1666, d (-), when the right of the Barony fell into abeyance, m after 1687, MICHAEL JOHNSTON of Twyzell Hall, co Durham, d 12 Ap 1714, and had issue 1a

1a *Mary Johnson, eldest da and in her issue* (12 Ap 1811), *sole h, a co-h to the Barony of Scrope,*[2] b 1689, d 8 *June* 1730, m 1st, c *Oct* 1716, *John Brockholes of Claughton Hall, co Lanc,* d 6 *Mar* 1719, 2ndly, 2 *Jan* 1721, *Richard Jones of Caton, co Lancaster,* d 23 *Nov* 1732, *and had issue* 1b *to* 2b

1b *Michael Jones of Caton, co Lancaster,* b 23 *Nov* 1729, d 24 *July* 1801, m 23 *Oct* 1773, *Mary, widow of Edward Cosney, da of Matthew Smith,* d 1811, *and had issue* 1c *to* 7c [2]

1c *Charles Jones, Capt 1st Dragoon Guards, who on the extinction of all the issue of the sisters of his grandmother by the death of Mary Bryer,* 12 Ap 1811, *became de jure 17th Baron Scrope of Bolton* [E 1371], *living May* 1825

2c *Michael Jones of Lincoln's Inn, Bar at Law, F S A, living May* 1825, m *Ann, da of Robert Etherington of Gainsborough, co Linc,* d s p 4 Ap 1804

---

[1] G E C's "Complete Peerage," vii 88

[2] See pedigree in Nicolas' "Synopses of the Peerage of England," i, Addenda, p 22

The Plantagenet Roll

3c *Edward Jones, Capt 29th Foot, living unm May 1825*

4c *James Jones, Major in the Army, K C S , &c , living s p May 1825, m Louisa Dacre, da of Peter Moore, M P*

5c *Mary Jones, living s p May 1825, m at St Omer's, Ap 1818, "Le Comte Pierre de Sandelin, Seigneur D'Halines, near St Omer's, in France"*

6c *Constantia Jones, living unm May 1825*

7c *Katherine Jones, d unm 1799*

2b *Katherine Brockholes, b 30 Ap 1718, d 21 Nov 1784, m 8 Nov 1739, Charles (Howard), 9th Duke of Norfolk [E], &c , d 31 Aug 1786, leaving an only son, who d s p 23 Dec 1815*

117 Descendants of Sir HENRY CHOLMLEY of Whitby and Roxby (Table XIII), *bur* at St John's, York, 13 Jan 1616, *m* MARGARET [descended from the Lady ANNE, sister to Kings Edward IV and Richard III], da of Sir William BAETHORPE, *b* 15 Ap 1628, and had issue

See the Exeter Volume, Table LVIII, and pp 607–679, Nos 51968–57332
[Nos 30311 to 35705]

118 Descendants, if any surviving, of JOHN (CONSTABLE), 2nd VISCOUNT DUNBAR [S], (Table XIII), *b c* 1615, *d c* 1667; will dated 15 Dec that year, *m* before 1649, MARY, da of Thomas (BRUDENELL), 1st Earl of Cardigan [E.]; and had issue 1a to 4a

1a *Robert (Constable), 3rd Viscount Dunbar [S], b c 1651, d 23 Nov 1714*

2a *William (Constable), 4th Viscount Dunbar [S], b c 1654, d s p l 15 Aug 1718*

3a *Hon Cecily Constable, d (–), m 5 Sept 1665, Francis Tunstall of Scargill and Wycliffe, co York and had issue, which apparently became extinct on the death of Francis Sheldon, alias Constable, of Burton Constable, 12 Feb 1821* [1]

4a *Hon Catherine Constable, d (–), m after 5 Sept 1665, John More of Kirklington, co Notts , and had issue 1b to 2b*

1b *John More,*   } *both living 30 Aug 1717, when they are named in the*
2b *Winifred More,* }   *will of the 4th Lord Dunbar* [2]

119 Descendants of the Hon CATHERINE CONSTABLE (Table XIII), *living* 1653, *d* (–), *m* WILLIAM MIDDLETON of Stockheld, co York, *d* 1658, and had issue

See the Exeter Volume, Table XXII, and pp 333–336, Nos 21284–24535
[Nos 35706 to 35957]

120 Descendants of the Hon ALATHEA FAIRFAX (XIV), *d* (–); *m c* Jan 1677, WILLIAM (WIDDRINGTON), 3rd LORD WIDDRINGTON [E], *d* 10 Feb 1695, and had issue 1a to 4a

1a *William (Widdrington), 4th Lord Widdrington [E], d 17 Ap 1743, having been attainted 7 July 1716 for his share in the "'15 ", m 1st (marriage bond dated*

---

[1] Foster's " Yorkshire Pedigrees "
[2] Balfour Paul's "Scots Peerage," III 298

220

13 *Ap*) 1700, *Jane, da and event* (1698) *h of Sir Thomas Tempest of Stella, 4th Bt* [E], d 9 *Sept* 1714, *and had issue which became extinct* 26 *May* 1792

2*a Hon Charles Widdrington, attainted* 31 *May-7 July* 1716 *and said to have d s p at St Omers* 1756

3*a Hon Mary Widdrington,* d *July* 1731, m *Richard Towneley of Towneley* [*descended from George, Duke of Clarence, K G*], b 1687, d *Aug* 1735, *and had issue*

See the Clarence Volume, Table XXXIV and pp 314-318, Nos 9083-9214

4*a Hon Elizabeth Widdrington,* d 7 *Jan* 1765, m *Marmaduke* (*Langdal*), 4*th Lord Langdale* [E] [*descended from the Lady Anne, sister to King Edward IV, &c*], d 8 *Jan* 1771, *and had issue*

See the Exeter Volume, pp 160-161, Nos 36724-37038

[Nos 35958 to 36304 100

121 Descendants, if any, of ALATHEA FAIRFAX (Table XIV), d (-), m JOHN FORCER

122. Descendants, if any, of the Hon PHILIP FAIRFAX, of the Hon MARY FAIRFAX, and of the Hon CATHERINE FAIRFAX, d 1715, m GEORGE METHAM of Metham, co York [1] (Table XIV)

123 Descendants of the Hon DAVID ERSKINE of Almondell, King's Advocate (Table XIV), b 1 Nov 1746, d 8 Oct 1817, m 1st, 30 May 1772, CHRISTIAN, da and h of George FULLERTON of Broughton Hall, d 1804, and had issue 1*a* to 3*a*

1*a Henry David* (*Erskine*), 12*th Earl of Buchan* [S], b *July* 1783, d 13 *Sept* 1857, m 1st, 28 *Sept* 1809, *Elizabeth Cole, da and co-h of Maj r-Gen Sir Charles Shipley, Gov of Grenada,* d 5 *Oct* 1828 2ndly, 26 *June* 1830, *Elizabeth, da of John Hervey of Castle Semple, co Renfrew,* d 17 *Dec* 1838, *and had issue* 1*b* to 5*b*

1*b Henry Erskine, Lord Cardross,* b 22 *Oct* 1812, d s p 21 *Dec* 1836, m 15 *May* 1832, *Jean Halliday, da of Archibald Terry of Edinburgh,* d 11 *Sept* 1886, *and had issue* 1*c*

1*c Hon John Berry Erskine of Dryburgh and Holmes, da and h of entail,* b 16 *Feb* 1833, d 16 *Mar* 1870, m 8 *Ap* 1856, *the Rev George Eden Biber, afterwards* (1856) *Biber-Erskine,* B 1, d 25 *July* 1866, *and had issue* 1*d to* 2*d*

1*d George Oswald Harry Erskine Biber-Erskine of Dryburgh and Newmains* J P, *heir-general of the Erskines, Earls of Buchan* (*Dryburgh Abbey, co Berwick Newmains, Dryburgh*), b 24 *May* 1857, m 15 *Aug* 1893, *Lucy da of T A Urwick of Corfe Mullen, co Dorset*

2*d Henry Erskine Biber-Erskine,* b 17 *July* 1858

2*b David Stuart* (*Erskine*), 13*th Earl of Buchan* [S], b 6 *Nov* 1815, d 3 *Dec* 1898, m 1st, 27 *Ap* 1819, *Agnes Graham, da of James Smith of Craigend, co Stirling,* d 2 *Sept* 1875, *and had issue* 1*c to* 2*c*

1*c Shipley Gordon Stuart* (*Erskine*), 14*th Earl of Buchan, &c* [S] (*Almondwell House, Linlithgow,* b *Aldford Street, Park Lane, W . Carlton*), b 27 *Feb* 1850, m 9 *Nov* 1876, *Rosalie Louisa, da of Capt Jules Alexander Sartoris of Hopsford Hall, Coventry, and has issue* 1*d* to 4*d*

1*d Ronald Douglas Stuart Mar Erskine, Lord Cardross, late Lieut Scots* Guards, b 6 *Ap* 1878

[Nos 36305 to 36308

---

[1] In Burke's " Extinct Peerage," p 194, she is confused with her aunt (see p 292), and is made to marry 2ndly Sir Arthur Ingram

The Plantagenet Roll

2d Lady Muriel Agnes Stuart Erskine, m 7 Jan 1903, Major the Hon Charles Strathavon Heathcote-Drummond-Willoughby, late Scots Guards [2nd son of Gilbert Henry, 1st Earl of of Ancaster [U K], P C, and a descendant of King Henry VII, &c] (19 Cheyne Walk S W), and has issue 1c to 2c

   1c Charles Peregrine Heathcote-Drummond Willoughby, b 13 Sept 1905

   2c Rosalie Heathcote-Drummond-Willoughby, b 10 July 1908

   3d Lady Marjorie Gladys Stuart Erskine

   1d Lady Evelyn Hilda Stuart Erskine, m 24 June 1903, Major the Hon Walter Edward Guinness, M P [3rd son of Edward Cecil, 1st Viscount Iveagh [U K], K P] (Knockmaroon, Castleknock, co Dublin, The Manor House, Bury St Edmunds, 11 Grosvenor Place., S W) and has issue 1c

   1c Bryan Walter Guinness, b 27 Oct 1905

   2c Hon Albany Mar Stuart Erskine, Capt 3rd Batt Duke of Wellington's Regt, b. 24 Feb 1852, m 16 May 1878, Alice Ellen, da of Alfred Keyser of Cross Oak, Berkhampstead, d 19 Sept 1902

3b Lady Christian Isabella Erskine, b Oct 1820, d 3 July 1886 m 4 June 1840, John Gordon of Aikenhead, co Lanark J P, D L, d 6 Aug 1897, and had issue 1c to 1c

   1c John Henry Gordon of Aikenhead, b 21 Oct 1842, d s p 7 Feb 1902

   2c Henry Erskine Gordon of Aikenhead, J P, D L, Major and Hon Lieut-Col Lanark Imp Yeo (Aikenhead House, Cathcart), b 11 Sept 1849, m 1 Oct 1895, Bertha Agnes, da of Major J Finlay of Castle Toward, co Argyll, and has issue 1d to 5d

      1d Jean Victoria Christian Erskine Gordon.

      2d Nancy Althea Gordon

      3d Dorothy Bertha Gordon

      4d Violet Erskine Gordon

      5d Barbara Isobel Gordon

   3c Charles Shipley Gordon (Ronerdenan, Merton Park, Surrey), b 12 Oct 1851, m 2 Aug 1875, Mary, da of Capt James Stirling Crawford-Stirling-Stuart [Bt of Pollok (1682) Coll], and has issue 1d to 4d

      1d John Stuart Gordon, b 13 Feb 1881

      2d Hamilton William Fortescue Gordon, b 1883

      3d Muriel Isabella Erskine Gordon

      4d Gwendoline Mary Harriet Gordon

   4c Hamilton Gordon (The Wildernesse, Hayward's Heath, Sussex), b 15 Feb 1856, m 3 Oct 1898, Alice Jane Erroll (see below), da of John Young of Westridge

4b Lady Alicia Diana Erskine, b Feb 1822, d 31 Oct 1891, m 1st, 6 June 1843 Rev the Hon Somerville Hay [E of Erroll Coll and a descendant of the Lady Anne, sister of King Edward IV (see Exeter Volume, p 682), d 25 Sept 1853, 2ndly, 5 July 1858 Capt James Young of Westridge, I W, d 1877, and had issue 1c to 3c

   1c Somerville Hay, b (posthumous) 19 Nov 1853

   2c John Harry Erskine Young, b 19 Aug 1859

   3c Alicia Jane Erroll Young, m 1898, Hamilton Gordon (see above)

5b Lady Margaret Erskine, b 15 Nov 1834, d 22 Nov 1872, m as 1st wife, 21 Ap 1860, Sir William Vincent of Stoke D'Alernon, 12th Bt [E], J P, D L, C A, Vice-Chairman Surrey C C and Deputy Chairman Surrey Quarter Sessions (Stoke D'Abernon Chase, Leatherhead, Surrey), and had issue 1c

   1c Francis Erskine Vincent, late Lieut 1st Life Guards (Ormesby, Great Yarmouth), b 24 Mar 1869 m 4 July 1893, Margaret Louisa, da of John Holmes of Brooke Hall, co Norfolk, and has issue 1d to 3d

      1d Anthony Francis Vincent, b 30 June 1894

      2d Victor Norman Erskine Vincent, b 9 Feb 1897

      3d Evelyn Joseph Vincent, b 25 Sept 1900   [Nos 36309 to 36334

# of The Blood Royal

2a *Elizabeth Compton Erskine*, d (–), m 21 Oct 1801, *Col George Callander of Craigforth, co Stirling, Lieut-Col Rifle Brigade*, b Mar 1770, d v p 18 Feb 1824, *and had issue 1b to 5b*

1b *James Henry Callander of Craigforth and Ardkinglas, M P*, b 18 Aug 1803, d 31 Jan 1851, m 1st, 29 Aug 1877, *the Hon Jane Plumer* (see p 227) *da of David Montague (Erskine), 2nd Lord Erskine [U K]*, d 30 May 1816, 2ndly, 1 July 1847, *Charlotte Edith Eleanora [descended from George, Duke of Clarence, K G* (see Clarence Volume, p 479)], *da of John George Campbell, Cadet of Islay, and had issue 1c to 5c*

1c George Frederick William Callander *of Craigforth and Ardkinglas, J P, D L (Craigforth House, Stirling, Ardkinglas Lodge, Inveraray Argyll)*, b 28 July 1848, m 20 Jan 1876, *Alice, da of John Cornelius Craigie-Halkett of Cramond*

2c Henry Barrington Callander (*Stone Hill Cottage, Ardkinglas, Argyll*), b 19 July 1849, m 9 Nov 1875, Sophia Leonora, da of Edward Clough Taylor of Kirkham Abbey

3c[1] Frances Jane Callander, 3rd Abbess of Cleever since 1892

4c[1] Mary Hermione Callander, m 1st, 16 Sept 1862, Charles Sartoris of Wilcote, co Oxon, J P, and High Sheriff for that co 1872, d 22 Sept 1881, 2ndly, 1886, George Henry Dawkins, J P [descended from George, Duke of Clarence, K G (see Clarence Volume, p 177)] (*Wilcote, Charlbury S O, Oxon*)

5c[1] Jane Sevilla Callander, m 12 Jan 1869, Lord Archibald Campbell, J P, D L [descended from Kings Henry VII and Edward IV (see Tudor Roll, p 230), George, Duke of Clarence, K G, &c &c] (*Coombe Hill Farm, Norbiton, Kingston-on-Thames*), and has issue 1d to 2d

1d Niall Diarmid Campbell (*28 Clarges Street, W*), b 16 Feb 1872

2d Elspeth Angela Campbell

2b *John Alexander Callander*, b 19 Sept 1809, d (–), m Aug 1837, *Emma, da of John Young of Westridge, I W, and had issue (2 sons and 5 das)*

3b *Elizabeth Anne Callander*, d 13 Ap 1839, m 11 Aug 1831, *Henry William Vincent of Lily Hill, co Berks [Bt of Stoke D'Abernon E 1620 Coll]*, b 5 Sept 1805, d 14 Feb 1865, *and had issue 1c to 2c*

1c *Susan Anne Vincent*, d 1 Oct 1899, m 28 Jan 1864, *John Henry Bagot Lane of King's Bromley, J P, Lieut-Col Coldstream Guards [descended from King Henry VII, &c]*, d 22 Mar 1886, *and had issue*

See the Tudor Roll, p 308, Nos 25856–25866, and the Exeter Volume, p 434, Nos 34998–35014

2c *Harriet Maria Vincent*, m 12 Ap 1860, James Carter Campbell of Ardpatrick, J P, D L, Capt (ret) R N (*Ardpatrick, Tarbert, co Argyll, The Hall, Filkins, co Oxford*), and has issue 1d to 3d

1d Henry Hervey Campbell, M V O, Capt R N, b 27 Feb 1865

2d Susan Eleanor Campbell, m 11 Jan 1888, Arthur Frederick Churchill Tollemache of Ballincor, King's Co, Heir to Baronetcy [G B 1793], J P [descended from King Henry VII, &c. (see Tudor Roll, p 202)] (*The Red House, Westgate-on-Sea*), and has issue 1e to 3e

1e Arthur Henry William Tollemache, b 5 Ap 1891

2e Eleanor Louisa Cornelia Tollemache

3e Hermione Edith Agnes Tollemache

3d Edith Elizabeth Campbell, m 26 Ap 1887, Capt Eustace Maudslay, *late 16th Lancers* (*Blaston Manor, Uppingham*), and has issue 1c to 5c

1e Colin Eustace Maudslay, b 3 Ap 1888

2e Ronald Vincent Maudslay, b 27 June 1889

3e Marjorie Edith Maudslay

4e Irene Isabel Maudslay

5e Vere Sybil Maudslay

[Nos 36335 to 36370

The Plantagenet Roll

4b Caroline Frances Callander, d (-), m 17 Jan 1832, Robert Dunmore Napier of Ballykinrain, co Stirling d 1846

5b Agnes Callander, d 1837, m 1836, William Dunmore, H E I C S

3a Henrietta Erskine d (-), m 11 May 1812, Peter Smith, M D

124 Descendants of THOMAS (ERSKINE), 1st BARON ERSKINE [U K], Lord Chancellor of Great Britain (Table XIV), b 21 Jan 1750, d 17 Nov 1823, m 1st, 29 May 1770, FRANCES, da of Daniel MOORE, M P, d 22 Dec 1805, 2ndly, 12 Oct 1818, SARAH [da of ——] BUCK, d 25 Oct 1825, and had issue 1a to 7a

1a David Montagu (Erskine) 2nd Baron Erskine [U K], b 1777, d 19 Mar 1855, m 1st, 16 Dec 1799, Frances, da of Gen George Cadwalader of Philadelphia, d 25 Mar 1843, and had issue 1b to 12b

1b Thomas Americus (Erskine), 3rd Baron Erskine [U K], b 3 May 1802, d s p 10 May 1877

2b John Cadwalader (Erskine), 4th Baron Erskine [U K], b 1804, d 28 Mar 1882, m 1st, 30 Ap 1829 Margaret, da of John Martyn, d 21 June 1862, and had issue 1c to 3c

1c William Macnaghten (Erskine), 5th Baron Erskine [U K], J P, D L (Spratton Hall, Northampton, Carlton), b 7 Jan 1841, m 2 July 1864, Caroline Alice Martha, da of William Grimble, and has issue 1d to 1d

1d Hon Montagu Erskine (Westwood Lodge, Windlesham, Surrey, Carlton), b 13 Ap 1865, m 16 Jan 1895, Florence, da of Edgar Flower of The Hill, Stratford-on-Avon, and Middlehall Park, co Worcester, and has issue 1e to 3e

1e Donald Flower Cardross Erskine, b 3 Jan 1899

2e Richard Alistan Erskine, b 8 Jan 1901

3e Victoria Esme Erskine, b 3 Jan 1897

2d Hon (Stuart Joseph) Ruandha Erskine (Tigh an Fhraoich, Banchory-Dwenich, Aberdeenshire), b 15 Jan 1869, m 1st, 18 July 1891, Muriel Lilias Colquhoun, da of Major-Gen George Farquhar Irving Graham, d 27 Ap 1895, 2ndly, 6 Aug 1902, Dona Maria Guadalupe Zaara Cecilia, da of Joseph Robert Heaven of the Forest of Buse, Aberdeenshire [by his wife, Mary Guadalupe Ignacia Antoinette, suo jure 1st Marchioness of Braceras [P S]], s p s

3d Hon Esmé Standish Erskine, b 5 Mar 1873

1d Hon Margaret Erskine, m 23 Oct 1890, Capt Henry Edmund Lacon, J P, late 71st Highlanders (Blythmore, Claydon, Ipswich)

2c Hon Frances Macnaghten Erskine, b 29 May 1839, d 5 May 1872, m 12 Jan 1861, Standish Grady Rowley of Sylvan Park, co Meath, LL D, D L, M R I A, d 1 May 1882, and had issue (with a son and da d unm) 1d to 2d

1d Clotworthy Rowley, b 12 Feb 1872, m s p

2d Georgie Alice Rowley, m 9 Nov 1892, Fanshawe Tower Tufnell (Marskalls, Felstead, Essex), and has issue 1e to 2e

1e Rowley Erskine Tufnell, b 30 Nov 1902

2e Fanshawe Edward Standish Tufnell, b 27 Ap 1904

3c Hon Margaret Catherine Erskine, m 1st, 30 Ap 1872, the Rev Evelyn Henry Villebois Burnaby, Rector of Burrough-on-the-Hill [marriage dissolved 1886], 2ndly, 7 June 1887, Sydney Beaumont Willoughby [B Middleton Coll,

[Nos 36371 to 36383

224

and a descendant of the Lady Anne, sister to King Edward IV &c (see Exeter Volume, p 615)] (63 *Goldington Road, Bedford*) and has issue 1*d* to 2*d*

1*d* Christopher John Willoughby, *b* 1889

2*d* Kathleen Riette Winifred Burnaby

3*b* Hon *David Erskine*, Major 21st and 51st *Regts*, and *Lieut-Col Comdg Natal Carabineers, Colonial Sec*, Natal, b 1816, d 21 *June* 1903, m 1st, 12 *Nov* 1839, *Anne Maria, da of Josiah Spode of Tasmania d at Pietermaritzburg 3 Nov* 1860, 2ndly, 26 *Sept* 1870, *Emma Florence* (*Sissinghurst, Kent*) *da of Capt Charles J Harford, 12th Lancers*, and had issue 1*c* to 8*c*

1*c* Stuart Townsend Erskine, *b* 23 Nov 1841, *m* 17 Jan 1864-6, Jessie Smith, da of David Dale Buchanan of Natal, Advocate

2*c* St Vincent Whitshed Erskine, *b* 22 Feb 1846, *m* 1870, Alice, da of David Dale Buchanan of Natal, Advocate

3*c* Herman Harford Erskine, Cape Colony Civil Service, *b* 21 Sept 1871, *m* 3 May 1899, Adela Eva, da of Richard Feilding Nevins, and has issue 1*d*

1*d* Angela Augusta Erskine

4*c* Robert Henry Erskine, H B M's Vice-Consul at Fredericia (*Fredericia, Denmark*), *b* 31 Dec 1873

5*c*¹ Fanny Cadwalader Erskine, *m* 22 Aug 1862 the Hon Sir Michael Henry Gallwey, K C M G, *formerly* Chief-Justice of Natal (*Pietermaritzburg*)

6*c*¹ Annie Barton Erskine, *m* 14 Aug 1872, Major Arthur Henry Pain, *formerly* 1st Batt Gordon Highlanders

7*c* Sevilla Florence Erskine, *m* 1 Aug 1908, George Glass Hooper, C E (30 *Palace Court, Bayswater Hill*, W), and has issue 1*d*

1*d* Mary Erskine Glass Hooper, *b* 24 May 1909

8*c* Gladys Kathleen Erskine, *m* 1903, Percy John Ling, Paymaster R N, and has issue 1*d*

1*d* David Erskine Ling, *b* 5 Sept 1908

4*b* Hon *Edward Morris Erskine*, C B, *Envoy Extra and Min Plen to Athens* 1864-72, and *to Stockholm* 1872-81, b 28 *Mar* 1817, d 19 *Ap* 1883, m 24 *July* 1847, *Caroline, widow of Andrew Loughnan, da of Robert Hamilton Vaughan, d 23 Oct* 1877, and had issue 1*c* to 4*c*

1*c* Mary Maud Erskine, *b* 19 *Ap* 1848, *d* 1892, *m* 1st, 16 *Ap* 1872, *William John Percy Lawton of Lawton Hall, co Chester, d 8 Nov 1883 2ndly,* 8 Sept 1885, *the Rev George William Charles Skene, M A, Rector of Barthomley*, and had issue 1*d* to 4*d*

1*d* John William Edward Lawton of Lawton (*Lawton Hall, Cheshire*), *b* 24 June 1873

2*d* Ralph Lupus Erskine Lawton, *b* 26 June 1878

3*d* Gwendolen Maud Lawton, *m* 21 Nov 1905, Edward Charles Crewe-Read (see below)

1*d* Mary Emily Lawton

2*c* *Elizabeth Steuarta Erskine*, b 3 *Feb* 1850, d 9 *Aug* 1905, m 2 *Mar* 1873, *Offley John Crewe-Read of Llandinam Hall co Montgomery, J P, Lieut-Col South Wales Borderers*, b 3 *Dec* 1848, and had issue 1*d* to 2*d*

1*d* Randolph Offley Crewe-Read, *late* of Llandinam, *b* 12 Ap 1876

2*d* Edward Charles Crewe-Read, *b* 15 June 1877, *m* 21 Nov 1905, Gwendolen Maud (see above), da of William John Percy Lawton of Lawton

3*c* Evelyn Constance Erskine, *m* 1 June 1876, Francis William White, F R G S, *late* Comr of Customs at Hankow, China, *d* (-), and has issue

4*c* Christina Edith Eleanor Erskine, *unm*

5*b* James (Erskine), 1st Baron Erskine (*Freiherr von Erskine*) [*Bavaria*], so cr 18 *Jan* 1872, b 4 *Sept* 1819 21, d 4 *Jan* 1904 m 27 Feb 1849, *the Countess Wilhelmina* (*Countess Lerchenfeld*), *da of Anthony Joseph Clements Count Toerring Minucci of Munich*, and had issue 1*c* to 2*c*   [Nos 36384 to 36404

The Plantagenet Roll

1c Herman David Montagu (Erskine), 2nd Baron Erskine (Freiherr von Erskine) [Bavaria], an Officer in the Bavarian Army, b 12 Feb 1854

2c Baroness Hermine Maria Erskine

6b *Hon Frances Erskine,* b 1801, d (?-p) 7 *June* 1876, m *Nov* 1824, *Gabriel Shawe,* d 11 *Feb* 1851

7b *Hon Mary Erskine,* b 28 Feb 1806, d 15 *Mar* 1874, m 16 *June* 1832, *Herrman, Count of Baumgarten (Graf von Baumgarten) [Bavaria],* d 11 *Jan* 1846

8b *Hon Sevilla Erskine,* d 12 *Mar* 1835, m *as 1st wife,* 23 *Dec* 1830, *Sir Henry Francis Howard, G C B [D of Norfolk Coll* (see Exeter Volume, p 559)], d 28 *Jan* 1898, *and had issue* 1c

1c Adela Howard, a Benedictine nun

9b *Hon Stuarta Erskine,* b Oct 1810, d *at Genoa* 17 *Sept* 1863, m 6 Oct 1828, *Yeats Brown of Stuppington, co Kent, H B M's Consul at Genoa,* d *before* 1863

10b *Hon Elizabeth Erskine,* b *Ap* 1812, d 19 *July* 1886, m 1 *Ap* 1832, *Sir St Vincent Keene Hawkins-Whitshed of Killincarrick, 2nd Bt [U K* 1834], d 1870, *and had issue* 1c to 3c

1c *Sir St Vincent Bentinck Hawkins-Whitshed, 3rd and last Bt [U K],* b 12 *Feb* 1837, d 9 *Mar* 1871, m 8 Dec 1858, *Anne Alice, da of Rev the Hon John Gustavus Handcock [B Castlemaine [I] Coll] [who re-m 2ndly,* 17 Dec 1885, *James Percival Hughes and]* d 1871, *and had issue* 1d

1d Elizabeth Alice Frances Hawkins-Whitshed, m 1st, June 1879, Col Frederick Augustus Burnaby, d Feb 1885, 2ndly, Mar 1886, John Frederick Main, d Ap 1892, 3rdly, June 1900, Francis Bernard Aubrey Le Blond of Roughetts, Hildenborough, co Kent (*Killincarrick House, Greystones, co Wicklow*), and has issue 1e

1e Harry Arthur Gustavus St Vincent Burnaby of Killincarrick (*Carlton*), b May 1880

2c *Elizabeth Sophia Hawkins-Whitshed,* d 4 *Jan* 1858, m *as 1st wife,* 18 *Feb* 1857, *Lieut Gen Arthur Cavendish-Bentinck [D of Portland [E] Coll],* d 11 *Dec* 1877, *and had issue* 1d

1d William John Arthur Charles (Cavendish Bentinck), 6th Duke [G B] and 7th Earl [E] of Portland, 2nd Baron Bolsover [U K], &c, K G, P C, G C V O, &c &c, Master of the Horse to H M the King 1886–1892 and 1895–1905 (*Welbeck Abbey, Worksop, Fullartn House, Troon, co Ayr, 3 Grosvenor Square, W, &c &c*), b 28 Dec 1857, m 11 June 1889, Winifred, a Lady of Grace of St John of Jerusalem, da of Thomas Yorke Dallas-Yorke of Walmsgate, Louth, and has issue 1e to 3e

1e William Arthur Henry Cavendish-Bentinck, Marquis of Titchfield, b 16 Mar 1893

2e Lord Francis Morven Dallas Cavendish-Bentinck, b 27 July 1900

3e Lady Victoria Alexandrina Violet Cavendish-Bentinck

3c *Renira Hawkins-Whitshed,* d 30 Aug 1894, m 18 *Nov* 1862, *Rear Adm Edwin John Pollard of Haynford Hall, R N, J P, D L,* d 15 *Sept* 1900, *and had issue* 1d to 6d

1d James Hawkins Whitshed Pollard, Major Royal Scots Fusiliers (*Haynford Hall, Norwich*), b 13 May 1866, m 18 Oct 1899, Clare Evelyn, da of G Hamilton Low, Royal Canadian Rifles, and has issue 1e to 2e

1e Hamilton Hawkins Whitshed Pollard, b 13 Ap 1903

2e Arthur Rodney Erskine Pollard, b 22 Aug 1906

2d Arthur Erskine St Vincent Pollard, Capt Border Regt, b 30 July 1869

3d Renira Elizabeth Pollard

4d Lucy Clara Pollard

5d Sevilla Florence Pollard

6d Grace Emily Pollard

[Nos 36405 to 36421

# of The Blood Royal

11b Hon Harriet Erskine, b Ap 1814, d 19 Nov 1855, m 29 Aug 1833, Charles Woodmass of Alveston, co Warwick

12b Hon Jane Plumer Erskine, b 9 May 1818, d 30 May 1846, m as 1st wife, 29 Aug 1837, James Henry Callander of Craigforth, M P, d 31 Jan 1851, and had issue

See p 223, Nos 36337-36341

2a Very Rev the Hon Henry David Erskine, Dean of Ripon, b 1786, d 27 July 1859, m 4 May 1813, Lady Harriet [descended from the Lady Anne, sister of Kings Edward IV and Richard III, &c] da of John (Dawson), 1st Earl of Portarlington [I], d 16 Dec 1827, and had issue

See the Exeter Volume, p 301, Nos 15216-15243

3a Right Hon the Hon Thomas Erskine, one of the Judges of the Court of Common Pleas, b 12 Mar 1788, d 9 Nov 1864, m 10 Dec 1814, Henrietta Eliza, da of Henry Traill, d 21 Aug 1865, and had issue 1b

1b Rev Thomas Erskine, Rector of Alderley, co Chester, b 12 Nov 1828, d 22 Feb 1878, m 8 Ap 1856, Emmeline Augusta (Cowley Street, Westminster, S W), da of Henry John Adeane of Babraham, and had issue 1c to 5c

1c Henry Adeane Erskine, Lieut-Col 3rd Northumberland Transport Supply Column, and Agent for Bank of England in Newcastle (Newcastle-on-Tyne), b 1 Mar 1857, m 8 July 1891, Florence Eliza Palmer, da of the Ven Frank Robert Chapman, Archdeacon of Sudbury, and has issue 1d to 4d

1d Henry David Erskine, b 17 Oct 1897
2d Margaret Helen Erskine, b 6 Oct 1892
3d Christian Mary Erskine, b 7 May 1894
4d Griselda Beatrice Erskine b 2 Jan 1900

2c Thomas Edward Erskine, H B M Consul at St Louis (British Consulate, St Louis, U S A), b 24 June 1859, m 17 Nov 1888, Amy Gertrude, da of Lieut-Gen Robert Bruce, and has issue 1d to 5d

1d Thomas Erskine, b 20 Feb 1897
2d John Steuart Erskine, b 8 Nov 1900
3d Marjory Rachel Helen Erskine
4d Diana Isobel Erskine
5d Violet Amy Erskine

3c Robert Steuart Erskine (10 Ovington Gardens, S W), b 15 Dec 1860, m 7 Mar 1899, Beatrice Caroline [descended from the Lady Anne, sister of Kings Edward IV and Richard III (see Exeter Volume, p 301), and also from Lady Elizabeth Percy, née Mortimer], da of Henry Linwood Strong, Bar-at-Law

4c Edward John Erskine, b 18 Ap 1864, m 1888, Gertrude, da of H or J Harding of Sydney, N S W, and has issue 1d to 3d

1d Steuart Edward Erskine, b 1902
2d Sybil Gertrude Erskine
3d Dona Maud Erskine

5c David Erskine, b 5 Ap 1873

4a Hon Hampden Erskine, b 5 Dec 1821

5a Hon Frances Erskine, d 25 Mar 1859, m 20 Jan 1802, the Rev Samuel Holland, D D, Prebendary and Precentor of Chichester and Rector of Poynings, Hurst Pierpoint, d 16 Ap 1857

6a Hon Elizabeth Erskine, d 2 Aug 1800, m 17 Nov 1798, Sir David Erskine [illegitimate son of the 11th Earl of Buchan]

7a Hon Mary Erskine, d 1864, m 29 Jan 1805, Edward Morris, a Master in Chancery, d 13 Ap 1815   [Nos 36422 to 36472

The Plantagenet Roll

125 Descendants of WILLIAM FRASER of Fraserfield [Lord Saltoun [S], Coll] (Table XIV), b 28 Sept 1725, d 31 Oct 1788; m 5 Jan 1752, RACHEL, da of the Rev Hugh KENNEDY of Rotterdam, d 3 June 1800, and had issue 1a to 4a

1a *Alexander Fraser of Fraserfield, on his elder brother's death, previously HEICS*, b 8 Jan 1761, d 18 July 1807, m 20 Ap 1795, *Mary Christina, da of George Moir, d 12 Sept 1813, and had issue (with another da who d unm)* 1b to 3b

1b *Margaret Fraser of Fraserfield*, d 19 Aug 1839, m 27 May 1816, *Henry David Forbes-Mitchell of Balgownie, J P, D L [Bt of Craigievar [S] Coll (see p 232)], d 21 July 1869, and had issue* 1c to 5c

1c *Henry Erskine Forbes-Mitchell of Kinmundy, co Aberdeen, J P, Lieut-Col and Major 21st Hussars*, b 11 July 1821, d 1891, m 12 Ap 1855, *Letitia Angelina da of Gen George St Patrick Lawrence, K C S I, C B, d 29 Oct 1857, and had issue* 1d to 2d

1d Margaret Isabella Forbes-Mitchell

2d Louisa Letitia Forbes-Mitchell, m 7 Oct 1879, Capt Christian Ernest Arp von During, *formerly Prussian Army*, and has issue 1e to 3e

1e Arp Henry George Louis Charles John von During, b 1880

2e Letitia Charlotte Helen von During, ⎰ twins

3e Isabelle Uda Catherine von During, ⎱

2c *Margaret Moir Forbes-Mitchell*, d 1 Nov 1904, m 25 Mar 1846, *Alexander Kinloch Forbes, Judge of the High Court, Bombay (see p 230), d at Poonah 30 Aug 1865, and had issue* 1d to 5d

1d *Rev John Fraser Forbes, M A (Oxon), Chaplain, Bombay*, b 17 June 1847, d 1887, m 13 June 1878, *Edith Palin, da of Henry Wenden of Barnes, Surrey, and had issue* 1e to 4e

1e Alistan Esme Buchan Forbes, an Engineer, b 1881

2e Agnes Dorothy Mary Forbes

3e Emmeline Brita Cahusac Forbes

4e Edith Margaret Lyndhurst Forbes

2d *Henry David Erskine Forbes, formerly Assist Sup in Revenue Dept, Bombay*, b 19 Ap 1849, m 1884 Alice Georgina, da of Henry Ingle

3d *Rev Edward Esme Forbes, Vicar of Roffey, formerly Capt I S C (Roffey Vicarage, Horsham)*, b 1 Sept 1855, m 1st, 10 July 1880, Frederica Maude, da of Brig-Gen George Frederick De Berry, d (-), 2ndly, 8 Ap 1902, Florence Emily Louise, da of Capt W Pemberton Hesketh, 42nd Highlanders

4d Margaret Theodora Lawrence Forbes

5d Emmeline Maria Elizabeth Forbes, m 1899, Charles Scott Chisholme

3c *Rachel Louisa Forbes Mitchell*, b at Balgownie 5 Ap 1826, d at Paris 6 Dec 1896, m at Balgownie 29 Mar 1846, *Major-Gen Francis Gregor Urquhart, C B [Cadet of Craigston], b at Aberdeen 28 Nov 1813, d at Bernay, Evre, 19 Sept 1889, and had issue (with a da, Margaret Isabella Mary, d unm 1 Sept 1891)* 1d

1d *Emily Henrietta Agnes Urquhart*, b at Cork 28 Sept 1852, m at Paris 24 Nov 1885, *Charles Koenig, sometime Artillery Instructor at the St Cyr Military School (Château de St Aubin de Scellon, par Thiberville, Eure), and has issue (with a da d young)* 1e

1e Paul Francis Louis Joseph George Koenig, now serving with the Artillery at Versailles, b at Plélan-le-Petit, Côtes du Nord, 12 Sept 1888

4c *Emmeline Forbes-Mitchell*, d 4 Ap 1881, m 29 Ap 1851, *the Rev John Gabriel Ryde, M A (Oxon), Incumbent of Trinity Church, Melrose, d there 7 Dec 1868, and had issue* 1d to 9d

1d William Erskine Curters Ryde, b 3 May 1855

2d Arthur John Ryde b 11 Feb 1857 [Nos 36473 to 36489

# of The Blood Royal

3d Rev Lewis Forbes Ryde, M A (Oxon) (89 *St Helen s Gardens, North Kensington*), b 10 Mar 1859

4d Francis Edward Ryde, Major *late* West Indian Regt , b 15 Nov 1862

5d Herbert George Ryde, b 16 Aug 1864

6d Cyril Alexander Ryde, b 21 May 1866

7d Henrietta Fraser Ryde

8d Caroline Elizabeth Ryde

9d Ada Margaret Ryde

5c *Georgina Mary Agnew Forbes*, d 2 May 1903, m 24 Dec 1857, *Robert Spottiswood Farquhar-Spottiswood of Muiresk, co Aberdeen*, d 2 Ap 1873, and had issue 1d to 3d

  1d Henry Alexander Farquhar-Spottiswood of Muiresk, J P (*Muiresk, Turriff co Aberdeen*), b 18 Aug 1859 m 1 June 1882, Elizabeth Agnes, da of Sir George Samuel Abercromby, 6th Bt [S], and has issue 1e to 2e

    1e Alistair Robert Farquhar-Spottiswood, Lieut R N , b 10 Aug 1885

    2e Violet Douglas Farquhar Spottiswood

  2d Thomas William Farquhar-Spottiswood, b 13 May 1874

  3d Mary Georgina Farquhar-Spottiswood (*Mount St Ternan, Banchory, Kincardineshire*)

2b *Rachael Fraser, da and co-h*, b 2 May 1798, d 13 Feb 1867 m 15 July 1828, *William Maxwell*, b 26 Aug 1791 d 17 Nov 1869, and had issue (with 4 sons and a da d unm) 1c to 2c

  1c *Wellwood Maxwell*, b 14 July 1830, d 6 Jan 1909, m 14 Ap 1861, *Isabella, da of William Moir of Park, co Aberdeen*, d 4 June 1898, and had issue 1d to 6d

    1d William George Maxwell, Solicitor, b 7 Mar 1870 *unm*

    2d Wellwood James Maxwell, Chartered Accountant (*Holmfield, Aigburth, Liverpool*), b 31 Mar 1872, *unm*

    3d Mary Elizabeth Maxwell, *unm*

    4d Rachael Maxwell, *unm*

    5d Isabella Margaret Maxwell, *unm*

    6d Catherine Louisa Maxwell, *unm*

  2c Katharine Isabella Maxwell, *unm*

3b *Mary Fraser, da and co-h*, d 23 Feb 1873, m 10 Feb 1825, *William Urquhart of Craigston, co Aberdeen, J P , D L*, d Mar 1847, and had issue 1c

  1c *Mary Isabella Urquhart of Craigston*. d 12 Dec 1873, m 20 Aug 1846, *William Pollard, afterwards (R L 11/24 June 1847) Pollard-Urquhart of Castle Pollard, co Westmeath, M P , J P , D L*, d 1 June 1871, and had issue 1d to 8d

    1d Walter William Dutton Pollard-Urquhart of Castle Pollard, J P , D L , b 10 July 1817, d s p 29 Dec 1892

    2d Francis Edward Romulus Pollard-Urquhart of Craigston and Castle Pollard, Lieut -Col (ret) R A , J P , D L , High Sheriff co Westmeath 1901 (*Castle Pollard, co Westmeath , Craigston Castle, Turriff, co Aberdeen*), b 8 Sept 1848 m 28 Nov 1888, Louisa Henrietta, da of Garden Duff of Hatton Castle, d 1 Oct 1908

    3d Rev Arthur de Capel Broke Pollard-Urquhart, b 1 Ap 1850

    4d *Michael Bruce Pollard-Urquhart*, b 25 Dec 1851, d 29 Ap 1879, m June 1875, *Florence Adeline, da of (--) Billings*, and had issue 1e

      1e Michael Bruce Pollard-Urquhart, Lieut Scottish Rifles, b 15 Aug 1879

    5d Montagu Alexis Pollard Urquhart, C E , b 9 May 1859, m July 1882, Honora Elizabeth, da of the Rev L A Buckley of Alderford, and has issue 1e to 3e

      1e William Edward Pollard-Urquhart

      2e Arthur Lewis Pollard-Urquhart

The Plantagenet Roll

6c Nora Mary Pollard-Urquhart, d 4 Aug 1909, m 16 Jan 1906, Arthur Herald Loughborough R A

6d Adah Mary Louise Pollard-Urquhart, m Oct 1882, Dudley Billings

7d Leonora Anna Maria Helen Pollard Urquhart

8d Octavia Harriet Pollard Urquhart, m July 1888, Charles Humphreys, M D (2 Avenue Crescent, Mill Hill Park, Acton, W), and has issue 1e to 2e

1e Frances Styles Humphreys, b 15 Jan 1896

2e Mildred Humphreys, b 7 June 1889

2a Henry David Fraser, an Officer in the British Army and a Brig -Gen in the Portuguese, b 27 Ap 1762, d 4 Aug 1810, m 6 Oct 1800, Mary Christina, da of John Forbes of Skellater G C B 4, G C C S, Field-Marshal and Gov of Rio de Jan no, &c, d at Lisbon and had issue (with 2 sons and a da who d s p) 1b to 2b

1b Sophia Maria Jane Fraser, d (-) m 1827, Count Henry Francis de Bombelles, d 1850, and had issue

2b Margaret Alexia Fraser, d (-), m the Marquis of Gargallo

3a Erskine Fraser of Woodhill, co Aberdeen, Col 109th Regt, b 23 June 1766, d 21 Jan 1804, m 3 May 1794, Elizabeth, da of Thomas Forbes of Ballogie, d 18 Aug 1813, and had issue 1b

1b William Fraser of Woodhill. Lieut -Col in the Army, b 21 Nov 1796, d 13 July 1872, m 20 Aug 1833, Mary Elizabeth, da of Thomas Starkie Shuttleworth of Ashton, co Lanc, and had issue 1c

1c Elizabeth Fraser

4a Katherine Anne Fraser, d 27 Dec 1836, m 27 Mar 1777, Duncan Forbes, afterwards (1772) Forbes-Mitchell of Thainstone, co Aberdeen [3rd son of Sir Arthur Forbes of Craigievar, 4th Bt [S 1620]], b 26 Mar 1757, d 6 Oct 1796, and had issue (with 3 elder sons, &c, who d s p) 1b to 3b

1b John Forbes Mitchell of Thainstone, b 21 Mar 1786, d in France 9 July 1822, m 8 Feb 1809, Ann, da of Lieut -Col George Powell, H E I C Art, d Sept 1861, and had issue 1c to 3c

1c Duncan Forbes-Mitchell of Thainstone, J P, D L, b 30 Oct 1812, d 13 Aug 1870, m 18 Feb 1824, Maria, da of Lieut -Col Robert Anthony Bromley, H E I C S, d 1892, and had issue 1d to 3d

1d John Forbes-Mitchell of Thainstone, J P, D L, F S A, b 25 June 1843, d s p 25 Ap 1882, m 28 July 1870, Jane Maria (Thainstone, Kintore, Queen's Cross, Aberdeen), da of Thomas James Rawson of Farrowville, co Carlow

2d Maria Forbes Mitchell, m 20 July 1878, John Alexander Stuart, late of the Admiralty and of the Office of the Secretary of State for War

3d Elizabeth Erskine Forbes-Mitchell (Dacca House, Colchester), m 20 Sept 1870, Lieut -Col John Nathaniel Gower, 78th Regt, d Sept 1905, and has issue 1e to 3e

1e John Forbes Gower, b 1877

2e Hugh Duncan Gower, b 1882

3e Alice Lilian Gower

2c John George Forbes, Major H E I C S, b 4 Mar 1814, d 29 Ap 1860, m 17 June 1837, Eliza Maria, da of John Lickie, d 10 July 1857, and had issue 1d

1d Charles Pulteney Forbes, Major-Gen, formerly Col and Lieut -Col Comdg 2nd Batt Leinster Regt (Fairlawn, Bath Road, Reading), b 29 Nov 1840, m 13 Jan 1864, Hannah, da of John Sims

3c Alexander Kinloch Forbes, Judge of the High Court of Bombay, b 7 July 1821, d at Poonah 31 Aug 1865, m 25 Mar 1846 Margaret Moir, da of Henry David Forbes-Mitchell of Balgownie, d 1 Nov 1904, and had issue

See p 228, Nos 36478-36485 [Nos 36515 to 36534

230

2b *Alexander Forbes*, Brazilian Merchant, b 13 Oct 1788, d 3 Feb 1813, m 11 Sept 1811, *Janet*, da of Sir William Forbes of Craigievar, 5th Bt [S], d 15 Feb 1846, *and had issue* 1c *to* 4c

1c *Duncan Forbes of Ernan Lodge, co Aberdeen*, b 7 Nov 1815, d 1894 m 14 Ap 1852, *Sarah*, da of Sir John Forbes of Craigievar, 7th Bt [S], d 6 Oct 1891, *and had issue* 1d *to* 5d

1d John Forbes, b 24 Mar 1855

2d Alexander Mansfield Forbes, b 28 Ap 1858, m 1887, May Antoinette, da of Alexander Forbes of Gallurs, co Aberdeen, and has issue 1e to 3e

1e Duncan Alexander Forbes, b 1888

2e Mansfield Duval Forbes, b 1889

3e Mhari Margaret Forbes

3d William Henry Forbes, b 26 Aug 1860

4d Charlotte Jessie Forbes

5d Katherine Elizabeth Forbes

2c *William Forbes*, Major Gen H E I C S, b 29 May 1820, d 6 May 1877, m 1st, *Sophia Adams*, da of (—) Fell, d (—), 2ndly, *Frances Helen*, da of R S M Spry, d 1896, *and had issue* 1d *to* 5d

1d¹ *John Forbes*, b at Agra 1853, d (? s p)

2d² William Alexander Forbes, *formerly* Capt 4th Batt Devonshire Regt, b 1861, m 1902, Katherina Fanny, da of the Rev E Royds of Brereton

3d² Duncan James Forbes, b 1864

4d² Henrietta Jessie Forbes

5d² Rachel Helen Forbes

3c *Sarah Forbes*, d 4 Ap 1851, m 20 Feb 1844, *Alexander Gordon of Newton, co Aberdeen*, d 8 Aug 1868, *and had issue* 1d *to* 4d

1d Alexander Morrison Gordon, b 14 July 1846, m 26 July 1870, Margaret, da of Capt James Crawford, Bombay Engineers, and has issue 1e

1e Margaret Helena Gordon

2d Duncan Forbes Gordon, Capt 92nd Gordon Highlanders, b 30 May 1849

3d Janet Forbes Gordon, m 10 June 1869, Frederick de Lemare Morrison, Col 1st Royal Scots, and has issue 1e to 2e

1e Alexander Edward Forbes Morrison

2e Isabel Gordon Morrison

4d Jane Margaret Gordon

4c *Katharine Anne Forbes*, d 3 Aug 1903, m 1 Dec 1840, *John Angus, J P, Advocate, Town Clerk of Aberdeen and Sheriff-Substitute for that co*, d 6 Nov 1878, *and had issue* 1d *to* 5d

1d Alexander Forbes Angus, J P (*Sydney, N S W, Junior Carlton*), b 25 Ap 1844, m 14 Mar 1883, Miriam Adelaide, da of the Hon Samuel Aaron Joseph of Sydney, M L A, s p s

2d John Angus, Lieut-Col Army Pay Dept, *formerly* York and Lancaster Regt (*Grosvenor Club*), b 9 Nov 1845, m 5 Sept 1870, Edith Mary, da of Edward Ronald Douglas, C I E, Dep Director-Gen Post Office of India, and has issue 1e

1e Ella Ernan Forbes Douglas Angus

3d William James Angus, *formerly* Lieutenant Highland L I Militia (*United Empire*), b 11 Jan 1856

4d Margaret Forbes Angus, m as 2nd wife, 17 July 1873, William John Renny of Danevale Park, Kirkcudbright, D L, d 25 Jan 1879, and had issue 1e to 3e
[Nos 36535 to 36558

231

The Plantagenet Roll

1e Percy Cyril Forbes-Napier Renny (*Bath Club*), b 1 Sept 1875

2e Angus Gordon Lyle Renny, } b (twins) 9 July 1876
3e Stanley Alexander Renny, }

5d Janet Christian Angus, m 3 Aug 1880, James Alexander Beattie, C E (*Dalbeattie, Murtle, co Aberdeen , Scottish Conservative*) , and has issue 1e to 2e

1e Rev Walter Roland Jardine Beattie, b 31 Dec 1883

2e Lilias Berkeley Beattie

3b Henry David Forbes-Mitchell of Balgownie, J P , D L , b 12 Nov 1790 , d 24 July 1869 , m 27 May 1816, Margaret, da and co-h of Alexander Fraser of Fraserfield, d 19 Aug 1839 , and had issue

See p 228, Nos 36473-36501   [Nos 36559 to 36593

126 Descendants of Lady FRANCES ERSKINE (Table XIV.), b 1700 , d 1774 , m 11 July 1726, Col JAMES GARDINER of Bankton, d (being killed at the battle of Prestonpans), 22 Sept 1745 , and had issue (with 9 others d young) 1a to 4a

1a David Gardiner, Cornet in Sir John Cope's Dragoons July 1747, b 1727

2a James Gardiner an Officer in the Army, b 1728

3a Frances Gardiner, d 7 Dec 1811 , m 1750, Sir William Baird of Saughton, 5th Bt [S], Capt R N , d 17 Aug 1771 , and had (with possibly other) issue 1b

1b Sir James Gardiner Baird, 6th Bt [S], Lieut Col 28th Light Dragoons, d 23 June 1836, m 1st, 1781 Henrietta, da of Wynne Johnston of Hilltown, and had issue 1c to 5c

1c William Baird, Capt in the Army, d v p , m 28 Mar 1809, Lucy, da of Thomas Dickson of Prospect House, co Hants , and had issue 1d to 6d

1d Sir James Gardiner Baird, 7th Bt [S], D L , Capt 10th Hussars, b 20 Aug 1813, d 6 Jan 1896, m 13 Mar 1845, Henrietta Mary, da of John Wauchope of Edmonstone, co Edin [Bt Coll (see p 233)], d 3 Nov 1896 , and had issue 1e

1e Sir William James Gardiner Baird of Saughton, 8th Bt [S], J P , *late* Lieut.-Col and Hon Col Lothians and Berwickshire Imp Yeo, *formerly* 7th Hussars (*The Knoll, North Berwick , Carlton , New (Edinburgh)*), b 23 Feb 1854 , m 3 Ap 1879, the Hon Arabella Rose, da of William Wallace (Hozier), 1st Baron Newlands [U K], and has issue 1f to 3f

1f James Hozier Gardiner Baird, Capt 4th Batt Argyll and Sutherland High-landers, b 25 Nov 1883

2f William Frank Gardiner Baird, *formerly* Lieut 7th Dragoon Guards, &c , b 18 Ap 1885

3f Frances Harriet Baird

2d David Baird, b 28 Ap 1815 , d (? unm s p)

3d Mackenzie William Baird, b 8 Dec 1816 (? s p)

1d Henrietta Jemima Baird, b 14 Jan 1810 , d 7 Feb 1889 , m 4 Feb 1836, John Hoskins of South Perrot, co Som

5d Mary Alicia Baird, b 18 Ap 1811 , d (? unm)

6d Frances Baird, b 26 Ap 1819 , d (? unm)

2c Richard Frederick Baird

3c Margaret Mary Baird

4c Henrietta Warrander Cecilia Baird, d 8 Nov 1826 , m Sept 1815, John Wauchope of Edmonstone, d 27 June 1837 , and had issue 1d to 2d

[Nos 36594 to 36597

232

# of The Blood Royal

1d *Sir John Wauchope, afterwards* (1862) *Don-Wauchope*, 8th *Bt* [S] 1667, *Chairman of the Board of Education for Scotland, &c* , b 10 *July* 1816 , d 12 *Dec* 1893 , m 26 *Ap* 1853, *Bethia Hamilton d 1 of Andrew Buchanan of Greenfield, co Lanark . and had issue* 1e *to* 6e

1e Sir John Douglas Don-Wauchope, 9th Bt [S] (*Edmonstone, Gilmerton, Midlothian , Newton House, Millerhill, Dalkeith*), b 15 *Sept* 1859

2e Andrew Ramsay Don-Wauchope (5 *Neville Street, Onslow Square*, S W), b 29 Ap 1861 , m 28 Oct 1903, Maizie, da of Major Gen Sir William Salmond, K C B

3e Patrick Hamilton Don-Wauchope, W S (13 *Saxe Coburg Place, Edinburgh , New Club*), b 1 *May* 1863 , m 10 June 1897, Georgiana Renira, da of George Fitzjohn , and has issue 1f

1f Patrick George Don-Wauchope, b 7 May 1898

4e Bethia Hamilton Don-Wauchope

5e Henrietta Cecilia Don-Wauchope, m 29 Nov 1882, Major Ernest Digby Mansel, *formerly* Highland L I [Bt of Muddlescombe [E 1621] Coll] (*Naval and Military*)

6e Clotilde Georgina Don-Wauchope (16 *Cheyne Court, Chelsea*), m 29 Jan 1886, the Hon Arthur Henry Browne [4th son of John Cavendish, 3rd Lord Kilmaine [I], and a descendant of Lady Anne, sister of King Edward IV (see Exeter Volume, p 432), d 3 May 1908, and his issue 1f *to* 3f

1f Clotilde Mary Hamilton Browne

2f Clementina Bethia Evelyn Browne

3f Gertrude Cicely Juliet Browne

2d *Henrietta Mary Wauchope*, d 3 Nov 1896 , m 13 *Mar* 1845, *Sir James Gardiner Baird of Saughton, 7th Bt* [S], d 3 *Nov* 1896 , *and had issue*
See p 232, Nos 36594–36597

5c *Alicia Sophia Baird*, d (? *unm*)

1a *Richenora Gardiner*, m *Lawrence Inglis , and had issue* [1]
[Nos 36598 to 36611

---

127 Descendants of ALATHEA FAIRFAX (Table XIV.), *d.* (-), *m.* RALPH PIGOTT of Whitton , and had issue [2] 1*a*.

1a *Nathaniel Pigott*, d 1804 , m *Anna Mathurina, da of* (—) *de Bertol, Grand Baillie of the Lordship of Aigemont Tavinque in the Austrian Netherlands*, d 1792 , *and had issue (with others)* 1b

1b *Charles Gregory Pigott afterwards* (*Act Parl* 1793) *Fairfax of Gilling Castle, co York, to which estate he suc on the death of his cousin, the Hon Anne Fairfax*, 8 *May* 1793 , *second son*, b c 1768 , d 29 *Dec* 1845, m 9 *June* 1791, *Mary, da of Henry Goodricke* [*eldest son and h-app of Sir John Goodricke, 5th Bt* [E 1641]], d 28 *Jan* 1845, *and had issue* 1c *to* 4c

1c *Charles Gregory Fairfax of Gilling*, bapt 14 *June* 1796 , d s p 21 *Ap* 1871

2c *Mary Ann Fairfax*, b 16 *Ap* 1795 , d (? *unm*)

3c *Harriet Fairfax*, bapt 15 *Dec* 1801 , d s p , m 22 *Feb* 1838, *Francis Cholmley of Bransby Hall, co York*, d s p 3 *Aug* 1855

4c *Lavinia Fairfax*, bapt 24 *Oct* 1802 , d (-), m *the Rev James Alexander Barnes, Rector of Gilling, living* 1874

---

[1] Paul's "Scots Peerage," ii 276
[2] Foster's "Yorkshire Pedigrees", Burke's "Commoners", ii. 113

128 Descendants, if any surviving, of Sir ROBERT LATON of East
Laton and Sexhow, co Yorks who granted a lease of East
Laton for 99 years to James Brook, 4 Sept 1669, and afterwards sold the said place to his brother Bryan, 21 Sept 1671 [1]
(Table XV), d (-), m ANNE, da of (——), and had issue
(with 3 elder sons, Thomas, Alexander, and John, who all
d s p) 1a to 5a

    1a *Robert Laton or Layton of Norwich, who was living 31 Jan 1703, when he
filed a Bill in Chancery claiming the Manor of East Laton against Sir James
Brook, Bt*
    2a *Charles Laton*
    3a *Elizabeth Laton, living 1691, m Anthony Dinby of Leek, co York*
    4a *Mary Laton, living 1691, m Thomas Brasse of Flasse, co Durham*
    5a *Catherine Laton, living a widow 1691, m (—) Leeke*

129 Descendants, if any, of BRYAN LATON of East Laton, co York,
which Manor he bought from his elder brother Robert for
£3000, 21 Sept 1671, and afterwards, 28 Mar 1678, sold to
Sir James Brook, Bt (Table XV), d (-), m and had
issue 1a

    1a *Charles Laton, son and h, living 31 Jan 1703, when he was one of the
defendants in a suit in Chancery on the complaint of his cousin Robert Laton*

130 Descendants of Sir WILLIAM FOULIS of Ingleby, co York, 5th
Bt [E] (Table XV), b. c 1680, bur 11 Dec 1756, m 1721,
MILDRED, da of Henry (DAWNAY), 2nd Viscount Downe [I],
bur 6 Feb 1780, and had issue 1a

    1a *Sir William Foulis, 6th Bt [E], b 1729, bur 17 June 1780, m 1758,
Hannah, da and h of John Robinson of Buckton, co York, d (a June) 1812, and
had issue 1b to 2b*
    1b *Sir William Foulis, 7th Bt [E], bapt 30 Ap 1759, d 5 Sept 1802, m
1789, Mary Anne [also descended from Edward III through Mortimer-Percy
(see p 397)], da of Edmund Turnor of Panton House, co Linc, d 18 Oct 1831,
and had issue 1c to 5c*
    1c *Sir William Foulis, 8th Bt [E], bapt 29 May 1790, d 7 Nov 1845, m
11 May 1825, Mary Jane, da of Gen Sir Charles Ross, 6th Bt [S] [by his wife,
Lady Mary, née FitzGerald], d 11 June 1852, and had issue 1d*
    1d *Mary Foulis da and h, d 11 June 1891, m as 1st wife, 23 Ap 1850,
Philip (Sidney), 2nd Baron de L'Isle and Dudley [U K] [senior representative and
heir of line of the Lady Anne Plantagenet, sister of Kings Edward IV and Richard
III (see Exeter Volume, p 77)], d 17 Feb 1898, and had issue 1e to 3e*
    1e *Philip (Sidney), 3rd Baron de L'Isle and Dudley [U K] [present senior
representative and heir of line of the Lady Anne Plantagenet, &c] (Penhurst Place,
Tonbridge, Kent, Ingleby Manor, Middlesbrough Carlton), b 14 May 1853, m
12 July 1902, the Hon Elizabeth Mary, widow of William Harvey Astell, J P,
D L, da of Standish Prendergast (Vereker), 4th Viscount Gort [I]*

                                     [No 36612

---

[1] Plantagenet Harrison's "History of York," p 530

# of The Blood Royal

2e Hon Algernon Sidney, Lieut-Col and Brevet-Col R A (*Marlborough*), b 11 June 1854

3e Hon William Sidney, Bar Inner Temple (107 *Sloane Street, S W*), b 19 Aug 1859, m 5 Dec 1905, Winifred, da of Roland Yorke Bevan, and has issue 1f to 2f

1f William Philip Sidney, b 23 May 1909

2f Mary Olivia Sidney, b 20 Nov 1906

2c *Rev Sir Henry Foulis of Ingleby, 8th and last¹ Bt* [*E*], bapt 15 *Sept* 1800, d s p 7 *Oct* 1876

3c *Hannah Foulis*, d 1869, m 28 *Nov* 1815, *the Rev Danson Richardson Roundell, sometime (1806-51) Currer, and finally (R L 21 Oct 1851) Roundell of Gledstone*, J P , D L , b 3 *Ap* 1784, d 10 *Mar* 1873, *and had issue* 1d to 3d

1d *William Roundell of Gledstone, High Sheriff co York* 1881, b 17 *July* 1817, d 21 *Oct* 1881, m 20 *Ap* 1864, *Harriet Jane*, da of *Francis Benyon Hackett of Moor Hall*, d 30 *Sept* 1895 *and had issue* 1e

1e Richard Foulis Roundell of Gledstone, J P , Capt 5th Batt Northumberland Fusiliers (*Gledstone, Skipton-in-Craven*), b 4 *Nov* 1872, m 29 *Nov* 1898, Beatrice Maud, da of Sir Matthew Amcotts-Wilson of Eshton Hall, 3rd Bt [U K], J P , and has issue 1f to 3f

1f Richard Henry Selborne Roundell, b 27 Sept 1901

2f Diana Georgina Amcotts Roundell, b 2 Jan 1900

3f Nancy Lea Roundell, b 25 Dec 1902

2d *Charles Savile Roundell, J P , D L , M P* 1880-95, *Private Sec to Earl Spencer while Lord-Lieut of Ireland*, b 19 *July* 1827, d 3 *Mar* 1906 m 10 *May* 1873, *Julia Anne Elizabeth* [*descended from King Henry VII* (see Tudor Roll, p 208)], *and had issue* 1e

1e Christopher Foulis Roundell (*Dorfold Hall, Cheshire*) b 11 July 1876

3d *Mary Anne Roundell*, d 20 *June* 1898, m as 2nd wife, 11 *Jan* 1855, *Capt John Hotham of Scraftwood, co Notts* [*Bt Coll*], d 1881, *and had issue* 1e to 3e

1e George Hotham, b 4 Ap 1856

2e Mary Hotham, *unm*

3e Lucy Hotham, *unm*

4c *Mary Ann Foulis*, d 1 *Feb* 1860, m 19 *Jan* 1822, *Sir Tatton Sykes of Sledmere, 4th Bt* [G B] [*descended from King Henry VII*] d 21 *Mar* 1863 *and had issue*

See the Tudor Roll, pp 389-390, Nos 29382-29406

5c *Sophia Frances Foulis*, d (-), m 21 *Aug* 1873, *Philip D Pauncefort Duncombe of Great Brickhill, co Bucks*

2b *John Robinson Foulis of Buckton*, ju d 29 *Ap* 1826, m 16 *Nov* 1795 *Decima Hester Beatrix* [*descended from King Henry VII* (see Tudor Roll, p 391)] d of *Sir Christopher Sykes, 2nd Bt* [G B], b 15 *Dec* 1775, d *Ap* 1843, *and had issue* (*with others who d s p*) 1c to 2c

1c *Elizabeth Foulis*, da and co-h, d (-), m *Vice-Adm George Edward Watts C B*, d 2 *Jan* 1860, *and had issue*²

2c *Lucy Dorothea Foulis*, d 1886, m 26 *Ap* 1827, *the Rev Charles Wastenys Eyre of Rampton, co Notts*, d 30 *Oct* 1862, *and had issue*

See the Exeter Volume, pp 612-613, Nos 52175-52180

[Nos 36613 to 36655

---

¹ See G E C's "Complete Baronetage," i 136

² Foster's "Yorkshire Pedigrees"

The Plantagenet Roll

131. Descendants of WILLIAM CHALONER of Guisboro', co York (Table XV), *bur* (? at St Maurice's, York) 14 July 1756 , m MARY, da of James FINNY of Finnyham, co Stafford, and had issue 1*a* to 4*a*.

1a *William Chaloner of Guisboro'*, *J P*, *D L*, b 14 *Aug* 1745, d 8 *May* 1793, m 8 *Aug* 1771, *Emma*, *sister of Adm Sir Eliab Harvey*, *G C B*, *da of William Harvey of Chigwell*, *and had issue* 1b *to* 3b

1b *Robert Chaloner of Guisboro'*, *J P*, *D L*, *M P*, *and Lord Mayor of York* 1817, b 23 *Sept* 1776, d 7 *Oct* 1842, m 24 *Jan* 1805, *the Hon Frances Laura* [*descended from the Lady Anne of Exeter*, *sister of King Edward IV*, *&c*], *da of Thomas (Dundas)*, 1st Baron Dundas [G B], d 27 *Nov* 1843, *and had issue*

See the Exeter Volume, p 260, Nos 9779-9798

2b *Charlotte Chaloner*, b (*twin*) 12 *Ap* 1787, d (-), m *Thomas Barton Bowen, Bar -at-Law*, *and one of the Commissioners of the Court of Insolvency*

3b *Williamina Chaloner*, b (*posthumous*) 6 *Nov* 1793, d (-), m *Col Alexander Wynch* [2nd son of *Alexander Wynch*, *Governor of Madras* 2 *Feb* 1773-*Dec* 1775 (see Supp)] b *at Cuddalore, Madras*, 10 *Aug* 1751, d (-), *and had issue* (2 *das*, *of whom one was* b *at Tunbridge Wells*, 3 *Mar* 1818)

2a *Edward James Chaloner of Lincoln Surgeon*, d (-), m *Theophania, da of* (—) *Burridge of Lincoln*, *and had issue* 1b *to* 3b

1b *Edward Chaloner*, *Capt in the Army*, d (*s p*) *of wounds received at the storming of Morne Fortune*, *St Lucia*, *bur at St Martin's, York*, 4 *July* 1807, m (—)[1]

2b *Theophania Chaloner*, b 23 *Jan* 1779, d 9 *June* 1857, m 12 *Aug* 1798, *Thomas Lodington Fairfax of Steeton and Newton Kyme*, *co York* d 1 *July* 1840 *and had issue*

See the Exeter Volume, pp 535-536, Nos 48976-49015

3b *Louisa Chaloner*, d (-), m *the Rev Edmund Edmonson*, *Vicar of Cokingham*

3a *Anne Chaloner*, d 22 *Feb* 1805, m 12 *May* 1761, *Edward (Lascelles)*, 1st *Baron Harewood* [G B], *so cr* 16 *June* 1796, *and Earl of Harewood* [U K], *so cr* 7 *Sept* 1812, d 3 *Ap* 1820, *and had issue* 1b *to* 3b

1b *Henry (Lascelles)*, 2nd *Earl of Harewood* [U K], *&c*, b 25 *Dec* 1767, d 24 *Nov* 1841, m 3 *Sept* 1794, *Henrietta* [*descended from the Lady Isabel Plantagenet*], *da of Lieut -Gen Sir John Sebright*, 6th *Bt* [E], d 15 *Feb* 1810, *and had issue*

See the Essex Volume, p 321, Nos 33493-33589

2b *Lady Frances Lascelles*, b 11 *June* 1762, d 31 *Mar* 1817, m 4 *Oct* 1784, *the Hon John Douglas*, b 1 *July* 1756, d 1 *May* 1818, *and had issue* 1c *to* 7c

1c *George Sholto (Douglas)*, 19th *Earl of Morton* [S], b 23 *Dec* 1789, d 31 *Mar* 1858, m 3 *July* 1817, *Frances Theodora* [*descended from the Lady Anne*, *sister to King Edward IV*, *&c*], *da of the Right Hon Sir George Henry Rose*, *G C H*, *P C*, *M P*, d 12 *July* 1879, *and had issue*

See the Exeter Volume, pp 645-646, Nos 55598-55673

2c *Rev the Hon Charles Douglas of Earlsgift*, *co Tyrone*, *who had a Royal Warrant of Precedency as son of an Earl* 23 *Aug* 1835, b 10 *Mar* 1796, d 28 *Jan* 1857, m 1st, 2 *Mar* 1816, *Lady Isabella, da of Arthur (Gore)*, 2nd *Earl of Arran* [I], d 30 *Nov* 1838, 2ndly, 28 *Dec* 1852, *Agnes Julia, da of Capt John S Rich of Woodlands, Castle Connell* [*who re-m* 2ndly, *Oct* 1862, *Lieut -Col Wills Croft Gason*], *and had issue* 1d *to* 7d

1d *William Grant Douglas, Comm R N*, b 25 *Feb* 1824, d 16 *Dec* 1898, m 1st, 16 *Dec* 1851, *Elizabeth, da of William Inglis*, d *May* 1865, 2ndly, 6 *June*

[Nos 36656 to 36888

# of The Blood Royal

1867, *Elizabeth Frances (37 South Parade, Southsea), da of Thomas Agmondesham Vesey of Caledon, co Tyrone, and had issue* 1e *to* 6e

  1e Sholto Osborne Gordon Douglas, B A (Oxon), *b* 11 Sept 1873

  2e[1] Bessie Henrietta Douglas, *m* 1st, 1 Feb 1875, Claud William Leslie Ogilby of Altnachree Castle, co Tyrone (see below), *d* 1891, 2ndly, 1895, Hugo Bartels

  3e[1] Ada Charlotte Douglas, *m* 1st, 1886, Harris St John Dick, *d* 1886, 2ndly, 1892, Frederick Gray Maturin

  4e[1] Mary Louisa Douglas, *m* 17 Jan 1877, Colin Bent Phillip

  5e[1] Margaret Caroline Douglas, *m* as 2nd wife, 1883, the Rev Edward Douglas Prothero (see below)

  6e[2] Maude Isabel Gore Douglas, *m* 23 Ap 1895, Capt Cuthbert Edward Hunter, R N

  2d *Gordon James Douglas of Poppleton House, York, b* 27 Aug 1835, *d* 1901, *m* 12 Aug 1858, *Louisa da of James Turbett of Owenstown, co Dublin, and had issue* 1e

  1e Isabella Sophia Frances Douglas, *m* 20 Sept 1883, Belford Randolph Wilson, Capt 4th Royal Irish Dragoons, *d* 1897

  3d *Augusta Frederica Douglas, b* 22 Nov 1819, *d* (-), *m* 15 Dec 1842, *Henry Poore Cox, d* 8 May 1876, *and had issue* 1e *to* 6e

  1e *William Douglas Cox, b* 1 June 1844, *d* 1905, *m* 2 Ap 1865, *Mary Anne Amelia Catherine (Tokio, Japan), da of the Rev Edward Pole [Bt (E 1628) Coll], and had issue* 1f *to* 2f

    1f Edward Pole Cox, *b* 28 Jan 1866

    2f Henry Augustus Cox, *b* 13 Nov 1876

  2e *Henry Poore Cox, b* 10 Dec 1846, *m* 4 Dec 1875, *Augusta Anne, da of Surgeon-Major William Walter Weld, and has issue* 1f

    1f Alice Frederica Cox, *b* 21 Nov 1878

  3e Charles Louis Hamilton Cox, *b* 27 Nov 1850

  4e George Nelson Cox, *b* 3 Feb 1861

  5e Caroline Marianne Cox

  6e Annie Elizabeth Georgiana Cox

  4d *Julia Mary Douglas, b* 18 Aug 1822, *d* (-), *m* 20 July 1818, *Lieut Col George James Montgomery, G C S, d at Agra 20 Sept* 1860, *and had issue* 1e *to* 3e

  1e *Isabella Montgomery, d* 15 May 1877, *m Charles Edward Macnamara, and had issue (a son and 2 das)*

  2e Elizabeth Charlotte Montgomery

  3e Georgiana Louisa Jane Montgomery

  5d *Caroline Douglas, b* 7 Dec 1826, *m* 17 Dec 1841, *Lieut Col Edward Prothero, 3rd West York L I Mil, d* 1887, *and has issue* 1e

  1e *Rev Edward Douglas Prothero, Rector of Turweston, d* (-), *m* 1st, 2 June 1877, *Anne, widow of Charles Church, da of John Cunningham of Grahamslaw, d* (-), 2ndly, 1883, *Margaret Caroline (see above), da of Capt William Grant Douglas, R N*

  6d *Adelaide Charlotte Douglas, b* 16 June 1830, *d* (-), *m* 30 Jan 1851, *William Ogilby of Altnachree Castle, co Tyrone, d* 1 Sept 1873, *and had issue* 1e *to* 7e

  1e *Claud William Leslie Ogilby of Altnachree Castle, Lieut 31st Regt, b* 1851, *d* 1891, *m* 17 Feb 1875, *Bessie Henrietta (see above), da of Capt William Grant Douglas, R N [who rem 2ndly,* 1895, *Hugo Bartels]*

  2e James Douglas Ogilby, *b* 1853

  3e Adelaide Charlotte Ogilby

  4e Isabella Caroline Ogilby

  5e Beatrice Emma Elizabeth Ogilby

  6e Louisa Ogilby

  7e Edith Sophia Ogilby

[Nos 36880 to 36912

2 H

The Plantagenet Roll

7d *Louisa Emma Douglas*, b 19 *Nov* 1831, d (–), m 29 *Sept* 1857, *Charles Burton Fox*, *and had issue* 1e *to* 6e

1e Charles Douglas Fox, *b* 21 Jan 1867

2e Constance Douglas Fox

3e Alice Louisa Fox

4e Beatrice Elizabeth Fox

5e Maude Cecilia Fox

6e Katherine Fox

3c *Edward Gordon (Douglas, afterwards (R L 25 Jan* 1841) *Douglas-Pennant)*, 1st *Baron Penrhyn [U K], so cr 3 Aug* 1866, b 20 *June* 1800, d 31 *Mar* 1886, m 1st, 6 *Aug* 1833, *Juliana Isabella Mary [descended from the Lady Anne, sister of King Edward IV , &c], da and co-h of George Hay Dawkins Pennant of Penrhyn Castle, co Carnarvon,* d 25 *Ap* 1842, 2ndly, 26 *Jan* 1846, *Lady Maria Louisa [descended from George, Duke of Clarence], da of Henry (FitzRoy), 5th Duke of Grafton [E], and had issue*

See the Exeter Volume, pp 457–458, Nos 36503–36558, and the Clarence Volume, p 339, Nos 10873–10881

4c *Lady Frances Douglas*, b 10 *Jan* 1786, d *Aug* 1833, m 21 *Ap* 1804, *Lieut -Gen the Hon Sir William Stewart, G C B [E of Galloway Coll],* d 7 *Jan* 1827, *and had issue*

See the Tudor Roll, pp 502–503, Nos 34122–34113

5c *Lady Harriet Douglas*, b 8 *June* 1792, d 26 *Aug* 1833, m 1st, 25 *Nov* 1809, *James Hamilton, Viscount Hamilton [son and h -app of John James, 1st Marquis of Abercorn [G B], K G]* d v p 27 *May* 1814, 2ndly, 8 *July* 1815, *George (Gordon), 4th Earl of Aberdeen [S], K G,* d 14 *Dec* 1860, *and had issue* 1d *to* 7d

1d *James (Hamilton), 1st Duke [I], 7th Marquis [G B], and 10th Earl [S] of Abercorn, 14th Duke of Chatellerault [F], &c , K G , P C , &c , b* 21 *Jan* 1811, d 31 *Oct* 1885, m 25 *Oct* 1832, *Lady Louisa Jane [descended from King Henry VII], da of John (Russell), 6th Duke of Bedford [E], K G,* d 31 *Mar* 1905, *and had issue*

See the Tudor Roll, pp 481–484, Nos 33416–33558

2d *Right Hon Lord Claud Hamilton, P C , M P , b* 27 *July* 1813, d 3 *June* 1884, m 7 *Aug* 1844, *Lady Emma Elizabeth [descended from Lady Anne, sister of King Edward IV], da of Granville Leveson (Proby), 3rd Earl of Carysfort [I],* d 24 *June* 1900, *and had issue*

See the Exeter Volume, p 185, Nos 6638–6645

3d–6d (Sons by 2nd husband) See the Tudor Roll, pp 463–465, Nos 32741–32797

7d *Lady Harriet Hamilton*, b 21 *Mar* 1812, d 19 *Mar* 1884, m 15 *May* 1836, *Admiral William Alexander Baillie-Hamilton, R N [E of Haddington Coll],* d 1 *Oct* 1881, *and had issue* 1e *to* 5e

1e Sir William Alexander Baillie-Hamilton, K C M G , C B , *late* Chief Clerk of the Colonial Office, and Officer of Arms of the Order of St Michael and St George, *formerly* Col Comdg Lothians and Berwickshire Yeo , &c &c (55 *Sloane Street*, *S W Carlton*), *b* 6 Sept 1844, *m* 21 June 1871, Mary Ayscombe, da of the Rev John Mossop, Rector of Hothfield, and has issue 1f *to* 2f

1f George Douglas Baillie-Hamilton, Capt 2nd Batt Royal Scots, *b* 26 Sept 1875

2f Walter Stuart Baillie-Hamilton, Private Sec to the Gov of S Australia (Adm Sir Day H Bosanquet, G C V O , K C B), *b* 9 Aug 1880

2e Charles Robert Baillie-Hamilton, *late* Clerk to the Treasury, *b* 24 Sept 1848

3e James Baillie-Hamilton, *b* 24 Ap 1851, *m* 10 Aug 1886, Lady Evelyn, da of John (Campbell), 8th Duke of Argyll [S], K G , K T

[Nos 36913 to 37218]

238

# of The Blood Royal

4c Harriet Eleanor Baillie-Hamilton (37 *Bedford Square, W C*), m 22 Sept 1863, Henry Samuel King of the Manor House Chigwell, co Essex, J P, d 17 Nov 1878, and has issue 1f to 6f

1f Arthur Hamilton King (12 *Cambridge Street, Hyde Park, W*), b 21 Jan 1866, m 26 Oct 1897, Charlotte Elizabeth, da of the Rev Charles Christopher Ellison of the Manse, Bracebridge, co Lanc

2f Violet Mary King, m 9 Feb 1898, Algernon Christian Baily (*Woodford Green, Essex*), and has issue 1g to 2g

1g Michael Henry Hamilton Baily, b 6 Dec 1901

2g Blanche Emma Violet Baily, b 1 Oct 1899

3f Harriet Frances Margaret King

4f *Katharine Douglas King*, d 26 May 1901, m 26 *June* 1900, *the Rev Edmund Godfrey Burr*, M A (*Oxon*), *Rector of Chatham* (*The Rectory, Chatham*), and had issue 1g to 2g

1g Katherine Veronica Mary Burr, } b (twins) 25 Mar 1901
2g Filumena Mary Douglas Burr, }

5f Honora Lilian King

6f Laura Beatrice King

5c Laura Frances Baillie-Hamilton, m as 2nd wife, 19 Oct 1901, Ralph Gooding, B A, M D, J P, D L (13 *Church Terrace, Blackheath, S E.*)

6c Lady Elizabeth Emma Douglas, b 8 Oct 1791, d 2 Feb 1857, m 10 *July* 1827, *William Hamilton-Ash of Ashbrook, co Londonderry, D L*, d 30 Nov 1866, and had issue 1d

1d *Caroline Hamilton-Ash*, d 13 Jan 1901, m as 2nd wife, 7 *July* 1853, *John Barre Beresford of Learmount, co Londonderry* [*E of Tyrone Coll*], d 30 Aug 1895, and had issue 1e to 6e

1e William Randall Hamilton Beresford, now (R L 26 June 1901) Beresford-Ash of Ashbrook, D L, Major Royal Welsh Fusiliers (*Ashbrook, Londonderry*), b 19 June 1859, m 23 Oct 1886, Florence Marion [descended from King Henry VII (see the Tudor Roll, p 412)], da of Lord Henry Ulick Browne [M of Sligo Coll], and has issue 1f

1f Douglas Beresford-Ash, b 3 Sept 1887

2e Marcus John Barre Beresford, Major South Wales Borderers, South African Medals and Clasps (*Sports*), b 10 Ap 1868

3e Emma Clara Beresford, m 20 Dec 1881, Francis Coffin Macky of Belmont, J P, D L, Capt *late* 3rd Dragoon Guards (*Belmont, Londonderry*), and has issue 1f to 4f

1f John Barre Beresford Macky, 2nd Lieut Royal Warwickshire Regt, b 5 Aug 1889

2f Eleanora Caroline Lucia Macky, m 28 Feb 1907, His Honour Judge (John Fitzpatrick) Cooke, Judge of Donegal County Court (*Glengollan, Fahan, co Donegal*), s p

3f Gladys Kathleen Macky

4f Emily Clara Macky

4e Barbara Caroline Beresford

5e Mary Elizabeth Beresford, m 6 Feb 1899, Henry John Cooke (*Boom Hall, co Londonderry*), and has issue 1f to 3f

1f John Sholto Fitzpatrick Cooke, b 1906

2f Frances Caroline Cooke

3f Clara Elizabeth Douglas Cooke

6e Louisa Gertrude Douglas Beresford, m 22 Aug 1894, Major John Edward Pine Coffin of Portledge, D S O, Royal N Lancashire Regt (*Portledge, near Bideford, Devon*), and has issue 1f to 3f   [Nos 37219 to 37241

The Plantagenet Roll

1f Edward Claude Pine Coffin, b 25 May 1895

2f Richard Geoffrey Pine Coffin, b 1 Dec 1908

3f Gertrude Beresford Pine-Coffin

1f Gwendolyn Mary Pine Coffin

7c Lady Caroline Douglas, b 17 De 1797 , d 7 Nov 1873 , m 31 Dec 1817, William Augustus Pitt Lane-Fox, d 1832 , and had issue

See the Exeter Volume, p 450, Nos 35654–35677

3b Lady Mary Anne Lascelles, b 22 Nov 1775 , d 10 June 1831 , m 20 Ap 1801 Richard York of Wighill Park, D L , Lieut-Col West Riding Yorkshire Hussar Yeomanry, High Sheriff co York 1832, d 27 Jan 1843 , and had issue 1c

1c Edward York of Wighill Park, J P , D L , b 6 Jan 1802, d 26 Jan 1861 , m 25 Nov 1835, Penelope Beatrix [descended from King Henry VII (see Tudor Roll, p 390)], da of the Rev Christopher Sykes, Rector of Roos, d June 1873 , and had issue 1d to 5d

1d Edward Christopher York of Hutton Hall, J P , b 14 Oct 1842, d 14 Dec 1885 , m 1st, 27 Jan 1870, Isabel Augusta [descended from Lady Anne, sister of King Edward and Richard III (see Exeter Volume, p 536)], da of Thomas Fairfax of Steeton, co York, J P , D L , d 21 Ap 1875 , 2ndly, 1876, Celina Rose, da of the Rev Charles Marsden, Vicar of Gargrave, and had issue 1e to 7e

1e Edward York of Hutton, J P , late Capt 1st Royal Dragoons (Hutton Hall, Long Marston, Yorks), b 16 Jan 1872 , m 10 May 1906, Violet Helen [descended maternally from Kings Henry VII and Edward IV (see Tudor Roll, p 502), and paternally from the latter's brother George, Duke of Clarence, K G (see Clarence Volume, p 270)], da of the Right Hon Sir Frederick George Milner, 7th Bt [G B], P C , M P , and has issue 1f to 2f

1f Christopher York, b 27 July 1909

2f Louise Violet Diana York

2e Richard Lister York, b 29 Mai 1880

3e Francis Stafford York, b 18 Sept 1883

4e Edwin Arthur York, b 27 Feb 1885

5e Beatrix Penelope Lucy York

6e Mabel Rose York

7e Sibell Marguerite York, m 1908, Leslie Reid, late 8th Hussars

2d Lucy Mary York, d 21 Feb 1893 , m as 1st wife, 16 Ap 1857, Edward Brooksbank of Healaugh, Lord of the Manor and Patron of that place, LL B (Camb), J P (Healaugh Manor, Tadcaster , Newton House, Whitby) , and had issue 1e to 4e

1e Edward Clitherow Brooksbank, B A (Camb), J P , Major late York Art , b 24 Nov 1858 , m 8 Ap 1885, Katharine Graham, da of Hugh Morris Lang of Broadmeadows, Selkirk , and has issue 1f to 4f

1f Stamp Brooksbank, b 17 Jan 1887

2f Edward York Brooksbank, b 16 Dec 1889.

3f Hugh Godfrey Brooksbank, b 24 Dec 1893

4f Margaret Graham Brooksbank

2e Philip Brooksbank (Nelson, British Columbia), b 5 Jan 1869

3e Laura Sophia Brooksbank, b 14 Nov 1861 , d 29 June 1887 , m 18 June 1885, Frederick William Slingsby (Red House Moor, Monkton, York) , and had issue 1f to 2f

1f Thomas Slingsby, Lancashire Fusiliers, b 18 Mar 1886

2f Henry Slingsby, b 13 June 1887

4e Lucy Hilda Brooksbank

3d Caroline Penelope York, m 28 Sept 1864, the Rev John Morland Rice, Rector of Bramber, Sussex, d s p 1894

4d Laura Marianne York, m 22 Sept 1870, Adm Ernest Rice, R N (Siberts-wold Place, Kent) , and has issue 1e to 3e

1e Arthur Rice, Lieut R N   [Nos 37245 to 37294

2e Laura Gwenllian Rice, m 4 Oct 1894, the Hon Walter John James, J P [son and h-app of Walter Henry, 2nd Baron Northbourne [U K], and descendant maternally of King Henry VII, &c (see the Tudor Roll, p 308)] (1 *Courtfield Road, S W , Travellers', Athenæum*), and has issue 1f to 4f

　　1f Walter Ernest Christopher James, b 18 Jan 1896
　　2f Dorothea Gwenllian James
　　3f Mary Beatrix James
　　4f Jane Margaret James

3e Beatrice Lucy Rice, m 1 June 1901, Major Eric Pearce-Serocold, King's Royal Rifles, and has issue 1f

　　1f Elizabeth Laura Pearce-Serocold, b 20 May 1903

5d Harriet York, m 3 Feb 1880, Richard Hewetson of York, and has issue 1e to 3e

　　1e Richard Stafford Hewetson
　　2e Mary Hewetson
　　3e Dorothy Hewetson

4a *Mary Chaloner, b 22 Dec 1743, d 2 Oct 1803, bur in Guisboro' Church with husband, m 11 June 1763, Gen John Hale of Plantation, near Guisboro', co York, Col 17th Light Dragoons and Gov of Londonderry* [4th son of *Sir Bernard Hale, Chief Baron of the Exchequer [I], b 1728, d 20 Mar 1806, and had issue* (with 6 other sons and 5 das who d ~ p) 1b to 10b

1b *Hon John Hale of Lower Canada, Paymaster-Gen to the Forces in Canada, Receiver-Gen of that Province, formerly Mil Sec to H R H the Duke of Kent, b 27 Mar 1764, d 21 Dec 1838, m 3 Ap 1799, Elizabeth Frances, sister to William Pitt, 1st Earl Amherst [U K], da of Lieut Gen William Amherst b 2 Ap 1774, d at Quebec 18 June 1826, and had issue* (with 3 sons and a da who d ~ p) 1c to 4c

1c *Edward Hale, Member of th Quebec Legislative Council, a godson of H R H the Duke of Kent, b in Quebec 6 Dec 1801; d there 26 Ap 1875, m there 10 Mar 1831, Elizabeth Cecilia, da of the Hon Mr Justice Bowen of Quebec, b 20 Feb 1813, d 19 Feb 1850, and had issue 1d to 6d

1d Edward John Hale (*30 Des Carrières Street, Quebec*), b in Quebec 14 Jan 1833, m there 17 Oct 1866, Justine Elise, da of James Sewell of Quebec, M D , and has issue 1e

1e Edward Russell Hale, Capt Army Service Corps (*Kingston, Ontario*), b in Quebec 10 Feb 1870, m 15 Aug 1893, Ethel, da of Frederick Montizambert, M D , and has issue 1f to 3f

　　1f Frederick Amherst Hale, b 26 Mar 1895
　　2f Jeffery John Hale, b 28 Ap 1897
　　3f Helen Justine Hale, b 19 Sept 1898

2d *Edward Chaloner Hale, Attorney-at-Law*, b 9 May 1814, d 9 Mar 1909, m 12 Mar 1873, Sarah Ellen, da of John Chillas, and had issue 1e to 2e

1e Edward Chaloner Hale (*Plantation, Lennoxville, Quebec, Canada*), b at Lennoxville 6 June 1884, m in Montreal 11 Mar 1909, Rae Blanch, da of Ambrose Hines Mudgett of Plymouth, New Hampshire, U S A

2e Frances Eliza Cecilia Hale, m at Lennoxville Ap 1905, Richard Trevor Buchanan (*Woodlands, Quebec*), and has issue 1f to 2f

　　1f Edward Trevor Buchanan, b 13 Ap 1906
　　2f John Hale Buchanan, b 23 Nov 1907

3d William Amherst Hale (*Sleepy Hollow, Sherbrooke, Quebec*), b at Sherbrooke 23 Feb 1847, m at Rivière du Loup, Quebec, 2 Aug 1884, Ellen, da of Stewart Derbishire, Private Sec to Lord Durham, and has issue 1e to 6e

　　1e Edward Amherst Forbes Hale, b 21 June 1894
　　2e Martha Gladys Forbes Hale
　　3e Mary Stewart Hale
　　4e Vera Derbishire Amherst Hale
　　5e Cecilia Montagu Hale
　　6e Elizabeth Alicia Amherst Hale　　　　　　[Nos 37295 to 37321.

The Plantagenet Roll

4d Ellen Frances Hale (*Sherbrooke, Quebec*), b in Quebec, unm

5d May Hale (*Sherbrooke, Quebec*) b in Sherbrooke, unm

6d Lucy Anne Hale, b in Sherbrooke, m there 16 Sept 1863, Henry Turner Machin, Assist Treasurer of the Province of Quebec (*Quebec*) s p

2c William Amherst Hale, Capt 52nd Regt, b 25 Jan 1809, d 25 Sept 1844, m Nov 1839, Caroline, da of Capt J Jenkins of New Brunswick [who m 2ndly, F S Stayner and] d 14 May 1876, and had issue 1d to 2d

1d May Louisa Hale (30 *Hereford Square, S W*), m 24 Jan 1865, Robert Bethune of Nydie, co Fife J P, Major 92nd Highlanders [2nd son of Lieut-Gen Alexander Bethune, *formerly Sharp, of Blebo*], b 29 July 1827, d 27 July 1901, and has issue 1e to 5e

1e Henry Alexander Bethune of Nydie and Mountquhanie, J P, Major 6th Vol Batt Black Watch, *formerly Gordon Highlanders* (*Nydie, co Fife*, *Naval and Military*), b 12 July 1866, m 2 Sept 1902, Elinor Mary, da of John Brown Witt of Sydney, N S W, and has issue 1f

1f Mary Sharp Bethune

2e Eleanor Mary Bethune, m as 2nd wife, 23 Sept 1901, Capt Frederick Campbell Maconchy, D S O, *late East Yorks Regt* (86 *Brook Street, S W*, *Naval and Military*)

3e Louisa Cecilia Bethune, m as 2nd wife 1903, Lieut-Col William Crawfurd Middleton, *late Royal Scots Greys*, and has issue 1f to 2f

1f Robert Campbell Middleton, b 3 July 1907

2f Doris Mary Middleton

4e Jane Millicent Bethune

5e Margaret Bethune, m 10 Nov 1900, the Rev Francis Walter Boyd, M A, and has issue 1f

1f Mary Cecilia Boyd

2d Caroline Henrietta Hale (14 *Eaton Square, S W*), m 19 Feb 1861, the Hon Pascoe Charles Glyn, M P, D L [6th son of George Carr, 1st Baron Wolverton [U K]], d 3 Nov 1904, and has issue 1e to 4e

1e Geoffrey Carr Glyn, D S O, Major N Somerset Yeo, and *late Mil Sec* to Governor of Madras (Sir Arthur Lawley, K C M G) (*White's, Marlborough*), b 19 Apr 1864, m 20 July 1889, the Hon Winifred [descended from the Lady Isabel Plantagenet (see Essex Volume, p 46)], da of Charles (Harbord), 5th Baron Suffield [G B], and has issue 1f

1f Louise Gwendoline Glyn, b 21 Sept 1891

. 2e Maurice George Carr Glyn, *late Lieut Dorset Yeo Cav* (21 *Bryanston Square, W*, *Albury Hall, Little Hadham*), b 12 Mar 1872, m 6 Oct 1897, the Hon Maud, da of Robert Wellesley (Grosvenor), 2nd Baron Ebury [U K], and has issue 1f to 3f

1f Christopher Pascoe Robert Glyn, b 8 Oct 1899

2f Francis Maurice Grosvenor Glyn, b 9 Aug 1901

3f Martin St Leger Glyn, b 5 Dec 1902

3e Maud Louisa Glyn, m 12 Oct 1887, Henry Percy St John, a Clerk in the House of Lords [V Bolingbroke Coll, a descendant of George, Duke of Clarence, K G (see Clarence Volume, p 489)] (64 *Eccleston Square, S W*), and has issue 1f to 3f

1f Geoffrey Robert St John, b 4 Jan 1889

2f Margaret Olivia St John

3f Ursula Mary St John

4e Agnes Mary Glyn, m 23 Feb 1884, Col Francis Onslow Barrington Foote, R A, *formerly Comdt Royal Mil School of Music* (*Manor House, Barnes, Surrey*), and has issue 1f to 4f

[Nos 37322 to 37346

# of The Blood Royal

1f Alan Wortley Barrington Foote, *formerly* Lieut 4th Hussars, b 1885

2f Philip Ward Barrington Foote, Lieut Royal Fusiliers b 1889

3f Randle Charles Barrington Foote, b 1890

4f Sibell Mary Barrington Foote

3c *George Carleton Hale*, b 30 Oct 1812, d 22 May 1892, m 1st, 1840, *Henrietta, da of Capt Thomas Trigge, Barrack-Master-Gen , Quebec, d s p Sept 1842 , 2ndly, 6 June 1847, Ellen, da of James Sampson of Kingston, Ont . M D , d 28 Feb 1854 , and had issue 1d to 4d*

1d Jeffery Hale (London, Canada), b 20 May 1850 , m 8 Sept 1881, Louisa Galt, da of Duncan Campbell of Simcoe , Ont , and has issue 1e to 2e

1e George Carleton Hale, b 30 June 1885

2c Jessie Campbell Hale, m 19 June 1909, George Stephen Hensley of the Bank of Montreal, Canada

2d Henrietta Hale } (*Forest House, Coleman's Hatch, Sussex*)
3d Frances Alicia Hale }

4d Mary Caroline Percy Hale, m 28 July 1886, the Rev Robert Percy Trevor Tennent, Vicar of Acomb (Acomb Vicarage, Yorks) , and has issue 1e to 7e

1e Jeffery Bernard Hale Tennent, b 6 Aug 1889

2e Oswald Moncrieff Tennent, b 16 June 1894

3e Mary Percy Clare Tennent

4e Frances Maud Tennent

5e Constance Hilda Madeline Tennent

6e Stephanie Millicent Tennent

7e Marjorie Augusta Tennent

4c *Elizabeth Harriet Hale*, d 31 May 1897, m at Quebec 5 Feb 1838, Rear-Adm John Orlebar, R N [3rd son of John Orlebar of Hinwick], b 18 Oct 1810 , d 11 May 1901 , and had issue 1d to 6d

1d Rev Henry Amherst Orlebar, Rector of King's Cliffe (King's Cliffe Rectory, Wansford, R S O), b 19 Nov 1844 , m 9 Aug 1894, Constance, da of the Rev Richard Bryans, M A , and has issue 1e to 3e

1e Ralph Chaloner Orlebar, b 6 Dec 1895

2e Constance Muriel Orlebar, b 5 Sept 1885

3e Dorothy Eleanor Orlebar, b 7 Oct 1889

2d John Hale Orlebar, Lieut R N , b 28 Sept 1846 , d (? unm) 1892

3d Rev Jeffrey Edward Orlebar, Vicar of Southsea (Southsea Vicarage, Camb), b 25 Nov 1857 , m 16 Jan 1877, China Albinia, da of Alexander Duff, and has issue 1e to 3e

1e Jeffrey Alexander Amherst Orlebar, b 3 Mar 1879

2e Marie Elspeth Maud Orlebar

3e Clarice Knightley Orlebar

4d Hotham George Orlebar, b 9 Nov 1853 , d (? unm) 1 Nov 1884

5d Harriot Orlebar

6d Frances Hale Orlebar

2b *Henry Hale*, H E I C Maritime Service, b 30 Oct 1765, d 16 May 1818 , m 27 June 1809, Elizabeth, da and co-h , and in her issue (24 June 1873) h of the Rev Henry Hildyard of Stokesley, co York, d 20 Feb 1856 , and had issue (with 2 sons who d s p) 1c to 4c

1c *Bernard Hale of Doncaster, Bar -at-Law*, b 6 Ap 1812 , d 13 May 1875 , m 5 Aug 1858, Elizabeth, da of William Gurley of Petershope, St Vincent, W I , d 11 May 1891 , and had issue 1d

1d Rev Bernard George Richard Hale, Vicar of Edenhall (Edenhall Vicarage, Langwathby, R S O , Cumberland), b 26 Oct 1859 , m 2 Aug 1893, Charlotte Sarah, da of John Bush of Beauthorn, Ullswater , and has issue 1e

1e John Bernard Windham Hale, b 4 Ap 1905   [Nos 37317 to 37375

243

The Plantagenet Roll

2c John Richard Westgarth Hale, afterwards (R L 19 June 1855) Hildyard of Horsley House and Unthank, J P , D L , High Sheriff (1883) co Durham, and Chairman of Quarter Sessions N R York, b 17 June 1813 , d 24 Oct 1888 , m 24 Aug 1860, Mary Blanche [descended from George, Duke of Clarence, K G (see Clarence Volume p 465)], da of Sir Richard Digby Neave, 3rd Bt [G B], and had issue 1d to 8d

1d John Arundell Hildyard of Horsley and Hutton-Bonville, J P , D L , High Sheriff co Durham 1900 (Horsley House, near Stanhope , Hutton-Bonville Hall, Northallerton , Carlton), b 24 Aug 1861

2d Edward Digby Hildyard, b 20 Aug 1864

3d Blanche Hildyard, m 19 Nov 1889, Charles Edward Leake Ringrose, Bar-at-Law, Registrar of Deeds for N R York (The Registrar House, Northallerton) , and has issue 1e to 2e

1e Christopher Hildyard Ringrose, R N , b 30 Nov 1890

2e Euphemia Blanche Ringrose

4d Phillis Mary Hildyard, m 5 Mar 1904, Capt Henry Grenville Bryant, D S O , Kings Shropshire L I

5d Elizabeth Muriel Hildyard

6d Venetia Dorothy Hildyard

7d Gertrude Isabel Hildyard

8d Cicely Frances Hildyard

3 George Charles Hale, Agent to the Earl of Derby, b 10 Jan 1818 , d Nov 1902 m 1 Aug 1862, Bessie Lizard [descended from the Lady Isabel Plantagenet (see Essex Volume, p 72)] (Knowsley), da of John Eyre of Eyre Court Castle, and had issue 1d to 6d

1d Wyndham Edward Hale, Agent for the Earl of Derby's Lancashire Estates (Mowbreck Hall, Kirkham), b 25 Oct 1864 , m 12 July 1894, Kezia, da of Major Cunliffe, 1st Bengal Fusiliers

2d George Duckworth Hale, b 3 June 1868

3d Robert Eyre Hale, b 2 July 1871 , m 7 Dec 1909, Elsie Emma, da. of Sir Lindsay Wood, 1st Bt [U K]

4d Lionel Hugh Hale, b 4 July 1875 , m 25 June 1899, Kathleen, da of (—) Kincaid of W Virginia

5d John Hale, b 8 Aug 1880 , m 14 Oct 1906, May Maud, da. of John Hughes, and has issue 1e

1e Ida May Armit Hale, b 29 July 1907

6d Muriel Alice Mary Hale

1c Elizabeth Anne Hale, b 13 Ap 1816 , d 26 May 1878 , m Feb 1846/7, the Rev John Burdon of Castle Eden, co Durham, Rector of English Bicknor, co Glos, b 14 Oct 1811 , d 12 Nov 1893 , and had issue 1d to 3d

1d Rowland Burdon of Castle Eden, J P , Lieut -Col and Hon Col 1st Vol Batt Durham L I (The Castle, Castle Eden, co Durham), b 19 June 1857 , m 17 Feb 1887, Mary Arundell, da of Wyndham Slade of Montys-Court, co Somerset, and has issue 1e to 4e

1e Rowland Burdon, b 6 Feb 1893

2e Frances Mary Burdon

3e Jean Burdon

4e Lettice Burdon

2d John George Burdon (Benwell Hall, Newcastle-on-Tyne), b 27 July 1859 , m Feb 1892, Blanche Louisa [descended from George, Duke of Clarence, K G (see Clarence Volume, p 331)], da of Gen Edward Arthur Somerset, C B [D of Beaufort Coll], and has issue 1e to 3e

1e Noel Edward Burdon, b 25 Dec 1893

2e John Burdon, b 10 Nov 1896

3e Elizabeth Alyson Blanche Burdon, b. 20 Ap 1895   [Nos 37376 to 37401.

# of The Blood Royal

3d Elizabeth Anne Burdon (*Munstone House, Hereford*)

3b *William Hale of Acomb, co York, Col N Yorkshire Mil,* b 17 *July* 1771, d 23 *Nov* 1856, m 18 *Nov* 1802, *Frances, da of Rowland Webster of Stockton-on-Tees,* d 25 *Mar* 1841, *and had issue (with a son and 4 das who d s p)* 1c *to 3c*

1c *Mary Emily Hale,* b 28 *Oct* 1803, m 31 *Aug* 1824, H *Charles Elsley of Patrick Brompton and Mt St John, and had issue (with 1 son and 5 das, of whom only one, Eliza, is living)*

2c *Frances Hale,* b 16 *Mar* 1805, d 18 *Oct* 1842, m *as 1st wife,* 8 *July* 1834, *Lamplugh Wickham Hird, afterwards* (1843) *Wickham, of Chestnut Grove, co York,* d 2 *Jan* 1863, *and had issue* 1d

1d William Wickham Wickham of Chestnut Grove, J P, *late* Capt Yorkshire Hussars (*Chestnut Grove, near Boston Spa, Yorks*), b 16 Sept 1835, m 27 Oct 1868, Katherine Louisa [descended from the Lady Anne, sister of King Edward IV], da of Thomas Fairfax of Newton-Kyme, d 4 July 1892, and has issue

See the Exeter Volume, p 535, Nos 48991–49004

3c *Harriot Emma Hale,* b 30 *May* 1814, d 30 *Ap* 1844, m 15 *Aug* 1838, *the Rev* H *Hawkins, and had issue (with a son and da d young)* 1d

1d Rev William Webster Hawkins (*Acomb, Yorks*), b 1842, m 1877, Kate L, da of P Leyburn d 1902, and has issue 1e to 5e

1e Charles Francis Hawkins, Capt R A, b 30 Jan 1880

2e Rose Mary Hawkins

3e Beatrice Hawkins

4e Harriet Emma Hawkins, m 12 Dec 1907, Thomas Bowman Henry Whytehead, Merchant Service (see p 314), and has issue 1f

1f Nancy Bowman Whytehead

5e. Olive Hawkins

4b *Vicissimus Hale,* H E I C S, b 6 *Mar* 1788, d *in Bombay Jan* 1826, m 17 *Mar* 1808, *Amelia* S, *da of* (—) *Dundas of co Stirling,* d (–), *and had issue (with 2 sons who d s p)* 1c *to* 4c

1c *William Dundas Hale,* b 25 *July* 1817, d 1879, m 13 *Ap* 1845, *Sarah, da of John Chisholm of Hamilton, Ont, and had issue (with 2 das who d s p)* 1d *to* 3d

1d John Hale

2d Alice Hale, m Joseph Cull (*Mitchell, Ont*), and has issue 1e to 2e

1e Henry Cull

2e Edith Cull

3d Florence Hale (6 *Classic Avenue, Toronto*), m Arthur Murton of Guelph, Ontario, d (–), and has issue 1e to 2e

1e Norman Murton

2e Edith Murton

2c *Elizabeth Jane Hale,* b 12 *May* 1814, d 15 *Jan* 1865, m 22 *Mar* 1834, *the Hon John Wetenhall,* M P P, *Canada, and had issue (with 3 sons d unm)* 1d *to* 2d

1d William Wetenhall, b 1836, m 1856, (—), da of Major Burrows, s p

2d *Frances Emilia Wetenhall,* b 12 *Dec* 1834, d 24 *May* 1887, m 1857, *Henry Seton Strathy* (71 *Queen's Park, Toronto, Canada*), *and had issue (with 1 son d unm)* 1e *to* 6e

1e *Philip John Neesham Strathy,* b 12 Dec 1861, d 2 *Jan* 1908, m *Frances, da of* (—) *Alley, and had issue* 1f *to* 3f

1f Hugh Strathy, b 15 Sept 1884

2f Donald Strathy, b 1903

3f Phyllis Strathy, b 1898

[Nos 37402 to 37432

2 I

The Plantagenet Roll

2c Emilius William Wetenhall Strathy, b 24 July 1867, d 23 Ap 1898, m 1892, Birdie (c/o Mrs Tempest, Port Hope, Ont) da of W S Tempest, and had issue 1f to 2f

    1f Edgar Strathy, b 3 July 1894

    2f Hugh Strathy, b 18 Sept 1898

3c Henry Edmund Breckenridge Strathy, M D, L R C P, F R C S (Edin) (171 Bolton Road, Bury, Lancs), b 23 July 1869, m 25 Ap 1908, Louie, da of John Edwards, s p

4c Frances Elizabeth Strathy, m 31 Jan 1888, the Rev Duncan Macalister Donald, M A, B D, Minister of Moulin (Moulin Manse, Pitlochry, co Perth), and has issue 1f to 3f

    1f Douglas Alan Donald, b 29 Dec 1888

    2f Ian Strathy Donald, b 21 Mar 1896

    3f Mary Theodora Donald, b 31 Oct 1891

5· Mary Theodora Strathy, m 22 Sept 1884 Augustus Henry Frazer Lefroy, K C, M A (Oxon), Professor of Roman Law and Jurisprudence, &c, at the University of Toronto [descended from King Henry VII, &c (see the Tudor Roll, p 401)] (171 Balmoral Avenue, Toronto), and has issue 1f to 3f

    1f Henry Cicherley Lefroy, b 23 July 1890

    2f Langlois Dundas Lefroy, b 16 June 1892

    3f Frazer Keith Lefroy, b 1 Feb 1895

6c Lilian Mabel Strathy, m 17 Oct 1894, Frederick Broughall (1 Elmsley Place, Toronto), and has issue 1f to 4f

    1f Dene Broughall, b 26 Oct 1896

    2f Seton Broughall, b 6 Oct 1897

    3f Jack Broughall, b 30 Nov 1899

    1f Gwyneth Broughall, b 16 Ap 1904

3c Emily Hale, b 22 Dec 1815, d at London, Ont, 19 Nov 1891, m 1842, William James Imlach, H E I C S, d at London, Ont, 20 Feb 1902, and had issue (with 3 other children who d s p) 1d to 4d

    1d William Dundas Imlach of London, Ont b 1845, d 1888, m Louise, da of Charles Smith of New York, and had issue (with a 3rd child, d young) 1e to 2e

        1e Bertram Dundas Imlach

        2e Grace Imlach, m (—) Ware of New York

    2d Eliza Imlach, d 2 Aug 1907, m 29 May 1866, the Rev Edward Edmund Newman, Canon of Huron, and had issue 1e to 2e

        1e Edward Newman, b 7 Nov 1867, m Matilda, da of (—) Carter of Simcoe, Ont, s p

        2e Charlotte Dundas Newman, m 15 Nov 1899, William George Hinds (14 The Ramparts, Quebec, Kingston, Ont), and has issue 1f

            1f Newman Hinds, b 3 July 1901

    3d Emily Catherine Imlach   } (222 Piccadilly Street, London, Ont), unm
    4d Gertrude Harriet Imlach   }

4c Harriet Margaret Hale, b 21 June 1819, d at Tenby, co Pemb, 26 Sept 1855, m 21 June 1838, Robert Anstruther Maingy of Guernsey, C E, d at the siege of Fredericksburg during the American War, 18 Nov 1862, and had issue 1d

    1d Emilia Sophia Dundas Maingy (11 Hirkmur Street, Hamilton, Ont), m at Stratford, Ont, 4 Sept 1862, James Edwin O'Reilly, B A (Toronto Univ), Barat-Law, and afterwards Judge of the Supreme Court in Hamilton, Ont, d there 27 Feb 1907, and had issue (with a son, Robert Miles, d young, and a da, Jane Alice, d unm 27 July 1907) 1e to 6e

        1e Edwin Patrick O'Reilly, B A (Toronto Univ), M D (M'Gill Univ, Montreal), d unm on service in South Africa 17 May 1901   [Nos 37433 to 37457

246

# of The Blood Royal

2e Lily Harriet O'Reilly, *unm*

3e Helen Brephine O'Reilly, *m* Ap 1895, Harry Webb (*Winnipeg*)

4e Ethel Dundas O'Reilly, *m* Ap 1905, Philip Alexander (*Hamilton, Ontario*), and has issue 1f

    1f Patricia Jane Alexander

5e Jessie Ford O'Reilly, *m* Nov 1908, Douglas Harington Chisholm (*Winnipeg*)

6e Anne Louise B O'Reilly, *m* Capt Duncan Frederick Campbell, D S O , Black Watch, *formerly* Lancashire Fusiliers, served in South Africa 1899-1901, including relief of Ladysmith, &c (despatches) (*Woodlands, Eldershe, Renfrewshire*), and has issue 1f to 2f

    1f Archibald Patrick Campbell

    2f John Dundas Campbell

5b *Mary Hale, twin,* b 10 May 1768, d 20 Nov 1837, m 2 Feb 1784, *Thomas Lewin of Ridgeway Castle and The Hollies, Eltham, co Kent,* b 19 Ap 1753, d 1843, *and had issue (with 3 sons and 2 das who d s p)* 1c to 7c

1c *Frederick Mortimer Lewin of the Hollies, co Kent,* b 30 Aug 1798, d 17 June 1877, m 9 Ap 1839, *Augusta Diana, da of Thomas Gisborne Babington of Rothley Temple, co Leic , J P,* d 25 May 1856, *and had issue (with 2 sons and 2 das who d s p)* 1d to 4d

1d Mortimer Lewin (*Little Bedwyn, Hungerford, Wilts*), b 13 Oct 1847, m Oct 1881, Louisa Mary, da of Major George Thompson, and has issue 1e to 2e

    1e Winifred Mary Lewin, *unm*

    2e Dorothy Babington Lewin, *unm*

2d Mary Hale Lewin, *m* 10 June 1865, Col Henry Masterman Thompson [son of Major George Thompson] (9 *Clarence Parade, Southsea*), and has issue 1e to 4e

1e Arthur Hale Thompson, Major 1st Goorkas, b 25 Ap 1866, m 21 Sept 1899, Eleanor, da of Dr Temple, D S O , *s p*

2e William Maxwell Thompson, Capt R E , b 18 Nov 1870, m 18 July 1900, Helen, da of (—) Bull, and has issue 1f to 2f

    1f Oliver Thompson, b 12 Jan 1906

    2f Margaret Helen Thompson, b July 1904

3e Noel Gillatt Thompson, in the Army, b 13 July 1872

4e Millicent Babington Thompson, *m* 18 Nov 1901, Capt Robert William Harling, and has issue 1f to 2f

    1f Katherine Elizabeth Harling, b 17 Jan 1905

    2f Helen Marjorie Harling, b 22 Mar 1908

3d *Diana Spencer Lewin,* b 15 *July* 1843, d 14 Nov 1903 m 10 Mar 1867, *Colonel Edward Spread Beamish, Bombay Artillery,* and had issue 1c to 6c

1c Frederick Chaloner Beamish, has settled in Orangia, South Africa, b 24 Nov 1870, m 17 Jan 1905, Elizabeth, da of John Campbell Dick , and has issue 1f

    1f Lisette Beamish, b 11 July 1906

2c Edward Percy FitzRoy Beamish (*Myburghsfontein, Orangia*), b 20 Dec 1873

3c Rev Charles Noel Bernard Beamish, Diocesan Missioner (*Wolvesey Palace, Winchester*), b 12 Feb 1877

    4c Augusta Diana Beamish, *unm*   ⎫

    5c Olive Mary Beamish, *unm*   ⎬ (*Myburghsfontein, Orangia*)

    6c Cecilia Hamilton Beamish, *unm*   ⎭

4d Julia Babington Lewin (66 *Church Road, St Leonards-on-Sea*)

2c *William Charles James Lewin, H E I C Bengal Art ,* b 15 *June* 1805, d

[Nos 37458 to 37485

247

The Plantagenet Roll

4 Dec 1846, m 18 June 1827, Jane Elizabeth, da of Stephen Laprimaudaye, b 11 May 1803, d 15 Aug 1877, and had issue (with 6 other children who d unm) 1d to 5d

1d Edward Pogson Lewin, b 31 Aug 1833, d (being killed at Lucknow) 1857, m Eliza, da of John Prior and had issue 1e

1e Ada Henrietta Lewin, m 3 Dec 1879, Alpin F Thompson, and has issue (with 3 others d young) 1f to 3f

1f Alpin Erroll Thompson, b 14 May 1893

2f Dorothea Bethune Thompson, b 3 Feb 1882

3f Vivian Irene Thompson, b 10 Jan 1891

2d Frederick Dedtry Lewin (14 Kidbrook Park Road, Blackheath, S E), b 9 Nov 1835, m 15 Oct 1879, Christina, da of Major-Gen Charles Scrope Hutchinson, R E, C B, and has issue (with a da, Christabel Harriet, who d young) 1e to 3e

1e Francis Hutchinson Laprimaudaye Lewin, Lieut R N, b 29 Oct 1880

2e Edward Hale Lewin, Capt 16th Punjabis, Indian Army b 27 Dec 1881

3e Rev William George Lewin, Curate of St John's, Bethnal Green, b 6 Jan 1883

3d William Henry Lewin, Comm (ret) R N (Down House, Frant, Tunbridge Wells), b 11 Nov 1843, m 5 Ap 1870, Caroline, da of Comm Edward George Elliott, R N, and has issue (with a da, Adelaide Laprimaudaye, who d unm 16 Feb 1893) 1e to 3e

1e Henry Frederick Elliott Lewin, Capt R F A, b 26 Dec 1872

2e Charles Laprimaudaye Lewin, Comm R N, b 23 Aug 1875

3e Honoria Caroline Lewin, m 21 Feb 1900, Comm Henry Cyril Royds Brocklebank, R N, , and has issue 1f to 3f

1f Thomas Anthony Brocklebank, b 5 June 1908

2f Margaret Petrina Brocklebank, b 1 Feb 1901

3f Elinor Joan Ida Brocklebank, b 10 Dec 1901

4d Jane Elizabeth Lewin (Haddenham Hall, Bucks)

5d Frances Gisborne Lewin (Haddenham Hall, Bucks), m 30 Ap 1861, Henry Green, d 7 June 1900, and has issue 1e to 10e

1e Richard Henry Green, b 17 June 1865, m 24 July 1894, Mary, da of Henry Mackeson of Hythe, Brewer, and has issue 1f to 4f

1f George Richard Green, b 4 Dec 1897

2f Margaret Mackeson Green, b 14 July 1895

3f Nancy Lawrie Green, b 23 Jan 1899

4f Rachel Mary Green, b 2 July 1903

2e John Frederick Ernest Green, Capt R N, b 8 Aug 1866, m 22 May 1901, Maud, da of Col Charles McInroy of The Burn, Edzell and has issue 1f to 2f

1f Henry Green, b 14 Nov 1906

2f Joan Green, b 30 June 1904

3e Walter Laprimaudaye Green, b 13 Aug 1872, m 26 Mar 1901, Christine, da of (—) Conybere, s p

4e Arthur Dowson Green, b 13 Ap 1874

5e Edward Cecil Green, b 29 Ap 1877

6e George Putzler Green, b 12 Nov 1881

7e Alice Mary Green, m 27 July 1889, Capt Charles Cooke, Merchant Service (ret), formerly Green's Blackwall Ships (Duclair, Seine Inf, France), and has issue 1f to 3f

1f Charles Henry Joseph Cooke, b 8 Dec 1898

2f Lavinia Mary Elizabeth Cooke, b 6 July 1890

3f Catherine Ella Laprimaudye Cooke, b 23 Dec 1892

[Nos 37486 to 37518.

248

# of The Blood Royal

8e Frances Elizabeth Green, *unm*

9e Mabel Lucy Green, *unm*

10e Margaret Helen Green, *m* 24 July 1900, George Henry Woolley, Solicitor (*Cossington, Leicester*), and has issue 1/ to 6/

1/ Stephen Woolley, *b* 9 Feb 1904

2/ Philip Woolley, *b* 23 Oct 1906

3/ Margaret Frances Woolley, *b* 3 Dec. 1901

4/. Honor Woolley, *b* 4 Mar 1903

5/ Lucy Sophia Woolley, *b* 10 May 1905

6/ Helen Mary Woolley, *b* 8 May 1906

3c *George Herbert Lewin, Attorney-at-Law*, b 1808, d 1857, m 1837, *Mary, da of John Friend of Birchington, Isle of Thanet*, d 1890, *and had issue* (*with a son d unm*) 1d to 4d

1d Thomas Herbert Lewin, Col Bengal Staff Corps, *late* 104th Regt (*Parkhurst, Abinger Common, Dorking*), b 1 Ap 1839, m 24 July 1876, Margaret, da of John Robinson McLean, F R S , M P , and has issue 1e to 3e

1e Charles McLean Lewin, Capt 4th Queen's Own Hussars, b 11 Ap 1880, m Sept 1908, Beatrice Emma, da of Henry Barlow Webb of Holmdale, Holmbury, co Surrey, and has issue 1/

1/ [da] Lewin, b 26 July 1909

2e Everest Hannah Grote Lewin, m 24 July 1901, Thomas Martin Macdonald [2nd son of Neil Macdonald of Dunach, Argyllshire] (*Barguillean, Taynuilt, Argyllshire*), s p

3e Audrey Hale Lewin, m 1902, Nicholas Edwin Waterhouse (*Feldemore, Holmbury, Surrey*)

2d *William C J Lewin*, b 1847, d 1879, m J, da of (—) Lewis, and had issue (2 sons and 1 da)

3d Harriet Lewin (17 *St Mildred's Road, Ramsgate*), m 1862, Bankes Tomlin of Dumpton Park, Thanet, Capt Dragoon Guards [2nd son of Robert Sackett Tomlin of Dane Court, co Kent, and Westgate House, co Northants, J P , D L], d 1908, and has issue 1e to 2e

1e Herbert Gore Tomlin, b 1873

2e Latham Julian Tomlin, b 1886

4d Isabella Charlotte Lewin, m 25 Sept 1872, Gen Nathaniel Stevenson, *late* Col Royal Inniskilling Fusiliers and Gov of Guernsey [2nd son of Nathaniel Stevenson of Braidwood, co Lanark, J P] (24 *Rutland Court, W* , *United Service*), and has issue 1e to 3e

1e Natalie Marguerite Stevenson, m 20 Jan 1896, Major Herbert Gordon, 93rd Highlanders (*Westhorpe, Marlow, Bucks*), and has issue 1/ to 2/

1/ Charles Gilbert Skerrow Gordon

2/ Joan Violet Gordon

2e Harriet Mary Stevenson

3e Edwina Katherine Isabel Stevenson

4c *Edward Bernard Hale Lewin of the G P O , London*, b at Bexley, Kent, 1 July 1810, d at Blackheath 3 Mar 1878, m 10 Oct 1850, Maria Matilda [also a descendant of King Edward III (*see the Mortimer-Percy Volume, Part II*)], da of Francis Rivaz, d at Shortlands, Kent, 12 Jan 1905, and had issue 1d to 5d

1d Arthur Hale Lewin (23 *Farnaby Road, Bromley, Kent*), b 14 June 1854, m 7 Oct 1884, Catherine Ann, da of James Chapman, d s p s 24 Nov 1885

2d Wilfred Hale Lewin, Col (ret) Indian Army (*Dorunda, Bromley, Kent*), b 18 May 1856, m 1st, at Poona, India, 31 Oct 1885, Kate, da of Thomas Weston Baggallay, d at Jalna, Deccan, 14 Dec 1888, 2ndly, at Shortlands, 10 Ap 1890, Isabella Marion, da of James Brown Alston, and has issue 1e to 3e

[Nos 37519 to 37513]

249

The Plantagenet Roll

1e Richard Alston Hale Lewin, Durand Scholar at Wellington College, b at Jalna 10 Dec 1891

2e Phyllis Margaret Lewin, b at Hingoli, Deccan, 3 Jan 1887

3e Mary Dorothea Lewin, b at Hingoli 24 Sept 1893

3d Harold Chaloner Lewin, Solicitor (*Birchdale, Bromley, Kent*), b 19 July 1859, m 21 July 1892, Frances Elizabeth, da of James Brown Alston, and has issue (with a son Kenneth Alston, b 26 Mar 1896, d unm 22 Feb 1908) 1e to 4e

  1e Edward Chaloner Lewin, now at Marlborough College, b 25 Sept 1893

  2e Francis Harold Lewin, now at Marlborough College, b 16 Mar 1895

  3e Mary Hope Lewin, b 10 Sept 1900

  4e Margery Theodora Lewin, b 12 Sept 1908

4d Marion Amy Lewin, m 9 Aug 1873, His Honour Judge Henry Tindal Atkinson [son of Henry Tindal Atkinson, Sergeant-at-Law] (*3 Clanricarde Gardens, Notting Hill Gate, W*) and has issue (with a da, Violet May, d young) 1e to 5e

  1e Edward Hale Tindal Atkinson, b 19 Sept 1878

  2e Ethel Marion Atkinson

  3e Amy Maud Atkinson

  4e Enid Katherine Atkinson

  5e Doris May Atkinson

5d Edith Gertrude Agnes Lewin (*23 Farnaby Road, Bromley, Kent*), unm

5c *Mary H Lewin*, b 1785, d 1825, m *Hippesley Marsh*, and had issue of whom 1d

  1d Hippesley Cunliffe Marsh, Col *formerly* Bengal S C (*Tunbridge Wells*)

6c *Harriet Lewin*, b 1 July 1792, d s p 29 Dec 1878, m 5 Mar 1820, *George Grote, Banker, D C L, LL D, M P for London, the Historian of Greece*, b 17 Nov 1794, d s p 18 June 1871

7c *Frances Eliza Lewin*, b 16 Feb 1804, d 21 Aug 1888, m 1832, *Nils Samuel von Koch, a Noble of Sweden* [1815, No 2244], *Attorney-General (Justitie-kanster) of Sweden*, b 10 Mar 1801, d *at Angerum* 13 June 1881, *and had issue 1d to 4d*

1d Nils Thomas Grote von Koch, a Noble of Sweden [1815, No 2244], Chamberlain (Kammarherren) to H M the King of Sweden, and Secretary of Legation, a Landed Proprietor (*Senate, Ludkoping, Sweden*), b 30 July 1833, m 28 June 1861, Hedvig Abela Isabella, da of Martin Vilhelm Rhedin, and has issue 1e to 2e

  1e Noble Nils Thomas Vilhelm von Koch, a Gentleman in-Waiting to H M the King of Sweden (*Rene, Sweden*), b 22 Feb 1861, m 5 Aug 1896, the Countess Jacquette Marie Anna, da of Gen Count Malcolm Walter Hamilton [Ct Hamilton [Sweden 1751] Coll], and has issue 1f to 6f

    1f Noble Nils Thomas Malcolm von Koch, b 11 Aug 1897

    2f Noble Jacques Bo Nils von Koch, b 9 Nov 1907

    3f Noble Hedvig Anna von Koch, b 13 June 1899

    4f Noble Marit Margareta von Koch, b 13 Nov 1900

    5f Noble Lilian Isabella von Koch, b 2 Dec 1901

    6f Noble Signe Jacquette von Koch, b 27 Jan 1903

  2e Noble Isabella Hedvig Frances Wilhelmina von Koch, an Artist, unm

2d Noble Fabian Wilhelm von Koch, *formerly* a Judge (*Halla, Falun, Sweden*), b 10 June 1837, m 17 Ap 1873, the Baroness Hedda Johanna, da of Major Baron Bengt Carl Fredrik Leijonhufvud [B Leijonhufvud [Sweden 1651] Coll], by his wife, Countess Anna Elisabeth Johanna, *née* Hamilton, and has issue 1e to 5e

  1e Noble Carl Fabian Richert von Koch, Civil Engineer and Dr of Elec (*Stockholm*), b 29 July 1879, m 22 Oct 1906, Elisabeth, da of George W Carpenter of Philadelphia, and has issue 1f to 2f

    1f Noble Sigfrid Fabian Richart von Koch, b 7 June 1909

    2f Noble Hedda Soldis Elisabeth von Koch, b 27 Oct 1907

[Nos 37544 to 37572

250

# of The Blood Royal

2e Noble Carl Wathier Gordon von Koch, Student, b 13 Aug 1887

3e Noble Nanny Frances Hedda von Koch, m 17 Aug 1905, Adolf August Emanuel Johansson, teol o filo Kand (teacher) (Gefle)

4e Noble Jane Marie Mathilda von Koch, m as 2nd wife, 11 Sept 1899 Baron Joseph Hermelin, Member of the Swedish Diet [B Hermelin [Sweden 1766] Coll] (Motala, Sweden), and has issue 1f to 5f

    1f Baron Peter Fabian Samuel Axel Hermelin, b at Ulfosa 2 Sept 1909

    2f Baroness Barbro Hedda Eugenia Hermelin, b 27 June 1900

    3f Baroness Karin Ebba Sofia Hermelin, b 9 Ap 1902

    4f Baroness Nanny Jane Ingeborg Hermelin, b 7 Feb 1904

    5f Baroness Birgitta Hermelin, b 17 Aug 1906

5e Noble Anna Mary Elvine von Koch, m 14 Ap 1909, Frithiof von Holmgren, Engineer (Zurich)

3d Noble Richert Vogt von Koch, Lieut Col , formerly Royal (Swedish) Horse Guards (12 Riddargatin, Stockholm) b 22 Dec 1838 m 4 July 1865 the Baroness Agathe Henriette, da of Gen Baron Fabian Jakob Wrede af Elma [B Wrede af Elma [Sweden 1653] Coll] , and has issue 1e to 7e

1e Noble Nils Fabian Helge von Koch, Professor of Mathematics (Djursholm, Sweden), b 25 Jan 1870, m 23 Sept 1893, Signe Sofia Charlotte, da of Magnus Neijber, and has issue 1f to 4f

    1f Noble Fabian Magnus von Koch, b 22 Oct 1894

    2f Noble Gunnar Magnus Richert von Koch, b 11 July 1897

    3f Noble Agnes Lisa Augusta Agathe von Koch, b 13 Oct 1899

    4f Noble Signe Maj von Koch, b 1 May 1908

2e Noble Richert Gerard Halfred von Koch, Editor of the Social Tidskrift (Stockholm), b 13 Jan 1872, m 11 July 1906, Carola Maria Euphrosyne, da of Dr Carl Sahl

3e Noble Nils Arne von Koch, Filos Kand (teacher) (Vasteras, Sweden), b 14 Jan 1875, m 6 Ap 1909, Ella, da of Isaac Neuendorff, Chief Pay Dept Swedish Admiralty

4e Noble Richert Sigurd Valdemar von Koch, Composer (Orno, Sweden), b 28 June 1879, m 8 Nov 1904, Karin Maria, da of Capt Carl Magnell

5e Noble Nils Ragnar von Koch, Jur Kand (Solicitor) (Stockholm), b 29 Ap 1881

6e Noble Harriet Ebba von Koch, Artist (Stockholm)

7e Noble Frances Aurore von Koch, m 26 Sept 1891, Count Hugo Hansson Wachtmeister af Johannishus [C Wachtmeister af Johannishus [Sweden 1687] Coll] (Gullbarna, Sweden), and has issue 1f to 3f

    1f Countess Ebba Frances Agathe Wachtmeister af Johannishus, b 26 Mar 1897

    2f Countess Signe Aurore Wachtmeister af Johannishus, b 3 June 1898

    3f Countess Sigrid Richissa Wachtmeister af Johannishus, b 27 June 1899

4d Noble Oscar Francis von Koch, Solicitor (Stockholm), b 7 Mar 1845, m 27 Nov 1876, Hanna, da of (——) Lundhquist

6b Ann Hale (twin), b 10 Mar 1768, d 5 Dec 1853, m 1st, as 2nd wife, 1785/7, Lieut -Col Henry Walker Yeoman of Woodlands. near Whitby, J P, b 1749, d 1801, 2ndly, 1801, Col Leon Smelt, Governor of the Isle of Man, and had issue 1c to 6c

1c Henry Walker Yeoman of Woodlands, J P, D L, b 13 July 1789, d 14 Sept 1875, m 5 Feb 1816, Lady Margaret Bruce [descended from Lady Anna, sister to King Edward IV , &c], da of Lawrence (Dundas), 1st Earl of Zetland [U K], &c , d 13 Sept 1860, and had issue

See the Exeter Volume, pp 257-258, Nos 9731-9740

[Nos 37573 to 37607.

251

The Plantagenet Roll

2c *Constantine Yeoman, Major in the Army (twin),* b 1791, d *July* 1852, m 28 *May* 1842, *Mary Smelt, da of the Rev Alexander Crigan, D D [who m 2ndly, Sheffield Cox of St Leonards],* and had issue (with 2 sons and a da who d young) 1d

1d *Mary Janette Hale Yeoman,* m 23 June 1861, the Rev Richard Edward Warner, Rector of Stoke and Canon of Lincoln (*Stoke Rectory, Grantham*), and has issue 1c to 7c

    1 Leonard Ottley Warner, b (—), m (—), da of (—), and has issue 1f to 4f

    1f Ashton Christopher Fenwick Warner.

    2f John Warner

    3f Audrey Elizabeth Cromwell Warner

    4f Joyce Trevor Warner

    2c Basel Hale Warner, b (—), m (—), da of (—), and has issue 1f.

    1f John Warner

    3c Richard Cromwell Warner, b (—), m (—), da of (—), and has issue 1f to 2f

    1f Oliver Martin Wilson Warner

    2f Grace Elinor Mary Warner

    4c Lawrence Dundas Warner

    5c Wynyard Alexander Warner

    6c Marmaduke Warner.

    7c Constance Emma Cromwell Warner, m (—) Weigall, and has issue 1f to 3f

    1f Richard Edward Cromwell Weigall

    2f Geoffrey Stephen Cormac Weigall

    3f Dulce Helen Weigall

3c *Bernard Yeoman, Capt R N (twin),* b 1791, d 23 *Ap* 1836, m 1823, *Charlotte, da of Sir Everard Home 1st Bt [U K],* d 21 *Jan* 1878, *and had issue*

    See p 116, Nos 10700-10723

    4c *Robert Smelt,* d 1817

    5c *Frances Smelt,* m (—) *Bacon*

    6c *Jessica Smelt,* m (—) *Cresnell*

7b *Harriot Hale,* b 16 *June* 1769, d 10 *Ap* 1834, m 21 *Ap* 1794, *Lawrence (Dundas), 1st Earl of Zetland [U K], 2nd Baron Dundas [G B] [descended from the Lady Anne, sister of King Edward IV, &c],* d. 19 *Feb* 1839, *and had issue*
See the Exeter Volume, pp 256-260, Nos 9689-9885

8b *Emma Hale,* b 16 *June* 1782, d *May* 1861, m *Oct* 1808, *Major Charles Lloyd, 66th Regt,* d (being drowned in Ireland) 5 Feb 1809, *and had issue* 1c

1c *Rev Charles Lloyd, Canon and Rector of Chalfont St Giles, co Bucks,* d 29 *Ap* 1883, m 20 *Ap* 1841, *Caroline Alicia, da of the Rev Charles Sheffield, M A [2nd son of Sir Robert Sheffield, 3rd Bt],* d 29 *June* 1893, *and had issue* (with 2 elder sons d unm) 1d to 10d

    1d *Francis Aylmer Lloyd (Hurstbury, Witley, Surrey, St Stephen's),* b 6 Sept 1845, m 2 Aug, 1883, Eugenie Alphonsene, widow of William Milner, da of Charles Gaudin, and has issue 1e to 3e

    1e Francis Charles Aylmer Lloyd, b 19 Aug 1884

    2e Florence Eugenie Aylmer Lloyd, b 2 Mar 1887

    3e Gerald Aylmer Lloyd, Welsh Regt, b 17 Ap 1888

    2d Robert Oliver Lloyd, Col R E, Chairman, County of Pembroke Territorial Force Association (*Treffgarne Hall, S O, Pembrokeshire*), b 20 Mar 1849, m 7 June 1877, Mary Isabella, da of Major-Gen Dillon Gustavus Pollard [also a descendant of King Edward III (see the Mortimer-Percy Volume, Part II)], and has issue 1e to 3e   [Nos 37608 to 37851.

252

# of The Blood Royal

1e Charles Whitworth Robert Lloyd, *b* 28 June 1879

2e Francis Oswald Lloyd, *b* 26 Ap 1883

3e Ursula Mary Vere Lloyd, *b* 16 Ma 1891

3d Leonard Sheffield Lloyd (*Holmcroft, Hampton Hill, Midx*) *b* 17 Jan 1851, *m* 11 June 1885, Mary Dora, da of Capt Charles Grigan, and has issue 1e

1e Dorothy Mary Vere Lloyd, *b* 3 May 1887

4d Cyril Hope Lloyd (*Morden, Manitoba, Canada*), *b* 28 Feb 1853, *m* 2 Mar 1878, Alice Augusta, da of Hartley Dunsford of Lindsay, Ontario, and has issue 1e to 7e

1e Digby Sheffield Lloyd, B A , *b* 31 July 1883

2e Cyril Geoffrey Lloyd, *b* 27 May 1887

3e Hartley Dunsford Lloyd, *b* 12 Nov 1889

4e Muriel Hope Lloyd *m* 27 Dec 1904, Robert Ernest Turnbull (2175 *Rae Street, Regina, Sask*), and has issue 1f to 3f

1f Alice Elizabeth Turnbull

2f Muriel Helen Turnbull

3f Mona Ruth Turnbull

5e Ruth Lloyd

6e Alice Marjorie Lloyd, *m* 20 Oct 1909, Arthur Hutchinson (*Morden, Manitoba*)

7e Kate Rubidge Lloyd

5d Marmaduke Bernard Lloyd (1016 *Pandora Avenue, Victoria, British Columbia*), *b* 11 July 1857, *m* 1882, Henrietta da of Hartley Dunsford of Lindsay, afsd , and has issue 1e to 2e

1e Leonard Rubidge Lloyd, *b* 1890

2e Violet Alicia Lloyd, *b* 1886

6d Giles William Lloyd, *b* 1 Dec 1860

7d Perceval Allen Lloyd F R C S , (Eng), L R C P (Lond), Dep Coroner S Div Pembrokeshire (*Chalfont House, Haverfordwest*), *b* 25 May 1863, *m* Feb 1906, Alice Auder Cecile, da of Arthur Say , and has issue 1e to 2e

1e John Perceval Auder Lloyd, *b* 10 May 1909

2e Marjorie Elizabeth Vere Lloyd, *b* 14 Dec 1906

8d Lucy Emma Julia Lloyd, *unm*

9d Caroline Octavia Mary Vere Lloyd, *m* 16 July 1874, the Rev Francis Amcotts Jarvis, M A (Camb), Vicar of Burton (*Burton Vicarage, Doncaster*), and has issue 1e

1e Charles Francis Cracroft Jarvis, Capt Yorks Regt (*Boodle's*), *b* 3 May 1875, *m* 9 June 1906, Helen Constance, widow of Capt Stan Hathorn Johnston Stewart of Physgill, da of Sir Edward Hunter-Blair, 4th Bt [G B] and has issue 1f

1f Ralph George Edward Jarvis *b* 1907

10d Margaret Alice Lloyd

9b Elizabeth Hale (*twin*), *b* 12 Feb 1784, *d* 19 Mar 1845, *m* at Kensington 2 Mar 1819, *the Rev Benjamin Puckle, Rector of Grafham, co Hunts, d at Bagnerre de Bigorres, in the Pyrenees, 1853, and had issue (with 2 das who d s p) 1c to 3c*

1c *Rev Benjamin Hale Puckle, Rector of Grafham*, b 1822, d 1892, m 1st, *Maria, da of (—) Nunn , 2ndly, 20 July 1853, Eleanor, da of the Right Hon Sir Maziere Brady, 1st Bt [U K], P C , Lord Chancellor [I], d s p 18 Feb 1891*

2c *Frederic Hale Puckle, settled in Australia*, b 24 Sept 1823 d 7 May 1909, *m* 4 *May 1858, Fanny, da of the Rev Edward Selwyn, Rector of Hemingford Abbots, d 30 Jan 1896, and had issue (with a da d unm) 1d to 3d*

[Nos 37852 to 37879

253   2 K

The Plantagenet Roll

1d Selwyn Hale Puckle, M B, C M (*Bishop's Castle, Salop*), b at Hamilton, Victoria, 9 June 1859 m 1 Sept 1888, Annie, da of B A Bremner of Morningside, Edinburgh, M D, and has issue (with 1 da d young) 1e to 5e

    1e Frederick Hale Puckle, b 8 June 1889

    2e Bruce Hale Puckle, b 10 Nov 1891

    3e George Hale Puckle, b 21 Dec 1892

    4e Phyllis Hale Puckle

    5e Mary Hale Puckle

    2d Louisa Hale Puckle   } (*Daphne Guildford*)
    3d Eleanor Hale Puckle }

    4c George Hale Puckle (*Nine Oaks, Windermere*), b 20 Dec 1845

10b *Jane Hale* (*twin*), b 12 Feb 1784, d 20 Aug 1821, m as 2nd *wife, at Kensington*, 25 May 1815, *the Rev Henry Budd, Rector of White Roothing, co Essex*, d 27 *June* 1850, *and had issue* (with another son and 2 das d s p) 1c

    1c *Richard Hale Budd of New Brighton, Melbourne, Australia, Inspector-General of Schools,* b 6 Mar 1816, d 27 Mar 1909, m 13 *June* 1843, *Elizabeth, da of Liddle Purves*, and had issue (with 4 sons and 2 das who d s p) 1d to 2d

    1d Mary Elizabeth Budd   } (*Roothing, Brighton, Victoria*)
    2d Emma Eliza Budd   }

[Nos 37880 to 37890

---

132 Descendants of the Rev WILLIAM CHALONER, M A, Queen's College, Cambridge (Table XV) b 17 May 1687, d (–), m 5 May 1724, ANNE, da of J HODGSON of Bishop Auckland, co Durham, and had issue (with 2 sons who d s p)[1] 1a to 2a

1a *Edward James Chaloner of Lincoln* (2nd son), d (–), m (–), and had (with possibly other) issue 1b

1b *Theophania Chaloner,* b 23 *Jan* 1779, d 9 *June* 1857, m 12 Aug 1799 *Thomas Lodington Fairfax of Steeton, co York,* d 1 *July* 1840, *and had issue*[2]

See the Exeter Volume, p 535, Nos 48976-49015

2a *Robert Chaloner of Bishop Auckland,* b 1 Feb 1729, d (–), m 12 *Sept* 1763, *Dorothy, da of Sir John Lister-Kaye, 4th Bt* [F], b 27 Feb 1741, and had issue 1b to 3b

1b *Rev John Chaloner, M A* (*Oxon*), *Rector of Newton Kyme* 1815-1830, b 3 June 1765, d 4 Nov 1830 m 12 Nov 1798, *Augusta Anne, da of Robert Sutton of Scofton, co Notts* d 3 Feb 1850, *and had issue* 1c to 2c

    1c *Rev. John William Chaloner, M A* (*Camb*), *Rector of Newton Kyme,* b 1 Sept 1811, d 12 Mar 1894, m 1st. *Marcella Louisa, da of Charles Legh of Adlington, co Chester,* d 22 Nov 1866, 2ndly, *Arabella, da of Joseph Harrison of Orgrave, co York,* and had issue (with a 3rd son d unm) 1d to 3d

    1d *Charles William Chaloner* (*Grove End Albion Crescent, Scarborough*), b 15 Oct 1840, m 26 Ap 1894, Florence, da of Capt John Rhind, s p s

    2d *John Erskine Chaloner,* settled in America, b 12 Feb 1842

    3d *Henry Edward Chaloner* (*Box 193, Johannesburg, Transvaal*), b 18 Sept 1845, m 23 July 1868, Louisa, da of W H Hodding of 84 Gloucester Place, Portman Square, London, W, M D, and has issue 1e to 3e

[Nos 37891 to 37933

---

[1] Foster's "Yorkshire Pedigrees," where, however, Edward, the 2nd son, is also said to have d s p

[2] Burke's "Landed Gentry," 1906, p 535, and Foster's "Yorkshire Pedigrees," Fairfax Pedigree

254

# of The Blood Royal

1e Cecil Erskine Sweet Chaloner, *b* at Lydenburg, Transvaal, 7 June 1880

2e Constance Marcella Chaloner, *m* at Doornfontein, Johannesburg, 22 Feb 1895, Edward Richard Headly Hutt, Mining Engineer, Manager, Dundee Coal Coy (*Talana, Dundee, Natal*), and has issue 1f to 2f

1f Joyce Chaloner Hutt, *b* at Johannesburg 15 Aug 1897

2f Myrtle Gwendoline Hutt, *b* at Wilbank, near Middelburg, 7 Aug 1905

3e Ada Gwendoline Chaloner, *m* at St Mary's Church, Johannesburg, 5 Feb 1902, Thomas Alexander Glenny, Land Agent and Accountant (*Rand Club, Johannesburg*), and has issue 1f to 2f

1f Harry Wallis Glenny, *b* at Crown Mine, Mayfair, Johannesburg, 15 Aug 1904

2f Alexander Hennen Glenny, *b* at Clifton Hill, London, 26 May 1906

2c *Augusta Maria Chaloner*, b 23 May 1809, d 19 July 1859, m 26 Nov 1831, *William Bennett Martin of Worsboro' Hall, co Yorks and Thurgarton Priory, co Notts, J P , D L , b 7 Oct 1790, d 6 Ap 1847, and had issue (with an elder son and 2 das who d unm)* 1d to 4d

1d *William Henry Michael Aloysius Martin-Edmunds of Worsboro' Hall, D L ,* b 8 May 1847, d 6 Oct 1899, m 5 Aug 1870, *Emily Frances [descended from the Lady Anne, sister to King Edward IV (see Exeter Volume, p 277)], da of John Hubert Washington Herbert of Bilton Grange [by his wife Julia, da of Sir Henry Joseph Tichborne, 8th Bt [E]], and had issue* 1e to 3e

1e Cecilia Elizabeth Mary Agnes Martin-Edmunds of Worsboro' (*Worsboro' Hall, Barnsley, York*)

2e Magdalen Mary Josephine Martin-Edmunds, *m* 11 Oct 1905, Ronald Charles Scott-Murray [3rd son of Charles Aloysius Scott-Murray of Hambleden]

3e Olyve May Evelyn Martin-Edmunds, *m* 9 Ap 1902, Eustace Theodore Heaven, Capt *late* Lancashire Art [2nd son of Joseph Robert Heaven of Forest of Birse by his wife Maria, 1st Marchioness of Bracers [Papal States]], and has issue (with an elder da *d* young) 1f to 5f

1f Eustace Joseph Benedict Heaven, *b* 16 Ap 1903

2f Mark Joseph Robert Severus Heaven, *b* 10 May 1904

3f Edgar Joseph Heaven, *b* 25 Sept 1908

4f Barbara Mary Josephine Heaven, *b* 2 May 1907

5f Merril Mary Teresa Tichborne Heaven, *b* 5 Dec 1909

2d *Maria Elizabeth Martin*, d 26 Sept 1891 , m 28 Aug 1855, *the Hon Francis Dudley Montagu Stuart-Wortley [2nd son of John, 2nd Baron Wharncliffe [U K] and a descendant of King Henry VII], d 21 Oct 1893, and had issue*
See the Tudor Roll, p 525, Nos 35120-35139

3d *Amelia Mary Martin*, b 21 July 1835, d 9 Oct 1895, m 29 Ap 1858, *Edward Chivers Bower of Broxholme, co York, J P , D L , Capt West Yorkshire Mil ,* b 22 Aug 1826, d 18 Ap 1896, *and had issue* 1e to 9e

1e Edward Thomas Chivers Bowers, *b* 9 Feb 1859

2e. George Chivers Bower, *b* 19 June 1860

3e Francis Chivers Bower, *b* 23 July 1861

4e Arthur Wentworth Chivers Bower, *b* 8 Nov 1866

5e Augusta Mary Chivers Bower

6e Amy Elizabeth Chivers Bower

7e Ethel Alice Chivers Bower

8e Cicely Maria Chivers Bower

9e Beatrice Lilian Chivers Bower

4d *Julia Constance Martin*, b 11 Sept 1837 , d (-), m 9 Aug 1863, *Stephen Soames, Bar -at-Law , and had issue*

2b *Charles Chaloner*, d (? s p) at Snaith   [Nos. 37934 to 37977]

255

The Plantagenet Roll

3b Dorothy Chaloner, b 25 May 1766, d (–), m the Rev Robert Greville, Rector of Bonsall and Winstone, co Dorset, and had (with possibly other) issue 1c

1c Robert Kaye Greville of George Square, Edinburgh, LL D, a Botanist of note, b 13 Dec 1794, d 4 June 1866, m 1816, Charlotte (see p 270), da and co-h of Sir John Eden 4th Bt [E], M P, and had issue 1d to 5d

2 1d Robert Greville, d (?) unm

2 2d Chaloner Greville

2 3f Charlotte Greville, m the Rev (—) Hogarth

2 4f Emmeline Greville, m (—) Drummond

2 5d [dr] Greville   [Nos 37978 to 37981]

133 Descendants, if any, of CATHERINE CHALONER (Table XV), d (–), m G MELTHORP of York

134 Descendants of KATHERINE LAMPLUGH, eldest sister and co-h of Thomas Lamplugh of Lamplugh (Table XV), d 1804, m in Belfray's Church, York, 1754, the Rev GODFREY WOLLEY, Rector of Thurnscoe and Wamsworth, co York, b 1722, d 1 May 1788, and had issue 1a to 7a

1a Edward Wolley. afterwards (R L 19 May 1810) Copley of Fulford Grange, co York, eldest son, d (–), m and had issue (with a da who d unm) 1b

1b Edward Thomas Copley of Nether Hall, co York, b c 1800, d 8 Oct 1849, m 3 Aug 1826, Emily Mary, da of Sir John Pennstone Milbanke, 7th Bt [E], d 1 June 1844, and had issue (with another son, John Milbanke, who d unm) 1c to 2c

1c George Edward Copley, b Ap 1831, d 27 Dec 1878, m Anna, da of Oswald Smithson of York, and had issue (a da)

2c Arthur White Copley (Casa Copley, Mentone, France), b 8 Aug 1836, unm

2a Thomas Wolley. Admiral R N, d (–), m Frances Edith, da of Gilbert Francklyn of Asp den Hall, co Herts, and had issue (with a da who d s p) 1b to 3b

1b Rev Thomas Lamplugh Wolley Rector of Portishead, co Som, d (–), m Emily, da of James Willis, and had issue (with a da, Rhoda Florence, d unm 1909) 1c

1c Arthur Lamplugh Wolley (5 Kildare Terrace, Bayswater Orotava, Teneriffe). b (—), m Annie, da of (—) Bernard, s p

2b Henry Wolley, R N, b 6 May 1810, d 3 Dec 1898, m 1st, 12 July 1838, Charlotte Elizabeth, da of Joseph Seymour Biscoe of Hempstead, co Glouc [and grandda of Vincent Biscoe of Austin Friars, London, by his wife Lady Mary, da of Edward (Seymour), 8th Duke of Somerset [E]], d 28 Feb 1851, and had issue 1c to 4c

1c Rev Henry Francklyn Wolley, Hon Canon of Canterbury, Vicar of St. Mary's Shortlands (St Mary's Vicarage, Shortlands, Kent), b 1 July 1839, m 5 July 1871, Emily, da of the Rev Frederick Brown, Rector of Nailsea, co Somerset, and his issue 1d to 4d

1d Hugh Seymour Lamplugh Wolley, Lieut 56th Punjabi Rifles, Indian Army, b 1882

2d Margaret Katharine Wolley

3d Mary Lilian Wolley

4d Mabel Stephana Wolley

2c Edith Emma Wolley, unm   [Nos 37982 to 37989.

256

# of The Blood Royal

3c Charlotte Louisa Wolley, b 12 June 1842 , m 1863, James Palladio Basevi, R E [son of George Basevi, the well known Architect], d 17 July 1871 , and has issue 1d to 2d

1d William Henry Basevi, Major A P Dept (Hill Lodge, Milverton Terrace, Leamington), b 24 May 1865 , m 20 Oct 1889, Ethel Wina, da of William Gill of Plymouth , and has issue 1e to 2e

1e James Basevi, b 21 Sept 1890

2e Doris Frances Basevi, b 27 May 1893

2d Rev Charles Lionel Basevi (The Oratory, Brompton, S W) b 30 Aug 1867

4c Alice Portia Wolley, m 3 Oct 1867, Thomas Monck-Mason, Bombay C S [descended from the Lady Isabel Plantagenet (see Essex Volume, p 97)], b 1 Sept 1837 , d 17 Feb 1871, and has issue (with a da who d young) 1d to 4d

1d Roger Henry Monck Mason, Capt Royal Munster Fusiliers, b 19 Feb 1871 , m 7 June 1901 (dissolved Aug 1909), Ethel Beatrice, da of Capt Cecil Strickland , s p

2d Thomas George Monck Mason (Masonbrook, Cranbrook, Western Australia), b 30 Sept 1872 , m Sept 1902, Jane, da of (—) Chmie of Ballochmyle, W Australia , and has issue 1e

1e Eileen Alice Portia Monck Mason, b Sept 1903

3d Edith Mary Monck Mason

4d Winifred Alice Monck Mason (93 Oakley Street, Chelsea, S W)

3o Frances Louisa Wolley, d 14 July 1874 m 9 Sept 1844, the Rev Robert Craufurd, afterwards (1812) Gregan Craufurd of Paris [Bt of Kilbirney [G B 1781] Coll], d 1868 , and had issue 1c to 3c

1c Henry Robert Gregan Craufurd, J P , late R A (Brightwood, Aldbury, Tring), b 13 Aug 1845 m 1st, 18 July 1872, Fanny, da of the Rev James Williams of Tring Park, d s p 16 Dec 1876 2ndly, 30 July 1878, Alice, da of the Rev Richard Mountford Wood, Rector of Aldbury , and has issue 1d to 4d

1d Robert Quentin Gregan Craufurd, Capt Royal Scots Fusiliers, b 9 Mar 1880 , m Oct 1909, Mildred, da of the Right Hon William Kenny, P C , Judge of the King's Bench Div , High Court of Justice [I]

2d Archibald Gregan Craufurd, Capt Gordon Highlanders, b 2 Aug 1881

3d James Gregan Craufurd, b 23 Feb 1886

4d Emma Katherine Gregan Craufurd

2c Charles Quentin Craufurd, Capt R N (Army and Navy) b 2 Dec 1847 m 1 June 1878, Esmeralda Culligary, da of Count Valsamachi of Corfu , and has issue 1d to 2d

1d Quentin Gregan Craufurd, b 1879 , m

2d Maud Gregan Craufurd, m (—) Dashwood (12 Tite Street, Chelsea)

3c Emma Katherine Gregan-Craufurd, m 26 Sept 1874, Edward Broughton Pillans of Milan, d 1889 , and has issue (with a son, Brian, who d s p) 1d to 4d

1d Robert Pillans

2d David Craufurd Pillans, R N

3d Mary Pillans, m 1908, Henri Chevallier (Paris)

4d Esme Katherine Pillans

3a Isaac Wolley, Adm R N , d s p

4a Rev Godfrey Wolley, M A , J P , Rector of Hawnby and Vicar of Hutton Bushel, co York, b 4 Mar 1760, d 20 Nov 1822, m 1st 28 Ap 1791, Ellice, da of Richard Cass of Snainton, co York [by his wife Ellice, da of William Stockdale of Scarborough], d 13 Mar 1800 , 2ndly, Frances, widow of (—) Spencer, da of (—) Barker , and had issue (with 4 other sons and 6 das by 2nd wife, who d s p) 1b to 6b   [37990 to 38013

257

1b¹ *Godfrey Wolley Adm R N*, b 15 *June* 1799, d 15 *Oct* 1870, m 17 *May* [?1830], *Mary, da of Bryan Taylor of Bridlington*, d 25 *July* 1863 *and had issue* (*with a da, Selina Louisa, d unm*) 1c to 2c

1c *Mary Charlotte Elluce Wolley*, b 5 *Nov* 1832, d 13 *Sept* 1861, m 30 *June* 1857, *Frederic Smith*, d 16 *Ap* 1882, *and had issue* 1d to 2d

1d *Godfrey Smith* (*Llanellen Court, Abergavenny*), b 28 *Jan* 1859, m 27 *Nov* 1884, *Eliza da of George Young of Longton, co Staff, Solicitor*, s p

2d Agnes Smith, *unm*

2c Katharine Emily Wolley, m 30 *July* 1864, the Rev Sackett Hope M A (Oxon), *Vicar of Chedworth* 1879 1898, &c (*Chedworth, The Leas, Folkestone*), and his issue (*with 4 others d young*) 1d to 9d

1d John Lamplugh Allen Hope M R C S (Eng), L R C P (Lond) (*Devonshire House, Addlestone*), b 14 *Oct* 1866, m 13 *Ap* 1896, Rose, da of Thomas Herring, and his issue 1e to 2e

1e Constance Katharine Mary Hope

2e Ruth Olga Margaret Hope

2d Godfrey Dawson Taylor Hope, M A (Oxon) (*Trowleigh, Bradford-on-Avon*), b 31 *Mar* 1868, m 21 *Dec* 1899, Ethel Jessie, da of William Dwyer Way, and his issue 1e to 2e

1e John Godfrey Adrian Hope, b 1 *May* 1907

2e Dorothea Katharine Esther Hope

3d Reginald Henry Walton Hope (*Greenmount, Cornwall Road, Uxbridge*), b 19 *Jan* 1872, m 29 *Aug* 1905, Mabel Constance, da of Edwin Beard, and has issue 1e

1e Monica Constance Alice Hope

4d Cyril Edward Wolley Hope, b 22 *Ap* 1876, *unm*

5d Rev Albin Sickett Hope, M A (Oxon) (*St Bartholomew's, Dover*), b 22 *June* 1877, *unm*

6d Noel Eustace Hope, B A (Oxon), A R C M, b 25 *Mar* 1880, *unm*

7d Mary Katharine Sackett Hope, *unm*

8d Beatrice Sarah Louisa Hope, *unm*

9d Isabel Ruth Duodecima Hope, *unm*

2b² *Thomas Wolley, C B, Chief Clerk in the Admiralty*, d (-), m *Matilda Frances, da of the Rev* (—) *Hatch, Rector of Kingston-on-Thames, and had issue* (*with an elder son who d s p*) 1c

1c Godfrey Lamplugh Isaac Wolley, "Godfrey Lamplugh," an Actor

3b¹ *Honor Wolley*, b 11 *Feb* 1792, d 28 *Oct* 1827, m *in the Abbey Church, St Albans, 28 Jan* 1812, the Rev *William Stockdale of Mears Ashby Hall, co Northants, J P, M A, and Fellow of Jesus Coll, Camb*, b 5 *Ap* 1767, d 17 *Feb* 1858, *and had issue* (*with 3 other sons and 2 das who d unm*) 1c to 4c

1c *Rev William Walter Stockdale, Rector of Wychling, co Kent*, b 6 *Mar* 1811, d 19 *Feb* 1893, m 1st, *Mary Martha Margaret, da of James Douglas of Rhydyfran, co Cardigan*, d *Oct* 1853, 2ndly, 16 *Ap* 1857, *Emma, da of James Ashenden*, d 15 *Feb* 1886, *and had issue* (*with a da d young*) 1d to 2d

1d¹ *Reginald Walter Stockdale*, b 9 *Jan* 1852, d (-), m *Adela, da of the Rev James John Douglas, Prebendary of Perth, and ha t issue* (*with 3 other children*) 1e to 2e

1e Reginald Walter Douglas Stockdale, b 11 *Ap* 1892

2e Mary Louisa Stockdale, b 11 *Dec* 1893

2d² Godfrey Henry Wolley Stockdale, Col R E, b 1 *Aug* 1858, m 15 *Nov* 1884, Ida Eliza, da of Gen Horatio Scott, and has issue 1e to 2e

1e Godfrey Eric le Scot Stockdale, b 1 *June* 1888

2e Dorothy Honor Stockdale, b 5 *May* 1893

2c Henry Minshull Stockdale of Mears Ashby Hall, M A (Camb), Bar-at-Law of Lincoln's Inn, J P , D L , and *late* Chairman Northants Quarter Sessions and Capt Northants Militia (*Mears Ashby Hall, Northampton*), b 30 Sept 1822 , m 12 Aug 1858, Sarah Emily, da of the Rev Robert Hervey Knight Rector of Weston Favell, d 15 May 1896 , and has issue (with a son and da who d *unm*) 1d to 5d

1d Henry Minshull Stockdale, J P , M A. (Camb), Bar-at-Law of the Inner Temple, *late* Major 3rd Batt Northants Regt (*Mears Ashby Hall, Northants*), b 8 Feb 1861 , m 7 July 1896, Florence Margaret Rose [descended from the Lady Isabel Plantagenet (see Essex Volume, p 269)], da of the Rev Charles Villiers, Rector of Croft, co York , and has issue 1e to 2c

    1e Henry Charles Minshull Stockdale, b 5 Ap 1902

    2e Edmund Villiers Minshull Stockdale, b 16 Ap 1903

2d Rev Robert William Stockdale, M A (Camb), Vicar of St Silas, Hunslet (*St Silas's Vicarage, Hunslet, Yorks*), b 31 Oct 1862 , m 1 Mar 1905, Emily, da of Israel Fozard , and has issue 1e to 2c

    1e Honor Stockdale

    2c Katherine Fozard Stockdale

3d Herbert Edward Stockdale, Major R H A , b 22 June 1867 , m. 4 Feb 1909, Margaret Frances, da of the Rev James Tufton Bartlet, Canon of Lincoln

    1d Emily Honor Stockdale, *unm*

    5d Mabel Katharine Mary Stockdale, *unm*

3c *Catherine Frances Stockdale*, b 22 *Jan* 1816 , d 27 *Sept* 1860 , m 23 *Mar* 1841, *the Rev Thomas Bury Wells, M A (Camb), Rector of Portlemouth, co Devon, formerly Lieut R N* , b *Jan* 1795 d 23 *May* 1879 , and had issue (with a son and da who d s-p) 1d to 6d

1d Lionel Bury Wells, M I C E (*Horsecombe, Salcombe, Devon*), b 12 Feb 1843 , m 11 Oct 1871, Mary Eliza, da of the Rev T P Kirkman, Rector of Croft, co Lanc , F R S , and has issue (with a da d young) 1e to 6c

    1e Lionel Fortescue Wells, C E , b 20 Oct 1877

    2e Katharine Edmina Wells, m 16 Aug 1901, Harry Augustus Whittall [son of Sir (James) William Whittall Founder and President of the British Chamber of Commerce of Turkey] (*Broussa, Hale, Altringham*) , and has issue 1f to 2f

        1f Lionel Harry Whittall, b 8 May 1907

        2f Katharine Marion Whittall, b 21 Feb 1906

    3e Mary Dorothea Wells

    4e Elizabeth Rose Wells

    5e Elinor Kirkman Wells

    6e Muriel Bury Wells

2d *Henry Lake Wells, C I E , Lieut-Col R E ,* b 8 *Mar* 1850 , d 1898 , m *Alice Bertha, da of the Rev Hugh Bacon of Baxterley, co Warwick , and had issue* 1e to 5e

    1e Lionel Salisbury Wells, Lieut Queen's Own Corps of Guides, b 1885 , d 1908

    2e Victor Horace Wells, b 1897

    3e Bessie Margaret Fortescue Wells

    4e Honor Lake Wells

    5e Kathleen Esther Wells

3d Thomas Bury Wells, b Oct 1856 , m Bertha, da of William Palmer of Montreal , s p

    4d Katherine Alicia Wells, m Robert Steine, Comm R N , s p

    5d Elizabeth Ellen Wells, *unm*

    6d. Caroline Emily Wells, *unm*   [Nos 38037 to 38063

The Plantagenet Roll

1c *Ellen Stockdale*, b 7 Jan 1826, d 9 Nov 1901, m 14 Ap 1860, *James Pain of Astley Guise, co Beds*, d 4 Jan 1878, *and had issue (with a son and 4 das d unm) 1d to 3d*

1d *John Athill James Pain*, b 2 Oct 1864, d 22 Dec 1899, m 29 Ap 1893, *Edith Jane, da of William Stagg*, d 13 Jan 1901, *and had issue 1e to 3e*

  1e James Crichton Pain, b 10 Sept 1895

  2e Catherine Mary Pain b 13 Mar 1891

  3e Mary Henrietta Pain, b 8 Sept 1897

2d Henrietta Mary Pain }
3d Amabel Barbara Pain } (*Woodlands, Woburn Sands*), *unm*

1b¹ *Catherine Wolley*, b 16 Mar 1793, d (–), m 15 Nov 1810, *the Rev Stephen Allen*, d (–), *and had issue 1c to 4c*

  1c *Rev Stephen Allen, D D*

  2c *Thomas Allen, m and had several children*

  3c *Godfrey Allen, emigrated to New Zealand*

  1c *Katharine Allen*, d (–), m in New Zealand, (–) Wray or Ray, *and had issue (a da)*

5b² *Isabella Wolley*

6b³ *Caroline Wolley*

5a *Honor Wolley*, d 1845, m as 2nd wife, *the Rev Anthony Fountaine Eyre of Baronburgh, co York*, d 14 Feb 1791, *and had issue (with a son and 3 das d unm) 1b*

1b *Rev Anthony William Eyre, Rector of Hornsea*, b 20 Nov 1783, d 1848, m *Sarah da of David Mapleton of Bath, M D*, d (–), *and had issue (with 2 sons and 2 das d unm) 1c to 3c*

1c *Edward John Eyre of the Grange, Staple Aston, co Oxon, sometime Governor of Jamaica*, b 5 Aug 1815, d 3 Nov 1901, m 3 Ap 1850, Adelaide Fanny, *da of Capt F Ormond, R N*, d 15 May 1905, *and had issue 1d to 7d*

1d Gervas Selwyn Eyre, Barrister-at-Law, Lieut-Col Indian Army, *formerly* Commissioner of Division, Burmah (*The Hudnalls, St Briavel's, S O, Glos*), b 25 July 1851, m 29 Jan 1874, Lucy Dorothea, da of the Rev E J Barnes, Vicar of Golding, co Kent, and has issue 1e

  1e Lucy Marguerite Eyre, b 9 Dec 1874

2d Edward Broughton Eyre, Lieut (ret) R N, b 23 Mar 1853, *unm*

3d Charles Ormond Eyre (*Fiji*), b 5 Dec 1856, m and has issue

4d Harry Eyre, *late Colonial Service, Gold Coast*, b 13 Feb 1861, *unm*

5d Sydney Frederick Eyre, b 30 Oct 1871, *unm*

6d Ada Austin Eyre (*Delamont, Killyleigh, co Devon*), m 15 Sept 1881, Alexander Hamilton Miller Haven Gordon of Florida Manor, and Delamont, co Devon, J P, D L, d 5 July 1910, and has issue 1e to 10e

  1e Alexander Robert Gisborne Gordon, Capt Roy Irish Reg, b 28 July 1882

  2e Eyre Gordon, Scholar Queen's College, Oxford, Indian C S, b 28 Feb 1884

  3e John de la Hay Gordon 67th Punjabis, Indian Army, b 30 Mar 1887

  4e Edward Ormond Gordon, b 1 Mar 1888

  5e Henry Gisborne Gordon, b 29 Aug 1889

  6e Eldred Pottinger Gordon, b 24 May 1891

  7e Ivy Dorothy Catherine Gordon, }
  8e Marjorie Frances Gordon }
  9e Honor Gordon, } *unm*
  10e Marion Alice Gordon, }

7d May Lilian Eyre, *unm*

2c *Caroline Eyre*, d 23 May 1863, m as 1st wife, 10 June 1839, *the Rev James Hare Wake Vicar of Sutton in Forest, co Yorks* [Bt (E 1621) Coll.], b 19 Feb 1805, d 5 Dec 1871, *and had issue 1d to 7d* [Nos 38064 to 38086

260

# of The Blood Royal

1d Rev Baldwin Eyre Wake, M A (Oxon) Vicar of Ruswarp (*Ruswarp Vicarage, Whitby, Yorks*), b 20 Mar 1840, m 16 June 1868. Adelaide Bowles, da of the Rev Henry Cleveland, Rector of Ronald Kirk, Darlington, and has issue 1e to 3e

1e Rev Hereward Eyre Wake, M A (Oxon), Vicar of Castle Cary (*Castle Cary Vicarage, Somerset*), b 8 June 1869 m 18 Ap 1899, Mary Frances, da of James Sealy Lawrence of 5 Upper Addison Gardens, W , and his issue 1f to 2f

1f Hereward Baldwyn Lawrence Wake, b 26 Aug 1900

2f Torfrida Marjory Wake, b 11 May 1902

2e Torfrida Mary Wake

3e Margaret Gladys Hermione Wake

2d Gervas Fountayne Wake (*Victoria, British Columbia*), b 15 Ap 1853 m 9 June 1881, his cousin, Amy Rosamond, da of Capt Baldwin Arden Wake, R N , and has issue 1e to 3e

1e Hereward Eyre Wake, b 16 July 1888

2e Rosamond Adelaide Alice Wake, m 14 Aug 1907, Frederick Paget Norbury (*The Norrest, Malvern*), and his issue 1f

1f Christopher Paget Norbury, b 8 Oct 1908

3e Gladys Maude Mary Wake

3d Emily Honor Wake, m 15 Sept 1868, Arthur Charles Cleveland (23 Eversley Road, *Bexhill*), and his issue 1e to 4e

1e Hereward Wake Cleveland b 1880

2e Ethel Mary Wake Cleveland

3e Blanche Seton Cleveland

4e Evelyn Eyre Cleveland

4d Lucy Joan Wake

5d Edith Caroline Wake, m 29 Nov 1864, Capt Martin Budd Lewin, *formerly* 51st Regt (78 Elliscombe Road, Old Charlton, Kent), and has issue 1e to 8e

1e *Robert Hutchinson Wake Lewin*, b 8 Jan 1869 d (s p)

2e Arthur Wyndham Wake Lewin, b 3 Mar 1871

3e Francis Ashby Wake Lewin, b 17 May 1873

4e Fenton Gervas Martin Lewin, b 20 Nov 1875,

5e George Edward de Montfleury Lewin, b 23 Dec 1876

6e Caroline Edith Constance Lewin

7e Gladys Bertha Joan Lewin

8e Torfrida Dorothy Wilhelmina Lewin

6d Bertha Charlotte Wake

7d Gertrude Maud Wake

3c *Fanny Eyre*, b 1820, d (-), m *Joshua Mashill of Pudsey, co York, Surgeon, and had issue 1d*

1d Clara Ruth Mashill, m H A Wickers, M D , and has issue (a da)

6a *Cordelia Wolley*, d (-), m *John Bower. and had issue*

7a *Katherine Wolley*, d (-), m *at Fulford 16 Oct 1789, John Raper of Abberford and Lotherton, co York, and Lamplugh, co Cumberland* (see p 262), d 3 July 1824, and had issue 1b to 3b

1b *John Lamplugh Raper, afterwards* (R L 10 Mar 1825) *Lamplugh Raper of Lamplugh*, b 19 July 1790, d s p 13 Ap 1867

2b *Henry Raper of Lamplugh*, b 12 Feb 1795, d s p 16 May 1867

3b *Anne Raper, da and in her issue* (16 May 1867) *sole h, d 19 Dec 1857, m 19 July 1815, James Brooksbank of The Batley, Durham, J P* [2nd son of Benjamin Brooksbank of Healaugh, co York, J P] b 21 Sept 1786, d 27 Feb 1870, and had issue 1c to 2c

1c James Brooksbank, Bar-at-Law, b 27 Sept 1816, d s p 27 Mar 1863, m 4 Feb 1824, Marianne, da of Thomas Edmonds of London, d 11 Oct 1852, and had issue 1d to 2d

261

The Plantagenet Roll

1d Walter Lamplugh Brooksbank, Lord of the Manor of Lamplugh and Patron of the Living, J P (*Lamplugh Hall, Cockermouth , Far Bank, Penrith, Cumberland*), b 4 Nov 1850 , m 8 Aug 1877, Mary Anne Madeleine, da of Francis Greenwell of Durham, J P , and has issue 1e to 5e

    1e James Lamplugh Brooksbank, b 21 Feb 1889

    2e Katherine Dorothy Aurora Brooksbank

    3e Honor Elizabeth Brooksbank

    4e Myrtle Philippa Brooksbank

    5e Una Frances Honora Brooksbank

2d Marianne Elizabeth Annie Brooksbank, m 26 Jan 1875, William Delisle Powles (40 *Sussex Gardens Hyde Park, W*) , and has issue 1e to 3e

    1e John Copley Powles, Lieut (ret) R N , b 22 Nov 1875

    2e Rev Robert Cowley Powles, M A (Oxon), b 22 June 1877

    3e Francis Brooksbank Powles, B A (Oxon), b 27 Ap 1882

2c *Rev Walter Brooksbank, M A , Rector of Lamplugh*, b 5 Aug 1830 , d 20 Oct 1908 , m 29 May 1855, *Elizabeth Jane, da of Stephen Poyntz Denning , and has issue* 1d to 6d

    1d Stephen Poyntz Brooksbank, C E , b 11 May 1856 , m and has issue (a da)

    2d Hugh Lamplugh Brooksbank, B A (Camb), b 25 Feb 1867 , m 27 Dec 1900, Sybil Lavallin, da of the Rev Herbert Boyne Lavallin Puxley of Lavallin House, Tenby, Rector of Caton

    3d Ethel Brooksbank, m 13 June 1882, the Rev Ernest Edward Stock, Vicar of Rocliffe (*Rocliffe Rectory, Carlisle*) , and has issue 1e to 8e

        1e Hugh Russell Stock, b 19 July 1883

        2e Reginald Walter Stock, b 4 Aug 1886

        3e Christopher Herbert Stock, b 5 July 1888

        4e Cecil Ernest Stock, b 23 Dec 1892

        5e Ethel Marjory Stock, b 5 May 1885

        6e Beatrice Mildred Stock, b 31 July 1889

        7e Gertrude Mary Stock   } (twins), b 11 May 1899
        8e Katharine Maud Stock }

    4d Gertrude Brooksbank (twin), m 29 Nov 1883, Samuel Taylor of Eccleston Hall and Birkdault, co Lancaster, J P , B A , Bar -at-Law, *late* Lieut 3rd Batt South Lancashire Regt (*Birkdault, Haverthwaite, near Ulverston*), and has issue 1e to 4e

        1e Rev Samuel Taylor, B A (Camb), b 6 Oct 1884

        2e Richard Brooksbank Taylor, Lieut Border Regt , b 8 Dec 1885

        3e Geoffrey Fell Taylor, b 8 Nov 1890

        4e Nancy Taylor

    5d Katherine Brooksbank (twin)

    6d Philippa Beatrice Brooksbank, m 28 July 1892, Anthony Gerard Salvin of Hawksfold, co Sussex, Capt Yorkshire R G A Militia (*Woodfold, Fernhurst*), and has issue 1e

        1e Philippa Malorie Salvin

                                       [Nos 38115 to 38143]

135. Descendants of ANNE LAMPLUGH, sister and co-h of the Rev Thomas Lamplugh of Lamplugh (Table XV), d (–) , m 8 Oct 1750, JOHN RAPER of Lotherton, co York , and had issue 1a to 4a

    1a *John Raper of Abberford and Lotherton, co York, and Lamplugh, co Cumberland,* d 3 July 1824 , m 16 Oct 1789, *Katherine, da of the Rev Godfrey Wolley , and had issue*

See p 261, Nos 38115-38143   [Nos 38144 to 38172]

# of The Blood Royal

2a Anne Raper, d aged 84, bur in Church of St Martin's, Coney Street, York, M.I , m George Townend , and had issue 1b

1b Anne Townend, only da and apparently only child,[1] b c 1762 d at Clapham Rise, 29 Dec 1858, aged 86 m 1st, John Moore, Capt 3rd Dragoon Guards, d (-) , 2ndly, Edmund Lally, Capt 4th Dragoon Guards [descended from George Plantagenet, Duke of Clarence (see Essex Volume, Clarence Supp , p 528)], and had issue (with a son, Edmund Lally, who d at Eton) 1c to 6c

1c Ann Moore, da and co-h, d (-) , m the Rev Jocelyn Wiley of Hexorth, co York

2c Frances Moore, da and co-h

3c Georgiana Moore, 3rd da[2] and co-h , d 1845, m 16 Dec 1824, her cousin, Henry Raper of Lamplugh (see p 261), d s p 16 May 1867

4c (—) Moore, da and co-h , d (-) , m Wynn Aubrey

5c Anna Katherine Lally, da and co-h, d 2 May 1900, m the Rev Edward John Speck, Sec Church Pastoral Aid Society, d (-) , and had issue 1d

1d Rev Jocelyn Henry Speck (St Martins Vicarage, Bedford), b 1857 , m Rosalie, da of Alexander Dalrymple , and has issue 1e to 3e

1e John Speck, b 1888

2e Gwendolen Lally Speck

3e Stella Speck

6c Augusta Lally, d 10 Sept 1898, m 11 Oct 1843, the Rev Henry Roxby Roxby, Rector of St Olave, Old Jewry, d 14 Jan 1860, and had issue 1d to 3d

1d Rev Edmund Lally Roxby, M A (Camb), Hon Canon of Gloucester, Rector of Cheltenham (The Rectory, Cheltenham), b 21 Aug 1844

2d Carus Wilson Roxby, b 26 Dec 1845

3d Herbert Roxby, Capt R N , b 9 Feb 1848

3a Honor Raper, d (-), bur in the Church of St Martin, Coney Street, York, m John Kendall of Hatfield, co York, d (-), bur in the Church of St Martin afsd , and had issue (with an eldest son John, lost at sea) 1b to 5b

1b Henry Edward Kendall of London, an eminent Architect d (-), m Anna Maria, da of (—) Lyon , and had issue 1c to 6c

1c Henry Edward Kendall of Brunswick Square, London, Architect, d (-), m Mary, da and h of Thomas Amery Cobham of Uckfield, co Sussex , and had issue 1d to 6d

1d Henry Robert John Edmunds Kendall, d (-)

2d Thomas Cobham John Kendall

3d Edward Herne Kendall

4d Arthur James Kendall

5d Anna Maria Mardow Kendall

6d Mary Leonora Kendall

2c George Kendall

3c John Kendall, Lieut 28th Bengal Native Infantry, d (? s p) 17 Ap 1852

4c Charles Kendall

5c Emma Kendall, d (-), m William Covey of Wilton Street, Belgrave Square, d (-), and had issue (with a son, Charles, Major Durham L I , d unm) 1d to 3d

1d Emma Covey, unm   [Nos 38173 to 38185

---

[1] "Outlines of the Genealogy of the Hassards and their Connections, York " (H Sotheran, Bookseller, Coney Street, 1858)

[2] Burke's "Landed Gentry," 1906, under Brooksbank of Lamplugh, p 206 This da is not mentioned in "Outlines of the Genealogy of the Hassards," &c, from which particulars of the other das are taken, unless, indeed, she is identified with the da (there called 3rd) who m Wynn Aubrey, in which case Henry Raper must have been her second husband

2d *Fanny Shelley Covey*, d 11 *Jan* 1908, m *Quintin William Francis Twiss of H M Treasury, d 7 Aug 1900, and had issue 1c to 5c*

1c Horace William Twiss, Solicitor (*Schiffbauerdamm* 15, *Berlin, N W*), b 24 Mar 1865, m in New York 8 Oct 1892, Lilian Beatrice, da of Henry Simms

2c Arthur Quintin Twiss, b 16 Nov 1867, *unm*

3c Ethel Fanny Twiss, *unm*

4c Annie Constance Twiss, m 6 Feb 1893, Ernest Blechynden Waggett, M A (Camb), M R C S , L R C P , Surgeon, Nose, Throat, and Ear Dept , Charing Cross Hospital, and Consulting Surgeon, London Throat Hospital (39 *Wimpole Street, W*), and has issue 1f

1f Judith Blechynden Waggett, b 4 May 1897

5c Mildred Caroline Twiss, *unm*

3d Myra Jane Covey, *unm*

6c *Sophia Kendall*, b 31 *Aug* 1811, d 17 *Feb* 1879 m 23 *Jan* 1830, *Lewis Cubitt* [*uncle of George (Cubitt), 1st Lord Ashcombe [U K] P C]*, b 29 *Sept* 1799, d 9 *June* 1883, *and had issue* 1d *to* 4d

1d *Lewis Cubitt of Orr House, Hastings, Capt 26th Cameronians,* b 5 *Dec* 1834 d 20 *Nov* 1872, m 31 *May* 1869, *Charlotte Anne, da of Robert William Kennard of Theobalds, co Herts, M P , J P , D L , and had issue* 1e

1e Thomas (Cubitt, now (R L 10 Dec 1904) Riccardi-Cubitt), 1st Count Riccardi-Cubitt [Italy, 27 May 1904] which title he had Royal Licence to use in the United Kingdom 16 Dec 1905 (*Eden Hall, Edenbridge, Kent*), b 8 May 1870, m 23 Nov 1895, Tede Maria, *suo jure* Countess Riccardi [Italy, 3 May 1904], da. and h of Adolfo, 3rd Count Riccardi [Sardinia, 2 Ap 1833], K M L , K C I , Col Italian R A , and Equerry to King Victor Emmanuel III , and has issue 1f to 4f

1f Charles Cyril Riccardi-Cubitt, heir to mother's title, b 28 Jan 1896

2f Vera Allen Maria Riccardi-Cubitt

3f Theodora Tede Maria Riccardi-Cubitt

4f Monica Yolanda Riccardi Cubitt

2d Ellen Cubitt, m as 2nd wife, 7 Dec 1858, Edgar Alfred Bowring, C B , *formerly* Librarian and Registrar to Board of Trade, and M P for Exeter 1868-1874 [son of Sir John Bowring, LL D , Min Plen to China] (30 *Eaton Place, S W*), and has issue 1c to 2c

1c Algernon Cunliffe Bowring (30 *Eaton Place, S W*), b 27 Sept 1859, *unm*

2c Victor Bowring now (D P) Bowring Hanbury (5 *Belgrave Square, S W , Ham Hall, Ashbourne*), b 26 Mar 1867, m 16 Feb 1904, Ellen, widow of the Right Hon Robert William Hanbury of Ham, P C , M P , President of the Board of Agriculture, da and h of Col Knott Hamilton

3d Agnes Cubitt, m 31 Oct 1855, Lieut -Col Henry Charles Cunliffe-Owen, R E , C B , V C , d 7 Mar 1867, and has issue 1e

1e Edward Cunliffe-Owen, C M G , Bar -at-Law, was Sec to the Fisheries, Health, and Inventions Exhibition, and Assist -Sec to Royal Commissioners of Colonial and Indian Exhibition 1886 (69 *Oxford Terrace, Hyde Park, W*), b 1 Jan 1857, m 18 Ap 1882, Emma Pauline, da of Sir (Francis) Philip Cunliffe-Owen, K C B , K C M G , C I E , and has issue 1f to 4f

1f Francis Edward Cunliffe Owen b 22 Dec 1884

2f Alexander Robert Cunliffe-Owen, b 25 Aug 1898

3f Dorothy Mary Cunliffe-Owen

4f Sybil Cunliffe-Owen

4d Ada Cubitt, *unm*

2b *George Kendall, Capt R M , served under Nelson at the Nile, Copenhagen, and Trafalgar, upon which last occasion he commanded the Marines on board the Neptune,* b c 1783, d (? s p) 8 May 1840

3b *Richard Kendall, Major R A* , b c 1808, d (? s p) *in Barbados* 3 *Sept* 1843 [Nos 38186 to 38207

4b *Honor Kendall,* d 3 June 1844, m 23 Ap 1805, *Thomas Shann of Tadcaster,* b 13 Mar 1768, d 9 Feb 1852, *and had issue (with 2 sons who d unm)* 1c

1c *George Shann of York,* M D, b 18 May 1809, d 3 Oct 1882, m 16 Ap 1845, *Jane, da of the Rev William Gray, Canon of Ripon and Vicar of Brafferton,* d at York 6 Sept 1899, *and had issue (with 2 other sons who d s p)* 1d *to* 9d

1d George Shann, M A (Camb), b 22 July 1846

2d Frederick Shann, B A (Camb), M R C S, L R C P, J P, V D (*Farnham, Knaresborough*), b 22 Ap 1849

3d Alfred Shann, b 1 July 1850

4d Henry Charles Shann, Surgeon (*Micklegate Hill House, York*), b 21 Feb 1852, m 23 July 1885, Caroline Mary, da of Sir William Henry Flower, K C B, F R S, and his issue 1e to 5e

1e Edward Warrington Shann, B Sc (St Andrews), b 6 Sept 1886

2e Gerald Davenant Shann, b 23 Dec 1888

3e Charles Douglas Shann, b 4 Mar 1907

4e Vera Flower Shann

5e Rosetta Mary Shann

5d Rev Reginald Shann, M A (Tri Coll, Camb), Rector of Chenies (*Chenies Rectory, Rickmansworth, Bucks*), b 18 July 1854, m 11 Sept 1879, Elizabeth, da of the Rev Edward Hoare, M A, Vicar of Holy Trinity Tunbridge Wells Canon of Canterbury [by his wife Maria Eliza, da of Sir Benjamin Collins Brodie, 1st Bt [U K], M D, F R S, D C L], and has issue 1e to 4e

1e Rev Charles Brodie Shann, M A (Camb), b 8 Dec 1884

2e Reginald Arthur Shann, b 26 June 1891

3e Lettice Mary Shann, B Sc (London)

4e Ethel Katharine Shann, M B (Camb)

6d William Arthur Shann, *formerly of St Anne's, Lowestoft* (*Camberley, Surrey*), b 10 June 1857, m 25 Ap 1900, Clara, widow of Capt V R Rae, West York Regt, da of Thomas Moss, s p

7d Thomas Lawrence Shann, M A (Camb) (*The Quarry Cottage, Farnham, near Knaresborough*), b 21 Sept 1858, m 4 Aug 1892, Lucy Fenwick, da of Joseph Watson of Gateshead, and has issue 1e to 4e

1e Kenneth Shann, b 22 Ap 1895

2e Honor Shann

3e Mary Grace Shann

4e Faith Shann

8d Lucy Honor Shann, *unm*

9d Laura Jane Shann, *unm*

5b *Mary Ann Kendall,* d 19 Oct 1851 m 26 Jan 1808, *Richard Samuel Hassard, afterwards* (R L 7 Aug 1807) *Short, Lord of the Manors of Edlington, East Keal, and part of Clerkenwell,* b 20 Ap 1751 d 24 Oct 1826, *and had issue (with an elder son and a da, Mrs Maitland, who d s p)* 1c *to* 7c

1c *John Hassard Short of Edlington Grove, co Lincoln,* J P, D L, b 18 Nov 1810, d 4 Dec 1893, m 24 Nov 1831, *Margaret, da of Lieut-Col Richard Elmhirst of Ashby Grove co Linc,* d 21 b 1881, *and had issue* 1d *to* 6d

1d Edward Hassard Short, now (D P 1 Jan 1899) Hassard, J P, co Lincoln (*Edlington Manor, Horncastle, co Lincoln*) b 22 Aug 1848, m 11 May 1873, Geraldine Rachel, da of John Henry Blagrave of Calcot Park, co Bucks, and Barrow Court, co Somerset, and has issue 1e to 2e

1e Hubert Edward Hassard, b 15 Oct 1877

2e Digby Valentine Hassard, b 14 Feb 1879

2d Algernon Lawson Hassard Short, *late Lieut Royal North Gloucestershire Militia, settled in North Carolina* (350 *West* 115*th Street, New York*), b 20 Feb 1852, m 13 Jan 1875, Routh Elizabeth, da of Col John Luther Bridgers of

[Nos 38208 to 38233

The Plantagenet Roll

Taboro, N Carolina, U S A , and has issue (with a son, Reginald Elmhirst Hassard Short, b 17 Mar 1878, d 30 Nov 1895) 1e

    1e Katharine Routh Bridgers Hassard Short

    3d Caroline Mary Short m 23 July 1868, Charles Godfrey Bolam, *late* 7th Royal Fusiliers (*Dunchurch, near Rugby*), and has issue 1e to 5e

    1e Rev Cecil Edward Bolam, Rector of St Mary Magdalene, Lincoln (*Lincoln*), b 7 Mar 1875, m 18 Nov 1902, Beatrice Helen, da of James Rhodes of Rotherham, co York , and has issue 1f

    1f Joyce Helen Bolam

    2c Mabel Marian Bolam, m 26 June 1901, John Edmonds, Land Agent (*The Manor House, Islip, Thrapston*), and has issue 1f

    1f Winifred Mary Edmonds

    3c Katharine Mary Bolam, *unm*

    4e Muriel Agnes Bolam, m 6 Ap 1899, the Rev Sydney Sparks Herington, M A , Rector of Heydour (*Heydour Rectory, near Grantham*)

    5e Beatrice Margaret Bolam, m 24 Jan 1907, the Rev Robert Harvey Baldwin Crosthwaite, M A , Rector of Calthorpe (*Calthorpe Rectory, near Rugby*)

    4d Frances Adela Short, m Dec 1879, Gen Thomas Augustus Carey, Bengal Staff Corps, d s p 23 May 1892

    5d *Katharine Jane Hassard Short*, b 26 Dec 184-, d 16 Feb 1902, m 24 Oct 1877, *the Rev Edwin Thomas James Marriner, BA* (*Camb*) (*The Pollards, Thurlow Hill, Torquay*), *and had issue* 1e

    1e Gwendolyn Marian Moulas Marriner

    6d Gertrude Elmhirst Short, now (D P 1 Jan 1899) Hassard

    2c *Rev Henry Short, afterwards Hassard,* b 21 Mar 1812, d 30 Jan 1885, m 1842, *Lucy, da of the Rev John Martin Butt, M A ,* d 17 May 1898, *and had issue* 1d *to* 4d

    1d Henry Hassard Hassard, b 21 Feb 1844 m 6 Nov 1872, Elizabeth Anna, da of Felix McKinnan , and has issue

    2d Rev Richard Samuel Hassard, M A (Oxon), Sub-Dean and Canon of Truro Cathedral (*Truro*), b 9 May 1818, m 7 Ap 1874, Edith, da of John Costeker

    3d Lucy Alice Hassard, m 1871, the Rev William Mason, D D , d (-), and has issue

    4d Emily Constance Hassard, m 5 Nov 1885, the Rev Robert Thomas Shea, M A (Camb), Vicar of Little Wakering (*Little Wakering Vicarage Southend*)

    3c. *William Short of Harrogate, M D ,* b 28 May 1813, d 1 Nov 1879, m 6 Aug 1837, Isabella, da of James Dixon of Cottingham Hall, co York [*and great-niece of the Rev William Mason the Poet*], *and had issue* (with 2 sons d s p) 1d *to* 8d

    1d William James Short, b 27 Aug 1840, m Emma, da of (—) Petley, d s p 13 Oct 1868

    2d Frederick Hugh Short, Chief Clerk of the Crown Office, Royal Courts of Justice, *late* Capt 3rd V B Royal West Kent Regt, b 19 Mar 1843 m 8 Oct 1872, Maud Eliza, da of John Downes of the City of London, Merchant, twice Master of the Salters' Company , and has issue (with a son killed in action in South Africa 25 June 1900) 1e to 2e

    1e Rev Frederick Winning Hassard-Short, M A (Ch Coll , Camb), Vicar of St Albans, Dartford (*99 East Hill, Dartford, Kent*), b 5 Aug 1873

    2e Adrian Hugh Short, *late* Midshipman R N , Associate King's Bench Div 1900-1908, now Court of Criminal Appeal, Royal Courts of Justice, b 3 Aug 1879, m 21 Sept 1908, Millicent Eliza, da of Capt. Thomas Renouf of Jersey

    3d Charles Mason Short, settled in South America, b 6 Mar 1848, m Mary, da of (—) Irwin

    4d John Locke Broadbent Short, Crown Office, b 8 Oct 1853, m 5 July 1881,

[Nos 38234 to 38255

# of The Blood Royal

Edith Constance, da of John James Harrison, J P , D L , Col 3rd West Yorkshire Militia, now 5th Batt West Yorkshire Regt , a Col 1st West Yorkshire Rifle Vol and has issue 1e to 6e

   1e William Hassard Short, b 18 May 1886

   2e James Hassard Short, b 2 June 1887

   3e John Hassard Short, b 23 Feb 1889

   4e May Short

   5e Violet Short

   6e. Daisy Blanche Short

   5d Frances Marion Short, m George Moncrieff Govan, M D , Brigade Surgeon (ret) Indian Medical Service , and has issue (with a da d s p) 1e to 6e

   1e Rev George William Govan Rector of Wittycombe (*Wittycombe Rectory, Carhampton, Taunton*), b 9 Aug 1861 , m 14 June 1892, Annie, da of John Rowland Howells of Cardiff , and has issue 1f

      1f Eileen Frances Govan, b 18 Oct 1897

   2e Henry Maitland Govan

   3e Douglas Moncrieff Govan, Lieut Indian Army, b 5 Oct 1875

   4e Ethel Mary Govan, m Major John Lampen, Indian Army

   5e Anne Maud Govan

   6e Frances Eleanor Govan, m Major Lewis Gordon Fisher, Indian Medical Service [son of William Lewis Ferdinand Fisher, Professor of Natural Philosophy and Mathematics, St Andrews], and has issue 1f to 5f

      1f Edith Fischer

      2f Nora Margaret Fischer

      3f Effie Govan Fischer

      4f Dorothy Tweedie Fischer

      5f Mary Eleanor Fischer

   6d Louisa Anne Short, m 29 Mar 1861, William Williams, M R C S , L S A , of Redcar, Yorks, d 2 May 1872 , and has issue 1e to 6e

   1e Edward Frederick Maitland Williams, b 26 Feb 1865 , m in Canada, Ada, da of (—) Hancock, and has issue 1f to 4f

      1f Guy Williams, b 1 Feb 1899

      2f Francis William Williams

      3f. Gwendoline Williams

      4f Violet Louise Williams

   2e Isabella Williams

   3e Louisa Williams

   4e Juliana Katherine Williams

   5e Gwladys Williams

   6e Gwendoline Williams

   7d *Annie Harriette Short*, d (—) , m *Capt Frederick Mills Harris, Indian Staff Corps* , and had issue 1e to 2e

   1e Maud Harris, m Henry Swayne

   2e Anne Harris, m Capt Rooke, R E

   8d Eleanor Theresa Short, m 10 May 1870, Capt Charles German Alison, *late* 91st Argyll and Sutherland Highlanders, *late* Chief Constable of Somerset , and has issue (with 3 das d young) 1e to 5e

   1e Charles Hugh Alison, b 5 Mar 1883

   2e Roger Vincent Alison, Lieut R N , b 22 Jan 1885

   3e Geoffrey Richard Alison, b 14 Ap 1886

   4e Laughton Hassard Alison, b 19 Ap 1890

   5e Eleanor Isabella Joan Alison   [Nos 38256 to 38293

267

4c *Mary Anne Short*, d (-) m 20 Nov 1832, *William Blanshard, M A, Bar-at-Law, Recorder of Doncaster, Chairman of Quarter Sessions*, d Nov 1872, and had issue 1d to 4d

    1d Henry Edward Blanshard, *b* 12 May 1816

    2d Caroline Marguretto Blanshard, *m* William Crawford, Bar-at-Law

    3d Edith Blanshard

    4d Florence Jane Blanshard

5c *Lucy Short*, d (-), m *Frederick Richard Lucas of Louth, co Lincoln*

6c *Jane Hassard Short*, d 9 Feb 1852, m Dec 1839, *William Garfit of Boston, co Linc*, b Feb 1810, d 2 Sept 1875, and had issue 1d to 1d

    1d William Garfit of West Skirbeck House, J P, D L, High Sheriff co Lincoln 1892, M P for Boston 1895–1906, and *formerly Capt 2nd Batt Lincolnshire R V (West Skirbeck House, Boston . 7 Chesham Place . S W Carlton, &)* b 9 Nov 1840, *m* 28 May 1868, Mary Krause, da of Conolly Norman of Fahan House, co Donegal, and his issue 1e

    1e Frances Mary Garfit, m 9 Feb 1892, Graham Lionel John Wilson of The Grove, M A (Oxon), Bar-at-Law, Capt 4th Batt North Staffordshire Regt *(The Grove, Market Drayton)*, and has issue 1f

        1f Lionel Garfit Wilson, *b* 6 Nov 1896

    2d Arthur Garfit, *b* 23 Sept 1847, *m* 7 Aug 1883, Frances, da of E Downe, and has issue 1e

        1e Stella Frances Garfit, *b* 16 Mar 1890

    3d Marianne Garfit

    4d Mary Louisa Garfit

7c *Maria Louisa Short*, d (-), m 5 Aug 1856, *Edgar John Meynell of Kilrington Hall, co York, J P, Judge of Durham County Court and Recorder of Doncaster [descended from Anne, Duchess of Exeter]*, d 15 Jan 1901, and had issue

See the Exeter Volume, p 337, Nos 24536–24543

4d *Margaret Raper*, d (-) m ( ) *Franks of Misterton, co Leic*

[Nos 38294 to 38312

136. Descendants, if any, of JANE LAMPLUGH (Table XV), d (-), m SAMUEL PAWSON of York, Merchant

137 Descendants, if any, of CORDELIA CHALONER (Table XV.), d (-), m at St Olave's, York, 4 May 1732, RICHARD GRAHAM of Whitewell, co York [3rd son of Sir Reginald Graham of Norton Conyers, 2nd Bt [E 1662]]

138 Descendants, if any, of MARY FOULIS (Table XV), d (-), m WILLIAM TURNER of Stainsby

139 Descendants of MARY FOULIS (Table XV.), *bur* (apparently) 19 Aug 1694, m as 2nd wife (contract dated July) 1660, ROBERT SHAFTO of Benwell Tower, Northumberland, *bapt* 30 May 1626, *d v p* 8 Nov 1668, and had issue 1a to 4a.[1]

1a *Robert Shafto of Benwell Tower, High Sheriff co Northbd* 1696, *bapt* 10 Mar 1664, d 1714, *shortly after* 14 May , m Dorothy da and (1700) co-h of Sir Thomas Heselrigge, 3rd Bt [E], d after 1715, and had issue 1b to 2b

[1] Surtees' "Durham," 1823, m 296

1b *Robert Shafto of Benwell Tower, High Sheriff* 1718, d 3 Nov 1735, m 1715, Mary, da and event sole h of Ralph Jenison of Elswick, and had issue (with a 2nd son, Jenison, who d s p 1771) 1c to 2c

1c *Robert Shafto of Benwell, co Northbd, and Wratling Park, co Camb, High Sheriff co Northbd* 1754, d 18 June 1780, m 14 Ap 1752, Camilla, da and co-h of Thomas Allan of the Flatts, Chester-le-Street, bur 19 June 1782, and had issue (with 2 sons who d s p) 1d

1d *Camilla Shafto of Benwell,* da and (30 Aug 1781) h, bapt 14 Feb 1756, liv 1822, m 23 Sept 1781, Hugh, otherwise William, Adair, Capt 25th Regt, liv 1822, and had issue then 1e to 3e

1e *Robert Shafto Adair,* b 26 June 1786

2e *William Adair*

3e *Alexander Adair*

2c *Thomas Shafto,* 3rd son

2b *Dorothy Shafto,* mentioned in father's will 14 Mar 1714

2a *Henry Shafto,* Bar-at-Law, bapt 13 Mar 1666, bur (? s p) 3 Feb 1711

3a *Jane Shafto,* bapt 5 Feb 1663, executer to will of her uncle, Mark Shafto, 19 Oct 1700, and then wife of James Sanderson of Durham, Clerk

4a *Mary Shafto,* mentioned in father's will 2 Nov 1668

---

140. Descendants of Sir JOHN EDEN **of West Auckland, 4th Bt [E.], M P** (Table XVI), b 16 Sept 1740, d 23 Aug 1812, m 2ndly, 9 Ap 1767, DOROTHEA, da and h of Peter JOHNSON, Recorder of Durham, d. 21 June 1792, and had issue 1a to 7a

1a *Sir Robert Eden, afterwards* (R L 15 Feb 1811) Johnson-Eden, 5th Bt [E], b 25 Oct 1771, d unm 4 Sept 1814

2a *Morton John Eden, afterwards* (R L 26 Oct 1812) Davidson Eden, of Beamish Park, b 30 June 1778, d unm 28 June 1841

3a *Dorothea Eden,* da and in her issue (1841) co h, d 1830, m 1st, 22 June 1790, Henry Methold, Capt Durham Fencible Cav 1798, d May 1799, 2ndly, Gen Daniel Seddon, and had issue (with 3 other sons who also d s p and a da who presumably did the same) 1b

1b *John Methold, afterwards* (R L 25 Sept 1844) Eden, of Beamish Park, co Durham, d unm 1885

4a *Catherine Eden,* da and co-h, b c 1770, d 19 May 1872 in her 102nd year, m Nov 1803, Robert Eden Duncombe Shafto of Whitworth Park, co Durham, M P., b 23 Mar 1776, d 17 Jan 1848, and had issue

See the Exeter Volume, pp 308-310, Nos 19416-19495

5a *Emmeline Eden,* da and co-h, d 21 July 1850, m as 2nd wife, 9 Nov 1809, Thomas Northmore of Cleve, M A , F R S (see p 52), d May 1851, and had issue 1b to 7b

1b *Emmeline Eden Northmore,* d (? unm)

2b *Charlotte Osgood Northmore,* d (-), m 4 Aug 1835, Capt John Whitlock, Madras Army, d 27 May 1849, and had issue

3b *Cornelia Risdon Northmore,* d 21 Aug 1870, m 8 May 1857, Benjamin Jones of Llanelly, and had issue

4b *Adelina Johnson Northmore,* d (? unm)

5b *Caroline Amelia Brunswick Northmore,* for whom Queen Caroline was Sponsor, d (-), m 17 Mar 1847, Capt George Longworth Dames, 66th Regt, d 20 Mar 1860, and had issue

6b *Elfrida St Aubyn Northmore*

7b *Gertrude Johnes Northmore*

[Nos 38313 to 38392

The Plantagenet Roll

6a Eleanor Eden, da and co-h, d at Bruges 22 Nov 1864, m 1813, the Rev Thomas Furness Wilson of Burley Hall, co York, and had issue

7a Charlotte Eden, da and co-h, d (-), m 1816, Robert Kaye Greville of Wyaston and Edinburgh, LL D, d 4 June 1866, and had issue

See p 220, Nos 37978–37981 [Nos 38393 to 38896

141 Descendants of Sir ROBERT EDEN, 1st Bt [G.B], so cr 19 Oct 1776, Governor of Maryland (Table XVI), b. c. 1741; d 2 Sept 1784, m 26 Ap 1763, the Hon. CAROLINE, sister and h of Frederick (CALVERT), 7th Baron Baltimore [I], da of Charles, 6th Baron Baltimore [I], d c 1803, and had issue 1a to 3a

1a Sir Robert Morton Eden, 2nd Bt [G B], b c 1767, d 14 Nov 1909, m 10 Jan 1792, Anne, da and h of James Paul Smith, of New Bond Street, d 14 July 1808, and had issue 1b to 7b

1b Sir Frederick Eden, 3rd Bt [G B], killed, unm, at New Orleans, 24 Dec 1814

2b Sir William Eden, 4th Bt, of Maryland [G B], and (1844) 6th Bt of West Auckland [E], b 31 Jan 1803, d 20 Oct 1873, m 23 Ap 1814, Elfrida Susanna Harriet, da of Col William Iremonger of Wherwell Priory, co Hants, d 8 July 1882, and had issue 1c to 4c

1c Sir William Eden, 7th Bt [E], and 4th Bt [G B], J P, D L, Hon Col 6th Batt Durham L I (Windlestone, Ferryhill, co Durham, 12n Waterloo Place, S W), b 4 Ap 1849, m 20 July 1886, Sybil Frances, da of Sir William Grey, K C S I [E Grey Coll], and has issue 1d to 5d

1d John Eden, b 9 Oct 1888

2d Timothy Calvert Eden, b 3 May 1893

3d Robert Anthony Eden, b 12 June 1897

4d William Nicholas Eden, b 14 Mar 1900

5d Elfrida Marjorie Eden, b 5 June 1887, m 29 Ap 1909, Leopold Guy Francis Maynard Greville, Lord Brooke, M V O [son and h-app of Francis Richard Charles Guy, 5th Earl of Warwick [G B], and a descendant of King Henry VII (see the Tudor Roll, pp 196–335)] (Warwick Castle, Warwick)

2c Morton Eden, b 25 June 1859, d 31 Mar 1909, m 1891, (—), whom he divorce 1896

3c Helen Eden, d 26 May 1878, m as 1st wife, 12 Aug 1871, Capt William St Lo Malet, 8th Hussars [Bt of Wilbury [G B 1791] Coll, also a descendant of King Edward III through the Mortimer-Percy marriage (see Part II)], b 20 Nov 1843, d 26 Aug 1885, and had issue 1d to 5d

1d Sir Edward St Lo Malet, 5th Bt [G B], &c (31 Corso d'Italia, Rome), b 14 Sept 1872, m 12 Nov 1901, Louise Michelle, da of Philibert Dubois, and has issue 1e

1e Charles St Lo Malet, b at Rome 1 Nov 1906

2d Henry Charles Malet, Capt 8th Hussars, formerly Cape Mounted Rifles, served in South Africa 1899-1902, Queen's Medal and 4 Clasps, King's Medal and 2 Clasps, b 21 Sept 1873, m 1 Feb 1906, Mildred Laura Lambert, da of Capt H Stephen Swiney of Gensing House, St Leonard's-on Sea, and has issue 1e to 2e

1e Edward William St Lo Malet, b 28 Nov 1908

2e Eimyntrude Virginia St Lo Malet

3d Elfrida St Lo Malet, m 1898, Capt Richard John Carey Oakes, Royal Garrison Regt, and has issue 1e to 2e

1e Elfrida Avice May Oakes

2e Marguerite Julia Oakes [Nos 38397 to 38410.

# of The Blood Royal

4d Helen Avice Harriet Malet (*Braham, Ray Park Avenue, Maidenhead*)

5d Hilda Mary Jeanne Malet, m 3 Ap 1900, Farquhar Celynn Lloyd [a descendant of Joan of Acre, da of King Edward I [1]] (*Marlands Court, Southwater, near Horsham, Yewlands, Crofton, Vancouver Island*), and has issue 1e to 2e

1e Richard Llewellyn Lloyd, b 1 Jan 1901

2e Stella Hilda Emily Lloyd, b 26 Mar 1908

4c Edith Eden, m 1st, as 3rd wife, 20 July 1875, William George (Eden), 4th Baron Auckland [I and G B], d 27 Feb 1890, 2ndly, 10 June 1897, Philip Symons (*Stonepitt Grange, Seal, Sevenoaks*)

3b *Right Rev Robert Eden, D D , Lord Bishop of Moray and Ross, Primus of Scotland*, b 2 Sept 1804, d 26 Aug 1886, m 17 Sept 1827, *Emma, da of Sir James Allan Park, a Justice of the Common Pleas*, d 24 Nov 1880 *and had issue* 1c to 9c

1c Frederick Morton Eden, Bar Lincoln's Inn, *formerly* Fellow of All Souls Coll, Oxford and Capt Oxford Militia (63 *Warwick Road, S W*), b 1 Nov 1829, m 1st, 23 May 1857, Louisa Ann (see p 274), da of Vice-Adm Hyde Parker, C B, d 9 Mar 1868, 2ndly, 4 Oct 1870, Fanny Helen, da of Edward Pomeroy Barrett-Lennard [Bt Coll], and has issue 1d to 6d

1d Morton Eden, b 8 Sept 1859

2d Frederick Charles Eden, b 6 Mar 1864

3d Rowland Frederick Eden (18 *Abingdon Villas, Kensington, W*), b 17 Aug 1874, m 1899, Marie Bernadette Anita, da of Col Henry George Saunders, Indian Army, and has issue 1e

1e Frederick Augustus Morton Eden, b 1 May 1901

4d Algernon Graham Eden, served in South Africa (Medals) 1901-02, b 1877

5d [1] Alice Eden, *unm*

6d [2] Dorothy Ione Helen Eden, m 1 Jan 1902 Arthur Dalrymple Forbes-Gordon, *late* 20th Hussars [B Sempill Coll] (*Langlea, co Roxburgh*)

2c Henley Eden (*Woodstock, As. ot*), b 8 Mar 1838, m 15 Ap 1871, Amy Frances [descended from King Henry VII (see Tudor Roll, p 169)], da of Lord Charles Lennox Kerr [M of Lothian Coll], and has issue 1d to 2d

1d Schomberg Henley Eden, Capt 1st Batt Black Watch, served in South Africa, Queen's Medal and 4 Clasps, b 18 Mar 1873

2d Charles William Guy Eden, Colonial C S, b 20 June 1874

3c Rev Robert Allan Eden, M A (Oxon), Vicar of Old St Pancras (58 *Oakley Square, N W*), b 27 Dec 1839, *unm*

4c William Alexander Eden, Col R A (ret) (*Oxer Cottage, Fawley, Hants*), b 16 June 1843, m 18 July 1885, Giovanna Anna Malvina, widow of Col Macbean of Tomatin, da of (—), s p

5c Lucy Eden, d (—), m 12 *June* 1849, *the Rev Herbert Samuel Hawkins, Rector of Beyton*, d 1893, *and had issue* 1d to 6d

1d Edward Robert Hawkins, b 6 May 1850, m 1888, Katie Clyde, da of Capt Edward Barkley, R N

2d Herbert Eden Hawkins, b 15 May 1852

3d Charles Henley Hawkins, b 21 Aug 1854

4d Mabel Ellen Hawkins

5d Margaret Mary Hawkins

6d Gertrude Lucy Hawkins

6c Caroline Eden (87 *Great King Street, Edinburgh*), m 11 Sept 1851, Col Arthur A'Court Fisher, C B, R E, d 2 Nov 1879, and has issue 1d to 6d

1d Arthur William Fisher, b 23 Sept 1852

2d Charles Sidney Dalton Fisher, Capt *formerly* 2nd Batt Mids Regt, served in South Africa, Queen's and King's Medals and 8 Clasps, mentioned in Despatches, b 20 Mar 1866   [Nos 38411 to 38437

---

[1] See Foster's "Noble and Gentle Families, &c," p 146

271

The Plantagenet Roll

3*d* Frederick A Court Fisher, *b* 1 Dec 1873, *m* 1902, Emma Lucy Athela, da of the Rev John Edward Alexander Inge, M A, Rector of Gayton

4*d* Alice Elizabeth Fisher (15 *Walker Street, Edinburgh*), *m* 19 Aug 1879, James Allan Park, 42nd (Black Watch) Royal Highlanders, *b* 20 Aug 1853, *d* from wounds received at Tel-el-Kebir 1882, and has issue (with a da *d* young) 1*e*

   1*e* Florence Ida Allan Park

5*d* Annie Caroline Ann Fisher, *m* 17 Nov 1887, William Macbean, and has issue 1*e* to 4*e*

   1*e* Ronald Eden Macbean *b* 19 July 1890

   2*e* Ian Gordon Macbean, *b* 24 Feb 1892

   3*e* Aileen Clelia Macbean

   4*e* Muriel Jean Macbean

6*d* Ethel Mary Fisher

7*c* *Alice Eden*, d 24 *Nov* 1894, m 5 *Dec* 1857, *the Right Hon George Ward Hunt, P C , M P* [*descended from the Lady Isabel Plantagenet*], d 29 *July* 1877; *and had issue*

See the Essex Volume, p 123, Nos 15690-15702

8*c* *Emma Selina Eden*, d (-), m 8 *June* 1861, *the Rev Dacres Olivier, Rector of Wilton and Canon of Salisbury*, d 12 *Sept* 1908, *and had issue* 1*d to* 10*d.*

   1*d* George Herbert Olivier, *b* 1863, d (? s p) Nov 1893

   2*d* Rev Henry Eden Olivier, M A (Oxon), Vicar of St James', Croydon (*St James' Vicarage, Croydon*), *b* 1866, *m* 2 July 1895, Gertrude Isabella [descended from the Lady Anne, sister to King Edward IV, &c (see Exeter Volume, p 173), da of the Rev Canon Edward Capel Cure, M A, Rector of St George's, Hanover Square, and has issue 1*e* to 3*e*

      1*e* Jasper George Olivier, *b* 20 Ap 1896

      2*e* Arthur Eden Olivier, *b* 6 July 1898

      3*e* Martin John Olivier, *b* 20 Feb 1900

   3*d* Alfred C S Olivier, *b* 1867, *m* 1900, Fanny Mary (Mrs Bernard Beere), widow of Capt Edward Cholmeley Dering [s and h app of Sir Edward Cholmeley Dering, 8th Bt], da of Francis Welby Whitehead

   4*d* Arthur Frank Olivier, *b* 1868

   5*d* Sidney Richard Olivier, Comm R N, *b* 1870, *m* 1897, Etheldred Mary, da of Capt Henry John Hodgson, R N, and has issue 1*e* to 5*e*

      1*e* Reginald Henry Dacres Olivier, *b* 1899

      2*e* Sidney John Olivier (twin), *b* 1905

      3*e* Joan Etheldred Olivier

      4*e* Lilian Rosemary Olivier

      5*e* Gillian Emma Olivier (twin)

   6*d* Reginald Ernest Olivier, *b* 1871

   7*d* Robert Harold Olivier, Capt 2nd Batt Duke of Cornwall's L I, served in South Africa 1899-1902, 2 Medals and 6 Clasps, *b* 1879

   8*d* Mary Olivier, *m* Jan 1895, Comm Charles James Collins, R N, *d* 12 Aug 1908

   9*d* Edith Maud Olivier

   10*d* Emma Mildred Olivier

9*c* Mary Eden

4*b* *George Morton Eden, Lieut-Gen in the Army,* b 10 *May* 1806, d *at Berne* 11 *Nov* 1862, m 18 *Jan* 1834, *Louisa Anne, da of George Robert Eyres,* d 5 *Nov* 1878, *and had issue* 1*c to* 3*c*

   1*c* *Morton Parker Eden, Lieut-Col R A,* b 11 *May* 1835, d 18 *Sept* 1880, m 4 *Ap* 1861, *Georgina Louisa Helen, da of Gen H Pester, R A,* d 22 *Ap* 1890, *and had issue* 1*d to* 4*d*   [Nos 38438 to 38477

# of The Blood Royal

1d Frederick Schomberg Eden, b 7 Mar 1872

2d Beatrice Caroline Eden, m 5 Oct 1889, Charles Cockburn Talbot, and has issue 1e to 3e

1e Robert Charles Talbot, b 2 Dec 1891

2e John Angelo Talbot, b 12 May 1893

3e Cecile Ione Talbot

3d Georgina Clarice Eden, m 25 Sept 1895, the Rev William Henry Pane, M A (37 Westminster Palace Gardens, S W)

4d Lilian Eden, m 16 May 1895, Capt William Nicolas McGachen, R N (ret) (see p 417), and has issue 1e

1e Armine Nicolas Eden McGachen

2c Charles Calvert Eden of Kingston Grange, H B M Diplo Ser, b 5 Nov 1837, d 10 Mar 1878, m 16 Dec 1862, the Baroness Cecile (The Grange, Kingston, Somerset), da of (—) Baron de Senner, of Merchligen, Switzerland, and had issue 1d to 3d

1d Morton Frederic Eden, b 16 June 1863

2d Evelyn Louisa Cecile Eden

3d Violet Cecile Eden, m 30 Aug 1899, Capt Arthur Street, A S C, and has issue 1e

1e John Noel Eden Street, b 1902

3c Fanny Evelyn Mary Eden (Hillside, Kingston, Taunton)

5b Sir Charles Eden, K C B, Vice-Adm R N, b 3 July 1808, d s p 7 Mar 1878

6b Marianne Eden, d 13 May 1859, m Nov 1812, Francis Mallet Sponge, d (² s p) Ap 1857

7b Caroline Eden, d 10 Nov 1854, m 11 July 1821, Vice-Adm Hyde Parker, C B, Senior Naval Lord of the Admiralty [Bt (1681) Coll], d 26 May 1854, and had issue 1c to 4c

1c Sir William Parker, 9th Bt [I.], Capt 44th Regt, D L, b 2 Sept 1826, d 24 May 1891, m 22 Nov 1855, Sophia Mary, da of Nathaniel Clarke Barnardiston of The Ryes, Sudbury, d 16 May 1903, and had issue 1d to 10d

1d Rev Sir William Hyde Parker, 10th Bt [I.], Lord of the Manor of Long Melford, M A (Camb), J P, C A, formerly Chaplain to the Bishop of Barbados (Melford Hall, Long Melford, Suffolk), b 8 Ap 1863, m 18 Nov 1890, Ethel, da of John Leech of Gorse Hall, Dukinfield, and has issue 1e to 3e

1e William Stephen Hyde Parker, b 23 Jan 1892

2e Harry Hyde Parker, b 17 Feb 1905

3e Mary Stephanie Hyde Parker

2d Edmond Hyde Parker, Capt R N, Flag Capt at Portsmouth, b 30 Jan 1868, m 1908, Helen Margaret, da of the Rev. George Raymond Portal, M A, Canon of Winchester

3d Laurence Hyde Parker (Smeatham Hall, Bulmer, Sudbury, Suffolk), b 23 Oct 1870, m 19 Ap 1906, Ada Letitia Moor, da of Joseph Alphonsus Horsford of Long Melford, M R C S, and has issue 1e to 2e

1e Mary Hyde Parker, b 19 Mar 1908

2e Dorothy Bridget Hyde Parker, b 6 Mar 1909

4d John Barnardiston Parker, 4th Class Medjidie, b 7 Ap 1879, m 31 Jan 1906, Dora Katherine, da of Canon Bromley of Newcastle-on-Tyne

5d Anne Hyde Parker, m 29 Ap 1886, Col Arthur Stamforth Hext, formerly Suffolk Regt (Trenarren, St Austell, Cornwall), and has issue 1e to 4e

1e Rhoda Marjorie Hext

2e Sybil Mary Hext

3e Margaret Hext } (twins)
4e Amy Hext

[Nos 38478 to 38504.

273

The Plantagenet Roll

6d Margaret Hyde Parker, m (her cousin) 15 Feb 1881, George Eden Hunt of Wadenhoe House, co Northants [son of the Right Hon George Ward Hunt (see above)] d 1892, and had issue

See p 272, Nos 38447-38449

7d Sophia Hyde Parker

8d Amy Hyde Parker

9d Mary Hyde Parker, m 25 Ap 1889 Charles Arthur Abraham [son of Canon Abraham] (Spire Hollin House, Glossop, Derby), and has issue 1c to 3c

   1c Christopher Charles Abraham, b 1 June 1893

   2c Geoffrey Austen Abraham, b 13 Feb 1899

   3c Doris Mary Abraham

10d Dorothy Hyde Parker, m 30 Dec 1903, Hugh Wilfrid Sherlock [son of the Rev Harry Sherlock of Bildeston] (56 West Park, Eltham, Kent), and has issue 1c

   1c Hugh Sherlock, b 1905

2c *Louisa Ann Parker*, d 9 Mar 1868, m 3 May 1857, *Capt. Frederick Morton Eden, and had issue*

See p 271, Nos 38417-38418, and 38422

3c *Caroline Maria Parker*, d 11 Nov 1890, m 12 Ap 1849, *Col John Home Purves, Equerry and Comptroller of the Household to H R H the Duchess of Cambridge* [Bt (1665) Coll], d 2 July 1867, and had issue 1d to 3d

   1d *Charles Hyde Home Purves*, D L, b 1850, d 19 Feb 1887, m 26 June 1877, *Frances Mabel (Purves, Greenlaw, R S O), da of Clement Archer of Hill House, Midx, and had issue 1e to 2e*

      1e Sir John Home Purves, now (1894) Home-Purves Hume-Campbell, of Marchmont, 8th Bt [S], Capt Lothians and Berwickshire Imp Yeo, *formerly Lieut 2nd Life Guards (Marchmont, Greenlaw, S O), b 9 Aug 1879, m 1 Oct 1901, Emily Jane* [descended from King Henry VII (see the Tudor Roll, p 166)], da of the Rev Robert Digby Ram, Preb of St Paul's, and has issue 1f to 2f

         1f Mabel Jane Home-Purves-Hume-Campbell

         2f Elsie Barbara Home-Purves-Hume-Campbell

      2e Alice Home Purves, m 6 July 1904, Major St John Louis Hyde du Plat Taylor, D S O, Brig-Major of a Territorial Force Inf Brigade, *formerly R A (Purves, Greenlaw), and has issue 1f*

         1f Frederica Mabel Joan du Plat Taylor

      2d Augusta Louisa Helen Purves   } (39 *Cheyne Walk, S W*)
      3d Alexandra Mary Caroline Purves }

   4c Fanny Letitia Parker (*Meaford, Ventnor, I W*)

2a *William Eden, Gen in the Army, d s p* [1]

3a [da] *Eden* [2]   [Nos 38505 to 38527

142 Descendants of WILLIAM (EDEN), 1st BARON AUCKLAND [I, 18 Nov. 1789] and 1st BARON AUCKLAND of West Auckland [G.B, 22 May 1793]. P C (Table XVI), d 28 May 1814, m 26 Sept 1776, ELEANOR, sister of Gilbert, 1st Earl of Minto [U K], da of the Right Hon Sir Gilbert ELLIOTT, 3rd Bt [S], P C, b 1758, d 18 May 1818 ; and had issue 1a to 6a

1a *George (Eden), 2nd Baron [G B and I] and (21 Dec 1839) 1st Earl of Auckland [U K], G C B, b 25 Aug 1784, d unm 1 Jan 1849*

---

[1] Foster's "Baronetage," 1880, p 186   [2] Burke's "Peerage," 1907, p 574

# of The Blood Royal

2a *Robert John (Eden), 3rd Baron Auckland [G B and I], Lord Bishop of Bath and Wells, D L , b 10 July 1799 , d 25 Ap 1870 , m 15 Sept 1825, Mary [descended from the Lady Isabel Plantagenet], da of Francis Edward Hurt of Alderwasley, d 25 Nov 1872 , and had issue*

See the Essex Volume, pp 360-361, Nos 35486-35531

3a *Hon Elizabeth Charlotte Eden, b 21 Mar 1780 , d 17 Ap 1847 , m 31 Mar 1800, Francis Godolphin (Osborne), 1st Baron Osborne [U K] [2nd son of the 5th Duke of Leeds [E], &c , descended from George, Duke of Clarence, K G], d 15 Feb 1850 , and had issue*

See the Clarence Volume, pp 627-629, Nos 28051-28117

4a. *Hon. Caroline Eden, b July 1781 , d 2 Mar 1851 , m 17 June 1806, Arthur Vansittart of Shottesbrooke and Clewer, co Berks, J P , D L , M P for Windsor 1804, Col Berks Militia [of the old Dutch family of Van Sittart, who settled in England under Charles II], bapt 28 Dec 1775 , d 31 May 1829 , and had issue (with 2 sons and a da who d unm)* 1b *to* 10b

1b *Arthur Vansittart of Shottesbrooke and Foot's Cray J P , Cornet 2nd Life Guards, b 2 May 1807 , d 22 Ap 1859 , m 26 May 1831, Diana Sara, da of Gen Sir John Gustavus Crosbie, G C H , d Sept 1881 , and had issue (with 2 sons who d s p)* 1c

1c *Rose Sophia Vansittart of Shottesbrooke, d 8 Jan 1892 , m 27 Nov 1856, Oswald Augustus Smith of Hammerwood, co Sussex, D L , b 21 Oct 1826 , d. 24 Aug 1902, and had issue* 1d *to* 3d

1d *Basil Guy Oswald Smith of Shottesbrooke (Shottesbrooke Park, Berks, 33 Grosvenor Street, W), b 28 Sept 1861 , m 15 Nov 1893, Rose Marguerite, da of Charles Bruce Henry Somerset [D of Beaufort Coll , and descended from George, Duke of Clarence, K G (see Clarence Volume, p 332)] , and has issue* 1e

1e *Nancy Oswald Smith, b 19 May 1896*

2d *Rupert Oswald Smith, b 29 Jan 1864*

3d *Maurice Oswald Smith, b 3 Ap 1866*

2b *Robert Vansittart of Driffield, co Berks, J P , Lieut-Col Coldstream Guards and a Page of Honour to H R H the Duchess of Gloucester and Edinburgh, b 21 Jan 1811 , d 2 May 1872 , m 4 Nov 1845, Elizabeth Harriet, da of John Willes Fleming of Stoneham Park, M P , d 3 Ap 1906, and had issue* 1c *to* 9c

1c *Robert Arnold Vansittart of Foot's Cray, J P , D L , Lord of the Manors of Ruxley and North Cray, late Capt 7th Dragoon Guards (Foot's Cray Place, Sidcup, Kent), b 21 Oct 1851 , m 30 July 1878, Alice, da of Gilbert James Blane of Foliejon Park, co Berks , and has issue* 1d *to* 6d

1d *Robert Gilbert Vansittart, M V O , 3rd Sec Diplo Service b 20 June 1881*

2d *Arnold Bealey Vansittart, b 24 Sept 1889*

3d *Guy Nicholas Vansittart, b 8 Sept 1893*

4d *Sibell Alice Vansittart*

5d *Honoria Edith Vansittart*

6d *Marjorie Marie Vansittart*

2c *Catherine Caroline Vansittart, m as 2nd wife, 14 Jan 1869, Thomas Campbell, Cadet of Golgirin , and has issue*

3c *Fanny Vansittart, m 26 Ap 1866, Walter Long of Preshaw and The Holt, co Hants, and Muchelney, co Som , J P , late 11th Regt (The Holt, Bishop's Waltham, Hants), and has issue (with a son and 2 das who d young)* 1d *to* 6d

1d *Walter Vansittart Long, b 27 Nov 1868 , m 25 Ap 1894, Mary Lilian, da of Col Philip Arthur Pleydell-Bouverie-Campbell-Wyndham of Dunoon [E of Radnor Coll]*

2d *Ethel Fanny Long, m 19 July 1892, Arthur Hildyard Robinson (The Mill House, Bishop's Waltham), and has issue*   [Nos 38528 to 38652

275

The Plantagenet Roll

3d Katharine Teresa Long, m 5 June 1895, Robert Eden Richardson, B A (Camb) [3rd son of John Crow Richardson of Glanbrydan Park (see p 278)] (*Morestead House, Hants*), and has issue 1e to 3e

    1e Douglas Courtenay Richardson, b 28 Dec 1905

    2e Katharine Doris Richardson, b 6 Jan 1900

    3e Maudo Eden Richardson, b 3 Oct 1901

1d Mildred Bertha Long, m 1 May 1900, Charles Hugh Finch (*Costessy House, Norwich*)

5d Moena Louisa Long, *unm*

6d Evelyn Alice Long, m 12 July 1904, Henri Ernst Armand Dehlle.

4c Bertha Vansittart

5c Edith Vansittart, m 25 Aug 1870, Robert Peel Wethered [5th son of Owen Wethered of Remnantz, J P], d 2 Nov 1873, s p s

6c Mary Emily Vansittart, m 19 Jan 1876, Henry Corry Fitzherbert, J P [4th son of Thomas Fitzherbert of Black Castle, J P , D L] (*Millbrook, Queen's Co*), and has issue 1d to 2d

    1d Arnold Vesey Fitzherbert, b 18 Mar 1878

    2d Edith Clare Fitzherbert, m 8 July 1897, Arthur Mildmay Hall-Dare, 3rd son of Robert Westley Hall-Dare of Newtonberry, J P , D L , and has issue 1e to 2e

        1e Derrick Arthur Hall Dare, b 4 Dec 1900

        2e Irene Clare Hall-Dare

7c Louisa Vansittart, m the Rev Alfred Cox

8c Constance Mary Vansittart, m Lieut -Col Charles Wigram Long, R A , M P for Evesham 1906 [2nd son of the Ven Archdeacon Charles Maitland Long] (*Severn Bank, Severn Stoke, Worc , Carlton*)

9c Evelyn Jane Vansittart, m 1 Nov 1882, Edward Strangways Neave [Bt (1795) Coll] (5 *Warwick Road, Ealing*), and has issue 1d to 7d

    1d Edward Arthur Neave, b 2 Aug 1883

    2d Gerald Vansittart Neave, b 2 Oct 1884

    3d Guy Mortier Neave, b 21 Oct 1886

    4d Digby Frank Neave, b 25 May 1892

    5d Hugh Alexander Neave, b 1 June 1893

    6d Eric Lloyd Strangways Neave, b 1898

    7d Evelyn Henriet Neave

3b William Vansittart of Brunswick Square, Brighton, H E I C S , D L , M P , Windsor, b 2 May 1813, d 15 Jan 1876, m 1st, 1 July 1839, Emily [descended from the Lady Anne, sister of King Edward IV , &c (see Exeter Volume, p 583)], da of Gen Robert Leslie Anstruther, d on her passage home from India 25 May 1841, 2ndly, 2 Dec 1847, Henrietta, da and co-h of John Humphreys, d 19 May 1852, 3rdly, 6 Feb 1866, Melanie [also descended from the Lady Anne (see Exeter Volume, p 235)], da of Sir Richard Jenkins, G C B , M P , &c (re-m Henry Pepys and), d 1891, and had issue 1c to 4c

1c William Henry Vansittart, b 25 May 1844

2c Charles Edward Bexley Vansittart, late Capt Antrim Rifles, b Dec 1867, m 28 July 1888, Constance Frances (who obtained a divorce 1904), da of Sir Thomas Macdonald Miller, 4th Bt [G B], and has issue 1d to 2d

    1d Constance Hilda Maude Bexley Vansittart

    2d Melanie Bexley Vansittart

3c¹ Emily Eden Vansittart, d 27 May 1905, m 1 Oct 1861, George Palmer of Nazing Park, co Essex, J P , Bengal C S , b 12 Nov 1828, d 13 Sept 1902, and had issue 1d

1d Emily Charlotte Palmer, d 1891, m 1889 Robert Francis Crawley [descended from George, Duke of Clarence (see Clarence Volume, p 155)], and had issue

[Nos 38653 to 38680.

# of The Blood Royal

4c[2] Caroline Betha Vansittart, m 1st, 21 Nov 1869, Reginald Wynyatt of Dymock, co Gloucester, d (–) 2ndly, 13 Sept 1882, Horace Drummond Dean

4b *George Nicholas Vansittart*, b *June* 1814, d 12 *May* 1889, m 1 *June* 1852, *Elizabeth Ann, da and co-h of James Mansfield of Midmar Castle, co Aberdeen,* d 19 Nov 1875 *and had issue* 1c *to* 3c

1c Arthur George Vansittart, H B M 's Consul-Gen at Port-au-Prince, *formerly* Diplo Ser (*British Consulate, Port-au-Prince, Haiti*), b 22 Nov 1854

2c Coleraine Nicholas Vansittart, *late* Lieut Berks Militia, b 3 Dec 1860, m 1886, Marie (who obtained a divorce 1896), da of Gustave Vincent, and has issue 1d to 2d

 1d Francis de Mansfield Vansittart, b 10 Feb 1891

 2d Violet Vansittart, b 15 Aug 1887

3c Emily Christina Vansittart (36 *Via Palestro, Rome*)

5b *Henry Vansittart, Civil and Session Judge, H E I C S,* b 3 *Nov* 1816, d 13 *Jan* 1896, m *Mary Amelia, da of Catt William Hugh Dobbie, R N,* d 18 *June* 1886, *and had issue* 1c *to* 7c

1c Henry Vansittart, Bar-at-Law, *late* Lieut R M A (*Saharanpur, India*), b 4 Aug 1849 m 1st, 19 Oct 1878, Mary Virginia, da of Francis Johnson Jessop of Derby, d 1886, 2ndly, 1888, Ellen, da of (—) Dianopolis, and has issue 1d to 2d

 1d[1] Amelia Mary Vansittart

 2d[2] Ellen Vansittart

2c Charles Vansittart, *late* a Clerk in the Finance Dept, India, b 1 Jan 1853, m 24 Feb 1881, Katherine Frances (see Part II), da of Lieut-Gen Charles Pollard, and has issue (with a son and da who d young) 1d

 1d Dorothy Mary Vansittart

3c Herbert Vansittart (9 *Portland Avenue Exmouth*), b 13 Ap 1854, m 12 Dec 1893, Mary Agatha, da of Adm William Dobbie, R N, and has issue (with a son d young) 1d to 2d

 1d Agatha Mary Vansittart, b 10 Oct 1895

 2d Hilda Florence Vansittart, b 23 May 1908

4c Eden Vansittart, Col Indian Army (*The Chalet, Bournemouth*), b 19 Ap 1856, m 16 Dec 1889, Ethel, da of R D Spedding, I C S, and has issue 1d

 1d Vera Mary Eden Vansittart

5c Edith Vansittart, m 26 Dec 1868, Major-Gen Newton Burton, Bengal Staff Corps (ret) (5 *Onslow House, South Kensington*)

6c Florence Mary Vansittart, m 24 Oct 1871, Lieut-Gen John Mackie Stewart, Bengal Army [Cadet of Cairnsmore] (*Carruchan, Dumfries, Naval and Military*), and has issue 1d to 1d

 1d John Henry Keith Stewart, Capt Indian Army, and D A A G India (*Naval and Military*), b 31 Aug 1872, m 30 Sept 1898, Frances Jane [descended from George, Duke of Clarence, K G, brother of King Edward IV, &c (see Clarence Volume, p 592)], da of the Hon George Augustus Hobart-Hampden [E. of Buckinghamshire Coll], and has issue 1e to 2e

  1e Florence Edith Keith Stewart, b 3 Sept 1899

  2e Julia Constance Keith Stewart, b 24 Sept 1903

 2d Patrick Alexander Vansittart Stewart, Capt K O Scottish Borderers (*Naval and Military*), b 29 June 1875

 3d James Montgomery Vansittart Stewart, Capt 10th Gurkha Rifles, b 12 July 1877

 4d Herbert William Vansittart Stewart, Lieut Royal Scots Fusiliers, b 15 Aug 1880

7c Rosamond Vansittart, *unm*

6b *Rev Charles Vansittart, M A, Rector of Shottesbrooke,* b 8 *Mar* 1820, d
[Nos 38681 to 38705

277 2 N

The Plantagenet Roll

14 *July* 1878 , m 27 May 1845, *Frances Rosalie, da and co h of Hens Busk of Glenalder, co Radnor, D L* , d 10 May 1899 , *and had issue (with a da who d unm)* 1c to 3c

    1c Sidney Nicholas Vansittart, *b* 10 Jan 1847

    2c Arthur Vansittart, in the Pontified Zouaves, has Medal and Mentana Cross, *b* 3 Nov 1849

    3c *Cyril Bexley Vansittart, Chamberlain of the Cape and Sword to Popes Pius IX and Leo XIII* , b 28 Aug 1851, d unm at Rome 22 Jan 1887

    7b *Caroline Vansittart,* d 30 *Sept* 1883, m 9 *July* 1828, *George Charles* (Mostyn), 6th Baron Vaux *of Harrowden [E 1523], who had that Barony called out of abeyance in his favour* 12 *Mar* 1838 *[descended from George, Duke of Clarence, K G (see Clarence Volume, p 421)],* d 28 *Jan* 1883, *and had issue*

    See the Clarence Volume, pp 421–422, Nos 16289–16303

    8b *Charlotte Eleanor Vansittart,* d (–) , m as 2nd *wife,* 1 Aug 1842, *the Rev Edward Serocold Pearce-Serocold (R L 30 July 1842), previously Pearce, of Cherry-hinton, co Camb , J P ,* d (–) , *and had issue* 1c to 2c

    1c Charlotte Pearce-Serocold, da and co-h of mother, *m* 1866, the Ven Hemming Robeson, Archdeacon of North Wilts

    2c Teresa Eden Pearce Serocold, da and co h of mother, *m* 1866, John Crow Richardson of Glanbrydan Park, co Carmarthen, and Pant-y-Gwydr, co Glamorgan, J P , D L , Col Comdg 3rd Glamorgan Rifle Vol , d 16 Nov 1903, and has issue 1d to 2d

    1d *Ernald Edward Richardson of Glanbrydan, &c , J P , Capt Royal Carmarthen Art Mil , M A (Oxon),* b 31 *July* 1869 d 7 *July* 1909 , m 9 *Feb* 1898, *Irene Caroline, da of Col Ynyr Henry Burges of Parkanaur, co Tyrone , and had issue* 1e to 4e

    1e Ernald Wilbraham Richardson (*Glanbrydan Park, Manordilo, Carmarthen , Pant-y-Gwydr, Swansea*), b 21 July 1900

    2e Llewellyn George Richardson, *b* 1902

    3e John Crow Richardson, *b* 4 Nov 1905

    4e Rose Eurene Ynyr Stella Richardson

    2d Robert Eden Richard Richardson, B A (Camb) (*Morestead House, Hants*), *b* 18 Dec 1872 , m 5 June 1895, Kathrine Teresa, da of Walter Long of Preshaw , and has issue

    See p 276, Nos 38654–38656

    9b *Martha Louisa Vansittart,* d 1877 , m 4 Aug 1841, *William Chapman of South Hill, co Westmeath, D L [3rd son of Sir Thomas Chapman, 2nd Bt [I]],* d 25 *Jan* 1889, *and had issue* 1c to 3c

    1c Thomas Robert Tighe Chapman of South Hill, J P , heir-presumptive to the Baronetcy, *b* 6 Nov 1846, *m* 24 July 1873, Edith Sarah Hamilton, da of George Augustus Rochfort-Boyd of Middleton Park, co Westmeath, D L , and has issue 1d to 4d

    1d Eva Jane Louisa Chapman

    2d Rose Isabel Chapman

    3d Florence Lina Chapman

    4d Mabel Cecile Chapman

    2c Francis Vansittart Chapman, J P (*South Hill, Delvin, co Westmeath*), *b* 9 Sept 1849

    3c Caroline Margaret Chapman (*Killua Castle, Clonmellon, co Westmeath*), m 9 Jan 1894, her cousin, Sir Montagu Richard Chapman, 5th Bt [I], *d s p* 22 Jan 1907

    10b *Sophia Vansittart,* d (–) , m 7 *Jan* 1841, *Thomas Andrew Anstruther, Madras C S [Bt of Balcaskie [S 1694] Coll],* d 14 *Ap* 1876, *and had issue* (with 3 sons who d s p) 1c   [Nos 38706 to 38739.

# of The Blood Royal

1c Philip Robert Anstruther, Lieut-Col 94th Regt, b 30 Jan 1841, d 26 Dec 1880, m 12 Jan 1875, Zaida Mary (Balchrystie, Colinsburgh, Fife), da of Sir Thomas Erskine of Cambo, 2nd Bt [U K], and had issue 1d to 3d

1d Philip George Anstruther of Thirdpart, Capt 2nd Batt Seaforth High-landers, served in South Africa, has Queen's and King's Medals and 4 Clasps, b 25 Oct 1875

2d Robert Abercrombie Anstruther, Capt R F A, served in South Africa, has Queen's Medal with Clasps, b 3 Aug 1879

3d Mary Rosamond Anstruther, m 21 Nov 1900, Edward Windsor Hussey of Scotney Castle, J P, D L, Bar-at-Law (Scotney Castle, Lamberhurst)

5a Hon Mary Louisa Eden, b 14 Sept 1788, d 2 Dec 1858, m 26 June 1806, Andrew Wedderburn, afterwards (R L 24 June 1811) Colville, d (2 s p) 3 Feb 1856

6a Hon Mary Dulcibella Eden, b 1 Sept 1793 d 20 Mar 1862, m 15 July 1819, Charles Drummond [V Strathallan [S] Coll, and a descendant of King Henry VII, &c], d 28 Aug 1858, and had issue

See the Tudor Roll, pp 534-535, Nos 35706-35742   [Nos 38740 to 38779

143 Descendants of THOMAS EDEN of Wimbledon, Deputy-Auditor of Greenwich Hospital (Table XVI), d 1 May 1805, m 7 July 1783, MARIANA, da of Arthur JONES of Reigate Priory, co. Surrey, and had issue 1a to 6a

1a Thomas Eden of The Bryn, co Glamorgan, Sec to Gov of Ceylon, b 29 Nov 1787, d 4 Nov 1845, m 4 Jan 1810, Frances Eliza, da of the Hon John Rodney [B Rodney Coll], d 5 Jan 1879, and had issue 1b to 8b

1b Rev John Patrick Eden, Hon Canon of Durham, b 6 July 1813, d 6 May 1885, m 3 May 1850, Catherine Frances, da of Col Henry Stobart, d 11 Sept 1898, and had issue 1c to 9c

1c John Henry Eden, Lieut-Col (ret) H M's Inspector of Constabulary, N Dist, &c (Bishopton Grange, Ripon, United Service), b 10 May 1851, m 12 Oct 1893, Lady Florence [descended from King Henry VII, &c (see Tudor Roll, p 259)], da of Somerset Richard (Lowry-Corry), 4th Earl of Belmore [I], and has issue 1d to 4d

1f Robert John Patrick Eden, b 26 Ap 1896

2d George Wilfrid Eden, b 13 Aug 1903

3d Christian Florence Eden

4d Norah Madeline Eden

2c Arthur Francis Eden (Penlan, Swansea), b 3 June 1852, m 5 July 1882, Frances, da of the Rev Robert Springett, Vicar of Brafferton

3c Right Rev George Rodney Eden, D D, 2nd Lord Bishop of Wakefield, formerly Bishop of Dover 1890-1897 (Bishopgarth, Wakefield), b 9 Sept 1853, m 4 July 1889, Constance Margaret, da of the Rev Henry John Ellison, Hon Canon of Canterbury and Chaplain-in-Ordinary to Queen Victoria, and has issue 1d to 5d

1d John Rodney Eden, b 4 July 1892

2d Gerald Balfour Eden, b 12 Aug 1896

3d. Margaret Agnes Eden

4d Dorothy Frances Eden

5d Mary Catharine Eden

4c Charles Hamilton Eden (Glynderwen, Black Pvl, S O, Glamorgan), b 2 Ap 1855, m 27 Jan 1885, Caroline Sophia, da of the Rev Charles Henry Ford, Vicar of Bishopston, and has issue 1d to 3f

1d Charles Henry Hamilton Eden, Royal Mil Acad, Woolwich, b 12 M n 1889

2d Frances Catherine Eden

3d Dulcibella Eden

[Nos 38780 to 38795

279

The Plantagenet Roll

5c Rev Frederick Nugent Eden, M A (Camb), Vicar of Rusthall (*Rusthall Vicarage, Tunbridge Wells*), b 3 Sept 1857, *unm*

6c Rev Henry Culley Eden, M A (Camb), Vicar of Holy Innocents', Hammersmith (205 *Goldhawk Road W*), b 4 Nov 1858, *unm*

7c Robert Gerald Rodney Eden (*Rhyd-yr-Helyg, Sketty, Glamorgan*), b 7 Jan 1860, m 11 Ap 1901, Elizabeth Anne, da of the Right Rev Thomas Bunbury, D D, Lord Bishop of Limerick, Ardfort, and Aghadoe

8c Frances Margaret Eden (*Selwyn Croft, Cambridge*) m 27 June 1893, the Rev Richard Appleton, Fellow of Trin Coll and 4th Master of Selwyn Coll, Camb, Hon Canon of Durham, d 1 Mar 1909

9c Mary Dulcibella Eden (*Rusthall Vicarage, Tunbridge Wells*)

2b *William Frederick Eden, Col in the Army*, b 31 Aug 1814, d. 14 Nov 1867, m 1 Jan 1838, *Marie Sidonie, da of Jean Isidor Deliselle, d 1891, and had issue (with 2 elder sons who d s p)* 1c

1c Henry Hamilton Forbes Eden, Major Army Motor Reserve, *formerly* Hon Lieut-Col 3rd Batt Norfolk Regt, served in South Africa, his Queen's Medal and 3 Clasps (*Eden Lodge, Cromer, Junior United Service, &c*), b 28 Oct 1856, m 11 Dec 1878, Emily Clara Charlotte, widow of S Bedford Edwards, da of (—)

3b *Louisa Frances Catherine Eden, d 26 Nov 1898, m 26 May 1859, the Rev John Robert Hall, Hon Canon of Canterbury, Rector of Hunton, d 1892, and had issue* 1c

1c Frances Caroline Hall

4b *Frances Marianne Eden, d 25 Ap 1862, m as 1st wife, 18 June 1850, Rev the Hon Lewis William Denman, d 6 May 1907, and had issue*
See p 166, Nos 17601–17606

5b *Sarah Frederica Eden, d 4 Nov 1903, m Aug 1841, Montign Wilmot of Norton House, co Glamorgan [Bt of Osmaston [G B] Coll], d 8 Dec 1880, and had issue*
See the Essex Volume, pp 135–136, Nos 16037–16055

6b *Caroline Elizabeth Eden, d 11 Nov 1872, m as 1st wife, 28 Ap 1859, Felix Hussey Webber* (see p 201), *a Clerk in the House of Commons, d 19 Ap 1905, and had issue* 1c to 4c

1c Gerald Rodney Webber, b 23 Feb 1863, m 24 Oct 1889, Eiteuse, da of Augustus Baylis, and has issue 1d to 2d

1d Arthur Rodney Webber, b 7 Sept 1890
2d Gladys Janthe Webber b 20 Sept 1892

2c *Felix Arthur Webber, M A, R N*, b 15 Ap 1866, d *unm* 17 July 1885
3c Helen Kate Webber, *unm*

4c Caroline Grace Webber, m 14 Jan 1901, Henry Fenwick Haszard, Comm R N d 31 Mar 1898 and has issue 1d to 2d

1d Gerald Fenwick Haszard, b 22 Oct 1894
2d Gladys Grace Haszard, b 19 Feb 1892

7b Emily Georgiana Eden (*The Bryn, Swansea*)

8b *Mary Dulcibella Eden, d 9 Ap 1909, m as 2nd wife, 17 July 1867 Captain Iltid Thomas of Glanmor, d 2 Sept 1889, and had issue* 1c to 4c

1c Iltid Edward Thomas (*Glanmor, Swansea*), b 1 July 1873

2c Isabel de Winton Thomas, m 24 Ap 1896, Francis William Gilbertson (*Glyn Leg, Pontardawe, Swansea*), and has issue 1d

1d Mary Dulcibella Frances Gilbertson

3c Dulcibel Iltuta Thomas

4c Amabel Charlotte Thomas, m 23 Sept 1902, Maurice Walter Henty, and has issue 1d

1d Richard Iltid Henty, b 25 June 1903   [Nos 38796 to 38841

# of The Blood Royal

2a *John Eden, C B , Gen in the Army*, b 25 Mar 1789 , d 6 Oct 1874 , m
1st, at Quebec, Aug 1829, Anne, da and in her issue (13 Oct 1858) co-h of Sir John
Caldwell of Castle Caldwell, 5th Bt [I], d at Montreal Nov 1841 , 2ndly, 4 July
1843, Charlotte Carse, da of Edmund Saul Prentice of Armagh, d (-) , and had
issue 1b to 5b

   1b William Thomas Eden, Col late Bombay S C , b 23 Ap 1838

   2b Frederick Morton Eden, Major late R M L 1 , Egyptian Medal with Clasps
and Bronze Star (Ivybridge, Devon). b 28 Dec 1847 , m 6 July 1881, Minnie Pitts,
da of Edward Allen of Stowford Lodge, Devon, J P , s p s

   3b George Henry Eden, Lieut R N (ret) (The Gull, Boundary Road, West
Worthing), b 7 Oct 1849 , m 1901, Miriam Sophia, da of W Farnham , and has
issue 1c

      1c Hugh Morton Eden, b 1903

   4b Frances Charlotte Eden, m 18 Sept 1872 Montagu St John Maule, B A ,
S C L , Solicitor (Chapel House, Park Street, Bath) . and has issue 1c to 3c

      1c Henry Noel St John Maule, b 1873

      2c Walter John Maule, b 1878

      3c Ethel Mary St John Maule

   5b Emily Elizabeth Eden, m 3 Sept 1874, Ernest Wallace Rooke, Solicitor
(Stratton House, Bath)

3a *Arthur Eden, Assist Comptroller of the Exchequer*, b 9 Aug 1793 , d 1871 ,
m 1821, Frances, widow of William Baring [Bt Coll], sister of Charles, 1st Baron
Sydenham [U K], and da of John Buncombe-Poulett-Thom on of Waverley Abb y,
co Surrey, d 25 Mar 1877 , and had issue 1c to 4c

   1c Arthur John Eden (19 Bedford Square, W ( ), b 1827 , unm

   2c Frederick Eden (Palazzo Barbarigo, Venice), b 1828 , m 28 Feb 1865,
Caroline, da of E Joseph L Joykill of Wargrave Hill , s p

   3c Mabel Eden, b 20 Jan 1837 , d 20 Ap 1889 , m 3 Ap 1861, Frederick
Cox, Banker and Army Agent (Stanswood Cottage, Fawley, Southampton) , and had
issue (with an elder son, Horace Frederick, d s p July 1899) 1f to 5f

      1d Reginald Henry Cox, Banker (26 Pont Street, S W), b 30 Dec 1865 m
3 May 1890, Sybil Mary, da of Thomas M Wequelin

      2f Hubert Arthur Cox, Banker (3 Grosvenor Crescent, S W), b 16 Feb 1871 ,
unm

      3d Algernon Charles Cox, Banker (57 Sloane Street, S W), b 23 Aug 1876
m 6 Nov 1901, Lilian Gertrude, da of William Grazebrook , and has issue
1e to 2e

         1c Frederick Cox, b 21 Nov 1902

         2e Isabel Valentine Cox, b 14 Feb 1906

      4d Lilian Cox, m 8 Mar 1888, Henry Vaughan Rudstow-Read [descended
from the Lady Anne, sister of King Edward IV (see Exeter Volume, p 532)]

      5f Mabel Horatia Cox

   4c Dulcibella Eden, d 25 Oct 1903 . m 23 Jan 1856, Hugh Hammersley of
Sun House, Chelsea, Army Agent, d Sept 1882 , and had issue 1d to 9d

      1d Arthur Charles Hammersley, Banker (56 Prince's Gate, S W ,), b 22 Dec
1856 , m 1st, 2 Sept 1882, Mary Louisa [descended from the Lady Anne, sister of
Edward IV (see the Exeter Volume, p 294)], da of George Herbert Frederick
Campbell, Cadet of Cawdor, J P , D L , d 12 Nov 1899 , 2ndly, 15 Ap 1902, Violet
Mary (see p 82), da of William Peere Williams-Freeman of Clapton, co Northants
and has issue 1e to 7e

      1e[1] Hugh Charles Hammersley, b 23 Feb 1892

      2e[2] Christopher Ralph Hammersley, b 4 Jan 1903

      3e[2] David Frederick Hammersley, b 15 July 1904

[Nos 38842 to 38863.

The Plantagenet Roll

4c[1] Gwendolen Mary Hammersley, m Jan 1908, George Henry Draper Post [son of Frederick A Post of 58 Eccleston Square], and has issue 1f to 2f

1f Pauline Post, b Dec 1908

2f Cynthia Alma Post, b 22 Dec 1909

5c[1] Cynthia Edith Hammersley, unm

6c[1] Doris Hammersley, unm

7c[2] Monica Violet Hammersley unm

2d Hugh Greenwood Hammersley, Banker (*The Grove, Hampstead, 16 Sackville Street, W*), b 1 July 1858, m 30 Aug 1889, Mary Frances [descended from the Lady Isabel Plantagenet (see the Essex Volume, p 289)], da of Owen Grant, and has issue 1e

1e *Eve Mary Hammersley, d unm*

3d Guy Frederick Hammersley, b 27 Jan 1871

4d Margaret Dulcibella Hammersley (51 *Iln Park Gardens, S W*), m 13 Jan 1883, Sidney Francis Godolphin Osborne [son of the Rev Lord Sidney Godolphin Osborne, and a descendant of George, Duke of Clarence, K G (see Clarence Volume, p 628)], d 22 Oct 1903, and has issue 1e to 3e

1e Francis D'Arcy Godolphin Osborne, Attaché Diplo Ser, b 16 Sept 1884

2e Sidney Hugh Godolphin Osborne, b 28 Dec 1887

3e Maurice Godolphin Osborne, b 1 July 1889

5d Dora Edith Hammersley, m 1880, Sir Francis Alexander Campbell of the Foreign Office and 7 Onslow Crescent, W, K C M G, C B [descended from the Lady Anne, sister of King Edward IV, &c (see Exeter Volume, p 294)]

1e Ronald Hugh Campbell a Clerk in the Foreign Office (33 *South Street, Brompton, S W*), b 1883 m Helen, da of (—) Graham, and has issue 1f

1f Mary Campbell, b 1908

2e Ivan Campbell, b 1887

3e Mabel Verena Campbell

6d Mabel Barbara Hammersley, m 27 Oct 1887, Walter Nassau Senior [son of Nassau John Senior (12 *Chichester Terrace, Brighton*), and has issue 1e

1e Oliver Nassau Senior, b 28 Nov 1901

7d Maud Emily Hammersley, m 26 Oct 1891, Henry William Duff-Gordon [descended from George, Duke of Clarence, K G (see the Clarence Volume, p 246)] (*Ivott Green, Welwyn, Herts*), and has issue (with a da d young) 1e to 3e

1e Douglas Frederick Duff-Gordon, b 12 Sept 1892

2e Cosmo Lewis Duff-Gordon, b 3 Mar 1897

3e Anne Maud Duff-Gordon, b 3 Jan 1903

8d Beatrice Hammersley, m 20 July 1898, Philip Apsley Treherne [son of Going Apsley Treherne] (*The Corner, Thursley, Surrey*)

9d Sylvia Hammersley, unm

4a Robert Eden, H E I C S, *Magistrate at Tinnevelly*, b 13 May 1800, d 23 Ap 1879, m 21 Ap 1829, *Frances Mary [descended from the Lady Anne, sister of King Edward IV*], da of the Rev Rowland Egerton Warburton, d 11 Jan 1898, and had issue

See the Exeter Volume, p 516, Nos 44910-44914

5a *Marianne Eden*, d 12 Jan 1865, m 1st, 19 Dec 1807, *John Spalding of Holme, co Kirkcudbright, M P*, d 26 Aug 1815, 2ndly, 1 Ap 1819, Henry (Brougham), 1st Baron Brougham and Vaux [U K], *Lord Chancellor of the United Kingdom 1830-34*, d at Cannes 7 May 1868, and had issue 1b to 2b

1b *John Eden Spalding of Holme, J P*, b 4 Oct 1808, d 29 Mar 1869, m 18 Aug 1831, the Hon Mary Wilhelmina, da of John Henry (Upton), 1st Viscount Templetown [I], d 20 Mar 1876, and had issue (with a son and da who d s p) 1c

[Nos 38864 to 38893

# of The Blood Royal

1c Augustus Frederick Montagu Spalding of Holme and Shurmers, J P , D L (*The Holme, New Galloway*, 11 Ashley Place, S W , Carlton, &c), b 23 Oct 1838 , *unm*

2b Marianne Dora Spalding, d 2 Jan 1891 , m 22 Dec 1834, Sir Alexander Malet, 2nd Bt [G B], K.C B , d 28 Nov 1886 *and had issue* 1c *to* 2c

1c Sir Henry Charles Eden Malet, 3rd Bt [G B], J P , Lieut Col Gren Guards, b 25 Sept 1835 , d 12 Jan 1904 , m 18 Feb 1873, *Laura Jane Campbell, da of John Hamilton of Hilston Park, co Mon , and had issue* 1d

1d Vera Jean Hamilton Malet, m 21 Jan 1903, Dorotheos Antoniadi [son of Michael Antoniadi of Constantinople]; and has issue 1e

1e Henry Edward Roger Fortuné Amédée Malet Antoniadi, b 1904

2c Right Hon Sir Edward Baldwin Malet, 4th Bt [G B], P C , G C B , G C M G , b 10 Oct 1837 , d s p 30 June 1908

6a Dora Eden, d (–), m Adm Sir Graham Moore, G C B , R N [brother of Sir John Moore, the hero of Corunna] [Nos 38894 to 38896]

144 Descendants of FREDERICK MORTON (EDEN), 1st Lord HENLEY [I], so cr 9 Nov 1799, having been Ambassador to the Courts of Vienna and Madrid (Table XVI), b 8 July 1752 , d 6 Dec 1830 , m 7 Aug 1783, Lady ELIZABETH, sister and h of Robert, 2nd and last Earl, and da of Robert (HENLEY), 1st Earl of Northington [G B], d 20 Aug 1821 , and had issue 1a to 2a

1a Robert Henley (Eden, afterwards (R L 31 Mar 1831) Henley), 2nd Baron Henley [I], b 3 Sept 1789 , d 3 Feb 1841 , m 11 Mar 1823, Harriet Eleanor, da of Sir Robert Peel, 1st Bt [G B], d 7 May 1869 , and had issue 1b to 2b

1b Anthony Henley (Henley), 3rd Baron Henley [I], M P , b 12 Ap 1825 , d, 27 Nov 1898, m 1st, 30 July 1846, Julia Augusta, da of the Very Rev John Peel D D , Dean of Worcester, d 15 Feb 1862 , 2ndly, 30 June 1870, Clara Campbell Lucy (9 Beaufort Gardens, S W), da of Joseph Henry Storie Jekyll , and had issue 1c to 6c

1c Frederick (Henley) 4th Baron Henley [I], J P (*Watford Court, near Rugby*), b 17 Ap 1849 , m 20 Oct 1900 Augusta Frederica, da of Herbert Langham of Cottesbrooke Park [Bt Coll], d s p 27 July 1905

2c Hon Anthony Ernest Henley, heir-presumptive, C E , b 3 July 1858 , m 1st, 17 Aug 1882, Georgiana Caroline Mary, da of Lieut -Col Richard Michael Williams [Bt Coll], d s p 26 Aug 1888 , 2ndly, 12 Sept 1889, Emmeline Stuart da of George Gammie Maitland , and has issue 1d

1d Joan Beryl Henley, b 1 Aug 1893

3c Hon Anthony Morton Henley, Capt 5th Lancers, served in South Africa 1900-02, Bar -at Law, &c (*Wellington , Cavalry*), b 4 Aug 1873 , m 21 Ap 1906, the Hon Sylvia Laura [descended from George, Duke of Clarence, K G (see Clarence Volume, p 442)] da of Edward Lyulph (Stanley), 4th Baron Stanley of Alderley [U K]

4c Hon Francis Robert Henley, M A (Oxon) (9 Beaufort Gardens, S W , *Wellington*), b 11 Ap 1877

5c[1] Hon Gertrude Augusta Henley, *unm*

6c[2] Hon Evelyn Henley, m 9 Aug 1881, John Langham Reed (*Thornby, Northants*) , and has issue 1d to 3d

1d Herbert Langham Reed, b 1882

2d Cecil Langham Reed, b 1884

3d Evelyn Langham Reed [Nos 38897 to 38906]

The Plantagenet Roll

2*b* Rev the Hon Robert Henley, M A (Oxon), *formerly* Vicar of Putney (*Eden Lodge, Putney*), *b* 7 Mar 1831, *m* 1 June 1852, Emily Louisa, da of Robert Aldridge of New Lodge, Horsham, *d* 20 Aug 1893, and has issue 1*c* to 7*c*

    1*c* Rev Robert Eden Henley, M A (Oxon), Vicar of Wharton (*Wharton Vicarage, near Winsford*), *b* 10 Sept 1861

    2*c* Charles Beauclerk Henley, *b* 7 Feb 1869

    3*c* Constance Laura Henley, *m* 16 Ap 1890, the Rev Robert Stewart Gregory, M A, Rector of Much Hadham (*Much Hadham Rectory, Herts*), and has issue 1*d* to 5*d*

        1*d* Robert Henley Gregory, *b* 3 Mar 1891

        2*d* Francis Stewart Gregory, *b* 3 Mar 1893

        3*d* John Stephen Gregory, *b* 26 June 1898

        4*d* Violet Emily Gregory

        5*d* Mary Noel Gregory

    4*c* Beatrice Mary Henley

    5*c* Ethel Maud Henley

    6*c* Mildred Caroline Henley

    7*c* Mabel Augusta Henley

2*a* *Rev the Hon William Eden Rector of Bishopsbourne, and Senior Preacher in Canterbury Cathedral*, *b* 9 Nov 1792, *d* 4 May 1859, *m* 19 Jan 1820, *Anna Maria, Dowager Baroness Grey de Ruthyn* [L], da of William Kelham, d. 23 Oct 1875, and had issue 1*b* to 5*b*

    1*b* Rev Arthur Eden Vicar of Ticehurst, *b* 3 Jan 1825, *d* 17 Nov 1908, *m* 24 Aug 1848, *Alice Julia*, da of Thomas Annesley Whitney of Merton, co Wexford, *d* 18 Dec 1897, and had issue 1*c* to 8*c*

    1*c* William Gaven Eden, late Lieut R N (*Tannygray, near Portmadre, N Wales*), *b* 26 July 1849, *m* 4 Jan 1876, Augusta Rose, da of Matthew Bell of Bourne Park, co Kent, and has issue 1*d* to 6*d*

        1*d* Cecil Eden, *b* 3 Oct 1876

        2*d* Morton Eden, *b* 9 Dec. 1881

        3*d* Constance Eden

        4*d* Nora Eden

        5*d* Hilda Eden

        6*d* Alice Nesta Eden

    2*c* Arthur Yelverton Eden, J P (*Granville House, Arundel*), *b* 19 Mar 1856, *m* 22 Nov 1888, Fanny Spencer, da and h of John Theodore Louis Le Blanch, of Beechfield, co Chester, and has issue 1*d* to 3*d*

        1*d* Barbara Yelverton Eden

        2*d* Lelgarde Edith Eleanor Eden

        3*d*. Dulcie Flora Eden

    3*c* Alice Lizzie Eden, *m* 27 Sept 1883, William Sherrard (*Pro Bank House, Fermoy, co Cork*), and has issue 1*d*

        1*d* Arthur William Eden Sherrard, *b* 17 Aug 1884

    4*c* *Mary Constance Eden*, *b* 11 May 1852, *d* 29 Mar 1884, *m* 30 Ap 1878, *Augustus Hills Cobbold* (*Brownhill, Nurseling, Southampton*), and has issue 1*d* to 2*d*

        1*d* Neville Eden Cobbold, *b* 15 Ap 1882

        2*d* Alice Mary Cobbold, *m* 12 Dec 1905, Comm Duncan Tatton Brown, R N

    5*c* *Eleanor Agnes Eden*, *b* 29 July 1853, *d* 4 Feb 1897, *m* 18 Dec 1879, *Vice-Adm Henry Bedford Woollcombe, R N*, *b* 25 Ap 1831, *d* 14 Feb 1904, and had issue 1*d*

        1*d* Eleanor Mary Woollcombe

    6*c* Edith Amelia Eden *m* 1st, 26 Oct 1876, Charles Davers Eden, R N,

# of The Blood Royal

d s p s 25 Feb 1895, 2ndly, 1 June 1901, Col Arthur Fred Eden-Perkins (*Dodwith, Bursledon, Hants*)

7c. Flora Colclough Eden

8c Julia Augusta Maria Eden

2b Robert Charles Eden, Lieut.-Col U S Army, *b* 31 Aug 1836, *m* 26 Jan 1863, Annie Gardner, da of Andrew Bain of Bonhill, co Dumbarton, and has issue 1c to 6c

1c Morton Edward Eden, *b* 17 Sept 1867, *m* 1894, Marie Elizabeth, da of James Stewart of Dansville, New York, and has issue 1d

1d Robert Henley Stewart Eden, *b* 1896

2c Reginald Yelverton Eden, *b* 15 Dec 1871, *m* 18—, Sophia, da of T Hart of Warren, U S A , and has issue

3c Mabel Wenonah Eden

4c Ethel Elizabeth Eden

5c Sybil Constance Eden

6c Charlotte Annie Maude Eden

3b Mary Yelverton Eden, *m* 4 July 1848, Samuel Lucas Lancaster-Lucas of Wateringbury Place, co Kent, *d* 1894, and has issue 1c to 5c

1c *William Matthias Lancaster-Lucas*, b 27 Ap 1849, d (*?s p*)

2c *Charles Eden Lancaster Lancaster-Lucas*, b 16 June 1851, d (*?s p*)

3c Mary Helewise Ursula Lancaster-Lucas

4c Flora Lancaster-Lucas

5c Katharine Elizabeth Lancaster-Lucas, *m* 1888, Col Ralph Bisnett Rastell Williamson, *formerly* 43rd L I , and has issue 1d to 3d

1d Ralph W B R Williamson, *b* 1890

2d Katherine Elizabeth Williamson

3d Ruth Mary Florence Williamson

4b Charlotte Maria Eden (*Glemham Hall, Wickham Market*), *m* 1st, 17 Oct 1850, Dudley, Lord North [son and h app of Francis 6th Earl of Guilford [G B]], *d v p* 28 Jan 1860, 2ndly, 10 July 1861, Major Alexander George Dickson, 3rd Hussars, M P , *d* 3 July 1889, and has issue 1c to 3c

1c *Dudley Francis (North), 7th Earl of Guilford [G B] and 9th Baron Guilford [E]*, b 14 July 1851, d 19 Dec 1885, m 4 May 1874, Georgiana (4 Lennox Gardens, S W) [descended from the Lady Anne sister of King Edward IV (see the Exeter Volume, p 322)], da of Sir George Chetwynd, 3rd Bt [G B] and had issue 1d to 2d

1d *Frederick George (North) 8th Earl of [G B] and 10th Baron Guilford [E] (Waldershare Park, Dover, Glemham Hall, Wickham Market), b 19 Nov 1876, m 25 June 1901, Mary Violet, da of William Hargrave Pawson of Shawdon, and has issue 1e to 2e*

1e Francis George North, Lord North, *b* 15 June 1902

2e Hon John Montagu North, *b* 28 Feb 1905

2d Lady Muriel Emily North

2c Hon *Morton William North*, b 31 Oct 1852, d 26 Ap 1895, m 3 Ap 1879, Hilda Hylton [descended from George, Duke of Clarence, K G (see Clarence Volume, p 189), da and co-h of Capt Hylton Joliffe [son and h app of 1st Lord Hylton [U K]], d 19 Feb 1902, and had issue 1d to 3d

1d Dudley John North, *formerly* Lieut 3rd Batt Norfolk Regt, *b* 9 Jan 1880

2d Hylton George Morton North, *b* 13 Sept 1885

3d Roger North, *b* 24 Sept 1888

3c *Lady Flora Mildred North*, b 25 Ap 1855, d 1 Mar 1886 m as 1st wife, 28 Dec 1880, Sir Robert Rodney Wilmot of Osmaston, 6th Bt [G B] [himself
[Nos 38937 to 38961

285   2 O

The Plantagenet Roll

a descendant of Edward III through the Mortimer-Percy marriage] (Binfield Grove, Bracknell, Berks), and had issue

See p 280, Nos 38811–38811 (also Essex Volume, p 135)

5b Flora Jane Eden (*Brokenhurst Park, Hants*). m as 2nd wife, 2 Ap 1866, John Morant of Brokenhurst, J P , D L High Sheriff co Hants 18— [descended from the Lady Anne, sister of King Edward IV , &c (see the Exeter Volume, p 685)], *d* 30 May 1899 , and had issue 1c to 3c

1c Edward John Harry Eden Morant of Brokenhurst, J P , Hon Attaché Diplo Ser (*Brokenhurst Park, near Lymington*), *b* 1868

2c Francis George Morant, *b* 1869

3c Mabel Caroline Flora Morant, *m* 1889, Herbert George Alexander , and has issue   [Nos 38962 to 38969

145 Descendants of DULCIBELLA EDEN (Table XVI), *d* (–), *m* 1767, MATTHEW BELL of Woolsington, Col. Northumberland Militia, *d.* 1811 , and had issue 1a to 7a.

1a Matthew Bell of Woolsington, M P , High Sheriff co Northbd 1797, d 18—, m 9 June 1792, Sarah Frances, da of Charles Brandling of Gosforth House, co Northbd , and had issue (with 4 elder sons and 2 das who all d s p) 1b to 3b

1b Rev John Bell, Vicar of Rothwell, Hon Canon of Ripon and Rural Dean, b 29 June 1805, d 21 Oct 1869, m 20 Nov 1828, Isabella Elizabeth, da of Sir Charles Loraine, 5th Bt [E], d 15 Mar 1881 , and had issue (with 5 other sons and a da who d young) 1c to 7c

1c Charles Loraine Bell of Woolsington, J P , D L , High Sheriff co Northbd 1895 (*Woolsington, Newcastle-on-Tyne*), b 3 July 1836, m 13 Ap 1871, Anna Roberta, da of Charles Bernard, 24th Regt , and has issue 1d to 4d

1d Walter Loraine Bell (*Woolsington, Newcastle-on-Tyne*), b 30 May 1877 , m 30 Nov 1890, Winifred Margaret, widow of John Loxley Firth of Hope, co Derby, da of Henry William Watson of Burnopfield, co Durham

2d Margaret Ellen Bell, *m* 12 June 1901, her cousin, Claude Henry Watson (see p 287) (*Sunnyside, Woolsington, Newcastle-on-Tyne*), and has issue 1e to 2e

1e Godfrey Charles Watson, *b* 9 Ap 1907

2e Dorothy Helen Watson, *b* 6 May 1902

3d Isabel Gertrude Bell (*Houndless Water, Haslemere, Surrey*), *m* 14 July 1898, Lieut Col Eustace Guinness of Burton Hall, co Dublin, R A , *d* (being killed in the Boer War) 30 Oct 1901, and has issue 1e to 2e

1e Eustace Francis Guinness, *b* Jan 1900

2e Humphrey Patrick Guinness, *b* Mar 1902

4d Dulcibella Mildreda Bell

2c William Bell, *b* 24 Mar 1839

3c Frank Bell, *b* 21 May 1842

4c Isabella Elizabeth Bell (*Palazzo Consiglio, Rione Amadeo. Naples*)

5c Frances Sarah Bell. b Ap 1835, d 23 Ap 1905, m 23 Ap 1863, the Rev Shepley Watson Hemmingway, afterwards Watson, Rector of Bootle, Cumberland, b 11 Jan 1827, d 23 Ap 1899, and had issue 1d to 4d

1d Rev Arthur Herbert Watson, Vicar of Long Preston (*Long Preston Vicarage, Leeds*), b May 1864, m Feb 1900, Louisa Caroline [descended from the Lady Anne, sister of King Edward IV , &c (see the Exeter Volume, p 568)], da of Thomas Edward Yorke of Beverley Hall, co York, J P , and has issue 1e to 5e

1e Edward Shepley Watson, *b* Feb 1901

2e Oliver Arthur Watson, *b* Sept 1902

3e Martin Yorke Watson, *b* Nov 1905

4e Beatrice Helen Frances Watson, *b* May 1907

5e. Joan Margaret Louisa Watson, *b* June 1909   [Nos 38970 to 38987

# of The Blood Royal

2d Cyril Francis Watson, Land Agent (*Greysouthen, Cockermouth, Cumberland*), b 23 Oct 1866, m 3 Jan 1900, Katharine Anna Keatinge, da of the Rev Canon Jeremy Taylor Pollock [a descendant of Bishop Jeremy Taylor], and has issue 1e to 3e

    1e George Loraine Pollock Watson, b 8 June 1902

    2e Cyril Jeremy Taylor Watson, b 28 Dec 1904

    3e Eileen Frances Katharine Watson, b 13 May 1901

3d Claude Henry Watson (*Sunnyside, Woolsington, Newcastle-on-Tyne*), b 4 Jan 1869, m 12 June 1901, his cousin, Margaret Ellen (see above), da of Charles Loraine Bell of Woolsington, and has issue

    See p 286, Nos 38973-38974

4d Loraine John Watson (*1 St George's Crescent, Stanwix, Carlisle*), b 23 Oct 1871, m Ap 1901, his cousin, Ethel Gertrude (see below), da of Richard Harrison, s p

6c Emma Rachel Bell, m 10 June 1869, Capt Albert Adams, 24th Regt (*Clyde House, Dawlish, South Devon*), and has issue (with 2 others, sons, who d young) 1d to 6d

    1d Algernon Frank Adams, b 8 Ap 1870, d unm in South Africa during the War, Sep 1901

    2d Reginald Shute Adams, farming in Canada, b 15 Sept 1872, m (—), da of (—), and has issue 1e to 3e

        1e Reginald Adams

        2e Walter Adams

        3e Una Adams

    3d Arthur Cecil Paget Adams, farming in the United States, b 21 Feb 1875, unm

    4d Gerald Colman Surtees Adams, b 21 July 1877, d unm (being killed in action at Magersfontein) 11 Dec 1899

    5d George Rorke Adams, farming in the United States, b 30 Ap 1880, unm

    6d Mildred Gertrude Adams

7c Gertrude Mary Bell, b c 1849, d 25 Oct 1878, m 1 Aug 1872, Richard Harrison, d June 1906, and had issue 1d to 6d

    1d John Harrison } (twins), b Oct 1878, unm
    2d Henry Harrison

    3d Ethel Gertrude Harrison, m Ap 1901, her cousin, Loraine John Watson (see above) (*1 St George's Crescent, Stanwix, Carlisle*), s p

    4d Evelyn Harrison

    5d Elsie Harrison

    6d Beatrice Harrison

2b William Bell, d (-), m *Jane, da of William Ridley of Park End, co Northbd*, d (-), and had issue 1c

    1c Sara Bell (*Castlehill, Middleham, S O, Bedale*), m Gen Ingilby, s p

3b Sarah Frances Bell, d 10 or 19 Aug 1874, m 25 May 1826, Sir John James Walsham of Knill Court, co Hereford, 1st Bt [U K], so cr 30 Sept 1831, D L and High Sheriff co Radnor 1870, b 6 June 1805, d 10 Aug 1874, and had issue 1c to 4c

    1c Sir John Walsham, 2nd Bt [U K], K C M G, M A (*Camb*). J P, D L, H B M's Envoy Extra and Min Plen to the Courts of Pekin 1885 1892 and Bucharest 1892-1894, b 29 Oct 1830, d 10 Dec 1895, m 5 Mar 1867, Florence, da of the Hon Peter Campbell Scarlett, C B [B Abinger Coll], and had issue 1d to 2d

        1d Sir John Scarlett Walsham, 3rd Bt [U K], an Inspector of Chinese Labour to Transvaal Govt (*Knill Court, Kington, Hereford, Germiston, Transvaal*), b

[Nos 38968 to 39011

The Plantagenet Roll

15 Oct 1869, m 20 Nov 1906, Bessie Geraldine Gundred (see pp 363 and 492), da of Vice-Adm John Borlase Warren, R N [Bt Coll], and has issue 1e

    1e Barbara Walsham

2f Percy Romilly Walsham, in Chinese Maritime Customs, b 1871, m 1899, Charlotte Cunningham, da of William Wykeham Myers of Formosa, M B, C M, and has issue 1e to 3e

    1e Percy Robert Stewart Walsham, b 6 Ap 1904

    2e Florence Mary Walsham

    3e Gladys Newell Walsham

2c *Rev Francis Walsham, M A (Durham), Rector of Knill,* b 9 Ap 1832, d (-), m 20 June 1865, *Marianne, da of Charles James Barnett of Bays Lawn, co Glouc M P, and had issue 1d to 3d*

1d John Charles Walsham *(Holmwood, Pannal Ash, Harrogate),* b 11 Sept 1866, m 22 May 1902, Alice Maude, widow of John Alfred Pike, Surgeon, da of John Headland

2d Florence Augusta Walsham, m 14 Sept 1892, John Cecil Thornhill of Castle Bellingham, co Louth *(Rathmullen House, Drogheda),* and has issue 1e to 4e

    1e Humphrey Thornhill, b 1894

    2e Kathleen Thornhill

    3e Phyllis Thornhill

    4e Sheila Thornhill

3d Mary Caroline Walsham, m 1897, Algernon Estcourt Keys-Wells *(28 Church Street, Walsham),* and has issue 1e

    1e William Yorke Keys-Wells, b 10 May 1908

3c *Anna Walsham,* d 18 Aug 1905, m 20 May 1855, *Major-Gen O'Bryen Bellingham Woolsey of Milestown and Prioryland, late R A, J P, D L, High Sheriff co Louth* 1889 *(Milestown Castle, Bellingham),* and had issue 1d

1d Alice Woolsey, m 21 Ap 1887, Cecil Butler, Bar-at-Law [B Dunboyne Coll], d 6 Dec 1901, and has issue 1e

    1e Cecilia Frances Butler

4c Fanny Walsham, m as 2nd wife, 30 Oct 1883, Thomas Edward Yorke of Bewerley and Halton Place, J P, High Sheriff co York [descended from the Lady Anne, sister of King Edward IV (see the Exeter Volume, p 568)] *(Bewerley Hall, Pateley Bridge, Leeds)*

2a *Stephen Bell,* d (? s p)

3a *Robert Bell of Fenham Hall, co Northbd, Mayor of Newcastle* 1822, d 1850, m *Anna Mildreda, da of Childers Walbanke-Childers of Cantley, co York,* d (-), and had issue 1b

1b Mildreda Eliza Bell, d 17 Mar 1850, m as 1st wife, 21 Sept 1846, *Matthew Robert Bigge, J P [8th son of Col Charles William Bigge of Linden, co Northbd, J P, D L],* d 17 July 1906, and had issue 1c

1c Anna Mildreda Bigge, m 7 Jan 1875, Albert George Legard, *late* H M Chief Inspector of Schools for Wales [Bt Coll, and himself a descendant of King Edward III through Mortimer-Percy (see p 193)] *(BrowHill, Batheaston, Somerset)*

4a *Henry Bell of Newbiggen House, co Northbd,* d 1830, m 2 June 1807, *Susannah Jane, da of Major Rowland Mainwaring of Four Oaks, co Warwick [who with her brother, Rear-Adm Rowland Mainwaring of Whitmore Hall, was 19th in descent from King Henry III],* d 11 Aug 1871, aged 83, and had issue 1b to 4b

    1b Matthew Bell, b 29 May 1814

    2b Rowland Mainwaring Bell, b 8 Dec 1821

    3b *Susanna Maria Bell,* b 13 Aug 1816, d 22 Jan 1904, m 26 Nov 1835,

[Nos 39012 to 39030

# of The Blood Royal

Samuel Gootin Barrett, d 20 *June* 1876 , *and had issue (with 3 sons and a da d unm)* 1c *to* 7c

    1c Henry Barrett, b 5 *Aug* 1838 , d 27 *Oct* 1895 , m 25 *July* 1878, *Julia Blanche* (18 *Inverna Gardens, London), da of Thomas Brace , and had issue* 1d *to* 3d

        1d Arthur Barrett, b 30 Nov 1880

        2d Charles Barrett, b 29 July 1886

        3d Evelyn Barrett

    2c Charles Rollo Barrett, J P (*Whitehill Hall, Pelton Fell, S O , co Durham*), b 26 May 1854 , m 6 July 1882, Mary Delmar, da of Alfred Bury of Newland Lodge, Sevenoaks , and has issue 1d to 5d

        1d Rollo Samuel Barrett, b 28 Ap 1883

        2d Kenneth Delmar Barrett, b 6 Nov 1886

        3d Lindsay Alfred Barrett, b 8 July 1891

        4d Dulcibella Mary Barrett

        5d Brenda de Courcy Barrett

    3c Robert Bell Barrett, J P (*Skipton Castle, Yorks*), b 29 Mar 1856 , m 12 Jan 1893, Frances Madeline, da of William Robinson of Reedley Hall, Burnley, J P , and has issue 1d to 4d

        1d Robin Coventry Barrett, b 17 Feb 1895

        2d Harry Eden Barrett, b 20 Sept 1903

        3d Monica Dulcibella Barrett

        4d Vera Doris Madeline Barrett

    4c *Maria Margaret Barrett*, b 5 *June* 1840 , d 5 *Aug* 1903, m 4 *June* 1868, *Adam Gillies-Smith of Agsacre, North Berwick*, d 8 *Jan* 1900 , *and had issue (with 2 sons who d s p)* 1d *to* 3d

        1d Margaret Gillies-Smith ⎫

        2d Coventry Barrett Gillies-Smith ⎬ (*Agsacre, North Berwick*), unm

        3d Adelaide Cathcart Gillies-Smith ⎭

    5c Jeannette Susanna Barrett, m 21 Dec 1865 Charles Tennant Couper (*Woolstone, Row, Dumbarton*) , and has issue 1d to 7d

        1d John Charles Couper, W S (15 *Rutland Street, Edinburgh*), b 10 Oct 1867 , m 17 Nov 1899, Elsie Winifred, da of Benjamin Hall Blyth of Edinburgh, C E , and has issue 1e to 3e

            1e Ian Charles Blyth Couper, b 11 May 1901

            2e Millicent Jeanette Couper

            3e Annabel Elsie Couper

        2d Samuel Barrett Couper, M D , M R C S (*Blaby, Leicester*), b 20 July 1876 , m 12 June 1899, Marjorie, da of J H W Davies of Minden, St John's Park, Blackheath

        3d Charlotte Maria Couper, m 26 May 1900, the Rev Charles Inglebert Baldwin, Vicar of Belper (*Christchurch Vicarage, Belper, Derby*), s p

        4d Edith Jeannette Couper, m 23 Dec 1901, George Edward Herne [son of Col George Edward Herne, 103rd Bombay Fusiliers] (*Balgarvie, St John's, near Woking*), and has issue 1e to 3e

            1e George Charles Barrett Herne, b 15 Aug 1895

            2e Dulcibella Jeannette Herne

            3e Edith Dorothea Margaret Herne

        5d Dulcibella Margaret Couper, *unm*

        6d May Coventry Couper, m 17 Oct 1905, Com Francis St George Brooker, R N , s p

        7d Maud Barrett Couper, m 3 Nov 1906, Henry John Bell Edge [son of

[Nos 39031 to 39001

The Plantagenet Roll

Adm William Henry Edge, R N] (*South Binns, Heathfield*), and has issue 1e to 2e

  1e Archibald Edge, *b* Jan 1907

  2e Elsie Edge

6c *Dulcibella Barrett*, b 11 Nov 1846, d 3 Dec 1879, m 11 *July* 1870, Collingwood Lindsay Wood of Freeland, Forgandenny, co Perth, d 10 *July* 1906, and had issue (*with a son d young*) 1d to 4f

  1d Dulcibella M Wood

  2f Ethel Wood

  3d Jeannette Wood

  4f Muriel Wood

7c *Emma Bassett Barrett*, b 20 Oct 1848, d 4 May 1891, m 25 *Sept* 1873, Sir Lindsay Wood, 1st Bt [U K 27 Sept 1897] (*The Hermitage, Chester-le-Street, Carlton*), and had issue 1d to 6f

  1d Arthur Nicholas Lindsay Wood, *b* 29 Mar 1875

  2d Henry Lindsay Wood, *b* 28 Oct 1878

  3f Collingwood Lindsay Wood, *b* 19 Nov 1881, *m* 30 Ap 1907, Lilian, da of William Sopper of 3 Upper Belgrave Street, S W, and Drummaglass, co Inverness, and has issue 1e to 2e

    1e Ian Lindsay Wood, *b* May 1909

    2e Heather Wood

  4d Robert Lindsay Wood, *b* 28 Feb 1884

  5f Maria Lindsay Wood, *m* 11 Ap 1899, the Hon Claud Eustace Hamilton-Russell, D L [son of Gustavus, 8th Viscount Boyne] (*Cleobury Court, Bridgnorth*) and has issue 1e to 3e

    1e Arthur Gustavus Lindsay Hamilton-Russell, *b* 30 Ap 1900

    2e Edric Claude Hamilton-Russell, *b* 24 Nov 1901

    3e Jean Katherine Hamilton-Russell

  6d Elsie Emma Lindsay Wood, *unm*

4b Janette Charlotte Bell, *b* 14 Nov 1818, *m* 22 Sept 1841, Robert M'Alpine, *d* 25 Dec 1866, and has issue 1c to 5c

  1c Cunyngham Martyn M'Alpine, *b* 24 Dec 1842, *s p*

  2c Henry Charles M'Alpine, *b* 6 May 1849, *d unm* 18 Oct 1894

  3c Robert Kyle M'Alpine, Adm R N (*Brighton*), *b* 29 Jan 1851, *m* 5 Jan 1899, Louisa Jane, da of James Leith-Hay, Younger of Rannes and Leith Hall, co Aberdeen, *s p s*

    1c Kenneth M'Alpine (*Loose, near Maidstone*), *b* 11 Ap 1858, *unm*

    5c Maria Louisa M'Alpine, *unm*

5a *Jane Bell*, d 14 Ap 1793, m as 1st wife, 7 Jan 1792, *William (Hay), 17th Earl of Erroll [S], &c [descended from the Lady Anne, sister of King Edward IV, &c], d 26 Jan 1819, and had issue*
See the Exeter Volume, p 682, Nos 57387–57391

6a *Dulcibella Bell*, d c 1857, m the Rev Robert Moore, Preb and Canon of Canterbury (see p 291), d Sept 1865, and had issue (*with 3 sons and 2 other d s who d s p*) 1b

  1b *Catherine Moore*, b c 1813, d 14 *July* 1888, m the Rev John Duncombe Shafto [*descended from the Lady Anne, sister of King Edward IV* (see Exeter Volume, p 308)], d 6 *Aug* 1863, and had issue 1c to 2c

    1c Catherine Mary Fitzwilliam Duncombe Shafto, *unm*

    2c Dulcibella Maria Duncombe Shafto (*St Martins, Sevenoaks*), *m* 11 Sept 1866, the Rev Arthur Majendie, Rector of Bladon, d 15 Jan 1895, and has issue
See the Exeter Volume, p 309, Nos 19110–19111

  7a *Maria Bell*, d (? *unm*)

[Nos 39062 to 39096

146 Descendants of CATHERINE EDEN (Table XVI), *d* (-), *m* as 2nd wife, 23 Jan 1770, the Most Rev JOHN MOORE, Lord Archbishop of Canterbury, *bapt* 13 Jan 1730, *d*. 18 Jan 1805, and had issue 1*a* to 1*a*.

1*a Rev George Moore, M A, Preb of Canterbury and Rector of Wrotham, d (-), m 1st, 19 June 1795, Lady Maria Elizabeth [descended from the Lady Anne, sister to Kings Edward IV and Richard III (see the Exeter Volume, p 687)] da of James (Hay, previously Boyd), 15th Earl of Erroll [S], &c, d 3 June 1804, 2ndly, 1806, Harriet Mary, da of Sir Brook Bridges, 3rd Bt [G B], M P [by his wife Fanny, née Fowler, a co-h of the Barons FitzWalter [E 1295]], and had (with possibly other issue by 2nd wife) 1b to 2b*

1*b Rev Edward Moore of Frittenden House, co Kent M 1, Hon Canon of Canterbury and Rural Dean, b 1811 d 1889, m 29 Mar 1842, Lady Harriet Janet Sarah Montagu [descended from Kings Henry VII and Edward IV, &c], da of Charles William Henry (Douglas Scott), 4th Duke of Buccleuch and 6th Duke of Queensberry [S], K T, d 16 Feb 1870, and had issue*

See the Tudor Roll, pp 161-162, Nos 19862-19899

2*b* Caroline Mary Moore

2*a Charles Moore, M P for Woodstock*
3*a Robert Moore, M A, Preb of Canterbury, b c 1778, d Sept 1865, m Dulcibella, da of Matthew Bell of Woolsington, d c 1857, and had issue*
See p 290, Nos 39090-39096

1*a John Moore*   [Nos 39097 to 39112

147 Descendants, if any, of ELIZABETH EDEN (Table XVI), *d* (-), *m* MATTHEW WHITFIELD of Whitfield, co Northumberland

148 Descendants, if any, of HANNAH EDEN (Table XVI), *d* (-), *m* JAMES MICKLETON of Durham

149 Descendants of JOHN EDEN of Newcastle, Merchant (Table XVI), *d*. (-), *m*. ELIZABETH, da of (—) HINDMARSH of Little Bentley, *d* (-), and had issue (a son and 2 das)[1]

150 Descendants of the Rev LATON EDEN, Rector of Hartborne, co Northumberland (Table XVI), *d* (-), *m* (—), da of the Rev (—) JOHNSON, and had issue (several sons and das).[1]

151 Descendants, if any surviving, of MARGARET LATON (Table XV.), *d* after 1664, *m* WILLIAM LATON or LAYTON of Dalemayne, co Cumberland, *b c* 1624, living and aged 40 in 1664, and had issue 1*a* to 8*a*[2]

1*a Thomas Laton, b c 1656, aged 8 in 1664*
2*a William Laton, b 1663*

---

[1] Brydges' "Collins," viii 288
[2] Foster's "Visitations of Cumberland and Westmorland"

The Plantagenet Roll

3a Mary Laton	4a Isabel Laton
5a Ann Laton	6a Margaret Laton
7a Katharine Laton	8a Elizabeth Laton

152 Descendants of the Hon. CATHERINE FAIRFAX (Table XIV), d
23 Feb 1666, m 1st, ROBERT STAPYLTON of Wighill, M P,
d 12 Mar 1634, 2ndly, as 2nd wife, Sir MATTHEW BOYNTON,
1st Bt [E], d (s p by her) Mar 1647, 3rdly, as 2nd wife,
Sir ARTHUR INGRAM of Temple Newsham, d 4 July 1655,
4thly, 1657, WILLIAM WICKHAM of Roxby [grandson of
William, Bishop of Winchester, by his wife Antonia, one of the
five das of John Barlow, Bishop of Chichester, who all married
Bishops], and had issue (with others whose lines all failed, two
das by 1st husband)

See Exeter Volume, Table XLIX, pp 535-536, Nos 48976-49015

[Nos 39143-39182

153 Descendants, if any, of the Hon JANE FAIRFAX (Table XIV),
m CUTHBERT MORLEY

154 Descendants of Sir THOMAS NORCLIFFE of Langton (Table XVII),
bapt 24 Feb 1641, d in France after 16 Sept 1684, m
(settl dated 1 2 Jan) 1670, FRANCES (Table VII), da and h
of Sir WILLIAM VAVASOUR of Copmanthorpe, 1st Bt [E], b in
Drury Lane 26 Oct 1654, d at Chelsea 12 Dec 1731, and
had issue

See p 119, Nos 10775-10977

[Nos 39183-39385

155 Descendants of JOHN GRIMSTON of Grimston Garth, co. York
(Table XVII), b 17 Feb 1725, d 21 June 1780, m 12 Mar
1753, JANE, da of Sir Thomas LEGARD, 4th Bt. [E], d 11 Nov
1758, and had issue

See p 196, Nos 29062-29142

[Nos 39386 to 39466

156. Descendants, if any, of DOROTHY GRIMSTON (Table XVII), b
9 July 1663, bur 24 July 1700, m. 4 Nov 1684, NATHANIEL
GOOCH of Hull, bur 17 June 1705, and of ANNE GRIMSTON,
b 18 Ap. 1669, m THOMAS RYDER

292

# of The Blood Royal

157 Descendants, if any surviving, of JOHN HATFEILD of Laughton, co York (Table XVI), *bapt* 24 Sept 1676, *d.* Nov 1751, *m* 17 Mai. 1698, MARY, da and event h of Elkana RICHE of Bullhouse, near Pemstone, *bur.* 30 July 1742, and had issue 1*a* to 2*a*

    1*a* *Aurengzebe Hatfeild of Laughton, bapt 1 June 1710, d Aug 1752, m Dec 1716, Susanna, da of John Hatfeild of Hatfeild (who m 2ndly, 24 June 1760, Capt William Marshall of Newton Kyme (see below) and), d 18 Nov 1793, and had issue which became extinct 11 Jan 1791*

    2*a* *Rosamond Hatfeild, da and in her issue (1791) h, d (–), m (—) Barker of Mansfield, and had issue (2 das)* [1]

158 Descendants, if any, of ANTONIA HATFEILD (Table XVII.), *d* (–), *m.* E. WILMOT of Dufheld, or of DOROTHY HATFEILD, wife of WILLIAM WOODHOUSE of Reresby, co Leic.

159 Descendants of WILLIAM MARSHALL of Newton Kyme, co York, Capt Heavy Dragoons (Table XVIII), *b* 1718; *d* 12 June 1775; *m* 24 June 1760, SUSANNA, widow of Aurengzebe HATFEILD of Laughton (see above), da of John HATFEILD of Hatfeild, *d* 18 Nov 1793, and had issue 1*a*

    1*a* *William Marshall of Newton Kyme and Laughton, Lieut.-Col West Yorkshire Militia, b 17 July 1764, d 17 Jan 1815, m 1793, Christiana, da and event h of Godfrey Higgins of Skellow Grange and Wadworth, near Doncaster, d 2 Oct 1832, and had issue 1b to 2b*

    1*b* *William Marshall, afterwards (R I. 26 Dec 1833) Hatfeild of Newton Kyme and Laughton, b 17 June 1799, d unm 7 Sept 1814*

    2*b* *Christiana Marshall of Laughton, Skellow Grange and Wadworth, d (–), m 9 Sept 1825, Randall Gossip, afterwards (R L 16 Oct 1844) Hatfeild of Thorp Arch, co Yorks, b 28 May 1800, d 1853, and had issue (with 3 sons and 4 das who d s p or whose issue is extinct) 1c to 2c*

    1*c* *John Hatfeild of Thorp Arch and Laughton, J P, b 15 June 1816, d 5 July 1889, m 10 June 1869, Mariana Frances da of Adolphe Davide, d 14 Oct 1894, and had issue 1d*

    1*d* *John Randall Hatfeild of Thorp Arch and Laughton (Edlington Hall, Horncastle, co Lincoln, Thorp Arch Hall, Tadcaster, Skellow Grange, Doncaster), b 21 Sept 1873, m 23 Oct 1901, Nest, da of W Hyde of Market Stainton Grange, co Line, and has issue 1e*

      1*e* Christine Joyce Hatfeild

    2*c* Lucy Hatfeild, *unm*   [Nos 39467 to 39469

160. Descendants of FRANCES NORCLIFFE (Table XVII), Executor to her mother in 1686, *m* after that year NICHOLAS RICHARDS of Westminster

---

[1] Foster's "Yorkshire Pedigrees"

The Plantagenet Roll

161 Descendants of Sir John Swinburne, 3rd Bt [E 1660] (Table XVIII), b 8 July 1698, d Jan 1745, m 1721, Mary, da of Edward Bedingfeld of Gray's Inn, Counsellor-at-Law [son of Sir Henry Bedingfeld, 1st Bt [E]], d 7 Feb 1761, and had issue 1a to 6a

1a Sir John Swinburne, 4th Bt [E], b 2 July 1724, d unm 1 Feb 1763

2a Sir Edward Swinburne, 5th Bt [E], b 24 Jan 1733, d 2 Nov 1786, m 1761, Christiana, da and h of Robert Dillon, d 13 Aug 1768, and had issue 1b to 2b

1b Sir John Edward Swinburne, 6th Bt [E], M P, F R S, b 6 Mar 1762, d 26 Sept 1860, m 8,13 July 1787, Emilia Elizabeth da of Richard Henry Alexander Bennet of Beckenham, d 28 Mar 1839, and had issue 1c to 4c

1c Edward Swinburne of Calgarth Park, Windermere, b 24 June 1788, d v p 14 Nov 1850, m 1st, 13 Dec 1819, Anna Antonia, da of Capt Robert Nassau Sutton, 58th Regt, d 1844, and had issue 1d to 5d

1d Sir John Swinburne, 7th Bt [E], Capt R N (ret), J P, High Sheriff co Northbl 1866, M P for Lichfield 1885-92 (Capheaton, Newcastle-on-Tyne), b 1831, m 1st, 1 Jan 1863, Emily Elizabeth, da of Rear-Adm Henry Broadhead, R N, d 23 July 1881, 2ndly, 10 Sept 1895, Mary Eleanor, da and h of John Corbett, d s p 16 May 1900, 3rdly, 7 June 1905, Florence Caroline, da of James Moffat of Windsor, D L, and has issue 1e to 5e

1e Hubert Swinburne, LL B (Camb), Capt Northumberland Imp Yeo (Wellington, Brooks'), b 24 Jan 1867, m 20 Sept 1905, Alice Pauline (see p 13), da of Nathaniel George Clayton of Chesters, co Northbl, and has issue 1f

1f Joan Swinburne, b 7 Aug 1906

2e Umfreville Percy Swinburne (Arthurs', Bachelors'), b 24 Nov 1868, m 31 July 1905, Arnoldine Georgiana, widow of (—) Peacocke, da of Thomas Arnold Marten of Oystermouth, co Glam

3e Robert Swinburne, b 10 Feb 1871

4e Marguerite Swinburne, unm

5e Ranee Theodora Swinburne (24 Wilton Street, S W, Lacie, Abingdon, Berks), m 19 July 1887, Richard Chamberlain of Oak Mount, Birmingham, d 2 Ap 1899, and has issue 1f

1f Richard Chamberlain, b 28 May 1888, drowned 26 May 1906

2d May Swinburne, m 11 Nov 1862, Capt William Ross, Gentleman Usher to Queen Victoria, d 1874

3d Ruth Swinburne, m 27 Oct 1858, William Edward Maude of Blawith, co Lancaster, d 1901

4d Jane Swinburne, m 1860, Professor Paul Thumann, d 1908, and had issue

5d Katherine Swinburne, d 16 July 1896, m 1863, Ferdinand Breymann, and had issue

2c Charles Henry Swinburne, Adm R N, b 2 Ap 1797, d 1 Mar 1877, m 19 May 1836, Lady Jane Henrietta [descended from King Henry VII (see the Tudor Roll, p 193)], da of George (Ashburnham), 3rd Earl of Ashburnham [G B], d 26 Nov 1896, and had issue (with others who d s p) 1d to 2d

1d Algernon Charles Swinburne, the Poet, b 5 Ap 1837, d unm 10 Ap 1909

2d Isabel Swinburne (61 Onslow Square, S W)

3c Emily Elizabeth Swinburne, d 19 Dec 1882, m 8 Ap 1824, Sir Henry George Ward, G C M G, Governor of Madras, d there 2 Aug 1860

4c Elizabeth Swinburne, d 1896, m 7 June 1828, John William Bowden, d 15 Sept 1844

[Nos 39170 to 39480.

# of The Blood Royal

2b Robert (Swinburne), 1st Baron Swinburne (*Freiherr von Swinburne*) [Austria], so cr 12 28 May 1863, a Gen in the Imperial Service and Gov of Milan, b 12 July 1763, d (-), m (—), and had issue which became extinct 25 June 1907

3a Henry Swinburne of Hamsterley, co Durham, Vendue Master at Trinidad, Author of "Travels through Spain," "Travels in the Two Sicilies," &c, b 19 July 1743, d at Trinidad Ap 1803, m 24 May 1767, Martha, da of John Baker of Chichester, Solicitor-Gen of the Leeward Islands, and had issue (with 4 sons and 2 other das who all d unm) 1b to 4b

1b Mary Frances Swinburne, d 1828, m 1793, Paul Benfield of Woodhall Park co Herts, and of Grosvenor Square, London, M P

2b Carolina Mariana Swinburne, d 1856, m Richard Walker of Michel Grove, co Sussex

3b Harriet Swinburne, d 1861, m 1814, John Walker of Purbrook Park, co Hants

4b Maria Antonia Swinburne, d 3 Sept 1869, m as 2nd wife, 20 Feb 1811, Major-Gen Oliver Robert Jones, 18th Hussars, 2nd son of Robert Jones of Fonman Castle, b 8 Sept 1776, and had issue 1c to 3c

1c Robert Oliver Jones of Fonman Castle, J P, D L, High Sheriff co Glamorgan 1838, and Chairman of the Quarter Sessions for that co, b 16 Dec 1811, d 13 Nov 1886, m 1st, 13 Sept 1843, Alicia, 2nd da of Evan Thomas of Llwynmadoc, co Brecon, &c, d 1 Ap 1851, and had issue 1d to 2d

1d Oliver Henry Jones of Fonmon Castle, Bar-at-Law, I T B A (Oxon), J P, D L, and Vice-Chairman Glamorgan Quarter Sessions (Fonman Castle, Cardiff, 39 Ashley Gardens, S W), b 7 Jan 1846, m 1900, Frances Beatrice, da of George Lyall of Hedley, co Surrey, J P, M P, Governor of the Bank of England

2d Edith Alicia Jones, m 14 Jan 1874, Robert Arthur Valpy of the Inner Temple, Bar-at-Law [eldest son of Robert Harris Valpy of Enborne Lodge, Newbury, J P, D L], and has issue

2c Oliver John Jones, Rear-Adm R N, b 15 Mar 1813, d 11 Jan 1878, m 23 July 1872, Annie Maria Louisa, widow of N E Vaughan, da of Edward Warnster Strangeways of Alne, co York

3c Rosa Antonia Jones, d (-), m 9 Aug 1838, the Rev John Montague Cholmeley, M A (Oxon), Vicar of Standen, co Herts, b 2 Dec 1812, d 31 Jan 1860, and had issue 1d to 3d

1d Henry John Cholmeley, Capt 16th Regt, b 10 May 1842

2d Antonia Cholmeley, m 4 Ap 1872, the Ven William Conybeare Bruce, M A (Oxon), Canon of Llandaff and Vicar of St Woolas [nephew of the 1st Lord Aberdare] (St Woolas' Vicarage, Newport, Monmouth), and has issue 1e to 2e

1e Montague William John Bruce, b 19 Jan 1873

2e Mary Rosa Bruce

3d Laura Selina Cholmeley

1a Teresa Swinburne, d Oct 1786, m 1716, Edward Charlton of Hesleyside and East Appleton, co Northbd, d 1767, and had issue 1b

1b William Charlton of Hesleyside, d 19 Feb 1797, m 1778, Margaret, da of John Fenwick of Morpeth, M D, d 12 Mar 1833, and had issue 1c

1c William John Charlton of Hesleyside, &c, High Sheriff co Northbd 1837, b 6 May 1784, d 25 Sept 1846, m 21 Oct 1809, Katherine Henrietta, da of Francis Cholmeley of Brandsby, co York, d 31 July 1819, and had issue 1d to 3d

1d William Henry Charlton of Hesleyside J P, D L, High Sheriff co Northbd 1857, b 22 Oct 1810, d 15 June 1880, m 20 June 1839, Barbara Anne [descended from George, Duke of Clarence, K G], da of Michael Tasburgh (R L 20 June 1810), previously Anne, of Burghwallis, d 30 Jan 1898, and had issue

See the Clarence Volume, p 385, Nos 14629-14643

2d Edward Charlton, D C L, M D, b 23 July 1814, d 14 Mar 1874, m

[Nos 39481 to 39502

295

The Plantagenet Roll

2ndly, 5 Ap 1864, Margaret, da of Mr Serjeant Bellasis, and had issue 1e to 6e

    1e Edward Francis Benedict Charlton R N , b 21 Mar 1865

    2e William Lancelot Stanislaus Charlton, b 7 May 1867 , m Theresa Mary, da of Thomas Walmesley of Lilystone, co Essex , and his issue

    3e Oswin John Charlton, b 15 Aug 1871

    4e George Victor Bellasis Charlton, b 16 Ap 1873

    5e Francis James Louis Charlton, b 1 Aug 1874

    6e Elsie Janet Charlton, m 30 Jan 1899, Edward Doran Webb (*Gaston House, Wardour, Tisbury, S O*)

    3d *Mary Charlton*, d 2 Aug 1854 , m 12 *June* 1850, *the Marquis Giuseppe Pasqualino of Palermo , and had issue*

    5a *Mary Swinburne*, d (–) , m 1754 *Edward Bedingfeld* [2nd son of Sir *Henry Arundell Bedingfeld, 3rd Bt* [E], *descended from King Henry VII , &c*], *and had issue*

    See the Tudor Roll, Table XLIV

    6a *Isabel Swinburne*, d (–) , m *at Horingham* 1755, *Thomas Crathorne of Ness, co York*, bur 2 Feb 1761 *and had issue* (*with 3 elder sons and 1 da who all apparently d s p*) 1b

    1b *George Crathorne, afterwards Tasburgh of Crathorne*, b 23 Ap 1761 , bur 9 Sept 1825 , m *Barbara, widow of George Tasburgh of Bodney, da of Thomas Fitzherbert of Swinnerton, co Staff* , d *July* 1808 , *and had issue*

    See the Clarence Volume, pp 384–385, Nos 14618–14643

[Nos 39503 to 39534

162 Descendants of THOMAS SWINBURNE (Table XVIII), *b.* 2 May 1705 , *d* (–) , *m.* MARY, widow of Thomas Thornton, da and co-h of Anthony MEABURNE of Pontop Hall, co Durham, *d* 1 Feb 1772 , and had issue 1a

    1a *Thomas Swinburne of Pontop Hall, co Durham*, d Oct 1825, m 1781, *Charlotte, da and co-h of Robert Sparman , and had* (*with possibly others*) *issue* 1b

    1b *Thomas Robert Swinburne of Pontop Hall, J P , D L , Lieut -Gen in the Army*, b May 1791, d 28 Feb 1864, m 1st, 8 Dec 1818, *Maria, da of the Rev Anthony Coates*, d 21 *July* 1820 , 2ndly, Oct 1826, *Helen, da of James Aspinall*, d 10 Mar 1860 *and had issue* 1c to 2c

    1c *Thomas Anthony Swinburne of Pontop Hall, and of Eilean Shona, co Inverness, Capt R N* , b 13 July 1820 , d 7 Dec 1893 , m 21 July 1852, *Mary Anne, da of Capt Edward Fraser*, d 21 Mar 1894 , *and had issue* 1d to 4d

    1d *Thomas Robert Swinburne, Major late R M A , Egyptian Medal and Bronze Star* 1882 and Soudan Clasp 1884-1885 (*Reeds, Liss, Hants , United Service*), b 4 Oct 1853 , m 9 Mar 1886, *Louisa Gertrude, da of Robert Stewart of Kinloch-moidart*, and has issue 1e to 2e

    1e Thomas Anthony Stewart Swinburne,, Lieut R E , b 6 Dec 1886

    2e Margaret Frances Troth Swinburne

    2d James Swinburne, F R S , an Engineer (*Woolhurst, Oxted, Surrey*, 82 Victoria Street, S W), b 28 Feb 1858 , m 1st, 28 Dec 1886, Ellen, da of R H Wilson of Gateshead-on-Tyne, M D , d 14 Jan 1893 , 2ndly, 25 May 1898, Lilian Gilchrist, da of Sir (Thomas) Godfrey Carey, Bailiff of Guernsey , and has issue 1e to 4e

    1e Anthony Swinburne, b 27 Dec 1887

    2e Spearman Charles Swinburne, b 8 Jan 1893

    3e Ida Swinburne, b 2 Dec 1899

    4e Marjorie Swinburne, b 19 Ap 1904

    3d. John Swinburne, *formerly* Lieut 3rd Batt Black Watch (*Hanarisburg, Transvaal*), b 18 Aug 1861   [Nos 39535 to 39543.

# of The Blood Royal

4d *Henry Swinburne*, b 9 *Oct* 1866, d 28 *Jan* 1900, m 21 *Aug* 1895, *Annie, da of Major Berkeley, and had issue 1e*

    1e Troath Swinburne

2c *James Swinburne of Marcus, co Forfar, D L, Lieut -Col late 4th Hussars*, b 29 *July* 1830, d 1881, m 20 *Ap* 1870, *Constance Mary [descended from the Lady Anne, sister of Kings Edward IV, &c], and had issue*

    See the Exeter Volume, p 548, Nos 49562-49564   [Nos 39544 to 39547

---

163 Descendants of ANNE SWINBURNE (Table XVIII), living 1708 , m (Settlement dated 2 Sept) 1687, NICHOLAS THORNTON of Netherwitton, co. Northbd , bur 13 Mar 1700 ; and had issue 1a to 8a

1a *John Thornton of Netherwitton, took part in the '15, for which he was convicted of high treason 7 July 1716, but reprieved 12 July following , bur 16 Ap 1742* , m (Settlement dated 22 *May*) 1708, *Margaret, da of Rowland Lyne , and had issue 1b to 7b*

    1b *Thomas Thornton of Netherwitton, d 26 Oct 1740 , m (Settlement dated 20 Ap) 1733, Mary, da and co-h of Anthony Meaburn of Pontop, co Durham (re-m 2ndly, Thomas Swinburne, 3rd son of Sir William Swinburne, 3rd Bt], b 4 Feb 1713 , bur 28 Ap 1786, and had issue 1c to 2c*

        1c *Anne Thornton of Netherwitton, d a 1761*

        2c *Catharine Thornton of Netherwitton, m as 2nd wife, 1758, William Salvin of Croxdale, d 21 Jan 1800, and had issue*

        See the Exeter Volume, p 529, Nos 48740-48777, and 48821-48835

    2b *Nicholas Thornton, 2nd son, living* 20 *Ap* 1733

    3b *James Thornton, will dated 27 May 1761, m Elizabeth, da of Roger Meynell, d 17 Sept 1762 , and had issue*

    See the Exeter Volume, pp 337-338, Nos 24570-24614

    4b *Rowland Thornton, living (and mentioned in father's will)* 1 *Dec* 1711

    5b *Margaret Thornton, d unm* 179-

    6b *Anne Thornton, living* 1740

    7b *Mary Thornton, d at Morpeth* 9 *Nov* 1773 , m *John Fenwick of Morpeth, M D , and had issue 1c to 2c*

        1c *James Fenwick of Netherwitton*

        2c *(—) Fenwick of Durham, M D*

    2a *Nicholas Thornton,*

    3a *William Thornton,*

    4a *Henry Thornton,*   } *living* 25 *Dec* 1688

    5a *Arthur Thornton,*

    6a *Anne Thornton,*

    7a *Catharine Thornton,* bur 3 *Oct* 1695

    8a *Isabella Thornton, will dated* 1711 [1]   [Nos 39548 to 39645

---

164 Descendants of Sir HENRY LAWSON of Brough, 2nd Bt [E] (Table XVIII), b c 1663. d 9 *May* 1726 , m. c 1688, ELIZABETH, da of Robert KNIGHTLEY of Offchurch, co Warwick, d. 1735 , and had issue 1a to 3a

1a *Sir John Lawson, 3rd Bt [E], b c 1689, d 19 Oct 1739 , m c 1712, Mary, da of Sir John Shelley of Michelgrove, 3rd Bt [E], d (-), and had issue 1b to 2b.*

---

[1] Hodgson's " Northumberland," I ii 318-319

The Plantagenet Roll

1b Sir Henry Lawson, 4th Bt [E] b c 1712, d Oct 1781, m Anastasia, da of Thomas Maire of Lartington Hall, co York, d 5 Nov 1764, and had issue

See the Clarence Volume, Table XXXIV, and pp 318-320, Nos 9215-9266, and Essex Volume Supp, p 510, Nos 9240 1-5

2b John Lawson of Bath, d 23 Jan 1791, m Elizabeth, da of Thomas William Selby of Biddleston, co Northumberland and had issue 1c to 2c

1c John Lawson of York, M D , d (-), m Clarina, widow of William Birmingham, da of John Fallon of Cloona, co Roscommon , and had issue 1d

1d Clarinda Lawson, da and h , d 10 Jan 1861 m 2 Oct 1825, Sir William Lawson (formerly Wright) of Brough, 1st Bt [U K], d 22 June 1865 , and had issue

See above, Nos 39657-39672, also Clarence Vol , pp 318-319, Nos 9225-9240

2c Elizabeth Lawson, d 6 Aug 1791, m as 1st wife, John Webbe, afterwards (1782) Webbe-Weston, of Sutton Place, co Surrey , and apparently had issue

See the Exeter Volume p 704, Note 2, Nos 58308-58327

2a Anne Lawson, d (-), m 20 Sept 1707, William Witham of Cliffe, co York, will dated 8 July 1723, and had issue

See the Exeter Volume, pp 558-560, Nos 19718-19913

3a Elizabeth Lawson bur 21 Dec 1732, m 1711, Stephen Tempest of Broughton, d 11 1p 1741, and had issue

See the Clarence Volume, pp 320-327, Nos 9267-9505

[Nos 39646 to 40143

165 Descendants of RALPH BLAKISTON of Chester-le-Street (Table XVIII), d (will dated 17 Mar. 1700, proved) 1704 , m MARY, da of (—) SAMPSON of Chester-le-Street , and had issue 1a to 6a [1]

1a William Blakiston, son and h 1700, bur 19 Feb 1710

2a Ralph Blakiston, 2nd son, 1700 , bur 6 Feb 1718

3a Michael Blakiston, 3rd son, 1700, bur at Chester-le-Street 6 June 1758, m (-), and had issue 1b to 2b

1b Anne Blakiston, bapt at Chester afsd 28 Feb 1739

2b Mary Blakiston, bapt there 9 Feb 1743

4a Anthony Blakiston of Loxford, Bishop Wearmouth, 4th son 1700, b c 1696 , living 1732 aged 36

5a Jane Blakiston, bur at Chester 23 Nov 1774, m c 1726, Sir Ralph Conyers of Hordon, co Durham, 5th Bt [E 1628], a Glazier in Chester-le-Street, bapt there 20 June 1697, d 22 Nov 1767, and had issue 1b to 1b

1b Sir Blakiston Conyers, 6th Bt [E], Capt R M , bapt at Chester 7 Dec 1721, bur there unm 1 Nov 1791

2b Sir Nicholas Conyers, 7th Bt [E], bapt 27 July 1729, d 1796, m (—) [said to have been a niece of Lord Cathcart], d at Greenock , and had issue 1c

1c Sir George Conyers, 8th Bt [E], d s p

3b Sir Thomas Conyers, 9th Bt [E], bapt 12 Sept 1731, d s p m s in the Workhouse at Chester-le Street 15 Ap 1810, m 24 Jan 1751, Isabel, da of James Lambton of Whitehall, co Durham, bur 10 Nov 1779, and had issue 1c to 2c

1c Jane Conyers, b 24 Jan 1758, d in 1813, m at St Margaret's, Crossgate, Durham, 19 Sept 1778, William Hardy of Chester-le-Street a working man [2]

2c Elizabeth Conyers, b 21 Nov 1758, living 1813, m at Chester-le-Street 1 July 1785, Joseph Hutchinson of Chester-le Street, a working man [2]

---

[1] Surtees' " Durham " ii 231

[2] Burke's " Vicissitudes of Families," 2nd Series, p 29

298

# of The Blood Royal

3c *Dorothy Conyers*, b 5 Ap 1762, *living at Sedgefield, co Durham*, 1813, m *at Richmond* 30 Nov 1795, *Joseph Barker, a working man* [1]

1b *William Conyers, Major Chatham Div R M*, bapt *at Chester* 11 July 1735, d *at Rochester c* 1800, m (—), *and had issue* 1c

1c *Jane Conyers, living near London, and then aged about* 13, 1800 [2]

6a *Elizabeth Blakiston, living unm* 1732, m *John Dunn of Tudhow, co Durham, and had issue* 1b to 2b [3]

   1b *John Dunn*
   2b *Margaret Dunn*

166 Descendants, if any surviving, of JAMES LAWSON (Table XVIII), d (–); m (—), and had issue 1a to 4a

   1a *Ralph Lawson*
   2a *Henry Lawson*
   3a *Mary Lawson*, m (—) *Paston of co Norfolk*
   4a *Elizabeth Lawson*

167 Descendants, if any, of ANNE LAWSON (Table XVIII.), d (–), m HENRY WIDDRINGTON of Bentland, co Northumberland

168. Descendants, if any, of MARGARET CONSTABLE (Table XIII), d. 1663, m Sir EDWARD STANHOPE of Edlington and Grimston, co York

169 Descendants of MARY CONSTABLE (Table XIII). will dated 17 Ap 1669, proved at York; m c 1610, Sir THOMAS BLAKISTON of Blakiston, 1st Bt [E] (see footnote, p 98), so cr 27 May 1615, d 1630, and had issue 1a to 2a

   1a *Margaret Blakiston*, b 1611
   2a *Mary Blakiston*, m *Sir Thomas Smith of Broxton, co Notts, and had issue* [4]

170. Descendants, if any surviving, of JOSEPH CONSTABLE of Upsall, co York (Table XIII), d (–), m MARY, da. of Thomas CRATHORNE of Crathorne, d ( ), and had issue

See the Essex Volume, Exeter Supplement, p 677

171 Descendants of JANE PUDSEY (Table XIX), bapt 14 Nov. 1683, bur 17 July 1708, m as 1st wife, 7 Aug 1705, WILLIAM DAWSON of Langcliffe, J P, Major Yorks Militia, d June 1762, and had issue 1a.

1a *Ambrose Dawson of Langcliffe Hall and Bolton, F R C P*, b Nov 1707, d 17 Dec 1794, m 1712, Mary, sister of Sir Willoughby Aston, 5th Bt [E], da of Richard Aston, and had issue 1b to 5b

---

[1] Burke's "Vicissitudes of Families," 2nd Series, p 29
[2] Surtees' "Durham," i 29   [3] Ibid ii 231
[4] Burke's "Extinct Baronetage," p 65

The Plantagenet Roll

1b *Pudsey Dawson of Langcliffe Hall, Major of Liverpool and Col Comdg Royal Liverpool Vol*, b 16 27 Feb 1752, d 19 Ap 1816, m 1774, *Elizabeth Anne, da of James Scott of Amsterdam*, d 2 Feb 1837, *and had issue (with 6 sons and 2 das who d unm)* 1c to 4c

1c *Richard Dawson of Liverpool*, b 11 Oct 1783, d 18 Feb 1850, m 2 June 1812, *Mary Anne, da of William Perkin of Cartmell, co Cumberland, and had issue* 1d to 2d

1d *Richard Pudsey Dawson of Delbury Hall, co Salop, and Hornby Castle, co York, &c, J P, D L*, b 10 Jan 1821, d (-) m *Louisa Elizabeth, da of Thomas Starkie Shuttleworth of Preston, and had issue* 1e to 7e

2e Richard Pudsey Dawson, b 30 Nov 1859
2e Willoughby Pudsey Dawson, b 30 Jan 1862
3e Charles Pudsey Dawson, b 11 Aug 1863
4e Ambrose Pudsey Dawson, b 4 July 1865
5e Thomas Starkie Pudsey Dawson, b 13 May 1867
6e Mary Louisa Pudsey Dawson
7e Lucy Margaret Pudsey Dawson

2d *Mary Seamand Dawson*, b 15 May 1814, d (-), m 7 Feb 1843, *Henry Ribton Hoskins, and had issue* 1e
1e Alexander Hoskins

2c *Edward Dawson*, b 1797, d in Bermuda Jan 1843, m *Eliza, da of (—) Liot*, d (-), *and had issue* 1d
1d *Elizabeth Anne Pudsey Dawson*, m *the Rev R Burrowes*

3c *Mary Dawson*, b 16 May (? Nov) 1779, d (-), m 1809, *Anthony Littledale of Liverpool*, b 2 Oct 1777, d 20 Jan 1820, *and had issue*

1c *Jane Dawson*, b 1795, d in childbirth 183-, m 1832, *the Rev. John Jennings, Canon of Westminster, and had issue* 1d
1d *Ambrose Dawson Jennings*, b 183-

2b *William Dawson of Caius Coll. Camb*, 1771, b 5 Sept 1753, d (-), m 1st, (—), *da of (—) O'Kill*, 2ndly, *at New York, Eleanor, da of (—) Lee, and had issue (with 2 other sons and 2 das who all d unm)* 1c to 3c

1c[1] *Rev Richard Dawson of Halton Gill, Rector of Belton by Bolland*, d (-), m 11 Aug 1774, (—), *da of the Rev William Hutton Long of Maids Moreton, and had issue 2 das who both d s p*
2c[2] *William Dawson of New York*, d (-), m (—), *da of (—) Jay, and had issue* 1d
1d *Mary Jay Dawson*, m 22 Sept 1870, Col Colville Frankland, *late 2nd Batt Royal Dublin Fusiliers [5th son of Sir Frederick William Frankland, 8th Bt [E]] (67 Brunswick Place, Hove, Junior United Service), and has issue* 1e to 6e

1e Robert Cecil Colville Frankland, Transvaal C S, *formerly* Lieut S Staffs Regt, b 7 July 1877
2e Thomas Hugh Colville Frankland, Lieut 2nd Batt Royal Dublin Fusiliers, b 17 Oct 1879
3e Katherine Marian Colville Frankland
4e Eleanor Colville Frankland, m 6 Ap 1905, Thomas Maberley Cobbe (*Newbridge House, Donabate, co Dublin*).
5e Beatrice Colville Frankland
6e Mary Olive Elsie Frankland

3c[2] *Frances Laura Dawson*, b 4 July 1814, d 25 July 1904, m 20 July 1847, *the Ven William Macdonald, M A, Archdeacon of Wilts and Canon Residentiary of Salisbury, Vicar of Bishops Canning*, b 10 Aug 1783, d 24 June 1862; *and had issue* 1d to 5d

[Nos 40144 to 40169

300

# of The Blood Royal,

1d Rev Frederick William Macdonald, Rector of Wishford and Rural Dean (*Wishford Rectory, Salisbury*), b 3 Ap 1848, m 6 Jan 1874, Frances Lucy, da of John Matthews of Pimperne, Dorset, s p

2d Robert Estcourt Macdonald, b 15 Aug 1854, m 1st, 10 Aug 1891, Agnes Gwyn, da of G Gwyn Elger, d 23 Aug 1895, 2ndly, 17 Ap 1900, Dorothy Horatia, da of Col Edmund Bacon Hulton, s p

3d Eleanor Frances Macdonald, *unm*

4d Flora Georgiana Macdonald, m 10 Ap 1879, the Rev Herbert William Sneyd Kynnersley, d s p 1 Nov 1886

5d Marion Kinneir Macdonald, *unm*

3b *Richard Dawson*, b 21 Ap 1755, d (-), m *Elizabeth, da of William Crosbie*, and had issue 1c to 3c

1c *Richard Crosbie Dawson*, b 7 Jan. 1799, d 1 June 1880, m 10 Ap 1828, *Annie, da of George Ashby Pritt*, d 7 Feb 1858, and had issue 1d to 5d

1d *Rev Richard Dawson, Vicar of Sutton Benger, co Wilts*, b 1 July 1829, d 19 July 1903, m 21 July 1863, *Alice, da of John Simmons of Moseley Heath, near Birmingham*, d 2 July 1879, and had issue (*with 3 das who d unm*) 1e to 3e

1e Richard Crosbie Dawson (*Sutton Benger, Chippenham*), b 21 May 1871, m 27 July 1908, Frances Sarah, da of John Collet of Draycott Cerne, co Wilts, and has issue 1f

1f Richard Pudsey Dawson, b 22 June 1909

2e Cyril John Dawson, b 16 Ap 1873, m 26 Sept 1904, Elizabeth, da of Peter Pockett, and has issue 1f

1f Richard Cyril Dawson, b 14 Aug 1905

3e Willoughby Crosbie Dawson (*Meadow Leigh, Fitton Road, Bristol*), b 25 Mar 1875, m 25 Ap 1905, Alice Mary, da of Sydney Herbert of Bristol, and has issue 1f

1f Alice Doreen Maud Dawson, b 17 Nov 1905

2d George James Crosbie Dawson of May Place (*May Place, Newcastle, Staffordshire*), b 30 Ap 1841, m 7 Aug 1872, Catherine Webber, da of the Rev. George Mackie, D D , and has issue 1e to 2e

1e George Crosbie Dawson, b 3 May 1873, *unm*

2e Constance Ethel Crosbie Dawson, *unm*

3d Rev Ambrose Pudsey Dawson, Rector of Harston (*Harston Rectory, Grantham*), b 30 Mar 1843, m Mary, da of the Rev J P Middleton, and has issue 1e to 7c

1e. Ambrose Middleton Dawson

2e Hugh Pudsey Dawson

3e Helen Mary Dawson

4e Annie Ruth Dawson

5e Margaret Pudsey Dawson

6e Elizabeth Pudsey Dawson

7e Rachel Irene Dawson

4d Annie Mary Dawson (12 *Warwick Crescent, London*)

5d Harriet Dawson, m 14 Sept 1873, Joseph Wagstaff Blundell, and has issue 1e

1e Benson Dawson Blundell, b (—), m and has issue

2c *William Ambrose Dawson*, b 21 Jan 1800, d Dec 1860, m June 1830, *Charlotte Jemima, da of (—) Clay*, and had issue (*with 2 sons who d unm*) 1d

[Nos 40160 to 40184

The Plantagenet Roll

1d Catherine Charlotte Dawson (18 *Pembroke Road, Kensington, W*), m as 2nd wife, Oct 1870 or 1874, Sylvester Frank Richmond [descended from the Lady Isabel Plantagenet (see Essex Volume, p 128)], *d s p* 4 Sept 1894

3c *Elizabeth Dawson*, b 1791, d 1867, m 1823, *Castel William Clay of Liverpool*, b 1795, d 1815, *and had issue (with a youngest son, Benjamin Sherard, d unm)* 1d to 2d

1d *Castel Pelham Clay*, b 1825, d 1863, m 1854, *Eva Emily, da of Charles Paul Berkeley, and had issue (with a da d young)* 1e to 2e

1e Evelyn Emily Clay, b Sept 1855

2e Charlotte Elizabeth Clay, b Oct 1857, m 1894, the Rev William Erskine

2d *Charlotte Elizabeth Clay*, b 12 Aug 1828, d 28 May 1901, m 19 Oct 1848, *the Rev Arthur Rawson of Bromley [3rd son of William Henry Rawson of Haugh End, co York]*, b 17 Sept 1818, d 18 May 1882, *and had issue (with a son d unm)* 1e to 9e

1e Herbert Evelyn Rawson (*Comyn Hill, Ilfracombe*), b 12 June 1852, unm

2e Henry Ernest Rawson, b 13 Ap 1854, m Ap 1894, Minna Alice, da of (—) Schwartz, and has issue 1f to 2f

1f Arthur Ernest George Rawson, b 8 Oct 1896

2f. John Sherard Rawson, b Jan 1900

3e Charles Selwyn Rawson, b 28 June 1855, m 18 Ap 1894, Alice Anne, da of (—) Cruickshank, and has issue 1f to 3f

1f Arthur John Selwyn Rawson, b 8 July 1896

2f Castel Duff Rawson, b 30 Mar 1906

3f Dorothea Alice Jennetta Rawson, b 30 Oct 1907

4e Sherard Rawson, b 19 Nov 1868, m 1904, Althea, da of (—) Turpie

5e Mary Sibella Rawson, unm

6e Emily Frances Rawson, unm

7e Charlotte Arabella Rawson, m 7 Feb 1905, Martin Chichester Harris [descended from the Lady Anne, sister of King Edward IV (see Essex Volume Supplement, p 630)] (43 *Cathcart Road, S W*)

8e Ellen Beatrice Rawson, unm

9e Ethel Rawson, m 24 Sept 1896, Capt Archibald Thomas Carter, R N, d 30 Nov 1899, and has issue 1f

1f Sybil Carter, b 17 June 1897

4b *Mary Dawson*, b 29 Ap 1717, d. (-), m 15 Dec 1778, *William Crosbie of Liverpool*

5b *Elizabeth Dawson*, b 18 Jan 1750, d (-), m 17 Oct 1776, *Col Charles Rooke, and had issue* [Nos 10185 to 10202

172 Descendants, if any surviving, of ELIZABETH PUDSEY, wife of JOHN WEBB (? WELD), of her aunt, ELIZABETH PUDSEY, wife of ROGER [son and h of John] TALBOT of Thornton, and of her great-uncles and aunts STEPHEN, *bapt.* at Bolton 11 Nov 1610, WILLIAM, *bapt* 1 Oct 1615, RALPH, *bapt* 19 Jan 1616, VALENTINE, *bapt* 18 Feb 1618, MARY, living 1620, ISABEL, *bapt* 9 Nov 1592, living 1620, TROTHE, *bapt* 9 May 1594, living 1620, ELIZABETH, living 1620, ANNE, *bapt.* 11 Nov. 1610, and JANE, *bapt* 25 Jan 1612 (Table XIX)

# of The Blood Royal

173 Descendants, if any, of MARY PUDSEY (Table XIX), *b* 24 May 1690, *d* (-); *m* at Houghton-le-Skerne 24 May 1708 WILLIAM HULLOCK of Barnard Castle, Merchant, *d* (-), and was father or grandfather of 1*a* [1]

    1*a Timothy Hullock of Barnard Castle, a Master Weaver and proprietor of a timber yard there, b c 1732, d 1805, aged 73,* [2] *m (—), and had issue at least 1b*

    1*b Sir John Hullock, Baron of the Exchequer, 16 Ap 1823, b 3 Ap 1767, d (²s p) 31 July 1829, m Mary, da of (—), d 18 Nov 1852* [3]

174 Descendants, if any, of CATHERINE PUDSEY (Table XIX), *m.* ROBERT PLACE of Picton, co York [2nd son of Christopher Place of Dinsdale, co. Durham], living 20 May 1696 [4]

175 Descendants of THOMAS PUDSEY of Hackfort, co. York (Table XIX), *b* 17 Aug 1567, *d* between 20 Feb 31 May 1620, *m* (—), and had issue (at least) 1*a*

    1*a Philippa Pudsey, living 1623, and a legatee under the will of her uncle, Ambrose Pudsey*

176. Descendants of CATHERINE TROTTER of Skelton Castle, co York (Table XIX), *d* (-), *m* JOSEPH HALL of Durham, *d* 1733, and had issue 1*a* to 4*a*

    1*a John Hall, afterwards Stevenson, of Skelton Castle, the "Eugenius" of Sterne, b c 1718, d 1785, m Anne, da and h of Ambrose Stevenson of Manor House, co Durham [by his wife Anne, da and event h of Anthony Wharton of Gilling Wood, co York], d 1790, and had issue 1b*

    1*b Joseph William Hall Stevenson of Skelton Castle, b c 1741, d 1786, m Anne, da and h of James Foster of Drumgoon, co Fermanagh, and had issue 1c to 5c*

    1*c John Hall, afterwards (R L 20 Nov 1807) Wharton of Skelton Castle, M P, b c 1766, d 2 June 1843, m Susan Mary Anne, da of Gen John Lambton of Lambton, d 19 Aug 1854, and had issue 1d to 2d* [5]

        1*d Susan Stevenson*

        2*d Margaret Stevenson*

    2*c James Hall, Major-Gen 21st Light Dragoons, d s p 1841*

    3*c Rev William Hall or Stevenson, afterwards Wharton, M 1, Vicar of Gilling, b c 1768, d 26 May 1842, m 19 Ap 1808, the Hon Charlotte [descended from the Lady Anne, sister of King Edward IV], da of Thomas (Dundas), 1st Lord Dundas [G B], d 5 Jan 1855, and had issue*

    See the Exeter Volume, pp 259-260, Nos 9764-9778

    4*c Margaret Hall*   [Nos 40203 to 40217

---

    [1] Foster's "Yorkshire Families," Pudsey Pedigree
    [2] *Gentleman's Magazine*, 1829, ii 275
    [3] D N B, *Notes and Queries*, 7th Series, viii 48, 197
    [4] Surtees' "Durham," iii 236, Hutchinson's "Durham," iii 147
    [5] Graves' "Cleveland," p 354

The Plantagenet Roll

5c *Francis Hall*, d (? s p), m 30 Oct 1792, *the Hon John Theophilus Rawdon* [2nd son of John, 1st Earl of Moira [I]], b 19 Nov 1757, d. May 1808, and, *according to some accounts, had issue*

2a *George Hall, a Col in the Army*, d (-), m (—), *natural da of Lord William Manners, M P* [2nd son of John, 2nd Duke of Rutland [E], K G], and *had issue (a da)* [1]

3a *Thomas Hall, a Gen in the Army*, d (-), m (—), *da of (—) Carter of co Cambridge, and had issue 1b to 2b* [1]

1b *John Hall*

2b *Elizabeth Hall*

1a *Frances Elizabeth Hall*, d ( ), m *Walter Ramsden, afterwards Hawksworth, of Hawksworth, co York*, d 12 Oct 1760, *and had issue 1b to 2b*

1b *Walter Ramsden Beaumont Hawksworth, afterwards* (R L 2 Sept 1786, *Fawkes, of Hawksworth and Farnley, High Sheriff co York* 1789, b 11 Aug 1746, d 17 Oct 1792, m 28 Dec 1768, *Amelia, da of James Farrer and had issue 1c to 6c*

1c *Walter Ramsden Hawksworth, afterwards* (R L 1 Dec 1792) *Fawkes, of Farnley, co York, M P, and High Sheriff* 1823, b 2 Mar 1769, d 1825, m 1st, 28 Aug 1794 *Maria, descended from the Lady Anne, sister of King Edward IV, &c], da of Robert Grimston of Neswick* d 10 Dec 1813, *and had issue*

See the Exeter Volume, pp 676-678, Nos 57242-57295

2c *Francis Ramsden Hawksworth, otherwise Fawkes, of Brambro Grange, Doncaster*, b 12 Oct 1774, d (-), m *Eliza Ann Mary [descended from the Lady Anne, sister of King Edward IV, &c], da of Robert Grimston of Neswick*, d (-), *and had issue*

See the Exeter Volume, pp 678-679, Nos 57296-57321

3c *Rev Ayscough Hawksworth, otherwise Fawkes, Rector of Leathley*

4c *Rev Richard Hawksworth, otherwise Fawkes*, b 17 Mar 1780, d (-), m *Isabella, da of Sir Michael Pilkington, 6th Bt [E], and had issue 1d to 3d*

1d *Isabella Frances Hawksworth, da and co-h*, d (-), m Mar 1824, *James Pickering Ord of Langton Hall, co Leicester and had issue (a da who d ? unm)*

2d *Amelia Hawksworth, da and co-h*, b 24 Sept 1807, d 17 June 1862, m 13 Sept 1827, *the Rev Charles Vanden Bempde Johnstone, M A, Canon of York, Vicar of Felixkirk* [2nd son of Sir Richard, 1st Bt [G B]], b 24 Aug 1800, d 15 May 1882, *and had issue 1e to 4e*

1e Rev *Charles Vanden Bempde Johnstone*, M A (Durham), Vicar of Hackness (*Hackness Vicarage, Scarborough*), b 17 June 1828

2e *Laura Georgiana Vanden Bempde Johnstone* (*Bayard's Lodge, Knaresborough*)

3e *Charlotte Frances Vanden Bempde Johnstone*, d 14 Mar 1888, m 8 Feb 1866, *Edmund Walker of Mount St John, Thirsk*, d 17 May 1873, *and had issue 1f to 2f*

1f *Arthur John Walker* (*Mount St John, Thirsk*), b 23 Dec 1869

2f *Frederick Edmund Walker* (*Ravensthorpe Manor, Thirsk*), b 29 Mar 1871

4e *Caroline Vanden Bempde Johnstone* (*Bayard's Lodge, Knaresborough*)

3d *Maria Hawksworth, da and co-h*, d (-), m 9 June 1828, *the Rev Thomas Dayrell of Shudy Camps, co Camb, M A, J P, D L, Rector of Long Marston*, b 28 May 1802, d 18 May 1866, *and had issue 1e to 7e*

1e *Marmaduke Frances Dayrell of Shudy Camp*, b 4 Jan 1834, d unm 1877

2e *Thomas Dayrell of Shudy Camps, Lieut -Col Bengal S C*, b 1 May 1838, d s p 1890   [Nos 40218 to 40302

---

[1] Graves' "Cleveland," p 351

304

3e *Rev Richard Dayrell of Shudy Camps*, Rector of *Lillingstone Dayrell*, b 8 *June* 1811 , d s p , m 27 *July* 1871, *Evangeline Elizabeth Adelaide* (*Shudy Camps Park, Linton*), da of *Samuel Orr of Innishannon, co Cork, M D*

4e Isabel Jane Dayrell, m 20 July 1869, Gerald Henry Band Young, *late 43rd Light Infantry* (*Fairlight House, Fawcett Street, S W*), and has issue 1f to 5f

  1f Isabel Mary Young, *unm*

  2f Edith Gertrude Young, *unm*

  3f Geraldine Frances Young, *unm*

  4f Isie Margaret Young, m 23 July 1902, Edward Henry Smith-Wright, and has issue 1g to 4g

    1g Edward Gerald Smith Wright

    2g John Evelyn Smith-Wright

    3g Henry Gordon Smith-Wright

    4g Josephine Margaret Smith-Wright

  5f Gwendolen May Young, m 5 Nov 1902, Capt Julian Mayne Young, A S C , and has issue 1g

    1g Dayrell Francis Mayne Young

5e Mary Anne Dayrell (*Leslie House, Spa Place, Cheltenham*), *unm*

6e Caroline Charlotte Dayrell, m 25 Ap 1876, the Rev Henry West (*103 Cheriton Road, Folkestone*)

7e Emily Elizabeth Dayrell, m 25 Ap 1878, Richard Samuel Bagnell (*Ryall Hill, Upton-on-Severn, Worcester*) , and has issue 1f to 2f

  1f Richard Dayrell Bignell, b 23 Ap 1879

  2f Myrtle Dayrell Bagnell, b 10 Aug 1887

5c *Amelia Hawksworth*, d 25 *June* 1834 , m 12 *May* 1791, *Godfrey Wentworth Wentworth* (*R L* 10 *Mar* 1789), *formerly Armytage, of Wooley, M P , J P , D L , High Sheriff co York* 1796 [*3rd son of Sir George Armytage, 3rd Bt* [S], *M P*], b 9 *May* 1773 , d 14 *Sept* 1834, and had issue 1d to 3d

  1d *Godfrey Wentworth of Woolley Park, co York, J P , D L , &c* , b 14 *Sept* 1797 , d 22 *Sept* 1865, m 20 *June* 1822, *Anne, da of Walter Fawkes of Farnley Hall, co York,* d 9 *June* 1842

  See p 304, Nos 40261–40298 (Exeter Volume, p 677 Nos 57285–57292)

  2d *Catherine Frances Wentworth*, d 1838 , m 27 *July* 1822, *John Marcus Clements of Glenb'y, co Leitrim, M P , Lieut -Col 18th Hussars* [*descended from the Lady Isabel Plantagenet*], d 1833 , and had issue

  See the Essex Volume, p 295, Nos 32334–32338

  3d *Dorothy Harriet Wentworth*, d (-), m 2 *July* 1831, *Sir Samuel Hancock, Senior Exon of the Yeomen of the Guard*

6c *Frances Elizabeth Hawksworth*, d (-), m *Charles John Brandling of Gosforth*

2b *Frances Hawksworth*, d Dec 1815 , m *Le Gendre Starkie of Huntroyde, co. Lancaster,* d 20 *Sept* 1791, and had (with possibly other) issue 1c

  1c *Le Gendre Pierce Starkie of Huntroyde, J P , Vice-Lieut co Lancaster and High Sheriff* 1806, b 1770 , d 25 *Oct* 1807, m *Charlotte, da of the Rev Benjamin Preely, D D , Rector of Brington,* d 30 *Ap* 1801, and had issue (with 2 elder sons and a da who d s p) 1d to 2d

    1d *Le Gendre Nicholas Starkie of Huntroyde, J P , D L , M P for Pontefract* 1826–1830, b 1 *Dec* 1799, d 15 *May* 1865, m *Feb* 1827, *Anne, da of Ambrose Chamberlain of Rylston-in Craven, co York,* d 27 *Dec* 1888, and had issue 1e to 4e

    1e *Le Gendre Nicholas Starkie of Huntroyde, J P , D L , and High Sheriff co Lancaster* 1868, *M P for Clitheroe* 1853–1856, *Col Comdg 3rd Batt E Lancashire Regt ,* b 10 *Jan* 1828 , d 13 *Ap* 1899, m 15 *Oct* 1867, *Jemima Monica Mildred* [*descended from George, Duke of Clarence, K G , brother of King Edward IV.* (see Clarence Volume, p 321]] (*Ribbleton Hall, Preston*), da of *Henry Tempest of Lostock Hall, co Lanc ,* and had issue 1f to 2f   [Nos 40303 to 40330

The Plantagenet Roll

1f Edmund Arthur Le Gendre Starkie of Huntroyde, J P , Capt 4th Batt E Lancashire Regt (*Huntroyde, Burnley, Lovely Hall, Blackburn*), *b* 10 Feb 1871, *m* 19 July 1898, Maud Margaret Dolores Anne [descended from the Lady Anne, sister of King Edward IV (see the Exeter Volume, p 465)], da of Major William Michael Ince Anderton of Euxton Hall, co Lanc , *s p s*

2f Pierce Cecil Le Gendre Starkie, Lieut Lancashire Hussars, *b* 11 Sept 1882

2e *John Pierce Chamberlain Starkie of Ashton Hall, co Lanc*, LL D , J P., *M P for N E Lancashire* 1868-1880, *b* 28 *June* 1830, d 12 *June* 1888, m 27 *June* 1861, *Anne Charlotte Amelia* (*Scarthwaite, near Lancaster*), da of Harrington George Frederic Hudson of Bessingby, co York , *and had issue 1f to 3f*

1f Francis Chamberlain Le Gendre Starkie (*Ashton Hall, Lancaster*), *b* 30 Mar 1863 , *m* Ellen, da of (—) Cooper

2f Charlotte Le Gendre Starkie, *m* as 2nd wife, 28 July 1885, James Edward Platt, J P (*Bruntwood, Cheshire*)

3f Susan Katherine Le Gendre Starkie, *unm*

3e Rev Henry Arthur Starkie, M A (Camb), *formerly* Rector of Radcliffe, Manchester, *b* 1 Jan 1838

4e *Anne Elizabeth Starkie*, d 24 *Jan* 1869 , m 19 *Aug* 1858, *the Rev George William Horton*, M A , *Vicar of Wellow, cadet of Horton of Howroyde, co York* [*and a descendant of King Henry VII* (see the Tudor Roll, p 465)], d 6 *May* 1886 , *and had issue 1f to 2f*

1f Rev Le Gendre George Horton, M A (Camb), Vicar of Wellow (*Wellow Vicarage, Bath*), *b* 12 July 1859 , *m* 3 Sept 1891, his cousin Mabel Augusta Hawksworth [descended from Edward III both through Lady Anne, sister of King Edward IV., and through Mortimer-Percy], da of the Rev Frederick Fawkes, and has issue 1g to 3g

    1g Le Gendre George William Horton *b* 14 June 1892

    2g Frederick Henry Le Gendre Horton, *b* 8 Aug 1894

    3g Dorothy Mary Horton

2f Anne Frances Horton, *m* 16 Aug 1888, the Rev Atherton Gwillym Rawstorne, Suffragan Bishop of Whalley 1909 and Rector of Croston (*Croston Rectory, Preston*) , and has issue 1g to 6g

    1g Richard Atherton Rawstorne, *b* 13 Mar 1893

    2g George Streynsham Rawstorne, *b* 22 Jan 1895

    3g Robert Gwyllim Rawstorne, *b* 16 Nov 1907

    4g Frances Marion Rawstorne

    5g Jennett Rawstorne

    6g Marjory Lila Rawstorne

2d *Charlotte Le Gendre Starkie*, d 13 *Dec* 1818, m *as 1st wife*, 12 *June* 1819, *Col Henry Armytage, Coldstream Guards* [*3rd son of Sir George Armytage, 4th Bt* [E]] b 29 *Oct* 1796 , d 30 *Oct* 1861, *and had issue 1e to 3e*

1e *Henry Armytage, Col Coldstream Guards*, b 1 Feb 1828 , d 18 *Ap* 1901, m 12 *Feb* 1851, *the Hon Fenella* [*descended from King Henry VII*], da of *Maurice Frederick* (*FitzHardinge Berkeley*), 1st *Baron FitzHardinge* [*U K*], *G C B* , d 20 *Nov* 1903 , *and had issue*

See the Tudor Roll, p 472, Nos 33061-33065

2e *Harriette Elizabeth Armytage*, d *Ap* 1901, m 15 *June* 1858, *Richard John Streatfeild* [*4th son of Henry Streatfeild of Chiddingstone co Kent, J P , D L*], b 7 *Nov* 1833 , d 22 *Mar* 1877, *and had issue 1f to 2f*

    1f Mervyn Armytage Streatfeild

    2f Roland Henry Armytage Streatfeild

3e *Emma Armytage*, d 27 *Dec* 1881, m *as 1st wife*, 11 *Oct* 1858, *Rev the Hon Henry Bligh* [*3rd son of Edward, 5th Earl of Darnley* [*I*], *and a descendant of George, Duke of Clarence, K G*], d 4 *Mar* 1905, *and had issue*

See the Clarence Volume, p 288, Nos 7788-7799   [Nos 10331 to 10366

# of The Blood Royal

177. Descendants, if any surviving, of CATHERINE TROTTER (Table XIX), d (-); m as 2nd wife, WILLIAM BOWER of Bridlington, co York, b. 1654, d (-), and had issue 1a to 4a[1]

    1a *Henry Bower of York, and afterwards of Killerby Hall, near Scarborough,* d unm 1770

    2a *George Bower of Bridlington,* d (-), m , *and had issue 1b*

    1b *Freeman Bower of Killerby Hall and Bawtry, co York, J P , D L*

    3a *Robert Bower of Sleights, near Whitby and Welham,* d s p 1777

    4a *Mary Bower,* d (-), m 1st, 1727, *Peter Whitton, Lord Mayor of York* 1728, d (-), 2ndly, 1712, *George Perrott, Baron of the Exchequer*

178 Descendants, if any, of MARGARET TROTTER, wife of GEORGE LAWSON, and of HANNAH TROTTER, wife of CHARLES PERROTT, of HUGH TROTTER, GEORGE TROTTER, and their sister MARY, wife of JOHN FULTHORPE of Tunstall co Durham, and of ELIZABETH TROTTER, wife of GEORGE NEVILL (Table XIX)

179 Descendants of ANTHONY MEYNELL of Kilvington, co York (Table XIX), b 1592, d 1669, m MARY, da of James TWAITES of Long Marston, co York, d 1669, and had issue 1a to 6a.

    1a *Thomas Meynell of Kilvington,* b 1615, d (-), m. 1637, *Gerard, da of William Ireland of Nostel Abbey, co York* [m 2ndly, *Capt Edward Saltmarshe*], *and had issue 1b to 5b*

    1b *Roger Meynell of Kilvington,* b 1639/10, bur 9 Nov 1683, m *Mary* [*descended from the Lady Anne, sister of King Edward IV*], *da and h of Sir John Middleton of Thurntofte,* bur 30 Ap 1685, *and had issue*

    See the Exeter Volume, Table XXII, and pp 336-338, Nos 21536-21611

    2b *John Meynell*

    3b *William Meynell*

    4b *Mary Meynell,* bur *at Goodramgate, co York, 9 Feb 1686,* m *John Brigham of Wyton.*

    5b *Elizabeth Meynell*

    2a *Winifred Meynell,* m 1st, *Thomas Killingbeck of Allerton Grange, co York,* 2ndly, *Thomas Barlow of Barlow, co Lanc*

    3a *Clare Meynell,* d (-), m. c 1658, *Sir Richard Foster, 2nd Bt* [E], d c (?) 1680, *and had issue 1b to 2b*

    1b *Sir Richard Foster, 3rd Bt* [E], b c 1653, d s p a 1714

    2b *Mary Foster,* d (-), m (—) *Collingwood of Hetton in the Hole, co Durham*

    4a *Collett Meynell*

    5a *Catharine Meynell*

    6a *Frances Meynell*   [Nos 40367 to 40445]

180 Descendants, if any, of MARY MEYNELL, wife of GEORGE POLE of Spinkhill, and of ANNE MEYNELL, wife of THOMAS GRANGE of Harlsey, co York (Table XIX).

---

[1] Burke's "Landed Gentry"

The Plantagenet Roll

181. Descendants, if any, of CATHERINE CHOLMLEY (Table XIII), d (-), m RICHARD DUTTON of Whitby

182 Descendants of CONYERS (DARCY), 1st EARL OF HOLDERNESS (1682), 5th Lord CONYERS (1509), and 2nd Lord DARCY and CONYERS (1641) [E] (Table XX), bapt 24 Jan 1599; d. 14 June 1689; m. a June 1619, GRACE, da and h of Thomas ROKEBY of Skiers, co York, bur. 4 Jan 1658, and had issue 1a to 4a.

1a Conyers (Darcy), 2nd Earl of Holderness, &c [E], b c 1620, d 13 Dec 1692, m 2ndly, 6 Feb 1650, Lady Frances, da of Thomas (Howard), 1st Earl of Berkshire [E], bur 10 Ap 1670, and had issue
See the Clarence Volume, Table LXXVIII, and pp 626–637, Nos 28010–28819

2a Lady Ursula Darcy, d (-), m Sir Christopher Wyvill, 3rd Bt [E], M P, bur 8 Feb 1681, and had issue
See the Exeter Volume, Table LII, and pp 549–553, Nos 19588–19656

3a Lady Elizabeth Darcy, bapt 8 Dec 1624, d (-), m 18 Oct 1650, Sir Henry Stapylton of Myton, 1st Bt [E], so cr 22 June 1660, M P, d 1679, and had issue
See pp 99–117, Nos 10149–10723

4a Lady Grace Darcy, d s p m a 1658, m as 1st wife, 18 Oct 1655, Sir John Legard of Ganton, 1st Bart [E], so cr 29 Dec 1660, d 1678, and had issue 1b
1b Grace Legard, aged 18, 31 Aug 1665 m John Hill of Thornton, co York
[Nos 30416 to 41899

183 Descendants, if any surviving, of the Hon Sir WILLIAM DARCY (Table XX), d (-), m DOROTHY, da of Sir George SELBY of Newcastle, and had issue [1]

184. Descendants of MARIA CATHERINE DARCY (Table XX), d. 21 Aug 1747, m. May 1738, Sir ROBERT HILDYARD of Winestead, 3rd Bt [E], M P., d. 1 Feb. 1781, and had issue 1a to 2a

1a Sir Robert Darcy Hildyard, 4th Bt [E], b 1743, d s p s 6 Nov 1814
2a Catherine Hildyard, d (-), m as 2nd wife, James Whyte of Denbies, co Surrey, d (-), and had issue 1b
1b Anne Catherine Whyte, da and event sole h, d (-), m May 1815, Col Thomas Blackborne Thoroton, afterwards (R L 23 May 1815) Hildyard of Flintham, co Notts, d July 1830, and had issue 1c to 8c
1c Thomas Blackborne Thoroton Hildyard of Flintham Hall, M P, J P, D L, High Sheriff co Notts 1862, and Chairman Quarter Sessions, b 8 Ap 1821, d 19 Mar 1888, m 3 May 1842, Anne Margaret, da of Col John Staunton Rochfort of Clogrenane, co Carlow, and had issue 1d to 1d
1d Thomas Blackborne Thoroton Hildyard of Flintham, J P, late Lieut Rifle Brigade (Flintham Hall, near Newark), b 10 Mar 1843, m 18 July 1871, Eleanor, da of the Right Hon Henry Herbert of Muckross, co Kerry, P C, s p
[No 41900

---

[1] Plantagenet Harrison's "History of Yorkshire," p 119

# of The Blood Royal

2d Robert Charles Thoroton Hildyard, Capt R E, b 3 Nov 1841, d (?s p)
25 Jan 1885, m 31 Aug 1871, Anne Catharine (see below), da of Robert D'Arcy
Hildyard of Colburn, d 1906, and had issue (with an elder son, Robert, who d unm
1908) 1e to 3e

   1e Cecil Thoroton Hildyard (Canada)
   2e Dorothy Anne Florence Thoroton Hildyard, m 8 Aug 1895, the Rev
Lyonel D'Arcy Hildyard, Rector of Rowley [himself descended from King Edward
III through Mortimer-Percy (Rowley Rectory, Hull), and has issue
    See p 155, Nos 16776–16777
   3e Kathleen Hildyard, unm

3d Sir Henry John Thoroton Hildyard, K C B, Col H L I, formerly Gen
Comdg Troops in South Africa 1904–1908, Director-Gen of Mil Education and
Training at Headquarters 1903–1904, &c, served in S Africa 1899–1902 in command
of 2nd Brigade and subsequently of 2nd Division, Egypt (Medal with Clasp and
Bronze Star) 1882, &c (United Service), b 5 July 1846, m 20 May 1871, Annette,
da of Adm James Prevost, and his issue 1e to 3e

   1e Harold Charles Thoroton Hildyard, Major R F A, b 16 July 1872, m
18 Aug 1909, Selina, da of the Rev Savile L'Estrange Malone
   2e Gerard Moresby Thoroton Hildyard, Bar-at-Law, b 3 June 1874
   3e Reginald John Thoroton Hildyard, Capt Royal West Kent Regt, b 11 Dec
1876

4d Edith Mary Thoroton Hildyard, m 28 Mar 1895, Edward Bromley, Clerk
of Assize (12 Eccleston Square)

2c Robert D'Arcy Hildyard of Coburn Manor, co York, b Sept 1823, d
23 Oct 1882, m 21 Sept 1842, Anna F J, da of Capt Lanford Burne, 3rd
Dragoon Guards, d 4 Mar 1896, and had issue 1d to 5d

1d Robert Maxwell Thoroton D'Arcy Hildyard of Coburn, Capt 68th Durham
L I, b 4 Oct 1867, d 11 Mar 1907, m Gertrude Mary (Coburn Manor, near
Richmond, Yorks), da of Edward Burdon, and had issue 1e to 3e

   1e Robert Vernon Saville D'Arcy Hildyard of Coburn Manor, b 2 Ap 1901
   2e Christopher John Ross Thoroton D'Arcy Hildyard, b 27 Jan 1907

2d Wilhelmina Catharine Hildyard, d 1896, m Charles Irwin, Royal Irish
Fusiliers, d (–), and has issue 1e to 4e

   1e Charles Irwin
   2e Frederick Irwin
   3e Annie Irwin
   4e Marie Elsie Irwin, m 1 Oct 1901, William Ashford, M D (Riversmeet,
Topsham, R S O, Devon), and has issue 1f
    1f Christopher Lee Ashford, b 4 Aug 1908

3d Anne Catharine Hildyard, d 1906, m 31 Aug 1871, Robert Charles
Thoroton Hildyard (see above), d 25 Jan 1885, and had issue
   See above, Nos 41901–41903

1d Mary Hildyard, m Major Charles Urquhart, late 87th Regt, d Nov 1909,
and has issue 1e to 2e
   1e Charles Frederick Urquhart, b (–), m Sybil, da of (–) Betherton
   2e Florence Urquhart, m Col Henry Denne Robson, formerly Col Comdg
Queen's Regt

5d Florence Sophia Ann Hildyard (Varnes, Lympstone, Devon), m 16 Nov
1886, Col William Robert Purchas, R E, d 23 Oct 1909, and has issue 1e to 2e
   1e Annie Florence Emily Purchas
   2e Dorothy Marian Purchas

3c Henry Charles Hildyard, d (?s p)
4c John George Bowes Hildyard of Winestead, J P (Cherry Burton House,
                        [Nos 41901 to 41929

The Plantagenet Roll

Hull), *b* 8 June 1828, *m* 12 Feb 1857, Caroline, da of Robert Dennison of Wapling-ton Manor, co York, *d* 5 Jan 1894, and has issue (with 2 sons who *d s p*) 1*d* to 2*d*

    1*d* Mabel Hildyard

    2*d* Evelyn Caroline Hildyard

    5*c* *Anne Catharine Hildyard*, d (? unm)

    6*c* Mary Anne Hildyard

    7*c* *Elizabeth Frances Hildyard*, d 3 Ap 1894, m 17 Mar 1741, *Sir John Charles Thorold, 11th Bt [E]*, b 26 June 1816, d 26 Ap 1866, and had issue (with a 4th son and da who *d s p*) 1*d* to 4*d*

    1*d* Sir John Henry Thorold, 12th Bt. [E], Hon LL D (Camb), J P, D L, High Sheriff co Linc 1876 and M P for Grantham 1865-1868 (*Syston Park, near Grantham Carlton*), b 9 Mar 1842, m 3 Feb 1869, the Hon Alexandrina Henrietta Matilda [descended from the Lady Anne, sister of King Edward IV, &c], da of Henry (Willoughby) 8th Baron Middleton [G B], and has issue

    See the Exeter Volume, p 613, Nos 52198-52203

    2*d* Montagu George Thorold, *formerly* Mid R N (*Honington Hall, Grantham, 1 Abbot s Court, Kensington Square, W*), b 23 Aug 1845, m 2 July 1881, Emmeline Laura, Dowager Lady Rivers [U K], da of Capt John Pownell Bastard (see p 73)

    3*d* *Cecil Thorold of Boothby*, co Linc, J P, D L, Capt 1st Life Guards, b 5 Oct 1847, d 26 Feb 1895, m 2 Sept 1875, *Anne Charlotte, da of Gen Edward Stopford Claremont, C B* [who m 2ndly, 25 Sept 1902, Ralph Henry Seymour Hall, d 29 Jan 1903], and had issue 1*c*

    1*c* Marguerite Thorold, m 21 Sept 1897, the Hon Maurice Raymond Gifford, C M G [4th son of Robert Francis, 2nd Baron Gifford [U K], and descended mater-nally from King Henry VII (see the Tudor Roll, p 170)] (*Boothby Hall, Grantham*) and has issue 1*f* to 4*f*

    1*f* Charles Maurice Elton Gifford, b 4 Mar 1899

    2*f* Diana Frederica Gifford

    3*f* Joan Gifford

    4*f* Vera Mary Gifford

    4*d* Edith Mary Thorold (9 *Wilbraham Place, S W*)

    8*c* Esther Sophia Hildyard   [Nos 41930 to 41947

185 Descendants of JAMES DARCY of Sedbury Park, co York, M P (Table XX), *b c* 1621, *d* (–); *m* ISABEL, da of Sir Marmaduke WYVILL, 2nd Bt. [E], and had issue

    See the Exeter Volume, Table LII, and pp 554-558, Nos 49657-49747

                              [Nos 41948 to 42038

186 Descendants of the Hon BARBARA DARCY (Table XX), *b* 3 May 1600, *bur* 31 Mar 1696, *m* 22 Ap 1617, MATTHEW HUTTON of Marske, co. York, a well-known Royalist, *b* 20 Oct 1597 *d* (–), and had issue 1*a* to 7*a*

    1*a* *John Hutton of Marske*, b 6 Oct 1625, d 21 Mar 1664, m (Articles dated 13 Sept) 1651, *Frances, da of Bryan Stapylton of Myton, co York*, bur 5 May 1684, and had issue

    See p 120, Nos 10978-11168

    2*a* *Dorothy Hutton*, b 22 July 1620, bur (?) 6 Aug 1644, m *as 1st wife, Sir Philip Warwick*

    3*a* *Elizabeth Hutton* b at Richmond 4 Mar 1630

    4*a* *Barbara Hutton*, b at Richmond 23 Oct (? Nov) 1630, m at Marske 16 25 Ap 1655, *Thomas Lister of Bawtry and of the Inner Templ.*, d at Bawtry 4 May 1670   [Nos 42039 to 42229

# of The Blood Royal

5a *Mary Hutton*, b at Marske 4 Feb 1637, m at Richmond a 1662 (not 12 June 1663), *Richard Peirse of Hutton Bonville*, and had issue 1b to 1b

1b *John Peirse of Lasenby Hall*, co York, b 1662, d s p 5 Oct 1694, m *Elizabeth*, da of Sir Henry Marwood, Bt, d 26 Mar 1726, and had issue 1c to 3c

1c *Henry Peirse of Bedale*, M P, b 1692, d. 1759, m *Anne*, da of (—) *Johnson*, and had issue 1d to 2d

1d *Henry Peirse of Bedale and Hutton Bonville*, M P, b 1754, d 1824, m 16 Aug 1777, *the Hon Charlotte Grace*, da of John (Monson), 2nd Baron Monson [G B], d 19 July 1793, and had issue

See the Exeter Volume, pp 244-246, Nos 9156-9241

2d *Anne Peirse*, d 6 Ap 1809, m *John Sawrey Morritt of Rokeby Park*, co York, d 3 Aug 1791, and had issue 1e to 2e

1e *John Bacon Sawrey Morritt of Rokeby Park*, M P, the well-known classical scholar and traveller, b 1771, d s p 12 July 1843

2e *Rev Henry Morritt*, d (—), m *Alice Margaret*, da of the Rev F Cookson, Vicar of Leeds, and had issue (with a da, Mrs Hely Hutchinson, d s p) 1f to 2f

1f *William John Sawrey Morritt of Rokeby Park*, M P, b 12 Sept 1815, d s p 13 Ap 1874

2f *Robert Ambrose Morritt of Rokeby Park*, J P, D L, b 9 May 1816, d 1890, m 11 Ap 1872, *Mary Blanche Mitchell* [a descendant of King Henry VII (see the Tudor Roll, p 550)], da of Alexander Mitchell Innes of Ayton Castle [by his wife Charlotte, da of Sir Thomas Dick Lauder, 7th Bt [S 1690], and had issue (with 2 sons d s p) 1g to 5g

1g *Henry Edward Morritt of Rokeby Park*, Lieut Royal Warwickshire Regt (Rokeby Park, Barnard Castle, Colton Lodge, Tadcaster, 17 Southwell Gardens, S W), b 3 Mar 1880, m 1903, Grace Lillia, da of (—) Chapman of Highland Park, Illinois

2g Charlotte Greta Morritt.

3g Florence Catherine Morritt

4g Hilda Mary Morritt

5g Linda Beatrice Morritt.

2c *Mary Peirse*, b 1686 [1]

3c *Dorothy Peirse*, b 1693 [1]

2b *Thomas Peirse of Hutton Bonville and Thimbleby*, will dated 9 Sept 1720, prov 9 June 1725, m 2 Ap 1700, Anne [descended from the Lady Anne, sister of King Edward IV (see the Exeter Volume, Table XVII)], da and co-h of Sir William Hustler of Acklam, d Dec 1758, and had issue (with others known to have d s p) 1c to 7c

1c *William Peirse of Hutton Bonville and Thimbleby*, bur 29 Jan 1753, m 1726, Dorothy [sister of Joseph, and] da of (—) Stillington of Kelfield, co York, and had issue 1d

1d *Mary Peirse*, da and event h, m the Rev Edward Stillingfleet of West Bromwich, co Stafford

2c *Richard Peirse of Hutton Bonville and Thimbleby*, d 26 June 1759, m Rachel [sister of William, and] da of (—) Bayne, d 24 Jan 1771, and had issue 1d to 2d

1d *Richard William Peirse of Hutton Bonville*, &c, b 20 Jan 1753, d 25 Nov 1798, m 1780, *Elizabeth*, da of Christopher Fawcett of Newcastle-on-Tyne, d 3 Sept 1791, and had issue 1e to 3e

1e *Richard William Christopher Peirse of Thimbleby Lodge*, b 28 June 1784, d 18 Dec 1844, m 29 Aug 1803, Maroa, da of the Rev Richard Clarke of Bedale, d 20 Aug 1859, and had issue 1f to 4f   [Nos 12230 to 12323]

---

[1] Foster's "Yorkshire Families"

The Plantagenet Roll

1*f* *Richard William Pearse of Northallerton, Capt 3rd Dragoon Guards and afterwards Registrar of Deeds for the North Riding,* b 14 Aug 1804, d 24 *July* 1872, m 23 Oct 1831, *Mary Anne Eliza, widow of J S Highatt of Lower Cheve, near Exeter, da of John Tharp of Chippenham Park, co Camb , and had issue* 1g

1*g* Arabella Georgina Pearse, d∴ and h , m. 27 July 1853, George Thomas Duncombe, now (R L 12 July 1887) Pearse-Duncombe of Winthorpe Hall, *formerly* Capt 11th Hussars, &c [nephew of Charles, 1st Lord Feversham, and a descendant of the Lady Anne, sister of King Edward IV (see the Exeter Volume, p 650)] (*Winthorpe Hall, Newark, 25 Queen's Gate, S W*) , and has issue (with a son and 2 das d unm) 1*h* to 8*h*

1*h* Charles Slingsby Pearse-Duncombe, b 18 May 1870

2*h* Richard Slingsby Pearse Duncombe, b 25 Aug 1872, m 1898, Josephine, da of (—) Foster

3*h* Elizabeth Slingsby Pearse-Duncombe

4*h* Georgiana Slingsby Pearse-Duncombe

5*h* Edith Slingsby Pearse-Duncombe

6*h* Ruth Slingsby Pearse-Duncombe, m 5 May 1892, Comm Richard Nigel Gresley, R N [Lt Coll] (*Ivy House Barton-under-Needwood, Burton-on-Trent*), and has issue 1*i* to 2*i*

1*i* Roger Gresley, b 26 Feb 1895

2*i* Dorothy Gresley

7*h* Mildred Slingsby Pearse-Duncombe, m 30 July 1888, Thomas Herbert Bindley, and has issue 1*i* to 2*i*

1*i* Herbert Duncombe Bindley, b 8 Feb 1891

2*i* Mildred Duncombe Bindley

8*h* Winifred Slingsby Pearse-Duncombe, *unm*

2*f* *Charles Milbank Pearse,* b 27 Aug 1811, d (-) m 1844, (—), *da of John George of co Kent*

3*f* *Ashford George Pearse,* b 6 Nov 1814, d 6 June 1873 m c 1842, *Marianna Emma, da of Major Brooke of Littlethorp, near Ripon , and had issue* (a da [1])

4*f* *Harriet Jane Pearse,* d (-), m 28 Feb 1832, *Henry Claridge of Jervaulx Abbey, co York and had issue*

2*c* *James Pearse, Lieut 23rd Foot,* b 12 Nov 1782, d *abroad Mar* 1813, m 9 July 1807 *Sophia, da of the Rev Richard Clarke of Bedale, d abroad and had issue*

3 *Elizabeth Peirse,* d (-), m 12 Oct 1812, *the Rev George Ford Clarke of Thornton Watlass co York*

2*d* *Anne Pearse,* b 15 Oct 1751, m *Joseph Williamson of Melton Hall, co York*

3*c* *Thomas Pearse, afterwards* (R L 8 May 1784) *Hustler, of Acklam, co York,* d 1784 m 2dly at York, 10 Feb 1769, *Constance, da of Ralph Hutton of Knapton* [by his wife, Constance, da of Sir Francis Boynton, 4th Bt [E 1618], M P] *and had issue*

See the Exeter Volume, pp 702-703, Nos 58067-58078

4*c* *Anne Peirse,* m *Richard Hodson of Witton-le-Wear, co Durham*

5*c* *Mary Peirse,* m 6 Feb 1728, *Joseph Stillington of Kelfield, co York*

6*c* *Dorothy Peirse*

7*c* *Elizabeth Peirse*

3*b* *Barbara* [2] *Peirse,* bur *at Bolton-on-Swale* 8 Oct 1690, m as 1st *wife at*
[Nos 42324 to 42348

---

[1] Foster's " Yorkshire Families "

[2] Not Katherine, as in Foster

# of The Blood Royal

Danby Wiske 13 *June* 1682, *John Wastell of Bolton-on-Swale and Ainderby Steeple* [*son of Leonard Wastell of Scorton, co York*] b 23 *Jan* 1660, bur 25 *Oct* 1738, *and had issue (with 3 sons, whose issue is extinct)* 1c *to* 3c

1c *John Wastell of London, Merchant*, b 21 *June* 1686, d *in Jamaica* 1717 m *Annabella, da of Thomas Williams, and had issue (with a son Philip*, d s p) 1d *to* 5d

1d *Elizabeth Wastell*, d 1774 m *at the Chapel Royal Whitehall*, 6 *Dec* 1748, *Gen Sir Philip Honeywood, K C B, Governor of Hull*, d 17 *June* 1752

2d *Barbara Wastell*, m (—) *O'Brien*

3d *Audrey Wastell*

4d *Mary Wastell*

5d *Catherine Wastell*, m (—) *Cotton*

2c *Rev Henry Wastell, M A (Camb), Rector of Simonburn, co Northbd*, b 19 *Feb* 1689, d 1771, m 1734, *Frances, da of William Bacon of Steward Peel, co Northbd*, d 1748, *and had issue (with an elder son d unm)* 1d *to* 3d

1d *John Wastell of Ainderby, co York, and Risby, co Suffolk, J P, D L, Winner of the Oakes* 1802, b 1736, d 1 *Dec* 1811, m *Hannah, da of* (—) *Chicken*, d *Oct* 1831, *and had issue (with 3 das of whom no issue survives)* 1e

1e *Rev John Daniel Wastell of Risby*, b 20 *July* 1782, bur 20 *July* 1874, m *Frances* (see p 316), *da of Bacon William Wastell*, d 26 *Aug* 1851, *and had issue (with 3 sons d unm)* 1f *to* 3f

1f *Eleanora Wastell, da and co h*, b c 1812, d 24 *Dec* 1838, m *as 1st wife, Thomas Stubbs Walker of Maunby, co York, and had issue* 1g *to* 2g

1g *Thomas Stubbs Walker of Maunby Hall*, b c 1840, d 11 *Jan* 1878 m 1st, 9 *Ap* 1861, *Jane, da of J G Lamb of Ryton, co Durham*, d 6 *July* 1865, 2ndly, 15 *Oct* 1867, *Mariann, da of Lawrence Oliphant of Condie and Newton, co Perth, M P, J P, D L* d 5 *Nov* 1903, *and had issue (with 2 sons by 2nd wife, Thomas Gerald, d unm at Cape Town during the S African War* 12 *May* 1901, *and Harry Grenville, d unm in British Columbia* 20 *Mar* 1898) 1h *to* 4h

1h¹ *Violet Eleanor Walker*, "*Sister Violet*" (*St Hilda's Home, Paddington*)

2h¹ *Constance Helen Walker, unm*

3h¹ *Florence Jane Walker*, m 20 *July* 1897, *the Rev Percy Wonnacott, Vicar of Waltham Cross* (*Waltham Cross Vicarage, Herts*), s p

4h² *Muriel Lilias Walker*, m 12 *Ap* 1902, *her cousin, Major Alan Hill Walker, V C* (see below) (*Maunby Hall, Thirsk*), *and has issue* 1i *to* 2i

1i *Gerald Alan Hill-Walker*, b 4 *Jan* 1903

2i *Thomas Harry Hill-Walker*, b 29 *Aug* 1904

2g *Frances Miriam Walker*, b 25 *July* 1835, d 30 *Ap* 1901 m 18 *Aug* 1858, *Capt Thomas Hill, Chief Constable of the North Riding* 1859–1898 [*son of Richard Hill of the Hall, Thornton, Pickering*], b 8 *Sept* 1822, d 5 *Nov* 1899, *and had issue (with a da d young)* 1h *to* 3h

1h *Alan Hill, now* (D P 10 *May* 1902) *Hill-Walker of Maunby Hall, V C, Major late Northants Regt, served at Lang's Neck, &c* (*Maunby Hall, Thirsk*), b 12 *July* 1859, m 12 *Ap* 1902, *his cousin, Muriel Lilias, da and co h of Thomas Stubbs Walker of Maunby Hall, and has issue*

See above, Nos 12353–42354

2h *Cecil Hill, Col R E* (*Wood Hill, Cork*), b 25 *Oct* 1861, m 30 *Nov* 1893, *Edith, da of Charles Lambert, and has issue* 1i

1i *Cecil Vivian Hill*, b 3 *Nov* 1908

3h *Maude Hill*, "*Sister Maude*" (*St Mary's Home, Wantage*)

2f *Frances Wastell, da and co-h*, b 13 *Feb* 1813 d 26 *Dec* 1858, m *as 1st wife*, 19 *July* 1836, *William Whytehead of York*, d 20 *Jan* 1888, *and had issue (with 2 sons and 3 das d s p)* 1g *to* 7g

1g *Thomas Bowman Whytehead*, b 16 *Mar* 1840, d 5 *Sept* 1907, m *at*

[Nos 42349 to 12360

The Plantagenet Roll

Auckland, N Z , 15 Sept 1870, *Caroline Forster* (24 *Gondar Gardens, West Hampstead) da of the Rev Thomas Drought of Punkstown House, co Kildare , and had issue (with an eldest son, William Wastell Drought, who fell in action in S Africa, 20 Ap* 1900) *1h to 8h*

 1h Thomas Bowman Henry Whytehead, Merchant Service, British India Coy , Bombay, *b* 22 Oct 1872 , *m* 12 Dec 1907, Harriet Emma (see p 245), da of the Rev William Webster Hawkins of Acomb , and has issue 1i

  1i Nancy Bowman Whytehead

 2h Hugh Richard Augustine Whytehead, Indian Army, *b* 17 May 1881 *unm*

 3h Christopher John Wastell Whytehead, *b* 26 Aug 1887

 4h Lionel Wanley Wastell Whytehead, *b* 3 Sept 1892

 5h Eleanora Frances Drought Whytehead

 6h Mary Alice Bayly Whytehead

 7h Isabella Margaretta Eliza Wastell Whytehead, *m* 3 Sept 1902, Herbert John Watson [eldest son of H E Watson of Petworth] (*St Helen's, Cockermouth*), and has issue 1i

  1i John Alexander Watson, *b* 29 May 1903

 8h Caroline Louisa Hinemoa Drought Whytehead

 2g William Wastell Whytehead, *b* 6 Feb 1848 , *m* 14 Aug 1889, Jessie, da of William Whytehead Boulton of Highgate House, Beverley , *s p*

 3g Rev Henry Robert Whytehead, M A (Camb), Vicar of Warminster (*The Vicarage, Warminster*), *b* 10 Oct 1849 , *m* 6 Sept 1876 Sarah May Louise [also descended from Edward III through Mortimer-Percy (see p 474)] da of the Rev Charles Clement Layard, and has issue (with an elder son, the Rev Wastell Layard, who *d unm* 1903) *1h to 3h*

  1h Henry Layard Whytehead *b* 31 May 1879

  2h John Layard Whytehead, *b* 19 Oct 1880

  3h Rev Ralph Layard Whytehead St John's Coll Oxon (*Church Road, Ilfracombe*), *b* 3 Oct 1883

 4g *Hugh Edward Whytehead, b* 30 Mar 1851 , *d* 11 *June* 1901, *m* 20 Jan 1886, *Maud, da of* (—) *Holtom, M D , and had issue 1h to 3h*

  1h Hugh Holtom Whytehead, *b* 11 Aug 1895

  2h Gladys Holtom Whytehead

  3h Doris Holtom Whytehead

 5g Alice Whytehead, *m* 6 June 1872, Arthur Horatio Poyser, M A (Oxon), Bar-at-Law (*Burniston, Sydenham, Kent*), and has issue 1h to 5h

  1h Arthur Hampden Ronald Wastell Poyser, B A (Oxon), Bar-at-Law, *b* 30 Sept 1884

  2h Alice Ianthe Poyser

  3h Ina Frances Poyser, *m* 6 June 1900, Gerald Edgell Mills, Bar-at-Law [2nd son of Sir Richard Mills, K C B , K C V O] (*Risby, Sanderstead, Surrey*) , and has issue 1i to 3i

   1i Gerald Hilary Mytton Mills, *b* 7 Jan 1904

   2i David Richard Poyser Mills, *b* 1 Mar 1907

   3i Ina Iris Mills

  4h Irene Grace Poyser *unm*

  5h Gwladys Isabelle Poyser, *m* 6 June 1901, Henry Clendon Dukes [2nd son of the Rev S Whitfield Dukes] (*Summer Hill, Norbury*)

 6g Louisa Frances Whytehead, *m* 6 June 1872, the Rev Canon Benjamin Lamb, Vicar of Clapham (*Clapham Vicarage, Lancaster*) and has issue (with 2 das *d unm*) 1h to 8h

  1h Rev Gilbert Henry Lamb, B A (Camb) (*Tuticorin, South India*), *b* 14 Sept 1875 , *unm*

[Nos 42361 to 42389

# of The Blood Royal

2*h* Charles Edward Lamb, Solicitor (*Vincent House, Kettering*), *b* 1 July 1878
m 19 Nov 1902, Alice, da of Samuel Hey, J P, F R C S, and has issue 1*i*

    1*i* Florence Mary Lamb, *b* 15 Sept 1904

3*h* Percy Hutchinson Lamb, Acting Govt Super of Cotton Culture, Uganda,
b 6 May 1883, *unm*

4*h* Harold Victor Lamb, *b* 6 May 1883, *unm*

5*h* Jesse Lamb, Physician and Surgeon (*Tarn Taran, India*), *unm*

6*h* Louisa Whytehead Lamb,

7*h* Maud Lamb,   } *unm*

8*h* Alice Margaret Lamb,

7*g* Emmeline Finny Whytehead *m* 12 Aug 1880, Marcus Valentine English
(*Orton Longueville, Peterborough*), and has issue 1*h* to 6*h*

    1*h* Marcus Claude English, B A (Camb), *b* 8 May 1886

    2*h* Guy Whytehead English, *b* 28 July 1888

    3*h* Reginald Wastell English, *b* 12 Ap. 1894

    4*h* Margaret English

    5*h* Olave English

    6*h* Phyllis English

3*f* *Mary Wastell*, *b* 18 May 1815 d 24 July 1863, *m* 24 Aug 1843, *John
Worlledge, M A (Camb). County Court Judge for Suffolk and Chancellor of the
Diocese of Norwich*, *b* 2 June 1809, d 19 July 1881 and had issue (with 2 sons
and a da d s p) 1*g* to 3*g*

1*g* Rev Arthur John Worlledge M A (Camb), Canon and Chancellor of
Truro Cathedral (*Truro*), *b* 29 May 1848, *unm*

2*g* Edward William Worlledge, M A (Camb), Solicitor and Registrar of
Yarmouth County Court (10 *Albert Square, Great Yarmouth*), *b* 27 Jan 1850, *m*
1 June 1876, Edith Georgiana, da of the Rev William Wigston, Vicar of Rushmere
St Andrew, Ipswich, and had issue (with 2 sons, Cyril Edward, *b* 15 July 1877,
d 5 Feb 1893, and Noel Arthur, Lieut 75th Carnatic Inf, *b* 23 May 1883, d
unm 7 Ap 1908) 1*h* to 3*h*

    1*h* Audrey Mary Worlledge

    2*h* Edith Cicely Worlledge

    3*h* Olive Margaret Worlledge

3*g* *Alfred Cranworth Worlledge* Major 4 P D, *b* 15 Nov 1857, d 24 Dec
1903, *m* 18 June 1885, Annabella Mary Garnons, da of the Rev Preb Garnons
Williams, d 18 Feb 1908, and had issue 1*h*

    1*h* John Penry Garnons Worlledge, Lieut R E, *b* 22 Sept 1887

2*d* *Henry Wastell of Newburgh*, d (-), *m* Anne, *widow of Middleton
Teisdale, da and coh of John Bacon [by his wife Jane, da and h of John Marshall
of Walltown]*, and had issue 1*e*

1*e* *Rev Henry Wastell of Walltown and Newburgh, co Northbd, Fellow of Clare
Hall, Oxon*, d (-), *m* Anne, da of (—) Henderson, d (-), and had issue 1*f*

1*f* *Anne Lindsay Wastell of Newburgh Hall, da and h*, d 12 May 1884, *m*
19 Dec 1843, *Gustavus Hamilton Coulson of Stonehouse, co Cumb, Capt R N,
J P, D L*, d 23 Nov 1868, and had issue 1*g* to 7*g*

1*g* Henry John Wastell Coulson of Walltown, J P, Bar-at-Law (*Langton
Lodge, Blandford*), *b* 13 Nov 1848 *m* 14 July 1875, Caroline Stewart, da of Henry
Unwin of the Bengal C S, and has issue (with a son, Gustavus Hamilton Blenkinsopp,
V C, D S O, Lieut King's Own Scottish Borderers, killed *unm* in action at Lam-
brechfontein 19 May 1901) 1*h* to 3*h*

    1*h* Florence Lindsay Coulson

2*h* Isabel Forbes Coulson, *m* 24 July 1902, Lisle March Philipps, *formerly*
Capt Remington's Guides

3*h* Inez Lisle Coulson, *m* 24 Ap 1906, Lieut Edward Tyrrell Inman, R N

[Nos 42390 to 42414

2*g* Anne Alicia Coulson

3*g* Mary Arabella Coulson

4*g* Frances Jane Wastell Coulson, *m* 10 Oct. 1876, Arthur Hamilton Unwin, B C S , and has issue

5*g* Theodosia Hamilton Coulson

6*g* Maud Maria Lisle Coulson

7*g* Margaret Lindsay Coulson

3*d Bacon William Wastell*, b 1740, d *Nov* 1821, m *Eleanor, da of William Fetherstonhaugh*, d 6 *Mar* 1818, *and had issue* 1*e to* 3*e*

1*e Mary Wastell*, m *John Forster*

2*e Eleanor Wastell*, m *William Hodgson*

3*e Frances Wastell*, b 1781, d 26 *Aug* 1851, m *the Rev John Daniel Wastell*, *and had issue*

See p 313 Nos 42349–42410

3*e Elizabeth Wastell*, bapt 22 *Sept* 1690, d a 1731, m *at York Minster*, 30 *Dec* 1712, *Christopher Bayles of Laxton, Chamberlain* (1714) *and Sheriff* (1717) *of Hull*, d 1744, *and had issue* 1*d*

1*d Deborah Bayles, da and event sole h*, b 1724, d 1782, m *at Dryfool, co York*, 12 *Aug* 1746, *Michael Inman of Beverley, Nidderdale*, d 1784, *and had issue* 1*e to* 2*e*

1*e Christopher Inman, afterwards Inman Whaley Bayles*, bapt 30 *Nov* 1748, d 8 Oct 1801 m *at St Saviour s, Jersey*, 12 May 1786, *Marie, da of Noe Gautier of St Helier, Jersey*, d 11 *Nov* 1843, *and had issue* (with 4 other sons who d *unm*) 1*f to* 2*f*

1*f Wastell Edwin Bayles*, b 25 *July* 1787, d 19 *Sept* 1868, m *Ann Luard, da of* (—) *Robert*, d 15 *Sept* 1865, *and had issue* (with 2 sons and 2 das who d s p) 1*g*

1*g Martha Bayles, unm*

2*f Gascoigne Noe Edwin Bayles of Guernsey* b 1793, d 3 *July* 1860, m *at St Peter Port*, 11 *Feb* 1826, *Charlotte, da of John Grut of Guernsey*, d 18 Oct 1882, *and had issue* (with a son d s p) 1*g to* 3*g*

1*g Mary Gautier Bayles*, b 23 *Mar* 1836; d 26 *Mar* 1896, m 17 *Aug* 1860, *the Rev Alfred John French, B A* (*Lond*) (*Grangewood, Princes Avenue, West Kirby*), *and had issue* (with a da d young) 1*h to* 9*h*

1*h Alfred Stead French*, b 13 Oct 1868

2*h. Herbert Noel French*, b 28 Feb 1871

3*h Reginald Ernest French*, b 17 Feb 1874

4*h Rosa Maria French*

5*h Marian Algeo French*

6*h Eliza Pulsford French*, b 6 *June* 1861, d 24 *Nov* 1903 m 5 *June* 1891, *John Howe Bourne* (*Montarina, Sea Bank Road, Liscard, Cheshire*), *and had issue* 1*i to* 2*i*

1*i John Pulsford Bourne*, b 12 *Nov* 1898

2*i Hilda Caroline Bourne*

7*h Emily Birchenall French*

8*h. Eleanor Elizabeth French*

9*h Maud Mary French*

2*g* Louise Charlotte Bayles, *m* John Fisher Le Page of Manchester and Cheadle, M D [son of William Le Page of Guernsey] (*The Poplars, Cheadle, Manchester*), and has issue 1*h* to 4*h*

1*h John Herbert Perceval De Jersey Le Page*, d young,

2*h Florence Bertha Louise De Wilton Le Page, M A*, unm

3*h Ethel Mabel Beatrice De Jersey Le Page*,

4*h Winifred Maud Mary d'Estelle Le Page*,

[Nos 42415 to 42497

316

# of The Blood Royal

3g Rose Algeo Bayles, b 8 May 1839, d 21 Ap 1886, m 14 Nov 1865 th.
Rev Edwin Webster, d 1892 and had issue (with a son d s p and 2 das d in
infancy) 1h to 7h

    1h Walter Pulsford Webster, b 10 Oct 1870, unm

    2h Howard Buchenall Webster, b 5 Mar 1875, unm

    3h Charles Frederick Smythe Webster, b 21 Dec 1880, unm

    4h Mary Gautier Webster, unm

    5h Elizabeth Overton Webster, unm

    6h Laura Inman Webster, m 28 Ap 1900, James MacKenzie, Engineer, H M
Postal Telegraph Dept (67 Langholm Crescent Darlington), and has issue 1i

        1i James Walter MacKenzie, b 14 July 1900

    7h Mabel Gwendoline Allen Webster

2e Whaley Charles Inman, b at Kingston-on-Hull b Aug 1751 d 1826, m
5 Sept /19 Dec 1783, Mary, da of (—) Oliver, d 1807, and had issue (with 4 sons
and a da d unm) 1f to 2f

    1f Deborah Inman, bapt at Bedale 25 May 1785 d 1826, m at Bedale
21 Dec 1808, the Rev Richard Inman, Rector of Todwick, near Sheffield, for
fifty years, bun 1826, and had issue (with 1 sons and 5 das who d s p) 1g
to 5g

        1g Rev Thomas Inman, B A, b 11 Nov 1818 d 12 Jan 1894, m Dec
1850, Lavinia Louisa, da of Col Burton, d 24 May 1856, and had issue (with a
da drowned at sea) 1h to 2h

            1h Lavinia Wyat Inman (Lanark Street, Balclutha, Otago, New Zealand) b
4 Nov 1851, m 16 Nov 1880, Andrew Purves of Kirkcaldy, co Fife, b 7 Dec
1844, d 12 Dec 1907, and has issue 1i to 3i

                1i Andrew Hope Purves, Watchmaker's Assistant, b 21 June 1883

                2i Thomas Burton Purves, University Student, Dunedin, formerly Headmaster
of Kelso School, N Z, b 14 July 1885, m 27 Jan 1908, Margaret, da of John
Faddes, and has issue 1j

                    1j Eva Mary Purves, b 16 Mar 1909

                3i Charles Evans Purves, Cycle Mechanic, b 30 June 1887, unm

            2h Mary Charlotte Inman (The Wilderness, Mitcheldean, Glos), unm

        2g Richard Inman of Manitoba, d (—). m Mary Ann, da of (—), and had
issue (a son and da) 1h to 2h

            1h Herbert Inman of Hamilton, Manitoba, b 30 Mar 1848, d 1903, m (—)
(Hamilton Manitoba), da of (—), and had issue (3 sons and 1 da)

            2h Marion Inman, d (-), m (—) Way of Australia, M D, and had issue
(2 sons and 2 das)

3g Mary Inman, b 15 Dec 1810, d 1 Mar 1892 m 5 Ap 1839, the Rev
Henry Austin Oram, b 17 Mar 1813, d 19 Feb 1880, and had issue (with a son
and 3 das d unm) 1h to 4h

    1h Rev Reginald Austin Oram, M A (Camb), Rector of Weeting (Weeting
Rectory Brandon, Suffolk), b 3 Jan 1846, m 14 July 1881, Fanny Forbes Becher,
da of Major-Gen Saxton, and has issue 1i to 2i

        1i Gladys Mary Oram

        2i Eileen Margaret Oram

    2h Catharine Inman Oram, b 9 Jan 1840, d 12 Ap 1909, m 28 Feb 1867,
Mander John Smyth (Bowles Lodge, Colchester), and had issue 1i to 9i

        1i Reginald Mander Smyth, M D (Linford Sanatorium), b (—), m June 1900,
Gladys, da of (—) Black-Hawkins, d s p Feb 1910

        2i Charles Inman Smyth (Highfield, Compton, Wolverhampton), b 12 Dec
1868, m Jessie, da of (—), and has issue 1j to 2j

            1j Kenneth Bowes Inman Smyth, b 31 Jan 1907

            2j Beatrice Lesbia Smyth, b 17 Aug 1908   [Nos 12498 to 12518

The Plantagenet Roll

3i Sydney Fairfax Smyth (*Livingstone Road, Hounslow*), b 13 Ap 1877, m 6 Jan 1898, Mary, da of (—) M'Carthy, and has issue 1j to 2j

    1j John Fairfax Smyth, b 28 Oct 1898

    2j Christine May Smyth, b 28 May 1900

    4i Sophia Smyth, *unm*

    5i Christine Smyth, *unm*

    6i Rachel Smyth, *unm*

    7i Janet Smyth, *unm*

    8i Dora Smyth, *unm*

    9i Gertrude Smyth, m Vincent Cook, and has issue 1j

    1j Phyllis Cook

3h Frances Lucy Oram, m 16 Jan 1873, the Rev Benjamin Hunter, B A (London), Vicar of Aukborough, *formerly* (1864–1870) a Solicitor (*Aukborough Vicarage, Doncaster*), and has issue 1i to 9i

    1i Herbert Austin Hunter (*West Hartlepool, Durham*), b 18 Jan 1875, m 27 Aug 1904, Annie, da of Robert Brown of Scarborough, and has issue 1j to 3j

        1j Oram Hunter, b 11 Mar 1907

        2j Marjory Eileen Hunter, b 9 Oct 1905

        3j Lucy Mabel Hunter, b 31 Oct 1908

    2i Edward William Baptist Hunter, b 24 June 1878, *unm*

    3i Marcus Charles Inman Hunter (*The Firs, Station Road, Bedford*), b 23 May 1882, m 27 July 1909, Edith Emily, da of (—) Cornelius

    4i Benjamin D'Arcy Hunter, b 26 June 1885, *unm*

    5i Helen Mary Hunter (*Papakaio, Oamaru, Otago, N Z*), *unm*

    6i Kate Angela Hunter, *unm*

    7i Annie Christabel Hunter, *unm*

    8i Lily Lucy Hunter, *unm*

    9i Dorothy Hunter, *unm*

4h Anne Elizabeth Oram (*Margaret Lodge, West Lyss, Hants*), m 20 Oct 1880, the Rev Charles Somes Saxton, M A, Rector of Beechamwell [eldest son of Major Gen Saxton], d 14 Jan 1893, and has issue 1i

    1i Walter Theodore Saxton, M A, F L S (South African College, Cape Town), b 16 Oct 1882, m 19 Dec 1906, Dorothy, da of the Rev E Apthorpe, and has issue 1j

        1j Dorothy Joyce Saxton, b 20 Sept 1908

4g Barbara Inman (*Oxford Parade, Cheltenham*), b 27 Oct 1816, living aged 94, *unm*

5g Annie Inman, b 6 Oct 1823, d 29 Dec 1905, m 7 Sep 1851, the Rev Anthony Edwards, Vicar of All Saints, Leeds, d 29 Mar 1874, and had issue 1h to 3h

    1h Ambrose Cadwallader Edwards, b 27 June 1858 ⎫ (21 *Prince of Wales*
    2h Anne Orah Edwards, *unm*   ⎬ *Terrace, Scarborough*)
    3h Kathleen Edwards, *unm*   ⎭

2f Barbara Inman, bapt at Bedale 22 Feb 1789, d Nov 1877, m at Bedale 23 July 1808, James Orton, M D, President of the Bombay Medical Board [son of the Rev James Orton of Hawkeswell, co York], b 20 Ap 1781, d Feb 1856, and had issue 1g to 4g

    1g Reginald Orton of Sunderland, Surgeon, b 27 Jan 1810, d 1 Sept 1862, m 1st, 4 Oct 1836, Caroline Agnes, da of Orton Bradley-Bradley, d (-), 2ndly, 25 Mar 1841, Mary Isabella, da of Turner Thompson, and had issue (*with others who d s p*) 1h to 4h

        1h¹ Reginald Orton, settled in New Zealand, b 22 Mar 1839, d 9 July 1895, m 2 Dec 1865, Jeannie (*The Bungalow, Pleasant Point, Timaru, Canterbury, N Z*), da of S Manson, and had issue 1i to 11i

            1i Reginald Orton (*Geraldine, N Z*), b 11 Sept 1866, m 17 June 1889, Rachel, da of W Ashby, and has issue 1j

                1j Isabella Jean Orton, b 13 Oct 1890   [Nos 12519 to 12550

2ı Malcolm Orton, Huntsman (*Claremont, Canterbury, N Z*), *b* 21 July 1871, *m* 1891, Louisa, da of W Cookson, and has issue 1ı to 6ı [1]

1ı Reginald Hunter Orton, *b* 29 Dec 1900
2ı Malcolm Manson Orton, *b* 21 June 1902
3ı Kenneth Orton, *b* 21 Aug 1904
4ı Stella Orton, *b* 28 Aug 1891
5ı Korita Orton *b* 16 Sept 1897
6ı Erica Linda Orton, *b* 15 Feb 1899

3ı *Bruce Orton*, b 10 *Jan* 1877, d 1906, m 1896, (—), *da. of J Brosnahaw*, *and had issue (with a da d young)* 1ı to 2ı

1ı Hilda Orton, *b* 13 July 1897
2ı Beatrice Orton, *b* 3 Jan 1906

4ı Allan Orton (*Cook Street, Heathcote Valley, Christchurch, N Z*), *b* 17 Jan 1684, *m* 11 Sept 1905, Robina, da of J Reid, and has issue (3 children) [1]

5ı Caroline Agnes Orton *m* 27 Dec 1893, T Mee (*Claremont, Timaru, N Z*), and has issue (with 2 others [1]) 1ı to 2ı

1ı Wellesley Thomas Mee, *b* 13 Aug 1894
2ı Alexander Reginald Mee, *b* 2 Oct 1896

6ı Marion Jeanne Orton, *m* 28 Dec 1892, Farquhar Macdonald (*Ashburton, N Z*), and has issue 1ı to 3ı

1ı Allan Farquhar Macdonald, *b* 19 Oct 1893
2ı Reginald Orton Macdonald, *b* 5 July 1895
3ı John William Macdonald, *b* 8 Nov 1898

7ı Bessie Anne Orton, *m* W White (*Kaikoura, N Z*), and has issue 1ı to 3ı

1ı Leo Orton White, *b* 20 Mar 1898
2ı Una Katherine White, *b* 30 Dec 1900
3ı Zeta Marion White, *b* 5 June 1905

8ı Mabel Ada Orton, *m* 9 Ap 1902, Holford Whittaker (*Hamilton, North Island, N Z*), and has issue 1ı

1ı Orton Whittaker, *b* 6 Dec 1906

9ı Jeannette Mary Orton, *m* 1907, Francis Edwin Lamb, Architect (78 *Church Street, Masterton, North Island, N Z*)

10ı Linda Ethel Orton, *m* 2 Oct 1905, John Nixon (*Waitomo Caves, North Island, N Z*), and has issue (2 children) [1]

11ı Cora Evelina Modlin Orton, *m* 19 Dec 1906, Alfred Andrew Sutherland Hintz (*Nelson, N Z*), and has issue (1 child) [1]

2h [1] Caroline Anne Orton, *m* 28 Sept 1858, Robert Modlin of Sunderland, M R C S, *formerly* 17th Lancers, and has issue 1ı

1ı Barbara Bessie Orton Modlin, *m* 29 Mar 1897, Percy Bayley of Beacon Hill, Brede, co Sussex, and has issue 1ı

1ı Cicely Conyers Bayley, *b* 20 Feb 1898

3h [2] Emma Catherine Orton, *m* 14 Nov 1877, Edward Sawer (*Isleworth*), and has issue 1ı to 3ı

1ı Edward Reginald Sawer, Civil Service (*Bulawayo*)
2ı Katharine Mary Sawer
3ı Rose Hilda Sawer

4h [2] *Ada Orton*, b 21 *Nov* 1853, d 28 Oct 1896, m *Ernest Reynolds* (*Marere, 12 Wanganui Avenue, Ponsonby, Auckland, New Zealand*), *and had issue* 1ı *to* 3ı

1ı Ernest Orton Reynolds (*Chicago*), *b* 6 Oct 1886
2ı Reginald Hugh Reynolds, *b* 13 Nov 1890
3ı Violet Mary Reynolds, *m* 10 Mar 1910, Leslie Radmall of Chingford, co Essex (*Canada*) [Nos 42551 to 42586

---

[1] See Appendix

319

The Plantagenet Roll

2g *Annie Inman Orton,* b 27 *Oct* 1816, d 11 *Nov* 1898, m *in Bombay* 6 *Dec* 1837, *Col Samuel Hennell, H E I C S , sometime H B M 's Resident, Persian Gulf* b 6 *July* 1799, d 13 *Sept* 1880, *and had issue (with others* d s p *)* 1h

1h *Arthur Reginald Hennell* Lieut -Col (ret) *formerly* 1st Batt Hants Regt (*Jenniscombe Tiverton, S Devon*), b at Bushire 27 Mar 1849, m 27 Mar 1879, Frances Elizabeth, da of John Phillips of Winsley Hall, co Salop, and his issue (with a son d young) 1i to 8i

 1i Arthur Samuel Hennell, b 29 Oct 1884
 2i Frederick John Hennell, b 12 May 1888
 3i James Reginald Hennell, b 5 Jan 1891
 4i Edward Biscoe Hennell, b 21 Nov 1893
 5i Frances Annie Emily Hennell
 6i Kathleen Rosa Hennell
 7i Lucy Ada Hennell
 8i Mary Edith Hennell

3g *Emma Orton* d 25 *Sept* 1889, m *as 2nd wife* 11 *Ap* 1839, *Col Bruce Seton, H E I C S* [3rd son of *Sir Alexander Seton of Abercorn, 5th Bt* [S 1663]], d 27 *Nov* 1876, *and had issue* 1h *to* 5h

1h *Alexander Reginald Seton, Lieut -Col R E ,* b 25 *May* 1840, d 12 *Nov* 1887, m 18 *Sept* 1862 *Emma Elizabeth* (see p 321) (156 *Croydon Road, Anerley, S E) da of Major William Loch, 1st Bombay Lancers, and had issue* 1i to 6i

 1i *Bruce Gordon Seton* Heir-presumptive to the Baronetcy [S 1663], Major Indian Med Ser and Sec to the Director-Gen Indian Med Ser , has Medal for the Waziristan Exp 1894-5 (severely wounded) and Tochi Field Force (1897) (*East India United Service*), b 13 Oct 1868, m 16 Mar 1895, Ellen Mary, da of Lieut - Col Frank Armstrong , and has issue 1j to 4j

  1j Alexander Hay Seton b 14 Aug 1904
  2j Bruce Lovat Seton, b 22 May 1909
  3j Jean Gordon Seton
  4j Marie de Seton Seton

 2i *Charles Monteath Seton,* Admiralty Victualling Dept , Sydney (*Royal Naval Yard, Sydney, N S W*), b 30 Mar 1880

 3i *Walter Warren Seton,* M A (Lond), is Sec Univ College, Gower Street, W C (*University College Hall, Ealing*), b 4 Oct 1882

 4i *Katharine Marion Seton* (*Glenrose, Croydon Road, Anerley, S E*)

 5i *Elsie Madeleine Seton,* m 8 May 1901, Algernon James Pollock (*Brackley, Charlton Road Weston-super-Mare*), and has issue 1j to 3j

  1j Erskine Reginald Seton Pollock, b 1 Jan 1905
  2j Alan Winton Seton Pollock, b 30 June 1907
  3j Aileen Marion Seton Pollock

 6i *Aileen Mary Seton,* m 22 Sept 1899, Frank Binford Hole (*The Mount, Edgfield, Melton Constable, Norfolk)*, and has issue 1j

  1j Bruce Binford Hole, b 24 Jan 1901

2h *Bruce Outram Seton, Lieut -Col R E ,* b 7 *May* 1841, d 29 *July* 1901, m 21 *July* 1880, *Louisa Harriet Manderson, da of Dep Surg -Gen Charles Thomas Paske,* d 31 *Mar* 1886, *and had issue* 1i *to* 3i

 1i *Evelyn Seton,* m 1 Oct 1902, Major Percy Molesworth Sykes, C M G , Indian Army, *formerly* 2nd Dragoon Guards (*British Consulate-Gen , Meshed, Persia*), and has issue 1j to 3j

  1j Arthur Frank Seton Sykes, b 1903
  2j Charles Mortimer Sykes, b 1907
  3j Edward Molesworth Sykes, b 10 Jan 1910

 2i *Ruth Mary Seton,* m 15 Feb 1905, Marmaduke Brian Sunderland, son of Lieut -Col Sunderland of Ravensden Grange, Beds, and his issue 1j to 2j

  1j Bridget Mary Sunderland
  2j Phyllis Joan Sunderland

[Nos 42587 to 42616

# of The Blood Royal

3ı Violet Adela Seton, *m* 18 May 1904 Charles Henry Seton (see below) (*Heath House, Aston-on-Clun, Salop*), and has issue 1ı to 2ı

1ı Christopher Bruce Seton, *b* 3 Oct 1909

2ı Joyce Phœbe Seton

3h Charles Compton Seton, *formerly* Lieut R E (*Heath Hous Hopton Heath, Salop*), *b* 24 July 1846, *m* 30 July 1868, Phœbe Elizabeth, da of Sır Henry William Ripley, 1st Bt [U K], and has issue 1ı to 2ı

1ı Charles Henry Seton (*Heath House, Aston-on Clun, Salop*), *b* 28 Ap 1869, *m* 18 May 1904, Violet Adela (see above), da of Lıeut -Col Bruce Seton, and has issue

See above, Nos 42618–42619

2ı Margaret Annie Phœbe Seton, *m* 12 Oct 1898, Capt Arthur Pelham Frankland, D S O [2nd son of Lieut -Col Sır William Adolphus Frankland, 9th Bt [E 1660], R E] (*Culford House, Felixstowe*), and has issue 1ı to 2ı

1ı Marion Anne Margaret Frankland

2ı Rosalind Lucy Seton Frankland

4h Henry James Seton, Major *formerly* 2nd Batt Royal Irish Rifles, served ın S Africa 1899 (Medal with 2 Clasps) (*Critchfield, Walton on-Thames*), *b* 27 Aug 1854, *m* 1st, 6 Dec 1888, Elizabeth da of Henry James Byron [B Byron Coll], *d* 2 Sept 1897, 2ndly, 3 May 1899, Marie Bowles, da of Percy Hale Wallace of Belfast, and has issue 1ı

1ı Marie Seton, *b* 20 Mu 1910

5h Emma Alice Seton, *d* 10 Jan 1884 *m* as 1st wife, 18 July 1876, Henry Ripley, J P [4th son of Sir Henry William Ripley, 1st Bt [U K], M P] (*Ashley Manor, Cheltenham*), and had issue 1ı to 3ı

1ı Henry Edward Ripley, *b* 6 Jan 1884

2ı Dorothy Alice Seton Ripley

3ı Martın Janet Ripley, *m* 14 Jan 1899, Thomas Herbert Littlejohn of Hampstead, F R C S Edin [son of Sır Henry Littlejohn of Edınburgh] *d* 4 Sept 1905

4g Catherine Orton, *b* 30 Ap 1821, *d* 11 June 1904, *m* 31 Aug 1841, m Col William Loch, 1st Lancers, Indian Army, *d* 19 Nov 1860, and had issue 1h to 4h

1h William Loch, Col ın the Army and Political Resident at Khakmandu, *b* 8 Nov 1846, *d* 8 Aug 1901, *m* 1st at Calcutta 6 Mar 1876, Edith Mary, da of the Hon James Gibbs, I C S , Member of the Viceregal Council *d* 12 May 1898, 2ndly, 8 Nov 1899, Grace, da of Major Sır George Wingate, K C S I , R E , and had issue 1ı to 2ı

1ı Percy Gordon Loch, ın the Foreign Office at Baghdad, *b* 14 Jan 1887, *unm*

2ı Kenneth Morley Loch, Cadet at Woolwich *b* 16 Sept 1891

2h Frederick Phayre Loch (*Harker Lodge Carlisle*), *b* 21 July 1857, *m* Feb 1886, Georgina, da of Charles Burn, C E and has issue 1ı to 3ı

1ı Charles William Loch, M E (*Lawless, West Australia*), *b* 12 Feb 1887, *m* 16 June 1908, Mary Elizabeth, da of the Rev Canon Deed, D D

2ı Frederick Sydney Loch (*Kırndeem, Culcairn, N S W*), *b* 24 Jan 1889

3ı Eric Erskıne Loch, Cadet at Sandhurst, *b* 1901

3h Emma Elizabeth Loch (156 *Croydon Road, Annerly, S E*), *m* 18 Sept 1862, her cousin, Lieut -Col Alexander Reginald Seton, R E , *d* 12 Nov 1887, and has issue

See p 320, Nos 42596–42609

4h Katharine Annie Louise Loch, *m* 5 Oct 1868, the Hon Sır George Edward Knox, a Judge of the High Court of Judicature of the United Provinces of India and formerly a Member of Bengal Council (*River View, Allahabad*), and has issue 1ı to 7ı   [Nos 42617 to 42653

321

The Plantagenet Roll

1ı Stuart George Knox, Major Indian Army, now Political Agent at Koweit on the Persian Gulf, *b* 7 Oct 1869, *m* 15 Mar 1893, Ethel, da of the Right Hon Sir John Edge, P C and has issue 1ʝ to 2ʝ

    1ʝ Stuart George Edge Inman Knox, *b* 27 Nov 1896

    2ʝ John Knox, *b* 26 Sept 1904

2ı Ernest Francis Knox, Major Indian Army, *b* 27 July 1871

3ı Robert Welland Knox, I M S, *b* 6 Sept 1873, *m* 31 Dec 1900, Lilian, da of Col John Loch, Bengal Cavalry, and has issue 1ʝ

    1ʝ Esmé Margaret Knox

4ı Kenneth Nevill Knox, I C S, *b* 21 July 1878

5ı Gordon Daniell Knox, Assist Editor *Times of India* (Bombay), *b* 10 July 1880

6ı Katharine Margaret Knox, *m* 16 Nov 1898, the Rev Percy Hugh Chapman, M A, LL D, Chaplain at Bareilly (*Bareilly, U P, India*), and has issue (with a son, Kenneth Hugh, *d* young) 1ʝ to 2ʝ

    1ʝ Winifred Margaret Chapman

    2ʝ Janet Marion Chapman

7ı Angel Dorothy Knox, *m* 17 Nov 1908, Spencer Pelham Flowerdew, A M I C E, Indian State Railways, and has issue 1ʝ

    1ʝ George Douglas Hugh Flowerdew, *b* 12 Jan 1910

1b *Dorothy Pease, m Thomas Stillington of Kelfield, co York*

6a *Elizabeth Hutton, b at Richmond 14 Mar 1638*

7a *Othy Hutton, bapt 8 Nov 1642*   [Nos 42651 to 42666

187   Descendants, if any surviving, of the Hon URSULA DARCY (Table XX), *d* (–), *m* JOHN STILLINGTON of Kelfield, co York, *d* 1658, and had issue (with 3 elder sons and a da who *d* unm) 1a to 5a [1]

1a *Thomas Stillington of Kelfield, aged 36, 22 Mar 1665, m Dorothy, da of Joseph Micklethwayte of York, M D, , and had issue 1b to 2b*

    1b *Thomas Stillington, aged 6 months, 22 Mar 1665*

    2b *Ursula Stillington*

2a *Margaret Stillington, m the Rev John Shaw of Rotheram, co York*

3a *Mary Stillington, m William Drake of Barnoldswicke Cotes, co York*

4a *Olive Stillington*

5a *Ursula Stillington, m George Tolson of Stakes, co York*

188   Descendants, if any, of the Hon. MARGARET DARCY (Table XX), *d* (–), *m* Sir THOMAS HARRISON

189   Descendants of the Hon DOROTHY DARCY (Table XX) *d* (–), *m* JOHN DALTON of Hawkswell, co York, *bapt* 17 Sept 1603, *d* of wounds received while conducting the Queen from Burlington to Oxford, *bur.* in York Minster 26 July 1644, and had issue 1a to 6a

1a *Sir William Dalton of Hawkswell, d 23 Mar 1675, m Elizabeth, da of Sir Marmaduke Wyvill, 2nd Bt [E], and had issue*

See Exeter Volume, pp 563–564, Nos 50255–50274   [Nos 42667 to 42686

[1] Foster's " Visitation of York "

# of The Blood Royal

2a Thomas Dalton of York, and afterwards of Bedale, admon 10 July 1710, m (Lic dated 16 Mar) 1665, Anne, da of Sir Marmaduke Wyvill, 2nd Bt [E], bur 28 Nov 1675, and had issue

See the Exeter Volume, p 561, Nos 50275-50680

3a Mary Dalton, d 1674, m as 2nd wife, John Beverley of Great Smeaton, co York, d 7 Oct 1680, and had issue [1] 1b to 6b

    1b John Beverley, aged 9, 19 Aug 1665
    2b Thomas Beverley
    3b Dorothy Beverley, aged 11, 19 Aug 1665
    4b Elizabeth Beverley
    5b Mary Beverley
    6b Anne Beverley

4a Barbara Dalton, d (-), m Charles Tancred of Arden, co York, High Sheriff for that co 1694, and had issue (24 children of whom [2]) 1b to 18b

    1b Henry Tancred
    2b William Tancred of Arden, d (-), m Elizabeth, da and co-h of Thomas Carter, Lord Mayor of York, and had issue 1c to 5c

        1c Charles Tancred of Arden d (-), m about 28 June 1734. Barbara, da of the Rev Darcy Dalton, Rector of Aston, and had issue
        2c Thomas Tancred
        3c William Tancred, bapt (?) at Belfrey's, York, 25 Nov 1694
        4c Henry Tancred
        5c Barbara Tancred, m William Stables of Pontefract

    3b Charles Tancred
    4b Jordan Tancred, m (—), da of (—) Holland
    5b John Tancred
    6b Charles Tancred
    7b James Tancred, m Catherine, da of (—) Sutherland
    8b Francis Tancred, m Catherine da of (—) Blitheman
    9b Christopher Tancred
    10b Richard Tancred
    11b Thomas Tancred
    12b Nicholas Tancred
    13b Dorothy Tancred
    14b Elizabeth Tancred
    15b Dorothy Tancred
    16b Barbara Tancred, m the Rev William Ellesley, Rector of Ryther
    17b Jane Tancred, m John Warcop of Gatenby
    18b Dorothy Tancred, m William Warwick of Atscough

5a Dorothy Dalton
6a Ursula Dalton   [Nos 42687 to 43092

190. Descendants of KATHERINE BEST (Table XX), m before Oct 1683, EDWARD GODDARD of Leatherhead, co Surrey, and had issue 1a to 2a

1a Edward Goddard, m 27 Nov 1705, Elizabeth, widow of (—) Place of Richmond, da of (—), and had issue [3]
2a Katherine Goddard, d (-), m at Gilling, 31 Jan 1705, Henry Darcy of Coburn Manor, and afterwards of Selbury, co York, and had issue
See pp 308-310, Nos 41900-41947   [Nos 43093 to 43110

---

[1] 'Visitation of York,' by Sir William Dugdale, 1665, Surtees Soc Pub xxxvi 35

[2] Foster's " Yorkshire Pedigrees "   [3] Foster's " Yorkshire Families "

323

The Plantagenet Roll

191. Descendants of WILLIAM MOLINEUX, Mayor of Doncaster 1721 [Bt of Teversal Coll] (Table XX), *b* 1681, *d* 1756, *m* KATHERINE, widow of William Squire of Doncaster, da of Richard SHEPHERD of the same place, and had issue 1*a* to 2*a*

1*a* *Darcy Molineux of Leeds, Merchant,* d 1789, m *and had issue 1b to 4b*

1*b* *Sir Darcy Molineux, 8th Bt [l. 1611] on the death of his remote kinsman,* 9 *June* 1812, d s p 1816

2*b* *William Molineux,* d s p 1813

3*b* *Elizabeth Molineux,* m *Edward Gray*

4*b* *Isabella Molineux,* m *John Holgate*

2*a* *Elizabeth Molineux,* b 1714

192 Descendants of JOHN MOLINEUX of Mansfield, co Notts, and Wolverhampton, co Stafford [Baronet of Teversal Coll] (Table XX). *d* 1754, *m* MARY, da of Richard BIRCH of Wolverhampton, *d* 1735, and had issue (with a son, William, who *d* young, 1726) 1*a* to 8*a*

1*a* *Thomas Molineux of Wolverhampton,* b 17 *Mar* 1704, d *about* 25 *Aug* 1791, m *at St Paul's Cathedral, London, Margaret, da of* (—) *Gisborne,* d 25 *Aug* 1791, *and had issue 1b to 3b*

1*b* *John Molineux of Wolverhampton,* b. 14 *May* 1736, d 28 *Ap* 1785, m *Margaret, widow of* (—) *Walker of Wolverhampton, da of* (—)*, and had issue 1c to 2c*

1*c* *Sarah Gisborne Molineux,* d Oct 1831, m *Isaac Scott of Wolverhampton, and had issue a da , Margaretta, who d unm* 9 *June* 1852

2*c* *Mary Anne Molineux,* m *John Lingard of Wolverhampton, and had issue (with a younger da d unm)* 1d *to* 2d

1*d* *John Lingard*

2*d* *Sarah Gisborne Lingard,* m *Charles S Stokes of Murrell's End, Newent, co Gloucester, and had issue* [1]

2*b* *Richard Molineux,* d 1784, m *Mary* (see p 328), *da of Benjamin Molineux of Wolverhampton, and had issue 1c to 3c*

1*c* *Mary Ann Molineux,* d (—) m *James Clutterbuck of Hyde House, co Gloucester, J P, D L [younger brother of Lewis Clutterbuck of Ford House, Wolverhampton]*

2*c* *Caroline Molineux,* d (—)*,* m *Robert Hodgson [son of Brian Hodgson of Swinscoe, co Stafford], and had issue 1d to 3d*

1*d* *Robert Molineux Hodgson of Paris,* d *at Versailles* 26 *July* 1876

2*d* *Caroline Hodgson*

3*d* *Ellen Hodgson*

3*c* *Elizabeth Molineux,* m *Thomas Brooke*

3*b* *Thomas Gisborne Molineux of London, Merchant,* d 13 *May* 1807, m *Mary, da of* (—) *Brice and had issue 1c to 2c*

1*c* *Francis Molineux of London, Merchant, Lieut London Vol* 1803, b 14 *Sept* 1785, d 15 *May* 1852, m 13 Oct 1819, *Sarah, d of Joseph Molineux of Lewes, Banker* (see p 326), *and had issue 1d to 3d*

---

[1] One of their granddaughters, Ada, m 28 Feb 1881, William Joshua, eldest son of William Goulding of Summer Hill, Cork, M P for that city 1877

# of The Blood Royal

1d Gisborne Molineux, Hon Sec of the Canada Coy, and one of the founders and Fellow and Member of Council of the Royal Colonial Institute, author of " Memoir of the Molineux Family," 1882, d s p

    2d Francis Molineux, d unm 1850

    3d Mary Elizabeth Molineux

2c Anne Molineux, m 13 Nov 1803, Josiah Rhodes of London, Merchant, Capt London Vol , and had issue 1d

    1d Mary Anne Rhodes, m William Fawcett of Yarm-on-Tees, co York, Solicitor, and had issue [1]

2a Richard Molineux of Cateaton (now Gresham) Street, London, a Common Councilman for the Cripplegate Ward, d 1762, m Sarah, da of Zachary Gisborne, d 1770, and had issue 1b

    1b Mary Molineux, d (—), m 24 June 1750, Capt George Barber of Somerford Hall, Brewood, co Stafford, d s p

3a John Molineux of Gainsborough, co Linc, m Elizabeth, da of (—) Wass and had issue 2 das whose issue is extinct

4a Joseph Molineux of Lewes, co Sussex, Receiver-Gen of Stamps and Taxes 1745-1764, b 1715, d 1771, m Ann, da of William Brett of Lewes, M D, d 1782, and had issue (with 2 sons and 2 das who d s p) 1b to 2b

    1b Joseph Molineux of Lewes, Banker, b 7 Mar 1754, d 1813, m 2 Dec 1777, Elizabeth, da of Thomas West of Southover, Lewes, d 20 July 1815, and had issue (with 2 sons and 2 das who d young) 1c to 7c

        1c George Molineux of Isfield and Lewes, Banker, J P, b 17 Mar 1791, d 27 Jan 1855, m 1815, Frances Ann, da of Thomas Ramsay of London, and had issue (with 3 sons and a da) 1d to 5d

            1d George Molineux of Isfield, J P, b 6 Aug 1816, d 20 Jan 1893, m 1st, 2 Oct 1840, Maria Ann, da and h of the Rev Joseph Hurlock, M A, d 11 Mar 1875 and had issue 1e to 6e

                1e George Fitzherbert Molineux, b 27 Aug 1841, unm

                2e Rev Charles Hurlock Molineux, Vicar of Staveley and Canon of Southwell (Staveley Vicarage, Chesterfield, Derby) b 28 Oct 1842, unm

                3e Philip Horace Molineux (Malling House, Lewes), b 12 Aug 1844, unm

                4e Rev Arthur Ellison Molineux, M A, Vicar of Minster (Minster Vicarage, Ramsgate), b 5 Feb 1846, m 16 July 1871, Eleanor Margaret, da of Matthew Bell of Bourne Park, co Kent, J P and has issue 1f to 2f

                    1f Agnes Irene Molineux

                    2f Evelyn Margaret Molineux

                5e Harold Parminter Molineux of Isfield, J P, Major formerly Essex Regt (The Cottage, Isfield, Sussex, Mornington, Eastbourne), b 16 Ap 1850, m 4 Jan 1881, Rosa Eugenie Katharine, da of Henry King of Isfield Place, J P , and has issue 1f to 5f

                    1f George King Molineux, 2nd Lieut 5th Fusiliers, b 15 Ap 1887

                    2f Henry Gisborne King Molineux, b 9 May 1891

                    3f Dorothy Eugénie Molineux

                    4f Katharine Augusta Molineux, m 7 Ap 1910, Lieut -Com Harold Ernest Sulivan, R N

                    5f Annie Rosa Molineux

                6e Mildred Constance Molineux

        2d Joseph Molineux, b 3 June 1818, d 1876, m 20 Oct 1857, Caroline, da of the Rev E Symons, Rector of Ringmer , and had issue several das

        3d Henry Molineux, b 23 July 1830   [Nos 43141 to 43154

---

[1] William Rhodes, the eldest son, of The Grange, Stainton in Cleveland, m Rosalie, da of Claude de Queiros of Calcutta Marianne, the second da , m Anthony Temple of Kington, co Hereford, son of the Rev W S Temple of Dinsdale, co Durham —"Memoirs of the Molineux Family," p 67

The Plantagenet Roll

4d *Frances Molineux*, b 11 May 1821, d 16 Nov 1868, m 22 *July* 1840, *her cousin, Job Smallpeice of Field Place, Compton, co Surrey*, d 21 May 1875, *and had issue* (see Appendix)

5d *Cordelia Molineux*, b 28 Jan 1827, d 20 July 1895, m Jan 1853, *Joseph Ewart of Manchster, Merchant* [*Cadet of Craigcleuch*], b 1807, d 1861, *and had issue* (*with a son, Russell*, d unm 19 Nov 1900) 1 *to 3e*

1e Ernest Molineaux Ewart, b 6 Nov 1853 *unm*

2e Emily Frances Ewart (*India*), *unm*

3e *Marianne Ramsay Ewart*, b 20 Dec 1856, d 5 April 1901, m 6 Dec 1888, *Henry James Richardson, and has issue* 1f

1f Gulielma Ewart Richardson, b 20 Nov 1890

2c *Elizabeth Molineux*, b 1779, d (—), m *C Chitty of Lewes*

3c *Cordelia Molineux*, b 1780, d 1859, m *Job Smallpeice of Northbrook, co Surrey*, d 1842, *and had issue* (*with 2 sons and 3 das* d *unm*) 1d *to* 4d

1d *Job Smallpeice of Field Place, Compton, co Surrey*, b c 1808, d 21 May 1875, m 22 July 1840, *Frances, da of George Molineux of Isfield and Lewis*, d 16 Nov 1868, *and had issue* (see above)

2d *Mark Smallpeice of Guildford*, b 29 Dec 1812, d 29 Sept 1901, m 1839, *Alicia, da of Heathfield Young of Dorking* d 15 June 1903, *and had issue* (*with 2 sons and 2 das* d *unm*) 1e *to* 6e

1e *Ferdinand Smallpeice* (*Cross Lanes, Guildford*), b 14 July 1843, m 13 May 1875, *Mary Jane, da of William Haydon Smallpeice of Guildford, and has issue* 1f

1f *Ferdinand William Smallpeice* (*Browning's Down, Guildford*), b 27 May 1877, m 7 June 1904, *Cecilia Mary Delves* [*descended from the Lady Anne, sister of King Edward IV* (see Exeter Volume, p 224)] *da of Col John Delves Broughton* [Bt Coll], *and has issue* 1g *to* 2g

1g Cecilia Lucy Smallpeice, b 29 June 1905

2g Rosemary Austice Smallpeice, b 18 Aug 1909

2e Humphry Smallpeice (*Guildford*), b 5 Dec 1818, *unm*

3e Stanley Smallpeice (*Haslemere*), b Feb 1852, *m* and has issue (1 da)

4e James Smallpeice (*Guildford*), b July 1854, *m* and has issue (4 das)

5e Alice Smallpeice, *unm*

6e Grace Smallpeice, *unm*

3d *Frederick Smallpeice*, d April 1855, m *Maria, da of* (—) *Keen, and had issue* (4 das)

4d *Emma Smallpeice*, d (—), m 1852, *James Ward, and had issue* (*with a da* d *unm*) 2 sons (*both* m, *one having a son and 2 das, the other a da*) *and* 3 das, *of whom one is* m *and has 2 sons*

4c *Sarah Molineux*, b 1783, d 16 Ap 1854, m 13 Oct 1819, *Francis Molineux of London, Merchant*, d 15 Mar 1852, *and had issue*

See p 324

5c *Jane Molineux*, b 1786, d (—), m *Joseph Browne of Holcombe House, co Glouc*

6c *Maria Molineux*, b 1789, d (—), m *Henry Sparkes of Shalford and Summerberry, co Surrey, and had issue* 1d

1d. *Maria Sparkes*, d s p 4 Sept 1863, m *as 1st wife*, 19 June 1860, *Sir John Charles Kenward Shaw, 7th Bt* [E], d s p

7c *Grace Molineux*, b 1793, d (—), m *William Browne of Minchinhampton, co Gloucester*

2b *Elizabeth Molineux*, d (—), m *A Verrall of Lewes*

5a *Benjamin Molineux of Molineux House, Wolverhampton, Banker*, d 1772, m *Elizabeth, da of George Fieldhouse*, d (—), *and had issue* 1b *to* 3b

1b *George Molineux of Wolverhampton, Banker and Iron Merchant, J P and High Sheriff co Stafford* 1791, d 22 Sept 1820, m *Jane, da of* (—) *Robinson*, d (—), *and had issue* (*with 5 younger sons and 3 das who all* d s p) 1c

[Nos 43155 to 43167.

# of The Blood Royal

1c Rev George Fieldhouse Molineux, M A , Rector of Ryton and Preb of St Peter's, Wolverhampton, J P, d 30 Sept 1840 , m Maria, da of William Hardman of Manchester, d 1858 , and had issue (with 4 sons and 4 das who d s p) 1d to 4d

1d Rev William Hardman Molineux, Rector of Elmsett, co Suffolk, b 1801 , d 11 May 1864 , m 12 Oct 1852, Elizab th, da of Edward Pemberton of Plas Isas, co Flint, J P , and had issue 1e to 2e

1e William Pemberton Molineux (Ashby Hall, Great Yarmouth), b 23 Oct 1853 , m Anna, da ot Robert Kidman , and has issue 1f

1f William Francis Pemberton Molineux, b 24 Jan 1899

2e Rev George Edward Francis Molineux, M A (Trinity Coll , Dublin), Vicar of Colyton (Colyton Vicarage, Devon), b 15 Ap 1855 , m 23 Sept 1890, Ada Louisa, da of the Rev Sackville Hamilton Berkeley , and has issue 1f to 6f

1f George Berkeley Molineux, b 16 Mar 1903

2f Laurence Perle Molineux, b 10 Aug 1908

3f Constance Hamilton Molineux

4f Mabel Elizabeth Sackville Molineux

5f. Frances Mary Pemberton Molineux

6f Muriel Berkeley Molineux

2d Charles Edward Molineux of Oakley Penkridge, co Stafford, J P , b 1810 , d 3 Nov 1880 , m 17 Mar 1845, Jane, da of Orson Bidwell of Albrighton, co Salop, d 5 Ap 1902 , and had issue 1e

1e Mary Jane Molineux, m 25 Ap 1867, Frederick John Staples-Browne of Brashfield House, J P , Bar at-Law (Brashfield House, Bicester , The Elms, Bampton, Oxford) , and has issue 1f to 2f

1f Richard Charles Staples Browne, M A (Camb), b 29 June 1881 , m 17 Feb 1909, Sylvia Maud, da of Sir Charles Philip Huntington, 1st Bt [U K], M P (14 Harrington Gardens, S W)

2f Mary Frederica Staples-Browne

3d Thomas Molineux of Beechfield, Bowden, co Chester, Silk Spinner, b 16 May 1807 , d 3 June 1855 , m 24 Jan 1839, Mary, da of William Lomas of Manchester, d 30 Jan 1851 , and had issue (with 2 sons and a da who d unm) 1e to 4e

1e George William Molineux (Betchworth House, Chideock, Bridport, Dorset), b 25 Dec 1848 , m 29 Sept 1883, Edith, da of John Eddowes Bowman, d 8 Aug 1909

2e Emily Molineux, b 15 Oct 1840 , d 7 June 1901 , m 3 Feb 1874, the Rev John Barratt Fawssett, M A , Rector of Laughton (Glebe Avenue, Enfield) , and had issue 1f to 3f

1f Richard Maurice Fawssett (Pinewoods, Ash, Surrey), b 11 May 1875 , m 30 Aug 1901, Sybil Wentworth, da of the Rev Henry Allen Steel, s p

2f John Leonard Fawssett, b 1 Mar 1877 , unm

3f Francis William Fawssett, M B (London) (260 Fore Street, Upper Edmonton, N), b 14 Oct 1878 , m 21 Ap 1904, Mildred Evelyne, da of the Rev Edward Pole Williams , and has issue 1g

1g Evelyne Mary Helen Fawssett, b 23 Mar 1905

3e Alice Mary Molineux, m 29 July 1869, the Rev John Trew, B A (Trinity Coll , Dublin), Vicar of Drighlington (Drighlington Vicarage, near Bradford) , and has issue (with a son who d young) 1f to 1f

1f John M'Cammon Trew, b 1 Ap 1870

2f Basil Molineux Trew, b 18 Aug 1885

3f Laura Mary Trew, m 30 Jan 1897, William Towler (Gildersome, Yorks), and has issue (with a da d young) 1g to 2g

1g Eric William Towler, b 28 Ap 1900

2g Cyril John Towler, b 20 Feb 1907

4f Mary Trew, unm

4e Fanny Molineux, unm

[Nos 43168 to 43192

327

The Plantagenet Roll

4d *Harriet Molineux*, b 18 *Aug* 1811, d *Ap* 1880, m 12 *Sept* 1844, *Thomas Lomas of Manchester*, b 20 *Oct* 1798, d *Oct* 1870, *and had issue* 1e

1e *George Henry Lomas*, b 24 *Aug* 1848, d 24 *Oct* 1906, m 14 *Aug* 1873, *Margaret Elizabeth, da of John Courtney Bluett of Gray's Inn, Bar-at-Law, and had issue* 1f *to* 3f

1f Alfred Lomas, M D (*Ashfield House, Castleton, near Manchester*), b 21 May 1874, m 2 Oct 1902, Alice Winifred, da of Frederick Price of Highfield, Sale, co Chester, Solicitor, s p

2f Harold Lomas, *b* 14 Sept 1875, *m* 25 Aug 1901, Virginia Washington, da of Gen Wager Swayne of New York, and Shinnecock, Long Island, and has issue 1g to 2g

1g Virginia Washington Lomas, b at Washington 7 Mai 1904

2g Elaine Margaret Lomas, b at Baltimore 15 Ap 1906

3f Ethel Mary Lomas, m 28 Oct 1905, Henry Cort Harold Carpenter, M.A (Oxon), Ph D (Leipzig), s p

2b *Sarah Molineux*, d (–), m *Lewis Clutterbuck of Ford House*

3b *Mary Molineux*, d (–), m *Richard Molineux of Wolverhampton, Banker,* d 1784, *and had issue*

See p 324

6a *Anne Molineux*

7a *Mary Molineux*

8a *Elizabeth Molineux*   [Nos 43193 to 43197

193 Descendants of LUCIUS CHARLES (CARY), 7th VISCOUNT FALK-LAND [S] (Table XX), d 27 Feb 1785, m 1st, 6 Ap 1734, JANE, widow of James Fitzgerald, Lord Villiers, da. of Richard BUTLER of London, Conveyancer, d in France 20 Dec 1751 and had issue 1a to 5a

1a *Lucius Ferdinand Cary, Master of Falkland, Commander of the British Forces in Tobago,* d *there v p* 20 *Aug* 1780, m *Mar* 1760, *Anne, da of Col Charles Leith, and had issue* 1b *to* 6b

1b *Henry Thomas (Cary), 8th Viscount Falkland [S],* b 27 *Feb* 1766, d *unm* 22 *May* 1796

2b *Charles John (Cary), 9th Viscount Falkland [S], Capt R N,* b *Nov* 1768, d *of wounds received in a duel* 2 *Mar* 1809, m 25 *Aug* 1802, *Christiana, da of* (—) *Anton,* d 25 *July* 1822, *and had issue* 1c *to* 3c

1c *Lucius Bentinck (Cary), 10th Viscount Falkland [S], 1st Baron Hunsdon* [U K], *P C,* b 5 *Nov* 1803, d s p 12 *Mar* 1884

2c *Plantagenet Pierrepoint (Cary), 11th Viscount Falkland [S], Adm R N,* b 8 *Sept* 1806, d s p 1 *Feb* 1886

3c *Hon Byron Charles Ferdinand Plantagenet Cary, Capt R N,* b 5 *Oct* 1808, d 21 *Feb* 1874, m 19 *Feb* 1814, *Selina Mary, da of the Rev Francis Fox of Fox Hall, co Longford,* d 10 *Aug* 1868, *and had issue* 1d *to* 4d

1d Byron Plantagenet (Cary), 12th Viscount Falkland and a Rep Peer [S], J P, D L, Lieut-Col and Hon Col (ret) 4th Batt Yorkshire Regt, *formerly* Royal Sussex Regt (26 *Upper Grosvenor Street, S W . Carlton, Marlborough, &c*), b 3 Ap 1845, m 25 Sept 1879, Mary, a Lady of Grace of St John of Jerusalem in England, da of Robert Reade of New York, and has issue 1e to 6e

1e Lucius Plantagenet Cary, Master of Falkland, Capt Grenadier Guards, served in South Africa 1900–1902 (139 *St James' Court, Buckingham Gate, S W*), b 23 Sept 1880, m 6 Ap 1904, Ella Louise, da of E W. Catford, and has issue 1f to 2f

1f Lucius Henry Charles Plantagenet Cary, b 25 Jan 1905

2f Byron Plantagenet Cary, b 28 June 1908   [Nos 43198 to 43201.

328

# of The Blood Royal

2e Hon Byron Plantagenet Cary, Lieut R N , *b* 25 Jan 1887
3e Hon Philip Plantagenet Cary, *b* 24 Sept 1895
4e Hon Catherine Mary Cary
5e Hon Mary Selina Cary
6e Hon Letice Cary

2d Hon Emma Amelia Cary, had Royal Warrant as a Viscount's da 29 Sept 1886, *m* 8 Mar 1869, Thomas Benyon Ferguson, Bar.-at-Law, *d* 12 Nov 1875, and has issue 1e to 2e

1e Annie Selina Emma Ferguson, *m* 1898, Hugh Wyndham Montgomery, *formerly* 17th Lancers
2e Edith Nora Ferguson

3d Hon Selina Catherine Cary, had Royal Warrant as a Viscount's da 29 Sept 1886, *m* 27 Sept 1877, Charles Edward Fox, Bar.-at-Law, Master of Equity, High Court of Bombay, *d* 6 Nov 1897 , and had issue 1e to 3e

1e Agnes Selina Fox
2e Dorothy Fox
3e Catherine Mary Fox, *m* 16 July 1908, Capt Alexander Adams, *late* R E (*Kingston, Canada*)

4d Hon Anne Christina Cary, had Royal Warrant as a Viscount's da 29 Sept 1886 , *m* June 1898, Capt Servante Morland, 7th Batt. Rifle Brig (*Heatle House, near Tonbridge, Kent*)

3b *Charlotte Maria Cary*, b Nov 1764, d (-), m *Samuel Charters*, and had issue

4b *Lucia Cary*, d (s p), m *at Calcutta* 10 Jan 1783, Major John Grattan, 100th Regt, Adj.-Gen to the Forces in India

5b *Lavinia Matilda Cary*

6b *Hon Emelia Sophia Cary, had Royal Warrant as a Viscount's da* 1834 , m 1798, *Major Charles Thomas Grant of Grant*

2i *Hon Mary Elizabeth Cary*, b 1738, d 1 Oct 1783, **m** *the Ven John Law, D D , Archdeacon of Rochester*, d 5 Feb 1827, aged 88

3a *Hon Frances Cary*
4a *Hon Mary Cary*
5a *Hon Charlotte Cary*, m *June 1799, Anthony Chapman*

[Nos 43202 to 43211

194 Descendants, if any, of DOROTHY MOLINEUX (Table XX), *d* (-), *m* TOBET HODGSON of Bishop Burton, co York

195 Descendants, if any surviving, of the Hon MARY DARCY (Table XX), *m* ACTON BURNELL of Winkburn Hall, co Notts , and had issue   Then apparently last surviving descendant 1a

1a *D'Arcy Burnell of Winkburn Hall, d s p leaving his estates to his widow, who d 1874, when they passed to his distant relative, Peter Pegge, afterwards Pegge-Burnell of Beauchief Abbey, co Derby* [1]

196 Descendants of Lady ELIZABETH CLIFFORD (Table VIII), *d* (-), *m*. 1533, Sir CHRISTOPHER METCALFE of Nappa, co York, J.P., *b c* 1513 , *d* 1574, and had issue 1a to 2a

1a *James Metcalfe of Nappa*, b c 1551, d 1580, m. *Joan, da of John Savile of Stanley, co. York*, and had issue 1b

[1] Burke's " Landed Gentry "

329

The Plantagenet Roll

1b Sir Thomas Metcalfe of Nappa, b c 1579, d 26 July 1650/5, m Elizabeth, da of Sir Henry Slingsby of Scriven, and had issue

See pp 72-74, Nos 9115-9381

2a Margaret Metcalfe, m as 2nd wife, George Middleton of Leighton, co Lanc, b 1522, d (-), and had issue (with 2 other sons and 3 das) 1b

1b Thomas Middleton of Leighton Hall, d (-), m Katharine, sister of Sir Richard Hoghton, 1st Bt [E], da of Thomas Hoghton of Hoghton Tower, co Lanc, and had issue (with 8 das) 1c to 2c

1c Sir George Middleton of Leighton, 1st Bt [E], so cr 21 June 1642, b 1600, d 27 Feb 1673, m 1st, Frances, da and h of Richard Rigg of Little Strickland, and had issue 1d

1d Mary Middleton of Leighton, da and h, d (-), m Somerford Oldfield of Somerford, co Chester, aged 35, 14 Sept 1663,[1] and had issue 1e to 6e

1e George Somerford (Middleton) Oldfield of Leighton and Somerford, which latter he sold, b 1660, being aged 3, 14 Sept 1663, d (-), m (?) Lady Clarke, and had issue 1f

1f [da] Oldfield of Leighton, da. and event sole h, m Albert Hodgson, ju of Leighton, attainted for his share in the '15, living 1740,[2] and had issue 1g to 2g

1g Anne Hodgson of Leighton, d s p, m Charles Townley of Townley

2g Mary Hodgson, d s p, m 1737, Ralph Standish of Standish

2e Anne Oldfield

3e Mary Oldfield

4e Elizabeth Oldfield

5e Catherine Oldfield

6e Frances Oldfield

2c Robert Middleton, d (-), m Jane, da and co-h of Thomas Kitson of Warton, and had issue (who resided until recently at Warton in very reduced circumstances[3] One of his sons) 1d

1d (—) Middleton, m and had (with possibly other) issue 1e to 2e

1e Robert Middleton, Mariner, d 1699, leaving issue a large family

2e Margaret Middleton, m Thomas Booker, Gent, and had (with possibly other) issue 1f

1f Robert Booker of Broughton, m and had issue 1g

1g Margaret Booker, da and h, m Robert Preston [son of Richard Preston of Cockerham]   [Nos 43215 to 43481]

197 Descendants, if any surviving, of the Hon. JOSCELINE PERCY (Table II), d 8 Sept 1532, m MARGARET, da of Walter FROST of Fetherstone, co York, d 15 Nov 1530, and had issue 1a

1a Edward Percy of Beverley, b c 1521, d 22 Sept 1590, bur at St Mary's Church, Beverley, m Elizabeth da of Sir Thomas Warton of Walton, J P, bur at St Mary's afsd 14 Dec 1607, aged 89, and had (with other) issue[4] 1b to 4b

1b Alan Percy of Beverley, M P 1603, b 1560, d 1632, m 1589, Mary, da of Ralph Moore of Beswick in Holderness, and had issue (with 4 sons, Henry (son and h, d c 1590-1), Jasper, Alan, and Francis, known to have d s p) 1c to 3c

1c Josceline Percy of Beverley, d 1653, m Elizabeth, da of William Fitzwilliam of Maplethorpe, co Linc, and had issue 1d to 4d

1d Alan (Percy), de jure 12th Earl of Northumberland [E] on the death of his remote kinsman the 11th Earl, 21 May 1670, d s p 1688, will dated 1687

2d John Percy

3d Charles Percy, living 1652, fate unknown

---

[1] Ormerod's "Cheshire," iii 60   [2] Burke's "Extinct Baronetcies," p 354
[3] Ibid   [4] See Appendix

4d Eleanor Percy, m William Farrand of West Hall, near Addingham, co Yorks[1]

2c Edward Percy, b 1594, d 27 Aug 1630, bur at Petworth

3c Frances Percy, m Ralph Elleker of Risby Park, co York, and had issue now extinct[2]

2b Thomas Percy, Constable of Alnwick and Auditor to the 9th Earl of Northumberland, one of the Conspirators in the Gunpowder Plot, killed at Holbeach 1605, m Martha, da of Robert Wright of Holderness, co York and had issue (with a da, Elizabeth, d young at Alnwick 1602) 1c to 2c

1c Robert Percy

2c [da] Percy, m Robert Catesby of Ashby Legers, co Northants, son of the Conspirator[3]

3b Ellen Percy, m Ralph Moore of Beswicke in Holderness and had issue[4]

4b [da] Percy, m John Berney of Dale Bank, co York[5]

198 Descendants of HENRY (STAFFORD), 1st Lord Stafford [E] (Table XXI), b 18 Sept 1501, d 30 Ap 1563, m 1518, the Lady URSULA, da of Sir Richard POLE, K G [by his wife Margaret (Plantagenet), suo jure Countess of Salisbury [E]], d 12 Aug 1570, and had issue

See the Clarence Volume, Table LXVII et seq, and pp 537-646, Nos 22808-31936   [Nos 43482 to 52610

199 Descendants of THOMAS (HOWARD), 21st or 14th EARL OF ARUNDEL, EARL OF SURREY, and EARL MARSHAL [E], K G (Table XXI), b 7 July 1585, d at Padua 26 Sept 1646, m 1606, Lady ALOTHEA, suo jure (1681) Lady FURNIVAL (1295), STRANGE of Blackmere (1309) and Talbot (1331) [E], da and event sole h of Gilbert (TALBOT), 7th Earl of Shrewsbury [E], &c, d 24 May 1654, and had issue

See the Exeter Volume, Table XVIII and pp 291-292, Nos 11740-14581   [Nos 52611 to 55452

200 Descendants of FREDERICK AUGUSTUS (HERVEY), 4th EARL OF BRISTOL [G B], and Lord Hervey (1799), 5th Lord Howard de Walden [E], Bishop of Derry [I.] (Table XXI), b 1 Aug 1730; d at Albano, near Rome, 8 July 1803, m 10 Aug 1752, ELIZABETH, da and event h of Sir James DAVERS, 3rd Bt [E], d 15 Dec 1800, and had issue 1a to 3a

1a John Augustus Hervey, Lord Hervey, b 1 Jan 1757, d v p 10 Jan 1796, m 4 Oct 1779, Elizabeth, da of Colin Drummond of Quebec, d 4 Sept 1818, and had issue 1b

1b Hon Elizabeth Catherine Caroline Hervey, b 1 Aug 1780, d 21 Jan 1803, m 2 Aug 1798, Charles Rose (Ellis), 1st Baron Seaford [U K], so cr 15 July 1826, b 19 Dec 1771, d 1 July 1845, and had issue 1c to 2c

---

[1] Brydge's "Collins," ii 303
[2] Brenan's "House of Percy" Collins says James, 2nd son of Ralph Elleker
[3] Ibid   [4] Ibid Omitted by Collins
[5] Brydge's "Collins," ii 303 Omitted by Brenan

The Plantagenet Roll

1c *Charles Augustus* (*Ellis*), *6th Baron Howard de Walden* [E] *in suc to his great grandfather, and 2nd Baron Seaford* [U K], *G C B*, *K T S*, b 5 *June* 1799, d 29 *Aug* 1868, m 8 *Nov* 1828, *Lady Lucy* [*descended from King Henry VII* (see Tudor Roll, p 2150], *da and event co h of William Henry* (*Cavendish-Bentinck*), *4th Duke of Portland* [*G B*]. &c, d 29 *July* 1899, *and had issue* 1d *to* 3l.

1d *Frederick George* (*Ellis*), *7th Baron Howard de Walden* [E] *and 3rd Baron Seaford* [U K], b 9 *Aug* 1830 d 3 *Nov* 1899, m 27 *Ap* 1876, *Blanche, da and co-h of William Holden of Palace House, co Lanc* [*rem 2ndly*, 25 *Mar* 1903, *Henry Ludlow* (*Lopes*), *2nd Baron Ludlow* [U K], *and had issue* 1e

1e *Thomas Evelyn* (*Ellis*), *8th Baron Howard de Walden* [E] *and 4th Baron Seaford* [U K], *and co h to the Barony of Ogle* [E 1461], *Capt 2nd County of London Yeo, form ds 10th Hussars* (*Kilmarnock*, *Audley End, Saffron Walden*, *Seaford House*, *37 Belgrave Square*, *S W*), b 9 *May* 1880

2d *Rev the Hon William Charles Ellis*, M A (*Oxon*), *Rector of Bothal-with-Hebburn* (*B thalhaugh, Morpeth*), b 22 *July* 1835, m 16 *Dec* 1873, *Henrietta Elizabeth, da of Henry Metcalfe Ames of Linden*, *and has issue* 1e *to* 6e

1e *Henry Guysulf Bertram Ellis*, b 7 *Mar* 1875

2e *Humphrey Cadogan Ellis*, b 21 *Jan* 1879

3e *Francis Bevis Ellis*, b 17 *Ap* 1883

4e *Roland Arthur Ellis*, b 7 *June* 1884

5e *Lucy Henrietta Katharine Ellis*, m 28 *July* 1908, *William Brabazon Lindesay* (*Graham Toler*), *4th Earl of Norbury* [I] (*Carlton Park, Market Harborough*)

6e *Henrietta Christobel Ellis*

3d *Hon Evelyn Henry Ellis, late R N* (*Rosenau, near Datchet*, 35 *Portland Plce*, *W*), b 9 *Aug* 1843, m 9 *Mar* 1882, *Albertha Mary* (p 333), *da of Gen the Hon Sir Arthur Edward Hardinge*, K C B, C I E *and his issue* 1e *to* 2e

1e *Arthur Evelyn Paul Ellis* b 27 *Ap* 1884

2e *Mary Ellis*

2c *Hon Augustus Frederick Ellis, Lieut-Col 60th Rifles, M P*, b 17 *Sept* 1800, d 16 *Aug* 1841, m 25 *June* 1828, *Mary Frances Thurlow, da of Sir David Cunynghame, 5th Bt* [S] [*rem 2ndly, William, Baron von Munster and*] d 12 *Sept* 1851, *and had issue* 1d *to* 5d

1d *Charles David Cunynghame Ellis, Major 60th Rifles*, b 25 *July* 1833, d 5 *Dec* 1906 m 17 *Nov* 1859, *Emily* (*Peebles Court, Holyport, Maidenhead*), *da of Major-Gen Sir Guy Campbell, 1st Bt* [U K], *C B*, *and had issue* 1e *to* 4e

1e *Augustus Frederick Guy Ellis* (*Fort George Penn, Annotta Bay, Jamaica*, *Stanford Wood, Bradfield, Berks*), b 10 *Dec* 1868, m 10 *Jan* 1899, *Mary Agnes, widow of the Hon E G Levy, da of the Hon Henry Westmorland, both of Jamaica*

2e *Mary Pamela Ellis* (*Larkfield, Holyport Road, Maidenhead*), m as 2nd wife, 2 *July* 1889, *Col David Milne-Home of Wedderburn*, D L, *late R H G*, d 19 *Nov* 1901, *and has issue* 1f

1f *Charles Alexander Milne-Home*, b 25 *Ap* 1891

3e *Helen Louisa Georgina Ellis*, m 16 *Ap* 1885, *James Grahame Stewart* (*Stonewall, Edenbridge Kent*), *and has issue* 1f *to* 2f

1f *John Cecil Graham Stewart*, b 1897

2f *Felicia Louise Marie Stewart*

4e *Lucy Emily Madeline Ellis* (*Pebbles Court, Holyport, Maidenhead*)

2d *Sir Arthur Edward Augustus Ellis*, G C V O, C S I, G C D, *Major-Gen Grenadier Guards, Equerry to H M the King and Comptroller in Lord Steward's Dept* 1901-1907, b 13 *Dec* 1837, d 11 *June* 1907, m 2 *May* 1864, *the Hon Mina Frances* (29 *Portland Place*, *W*), *da and co-h of Henry* (*Labouchere*), *1st Baron Taunton* [U K], *and had issue* 1e *to* 7e.

1e *Henry Arthur Augustus Ellis, a Clerk in the House of Commons*, b 13 *Feb* 1866

[Nos 55453 to 5547]

332

# of The Blood Royal

2e Gerald Montagu Augustus Ellis, Capt (ret) Rifle Brigade, *formerly* a Page of Honour to Queen Victoria, served in India 1897-1898 (Medal with Clasps) and in S Africa 1899-1901 (Medal with 5 Clasps), *b* 13 Sept 1872

3e Mary Evelyn Ellis, *m* 17 Dec 1885, Ralph Sneyd of Keele [descended from King Henry VII (see Supplement to Essex Volume, p 176] (*Keele Hall, Newcastle-under-Lyme*)

4e Albertha Lilian Magdalen Ellis, for whom H M King Edward was Sponsor

5e Alexandra Mina Ellis, for whom H M Queen Alexandra was Sponsor, *m* 4 Nov 1899, Sir Arthur Hardinge, K C B , K C M G , H B M's Minister at Brussels (see below) (*British Legation, Brussels , Bencombe, Dursley, Glouc*) , and his issue 1*f*

1*f* Henry Arthur Mina Hardinge, *b* 1 Oct 1904

6e Evelyn Mary Ellis, *m* 22 June 1898, Walter William Kerr [M of Lothian Coll and a descendant of King Henry VII (see Tudor Roll, p 168)]

7e Dorothy Ellis, *m* 10 Aug 1899, Charles Theodore Halswell Kemeys-Tynte of Cefn Mably and Halswell (*Cefn Mably, Cardiff, &c*) , and has issue 1*f*

1*f* Elizabeth Dorothy Kemeys-Tynte (same as Nos 28553-28554, p 184)

3d Mary Georgiana Frances Ellis, a Woman of the Bedchamber to H M Queen Alexandra when Princess of Wales, 1867-1901, *m* 30 Dec 1858, Gen the Hon Sir Arthur Edward Hardinge, K C B , C I E , G C D [Vt Hardinge Coll], *d* 15 July 1892 , and has issue 1e to 3e

1e Sir Arthur Henry Hardinge, K C B , K C M G , H B M's Minister to the Court of Brussels, *formerly* at Teheran (*British Legation, Brussels , Bencombe, Dursley, Glouc*), *b* 12 Oct 1859 , *m* 1 Nov 1899, Alexandra Mina (see above), da of Sir Arthur Edward Augustus Ellis, G C V O , &c , and has issue 1*f*

1*f* Henry Arthur Mina Hardinge, *b* 1 Oct 1904 (same as No 55476, above)

2e. Albertha Mary Hardinge, *m* 9 Mar 1882, the Hon Evelyn Henry Ellis (*Rosenau, near Datchet, &c*) , and has issue

See p 332, Nos 55462-55463

3e Hon Mary Ellis, *formerly* Maid of Honour to Queen Victoria, *m* 17 July 1894, Major Ivone Kirkpatrick, S Staffordshire Regt , and an A D G in India

4d Annie Eliza Margaret Ellis (5 *Piazza Madonna degli Aldobrandini, Florence*), *m* 13 June 1859, Col Sir Charles Edward Mansfield, K C M G , *formerly* H B M's Minister and Consul-Gen at Lima [younger brother of William Rose, 1st Baron Sandhurst [U K], G C B], *d* 1 Aug 1907 , and has issue 1e to 3e

1e John Charles Ellis Mansfield, a Pasha and Major-Gen in the Egyptian Army (*Cairo*), *b* 8 Aug 1860 , *m* 20 Oct 1889, Lina Marie Eugenie, da of Alexander Lubstoff, and has issue 1*f*

1*f* John Charles Mansfield, *b* 21 Sept 1890

2e Frederick Henry Edward Mansfield (*Rhodesia, S Africa*), *b* 1 Nov 1864 , *m* 1904, Kate, da of Stephen Dorey of Wool, co Dorset

3e Mildred Mary Blanche Mansfield

5d Augusta Louisa Caroline Ellis, a Lady-in-Waiting to H I and R H the Dow -Duchess of Saxe-Coburg-Gotha (Duchess of Edinburgh) (*The King's Cottage, Kew*), *m* 25 Dec 1861, Debonnaire John (Monson), 8th Baron Monson [G B], C V O [descended from Anne, Duchess of Exeter], *d* 18 June 1900 , and his issue

See the Exeter Volume, p 243, Nos 9109-9115

2a Frederick William (Hervey), 5th Earl [G B] and (30 *Jun* 1826) 1st *Marquis of Bristol [U K] 5th Lord Hervey [E], &c*, F R S , *b* 2 Oct 1769 , *d* 15 Feb 1859 , *m* 20 Feb 1798, *the Hon Elizabeth Albana, da of Clotworthy* (*Upton*), 1st *Baron Templetown [I], d* 25 May 1844 , *and had issue 1b to 8b*

1b *Frederick William (Hervey), 2nd Marquis [U K] and 6th Earl [G B] of Bristol, and 6th Baron Hervey [E],* b. 15 *July* 1800 , *d* 30 Oct 1864 , *m* 9 *Oct*

[Nos 55472 to 55500

The Plantagenet Roll

1830, *Lady Katherine Isabella* [*descended from King Henry VII*], *da of John (Manners), 5th Duke of Rutland* [*E*], *K G*, *d 20 Ap 1848, and had issue*

See the Tudor Roll, pp 296-297, Nos 25460-25479

2b Lord *William Hervey, C B*, b 27 Sept 1805, d 6 May 1850, m 8 Sept 1844, *Cecilia Mary, da of Vice-Adm Sir Thomas Fremantle, G C B*, d 24 Nov 1871, *and had issue* 1c to 3c

1c Sir George William Hervey, K C B, Sec and Comptroller-Gen of the National Debt (*Finchley House, Finchley, Carlton, &c*), b 16 June 1845, m 9 Feb 1881, Emily Dora [descended from George, Duke of Clarence, K G (see the Clarence Volume, p 176)], da of Lord Charles Pelham Clinton [D of Newcastle Coll], and has issue 1d to 4d

2d Gerald Edward William Hervey, *formerly* Lieut Suffolk Regt, b 5 Dec 1881

2d Philip Henry Charles Hervey, b 13 Jan 1883

3d Eric George Hervey, b 6 Dec 1884

4d Claude Arthur Hervey, b 16 Mar 1891

2c *Francis Arthur Hervey*, b 11 Mar 1849, d 13 Jan 1905, m 1 June 1876, *Louisa Maude* (*Hedgerley, Esher*), *da of Richard Rice Clayton of Hedgerley Park, co Bucks, and had issue* 1d to 3d

1d Richard George Hervey, Lieut R N, b 17 July 1879

2d Alec Francis Hervey, b 8 Oct 1885

3d Lionel Arthur Hervey, b 24 June 1889

3c Augusta Elizabeth Hervey (12 *Moore Street, Cadogan Square, S W*)

3b *Right Rev Lord Arthur Charles Hervey, Lord Bishop of Bath and Wells 1869-1894*, b 20 Aug 1808, d 9 June 1894, m 30 July 1839, *Patience, da of John Singleton, d 14 Dec 1904, and had issue* 1c to 8c

1c Rev John Frederick Arthur Hervey, M A (Camb), Rector of Shotley and + C A Suffolk (*Shotley Rectory, Ipswich*), b 11 Nov 1840, m 22 Ap 1885, Emily, da of Thomas Ely, and has issue 1d to 4d

1d Arthur Charles Constantine Hervey, b 18 Dec 1886

2d Margaret Caroline Hervey

3d Mary Edith Emily Hervey

4d Patience Gertrude Hervey

2c George Henry William Hervey (*Church House, Tendring, Essex*), b 17 Feb 1843, m 1st, 13 July 1876, Emma, da of William Arkwright of Sutton Scarsdale, co Derby, d 29 Ap 1877, 2ndly, 3 July 1879, Mary, da of William Wells Cole, d 21 Aug 1900, and has issue 1d to 5d

1d Douglas George Hervey, b 3 Ap 1880

2d Gerald Arthur Hervey, B A (Camb), b 3 Oct 1881

3d [1] Gwendolen Emma Hervey

4d [2] Geraldine Mary Hervey

5d [2] Eveline Victoria Hervey

3c Rev Sydenham Henry Augustus Hervey, *formerly* Vicar of Wedmore (*Angel Hill, Bury St Edmunds*), b 20 Dec 1846, *unm*

4c Constantine Rodney William Hervey, *late* Col R A (*Thurston Cottage, Bury St Edmunds*) b 6 Dec 1850, m 12 Aug 1886, Mary Frances, da of William Hanford Flood of Flood Hall and Farmley, co Kilkenny, and has issue 1d

1d Alice Lucy Patience Hervey

5c Rev James Arthur Hervey, Rector of Chipstead (*Chipstead Rectory, Surrey*), b 26 Sept 1854, m 15 July 1886, Margaret Augusta, da of Sir Robert Percy Douglas, 4th Bt [G B], and has issue 1d

1d Thomas Arthur Percy Hervey, b 23 July 1887

6c Katherine Patience Georgiana Hervey (*Purbrook Park, Cosham, Hants*),

[Nos 55501 to 55546

334

# of The Blood Royal

m 9 Ap 1872, Charles Hoare [descended from King Henry VII (see the Tudor Roll, p 273)]. *d* 30 Mar 1898, and had issue 1*d* to 7*d*

 1*d* Charles Hervey Hoare, Capt Glamorgan Imp Yeo (*Hockridge, Cranbrook, Kent*), *b* 16 Dec 1875, *m* 1909, Marie, widow of Sir Lepel Henry Griffin, K C S I, da of Ludwig Leupold of La Coronato, Genoa

  2*d* Arthur Hervey Hoare, *b* 25 July 1877

  3*d* Guy Hervey Hoare, *b* 16 Oct 1879

  4*d* Reginald Hervey Hoare, 3rd Sec Dip Ser, *b* 1882

  5*d* Patience Mary Hoare

  6*d* Constance Sarah Hoare

  7*d* Katherine Angela Adeleza Hoare

 7*c* Patience Mary Hervey, *m* 17 July 1873, Charles Rowland Palmer Morewood of Alfreton J P, D L, High Sheriff co Warwick 18— (*Alfreton Park, Derby, Ladbroke Hall, Southam*, 66 *Queen's Gate, S W*), and has issue 1*d* to 2*d*

 1*d* Rowland Charles Arthur Palmer-Morewood, J P (*Ladbroke Hall, Southam, co Warwick*), *b* 9 Jan 1877

 2*d* Clara Winifred Sarah Palmer, *m* 27 Ap 1905, Alwyne Mason [eldest son of Robert Harvey Mason of Necton Hall] (*Necton Hall, Norfolk*)

 8*c* Caroline Augusta Hervey (*The Grove, Alfreton*)

 4*b* *Rev Lord Charles Amelius Hervey, D D* b 1 Nov 1814 d 11 Ap 1880, m 15 Aug 1839, *Lady Harriet Charlotte Sophia* [descended from King Henry VII], da of Dudley (Ryder), 1st Earl of Harrowby [U K], d 25 Sept 1899, and had issue

See the Tudor Roll, p 526, Nos 35149–35173

 5*b* *Lord Alfred Hervey, M P*, and a Lord of the Treasury, &c, b 25 June 1816, d 15 Ap 1875, m 5 Aug 1845, *Sophia Elizabeth* (see p 151), da of Lieut -Gen John Chester Bagot [Bt Coll], d 20 Sept 1892, and had issue 1c to 3c

 1*c* Rev Frederick Alfred John Hervey, C V O, M A (Camb), Canon of Norwich and Domestic Chaplain and Chaplain-in-Ordinary to H M King Edward, &c, *formerly* Rector of Sandringham and Chaplain to Queen Victoria (*The Close, Norwich*), b 18 May 1846, m 13 Oct 1881, Mabel Elizabeth [descended from King Henry VII (see the Tudor Roll, p 466)], da of Major-Gen Augustus Frederick Francis Lennox [D of Richmond and Lennox Coll], and has issue 1*d*

 1*d* Alexandra Leila Hervey, for whom H M Queen Alexandra stood Sponsor

 2*c* Algernon Charles George Hervey (*Church Walk House, Hunstanton*), b 28 Sept 1851, *unm*

 3*c* Mary Frederica Sophia Hervey (22 *Morpeth Mansions, S W*)

 6*b* *Lady Augusta Hervey*, b 29 Dec 1798 d 17 Mar 1880, m as 2nd wife, 18 Sept 1832, *Frederick Charles William Seymour* [M of Hertford Coll], d. 7 Dec 1856, and had issue

See the Clarence Volume, p 137, Nos 1810–1807 and 1810–1814

 7*b* *Lady Georgiana Elizabeth Hervey*, d 16 Jan 1869, m as 1st wife, 12 July 1836, Rev the Hon John Grey [E Grey Coll], d 11 Nov 1895, and had issue

See the Essex Volume, p 183, Nos 24013–24014

 8*b* *Lady Sophia Elizabeth Caroline Hervey*, b 26 Ap 1811 d 30 Sept 1863, m 1st, 18 July 1835, William Howe Windham of Felbrigg Hall, co Norfolk, d 22 Dec 1855, 2ndly, 10 May 1858, (—) Giubilio

 3*a* *Lady Mary Caroline Hervey*, d 10 Jan 1812, m as 2nd wife, 22 Feb 1776, John (Creichton), 1st Earl of Erne [I], P C, d 15 Sept 1828, and had issue 1*b*

 1*b* *Lady Caroline Elizabeth Mary Creichton*, b 1778, d 23 Ap 1856, m 30 Mar 1799, James Archibald (Stuart-Wortley-Mackenzie), 1st Baron Wharncliffe [U K], d 19 Dec 1845, and had issue

See the Exeter Volume, pp 297–298, Nos 11808–14882

[Nos 55547 to 55675

The Plantagenet Roll

201 Descendants of the Hon LEPEL HERVEY (Table XXI), *b* Jan 1723, *d* 11 Mar 1780, *m* 26 Feb 1743, CONSTANTINE (PHIPPS), 1st BARON MULGRAVE [I], *bapt.* 22 Aug 1722, *d* 13 Sept 1775, and had issue

See the Exeter Volume, Table XII, and pp 236-237, Nos 8448-8702

[Nos 55676 to 55939

202 Descendants of the Hon MARY HERVEY (Table XXI), *b* 1726, *d* 9 Ap 1815, *m* 31 Oct 1745, GEORGE FITZGERALD of Turlough, co Mayo. Capt in the Austrian Service, *d* 23 June 1782, and had issue 1*a* to 2*a*

1*a* *George Robert FitzGerald of Turlough, d* (-), *m* 1st *(sett. dated 10 Feb)*, 1770, *Jan , da of the Right Hon William Conolly of Castletown, co Kildare [by his wife Lady Anne, nee Wentworth], d 1780 , and had issue 1b*
1*b* *Mary Anne FitzGerald*

2*a* *Charles Lionel FitzGerald of Turlough, Lieut-Col N Mayo Militia, d 29 Ap 1805, m 1777, Dorothea, da of Sir Thomas Butler, 6th Bt [I], M P d 11 Ap 1829 and had issue 1b to 4b*

1*b* *Thomas George FitzGerald of Turlough Park, co Mayo, and Maperton House, co Som , Lieut-Col in the Army D L, b 5 June 1778 , d (-), m 1st, 6 Sept 1800, Delia, da of Joshua Field of Heaton, co York, d (-) , 2ndly, 29 Ap 1819, Elizabeth, da of James Crowther of Bolshay Hall, co York, d 15 Sept 1838, and had issue 1c to 4c*

1*c* *Charles Lionel William FitzGerald of Turlough Park, d 9 Nov 1834, m Dorothea Julia (see p 340), da of Patrick Kirwan of Dalgin, d (-), and had (with possibly other) issue 1 t*
1*d* *Charles Lionel FitzGerald of Turlough, J P , D L , b 24 Aug 1833, d s p 28 Dec 1902.*

2*c* *Henry Thomas George FitzGerald of Maperton House, co Som , J P , Major sometime 1st Life Guards b 5 Mar 1820 , d 25 May 1890, m 23 May 1839, Elizabeth Harriott, da of the Rev Samuel Wallman Yates, Vicar of St Mary's, Reading d 26 Nov 1884 , and had issue 1d to 4d*
1*d* *George Wildman Yates FitzGerald, b 29 Mar 1840 , d v p at sea 29 June 1873 , m at Christ Church, Sydney N S W , 13 Oct 1869, Frances Isabella, da of Sprott Boyd, M D , d 23 Mar 1900 and had issue 1e*
1*e* *Elizabeth Harriot FitzGerald, m 8 June 1898, Freeman Roper, J P (Forde Abbey, Chard, Somerset) , and has issue 1f to 3f*
1*f* *George FitzGerald Roper, b 19 Ap 1899*
2*f* *Geoffrey Desmond Roper, b 26 Feb 1901*
3*f* *Isobel Katharine Roper, b 23 May 1904*

2*d* *Charles Lionel Wingfield FitzGerald of Turlough, b 26 Dec 1841 , d s p 7 Jan 1909, m 1893, Adolphine Caroline Annie Helena Marie (Turlough Park, Castlebar, co Mayo , Winterton Hall, Hythe, Southampton), da of Capt Schmitz, Imperial German Army*

3*d* *Charlotte Elizabeth Harriott FitzGerald, m 14 Nov 1867, Major-Gen John Talbot Coke, J P [descended from George, Duke of Clarence, K G] (Trusley, co Derby , Debdale Hall, Mansfield), and has issue*

See the Clarence Volume, pp 183-184, Nos 3043-3058

4*d* *Frances Geraldine FitzGerald, m 30 Ap 1868, Sir Richard George Glyn, 3rd Bt [G B] late Capt 1st Dragoons, J P , D L , C C , and High Sheriff co Dorset 1869 (Gaunt's House, Wimborne) , and has issue 1e to 2e*

[Nos 55931 to 55952

336

# of The Blood Royal

1e Richard FitzGerald Glyn, Lieut Army Motor Reserve, *formerly* 1st Dragoons, served in S Africa 1900 (*Fontmell Magna, Shaftesbury*), b 13 May 1875, m Dec 1906, Edith Hilda, da of Douglas George Hamilton Gordon [E of Aberdeen Coll] and has issue 1f to 2f

1f Richard Hamilton Glyn, b 12 Oct 1907

2f Gerald Glyn, b Jan 1909

2e Geraldine Mary Glyn, m 30 Nov 1898, Ralph Paget [M of Anglesey Coll and a descendant of the Lady Isabel Plantagenet (see Essex Volume, p 110)] (*St Mary's Grange, Salisbury*)

3c² Elizabeth Geraldine FitzGerald, m Ap 1840, John Eveleigh Wyndham of Stock Dennes, co Som, M A, J P, b 25 May 1814, d 9 Nov 1887, and has issue (with an eldest da, Mary Geraldine, d young 1851) 1d to 10d

1d *Thomas Heathcote Gerald Wyndham, M A, Fellow of Merton College*, b 1842, d (? unm) 11 Nov 1876

2d Edward John Eveleigh Wyndham, b 1846, m 1886, Amy, da of J K Huntley of West Hall, co Flints

3d Charles Hugh Wyndham, *late* 21st Fusiliers, b 1848

4d Francis Wadham Wyndham, b 1851

5d Jane Florence Wyndham

6d Alice Wyndham

7d Blanche Wyndham

8d Eva Wyndham

9d Isabel Wyndham

10d Geraldine Wyndham

4c² Mary Dorothea FitzGerald, m the Rev Edward Newton Dickenson, and has issue 1d to 4d[1]

1d Edward Newton Dickenson

2d. Clara Dickenson

3d Cecil Dickenson

4d Lily Dickenson

2b *Edward Thomas FitzGerald, Lieut-Col in the Army and A Q M G with the Guards at Waterloo,* b 22 Dec 1784, d 19 Sept. 1845, m 20 Nov 1811, Emma, da of Edmond Green of Medham, I W, d 1862, and had issue 1c to 6c

1c *Lionel Charles Henry William FitzGerald, K T S, 2nd W I Regt, served with Doña Maria's Forces in Portugal* 1832–1834, b 9 Sept 1812, d 21 Dec 1894 m 31 Jan 1839, Sarah Caroline, da of the Hon Patrick Brown of Nassau, N P, d 19 Nov 1856, and had issue 1d to 2d

1d Desmond FitzGerald, C E (*Brookline, Boston, Mass, U S A*), b 20 May 1840, m 21 June 1870, Elizabeth Parker Clarke, da of Stephen Salisbury of Brookline afsd, M D, and has issue 1e to 4e

1e Harold FitzGerald (127 *East 56th Street, New York*), b 19 May 1877, m 3 Oct 1903, Eleanor, da of Gen Lewis FitzGerald of New York, and has issue 1f

1f Eleanora FitzGerald

2e Stephen Salisbury FitzGerald, b 19 Sept 1878, m 9 Sept 1906, Agnes, da of Francis Blake of Weston, Mass

3e Caroline Elizabeth FitzGerald, m 12 Dec 1899, Charles Augustus van Rensselaer (130 *East 56th Street, New York*), and has issue 1f to 2f

1f Charles Augustus van Rensselaer, b 28 Sept 1902

2f Stephen van Rensselaer, b 29 Nov 1905

4e Harriot FitzGerald, m 18 Nov 1897, Robert Jones Clark (*Dedham, Mass*) and has issue 1f to 2f   [Nos 55953 to 55979

---

[1] Burke's " Landed Gentry of Ireland," 1899, p 144

The Plantagenet Roll

1f Robert FitzGerald Clark *b* 13 Sept 1898

2f Geraldine Clark

2d Ormond Edward FitzGerald, *b* 6 July 1849 *unm*

2c Edgar Thomas FitzGerald, *b* 19 S. bt 1817 d (-) m 1856 Ivnte
Frances, or da of Leonard S Cox and had issue 1d to 2d

1d Edgar Leonard FitzGerald, *b* 17 Jun. 1859 d 1896 m 3 Aug 1882,
Florence Elizabeth Sophia da of Roger J Hunter and had issue 1e to 6e

1e Edward Walter FitzGerald *b* 19 Jan 1885, *unm*

2e Desmond FitzGerald *b* 1 Sept 1893

3e Florence FitzGerald ⎫

4e Marjorie FitzGerald ⎪

5e Dorothy FitzGerald ⎬ *unm*

6e Audrey FitzGerald ⎭

2d Anne FitzGerald,

3c Desmond Gerald FitzGerald *b* 28 Dec. 1834, d 5 Jan 1908 m 20 May
1862 Louisa, da of Matthew Crawford of Crowlin co Westmeath d 30 Nov 1906
and had issue 1d o 5i

1f Desmond Gerald FitzGerald of Turlough High Sheriff co Mayo 1909
(Turlough Park Castlebar co Mayo) *b* 25 May 1863

2f Ormonde Edward FitzGerald (Charleville, Turlough co Mayo), *b* 1 Mar
1865 *m* 16 June 1900 Rebecca Susannah da of Becher Lionel Fleming of New-
court co Cork and has issue 1e to 2e

1e Gerald FitzGerald *b* Ap 1904

2e Elizabeth Cicely FitzGerald

3f Cecil Henry FitzGerald C E *b* 5 Jan 1871 *m* May 1904, Mary, da of
(—) Rinter of Lydenburg Transvaal and has issue 1e to 2

1e Cecil FitzGerald, *b* Ap 1905

2. Sheelah Nesta FitzGerald

4f Emma Louisa Hope FitzGerald *m* Oct 1902 Duncan A MacLeod [2nd,
son of the Rev John MacLeod D D, Rector of Govan] d 11 Dec 1907, and has
issue 1e to 2.

1e Duncan Crawford MacLeod, *b* 24 Ap 1907

2e Deirdre Hope Gwendolen MacLeod

5f Ruby Gwendoline FitzGerald

4c Louisa FitzGerald, d (—) m 1841 the Rev Edward Powell d (-), and
had issue (with a da, Mrs Trempson d s p) 1d to 4d

1d Robert Powell, *b* 1812 d 1904 m 1863, Julia, da of Joshua F Whitell
of Helmsley Long. co York and had issue 1e to 5e

1e Joshua Edward Powell *b* (—) m 1905, (—), da of (—), and has issue 1f

1f [da.] Powell

2e Robert Powell, *b* (—) *m* 1909 Kathleen da of W J Shannon of Killine,
co Dublin

3e Louisa Powell, *unm*

4e Annie Florence Powell *unm*

5e Henrietta Powell *unm*

2d Edward FitzGerald Powell, *b* (—) d 1878 m Frances da of (—) Darley
of co York and had issue 1e to 2e

1e Edward Darley Powell C E, *b* 1877 *m* 1909, (—), da of (—)

2e Marian Powell *unm*   [Nos 55980 to 56008

¹ Ex inform D G FitzGerald of Turlough

3d Henry Powell, b (—), m Frances, da of Winter Irving of Australia, and has issue 1c

1c Henry Irving FitzGerald Powell, b

4d Louisa Powell, d (—), m Henly J Edwards, Lieut Indian Navy, d (—) and had issue 1e to 5e

1e Arthur Edwards, b (—), m and has issue

2e [son] Edwards

3e [son] Edwards

4e Gerald Edwards, unm

5e Geraldine Spencer Edwards, m 6 Jan 1891, Mountifort Longfield, J P (see p 398) (Sea Court, Timoleague, co Cork)

5c Catherine Dorothea FitzGerald, d 1873, m 1848, Frederick Barry, c (—), and had issue [1] 1d to 2d

1d Mary Barry, unm

2d Amy Barry, m Horatio Francis Hoskins, and has issue 1e to 2e

1e Noel Hoskins

2e Francis Desmond Hoskins

6c Dorothea Frances FitzGerald, d (—), m 1847 Peter Bourke, d (—), and had issue (with other sons and 2 das who both m and left issue) 1d to 3d

1d John Bourke, d (—) m and had issue

2d Peter Bourke, b (—)

3d Desmond Bourke b (—)

3b Charles Lionel FitzGerald, Lieut Col and Hon Brig Gen in Peninsular War, d (—), m Marianne, da of Lieut-Col Breeton, R I , and had issue (all settled in the Colonies) 1c to 6c

1c Charles Lionel FitzGerald, Lieut-Col R I , d (—), m (—), da of Lieut Col Petter, R A , and had issue (with other sons) 1d to 3d

1d Charles Lionel FitzGerald ⎫
2d Ormonde FitzGerald,   ⎬ all resident in Canada
3d Olive FitzGerald,   ⎭

2c Henley FitzGerald d (—), m and had issue 1d

1d Hervey FitzGerald

3c Alfred John FitzGerald, Lieut Col 60th Rifles b 5 Nov 1842 d s p

4c Ormonde FitzGerald, d (—) m and had issue (with other sons) 1d to 3d

1d Henry FitzGerald, Indian Frontier Police

2d Ormonde FitzGerald

3d Augusta FitzGerald, m

5c Henry FitzGerald, d (—) m (—), da of (—) Knott, and had issue (several sons and das)

6c Augustus FitzGerald d (—), m and had issue 1d to 4d

1d Hervey FitzGerald, b (—) m (—)

2d Desmond FitzGerald, b (—)

3d Florence FitzGerald

4d Gertrude FitzGerald

4b Dorothea Mary FitzGerald d (—), m 1890 × Patrick Kirwan of Dalgin Park co Mayo, d 1854, and had issue 1c to 6c

1c Charles Lionel Kirwan, afterward, Maitland-Kirwan, of Dalgin, J P , D L , High Sheriff co Mayo 1846, b July 1811 d 1862 m 25 Oct 1842, Martha Elizabeth, da of William Maitland of Inchlone and Gelston, and had issue 1d to 9d

1d Charles Lionel Maitland-Kirwan of Gelston Castle b 9 July 1843, d s p 11 Nov 1889   (Nos 55069 to 55042)

---

[1] Ex inform D G FitzGerald of Turlough

The Plantagenet Roll

2d William Francis Maitland-Kirwan of Gelston Castle, J P , D L , Lord of the Barony of Gelston, *late* Capt 78th Highlanders (*Gelston Castle, Castle Douglas, Kircudbright*), b 1845 , m 20 Nov 1879, Mary Alice da of James Tyrrell of Auchangreagh, co Longford , s p

3d Lionel Maitland-Kirwan, b Ap 1849 , m 29 Aug 1878, Agnes, da of Wellwood Herries Maxwell of Munches, J P , D L , M P , and has issue 1e to 3e

    1e Lionel FitzGerald Maitland-Kirwan, Lieut R N , b 1879

    2e Matilda Rowe Maitland-Kirwan

    3e A Marguerite Maitland Kirwan.

4d James Maitland Maitland-Kirwan, b 1853, d 1907 , m 2 June 1876, Edith Mary O Sullivan, da of J Bateman and had issue 1e to 3e

    1e James Douglas Maitland-Kirwan, b 1889

    2e Mary Douglas Maitland-Kirwan

    3e Edith Valerie Maitland-Kirwan

5d Gerald Maitland-Kirwan, b 1862 , m (—), and has issue 1e

    1e Gerald Maitland-Kirwan, b 1897

6d Mary Agnes Maitland-Kirwan, m 25 June 1868, Lieut -Col Hamilton Campbell , and has issue 1e

    1e Charles Lionel Kirwan Campbell, Major 16th Lancers, b 1 Nov 1873

7d Dorothea FitzGerald Maitland-Kirwan, m 29 Mar 1877, William Jardine Herries Maxwell of Munches, M A (Oxon), J P , D L , M P for co Dumfries 1892-1895 and 1900-1906, Convener of the Stewartry of Kircudbright (*Munches, near Dalbeattie , Terraughty, near Dumfries*) , and has issue 1e to 7e

    1e William Jardine Herries Maxwell, Lieut Cameron Highlanders, b 8 June 1882

    2e Charles Lionel Maxwell, b Aug 1883

    3e Desmond Maxwell, Lieut R N , b Oct 1886

    4e John Maxwell, b June 1889

    5e Matilda Elizabeth Maxwell

    6e Jean Helen Maxwell

    7e Victoria Maxwell

8d Matilda Douglas Maitland Kirwan, m Major-Gen Oldfield , and has issue 1e

    1e Henry Oldfield, b 1880

9d Eva Maitland-Kirwan, m 24 July 1895, Major the Hon Percy Cecil Evans Freke, D L [2nd son of Algernon William George, 9th Baron Carbery [I] , and a descendant of George, Duke of Clarence, K G (see Clarence Volume, p 262)] (*Bisbrook Hall, Uppingham*) . and has issue 1e

    1e Maida Cecil Evans-Freke

    2e Martin Frances Kirwan

    3e Caroline Kirwan

    4e *Dorothea Julia Kirwan*, d (-) , m. *Charles Lionel William FitzGerald of Turlough*, d 9 Nov 1834 , and had issue

    See p 336

    5e *Mary Kirwan*

    6e *Julia Emma Kirwan*   [Nos 56033 to 56058

203 Descendants of the Hon THOMAS HERVEY, M P (Table XXI), b 20 Jan 1699 , d 10 Jan. 1775 , m 1744, ANNE, da and co-h of FRANCIS COGHLAN, Councillor of Law, Ireland, d 27 Dec 1761 , and had issue 1a.

1a *William Thomas Hervey, Col in the Guards,* d (-) , m *Elizabeth, da and h of Francis Marsh*

# of The Blood Royal

204 Descendants of Rev the Hon. HENRY HERVEY, *afterwards* (Act Parl. 22 Mar 1744) ASTON, D D (Table XXI), *b* 5 Jan. 1700, *d* (–), *m.* 2 Mar. 1730, CATHERINE, sister and h of Sir Thomas Aston of Aston, 4th Bt [E], da. of Sir Thomas ASTON, 3rd Bt [E], *d* (–); and had issue 1*a*

1*a* *Henry Hervey Aston of Aston, co Chester,* d (–), m (–), *da of* (—) *Dickinson, and had issue* 1*b to* 2*b*

1*b* *Henry Hervey Aston of Aston, Col in the Army,* d 23 Dec 1798, m 16 Sept 1789, *the Hon Harriet, da of Charles (Ingram-Shepherd), 9th Viscount Irvine* [S], *and had issue*

See the Essex Volume, p 150, Nos 17211–17243

2*b* *Anna Sophia Aston,* d (–), m 1782, *Anthony Hodges*

[Nos 56059 to 56091]

205 Descendants of the Hon. FELTON HERVEY, M P (Table XXI), *b* 12 Feb 1712, *d* 18 Aug 1773, *m* DOROTHY, widow of Charles PITFIELD, da of Solomon ASHLEY, *d.* 8 Nov 1761; and had issue 1*a* to 4*a*.

1*a* *Felton Lionel Hervey, Lieut R H G,* d 9 *Sept* 1785, m 2 *Mar* 1779, *Selina Mary, da and h of Sir John Elwill, 4th Bt* [G B] [m 2ndly, 21 Sept 1797, *the Right Hon Sir William Henry Fremantle, G C H, P C, and*] d 23 Nov. 1841, *and had issue*

See the Essex Volume, pp 56–59, Nos 5620–5713

2*a* *Emily Hervey,*
3*a* *Caroline Hervey,* } d (? unm)
4*a* *Elizabeth Hervey,*

[Nos 56092 to 56185.

206 Descendants, if any surviving, of Lady LOUISA CAROLINE ISABELLA HERVEY (Table XXI), *b* 1715, *d* 11 May 1770; *m* 23 Sept 1731, Sir ROBERT SMYTH of Smith Street, Westminster, 2nd Bt [G B 1714], *d* 10 Dec 1783; *bur* at West Ham Church; and had issue 1*a* to 2*a*

1*a* *Sir Hervey Smyth, 3rd Bt* [G B], *Col Foot Guards, 1 D C to Gen Wolfe,* b 1734, d *unm* 2 *Oct* 1811

2*a* *Anna Mirabella Henrietta Smyth* b 1738, *d* (–), m 1761, *William Beale Brand of Polsted Hall, co Suffolk*

207 Descendants, if any surviving, of GEORGE (HOWARD), 4th EARL OF SUFFOLK [E] (Table XXI), *b c* 1625, *d* 21 Ap 1691, *m* 1st, CATHERINE, da of John ALLEYNE of Northanger in Blenham, co. Beds, *d a* July 1683, and had issue 1*a* to 2*a*

1*a* *Lady Mary Howard, da and co-h,* d 1712, m *Lieut-Gen Percy Kirke, Col of "Kirke's Lambs," Keeper of Whitehall Palace, Governor of Tangiers 1682– 1684,* d *at Brussels* 31 *Oct* 1691, *and had (with other) issue* 1*b to* 2*b* [1]

The Plantagenet Roll

1b Percy Kirke, Lieut-Gen and Col of "Kirke's Lambs," Keeper of White-hall Palace, b 1684, d s p 1 Jan 1741, eldest surv son

2b Diana Kirke, m John Dormer of Rousham, co Oxford, and had issue 1c

1c Diana Dormer, sole h to uncle, d unm 22 Feb 1743, bur in Westminster Abbey with uncle and grandfather

2a Lady Anne Howard, da and co-h, m William Jephson, M P, Marlow

208 Descendants if any, of Lady DIANA HOWARD (Table XXI), d June 1710, bur at Walden, m Col JOHN PITT

209 Descendants of Lady CATHERINE HOWARD (Table XXI), d at the Hague 1650, m 1st, GEORGE (STUART), 8th Lord d'Aubigny [F] [2nd surviving son of Esmé, Duke of Lennox [S]], d (being slain ex parte Regis at the Battle of Edgehill) 23 Oct 1642, 2ndly, as 1st wife, c 1649, JAMES (LIVINGSTON), 1st EARL OF NEWBURGH [S], d 26 Dec 1670, and had issue 1a to 2a

1a Charles (Stuart), 6th Duke of Lennox [S] and 3rd Duke of Richmond and 6th Baron Clifton of Leighton Bromswold [E], b 7 Mar 1640, d s p s 12 Dec 1672

2a Katherine (Stuart), suo jure 7th Baroness Clifton of Leighton Bromswold [E], sister and h, bapt 5 Dec 1640, bur 11 Nov 1702, m 1st, c 1661, Henry O'Brien, Viscount Ibrackan [son and h-app of Henry (O'Brien), 7th Earl of Thomond [I]], d s p Sept 1678, and had issue 1b

1b Katherine (O'Brien), suo jure 8th Baroness Clifton, &c [E], b 29 Jan 1673, d in New York 11 Aug 1706, m 10 July 1688, Edward (Hyde), 3rd Earl of Clarendon [E], d 31 Mar 1723, and had issue

See the Exeter Volume, Table XXVII, and pp 387–396, Nos 32552–33533

[Nos 56186 to 57167

210. Descendants of Lady ELIZABETH HOWARD (Table XXI), d. 11 Mar. 1705, m as 2nd wife, 1 Oct 1642, ALGERNON (PERCY), 10th EARL OF NORTHUMBERLAND [E]., K G., K B, bapt 13 Oct 1602, d. 13 Oct 1668, and had issue

See pp 66–71, Nos 749–1999   [Nos 57168 to 58418

211 Descendants of ROGER (BOYLE), 2nd EARL OF ORRERY [I] (Table XXI.), bapt 24 Aug 1646, d 29 Mar 1682, m 6 Feb 1665, Lady MARY (see p 431), da of Richard (SACKVILLE), 5th Earl of Dorset [E], d. 4 Nov 1710, and had issue 1a to 2a.

1a Lionel (Boyle), 3rd Earl of Orrery [I], b 1670, d s p s 31 Aug 1703

2a Charles (Boyle), 4th Earl of Orrery [I] and 1st Baron Boyle of Marston [G B], so cr 5 Sept 1711, b 28 July 1674, d 28 Aug 1731, m 30 Mar 1706, Lady Elizabeth, da of John (Cecil), 5th Earl of Exeter [E], d 12 June 1708, and had issue

See the Tudor Roll, Table XCVII and pp 418–428, Nos 30324–30994

[Nos 58418 to 59088

# of The Blood Royal

212 Descendants of HENRY (BOYLE), 1st EARL OF SHANNON [I] (Table XXI), d 28 Dec 1764 , m 2ndly, Sept 1726, Lady HARRIET, da of Charles (BOYLE), 3rd Earl of Cork [I] and 2nd Earl of Burlington [E], d. 13 Dec 1746 ; and had issue

See the Tudor Roll, Table XLV, pp 252-263, Nos 23255-23604

[Nos 59089 to 59438

213 Descendants of Capt WILLIAM BOYLE, Commissioner of Appeals [I] (Table XXI), d 1725 , m 1711, MARTHA BEAUFOY, da of Sir Samuel GARTH, Physician to the Forces in Ireland , and had issue (with 2 sons who d s p) 1a to 3a

    1a *Beaufoy Boyle*, b c 1714 d 17 May 1765, m 11 June 1736, *John Wilder of Nunhide, co Berks, and Shiplake, co Oxford, J P , D L* , bur 13 July 1772 , and had issue 1b to 4b
    1b *Rev Henry Wilder of Purley Hall, co Berks, Rector of Sulham, D C L and Fellow of St John's Coll , Camb* , b Sept 1714 , d 22 Jan 1814 , m *Joan, da of William Thoyts of Sulhamstead, d 1837* , and had issue 1c to 8c
    1c *John Wilder of Purley and Sulham, J P , D L* , bapt 30 Oct 1769 , d 22 Feb 1834 , m 22 Nov 1797 *Harriet, da of the Rev Edward Beadon, Rector of North Stoneham, d 4 Oct 1825* and had issue 1d
    1d *Rev Henry Watson Wilder of Purley, Rector of Sulham,* b 3 Nov 1798 , d (*being drowned off Yarmouth), I W , 2 July 1836* , m 8 Ap 1828, *Augusta, sister of Sir Charles Joshua Smith, 2nd Bt [U K], da of Charles Smith of Suttons, M P ,* d (*being drowned with her husband) 2 July 1836 , and had issue* 1e to 2e
    1e *Frederick Wilder of Purley and Sulham J P* , b 2 July 1832, d s p 13 May 1899
    2e *Rev Henry Beaufoy Wilder of Purley and Sulham, M A L S I , M R C S (Eng), Rector of Sulham,* b 25 Oct 1831, d 25 Ap 1908, m 1 July 1858, *Augusta, da of Langham Christie of Preston Deanery, co Northants, d 17 Nov 1892, and had issue* 1f to 5f
    1f *Rev Henry Charles Wilder, M A , Rector of Sulham (Purley Hall, Berks , Sulham House, Reading, Athenæum),* b 7 July 1860 , m 20 Ap 1893, *Cicely Helen* [descended from the Lady Anne, sister of King Edward IV , &c (see Exeter Volume, p 133)], da of the Rev Arthur Bourchier Wrey, M A [Bt Coll], and has issue 1g to 4g
        1g Henry Arthur John Wilder, b 26 May 1894
        2g Frederick Wrey Wilder, b 23 Sept 1899
        3g Augusta Helen Mary Wilder, b 29 Aug 1895
        4g Alice Victoria Wilder, b 20 Mar 1897

    2f *Francis Langham Wilder (Underwood, Whitchurch, Oxon),* b 26 July 1863 , m 28 Oct 1903, *Beatrice* [descended from George, Duke of Clarence, K G , brother of King Edward IV (see Clarence Volume, p 497)], da of Lieut -Col Frederick Drummond Hibbert , and has issue 1g to 3g
        1g John Charles Wilder, b 18 Oct 1904
        2g Frances Elizabeth Wilder
        3g Augusta Beaufoy Wilder
    3f Augusta Mary Wilder
    4f Helen Margaret Wilder
    5f Eveline Irene Wilder

    2e *William Wilder, living unm* 1857.

[Nos 59439 to 59450

343

3c *George Lodowick Wilder*, d (-), m *Augusta Ivy Mary, da. of Edmund Walcot of Winckton, co Hants, d (-), and had issue 1d to 2d*

  1d Edmund Wilder

  2d George Wilder

1c *Francis Boyle Shannon Wilder of Busbridge Hall, co Surrey*, b 18 Dec 1785, d (? s p) (-), m 4 Sept 1831, *Augusta, da of John Cornwall of Hendon [by his wife the Hon Susannah Hall, née Gardner]*

5c *Mary Anne Wilder*, d (-) m *the Rev Frederick Beaton, Rector of North Stoneham, co Hants, and had issue (1 son and 2 das)*

6c *Harriet Wilder*, d (? s p), m *Charles Dixon of Stanstead, co Sussex*

7c *Lucy Wilder*, d (-), m *the Rev John Pannel of Aldsworth, co Sussex, and had issue (1 son and 1 da)*

8c *Charlotte Beaufoy Wilder*, d (-), m *William Blackwood of London, and had issue (1 da)*

  2b *Harryot Anne Wilder*,

  3b *Mary Wilder*,   } b *at Shiplake, living unm 1766*

  4b *Lucy Wilder*,

2a *Henrietta Boyle*, d (? s p), m 9 Dec 1736, *William Nichols of Froyle, co Bucks*

3a *Elizabeth Boyle*, b 1715, d (-), m 9 Oct 1736, *Matthew Graves of Chiswick, and had issue 1b*

1b *Elizabeth Graves, living at Huglescote 18 Oct 1802*, m *as 3rd wife, William Bainbridge of Palsgrave, Head Street, Southampton Buildings, Chiswick, and Newark, co Leic*, b 7 Jan 1720, d 22 Ap 1780, *and had issue (with a son, Henry, d young) 1c*

1c *Matthew Bainbridge of Huglescote Grange, co Leic*, b 14 Ap 1763, d 6 June 1802, m *Elizabeth, da of Isaac Dawson of Huglescote*, d (-), *and had issue (with a son, Matthew, d young 1792) 1d to 3d*

  1d *Henry Bainbridge* } (twins)

  2d *Isaac Bainbridge* }

  3d *Mary Elizabeth Bainbridge*   [Nos 59451 to 59452

214 Descendants of the Right Hon and Most Rev JOSEPH DEANE (BOURKE), 3rd EARL OF MAYO [I.], Lord Archbishop of Tuam (Table XXI), d 20 Aug 1794, m 1760, ELIZABETH, sister of John, 1st Earl of Clanwilliam [I], da of Sir Richard MEADE, 2nd Bt [I], d 13 Mar 1807, and had issue 1a to 7a.

1a *John (Bourke), 4th Earl of Mayo [I], P C, G C H*, b 18 June 1766; d s p 23 May 1849

2a *Right Rev the Hon Richard Bourke, Lord Bishop of Waterford and Lismore*, b 22 Ap 1767, d 15 Nov 1832, m 20 Mar 1795, *Frances, da of the Most Rev Robert Fowler, Lord Archbishop of Dublin*, d 10 Jan 1827, *and had issue 1b to 3b*

1b *Robert (Bourke), 5th Earl of Mayo [I]*, b 12 Jan 1797, d 12 Aug 1867, m 3 Aug 1820, *Anne Charlotte, da and h of the Hon John Jocelyn [E of Roden Coll]*, d 26 Jan 1867, *and had issue*

See the Clarence Volume, pp 299-300, Nos 8366-8393

2b *Lady Mildred Bourke, had Royal Warrant as an Earl's da* 19 Oct 1849, b 18 Dec 1795, d 29 July 1869, m 2 Aug 1821, *Robert John Uniacke of Woodhouse, co Waterford, J P, D L*, d 29 Mar 1851, *and had issue*

See the Essex Volume, p. 295, Nos 32358-32365

                                       [Nos 59453 to 59458.

# of The Blood Royal

    3b Lady Catherine Bourke, b 19 *July* 1804, d 12 *Sept* 1876, m 8 *June* 1830, *the Rev Henry Prittie Perry, Rector of Newcastle, co Limerick* [2nd *son of Samuel Perry of Woodrooff, co Tipperary*], *and had issue* 1c *to* 8c

    1c *Samuel William Perry,* b 1831, d (s p) 14 *Aug* 1898, m *Elizabeth Jane, da of Hastings Otway, Recorder of Belfast*

    2c *Henry Robert Prittie Perry,* d (s p) 24 *Aug* 1903

    3c-8c 6 das

    3a Very Rev the Hon Joseph Bourke, Dean of Ossory, b 24 *Dec* 1771, d 3 *May* 1843, m 23 *Ap* 1799, *Mary, da and co-h of Sackville Gardiner* [*uncle of the* 1st *Viscount Mountjoy* [I]], d (-), *and had issue* 1b

    1b *Rev Sackville Gardiner Bourke, Rector of Hatherop, co Glouc,* b 1 *May* 1805, d 30 *Jan* 1860, m 6 *June* 1839, *Lady Georgiana Sarah* [*descended from King Henry VII* (see Tudor Roll, p 237)], *da of John William (Ponsonby),* 4th *Earl of Bessborough* [I], d 25 *June* 1861, *and had issue* 1c *to* 2c

    1c *Ven Cecil Frederick Joseph Bourke, Archdeacon of Buckingham* (*Hill House, Taplow*), b 1 Sept 1841

    2c *Lucy Josepha Maria Bourke*

    4a Rev the Hon George Theobald Bourke, b 15 *Ap* 1770, d 22 *Dec* 1847, m 1808, *Augusta Georgiana, da of Thomas Webster,* d 7 *Oct* 1863, *and had issue* 1b *to* 3b

    1b *Richard Bourke, Bar-at-Law,* b 22 *Feb* 1811, d 21 *May* 1876, m 20 *June* 1849, *Gertrude, da of Robert Borrowes of Gilltown, co Kildare* [re-m 2ndly, 12 *Aug* 1858, *Anthony North Peat*], *and had issue* 1c *to* 3c

    1c *Southwell George Theobald Bourke, Bar-at-Law,* M T, *formerly Lieut* R N, J P, *and Acting Police Magistrate, Georgetown* (*Georgetown, British Guiana. Junior United Service*), b 23 July 1851, m 27 July 1881, *Catherine Jane, da of William Cameron of Tudor House, Lee, co Kent*

    2c *Hubert Edward Madden Bourke,* Lieut (ret) R N (*Naval and Military*), b 7 Dec 1853, m 4 Aug 1881, Rose, *da of Henry Blackett, and has issue* 1d *to* 3d

    1d *Dermot Southwell Richard Bourke,* b 14 *Ap* 1884

    2d *Cecil Hugh Bourke,* b 24 *Jan* 1892

    3d *Vivian Margaret Nellie Bourke*

    3c Augusta Georgiana Clara Bourke, b 1850, d 29 *Feb* 1870, m 6 *Dec* 1867, *Charles de Gannes of Pierrefonds, and had issue* 1d

    1d *Charlotte de Gannes,* m 1889, *Paul Revoil, French Ambassador to the Court of Madrid* (*French Embassy, Madrid*)

    2b Rev John Bourke, Rector of Kilmeaden, co Waterford, b 15 *Aug* 1812, d 15 *Mar* 1891, m 8 *Feb* 1842, *Louisa Maria, da of James David Potts,* d 14 *Nov* 1870, *and had issue* 1c *to* 5c

    1c *Arthur Edward Desborough Bourke,* B A (T C D), *Bar-at-Law, Inspector Local Govt Board, Ireland,* b 3 *Dec* 1852, d 31 *Jan* 1903, m 2 *Ap* 1888, *Maude Margaret* (21 *Lincoln Place, Dublin*), *da of Henry Blake Mahon of Belleville, co Galway, and had issue* 1d *to* 2d

    1d *Arthur John Henry Bourke,* b 9 *May* 1897

    2d *Eleanor Louise Bourke*

    2c *Henry Beresford Bourke,* D S O, *Lieut-Col formerly* 3rd *West India Regt* (*United Service*), b 2 June 1855

    3c *Elizabeth Margaret Bourke*

    4c *Louisa Mary Josephine Bourke*

    5c *Alice Mildred Bourke*

    3b Thomas Joseph Deane Bourke, Lieut-Col 34th *Regt,* b 7 *Mar* 1815, d 25 *Feb* 1875, m *Jan* 1849, *Mary, da of the Ven Robert Wallis, Archdeacon of Nova Scotia,* d 1895, *and had issue* 1c *to* 5c   [Nos 59189 to 59502

345

The Plantagenet Roll

1c George Deane Bourke, C B, Col R A M C, L R C S I, Principal Med Officer, Irish Command, his Nile (1884-1885) and Burmah (1888-1889) Medals with Clasps, &c (*Dublin*), b 15 Oct 1852, m 24 Jan 1883, May Morrow, da of John Stairs of Fairfield, Halifax, N S, J P, and his issue 1d

1d Ulick John Deane Bourke, Lieut 2nd Batt Oxfordshire and Bucks L I, b 13 Ap 1884

2c Robert John Bourke (*Boodle's*), b 18 Ap 1854

3c Frederick Arthur Deane Bourke (*Battleford, Saskatchewan, Canada*), b 6 July 1856, m 1887, Anne Caird, da of Col Hutchinson of Cheltenham

4c Margaret Augusta Deane Bourke

5c May Josephine Deane Bourke

5a *Lady Mary Anne Bourke*, d 24 Mar 1830, m as 2nd wife, 1806, *Admiral Thomas Sotheby*, d 1832, and had issue (*with a younger da who d s p*) 1b to 4b

1b *Rev Thomas Hans Sotheby, Vicar of Milverton*, b 1809, d 1888, m 27 Dec 1838, Jane, da of the Ven Anthony Hamilton, Archdeacon of Colchester [B Belhaven Coll], d 1842, and had issue 1c

1c Rev Walter Edward Hamilton Sotheby, Vicar of Gillingham and Rural Dean (*Gillingham Rectory, Dorset*), b 23 Feb 1842, m 24 Oct 1893, the Hon Frederica Spring [descended from George, Duke of Clarence, K G, brother of King Edward IV (see the Clarence Volume, p 562)], sister of Thomas, 2nd Baron Monteagle [U K], da of the Hon Stephen Edmond Spring Rice

2b *Sir Edward Southwell Sotheby, K C B, Admiral R N*, b 14 May 1813, d 6 Jan 1902, m 24 June 1864, Lucy Elizabeth, da of Henry John Adeane of Babraham, co Camb, d 6 Jan 1901, and had issue 1c to 3c

1c William Edward Sotheby (*Purcian, Llanengrad, Menai Bridge, Anglesey*), b 18 Dec 1865, m 24 Oct 1891, Margaret, da of William Williams of Purcian, co Anglesey, and his issue 1d to 2d

1d Lionel Frederick Southwell Sotheby, b 16 Aug 1895

2d Nigel Walter Adeane Sotheby, b 19 Sept 1896

2c Herbert George Sotheby, of H M Privy Purse Office, Buckingham Palace (*26 Green Street, Park Lane, W*), b 9 Nov 1871, m 23 Sept 1909, Catharine Barbara, da of Sir Baldwyn Leighton, 8th Bt [E]

3c Alfred Frederick Sotheby, of H M Probate Office, Somerset House (*26 Green Street, Park Lane, W*), b 22 Nov 1874 unm

3b *Mary Anne Sotheby*, d 19 Aug 1881, m as 2nd wife, her cousin, 1830, *Charles Sotheby of Sexandstone, Rear-Admiral of the Blue*, d 26 Jan 1854, and had issue (*with a son, Major Gen Frederick Edward Sotheby, and a da d unm*) 1c to 3c

1c Eleanor Catherine Sotheby (*The Grange, Weston Park, Bath*)

2c Jane Louisa Sotheby, m 18 Nov 1873, Lieut-Col Thomas William Cator [descended from the Lady Anne, sister of King Edward IV (see Exeter Volume, p 633)], d s p 14 Jan 1900

3c Cecilia Elizabeth Sotheby (*The Grange, Weston Park, Bath*)

4b *Charlotte Sotheby*, d 15 Jan 1845, m as 1st wife, 9 Mar 1837, *the Rev Robert Boothby Heathcote, J P* [descended from the Lady Anne, sister of King Edward IV], d 19 Sept 1865, and had issue

See the Essex Volume, p 675, Nos 57679/11-12

6a *Lady Charlotte Bourke*, d 15 June 1806, m as 1st wife, 27 July 1793, *William Browne of Browne's Hill, M P, J P and Custos Rotulorum, co Carlow*, b Jan 1793, d 1 Ap 1840, and had issue 1b to 4b

1b *Robert Clayton Browne of Browne's Hill, J P, D L, High Sheriff co Carlow 1831*, b 28 Jan 1799, d 22 July 1888, m 28 Oct 1834, Harriette Augusta, da of Hans Hamilton of Dublin, M P, d Jan 1908, and had issue 1c to 3c   [Nos 59503 to 59519

346

# of The Blood Royal

1c *William Clayton Browne (afterwards R L 2 Mar 1889) Browne-Clayton, of Browne's Hill, J P , D L , and High Sheriff co Carlow* 1859, b 20 Nov 1835 , d 13 Jan 1907 , m 10 Jan 1867, *Caroline, da of John Watson Barton of Stapleton Park, co York, and had issue* 1d *to* 12d

1d Robert Clayton Browne Clayton, *late Major 5th Lancers (Browne's Hill, co Carlow),* b 24 Feb 1870, m 16 Nov 1905, May Magdalene, da of Edward Wienholt of Jondaryan, Queensland , and has issue 1e to 2e

1e William Patrick Browne-Clayton, b 27 Sept 1906

2e Annette Mary Browne-Clayton, b 28 Ap 1908

2d *William Clayton Browne-Clayton, 2nd Lieut Royal West Kent Regt ,* b 29 July 1873 , d unm (being killed in action at Agrah Malakan) 30 Sept 1897

3d Lionel Denis Browne-Clayton, b 10 Aug 1874

4d Mary Caroline Browne-Clayton, *m as 2nd wife,* 6 Oct 1898, Thomas Henry Bruen Ruttledge of Bloomfield, J P , D L , High Sheriff co Mayo 1902 (42 *North Great George Street, Dublin , Bloomfield, Hollymount, co Mayo),* and has issue 1e to 2e

1e Robert Francis Ruttledge, b 11 Sept 1899

2e William Ruttledge, b 29 July 1901

5d Annette Constance Browne-Clayton

6d Margaret Frances Browne-Clayton

7d Florence Hope Browne-Clayton, m 28 Ap 1904, Col Horace James Johnston, D S O , 3rd Batt West Riding Regt (*Watch Hill House, Canonbie, Dumfries),* and has issue 1e to 2e

1e Francis William Johnston, b 19 Aug 1905

2e Patrick James Johnston, b 7 Jan 1908

8d Kathleen Octavia Louisa Browne-Clayton

9d Madeline Emma Browne-Clayton

10d Lucy Victoria Browne-Clayton, m 12 Dec 1901, Claud Edward Pease (*Cliff House, Marske-by-the-Sea, Yorks),* and has issue 1e to 3e

1e Diana Vere Pease, b 4 Oct 1902

2e Lucy Margaret Pease, b 3 Feb 1904

3e Olive Mary Caroline Pease, b 16 May 1906

11d Juliet Harriet Vere Browne-Clayton.

12d Caroline Zoe Browne-Clayton, m 14 Dec 1905, Capt Herbert Chase Hall, Northumberland Fusiliers, s p

2c Robert Clayton Browne, b 3 May 1839

3c Annette Caroline Browne, d 16 Feb 1892, m 12 Feb 1863, Denis William Pack-Beresford of Fenagh Lodge, M P [descended from the Lady Isabel Plantagenet (see Essex Volume, p 159), d 28 Dec 1881 , and had issue 1d to 7d

1d Denis Robert Pack-Beresford of Fenagh, J P , D L , High Sheriff co Carlow 1890 (*Fenagh House Lodge, Bagnalstown, co Carlow),* b 23 Mar 1864 , m 11 Aug 1891, Alice Harriet Cromie [descended from George, Duke of Clarence, K G (see Clarence Volume, p 280)], da of James Acheson Lyle of Portstewart

2d Charles George Pack-Beresford, Major Royal West Kent Regt , b 21 Nov 1869

3d Henry John Pack-Beresford, Capt Highland L I , b 22 Aug 1871, m 28 July 1904, Sybil Maud, da of John Bell of Rushpool Hall, co York , and has issue 1e to 2e

1e Denis John Pack-Beresford, b 27 Oct 1905

2e Tristram Anthony Pack-Beresford, b 8 May 1907

4d Reynell James Pack-Beresford, b 21 Dec 1872 , m 17 June 1899, Florence, da of Frederick Leith of Walmer, co Kent , and has issue 1e to 2e

1e Arthur Reynell Pack-Beresford, b 28 Ap 1906

2e Joyce Annett Pack-Beresford, b 27 July 1900   [Nos 59520 to 59548

The Plantagenet Roll

5d Hugh de la Poer Pack-Beresford, b 11 July 1874

6d Elizabeth Harriet Pack-Beresford

7d Annette Louisa Pack-Beresford

2b *Joseph Deane Browne*, *Capt Carabineers*, d 1 *Jan* 1878, m *Georgina, da of (—) Thursby*

3b *Elizabeth Browne*, d 15 *Jan* 1871, m 31 *Jan* 1844, *Sir Jonah Denny Wheeler-Cuffe of Leyrath, 1st Bt* [I], d 9 *May* 1853, *and had issue* 1c *to* 5c

1c *Sir Charles Frederick Denny Wheeler Cuffe, 2nd Bt* [I], D L, *formerly Major 66th Regt*, served as A A G during Indian Mutiny 1858–1859, &c (*Leyrath, co Kilkenny United Service*), b 1 Sept 1832, m 2 July 1861, the Hon Pauline, da of Henry (Villiers-Stuart), 1st Baron Stuart de Decies [U K], *d s p* 5 July 1895

2c *Otway Wheeler Cuffe, formerly Capt R M Artillery and Hon Major Waterford Art*, b 1 *Mar* 1836, d 30 *Dec* 1908, m 14 *Sept* 1865, *Louisa Frances Florence* (*Woodlands, Waterford*) *da of the Rev Luke Fowler, Preb of Aghour*, d 22 *Dec* 1906, *and has issue* 1d *to* 2d

1d Otway Fortescue Luke Wheeler Cuffe, Lieut Indian Army Reserve, M I C E, P W D, Burmah (*Rangoon*), b 9 Dec 1866, m 3 June 1897, Charlotte Isabel, da of William Williams, s p

2d *Pauline Florence Elizabeth Wheeler-Cuffe*, m 29 Ap 1897, Frederick Richard Cowper Reed, Trin Coll, Camb (*Gaultier, Madingley Road, Cambridge*), s p

3c *Rosetta Wheeler-Cuffe*, d 27 *May* 1901, m *as 2nd wife*, 8 *Jan* 1853, *Admiral of the Fleet Sir Thomas John Cochrane, G C B* [E *of Dundonald Coll*], d 19 *Oct* 1872, *and had issue*

See the Exeter Volume, p 626, Nos 53011–53013

1c *Elinor Mildred Wheeler Cuffe*, d 14 *Oct* 1884, m 5 Dec 1840, *her cousin, Richard Wheeler of the Rocks, co Kilkenny, J P*, d 9 *Ap* 1861, *and had issue* 1d *to* 3d

1d Edward Wheeler, Lieut -Col (ret) R M Art (*The Rocks, Kilkenny*), b 18 Aug 1850, m 3 July 1888, Isabel Charlotte, da of Major James Palliser Costobadie, 70th Regt, and his issue 1e to 2e

1e Charles Palliser Wheeler, Royal Military College, Sandhurst, b 10 July 1889

2e Pauline Gladys Laura Wheeler

2d John William Wheeler (6 *Gardiner's Row, Dublin*), b 23 May 1859, *unm*

3d Minnie Wheeler (6 *Gardiner's Row, Dublin*), *unm*

5c *Frances Letitia Wheeler-Cuffe*, d 29 *Dec* 1908, m 20 *Aug* 1846, *Capt Charles William Tupper, late 7th Fusiliers, and had issue* 1d *to* 2d

1d Sir (Charles) Lewis Tupper, K C I E, C S I, Pres Indian Telegraph Committee since 1906, and *formerly an additional member of Gov Gen's Council 1900–1903, and temporary member Executive Council 1905–1906, Vice-Chancellor Punjab Univ*, &c (*Glenlyn, East Molesey*), b 16 May 1848, m 2 Oct 1875, Jessie, da of Major-Gen Henry Campbell Johnstone, C B and has issue 1e to 3e

1e Geoffrey Tupper, b 11 Dec 1878

2e Frank Gaspard Tupper, b 11 Aug 1886

3e Ruth Tupper, m 16 Feb 1905, Lewis French, M A (Oxon), I C S, Assist Commr, Punjab, and has issue 1f

1f Dorothy Margaret French, b 14 Nov 1905

2f Reginald Godfrey Otway Tupper, Capt R N, H M S *Excellent*, an A D C to H M. the King, &c, b 16 Oct 1859, m 1888, Emily Charlotte, da of Lieut -Gen H Green, C B

1b *Charlotte Browne*, d (–), m 1835, *William Brownlow of Knapton House, Queen's Co*, and *Loughderry, co Monaghan, J P, D L* [*descended from the Lady Anne, sister of King Edward IV* (see Exeter Volume, p 206)], b 1802, d 18 *July* 1881, *and had issue* (*with a da*) 1c *to* 2c [Nos 59549 to 59568

3+8

# of The Blood Royal

1c Francis Brownlow, C B , Lieut-Col 72nd Highlanders served in Crimean and Afghan Wars, b 19 July 1836 , d (being killed in action at Kandahar) 31 Aug 1880 , m 1878, Effie Constance, da of Col Robert Christopher Tytler [m 2ndly, 1 Aug 1885, Alfred (Porcelli), Baron Porcelli di Sant Andrea [Sicily], Col (ret) R E] , and had issue 1d

1d Norman Francis Brownlow, b 31 Oct 1879

2c William Vesey Brownlow, Major-Gen and Col 1st Dragoon Guards, C B , J P , High Sheriff co Monaghan 1907, served in Zulu (1879) and Boer (1880-1881) Wars, formerly Col Comdg 22nd Regt Dist 1889-1894 (Freeley Liphook, Hants), b 12 June 1841 , m 1st, 19 Nov 1881, Lady Anne Henrietta, da of John Hamilton (Dalrymple), 10th Earl of Stair [S] d 18 Feb 1898 . 2ndly, 1 June 1904, Lady Kathleen Susan Emma, da of John Sturt (Bligh), 6th Earl of Darnley [I]

7a Lady Theodosia Eleanor Bourke, b a 1781 , d 23 Aug 1815 , m 1807, Robert Hale Blagden Hale of Alderley, co Glouc , d 20 Dec 1855, and had issue 1b to 4b

1b Robert Blagden Hale of Alderley, M P , J P , High Sheriff co Glouc 1870, b 29 Sept 1807 , d 22 July 1883 , m 17 Aug 1832, Anne Jane, da of George Peter Holford of Westonbirt, co Glouc , d 18 Ap 1879 , and had issue 1c to 5c

1c Robert Hale of Alderley, J P , Major-Gen , formerly Col 7th Hussars, A D C to H R H the Duke of Cambridge 1879-1886, b 9 July 1834 , d unm 12 May 1907

2c Mathew Holford Hale (Alderley, near Wooton-under-Edge) Col formerly 26th Cameronians, b 26 July 1835 , unm

3c Anne Hale (Dunachton House, Inverness), m 24 Nov 1859, Thomas Henry Sherwood, Lieut 21st Fusiliers, b 2 May 1832 , d 7 May 1895 , and has issue 1d to 5d

1d Thomas Edward Sherwood (Makarika, Waipiro Bay, New Zealand), b 28 Feb 1861 , m 9 Sept 1893, Mary Sophia, da of Frederick Addington Goodenough of Calcutta , and has issue 1e to 2e

1e Robert Goodenough Sherwood b 21 June 1894

2e Frederick Hale Sherwood, b 15 Ap 1900

2d Arthur Robert Sherwood (Victoria, British Columbia), b 4 Aug 1862 , m 14 Sept 1895, Elizabeth Lucy, da of W Crickmay of Vancouver , and has issue 1e to 2e

1e Thomas Mathew Sherwood, b 20 May 1902

2e Agnes Anne Florence Sherwood, b 6 Jan 1901

3d Harold Joseph Sherwood, Major R E b 22 June 1865 , d at Roorkee, India, 24 Jan 1907 , m 10 May 1906, Margaret Emily, da of the Rev W Millar Nicolson, D Sc , and had issue 1e

1e Anne Josephine Hale Sherwood, b 29 Ap 1907

4d Eveline Anna Sherwood, m 6 June 1899, Robert East Hedley (Nelson, British Columbia) , and has issue 1e to 3e

1e Robert Hale Hedley, b 29 Ap 1900

2e Mathew Sherwood Hedley, b 2 May 1905

3e Anne Hedley, b 6 Aug 1901

5d Ethel Georgina Theodosia Sherwood, m 1 Aug 1895, the Very Rev Vernon Staley, Provost of St Andrew's Cathedral Inverness, Author of " Plain Words on the Holy Catholic Church," " The Catholic Religion," " The Natural Religion," " The Practical Religion," and many works on liturgiology (Dunachton House, Inverness) , and has issue 1e

1e Edward Vernon Staley, b 6 Jan 1899

4c Theodosia Hale } (Alderley, near Wooton-under-Edge)
5c Georgina Hale

2b John Richard Blagden Hale of Bradley Court, co Glouc , Col 1st Life
[Nos 59569 to 59587

349   2 Y

The Plantagenet Roll

Guards and 3rd King's Own Light Dragoons, b 5 June 1810, d 13 Oct 1864, m 27 Ap 1848, Jane, da of the Rev Thomas George Clare, Vicar of Walmer, co Kent and Rector of St Andrew's, Holborn, d 4 Mar 1861, *and had issue 1c to 3c*

1c Jane Clare Hale of Bradley Court (*Bexley House, Melrose Road, Southfields, S W*), m 1st, 11 Feb 1873, Col Alfred Cook, 40th Regt, d s p s 20 June 1885, 2ndly 27 Ap 1887 the Rev John Gregory, M A, Vicar of St Mary's, Far Cotton, co Northants, d s p 2 July 1905

2c Edith Harriet Blagden Hale (*Waverley, Albemarle Road, Beckenham*), m 23 Jan 1877 Col Hugh Hulse Ley of Penzance, co Cornwall, 3rd Batt Duke of Cornwall's L I, b 1 Aug 1851, d 5 Dec 1906, and has issue 1d to 4d

1d Arthur Edwin Hale Ley, Capt 20th Deccan Horse, Indian Army, b 18 June 1879, m 15 Feb 1909, Ena Doris, da of Capt Gwynne Harrison, niece of Sir Frederick Gwynne-Harrison

2d Lindsay Hugh Ley, Tea Planter (*Travancore, S India*), b (twin) 1 Sept 1881

3d Richard Hulse Ley, Mining Engineer (*Nelson, Victoria, B C*), b (twin) 1 Sept 1881, m 3 July 1907, Jessie, da of William Blakemore, d at Nelson afsd 15 Mar 1909, and has issue 1e

1e Margaret Jessie Ley, b 3 Mar 1909

4d Victoria Eleanor Joan Ley, m 22 Ap 1909, Carlos Bovill, Lieut R A

3c Constance Eleanor Blagden Hale, *unm*

3b Right Rev Mathew Blagden Hale, D D, M A (*Camb*), Lord Bishop of Brisbane 1875-1885, *previously* 1st Lord Bishop of Perth, W A, 1857-1875, *and Archdeacon of Adelaide* 1847-1857, b 18 June 1811, d 3 Mar 1895, m 1st, 25 Feb 1840, Sophia, da of George Clode of London, Merchant, b 20 Jan 1813, d 27 Mar 1845, 2ndly, in W Australia 1848, Sabina Dunlop, da of Col John Molloy, Rifle Brigade (*Waterloo Medal*), b at Augusta, W A, 7 Nov 1831, d in Tasmania Aug 1905, *and had issue 1c to 8c*

1c² Robert Dalton Hale, Assayer (*Broken Hill Silver Mine, Australia*), b at Poonindee, Port Lincoln, South Australia, 11 Ap 1853, *unm*

2c² Edward Mathew Hale, Comm R N (*Leonard Stanley, Glouc*), b 11 May 1865, m 21 Nov 1905, Helen Ethel, da of William Denis-Browne of Leamington, and has issue 1d to 2d

1d Mathew Blagden Hale, b 9 Sept 1906

2d Theodosia Hale

3c² Harold Hale (*Cotswold, New Norfolk, Tasmania*), b Mar 1869, m 1901, Georgina, da of Gen Officer of Melbourne, Vic, and has issue 1d to 4d

1d Harold Mathew Officer Hale, b 28 Sept 1902

2d Robert Blagden Hale

3d Margaret Georgiana Hale

4d Muriel Constance Hale

4c² Ernest Nathaniel Hale, B A (*Camb*) and Assistant Master Uppingham School (*Uppingham School*), b 11 July 1871

5c² Arthur Frederick Hale (*Glandore, Eidsvold, Queensland*), b 25 Sept 1873, *unm*

6c¹ Amy Hale, m 15 June 1869, the Rev Willoughby Balfour Wilkinson, Vicar of Bishop's Itchington, *formerly* of St Paul's, Stonehouse, and St Luke's, Birmingham (*The Vicarage, Bishop's Itchington, near Leamington*), and has issue (with 2 sons d in infancy) 1d to 4d

1d Mathew Hale Wilkinson (*Glandore, Eidsvold, Queensland*), b 12 Aug 1879, *unm*

2d George Jerrard Wilkinson, B A (*Camb*), b 16 Aug 1885, *unm.*

3d Amy Hale Wilkinson, m 10 Aug 1901, Arthur Joseph Burder Rankin of

[Nos 59588 to 59610

# of The Blood Royal

Birmingham, Solicitor (*Harborough House, Kingswood, Warwickshire*), and has issue 1e to 2e

* 1e Arthur Christian Rankin, *b* 9 May 1902
  2e Janice Mary Rankin

4d Clementina Wilkinson, *unm*

7c¹ Mary Hale, *m* 15 Ap 1868, the Rev George Christian, Vicar of Billesdon (*Billesdon Vicarage, Leicestershire*) *s p*

8c² Georgina Theodosia Hale, *m* 1904, Capt John Hutton Bisdee, V C (*Hutton Park, Tasmania*), *s p*

4b Theodosia Eleanor Hale, *d* 23 Aug 1857, *m* 27 Sept 1842, *Thomas George Wills-Sandford* (see p 371) *of Willsgrove and Castlerea, co Roscommon, J P, D L*, b 15 Aug 1817, d 13 Ap 1887, *and had issue 1c to 6c*

1c *William Robert Wills-Sandford of Willsgrove and Castlerea, J P*, Capt 2nd Dragoons and Royal Scots Greys, b 12 Ap 1844, d 3 Ap 1889, m 26 Mar 1874 Adelaide Elizabeth, da of Henry Jephson of Glenbrook, co Wicklow, by his wife Adelaide, da of Sir Philip Crampton, 1st Bt [U K], M D, F R S, d 29 June 1880, *and had issue 1d to 3d*

1d Thomas George Wills-Sandford of Willsgrove and Castlerea (*Willsgrove, Castlerea*, both co Roscommon), b 9 Nov 1879, m 12 Feb 1907, Kathleen Fanny, da of Robert Burrowes of Stradone, co Cavan, and has issue 1e

1e William Robert Wills-Sandford, b 3 Feb 1909

2d Charlotte Georgina Wills-Sandford, m 17 Mar 1898, Charles Wood, Fellow of Gonville and Caius Coll, Camb (*17 Cranmer Road, Cambridge*), and has issue 1e to 4e

1e Patrick Bryan Sandford Wood, b 18 Feb 1899
2e Edward Mathew Sandford Wood, b 19 Ap 1900
3e Catherine Elizabeth Sandford Wood, b 8 Dec 1902
4e John Kathleen Sandford Wood, b 13 Feb 1907

3d Mary Adelaide Wills Sandford, *unm*

2c Edward Wills-Sandford, now (R L 12 Jan 1889) Sandford-Wills, J P (*Cashlieve, Ballinlough, co Roscommon, Kildare Street*), b 20 Feb 1851, m 28 May 1889, Amy Henrietta, da of Henry Guinness of Burton Hall, Stillorgan, co Dublin, and has issue 1d to 2d

1d Lucy Eleanor Sandford-Wills
2d Mary Grace Sandford-Wills
3c Godfrey Robert Wills-Sandford, b 5 Oct 1852
4c Theodosia Eleanor Wills-Sandford
5c Alice Mary Wills-Sandford

6c Evelyn Louisa Wills-Sandford, m 20 July 1881, William Frederick Hammersly Smith Hamilton (*Dromahaere, co Leitrim*), and has issue 1d

1d Evelyn Eleanor Smith, m 16 Feb 1904, George H Mercer, R I C (*The Barracks, Galway*), and has issue 1e to 2e

1e Evelyn Alice Violet Mercer, b 7 Feb 1905
2e Olive Mary Nora Mercer, b 13 Mar 1906   [Nos 59611 to 59633

215 Descendants of CATHERINE DEANE (Table XXI), *d* 5 July 1743, *m.* as 1st wife, 17 Dec 1735, JOHN (LYSAGHT), 1st BARON LISLE [I.], so cr 18 Sept 1758, *d* 15 July 1781, and had issue 1*a* to 2*a*.

1a *John (Lysaght), 2nd Baron Lisle [I]*, d 8 Jan 1798, m 1778, *Marianne, da of George Connor of Ballybricken, co Cork*, d 19 Oct 1815, *and had issue 1b to 4b*

351

The Plantagenet Roll

1b John (Lysaght), *3rd Baron Lisle* [I], b 6 Aug 1781, d s p 26 Nov 1834

2b George (Lysaght), *4th Baron Lisle* [I], b 6 June 1783, d 7 July 1868, m 1st, 11 Oct 1810, Elizabeth, da of Samuel Knight, d 12 Ap 1815, 2ndly, 14 Oct 1816, Elizabeth Anne, da of John Davy Foulkes, d 1 Nov 1825, and had issue 1c to 2c

  1c John Arthur (Lysaght), *5th Baron Lisle* [I], b 12 Oct 1811, d 18 Ap 1898, m 6 Mar 1837, Henrietta, da of John Church, d Ap 1860, and had issue 1d to 4d

    1d George William James (Lysaght), *6th Baron Lisle* [I], formerly Lieut Devon Mil Art and Jackson Forest Rangers, Waikato Militia, served during Maori War 1864-1865 (Annabella Terrace, co Cork), b 29 Jan 1840, m 31 Oct 1868, Amy Emily, da of Ayliffe Langford of Ventnor and St Heliers, Jersey, and has issue 1e to 2e

      1e Hon Horace George Lysaght, J P (Newmarket Cottage, co Cork), b 16 Feb 1873, m 28 June 1899, Alice Elizabeth, da of Sir John Wrixon-Becher, 3rd Bt [U K], and has issue 1f to 3f

        1f John Nicholas Horace Lysaght, b 10 Aug 1903

        2f Horace James William Lysaght, b 22 Sept 1908

        3f Alice Amy Lysaght

      2e Hon Kathleen Eily Lysaght

    2d Hon Frederick Lysaght, formerly Lieut Devon Art Mil, b 27 May 1841, m 1st, 31 Dec 1867, Annie Elizabeth, da of Ayliffe Langford of Ventnor afsd, d 24 May 1868, 2ndly 10 Nov 1868, Elizabeth Lavinia, da of D Le Couteur of St Peter's, Jersey and has issue 1e

      1e Frederick Edward John Lysaght, b 1868

    3d Rev the Hon Henry Lysaght, late Vicar of St Mary's, Middleton (53 Banbury Road, Oxford), b 10 Mar 1847, m 14 Jan 1875, Susan Isabelle, da of Philip Scott of Hill House Queenstown, and has issue 1e

      1e Rev John Arthur Constantine Lysaght, B A, Vicar of Carham (The Elms, Kennington Oxford) b 13 Sept 1876, m 8 Ap 1902, Mary Nicholl, da of Adam Feltiplace Blundy of The Warren, Abingdon, and has issue 1f to 3f

        1f Winifred Joyce Lysaght

        2f Kathleen Mary Lalage Lysaght

        3f Renee Primrose Lysaght

    4d Hon Philippa Charlotte Lysaght, m 1884, Arthur Octavius Marwood (25 Westbourne Gardens, Folkestone), and has issue 1e to 3e

      1e Arthur Henry Lysaght Marwood, Lieut 1st Batt York and Lancaster Regt, b 1885

      2e Charles Philip Lysaght Marwood, Lieut Royal Warwickshire Regt, b 1888

      3e Edith Marion Lysaght Marwood

  2c Hon Catherine Charlotte Lysaght, b 25 Sept 1822, d 22 Dec 1905, m 19 Dec 1841, the Rev John Eyre Yonge, M A, Rector of Hempstead, d 11 June 1890 and had issue

  See the Clarence Volume, p 159, Nos 2169-2487

  3b Hon Elizabeth Lysaght, d 1813, m James Hall

  4b Hon Catharine Lysaght, d (-), m. 1803, Thomas Delany Hale

2a Hon Mary Lysaght, d (-), m Kingsmill Pennefather, M P for Cashel 1753, 1761, 1771, d s p May 1771, and had issue 1b to 6b

  1b Richard Pennefather of New Park, M P, Lieut -Col Tipperary Militia, d May 1831, m 1st, 1782, Anna, da and h of Matthew Jacob of St Johnstown, co Tipperary, and had issue 1c to 7c

    1c Kingsmill Pennefather, Lieut -Col Tipperary Militia, d v p 1819, m 1st, Maria, da of Burton Persse of co Galway, d (-), 2ndly, Grace, da of Thomas Burton of Groie, d (-), and had issue 1d to 2d   [Nos 59634 to 59669

# of The Blood Royal

1d¹ *Anna Pennefather*, d 31 *Dec* 1887 , m 25 *May* 1833, *Stephen Charles Moore of Barne, co Tipperary, J P, D L , High Sheriff for that co* 1867, b 12 *Mar* 1808 , d 10 *Ap* 1873, *and had issue* 1e *to* 6e

1e *Stephen Moore of Barne, J P, D L , M P co Tipperary* 1875-1880, *and High Sheriff for that co* 1885, *formerly Capt* 63rd *Regt ,* b 23 *Aug* 1836 , d 9 *July* 1897 , m 1st, 1 *Oct* 1867, *Anna Maria, da and h of Wilmer Wilmer of* 24 *Wilton Crescent, London,* d 22 *Dec* 1886 , 2ndly, 11 *July* 1888, *Martha Mary, da of the late John Morgan of Brampton Park, co Hunts and had issue* 1f *to* 6f

1f Randal Kingsmill Moore of Barne J P , D L , *formerly* Lieut 3rd Batt Leinster Regt (*Barne, near Clonmel*), b 12 Feb 1873

2f Stephen Thomas Moore, now (R L 6 Feb 1903) Wilmer, Lieut 16th Lancers, b 7 Feb 1881

3f Anna Eleanor Isabel Moore, m 11 Mar 1895, Francis Simon Low, *formerly* 2nd Life Guards [only son and h of Francis Wise Low of Kilshane, J P] (37 *Cadogan Square, S W*), and has issue 1g

1g [da] Low

4f Geraldine Elena Moore

5f Mary Augusta Moore, m 11 Mar 1903, Capt Noel Arbuthnot Thomson, Seaforth Highlanders

6f Stephanie Hilda Grace Moore, m 21 Nov 1901, the Rev John Carleton Steward, Rector of Mulbarton (*Mulbarton Rectory, Norfolk*)

2e Richard Albert Moore (*Queensland*), b 19 May 1848 , m

3e Charles Henry Algernon Moore, b 8 Aug 1851 , m May, da of Gen Foster

4e Anna Maria Moore, m Dec 1866, Col Charles Thornhill, R A , and has issue 1f

1f Charles Thornhill

5e Katherine Grace Moore, m 25 Aug. 1870, Sir Francis John Milman of Levaton, 4th Bt [G B], *formerly* Hon Major and Adj 2nd Brig Welsh Div R A (*Woodlands, Bexley Road, Erith*), and has issue 1f to 7f

1f Francis Milman, b 27 Oct 1872

2f William Ernest Milman, b 11 Aug 1875

3f Lionel Charles Patrick Milman, Lieut R A , b 23 Feb 1877

4f Stephen Walter Milman, b 15 Nov 1879

5f Henry Augustus Milman, b 1882

6f Hugh Milman, b 1884

7f Violet Grace Milman

6e Elmina Constance Moore, m 5 Jan 1875, Henry Burrough (*Boston, Mass ,* U S A), and has issue

2d *Catherine Pennefather*, d 1 *Jan* 1843, m 17 *Aug* 1840, *the Hon Henry Alexander Savile* [2nd *son of John,* 3rd *Earl of Mexborough* [*I*]], d 1 *Mar* 1850, *and had issue* 1e

1e *William Savile, Capt* 9th *Lancers, D L ,* b 8 *Oct* 1841 , d 4 *Ap* 1903, m 12 *June* 1865, *Emily* [*descended from Georg., Duke of Clarence, K G* (see the Clarence Volume, p 131)] (20A *St James' Place, S W*), *da of Capt Delmé Seymour Davies of Penlan , and had issue* 1f *to* 2f

1f John Herbert Drax Savile, Capt *late* Rifle Brigade

2f Beatrice Anne Louisa Savile

2c *Matthew Pennefather of New Park, M P , J P , D L , High Sheriff co Tipperary* 1826, b 1784, d (-) . m 1814, *Anna, da of Daniel Connor of Ballybricken, co Cork, and had issue* 1d *to* 4d

1d Daniel Francis Pennefather, b 1816

2d Richard Pennefather

3d Mary Pennefather

4d Anna Pennefather

[Nos 59670 to 59695

353

The Plantagenet Roll

3c *William Pennefather of Lakefield*, d 4 *Feb* 1872, m 1819, *Charity Maria, da of Richard Long of Longfield, co Tipperary*, and had issue 1d to 4d

1d *Richard Pennefather of Lakefield, J P*, b 19 *Jan* 1826, d 1876, m 24 *Feb* 1857, *Emma Elizabeth, da of Robert Darwin Vaughton of Ashfurlong House, co Warwick*, and had issue 1e to 5e

1e William Vaughton Pennefather of Lakefield (*Stoke Lodge, Milborough, Lakefield*), b 14 *Jan* 1862, m 17 *Nov* 1891, Louisa May [descended from George, Duke of Clarence, K G (see Clarence Volume, p 164)], da of William John Bankes, *formerly Murray, of Winstanley*, and has (with other) issue 1f

1f Richard Pennefather, b 1893

2e Richard Dymoke Pennefather, b 1865

3e Maria Emma Pennefather

4e Harriet Lavinia Pennefather

5e Anna Louisa Pennefather

2d William Pennefather.

3d *Matthew Pennefather*, d 1859

4d *William John Copley Lyndhurst Pennefather*, d 1865

4c *Dorothea Pennefather* d (? s p) 1845, m 1st, *Richard Lockwood of Cashel*, d (—), 2ndly, as 2nd wife, 1 Oct 1827, *Capt Thomas Sadleir of Castletown, co Tipperary*, 99th Regt, d (s p by her) 22 Oct 1842

5c *Catherine Pennefather*, d (—), m 31 *Dec* 1801, *Lieut -Col Owen Lloyd of Rockville, co Roscommon*, d 12 *Ap* 1810, and had (with oth r) issue 1d to 2d

1d *William Lloyd of Rockville* (eldest son), b 28 *Feb* 1803, d 7 *Jan* 1870, m 22 *Sept* 1829, *Anne* (see p 356), da of Major *Acheson Montgomery Moore*, d (—), and had issue 1e to 2e

1e *Owen Richard Nathaniel Lloyd of Rockville, Major in the Army*, b 7 *July* 1830 d 17 *Nov* 1863, m 20 *Sept* 1855, *Frances Maria, da of William Hutchinson of Carrick on Shannon*, M D, d 2 Oct 1885, and had issue 1f to 3f

1f William Lloyd of Rockville, J P, D L, High Sheriff co Roscommon 1889, *formerly Capt and Hon Major 5th Batt Connaught Rangers* (*Rockville, Drumsna, Roscommon, Kildare Street*), b 8 July 1858, m 28 *Jan* 1884, Mary Brodribb, da of Major William Lancelot Hutchinson, and has issue 1g to 3g

1g William Hutchinson Lloyd, b 2 Ap 1885

2g Coote Richard FitzGerald Lloyd, b 2 July 1887

3g Gwendoline Elizabeth May Lloyd

2f John Charles Lloyd, b (—), m Margaret, da of (—) Waldron, and has issue 1g to 2g

1g Owen John Montgomery Lloyd

2g Frances Maria Lloyd

3f *Anna Montgomery Lloyd*, d 190-, m the Rev *William Kennedy Brodribb*, B A, Rector of Putley, co Herts, d (—), and had issue 1g to 2g

1g Owen Adams Kennedy Brodribb

2g *Eanswith Alice Kennedy Brodribb*, d (—)

2e Acheson Montgomery Lloyd, b 26 Oct 1831, m 18 *Jan* 1865, Catherine (see p 355), da of the Rev James Wentworth Mansergh, and has issue 1f

1f William Owen Lloyd, b 29 July 1866

2d *Catherine Lloyd* (3rd da), d 27 *Sept* 1891, m 31 *Oct* 1835, the Rev *James Wentworth Mansergh* (see p 361), Rector of Kilmore [Cadet of Grenane], d 1845, and had issue (with 2 other sons who d s p) 1e to 2e

1e *Daniel James Mansergh of Grallagh Castle, co Tipperary, J P*, Col Comdg South Tipperary Art Mil, formerly 19th Regt, b 3 Nov 1836, d (—), m 3 July 1866, Margaret, da of Justin Cooper of Camas

[Nos 59696 to 59712.

354

# of The Blood Royal

2c Catherine Mansergh, m 18 Jan 1865, Acheson Montgomery Lloyd (see p 354), and has issue

See p 354, No 59712

6c *Margaret Pennefather*, d 1874, m *Feb* 1811, *Ambrose Going of Bally-philip*, co *Tipperary*, b Oct 1785, d *Aug* 1857, *and had issue 1d to 7d*

1d *William Going of Ballyphilip*, J P , D L , b *June* 1815, d 1878, m *Oct* 1841, *Jane Eliza, da of Benjamin Frend of Rocklow, co Tipperary*, d 2 Oct 1892, *and had issue (with a son and da d s p) 1e to 3e*

1e *Benjamin Frend Going of Ballyphilip J P , D L , High Sheriff co Tippe-rary* 1883, b 17 Ap 1852, d 7 Mar 1885 m 16 Jan 1879, *Florence Isabella Anna, da of Richard Fitzroy Creagh of Millbrooke and Athassel, co Tipperary*, and had issue 1f to 3f

1f *William Ambrose Going of Ballyphilip*, b 31 Oct 1881, d s p 7 Mar 1897

2f Mabel Anna Going of Ballyphilip, m 25 Jan 1908 Capt Charles Morris Thielfell, *late* 8th Hussars (*Nun Monkton, York*), and has issue 1g

1g Charles Reginald Morris Thielfell, b 15 Oct 1908

3f Bena Going of Ballyphilip (*Ballyphilip, Killenaule, Tipperary*)

2e Eliza Going, m 5 Nov 1873, Major Alexander W Bailey, Fermanagh L I , s p

3e Arabella Jane Going, *unm*

2d *Richard Pennefather Going*, J P , b 1821, d s p 1872, m 1862, *Letitia Elizabeth, da of the Rev Robert Bury of Killora, co Cork*

3d *John Going of Wilford, co Tipperary*, b Aug 1822, d s p 1873

4d *Anna Going*, d 1865, m 1835, *the Rev Anthony Armstrong, Rector of Killorskully*, and had issue a da , *Meta*, d 1908

5d *Margaret Isabella Going*, d 12 June 1858, m 1841, *Christopher F Tuthill of Dublin, M D*, and had issue, George and Ambrose both *(d s p)*

6d *Elizabeth Frances Going*, d 25 July 1867 m as 1st wife 30 Ap 1846, *John Hervey Adams of Northlands, co Cavan, Bar at Law, J P , High Sheriff for that co and Monaghan* 1854, b 28 Ap 1818, d 8 May 1871, *and had issue 1e to 4c*

1e Samuel Allen Adams of Northlands, J P , *formerly* Lieut Tipperary Art Mil (*Northlands, Carrickmacross*), b 1 Mai 1817, m 13 June 1871, Frances Dorothea [descended from the Lady Anne, sister of Kings Edward IV and Richard III (see Exeter Volume, p 542)], da of the Rev Decimus William Preston, M A , Rector of Killinkere [and grandda of William Preston, a Judge of the Court of Appeal, by his wife the Hon Frances Dorothea, da and co-h of John (Evans), 5th Baron Carbery [I]], and has issue (with 3 das d young) 1f to 6f

1f John Hervey Stuart Adams, b 30 Dec 1875

2f Samuel Allen Adams, b 11 Ap 1882

3f Ambrose Douglas Adams, b 9 May 1889

4f Olive Mildred Adams

5f Mary Henrietta Mabel Adams

6f Hazel Gertrude Adams

2e *Ambrose Going Adams*, J P , b 22 Mar 1850, d 11 Jan 1888, m 3 Oct 1872, *Anne Jane Foster, da of the Rev William Watkyns Deering, M A* , and had issue 1f to 2f

1f Clara Elizabeth Charlotte Adams, m 1 June 1894, Frederick Foster McClintock

2f. Ethel Annie Adams

3e Margaret Anna Adams, m 4 Ap 1871, Ormsby Colville McClintock Jones of Mount Edward, co Sligo, J P (*Mount Edward, Drangan, Fovrock, co Dublin*), and has issue (with 2 sons d s p) 1f to 5f

1f Percy James Colville Jones, b 22 Nov 1872

2f John Henry Colville Jones, b 28 Aug 1874 [Nos 59713 to 59731

The Plantagenet Roll

3/ William Ambrose Colville Jones, b 16 Sept 1886

4/ Digby Colville Jones, b 1892

5/ Dorothy Colville Jones

4c Elizabeth Frances Adams, m 3 Sept 1872, Robert Edward Follett Jones [son of Major James Jones of Mount Edward] (*Iherstoke, Forrock, co Dublin*), and has issue (with 3 sons d young) 1/ to 2/

1/ Sidney Follett Jones, b 20 June 1879

2/ Elsie Noel Jones

7d *Dorothea Going, d 1873, m May 1848, Samuel Murray Going of Liska-teen House, co Tipperary, and had issue, John, d (-), and Margaret and Mary, one of whom m as 2nd wife, Nov 1883, Owen Lloyd Mansergh, afterwards Going, J P , d s p 3 Oct 1892*

7c *Eliza Pennefather, d 26 Ap 1835, m 1st, 1813, Major Acheson Montgomery-Moore [Cadet of Garvah, co Tyrone], b 17 Oct 1788, d (-), 2ndly, as 1st wife, 10 Aug 1816, Sir John Judkin-FitzGerald of Lisheen, 2nd Bt [U K], b 27 Aug 1787, d 28 Feb 1860, and had issue 1d to 2d*

1d *Sir Thomas Judkin FitzGerald, 3rd Bt [U K], b 20 July 1820, d 27 Ap 1864, m 25 Jan 1845, Emma Louisa Maunsell, da of Henry White of Golden Hills, co Tipperary, and had issue 1e to 5e*

1e Sir Joseph Capel Judkin-FitzGerald of Lisheen, 4th Bt [U K], b 9 Aug 1853, m 5 June 1872, Constance Sarah, da of Capt William Augustus Hyder, 10th Hussars, and has issue 1/ to 2/

1/ Thomas Judkin Judkin-FitzGerald, b 1873

2/ Evelyn Constance Hyder Judkin-FitzGerald

2e Robert Unricke Judkin-FitzGerald, b 1855

3e Eliza Anne Judkin-FitzGerald, m 1872, John E Roberts of Clifton, Bristol

4e Emma Augusta Judkin-FitzGerald, m 1872 Edmund T Hale, *formerly of* The Grange, co Somerset

5e Henrietta Mary De la Poer Judkin-FitzGerald, m 1874, William Powell Keale, *formerly of* Nelson Lodge, Bristol, d (-)

2d *Anne Montgomery-Moore, d (-), m 22 Sept 1829, William Lloyd of Rockville, d 7 Jan 1870, and had issue*
See p 354, Nos 59703-59712

2b *Rev John Pennefather, D D , Rector of St John's, Newport, co Tipperary, d (-), m Elizabeth, da of Major Perceval, d (-), and had issue 1c to 9c*

1c *Kingsmill Pennefather, Major Limerick Militia, d 1860, m 1st, Frances, da of Major Townsend of Monckton Hall, d (-), 2ndly, 1842, Jane Catherine Patricia [descended from George, Duke of Clarence, K G (see the Essex Volume Supplement, p 558)], da of Thomas de Grenier de Fonblanque, K H , d 6 May 1886, and had issue 1d to 8d*

1d ¹ John Pennefather

2d ² Charles Edward de Fonblanque Pennefather, b 23 June 1848, m Maizie, da of C Seward of Melbourne, and has issue 1e to 3e

1e John Pennefather

2e Charles Pennefather

3e Edward Pennefather

3d ² De Fonblanque Pennefather, J P (*Kinnersley Castle, co Hereford*), b 29 Mar 1856, m 28 Ap 1886, Madeline, da of Sir Robert Prescott Stewart, s p

4d ¹ Elizabeth Pennefather

5d ¹ Fanny Pennefather

6d ¹ Caroline Pennefather

7d ¹ Clare Pennefather   [Nos 59732 to 59764

356

# of The Blood Royal

8d² *Ruth Pennefather*, d Sept 1906, m *William Nimo (Oakhill Park, near Liverpool)*, *and had issue* 1e *to* 4e

    1e William Pennefather Nimo, *b* 6 Sept. 1881

    2e *Charles Nimo*, b 4 Aug 1883, d 20 Ap 1909

    3e *Kingsmill Nimo*, *b* 23 June 1885

    4e Dorothea Nimo

2c *William Westby Pennefather, Lieut R N*, d (? s p), m *Elizabeth, da of William Harding*

3c *Sir John Lysaght Pennefather, K C B, G C L H, K C M L, Gen and Col 22nd Foot*, d 1872, m 1830, *Margaret, da of John Carr of Mountrath*

4c *Joseph Lysaght Pennefather, Bar -at-Law*, d (—), m *Elizabeth, da of (—) Rea of Barnwood, co Glouc*, *and had issue* 1d

    1d Julia Pennefather

5c *Robert Perceval Pennefather, Lieut and Adj 3rd Bengal Cav*, d (–), m *Elizabeth, da of (—) Benson*, d 28 Mar 1887, *and had issue* 1d *to* 2d

    1d *Henry Vansittart Pennefather, Capt 41st Foot*, b 1791, d in Natal 9 Aug 1888, m 23 Oct 1860, *Margaretta Luchesa Jane Maria, widow of Col John Temple West, da and h of Sir John George Reeve De la Pole, 8th Bt [E]*, d (–)

    2d *Laura Pennefather*, d. (–), m *George Rae, M D, Bengal Med Estab*

6c *Anne Pennefather*, d Dec 1863, m Sept 1814, *William Ryan of Bally-mackeogh, co Tipperary*, d 27 Nov 1835, *and had issue* 1d *to* 8d

– – 1d *William Ryan of Ballymackeogh, J P*, b 1 Dec 1815, d 13 Feb 1890, m 29 Nov 1842, *Jane, sister of Sir Edward Grogan, 1st Bt [U K], M P, da of John Grogan, Bar -at-Law*, d 17 Nov 1895, *and had issue* 1e *to* 3e

    1e Charles Arthur Ryan of Ballymackeogh, J P (*Ballymackeogh, Newport, Tipperary*), *b* 7 Nov 1853, m 24 Feb 1903, *Mary, da of Henry Ormsby Rose of Ballyculleen, co Limerick*

    2e Anne Alicia Susanna Ryan, m 8 Jan 1881, *Ringrose Drew [Cadet of Drewscourt]*, d 23 Dec 1895, *and has issue* 1f *to* 4f

        1f Francis William Massy Drew

        2f Ringrose Charles Wellington Drew

        3f Alicia Jeannette Drew

        4f Anna Evelina Margaret Drew

    3e Jeannette Ryan, m 10 Aug 1886, Edward Herbert Maunsell (*Macleod, Alberta, Canada*), *and has issue*

    2d *John Ryan*, d Sept 1873, m 1843, *Louisa Ricarda, da of Major Kingsmill Pennefather of Knockinglass, co Tipperary*, *and had issue* 1e *to* 4e

        1e *Rev William Ewer Ryan, M A*, d (–)

        2e *John Pennefather Ryan, M D*, d (–)

        3e *Frances Elizabeth Ryan*, d (? unm)

        4e *Louisa Mary Ryan*, d (? s p), m 1885, *Townsend Hall of Pilton, co Devon*

    3d *George Henry Ryan, M D, Surg R N*, d s p

    4d *Robert Perceval Ryan*, d (? s p)

    5d *Edward Ryan*, d (? s p)

    6d *Elizabeth Ryan*, d (? s p)

    7d *Clara Ryan*, d (? s p)

    8d *Laura Ryan*, d (? s p)

7c *Mary Charity Pennefather*, d 2 July 1834, m *as 1st wife*, 15 May 1809, *Henry Vansittart of Eastwood, Woodstock, Canada, Vice-Adm R N [5th son of George Vansittart of Bisham Abbey, co Berks, M P, J P, D L (see p 453)]*, d 14 Mar 1842, *and had issue* 1d *to* 4d

    1d *John George Vansittart of Woodstock and Ottawa, Canada*, b 15 Ap 1813,

[Nos 59765 to 59775

2 z

The Plantagenet Roll

d 13 *Oct* 1869 , m 11 *Aug* 1835, *Isabella Carrick, da of James Rovse Yelding of Tralee, co Kerry,* d 7 *Feb* 1903, *and had issue* 1e *to* 3e

1e *John Pennefather Vansittart, P W D , India,* bapt 22 *Oct* 1837 , d 1887 , m 1 *Oct* 1879, *Isabella Maud (Toronto, Canada), da of the Hon John Alexander, a Canadian Senator , and had issue* 1f *to* 2f

1f. George Edward Vansittart, *b* 1884

2f Cecil Isabella Vansittart, *b* at Mussooree, N W P , India, 12 June 1880

2e *James Graham Vansittart of Osgood Hall, Bar, Medal, and Clasps for Fenian Raid of* 1866, b 18 *June* 1839, d 22 *June* 1901, m 1868, *Letitia, da of Henry Prittie Bayly of Ballykeefe, Limerick , and had issue* 1f

1f Frances Isabella Linda Vansittart, *m* 6 June 1900, Lorne Bruce Chadwicke Livingstone, Bar-at-Law [son of William Livingstone of Musselburgh, Scotland] (*Osgood Hall, Tilsonburg, Ontario*) , and has issue 1g to 3g

1g John Pennefather Livingstone, *b* 6 June 1902

2g Margaret Vansittart Livingstone, *b* 7 Mar 1901

3g Isobel Kingsforth Livingstone, *b* 4 Jan 1910

3e *Charles Edward Vansittart, Lieut-Col Army Ordnance Dept* , b 3 *Mar* 1847, d 16 *Aug* 1898, m 12 *May* 1894, *Teresa, widow of the Rev Joseph Wolstenholme, da of* (—), d 15 *May* 1905 , *and had issue* 1f

1f Mignon Vansittart

2d *Henry Vansittart of Canada,* b 26 *May* 1815, d 1 *Nov* 1868, m 4 *Oct* 1848, *Emily Louisa, da of Edward Huggins of The Old Manor Estate, Nevis, W.I* , d 1 *July* 1869 , *and had issue* (with 2 sons and 2 das d s p) 1e

1e Fanny Georgina Vansittart, *m as* 2nd *wife,* 18 Oct 1883, the Rev John Wynn Wernnck (see p 359), *Rector of Weston Bampfylde, formerly Vicar of Stanton Drew* (*Weston Bampfylde Rectory, Sparkford, Som*) , and has issue 1f to 5f

1f Pelham Vansittart Wynn Wernnck, *b* 20 Sept 1884

2f Henry Vansittart Wynn Wernnck, *b* 12 Mar 1877

3f Kathleen Marjorie Wynn Wernnck

4f Fanny Gladys Wynn Wernnck

5f Alice Maude Wynn Wernnck

3d *Elizabeth Vansittart,* d 8 *Aug* 1873 , m 4 *Ap* 1836, *Robert Riddell* [Bt [S 1628] *Coll*], d 18 *Nov* 1864 , *and had issue* 1e *to* 6e

1e *Robert Vansittart Riddell, Col late* R E, *sometime Master of* H M's *Mint, Bombay* (*Essex Lodge, Liverpool Gardens, Worthing*), b 12 *Mar* 1840, m 27 *Ap* 1870, *Louisa Flora Steel, da of Gen Alexander Dick , and has issue* 1f to 4f

1f Robert Buchanan Riddell, Capt and Brevet-Major R A , served in S Africa 1899–1900, Medal and 5 Clasps, *b* 1 Ap 1872

2f Edward Vansittart Dick Riddell, Capt and Brevet-Major R A , served in S Africa 1899–1900, *b* 30 Mar 1873, *m* 20 Feb 1902, Edith Mary, da. of Major-Gen E P Bingham Turner, R A , and has issue 1g

1g Edward Alexander Buchanan Riddell, *b* 8 Feb 1903

3f John Balfour Riddell, Capt R F A , *b* 2 May 1880, *m* 5 Aug 1908, Margaret Alice, da of John William Smith of The Rectory, Oundle

4f Ethel Riddell, *m* 27 July 1901, Charles Dingwall Williams , and has issue 1g

1g Charles Dingwall Williams, *b* 1902

2e *Henry Vansittart Riddell, Col Bengal N I ,* b 9 *Oct* 1841 , d 14 *Jan* 1888 , m 1st, 1 *Nov* 1864, *Alice, da of Richard Attwood,* d 1884 , 2ndly, 1886, *Annie, da of Stephen Francis Shairp of St Maur* (see Supp) . *and had issue* 1f *to* 3f

1f[1] Laurie Archibald Riddell, *b* 1877.

2f[1] Mary Alice Riddell, *m* 1st, 17 Feb 1885, Capt John Hawley Burke, W Yorks Regt, d 24 Oct 1887, 2ndly, 1890, John Burke, and his issue 1g to 4g
[Nos 59776 to 59797

358

# of The Blood Royal

1g Noel Hawley Michael Burke, b 1885

2g Arthur Laurie Burke, b 1887

3g John Lawrence Burke, b 1891

4g Yvonne Lilian Gervaise Burke

3f Clara Edith Riddell

3e *Walter Riddell, Lieut Col R A*, b 27 Ap 1845, d 15 Oct 1895 m 27 Sept 1877, *Charlotte Margaret, da of Brig -Gen James George Nuill, C B , and had issue 1f*

1f Florence Agnes Isabel Riddell

4e Mary Clare Riddell (*St Cuthberga, Rushton Crescent, Bournemouth*), m 1883, John Broughton, *d s p* 5 Mar 1906

5e Elizabeth Janet Riddell, *unm*

6e *Caroline Edith Westby Riddell*, d ~ p 28 *Nov* 1881, m *as 1st wife*, 2 Sept. 1880, *the Rev John Wynn Werninck* (see p 358)

4d *Mary Charity Vansittart*, d 3 Sept 1866, m 11 *June* 1838, *Spencer Mackay of Blandford, Canada*, d 1860, *and had issue 1e to 6e*

1e *Spencer Henry Mackay, Major 101st Royal Munster Fusiliers*, b 21 *Jan* 1842, d 20 *Ap* 1905 m *Mary Horan, da of J Thompson , and had issue 1f to 3f*

1f Spencer Edward Mackay, b Aug 1878, m 19 Sept 1910, May, da of Col Penton

2f William Mackay, b Nov 1879

3f Ethel Maud Mackay

2e Edward Vansittart Mackay, *late* Indian Police (*10 College Road, Clifton*), b 11 July 1849, m 1886, Nina, da of J C Whitty, and has issue 1f to 3f

1f Eric Vansittart Mackay, b Sept 1891

2f Claude Lysaght Mackay, b Oct 1894

3f Verna Maude Vansittart Mackay

3e Louisa Mary Mackay, *unm*

4e Elizabeth L Mackay, m 1892, the Rev John Watson Gordon Bishop, *formerly* Chaplain at Grasse 1883–1886 (*Dudley House, Sandown, I W*), s p

5e Rosa M Mackay (*26 St James' Road, Tunbridge Wells*), m C Stanley of Roughan Park, Dungannon, d s p

6e Gertrude Mackay, m 14 Aug 1873, Arthur H Bowles (*Temple Court, near Guildford*), and has issue (with a da , Florence Maud Ethel, b *unm*) 1f to 6f

1f *Arthur Frederick Vansittart Bowles*, b 10 Nov 1875, d 1 Dec 1908, m 1903, *Edith, da of W C Prangley*, and had issue (a da , Edith)

2f *Charles Edward Bowles, M E* (*South Africa*), b 27 Nov 1876

3f *Rosa Gertrude Eleanor Bowles*, m 1902, Henry Clutton Broock (*Lake View, Northwood, Midx*), and has issue (2 sons)

1f Mary Edith Bowles, m 1905, Guy Fleming (*Mexico*)

5f Lilian Maude Bowles, m 1908, Hugh Merriman (*Hall Dene, Marrow, near Guildford*)

6f Margaret Irene Bowles, *unm*

8c *Clare Pennefather*, d (–), m *Thomas Evans of Ashore, co Tipperary, Lieut R N*

9c *Laura Pennefather*, d (–), m (—) *Philips of Mount Philips*

3b *William Pennefather, M P for Cashel* 1783–1797, *Surveyor Gen in Ireland, &c*, d (–), m *Frances, da of Francis Nisbett of Derrycarne, co Leitrim , and had issue 1c to 5c*

1c *William Pennefather, H E I C S*, d *unm* 1826

2c *Richard Daniel Pennefather of Kilbracken, co Leitrim, J P , D L , Col E Kent Militia*, b 13 Aug 1818, d 7 Sept 1881, m 7 Oct 1868, *the Hon Sarah Anna, da of Hervey (de Montmorency), 4th Viscount Mountmorres* [I], *LL D , Dean of Achonry, and had issue 1d to 3d* [Nos 59798 to 59821

The Plantagenet Roll

1d Rev William de Montmorency Pennefather, M A (Oxon) (*Lincoln College, Oxford*), *b* 27 Aug 1869, *unm*

2d Anna de Montmorency Pennefather, *m* 1st, as 3rd wife, 26 Sept 1900, Col George Fleming of Higher Leigh, co Devon, C B, LL D, *d* 13 Ap 1901, 2ndly, 11 Sept 1905, Alfred Moore, *otherwise* More, now (D P 24 Ap 1906) Alfred Thomas More, B Sc (*Moscot, Abingdon*), and has issue (with Daniel de Montmorency Thomas More, *b* 24 Nov 1907, *d* 29 Jan 1908) 1e

1e David Pennefather Thomas More, *b* 24 June 1906

3d Mary Eva de Montmorency Pennefather

3c *Margaret Pennefather*, d *Dec* 1873, m 1824, *Richard Warren of Lisgoold, M D [Bt Coll (see p 363)], d Dec 1870, and had issue 1d to 2d*

1d *Frances Warren*, d (–), m 1st, *Capt Oldham, 2nd Regt, d (being killed in Kaffir War)* 18—, 2ndly, 1859, *William Connor of Milton, co Cork*

2d *Augusta Warren*, d 1 Dec 1873, m as 1st wife, 22 Aug 1854, *her kinsman Richard Lane Warren, 35th Regt, b 29 Jan 1828, d (–), and had issue 1e to 6e*

1e William Pennefather Warren, *b* 16 Ap 1860

2e Richard Warren, *b* 5 Dec 1861

3e Ethel Warren, *m* Henry Daunt of Kinsale [4th son of Achilles Daunt of Tracton Abbey, co Cork]

4e Augusta Julia Warren

5e Cherry Frances Warren

6e Violet Laura Warren

4c *Elizabeth Pennefather*, d (–), m as 2nd wife, *Phineas Bury of Little Island, co Cork, J P, Capt 7th Dragoons, d 1853, and had issue 1d to 3d*

1d *Phineas Bury of Little Island, J P, Capt 15th Hussars, b 7 Mar. 1841, d s p 9 May 1895*

2d *William Phineas Bury of Curraghbridge, co Limerick, b 27 Nov 1842, d (–), m Harriet, da of Arthur Forbes of Newstone, co Meath, and had issue 1e*

1e William Phineas Bury of Curraghbridge and Little Island (*Carrigrenane, Little Island, co Cork, Curraghbridge, Adare, co Limerick*)

3d Frances Jane Bury, *m* Major C T Tuckey, 41st Regt

5c *Frances Mary Pennefather*, d (? s p) 1848, m *Col Arthur St George Herbert Stepney, C B, Coldstream Guards*

4b *Mary Pennefather*, d (–), m *Daniel Conner of Ballybricken, co. Cork, and had (with possibly other) issue 1c*

1c *Daniel Conner of Ballybricken, J P, d (–), m his cousin Anna, da of William Pennefather, and had (with possibly other) issue 1d*

1d *Richard Conner of Ballybricken, d 1862, m 1833, Elizabeth, da of (—) Perrott, d 1853, and had issue 1e to 4e*

1e *Daniel Conner of Ballybricken, J P, b 27 Sept 1835, d 31 Dec 1899, m 14 June 1866, Emily, da of Henry Steigen Berger of 30 Cleveland Square, Hyde Park, W, and had issue 1f to 6f*

1f Daniel Henry Conner of Ballybricken (*Ballybricken, co Cork*), *b* 5 Ap 1867, m 14 Jan 1902, Florence Jane, da of Capt Horace Townshend, 99th Regt

2f Richard Conner, Major Gloucester Regt, *b* 29 Dec 1868

3f Henry Conner } (twins), *b* 17 Sept. 1872
4f Samuel Conner, Staff Surgeon, R N }

5f Emily Conner

6f Kathleen Louisa Conner

2e William Conner, M D, m 6 June 1872, Ellen Lawrence, da of William Colbourne of Monkstown, co Cork

3e *George Conner, Col 28th Regt, d (–)*

4e. Elizabeth Mary Conner, *m* 28 Ap 1870, Samuel Willy Perrott

[Nos 59822 to 59841.

# of The Blood Royal

5*b* *Catherine Pennefather*, d 17 Nov 1831, m *June* 1788, *Daniel Mansergh of Cashel, High Sheriff co Tipperary* 1789 [*Cadet of Grenane*], b c 1773, d 10 *June* 1823, and had issue 1c *to* 5c

1c *Nicholas Mansergh of Macrony Castle, co Cork, J P, M A, last Recorder of Cashel* 1836, b 20 *May* 1789, d (? s p) *Oct* 1865

2c *Daniel Mansergh of Ballyshean, Cashel, Capt in the Army*, d (—), m 1*st*, 22 *Aug* 1836, (—), *da of* (—) *Budd of Kilkenny*, d (—), 2ndl*v*, *Eleanor Jane, da of George Riall of Parsonstown*, d 21 *Aug* 1893, and had issue 1d *to* 5d

1*d*[1] Henry Mansergh, d 1889

2*d*[1] [son] Mansergh

3*d*[1] [da] Mansergh

4*d*[1] [da] Mansergh

5*d*[2] Helen Elizabeth Frances Mansergh

3c *Rev James Wentworth Mansergh, Rector of Kilmore*, d 1845, m 31 *Oct* 1835, *Catherine, da of Col Owen Lloyd of Rockville*, d 27 *Sept* 1891, and had issue

See p 354, Nos 59713-59711

4c *Mary Mansergh*, d (—), m *Edward Pennefather of Marlow, near Cashel*, and had issue 5 sons, of whom one was father of *Richard Lloyd Pennefather of Marlow, Goold's Cross, co Tipperary*

5c *Catherine Mansergh*, b 5 *Ap* 1805, d 25 *Sept* 1898, m 10 *July* 1840, *Richard Martin of Castle Jane, co Cork*, b 15 *Dec* 1786, d 16 *Ap* 1870, and had issue 1d *to* 3d

1d Richard Mansergh Martin of Castle Jane (*Castle Jane, Glanmire, co Cork*), b 22 Mar 1813, m 3 Oct 1905, Leonarda, da. of Capt. John Crawford Langford of Kingstown, co Dublin, s p

2d Daniel Nicholas Martin, M D, Lieut -Col (ret) Indian M S (*Churston, co Devon*), b 4 Aug 1844, m 15 Jan 1895, Etheldreda, da of the Rev J W Hardman of Cadbury House, Yatton, LL D , and has issue 1e

1e Viola Martin, b 25 Mar 1896

3d James Wentworth Martin, *formerly Madras P W Dept* (*Banisters, Finchampstead, Berks*), b 24 Jan 1847, m 13 Dec 1900, Violet, da of the Rev Canon Joseph Hammond of New Beckingham, and has issue 1e to 2e

1e James Mansergh Wentworth Martin, b 5 Aug 1902

2e [son] Wentworth Martin, b 10 Feb 1906

6*b* *Margaret Pennefather*, d 1833, m *the Rev Robert Warren of Crookstown House, co Cork* [*5th son of Sir Robert Warren of Warren's Court, 1st Bt* [*I* 1784]], d 1830, and had issue 1c *to* 3c

1c *Rev Robert Warren, Rector of Cannoway, co Cork*, b 7 *Mar* 1794, d 7 *May* 1879, m 26 *May* 1824, *Mary, da of David Crawford of Ballyshannon, J P, R N* , and had issue 1d to 4d

1d *Robert Warren of Crookstown*, b 8 *Oct* 1826, d 6 *May* 1903, m 6 *Sept* 1859, *Sophia* (*Crookstown, co Cork*), *da of Henry Braddell of Mallow*, and had issue 1e *to* 5e

1e Robert Warren of Crookstown (*Crookstown House, co Cork*), b 22 May 1870, m 1 Jan 1901, Maria Frances Lumley, da of William Lumley Perrier of Maryborough, Douglas, co Cork, and has issue 1f to 2f

1f Augustus John Warren, b 9 Sept 1909

2f Gladys Irene Warren, b 20 May 1908

2e Mary Frances Warren, *unm*

3e Sophia Louise Clowser Warren, m 17 June 1891, Jasper Drury, *formerly* of the Bush, Youghal, co Cork (*Douglas, Isle of Man*) , and has issue 1f to 2f

1f Jasper Drury, b 17 Feb 1893.

2f Robert Warren Drury, b 27 Oct 1894   [Nos 59812 to 59860

The Plantagenet Roll

4c Alice Sarah Warren, m 1893, Major Arthur Phelps, Army Ser Corps, *formerly* Dept Assist Dir of Quartering H Q 1901-1908, and D A A G South Africa 1901-1902 (*Modern Imperial Hotel, Lliema, Malta*)

5c Maude Warren

2d Richard Warren, Major Gen (ret) R E (12 *Portland Terrace, Southsea, Junior United Service*), b 31 May 1828, m 1st, 24 Feb 1852, Emily, da of William Lauder of Dominica, d 7 Aug 1891, 2ndly, 27 Dec 1893, Martha Elizabeth, widow of Robert Pitcairn of Sydney, Bar-at-Law, dr of Stephen Hawley Dunstall of Wolverhampton, and has issue (with others who d s p) 1c to 7c

1c *Herbert Lauder Warren, Staff Paymaster R N*, b 1 Ap 1855, d 9 Jan 1897, m 7 Nov 1885, Ella Christian (*Vectis Lodge, Victoria Road South, Southsea*), da of Christian Hoyer Millar of Blair Castle, co Perth, and had issue 1f to 2f

1f Ella Christian Louise Lauder Warren

2f Kathleen Pelham Lauder Warren

2c *Albert Edward Warren*, b 29 May 1856, d 27 Feb 1899, m 1884, Emily, da of Talbot Palmer of Waterloo Ville, co Hants, and had issue 1f to 6f

1f Edward Richard Warren, b 28 Oct 1888

2f Henry Charles Herbert Warren, b 3 Nov 1898

3f Emily Ruth Warren, m 1907, (—) Hardy (*Cape Town*)

4f Dorothy Talbot Warren, m 1907, Bernard Twedale

5f Winifred Mary Warren, m the Rev E W Witt

6f Marjorie Anne Warren

3c Henry Herrick Warren, b 22 Dec 1857, m 1908, Elizabeth, da of John Leader of Keale, co Cork

4c Richard Augustus Warren, H M's Customs, Natal (*Durban, Natal*), b. 31 Mar 1862, m 12 Ap 1898, Marie Charlotte Alice, da of Attwell Hayes Allen of Sea View, Queenstown, co Cork, s p

5c Percy Bliss Warren, Lieut-Col Indian Army, has Medal and Clasp for Chin-Lushai Exped 1889-1890 (*Junior United Service*), b 23 Ap 1864, m 11 Jan 1892, Margaret Ellen, da of William Langdon Martin of Windsor Villas, Plymouth, and has issue 1f to 4f

1f Richard Crawford Warren, b 25 Sept 1898

2f Wallis Langden Warren, b 13 Feb 1900

3f Geoffrey Martin Warren, b 3 Mai 1908

4f Margaret Joan Warren

6c William Waldegrave Warren, Lieut R N R, b 5 Sept 1867, m 4 Sept. 1901, Alice Matilda, da of the Rev Joseph Barton of East Leigh, Havant, and has issue 1f

1f Arthur Lionel Waldegrave Warren, b 15 July 1902

7c Emily Margaret Warren, m 21 Jan 1891, Major Arthur Gambier Norris, R G A

3d *Sarah Warren*, d (–), m 15 *July* 1852, her cousin, *John Warren Payne-Sheares*, d 14 Jan 1902, and had issue 1e to 2e

1e Somers Henry Payne, J P, D L (*Carrigmahon, Monkstown*), b 27 June 1853, m 23 May 1878, Edith Anne, da of James Leslie of Lecaron, co Cork, and has issue 1f to 4f

1f Robert Leslie Payne, Capt Connaught Rangers, b 7 May 1880

2f James Cecil Warren Payne, b 9 Oct 1882

3f Edith Elizabeth Payne

4f Margery Warren Payne

2e Mary Helen Payne, m 1889, the Very Rev William Joseph Wilson, M A (T C D), Dean of Cloyne and Canon of Kilbrogan in Cork Cathedral (*The Deanery, Cloyne, co Cork*)   [Nos 59861 to 59887]

# of The Blood Royal

4*d* Margaretta Warren (*Bellmount, Crookstown, co Cork*), *m* 19 Jan 1858, Capt Edward Herrick of Bellmount, co Cork, J P, 12th Regt, *d* 28 May 1879, and has issue 1*e* to 2*e*

1*e* John Edward Henry Herrick of Bellmount, *formerly* Capt 3rd Batt Royal Munster Regt (*Bellmount, Crookstown co Cork*), *b* 28 Jan 1862, *m* 12 Dec 1883, Emily Frances, da of James Low Holmes of Carrigmore, co Cork

2*e* Robert Warren Herrick, M D (30 *Regent Street, Nottingham*), *b* 23 Jan 1864, *m* 25 June 1891, Edith, da of Joseph Whitaker of Ramsdale, Notts, and has issue 1*f* to 2*f*

1*f* John Riversdale Warren Herrick, *b* 22 May 1893

2*f* Robert Lysle Warren Herrick, *b* 26 May 1895

2*c* *Richard Warren of Lisgoold, M D*, *b* Feb 1795, *d* Dec 1870, *m* 1824, *Margaret, da of William Pennefather, M P, Surveyor-Gen. of Ireland, d Dec 1873, and had issue*

See p 360, Nos 59826–59831

3*c* *Mary Warren*, *d* (–), *m* 23 *Nov* 1823, *Sir John Borlase Warren of Warren's Court, 4th Bt [I], d* 4 *Dec* 1863, *and had issue* 1*d* to 8*d*

1*d* Sir Augustus Riversdale Warren, 5th Bt [I], J P, D L, High Sheriff co Cork, Hon Col 4th Batt Royal Munster Fusiliers, *formerly* 20th Regt, Crimea and Indian Mutiny Medals and Clasps (*Army and Navy*, *Hurlingham*), *b* 24 Aug 1833, *m* 1st, 28 Ap 1861, Georgina, da of the Rev John Blennerhassett, M A, *d* 10 Nov 1893, 2ndly, 5 Feb 1898, Ella Rosa [descended from the Lady Anne, sister of Kings Edward IV and Richard III (see Essex Volume, p 636)], *formerly* wife of Col Frederick William Clarkson (whom she divorced 1887), da of Major-Gen John Octavius Chichester, and has issue 1*e*

1*e* Augustus Riversdale John Blennerhassett Warren, J P, *formerly* Lieut 3rd Batt Royal Munster Fusiliers (*Warren's Court, Lisarda, co Cork*), *b* 11 Mar 1865, *m* 12 Jan 1898, Agnes Georgina, da of George Maurice Ievers of Inchera, Glanmire, co Cork, and has issue 1*f*

1*f* Augustus George Digby Warren, *b* 23 Oct 1898

2*d* John Borlase Warren, Vice-Adm R N, Crimea and Chinese Medals (*United Service*), *b* 27 Mar 1838, *m* 12 Sept 1874, Mary Elizabeth St Leger, da of Major Robert St Leger Atkins of Water Park, co Cork, and has issue 1*e* to 3*e*

1*e* Bessie Geraldine Gundreda Warren, *m* 20 Nov 1906, Sir John Scarlett Walsham, 3rd Bt [U K] (see p 287) (*Knill Court, Kington, co Hereford, Germiston, Transvaal*), and has issue 1*f*

1*f* Barbara Walsham

2*e* Mary Detta St Leger Warren

3*c* Louisa Ursula Warren

3*d* Mary Warren (*Ashburn, Knock, Belfast*), *m* 10 May 1859, the Rev Thomas Robert Hamilton, Chaplain R N, and Rector of St Mark's, Dundela, *d* 1905, and has issue 1*e* to 4*e*

1*e* *Hugh Cecil Waldegrave Hamilton, Lieut Queensland Permanent Forces, formerly 2nd Brig N Irish Div R A*, *b* 17 *Nov* 1864, *d* (*e*)

2*e* Augustus Warren Hamilton, a Partner in the Firm of Hamilton & McMaster of Belfast (*Canadian Villa, Knock, Belfast*), *b* 12 Aug 1866, *m* 1897, Annie Sergeant, da of William Hailey of Newcastle, Miramichie, New Brunswick, and has issue 1*f* to 3*f*

1*f* John Borlase Warren Hamilton, *b* 1905

2*f* Ruth Sergeant Hamilton

3*f* Annie Hailey Hamilton

3*e* Lilian Frances Hamilton, *m* 1882, William Sufferin, LL D (*Gundreda Cottage, Cockenzie, Prestonpans*)

4*e* Florence Augusta Hamilton   [Nos 59888 to 59913

The Plantagenet Roll

4d *Margaret Warren*, d 1881; m 14 *Aug* 1851, *Charles Bosworth Martin, J.P co Cork, Leic Yeo Cav (Clonmoyle House, Aghabullogue, Cork)*, and had issue 1c to 3c

  1c Charles Augustus Martin, *b* 29 Oct 1855

  2c William John Borlase Martin, *b* 11 Feb 185-

  3c Anne Margaretta Martin

5d *Charlotte Warren*, d 22 *Ap* 1886, m 8 Feb 1848, *Robert Heard of Kinsale and Pallastown, co Cork, High Sheriff for that co* 1870, *Capt S Cork Mil*, d 12 *Sept* 1896, and had issue 1c to 5c

  1c *Robert Wilkes Heard of Kinsale and Pallastown*, b 17 *July* 1852, d 17 *Ap* 1897, m 20 *June* 1888, *Charlotte Amyand Powys [descended from the Lady Isabel Plantagenet (see the Essex Volume, p 382)] (10 Fisher Street, Kinsale, co Cork), da of Henry Atherton Adams of Wynters, co Essex, J P [who re-m 16 Aug. 1898, Richard Charles Pratt]*, and had issue 1f to 5f

    1f Robert Henry Warren Heard of Kinsale and Pallastown (*Pallastown and Ballydaly, Kinsale, The Lodge, Lackamore, co Tipperary*), b 6 Mar 1895

    2f Margaret Marion Atherton Heard

    3f Evelyn Mary Warren Heard

    4f Kathleen Vittorra Fiorenza Servatt Heard

    5f Amyand Dorothy Heard.

  2c Augustus Riversdale Heard

  3c Mary Warren Heard, m 23 May 1876, Sir William Quartus Ewart, 2nd Bt [U K], J P, D L, High Sheriff co Antrim 1907 (*Glenmachan, Strandtown, Belfast, Junior Carlton*), and has issue 1f to 5f

    1f Robert Heard Ewart, *b* 5 Nov 1879

    2f Charles Gordon Ewart, *b* 1885

    3f Charlotte Hope Ewart

    4f Isabella Kelso Ewart

    5f Margaret Gundred a Ewart

  4c *Charlotte Heard*, d 18 Feb 1892, m *as 1st wife*, 6 Dec 1888 (*Gilbert King, who afterwards (1895) suc his father as*) *Sir Gilbert King, 4th Bt [U K], M A, High Sheriff cos Roscommon* 1892 *and Leitrim* 1894 *and* 1904, &c [*a descendant of King Edward I] (Charlestown, Drumsna, Roscommon, 21 Fitzwilliam Square South, Dublin)*, and has issue 1f

    1f Mary Rowley King

  5c Catherine Jane Heard, m Sept 1887, Major Herbert Eyre Robbins, R M (*Winkleigh, Queen's Road, Tunbridge Wells*), and has issue

6d *Esther Warren*, d 12 *Mar* 1877, m 1867, *Ralph Fuller of Kilkondy House, Lisardu, co Cork*, and had issue 1f

  1f George Robert Fuller, *b* 1867

7d *Elizabeth Warren*, d 1899, *William Massy Hutchinson Massy of Mount Massy, J P (Mount Massy, Macroom)*, and had issue 1c to 4c

  1c Hugh Hutchinson Massy, *b* 1869

  2c John Warren Massy, *b* 1870

  3c Rose Catherine Massy

  4c Alice Massy

8d Frances Augusta Warren, m 10 Ap 1867, Capt Charles Henry Chauncy, *formerly 22nd and 41st Regts (44 Lee Park, Blackheath, S E)*, and has issue 1c to 7c

  1c Augustus Charles Chauncy, Dist Agent G E R C, Major 20th Batt co of London Div (*19 Henry Road, West Bridgford, Nottingham*), b 11 Dec 1867, m 1897, Rebecca Mary St Clair, da of Major W R Isles, 19th Regt, and has issue 1f

    1f. Francis Charles Martin Chauncy   [Nos 59914 to 59938

2e John Borlase Warren Chauncy (16 *Craigerne Road, Blackheath*), b 22 Jan 1869 , m 20 Ap 1899, Emily, da of Col Bayley, R A and has issue 1/ to 3/

1/ Charles Frederick Chauncy, b 6 May 1900

2/ Robert Augustus Chauncy, b 6 July 1906

3/ Anna Frances Chauncy

3e Charles Henry Kemble Chauncy, Capt Indian Army, 124th Infantry, b 21 Dec 1873 , m 3 Jan 1902, Constance Margaret, da of G W Sealy , and has issue 1/ to 2/

1/ Leslie Chauncy

2/ Helen Chauncy

4e James Hornidge Chauncy, M R C S (Eng), L R C P (Lond) (*St Mary's, near Sidney , Delegate, New South Wales*), b 1880 , m 1907, Adela, da of (—) Newton

5e Edith Julia Frances Rose Chauncy, m 1901, Major Arthur Gosset Crawford, 84th Punjabis, Indian Army , and has issue 1/ to 2/

1/ George Oswald Crawford, b 1902

2/ Dick Crawford, b 1909

6e Eleanor Aufride Mary Chauncy

7e Kate Isabel Chauncy   [Nos 59939 to 59951.

216 Descendants of MARGARET DEANE (Table XXI), d (–), m JOHN FITZGERALD of Innishmore, co Kerry, 15th Knight of Kerry, M P , d June 1741, and had issue (with 3 other children Maurice, 16th Knight, b 1733, Joseph, and Margaret, who all d s p) 1a

1a Elizabeth FitzGerald, da and event h , d (–), m Oct 1752, Richard Townsend, otherwise Townshend, of Castle Townsend, co Cork, M P , and High Sheriff for that co 1753, Col Cork Militia, d Dec 1783 , and had issue 1b

1b Right Hon Richard Boyle Townsend, otherwise Townshend, of Castle Townsend, P C , M P , High Sheriff co Cork 1785, b 1756 , d 26 Nov 1826 , m 16 May 1784, Henrietta, da of John Newenham of Maryborough, co Cork, d Dec 1848 , and had issue (with 4 other sons and a da who d s p) 1c to 2c

1c Rev Maurice FitzGerald Stephens Townsend afterwards (1870) Townshend of Castle Townshend, J P , D L , Vicar of Thornbury, co Glouc , b 7 May 1791, d 21 Mar 1872, m 16 May 1826, Alice Elizabeth, da and h of Richmond Shute of Iron Acton, co Glouc [by his wife Harriet, sister and h of Henry Hankes Willis Stephens of Eastington and Chavenage House, co Glouc], d 21 May 1872, and had issue 1d to 3d

1d Henry John Townshend, J P , 2nd Life Guards, b 1 Nov 1827 d v p 7 Sept 1869, m 29 Sept 1864, Jane Ideliza Clementina, da of John Hamilton Hussey de Burgh of Kilfinnan Castle, co Cork, J P , and had issue 1e to 2e

1e Maurice FitzGerald Stephens Townshend of Shute Court, formerly of Castle Townshend (*Riviere Lodge, Glandore, Cork*) b 4 Nov 1865 , unm

2e Hubert de Burgh FitzGerald Stephens Townshend, J P , late Capt 4th Batt Essex Regt , has South African Medal with 2 Clasps (*Shepperton Park, Leap, co Cork*), b 4 Ap 1867 , unm

2d Geraldine Henrietta Townshend (*Thornbury House, Thornbury, R S O , co Glouc*), m as 2nd wife, 30 Ap 1870, Major-Gen Pierrepont Henry Mundy of Thornbury House, co Glouc , J P R H A [6th son of Gen Godfrey Basil Mundy (2nd son of Edward Miller Mundy of Shipley, M P), by the Hon Sarah Brydges, d i of George Brydges (Rodney), 1st Baron Rodney [G B], Adm R N] d s p 16 Feb 1889

3d Alice Gertrude Townshend (*Compton, Guildford*), m 25 May 1856, Rev   [Nos 59952 to 59955

The Plantagenet Roll

the Hon Courtenay John Vernon [3rd son of Robert, 1st Baron Lyveden [U K]], d 2 July 1892, and had issue 1e to 3e

1e Courtenay Robert Percy (Vernon), 3rd Baron Lyveden [U K], *formerly* Capt 3rd Batt Highland L I , is President of the British Committee for the Study of Foreign Municipal Institutions (3 *Earl's Avenue, Folkestone*), b 29 Dec 1857, m 12 Feb 1890, Fanny Zelie, da of Major Hill of Wollaston Hall, co Northants, and has issue 1f to 2f

    1f Hon Robert FitzPatrick Courtenay Vernon, b 1 Feb 1892

    2f Hon Victoria Wyndham Dorothy Vernon

2e Hon Sydney Charles FitzPatrick Vernon (*High Wycombe, Bucks*), b 14 July 1862, m 7 Jan 1897, Emilie Louise, da of Charles Lorkin of Hockley, co Essex

3e Hon Evelyn Mary Geraldine Vernon, m 7 Aug 1877, the Rev Hugh Hodgson Gillett M A , Rector of Compton and Canon of Peterborough (*Compton Rectory, Guildford*), and has issue 1f to 5f

    1f Hugh Vernon Gillett, b 12 June 1878

    2f Charles Richard Gillett, Lieut R A and Instructor in Gunnery at Malta, b 21 Aug 1880, m 8 Feb 1906, Gwynne, da of Robert Keate of 14 Rosary Gardens, S W

    3f George Maurice Gerald Gillett, b 17 Nov 1882

    4f Sybil Evelyn Gillett

    5f Gertrude Mary Gillett

2c Henrietta Augusta Townsend, d Dec 1869, m 12 Oct 1822, Thomas Somerville of Drishane, co Cork, J P , D L , and High Sheriff for that co 1863, d 19 May 1882, and had issue 1d to 2d

1d Thomas Henry Somerville of Drishane, J P D L , and High Sheriff co Cork 1888, Lieut Col 3rd Buffs, b 29 Oct 1824, d 15 Mar 1898, m 29 June 1857, Adelaide Eliza, da of Adm Sir Josiah Coghill, 3rd Bt [G B], d 3 Dec 1895, and had issue 1e to 7e

1e Thomas Cameron FitzGerald Somerville of Drishane, Col Comdg King's Own Royal Lancaster Regt (*Drishane, Skibbereen, co Cork*), b 30 Mar 1860

2e Henry Boyle Townsend Somerville, Capt R N (*Maraelton, The Hale, Edgware*) b 7 Sept 1863, m 7 Ap 1896, Helen Mabel, da of Sir George Wigram Allen of Toxteth, Sydney, K C M G , and has issue 1f to 4f

    1f Raymond Thomas Somerville, b 14 Mar 1897

    2f Brian Aylmer Somerville, b 27 Jan 1900

    3f Michael Fitzgerald Somerville, b 13 Sept 1908

    4f Diana Marian Somerville

3e Aylmer Coghill Somerville, J P , Capt S of Ireland Imp Yeo (*Penleigh House, Westbury, Wilts Castle Townshend, co Cork*), b 23 Sept 1865, m 1st, 1 Oct 1888 Emmeline Sophia, da of Daniel Sykes of Oaklands, co Glouc, d 13 Feb 1900, 2ndly, 3 July 1901, Nathalie Adah, da of William Barrow Turner of Ponsonby Hall, co Cumberland, and has issue 1f to 4f

    1f¹ Desmond Henry Sykes Somerville, b 6 Aug 1889

    2f² Thomas Henry Gilbert Somerville, b 29 Ap 1907

    3f¹ Gillian Margaret Hope Somerville

    4f² Elizabeth Geraldine Aylmer Somerville

4e John Arthur Coghill Somerville, Major Royal Sussex Regt (*Junior Naval and Military*), b 26 Mar 1872

5e Hugh Gualter Coghill Somerville, Capt R N (*Junior Naval and Military*), b 10 July 1873, m 1900, Mary, da of W Hancock of Patris

6e Edith Anna Ænone Somerville

7e Elizabeth Hildegarde Augusta Somerville, m 11 July 1893, Sir Egerton Bushe Coghill, 5th Bt [G B], J P (*Glen Barrahan., Castle Townshend, co Cork*), and has issue 1f to 4f   [Nos 59956 to 59980

# of The Blood Royal

1/ Marmaduke Nevill Patrick Somerville Coghill, *b* 17 Mar 1896
2/ Nevill Henry Kendal Aylmer Coghill, *b* 19 Ap 1899
3/ Joscelyn Ambrose Cramer Coghill, *b* 30 Sept 1902
4/ Katherine Adelaide Hildegarde Coghill
2*d* Henrietta Somerville   [Nos 59981 to 59985

217 Descendants of WILLIAM (O'BRIEN), 4th EARL OF INCHIQUIN
   (Table XXI), *d* 18 July 1777, *m* 1st, 28 Mar 1720, ANNE
   (HAMILTON) *suo jure* 2nd COUNTESS OF ORKNEY [S], *d*. 7 Dec
   1756, and had issue 1*a*.

1*a* Mary (O'Brien), *suo jure* 3rd *Countess of Orkney* [S], b *a* 1721, d
10 May 1791, m 5 Mar 1753, *Murrough (O'Brien), 1st Marquis of Thomond* [I]
(see below), d 10 Feb 1808, *and had issue* 1b
   1*b* Mary (O'Brien), *suo jure* 4th *Countess of Orkney* [S], b 1755, d 20 Dec
1831, m 21 Dec 1771, *the Hon Thomas Fitzmaurice of Llewenny, co Denbigh*
[2nd son of John, 1st Earl of Shelburne [I]], d 28 Oct 1793, *and had issue* 1c
      1*c* John Fitzmaurice, Viscount Kirkwall, b 9 Oct 1778, d v p 3 Nov 1820,
m 11 Aug 1802, *the Hon Anna Maria, da of John (de Blaquiere), 1st Baron de
Blaquiere* [I], d 31 Jan 1843, *and had issue* 1d *to* 2d
      1*d* Thomas John Hamilton (Fitzmaurice), 5th *Earl of Orkney* [S], b 8 Aug
1803, d 16 May 1877, m 14 Mar 1826, *the Hon Charlotte Isabella, da of George
(Irby), 3rd Baron Boston* [G B], d 7 Sept 1883, *and had issue*
      See the Essex Volume, pp 116-118, Nos 15509-15556
      2*d* Hon William Edward Fitzmaurice, M P, co Bucks, Major 2nd Life
Guards, b 21 Mar 1805, d 18 June 1889, m 1st, 3 Aug 1837, *Hester, da of
Henry Harford of Down Place, co Berks, d 24 Aug 1859, and had issue* 1e *to* 3e
         1*e* Cecil Henry Fitzmaurice, late R N, b 25 Aug. 1844, m 1870, Elizabeth
Maria, da of (—) Hatton, d 1902, and has issue 1f
            1*f* Cecil Edward Fitzmaurice, b 27 July 1871
         2*e* Agnes Isabella Fitzmaurice, d 5 Dec 1863, m 27 Nov 1860, *William
Reginald Hesketh of Gwyrch Castle, co Denbigh*
         3*e* Flora Louisa Fitzmaurice, m 4 Nov 1869, *Arthur William Baker, formerly
60th Regt*, and has issue   [Nos 59986 to 60036

218 Descendants of the Hon JAMES O'BRIEN, M P (Table XXI),
   d (-), *m* MARY, da. of the Very Rev William JEPHSON,
   Dean of Kilmore, *d* (-), and had issue 1*a* to 5*a*

• 1*a* Murrough (O'Brien), 5th *Earl of Inchiquin* [I] *and 1st Marquis of
Thomond* [I 29 Dec 1800] *and 1st Baron Thomond of Taplow* [U K 2 Oct 1801],
d 9 Feb 1808, m 1st, 5 Mar 1753, *Mary (O Brien), suo jure 3rd Countess of
Orkney* [S], d 10 May 1791, *and had issue*
   See above, Nos 59986-60036
   2*a* Edward O'Brien, d Mar 1801, m *Mary, da of (—) Carrick, and had
issue* 1b *to* 5b
      1*b* William (O'Brien), 2nd *Marquis of Thomond and 6th Earl of Inchiquin*
[I], 1st *Baron Tadcaster* [U K 3 July 1826], d 21 Aug 1846, m 16 Sept 1809,
Elizabeth, da and h of Thomas Trotter of Duleck, d 3 Mar 1852, and had issue
1c *to* 3c
         1*c* Lady Susan Maria O Brien, d 25 Mar 1857, m 12 Aug 1821, *Rear-
Adm the Hon George Frederick Hotham, R N* (p 522), d 19 Oct 1856, *and had
issue* 1d *to* 3d   [Nos 60037 to 60087

The Plantagenet Roll

1d *Charles (Hotham), 4th Baron Hotham [I] and 14th Bt [E], d unm 29 May 1872*

2d *John (Hotham), 5th Baron Hotham [I] and 15th Bt [E], b 13 May 1838, d unm 13 Dec 1907*

3d Hon *Susan Frances Hotham (46 Belgrave Road, S W), m 6 June 1877, the Rev Alexander Cosby Jackson, d 23 Feb 1907, and has issue 1e*

1e Augusta Frances Cyrilla Jackson

2c *Lady Sarah O'Bryen, d 9 Feb 1859, m 3 Ap 1830, Major William Stanhope Taylor [son of Thomas Taylor of Sevenoaks by his wife Lady Lucy Rachel, née Stanhope], d (−), and had (with possibly other) issue 1d*

1d *O'Bryen Taylor, Major and Standard Bearer H M's Body-Guard of Gentlemen-at-Arms, d (−), m (−−) and had (with possibly other) issue 1e*

1e Mabel O'Bryen Taylor, m 16 June 1896, Sir Sydney James O'Bryen Hoare, 6th Bt [I], and has issue

See p 369, Nos 60108–60109

3c *Lady Elizabeth O'Brien, d 9 May 1870, m as 1st wife, Sir George Stucley Stucley (R L 27 July 1858), previously Buck 1st Bt [U K 26 Ap 1859], M P, J P, D L, Col Com'tg Devonshire Lit, b 17 Aug 1812, d 13 Mar 1900, and had issue*

See p 453, Nos 103413–103414

2b *James (O Brien), 3rd and last Marquis of Thomond and 7th Earl of Inchiquin [I], &c Adm R N d s p 3 July 1855*

3b *Lord Edward O Bryen, Capt R N, d 9 Mar 1821 2ndly, 11 Ap 1815, Gertrude Grace, sister of Paul, 1st Baron Methuen [U K], da of Paul Cobb Methuen of Corsham, d 1 May 1817 and had issue 1c to 2c*

1c *Gertrude Matilda O'Bryen, d 17 Dec 1869, m 17 June 1840, the Rev Thomas Plumptre Methuen, M A [nephew of Paul, 1st Baron Methuen], b 14 Aug 1811, d 17 Dec 1869, and had issue 1d to 2d*

1d Rev Paul Edward O Bryen Methuen (*Bicknoller, Mount Beacon, Bath*), b 15 May 1841

2d *Charles Lucas Methuen, Lieut 79th Highlanders, b 25 Sept 1842, d 17 Aug 1905 m 25 June 1872, Eleanor Mary, da of the Rev Alfred Harford of Locking, co Som*

2c *Mary Catherine O'Bryen d 10 May 1885, m 20 Jan 1842, the Rev John Hamilton Forsyth, d 25 June 1848, and had issue (with another son who d s p) 1d*

1d *Thomas Hamilton Forsyth, Col late 62nd Regt (Northwold, Bournemouth), b 29 Dec 1843, m 5 Aug 1873, Anne Noel [descended from Lady Anne, sister of King Edward IV, &c (see Exeter Volume, p 194)], da of Edward Andrew Noel, J P D L [E of Gainsborough Coll], and has issue 1e to 3e*

1e Ronald Graham Hamilton Forsyth, b 1 Dec 1875, m 30 Dec 1904, Helen Crosbie, da of Crosby Stewart Sawyer of St Barbara, California, and had issue 1f

1f Thomas Hamilton Forsyth, b 1 Sept 1905

2e Anne Cecilia Noel Forsyth

3e Mary Beatrice Gertrude Forsyth

2d *Douglas Methuen Forsyth, Comm (ret) R N (Leavington House, Ryde, I W), b 19 Ap 1847, m 1 Oct 1874, Kate, da of Capt William O'Brien, 53rd Regt, and has issue 1e to 3e*

1e Douglas William O'Bryen Forsyth, b 6 Oct 1880

2e Archibald Hamilton O'Bryen Forsyth, b 16 May 1884

3e Katharine Mary O'Bryen Forsyth

4b *Lady Mary O'Bryen, d 28 June 1840, m 1st, 2 Feb 1780, Sir Richard*

[Nos 60088 to 60104

368

# of The Blood Royal

Cox, 4th Bt [I], d 6 Sept. 1784 (by whom she had an only da, Maria who apparently d young) 2ndly, Jan 1786, the Right Hon William Saurin, P C, Attorney-General [I], d (–), and had issue 1c to 3c

1c *Edward Saurin, Adm R N, d 28 Feb 1878, m 15 July 1828, Lady Mary [descended from King Henry VII (see Tudor Roll, p 524)] da of Dudley (Ryder), 1st Earl of Harrowby [U K], and had (with other) issue 1d*

1d *William Granville Saurin, eldest son, d 1893, m 2 Aug 1865, Madine Nicolaicvora, da of (–) de Smirnoff, P C and a Senator of Russia, and had (with other) issue (an eldest da, Susan Marcia, who d unm 3 Ap 1878)*

2c James Saurin, } both living May 1819
3c Mark Anthony Saurin }

5b *Lady Harriet O'Bryen, d 1 May 1851, m 17 Ap 1800, Sir Joseph Wallis Hoare of Annabella, 3rd Bt [I], d 26 Nov 1852, and had issue 1c to 7c*

1c *Sir Edward Hoare, 4th Bt [I], b 23 Dec 1801, d 15 Nov 1882, m 24 Ap 1824, Harriet, da and co-h of Thomas Hercy Barritt of Garland Hall, co Surrey, d 25 Jan 1880, and had issue 1d to 2d*

1d *Sir Joseph Wallis O'Bryen Hoare, 5th Bt [I], J P D L, b 11 Nov 1828, d 30 Ap 1904, m 6 Aug 1857, Cecilia Eleanor Selina, da of James Ede of Ridgeway Castle, co Hants, d 7 Jan 1888, and had issue 1e to 3e*

1e *Sir Sydney James O'Bryen Hoare, 6th Bt [I] formerly Lieut Mdx Regt (16 The Grange, Wimbledon), b 2 July 1860, m 16 June 1896, Mabel O'Bryen, da of Major O'Bryen Taylor, Standard-Bearer to H M's Body-Guard of Gentlemen-at-Arms, and has issue 1f to 2f*

1f Edward O'Bryen Hoare, b 29 Ap 1898
2f Terence O'Bryen Hoare, b 21 Jan 1904

2e Kathleen Henrietta Hoare
3e Norah Cecile Helen Hoare (Rostellan, Pear Tree Avenue, Itchen, Hants)

2d *Anne Hoare, d 24 Feb 1910, m 4 June 1856, Thomas Leslie, M A, Bar-at-Law [son of the Right Rev John Leslie, D D, Lord Bishop of Kilmore], d 15 Feb 1880, and had issue 1e to 5e*

1e *Rev Edward Charles Leslie, M A (Oxon), Rector of Winterborne-Came, (Winterborne-Came, Dorset), b 15 July 1858, m 6 Nov 1906, Margaret Elizabeth, da of Henry Joseph Moule of Dorchester*

2e *Arthur Trevor O'Bryen Leslie, Capt formerly 3rd Vol Batt E Surrey Regt (46 Comeragh Road, West Kensington, W) b 23 May 1868, m 7 Oct 1896, Guendolen Amy, da of Sir Charles Rugge-Price, 6th Bt [U K], s p s*

3e Harriet Eleanor Josephine Leslie
4e Annie Isabella Leslie
5e Frances Emily Clotilda Leslie

2c *William O'Bryen Hoare, Capt R N, b 23 Mar 1807, d 20 May 1886, m 2 May 1834, Caroline, da of John Hornby of The Hook, co Hants, d 9 Jan 1891, and had issue 1d*

1d Elizabeth Clotilda Hoare (1 Liverpool Gardens, Worthing)

3c *Joseph James Parish Hoare, b 22 Mar 1811, d 17 Dec 1889, m 17 Ap 1834, Helen Moritz Dillon, da of Henry Arthur Hardman of Mount Hardman Grenada, and had issue 1d to 7d*

1d *Rev James O'Bryen Dott Richard Hoare, M A (Camb), Vicar of Papanui (Christchurch, New Zealand), b 12 Mar 1835, m 23 Feb 1865, Frances Eleanor, da of the Rev Thomas Henderson, and has issue 1e to 7e*

1e *Arthur Hoare, Electrical and Mechanical Engineer (Bombay), b 30 Nov 1866*

2e *Philip Hoare, Public Accountant (New South Wales), b 28 Nov 1871, m 1897, Florence, da of F Evans, and has issue 1f*

1f Donovan O'Bryen Hoare

369   [Nos 60105 to 60121

The Plantagenet Roll

3c John Hoare, Mechanical Engineer (*Queensland*), b 23 Dec 1873, m 1904, Margaret Jane, da of E S Leversedge, and has issue 1f to 2f

　1f James O'Bryen Hoare

　2f John Mary Hoare

4c Denys Hoare, Accountant and Coy Manager (*Brownlow, 21 Mansfield Avenue, Christchurch, N Z*), b 30 Nov 1875, m 17 Jan 1906, Frances, da of Thomas York, and has issue 1f

　1f Norah Frances O'Bryen Hoare

5c Mary Hoare, *unm*

6c Janet Hoare, m 1899, Geoffrey John Phillips, C E (*Cape Town*), and has issue 1f to 2f

　1f Geoffrey O'Bryen Phillips

　2f Marjory O'Bryen Phillips

7c Helen Hoare, m Ap 1910, Hugh Mostyn Trevor

2d *Joseph George Wallis Hoare*, R N, b 26 July 1838, d 14 May 1883, m 1st, 1 June 1865, Susan Mary, da of Capt F W Paul, R N, d 13 Sept 1874, 2ndly, 9 Ap 1878, *Mary Martha*, da of H White England of Kingsbury, co Som, and had issue 1c to 5c

1c Helen Susan Kathleen Hoare (*La Floresta, Barranquilla, Colombia*), m m Barranquilla 2 Ap 1894, John Meek of Liverpool and Barranquilla, Jr, d 6 Oct 1907, and has issue 1f to 2f

　1f John Wallace Meek, b 22 Dec 1902

　2f Francis Forwood O'Bryen Meek, b 2 July 1905

2c Lily Hoare (8a *Nevern Road, Earl's Court, S W*), *unm*

3c Edith Mary Hoare, m in Barranquilla 25 May 1897, Fritz Rudolf Fuhrhop, and has issue (see Appendix)

4c Marie Violet Hoare, *unm*

5c Olive Buchanan Hoare, m 21 June 1904, William Gerald Morris, M I C E (*Muchelney, Broxbourne, Herts*), and has issue 1f to 3f

　1f William Arabi Morris ⎱ (twins), b 3 Ap 1905
　2f Wallace Gerald Morris ⎰

　3f Mary Daphne Morris, b 15 Nov 1907

3d *Arthur Calvert Hoare*, b 24 Mar 1810, d 4 Ap 1898, m 29 Jan 1869, *Charlotte Rosina*, da of Joseph Robinson, otherwise Robertson, of co Banff, and had issue 1c to 4c

1c Arthur Carrick Dickson Hoare (*Isthmian*), b 23 Oct 1874

2c Helen Brownlow Hoare, m 21 Sept 1904, Wilhelm Ernst Harald Solger, Lieut 7th E Prussian Inf

3c Brenda Marie Hoare, m 18 Oct 1905, Charles Henry Dorward Moberly, Agent, Bank of Bengal (*Hyderabad, Deccan, India*), and has issue 1f

　1f Brenda Winifred Moberly

4c Sidney Josephine Fitzmaurice Hoare, m 29 May 1909, Walter Granville Warburton of Bombay and Karachi, East India Merchant (*Sind Club, Karachi*)

4d Charles Campbell William Hoare, *formerly* one of H M's Inspectors of Factories (*Gulistan, 65 Laurie Park Road, Sydenham, S E*), b 31 Dec 1841, m 25 July 1867, Blanche, da of Frederick Richard Phayre of Killoughram, co Wexford, and had issue 1c to 3c

1c Carl Frederick Hoare, b 21 Sept 1869

2c Mary Annesley Hoare, m 1890, Charles Frederick Edwards, C E

3c Blanche Evelyn Hoare

5d *Oliver William Simpson Hoare*, Capt Lanark Militia, b 3 Oct 1843, d Oct 1902, m 27 Oct 1864, *Anne*, da of George James of Ridgeway, co Hants, d 1881, and had issue 1c to 7c　　　　　　　　　　[Nos 60122 to 60150

370

# of The Blood Royal

1e Oliver George St Clair Hoare (*Santa Rosa, S America*), *b* 18 Sept 1866, *m* 1892, Helen, da of Robert Lloyd Peel

2e Basil O'Bryen Hoare, *b* 1 Mar 1870

3e Walter James Hoare, *b* 4 Oct 1871

4e Gerald Robbin O'Bryen Hoare, *b* 11 Nov 1879

5e Isabella Hoare, *m* 1897, Isaac Benjamin Oyles

6e Constance Helen Hoare, *m* 1901, Major Philip L. Stevenson, *late* 5th Lancers

7e Geraldine Erin Hoare, *m* 26 Sept 1893, Edmund Beverly Blan McKean (*New Park, co Herts*)

6d *Edward Senior Hoare, b* 15 *July* 1851, d 21 *Aug* 1895, m 16 *Aug* 1870, *Sophia Elizabeth, da of the Rev J S Hird of Sunningdale, and had issue 1e*

1e Cyril Bertie Edward Hoare (*Bleak House, Dyke Road, Brighton*), *b* 29 Sept 1882, *m* 24 Oct 1907, Isabel Mary, da of Edward Fielder of Anerley, S E, and has issue 1f

1f Hermione Sophia O'Bryen Hoare, *b* 27 Feb 1910

7d *Marion Maria Dorothea Hoare*, d 14 *Oct* 1896, m 20 *Feb* 1855, *John Turner-Turner, formerly Phillipson, of Avon, co Hants*, d 8 *Feb* 1874, *and had issue 1e to 2e*

1e John Edmund Unett Phillipson Turner (*Avon Castle, Ringwood, Hants*), *b* 19 Feb 1856

2e Gwendoline Evelyn Fitzmaurice Turner, *m* 28 Oct 1878, John Aitken of Mount Aitken (*Wyke Hall, Gillingham, Dorset*)

4c *John Lynam Parish Hoare, Major 13th Bombay N I* d (*?* s p) 12 *June* 1882, m 4 *May* 1840, *Jane Ellis, da of Lieut -Col Charles Payne*

5c *Harriet Hoare*, d 8 *Oct* 1827, m 17 *Oct* 1826, *Francis Hurt Sitwell of Ferney Hall, co Salop*, d 22 *Aug* 1835, *and had issue 1d*

1d William Willoughby George Hurt Sitwell of Ferney Hall, J P, High Sheriff co Salop 1855 (*Ferney Hall, Craven Arms, Salop*), *b* 2 Oct 1827, *m* 1st, 29 Sept 1853, Harriet Margaret, da of William Henry Harford of Barley Wood, d 18 May 1855, 2ndly, 8 July 1858, Eliza Harriet, da of Richard Burton Phillipson of Dunston Hall, Stafford, d 21 June 1888, and has issue 1e to 2e

1e Willoughby Harford Sitwell, J P, Lieut 6th Dragoons, *b* 18 May 1855, *m* 7 Sept 1880, Rose Augusta Cecil, da of James Henry Brabazon of Mornington [E of Meath [I] Coll], and has issue 1f

1f Willoughby Hurt Sitwell, *b* 30 Ap 1881

2e Francis Hurt Sitwell, J P, Lieut -Col *late* Shropshire I Y, *b* 14 Jan 1860

6c *Mary Hoare*, d (*?* s p) 11 *Dec* 1836, m 1832, *Capt Matthew Charles Forster, R N*, d 1 *Feb* 1897

7c *Elizabeth Hoare*, d 21 *Sept* 1872, m 1838, *the Rev James Payne Hersford, Colonial Chaplain, Ceylon Ecclesiastical Estab, and had issue*

3a *Mary O'Bryen*

4a *Anne O'Bryen*, d 19 *Jan* 1745, m as 2nd *wife*, 23 *Mar* 1744, *the Most Rev Michael Cox, D D, Lord Archbishop of Cashel 1754-1779 [Bt [I 1706] Coll]*, b 2 *Nov* 1691, d 28 *May* 1779, *and had issue 1b*

1b *Richard Cox of Castletown*, b 15 *Jan* 1745, d *July* 1790, m 25 *Jan* 1766, *Mary, da of Francis Burton [Bt of Pollerton Coll]*, d (-), *and had issue 1c to 6c*

1c *Michael Cox of Castletown*, b 14 *Ap* 1768, d 1836, m *the Hon Mary, da of Henry (Prittie), 1st Baron Dunalley [I]*, d 12 *Feb* 1859, *and had issue 1d to 2d*

1d *Sir Richard Cox, 8th Bt [I]*, d 7 *May* 1846

2d *Catherine Cox*, d 14 *Sept* 1879, m 1st, *June* 1833, *Capt William Villiers-Stuart, M P [M of Bute Coll]*, d 7 *Nov* 1873, *and had issue*

See the Clarence Volume, pp 146-147, Nos 2097-2103

[Nos 60151 to 60174

371

The Plantagenet Roll

2c Sir Francis Cox, 9th Bt [I], b 23 July 1769, d s p 6 Mar 1856

3c Rev Richard Cox, Rector of Cahirconlish, co Limerick, b 20 Sept 1771, d 1834, m Sarah, da of the Rev Ralph Hawtrey, d (–), and had (with other) issue 1d to 5d

    1d Sir Ralph Hawtrey Cox, 10th Bt [I], b 1808, d s p 12 Ap 1872

    2d Sir Michael Cox, 11th Bt [I], b 1810, d unm, 15 June 1872

    3d Sir Francis Hawtrey Cox, 12th Bt [I], b c 1816, d s p 17 Oct 1873

    4d William Saurin Cox, sometimes said to have succ as 13th Bt, d s p s

    5d Anne Cox, m the Rev Thomas Lyon

4c William Cox, b 6 Jan 1773,   } d s p m and presumably s p
5c Benjamin Cox, b 20 Jan 1775 }

6c Rachel Cox, b 9 Nov 1770, d (–), m Ponsonby Hore of Harperstown, co Wexford [son of Walter Hore of the same by his wife Lady Anne, née Stopford]

5a Lady Henrietta O'Brien, d 17 Nov 1797, m 1st, Terence O'Loghlin, d (–), 2ndly, 5 Oct 1769, Sir William Vigors Burdett of Dunmore, 2nd Bt [I], d 17 Dec 1798, and had issue (with a younger son d unm) 1b to 2b

1b Sir William Bagenal Burdett, 3rd Bt [I], bapt 16 July 1770, d 14 Dec 1810, leaving issue an only da, who d s p

2b Mary Orkney Burdett, d at Radipole, co Dorset, 17 Dec 1857, m 1800, Burton Newenham [son of Sir Edward Newenham, Cadet of Coolmore, co Cork], d (–), and had issue (with 6 children, of whom no issue survives) 1c to 3c

1c William Burton Newenham of Fitzwilliam Square, Dublin, b 2 June 1806, d May 1877, m 15 Oct 1853 Frances Louisa, da and h of Francis Wortham of S:eaversy, co Camb, and had issue 1d

    1d Francesca Louise Newenham, m 19 Dec 1882, George Reginald Trappes [Cadet of Nidd (see Essex Volume, p 673)] (The Hawthornes, Hanley Swan, Worcestershire), s p

2c Rev Bagenal Burdett Newenham, Vicar of Bilton, co York, b in Dublin 3 Mar 1816, d 19 Oct 1901, m in London 19 Feb 1857, Helen Louisa, da of Hambly Knapp, and had issue 1d to 3d

    1d Edward Burdett Newenham, B A (Oxon) (Provincerssingel 20, Rotterdam), b 29 Sept 1858, m Dec 1891, Susan Frances, da of William Joy of London and has issue 1e to 4e

        1e William Edward Burdett Newenham, b Feb 1890

        2e Frederick Alfred Joy Newenham, b Jan 1902

        3e Robert O'Brien Newenham, b June 1903

        4e Emily Frances Newenham, b 31 Dec 1892

    2d Frederick George Newenham (New Zealand), b 29 June 1860, unm

    3d Rev Arthur O'Brien Newenham, M A (Oxon), Rector of Cowthorpe (Cowthorpe Rectory, Wetherby), b 15 Feb 1862, m 13 June 1889, Eliza Ada, da of William Thompson, and has issue 1e to 2e

        1e Gerald Arthur Burdett Newenham, b 25 Jan 1898

        2e Irene Ada Newenham, b 29 June 1893

3c Grace Anna Newenham, b 4 Feb 1805, d Mar 1887, m 3 Mar 1827, James Stuart Brownrigg [nephew of Lieut-Gen Sir Robert Brownrigg, 1st Bt [U K 1816], G C B], d in Paris Nov 1879, and had issue (with a son and a da, Mrs Dillon-Trant, who d s p) 1d to 3d

    1d Grace Anna Maria Brownrigg, da and co-h, b 1 Feb 1831, d 1 Ap 1890, m 12 July 1849, Henry Alexander Leishman of the Mauritius, b 16 Sept 1821, d 19 Mar 1881, and had issue (with 2 sons d young) 1e to 6e

        1e Henry James Charles Leishman (Nanarup, Western Australia), b 12 July 1850, m 12 July 1880, Alice, da of Judge Bunny of Melbourne, and has issue 1f to 3f

            [Nos 60175 to 60185

# of The Blood Royal

1f Hugh Arthur Leishman, *b* Aug 1886

2f Lilian Leishman }
3f Grace Leishman } (twins), *b* 8 May 1882

2e Stuart Brownrigg Leishman (*Queensland*), *b* 12 Sept 1862, *m* 1st at Melbourne, June 1888, Augusta Nicola, da of Dr G A Mein, *d* 1897, 2ndly, at Brisbane, 8 July 1901, Gertrude Isobel, da of (—) Blakeney, and has issue 1f

1f George Alexander Burdett Leishman, *b* 11 Nov 1892

3e Grace Augusta Matilda Leishman, *m* 21 Feb 1878, the Rev Alfred Edward Beavan, M A (Oxon), Chaplain of Normanfield, Hampton Wick (*The Grange, King Charles Road, Surbiton Hill, Surrey*), *s p*

4e Eliza Mary Leishman, *m* 26 Ap 1883, the Rev Arthur Adam Farnell, *d s p* 22 Sept 1902

5e Lilian Louisa Leishman, *m* 15 June 1886, Harry Frank Dibben, and has issue 1f to 3f

1f Arthur Douglas Harry Dibben, *b.* 15 May 1887.

2f Eric Dibben, *b* 7 Dec 1894

3f Muriel Dibben, *b* 22 Oct 1892

6e Rose Elmyra Alexandrina Leishman, *unm*

2d *Augusta Henrietta Anne Brownrigg*, da and co-h, b 24 May 1833, d at Trouville 10 July 1900, m 12 July 1849, *Hambly Knapp of Upton Park, Slough,* d (—), and had issue (*with a son and 2 das d unm*) 1e to 5e

1e Charles Cornwallis Knapp (*St Helen's Cottage, Byfleet, Surrey*), *b* 25 Aug 1852, *m* 30 Oct 1882, Georgina Harriet, da of George Augustus Pollard of Rostrevor, co Devon, J P, and has issue (with a son, Cedric Jerome, *b* 7 Ap 1890, *d* 11 June 1896) 1f

1f Florence Helen Knapp

2e Rev Ashley Henry Arthur Knapp, in Holy Orders of the Roman Catholic Church, *b* 16 Sept 1866

3e Augusta Emma Grace Knapp, *m* 6 Feb 1873, Frederic Shenstone (*Sutton Hall, Barcombe, Sussex*), and has issue (with a son, Frederick Wyattville Smith, *b* 17 June 1876, *d* young) 1f

1f Adela Shenstone

4e Georgina Annie Ashley Knapp, *unm*

5e Rosalie Violet Olympe Knapp, *unm*

3d *Caroline Malcy Matilda Brownrigg*, da and co h, b at the Cape 12 May 1839, d 1 Jan 1900, m 15 July 1865, *George Harvey Jay of Sherlocks Hall, co Kent, and* 16 Westbourne Street, London, W, d 5 Nov 1881, and had issue 1e to 3e

1e Harvey Brownrigg Jay, late D C L I (*The White Lodge, Purton, Wilts*), *b* 13 Mar 1868, *m* 22 July 1893, Kate Bellville, da of Francis John Bucelle, and has issue 1f to 5f

1f George Harvey Brownrigg Jay, *b* 3 Aug 1894

2f Judith Malee Brownrigg Jay

3f Marjorie Grace Brownrigg Jay

4f Gwyneth Mary Brownrigg Jay

5f Myra Kathleen Brownrigg Jay

2e *Grace Isabel Brownrigg Jay*, b 30 Nov 1866, d 13 June 1897, m 18 July 1887, *the Rev Henry John Claude Torry*, M A (Camb), Rector of Streat (*Streat Rectory, Hassocks*) and had issue 1f

1f John Shirley Archibald Torry, *b* 17 July 1889

3e Ethel Rose Brownrigg Jay, *m* 1 Feb 1897, Major Walter Dougall, *formerly* "The Carabineers," 6th Dragoon Guards (*Silton Hall, Neth r Silton, Northallerton*), and has issue 1f to 2f

1f Ferrers Mackintosh Dougall, *b* 1 Nov 1897

2f Eustace Melville Dougall, *b* 7 Feb 1903   [Nos 60186 to 60214

The Plantagenet Roll

219 Descendants of Lady HENRIETTA O'BRIEN (Table XXI.), *d* 1730, *m*. 1717, ROBERT SANDFORD of Castlerea, M P co. Roscommon, and had issue 1*a* to 5*a*

1*a* *Henry Sandford of Castlerea, d* 12 Feb 1797, m 21 Sept 1750, *the Hon Sarah, da of Stephen (Moore), 1st Viscount Mountcashell [I], d* 3 Oct 1764, *and had issue* 1*b* to 2*b*

1*b* *Henry Moore (Sandford), 1st Baron Mount Sandford [I], d s p* 14 June 1811

2*b* *Rev William Sandford,* b 1752, d 17 Aug 1809, m 1789, *Jane, da of the Right Hon Silver Oliver of Castle Oliver, co Limerick, d.* (–); *and had issue* 1*c* to 3*c*

1*c* *Henry (Sandford), 2nd Baron Mount Sandford [I], d s p,* m 11 June 1828

2*c* *Mary Grey Sandford, da and event* (1828) *co-h,* b 1791, d 1851, m *as 2nd wife,* 11 Oct 1816, *William Robert Wills, afterwards* (R.L 13 Sept 1847) *Wills-Sandford of Willsgrove, co Roscommon, J P, D L, d* 11 Aug 1859, *and had issue (with 2 das unm)* 1*d* to 4*d*

1*d* *Thomas George Wills-Sandford of Willsgrove and Castlerea, J P, D L,* b 15 Aug 1817, d 13 Ap 1887, m 29 Sept 1844, *Theodosia Eleanor Blagden, da of Robert Blagden Hale of Alderley, co Glouc, d* 23 Aug 1857, *and had issue*
See p 351, Nos 59616–59633

2*d* *William Sandford Wills-Sandford of Garryglass, Queen's Co, and Compton Castle, co Somerset, J P,* 83rd Regt, b 26 Mar 1822, d 8 Feb 1882, m 30 May 1849, *Julia, da of William Foster of Stourton Court, co Worc, d* May 1883, *and had issue* 1*e* to 5*e*

1*e* *Arthur Pakenham Wills-Sandford of Garryglass, &c (The Priory House, Sherborne, Dorset),* b 7 Jan 1856

2*e* *Reginald Wills-Sandford* (2802 *Garber Street, Berkeley, California, U S A*), b 3 May 1862, m 9 Mar 1892, Mary Woods, da of Chauncey Hatch Phillips, and has issue 1*f*

1*f* *Georgina Maude Wills-Sandford*

3*e* *Florence Mary Wills-Sandford,* m 8 Feb 1872, John Graham Carrick Moore, Lieut R H G, s p

4*e* *Geraldine Wills-Sandford,* m 1st, 19 Oct 1899, Arthur Dendy, d Jan 1900, 2ndly, Nov 1908, Loftus Moller le Champion (*Wickenthorp, Templecombe*), s p

5*e* *Maude Wills-Sandford,* m 14 June 1890, John Hunter-Blair [7th son of Sir Edward Hunter Blair, 4th Bt [G B], J P, D L] (*Elmbank, Halliford-on-Thames*), and has issue 1*f*

1*f* Colin Edward Hunter-Blair, b 13 Feb 1898

3*d* *Elizabeth Sydney Wills-Sandford, d* 21 Feb 1873, m 18 July 1844, *Godfrey Wills, d Sept 1866, and had issue (with a son, Ormond Kingsley, d s p)* 1*e*

1*e* *Jane Mary Wills,* b Nov 1861, d 7 Mar 1897, m 17 Oct 1882, *Charles Edward Wynne Eyton [Cadet of Leeswood] (The Tower, Mold, N Wales), and had issue* 1*f* to 5*f*

1*f* Robert Mainwaring Eyton (*South Africa*), b Jan 1886

2*f* Charles Sandford Wynne Eyton (*South Africa*), b Oct 1888

3*f* Dorothy Elizabeth Eyton

4*f* John Katherine Eyton

5*f* Aline Margaret Eyton

4*d* *Caroline Julia Wills Sandford* (2 *St Paul's Place, St Leonards-on-Sea*)

3*c* *Eliza Catherine Sandford, da and* (1828) *co-h,* b 1796, d 1867, m 15 Jan 1822, *Very Rev the Hon Henry Pakenham, Dean of St Patrick's [5th son of the 2nd Baron Longford [I], d* 26 Dec 1863, *and had issue* 1*d* to 2*d*

[Nos 60215 to 60215

374

# of The Blood Royal

1d *Henry Sandford Pakenham*, now (*R L* 26 *May* 1847) *Pakenham-Mahon of Strokestown, J P, D L, 8th Hussars*, b 6 *Feb* 1823, d 28 *Mar* 1893, m 11 *Mar* 1847, *Grace Catherine* [*descended from the Lady Isabel Plantagenet* (*Westbrook, Ryde, I W*), *da and h of Major Denis Mahon of Strokestown, co Roscommon and had issue*

See the Essex Volume, p 82, Nos 6183-6189

2d *William Sandford Pakenham*, b 10 *Jan* 1826, d 26 *Nov* 1886, m 15 *Jan* 1857, *Constantia Henrietta Frances, da of Sir William Verner, 1st Bt* [*U K*], *and had issue* 1e *to* 6e

1e *William Wingfield Verner Pakenham, formerly* Lieut.-Col Indian Army, b 11 Nov 1857, m 1 *Jun* 1883, *Frances Josephine, da of* Dep Surg.-Gen *Joseph Marcus Joseph*, M D, Madras Med Ser , *and has issue* 1f *to* 2f

1f William Henry Verner Pakenham, b 2 June 1885

2f Ida Constance Pakenham

2e *Frederick Edward Sandford Pakenham*, b 15 Ap 1859 , m 1898, *Margarita Louisa, da of Maurice Ceely Maude* [V Hawarden Coll], *and has issue* 1f

1f Michael Ceely Sandford Pakenham, b 26 Ap 1903

3e Francis Henry Godfrey Pakenham, b 21 Jan 1865, m 1890, (—), da of (—) Russell

4e Robert Sandford Pakenham, b 1 May 1866

5e Hamilton Richard Pakenham, b 25 Nov 1867, m 18—, (—), da of (—) Strickland

6e Constance Selena Pakenham

2a *Robert Sandford, Gen in the Army*, d (ˀs p) 1793

3a *Mary Sandford*, d (ˀs p), m *Robert Cooke*

4a *Anne Sandford*, d (ˀs p), m *John Bourne*

5a *Henrietta Sandford*, d (ˀs p), m *Edward Nicholson*

[Nos 60216 to 60261.

---

220 Descendants of Lady MARY O'BRIEN (Table XXI), b in London 12 Feb 1692 , d Feb 1780, m. 7 Mar 1709, ROBERT (FITZ-GERALD), 19th EARL OF KILDARE [I], P C , b 4 May 1675 , d 20 Feb 1744 , and had issue 1a to 2a

1a *James (FitzGerald), 20th Earl of Kildare and* (26 *Nov* 1766) 1st *Duke of Leinster* [*I*], 1st *Viscount Leinster* [*G B* 21 *Feb* 1717], b 29 *May* 1722 , d 19 *Nov* 1773, m 7 *Feb* 1747, *Lady Emilia Mary, da of Charles* (*Lennox*), 2nd *Duke of Richmond* [*E*] *and Lennox* [*S*] [*rem* 2ndly, 1774, *William Ogilvy and*] d 27 *Mar* 1814, *and had issue*

See the Exeter Volume, pp 468-477, Nos 41433-41780, and Supplement, 41759'1-19

2a *Lady Margaretta FitzGerald*, b 2 *July* 1729 , d *at Naples* 19 *Jan* 1766, m as 1st *wife*, 1 *Mar* 1748, *Wills* (*Hill*), 1st *Earl of Hillsborough* [*I*], *and afterwards* (20 *Aug* 1789) 1st *Marquis of Downshire* [*I*] *and* (28 *Aug* 1772) *Earl of Hillsborough* [*G B*], P C , d 7 *Oct* 1793, *and had issue* 1b *to* 3b

1b *Arthur* (*Hill*), 2nd *Marquis of Downshire, &c* [*I*], *and Earl of Hillsborough* [*G B*], b 3 *Mar* 1753, d 7 *Sept* 1801, m 29 *June* 1786, *Mary, afterwards* (29 *June* 1802) suo jure 1st *Baroness Sandys* [*U K*] *da of the Hon Martin Sandys*, d 1 *Aug* 1836, *and had issue*

See the Essex Volume, pp 142-144, Nos 16212-16318

2b *Lady Mary Amelia Hill*, b 16 *Aug* 1750, d (*being burnt to death at Hatfield House*, 28 *Nov* 1835, m 2 *Dec* 1773, *James* (*Cecil*), 1st *Marquis* [*G B*] *and 7th Earl* [*E*] *of Salisbury*, K G d 13 *June* 1823, *and had issue*

See the Exeter Volume, pp 216-219, Nos 7652-7738   [Nos 60262 to 60822

The Plantagenet Roll

3b *Lady Charlotte Hill*, b 18 Mar 1754, d 17 Jan 1804, m 7 May 1776, *John Chetwynd (Talbot, afterwards (R L 19 Ap 1786) Chetwynd-Talbot), 1st Earl and 3rd Baron Talbot [G B], d 19 May 1793, and had issue 1c*

1c *Charles (Chetwynd-Talbot), 2nd Earl Talbot, &c [G B], K G*, b 25 Ap 1777, d 10 Jan 1849, m 28 Aug 1800, *Frances Thomasina, da of Charles Lambart of Beau Parc, co Meath*, d 30 Dec 1819, *and had issue*

See the Essex Volume, pp 220-223, Nos 29531-29713

[Nos 60823 to 61005.

221 Descendants, if any, of Lady CATHERINE BOYLE (Table XXI.), b c 1653, d 3 Sept 1681, aged 28, *bur* at Richmond, co Surrey, *m* RICHARD BRETT of co Somerset

222 Descendants of Lady ANNE HOWARD (Table XXI), d (-); *m a* 1646, THOMAS WALSINGHAM of Scadbury, co Kent (sold about 1619), and of Little Chesterford, co Essex, d 22 Nov 1691, and had issue (with another da., Lady Osborne, who *d s p*) 1a to 3a[1]

1a *James Walsingham of Little Chesterford*, d s p 28 Oct 1728, aged 82

2a *Barbara Walsingham*, d 23 Nov 1723, m a 1685, *Henry (Browne), 5th Viscount Montagu [E]*, d 25 June 1717, *and had issue*

See the Clarence Volume, pp 391-396, Nos 15001-15122

3a *Frances Walsingham*, d a 1728, m *John Rossiter of Somersby, co Linc* , *and had issue 1b*

1b *Arabella Rossiter, da and h* , m *as 1st wife, Henry Villiers* (see p 377), d 1753
[Nos 61006 to 61127

223 Descendants of Lady FRANCES HOWARD (Table XXI), *bur* in Westminster Abbey 27 Nov 1677; *m* as 1st wife, Sir EDWARD VILLIERS, Knight-Marshal of the Royal Household and Governor of Tynemouth Castle [V Grandison [I] Coll], *bur* with wife, 2 July 1689; and had issue 1a to 7a

1a *Edward (Villiers), 1st Earl of Jersey [E]*, b 1656, d 25 Aug 1711, m 17 Dec 1781, *Barbara (who was cr by King James III in exile, Ap 1716)[2] Countess of Jersey [E], da of William Chiffinch of Febbers, co Berks*, d in Paris 22 July 1735, *and had issue 1b to 2b*

1b *William (Villiers), 2nd Earl of Jersey [E]*, b c 1682, d 13 July 1721; m 22 May 1705, *Judith, da and h of Frederick Herne, bur 31 July 1735, and had issue 1c to 2c*

1c *William (Villiers), 3rd Earl of Jersey [E] and (1766) 6th Viscount Grandison [I]*, d 28 Aug 1769, m 23 June 1733, *Anne, Dowager-Duchess of Bedford [L], da and in her issue (1803) co-h of Scroop (Egerton), 1st Duke of Bridgewater [G B]*, d 16 June 1762, *and had issue*

See the Tudor Roll, pp 358-371, Nos 27543-28029

2c *Thomas (Villiers), 1st Earl of Clarendon [G B 14 June 1776]*, b 1709, d 11 Dec 1786, m 30 Mar 1752, *Lady Charlotte, da of William (Capel), 3rd Earl of Essex [E]*, d 3 Sept 1790, *and had issue*

See the Exeter Volume, pp 379-381, Nos 26875-27057

[Nos 61128 to 61797

---

[1] Manning and Bray's "Surrey," ii 540

[2] Ruvigny's "Jacobite Peerage," p 63

# of The Blood Royal

2b Lady Mary Villiers, d 17 Jan 1735, m 1st, 1709, Thomas Thynne of Old Windsor (see p 435), d 21 Ap 1710, 2ndly, 1711, George (Granville) 1st Baron Lansdowne [G B] and 1st Duke of Albemarle [E], so cr by King James III in exile 3 Nov 1721[1] (see p 465), d 30 Jan 1735, and had issue 1c to 3c

1c Thomas (Thynne), 2nd Viscount Weymouth [E], b posthumous 21 Mar 1710, d 13 Jan 1751, m 2ndly, 3 July 1733, Lady Louisa, da of John (Carteret), 1st Earl Granville [G B], K G, d 26 Dec 1736, and had issue

See the Tudor Roll, Table XXXVI, pp 212-222, Nos 21654-22022

2c Lady Mary Granville, d Nov 1735 m 1730, William Graham of Platten, near Drogheda

3c Lady Grace Granville, d 1 Nov 1769, m 28 May 1740, Thomas (Foley), 1st Baron Foley [G B], d 14 or 18 Nov 1777, and had issue

See the Essex Volume, pp 320-322, Nos 33109-33411.

2a Henry Villiers, Col in the Army and (8 July 1702) Governor of Tynemouth Castle, d. 18 Aug 1707, m (—), da of (—), and had issue. 1b

1b Henry Villiers, Governor of Tynemouth Castle, d (s p) 29 May 1753, m 1st, Arabella (see p 376), da and h of John Rossiter of Somersby, co Linc, 2ndly, Mary, sister of Lieut Gen Thomas Fowke, da of (—) Fowke

3a Elizabeth Villiers, d 19 Ap 1733, m 25 Nov 1695, George (Hamilton), 1st Earl of Orkney [S], K T, d 29 Jan 1737, and had issue 1b to 3b

1b Anne (Hamilton), suo jure 2nd Countess of Orkney [S], d 7 Dec 1756, m 29 Mar. 1720, William (O'Brien), 4th Earl of Inchiquin [I], d 18 July 1777, and had issue

See p 367, Nos 59986-60036

2b Lady Frances Hamilton, d 27 Dec 1772, m 27 June 1724, Thomas (Lumley), 3rd Earl of Scarbrough [E] and 4th Viscount Lumley [I], K B (see p 431), d 15 Mar 1752, and had issue

See the Exeter Volume, pp 632-635, Nos 53563-53667

3b Lady Henrietta Hamilton, d 22 Aug 1732, m as 1st wife, 9 May 1728, John (Boyle), 5th Earl of Cork and Orrery [I], d 23 Nov 1762, and had issue

See p 312, Nos 58509-58552

4a. Catherine Villiers, living 1702, m 1st, 20 July 1685, James Louis (Le Vasseur-Cougnée), 1st Marquis of Prissac [F], Col 24th Regt 1695, d app s p. 1701,[2] 2ndly, 1702, Col William Villiers

5a Barbara Villiers, d 19 Sept 1708, m John (Berkeley), 4th Viscount Fitzhardinge [I], d 19 Dec 1712, and had issue which became extinct on the death of Sir Thomas Charges, 4th Bt, 1831

6a Frances or Ann. Villiers, d Nov 1688, m as 1st wife, Feb 1678, Hans William (Bentinck), 1st Earl of Portland [E], K G, d 23 Nov 1709, and had issue 1b to 4b

1b Henry (Bentinck), 2nd Earl [E] and (6 July 1716) 1st Duke of Portland [G B], b 17 Mar 1682, d 4 July 1726, m 9 June 1704, Lady Elizabeth, da of Wriothesley (Noel), 3rd Earl of Gainsborough [E], d Mar 1733, and had issue

See the Essex Volume, pp 156-160, Nos 18189-19078

2b Lady Mary Bentinck, b 1679, d 20 Aug 1726 m 1st, 28 Feb 1698, Algernon (Capel), 2nd Earl of Essex [E], d 10 Jan 1710, and had issue

See the Exeter Volume, pp 374-385, Nos 26717-27271

3b Lady Anna Margaretha Bentinck, b at the Hague and bapt there 19 Mar 1683, d there 3 May 1763, m 1701, Arent, Baron van Wassenaer, Lord of Duvenvoirde, Voorschoten, Veur, T'Woud, Rosande, and Harsselo, Ambassador Extraordinary for the States-General to the Court of St James, bapt at the Hague 1 Dec 1669, d there 15 Dec 1721, and had issue 1c to 2c   [Nos 61798 to 64081

---

[1] Ruvigny's "Jacobite Peerage," p 3
[2] Ruvigny's "Nobilities of Europe," p 108

377

The Plantagenet Roll

1c *Baroness Jacoba Maria van Wassenaer, Lady of Duvenvurde, &c*, b at the Hague 4 Oct 1709, d at Duvenvoorde Castle, Voorschoten, 1 Oct 1771, m at the Hague 20 Oct 1732, *Frederik Willem (Torck), Baron Torck, Lord of Heerjansdam and Pethum and heir of Rosendael*, b 6 Sept 1691, d at Arnhem 1 Nov 1761, and had issue 1d

1d *Assueer Jan (Torck), Baron Torck, Lord of Rosendael, &c*, b at the Hague 11 July 1733, d at Wageningen 21 Feb 1793, m at Rosendael Castle 8 June 1758, *Baroness Eusebia Jacoba, da of Baron (—) de Rode van Heeckeren tot Overlaer*, b at Overlaer Castle, Laren, 16 Mar 1740, d at Wageningen 3 Dec 1793, and had issue 1e to 2e

1e *Reinhard Jan Christiaan (Torck), Baron Torck, Lord of Rosendael, &c*, b at Rosendael Castle 2 Aug 1775, d there 2 Jan 1810, m at Eck en Wiel 9 Sept 1800, *Baroness Gooswina Geurdina, da of Baron (—) van Neukirchen genaamd van Nyvenheim [H R E]*, b at Arnhem 25 May 1781, d at Utrecht 6 Dec 1830, and had issue 1f to 2f

1f *Assueer Lubbert Adolf (Torck), Baron Torck van Rosendael*, b at Roesendael Castle 23 Nov 1806, d there 18 Aug 1842, m at the Hague 29 Aug 1834, *Jkvr Louise Catharina Wilhelmina, da of Johan Willem (Huyssen), 1st Baron Huyssen van Kattendijke [Netherlands, 16 Oct 1827]*, b at Brunswick 20 July 1812, d at the Hague 5 Mar 1843, and had issue 1g

1g *Baroness Ada Catharina Torck van Rosendael*, b at Rosendael Castle 26 Oct 1835, d there 13 Jan 1902, m at the Hague 14 Dec 1851, *Reinhard Jan Christiaan (van Pallandt), 7th [H R E 1675] and 4th [Neth 1814] Baron van Pallandt, Burgomaster of Rosendael (see p 379)*, b there 7 July 1826, d there 24 Dec 1899, and had issue 1h to 3h

1h Reinhard Adolf (van Pallandt), 8th [H R E] and 5th [Neth] Baron Torck van Pallandt (*Rosendael Castle*), b 24 Dec 1857, unm

2h Baron Frederik Jacob Willem van Pallandt (*Rosendael*), b at Rosendael Castle 11 Sept 1860, m there 20 May 1886, Constantia Alexine Loudon, da of Hugh Hope [by his wife Baroness Jacoba Cornelia Wilhelmina, née van Pallandt], and has issue 1i to 5i

   1i Baron Reinhard Jan Christiaan van Pallandt, b 24 Jan 1888

   2i Baron Hugh Hope Alexander van Pallandt, b 30 May 1891

   3i Baron Willem Frederick Torck van Pallandt, b 4 Sept 1892

   4i Baroness Helena Susanna Cornelia van Pallandt, b 20 Jan 1895

   5i Baroness Cecilia Emelie Louisa van Pallandt, b 3 Nov 1899

3h Baron Werner Karel van Pallandt, Lord of (Heer van) Petkum (*Rosenheuvel te Rosendael*), b 26 Dec 1863, m at the Hague 17 May 1888, Baroness Adolphine Wilhelmine Charlotte, Lady van Nyenhuis and Ammerfelde (see p 379), da of Hendrik Antoni Zwier (van Knobelsdorff), 2nd Baron van Knobelsdorff [Neth 18 Ap 1837], and has issue 1i to 5i

   1i Baron Assueer Lubbert Adolf van Pallandt, b 11 July 1889

   2i Baron Emilius Johan van Pallandt, b 17 May 1893

   3i Baron Karel Werner van Pallandt, b 23 Aug 1900

   4i Baroness Henriette Jeanne Adelaide van Pallandt, b 25 Aug 1890

   5i Baroness Adolphine Wernardine Charlotte Wilhelmine van Pallandt, b 13 June 1902

2f *Baroness Henriette Jeanne Adelaide Torck*, b at Rosendael 14 Aug 1802, d at Keppel Castle 30 Nov 1877, m at Rosendael 19 Aug 1824, *Adolph Werner Carel Willem (van Pallandt), 5th Baron van Pallandt, H R E [12 July 1675], and 2nd Baron van Pallandt [Neth 28 Aug 1814], Lord of (Heer van) Keppel, Barlham, &c*, b at the Hague 25 June 1802, d at Keppel Castle 22 Jan 1874, and had issue 1g to 6g

1g Frederik Jacob Willem (van Pallandt), 6th [H R E] and 3rd [Neth] Baron van Pallandt, b 3 June 1825, d s p 17 May 1888

2g Reinhard Jan Christiaan (van Pallandt), 7th [H R E] and 4th [Neth]

[Nos 61085 to 64097

# of The Blood Royal

Baron van Pallandt, b at Rosendael Castle 7 July 1826, d there 21 Dec 1899, m at the Hague 14 Dec 1854, Baroness Ada Catherine, da and h of Assueer Lubbert Adolph (Torck), Baron Torck van Rosendael, d at Rosendael Castle 13 Jan 1902, and had issue

See p 378, Nos 64085-64097

3g Baron Emilius Joan van Pallandt (Keppel Castle), b at Rosendael Castle 18 Sept 1829, unm

4g Baron Floris van Pallandt, Lord of (Heer van) Hagen, b at the Hague 25 Feb 1835, d 29 Dec 1902, m at the Hague 15 May 1863, Johanna Wilhelmina, da of Mr Pieter François van Hoogstraten, d at Almen 18 Aug 1901, and had issue 1h to 2h

1h Baron François Johan van Pallandt (Hastière, Belgium), b 3 Feb 1866, m at Brussels 25 Ap 1908, Marie Louise Ghislaine, da of (—) Defays

2h Baroness Henriette Jeanne van Pallandt, m at the Hague 9 Oct 1884, Jonkheer Vincent Johan Gerard Beelaerts van Blokland [Jhr Neth 15 Ap 1815 Coll] (The Hague), and has issue 1i

1i Jkr Vincent Pieter Adriaan Beelaerts van Blokland, b at the Hague 7 June 1889

5g Baroness Adelaide Jeanne Henriette van Pallandt, Lady of the Palace to H M the Queen (Nyenhuis onder Heine en s'Gravenhage), m at Keppel 10 Oct 1863, Hendrik Antoni Zwier (van Knobelsdorff, 2nd Baron van Knobelsdorff [Neth 18 Ap 1837], Heer van de Gelder, Nyenhuis, &c, b at Gelder Castle 28 June 1840, d at the Hague 24 Feb 1905, and has issue 1h to 2h

1h Frederik Willem Adriaan Karel (van Knobelsdorff), 3rd Baron van Knobelsdorff van de Gelder [Neth] (The Hague), b at Keppel 2 Sept 1865

2h Baroness Adolphine Wilhelmine Charlotte van Knobelsdorff, Lady van Nyenhuis, &c, m 17 May 1888, Baron Werner Karel van Pallandt, Lord of Petkum [B (H R E) Coll] (Rosenheuvel te Roosendaal), and has issue

See p 378, Nos 64093-64097

6g Baroness Catharine Louise Wilhelmine van Pallandt (The Hague), m 15 May 1863, Baron Henri van Pallandt, Lord of (Heer van) Wolfswaard [B van Pallandt (H R E 12 July 1675) Coll], b at Arnhem 14 Jan 1841, d at the Hague 1 Nov 1901, and had issue 1h to 2h

1h Baroness Everdine Susette van Pallandt, m at the Hague 14 July 1887, Guillaume Charles, Baron Snouckaert van Schauburg [Neth 24 Nov 1816], Chamberlain and Treasurer of the Household to H M the Queen, formerly to King William III (The Hague), and has issue 1i

1i Baron Willem Carel Snouckaert van Schauburg, b at the Hague 21 Aug 1888

2h Baroness Adolphine Wernardine van Pallandt (The Hague), unm

2e Baroness Henriette Christine Alexandrine Torck, Lady of (Vrouwe van) Duvenvoorde, Voorschoten, Veur, and Heeriansdam, b at the Hague 31 Mar 1764, d 11 Aug 1792, m at Rosendael Castle 5 Oct 1788, Adolph Hendrik, Count van Rechteren [H R E], Heer van Collendoorn, b at the Hague 26 Oct 1738, d there 3 Dec 1805, and had issue 1f

1f Countess Maria van Rechteren, Vrouwe van Pettkum, Duvenvoorde, &c, b at Zutphen 27 July 1789, d at s'Gravenhage 30 Ap 1808, m as 1st wife 5 Oct 1806, Jan Gijsbert Ludolf Adriaan (van Neukirchen), 1st Baron van Neukirchen gen Nyvenheim [Neth 25 Mar 1822], Heer van Eck en Wiel, b at Arnhem 12 Dec 1783, d at Paris 21 Dec 1818, and had issue 1g

1g Baroness Henriette Jeanne Christine van Neukirchen, Vrouwe van Duvenvoorde, Voorschoten, &c, b at Eck 19 Sept 1807, d at Hyères 16 Nov 1849, m at Roosendaal 8 July 1830 (3rl) Jhr Nicolaas Johan Steengracht [Neth 1 July 1816], Heer van Moyland, Till, &c, b 13 Jan 1806, d at Moyland, near Cleves, 4 Oct. 1866, and had issue 1h to 3h.   [Nos 64098 to 64126

379

The Plantagenet Roll

1h. Nicolaas Adriaan (*Steengracht*), 1st Baron Steengracht van Moyland [Neth 19 Dec 1888], *Heer van Moyland en Till, Chamberlain of the Household to King William III*, b 29 Mar 1834, d at Moyland Castle 29 June 1906, m 1st, 3 Dec 1868, *Jkvr Maria Theodora, da of Willem Frans (van Herzeele)*, 2nd Baron van Herzeele [Neth 30 Mar 1820], d 29 Oct 1895, 2ndly, 3 Aug 1901, *Irene Theresia Ludvina Christine Paule Clara, da of Edler Hugo Heinrich Raphael Jacob von Kremer-Auenrode*, and had issue 1i to 2i

1i Hendrik (Steengracht), 2nd Baron Steengracht van Moyland [Neth] (*Moyland bij Cleve*), b 1 Dec 1869, m 24 Nov 1897, Helene, da of Charles de Struve, 2ndly, in London 1905, Olga Louisa Charlotta, da of Jacob Pieter van Braam, and has issue 1j

  1j Jhr Henry Adolf Adriaan Gustav Steengracht, b at Cleves 28 July 1905

  2i Jhr Gustav Adolph von Steengracht-Moyland, b 15 Nov 1902

2h *Jkvr Cornelia Maria Steengracht, Lady of the Palace to the Queen Mother*, b 24 May 1831, d at Duivenvoorde Castle 7 Sept 1906, m at Voorschoten 19 Dec 1855, *William Assuear Jacob (Schimmelpennick)*, 2nd Baron Schimmelpennick van der Oye [Neth 22 Aug 1820], LL D, b at Karlsruhe 26 July 1834, d at Cadenabbia 2 June 1886, and had issue 1i to 5i

1i Alexander Willem (Schimmelpennick), 3rd Baron Schimmelpennick van der Oye [Neth], LL D (*Oud-Clingendaal te Wassenaer*), b 10 July 1859, m 1st, 24 Aug 1888, Baroness Cornelia Elizabeth, da of Gen Baron Gijsbert Jan Anne Adolph van Heemstra [B v Heemstra [Neth 2 Ap 1826] Coll], d at Nordrach, Baden, 29 Dec 1901, 2ndly, 19 Ap 1905, Jeanne Françoise, da of Leon Chassagnard, and has issue 1j to 3j

  1j Baron Willem Anne Assuerus Jacob Schimmelpennick van der Oye, b at Rome 5 Oct 1889

  2j Baron Leon Frans Carel Schimmelpennick van der Oye, b at Wassenaer 26 Oct 1905

  3j Baroness Ludolphine Henriette Schimmelpennick van der Oye, b at St Petersburg 20 July 1891

2i Baron Hendrik Nicolaas Schimmelpennick van der Oye (*Amersfoort*), b 4 Ap 1862, m 10 Feb 1887, the Countess Cécile Eugenie Marie Desirée, da of Count du Monceau, and has issue 1j to 8j

  1j Baron René Henri Schimmelpennick van der Oye, b at Kloetinge 7 Feb 1893.

  2j Baron Felix Cornelius Schimmelpennick van der Oye, b there 14 May 1901

  3j Baron Henri Felix Marie Schimmelpennick van der Oye, b at Goes 16 Jan 1903

  4j Baroness Marie Cornelie Annee Schimmelpennick van der Oye, b at Goes 29 Nov 1887

  5j Baroness Felicia Maria Schimmelpennick van der Oye, b at Kloetinge 6 July 1889

  6j Baroness Cornelie Marie Henriette Antonia Gustavine Schimmelpennick van der Oye, b there 24 Oct 1895

  7j Baroness Cécile Emelie Alexandrine Schimmelpennick van der Oye, b there 25 May 1899

  8j Baroness Ida Henriette Schimmelpennick van der Oye, b at Amersfoort 19 Nov 1904

3i Baroness Henriette Marie Sophie Schimmelpennick van der Oye, m 21 July 1881, Jhr Mr Dirk Arnold Willem van Tets [Neth 26 Aug 1837], *Heer van Goudriaan, &c* (*'s Gravenhage*), and has issue 1j to 3j

  1j Jhr George Catharinus Willem van Tets, b 31 Aug 1882, m at Noordwykerhout 6 May 1909, Jkvr Pauline Johanna, da of Jhr Mr Abraham Daniel Theodore Gevers [Neth 27 Oct 1812]

  2j Jkvr Henriette van Tets, b in Constantinople 31 Mai 1888

  3j Jkvr Digna Hendrika van Tets, b in Constantinople 31 Mai 1889

[Nos 64127 to 64146.

# of The Blood Royal

4i Baroness *Maria Cornelia Schimmelpenninck van der Oye*, b at s'Gravenhage 30 Oct 1857, d there 11 Dec 1897, m there as 1st wife 14 Mar 1878, *Jhr Mr Sir Jacob Willem Gustaaf Boreel van Hogelanden*, 10th Bt [E 21 Mar 1645], *Burgomaster of Haarlem, Chamberlain to H M Queen Wilhelmina and formerly a Gentleman of the Privy Chamber to King William III (Waterland, Velsen, en Haarlem)*, and had issue 1j to 2j

1j Jkvr *Cornelia Maria Boreel*, m 27 Nov 1902, Baron Frederik Willem van Tuyll van Serooskerken [B van Tuyll van Serooskerken [Neth 21 Mar 1822] Coll] (*Villa Edison te Aerdenhout-Bloemendaal*), and has issue 1k to 3k

1k Baron *Jacob Willem Gustaaf van Tuyll van Serooskerken*, b 4 Aug 1906

2k Baroness *Marie Cornelie van Tuyll van Serooskerken*, b 5 Oct 1903

3k Baroness *Aleni Theela Ann van Tuyll van Serooskerken*, b 28 Feb 1905

2j Jkvr *Agnes Boreel*, m at Velsen 17 Oct 1907, Ernest Cremers (*Villa la Canetta te Noordwijk aan Zee*)

5i Baroness *Cornelia Schimmelpenninck van der Oye*, m 1st, 9 July 1889, Jhr Ernst Hendrik van Loon [Neth 2 June 1822, Coll] (*s'Gravenhage*), and has issue 1j to 2j

1j Jhr *Louis Charles van Loon* (*Noordhey, Voorschoten*), b 15 Feb 1891

2j Jkvr *Antoinette Cornelie van Loon*, b 5 June 1893

3h Jhr Mr *Hendricus Adolphus Steengracht, Heer van Duivenvoorde Voorschoten en Veur, Gentleman of the Chamber and afterwards Special Chamberlain to King William III and ex-Member of the States for South Holland* (*K Duivenvoorde te Voorschoten, s'Gravenhage, Nice*), b 25 Ap 1836

2c Baroness *Louise Isabella Hermeline van Wassenaer*, da and co-h, bapt at the Hague 19 Feb 1719, d at Amerongen 23 Ap 1756, m at Voorschoten 2 May 1742, *Frederik Willem (van Reede), 4th Earl of Athlone* [I], *5th Baron van Reede* [Denmark 1671], b 1 Apr 1717, d at Arnhem 1 Dec 1717, and had issue 1d

1d *Frederik Christiaan Reinhard (van Reede), 5th Earl of Athlone* [I], *6th Baron* [Denmark] *and 1st Count* [H R E 25 Sept 1790] *van Reede, Lord of Amerongen, Middachet Elst, Ginkell, &c, in Utrecht, Ranger of that Province*, b at the Hague 31 Jan 1713, d at Teddington, co Mids, 13 Dec 1808, m at the Hague 29 Dec 1765, *Baroness Anna Elizabeth Christina*, da of Jan (van Tuyll), Baron van Tuyll van Serooskerken [Neth], Heer van Zuylen en Westbroek, b at Zuylen Castle 9 Sept 1745, d at the Hague 16 Jan 1819, and had issue 1e to 4e

1e *Frederick William (van Reede), 6th Earl of Athlone* [I], *&c*, b at Utrecht 22 Oct 1766, d s p at Greenwich 5 Dec 1810

2e *Reynoud Diederik Jacob (van Reede), 7th Earl of Athlone* [I], *&c*, b at Utrecht 2 July 1773 d at the Hague 31 Oct 1823, m at Paris 19 Mar 1818, *Henrietta Dorothea Maria*, da and event h of John Williams Hope of Amsterdam, d 30 Sept 1830, and had issue 1f

1f *George Godard Henry (van Reede), 9th Earl of Athlone* [I], *&c*, b at Utrecht 21 Nov 1820, d unm at Bath 2 Mar 1843

3e *William Gustaf Frederik (van Reede), 9th and last Earl of Athlone* [I], *&c*, *5th Count* [H R E] *and 10th Baron* [Denmark] *van Reede, Lord of Ginkell, Amerongen, &c, in the Netherlands*, b at Utrecht 21 July 1780, d s p at the Hague 4 May 1844

4e Lady (Countess) *Jacoba Helena van Reede-Ginkell*, da and in her issue (21 May 1844) sole h, b 21 Dec 1767, d 6 Sept 1839, m 20 Mar 1785, *Count John Charles Bentinck, Maj r-Gen British Army* [E of Portland [E 1689] and C Bentinck [H R E 1732] Coll], d 22 Nov 1833, and had issue 1f to 2f

1f *William Christian Frederick (Bentinck), 4th Count Bentinck* [H R E], *&c, K C Teutonic Order, Chamberlain to King William I, &c*, b 15 Nov 1787, d 8 June 1855, m 16 Ap 1841, the Countess Pauline Albertine, da of Friedrich Franz, Count of Manmich, d 12 Oct 1898, and had issue 1g

1g Countess *Jacqueline Christine Anne Adelaide Bentinck*, m at s Gravenhage [Nos 64117 to 64156.

381

3 c

The Plantagenet Roll

6 Nov 1874, Frederick Magnus, Sovereign Count of Solms-Wildenfels, Knight of Malta, Hereditary Member of the Upper House of the Saxon Diet, &c , &c (*Castle of Wildenfels, near Dresden*) , and has issue 1*h* to 5*h*

    1*h* Frederick Magnus, Hereditary Count, *b* 1 Nov. 1886

    2*h* Countess Sophie von Solms-Wildenfels, *b* 9 Feb 1877

    3*h* Countess Magna Marie Augustine Adele van Solms-Wildenfels, *b* 31 Aug 1883

    4*h* Countess Anne von Solms-Wildenfels, *b* 14 June 1890

    5*h* Countess Gesele Clementina Christophera Carola von Solms-Wildenfels, *b* 30 Dec 1891

    2*f* *Charles Anthony Ferdinand (Bentinck), 5th Count Bentinck [H R E], Lord of Middachten, K C Teutonic Order, Lieut -Gen in the British Service, b 4 Mar 1792, d 28 Oct 1864, m 30 Jan 1816, the Countess Caroline Mechtild Emma Charlotte Christine Louisa, da of Charles, Reigning Count of Waldeck and Pyrmont, d 28 Feb 1899, and had issue* 1*g* to 5*g*

    1*g* *Henry Charles Adolphus Frederick William (Bentinck), 6th Count Bentinck [H R E], which title he resigned to his next brother 1874, K C Teutonic Order, Lieut -Col Coldstream Guards, b 30 Dec 1846 , d 18 June 1903 , m 8 Dec 1874, Henrietta Eliza Cathcart (53 Green Street, Park Lane, W), da of Robert McKerrell of Hillhouse , and had issue* 1*h* to 7*h*

    1*h* Count Robert Charles Bentinck, Lieut Derbyshire Imp Yeo (*Bath Club*), *b* 5 Dec 1875

    2*h* Count Charles Henry Bentinck, 2nd Sec Diplo Ser (*H B M 's Legation, The Hague , St James' , National*), *b* 23 Ap 1879

    3*h* Count Henry Duncan Bentinck, B A (Camb), Lieut Coldstream Guards (*Guards*), *b* 24 June 1881

    4*h* Count Arthur William Douglas Bentinck, B A (Camb), 2nd Lieut Coldstream Guards (*Guards*), *b* 24 July 1887

    5*h* Countess Renira Christine Bentinck, *m* 6 Dec 1898, Baron Alexander van Heeckeren van Kell [B van Heeckeren [Neth 28 Mar 1815] Coll], LL D , Burgomaster of Ede, Gelderland (*Wielbergen, onder Angerlo*), and has issue 1*i* to 6*i*

    1*i* Baron Alexander William Henry Walraven van Heeckeren van Kell, *b* (twin) 19 Mar 1906

    2*i* Baron Henry Robert van Heeckeren van Kell, *b* 9 Dec 1907

    3*i* Baroness Albertine Renira Alexandra Henrietta Mechtild Ottoline van Heeckeren van Kell, *b* 29 Sept 1899

    4*i* Baroness Renira Sophia Louise Rudolphine van Heeckeren van Kell, *b* 6 Aug 1901

    5*i* Baroness Henrietta van Heeckeren van Kell, *b* 12 July 1903

    6*i* Baroness Lilian Gunnevere Justine May van Heeckeren van Kell, *b* (twin) 19 Mar 1906

    6*h* Countess Ursula Victoria Henrietta Bentinck

    7*h* Countess Naomi Mechtild Henrietta Bentinck

    2*g* William Charles Philip (Bentinck), 7th Count Bentinck [H R E] on his brother's resignation, Count and Baron of Aldenburg and Count of Waldeck-Limpurg, which latter title he assumed by letters patent 1889, obtained Royal Licence for himself and the other descendants of his father to assume and use their foreign honours in the United Kingdom 22 Mar 1886, is a K M , K C T O , and a Hereditary Member of the Wurtemberg Upper House, 3rd Sec H B M 's Diplo Service (*Middachten Castle, near Arnhem , and 13 Voorhout, The Hague, Holland , Gaildorf, Wurtemberg , St James' Club, London, &c &c*), *b* 28 Nov 1848 , *m* 8 Mar 1877, the Baroness Mary Cornelia, Vrouwe (Lady) van Obdam, &c , da. of Baron Jacob Derk Carel van Heeckeren, LL D , Grand Master of the House to King William III [B van Heeckeren [Neth 28 Mar 1815] Coll] , and has issue 1*h* to 4*h*

[Nos 64157 to 64175

# of The Blood Royal

1*h* William Frederick Charles Henry, Hereditary Count, K C T O, Lieut. Prussian Gardes du Corps (28 *Burggrafenstrasse, Potsdam*), *b* 22 June 1880

2*h*. Count Frederick George Unico William Bentinck, *b* 21 June 1888

3*h* Countess Mechtild Corisande Renira Mary Bentinck, *m* 1 Sept 1905, Casimir Frederick, Hereditary Count of Castell, Capt 5th Prussian Lancers [son and h-app of H S H the Reigning Prince of Castell-Rüdenhausen] (*Rüdenhausen, Upper Franconia, Bavaria*), and has issue 1i

1*i* Countess Marie Emma Agnes Victoria Elizabeth Caroline Mechtilde of Castell, *b* at Dusseldorf 8 Mar 1907

4*h* Countess Isabella Antoinette Mary Clementina Bentinck

3*g*. Count Charles Reginald Adelbert Bentinck, K C T O, *late* Capt 2nd Prussian Dragoon Guards (*Zuylestein, Utrecht*), *b* 9 Feb 1853, *m* 28 Sept 1878 (dissolved 1885), Countess Helena Agnes Alexandrina Amelia Caroline, da of Count Charles of Waldeck-Pyrmont, and has issue 1*h*

1*h* Countess Mary Amelia Mechtild Agnes Bentinck, *b* 16 Sept 1879

4*g* Count Godard John George Charles Bentinck, Lord of Amerongen, Ginkel, Elst, Zuylestein, &c, K C T O (*Amerongen Castle, Utrecht*), *b* 3 Aug 1857, *m* 12 June 1884, the Countess Augustine Wilhelmina Louise Adrienne, da of Count Jules Auguste von Bylandt [C of Bylandt [H R E 19 May 1678] Coll], &c, and has issue 1*h* to 5*h*

1*h* Count Charles Arthur Renaud William Godard Augustus Bentinck, *b* 16 Aug 1885

2*h* Count Godard Adrian Henry Jules Bentinck, *b* 21 Feb 1887

3*h* Count John Victor Richard Rudolph Bentinck, *b* 5 Feb 1895

4*h* Count William Henry Ferdinand Godard Bentinck, *b* 20 Dec 1900

5*h* Countess Elizabeth Mechtild Marie Sophia Louise Bentinck

5*g* Countess Victoria Mary Frederica Mechtild Bentinck (*Zuylestein, Utrecht*)

4*b* *Lady Isabella Bentinck*, b 4 May 1688, d *at Paris 23 Feb 1728, m as 2nd wife*, 2 *Aug* 1714, *Evelyn* (*Pierrepont*), 1st *Duke of Kingston* [*G B*], *K G , d 5 Mar 1726, and had issue 1c*

1*c Lady Caroline Pierrepont*, m 1712, *Thomas Brand*

7*a Mary Villiers*, d 17 *Ap* 1753, m *as 2nd or 3rd wife, Ap* 1691, *William* (*O'Brien*), 3*rd Earl of Inchiquin* [*I*], d 24 *De.* 1719, *and had issue*

See pp 367-376, Nos 59986-61005   [Nos 61176 to 65209

---

224 Descendants of THOMAS (HOWARD), 1st EARL OF BERKSHIRE [E], K G , K B (Table XXI), *b c* 1590, *d* 16 July 1669, *m*. 26 May 1614, Lady ELIZABETH, da and co-h of William (CECIL), 2nd Earl of Exeter [E], *bur*. 24 Aug 1672 , and had issue

See the Clarence Volume, Table LXXVII , and pp 624-637, Nos 27996-28819
[Nos 65210 to 66063

---

225 Descendants, if any surviving, of the Hon Sir CHARLES HOWARD (Table XXI), *d* **(-)**, *m* MARY, widow of the Hon THOMAS DARCY [son and h of Thomas, 1st Earl of Rivers [E]], and previously of Sir ALAN PERCY, K B , da. and h of Sir John FITZ of Fitzford and Cavistock, co Devon , and had issue 1*a*

1*a Elizabeth Howard, da and h*

The Plantagenet Roll

226 Descendants of EDWARD (HOWARD), 1st BARON HOWARD of Escrick [E 12 Ap. 1628] K B (Table XXI), d 24 Ap 1675; m 30 Nov 1623, the Hon MARY, da and co-h of John (BOTELER), 1st Baron Boteler of Bramfield [E.], bur 30 Jan. 1634; and had issue 1a to 3a

> 1a Thomas (Howard), 2nd Baron Howard of Escrick [E], d s p s at Bruges 24 Aug 1678
>
> 2a William (Howard), 3rd Baron Howard of Escrick [E], bur 24 Ap 1694, m Frances da of Sir James Bridgman of Castle Bromwich, co Warwick, d 19 Dec 1716, and had issue 1b
>
> 1b Charles (Howard), 4th and last Baron Howard of Escrick [E], d s p 29 Ap 1715
>
> 3a Hon Anne Howard, da and in her issue (29 Ap 1715) sole h, bur. 4 Sept 1703, m Charles (Howard) 1st Earl of Carlisle [E], P C (see p 398), d 24 Feb 1685, and ha l issue 1b
>
> 1b Edward (Howard), 2nd Earl of Carlisle [E], b c 1646, d 23 Ap 1692, m (lic dated 27 Ap 1668), Elizabeth, widow of Sir William Berkeley, da and co-h of Sir William Uvedale of Wickham, co Hants, bur there 30 Dec 1696, and had issue 1c
>
> 1c Charles (Howard), 3rd Earl of Carlisle [E], b 1669 d 1 May 1738, m 25 July 1683, Lady Anne, da of Arthur (Capell), 1st Earl of Essex [E], d 14 Oct. 1752, and had issue
>
> See the Exeter Volume, Table XXVII, and pp 385-386, Nos 27272-28169
>
> [Nos 66064 to 66961.

227 Descendants of Lady ELIZABETH HOWARD (Table XXI), bapt 11 Aug 1586, d. 17 Ap 1658, m 1st, as 2nd wife (settl dated 23 Dec 1605), WILLIAM (KNOLLYS), 1st EARL OF BANBURY [E], K.G, b. c 1547, d. 25 May 1632, 2ndly, before 2 July 1632, EDWARD (VAUX), 4th BARON VAUX of Harrowden [E], d s p 8 Ap 1661, and had issue (whose legitimacy is disputed)

228 Descendants of Lady FRANCES HOWARD (Table XXI), b 30 Sept. 1589; d 23 Aug 1632, m 1st, 5 Jan. 1606, ROBERT (DEVEREUX), 3rd EARL OF ESSEX [E] (from whom she was divorced Oct 1613), d s p s. 14 Sept 1646, 2ndly, 26 Dec 1613, ROBERT (KERR, alias CARR), 1st EARL OF SOMERSET [E], K G., d 17 July 1645, and had issue 1a

> 1a Lady Anne Carr, da and h, b 9 Dec 1615, d 10 May 1684, m 11 July 1637, William (Russell), 5th Earl and (11 May 1694) 1st Duke of Bedford [E], K.G, K B, d 7 Sept 1700, and had issue 1b to 2b
>
> 1b William Russell, Lord Russell, M P, b 29 Sept 1639, d v p (being executed for high treason) 21 July 1683, m (lic dated 31 July) 1669, Lady Rachel, widow of Francis Vaughan, Lord Vaughan, da and co-h of Thomas (Wriothesley), 4th Earl of Southampton [E], K G (by his wife Rachel, sister of Henry (de Massue), 1st Marquis of Ruvigny and Raineval [F], P C.], d 29 Sept 1723, and had issue
>
> See the Essex Volume, Table XIII, and pp 173-190, Nos 21135-25217
>
> [Nos 66962 to 71044

# of The Blood Royal

2b *Lord James Russell*, d¹ 22 June 1712, m *Elizabeth, da of (—) Lloyd* [re-m 2ndly, 14 Ap 1721, Sir Henry Houghton, 5th Bt [E] and] d 1 Dec. 1736, and had issue 1c

1c *Tryphena Russell of Maidwell, co Northants, da and h*, d (–), m 1725, *Thomas Scawen of Carshalton Park, co Surrey, M P*, d 11 Feb 1774, and had issue 1d to 2d

1d *James Scawen of Carshalton Park, M P*

2d *Tryphena Scawen*, b 31 Dec 1730, d 2 Dec 1807, m *as 2nd wife, 14 June 1759, Henry (Bathurst), 2nd Earl Bathurst [G B] and Lord High Chancellor [G B]*, d 6 Aug 1794, and had issue 1e

1e *Henry (Bathurst), 3rd Earl Bathurst [G B], K G , P C* , b 22 May 1762, d 27 July 1834, m 1 1p 1789, Lady *Georgina, da of Lord George Henry Lennox*, d 20 Jan 1841, and had issue

See the Clarence Volume, pp 636-637, Nos. 28837-28849

[Nos 71015 to 71057]

229. Descendants of JAMES (CECIL), 3rd EARL OF SALISBURY [E], K.G. (Table XXII), b. 1648, d June 1683, m 1665, Lady MARGARET, da. of John (MANNERS), 8th Earl of Rutland [E], d. at Paris 30 Aug 1682; and had issue

See the Exeter Volume, Table XI , and pp 216-236, Nos 7652-8318, Essex Volume, p 378, Nos 36474-36480 [Nos 71058 to 71731]

230 Descendants of the Hon FRANCES CECIL (Table XXII). d 15 June 1723, m (lic dated 24 Dec 1679) Sir WILLIAM BOWYER, 2nd Bt [E], M P , d 13 Feb 1722, and had issue 1a to 3a

1a *Cecil Bowyer*, b 1 June 1681, d v p 5 Dec 1720, m 22 July 1707, *Juliana, da of Richard Parker of Hedsor [Bt Coll], and had issue (with another son and da known to have d young) 1b to 4b*

1b *Sir William Bowyer, 3rd Bt [E]* b c 1710, d 12 July 1768, m 21 Aug 1733, *Anne, da of the Right Hon Sir John Stonhouse, 7th Bt (1628) and 4th Bt (1670) [E], P C , M P*, d 22 May 1785, and had issue 1c to 4c

1c *Sir William Bowyer, 4th Bt [E]*, b c 1736 , d s p Ap 1799

2c *Sir George Bowyer, 5th Bt of Denham [E] and (8 Sept 1791) 1st Bt of Radley [G B], Admiral of the Blue, M P*, b 1739 , d 6 Dec 1799, m 2ndly, 4 June 1782, *Henrietta da and h of Sir Piercy Brett, M P , Admiral of the White*, d Nov 1845 , and had issue 1d to 2d

1d *Sir George Bowyer, 6th [E] and 2nd [G B] Bt, M P*, b 3 May 1783 d 1 July 1860, m 19 Nov 1808, *Anne Hammond, da of Capt Sir Andrew Snape Douglas, R N*, d 1844, and had issue 1e to 3e

1e *Sir George Bowyer, 7th [E] and 3rd [G B] Bt, K M , G C S G , M P*, b 8 Oct 1811 , d unm 7 June 1883

2e *Sir William Bowyer, 8th [E] and 4th [G B] Bt*, b Oct 1812 , d s p 30 May 1893

3e *Henry George Bowyer, one of H M 's Inspectors of Schools*, b 3 Jan 1813, d 25 Sept 1883, m 20 Feb 1855, *Katherine Emma (1 Clarendon Crescent, Leamington), da and h of the Rev George Sandby*, and had issue 1f to 3f

1f *Sir George Henry Bowyer, 9th Bt of Denham [E] and 5th Bt of Radley [G B] (1 Clarendon Crescent, Leamington)*, b 9 Sept 1870, m 4 May 1899, *Ethel, da of Francis Hawkins (which m was dissolved 7 Nov 1900)*

[No 71732

¹ Burke's "Peerage" has s p

The Plantagenet Roll

2/ Beatrice Mary Bowyer, m 1890, James Frederick Shaw, and has issue 1g

1g Charles Henry Shaw, b 1893

3/ Helen Gertrude Bowyer, a Nun of the Order of the Assumption

2d Henrietta Bowyer, d 1864, m 10 Oct 1812, Charles Sawyer of Heywood Lodge, co Berks, J P, D L, d 2 June 1876, and had issue (with others who all d s p) 1e to 3c

1e Rev George Herbert Sawyer, LL B, B C L (152 Caversham Road, Reading), b 29 Mar 1826, unm

2e Rev William George Sawyer, M A (Camb), Rector of Taplow 1890-1897, &c (Stanlow, Maidenhead), b 24 Nov 1829, m 29 Ap 1862, Margaret, da of the Rev C A Sheppard of Great Milton, co Oxon, and has issue 1f to 7f

1f Edmund Charles Sawyer of Heywood (Heywood Lodge, Maidenhead), b 2 Mar 1871

2f Herbert William Sawyer, b 1 Ap 1874

3f William Ellis Sawyer, b 4 May 1878

4f Guy Henry Sawyer, b 18 May 1882

5f Agnes Elizabeth Sawyer

6f Margaret Henrietta Sawyer

7f Dorothy Alice Sawyer

3c Charlotte Sawyer

3c Richard Bowyer afterwards Atkins-Bowyer, of Clapham, d 21 Nov 1820, m 1773, Elizabeth, da of (——) Brady, and had issue 1d to 3d

1d William Bowyer, afterwards (R L 16 Nov 1835) Atkins-Bowyer of Braywick Grove, co Berks, and Clapham, co Surrey, Brigade-Major to the Forces at Halifax, N S, b 1779, d 9 Feb 1844, m 1803, Frances, da of the Hon Behning Wentworth, Colonial Secretary for Nova Scotia, d 24 Jan 1856, and had issue 1e to 7e

1e Henry Atkins-Bowyer of Steeple Aston and Clapham, D L, Lieut-Col 1st Oxford Univ Rifle Vols, previously 11th Hussars, b 1805, d 29 July 1871, m 15 Jan 1833, Isabella Duncan, da of James H Byles of Bowden Hall, co Glouc, d 12 Nov 1841, and had issue (with 3 sons who d s p) 1f

1f Isabel Caroline Eliza Atkins-Bowyer, m 23 June 1873, Bertie Wentworth Vernon of Harefield and Stoke Bruerne Park, J P, High Sheriff co Northants 1892 (Stoke Bruerne Park, Towcester, Harefield Park, near Uxbridge), s p s

2e Rev William Henry Wentworth Atkins-Bowyer, Rector of Clapham, b 3 Feb 1807, d 25 Feb 1872, m 1st, 1831, Emily, da of Henry Harford of Downe Place, Maidenhead, d 1839, 2ndly, 1844 Charlotte [descended from King Henry VII (see Essex Volume Supplement, p 469)], da of Capt William Wells, R N [by his wife, Lady Elizabeth, née Proby], d 3 May 1862, and had issue 1f to 7f

1f Wentworth Grenville Bowyer, Lieut-Col R E, heir-presumptive to the Baronetcies (1660 [E] and 1794 [G B]) (Weston Manor, Olney, Bucks), b 10 Nov 1850, m 29 Oct 1885, Eva Mary [a descendant of the Lady Anne, sister of Kings Edward IV and Richard III], da of Major-Gen Charles Stuart Lane, C B, Cadet of King's Bromley, and has issue 1g to 5g

1g George Edward Wentworth Bowyer, b 16 Jan 1886

2g Richard Grenville Bowyer, R N, b 18 May 1890

3g John Francis Bowyer, b 11 Jan 1893

4g Hilda Mary Bowyer, b 2 Ap 1887

5g Mildred Elizabeth Bowyer, b 16 Ap 1898

2f Edward Wentworth Bowyer (The Manor House, Wellington, Salop), b 25 June 1862, m 8 Jan 1895, the Hon Georgina Harriet, da of Richard Assheton (Cross), 1st Viscount Cross [U K], G C B, and has issue 1g to 2g

1g Richard Wentworth Bowyer, b 27 Dec 1895

2g Helen Georgiana Bowyer, unm   [Nos 71733 to 71755.

386

# of The Blood Royal

3f[1] *Frances Emily Atkins-Bowyer*, d (-), m 26 *Aug* 1865, *Edward Till of Clapham Common, co Surrey, and had issue* 1g *to* 2g

    1g Violet Beatrice Tell

    2g Ruth Felicity Tell, *m* Herbert Jackson, and has issue (3 sons)

4f *Beatrice Ann Bowyer*, d *Oct* 1907, m 16 *Nov* 1878, *the Rev Henry Ley Greaves*, d 27 *Dec* 1899, *and had issue* 1g *to* 3g

    1g Humphrey Grenville Ley Greaves, b 22 Mar 1887

    2g Dorothy Charlotte Ley Greaves, *m* 1905, Francis Quailes Harrison

    3g Marjorie Beatrice Millicent Ley Greaves *m* 20 July 1904, William Arthur Newcombe (*Wooton Court, Canterbury*), and has issue 1h to 2h

        1h Arthur Peter Ley Newcombe, b 31 July 1905

        2h Hilda Violet Marjorie Lockhart Newcombe, b 20 Dec 1906

5f Marion Frances Bowyer (*Weston Underwood, Olney, Bucks*)

6f Cecil Bowyer

7f Lilian Bowyer, *m.* 11 July 1876, Henry Charles Zerffi (47 *Warrington Crescent, W*), and has issue 1g

    1g Henry Gustavus Wentworth Zerffi, b 12 July 1881

3e *Frances Augusta Atkins-Bowyer*, b *at Halifax, Nova Scotia*, 1804 , d 16 *Nov* 1869, m 1st, 20 *Aug* 1825, *the Rev George Augustus Legge* [*E of Dartmouth Coll*], d s p 16 *June* 1826, 2ndly, 28 *Oct* 1828, *the Rev Samuel Wyatt Cobb, M A* (*Oxon*), *Rector of Ightham, co Kent* [*son of the Rev Thomas Cobb, Rector of the same*], d 22 *Dec* 1856, *and had issue* (*with 4 sons d young*) 1f *to* 4f

1f *Augusta Louisa Cobb*, b 8 *Oct* 1829, d 31 *Jan* 1897, m 26 *Oct* 1858, *the Rev David Payne Williams, Senior Chaplain, Bengal* [*son of the Rev David Williams, Rector of Bleadon and Kingston Seymour, co Som*], *and had issue* (*with a son and da d young*) 1g *to* 3g

    1g Henry Llewellyn Williams, Indian Police, b at Delhi 14 Aug 1862, *m* Ap 1884, Mary Elizabeth, da of Cecil Burton, Cantonment Magistrate, Jullunder, and has issue 1h to 5h

        1h Cecil Walter Hackett Williams, b at Saharanpur, 11 June 1885 ·

        2h Edward Williams, b in India, 17 Feb 1895

        3h David Williams, b at Murree, Sept 1898

        4h Evelyn Amy Williams, b in India, 22 Feb 1888

        5h Phyllis Williams, b 29 June 1893

    2g Lilian Augusta Williams, b at Delhi, *m* at Simla, 4 June 1904, William George Goldney, Indian Police [son of Samuel Alfred Goldney of Langley Furse, co Bucks]

    3g Evelyn Helen Catherine Williams, b at Murree, *m* Nov 1902, Robert Donald Spencer, Indian Police [son of Robert Spencer of Lahore], and has had issue, Helen Monica, d in infancy

2f *Katharine Mary Cobb*, b 11 *Sept* 1832, d 4 *Nov* 1905, m 26 *Oct* 1858, *Henry Walmesley Hammond, Bengal C S* [*son of the Rev John Hammond, Rector of Priston, co Som*], *and had issue* (*with a son, William John, d unm* 24 *Aug* 1901) 1g *to* 5g

    1g Rev Anthony Hammond, M A (Oxon), Rector of St Anthony's, Stepney (*St Anthony Rectory, Stepney, E*), b 29 Nov 1861, *m* 27 Aug 1891, Isabel Sarah Catherine Mary, da of the Rev H Martin, Vicar of Thatcham , and has issue (with a son d young) 1h to 3h

        1h Anthony Hammond, b 5 June 1893

        2h Cicely Margaret Hammond, b 19 Apr 1896

        3h Evelyn Dorothea Hammond, b 25 Oct 1905

    2g Henry Edward Denison Hammond, M A (Oxon), b 26 Nov 1866, *unm*

    3g Robert Francis Frederick Hammond, b 15 Oct 1868 , *unm*

    4g Mary Katharine Hammond ⎱ (1 *St Stephen's Road, Bayswater*)
    5g Isabel Bowyer Hammond ⎰

[Nos 71756 to 71782

The Plantagenet Roll

3f Alice Cobb, a Sister of Mercy (*St Wilfrid's, Exeter*)

4f Margaret Katharine Cobb, m 22 June 1880, Ivan Vernon Watson [son of Dr J F Watson, F R G S, K C Charles III of Spain], and has issue 1g to 2g

1g George Ivan Augustine Watson, b 25 July 1887

2g Luna Cicely Watson.

4e *Henrietta Elizabeth Atkins-Bowyer*, d. 1849, m *Charles Vincent Eyre of Calais and had issue (at least)* 1f

1f [da] Eyre, m (—) Perret, and had issue

5e *Penelope Maria Atkins-Bowyer*, d. 1859, m *the Rev William Francklin, Rector of Thursley, co Surrey, d (-), and had issue (with 3 sons d unm)* 1f

1f Emily Wentworth Francklin, b 4 Aug 1815, d 23 Feb 1889, m 13 Feb 1866, *Florance Wyndham of Great Marlow, co Bucks* [youngest son of Wadham Wyndham of Great Marlow], d 27 Dec 1897, and had issue 1g to 3g

1g Emily Wentworth Wyndham (175 *Clive Road, West Dulwich*), unm

2g Alice Mary Wyndham, b 19 May 1871, d 18 Dec 1906, m 16 June 1881, Arthur Edmund Little of Ireland, and had issue 1h to 2h.

1h Kathleen Mary Little.

2h Dorothy Little

3g Edith Constance Wyndham, m 21 Sept 1887, Charles Crouch, Cashier, London & County Bank (*East Finchley*), and has issue 1h to 2h

1h Harold Wyndham Crouch, b 4 June 1900

2h Dora Edith Crouch

6e *Anne Elizabeth Atkins-Bowyer*, b 27 Oct 1818, d 13 Nov 1890, m 13 Feb 1850, *the Rev Henry William Hodgson, Rector of Ashwell, co Herts*, b. 22 Jan 1821, d 23 Ap 1898, and had issue 1f to 2f

1f Rev Hugh Alexander Hodgson, M A (Camb), Rector of Beddington since 1891 (*Beddington Rectory, Croydon*), b 17 Mar 1856, m 19 Oct 1880, Kate Alice, da of Thomas Hill Barrows of the Grange, Great Malvern, and has issue 1g to 6g

1g Douglas Bowyer Hodgson, b 4 Jan 1882

2g Christopher Michael Hodgson, b 29 Sept 1883

3g Grenville Henry Hodgson, b 27 Aug 1885

4g Ruth Christabel Hodgson, b 26 Sept 1887

5g Winifred Mary Hodgson, b 7 July 1889

6g Noel Wentworth Hodgson, b 24 Dec 1898

2f Margaret Annie Hodgson, m 1st, 8 July 1879, Henry Dent Hinrich-Dent of Hallaton Manor, Uppingham, d 31 May 1883, 2ndly, 27 June 1888, Richard Cotton Rowley (*The Wrekin, Milton Road, Harpenden*), and has issue 1g

1g Balbirie Thomas Cotton Rowley, b 7 Ap 1889

7e *Eleanor Catherine Atkins-Bowyer*, b 27 Nov 1822, d 7 Oct 1892, m 2 May 1846, Beaumont Hankey of 15 *Southwell Gardens, S W*, and 71 *St James' Street, S W*, d 18 Feb 1909, and had (with a son, the Rev Wentworth Beaumont Hankey, d unm 16 June 1905) issue 1f to 4f

1f Douglas Hankey, b 6 Mar 1856, unm

2f Evelyn Mary Hankey (13 *Lexham Gardens, W*)

3f Helen Frances Hankey, b 18 Sept 1857, d 9 Mar 1906, m 1st, 1879, William Roderick Hallett Edwards, Lieut R N, d 10 Dec 1885, 2ndly, 1888, Major Henry Wyndham Davidson, 103rd Regt, d 21 July 1899, and had issue 1g

1g Lilian Helen Davidson, b 22 Aug 1890

4f Mabel Hankey, m 1 July 1878, Martin Fletcher Luther, Lieut (ret) R N. (*Adelaide Crescent Brighton*), and has issue 1g to 3g

1g Guy Fletcher Luther, Capt Sherwood Foresters, b 13 Aug 1879

2g Alan Charles Grenville Luther, Capt K O Yorkshire Light Infantry, b 17 Sept 1880

3g John Wentworth Luther, b 16 July 1886   [Nos 71783 to 71809.

# of The Blood Royal

2d *Cornelius Atkins-Bowyer*, C B , Col in the Army, d (-) , m *Sophia, da of* (—) *Hopkinson, Comm R N* , and had issue 1e to 3e

1e *William Atkins-Bowyer*, d (? s p)

2e *Henry Atkins-Bowyer*, d (? s p) in India

3e *Augusta Atkins-Bowyer*, d (? unm)

3d *Frances Penelope Atkins-Bowyer*, d 1836 , m as 1st wife, 24 Aug 1807, Lieut -Col James Forest Fulton, K H 92nd Foot, A D C to Sir George Prevost Gov -Gen of Canada, b 30 Sept 1780 , d Dec 1854 and had issue (with 3 eld r sons and a da who all d s p) 1e

1e *Richard Robert Fulton, formerly* 44th Regt and afterwards R I C (*Parsonstown, King's Co*), b 7 May 1823 , m 10 Nov 1857, Margaret Ormsby, da of Robert Twiss of Parteen, co Tipperary, and has issue 1f to 2f

1f *Elizabeth Frances Fulton*, m 10 Jan 1883, Capt John Edward Maxwell Pilkington, 28th Regt , d 12 July 1898 , and had issue 1g to 2g

1g Ulick Wetherall Pilkington, b 7 May 1898

2g Eileen Mary Pilkington, b 7 Nov 1883

2f *Mary Ormsby Fulton*, m 21 June 1888, Lieut -Col Alfred Ruttledge, 14th Regt , and has issue 1g to 3g

1g John Forrest Ruttledge, b 1 Aug 1894

2g Richard Theodore Ruttledge, b 14 Dec 1897

3g Eric Peter Knox Ruttledge, b 24 Aug 1899

4c *Penelope Bowyer*, d 9 June 1820 , m 1st, 5 Aug 1765, George John Cooke of Harefield Park, co Midx , M P , 2ndly, Major-Gen Edward Smith [uncle of Adm Sir Sydney Smith, G C B], and had issue 1d to 5d

1d Sir George Cooke, K C B , K S G , K T S , &c , Lieut -Gen and Col 77th Regt , d unm 3 Feb 1837

2d Sir Henry Frederick Cooke, K C H , C B , K M M , K S G , M P , Major-Gen , d s p 10 Mar 1837

3d *Kitty Cooke*, d (-) , m 1st, George Bond, Serge nt-at Law , 2ndly, James Trebeck, and had issue 1e

1e *Elinor Bond, da and h* , d 7 Dec 1862 , m at St George's, Hanover Square, 1826, Capt Richard Kirwan, 94th Regt [3rd son of Hyacinth Kirwan of Cregg Castle], d 6 Jan 1853 , and had issue (with a 3rd son and a da , Mrs Cooch, d s p) 1f to 2f

1f *Rev Richard Kirwan*, b 11 Dec 1828 , d 2 Sept 1872 , m 29 Oct 1859, Rose Helen, da of the Rev Barrett Lampet of Great Bardfield , and had issue 1g to 6g

1g Rev Robert Mansel Kirwan, M A (Oxon), Chaplain Bengal Eccles Estab , b 13 Mar 1861 , m 29 Oct 1902, Marguerite Theodora, da of Henry Trenton Wadley , s p

2g Rev Ernest Cecil Kirwan, M A (Oxon), Rector of Holy Trinity, Guildford (*Holy Trinity Rectory, Guildford*), b 10 Sept 1867 , unm

3g Lionel Edward Kirwan (*Madras*), b 12 Feb 1869 , m 3 Feb 1903, Evelyn Willet, da of Edward W Stoney of Madras, C I E , and has issue 1h to 3h

1h Patrick Lionel Kirwan, b 19 Dec 1905

2h Ralph Bertram Kirwan, b 17 Dec 1908

3h Hyacinth Ethel Kirwan, b 22 Oct 1903

4g Bertram Richard Kirwan, Major R A (12 *York Mansions, Battersea Park, S W*), b 17 May 1871 , m 20 Oct 1897, Helen, da of Col Hogg, Indian Army , and has issue 1h to 2h

1h Rudolph Charles Hogg Kirwan, b 22 May 1903

2h Kathleen Helen Kirwan, b 2 Jan 1899

5g Gerald William Claude Kirwan, b 3 Aug 1872 , unm

6g Eleanor Augusta Mary Kirwan, m 9 Feb 1897, Reginald Barlow Plumer, Mysore C S , s p

[Nos 71810 to 71828

The Plantagenet Roll

2f George Kirwan, Capt 25th Regt, b 1830, d 1899, m *Ellen Ewbank, da of Lieut-Col R G Chambers, 5th Bengal Cavalry*, d 1 May 1897, *and had issue (with 5 others d s p)* 1g to 6g

    1g George Brudenell Kirwan (*Texas, U S A*), m (—)

    2g Francis Vernon Brudenell Kirwan, Lieut A S C (*Portsmouth*), b 15 May 1878, *unm*

    3g Noel Gerald Brudenell Kirwan (*Santaizri, Mysore*). b 25 Dec 1880

    4g Ella D'Arcy Kirwan, m 1896, the Rev Christopher Frederic Wellesley Hatchell M A (Camb), Chaplain Madras Eccles Estab (*Vepery, Madras*), and has issue 1h to 2h

        1h Eric Wellesley Hatchell, b Oct 1898

        2h Sheila D'Arcy Hatchell

    5g Katherine Brudenell Kirwan, m Charles Ievers Lopdell, A M I C E, and has issue 1h to 2h

        1h Eileen Lopdell

        2h Hyacinthe Lopdell

    6g Florence Sydney Brudenell Kirwan, *unm*

4d Penelope Anne Cook, b c 1760, d 2 Feb 1826, m 8 Mar 1794, *Robert (Brudenell), 6th Earl of Cardigan [E]*, d 14 Aug 1837, *and had issue*

See the Tudor Roll, Table XXI and pp 171-178, Nos 20337-20447

5d Maria Cooke, d at Geneva 3 Oct 1827, m 28 Feb 1804, *Major-Gen Henry Charles Edward Vernon of Hilton Park*, co Stafford, C B, d 22 Mar 1861, *and had issue 1e to 3e*

    1e *Henry Charles Vernon of Hilton Park, J P, D L, High Sheriff co Stafford* 1867, b 9 Jan 1805, d 26 Feb 1886, m 15 Mar 1828, *Catherine, da of Richard Rice Williams of Hendredenny, co Glam*, d 29 May 1884, *and had issue (with 2 sons and 2 das d unm)* 1f to 4f

    1f *Augustus Leveson Vernon of Hilton, J P, D L, High Sheriff co Staff* 1899 (*Hilton Park, Wolverhampton, Carlton, &c*), b 30 Sept 1836, m 17 Nov 1864, Selma Anne [descended from George, Duke of Clarence, K G (see the Clarence Volume, p 395)], da of Walter Peter Giffard of Chillington, and has issue 1g to 4g

    1g Henry Arthur Leveson Vernon of Culmleigh, Stoke Canon, Exeter, D L, b 3 Sept 1868, d v p 28 Dec 1899, m 2 June 1896, Georgiana Frances D'Anyers, da of Henry Rodolph d'Anvers Willis of Halsnead, J P, D L, and had issue 1h

        1h Dorothy Vernon, b 28 Jan 1898

    2g Walter Bertie William Vernon, b 18 Oct 1871, m 15 Sept 1897, Esther Hodgson, widow of Francis Robinson Hartland Atcherley of Marton Hall, da of John Mills, and has issue 1h

        1h Richard Leveson Vernon, b 26 Nov 1900

    3g Henrietta Catherine Vernon

    4g Selma Mary Vernon

    2f Rev Frederick Wentworth Vernon, Vicar of Rangeworthy, b 8 Jan 1839, d 20 May 1906, m 1st, 6 June 1867, Ellen Mary Woodhouse, da of Hugh Woolhouse Acland, d June 1883, 2ndly, 13 Aug 1885 Edith Serena Hill (Cleveden), da of the Rev William Henry Boothby, Vicar of Hawkesbury [Bt Col?], and has issue (with 2 sons and 5 das, d young) 1g to 7g

    1g Hugh Woodhouse Vernon, b 9 Oct 1872

    2g Charles Percy Vernon (*The Highlands, Symonds, Yat, co Hereford*), b 22 Sept 1873

    3g Richard Francis Vernon (*26 Banbury Road, Oxford*), b 13 Sept 1871

    4g Evelyn Vernon b 31 May 1889

    5g Roger Vernon, b 27 Oct 1893

    6g Peter Wentworth Vernon, b 12 Ap 1895

    7g Millicent Eleanor Vernon, b 8 Ap 1887   [Nos 71829 to 71962

# of The Blood Royal

3/ Rev William George Vernon, M A (Camb), *formerly* Vicar of St John's, Kenilworth (*The Croft, Avenue Road, Malvern*), *b* 8 Ap 1840 , *m* 8 Feb 1866, Alexandrina Adelaide, da of William Davey Sole of Devonport , and his issue 1g

1g Cecil Charles William Vernon (*The Firs, Llandrinio, Llanvmynech, S O*), *b* 21 July 1868 , *m* 29 Oct 1893, Charlotte Isabel Leane, da of R W Flick of Banbury , and has issue 1h to 4h

    1h Eric Cecil Wentworth Vernon, *b* 1896.

    2h Leveson George Vernon, *b* 1898

    3h Sidney Richard Wentworth Vernon, *b* 1900

    4h Isabel Adelaide Vernon, *b* 1907

4/ Rev Edward Hamilton Vernon, Rector of Burnett (*Burnett Rectory, Clifton, Bristol*), *b* 16 Jan 1844 , *m* 1st Fanny, da of (—) Ibbotson of Sunderland , 2ndly, Miriam, da of the Rev Henry Fisher of Leamington , 3rdly, (—), and has issue (2 sons and 2 das)

2e *William Frederick Vernon of Harefield Park, co Midx , J P , D L* , *b* 7 Nov 1807 , *d s p Sept* 1889

3e *George Augustus Vernon of Harefield Park, J P , D L , Lieut-Col Cold-stream Guards*, *b* 31 May 1811 , *d* 25 Nov 1896 , *m* 1 *June* 1842, *Louisa Jane Frances, da of Admiral Bertie Cornelius Cator, R N* , *d* 20 Dec 1880 , *and had issue (with an elder son d young)* 1f *to* 7f

1f Bertie Wentworth Vernon of Harefield and Stoke Bruerne, J P and High Sheriff co Northants 1892, *formerly* R N (*Harefield Park near Uxbridge , Stoke Bruerne Park, Towcester*), *b* 26 Oct 1846 , *m* 23 June 1873, Isabel Caroline Eliza (see p 386), da of Lieut-Col Henry Atkyns-Bowyer of the Grange, Steeple Aston , *s p s*

2f *Herbert Charles Erskine Vernon, I C S* , *b* 28 Sept 1851 , *d* 15 *Feb* 1893 , *m Helen Mayne, da of Gen Liptrott, and had issue* 1g *to* 3g

    1g Henry Albemarle Vernon, *b* 5 Dec 1879

    2g Grenville Bertie Vernon, *b* Sept 1884

    3g Louisa Muriel Vernon, *m* 20 Oct 1906, Edward Harington, J P , B A (Oxon), Bar-at-Law, County Court Judge, Circuit No 45 [3rd son of Sir Richard Harington, 11th Bt [E 1611] (20 *Ovington Square, S W*), and has issue 1h

        1h Edward Henry Vernon Harington, *b* 13 Sept 1907

3f Mary Vernon, *m* Charles Pringle , *s p s*

4f Edith Henrietta Sophia Vernon

5f Louisa Jane Vernon, *m* 1st, 26 July 1870, Gen Edward Westby Donovan, K L H , East Yorkshire Regt [2nd son of Richard Donovan of Ballymore, co Wexford], *d* Jan 1897, 2ndly, 16 Mar 1898, Com Frederick E Thomas, R N , and has issue 1g

    1g Edward Herbert Donovan, Lieut R N , *b* 8 Oct 1874

6f Lizzie Vernon, *m* 1st, 22 Ap 1873, Capt Henry Bowyer of the Grange, Steeple Aston [Bt Coll], *d s p* 6 May 1882 , 2ndly, 1882, William Frederick Gore-Langton (*Padbury Lodge, Bucks*) , and has issue 1g to 3g

    1g Francis Wilfrid Gore-Langton, Lieut Coldstream Guards, *b* 14 Ap 1884

    2g Gerald Wentworth Gore-Langton, Lieut 18th Hussars, *b* 23 Aug 1885

    3g Montagu Vernon Gore-Langton, Lieut Irish Guards, *b* 28 Aug 1887

7f Muriel Isabel Vernon

2b *Richard Bowyer*, d (? *unm*)

3b *Thomas Bowyer*, d (? *unm*)

4b *Charlotte Bowyer*, d (? *unm*)

2a *William Bowyer*, *b* 14 *July* 1688 , *d* (—) , *m Elizabeth, da of Richard Parker of Hedsor afsd , and had issue* 1b *to* 3b

    1b *Richard Bowyer*, bapt *at Woburn* 4 *Ap* 1718

    2b *William Bowyer*

[Nos 71963 to 71983

ob *Juliana Bowyer*, m *the Rev George Burville of Bexley, co Kent ; and had issue* [1]

3a *Diana Bowyer*, bapt 7 Oct 1680 , d (-) , m *Philip Jennings of Duddles ton co Salop and had issue* [2] 1b

1b *Edward Jennings*, b 23 Oct 1706

231 Descendants, if any, of the Hon ROBERT CECIL, d (-) ; m (—), da of (—) HOPTON , of the Hon PHILIP CECIL, d (-) , m (—), da of (—) ALLEN , and of the Hon WILLIAM CECIL d (-) , m ELIZABETH, da of Sir Thomas LAWLEY of Spoonhill, 1st Bt [E], M P [3] (Table XXII)

232 Descendants of EDMUND TURNOR of Stoke Rochford and Panton, co Lincoln (Table XXII), b. c 1708 , d 5 Jan 1769 , m ELIZABETH, da and event co-h of Henry FYNES of Snitterton, co Derby, d 4 Dec 1765 , and had issue 1a to 5a.

1a *Edmund Turnor of Stoke Rochford, &c*, d 1805 , m *Mary da of John Disney of Lincoln , and had issue* 1b *to* 8b

1b *Edmund Turnor of Stoke Rochford, &c*, FRS, FSA, MP *for Midhurst, Author of a History of Grantham, and an eminent Antiquary* b 1755 , d 19 Mar 1829 , m 1st 7 May 1795, *Elizabeth, da of Philip Broke*, d 1801 *2ndly, Dorothea da of Lieut Col Tucker, d May 1854 , and had issue (with another son and 2 das , of whom no issue survives)* 1c *to* 5c

1c *Christopher Turnor of Stoke Rochford, JP, DL , and High Sheriff co Lincoln* 1833, M P *for S Lincoln* 1841-47, b 4 1p 1809 d 7 Mar 1886, m 2 Feb 1837, *Lady Caroline [herself a descendant of Edward III through Mortimer-Percy], da of George William (Finch-Hatton), 9th Earl of Winchilsea [E]*, d 13 Mar 1888 , *and had issue*

See p 130, Nos 12182-12211

2c *Cecil Turnor*, d (? s p)

3c *Rev Algernon Turnor*, d Aug 1842 , m 9 Jan 1840, *Sophia* (see p 151), *da of Sir Thomas Whichcote, 6th Bt [E]*

4c *Henry Marten Turnor, Capt King's Dragoon Guards*, d (-), m 28 *July* 1840, *the Hon Marianne [descended from the Lady Anne, sister of King Edward IV], da of Godfrey (Macdonald), 3rd Baron Macdonald [I]* d 12 *July* 1876 , *and had issue* 1d *to* 4d

1d *Reginald Charles Turnor, late Major 1st Life Guards (Tidmarsh, Berks),* b 26 Sept 1850 , d 11 June 1910, m 1st, *Gabrielle, da of the Marquis Sampieri ,* 2ndly, *Laura, da of J Lucas , and had issue* 1e *to* 3e

1e [2] *Christopher Turnor*

2e [1] *Rence Turnor*

3e [2] *Joan Turnor*

2d *Harriet Mary Turnor*, m 1 July 1869, John (Scott), 3rd Earl of Eldon
[Nos 71984 to 72018

---

[1] Lipscombe's " Bucks," iv 446

[2] Ibid According to Burke's " Royal Descents " (ii xcv) and " Landed Gentry " (1906, p 1718) she had also a da Jane, who m Thomas ap John Vaughan of Plas Thomas, co Salop whose alleged *great grandson* by her, Philip Vaughan of Burlton, ancestor of the present family, was bapt 10 Oct 1690 As the said Jane's mother was bapt 7 Oct 1680, this descent is impossible

[3] Brydges' " Collins," ii 491 Wotton's " Baronetage," ii 262

# of The Blood Royal

[U K] (*Stowell Park, Northleach, co Glouc,, 13 Portman Square W*), and has issue

See the Exeter Volume, p 591, Nos 51408-51415

3*d* Florence Turnor, *m* (—) Neville of (—), and has issue 1*e*
1*e* [*da*] Neville, *m* (—) Wheeler
4*d* Mabel Turnor, *m* (—) Morgan, *s p*
5*c* *Elizabeth Edmund Turnor*, d 1868, m *Frederick Manning*

2*b* *George Turnor*, d (-), m *Eleanor*, da of (——) *Henmer*, and had issue[1]
3*b* *John Turnor*
1*b* *Charles Turnor*

5*b* *Elizabeth Frances Turnor*, d 27 Ap 1835, m 2 Dec 1783, Samuel Smith of Woodhall Park, co Herts [next younger brother of Robert, 1st Baron Carrington [I and G B] b 14 Ap 1754, d 12 Mar 1831, and had issue 1c to 9c

1*c* Abel Smith of Woodhall J P , M P co Herts 1835-47, b 17 July 1788, d 23 Feb 1859, m 2ndly, 12 July 1826 Frances Anne [descended from the Lady Isabel Plantagenet, da of Gen Sir Harry Calvert, 1st Bt [U K], G C B, d 18 Nov 1885, and had issue

See the Essex Volume, pp 303-306, Nos 32716-32817

2*c* Samuel George Smith of Sacombe Park, co Herts M P, b 19 July 1789, d 4 Oct 1863, m 4 July 1821, Eugenia [descended from the Lady Isabel Plantagenet], da of the Rev Robert Chatfield, D C L, d 5 Jan 1838, and had issue

See the Essex Volume, pp 264-266, Nos 30974-31025

3*c* Henry Smith of Wilford House, co Notts, b 12 Dec 1794, d 7 Feb 1874, m 14 July 1824, Lady Lucy [descended from George, Duke of Clarence, K G], da of Alexander (Leslie-Melville), 10th Earl of Leven and 7th Earl of Melville [S], d 23 Dec 1865, and had issue

See the Essex Volume, Clarence Supplement, p 525, Nos 1324/291-308

4*c* Sophia Smith, d 2 Ap 1844, m 19 July 1803, William Dickinson of Kingweston, co Som, M P for that co in seven successive Parliaments, b 1 Nov 1771, d at Naples 19 Jan 1837, and had issue 1d to 4d

1*d* Francis Henry Dickinson of Kingweston, J P , D L , High Sheriff co Som 1853, M P West Som 1841-1847, b 6 Jan 1813, d 17 July 1890, m 8 Sept 1835, his cousin (see p 397) Caroline, da of Major-Gen Thomas Cary, d 19 Ap 1897, and had issue (with others who d s p) 1e to 8e

1*e* William Dickinson of Kingweston, late Somerset Militia (Kingweston, Somerton Somerset), b 20 Aug 1839, m 1st, 31 Mar 1875, Helen Isabella, da of George Barnsfather, H E I C S, d 19 Ap 1888, 2ndly, 1 Jan 1896, Isabel Frances, da of Col Evanson Harrison, R A , and has issue 1f to 4f

1*f* William Francis Dickinson, b 20 Mar 1877
2*f* John McLennan Dickinson, b 20 Mar 1881
3*f* Hugh Cary Dickinson, b 19 Oct 1884
4*f* George Barnsfather Dickinson, b 4 Jan 1886

2*e* Reginald Dickinson (121 St George's Square, London, S W), b 27 Jan 1841

3*e* Arthur Dickinson (Somerton Somerset), b 18 Jan 1847, m 16 Ap 1873, Alice Berkeley, widow of the Rev George Goodden, da of Augustus Woodforde of Ansford, co Som , and has issue 1f to 2f

1*f* Francis Arthur Dickinson, Capt Duke of Cornwall's L I , and attached to Egyptian Army, b 6 Feb 1874

2*f* Stephen Carey Dickinson, b 9 Aug 1875, m 1 Feb 1905, Hilda Grace, da of Arthur Leckconby Phipps

4*e* Sophia Caroline Dickinson
5*e* Frances Dickinson   [Nos 72019 to 72212

---

[1] Burke's "Commoners," i 301

The Plantagenet Roll

6e Lucy Dickinson, m 1st, 5 Ap 1866, William Henry Dorrien-Magens, d 4 Ap 1875, 2ndly, 16 May 1888, the Rev Llyd Jenkin Rosser, Vicar of Austrey (*Austrey Vicarage, Atherstone*), and has issue 1f

1f Constance Lucy Dorrien-Magens, m 6 Sept 1892, the Rev Francis Henry Greville Knight, M A (Oxon), Rector of Leadenham (*Leadenham Rectory, Lincoln*), and has issue 1g to 2g

   1g Ruth Constance Dorrien Knight

   2g Katharine Lucy Knight

7e Mary Dickinson, m 14 Ap 1878, Thomas Charles (Agar-Robartes), 6th Viscount Clifden [I], 6th Baron Mendip [G B] and 2nd Baron Robartes [U K], J P , D L [descended from George, Duke of Clarence, K G , brother of Edward IV] (*Lanhydrock House, Bodmin , 1 Great Stanhope Street, W*), and has issue

See the Clarence Volume, p 640, Nos 30079-30087

8e Edith Dickinson

2d Edmund Henry Dickinson of Chapmanslade, co Wilts, J P , b 30 June 1821, d 22 Ap 1897, m 11 May 1861, Emily Dulcibella [descended from Edward III through Lady Isabella Plantagenet (see Essex Volume, p 361), and also through Mortimer Percy (see this Volume, p 275)], da of Robert John (Eden), 3rd Baron Auckland [G B and I], Lord Bishop of Bath and Wells, d 27 Jan 1893, and had issue 1c to 4c

   1c Robert Edmund Dickinson M P for Wells 1899-1906, b 1 Aug 1862, unm

   2c Philip Francis Dickinson, b 2 Aug 1863 unm

   3c Oswald Eden Dickinson, b 17 Nov 1864, unm

   4c Violet Mary Dickinson (21 *Manchester Street, W*), unm

3d Sophia Gertrude Dickinson, b 13 Nov 1841, d 20 June 1902, m 22 Sept 1870, the Rev John Stuart Hippisley Horner of Mells Park, co Som , Preb of Wells and Rector of Mells, b 9 Oct 1810, d 9 Ap 1874, and had issue 1c to 8e

1c Sir John Francis Fortescue Horner of Mells, K C V O , M A , J P , D L , and High Sheriff 1885 co Som , Bar at Law, formerly (1895-1907) Commissioner of Woods and Forests (*Mells Park, Frome , 9 Buckingham Gate, S W*), b 28 Dec 1842, m 18 Jan 1883, Frances, da of William Graham, formerly M P for Glasgow , and has issue (with a younger son d young) 1f to 3f

   1f Edward William Horner, b 3 May 1888

   2f Cicely Margaret Horner, m 7 Dec 1908, Hon George Lambton, 5th son of George Frederick, 2nd Earl of Durham [U K] (*Mesnil Warren, Newmarket*), and has issue 1g

      1g John Lambton, b 31 July 1909

   3f Katharine Frances Horner, m 25 July 1907, Raymond Asquith, Bar at Law [son of the Right Hon Herbert Asquith, P C , M P] (*49 Bedford Square, W C*), and has issue 1g

      1g Helen Frances Asquith, b 22 Oct 1909

2c Rev George William Horner, Editor of the Coptic New Testament (*12 St Helen's Place, E C*), b (twin) 10 June 1849

3c Maurice Horner, J P co Som (*12 St Helen's Place, E C*), b (twin) 10 June 1849

4c John Stuart Horner (*Caverleigh, Surbiton*), b 30 Aug 1855, m 26 July 1887, Emily Green, da of Col James Francis Birch, 3rd West India Regt , and has issue 1f to 4f

   1f Bernard Stuart Horner, b 5 Dec 1889

   2f Maurice Stuart Horner, b 18 Dec 1893

   3f David Stuart Horner, b 29 July 1900

   4f Olivia Stuart Horner

5c Elizabeth Gertrude Horner

6c Margaret Maria Horner

7c Caroline Sophia Horner

8c Alice Muriel Horner

[Nos. 72213 to 72248.

# of The Blood Royal

4d *Caroline Dickinson*, b 7 *July* 1817, d 18 *July* 1886, m 6 *July* 1843, *William Bence-Jones of Lisselan, co Cork, M A , J P , Bar at Law*, b 5 *Oct* 1812 , d 22 *June* 1882, *and had issue* 1e *to* 5e

  1e *William Francis Bence-Jones of Lisselan*, b 9 *Mar* 1856, d *unm* 20 *Nov* 1883

  2e Reginald Bence-Jones of Lisselan, J P , D L , High Sheriff co Cork 1894 (*Lisselan, Clonakilty, co Cork*), b 4 *Nov* 1865 , m 9 *Oct* 1890, Ethel Annie, da of D C da Costa of Barbados, W I , and has issue 1f to 2f

    1f Campbell William Winthrop Bence Jones, b 21 Ap 1891

    2f Philip Reginald Bence-Jones, b 12 Jan 1897

  3e Caroline Sophia Jones, m 16 Aug 1877, Francis Henry Blackburne Daniell [only son of Capt George Daniell, R N , by his wife Alice Catherine, da of the Right Hon Francis Blackburne, Lord Chancellor of Ireland] (19 *Nevern Place Earls Court Road, S W*), and has issue (with a son, Francis Reginald, b 23 Sept 1882, d unm 21 Sept 1903) 1f to 4f

    1f George Francis Blackburne Daniell, b 8 June 1878

    2f William Arthur Blackburne Daniell, Capt Royal Fusiliers, b 26 Jan 1881.

    3f Henry Edmund Blackburne Daniell, b 11 Feb 1885

    4f Alice Caroline Blackburne Daniell, m 20 June 1906, Edward Granville Browne, Sir Thomas Adams' Professor of Arabic in the University of Cambridge and Fellow of Pembroke College, Author of " A Literary History of Persia," " A Year among the Persians," and other works and papers on Oriental subjects [son of Sir Benjamin Chapman Browne, D C L] (*Cambridge*) , and has issue 1g

      1g Patrick Reginald Evelyn Browne, b 28 May 1907

  4e Mary Lilias Jones, m 1 Feb 1886, the Rev Robert Henry Charles, D D , M A , Professor of Biblical Greek at T C D 1898 1906 Fellow of the British Academy, Grinfield Lecturer, Oxford University, 1905-1910, Author of many well known works (24 *Bardwell Road Oxford*)

  5e Philippa Frances Jones, m as 2nd wife, 12 Aug 1885, Sir Frederick Albert Bosanquet, K C , J P , Common Serjeant of the City of London since 1900, *formerly* Recorder of Worcester 1879-1891 and of Wolverhampton 1891-1900, &c (12 *Grenville Place, S W , Cobbe Place Lewes*) , and has issue 1f to 2f

    1f William Sidney Bence Bosanquet, b 9 May 1893

    2f Edith Madeline Bosanquet

5c *Frances Anne Smith*, d 20 *Feb* 1862, m 18 *Ap* 1806, *Claude George Thornton of Marden Hill, co Herts, High Sheriff for that co* 1838, b 20 *Jan* 1776 , d 4 *Aug* 1866, *and had issue* 1d *to* 2d

  1d *George Smith Thornton of Marden Hill, J P* , b 20 *Nov* 1808, d *May* 1867, m 16 *Oct* 1839, *Agnes, da of the Rev Henry Pole of Altham Place, co Berks* [who m 2ndly, 1869, *John Henry Blagrave of Calcot Park and*] d 27 *Jan* 1895, *and had issue* 1e

    1e Godfrey Henry Thornton, b 16 Aug 1856

  2d *Rev Spencer Thornton, M A , Vicar of Wendover*, b 12 *Oct* 1813, d 12 *Jan* 1850, m 7 *Sept* 1839, *Caroline Adelaide, da of James Du Pré of Wilton Park, co Bucks*, d 17 *Feb* 1898 , *and had issue* (*with an elder son* d s p) 1e *to* 3e

    1e Henry Edward Thornton (58 *The Rofewalk, Nottingham*), b 31 Aug 1842 , m 1st, 15 Feb 1871, Katherine Charlotte, sister to Field-Marshal the 1st Baron Grenfell [U K], P C , G C B , da of Pascoe St Leger Grenfell of Maesteg, co Glamorgan, d 16 Jan 1906, 2ndly, 19—, Isabel Mary [descended from the Lady Isabel Plantagenet (see the Essex Volume, p 304)], da of Robert Smith of Goldings, co Herts, J P , D L , and has issue 1f to 2f

      1f Henry Grenfell Thornton, b 9 Feb 1873

      2f Pascoe Spencer Thornton, b 3 Mar 1877

      3f Rev Claude Cyprian Thornton, M A (Camb), Vicar of Greasley (*Greasley*
                               [Nos 72249 to 72266

The Plantagenet Roll

Vicarage, Notts), *b* 2 July 1878, *m* 12 Sept 1905, Alice May, da of Frederick Sillery Bishop of Northwood co Mdlx , and has issue 1g

1g Piscoe Cyprian Thornton, *b* 20 Jan 1907

4/ Godfrey St Leger Thornton, Capt R F A , *b* 21 Mar 1881

5/ Rev John Gordon Thornton, B A , Curate of St Andrews, Auckland (*Castle Lodge, Bishop Auckland*), *b* 23 Dec 1884

6/ Robert Henry Thornton, *b* 6 Oct 1909

7/ Nina Katherine Thornton, *m.* 15 June 1898, the Rev Frank Theodore Woods, M A (Camb), Vicar of Bishop Auckland (*The Vicarage, Bishop Auckland*)

8/ Susan Theresa Thornton, *m* 31 July 1895, the Rev John Bernard Barton, M A (Camb), Rector of St Pancras (*St Pancras Rectory, Rousdon, Devon*), and has issue 1g to 4g

1g Bernard Cecil Leslie Barton

2g Arthur Grenfell Barton

3g Raymond Henry Barton

4g Nina Joyce Katherine Barton

9/ Gertrude Fanny Thornton, *m* as 2nd wife, 2 Oct 1907, Frank Evelyn Seely, J P, Major and Hon Lieut-Col S Notts Hussars T D Yeo [2nd son of Sir Charles Seely, 1st Bt [U K] (*Calverton Hall, Nottingham*), and has issue 1g

1g Sheila Katherine Seely

2e Rev Claude Cecil Thornton, M A (Camb), Rector of Northwold (*Northwold Rectory, Norfolk*), *b* 21 Jan 1841, *m* 1st, 10 July 1866, Fanny, da of John Barton of East Leigh, Havant, *d* 28 Dec 1878, 2ndly, 19 Sept 1882, Alice Henrietta, da of Christopher William Giles Puller of Youngsbury Ware, co Herts, M P, J P , and has issue (with a son *d unm*) 1f to 12f

1f Claude Du Pre Thornton, *b* 27 Sept 1867, *m* 9 Sept 1909, Fanny Theodosia Savignac, da of (—) Stedman

2f *Douglas Montagu Thornton, b* 18 Mar 1873, *d* 8 Sept 1907, *m* 7 Nov 1899, Elsie, da of Sir William Anderson, K C B , and had issue 1g

1g Cecil Anderson Montagu Thornton, *b* 11 May 1901

3f Reginald Christopher Thornton, *b* 18 July 1883

4f Rev Lionel Spencer Thornton, B A (Camb), Curate of Langfield, Surrey, *b* 27 June 1884

5f Bernard Giles Thornton, *b* 22 Sept 1885

6f [1] Adelaide Frances Thornton,

7f [1] Evelyn Maude Thornton,

8f [1] Katharine Emily Cecilia Thornton,

9f [2] Winifred Mary Thornton,   *unm*

10f [2] Elsie Caroline Thornton,

11f [2] Alice Nora Thornton,

12f [2] Christabel Monica Thornton,

3e *Rev George Ruthven Thornton, Vicar of St Barnabas, Kensington, b* 23 Mar 1815, *d* 19 June 1895, *m* 12 Oct 1869, Theresa (18 Craven Hill Hyde Park, W), da of John Labouchere of Broom Hall, co Surrey, and had issue (with a da Theresa, *d unm*) 1f to 8f

1f Edward Labouchere Ruthven Thornton, I C S , District and Session Judge (*Madras*), *b* 10 July 1870, *m* 13 Nov 1893, Mabel, da of (—) Higgenbotham, *d* (-), and has issue 1g

1g Dorothy Mabel Thornton, *b* 25 Ap 1896

2f Spencer Ruthven Thornton, *b* 10 Aug 1871 *unm*

3f Arthur Ruthven Thornton, served in Lumsden's Horse, S Africa, *b* 10 Sept 1876

4f Maxwell Ruthven Thornton, Solicitor (*Penang*), *b* 11 July 1878, *m* Nov 1909, Kathleen, da of (—) Yates of co York   [Nos 72267 to 72296

5*f* Rev George Ruthven Thornton, M A, Org Sec S Amer M S for S E Dist (33 *Melville Road, Barnes*), *b* 30 Sept 1882, *m* 22 Ap 1908, Frances Penelope [descended from the Lady Isabel Plantagenet (see the Essex Volume, p 346)], da of Jacob Phillipps of 21 Addison Gardens, W

6*f* Francis Ruthven Thornton, *b* 5 Aug 1884, *unm*

7*f* Cicely Ruthven Thornton, *m* 1 Sept 1903, the Rev. Charles Ransford, Vicar of All Saints, Hertford

8*f* Mary Louisa Ruthven Thornton, *unm*

4*e* *Julia Frances Thornton*, d (-), m 1868, *the Rev William Thomas Henry Wilson, formerly Rector of Burlingham* (1 *Holmesdale Gardens, Hastings*), *and had issue 1f to 4f*

1*f* William Thornton Pender Wilson, Lieut R N

2*f* John Wilson

3*f* [da] Wilson, *m* A F (?) Ives

4*f* [da] Wilson, *m* M (?) Webster

5*e* Caroline Sophia Thornton, *unm*

6*e* Emily Montagu Thornton, *unm*

6*c* *Mary Smith*, d (-), m 25 Jan 1811, *Thomas Daniel of Aldridge Lodge, co Stafford*

7*c* *Caroline Smith*, d 17 Feb 1816, m 1814, *Major-Gen Thomas Cary*, d 9 Nov 1821, *and had issue 1d*

1*d* *Caroline Cary*, b at Eltham Palace, co Kent, 29 Jan 1816, d at Kingweston 19 Ap 1897, m 8 Sept 1835, *Francis Henry Dickinson of Kingweston, J P, D L, M P*, d 17 July 1890, *and had issue*
See p 393, Nos 72202-72227

8*c* *Barbara Smith*, d 9 Jan 1861, m 25 Oct 1836, *Lieut James John Gordon of Hadlow House, co Kent, R N*

9*c* *Charlotte Smith*, d 26 Ap 1879, m 19 Oct 1825, *the Hon Alexander Leslie-Melville* [*E of Leven and Melville Coll*], d 19 Nov 1881, *and had issue*
See the Essex Volume, Clarence Supplement, pp 523-524, Nos 1324/289-291

6*b* *Mary Turnor*, d 18 Oct 1831, m 1789, *Sir William Foulis of Ingleby, 7th Bt* [*E*], d 5 Sept 1802, *and had issue*
See p 234, Nos 36612-36649

7*b* *Diana Turnor*, b c 1763, d 4 Feb 1821, m 21 June 1785, *Sir Thomas Whichcote, 5th Bt* [*E*], d 22 Sept or 4 Oct 1828, *and had issue*
See p 150, Nos 16642-16722

8*b* *Frances Turnor*, d (? um)

2*a* *John Turnor, Capt of Dragoons*, d (? s p) 1752

3*a* *Diana Turnor*, b c 1712, d 1793, m *Bennet Langton of Langton, co Linc*, d 1769, *and had issue*
See the Clarence Volume, Table LXIX, and pp 515-550, Nos 23355-23486

4*a* *Elizabeth Turnor*, d (? s p), m *Edward Andrewes of Brockhill House, co Glouc*

5*a* *Isabella Turnor*, d (? s p), m *Lieut-Gen Alexander Drewry*
[Nos 72297 to 72666

233. Descendants of Lady ANNE CECIL (Table XXII), *b* 1612; *d* 6 Dec 1637, *m* as 1st wife *a* 1630, ALGERNON (PERCY), 10th EARL OF NORTHUMBERLAND [E.], K.G, K B, *bapt* 13 Oct. 1602, *d.* 13 Oct 1668, and had issue

See p 71, Nos 2000-3122   [Nos 72667 to 71089

The Plantagenet Roll

234 Descendants of Lady ELIZABETH CECIL (Table XXII.), *d* 19 Nov 1689, *m* (lic 4 Mai) 1639, WILLIAM (CAVENDISH), 3rd EARL OF DEVONSHIRE [E], *b* 10 Oct 1617; *d* 23 Nov 1684, and had issue 1*a* to 2*a*

1*a* *William (Cavendish), 4th Earl and* (12 *May* 1694) 1*st Duke of Devonshire* [E], *K G*, *b* 25 *Jan* 1641, *d* 18 *Aug* 1707, *m* 26 Oct 1662, *Lady Mary, da of James (Butler), 1st Duke of Ormonde* [E *and* I], *K G*, *d* 31 *July* 1710, *and had issue* 1*b to* 2*b*

1*b* *William (Cavendish), 2nd Duke of Devonshire, &c* [E], *K G*, *b c* 1672, *d* 4 *June* 1729, *m* 21 *June* 1688, *Lady Rachel, da of William Russell, Lord Russell, d* 28 *Dec* 1725, *and had issue*

See the Essex Volume, Table XIII, and pp 174–190, Nos 22908–24381

2*b* *Lord James Cavendish of Stapley Park, co Devon, M P, d* 14 *Dec* 1751, *m Anne, da of Elihu Yale, Governor of Fort St George, in the East Indies d* 27 *June* 1734, *and had issue* 1*c*

1*c* *Elizabeth Cavendish, da and after the death* (30 *June* 1751) *of her brother William, sole h, d* 1 *Aug* 1779, *m Feb* 1732, *Richard Chandler, afterwards* (*Act Parl* 26 *Mar* 1752) *Cavendish, M P* [*son and h of the Right Rev Edward Chandler, Lord Bishop of Durham*], *d* (*apparently s p*) 22 *Nov* 1769 [1]

2*a* *Lady Anne Cavendish, b c* 1649, *d* 18 *June* 1703, *m* 2*ndly* (lic 4 *May*), 1670, *John (Cecil), 5th Earl of Exeter* [E], *d at Issy, near Paris, 29 Aug* 1700, *and had issue*

See the Tudor Roll, Table XCVII, and pp 414–428, Nos 30220–30994

[Nos 71090 to 76338

235 Descendants of Lady CATHERINE CECIL (Table XXII), *d.* 18 Aug. 1652, *m* 9 May 1645, PHILIP (SYDNEY), 3rd EARL OF LEICESTER [E], *d* 6 Mar 1698, and had issue

See the Essex Volume, p 88, Nos 9363–9375   [Nos 76339 to 76351

236. Descendants of CHARLES (HOWARD), 1st EARL OF CARLISLE [E] (Table XXIII), *b* 1629, *d* 24 Feb 1685, *m* the Hon. ANNE, da of Edward (HOWARD), 1st Baron Howard of Escrick [E], *bur* 4 Sept 1703, and had issue

See p 384, Nos 66061–66961   [Nos 76352 to 77249

237 Descendants of MARY HOWARD (Table XXIII), *d* (–), *m* Sir JONATHAN ATKINS, Governor of [Jersey and *afterwards*] of Barbados, *d* there 1702, aged 99, and had issue (with apparently other das)[2] 1*a*.

1*a* *Frances Atkins, styled co-h to brother, b* 20 *Mar* 1659, *d* (–), *m* 1*st*, *Sir Robert Hackett, d* 31 *Mar* 1679, 2*ndly, Col Thomas Walrond* [*a younger son of Humphrey (Walrond), 1st Marquis of Vallado* [Sp 1653], *Governor of Barbados*], *d* 1694, *and had* (*with other*) *issue* 1*b*

1*b* *Frances Walrond, elder da and co-h, b in Barbados* 1680, *d in London* 1716, *m* 1*st, George Grame of Barbados,* 2*ndly, William Adams of the same Island, and had* (*with possibly other*) *issue* 1*c*

---

[1] *Gentleman's Magazine*, 1793, pp 974, 1000, 1131

[2] Burke's "Royal Families," ii cent, from which all these particulars are taken

    1c Thomas Adams, a Master in Chancery at Barbados, b 1699, d 1761, m *Margaret, da of Lieut-Gen Thomas Maxwell, and had (with possibly other) issue 1d*

    1d William Adams of Barbados, d in Jamaica 1781, m Elizabeth Ann, da of th: Rev Thomas Coverer, and had (with possibly other) issue 1e

    1e Edward Hamilton Adams of Middleton Hall, co Carmarthen, M P and High Sheriff for that co, d 2 June 1842, m *Amelia Sophia, da of Capt John Macpherson, and had issue 1f to 6f*

    1f Edward Adams of Middleton Hall

    2f William Adams

    3f Mary Adams

    4f Sophia Adams

    5f Caroline Adams

    6f Matilda Adams   [Nos 77250 to 77255]

238. Descendants of CATHERINE **H**OWARD **(Table XXIII),** *d* 4 July 1668, *m c* 1660, Sir J**OHN** L**AWSON** of Brough, 1st Bt [E], *d* 26 Oct 1698, and had issue.

    See pp 297-298, Nos 39646-40113   [Nos 77256 to 77753]

239 Descendants of F**RANCES** D**OWNING** (Table XXIII), *d* (-), *m* J**OHN** C**OTTON**, son and h of Sir John Cotton, 1st Bt [E], M P, *b c* 1650, *d i p* 1681, and had issue 1*a* to 3*a*

    1a Sir John Cotton, 3rd Bt [E], *M P*, d s p 5 *Feb* 1731

    2a Thomas Cotton, d (-), m *Frances, da and h of William Langton of Peterborough, and had issue a da*, Mary, *who must have d unm*

    3a Frances Cotton, da and event h, having the privilege of appointing successive Cottonian Family Trustees to the British Museum, vested in her and the male issue of her four das in succession, according to their seniority, by Act of Parliament, 1752, b 1675 7, d 21 *Nov* 1756, m *William Hanbury of Little Marcle, co Hereford* [son of Sir Thomas *Hanbury*], d 19 Oct 1737, *and had issue (with 2 other das who d s p) 1b to 2b*

    1b Mary Hanbury, da and co-h, b 1708, d 20 *Dec* 1796, m 12 *Dec* 1732, *the Rev Martin Annesley D D, Preb of Sarum [V Valentia Coll]*, b 5 *Oct* 1701, d 4 *June* 1749, *and had issue (with 4 other sons and 1 da who d s p) 1c to 3c*

    1c Rev Arthur Henry Annesley, D D, Vicar of Chewton Mendip, b 8 *May* 1735, bur 12 *July* 1792, m 7 *Nov* 1761, *Alice, da and h of Francis Keyte Dighton of Clifford Chambers, co Glouc*, d 29 *Nov* 1790, *and had issue (with a da who d s p) 1d*

    1d Rev Arthur Annesley, Rector and Lord of the Manor of Clifford Chambers, a Cottonian Family Trustee of the British Museum, b 30 *Oct* 1768, d 9 *Feb* 1845, m 14 *Jan* 1800, *Elizabeth Vere, da of George Booth Tyndale of Bathford [descended from George, Duke of Clarence, K G]*, d 15 *June* 1865, *and had issue*

    See the Clarence Volume, pp 542-544, Nos 23283-23354

    2c Katherine Annesley, b 20 *Mar* 1738, d 22 *Ap* 1826 m *as 2nd wife*, 1 *Jan* 1761, *the Rev John Trollope, D D [Bt (E 1641) Coll]*, d 10 *July* 1794, *and had issue 1d to 2d*

    1d Arthur William Trollope, Capt 40th Regt, b 15 *Dec* 1771 d 20 *Sept* 1799, m 26 *Dec* 1797, *Mary, da of Barnard Foord of Beverley, M D*, d 19 *July* 1822, *and had issue 1e to 2c*

    1e Barnard Trollope, afterwards (R L 30 Oct 1861) Foord-Bowes, of Cowlam, co Yorks, b 25 *Oct* 1798, d 10 *June* 1870, m 27 *July* 1818, *Mary, da of Samuel Greathed*, d 7 *Jan* 1861, *and had issue a da who d s p*   [Nos 77751 to 77825]

The Plantagenet Roll

2c *William Henry Trollope, Capt H E I C S*, b 4 Ap 1800, d 21 Sept 1873 m 30 July 1834, *Mary Arthur, da of John Arthur Worsop of Landford House, co Wilts*, d 1891, *and had issue 1f to 3f*

1f *Edward Charles Trollope, Major R A*, b 20 Aug 1849, d 23 Feb 1904, m 1st, 5 Oct 1871, *Louisa Sarah, da of Robert Pipon of Beaumont, Jersey*, d 19 Aug 1882, 2ndly, 27 May 1886, *Eva Annie Noel (45 Lower Belgrave Street, S W), da of Capt Frederick Dampier Rich, R N [Bt Coll], and had issue 1g to 2g.*

1g[1] Mary Emily Arthur Trollope

2g[2] Constance Zara Trollope

2f *Mary Anne Trollope*, d 15 Sept 1897, m 19 Aug 1862, *Frederick Ashe Bradburne of Lyburne, co Hants (Bramshaw Lodge, Lyndhurst, Hants), and had issue 1g to 4g*

1g Frederick Arthur Bradburne, b 1863

2g Henry Humphrey Brucker Bradburne, b 1869

3g John Edward Bradburne, b 1875

4g Charles Wyndham Bradburne, b 1879

3f *Eliza Maria Trollope (19 Montague Road, Richmond Hill, Surrey)*, m 19 Aug 1862, the Rev *George Goodwin Pownall Glossop*, Rector of West Dean, co. Hants d 23 Ap 1871, and had issue 1g to 9g

1g Rev *Charles Henry James Glossop, M A (Camb)*, Rector of Brympton *(Brympton Rectory, Yeovil)*, b 25 July 1864, m 27 June 1894, *Ada, da of the Rev Richard George Watson*, and has issue 1h

1h George Charles William Glossop, b 26 Mar 1906

2g Francis Edward Glossop, Major 1st Batt Leicestershire Regt, b 25 Aug. 1866 m 1 Oct 1902, *Ellen Sabine, da of Capt Thomas Malcolm Sabine Pasley, R N [Bt Coll]*

3g Rev *Arthur George Barnard Glossop, M A (Oxon)*, a Missionary of the Universities Mission to Brit Central Africa *(Likoma, Nyassaland, 19 Montague Road, Richmond Hill, S W)*, b 9 Nov 1867

4g William Richard Newland Glossop, b 26 Nov 1868

5g John Collings Taswell Glossop, Comm R N, b 23 Oct 1871

6g Harry Anthony Pownall Glossop, Lieut R N, b 14 Jan. 1873

7g Mary Eliza Glossop, m 20 May 1886, *Campbell Fortescue Stapleton Sanctuary (Mangerton, Melplash, R S O, Dorset), and has issue 1h to 5h*

1h Campbell Thomas Sanctuary, b 31 July 1889

2h Arthur George Everard Sanctuary, b 8 Nov 1892

3h Harry Nicholson Sanctuary, b 11 June 1898

4h Mary Frances Alice Sanctuary

5h Isabel Gemma Sanctuary

8g Ellen Maria Glossop

9g Alice Emma Harriet Glossop

2d *George Barne Trollope, Rear-Adm R N, C B*, b 17 Ap 1779, d 31 May 1850, m 18 Mar 1813, *Barbara, da of Joseph Goble*, d 11 July 1874, *and had issue 1c to 3c*

1c Rev *John Joseph Trollope, M A (Oxon)*, Preb of Hereford, b 15 Nov 1817, d 8 Jan 1893, m 7 Dec 1850, *Anne Mary Theresa, widow of Capt Henry Frederic Alston, 99th Regt, da of John Walsh of Anne Mount, co Kilkenny*, d. 22 Nov 1905, *and had issue 1f to 2f*

1f Helen Lucy Trollope

2f *Catherine Annesley Trollope (Montpelier Grove, Cheltenham)*, m 1902, the Rev *James Albert Owen, d 16 July 1907*

2c Rev *Charles Trollope, Rector of Stibbington, Hon Canon of Ely*, b 4 Feb 1819, d 8 Sept 1907, m 30 Oct 1872, *Eleanor, da of the Rev William Hiley Bathurst of Lydney Park, co Glouc*, *and had issue 1f to 2f* [Nos 77826 to 77849

400

# of The Blood Royal

1/ Rev Charles Henry Bathurst Trollope, M A (Camb), Rector of Escrick (*Escrick Rectory, York*), b 27 Ap 1876

2/ Eleanor Mary Trollope

3e *Frederick Trollope*, Capt Bengal S C, b 20 July 1820, d 11 Sept 1857, m 24 Oct 1844, *Mary Victoria, da of Charles Francis, and had issue 1f to 2f*

1f *George Frederick Trollope*, b 31 July 1845, d 21 June 1871, m 18 June 1870, *Clara Sophia, da of (—) Hudswell, and had issue 1g*

1g Frederick William Trollope, b 11 Feb 1871

2f Charles William Annesley Trollope, a Clerk in the Exchequer and Audit Dept (*Morningside, Marryat Road, Wimbledon*), b 20 Jan 1850, m 23 Aug 1877, Marian Eirene, da of the Rev William Watson, and has issue 1g to 3g

1g George Henry Annesley Trollope, b 12 Dec 1879

2g Leonard Edward Annesley Trollope, b 13 Mar 1892

3g Dorothy Marion Annesley Trollope

3c *Elizabeth Annesley*, bapt 5 Oct 1715, d 21 July 1816, m 20 June 1771, *George Booth Tyndale of Bathford, co Som, d 28 Dec 1779, and had issue*

See the Clarence Volume, pp 538–544, Nos 23152–23354

2b *Catherine Hanbury, da and co-h, b 1711, d 1779, m as 3rd wife, 2 Ap 1737, Velters Cornewall of Moccas Court, co Hereford, M P, d 3 Ap 1768, and had issue 1c*

1c *Catherine Cornewall of Moccas Court, da and h, b 15 Mar 1752, d 17 Mai 1835, m 15 July 1771, Sir George Armyard, afterwards (1771) Cornewall, 2nd Bt [G B], M P, b 8 Nov 1748, d 26 Sept 1819, and had issue 1d to 4d*

1d *Sir George Cornewall, 3rd Bt [G B], b 16 Jan 1774, d 27 Dec 1835, m 26 Sept 1816, Jane, niece of James, 1st Baron Sherborne [G B], da of William Naper of Loughcrew, co Meath, d 13 Feb 1853, and had issue 1e to 4e*

1e *Sir Velters Cornewall, 4th Bt [G B], b 20 Feb 1824, d unm 14 Oct 1868*

2e *Rev Sir George Henry Cornewall, 5th Bt [G B], J P, D L, Rector of Moccas, b 13 Aug 1833, d 25 Sept 1908, m 4 June 1867, Louisa Frances, da of Francis Bayley, Judge of the Westminster County Court, d 2 Feb 1900, and had issue 1f to 3f*

1f Sir Geoffrey Cornewall, 6th Bt [G B], J P., D L, Barrister I T., &c. (*Moccas Court, Hereford*), b 7 May 1869, *unm*

2f William Francis Cornewall, Barrister I T (*1 Hare Court, Temple, E C.*), b 16 Nov 1871

3f Mary Louisa Cornewall

3e *Catherine Elizabeth Cornewall, d 1896, m 7 Ap 1840, Thomas William Chester Master of Knole Park and The Abbey, Cirencester, M P, d 30 Jan. 1899, and had issue*

See the Tudor Roll, p 385, Nos 29174–29190

4e *Henrietta Cornewall, d 25 June 1900, m 29 July 1858, the Rev Augustus Chester Master, d 10 Dec 1887, and had issue*

See the Tudor Roll, p 386, Nos 29199–29303

2d *Frances Elizabeth Cornewall, d 20 Feb 1864, m 12 Dec 1805, Henry (Devereux), 14th Viscount Hereford [E], d 31 May 1843, and had issue*

See the Essex Volume, pp 363–364, Nos 35571–35605

3d *Harriet Cornewall, d 11 Aug 1838, m as 1st wife, 11 Mar 1805, the Right Hon Sir Thomas Frankland Lewis, 1st Bt [U K], P C, M P, b 14 May 1780, d 22 Jan 1855, and had issue 1e to 2e*

1e *Right Hon Sir George Cornewall Lewis, 2nd Bt [U K], P C, M P, the eminent Statesman and Author, b 21 Oct 1806, d s p 13 Ap 1863*

2e *Rev Sir Gilbert Frankland Lewis, 3rd Bt [U K], M A, Canon of Wor-*
[Nos 77850 to 78116

The Plantagenet Roll

cester, b 21 July 1808, d 18 Dec 1883, m 3 Aug 1843, Jane [descended from George, Duke of Clarence, K G (see Clarence Volume, p 217)], da of Sir Edmund Antrobus 2nd Bt [U K] d 20 Oct 1899, and had issue 1f to 3f

1f Sir Herbert Edmund Frankland Lewis, 4th Bt [U K], J P, D L (Harpton Court, near Kington, co Radnor), b 31 Mar 1816, m 4 May 1880, Maria Louisa, widow of Col George Frederick Dallas, K L H [Bt Coll], da of James Arthur Taylor of Strensham Court

2f Mary Anna Lewis

3f Elinor Lewis, m is 2nd wife, 7 Jan 1890, Col Sir St Vincent Alexander Hammick, 3rd Bt [U K] (Little Stodham, Liss, Hants)

1d Caroline Cornewall, d 23 Ap 1875, m 15 Feb 1810, Sir William Duff Gordon, 2nd Bt [U K], d 8 Mar 1823, and had issue

See the Clarence Volume, p 246, Nos 5867–5886   [Nos 78117 to 78139

240 Descendants, if any surviving, of Mary Downing (Table XXIII), d (-); m 28 June 1705, Thomas Barnardiston of Bury and Wyverstone, co Suffolk, and had issue 1a to 3a [1]

1a Thomas Barnardiston, Sergeant-at-Law, b 1706 d unm 1752

2a Mary Barnardiston, m Edward Goate of Brenteleigh, co Suffolk

3a Elizabeth Barnardiston, d after 1771, m 14 Sept 1713, the Right Rev John Ewer, D D, Lord Bishop of Landaff 1761–1768 and Bangor 1768–1774, d 28 Oct 1774, leaving issue 1b

1b Margaret Frances Ewer

241 Descendants of Alathea Howard (Table XXIII), d. 3 Sept 1677, m Thomas (Fairfax), 2nd Viscount Fairfax [I], d 24 Sept 1641, and had issue

See pp 220–221, Nos 35958–36304/100   [Nos 78140 to 78586

242 Descendants of Sir Francis Howard of Corby Castle, co Cumberland (Table XXIII), b 29 Aug 1588, d 11 Ap 1660, m 1st, Margaret, da of John Preston of Furness, co Lancaster, d 7 Sept. 1625, 2ndly, Mary, da of Sir Henry Widdrington of Widdrington, d 22 July 1672, and had issue 1a to 4a

1a [2] Francis Howard of Corby Castle, Gov of Carlisle, b 29 June 1635, d 1702, m 1st, Ann, da of William Gerard of Bryn, d 1679, 2ndly, Mary Ann Dorothy, da of Richard Towneley of Towneley, and had issue (with two elder das by 1st wife, whose issue failed in 1711, and a younger da who d unm) 1b

1b Anne Howard, da and in her issue (if any) sole h , m Marmaduke Langdale of Houghton

2a [2] William Howard of Corby Castle, d 1708, m Jane, da of John Dalston of Acombank, co Westmorland, and had issue 1b to 4b

1b Thomas Howard of Corby Castle, d (-), m 2ndly, 1724, Barbara, da of Philip Musgrave, and had issue

See p 216 (Sec 111), Nos 30187–30304

2b William Howard

3b John Howard   [Nos 78587 to 78704

[1] " Proceedings of the Suffolk Institute of Archæology," iv 155

1b *Elizabeth Howard*, m *William Sanderson of Armathwaite*

3a[1] *Elizabeth Howard*, d (-), m 11 *Nov* 1632, *Edward Standish of Standish, co Lancaster, aged 47, 22 Sept* 1664, d (-) *and had issue* 1b *to* 3b

  1b *William Standish of Standish*, b c 1638, d 8 *June* 1705 m *Cecilia, da and h of Sir Robert Bindlosoe, 1st Bt* [E], d 19 *Jan* 1730, *and had issue* 1c

  1c *Ralph Standish of Standish, forfeited for his share in the* '15, d (-) m *Lady Philippa, da of Henry* (*Howard*), *6th Duke of Norfolk* [E], d 5 *Ap* 1731, *and had issue*

  See the Exeter Volume, p 291, Nos 13756–13799

  2b *Mary Standish*, d (-) m (--) *Daniel of Heton Place, Sudbury, co Suffolk*

  3b *Elizabeth Standish*, d (-), m *as 1st wife* (*cont dated* 18 *Jan*) 1678, *John Witham of Cliffe, co York, and had issue*

  See the Exeter Volume, pp 558–560, Nos 49718–49913

4a[2] *Margaret Howard*, d (-), m *as 1st wife, Sir Thomas Haggerston of Haggerston, 2nd Bt* [E], d c 1710, *and had issue* (9 *sons and a da of whom only one left issue, viz*) 1b

  1b *William Haggerston* d v p (-), m *Anne, da and event h of Sir Philip Constable, 3rd Bt* [E], *and had issue*

  See the Exeter Volume pp 529–530, Nos 48488–18835

[Nos 78705 to 79262

243 Descendants of Sir CHARLES HOWARD (Table XXIII), d (-), m. DOROTHY, da of Sir Henry WIDDRINGTON, and had issue [1]

244. Descendants of THOMAS HOWARD (Table XXIII), d (-), m ELIZABETH, da of Sir William EURE, and had issue (with a son, Thomas, who d unm) 1a to 2a

  1a *Frances Howard*, } one of whom m (—) *Fetherston* [2]
  2a *Mary Howard*, }

245 Descendants, if any, of MARY HOWARD (Table XXIII), d (-), m Sir JOHN WINTOUR of Lydney, co Glouc

246 Descendants of Sir JOHN COTTON, 3rd Bt [E], M P (Table XXIII), b 1621, d 12 Sept 1702, m 1st, DOROTHY, da. and h of Edmund ANDERSON of Stratton and Egworth, co Bedford; 2ndly, 20 Oct 1658, ELIZABETH, da and h of Sir Thomas HONYWOOD, d 3 Ap 1702, and had issue 1a to 4a

  1a[1] *John Cotton, son and h*, b 1650, d v p. 1681, m *Frances, da and in her issue* (6 *Feb* 1761) *co-h of Sir George Downing, 1st Bt* [E], *M P, and had issue*
  See pp 399–402, Nos 77754–78139

  2a[2] *Sir Robert Cotton, 5th Bt* [E], b c 1679, d 12 *July* 1749, m 1st, *Elizabeth, da of* (—) *Wigston, and had issue* 1b   [Nos 79263 to 79618

---

  [1] A son, William, is mentioned in Brydges' "Collins," m 502, and a 4th son is supposed to have been the Henry Howard who settled at Conway in the middle of the seventeenth century, and was ancestor of the Howards of Wygfan, co Denbigh See Burke's "Landed Gentry," 1906, p 863

  [2] Brydges' "Collins," m 502

1*b* Sir John Cotton, 6th Bt [E], d 27 Mar 1752, m Jane, da of Sir Robert Burdett, 3rd Bt [E], d 1769, and had issue 1c to 1c

  1*c* Jane Cotton, m Oct 1741, Thomas Hurt of Warfield, co Berks
  2*c* Elizabeth Cotton
  3*c* Frances Cotton
  1*c* Mary Cotton

  3*a*[1] Dorothy Cotton, d (–), m William Dennis of co Glouc

  4*a*[2] Elizabeth Cotton, d (–), m 1st, Lyonel Walden of Huntingdon, 2ndly, (—) Smith of Westminster, and had issue (with a son who d unm and possibly other children by 2nd husband) 1b to 2b

  1*b* Elizabeth Walden, d (–), m 1st, Charles Pitfield, 2ndly, Talbot Touchet, and had issue (with possibly others by 2nd husband, a son Charles and da Elizabeth, 1st wife of Edward Digland of Long Whatton, co Leic, who both d s p)

  2*b* Hester Walden, d (–), m Humphrey Orme of Peterborough, Capt R N, and had (with possibly other) issue 1c[1]

  1*c* Walden Orme of Peterborough, son and h, d (–), m Sarah, da of Adland Squire Stukeley of Holbeach, co Linc, and had (with possibly other issue) 1d

  1*d* Walden Orme of Peterborough, son and h, d 1809, m (—), da of Robert Tomlin of Edith Weston, co Rutland, and had (with possibly other) issue 1e

  1*e* Humphrey Orme of Peterborough, Capt 11th Light Drag, served at Waterloo

247 Descendants of Sir ARMINE WODEHOUSE, 5th Bt [E], M P. for Norfolk 1737–68 (Table XXIII.), b 1714, d 21 May 1777; m 3 Oct 1738, LETITIA, da. and co-h of Sir Edmund BACON, 6th and Premier Bt [E.], bm. 7 Ap 1758; and had issue 1*a* to 3*a*.

  1*a* John (Wodehouse), 1st Baron Wodehouse [G B], so cr 26 Oct 1797, b 4 Ap 1741, d 29 May 1834, m 30 Mar 1769, Sophia, da and h of the Hon Charles Berkeley of Bruton Abbey, co Som [B Berkeley of Stratton Coll], d 16 Ap 1825, and had issue 1b to 3b

  1*b* John (Wodehouse), 2nd Baron Wodehouse [G B], b 11 Jan 1771, d 29 May 1846, m 17 Nov 1796, Charlotte Laura, da and h of John Norris of Witton Park and Witchingham, co Norfolk, d June 1845, and had issue 1c to 5c

  1*c* Hon Henry Wodehouse, b 19 Mar 1799, d v p 29 Ap 1831, m 7 Ap 1825, Anne, da of Theophilus Thornhaugh Gurdon of Letton, co Norfolk, d 29 Ap 1834, and had issue 1d

  1*d* John (Wodehouse), 3rd Baron Wodehouse [G B] and (1 June 1866) 1st Earl of Kimberley [U K] K G, P C, Lord President of the Council 1892–1894, Secretary of State for India 1882–1885, 1886, and 1892–1894, and for Foreign Affairs 1894–1895, Lord-Lieutenant of Ireland 1864–1866, Ambassador at St Petersburg 1856-1858, &c, a distinguished Statesman, b 7 Jan 1826, d 8 Ap 1902, m 16 Aug 1847, Lady Florence, C I, da and co-h of Richard (FitzGibbon), 3rd Earl of Clare [I], d 4 May 1895, and had issue 1e to 1e

  1*e* John (Wodehouse), 2nd Earl of Kimberley [U K], 4th Baron Wodehouse [G B] and 9th Bt [E], &c (Kimberley House, Wymondham, Norfolk, Witton Park, North Walsham, &c), b 10 Dec 1848, m 22 June 1875, Isabel Geraldine, da of Sir Henry Josias Stracey, 5th Bt [U K], and has issue 1f to 4f.

  1*f* John Wodehouse, Lord Wodehouse, M P (Witton Park, North Walsham), b. 11 Nov 1883

  2*f* Hon Philip Wodehouse, b 1 Oct 1886

  3*f* Hon Edward Wodehouse, b 12 Ap 1898

  4*f* Lady Isabel Wodehouse   [Nos 79649 to 79653.

---

[1] Burke's "Royal Families," i LIX

2e *Hon Armine Wodehouse*, C B , M P , b 24 *Sept* 1860 , d 1 *May* 1901 , m 6 *June* 1889, *Eleanor Mary Caroline* (21 *Sloane Gardens, S W*), *da of Matthew Arnold , and had issue* 1f

1f Roger Wodehouse, b 24 Sept 1890

3e Lady Alice Wodehouse (41 *Charles Street, Berkeley Square, W*), m 14 Aug 1872, Hussey Packe of Prestwold Hall, J P , D L, Chairman Leicester County Council [descended from the Lady Anne, sister of King Edward IV (see Essex Volume Supplement, p 676)], d 8 Oct 1908 , and has issue 1f to 3f

1f Edward Hussey Packe of Prestwold Hall, J P , D L (*Prestwold Hall, Loughborough Caythorpe Hall, Grantham*), b 6 Jan 1878 , m 11 Dec 1899, the Hon Mary Sydney, da of Edward Arthur (Colebrooke), 1st Baron Colebrooke [U K], C V O

2f Florence Marion Packe, m 10 Aug 1905, Capt the Hon Cuthbert James [2nd son of Walter Henry, 2nd Lord Northbourne [U K]] (*Junior United Service , Garrick*), and has issue 1g to 2g

1g Thomas James, b 10 July 1906

2g Olivia Mary James, b 11 Dec 1909

3f Sybil Alice Packe

4e Lady Constance Wodehouse (*Beechey Grange, Parkstone, Dorset*)

2c *Hon Edward Wodehouse, afterwards* (R L 21 *Sept* 1838) *Thornton-Wodehouse, Vice-Adm R N* , b 5 *June* 1802, d 17 *Mar* 1874 , m 10 *Nov* 1838, *Diana, da of Col Thornton of Falconer's Hall, co Yorks*, d 13 *Mar* 1884, *and had issue* 1d *to* 3d

1d Albert Wodehouse, Col R A (ret) (*United Service*), b 5 Feb 1840 , m 1 July 1874, Elizabeth Katherine, da of the Hon George Edgcumbe

2d Cecilia Wodehouse, m 24 July 1879, Baron Ferdinand von Liliencron [Baron Liliencron [H R E 5 June 1673] Coll] (*Florence*)

3d Mary Drina Wodehouse (17 *Montpelier Square, S W*), m 4 Ap 1878, Charles Conway Thornton of the Diplo Service, d 17 May 1902 , and has issue 1e

1e Charles Edward Conway Thornton, b 25 Mar 1879

3c *Hon Berkeley Wodehouse*, C M G , Col E *Norfolk Mil* , H B M 's *Consul at Dunkirk*, b 14 *May* 1806, d 13 *Sept* 1877, m 5 *June* 1837, *Fanny, da of Alexander Holmes of Curragh, co Kildare*, d 2 *Ap* 1871 , *and had issue* 1d *to* 2d

1d Killegrew Reginald Berkeley Wodehouse, Col late 1st Batt Highland L I (*Leyden House, Colchester Wellington &c*), b 9 Sept 1843 , m 22 Feb 1881, Katharine Elizabeth, da of James Marke Wood of Liverpool , and has issue 1e to 3e

1e Reginald Berkeley Wodehouse, b 13 Ap 1886

2e Philip Edward Berkeley Wodehouse, b 20 Nov 1887

3 Laura Mary Katherine Wodehouse

2d Charles Francis Berkeley Wodehouse, a Dist Comm of Cyprus, *formerly Lieut* 77th Regt (*Papho, Cyprus , Llaynbedw, B neat, R S O , South Wales*) b 1 Aug 1855 , m 21 July 1881, Francie, da of Arthur H Sanders Davies of Pentre, co Pemb , and has issue 1e to 4e

1e Clarence John D'Everton Berkeley Wodehouse, Inspector Cyprus Mil Police, Acting A D C to High Comm of Cyprus and Lieut 3rd (Reserve) Batt Norfolk Regt (*Government House, Nicosia , Auxiliary Forces Club, &c*), b 31 May 1882

2e Mary Jessie Gwyn Berkeley Wodehouse

3e Kitty Dagmar Berkeley Wodehouse

4e Armine Frances Berkeley Wodehouse

4c *Rev the Hon Alfred Wodehouse*, b 10 *June* 1814, d 6 *Sept* 1848, m 21 *Ap* 1840, *Emma Hamilla, da of Reginald George Macdonald of Clanranald, M P* [*by his wife Lady Caroline, nee Edgcumbe, des ended from the Lady Anne, sister of King Edward IV* (see the Exeter Volume, p 664)], d 5 *Ap* 1852, *and had issue* (*with a da , Mrs Wyndham,* d s p) 1d *to* 4d   [Nos 79654 to 79674

The Plantagenet Roll

1d Hobart Wodehouse, b 23 Ap 1842

2d Henry Wodehouse b 2 Jan 1849

3d Hamilla Caroline Wodehouse b Jan 1841, d 1879 m 8 Nov 1876, Edward Taylor H B M 's Vice-Consul at Dunkirk, d (-), and had issue 1e to 2e

1e Laura Taylor, m (—) Lawford of Shanghai

2e Mary Taylor, m (—) Hornby

4d Ernestine Emma Wodehouse (The Island, Derwentwater, Keswick), m 17 May 1866, John Marshall, d 1894, and has issue (3 sons)

5c Hon Laura Sophia Wodehouse, b 13 Jan 1801, d 17 Feb 1869, m 28 June 1825, Raikes Currie of Bush Hall, co Midx, and Minley Manor, co Hants, M P , J P , D L , b 15 Ap 1801, d 16 Oct 1881, and had issue (with 2 sons and 2 das who d s p) 1d to 2d

1d Bertram Wodehouse Currie of Minley Manor, J P , High Sheriff for London 1892, b 23 Nov 1827, d 29 Dec 1896, m 30 Oct 1860, Caroline, da of Sir William Lawrence Young, 4th Bt [G B], M P, d 16 Ap 1902, and had issue 1e

1e Laurence Currie of Minley and Coombe Warren, J P (Minley Manor, Farnboro , Coombe Warren, Kingston-on-Thames, 1 Richmond Terrace, Whitehall S W), b 7 Nov 1867, m 23 Feb 1895, Edith Sibyl Mary [descended from King Henry VII (see Tudor Roll, p 522)], da of the Right Hon George Henry Finch, P C , M P , and has issue 1f to 3f

1f Bertram Francis George Currie, b 18 June 1899

2f Edith Catherine Currie

3f Daphne Mary Currie

2d Philip Henry Wodehouse (Currie), 1st Baron Currie [U K], so cr 25 Jan 1899, P C , G C B H B M 's Ambassador at Rome, 1898-1903, &c , b 13 Oct 1831, d s p 13 May 1906

2b Hon Philip Wodehouse, Vice-Adm of the White, b 16 July 1773, d 21 Jan 1838, m 7 May 1814, Mary Hay [descended from the Lady Anne, sister of King Edward IV] da of Charles Cameron, d 1 Oct 1854, and had issue

See the Essex Volume, pp 664 665, Nos 57522/1-9

3b Rev the Hon William Wodehouse, M A , b 4 Aug 1782, d 3 Ap 1870, m 11 Feb 1807, Mary, da of Thomas Hussey of Galtrim, co Meath [by his wife, Lady Mary, née Walpole, descended from the Lady Isabel Plantagenet (see Essex Volume, p 190)], d 29 Nov 1865, and had issue 1c to 3c

1c George Wodehouse, Vice-Adm R N , b 8 July 1810, d 15 Feb 1900, m 20 July 1848, Eleanor Charlotte, da of Andrew Mortimer Drummond [E of Perth Coll] by his wife, Lady Emily, née Percy [a descendant of King Henry VII (see Tudor Roll, p 194)], d 27 Mar 1888, and had issue 1d to 2d

1d Sir Josceline Heneage Wodehouse, K C B , C M G , Lieut -Gen R A , Comdg N Army India 1908, formerly Gov and Com -in-Chief of Bermuda, a Major-Gen in the Egyptian Army and Gov of Egyptian Frontier Provinces 1889-1893, &c , &c (Minies, Punjab), b 17 July 1852, m 1st, 1 Oct 1885, Constance, da of Sir Charles D'Aguilar, K C B , d s p 21 Aug 1886, 2ndly, 15 May 1901, Mary Joyce, da of Robert Sicheverell Wilmot Sitwell of Stainsby House, co Derby, and has issue 1e

1e Armine George Wodehouse, b 25 May 1904

2d Evelyn Georgiana Susan Wodehouse (10 Palace Mansions, Addison Bridge, Kensington, W)

2c Arthur Wodehouse of Saltville, Toronto, b 17 Jan 1813, d Feb 1893

3c Rev Algernon Wodehouse, M A b 13 May 1814, d 2 May 1882, m 26 Nov 1844, Lady Eleanor da of George (Ashburnham), 3rd Earl of Ashburnham [G B], K G d 6 Mar 1895, and had issue

See the Tudor Roll, p 193, Nos 21169-21176

2a Rev. the Hon Philip Wodehouse, M A , Preb of Norwich, b 1 May 1745,
[Nos 79675 to 79703

406

d 14 Feb 1811 m 29 July 1775, Apollonia, da and co h of John Nourse of Woodeaton, co Oxon, d 21 Mar 1817 and had issue 1b to 4b

1b Philip Wodehouse, Col in the Army, b 6 Aug 1788, d 15 Dec 1846, m 13 June 1832, Lydia, da of Joseph Lea, d 8 May 1892, and had issue 1c to 8c

1c Rev Philip John Wodehouse, M A (8th Wrangler 1859, and Fellow Caius Coll) (Camb), Preb of Exeter and Rector of Bratton Fleming (Bratton Fleming Rectory, N Devon), b 6 Oct 1836, m 1st, 29 Jan 1876, Constance Helen, da of Wade Browne of Monkton Farleigh, d s p 23 Feb 1877 2ndly, 25 Sept 1879, Marion Bryan, da of the Rev Gilbert J Wallas of Shobrooke, and has issue 1d to 4d

    1d Philip George Wodehouse, Lieut R N, b 26 Nov 1883

    2d Charles Gilbert Wodehouse, b 28 Dec 1885

    3d Helen Marian Wodehouse

    4d Christine Lucy Wodehouse

2c Charles Wodehouse, C I E, Col I S C, b 8 May 1838, d 18 Aug 1893, m 3 Dec 1862, Jemima, da of George Forbes, d 11 Aug 1886, and had issue 1d to 3d

    1d Frederick William Wodehouse, Major Indian Army, now attached to Bombay Political Dept, has Chin-Lushai (1889-1890) and Delhi Durbar Medals (The Residency, Kolhapur), b 7 Ap 1867, m 5 Ap 1893, May Helen, da of George Nugent Lambert, Sup Engineer, Sind, and has issue 1e to 3e

        1e Constance Mary Wodehouse

        2e Kathleen Doris Letitia Wodehouse

        3e Sybil Margaret Wodehouse

    2d Ernest Charles Forbes Wodehouse, D S O, Major Worcestershire Regt, served in S Africa 1900-1902, has Queen's Medal with 3 clasps and King's Medal with 2 clasps (United Service), b 5 Aug 1871, m 18 Ap 1906, Amy Violet, da of Swinton Isaac of Boughton Park, co Worc

    3d Amabel Lucy Wodehouse (42 Courtfield Gardens, W), m as 2nd wife, 13 Ap 1898, Gen John Augustus Fuller, C I E, R E

3c Rev Frederick Armine Wodehouse, B A (Camb), Rector of Gotham and Vicar of Ratcliff-on-Soar (Gotham Rectory, near Derby), b 1 July 1842, m 7 Sept 1880, Alice Elizabeth Juliana [descended from King Henry VII (see Tudor Roll, p 300)], da of Rev the Hon Atherton Legh Powys [B Lilford Coll], and has issue 1d to 4d

    1d Arthur Powys Wodehouse, Lieut Indian Army, b 2 June 1881

    2d Frederic Armine Wodehouse, b 23 June 1884

    3d Norman Atherton Wodehouse, Lieut R N, b 18 May 1887

    4d Mabel Evelyn Wodehouse

4c Henry Ernest Wodehouse, C M G, formerly Hong-Kong C S and a Member of Executive Council, and Pol Magistrate there (1 Royal Crescent Cheltenham), b 14 July 1845, m 3 Feb 1877, Eleanor, da of the Rev J Bathurst Deane, M A, and has issue 1d to 4d

    1d Philip Peveril John Wodehouse Assist Sup of Police, Hong-Kong b 26 Sept 1877

    2d Ernest Armine Wodehouse, Prof Eng Lit Elphinstone College, Bombay, b 11 May 1879

    3d Pelham Grenville Wodehouse, Author and Journalist, b 15 Oct 1881

    4d Richard Launcelot Deane Wodehouse, b 30 May 1892

5c Albert Philip Wodehouse, Col late Royal Inniskilling Fusiliers b 9 Nov 1846, m 1881, Amy, da of Henry Villiers

6c Lydia Josephine Wodehouse

7c Lucy Apollonia Wodehouse, m 18 June 1867, the Rev Edward Whitmore Isaac (Hanley Castle Vicarage, Worcester) and has issue 1d to 3d

[Nos 79704 to 79727

The Plantagenet Roll

1d Edward Swinton Wodehouse Isaac, b 1871

2d Gwendoline Lucy Isaac

3d Gertrude Harriet Isaac

4d Mary Charlotte Lydia Isaac

8c Harriet Elizabeth Wodehouse (*Burfield Christchurch, New Zealand*), m 25 July 1861, the Rev Henry Bromley Cocks, Vicar of Sydenham, NZ [B Somers Coll], d 1894 and has issue 1d to 10d

1d Reginald Wodehouse Cocks, b 31 Aug 1863 m 1883 Mary Myra, da of (—) Thompson of Alabama, USA

2d *Henry Somers Cocks* b 16 *June* 1865, d (? s p) 1897

3d Rev Philip John Cocks, Vicar of Sydenham, NZ (*Sydenham Vicarage, Canterbury, NZ*), b 31 Oct 1866 m 20 June 1895, Mary, da of John Gebbie, and has issue 1e to 5e

1e Henry Bromley Cocks b 15 Ap 1896

2e John Reginald Cocks, b 19 May 1898

3 Edgar Basil Cocks, b 22 June 1899

4e Hubert Maurice Cocks, b 6 Aug 1901

5e Edith May Somers Cocks, b 2 Dec 1905

4d Frederick Armine Cocks (*Latt Street Spreydon, Christchurch*), b 27 Jan 1871 m 1899 Mary Louisa, da of Capt Parsons of Rangoria, NZ, and has issue 1e to 4e

1e Douglas Edgar West Cocks, b 1899

2e Armine Christopher Somers Cocks, b 1903

3e Charles John Somers Cocks, b Ap 1904

4e Patrick Somers Cocks, b Sept 1905

5d Charles Richard Cocks, b 31 Dec 1877

6d Arthur Eustace Cocks, b 23 Dec 1882

7d Frances Mercy Cocks, m 1894, Walter Septimus Fisher, Official Assig NZ (*Forbury Road, Cave, Dunedin, NZ*), and has issue 1e to 2e

1e Harriet Mercy Fisher

2e Margaret Agatha Fisher

8d Harriet Lydia Muriel Cocks

9d Katharine Agatha Cocks

10d Monica Cocks

2b *Ven Charles Nourse Wodehouse, Archdeacon of Norwich*, b 8 Sept 1790, d Mar 1870, m 19 Dec 1821, *Lady Dulcibella Jane, da of William (Hay), 17th Earl of Erroll [S], d 10 Jan 1885, and had issue*

See the Exeter Volume, pp 682–684, Nos 57387–57428

3b *Letitia Wodehouse, d 1861, m 9 June 1801, George Boulton Mainwaring*

4b *Lucy Wodehouse, d 21 June 1829, m 26 June 1809, Edmund Wodehouse of Sennow Lodge, MP* (see p 409), d 21 Aug 1855, and had issue (with 6 other sons and 2 das who d s p) 1c

1c Sir Philip Edmund Wodehouse, K C B, G C S I, *Governor of the Cape of Good Hop*, 1861–1871, &c, &c, b 26 Feb 1811, d 25 Oct 1887, m 19 Dec 1833, *Katherine Mary da of Francis James Templer, Treasurer of Ceylon, d 6 Oct 1866, and had issue 1d*

1d Right Hon Edmond Robert Wodehouse, P C, M A (Oxon), Bar-at-Law, M P for Bath 1880–1906, &c (56 *Chester Squar., S W , Minley Grange, Farnborough*), b 3 June 1835, m 1 June 1876, Adela Harriett Sophia [descended from King Henry VII (see Tudor Roll, p 369)], da of the Rev Charles Walter Bagot [B Bagot Coll]

3a *Hon Thomas Wodehouse of Sennow, co Norfolk, Bar-at-Law,* b Feb
[Nos 79728 to 79795

408

1747, d c 1803, m 12 *Sept* 1782, *Sarah sister of John, 1st Baron Cawdor* [*G B*], *da of Pryce Campbell of Sta kpole Court, co Pemb*, d (-), *and had issue* 1b to 4b

1b *Edmond Wodehouse of Sennow, M P F Norfolk,* b 26 *June* 1784, d 21 *Aug* 1855, m 26 *June* 1809, *Lucy, da of the Rev Philip Wodehouse,* d 21 *June* 1829, *and had issue*

See p 408, No 79795

2b *Rev Thomas Wodehouse, Can n of Wells an l Rector of Norton, Kent,* b 13 *Oct* 1788, d 22 *Mar* 1840, m 3 *June* 18—, *Anne, da of the Right Rev Walker King, D D, Lord Bishop of Rochester,* d 6 *Mar* 1851, *and had issue* 1c to 5c

1c *Francis Arthur Wodehouse* b 18 June 1831, m 1879, Frances (see below), da of the Rev Nathaniel Wodehouse d s p 30 Dec 1891

2c *Edmond Henry Wodehouse, C B, M A (Oxon), Bar at Law and sometime* a Commr of Inland Revenue (*Oxford and Cambridge*), b 17 Feb 1837, m 26 May 1864, Louisa Clara (see below), da of the Rev Nathaniel Wodehouse

3c *Sarah Frances Wodehouse,* m 15 May 1850, William Spencer Dawson of Cobham, co Kent

4c Anne Wodehouse, m 13 Ap 1852, the Rev James Culeton King

5c *Agnes Wodehouse,* d (-), m 11 *Feb* 1865, *George Sardes Williams, Ceylon C S* , and has issue 1d

1d John Wodehouse Williams

3b *Rev Nathaniel Wodehouse, Vicar of Dulverton,* b 2 *Nov* 1802, d 23 *Oct* 1870, m 27 *Sept* 1829, *Georgiana [descended from the Lady Ann, sister of King Edward IV], da of Rev the Hon William Capell,* d 1892 *and had issue*

See the Exeter Volume, pp 378-379, Nos 26853-26874

1b *Susan Wodehouse,* d 2 *Nov* 1834, m 13 *June* 1822, *Thomas John Dashwood, Senior Merchant on the Bengal Establishment [Bt of Kirtlington Coll],* d 17 *June* 1836, *and had issue* 1c to 3c

1c *Thomas Alexander Dashwood, J P, B A (Oxon) Bar-at-Law,* b 22 *Feb* 1826, d 9 *Jan* 1909, m 3 *Oct* 1866, *Charlotte Eliza (Everton House, Shanklin, I W), da of the Rev Charles Knyvett, and had issue* 1d to 6d

1d *Thomas Henry Knyvett Dashwood* b 3 Jan 1876, m 5 Ap 1910, Florence Kathleen, da of J F Hugh Smith, F R C S

2d Mary Susan Dashwood, m 19 Jan 1892, Arthur Geoffry Robins, d (-), and has issue 1e to 4e

1e Henry Duryll Geoffry Dashwood Robins, b 1892

2e Arthur Prichard Townsend Robins, b 1902

3e Audrey Maud Mary Robins

1e Stella Rose Robins

3d Maud Dashwood

4d Florence Dashwood

5d Rose Dashwood

6d Alice Katherine Dashwood

2c Ellen Catherine Dashwood $\Big\}$ (*Sonning, Reading*)
3c Louisa Blanch Dashwood

[Nos 79796 to 79835

248 Descendants of SOPHIA WODEHOUSE (Table XXIII) d. Ap 1738, m 2ndly, as 2nd wife, 7 July 1730, Sir CHARLES MORDAUNT, 6th Bt [E 1611], d 11 Mar 1778, and had issue 1a to 2a

1a *Sir John Mordaunt, 7th Bt [E], M P, LL D,* b c 1735, d 18 *Nov* 1806, m 3 *Jan* 1769, *Elizabeth, da and co-h of Thomas Prowse of Axbridge, co Somerset,* d. 5 Oct 1826, *and had issue* 1b to 8b

1b *Sir Charles Mordaunt, 8th Bt* [E], *M P*, b c 1771, d 30 May 1823, m 1807, *Marianne, da of William Holbech of Farnborough, co Warwick, d 1842, and had issue* 1c *to* 2c

1c *Sir John Mordaunt, 9th Bt* [E], b 21 Aug 1808, d 27 Sept 1845, m 7 Aug 1834, Caroline Sophia [*descended from King Henry VII, da of the Right Rev George Murray D D , Lord Bishop of Rochester*], *and had issue*

See the Tudor Roll, pp 449-450, Nos 31677-31702

2c *Mary Mordaunt*, d 11 June 1851, m *as 1st wife*, 14 Mar 1841, *the Right Hon Sir Thomas Dyke Acland, 11th Bt* [E], P C , *M P , D C L* , d 29 May 1898 *and had issue* 1d *to* 7d

1d Sir (Charles) Thomas Dyke Acland, 12th Baronet [E], J P , D L , M A (Oxon), M P for E Cornwall 1882-1885 and for N E Cornwall 1885-1892, Parl Sec to the Board of Trade and Church Estate Commr 1886, &c (*Killerton, Exeter, Holnicote, Taunton*), b 16 July 1842 , m 1 Nov 1879, Gertrude, sister to William, 1st Lord Waleran [U K], P C , da of Sir John Walrond Walrond, 1st Bt [U K]

2d Right Hon Arthur Herbert Dyke Acland, P C, Hon Fellow of Balliol Coll , Oxon , Vice-President of the Committee of Council on Education 1892-1895, M P for Rotheram 1885-1892, offered but declined a Peerage 1908, &c, &c (*Dunkerry House, Felixstowe*, 29 *St James' Court, Buckingham Gate, S W*), b 13 Oct 1847 , m 14 June 1873, Alice Sophia, da of the Rev Francis Macaulay Cunningham, M A , Rector of Brightwell, and has issue 1e to 2e

1e Francis Dyke Acland, M P , Financial Sec to War Dept , and a Member of the Army Council, &c (*Colby Hall, Askrigg, Yorks* , 118 *Grosvenor Road, S W*), b 7 Mar 1874 , m 31 Aug 1905, Eleanor Margaret, da of Charles James Cropper of Ellergreen, co Westmorland [by his wife the Hon Edith Emily, née Holland]

2e Mabel Alice Acland

3d Mary Lydia Acland, m 30 Oct 1872, the Rev Richard Hart Hart-Davis, *formerly Vicar of All Saints, Dunsden* (*The Ridgefield, Caversham, Reading*), and has issue 1e to 8e

1e Hugh Vaughan Hart-Davis (twin), b 25 July 1883

2e Katherine Lucy Hart-Davis

3e Mary Hart-Davis

4e Dorothy Hart-Davis.

5e Agnes Cecily Hart-Davis

6e Stella Frances Hart-Davis

7e Helen Verena Hart-Davis (twin)

8e Sylvia Charity Hart-Davis

4d Agnes Henrietta Acland, m 11 Aug 1885, Frederick Henry Anson [*descended from the Lady Anne, sister of King Edward IV (see Exeter Volume, p 91), and also through Mortimer-Percy*] (72 *St George's Square, S W*), and has issue 1e to 2e

1e Mary Acland Anson

2e Frances Gertrude Anson

2b *Rev John Mordaunt, Rector of Wickham, co Bucks*, d 1806

3b *Elizabeth Mordaunt*

4b *Sophia Mordaunt*

5b *Mary Mordaunt*, d 17 July 1821 , m 1802, *John Erskine, Comptroller of Army Accounts* [*younger brother of James, 2nd Earl of Rosslyn* [U K]], d 10 Feb 1817 , *and had issue (a da , Lady Acland, who d s p 14 May 1892*)

6b *Catherine Mordaunt* d 7 May 1852, m 26 Oct 1811, *the Rev Francis Mills of Pillerton, M A* (Oxon), *Rector of Barford, co Warwick* [*younger brother of William Mills of Bisterne, M P*], b 29 June 1759 , d 23 Ap 1851 , *and had issue*

See p 146, Nos 16540-16555

7b *Charlotte Mordaunt*, d May 1848, m 15 Ap 1800, *Richard Hippisley Tuckfield of Fulford, co Devon*   [Nos 79886 to 79893

# of The Blood Royal

8b *Susan Mordaunt*, d s p 5 Feb 1830, m *as 4th wife*, 30 Aug 1814 *William (Eliot), 2nd Earl of St Germans [U K]*, d 19 Jan 1845

2a *Rev Charles Mordaunt, Rector of Massingham*, d 22 Jan 1820, m 1774, *Charlotte, da of Sir Philip Musgrave, 6th Bt [E]*, and had issue

See p 200, Nos 29642-29651   [Nos 79894 to 79903

249 Descendants of ARMINE L'ESTRANGE of Hunstanton, co Norfolk, da and event co-h of Sir Nicholas L'ESTRANGE, otherwise LE STRANGE, 4th Bt [E], M P, a co-h to the Baronies of Hastings and Camois [E 1383] (Table XXIII), d 29 May 1768, m NICHOLAS STYLEMAN of Snettisham, co Norfolk, d 6 Jan. 1746, and had issue 1a to 2a

1a *Nicholas Styleman of Hunstanton and Snettisham D L*, d s p 9 Jan 1788
2a *Rev Armine Styleman M A , (Camb), Rector of Ringstead*, d 3 Ap 1803, m *Anne, da of Capt James Blakeway, R N* , and had issue 1b to 1b

1b *Henry Styleman of Hunstanton, &c , High Sheriff co Norfolk* 1801, d 25 Mar 1819 m 2ndly 5 Dec 1809, *Emilia, da of Benjamin Preedy of St Albans*, d 20 Feb 1873, and had issue 1c to 3c

1c *Henry L'Estrange Styleman, afterwards (R L 23 July 1839) Styleman-le Strange of Hunstanton, J P , D L , Capt 1st W Norfolk Militia*, b 25 Jan 1815, d 27 July 1862, m 25 July 1839, *Jamesina Joyce Ellen, da and event co-h of John Stewart of Belladrum, co Inverness M P [who m 2ndly, 7 Sept 1863, Charles Wynne Finch of Voelas and]*, d 6 July 1892, and had issue (with a son and da who d s p) 1d to 4d

1d Hamon Styleman-le Strange, now (D P 1 May 1874) le Strange of Hunstanton, M A F S A , J P , D L , C A , a Chairman of the Norfolk Quarter Sessions and High Sheriff for that co 1880, *formerly Sec Diplo Ser (Hunstanton Hall, Norfolk , 1 Eaton Place, S W)*, b 25 Nov 1840, m at Boston, 20 Dec 1866, Emmeline, da of William Austin of Boston, Mass, U S A , and has issue 1e to 6e

1e Roland le Strange, J P , D L , Lieut P W O Norfolk Art (*Hunstanton Hall, Norfolk*), b 5 Mar 1869, m 22 Oct 1891, the Hon Agneta Frances Delaval (see p 122), da of Delaval Loftus (Astley), 10th Baron Hastings [E], and has issue 1f to 2f

1f Charles Alfred le Strange, for whom H R H Alfred, Duke of Saxe Coburg-Gotha (Duke of Edinburgh), was Sponsor, b 9 Dec 1892

2f Bernard le Strange, b 23 Aug 1900

2e Rev Austin le Strange, M A (Oxon), Rector of Great Ringstead (*Ringstead Rectory, Kings Lynn*), b 22 May 1874, m 16 Ap 1903, Katharine Ellen Grey, da of Rev the Hon Hugh Wynne Lloyd Mostyn [B Mostyn Coll], and has issue 1f to 3f

1f Hamon le Strange, b 5 June 1904
2f Viola le Strange, b 30 Sept 1905
3f Dorothy le Strange, b 1 Nov 1907

3e Eric le Strange (*Eaton, Sedgeford, King's Lynn*), b 20 Jan 1878, m 17 Oct 1906, Nita Florence, da of Francis Frederick Gordon [M of Huntly Coll] and has issue 1f

1f Gordon le Strange, b 4 Oct 1907

4e Emmeline le Strange, m 22 Jan 1898, Capt Charles Harcourt Gam Wood, *late 15th Hussars (Caerberis Builth, S Wales)*, and has issue 1f to 3f

1f Eric Harcourt Wood
2f David Sam Wood
3f Beris Harcourt Wood.

5e Maud le Strange, }
6e Sybil le Strange, } twins   [Nos 79904 to 79919

411

The Plantagenet Roll

2d Guy Styleman le Strange now (D P 1875) le Strange (*Athenæum*), *b* 21 July 1851, *m* 4 Aug 1887, W.... Irene, da of William Cornwallis Cartwright Aynhoe, M P, *d s p* 3 Feb 1907

3d Jamesina Styleman le Strange (*Hunstanton, Norfolk*), *m* 19 July 1866, the Rev Adolphus Waller, M A [younger son of Sir Thomas Wathen Waller, 2nd Bt [U K] (see p 536)], *d* 16 July 1890, and has issue 1e

1e Rev Wathen Henry Waller, M A (Camb), Town Chaplain, St Mary's, Mandalay, *formerly* R N Iess Egyptian (1882) Medal with Bronze Star (*Civil Lines, Mandalay Burma*), *b* 4 June 1867, *unm*

1d Ida Styleman-Le Strange, *b* 17 Sept 1848, *d* 28 Sept 1873, *m* as 1st aif., 9 June 1870 Edward Heneage Wynne Finch of Stokesley, J P (*Stokesley, co Yorks*), *and had issue* 1e

1e Heneage Wynne-Finch, B A (Oxon), *b* 30 Ap 1871

2c *Emiha L'Estrange Styleman,* *d* 5 Ap 1901, *m* 29 May 1834, *the Rev Fredrick Thomas William Coke Fitzroy, M A [B Southampton Coll], d* 20 Feb 1862 *and had issue*

See the Clarence Volume, pp 315-346, Nos 11286-11289

3c *Armine L'Estrange Styleman* *b* 3 Oct 1819, *m* 28 July 1840, *Capt William Charles James Campbell, 3rd Dragoon Guards, 3rd son of Col William Campbell of Lasty Island, Harris d at Hastings,* 18 Ap 1880, *and had issue* (*with a son d young*) 1d *to* 3d

1d *Rev William Fraser Campbell, Rector of Kintbury, co Berks b* 11 Jan 1843 *d* 29 Jan 1886, *m* 9 Sept 1869 *Georgina Jane, da of Lionel Oliver of Heacham, co Norfolk and had issue (with a da d young)* 1e *to* 5e

1e James Fraser Campbell (*Penticton, British Columbia*), *b* 30 Nov 1870, *m* 23 Nov 1909, Dora Whates, da of Arthur Brown of Norwich

2e William McLeod Campbell, Suffolk Regt , *b* 30 May 1879

3e Donald Fraser Campbell, *b* 21 Dec 1881

4e Armine le Strange Campbell, } *unm*
5e Katharine Grant Campbell, }

2d Archibald Campbell (*The Limes Shrewsbury*), *b* 21 July 1853 , *m* 28 July 1904, Katharine, da of Samuel Poultney Smith

3d Flora Campbell, *m* 30 Ap 1873, John Windsor Stuart, Col Argyle and Bute Vol Art [M of Bute Coll , and a descendant of the Lady Anne, sister of Kings Edward IV and Richard III (see the Exeter Volume, p 295)], and has issue 1e to 3e

1e Henry Campbell Stuart (*West Glen, Fyles of Bute*), *b* 2 Mar 1874 , *m* 20 Ap 1904, Laleen Barbara, da of Major H G Fenton-Newall, and has issue 1f to 3f

1f Mary Barbara Stuart, *b* 13 Jan 1905

2f Margaret Windsor Stuart, *b* 15 Oct 1908

3f Flora Emily Windsor Stuart, *b* 26 Feb 1910

2e John Dudley Stuart (*Pontcanna House, Cardiff*), *b* 1 Sept 1875 , *m* 30 Ap 1902 Florence Emily, da of Charles Hunter, Ch Eng Bute Docks, Cardiff

3e Elizabeth Ada Mary Stuart, *m* 20 Oct 1908, Francis Gerald Cradock-Hartopp [Bt Coll] (*Edensor Bakewell*), and has issue 1f

1f Gwendolen Mary Cradock-Hartopp, *b* 29 Dec 1909

2b *Catherine Styleman,* *b* c 1759, *d* 29 Ap 1823, *m* 1st, the Rev Edward Rogers North Vicar of Harlow, co Essex, and Rector of Ringstead, co Norfolk, d (s p), 2ndly as 2nd wife, 4 Aug 1808, Sir Mordaunt Martin, 4th Bt [E], d (s p by her) 24 Sept 1815

3b *Anne Styleman* *b* at Ringstead 20 Dec 1760, *d* 20 Oct 1823, *m* 1st, as 2nd wife, 16 May 1789, Tomkyns Dew of Lincoln's Inn Fields and of Portland

[Nos 79920 to 79941

412

Place, London, and of Whitney Court, co Hereford, Lord of the Manors of Clifford and Whitney and High Sheriff co Hereford, b 1720, bur at Marylebone 6 Nov 1799, 2ndly, 29 Mar 1806, Lieut.-Col Thomas Powell, 11th Regt, d 20 Mar 1856, and had issue 1c to 3c

1c Tomkyns Dew of Whitney Court, High Sheriff co Hereford, b 9 July 1791, d 1 Feb 1853, m 29 Ap 1813, Margaret Beatrice, da of the Rev Timothy Napleton, Rector of Powderham, d 11 July 1877, and had issue (with 3 sons and 1 das who d s.p) 1d to 7d

1d Tomkyns Dew of Whitney Court, J P, D L, High Sheriff co Hereford 1868, Bar.-at-Law I T, &c, b 10 Sept 1816, d 26 Jan 1891, m 13 May 1879, Ada Isabella, da of Capt Edward Ruiston Read, 9th Lancers (who m 2ndly, 1 Feb 1892, Charles Joseph Brown), and had issue 1e

1e Rosamond Clifford Dew, b 11 Sept 1887

2d Rev Henry Dew, B A (Camb), J P, Rector of Whitney, b 18 Mar 1819, d 16 Nov 1901, m 16 Sept 1845, Mary Elizabeth, da of Thomas Monkhouse of London, d 30 Jan 1900, and had issue 1e to 10e

1e Henry Monkhouse Dew (1 Wilbury Villas, Nelson Street, Hereford), b 14 Jan. 1850, m 1st, 3 Nov 1881, Minnie Phœbe, widow of Arthur Stenning, da of (—) Jackson of Whittlesea, co Camb, d s p 14 May 1899, 2ndly, 5 Feb 1902, Lena Mary Meta, da of Rev T J Bewsher, Rector of Cley-next-the-Sea, s p

2e Arthur Tomkyns Dew, formerly R M for Matang, Perak (Monkerton Manor, Pinhoe, Devon), b 5 Mar 1853, m at the English Church, Taiping, Straits Settlements, 31 Dec 1891, Lucy Elizabeth (see p 417), da of the Rev Charles Amphlett of Four Ashes Hall, Bridgnorth, co Salop, s p

3e Rev Edward Napleton Dew, M A, B D (Oxon), Vicar of St Michael and All Angels, Gallywood (Gallywood Vicarage, Chelmsford), b 30 Mar 1859, m 3 Jan 1888, Caroline, da of Lieut.-Gen Edward William Boudier, Madras S C, and has issue 1f

1f Harry Edward le Strange Dew, b 27 Ap 1889

4e Walter Frederick Dew, Tea Planter (Ceylon), b 3 Jan 1863 4, m 1st, 28 Feb 1895, Ethel Grace, da of the Rev Charles Down, d 31 May 1898, 2ndly, 2 Oct 1907, Nancy, da of the Rev Edward Smith, and has issue 1f

1f Sylvia Grace Alice Temple Dew, b 6 Nov 1896

5e Emily Mary Dew, b 2 Sept 1846, unm

6e Jane Beatrice Dew, b 30 Ap 1848, unm

7e Armine Dew, b 12 Sept 1854, m 30 June 1874, Col George William Furlonge (see p 417), late 21st Royal Scots (formerly North British) Fusiliers (Seaton, Devonshire), and has issue 1f to 2f

1f George Henry Stuart Furlonge, P & O Coy Service, Lieut R N R, served in China 1900 (Medal), b 29 Mar 1875

2f Charles le Strange Furlonge, C E, Lieut R N R, served throughout South African War (2 Medals and Clasps), b 7 Oct 1878

8e Helen Frances Dew, unm

9e Alice Horrocks Dew, unm

10e Louisa Margaret Dew, m 1st, 28 Feb 1889, Edward Ayton Safford of London, Solicitor, 2ndly, (—), s p

3d Frederick Napleton Dew, Major 88th Connaught Rangers, served in Crimea 1855-1856 and Indian Mutiny 1857-1858, Medals and Clasps, J P, D L, co Hereford, b 29 Mar 1836, d Aug 1908, m 24 Ap 1861, Henrietta Lucy, da of the Rev Charles David Brereton of Little Massingham, and had issue 1e to 7e

1e Armine Brereton Dew, Major I S C, Political Agent at Gilgit, Kashmir, served in Black Mountain Expedition 1891 (Medal with Clasp), b 27 Sept 1867, m 15 Sept 1900, Esmé Mary Dorothea [descended from the Lady Anne, sister of Edward I V (see Exeter Volume, p 221)], da of Sir Adalbert Talbot, and has issue 1f

1f Armine Roderick Dew, b 20 Mar 1906   [Nos 79942 to 79958

The Plantagenet Roll

2c. Rev Roderick Dew, M A (Oxon), Rector of Kilkhampton (*Kilkhampton Rectory, Cornwall*), b 21 Oct 1872, m 26 Sept 1905, Gladys Mary, da of Col Gerveys Richard Grylls, and has issue 1f to 3f

1f Gerveys Roderick Dew, b 20 Dec 1909

2f Mary Lucy Agnes Dew, b 5 Oct 1906

3f Frances Evelyn Margaret Mary Dew, b 2 Feb 1908

3c Gertrude Frances Dew, b at Futtyghur, N W P (*28 Bramham Gardens, S W*), m Arthur Clegg Stratten, d s p 18 June 1907

4c Isabel Mary Dew, m 6 Feb 1890, John Cockburn (*The Abbey, North Berwick*), and has issue 1f to 3f

1f Archibald Frederick Cockburn, b 21 Nov 1890

2f Isabel Stella Cockburn, b 15 Jan 1892

3f Laelia Armine Cockburn, b 23 Mar 1894

5c Annette Beatrice Dew, m 5 Ap 1899, Moncrieff Cockburn (*2 Ashburn Gardens, S W*), and has issue 1f to 3f

1f Archibald Moncrieff Cockburn, b 3 May 1900

2f Frederick Armine Cockburn, b 19 June 1902

3f Elizabeth Lucy Mary Cockburn, b 11 June 1908

6c Alice Henrietta Dew, m 23 Jan 1908, Col Richard Prescott Decie (*Pontrilas Court, Hereford*), s p

7c Margaret Louise Dew, m 18 Nov 1902, Capt Philip James Stopford, R N [E of Courtown Coll], s p

4d Elizabeth Sophia Dew, b 17 *Jan* 1815, d 8 *Oct* 1898, m 23 *Aug* 1841, Arthur Pryor of Hylands, co Essex, J P, D L, and High Sheriff for that co 1866, b 7 *Jan* 1816, d 25 Sept 1901, and had issue (with a da d s p) 1e to 8e

1e Arthur Vickris Pryor of Hylands, co Essex, J P, D L, B A (Oxon) (*Egerton Lodge, Melton Mowbray, Carlton, Travellers', &c*), b 3 Aug 1846, m 11 Sept 1886, Elizabeth Charlotte Louisa, Dow-Countess of Wilton [U K], da of William (Craven), 2nd Earl of Craven [U K], s p

2e Roderick Pryor (*Weston Lodge, Stevenage, Berks*), b 1 Mar 1854, m 11 Sept 1906, Caroline [descended from King Henry VII (see Tudor Roll, p 450)], da of the Rev Osbert Mordaunt [Bt Coll], and has issue 1f

1f Peter Pryor, b 25 Sept 1907

3e Edmund Pryor, b 4 Oct 1850, d Feb 1885, m 28 Feb 1876, Evelyn Horatia (*Chagford, S O*), da of Rev the Hon Francis Sylvester Grimston [E of Verulam Coll], and had issue (with a son, Guy Francis, b 5 Nov 1876, d unm 28 July 1902) 1f to 3f

1f John Arthur Pryor, b 5 Nov 1884, m Blanche Marion, da of Major Burrell, and has issue 1g

1g Blanche Evelyn Marion Pryor, b 27 Feb 1908

2f Katharine Pryor, m E Scott James, and has issue 1g to 2g

1g Edward John James, b 4 Oct 1906

2g Angela Horatia Emma James, b 28 Sept 1902

3f Elizabeth Pryor, unm

4e Robert Pryor, b 17 Mar 1852, d 5 July 1905, m 8 Jan 1884, Matilda, da of Vincent Eyre, and had issue 1f

1f Phyllis Olive Barbara Pryor, m 25 Sept 1909, Capt Evelyn George Harcourt Powell, Grenadier Guards

5e Lucy Elizabeth Pryor, b 3 Mar 1845, d 21 Nov 1902, m July 1867, David Powell, Governor of the Bank of England 1892-1895, b 16 Ap 1810, d 2 Sept 1897 and had issue (with a son d young) 1f to 4f

1f David Powell, M A (Camb), a Director of the New River Coy (*Overstrand, Grove Park Road, Chiswick, W, Travellers*) b 13 June 1868

[Nos 79959 to 79981

414

# of The Blood Royal

2/ Albert Laurence Powell, Major 19th Hussars, b 29 Nov 1869, m 10 Mar 1897, Ella Eugenie Elizabeth, da. of Charles Augustus T Breul, and has issue (with a da d young) 1g to 2g

1g John Augustus Laurence Powell, b 24 Jan 1898

2g Elizabeth Evelyn Powell, b 25 Dec 1906

3/ Felix Edmund Powell, Chief Inspector of Cleansing Service, Egyptian Public Health Dept (Cairo), b 24 July 1873

4/ Robert Montagu Powell, Capt R A, b 19 May 1881, m 18 Nov 1905, Kathleen Mary Douglas, da of Frederic de Pledge

6e Edith Louisa Pryor, m 1881, Francis Richard Sutton [descended from the Lady Anne, sister of King Edward IV (see the Exeter Volume, p 160)] (The Canons, Thetford, Norfolk), and has issue 1/ to 4/

1/ Richard Coningsby Sutton, b 12 Mar 1882, d 12 Sept 1905, m 9 May 1904, Frances Olive (? Katherine Helen), da of Francis Foljambe Anderson of Lea, co Lincoln, and had issue 1g to 3g

1g Francis Richard Heywood Sutton, b 10 Feb 1905

2g Olinda Margaret Sutton
3g Olivia Katherine Sutton } (twins), b 4 May 1906

2/ Francis Arthur Sutton, b 15 Feb 1884

3/ Olinda Emily Sutton, m July 1909, Arthur Campbell Watson, Lieut 7th Hussars

4/ Sylvia Katherine Sutton, m Ap 1909, John St Vigor Fox

7e Emily Pryor, d 1 Feb 1884, m 19 June 1872, Walter Edward Grimston of Bures, co Essex [E of Verulam [U K] Coll, and a descendant of George, Duke of Clarence (see the Clarence Volume, p 157)] (Earls Colne, Essex), and had issue 1/ to 4/

1/ Susan Edith Grimston, m 14 June 1899, Major Arthur Faulconer Poulton, late Suffolk Regt, Chief Constable of Berkshire (Highgrove, Reading)

2/ Cecilia Grimston, m 11 June 1904, Capt Forrester Colvin Watson, 7th Dragoon Guards and Adj Essex Yeo

3/ Mary Noel Grimston, m 11 Jan 1905, Henry Hamilton Gepp, Lieut Essex Yeo (Hill House, Hatfield Peverel, Essex), and has issue 1g

1g Miriam Helen Gepp, b 5 Feb 1906

4/ Eleanor Vera Grimston, m 1908, Arthur Mervyn Toulmin

8e Katherine Pryor

5d Louisa Dew, b 15 Nov 1820, d 23 Nov 1909, m 19 June 1849, the Rev William Latham Bevan, M A, Vicar of Hay, Canon of St Davids and Archdeacon of Brecon [elder son of William Hibbs Bevan of Crickhowell, J P, High Sheriff co Brecon 1841], b 1 May 1821, d 21 Aug 1908, and had issue 1e to 6e

1e William Armine Bevan (11 The Boltons, South Kensington) b 20 June 1855, m 22 Aug 1885, Amy, da of the Rev F Wayet, d s p 16 May 1909

2e Ven Edward Latham Bevan, Vicar and Archdeacon of Brecon (Brecon), b 1861, unm

3e Mary Louisa Bevan m 16 Nov 1886, Henry Philip Dawson of Hartlington Hall Capt R A [eldest son of Capt Henry Dawson by his wife, Harriet Emma, da of Sir Philip Bainbridge, K C B [also a descendant of Edward III (see the Mortimer-Percy Volume, Pt II)] (Hartlington Hall, Skipton), and has issue 1/ to 2/

1/ Henry Christopher Dawson, b 12 Oct 1889

2/ Gwendoline Mary Dawson

4e Alice Catherine Bevan, m 14 Aug 1883, Capt Thomas Llewellyn Morgan, R H A [son of Col Morgan of St Helens, Swansea] (The Poole, Hereford), and has issue 1/ to 2/

1/ Jeffrey Morgan, b 14 Ap 1890
2/ Sibell Morgan, b 18 Dec 1891

[Nos 79985 to 80010

415

The Plantagenet Roll

5e Frances Emily Bevan, m 1 June 1897, the Rev Lewis Davies, Vicar of Talgarth [son of J M Davies of Antiron, co Cardigan, J P, D L] (*Talgarth Vicarage Brecon*)

6e Ellen Bevan, *unm*

6d *Emily Dew*, b 21 May 1825, d 17 Dec 1889, m *at Whitney*, 16 Aug 1849, Indrica Amédée Miéville of London [*of an old Swiss family, formerly of Yverdon*], d 23 Mar 1873, *and had issue* 1e *to* 5e

1e Edward Amédée Miéville, b 25 Sept 1851, m at Oswego, U S A, 22 May 1873, Helena Maude da of Charles C Mattoon, d 1902, and has issue 1f

1f Charles Amédée Miéville, b in New York 8 July 1876, m Maybelle Louise, da of (—) Thomas, and has issue 1g

1g Olive Vivian Miéville, b 16 June 1901

2e Sir Walter Frederick Miéville, K C M G, F R G S, late President of the Egyptian Maritime and Quarantine Board of Health (68 *Wilbury Road, Hove, Sussex*), b 17 July 1855, m 28 Mar 1882, Theodora Johanna, da of Henry Frederick Taylor of Alexandria, *s p*

3e Charles Ernest Miéville, Hon Sec Professional Golfers' Association (1 *Freeland Road, Ealing Common*), b 7 May 1858, m 16 Nov 1882, Alice Huleatt Garcia, da of Major William John Bampfield, and has issue 1f *to* 4f

1f Ernest Frederick Miéville, b 25 Feb 1891

2f Eric Charles Miéville, b 31 Jan 1896

3f Alice Dusie Miéville

4f Gladys Miéville

4e Herbert Le Strange Miéville, served through Boer War with 1st City (Grahamstown) Vols, Medals and 2 Clasps (*Johannesburg*), b 31 Mar 1866, m 6 Aug 1902, Edith Ellen Goddard, da of (—) Watson, *s p s*

5e Emily Frances Miéville, m 28 July 1874, Edward Stone, F S A, Solicitor (3 *Lansdowne Place, Blackheath, S E*), and has issue 1f *to* 10f

1f Edward Stone, Lieut 2nd Dragoon Guards, served in S Africa with W Australian Imperial Bushmen's Corps (Medal with 3 Clasps), b 14 Mar 1876

2f Arthur Stone, M A (Camb), b 27 June 1877

3f Reginald Guy Stone, Lieut R N, b 9 Feb 1880

4f Francis le Strange Stone, Solicitor, b 14 June 1886

5f Walter Napleton Stone, b 7 Dec 1891

6f Edith Emily Stone, m 1 Jan 1908, Cyril Arthur Priday (23 *Langlands Road, Sidcup*), and has issue 1g

1g Joan Priday, b 27 Sept 1908

7f Dorothy Stone

8f Marjorie Armine Stone

9f Phyllis Louisa Stone, m 14 Ap 1910, William Henry Strickland Ball, Lieut R N

10f Eleanor Whitney Stone

7d *Lucy Beatrice Dew*, b 8 Ap 1829, d 9 Mar 1907, m 10 Ap 1855, *the Rev Charles Amphlett* (R L 19 Mar 1855), *formerly Dunne of Four Ashes Hall, Bridgnorth, co Salop. Lord of the Manor of Earl's Croome, co Worc, M A (Oxon), &c* [*2nd son of Thomas Dunne of Gatley Park, co Hereford, J P, D L*], b 25 Ap 1818, d 5 Mar 1891, *and had issue (with a son and da d young)* 1e *to* 4e

1e Charles Grove Amphlett, D S O, Major (ret) South Staffordshire Regt, served in S Africa in command of 1st Batt Mounted Inf (*Four Ashes Hall, near Stourbridge*), b 8 Mar 1862, *unm*

2e Rev George Le Strange Amphlett, Rector of Earl's Croome and Hill Croome (*Earl's Croome Rectory, Worcestershire*), b 3 Sept 1868, m 6 Jan 1904, Blanche Katherine Adine, da of the Rev Canon Henry William Coventry, J P [E of Coventry Coll], and has issue 1f *to* 3f

1f Leah Blanche Amphlett, b 19 Oct 1905   [Nos 80011 to 80037

416

# of The Blood Royal

2f Ann Elizabeth Amphlett, b 29 Jan 1907

3f Justina Alice Amphlett, b 22 Sept 1908

3e Lucy Elizabeth Amphlett, m 31 Dec 1891, Arthur Tomkyns Dew, R M (see p 413), s p

4e Mabel Amphlett, m 19 Nov 1895, Arthur Edward Lloyd Oswell, A R I B A (Coton Hill Cottage, Berwick Road, Shrewsbury), s p

2c Ann Dew, b 10 Jan 1790, d at Cheltenham 18 1p 1873, m at Paris c 1820, John McGachen, Capt 72nd (Seaforth) Highlanders, d (—), and had issue (with 4 other sons) 1d

1d Rev Nicolas Howard McGachen, B A (Oxon), formerly (1881-1899) Vicar of Littlebourne (12 Marine Parade, Dover), b (—), m (—), da of (—), and has issue (with 4 other children) 1e to 2e

1e William Nicolas McGachen, Comm (ret) R N, b (—), m 16 May 1895, Lilian, da of Lieut.-Col Morton Parker Eden, R A, and has issue

See p 273, No 38485

2e Anne McGachen, m the Rev J Bowen, formerly in Army Chaplain

3c Armine Dew, b 14 Oct 1794, d at Bath 2 Sept 1856, m as 1st wife, at the British Embassy, Paris, 29 Dec 1819, Lieut.-Col Charles John Furlonge, 21st Royal North British Fusiliers, b 9 Jan 1793, d 27 Dec 1872, and had issue (with 3 das who d unm) 1d to 3d

1d Charles George Henry Furlonge, J P and Coroner, formerly a Chief Clerk W O (Lisle, Tasmania), b 17 June 1829, m 10 Dec 1868, Laura, da of Capt Herbert Ryves, R N, and has issue (with a son, Charles, b Aug 1869, d (?) unm) 1e to 9e

1e Charles George Herbert de Lisle Furlonge, b 29 Dec 1879, unm

2e George Le Strange Furlonge (Hunstanton, Lisle Road Station, Tasmania), b 1 Ap 1883, unm

3e Laura Eliza Armine Furlonge,

4e Armine Furlonge,

5e Marian Elizabeth Furlonge,

6e Annie Styleman Furlonge,　} unm

7e Elizabeth Adelaide Furlonge,

8e Caroline Grace Ryves Furlonge,

9e Isabel Arundel Rosaline Furlonge,

2d George William Furlonge, Col (ret) formerly 21st Royal Scots Fusiliers, served in the Crimea, has Medal and Clasps (Lynwood, Seaton, Devonshire), b 31 July 1834, m 30 June 1874, Armine, da of the Rev Henry Dew of Whitney, and has issue

See p 413, Nos 79952-79953

3d Caroline Warner Furlonge, m 3 July 1851, Nelson Girdlestone of the Admralty [great-nephew of Admiral Lord Nelson] (24 Church Road, St Leonards-on-Sea), and has issue (with 2 sons and a da d s p) 1e to 8e

1e Nelson Styleman Girdlestone, late R N (Port Elizabeth, Cape Colony), b 5 May 1852, m 1876, Marra, da of John Thornhill, d 1909, s p

2e Charles Henry Girdlestone, b 13 June 1857, d 1884, m 18—, Alice (7 Cora Terrace, Grahamstown, Cape Colony), da of Benjamin Roberts of Grahamstown, and had issue 1f to 2f

1f L'Estrange Girdlestone

2f Hugh Bertie Girdlestone

3e Francis Crawford Girdlestone (Port Elizabeth, Cape Colony), twin, b 15 May 1861, m 1882, Norah, da of Colonel Richard Athol Nesbitt, C B, and has issue 1f to 4f

1f Cedric Girdlestone, b 1897

2f Hilary Girdlestone, b 1898

3f Ronald Girdlestone, b 1904

4f Violet Girdlestone

[Nos. 80038 to 80067

The Plantagenet Roll

4e Armine Horatia Josephine Girdlestone (*Grahamstown, Cape Colony*), b 30 Oct 1853, m Feb 1876, Edwin Atherstone of Grahamstown, S Africa, M D, d (-), and has issue (with 2 sons d s p) 1f to 2f

    1f Roderic Atherstone

    2f Alice Armine Atherstone

5e Maria Adelaide Frances Girdlestone, b 4 Aug 1855, m Herbert Rees, S African Civil Ser , Clerk to the Mines Office (*Barkly West, Cape Colony*), s p.

6e Grace Geraldine Girdlestone, b 4 Mar 1860 m William (? A H) Holland (*Upper Bell Street, Grahamstown, Cape Colony*), and has issue 1f to 4f

    1f Frederic Holland

    2f Lionel Holland

    3f Doris Holland

    4f Cecile Holland

7e Florence Nelson Girdlestone, m 6 Feb 1890, Edward John Bishop Gardner, Attorney-at-Law (*Barkly West, Cape Colony*), and has issue 1f to 4f

    1f Reginald (Rex) Llewellyn Gardner, b 5 Oct 1891

    2f Nelson Percy Edward Gardner, b 2 Feb 1895

    3f Dorothy Florence Gardner

    4f Grace Maud Gardner

8e Lilian Rose Madelaine Girdlestone, b 28 Oct 1868 m Llewellyn Powys Jones, *formerly* Resident Magistrate at Buluwayo (*Fife Street, Buluwayo, Rhodesia*), and has issue 1f

    1f Lionel Powys Jones, b 1894

4b *Lucy Styleman*, b 1 July 1766, d (-), m *William Herring of St Faith's House, Norwich, J P [eldest son of the Rev J Herring, D D, Dean of St Asaph, and great-nephew of Thomas Herring, Archbishop of Canterbury 1747-1757], d 1827, and had issue (with a da , Lucy, d unm)* 1c to 2c

    1c *William Herring of St Faith's House, J P*, b 1798, d 1853, m *Maria Elizabeth, sister of Sir Henry Robinson, C B , J P , D L , da of George Robinson of Knapton House, co Norfolk, J P , d 29 Feb 1896, and had issue (with a son and da d young)* 1f to 4f

        1f William Herring, J P , Lieut-Col *late* 27th Inniskillings (*Narborough House, Norfolk*), b 20 Mar 1839, m Nov 1876, Jessie, da of Col William Welsby, J P , *formerly* 3rd Batt Liverpool Regt , and has issue (with 2 other sons who d unm) 1g to 3g

            1g *William Henry Armine Herring, B A (Camb), Lieut R F A*, b Feb 1882, d unm 10 Sept 1909

            2g Margaret Styleman Herring

            3g Elsie le Strange Herring

        2f *Maria Elizabeth Herring*, b c 1834, d 14 Jan 1871, m 1852, *Capt Joseph Edwin Day of Swardestone, co Norfolk, West Norfolk Mil [son and h of James Day of Horsford, co Norfolk]*, b 16 July 1830, d 16 Sept 1864, *and had issue (with a son and da d unm)* 1g to 2g

            1g James L'Estrange Day, b 20 Aug 1855 *unm*

            2g Augusta Maud Mary Day (*Tanglewood, Brownshill, Glos)* unm

        3f Frances Henrietta Herring (*31 Cambridge Road, Southend-on-Sea*), m 10 Jan 1861, the Rev George Metcalfe, Rector of Christ Church, Upwell, d 10 Oct 1888, 2ndly, 23 Ap 1898, John Major, d 1910, and has issue 1g to 6g

            1g Herbert Charles Metcalfe, Capt 2nd Batt Northants Regt , Chief Constable of Somerset (*Rowford Lodge, Cheddon, Fitzpaine, Taunton*), b 9 May 1864, m 3 Jan 1899, Dorothea Maud, da of Capt Brodnex Knight, Queen's Bays [and grand-da of Edward Knight of Chawton House, co Hants, by his 1st wife, Mary Dorothea, da of the Right Hon Sir Edward Knatchbull, 9th Bt [E], P C], and has issue 1h to 3h

                [Nos 80068 to 80090.

# of The Blood Royal

1*h* Christopher Le Strange Metcalfe, *b* 23 May 1907

2*h* Violet Beatrice Armine Metcalfe

3*h* Daphne Geraldine Dorothea Metcalfe

2*g* Rev Armine George Metcalfe, B A (Camb), Rector of Norbury (*Norbury Rectory, Ashbourne, Derbyshire*), *b* 2 Aug 1868, *m* 23 Jan 1901, Mary Bernina, da of Frederick Charles Millar, Q C, Bencher of the Inner Temple, and has issue 1*h* to 2*h*

1*h* Armine Ernest George Metcalfe, *b* 7 Oct 1901

2*h* Harold Guy Metcalfe, *b* 28 Sept 1905

3*g* Harold William Metcalfe, Partner, Messrs Osborne & Chappel, Mining and Consulting Engineers (*Ipoh, Perak, Federated Malay States*), *b* 11 Aug 1876 *m* 30 Sept 1908, Edith, da of J Cresswell, M D, and has issue 1*h*

1*h* Nigel William Metcalfe, *b* 25 Sept 1909

4*g* Edith Augusta Metcalfe, *m* 12 Ap 1882, the Rev Henry Teasdale Hutchinson, Vicar of Sancton (*Sancton Vicarage, R S O, York*), and has issue 1*h* to 3*h*

1*h* Charles Hilton Hutchinson, *b* 28 Aug 1885

2*h* Henrietta Styleman Hutchinson

3*h* Beatrice Lilian Mary Hutchinson

5*g* Anna Georgina Metcalfe, } *unm*
6*g* Katherine Alice Mary Metcalfe, }

4*f* Lucy Styleman Herring (*Stanhoe, Bitterne Park, Southampton*), *m* as 2nd wife, Major-Gen Henry Vincent Mathias, B S C (see p 420), *d* 3 Feb 1901, and has had issue (2 children *d* in infancy in India)

2*e* *Rev Armine Herring, Patron and Rector of Thorpe Episcopi, Norwich, b 28 Ap 1801, d 21 Jan 1867, m June 1830, Mary Elizabeth, da of George Robinson of Knapton House, co Norfolk, d 17 Dec 1856, and had issue (with a son, the Rev Armine Styleman Herring, Vicar of St Paul's, Clerkenwell, d s p 5 June 1896) 1f to 2f*

1*f* Henry Le Strange Herring, *late Capt 87th Royal Irish Rifles*, served in the Crimea with 30th Regt (*The Old Rectory, Thorpe, Norwich*), *b* 5 Dec 1832, *m* 1st, 21 June 1865, Mary Elizabeth, da of John Bell of Toronto, Q C, *d* 21 Jan 1871, 2ndly, 27 Ap 1881, Emma, da of Col William Welsby of Southport, J P, and has issue 1*g* to 5*g*

1*g*¹ Armine Bell Le Strange Herring (*Canada*), *b* 11 Aug 1866, *m* in Ontario 1903, Maud Olive, da of (—) Farriol, *s p*

2*g*¹ Styleman Percy Bell Le Strange Herring, Solicitor (*Croft House, Belaugher, Wroxham, Norfolk*), *b* 28 Aug 1868, *m* 24 May 1897, Frederica Sydney, da of Capt Herbert, R N, *s p*

3*g*² Henry William Herring, Lieut R E, *b* 29 July 1882, *unm*

4*g*¹ Alice Henrietta Le Strange Herring, *unm*

5*g*² Coela Elizabeth Le Strange Herring, *m* 18 Sept 1907, Capt Arthur Howarth Pryce Harrison, 33rd Punjabis, Indian Army, and has issue 1*h*

1*h* Hugh Devereux Harrison, *b* 24 June 1908

2*f* Alice Elizabeth Herring, *m* 4 June 1872 Capt Charles Sumner Pinwill, 27th Inniskillings Regt, *d* 30 Aug 1889, and has issue 1*g*

1*g* Alice Stackhouse Pinwill, *m* 4 Aug 1897, the Rev Raymond Williams, M A (Oxon), Vicar of Fisherton Delamere (*Fisherton-Delamere Vicarage, Wylye, S O, Wilts*)

3*e* *Henrietta Herring, d Oct 1832, m as 1st wife, 1827, Capt George Mathias, 79th Highlanders, afterwards in Holy Orders and one of the Chaplains to Queen Victoria, d 10 Mar 1884, and had issue (with das who d s p) 1f to 2f*

1*f* *Henry Vincent Mathias, Major-Gen B S C, previously 5th Bengal N I,*

[Nos 80091 to 80114

The Plantagenet Roll

b 20 Nov 1830, d 3 Feb 1901, m 1st at Dinapore, India, 8 Mar. 1854, Eleanor Matilda, da of Capt Edward Mathias, 44th Regt, d 19 June 1867, 2ndly, 22 June 1869, Lucy Styleman, da of William Herring of St Faith's House, J P (see p 419), and had issue (with 4 sons and a da who d young or s p) 1g to 5g

1g Leonard John Mathias, Lieut.-Col Indian S C, b 26 Nov 1860, m at Calcutta, 29 Jan 1890, Sarah, da of J Swinhoe, and has issue 1h to 3h

    1h Leonard William Henry Mathias, b 31 Oct 1890

    2h George Edwin Mathias, b 29 Ap 1895

    3h Pearl Glory Mathias

2g Hubert Mathias, Duke of Cornwall's L I, served in Boer War, b 1863

3g Eleanor Marion Mathias, m 4 Oct 1878, George Waddington, Bombay C I., and has issue 1h

    1h George O'Neill Waddington, b 17 Oct 1879

4g Susan Constance Mathias, m Dec 1876, Robert Login, Bengal C S., and has issue 1h to 3h

    1h Robert Hector Login, b 1877

    2h Guy L'Estrange Login, b 1882

    3h Constance Ruby Login

5g Lilla Mae Mathias, m Nov 1885, Col Robert Drury, R A M C, and has had issue (two das d young)

2f Rev George Henry Duncan Mathias, Fellow of King's Coll, Camb, b 5 Oct 1832, d 7 June 1869, m 21 Ap 1857, Fanny, da of William Brown Lockwood of Bury St Edmunds, d (—), and had issue 1g to 8g

1g Duncan L'Estrange Mathias, in Coutts' Bank (440 Strand), b 31 Mar 1860, unm

2g George Mathias (South America), b 26 June 1861, m 25 May 1890, Caroline, da of (—) Evans, and has issue (with a son d young) 1h to 2h

    1h George Harold Duncan Mathias, b 15 Jan 1901

    2h Geraldine Mathias, b 28 Mar 1903

3g Marian Ella Mathias, unm

4g Ida Mathias, m 23 Ap 1879, Gustav Lahusen of Bremen, Merchant (Breitenaeg 8, Bremen), and has issue 1h to 7h

    1h Christian Heinrich Lahusen, 13th Dragoons, German Army, b in Buenos Ayres 31 May 1881, m 16 Ap 1907, Ida, da of Oscar Caro, and has issue 1i to 2i

        1i Johann Gustav Leberecht Lahusen, b in Metz 18 Ap 1908

        2i Ida Leonore Lahusen, b in Bremen 16 Jan 1907

    2h Friedrich George Henry Duncan Lahusen, b in Bremen 15 Aug 1888

    3h Diedrich Henry Fritz Gerald Lahusen, b in Uruguay 6 Mar 1894, unm

    4h Violet Fanny Anna Lahusen, m 23 Jan 1903, Friedrich Wilhelm Vincenz Meyer, now Meyer-Lahusen, Merchant (Bremen), and has issue 1i to 2i

        1i Hans Gustav Reinhold Meyer-Lahusen, b in Bremen 12 Feb 1908

        2i Ida Marie Helene Meyer-Lahusen

    5h Marie Lahusen, m 22 June 1906, Reinhold Kulenkampff-Pauli

    6h Charlotte Lucy Anne Lahusen, m 22 June 1906, Reginald Calvert Booth (Estancia San Juan, Conchillas, Uruguay), and has issue 1i

        1i Violet Ida Maria Booth, b 7 Feb 1908

    7h Armine Therese Margaret Lahusen, unm

5g Lucy Angela Mathias, m 21 May 1901, Francis Thackeray Green, of the Bank of England (21 Putney Common South, S W)

6g Amy Mathias, m 27 Ap 1897, Hugh Henry Mathias [son of Archdeacon Mathias of Christchurch, New Zealand], and has issue (with a da d young) 1h to 2h

    1h Lionel Armine Mathias, b 23 Jan 1907

    2h Judith Amy Duncan Mathias

[Nos 80115 to 80148

420

# of The Blood Royal

7g Geraldine Mathias, m 21 Nov 1897, Eduard Seemann, and has issue 1h to 5h

    1h Eduard Duncan Christian Franz Seeman, b June 1900

    2h Julia Angela H A Seemann, b 8 Jan 1899

    3h Mary A Ida Seemann, b 3 May 1900

    4h Margaret Olga Gladys Seemann, b 21 July 1901

    5h Inez Geraldine Constance Seemann, b 2 Ap 1903

8g Armine Mathias, m 5 Oct 1887, Johann Carl Lahusen of Bremen, Merchant (*Delmenhorst, Germany*), and has issue (with a son, Carl Wilhelm, d young) 1h to 8h

    1h (Christian Friedrich Georg) Carl Lahusen, b Delmenhorst 17 July 1888

    2h Diedrich (Duncan) Lahusen, b at Delmenhorst 1 Sept 1889

    3h (Johann Heinrich) Gustav Lahusen, b in Bremen 5 Dec 1890

    4h Johannes (Christian) Lahusen, b in Bremen 21 Feb 1892

    5h Heinrich (Ludwig) Lahusen, b at Delmenhorst 14 Sept 1894

    6h Friedrich (Johannes) Lahusen, b at Delmenhorst 2 June 1900

    7h (Fanny Marie) Armine Lahusen, b at Delmenhorst 26 Nov 1898

    8h Anna Agnes Clara Lahusen, b at Delmenhorst 11 Mar 1905

[Nos 80149 to 80163

250 Descendants of LUCY L'ESTRANGE, otherwise LE STRANGE, da and event co-h of Sir Nicholas L'Estrange, otherwise Le Strange, 4th Bt [E], M P, co-h. to the Baronies of Hastings (1290) and Camoys (1383) [E] (Table XXIII), *bapt.* 23 Jan 1699, d 25 July 1739, m as 1st wife, 1721, SIR JACOB ASTLEY, 3rd Bt [E] (see p 428), b 3 Jan 1692, d 5 Jan. 1760, and had issue 1a to 3a

    1a *Sir Edward Astley 4th Bt [E], M P* bapt 26 Dec 1729, d 27 Mar 1802, m 1st, 1751, *Rhoda, da of Francis Blake Delaval of Seaton Delaval, co Northbd,* d Oct 1757, *2ndly, 24th Feb 1759, Anne, da of Christopher Milles of Nackington co Kent,* d 11 July 1792, *3rdly Elizabeth, da of (——) Bullen,* d s p m 1810, *and had issue (with apparently a da or das by 3rd wife)* 1b to 2b

    1b *Sir Jacob Henry Astley, 5th Bt [L] M P,* b 12 Sept 1756 d 28 Ap 1817, m 14 Jan 1789, *Hester, da and co-h of Samuel Browne of King's Lynn,* d 13 Jan 1855, *and had issue* 1c to 5c

    1c *Jacob (Astley) 16th Baron Hastings [E 1290] having the abeyance of that Barony terminated in his favour* 18 May 1841, b 13 Nov 1797 d 27 Dec 1859, m 22 Mar 1819, *Georgiana Carolina, da of Sir Henry Watkin Dashwood, 3rd Bt [E],* d 28 June 1835, *and had issue* 1d to 2d

    1d *Jacob Henry Delaval (Astley), 17th Baron Hastings and 7th Bt [E],* b 21 May 1822 d s p 8 Mar 1871

    2d *Delaval Loftus (Astley), 18th Baron Hastings and 8th Bt [E], Rector of East Barsham* b 24 Mar 1825, d 28 Sept 1872, m 8 Aug 1848, *the Hon Frances Diana [descended from th Lady Anne sister of King Edward IV (see Exeter Volume, p 163)], da of Charles (Manners Sutton), 1st Viscount Canterbury [U K], G C B and had issue* 1e to 3e

    1e *Bernard Edward Delaval (Astley), 19th Baron Hastings &c [E],* b 9 Sept 1855, d unm 22 Dec 1875

    2e *George Manners (Astley), 20th Baron Hastings and 10th Bt [E],* b 1 1p 1857, d 18 Sept 1904, m 17 Ap 1880 *the Hon Elizabeth Evelyn (Melton Constable, Norfolk, Delaval, Newcastle on-Tyne, 9 Seymour Street, Portman Square, W), da of Charles (Harbord), 5th Baron Suffield [E], and had issue* 1f to 5f

3 H

The Plantagenet Roll

1f Albert Edward Delaval (Astley), 21st Baron Hastings and 11th Bt [E] (*Melton Constable, Norfolk*, *Seaton Delaval, Newcastle-on Tyne*), b 24 Nov 1882 (King Edward sponsor), m 11 Feb 1907, Marguerite Helen, da of Lord Henry Gilbert Ralph Nevil [M of Abergavenny Coll], and has issue 1g

   1g Hon Helen Elizabeth Delaval Astley, b 12 Nov 1907

   2f Hon Jacob John Astley, Lieut 16th Lancers, b 5 May 1884

   3f Hon Charles Melton Astley, b 5 May 1885

   4f Hon Alexandra Rhoda Astley (Queen Alexandra sponsor), b 28 Sept 1886

   5f Hon Hester Astley b 17 May 1899

   3e Hon Agneta Frances Delaval Astley, m 22 Oct 1891, Roland le Strange, J P, D L (*Hunstanton Hall, Norfolk*), and has issue

   See p 411, Nos 79906–79907

2c Francis L'Lstrange Astley, Lieut-Col in the Army, b 27 Feb 1801, d 9 Ap 1866, m 1st, 28 July 1836, Charlotte, da of Nathaniel Micklethwaite of Taverham, co Norfolk, d 29 July 1848, 2ndly, 7 Sept 1854, Rosalind Alicia [descended from King Henry VII. (see Tudor Roll, p 455)], da of Sir Robert Frankland Russell, 7th Bt [E], d 27 Aug 1900, and had issue 1d to 6d

   1d Francis Nathaniel Astley, Capt Carabineers, b 26 May 1837, d 1868, m 25 Mar 1863, Jane, da of W H Binney and had issue 1e to 3e

      1e Francis Jacob L'Estrange Astley, b 17 Ap 1866

      2e Edward Henry Nathaniel Astley, b 25 Nov 1868

      3e Charlotte Mabel Astley

   2d Frederic Bernard Astley, b 18 Aug 1843, d 19 Aug 1876, m 4 Oct 1866, Emma Augusta da of Charles Schreiber of Roundway Park, Suffolk [who m 2ndly, 25 Jan 1879, Major Ludovic Montefiore Carmichael and] d 1883, and had issue 1e to 4e

      1e Delaval Graham L'Estrange Astley, formerly Major N Somerset Yeo Cav (*Plumstead Hall, Norwich*), b 7 Dec 1868, m 1 July 1897, Kate, da of J K Clark of Ghoolendaadi, N S W, and has issue 1f to 2f

         1f Joan Doreen Astley, b 19 Jan 1901

         2f Betty L'Estrange Astley, b 8 Oct 1902

      2e Bernard Armine Frederick Astley, b 4 Aug 1873

      3e Lilian Augusta Muriel Astley

      4e Blanche Rhoda Delaval Astley, m 2 Dec 1897, Thomas John Green (*Watford*)

   3d Bertram Frankland Astley, afterwards (R L 1901) Frankland-Russell-Astley of Chequers Court, co Bucks, J P, D L, b 27 Feb 1857, d 11 Feb 1904, m 30 Ap 1887, Lady Florence [descended from King Henry VII (see Tudor Roll, p 365)] (21 Eaton Place, S W), da of George (Conyngham), 3rd Marquis Conyngham [I] [who m 2ndly, 17 June 1905, Capt the Hon Claud Heathcote-Drummond-Willoughby], and had issue 1e to 2e

      1e Henry Jacob Delaval Astley of Chequers Court (*Chequers Court, Bucks*), b 3 May 1888, m

      2e Olive Joan Astley

   4d Rev Hubert Delaval Astley, M A (Oxon), formerly Rector of Ellesborough (*Benham Valence, Newbury, Bucks*), b 14 July 1860, m 30 July 1895, Constance Edith, widow of Sir Richard Francis Sutton, 5th Bt [G B], da of Sir Vincent Rowland Corbet, 3rd Bt [U K], and has issue 1e to 2e

      1e Philip Reginald Astley, b 9 June 1896

      2e Ruth Constance Astley

   5d Reginald Basil Astley (*Bachelor's*), b 8 Jan 1862

   6d Charlotte Laura Astley, d 18 Nov 1905, m 12 Feb 1867, the Hon Graham Edward Henry Manners Sutton [V Canterbury Coll], d 30 May 1888, and had issue

   See the Exeter Volume, p 162, Nos 2901–2903   [Nos 80164 to 80190

# of The Blood Royal

3c *Anne Astley*, d 1833, m 1820, *Thomas Potter Macqueen of Ridgemount, co Bedford, and had issue*

4c *Editha Astley*, d 27 Mar 1871, m 23 Mar 1825, *Warden Sergison of Cuckfield Park, co Sussex, J P, D L*, d 22 May 1868, *and had issue* 1d to 2d

1d *Warden Sergison of Cuckfield Park, J P, D L, Capt 4th Hussars*, b 13 July 1835, d 16 July 1888, m 8 Jan 1867, *Emiho, da of Sir William Gordon Gordon-Cumming, 2nd Bt [U K] [who m 2ndly, 12 Sept 1891, the Rev Seymour Edgell], and had* 1e to 2e

1e *Charles Warden Sergison of Cuckfield Park, J P, D L, formerly Capt Scots Guards, served in South Africa 1899-1900 (Cuckfield Park, Sussex, Slaugham Place, Sussex)*, b 25 Nov 1867, m 21 June 1891, the Hon Florence Emma Louisa [descended from King Henry VII (see Tudor Roll, p 201)] da of Charles (Hanbury-Tracy), 4th Baron Sudeley [U K], and had issue 1f to 2f

　1f Prudence Ida Evelyn Sergison, b 2 Sept 1892

　2f Cynthia Mary Sergison, b 10 May 1897

2e *Editha Elma Sergison*, m 6 Aug 1890, Joseph Henry Russell (Bailey), 2nd Baron Glanusk [U K], D S O, Lord-Lieut co Brecon, and Pres co Brecon Territorial Force, and *Hon Col and Lieut-Col Commdg 3rd Batt S Wales Borderers, formerly Gren Guards (Glanusk Park, near Crickhowell, Peterstone Park, Brecon, Hay Castle and Llangoed Castle, Brecon), and has issue* 1f to 4f

　1f Hon Wilfred Russell Bailey, b 27 June 1891

　2f Hon Gerald Sergison Bailey, b 1893

　3f Hon Bernard Michael Bailey, b 1899

　4f Hon Dulcie Editha Bailey

2d *Editha Agnes Sergison (Rendcomb Park, Cirencester), m as 2nd wife, 5 May 1888, James Taylor of Rendcomb, J P, d s p 1 Nov 1896*

5c *Agnes Astley*, d 30 July 1871, m Sept 1825, *the Rev John Henry Sparke of Gunthorpe Hall, M A, Canon of Ely and Chancellor of the Diocese*, d 8 Feb 1870, *and had issue (with an elder son, Henry Astley, killed in the charge of the Light Brigade at Balaclava)* 1d to 3d

1d *Edward Bowyer Sparke of Gunthorpe, M A, J P, D L, High Sheriff co Norfolk 1877*, b 28 July 1832, d 1 June 1910, m 4 July 1872, Annie (Gunthorpe Hall, Brimingham, Norfolk 66 Eaton Square, S W) [descended from the Lady Anne, sister of King Edward IV (see Supp)], da of Lieut-Col John Marcon of Wallington Hall, co Norfolk, and had issue 1e to 2e

1e *Henry Bowyer Sparke of Gunthorpe, J P, formerly Scots Guards, served in South Africa 1900-1902 (Gunthorpe Hall, Brimingham, Norfolk, Carlton, Bachelors')*, b 10 Feb 1875, m 12 Oct 1904, Eileen, da of the Right Hon Sir Charles Stewart Scott, P C, G C B, G C M G, and has issue 1f to 2f

　1f Michael Edward Bowyer Sparke, b 5 Aug 1905

　2f Reginald Charles Bowyer Sparke, b 22 Feb 1908

　2e Ethel Agnes Sparke, *unm*

2d *John Frances Sparke, Major 68th and 84th Regts*, b 25 July 1835, d 27 Feb 1888, m 2ndly, *Mary Adela, da of George Edwin Taunton of The Marfords, co Chester (marriage dissolved), and had issue* 1e

　1e Agnes Violet L'Estrange Astley Sparke, *unm*

3d *Agnes Sparke*, b 4 June 1831, d 18 June 1892, m 20 Jan 1870, *the Rev Robert Arbuthnot Law, Rector of Gunthorpe-cum-Bale*, d 11 Dec 1889, *and had issue* 1e to 3c

　1e Arbuthnot Patrick Astley Law, b 5 July 1872

　2e Herbert Henry Bingham Law, b 23 Oct 1873

　3c Alexander Delaval Hamilton Law, b 18 Oct 1874

2b *Rev Henry Nicholas Astley*, b 5 Jan 1767, d 14 Aug 1834, m 20 Feb 1798, *Sarah, da of the Rev J Pitman, and had issue* 1c to 3c

[Nos 80191 to 80207

The Plantagenet Roll

1c *Rev Henry L'Estrange Milles Astley, Rector of Foulsham*, b 27 Dec 1804, d (–), m 1841, *Dulcibella, da of Col William Gooch of Carleton, co York*, and had issue 1d to 3d

    1d William Henry L'Estrange Milles Astley, *bapt* 2 Ap 1838 [1] (sic)

    2d Evelyn Astley, m (–)

    3d Dulcibella Louisa Astley, m (—) [3rd son of the Viscount of Kersebrique]

2c *Jane Mary Astley*, d 16 Aug 1904, m 1 Oct 1833, *the Rev William Frank Cubitt, M A, Rector of Fritton, co Suffolk*, d 22 June 1882, *and had issue* 1d to 6d

    1d Frank Astley Cubitt of Thorpe Hall, &c, J P, *formerly* Capt 5th Fusiliers (*Thorpe Hall, Norwich. Fritton House, Great Yarmouth*), b 20 Nov 1834, m 16 Oct 1861, Bertha Harriett, da of Capt Thomas Blakiston, R N [Bt Coll], and has issue 1e to 4e

        1e Bertram Blakiston Cubitt, a Principal Clerk in the War Office (*Hillstead Brentwood Essex*) b 20 Aug 1862, m 21 Ap 1897, Leila, da of Capt W Norman Leslie, Gordon Highlanders, and has issue 1f to 2f

            1f Frank Leslie Cubitt, b 19 Jan 1898

            2f Alan Blakiston Cubitt, b 24 Feb 1903

        2e Julian Francis Cubitt, b 16 Aug 1869

        3 Thomas Astley Cubitt, D S O, Major R F A, b 9 Ap 1871

        4e Theresa Helen Cubitt, m 7 Sept 1905, Dr Moritz Julius Born, a Professor at Munich University (*Munich*)

    2d *Rev Spencer Henry Cubitt, Rector of Scarning*, b 7 Nov 1839, d 1879, m *Catherine, da of William Garforth of Steeton, co Yorks*, d 1879, *and had issue* 1e to 3e

        1e Rev Spencer Henry Cubitt, M A (Camb), Rector of Fritton (*Fritton Rectory, Great Yarmouth*) b 7 Nov 1869, m 9 Nov 1904, Jeanie Blythe, da of E W Bacon of Oldbury Grange, Bridgnorth

        2e Ida Cubitt, m John R Pearson (*Ripon, Yorks*), and has issue

        3e Mabel Cubitt, m 10 Feb 1892, Major William Thwaites, R F A

    3d Lucy Cubitt

    4d Emily Jane Cubitt

    5d Sophia Anne Cubitt (*Wistow Lodge, Huntingdon*), m 1869, Charles de La Pryme, M A, J P, Bar-at-Law, and has issue 1e to 5e

        1e Alexander George de La Pryme M A, Universities Mission, Central Africa, b Nov 1870

        2e Percy Christopher de La Pryme, Capt A S C, b 21 Sept 1875

        3e William Henry Astley de La Pryme, Lieut P W O Yorkshire Regt, b 20 Feb 1880

        4e Louis de La Pryme

        5e Helen de La Pryme

    6d Georgiana Helen Cubitt, m 14 Sept 1876, John Rochfort Blakiston [Bt Coll] (*The Wilderness, Westend Southampton*), and has issue 1e to 4e

        1e John Francis Blakiston, b 21 Nov 1882

        2e Margaret Blakiston

        3e Catherine Blakiston

        4e Mary Helen Blakiston

3c *Anne Astley*, b 14 Jan 1808, d 26 May 1878 m 15 Oct 1835, *the Rev Henry James Lee-Warner of Thorpland Hall, co Norfolk, Hon Canon of Norwich*, d 10 July 1885, *and had issue* 1d to 9d

    1d Rev James Lee-Warner of Thorpland Hall, M A (Oxon), *formerly* Rector
                                      [Nos 80208 to 80234

---

[1] Lodge's "Peerage," 1909, p 943

# of The Blood Royal

of Beckley (*Thorpland Hall, Norfolk*), b 13 Aug 1836 m 7 May 1874, Agnes Louisa, da of the Rev Henry Philip Marsham of Rippon Hall, and has issue 1e to 4e

    1f George Lee-Warner (*Innerfail, Spruce Coulee, Alberta, Canada*), b 8 Feb 1875, m 6 Nov 1905 Margaret da of Grant Ogilvie, and has issue 1f to 2f

        1f George Lee Warner, b 16 July 1906

        2f Edgar Lee-Warner, b 10 June 1909

    2e Rev Alfred Lee-Warner, M A (Oxon) (17 *Gordon Road, Ilverstoke*), b 6 Oct 1877

        3e James Lee-Warner, b 29 Ap 1889

        4e Caroline Lee-Warner

    2d Henry Lee-Warner, J P (*The Paddocks Swaffham*) b 3 Jun 1842, m 29 Dec 1868, Eleanor, da of Robert Blake-Humfrey of Wroxham, J P, D L

    3d John Lee-Warner (25 *Courtfield Road S W*), b 27 Jan 1843, m 17 Nov 1880, Blanche, da of Henry Hall Dare and has issue 1e to 5e

        1e Henry Granville Lee-Warner, Lieut R F A, b 1 Jun 1883

        2e Anne Agatha Lee-Warner, m 27 Jan 1904 Eustace Gurney of Sprowston Hall, J P, M A (Oxon) (*Sprowston Hall, Norwich*), and has issue 1f to 4f

            1f John Gurney, b 3 July 1905

            2f Jocelyn Eustace Gurney, b 24 Feb 1910

            3f Catherine Gurney

            4f Rosamond Agatha Gurney

        3e Ruth Veronica Lee-Warner

        4e Gilian Cicely Lee-Warner

        5e Blanche Maud Lee-Warner

    4d Edward Lee-Warner (67 *St Georges Square, S W*) b 10 Jun 1845, m 12 Feb 1884, Maria Harvey, da of Onley Savill-Onley of Stisted Hall, co Essex, J P, D L , and has issue 1e to 2e

        1e Edward Henry Lee-Warner, b 22 Jan 1887

        2e Maria Gladys Lee-Warner, b 20 Feb 1889

    5d Sir William Lee-Warner, K C S I, J P, M A, and a Member of Council of India, *formerly* Sec in Political and Secret Depts of India Office 1895-1902, &c, &c (*Eaton Tower, Caterham, Surrey*), b 18 Ap 1846, m 2 Aug 1876, Ellen Paulina, da of Gen Henry William Holland, C B and has issue 1e to 3e

        1e Philip Henry Lee Warner, b 5 June 1877, m 21 June 1907, Mary King, da of Gen Thomas Sherwin of Boston, Mass , and has issue 1f

            1f Isabel Ellen Lee-Warner

        2e William Hamilton Lee-Warner, Assist Resident, Brunei, b 14 Oct 1880

        3e Roland Paul Lee Warner, b 4 Jan 1892

    6d Lucy Lee-Warner

    7d Anne Lee-Warner

    8d Maria Lee-Warner (*Bolwick Hall, Marsham, near Aylsham*), m 3 July 1873, Charles Louis Buxton, J P, C C [6th son of Sir Edward North Buxton, 2nd Bt [U K], M P], d 23 Ap 1906, and has issue 1e to 4e

        1e Walter Louis Buxton, B A (Camb), J P, *formerly* Capt King's Own Norfolk Imp Yeo (*Brooks'*), b 6 May 1875

        2e Norah Louis Buxton, b 14 Ap 1874, d 17 Ap 1907, m 22 Nov 1904, *William Done Bushell, and had issue 1f*

            1f Maurice Done Bushell, b 6 Ap 1907

        3e Amy Louis Buxton

        4e Millicent Louis Buxton, m 16 Nov 1909, Gerard Anstruther Withen

    9d Emma Lee-Warner, *unm*   [Nos 80237 to 80267

425

The Plantagenet Roll

2a *Rev John Astley*, b 1734, d 1803 m 1762, *Catherine, da of Philip Bell of Wallington, co Norfolk, and had issue* 1b to 2b [1]

1b Catherine Astley

2b Lucy Astley

3a *Blanch Astley*, b 1726, d 3 May 1805, m 1751 *Edward Pratt of Ryston, co Norfolk, d 18 June 1784 and had issue* 1b to 3b

1b *Edward Roger Pratt of Ryston, High Sheriff co Norfolk* 1798, b 24 Oct 1756, d 5 Mar 1838, m 3 Dec 1788, *Pleasance, da and co h of Samuel Browne of Kings Lynn, d 3 Oct 1807, and had issue (with 4 other sons and 2 das who d s p) 1c to 4c*

1c *Rev Jermyn Pratt of Ryston*, b 6 Feb 1798, d 15 May 1867, m 4 May 1817, *Mary Louisa [descended from King Henry VII (see the Tudor Roll, p 150)], da of the Right Rev Lord George Murray, Bishop of Rochester [younger son of the 3rd Duke of Atholl [S]], d 5 May 1878, and had issue (with 2 other das d s p) 1d to 6d*

1d Edward Roger Murray Pratt of Ryston, J P, C C, Col *formerly Norfolk Art* (*Ryston Hall, near Downham, Norfolk*), b 3 Dec 1847, m 12 July 1881, the Hon Louisa Frances, da of John (Mulholland), 1st Baron Dunleath [U K], and has issue 1e to 5e

1e Edward Roger Pratt, b 2 June 1882

2e Jermyn Harold Pratt, b 12 July 1883

3e Lionel Henry Pratt, b 17 Dec 1889

4e Dorothy Louisa Pratt

5e Ursula Frances Pratt

2d Walter Jermyn Murray Pratt (*Wallington Lodge, Baldock, Herts*), b 6 Feb 1853, m 1878, Elizabeth, da of the Rev Henry George

3d Reginald Henry Murray Pratt (*Portagela Prairie, Canada*), b 29 May 1854, m 1887, Maria, da of the Rev Henry George, and has issue 1e to 5e

1e Horace Reginald Pratt, b 26 Jan 1888

2e Cecil Arden Pratt, b 29 Nov 1889

3e Alwyn Murray Pratt, b 7 Sept 1892

4e Gerald Henry Pratt, b 20 May 1895

5e Bernard Edward Pratt b 1 Mar 1901

4d Blanche Eleanor Murray Pratt, m 30 Ap 1891, Capt James Boyle, M V O, H B M Consul for Madeira 1907, *formerly at Copenhagen*, &c [E of Glasgow Coll] (*British Consulate, Funchal, Madeira*)

5d Henrietta Mary Murray Pratt, m 24 Jan 1895, Cecil Henry Spencer Perceval [E of Egmont Coll and a descendant of George, Duke of Clarence, K G (see the Clarence Volume, p 209] (*Longwitton Hall, co Northumberland*)

6d Alice Rosalind Murray Pratt, m 14 July 1885, the Rev Charles Francis Townley of Fulbourne, co Camb, Rector of Christchurch, Wisbech [descended from King Henry VII (see the Tudor Roll, p 393)] (*Christchurch Rectory, Wisbech*), and has issue 1e to 4e

1e Charles Evelyn Townley, b 22 Jan 1888

2e Gladys Mary Townley

3e Rosalinde Cecil Townley

4e Selma Georgiana Townley

2c *Rev William Pratt, Rector of Harpley-cum-Bircham*, b 2 Nov 1803, d 2 Nov 1874, m 1835, *Louisa, da of William Coxhead Marsh of Gaynes Park, co Essex, d 7 June 1877, and had issue (with 2 other sons who d s p) 1d to 9d*

1d William Roger Pratt, Indian C S (ret) (41 *Hill St, Berkeley Square*), b 27 Ap 1837   [Nos 80268 to 80288

[1] Betham's "Baronetage," 1802, ii 76

# of The Blood Royal

2d Henry Marsh Pratt, C B , Col (ret) Indian Army (43 *Courtfield Gardens, S W*), b 24 Oct 1838, m 7 May 1891, Evelyn Margaret, da of Clayton William Freake Glyn of Durrington House, Harlow [Bt Coll], and has issue 1e to 2e

1e Pleasance Millicent Mary Pratt

2e Evelyn Lucy Pratt

3d William Dering Pratt, *formerly* Dep Inspector-Gen of Police, Bengal (36 *West Cromwell Road, S W*), b 5 Sept 1842 , m 30 Nov 1867, Louisa Constance, da of Henry Steel, H E I C S , and has issue 1e to 2e

1e Henry Roger Evelyn Pratt D S O , Capt 36th Sikhs, Indian Army, b 8 Dec 1875 , m 20 Dec 1909, Yolande, da of Edmund Tower

2e Amy Pratt

4d Rev Dashwood Pratt, B A (Camb), Vicar of Barney (*Barney Vicarage, East Dereham, Norfolk*), b 5 Oct 1845 unm

5d *Emily Blanche Pratt* b 19 Ap 1847 , d 24 *June* 1871, m 1870, *Henry John Denis Dugmore of Bagthorpe Hall, co Norfolk*, d 1883 , and had issue 1e

1e Henry Norris Pratt Dugmore of Bagthorpe (*Bagthorpe Hall, King's Lynn*), b (—), unm

6d Hester Sophia Astley Pratt, unm

7d Harriett Pratt, unm

8d Laura Louisa Pratt, m 19 May 1886, Arthur Hussey of 11 Stone Buildings, Lincoln's Inn, Solicitor (15 *Grange Road Ealing*), and has issue 1e to 2e

1e William Jermyn Hussey, b 2 Ap 1887

2e Emily Blanche Hussey

9d Eveline Pratt, m 14 May 1885, Major-Gen Charles Grant Mansell Fisken, C B , Indian Army, now Comdg Bannoo Brigade, India (*Bannoo Punjab, India*), and has issue 1e to 3e

1e Douglas Fasken, b 16 Sept 1896

2e Grace Evelyn Fasken

3e Myrtle Annie Fasken

3c *Maria Pratt*, d 14 Jan 1856 , m 1831, *Henry W Coldham of Anmer Hall, co Norfolk, D L , d Nov 1871 , and had issue 1d to 3d*

1d *Henry James Coldham of Anmer Hall*, d 13 July 1887 , m *Agatha Geraldine de Courcy (Essenden, near Hatfield, Herts), da of (—) Ham l'on , and had issue (2 sons and 5 das)*

2d Maria Elizabeth Coldham, m Capt James Mason, 94th Regt , d July 1901

3d Lucy Coldham (*Preston Cottage, near Uppingham*), m Rev H Lucas

4c *Lucy Pratt, d s p 12 May* 1854 , m 1st, 10 Jan 1826, *William (Thellusson), 3rd Baron Rendlesham [U K] d s p 13 Sept 1839, 2ndly, 2 Feb 1841 Stewart Marjoribanks of Bushey, co Herts, M P , J P , d Sept 1863*

2b *Sarah Maria Pratt*, d (—), m *the Rev Charles Collyer of Gunthorpe Hall, co Norfolk*, d (—) , and had issue (with possibly others) 1c

1c *Harriet Collyer*, d (—), m *her cousin-german, Lieut Col William Collyer of Gunningham, co Norfolk, J P H E I C S , d 1861*

3b *Lucy Pratt*, d (—) , m *Hadmond Alpe of Hardingham*

[Nos 80289 to 80307]

251. Descendants of EDMOND WODEHOUSE of East Lexham, co Norfolk (Table XXIII), d (—), m 1st, MARY, widow of WILLIAM GUYBON, da. of Sir Philip PARKER; and had issue (with a son and 2 das who d s p) 1a

1a *Lucy Wodehouse*, d (—), m *Lewis Monnoux of Sandy*

427

The Plantagenet Roll

252. Descendants of JOHN WODEHOUSE of Fettwell (Table XXIII), *d* (–), *m* ANNE, widow of WILLIAM SAMWELL, da of Sir Denner STRUTT, 1st Bt [E 1642] *d* (–), and had issue 1*a*.

    1*a* *Elizabeth Wodehouse*

253 Descendants of BLANCHE WODEHOUSE (Table XXIII.), *d* (–), *m* 6 Feb 1661, Sir JACOB ASTLEY, 1st Bt [E 25 Jan 1660]. M P, co Norfolk 1685 1722, *d* 17 Aug 1729, and had issue 1*a*.

    1*a* *Sir Jacob Astley, 2nd Bt [E], b 20 July 1667, d 7 July 1739 m 2 Dec 1690, Elizabeth, da and h of Thomas Bransby of Carton, co Norfolk, d 30 May 1738, and had issue* 1*b to* 3*b*

    1*b Sir Jacob Astley, 3rd Bt [E], b 3rd Jan 1692, d 5 Jan 1760, m 1st, 1721, Lucy, da and event co-h of Sir Nicholas L'Estrange, 4th Bt [E], d 25 July 1739, and had issue*

    See pp 421–427, Nos 80164–80307

    2*b Elizabeth Astley, d* (–), *m Caleb Elwin of Thurning*

    3*b Jemima Astley, d* (–), *m* 1st, 1731, *Roger Metcalfe of St Giles-in-the-Fields, co Midx M D, b 8 Mar 1680, d* (–). 2ndly, *Henry Groom, of the City of London and had issue (with 2 sons d s p)* 1*c*

    1*c Christopher Metcalfe of Hawstead, a literary friend of the poet Dryden, b 1 Ap 1732 d 24 June 1794, m 19 May 1753, Ellen, da and h of Christopher Barton of Bromley co Midx, and Hawstead co Suffolk, d 6 Mar 1775, and had issue (with a son and 6 das d unm)* 1*d to* 2*d*

    1*d Christopher Barton Metcalfe of Hawstead, b 28 Aug 1759, d 15 Aug 1851, m Sophia, da of Robert Andrews of Averics, co Essex, d 27 Feb 1815 and had issue* 1*e to* 4*e*

    1*e Henry Metcalfe of Hawstead, b 10 Ap 1791, d 1849, m 1820 Frances Jane, da of Martin Whish, Commr of Excise d 29 Ap 1830, and had issue (with a da d young)* 1*f to* 3*f*

    1*f Henry Christopher Metcalfe of Hawstead, 91st Regt, b 4 Sept 1822, d 16 Ap 1881, m 5 Dec 1845, Mary, da of George Price of Grahamstown, South Africa, 21st Light Dragoons and had issue (with a da d unm)* 1*g to* 4*g*

    1*g Henry George Price Metcalfe of Hawstead, b 16 Sept 1846, d* (–), *m* (—), *da of* (—), *and had issue* 1*h to* 6*h*

        1*h* Henry Christopher Metcalfe, *b* 1873

        2*h* George Harry Price Metcalfe

        3*h* John Joseph Metcalfe

        4*h* Frederica Sophia Metcalfe

        5*h* Daisy Emma Whish Metcalfe

        6*h* Alice Georgina Metcalfe

    2*g* Christopher Barton Metcalfe, *b* 6 Jan 1860

    3*g Frances Jane Whish Metcalfe, m* 25 Feb 1873, Col Thomas George Booth of Hawstead House, A P D, *late* 10th Regt (*Hawstead House, Bury St Edmunds*), *s p*

    4*g Ellen Marie Metcalfe, d* 22 Mar 1877, *m Edward Beall, and had issue* 1*h to* 2*h*

        1*h* Edward Beall, *b* Feb 1877

        2*h* Lucy Beall

    2*f Philip Roger Colville Metcalfe of Erith, co Kent b 12 May 1827, d* (–), *m 11 Aug 1860, Martha, da of William James Mostnan of Bury St Edmunds, and had issue (with 2 das d unm)* 1*g to* 1*g* [Nos 80308 to 80461

# of The Blood Royal

1g Harry Philip Metcalfe, *b* 22 Aug 1865

2g Clarissa Kate Metcalfe

3g Anne Florence Metcalfe

4g Frances Martha Metcalfe

3f *Walter Charles Metcalfe of Epping, co Essex,* b 26 *May* 1828, d (–), m 1850, *Mary, da of Richard B Andrews of Epping, and had issue 1g to 2g*

1g Gilbert Metcalfe, *b* 1851

2g Clara Metcalfe

2e *Ellen Metcalfe,*

3e *Frances Sophia Metcalfe,* } d (?) *unm*

4e *Emma Metcalfe,* d 14 *Feb* 1810, m *as 1st wife, the Rev. Nathaniel Colvile, M A, Rector of Little Livermere, co Suffolk, and had issue 1f to 2f*

1f Augusta Letitia Colvile

2f Clara Harriet Emma Colvile

2d *Frederica Sophia Metcalfe,* b 3 *Nov* 1763, d 5 1*p* 1834, m *James Mure of Cecil Lodge, co Herts* [2nd *son of William Mure of Caldwell, M P, a Baron of the Exchequer], and had issue (with an elder son d s p* [1]) *1e to 6e*

1e *James Mure,* d (–) m *Harriet, da of Brice Pearce of Munkham, co Essex*

2e *Philip William Mure,* d (–), m *Louisa, da of Sir Thomas Andrew Strange, Chief Justice of Madras*

3e *Frederica Mure,* d (–), m *Col Horatio George Broke* [3rd *son of Philip Bower Broke of Nacton, co Suffolk], and had issue 1f*

1f Horace Broke, *b* 26 Sept 1827

4e *Catherine Mure,*

5e *Ellen Mure,* } d (? *unm*)

6e *Harriet Mure,*

[No~ 80462 to 80470]

---

254 Descendants, if any surviving, of MARGARET WODEHOUSE (Table XXIII), d. (–), m THOMAS SAVAGE of Elmley Castle, co. Worcester,[2] and had issue 1a to 4a

1a *Thomas Savage of Elmley Castle,* bur 22 *Ap* 1694, m *and had issue 1b*

1b *Thomas Savage of Elmley Castle,* d 7 *May* 1712, m *May* 1700, *Elizabeth, widow of Thomas (Coventry), 1st Earl of Coventry* [E], *da of Richard Graham or Grimes,* bur 10 *Ap* 1724, *and had issue 1c to 3c*

1c *Elizabeth Savage, da and co h, m William Byrche of Leacroft, co Staff, LL D, Chancellor of Worcester, and had issue 1d to 3d*

1d *Thomas Byrche, afterwards Savage of Elmley,* d s p 1776

2d *Elizabeth Byrche,* m *John Perrot, and had issue (with app other) issue 1e to 2e*

1e. *Thomas Perrot*

2e *Mary Perrot*

3d *Jane Byrche,* m *Richard Clavering of co Northbd, and had (with app other) issue 1e to 2e*

1e *Robert Clavering, afterwards (R L 21 Oct 1797) Savage*

2e. *Jane Clavering*

2c *Margaret Savage,* d (–), m *Thomas Coventry, Bar-at-Law, M P for Bridport* 1762, 1768, *and* 1774 [*nephew of William, 5th Earl of Coventry*], d *app* s p

---

[1] Gage's "Suffolk," p 416   [2] Nash's "Worcester," 1 383

3c *Mary Savage*, d (-), m *Humphrey Monnoux of Sandy, co Beds, a Bencher of Gray's Inn, and had issue* 1d

1d *Sir Philip Monnoux, 5th Bt* [E 4 Dec 1660], b c 1739, d 17 Ap 1805, m 22 June 1762, *Elizabeth, da of Ambrose Riddell of Eversholt, co Beds*, d 12 Sept 1770, *and had issue (with 2 other das* [1]*)* 1e *to* 3c

1e *Sir Philip Monnoux, 6th Bt* [E], d *unm* 27 Feb 1809

2c [*da*] *Monnoux*, m *1st, Sir John Payne, 2ndly, Col Buckworth*

3c *Frances Monnoux*, m 3 Oct 1809, *the Hon Samuel Henry Ongley* [2nd *son of Robert*, 1st *Baron Ongley* [I 1776], d *certainly* s p m *and app* s p 1822.

2a *Anne Savage*, m *Samuel Bracebridge of Lindley, co Leic* [2nd *son of Abraham Bracebridge of Atherston, co Warwick*], *and had issue (with Abraham, Thomas, and Elizabeth)* 1b *to* 6b

1b *Samuel Bracebridge M P for Tamworth*, b c 1716, *aged* 14, 1730,[2] d *in the Isle of Scio* 1786[3]

2b *Robert Bracebridge*, b c 1723, *aged* 7, 1730[2]

3b *Rev Philip Bracebridge*, b c 1721, *aged* 6, 1730,[2] d 1762, *and had issue* 1c *to* 2c

1c *Anne Bracebridge of Lindley Hall*, m *Robert Abney of Lindley Hall, High Sheriff* (?) *co Leic*, *and had issue* 1d

1d [*da*] *Ibney*, m *the Rev Samuel B Heming*

2c *Amicia Bracebridge*, m *George Heming*, *and apparently had issue at least one son* (see above)

4b *James Bracebridge*, b c 1725, *aged* 5, 1730[2]

5b *Maria Bracebridge*, b c 1710, *aged* 20, 1730[2]

6b *Mary Ann Gratia Bracebridge*, b c 1719, *aged* 11, 1730[2]

3a *Lucy Savage*, d 21 May 1721, m *Thomas Adderly of Woddington, co Warwick*, *and had issue* [4] (*with a son, Gilbert*, d *young*) 1b *to* 2b.

1b *Thomas Adderly*

2b *Elizabeth Adderly*

4a [*da*] *Savage*, m (—) *Reed of Luggardine*

255 **Descendants of Lady MARGARET HOWARD** (Table XXI), *d.* 4 Sept 1591, *m* as 1st wife (lic 4 Feb) 1580, ROBERT (SACKVILLE), 2nd EARL OF DORSET [E.], *d* 27 Feb 1609, and had issue 1*a* to 4*a*.

1a *Richard (Sackville), 3rd Earl of Dorset* [E], b 28 Mar 1589, d 28 Mar 1624, m 25 Feb 1609, *Anne, suo jure 14th Baroness de Clifford* [E], d 22 Mar 1676, *and had issue* 1b

1b *Lady Margaret Sackville, da and event sole h*, b c 1614, d 14 Aug 1676, m 21 Ap 1629, *John (Tufton), 2nd Earl of Thanet* [E], d 6 May 1664, *and had issue*

See pp 128-131, Nos 11638-13475

2a *Edward (Sackville), 4th Earl of Dorset* [L], K G, b 1590, d 17 July 1652, m a 12 Mar 1612, *Mary, da and h of Sir George Curzon of Croxall, co Derby*, bur 3 Sept 1645, *and had issue* 1b

1b *Richard (Sackville), 5th Earl of Dorset* [E], b 16 Sept 1622, d 27 Aug 1677, m a 1638, *Lady Frances, da and event h of Lionel (Cranfield), 1st Earl of Middlesex* [E], *and had issue* 1c *to* 2c   [Nos 80471 to 82308

---

[1] Burke's " Extinct Baronetcies "
[2] Dugdale's "Worcester," 1730, p 1057
[3] Burke's "Commoners," i 273
[4] Nash's "Worcester," p 1096

# of The Blood Royal

1c Richard (Sackville), 6th Earl of Dorset [E], K G, b 24 Jan 1638, d 29 Jan 1706, m 2ndly, 7 Mar 1685, Lady Mary, da of James (Compton), 3rd Earl of Northampton [E], d 6 Aug 1691, and had issue
See the Clarence Volume, Table XX and pp 223-227, No 1502-4613

2c Lady Mary Sackville, bapt 11 Feb 1648, d 4 Nov 1710, m 6 Feb 1665, Roger (Boyle), 2nd Earl of Orrery [I], d 29 Mar 1682, and had issue
See p 342, Nos 58418-59088

3a Lady Cecily Sackville, d (-), m the Hon Sir Henry Compton, K B, and had issue (with 3 sons who d unm) 1b to 3b

1b Cecily Compton, b c 1608, d 21 Mar 1675, m 1st, Sir John Fermor of Somerton, co Oxon, d v p s p 1625, 2ndly, a 18 May 1629, Henry (Arundell), 3rd Baron Arundell of Wardour [E] and Count Arundell [H R E], P C, K B, d 28 Dec 1694, and had issue (by 2nd husband)
See the Clarence Volume, Table LVI and pp 462-471, Nos 20213-20851

2b Mary Compton, d (-), m the Hon John Lumley, d v p Oct 1658, and had issue 1c to 2c

1c Richard (Lumley), 2nd Viscount Lumley [I] and (10 Ap 1689) 1st Earl of Scarbrough [E], b c 1650, d 17 Dec 1721, m 17 Mar 1685, Frances, da and h of Sir Henry Jones of Aston, co Oxon, d 7 Aug 1722, and had issue 1d to 3d

1d Richard (Lumley), 2nd Earl of Scarbrough [E], &c, K G, d unm 29 Jan 1740

2d Thomas (Lumley, afterwards (4 P 1723) Lumley-Saunderson), 3rd Earl of Scarbrough [E], &c, K B, b c 1690, d 15 Mar 1752, m 27 June 1724, Lady Frances, da of George (Hamilton), 1st Earl of Orkney [S], d 27 Dec 1772, and had issue
See p 377, Nos 62521-62625

3d Lady Mary Lumley, d 10 Dec 1726, m as 2nd wife, George (Montague), 1st Earl of Halifax [E], K B, d 9 May 1739, and had issue
See the Clarence Volume, Table LXXVI and pp 615-619, Nos 26908-27008

2c Elizabeth Lumley, d (-), m Richard Cotton of Water Gates, co Essex

3b Margaret Compton, d (-), m Col Thomas Sackville of Selscombe, co Sussex [1]

4a Lady Anne Sackville, d (-), m 1st, 21 June 1609, the Hon Sir Edward Seymour, K B [gd-son and h-app of Edward, 1st Earl of Hertford [E]], d s p s Sept 1618, 2ndly, 7 Oct 1622, Sir Edward Lewes   [Nos 82309 to 83906

256 Descendants of Lady JANE HOWARD (Table XXI) d. 1593, m a 1564, CHARLES (NEVILL), 6th EARL OF WESTMORLAND [E], K.G., d. 16 Nov 1601, and had issue

See the Exeter Volume, Table XXII and pp 333-338, Nos 24284-24614
[Nos 83907 to 84237

257 Descendants of GEORGE (BERKELEY), 1st EARL OF BERKELEY [E], P C, F R.S (see Table XXI), b c 1627, d 14 Oct 1698, m 11 Aug 1646, ELIZABETH, da and co-h. of John MASINGBERD of London, Treasurer of the East India Coy, bur. 10 Dec 1708, and had issue 1a to 6a

1a Charles (Berkeley), 2nd Earl of Berkeley [E], K B, b 8 Ap 1649, d 24 Sept 1710, m (lic dated 16 Aug) 1677, the Hon Elizabeth, da of Baptist (Noel), 3rd Viscount Campden [E], d 30 July 1719, and had issue 1b to 3b

---

[1] Berry's "Sussex Genealogies," p 300

The Plantagenet Roll

1b James (Berkeley), 3rd Earl of Berkeley [E], KG, d at Aubigny Castle, near La Rochelle, Aug 1736, m Lady Louisa, da of Charles (Lennox), 1st Duke of Richmond [E] and Lennox [S], d 15 June 1717, and had issue

See the Exeter Volume, pp 482-487, Nos 42058-42430

2b Hon Henry Berkeley, MP, Col 4th Foot, b 1690, d May 1736, m Mary, da of Henry Cornwall of Breckwardine Castle, co Hereford, d 25 Ap 1741, and had issue (with a son and 3 das who d s p) 1c to 3c

1c Lionel Spencer Berkeley, d (–), m Margaret, da. of James Whitefield of Twickenham, co Midx, and had issue (with 2 sons d young) 1d to 4d.

1d Velters Cornwall Berkeley, Capt R N
2d Henry Nicholas Lionel Berkeley
3d James Berkeley
4d George Berkeley

2c Mary Berkeley, d 10 Mar 1755, m Charles Morton, MD, FSA, Sec. to the Royal Society, Keeper of MSS and Medals at the British Museum

3c Elizabeth Berkeley, d (–), m (—) Martin

3b Lady Mary Berkeley, d (–), m Thomas Chambers of Hanworth, co Midx

2a Rev the Hon George Berkeley, Prebendary of Westminster, d Oct 1694, m 4 Mar 1689, Jane, da of George Cole of co Devon, d (–), and had issue 1b

1b Elizabeth Berkeley, da and h, bapt 22 Mar 1691, d 8 Ap 1730, m John Brome of Tuppinden, co Kent, d 22 Feb 1747, and had issue[1] (Thomas, Elizabeth, Maria, Arethusa, William, and Jane, of whom only 2 das survived, viz) 1b to 2b

1b [da] Brome m (—) Clarke, MD

2b [da] Brome, m John Hamond, Surgeon H M Dockyard at Chatham, d Jan 1774, and had issue who inherited Tuppinden

3a Lady Elizabeth Berkeley, d c 1681, m William Smith, of the Inner Temple, and had issue (a da)

4a Lady Theophila Berkeley b 1650, d 26 Jan 1707, m 1st, 14 May 1668, Sir Kingsmill Lucy, 2nd B' [E 1618], FRS, DCL, MP, b c 1649, bur. 20 Sept 1678, 2ndly, 23 Nov 1682, Robert Nelson, the well-known author of "Festivals and Feasts of the Church," d 16 June 1715, and had issue 1b to 2b

1b Sir Berkeley Lucy, 3rd Bt [E], FRS, b c 1672, d 19 Nov 1759, m. Catherine, da of Charles Cotton of Beresford, co Stafford, bar 22 June 1710, and had issue 1c to 2c

1c Mary Lucy, da and co-h, bapt 9 Nov 1709, d (–), m 14 Aug. 1727, the Hon Charles Compton, MP, d 20 Nov 1755, and had issue

See the Clarence Volume, Table XX and pp 199-219, Nos. 3458-4434

2c Elizabeth Lucy da and co-h, d (–), m William Thompson of Leicester Square, London, d (–), and had issue (at least) 1d

1d Lucy Thompson, d 4 July 1765, m 20 July 1755, Edmund Plowden of Plowden, co Salop, d 9 Jan 1768, and had issue

See the Exeter Volume, Table XVI and pp 274-280, Nos 10900-11110.

2b Theophila Lucy, b 24 Jan 1671, d 30 July 1721, m 27 Oct 1691, Sir William Ingoldsby, 3rd Bt [E], d 25 Ap 1726, and had issue 1c

1c Elizabeth Ingoldsby, had admon to father 10 May 1726, and then wife of the Hon Col Thomas Foulkes

5a Lady Mary Berkeley, d 19 May 1719, m 1st, Ford (Grey), 3rd Baron Grey of Werke [E] and (11 June 1695) 1st Earl of Tankerville [E], PC, d 24 June 1701, 2ndly, (—) Booth of Epsom, co Surrey, and had issue 1b

[Nos 84238 to 85798

---

[1] Hasted's "Kent," i 115

432

# of The Blood Royal

1b Lady Mary Grey, d 31 May 1710, m 3 July 1695, Charles (Bennet), 3rd Baron Ossulston [E] and (19 Oct 1714) 1st Earl of Tankerville [G B], b 1674, d 21 May 1722, and had issue 1c to 4c

1c Charles (Bennet), 2nd Earl of Tankerville [G B], 4th Baron Ossulston [E], K I , d 14 May 1753, m a Nov 1715, Camilla, da of Edward Colville of White-house, co Durham, d 8 Oct 1775, and had issue 1d to 3d

1d Charles (Bennet), 3rd Earl of Tankerville [G B], 5th Baron Ossulston [E], b 6 Sept 1716, d 27 Oct 1767, m 23 Sept 1742, Alicia, da and co-h of Sir John Astley, 2nd Bt [E], bur 7 Mar 1791, and had issue 1e to 1e

1e Charles (Bennet), 4th Earl of Tankerville [G B], 6th Baron Ossulston [E], b 15 Nov 1743, d 10 Dec 1822, m 7 Oct 1771, Emma, da and co-h of Sir James Colebrooke, 1st Bt [G B], d 20 Nov 1836, and had issue 1f to 1f

1f Charles Augustus (Bennet), 5th Earl of Tankerville [G B], 7th Baron Ossulston [E], b 28 Ap 1776, d 25 June 1859, m 28 July 1806, Corisande Armandine Sophie Leonice Etienne, da of Anthony Louis Marie (de Gramont), 8th Duke of Gramont [F 1643], d 23 Jan 1865, and had issue 1g

1g Charles Augustus (Bennet), 6th Earl of Tankerville [G B], 8th Baron Ossulston [E], P C , b 10 Jan 1810 d 18 Dec 1899, m 29 Jan 1850, Lady Olivia [descended from George, Duke of Clarence, K G], da of George (Montagu), 6th Duke of Manchester [G B], and had issue

See the Clarence Volume, pp 242-243, Nos 5312-5319

2f Hon Henry Grey Bennet, b 2 Dec 1777, d 29 May 1836, m 15 May 1816, Gertrude Frances, da of Lord William Russell [Duke of Bedford Coll , a descendant of King Henry VII (see Tudor Roll, p 360)], d 23 Jan 1841, and had issue 1g to 2g

1g Charlotte Emma Georgiana Bennet, m 20 Nov 1839, the Right Hon Patrick Fitz Stephen French, P C , M P [brother of Arthur, 1st Baron De Freyne, &c], d 4 June 1873, and had issue 1h to 2h

1h Louisa Emma Corisande French, m 18 June 1868, Capt George H Bridges, A D C

2h Augusta Sarah French

2g Gertrude Frances Bennet, m 1 Aug 1839, Hamilton Gorges of Kilbrew, co Meath, d 1860

3f Lady Caroline Bennet, b 2 Oct 1772, d 7 Mar 1818, m as 1st wife, 23 June 1795, John (Wrottesley), 1st Baron Wrottesley [U K], d 16 Mar 1841, and had issue

See the Tudor Roll, pp 333-334, Nos 26544-26576

4f Lady Anna Bennet, b 28 Ap 1774, d Sept 1836, m 19 July 1804, Rev the Hon William Beresford [3rd son of William, 1st Baron Decies [I], Archbishop of Tuam], d 27 June 1830, and had issue 1g to 2g

1g William Henry Beresford, Capt Rifle Brigade, b 1810, d 26 Feb 1875, m 10 July 1850, Emma Catherine [da of (—)] Laurence of Montreal, Canada, and had issue 1h

1h Henrietta Beresford

2g Alicia Beresford, d 27 Mar 1882, m 12 Sept 1834, Horace Hamond, K H , Consul at Cherbourg, d (—), and had issue (a son and 2 das)

2e Hon Henry Astley Bennet, Lieut-Gen and Lieut-Col 85th Foot, b 3 Ap. 1757, d (?s p) 1815

3e Lady Camilla Elizabeth Bennet, b 22 May 1747, d 2 Sept 1821, m 1st, 5 Sept 1764, Count Dunhoff, of Poland, d 25 Sept 1764, 2ndly, 1778, Robert Robinson

4e Lady Frances Alicia Bennet, d (—), m 1st, William Aslong, 2ndly, 1781, the Rev Richard Sandys [eldest son of Richard Sandys of Northborne Court, co Kent], 3rdly, the Rev Edward Beckingham Benson, Rector of Deal

[Nos 85799 to 85814

+33

2d Hon George Bennet, a godson of George II, b 1727, d (² s p) 1799

3d Lady Camilla Bennet, d 7 Feb 1785, m 1st, 11 Jan 1754, Gilbert Fane Fleming, 2ndly, 9 Oct 1779, (—) Wake of Bath, and had issue (by 1st marriage)

2c Lady Bridget Bennet, d 12 Oct 1738, m as 1st wife, 20 Jan 1716, John (Wallop), 1st Earl of Portsmouth [G B], d 23 Nov 1762, and had issue

See the Essex Volume, pp 237–240, Nos 30015–30098

3c Lady Annabella Bennet, d 27 Nov 1769, m Feb 1721, William Paulet, M P [D of Bolton Coll], d (-), and had issue

See the Exeter Volume, Table XXXVII, the Essex Volume Supplement, p 638, and the Essex Volume, p 239, Nos 30085–30098

4c Lady Mary Bennet, d 24 May 1729, m 6 Aug 1729¹ or 1720,² William Willmer of Sywel Park, co Notts, M P

6a Lady Arethusa Berkeley, d 11 Feb 1743, m as 2nd wife, Charles (Boyle), 3rd Baron Clifford of Lanesborough [E], styled Viscount Dungarvan [I], d v p 12 Oct 1794, and had issue 1b

   1b Hon Arethusa Boyle, m James Younger   [Nos 85845 to 85942

258 Descendants, if any surviving, of the Hon MARY BERKELEY (Table XXI), *d* **(-)**, *m* Sir JOHN ZOUCH of Codnore, co Derby, who was knighted 23 Ap 1604 and was living 1615, and had issue ¹ 1*a* to 3*a*.

   1a John Zouch, son and h -app, joined father in sale of Codnore, m Isabella, da of Patrick Lowe of Denby

   2a Maria Zouch

   3a Isabella Zouch

259 Descendants of the Hon. FRANCES BERKELEY (Table XXI), *b. c.* 1564, *d* 29 Dec 1595, *m* as 1st wife (settl 21 Feb), 1587, Sir GEORGE SHIRLEY, 1st Bt [E. 22 May 1611], *d*. 27 Ap 1622 ; and had issue 1*a* to 2*a*

   1a Sir Henry Shirley, 2nd Bt [E], b c 1588, d 8 Feb 1633 m 1 Aug 1616, Lady Dorothy, da of Robert (Devereux), 2nd Earl of Essex [E] (who m 2ndly, 1634, William Stafford of Blatherwick, co Northants, and) d 30 Mar 1636, and had issue

See the Essex Volume, Table III and pp 36–88, Nos 4544–6687

   2a Sir Thomas Shirley of Botolph Bridge, co Hants, the Antiquary, bur at St Peter's, Paul's Wharf, London, 4 Feb 1654, m Mary, da of Thomas Harpar of Rushall, co Stafford, living Sept 1650, and had issue (all living Sept 1650) 1b to 7b

   1b Henry Shirley, b a 1629

   2b George Shirley

   3b John Shirley

   4b Francis Shirley

   5b Thomas Shirley, probably the Capt Thomas Shirley living 1669, and then next h to the Baronetcy

   6b Mary Shirley

   7b Anne Shirley   [Nos 85943 to 88086

---

¹ Brydge's " Collins," iii 130   ² Burke's " Peerage," 1907, p 1620

# of The Blood Royal

260 Descendants of Lady Margaret Howard (Table XXI), *bapt* 30 Jan. 1543, *d* 17 Mar 1590; *m*. as 2nd wife, Henry (Scrope), 9th Baron Scrope of Bolton, K G, *d* 10 May 1591, and had issue, which became extinct 30 May 1630

261 Descendants, if any, of the Hon Douglas Howard (Table XXIV), *bapt* at Stratford-le-Bow 29 Jan. 1572, *d* (–), *m* as 1st wife, Sir Arthur Gorges of Chelsea, *d* 1625, and had (with possibly other [1]) issue 1*a*

1*a Dudley Gorges*, d *(will proved* 17 *Sept*) 1667, m *at Chelsea* 12 *Aug* 1610, *Sir Robert Lane*, d *(will proved* 2 *Oct*) 1624

262 Descendants of Thomas (Thynne), 1st Viscount Weymouth [E 11 Dec 1682] (Table XXIV), *b. c* 1640, *d*. 28 July 1714, *m*. Lady Frances, da of Heneage (Finch), 3rd Earl of Winchilsea [E], *d* 17 Ap 1712, and had issue

See the Tudor Roll, Table XXIV and pp 186–240, Nos 20946–22550
[Nos 88087 to 89691

263 Descendants of Thomas Thynne of Old Windsor (Table XXIV), *d* 24 Ap 1710, *m* 1709, Lady Mary, da of Edward (Villiers), 1st Earl of Jersey [E] (who *m* 2ndly, 1711, George (Granville), 1st Baron Landsdowne [G B] and) *d* 17 Jan 1735, and had issue

See p 377, Nos 61798–62166 [Nos 89692 to 90060

264. Descendants of Dorothy Thynne (Table XXIV), *bapt* 21 Sept 1692, *d* 14 Feb 1777, *m* John (Howe), 1st Baron Chedworth [G B], *d* Ap 1742, and had issue 1*a* to 5*a*

1*a John Thynne (Howe)*, 2nd Baron Chedworth [G B], b 18 *Feb* 1714, d s p 9 *May* 1762
2*a Henry Frederick (Howe)*, 3rd Baron Chedworth [G B], b 17 *Feb* 1715, d *unm* 7 *Oct* 1781
3*a Rev the Hon. Thomas Howe, Rector of Wishford, co Wilts*, d (–), m *Frances, da of Thomas White of Tattingstone Place, co Suffolk, and had issue* 1b
1b *John (Howe)*, 4th and last *Baron Chedworth* [G B], b 22 *Aug* 1754, d *unm* 29 *Oct* 1804.

---

[1] Sir Arthur Gorges had, in addition to the da named above (1) Sir Arthur, whose only son d s p 1668, (2) Elizabeth (by 2nd wife), who m 1st, Sir Robert Stanley, and 2ndly, Theophilus, 4th Earl of Lincoln [E], (3) Timoleon (4) Egremont, (5) Carew, and (6) Henry—but, with the exception of the da Elizabeth, it does not appear clear whether they were the issue of the Howard marriage or of his 2nd wife, Lady Elizabeth Clinton

The pedigree given in Berry's "Buckingham Genealogies," deducing the Ouseleys from this Sir Arthur, is incorrect

4a Hon Mary Howe, da and in her issue, if any (1804), co-h, d (-); m *Alexander Wright*

5a Hon Anne Howe, da and in her issue (1804) h or co-h, d (-), m *Roderick Gwynne of Glanbrâne, co Brecon*, and had (with possibly other) issue[1] 1b to 2b

1b *Sackville Gwynne of Glanbrâne*, d 1791, m 1st, Catherine, da of (—) *Prytherch*, and had issue 1c to 5c

1c *Sackville Frederick Henry Gwynne of Glanbrâne*, b 14 Aug 1778, d (-) m twice, and had issue

2c *John Gwynne of Gwernvale House, co Brecon, J P, D L, High Sheriff co Brecon 1819*, d (s p), m Arabella [da of (—)] Gorges of Alscott Manor, co Oxon

3c David Gwynne, d (-), m Catherine, d of Humphrey Jones

4c }
5c } 2 das

2b *Thomas Howe Gwynne of Buckland, co Brecon*, d (-), m (—), da and h of (Matthew of Lundock Castle, co Glamorgan, and had (with possibly other) issue 1c

1c Roderick Gwynne, son and h, d v p, m Eliza Ann, da and co-h of (—) *Hughes of Tregunter*, and had issue 1d

1d *Anna Maria Eleanor Gwynne*, d 7 Aug 1881, m 4 Sept 1830, James *Price Holford of Kilgwyn, co Carmarthen, J P*, and High Sheriff co Brecknock 1840, Lieut-Col in the Army, b 25 Sept 1791, d Aug 1846, and had issue 1e to 3e

1e James Price William Holford, now Gwynne-Holford, of Kilgwyn and Buckland, J P, D L, M P for Brecon 1870–1880, and High Sheriff 1857, formerly 16th Lancers (Kilgwyn, co Carmarthen, Buckland, Bwlch, Tie Holford, co Brecon, Carlton), b 25 Nov 1833 m 14 Ap 1891, Mary Eleanor, da of Captain Patrick Robert Gordon-Cumming of Hartpury, co Glouc, and has issue 1f

1f Eleanor Mary Gwynne-Holford, b 18 Nov 1899

2e Jane Eliza Anna Maria Holford

3e *Louisa Mary Ermine Eleanor Holford*, d 10 Jan 1876, m as 1st wife, 21 Oct 1865, *Major Edmund Philip Herbert (R L 27 Sept 1848), formerly Jones, of Llansanffraed Court, Chief Constable co Monmouth [descended from George, Duke of Clarence, K G, brother of King Edward IV* (see Clarence Volume, p 456)] (Llansanffraed Court, Abergavenny), and had issue 1f

1f Edmund Arthur Herbert, M V O, Lieut-Col Comdg 6th Inniskilling Dragoons, b 5 Aug 1866, m 8 Jan 1898, Ethel, da of John Pickersgill Rodger of Hadlow Castle, co Kent, and has issue 1g to 2g

1g Eleanora Herbert

2g Mary Catherine Herbert   [Nos 90061 to 90066

265 Descendants, if any surviving, of the Hon MARY LOWTHER (Table XXIV), d (-), m Sir JOHN WENTWORTH

266 Descendants of the Hon ELIZABETH LOWTHER (Table XXIV.), bur 9 Oct 1764, m 6 Aug. 1696, Sir WILLIAM RAMSDEN, 2nd Bt [E], bapt 22 Oct 1672, d 27 June 1736; and had issue 1a to 4a

1a *Sir John Ramsden, 3rd Bt [E], M P*, bapt 21 Mar 1699, d 10 Ap. 1769, m (lic dated 8 Aug) 1748, Margaret, widow of Thomas Bright, formerly Liddell of Badsworth, co York, da and h of William Norton of Sawley, bur 7 June 1775, and had issue 1b to 2b

---

[1] Burke's "Royal Families, i –cxxix

# of The Blood Royal

1b *Sir John Ramsden*, 4th Bt [E], bapt 1 Dec 1755, d 15 July 1839, m 5 June 1787, the Hon *Louisa Susan*, da of Charles Ingram (*Shepherd*), 10th Viscount Irvine [S], d 21 Nov 1857, *and had issue*

See the Essex Volume, pp 151-152, Nos 17244-17285

2b *Elizabeth Ramsden*, d (-), m 1771, *William Weddell of Newby*, M P

2a *Robert Ramsden of Osberton*, co Notts, *an Officer in the Army*, b 1708, d 9 Feb 1769, m 13 Jan 1753, *Elizabeth*, da and event h of John Smyth of Heath Hall, co York, *and had issue* 1b *to* 1b

1b *Robert Ramsden of Carlton Hall*, co Notts, bapt 22 Nov, 1753, d 27 Ap 1830, m 1783, *Elizabeth, widow of Abel Smith of Wilford*, co Notts, M P, da of Charles Appleby of Wooton, co Linc, d 21 Nov 1807, *and had (with other) issue* 1c

1c *Robert Ramsden of Carlton Hall*, J P, *elder son*, b 29 Mar 1784, d 1865, m 29 July 1816, *Frances Matilda*, da of John Plumptre, d 22 Ap 1837, *and had issue* 1d *to* 5d

1d *Robert John Ramsden of Carlton Hall*, J P, b 12 June 1817, d 20 Mar 1892, m 10 Dec 1844, *Mary Matilda*, da of the Rev Henry Gipps of Elmley, d 4 July 1874, *and had issue* 1e *to* 8e

1e *Robert Henry Ramsden*, b 10 Sept 1845, d v p 19 May 1874, m 31 May 1871, *Francesca Romana Maria*, da of Charles William Jebb of Clifton, co Glouc, *and had issue* 1f *to* 2f

1f Robert Charles Plumptre Ramsden of Carlton Hall, J P, LL B, B A (Camb), Bar-at-Law (*Carlton Hall, Worksop, Oxford and Cambridge Club*), b 9 Feb 1874, *unm*

2f Frances Alice Mary Ramsden, m 16 Ap 1896, the Rev John Alfred James, Rector of Dodington, d 21 Jan 1910, *and has issue* 1g *to* 3g

    1g Robert Charles Patrick James, b 17 Mar 1898

    2g George Herbert Gladwyn James, b 13 Jan 1901

    3g John Cecil James, b 2 Mar 1904

2e Edward Plumptre Ramsden (*Croyde, Cape Patton, Australia*) b 21 Mar 1848, m 3 Sept 1875, *Frances Elizabeth*, da of William Kelly of Blackheath, *and has issue* 1f *to* 7f

    1f John Edward Cecil Ramsden, b 5 July 1881

    2f William Eustace Ramsden, b 4 July 1882

    3f-7f 5 das

3e *Charles Arthur Ramsden*, b 4 Ap 1849, d 3 Jan 1902, m 15 Sept 1875, *Elizabeth Mary* (*Harkaway, Berwick, Melbourne*), da of John Leckenby of Scarborough, *and had issue* 1f *to* 3f

    1f Edith Elizabeth Mary Ramsden, m 14 Ap 1897, Walter Henry Fossey (*Melbourne*), and has issue

    2f Emily Gertrude Ramsden, m 21 Dec 1899, Albert Walter Chartress (*Melbourne*), and has issue

    3f Maud Ramsden, *unm*

4e Algernon Feilden Ramsden (*Dunmore, 9 Avenue Victoria, Scarboro'*), b 11 Sept 1850, m 4 May 1892, *Mary Smith*, da of Thomas Purdom of Hawick, *and has issue* 1f

    1f Edward Feilden Ramsden, b 29 May 1893

5e John Pemberton Ramsden, B A (Camb) (*Fridhem, Bath*), b 28 Jan 1851, m 23 Aug 1883, *Alice Louisa*, da of Arthur Malet, Bombay C S [Bt Coll], *and has issue* 1f *to* 7f

    1f Arthur Amherst Ramsden, b 11 Feb 1889

    2f Ralph Western Ramsden, b 10 Oct 1890

    3f Evelyn Charlotte Ramsden

    4f Alice Frida Ramsden

    5f Guendolen Ebba Ramsden

    6f Frances Teresa Ramsden

    7f Monica Hilda Ramsden

[Nos 90067 to 90129.

The Plantagenet Roll

6e Mary Emma Frances Ramsden, m 16 Nov 1876, Thomas Eadie Purdom, M D (*Ellershe, Park Hill Road, Croydon*), and has issue

7e Elizabeth Emily Cecilia Ramsden } (16 *West Mall, Clifton, Bristol*)
8e Frances Eleanor Matilda Ramsden }

2d *Rev Charles Henry Ramsden, M A , Vicar of Chilham, co Kent*, b 6 June 1818, d 18 May 1893, m 21 May 1846, *Mary Hamilton, da of the Rev Henry Hamilton Beamish of Mount Beamish, co Cork*, d 14 Aug 1902, and had issue 1e to 7e

1e Charles Hamilton Ramsden, b 27 Mar 1847, m 1873, Caroline Augusta, da of James McEwen of San Francisco, and has issue 1f to 2f

1f Charles Harold Lowther Ramsden, B Sc , b 1883

2f Percival Scott Webber Ramsden, b 1886

2e *Rev Henry Plumptre Ramsden, B A (Oxon), Rector of Cottingham*, b 7 Ap 1848 d 6 Dec 1901, m 26 July 1887, *Ethel Frances Alice (Heathfield, Weston, Bath), da of William Henry Havelock, Bombay C S* , and had issue 1f to 2f

1f William Havelock Chaplin Ramsden, b 3 Oct 1888

2f Elaine Margaret Frecheville Ramsden

3e *Francis Edward Ramsden of Colorado, U S A , Comm R N* , b 24 July 1819, d 2 Ap 1882, m 7 June 1879, *Emma Elizabeth, da of Col F H Birch* , and had issue 1f

1f Francis Charles **Home** Ramsden (*Seattle, Washington, U S A*), b 3 Dec 1880

4e Herbert Frecheville Smyth Ramsden, Col Indian Army (*Stone Cross House, Wadhurst, Sussex*), b 6 Mar 1856, m 20 Aug 1889, the Hon Edwyna Susan Elizabeth, da of John Fiennes (Twisleton-Wykeham-Fiennes), 14th Baron Saye and Sele [E], and has issue 1f to 2f

1f Geoffrey Charles Frecheville Ramsden, b 21 Ap 1893

2f Mary Edwyna Ramsden

5e Ernest Western Ramsden (*Port Darwin, Northern Territory, S Australia*), b 27 Jan 1863

6e *Frances Matilda Anne Ramsden*, d 31 Dec 1909, m 19 Ap 1876, *Stafford O'Brien Hoare of Turville Park, co Bucks, J P , D L* , d 9 Sept 1906, and had issue 1f

1f Lilias Hoare, sometime (D P 1897) Stafford O'Brien Hoare, of Turville Park, co Bucks, m 23 Jan 1908, Major Edward Spencer Nairne, now (D P Mar 1910) Hoare-Nairne, R A (*Turville Park, Henley-on-Thames*), and has issue 1g

1g. Lilias Hoare-Nairne, b 6 June 1909

7e Gertrude Mary Ramsden (*The Rookery, Yarlington, Wincanton*), m 1887, the Rev Arthur Johnson Rogers, Rector of Yarlington, d 15 Ap 1908, and has issue 1f

1f Mary Ramsden Rogers

3d *Rev Frederick Selwyn Ramsden M A* , b 12 July 1830, d 17 Jan 1865, m 23 Ap 1862, *Mary Jane, da of the Rev Joseph Parker, M A , Rector of Wyton* , and had issue 1e

1e Frederick Plumptre Ramsden, B A (Oxon), b 1863, m Mar 1906, Norah, da of (--) White

4d *Emma Louisa Ramsden*, d 8 Oct 1901, m 29 Sept 1853, *the Rev Henry Gladwin Jebb of Firbeck Hall, co Yorks*, d 19 Ap 1898, and had issue 1e to 3e

1e Henry Scrope Frecheville Jebb, J P , formerly Lieut 3rd Hussars (*Tulloch Lodge, Ballater, Aberdeen , Athenæum*), b 17 July 1867, m 1st, 11 Aug 1888, Evelyn Lucy, widow of Capt Francis Michael Goold-Adams, R A , da of the Rev Edward Bristow Philips Wynne, d 2 Mar 1907, 2ndly, 25 Ap 1908, Winifred, da of Thomas Marriott Dodington of Horsington House, co Som , and has issue 1f to 2f   [Nos 90130 to 90148

438

# of The Blood Royal

1/ Henry Cecil Edward Jebb, *b* 14 July 1889

2/ Samuel Henry Jebb, *b* 12 Mar 1909

2c Florence Emily Dorothy Jebb (*East Liss, Hants*)

3e Edith Fanny Maud Jebb, *m* 25 Ap 1889, John Sydney Burton Borough of Chetwynd Park, M A (Oxon), J P , High Sheriff co Salop 1901 (*Chetwynd Park, Newport, Salop , Carlton*) , and has issue 1/ to 4/

    1/ John George Burton Borough, *b* 13 Sept 1890

    2/ Alaric Charles Henry Borough, *b* 9 Ap 1892

    3/ Elizabeth Honora Borough

    4/ Cynthia Mabel Borough

5d Emily Anna Ramsden (*North House, Carlton, Worksop*)

2b *Rev John Ramsden, Rector of Crofton and Vicar of Arksey*, d 12 Oct 1807 m 8 Oct 1790, *Frances Elizabeth, da of Sir George Cooke, 7th Bt* [E], d 13 Dec 1817, *and had issue 1c to 2c*

1c *John Ramsden*, b 3 Jan 1793, d 19 Mar 1861, m 28 Oct 1828, *Maria, da of* (—) *Jackman, d July 1859, and had issue 1d*

1d *William John Plantagenet Ramsden, b 30 Sept 1837, m 2 July 1861,* Emma Mary, da of Thomas Fairland, *d s p 9 Sept 1878*

2c *George Ramsden*, b 13 Jan 1796, *d* (-), *m* 6 Jan 1825, *Anna, da of John Fullerton of Thriberg, d 3 Jan 1837, and had issue 1d*

1d *Rev Frederick John Ramsden, M A* (Oxon), *Rector of Uffington*, b 5 Aug 1836, d 26 Nov 1903 *m* 22 Aug 1865, *Anna Cassandra, da of Rear-Adm the Hon Major Jacob Henniker, d 5 May 1906, and had issue 1e to 4e*

1e Frederick Frank Ramsden (*Bishop Thornton Grove, Ripley, Yorks*), *b* 8 Dec 1867, *m* 1893, Selina Lucinda, da of Capt Edmund Mackinnon, 2nd Life Guards

2e Cassandra Ramsden, *m* 14 Ap 1898, George William Staunton

3e Julia Selina Ramsden   } (58 *Cornwall Gardens, S W*)
4e Frances Georgiana Ramsden }

3b Catherine Ramsden

4b Charlotte Ramsden

3a *Thomas Ramsden, Latin Sec in the Office of Sec of State*, bapt 22 July 1709, d (*will dated 2 Sept 1785, pr 31 May*) 1791, *m* 14 July 1743, *Anne, da of Sir Philip Medowes, Knight Marshal*

4a *Frecheville Ramsden, Lieut -Col Grenadier Guards, Lieut -Gov of Carlis'e,* bapt 11 Ap 1715, d 24 Dec 1804, *m* 17 Mar 1761, *Isabella* [*descended from the Lady Isabella Plantagenet*], *da of Col Charles Ingram* [*Vt Irvine Coll*], d 25 Feb 1762, *and had issue 1b*

1b *George Ramsden, Capt 15th Light Dragoons,* b c 1761, d 1793, m *Lucy, da and co-h of Gen Bryn Carpenter,* d 17 Aug 1842, *and had issue* (*with a younger son d s p*) 1c to 2c

1c *George Ramsden, Lieut -Col 1st Foot Guards,* d (? s p) 9 Oct 1820

2c *Rev William Ramsden, Rector of Ashurst, Kent, and Linwood, co Linc ,* b 1787, d 4 Nov 1860, m 5 Ap 1815, *Elizabeth Jane, da of Richard Bell of Selby, co Yorks,* d 11 Ap 1888, *and had issue* (*with 2 sons and a da d unm*) 1d

1d *Arthur Charles Ramsden of Stoneness, co Kent, J P , Hon Col 2nd Vol Batt The Buffs,* b 1 Ap 1825, d 11 Dec 1891, m 21 Jan 1855, *Frances Elizabeth, da of John Deacon of Mabledon, co Kent,* d 8 Oct 1892 *and had issue 1e to 3e*

1e Arthur John Ramsden, J P , *formerly Capt and Hon Major 1st Vol Batt* Queen's Own (*Great Budlake, Bridstowe, Devon*), b 10 June 1855 *m* 26 Ap 1883, Elizabeth Alice, da of Henry William Hawkins of Martinstown, Dorset, and his issue 1/ to 4/

[Nos 90149 to 90165

The Plantagenet Roll

1/ Arthur Geoffrey Francis Ramsden, *b* 13 Aug 1887.

2/ John Hope Frecheville Ramsden, *b* 26 July 1896

3/ Elizabeth Joan Ramsden, *m* 12 Oct 1910, Julian Baring-Gould [2nd son of the Rev Sabine Baring-Gould and a descendant of Lady Isabel Plantagenet (see Essex Volume, p 127)]

1f Frances Honor Ramsden

2e Rev William Frecheville Ramsden, M A (Oxon), Vicar of St Saviour's, Scarborough (*St Saviour's Parsonage, Scarborough*), *b* 16 July 1857 *unm*

3 Rev George Ramsden, Chaplain of Walmsgate (*The Priory, Burwell, Louth, Lincoln*) *b* 8 Mar 1862, *m* 27 Sept 1886, Elizabeth Jane, da of John Wykes of Diventry, *d s p* 8 Oct 1905 [Nos 90166 to 90171]

267 Descendants of the Hon MARGARET LOWTHER (Table XXIV), *d* 15 Sept 1738 , *m* 20 Mar 1706, Sir JOSEPH PENNINGTON, 2nd Bt [E], *d* 3 Dec 1744 , and had issue

See the Exeter Volume, pp 536–537, Nos 49016–49258

[Nos 90172 to 90414]

268 Descendants, if any, of ELIZABETH THYNNE (Table XXIV), *d* (–) , *m* Sir THOMAS NOTT of Richmond, co Surrey

269 Descendants, if any, of the Hon GRACE HOWARD (Table XXIV), *d* (–) , *m* JOHN [son and h of Sir John] HORSEY of Clifton, co Dorset

270 Descendants of HENRY (NEVILL), 5th EARL OF WESTMORLAND [E], K G (Table XXV), *b* 1525, *d* Aug 1563, *m* 1st, 3 July 1538, Lady ANNE, da of Thomas (MANNERS), 1st Earl of Rutland [E], 2ndly, JANE, da. of Sir Roger CHOLMELEY, 3rdly MARGARET, widow of Sir HENRY GASCOIGNE, da of Sir Roger CHOLMELEY, *bur.* 2 Ap 1570, and had issue 1*a* to 5*a*

1a *Charles (Nevill), 6th Earl of Westmorland [E], K G, b 1543 d 16 Nov 1601 m a 1564, Lady Jane da of Henry (Howard), Earl of Surrey [E], K G, d c 1593 and had issue*
See the Exeter Volume, Table XXII and pp 333–338, Nos 24284–24614

2a[1] *Lady Eleanor Nevill m as 1st wife, Sir William Pelham, P C, d 1587, and had issue*
See the Exeter Volume, Table XXIII and pp 339–346, Nos 24615–25204

3a[1] *Lady Katherine Nevill, d s p , m Sir John Constable of Kirby Knowle, co York*
4a[2] *Lady Margaret Nevill*
5a[2] *Lady Elizabeth Nevill* [Nos 90115 to 91535]

271 Descendants of Lady KATHERINE DE VERE (Table XXV.), *d* 17 Jan 1599 , *m* EDWARD (WINDSOR), 3rd BARON WINDSOR [E], *d* 24 Jan 1575 , and had issue 1*a* to 6*a*.

1a *Frederick (Windsor), 4th Baron Windsor [E], b 1559 , d unm 24 Oct 1585*
2a *Henry (Windsor) 5th Baron Windsor [E], b 1562, d 6 Ap 1605, m*

440

# of The Blood Royal

1590, *Anne, da and co-h of Sir Thomas Revett of London, d 27 Nov 1615, and had issue 1b to 3b*

1b *Thomas (Windsor), 6th Baron Windsor [E] K B , b 29 Sept 1591, d s p 6 Dec 1642*

2b *Hon Elizabeth Windsor, da and co-h , d (–), m 21 July 1616, Dixie Hickman of Kew, co Surrey , and had issue 1c to 3c*

1c *Thomas (Hickman), 7th Baron Windsor and (6 Dec 1682) 1st Earl of Plymouth [E], d 3 Nov 1687 m 1st, 12 May 1656, Anne, da of Sir William Savil. of Thornhill, 3rd Bt [E 1611], d 22 Nov 1666 , 2ndly, 9 Ap 1668, Ursula, da and co-h of Sir Thomas Widdrington of Sherburne Grange, co Northbd d 22 Ap 1717 and had issue 1d to 3d*

1d[1] *Other Hickman, Lord Windsor, b 12 Sept 1659, d v p 11 Nov 1684, m 20 Oct 1673, Elizabeth, da and h of Thomas Turvey of Walcote, co Worc [who m 2ndly, Edward Wyke and was] bur 29 Jan 1688 , and had issue*

See the Exeter Volume, Table XXI and pp 321-333, Nos 23949-24283

2d[2] *Thomas (Hickman), 1st Viscount Windsor [I], so cr 19 June 1699, and Baron Mountjoy [G B], so cr 1 Jan 1712, d 8 June 1738, m 28 Aug 1703, Charlotte, widow of John (Jeffreys), 2nd Baron Jeffreys [E], da and h of Philip (Herbert), 7th Earl of Pembroke [E], d 13 Nov 1733 , and had issue 1e to 5e*

1e *Herbert (Hickman), 2nd Viscount Windsor [I] and Baron Mountjoy [G B], d 25 Jan 1758 , m 12 Aug 1735, Alice, sister and co-h of Sir James Clavering, 4th Bt [E] d 24 Nov 1776 , and had issue 1f*

1f *Hon Charlotte Jane Hickman, da and (11 Nov 1772) sole h , d 28 Jan 1800 , m as 1st wife, 12 Nov 1766 John (Stuart), 4th Earl [S] and (27 Feb 1796) 1st Marquis [G B] of Bute, d 16 Nov 1814 , and had issue*

See the Exeter Volume, pp 294-297, Nos 14684-14791

2c *Hon Ursula Hickman, d (–), m as 1st wife, 20 Mar 1736, John Wadman of Imber, co Wilts, d 1793 , and had issue 3 children who d s p* [1]

3e *Hon Charlotte Hickman, d (–), m 18 Ap 1736, John Kent of Salisbury*

4e *Hon Catherine Hickman, b in London 1716 , d s p at Frankfort-on-Main 26 May 1742, m as 1st wife, 10 Feb 1741, Matthews Lestevenon, Lord of Berkenrode and Strijen, in Holland, LL D Secretary to the City of Amsterdam 1729-1745, and Sheriff 1715-1748, and Ambassador to France 1749-1792, d at the Hague 13 Jan 1797*

5e *Hon Elizabeth Hickman*

3d *Lady Ursula Hickman, d 20 Aug 1737 m 28 Mar 1703, Thomas Johnson*

2c *Mariana Hickman, b 1620 , bur at Worcester 7 Feb 1670, m 1st, June 1644, Sir Henry Hunloke, 1st Bt [E 28 Feb 1642], d 13 Jan 1647, 2ndly, 25 May 1655, Col William Michell, d c (will proved 26 June) 1673, and had issue (with a da by 2nd husband who d s p) 1d*

1d *Sir Henry Hunloke, 2nd Bt [E], b 20 Nov 1645, d 3 Jan 1714, m. 28 Jan 1674, Katherine, da and h of Francis Tyrwhitt of Kettleby, co Linc , and had issue*

See the Exeter Volume, Table II , and pp 77-78, Nos 1-106

3c *Catherine Hickman, d (–), m John Columbine* [2]

3b *Hon Elizabeth Windsor, da and co-h , m 1st, Sir Andrew Windsor, 2ndly, Sir James Ware, Auditor-Gen of Ireland , and had issue of whom descendants of the name of Ware survived in Ireland in the eighteenth century* [3]

[Nos 91336 to 91887

---

[1] Hoare's "Wilts," 1 ii 165

[2] Not mentioned in the Columbine pedigree in Carthew's "West and East Bradenham," p 160

[3] Brydge's "Collins," iii 682

3a Hon *Edward Windsor*, m *Elizabeth [da of (—)] Ardington*

4a Hon *Andrew Windsor*, m *Anne [da of (—)] Peche*

5a Hon *Margaret Windsor*, d s p[1], m as 2nd wife, *John Talbot of Grafton*, co *Worc*

6a[1] Hon *Catherine Windsor*, b c 1568, d 15 *Dec* 1641, m *Robert Audley of Berechurch, co Essex*, b 11 *Mar* 1556, d 27 *Sept* 1624, and had issue 1b to 5b[2]

1b Sir *Henry Audley of Berechurch*, aged 19 and over 1624, m *Anne, da of Humphrey Porkington of Horsington, co Worc*, and had issue (at least 2 sons)[3] 1c to 2c

1c *Thomas Audley of Berechurch*, d s p 1697

2c *Henry Audley* d 1 *Sept* 1711, after having sold his estates

2b *Robert Audley of Colchester*, living 1634

3b *Richard Audley*

4b *Catherine Audley*, m *John Thatcher*

5b *Mary Audley*

272 Descendants, if any, of Lady MARY NEVILL (Table XXV), d. 14 Mar 1596, *m* Sir THOMAS DANBY of Farnley, co York, knighted Sept 1547, d 13 Sept 1590, and had issue (with others who all app *d s p*) 1a

1a *Thomas Danby of Farnley, &c, co York*, d s p 3 *Jan* 1584 m *Elizabeth, da of Thomas Wentworth of Wentworth Woodhouse*, d 1629, and had issue 1b

1b *Christopher Danby of Farnley and Leighton*, d 18 *July* 1624, m the Hon *Frances, da of Edward (Parker), 6th Baron Morley [E]* (who re-m 2ndly, *William Richards* ond) d 20 *Sept* 1654, and had issue 1c to 2c

1c Sir *Thomas Danby of Farnley and Leighton, High Sheriff co York* 1625, and a Col in the Royal Army, d 5 *Aug* 1660, m *Katherine, da of Christopher Wandesford, Lord-Deputy of Ireland*, d 22 *Sept* 1645[4], and had issue 1d to 3d

1d *Thomas Danby of Farnley, 1st Mayor of Leeds*, d 1667, leaving issue, which became extinct 1683

2d *Christopher Danby of Farnley*, d *Nov* 1689, m *Anne, da of Col Edward Colepepper* and had issue 1e to 4e

1e Sir *Abstrupus Danby, J P, D L, co York*, b 1655, d 24 *Mar* 1727, m and had issue, which became extinct in or about 1792

2e *Wandesforde Danby*

3e *Francesca Danby*

4e *Eleanor Danby*

3d *Katharine Danby*, d 1688, m *Henry Best of Gray's Inn*

2c *Katharine Danby*, bapt at Leeds 29 *Nov* 1612, bur 13 *Jan* 1666, m 1629, Sir *Francis Armytage of Kirklees, 1st Bt [E 15 Dec 1611]*, d s p (bur 12 *June*) 1644 and had issue 1d to 5d

1d Sir *John Armytage, 2nd Bt [E]*, bapt 15 *Dec* 1629 bur 9 *Mar* 1677, m c 1651, *Margaret, da of Thomas Thornhill of Fixby, co York*, bur 10 *Feb* 1695, and had issue 1e to 6e

1e Sir *Thomas Armytage, 3rd Bt [E]*, bapt 10 *May* 1652, d unm 1694

---

[1] Brydge's "Collins," III 36   [2] Berry's "Essex Pedigrees," p 134

[3] Morant's "Essex," II 205

[4] Whitaker's "Richmond," II 98   In Thoresby's *Ducatus Leodiensis* (p 202), however, she is said to have died of her fifteenth child in the thirtieth year of her age, 1629

# of The Blood Royal

2e *Sir John Armytage, 4th Bt* [E], bapt 14 Ap 1653, d unm 2 Dec 1732

3e *Christopher Armytage of Hartshead Hall, whose only son d s p 1732*

4e *Sir George Armytage, 5th Bt* [E], bapt 23 Aug 1660, d unm. (bur 24 Ap) 1736

5e *Margaret Armytage,* bapt 24 Sept 1650, d (-), m 27 May 1672, *Francis Neville of Chevet, co York,* bur 5 June 1707, *and had issue, which became extinct 1765*

6e *Catherine Armytage,* bapt 7 Ap 1654, d (-), m *as 1st wife,* 19 Nov 1679, *Christopher Tancred of Whexley, co York, M P, High Sheriff* 1685, d 21 Nov 1705, *and had issue*

See the Exeter Volume, pp 551-553, Nos 49618-49656

2d *Francis Armytage of South Kirby, co York,* bapt 3 Jan 1632, d *between* 1695 and 1728 m *Mary, da of Robert Trappes of Nidd, co York, and had issue* 1e

1e *Sir Thomas Armytage, 6th and last Bt* [E], bapt 31 July 1673, d unm 12 Oct 1737

3d *William Armytage of Killinghall, co York, living* 1660, m *Elizabeth, da of Robert Trappes*

4d *Anne Armytage,* m (—) *Smith of London*

5d *Winifred Armytage,* m *Thomas Lacy*   [Nos 91888 to 91926

273 Descendants of Lady MARGARET NEVILL (Table XXV), *d* 13 Oct 1559, *m* as 1st wife, 3 July 1536, HENRY (MANNERS), 2nd EARL OF RUTLAND [E], K G, *d* 17 Sept 1563, and had issue.

See the Exeter Volume, Table II, and pp 77-159, Nos 1-2470, and Essex Volume Supplement, pp 606-613, Nos 2470 1-183   [Nos 91927 to 94580

274 Descendants of JOHN (VERNEY, *afterwards c* 1772 PEYTO-VERNEY), 14th BARON WILLOUGHBY DE BROKE [E] (Table XXV), *b* 1738; *d* 15 Feb 1816, *m* 8 Oct 1761, Lady LOUISA, da of Francis (NORTH), 1st Earl of Guildford [G B], *b* 23 Mar. 1737, *d.* 2 Ap 1798, and had issue 1*a* to 3*a*

1a *John Peyto (Verney), 15th Baron Willoughby de Broke* [E], b 28 June 1762, d s p 1 Sept 1820

2a *Henry (Verney), 16th Baron Willoughby de Broke* [E], b 5 Ap 1773, d s p 16 Dec 1852

3a *Hon Louisa Verney,* b 20 June 1769, d 3 Feb 1835, m 31 Oct 1793, *the Rev Robert Barnard, Preb of Winchester,* d 25 Feb 1835, *and had issue* 1b

1b *Robert John (Barnard, afterwards (R L 17 May 1853) Verney), 17th Baron Willoughby de Broke* [E], b 7 Oct 1809 d 5 June 1862, m 25 Oct 1842, *Georgiana Jane, da of Major Gen Thomas William Taylor of Ogwell, co Devon, C B,* d 7 Mar 1889, *and had issue* 1c to 6c

1c *Henry (Verney), 18th Baron Willoughby de Broke* [E], b 14 May 1844, d 19 Dec 1902, m 17 Oct 1867, *Geraldine, da of James Hugh Smith-Barry of Marbury Hall, co Chester,* d 21 Dec 1894, *and had issue* 1d to 3d

1d *Richard Greville (Verney), 19th Baron Willoughby de Broke* [E] *and also de jure Baron Latimer* [E 1299], J P, D L, &c (*Kineton House, Warwick, Compton Verney, Warwick, Woodley House, Kineton, Carlton*), b 29 May 1869, m 2 July 1895, Marie Frances Lisette, da of Charles Addington Hanbury, s p s
                                                              [No 94581.

443

The Plantagenet Roll

2*d* Hon Blanche Verney, *m* 13 Ap 1898, Richard Granville Lloyd Baker, J P [eldest son and h of Granville Edward Lloyd Baker of Hardwicke Court] (*The Cottage, Hardwicke, Glos*), and has issue 1*c* to 3*e*

    1*c* Hylda Blanche Lloyd Baker

    2*e* Olive Katharine Lloyd Baker

    3*e* Audrey Pamela Lloyd Baker

3*d* Hon Patience Verney, *m* 4 June 1896, Basil Hanbury (*The Lodge Farm, Compton Verney, Warwick*), and has issue 1*e*

    1*c* Harold Greville Hanbury, *b* 1898

2*c* Rev the Hon Walter Robert Verney, M A (Oxon), Vicar of Chesterton, late Rector of Lighthorne (*Lighthorne, Warwick, Junior Carlton*), *b* 18 Mar 1846, *m* 5 June 1879, Elizabeth Georgina, da of Major Robert Wilberforce Bird of Barton House, Shipston-on-Stour, and has issue 1*d* to 3*d*

    1*d* Robert Barnard Verney, *b* 5 Nov 1882

    2*d* Reynell Henry Verney, *b* 12 Jan 1886

    3*d* Clare Verney

3*c* Hon Margaret Louisa Verney (23 *Hans Place, S W , Sandwell, S Devon*), *m* 30 Sept 1874, Jervoise Smith, M P , *d* 21 July 1884, and has issue 1*d*

    1*d* Dorothy Anne Smith

4*c* Hon Alice Jane Verney, *b* 3 Feb 1849, *d* 8 *Jan* 1882, *m* 20 *Sept* 1874, *Edward William Tritton, d Jan* 1902, *and had issue* 1*d to* 4*d*

    1*d* Oswald Tritton, Officers' Reserve Territorial Force.

    2*d* Louis Tritton

    3*d* John Tritton, I C S , d in India

    4*d* Claude Tritton

5*c* Hon Susan Emma Verney (*Banks Fee, Moreton-in-Marsh*), *m* 11 June 1885, Edmund Temple Godman of Banks Fee, co Glos , J P , D L , High Sheriff for that co 1882, *d* 22 Mar 1891, and has issue 1*d*

    1*d* John Godman, Lieut 15th Hussars, *b* 9 May 1886

6*c* Hon Mabel Verney (*Craddocks, Kineton, Warwick*)

[Nos 94582 to 94599

275 Descendants, if any of the Hon Mary Verney ('Table XXV), *d* (-), *m* Samuel Davenport of Calverley, co Cheshire

276 Descendants of the Hon Diana Verney (Table XXV), *d* 28 Sept 1725 , *m* as 2nd wife (he dated 26 Oct), 1684, Sir Charles Shuckburgh, 2nd Bt [E 1660], M.P , *b* Nov. 1659 ; *d* 2 Sept 1705 , and had issue 1*a* to 4*a*

    1*a Charles Shuckburgh of Longborough, co Glos , b* 1694, *d* 1752, *m* 1718, *Sarah, da of Col Henry Hunt , and had issue* 1*b to* 2*b*

    1*b Sir Charles Shuckburgh, 5th Bt* [E] *on the death of his cousin* 1759, *d s p* 10 *Aug* 1773

    2*b Richard Shuckburgh, Lieut Col in the Army, b* 1727, *d* 3 *Sept* 1772 *m* 1750, *Sarah, widow of Edward Bate, da of Capt Hayward, R N , and had issue* 1*c to* 3*c*

    1*c Sir George Augustus William Shuckburgh, afterwards* (4 P 1794) *Evelyn, 6th Bt* [E], *M P , a distinguished scientist, b c* 1752, *d* 11 *Aug* 1804, *m* 2ndly, 6 *Oct* 1785, *Julia Annabella, da and h of James Evelyn of Felbridge, co Surrey, bur* 23 *Sept* 1797 *and had issue* 1*d*

    1*d Julia Evelyn Medley Shuckburgh Evelyn, b* 6 *Oct* 1790 , *d* 8 *Ap* 1814, *m* 19 *July* 1810, *Charles Cecil Cope* (*Jenkinson*), *3rd Earl of Liverpool and Baron*

444

# of The Blood Royal

Hawkesbury [G B], &c., G C B, *Lord Steward of the Household,* d 3 Oct 1851, *and had issue (with an elder son who d s p) 1e to 2c*

1e *Lady Selina Charlotte Jenkinson,* b 3 July 1812, d 24 Sept 1883, m 1st, 15 Aug 1833, *William Charles Wentworth Fitzwilliam, Viscount Milton* [s and h of Charles, 5th Earl Fitzwilliam [I and G B], K G, and a descendant of the Lady Anne, sister of King Edward IV], d v p 8 Nov 1835, *2ndly, as 2nd wife, 28 Aug 1845, George Savile Foljambe of Osberton and Aldwarke* [also descended from the Lady Anne, sister of King Edward IV], d 18 Dec 1869, *and had issue 1f to 6f*

    1f-2f Sons by 2nd husband   See the Exeter Volume, p 673, Nos, 57148-57160

    3f Da by 1st husband   See the Exeter Volume, p 253, Nos 9608-9631

    4f-6f Das by 2nd husband   See the Exeter Volume, p 674. Nos 57161-57172

    2e *Lady Louisa Harriet Jenkinson,* b 28 Mar 1814, d 5 Feb 1887, m 5 Sept 1839, *John Coles of Woodcote Hall, co Salop, M P,* d 1874, *and had issue*
See the Tudor Roll, pp 324-325, Nos 26303-26318

    2c *Sir Stewkley Shuckburgh, 7th Bt* [E], b c 1760, d 21 July 1809, m 5 Sept 1786, *Charlotte Catherine, da of Thomas Tydd,* d 8 Feb 1837, *and had issue (with 2 sons and 8 das d s p) 1d to 3d*

    1d *Sir Francis Shuckburgh, 8th Bt* [E], F R S, b 12 Mar 1789, d 29 Oct 1876, m 27 Oct 1825, *Anne Maria Draycott, da of Peter Denys of Chelsea* [by his wife Lady Charlotte, née Fermor], d 8 Nov 1846, *and had issue 1e to 2e*

    1e *Sir George Thomas Francis Shuckburgh, 9th Bt* [E], J P, D L, Major *Scots Guards,* b 23 July 1829, d 12 Jan 1884, m 24 June 1879. *Ida Florence Geraldine, da of the Rev Frederick William Robertson* [who m 2ndly 25 Nov 1886, *Major Henry James Shuckburgh (eldest son of Col Henry Adolphus Shuckburgh* see below), who d s p, and] d 12 Jan 1906, *and had issue 1f to 2f*

    1f *Sir Stewkley Frederick Draycott Shuckburgh, 10th Bt* [E] (*Shuckburgh, near Daventry*), b 20 June 1880

    2f *Gerald Francis Stewkley Shuckburgh,* b 28 Feb 1882, m 2 Mar 1909, *Honor Zoe, da of Neville Thursby of Harlestone, co Northants, and has issue 1g*

    1g *Evelyn Honor Shuckburgh,* b 21 Feb 1910

    2e *Charlotte Georgiana Amelia Shuckburgh,* b 21 Aug 1826, d 11 June 1902, m 24 Ap 1860, *the Rev John Richard Errington, M A, Rector of Ladbrooke and Hon Canon of Worcester,* d 4 Oct 1882, *and had issue (with a son d young) 1f to 4f*

    1f *Frederick Francis Errington,* b 30 July 1861

    2f *Wilfred John Errington,* b 10 Aug 1865, d (?)

    3f *Walter Alfred Errington,* b 24 Feb 1868

    4f *Eliza Margaret Errington*

    2d *Henry Adolphus Shuckburgh, Col 10th Bengal N I,* b 25 Nov 1800, d 22 Dec 1860, m 2ndly, 5 May 1854, *Catherine Lowthy, da of Daniel J Cloete, High Sheriff of Cape Town,* d 17 Ap 1866, *and had issue (with a son and da d s p) 1e to 2e.*

    1e *George Stewkley Shuckburgh, Capt R N (Falmouth),* b 5 Aug 1860, m 9 Sept 1898, *Amy Mary, da of John Robertson of Coromooke, Colac, Victoria, and has issue 1f to 2f*

    1f *Mabel Evelyn Shuckburgh*

    2f *Lorna May Shuckburgh*

    2e *Caroline Emma Shuckburgh* (*36 Lexham Gardens, W*)

    3d *Mary Amelia Shuckburgh,* b 17 Ap 1793, d 19 Feb 1858, m 1820, *Thomas Lamb Polden Laugharne, Comm R N, and had issue 1e to 2e*

    1e *Rev Thomas Robert John Laugharne, Vicar of Rhayader, co Radnor,* b 24 Mar 1821, d 8 July 1891, m 1st, 1 Mar 1859, *Ellen Maria, da of (—) Wilkes,* d 10 Aug 1868, 2ndly, *Easter Tuesday, 1873, Elizabeth Emily, wid w (with issue) of Henry Campbell of Dunmorn, da of William Henry Cooke of Darfield, co Yorks,* d 12 Jan 1906, *and had issue 1f to 1f*   [Nos 94600 to 94674

445   3 L

The Plantagenet Roll

1f Roland Lamb Polden Laugharne, b 10 June 18—, m 9 June 1890, Alexandra Beatrix, da of (—) Cox, and has issue 1g to 3g

    1g Ronald Hugh Polden Laugharne, Mid R N

    2g Knightley Owen Shuckburgh Laugharne

    3g Beatrix Laugharne, unm

2f¹ Ellen Mary Julia Laugharne, m 8 Nov 1888, William Arthur Allen of Gosport House, Laugharne, co Carmarthen, Manager North and South Wales Branch of London City and Midland Bank, Ltd (100 *South Road, Waterloo, Liverpool, W*), and has issue 1g to 5g

    1g Cyril Allen, b Dec 1896

    2g Arthur Allen, b Aug 1898

    3g Ruth Allen

    4g Barbara Allen

    5g Gladys Allen

3f¹ Margaret Maria Meliora Laugharne, unm

4f² Emily Ruth Laugharne, m 20 June 1904, Daniel Howell Roland Thomas of Puke, Whitland, co Carmarthen, Solicitor (*Blaencorse, St Clears, S Wales*), and has issue 1g

    1g Elizabeth Orpah Gwenneth Thomas

2e *Julia Charlotte Laugharne*, b 18 Feb 1829, d 4 Mar 1905, m 9 Ap 1863, *the Rev Percival Alfred Fothergill, B A, F R A S, Rector of South Heighton with Tarring Neville, co Sussex, Dom Chaplain to the Earl of Limerick, previously R N*, d 24 Aug 1888, *and had issue (with a son and da d unm)* 1f to 1f

    1f Percival Guy Laugharne Fothergill, ⎫

    2f Frederick Henry Gaston Fothergill, ⎪ *unm*

    3f Henryetta Mary Bertha Fothergill, ⎬

    1f Ernestine Gertrude Frances Fothergill, ⎭

3c *Sarah Shuckburgh*, d (–), m *John Cleveland of Tapley, co Devon, M P for Saltash 1761, for Barnstaple 1766*

2a *Grace Shuckburgh*, d (–), m *the Rev* (—) *Crabb*

3a *Sophia Shuckburgh*, d Mar 1739, m *Francis Loggin*

4a *Diana Shuckburgh*, d (–), m *the Rev Nicholas Webb*

[Nos 94675 to 94691

277. Descendants, if any, of ELIZABETH VERNEY (Table XXV), d (–), m WILLIAM PEYTO of Chesterton, co Warwick

278. Descendants, if any, of GEORGE VERNEY (Table XXV), d (–), m. Lady TRYPHENA, da. of Edmund (SHEFFIELD), 1st Earl of Mulgrave [E.]

279. Descendants of Sir THOMAS SAMWELL of Upton and Gayton, 1st Bt [E 1675], M P (Table XXV.), *bur* 3 Mar. 1694, m 1st, 1673, ELIZABETH, da and h of George GOODAY of Bowerhall, co Essex, *bapt* 3 Mar 1651, living 1678, 2ndly, 1685, ANNE, da and h of Sir John GODSCHALK of Atherston, co Warwick, and had issue 1a to 3a.

1a *Sir Thomas Samwell, 2nd Bt [E], M P*, bapt 14 Ap 1687, d 16 Nov. 1757, m 1st, 22 Mar 1710, *Millicent, da and h of the Rev Thomas Fuller, D D*,

Rector of Hatfield, co Herts, bu 11 May 1716, 2ndly, 26 Jan 1721, Mary, da of Gilbert Clarke of Chilcot, co Derby, d 1 Aug 1758, and had issue 1b to 1b

1b *Sir Thomas Samwell, 3rd Bt* [E], b 28 May 1711, d s p 3 Dec 1779

2b *Sir Wenman Samwell 4th and last Bt* [E], b 24 Oct 1728, d s p 18 Oct 1789

3b *Mary Samwell, da and in her issue (1789) co-h*, bapt 28 Oct 1715, d (-), m 24 July 1739, *the Rev Stephen Langham, Rector of Cottesbrook* (see below), d 1 Mar 1755, *and had issue (with a son and da known to have d s p) 1c to 3c*

1c *Millicent Langham, da and co-h, d at Northampton 8 Ap 1808, m William Drought of Oxford, and had issue 1d to 3d*

    1d *Thomas Fuller Drought of Oxford*

    2d *Frances Drought*

    3d *Juliana Drought*

2c *Frances Anne Langham, da and co-h* [1]

3c *Phillis Langham, da and co-h* [1]

1b *Catherine Samwell, da and co-h* b 27 May 1724, d 25 July 1790, m 6 Mar 1754, *Thomas Atherton Watson of Bedlington, co Northbd,* b 18 Aug 1714, d 1 Oct 1793, *and had issue 1c to 3c*

1c *Thomas Samwell Watson, afterwards (Act of Parl 1790) Samwell of Upton,* d s p 15 Jan 1831

2c *Wenham Langham Watson, afterwards (Act of Parl 1832) Samwell of Upton,* d s p

3c *Charlotte Felicia Watson,* d (-), *m at Chesterfield 14 Aug 1792, the Rev Benjamin Tinley of Whissendine, co Rutland, B D,* d 27 Jan 1804, *and had issue 1d to 3d*

    1d *Clarissa Felicia Tinley,* b 27 June 1795

    2d *Frances Anne Tinley,* b 3 May 1798

    3d *Charlotte Henrietta Tinley,* b 3 Ap 1800

2a *Elizabeth Samwell,* bapt 24 Mar 1674, d 1715, m *as 1st wife,* 11 June 1691, *Sir John Langham, 4th Bt* [E], d May 1747, *and had (with other) issue 1b to 3b*

1b *Sir James Langham, 5th Bt* [E], d s p 12 Aug 1749

2b *Sir John Langham, 6th Bt* [E], d s p Sept 1766

3b *William Langham of Rance, co Northants,* d (-), m *Mary, da of Anthony Drought, and had issue 1c to 2c*

1c *Sir James Langham, 7th Bt* [E], M P, b 31 Jan 1736, d 7 Feb 1795, m 2 June 1767, *Juliana, sister and h of Thomas Musgrave of Old Cleve, co Som,* d 21 Mar 1810, *and had issue 1d to 3d*

1d *Sir William Langham, 8th Bt* [E], b 10 Feb 1771, d 8 Mar 1812, m 1st, 20 Aug 1795, *Henrietta Elizabeth Frederica, da and h of the Hon Charles Vane* [B Barnard Coll], d 11 Nov 1809, *and had issue*

See the Clarence Volume, Table LXXIII and pp 585-586, Nos 24544-24573

2d *Sir James Langham, 10th Bt* [E], M P, b 21 Aug 1776, d 11 Ap 1833, m 26 May 1800, *Elizabeth, sister of Sir Francis Burdett, 5th Bt* [E], *da of Francis Burdett,* d 30 Nov 1855 *and had issue 1e to 2e*

1e *Sir James Hay Langham, 11th Bt* [E], b 13 Nov 1802, d s p 13 Dec 1893

2e *Herbert Langham,* b 12 June 1804, d 27 Feb 1874, m 25 June 1839, *Laura Charlotte, da of Nathaniel Micklethwait of Taverham Hall, co Norfolk [by his 2nd wife Lady Charlotte, née Rous]* d 3 Sept 1861, *and had issue (with a son and 2 das d s p) 1f to 2f*

1f *Sir Herbert Hay Langham, 12th Bt* [E], J P, D L, *late Lieut 1st Life* [Nos 94692 to 94721

1 Baker's "Northants," i 221

The Plantagenet Roll

Guards, b 28 Ap 1840, d 13 Dec 1909, m 25 Aug 1868, the Hon Anna Maria Frances [descended from the Lady Isabel Plantagenet (see the Essex Volume, p 143)], da of Arthur Marcus Cecil (Sandys), 3rd Baron Sandys [U K] P C , d 27 May 1876 , and had issue 1g to 2g

1g Sir Herbert Charles Arthur Langham, 13th Bt [E] *(Cottesbrooke Park, Northampton , Tempo Manor, co Fermanagh), b* 21 Mar 1870 , *m* 1 June 1893, Ethel Smith, da of Sir William Emerson-Tennent, 2nd Bt [U K], and has issue 1h

1h John Charles Patrick Langham, *b* 30 June 1894

2g Cecily Langham

2f *Francis Nathaniel Langham (Spratton, Northampton), b* 9 June 1841

3c *Henrietta Langham, d* 25 *May* 1909 , *m* 16 *Sept* 1851, *the Right Hon Sir Arthur John Otway, 3rd Bt [U K], P C , formerly an M P and* (1868–1871) *Under-Sec of State for Foreign Affairs (31 Eaton Square, S W) , and had issue 1f*

1f Henrietta Evelyn Otway, *m* 18 Nov 1880, Edward Garrow-Whitby, *d* 1900, *and has issue* 1g *to* 2g

1g Humphrey Otway Garrow Whitby, b 1883

2g Phœbe Eleanora Otway

3d Charlotte Langham, *m* Capt P R Minster, R N

2c *Sir William Langham, afterwards Jones, 1st Bt [G B* 1774], d s p *3 May* 1791

3a *Frances Samwell, bapt* 5 *Dec* 1676 , *d* 1 *Dec* 1730 , *m Sir Richard Newman of Fifehead Magdalen, co Dorset, 1st Bt [E* 20 *Dec* 1699], d 30 Dec 1721 , *and had issue which became extinct 25 Aug 1775*　　　　[Nos 94722 to 94729

280　Descendants, if any surviving, of MARGARET SAMWELL (Table XXV), *bapt* 6 Oct. 1640 , *d* 12 Jan. 1727 ; *m.* 1665, THOMAS CATESBY of Ecton and Whiston, *d* 20 Feb 1700 ; and had issue [1]

281.　Descendants, if any, of PENELOPE SAMWELL (Table XXV), *bapt.* 4 Sept. 1641 , *d* (-) , *m* 1678, SIR WILLIAM YORKE of Lessington, co Lincoln [2]

282　Descendants of AGNES SAMWELL (Table XXV), *d* 25 Oct. 1717 , *m* ROBERT CODRINGTON of Codrington, co Gloucester, *d* 11 June 1717 , and had issue.[3]

283　Descendants of SIR WALTER WAGSTAFFE BAGOT, 5th Bt [E], LL.D., M P. (Table XXV), *b.* 3 Aug 1702 , *d.* 20 Jan 1768 ; *m* 27 July 1724, Lady BARBARA, da. of William (LEGGE), 1st Earl of Dartmouth [G B], *d* 29 Aug. 1765, and had issue 1*a* to 5*a*

1a *William (Bagot), 1st Baron Bagot [G B], so cr 17 Oct 1780, b 28 Feb 1728 , d 22 Oct 1798, m 20 Aug 1760, the Hon Elizabeth Louisa, da. of John (St John), 2nd Viscount St John [G B], d 4 Feb 1820 , and had issue*
See the Clarence Volume, pp 492–493, Nos 21328–21515
　　　　　　　　　　　　　　　　　　　[Nos 94730 to 94917

---

[1] Baker's "Northants," i 224　　　[2] Ibid　　　[3] Ibid

448

# of The Blood Royal

2a *Charles Bagot, afterwards (Act of Parl.) Chester of Chicheley, co Bucks*, b 1 Sept 1730, d 2 Ap 1792, m 3 Oct 1765, *Cathrine, da of the Hon Heneage Legge*, d 29 Oct 17—, *and had issue* 1b to 5b

1b *Anthony Chester-Bagot, Capt 13th Regt*, b 5 May 1773, *killed in Egypt* 1802, m 1799, *Anne Eliza, da of Hamlet Obins of Castle Obins, co Armagh*, d 1867, *and had issue* 1c

1c *Rev Anthony Chester Bagot of Chicheley Hall, co Bucks*, b 1800, d 10 Dec 1858, m 1834, *Henrietta, da and h of William Brown of Lisbon*, d Oct 1851 *and had issue* 1d

1d *Henrietta Mary Chester Bagot*, d 15 May 1895, m 16 Ap 1861, *Richard Purefoy Fit:Gerald of North Hall, Preston Candover, J P , Hon Col Bucks Yeo*, b 7 Jan 1837, d 28 Feb 1895, *and had issue* 1e to 6e

1e *Richard Purefoy FitzGerald, now (R L 26 Dec 1899) Purefoy of Shalstone, M V O , J P , Capt R N (Shalstone, Manor, Buckingham)*, b 26 May 1862, m 23 Dec 1895, *Mary Lillias da of the Rev Francis Gordon Sandys Lumsdaine of Lumsdaine, J P , and has issue* 1f

1f Mary Lillias Geraldine Purefoy, b 27 Mar 1897

2e Rev Henry Purefoy FitzGerald (*Lidwells, Goudhurst, co Kent*), b 27 May 1867, m 16 Ap 1895, *Lilian Mary, da of Walter Langton of Gatcombe Park, I W , and has issue* 1f to 4f

1f Knightley Purefoy FitzGerald, b 12 July 1899

2f Cicely Purefoy FitzGerald, b 4 Jan 1897

3f Marjorie Purefoy FitzGerald, b 11 Ap 1898

4f Geraldine Purefoy Fit:Gerald, b 14 July 1901

3e Mary Frances Purefoy FitzGerald, *unm*

4e Laura Purefoy FitzGerald, *unm*

5e Catharine Purefoy FitzGerald, *unm*

6e Mabel Purefoy FitzGerald, *unm*

2b *Rev William Chester, M A , Rector of Denton*, b 27 May 1775, d 22 Nov 1838, m 1810, *the Hon Elizabeth, da of Henry (Wilson), 4th Baron Berners [E]*, d 10 Feb 1865, *and had issue* 1c to 3c

1c *Charles Montague Chester of Chicheley Hall, co Bucks, J P , D L , Lieut-Col in the Army*, b 18 Jan 1815, d 17 Nov 1879, m 7 Sept 1843, *Maria, da of Major Sandham, R I*, d 8 Ap 1895, *and had issue* 1d to 7d

1d Rev John Greville Chester, M A , Vicar of Gilling (*Gilling Vicarage, Richmond, Yorks*), b 15 May 1852, m 26 Sept 1883, *Amy, da of Arthur Hughes, and has issue* 1e to 7e

1e Greville Arthur Bagot Chester, b 3 Ap 1891

2e Anthony James Bagot Chester, b 29 Dec 1892

3e George Bagot Chester, b 6 Sept 1894

4e Henry Montagu Bagot Chester, b 31 July 1896

5e Lewis Charles Bagot Chester, b 29 Aug 1898

6e Dorothy Mary Bagot Chester

7e Kathleen Agnes Bagot Chester

2d Rev Algernon Stewart McKenzie Chester, Rector of Elford and Rural Dean (*Elford Rectory, Tamworth*), b 30 Dec 1853, m 11 June 1884, *Emily Mary, da of the Rev Edward Manners Dillman Pyne, and has issue* (with a son and da d unm) 1e to 2e

1e Walter Greville Chester, Cadet Royal Mil Coll, b 15 May 1887

2e Muriel Bagot Chester

3d Fanny Maria Chester, m 19 Sept 1876, *Lieut -Col Charles William Selby-Lowndes* [descended from George, Duke of Clarence, K G , and entitled to quarter the Royal Arms (see the Clarence Volume, p 476)] (*The Lunes, Bexhill-on-Sea*), and has issue 1e to 5e   [Nos 94918 to 94940

The Plantagenet Roll

1c Charles Henry Chester Selby-Lowndes, *formerly Lieut 4th Batt. Bedford-shire Regt*, has S African Medal with 3 Clasps, *b* 17 Oct 1880

2c Rev George Noel Selby-Lowndes, *b* 25 Dec 1886

3c Laura Fanny Mary Selby-Lowndes

4c Ella Louisa Selby-Lowndes

5c Mary Isabella Selby-Lowndes

4d Louisa Grace Chester

5d Mary Isabella Chester

6d Catherine Chester

7d Margaret Isabel Chester

2c *Fanny Chester*, d 30 *July* 1890 m 2 *June* 1840, *the Rev Francis Edward Paget, Rector of Elford [E of Uxbridge Coll], d 4 Aug 1882, and had issue*
See the Clarence Volume, p 493, Nos 21499-21515

3c *Charlotte Chester*, d 1887, m 1836, *the Rev Salisbury Everard, Rector of Burgate, co Norfolk, Hon Canon of Norwich, and had issue (5 sons and 4 das)*

3b *John Chester of Ashstead, co Surrey, a Lieut-Gen in the Army, b 3 Aug 1779, d 19 May 1857*, m. 17 *May* 1821, *Sophia Elizabeth, da of Charles Stuart of Airdroch, d 19 May 1879, and had issue 1c to 5c*

1c *John Chester, afterwards (R L 1 Ap 1863) St Leger, of Park Hill, co York, J P , D L , Col 53rd and 85th Regts*, b 6 *May* 1823, *d 9 Aug 1905*, m 8 *Ap* 1858, *Philippa, da of John Bonfoy Rooper of Abbot's Ripton Hall, M P , d 27 Dec 1909, and had issue 1d to 6d*

1d Arthur John Bonfoy St Leger of Park Hill, *formerly* Capt King's Royal Rifle Corps (*Park Hill, Rotherham*), b 25 Nov 1859, m 8 Ap 1896, Hilda Geraldine, da of Col Sir Gerard Smith, K C M G , *late Gov of West Australia*, and has issue 1e to 2e

1e Brenda May St Leger, *b* 11 July 1897

2e Vera St Leger, *b* 29 July 1900

2d Henry Berners St Leger, Bengal Police, *b* 26 Oct 1861

3d Reginald Wadham Anthony St Leger, *b* 15 Feb 1868

4d Gwendolene May Hope St Leger, m 9 Ap 1885, Frederic William Brooke of Glenbrook, *formerly* Capt 3rd Batt Suffolk Regt (*Glenbrook, Shanklin, I W*), and has issue 1e to 3e

1e Gerald Douglas Brooke, *b* 20 Mar 1891

2e Gladys Beatrice Brooke

3e Dulce Brooke

5d Georgina Harriet St Leger, m 1888, John Walter Parry-Crooke of Darsham House, co Suffolk, J P (*Carlton, Bournemouth*), and has issue 1e to 3e

1e Douglas John Parry-Crooke, *b* 1889

2e Lionel Walter Parry Crooke, *b* 1891

3e Charles Philip Parry Crooke, *b* 1896

6d Ursula Beatrice Philippa St Leger, m 19 Dec 1888, Frances Egbert Hollond, J P (*Satis House, Yoxford, Suffolk*), and has issue 1e to 5e

1e Raymond Claude Hollond, *b* 1891

2e George Egbert Hollond, *b* 1895

3e Hugh Ernest Hollond, *b* 1897

4e Marjorie Hollond

5e Nancy Ursula Hollond

2c Heneage Charles Bagot-Chester, Col Reserve Forces, served throughout Indian Mutiny, has Medal with Clasps (*Zetland House, Maidenhead, Centre Cliff, Southwold, &c*), *b* 12 Feb 1834, m 11 Mar 1865, Madeline Elizabeth, widow of T B Sheriffe of Henstead Hall, co Suffolk, da of Richard Mansel Oliver Massey of Tickford Abbey, co Bucks, and has issue 1d to 2d   [Nos 94941 to 91986

# of The Blood Royal

1d Greville John Massey Bagot-Chester, *formerly* Capt 1st Scots Guards, has S African Medals and Clasps, *b* 20 Oct 1866

2d Hugh Augustus Bagot-Chester, *formerly* Capt 3rd Batt Royal Lancaster Regt., has S African Medal and Clasps, *b* 21 Ap 1871, *m* 13 Jan 1895, Margaret Kathleen Juliana (who obtained a div 1908), da of Col R E Oakes, B S C

3c Sophia Elizabeth Chester, d 20 Sept 1892, m 5 Aug 1845, Lord Alfred Hervey, d 15 Ap 1875, and had issue.

See p 335, Nos 55583–55586

4c. Mary Chester, d 15 Ap 1899, m 18 Feb 1846, her cousin the Rev Charles Walter Bagot, Chancellor of Bath and Wells, d 10 Sept 1884, and had issue

See the Tudor Roll, p 369, Nos 27951–27963

5c Barbara Frances Wilhelmina Chester (Roydsmoor, East Molesley), m 12 Feb 1862, Rev the Hon William Howard [E of Effingham Coll.], d s p 12 May 1881

4b Barbara Chester, b 28 Feb 1769 d 9 Aug 1832, m John Drummond, *d 28 May 1833*

5b Frances Chester, b 26 Oct 1770, d (–), m 6 Aug 1803, Thomas Richmond-Gale-Braddyll of Highhead Castle, and Conishead Priory, co Lancaster, J P., D L, b 14 Nov 1776, d (–), and had issue 1c to 2c

1c Edward Stanley Bagot Richmond-Gale-Braddyll of Highhead Castle and Conishead Priory, d 2 Sept 1871, m 7 Dec 1837, Sophia Frances Anne, da of William Hulton of Hulton Park, co Lanc, and had issue 1d to 3d

1d Henry John Richmond-Gale-Braddyll of Highhead Castle, b 29 Oct 1837, d s p 24 Dec 1886, m 2 June 1875, Mary (Amberwood, Christchurch, Hants), da of William Birch of Barton under-Needwood, co Stafford.

2d Edward Sotheron Richmond-Gale-Braddyll of Southport, b 3 Jan. 1839, d 26 Nov, 1882, m 21 Feb 1861, Anna Cecilia, da of Edward Willis of Cleevemount, co Glouc, d 1874, and had issue 1e to 6e

1e Hubert Edward Richmond-Gale-Braddyll (East Court, Oxton, Cheshire), b 20 Nov 1861, m 1884, Mary, da of H M Lennard of Leven House, co York, and has issue 1f to 3f

    1f Hubert Stanley Richmond-Gale-Braddyll, R N, b 25 Aug 1886

    2f Edward Clarence Richmond Gale-Braddyll, 19th Lancers, b 18 Oct 1888

    3f Mary Alice Richmond-Gale-Braddyll

    2e Florence Richmond-Gale-Braddyll

    3e Maude Richmond-Gale-Braddyll, m William Rampling Rose

4e Ethel Marguerite Richmond-Gale-Braddyll, m 31 July 1890, Sir William Rothwell Hulton, 2nd Bt [U K] (Worden Lodge, Leyland, near Preston), and his issue 1f to 2f

    1f Roger Braddyll Hulton, b 30 Mar 1891

    2f Leslie Florence Hulton

5e Evelyn Cecilia Richmond Gale-Braddyll, m 30 Mar 1892, Edward Dennison Hargreaves (Achnasgiach, N B, Harefield, near Romsey, Hants), and has issue 1f to 3f

    1f Dennison Braddyll Hargreaves, b 5 Ap 1893

    2f John Dennison Hargreaves, b 5 Nov 1905

    3f Audrey Dennison Hargreaves, b 20 Feb 1898

6e Lilian Richmond-Gale-Braddyll, m 1 Nov 1893, Llewellyn Caradoc Picton-Jones [4th son of G T Picton-Jones of Yoke House, co Carnarvon], and has issue 1f.

    1f Esmé Doris Picton Jones, b 30 Sept 1896

3d Harriet Georgiana Richmond-Gale-Braddyll (5 Albert Road, Birkdale)

2c Clarence Richmond-Gale-Braddyll, for whom King William IV was sponsor
[Nos 94987 to 95022

451

The Plantagenet Roll

3a Rev Walter Bagot of Pipe Hall, co Stafford, b 2 Nov 1731, d 1806, m 1st, 7 Sept 1773, Anne, da of William Swinnerton of Butterton, co Stafford, 2ndly, Mary [da of (—)] Ward, and had issue 1b to 8b

1b² Rev Ralph Bagot, Vicar of Erdington, d 20 July 1866, m 3 Sept. 1815, Mary [da of (—)] Adams d 8 Mar 1890, and had issue 1c

1c William Walter Bagot of Pipe Hayes Hall, b 21 Jan 1847, d 23 Jan 1893, m 4 Feb 1868 Lucy Matilda, da of the Rev Robert Loftus Tottenham, d 1895, and had issue 1d

1d Frances Anna May Bagot (Chambers' Court, Tewkesbury), m 25 Mar 1890, Henry Richard Reginald Bagot [B Bagot Coll], d s p 17 July 1908

2b¹ Honora Bagot, b 20 June 1775, d 2 Oct 1863, m 15 Dec 1795, Rev the Hon Augustus George Legge, Preb of Winchester [L of Dartmouth Coll] d 21 Aug 1828, and had issue (with 4 sons who d s p) 1c to 4c

1c Rev Henry Legge of Mareland, co Surrey, and Bramdean, co Hants, b 29 June 1803, d 8 Nov 1879, m 4 May 1830, Elizabeth Louisa, da of Rear-Adm Stair Douglas [M of Queensberry Coll], d 28 Oct 1840, and had issue 1d to 2d

1d Rev Augustus George Legge, M A (Oxon), Vicar of North Elmham, co Norfolk, b 20 Jan 1835, d 9 Jan 1906, m 25 Aug 1861, Alice Mary, da of John Greenwood of Broadhanger, co Hants, Q C, d 21 Feb 1885, and had issue 1c to 5c

1c Walter Douglas Legge (Hove Lawn, Hove, Sussex), b 31 Oct 1865, m 24 Sept 1907, Rebecca Lang, da of Theophilus Hoskin of Calstock, co Cornwall

2c Honora Alice Charlotte Legge ⎞
3c Beatrice Louisa Legge   ⎟ (Littledean, Bramdean, Alresford)
4c Frances Mary Legge   ⎟
5c Alice Georgina Legge   ⎠

2d Charles Egerton Legge, J P, D L, High Sheriff co Sussex 1901 (Ashling House, Chichester), b 22 May 1840, unm

2c Charlotte Anne Legge, b 5 June 1799, d 21 June 1856, m 15 Dec 1825, Rev the Hon Arthur Philip Perceval [E of Egmont Coll], d 11 June 1853, and had issue

See the Clarence Volume, pp 203-204, Nos 4024-4049

3c Honora Augusta Legge, b 1 May 1816, d 27 Dec 1897, m 12 Ap 1855, Gen William Cowper Coles, d 27 Aug 1867

4c Louisa Frances Catherine Legge, b 14 July 1817, d 4 June 1893, m 4 Ap 1866, the Rev Alfred Bishop, Rector of Martyr Worthy, co Hants, d 29 Sept 1885

3b¹ Elizabeth Bagot, b 25 May 1780, d 24 Feb 1855, m 19 Mar 1807, Joseph Phillimore of Shiplake House, D C L, M P, Regius Professor of Civil Law in the University of Oxford, Chancellor of the Dioceses of Oxford, Worcester, and Bristol, b 14 Sept 1775, d 24 Feb 1855, and had issue 1c to 3c

1c John George Phillimore of Shiplake House, Q C, M P, b 5 Jan 1808, d 27 Ap 1865, m 4 Aug 1839, Rosalind Margaret, da of the Right Hon Sir James Lewis Knight Bruce, Vice-Chancellor of England and Lord Justice of the Court of Appeal, d 22 Sept 1871, and had issue 1d

1d Egerton Grenville Bagot Phillimore of Shiplake House (Shiplake House, Oxon), b 20 Dec 1856, m 22 Jan 1880, Susan Eliza, da of Richard Barnes Roscow of Church, near Accrington, M R C S, and has (with other) issue 1c to 2c.

1c John George Phillimore, B A (Oxon), b 24 Oct 1880

2c Margaret Phillimore, b 24 Nov 1881

2c Sir Robert Joseph Phillimore, 1st Bt [U K 21 Dec 1881], P C, M P D C L, b 5 Nov 1810, d 4 Feb 1885, m 19 Dec 1844, Charlotte Anne, sister of John Evelyn, 1st Viscount Ossington [U K], da of John Denison of Ossington Hall, co Notts, M P, d 19 Jan 1892 and had issue 1d to 3d

[Nos 95023 to 95058

# of The Blood Royal

1d Sir Walter George Frank Phillimore, 2nd Bt [U K], D C L, Hon LL D (Edin), a Judge of the High Court of Justice (Queen's Bench Div), Bencher of the Middle Temple, *formerly* Chancellor of Lincoln and Fellow of All Souls' Coll Oxon, Mayor of Kensington 1910, &c (*The Coppice, Henley-on-Thames, Cam House, Campden Hill, W*), b 21 Nov 1845, m 26 July 1870, Agnes, da of Charles Manners Lushington, M P, and has issue 1e to 6e

1e Robert Charles Phillimore, B A (Oxon), Bar M T, J P (*Radlett, St Albans*), b 19 Aug 1871, m 12 Dec 1895 Lucy, da of William FitzPatrick

2e Godfrey Walter Phillimore, M A (Oxon), b 29 Dec 1879 m 5 July 1905, Dorothy Barbara, da of Lieut.-Col Arthur Balfour Haig, C V O, C M G, and has issue 1f

1f Anthony Francis Phillimore, b 2 Feb 1907

3e Stephen Henry Phillimore, M A (Oxon), b 14 Dec 1881

4e Eleanor Mary Phillimore, m 17 Sept 1895, Francis John Kynaston Cross, J P, Bar-at-Law (*Aston Tirrold Manor, Wallingford*), and has issue 1f to 5f

1f Philip Kynaston Cross, b 3 Jan 1898

2f Michael Robert Cross, b 8 Ap 1899

3f Christopher Francis Cross, b 7 May 1902

4f Geoffrey John Cross, b 2 Feb 1910

5f Hannah Margaret Cross, b 25 Ap 1908

5e *Margaret Blanche Phillimore, d 19 Oct 1901, m 29 July 1899, Eustace Gilbert Hills, Bar-at-Law (22 Cheyne Gardens, S W, Library Chambers, Temple, E C), and had issue 1f to 2f*

1f Elizabeth Anna Hills, b 9 Nov 1900

2f Katharine Agnes Hills, b 11 June 1902

6e Grace Agnes Phillimore

2d Catherine Mary Phillimore }
3d Lucy Phillimore   } (*Shiplake House, Henley-on-Thames*)

3c *Sir Augustus Phillimore, K C B, Admiral R N, b 24 May 1822, d 25 Nov 1897, m 29 Mar 1864, Harriet Eleanor (Shedfield House, Botley Hants), da of the Hon George Matthew Fortescue [descended from King Henry VII (see Tudor Roll, p 282)], and had issue 1d to 7d*

1d Richard Fortescue Phillimore, M V O, R N, Capt H M S *Aboukir* (*Portsmouth, United Service*), b 23 Dec 1864 m 21 Dec 1905, Violet Gore, da of Henry Hobhouse Turton, and has issue 1e to 2e

1e Richard Augustus Phillimore, b 9 Jan 1907

2e John Gore Phillimore, b 16 Ap 1908

2d George Grenville Phillimore, M A (Oxon), Bar M T, is an Assist Charity Commr (*Maplecroft, Wargrave, Marlborough House Tunbridge Wells, 1 Mitre Court Buildings, Temple*), b 28 Oct 1867, m 30 Aug 1893, May Melba, da of Henry William Franklyn of Shedfield Lodge, co Hants, and has issue 1e to 3e

1e Henry Augustus Grenville Phillimore, b 31 July 1894

2e Matthew Arden Phillimore, b 17 Mar 1896

3e Hester Mary Melba Phillimore, b 7 Oct 1900

3d Charles Augustus Phillimore, M A (Oxon), a partner in Coutts' Bank (*Oxford and Cambridge*), b 11 Aug 1871, m 8 Dec 1908, Alice (see p 513), da of William Henry Campion of Danny, C B, and has issue 1e

1e Violet Alice Valentine Phillimore, b 10 Dec 1909

4d John Swinnerton Phillimore, M A (Oxon), Professor of Humanity in Glasgow University (*5 The College, Glasgow*), b 26 Feb 1873, m 26 July 1900, Margaret Cecily, da of the Rev Spencer Compton Spencer-Smith [Bt Coll], and has issue 1e to 2e

1e John Michael Fortescue Phillimore, b 9 Sept 1903

2e Cynthia Mary Louisa Phillimore, b 18 May 1901   [Nos 95059 to 95086

The Plantagenet Roll

5d Valentine Egerton Bagot Phillimore, D S O, Comm R N, b 14 Feb 1875, m 16 June 1908 Mary Kathleen, da of George Robinson of Overdale, Shipton-in-Craven, d 23 Mar 1909

6d Rev Edward Granville Phillimore, B A (Oxon), is Priest in Charge of Kingsley (Kingsley, Hants), b 7 Sept 1876, m 14 July 1903, Mabel von Essen, da of William Henry Moberly of Beechwood, Bitterne, and has issue 1e to 2e

    1e Barbara Louisa Agnes Phillimore, b 27 Mar 1906

    2 Audrey Magdalen Dominica Gwladys Phillimore

7d Violet Elizabeth Annie Phillimore, m 1 June 1893, John Edward Arthur Willis-Fleming of Chilworth and Stoneham, J P, D L, High Sheriff co Hants 1901 (Chilworth Manor Romsey, Stoneham Park, Southampton) and has issue 1e to 5e

    1e John Baynes Phillimore Willis-Fleming, b 2 June 1895

    2e Richard Thomas Cyril Willis-Fleming, b 3 Aug 1896

    3e Edward Charles Augustus Willis Fleming, b 22 Ap 1903

    4e Ida Harriet Willis-Fleming

    5e Elizabeth Katherine Willis-Fleming

4b [1] Louisa Bagot, d Mar 1864, m 16 Jan 1804, the Rev Richard Levett of Milford Hall, co Stafford, b 17 Nov 1772, d 25 Aug 1843, and had issue 1c

    1c Richard Byrd Levett of Milford Hall, J P, D L, Lieut-Col Comdg 3rd Batt Staffordshire Rifles, b 24 Nov 1810, d 8 July 1887, m 1 Aug 1848, Elizabeth Mary, da of John Mirehouse of Brownslade, co Pemb, Common Sergeant of London [by Elizabeth, da of the Right Rev John Fisher, D D, Bishop of Salisbury], and had issue 1d to 7d

    1d Richard Walter Byrd Mirehouse, formerly (R L 17 Mar 1865) Levett of Angle, C M G, J P and High Sheriff co Pembroke 1886, Hon Col and Lieut-Col Comdg 4th North Stafford Regt (The Hall, Angle, co Pemb, Junior Carlton), b 5 May 1849, m 22 June 1881, Mary Beatrice, da of Thomas Entwisle of Wolhayes, co Hants, and has issue 1e to 3e

        1e Gladys Sybil Evelyn Mirehouse, b 18 Ap 1882

        2e Ruth Violet Esther Mirehouse, b 5 June 1883, m (—)

        3e Cecil Elinor Mirehouse, b 7 Ap 1886

    2d William Swinnerton Byrd Levett of Milford Hall, J P, D L, late Capt Royal Inniskilling Fusiliers (Milford Hall, Stafford), b 22 Jan 1856, m 8 July 1896, Maud Sophia [descended from the Lady Isabel Plantagenet (see Essex Volume, p 338)], da of Major Edward Levett, 10th Hussars, and has issue 1e to 2e

        1e Richard William Byrd Levett, b 30 May 1897

        2e Dyonese Levett, b 13 Ap 1900

    3d Egerton Bagot Byrd Levett Scrivener (D P 6 Ap 1889), formerly Levett of Sibton, J P, Comm R N (ret), formerly Bursar Keble Coll (Oxon) (Sibton Abbey, Yoxford, Suffolk), b 11 Feb 1857, m 1st, Mar 1884, Mabel Desborough, da of Sir Harry Smith Parkes, G C M G, K C B, d May 1890, 2ndly, 3 Sept 1891, Mary, da of Henry John Mirehouse of St George's Hill, co Somerset, and has issue 1e to 5e

        1e Evelyn Harry Byrd Levett Scrivener, b 11 Dec 1884

        2e Alaric Parkes Levett Scrivener, b 12 Ap 1886

        3e [2] Iris Theodora Levett Scrivener

        4e [2] Winifred Violet Levett Scrivener

        5e [2] Pamela Levett Scrivener

    4d Walter Leveson Byrd Levett, J P (Oleton, Wellington, Salop), b 1 Aug 1859, m Oct 1884, Helen, da of Charles Lambert of Park Lane, London, and has issue 1e to 3e

        1e Richard Walter Levett, b 19 Jan 1890   [Nos 95087 to 95111

2*e* Mary Beatrice Levett, *b* 28 June 1886, *m* Jan 1909, John Benson [son of the Rev George Riou Benson], and has issue 1*f*

1*f* John Benson

3*e* Rachel Helen Levett, *b* 13 Mar 1900

5*d* Louisa Mary Levett

6*d* Evelyn Honora Levett

7*d* Isabel Mary Levett, *m* 6 July 1898, Harry Robert Bruxner (*Chartley Castle, co Stafford*), and has issue 1*e* to 2*c*

1*e* George Mervyn Bruxner, *b* 4 June 1899

2*e* Alistair Egerton Bruxner, *b* 11 Feb 1905

5*b*[2] *Caroline Bagot*, b *c* 1797, d 5 Feb 1886, m 1828, *Edmund R Daniel, Bar-at-Law*

6*b*[2] *Charlotte Bagot*, d 24 Feb 1865, m 5 May 1830, *Rev the Hon William Somerville*, d 6 July 1857, *and had a son who d unm*

7*b*[2] *Jane Margaret Bagot*, d 24 Sept 1889, m 1826, *the Right Hon Sir Edward Vaughan Williams, Judge of the Court of Common Pleas*, d 1875, *and had issue*

8*b*[2] *Agnes Bagot*, d (–), m *John Farquhar Fraser*

4*a Barbara Bagot*, b 29 Mar 1725, d 1797, m 1749, *Ralph Sneyd of Keele*, d 10 Dec 1793, *and had issue*

See the Essex Volume Supplement, pp 476–479, Nos 27542.1–27542/116

5*a Maria Bagot*, d (–), m *Rowland Wingfield*   [Nos 95112 to 95235

284   Descendants of ANNE NEALE, Maid-of-Honour to Queen Caroline (Table XXV.), *b* Feb 1721, *d.* 1 Dec 1747, *m* as 1st wife, c. 1744, the Rev SIR JAMES STONEHOUSE, 10th (1628) and 7th (1670) Bt [E], *b* 9 July 1716; *d* 8 Dec 1795, and had issue 1*a* to 2*a*

1*a Sir Thomas Stonehouse, 11th and 8th Bt [E]*, b 1744, d unm 1810

2*a Sarah Stonehouse*, d 1819, m 24 Oct 1767, *George Vansittart of Bisham Abbey, co Berks, J P, D L, M P, a Member of the Supreme Council of Bengal*, b 15 Sept 1745, d 20 June 1825 *and had issue* 1*b* to 4*b*

1*b. George Henry Vansittart, Gen in the Army, D C L*, b 16 July 1768, d v p 4 Feb 1824 m 29 Oct 1818, *Anna Maria, da and co-h of Thomas Copson of Sheppey and Sutton, co Leic*, d 1874, *and had issue two sons who both d unm*

2*b Rev Edward Vansittart, afterwards (R L 14 Oct 1805) Vansittart-Neale, M A, B C L, Rector of Taplow*, bapt 4 Nov 1769, d 21 Jan 1850, m 2ndly, 3 Jan 1809, *Anne da of Isaac Spooner of Elmdon, co Warw*, *and had issue*

See the Essex Volume Supplement, p 661, Nos 56226/253–271

3*b Henry Vansittart of Eastwood, Woodstock, Canada, Vice-Admiral of the Blue*, b 7 Ap 1777, d 14 Mar 1843, m 1st, 15 May 1809, *Mary Charity, da of the Rev John Pennefather, D D*, d 2 July 1834, *and had issue*

See p 357, Nos 59776–59821

4*b Laura Vansittart*, d 8 Feb 1844, m 26 Nov 1809, *Fulwar Craven of Brockhampton, co Glouc [B Craven Coll]*, d 14 Ap 1860, *and had issue* 1*c* to 2*c*

1*c Fulwar William Craven*, b 12 Sept 1810, d 7 Mar 1844 m 11 Nov 1831, *Louisa, da of the Rev John Orde*, d 19 Ap 1856, *and had issue* 1*d* to 3*d*

1*d Edmund Filmer Craven, a Police Magistrate and J P for Queensland, formerly R N (The Oasis, Hughenden, via Townsville, Queensland)*, b 21 Nov 1836, m 10 Mar 1866, Caroline, da of William Smith of Bedford, *and has issue* 1*e* to 10*e*

1*e Fulwar Craven*, b 26 May 1873   [Nos 95236 to 95302

2e Edmund Cecil Colrington Craven, served in South Africa 1901–1902 with Queensland Mounted Inf , *b* 2 Ap 1875

3e Ethel Laura Craven *m* 1889, John Cowper Linedale, Mining Registrar (*Paradise, Bundaberg, Queensland*) and has issue 1*f*

1*f* [da] Linedale, *b* 1890

4e Georgiana Louisa Craven

5e Evelyn Caroline Jocelyn Craven

6e Constance Talran Craven

7e Florence Lucy Craven, *m* 1899, Edward Goddard Blume (*Bexley, Long-reach, Queensland*) and has issue 1*f* to 2*f*

1*f* Edward Craven Blume, *b* 1900

2*f* [son] Blume, *b* 1905

8e Beatrice Violet Craven, *m* Dec 1905, Eldred Pringle , and has issue (a da)

9e Mabel Carleton Craven, *m* Dec 1909, the Rev Ernest Clarence Sandeman

10e Blanche Guendolene Craven

2d Laura Louisa Craven (*27 Pen y wern Road, Earl's Court, S W*), *m* 7 Jan 1862, Major Edmund Garland Horne, 25th Regt , *d* 15 Oct 1905 , and has issue 1e to 2e

1e Beatrice Charlotte Maria Horne, *m* 2 Dec 1886, Alfred Harry Veitch, Paymaster R N (*Hartland, Victoria Road North, Southsea*) , and has issue 1*f* to 3*f*

1*f* Harry Cecil Craven Veitch, *b* 5 June 1891

2*f* Hyacinth Laura Guendolyn Veitch

3*f* Nesta Phyllis Alfreda Veitch

2e Amelia Eliza Eleanor Gwendohne Horne, *m* 13 Ap 1889, Grismond Philipps (*20 Victoria Road, Tenby*), and has issue 1*f*

1*f* Frances Gwendohne Horne

3d *Georgina Craven*, d 15 *Jan* 1887 , m *as 2nd wife*, 28 *July* 1863, *the Rev Thomas Grey Clarke, Vicar of Oldham , and had issue* 1e *to* 2e

1e William Edmund Grey Clarke (*61 Manor Park, Lee, S E*), *b* 4 Ap 1864 , *m* 19 Dec 1886, Emily, da of Charles Frewen Lord, of Clifford's Inn, Solicitor , and has issue (with a son *d* young) 1*f* to 3*f*

1*f* Edmund Frewen Grey Clarke, *b* 25 Feb 1892

2*f* Charlotte Phyllis Georgina Clarke, *b* 26 June 1888

3*f* Enid Jocelyn Clarke, *b* 11 Dec 1895

2e Evelyn Georgiana Maria Clarke, *m* 10 Jan 1897, the Baron Arturo Lombardi (*Via Araceli 3, Palazzo Muti, Rome*), and has issue 1*f* to 2*f*

1*f* Baron Achille Grey Lombardi, *b* 4 Sept 1897

2*f* Baroness Georgina Amelia Lombardi, *b* 14 June 1903

2c *Georgina Maria Craven*, d 10 *Ap* 1878 , m 17 *June* 1841, *Goodwin Charles Colquitt, sometime (R L* 10 *Feb* 1842) *Goodwin and finally (R L* 12 *Dec* 1860) *Colquitt-Craven of Brockhampton Park, co Glos , J P , D L , d* 29 *Jan* 1899, *and had issue* 1d *to* 3d

1d *Fulwar John Colquitt-Craven, Capt Grenadier Guards, J P ,* b 19 *Sept* 1819 , d v p 1890, m 23 *Jan* 1873, *Sarah Llewellyn, da of Lewis Llewellyn Dillwyn of Hendrefoilan, M P , d* 1893, *and had issue* 1e *to* 5e

1e Lewis Fulwar George Colquitt-Craven of Admington and Burton (*Admington Hall Shipton-on-Stour , Burton Hall, Cheshire*), *b* 14 Nov 1873 , *m* 2 Oct 1900, Rose Macey, widow of (—) Freeman, da of Richard Taylor

2e George Fulwar Llewellyn Colquitt-Craven, *b* Jan 1875 , *m* in Australia

3 Nigel Fulwar de la Beche Colquitt-Craven, *b* 6 Nov 1881 , *m* 1909

4e Arabel Laura Colquitt-Craven, *m* 23 Ap 1902, Llewellyn H Prichard (*Penmaen House, Penmaen, Glamorgan*) , and has issue (a da)

[Nos 95303 to 95332

# of The Blood Royal

5c Hilda Charlotte Colquitt-Craven, m 10 Sept 1900, Robert Picton-Warlow [descended from the Lady Isabel Plantagenet (see the Essex Volume, p 384)] (*Coity Maur, Talybout-on-Usk, Brecon*), and has issue 1f to 2f

    1f John Fulwar Picton-Warlow, *b* 30 Jan 1903

    2f Robert Wallace Picton-Warlow, *b* 13 Oct 1904

2d Leila Louisa Colquitt-Craven, d 9 Oct 1899, m 21 Ap 1868, *the Rev Henry William Coventry* [*E Coventry Coll*], *Rector of Severn Stoke and Hon Canon of Worcester, J P* (*Severn Stoke Rectory, Worcester*), and had issue 1e to 4e

    1e Fulwar Cecil Ashton Coventry, *b* 14 July 1874

    2e Blanche Katherine Adine Coventry, m 6 Jan 1904, the Rev George Le Strange Amphlett, Rector of Earl's Croome and Hill Croome (*Earl's Croome Rectory, co Worcester*), and has issue 1f to 3f

        1f Leila Blanche Amphlett

        2f Ann Elizabeth Amphlett

        3f Justina Alice Amphlett

    3e Sybil Augusta Coventry, m 3 Feb 1904, Capt Ferdinando Dudley William Lea-Smith [descended from King Henry VII, whose arms he is entitled to quarter (see the Tudor Roll, p 313)] (*Halesowen Grange, Worcester*), and has issue 1f

        1f Barbara Amy Felicity Lea-Smith

    4e Winifred Leila Coventry, m 14 Nov 1906, the Rev Francis Herbert Horne, Rector of Beyton (*Beyton Rectory, Bury St Edmunds*) and has issue 1f

        1f Henry Francis Coventry Horne, *b* 22 Aug 1908

3d Arabella Catherine Colquitt-Craven (*Court House, Malvern*), m 9 Feb 1873, Sir James Buchanan, 2nd Bt [U K], Comm R N [eldest son of the Right Hon Sir Andrew Buchanan, 1st Bt [U K], G C B, H B M Ambassador at Vienna], *d s p* 14 Oct 1901   [Nos 95313 to 95315

285 Descendants of FRANCES NEALE (see Table XXV), *b.* 1723, *d* 7 Mar 1748, *m* 17 Oct 1742, Sir JOHN TURNER of Warham, 3rd Bt [G B 1721], M P in six Parliaments 1739–1774 and a Lord of the Treasury 1762–1765, *b* 1712, *d* 4 June 1780, and had issue 1a to 2a

    1a Ann Turner, *da and co-h*, b c 1747, d 26 July 1822, aged 75, m 27 July 1772, Robert Hales, *Collector of Customs at King's Lynn*, d 12 Sept 1789, aged 48, and had issue (with 2 elder sons who d s p) 1b

    1b James Hales *of Norwich, Solicitor*, *b* 11 Ap 1785, *d* 6 Ap 1831, m 13 June 1810, Barbara, da of John Greene Baseley, *Mayor of Norwich*, d 9 Dec 1850, *and had issue (with 4 sons and 3 das who d unm)* 1c to 6c

    1c John Hales, *afterwards* (1p 1892) *Hales-Tooke of Copdock and Washbrook, co Suffolk, and of Holt, co Norfolk, M R C S E*, *b* 26 Sept 1820, *d* 7 Mar 1899 m 1st, 16 Sept 1846, Sarah, da and h of John Clark of Holt, d 8 Aug 1895, *and had issue* 1d to 2d

    1d John Baseley Tooke Hales of Copdock and Washbrook, B A (Camb) (*The Close, Norwich*), *b* 9 Dec 1849, m 19 Ap 1888, Elizabeth Blanche Mary, da of the Rev William Bagnall-Oakeley of Newland, co Glouc, and has issue 1e to 2e

        1e John Baseley Hales, B A (Camb), *b* 23 Jan 1889

        2e Mary Barbara Hales

    2d Robert Turner Hales, M D, C M, M R C S E (*Holt, Norfolk*) *b* 1 Sept 1853, m 26 Sept 1889, Alice Mary, da of Henry Ward of Rolleston, co Stafford and has issue 1e to 4e

        1e Henry Ward Hales, *b* 11 Nov 1890

        2e Robert Neale Hales, *b* 7 Nov 1894

        3e Margaret Frances Turner Hales, *b* 22 Mar 1893

        4e Mabel Alice Jane Hales, *b* 9 Jan 1904   [Nos 95346 to 95353

The Plantagenet Roll

2c Rev George Hales, LL B (Camb), *late* Rector of Rickinghall (6 *Westgate, Bury St Edmunds*), b 15 Ap 1827, m 1st, 18 Aug 1851, Ann Holt, da of James Horrox, d 2 Feb 1892, 2ndly, 26 Oct 1892, Mary Seton, da of John Dury, and has issue (by 1st wife) 1d to 10d

1d Rev George Henry Hales, B A (Camb), Rector of Stickney (*Stickney Rectory, Lincolnshire*). b 20 May 1854

2d Herbert Martyn Hales (*Carshalton*) b 16 Mar 1856, m 3 Feb 1887, Marion Barrow, da of W Barrow Simonds of Abbots Barton, Winchester, J P, D L, and his issue 1e to 2e

1e Helen Barbara Hales, b 22 Jan 1888

2e Rhona Brunwin Hales, b 19 Ap 1894

3d Rev Canon Greville Turner Hales, now (1905) Brunwin-Hales, of Bradwell, near Braintree (*St Mary s Rectory, Colchester*), b 23 Nov 1859, m 30 Nov 1886, Eva Caroline, da of John Oxley Parker of Woodham Mortimer, co Essex, and has issue 1e to 3e

1e Greville Oxley Brunwin-Hales, b 21 Nov 1889

2e Henry Tooke Brunwin-Hales, b 12 Nov 1892

3e Eva Elizabeth Brunwin-Hales, b 8 June 1888

4d Rev James Tooke Hales, Chaplain served in S Africa 1901–1902, Medal and 3 Clasps (*Trentsia*), b 7 Sept 1863, *unm*

5d Ernest Baseley Hales, Major Durham Light Infantry, served in South Africa, Medal and 2 Clasps, b 2 Feb 1867, *unm*

6d Rev John Percy Hales, Rector of Cotgrave (*Cotgrave Rectory, Nottingham*), b 7 Oct 1870, m 8 July 1898, Augusta Margaret, da of Col Albert Cantrell Cantrell-Hubbersty, and has issue 1e to 3e

1e George Frederick Hales, b 21 Mar 1901

2e Aline Holt Hales, b 10 Jan 1900

3e Helen Margaret Hales, b 2 Nov 1907

7d Caroline Durnford Hales, m 31 May 1880, the Rev Harry Edward Beck, M A (Camb), Rector of Harpley, *formerly a Bar-at-Law* (*Harpley Rectory, Kings Lynn*), and has issue 1e to 5e

1e Anthony Horace Beck, b 3 Nov 1884

2e Annie Caroline Beck,
3e Mabel Constance Beck, } *unm*
4e Amy Sybil Beck,
5e Charlotte Herris Beck

8d Amy Wilson Hales, m 1 June 1882, Rowland Holt Wilson, Solicitor (see p 459) (*Bury St Edmunds*), and has issue 1e to 3e

1e Thomas Wilson, Solicitor, b 12 July 1883

2e George Wilson, Lieut R N, b 12 May 1885

3e Edward Rowland Wilson, Indian Army, b 13 June 1887

9d Annie Maud Hales, *unm*

10d Mary Hales, *unm*

3c Barbara Hales, b 16 *June* 1812, d 13 *Jan* 1875, m 26 Nov 1839, *the Rev Thomas Daniel Holt Wilson, M A, Rector of Redgrave [2nd son of George Wilson of Redgrave Hall, co Suffolk Admiral of the Red]*, d 4 *Jan* 1881, and had issue 1d to 5d

1d Rev Charles Holt Wilson, M A, Vicar of Dilton Marsh and Rural Dean of Heytesbury (*Dilton Marsh Rectory, Wilts*), b 2 Dec 1841, m 12 Jan 1871, Catharine Ellen, da and coh of the Rev Thomas Thorogood Upwood of Lovell's Hall, Lynn, J P, D L

2d Rev Thomas Holt Wilson, M A (Camb), Rector of Brayosworth 1901–1909, *formerly* of Redgrave and Botesdale (*Briarfield, Great Malvern*), b 4 June

[Nos 95354 to 95382

+458

# of The Blood Royal

1843, *m* 1st, 13 Sept 1870, Helen Emily [herself a descendant of King Edward III through the Mortimer-Percy marriage (see p 127)], da of Edward Greene of Nether Hall, M P, *d* 25 Oct 1880, 2ndly, 29 Aug 1882, Alice Bertha, widow of Henry John Smith [Bt Coll], da of the Rev Edmund Dawe Wickham, *d* 5 Mar 1883 3rdly, 8 July 1890, Mary Isabella, da and h of the Rev Michael Turner, Rector of Cotton, and has issue 1*e* to 8*e*

1*e* Eric Edward Boketon Wilson, now Holt Wilson, D S O, Capt R E, Instructor at the Royal Military Academy, Woolwich, *b* 26 Aug 1875, *m* 19 Jan 1903, Susannah Mary, da of Charles George Shaw of Ayr and has issue 1*f* to 2*f*

    1*f* Daniel Shaw Holt Wilson, *b* 10 Dec 1903

    2*f* Charles George Holt Wilson, *b* 12 July 1905

2*e* Michael Carlyon Holt Wilson, *b* 19 Sept 1892

3*e* Algernon Charles Winstanley Wilson, *b* 3 Jan 1896

4*e*[1] Muriel Barbara Wilson, *m* 9 Feb 1897, Robert Purdon Robertson-Glasgow of Craigmyle, co Aberdeen, J P, D L co Ayr, *late* Lieut-Col 2nd Vol Batt Royal Scots Fusiliers [descended from the Lady Isabel Plantagenet (see the Essex Volume, p 180)] (*Craigmyle, Aberdeen*), and has issue 1*f* to 2*f*

    1*f* Robert Wilson Robertson-Glasgow, *b* 7 Nov 1899

    2*f* Raymond Charles Robertson-Glasgow, *b* 15 July 1901

5*e*[1] Helen Ursula Wilson, *m* 5 June 1900, Philip Armstrong Shaw (*Hemington Hall, Derby*), and has issue 1*f* to 3*f*

    1*f* Eric Charles Holt Shaw, *b* 6 June 1903

    2*f* Alexander Armstrong Shaw, *b* 7 Sept 1907

    3*f* Ursula Flora Shaw, *b* 12 Mar 1901

6*e*[2] Amica Nelson Washington Wilson.

7*e*[2] Joyce Philippa Turner Wilson

8*e*[2] Rachel Edmunda Holt Wilson

3*d* *Algernon George Wilson*, b 25 *July* 1844, d (*s p*) *at Melbourne*, 7 *Sept* 1877, m *Mar* 1872, *Charlotte, da of* (—) *Parsons,* d 1879

1*d* Edward Hales Wilson, C B, Col Indian Army (*Junior United Service*), *b* 17 Sept 1845, *m* at Agra, Ap 1874, Rose Mackenzie, da of John Alone, and has issue 1*e* to 5*e*

    1*e* Geoffrey Edward Holt Wilson, Capt 34th Pioneers, *b* 27 Ap 1879

    2*e* William Holt Wilson, *b* 27 July 1888

    3*e* Barbara Emily Holt Wilson, *unm*

    4*e* Cicely Catherine Wilson, *m* Oct 1901, Capt John Ovans, King's Own Scottish Borderers, and has issue 1*f* to 5*f*

        1*f* John Malcolm Ovans, *b* 21 Dec 1905

        2*f* David Lambert Ovans, *b* 29 June 1908

        3*f* Geoffrey Hornby Ovans, *b* 26 Aug 1909

        4*f* Joyce Rosemary Ovans, *b* 14 Oct 1904

        5*f* Katherine Mary Ovans, *b* 16 Feb 1907

    5*e* Rose Marion Wilson, *unm*

5*d* Rowland Holt Wilson, Solicitor (*Bury St Edmunds*), *b* 4 Nov 1846, *m* 1 June 1882, Amy Wilson (see p 158), da of the Rev George Hales, LL B, and has issue

See p 458, Nos 95376-95378

4*c* *Fanny Hales*, *b* 12 Dec 1813, *d* 23 *July* 1879, m 28 *Aug* 1834, *the Rev Charles Herbert Jenner, M 1, Rector of Wenve* [*2nd son of the Right Hon Sir Herbert Jenner-Fust, P C, LL D*], b 26 *July* 1809, *d* 6 *Oct* 1891, *and had issue* (*with 5 others who d young*) 1*d* to 3*d*

1*d* Henry Augustus Jenner, District Probate Registrar H M High Court of Justice, Chester (11 *Whitefriars, Chester*), *b* 15 Nov 1846, *unm*

[Nos 95383 to 95413

The Plantagenet Roll

2d Edwin Arthur Jenner of the Bank of England, b 3 Dec 1850, d 22 Feb 1908, m 8 May 1879, Edith Sarah, da of Fredrick Halsey Janson of Chislehurst, and had issue 1c to 6c

1c Montague Arthur Jenner, b 17 Oct 1883
2c Charles Herbert Jenner, b 31 Oct 1888
3c Violet Edith Jenner
4c Muriel Agnes Jenner
5c Cicely Frances Jenner, m 14 July 1908, Sidney Preston (Wallington, Surrey).
6c Evelyn May Jenner

3d Rev George Herbert Jenner, M A (Oxon), Rector of Wenvoe (Wenvoe Rectory, Glamorgan), b 17 Aug 1852, m 1st, 25 Sept 1877, May Hales (see p 461), da of the Rev William Grigson, d 11 June 1905, 2ndly, 9 Ap 1907, Julia, da of the Rev Arthur Thomas Whitmore Shadwell and his issue 1e to 6c

1c Herbert Lancelot Jenner, b 9 Sept 1885
2c Raymund Francis Jenner, b 30 Aug 1890
3c Caroline Elizabeth Mary Jenner
4c Fanny Jenner, m 19 Ap 1906, Lancelot Horace Augustus Shadwell (Durban, Natal)
5c Norah Margaret Jenner
6c Hilda Mary Lascelles Jenner

5c Margaret Hales b 25 Nov 1817, d 26 Jan 1887, m 9 July 1844, the Rev William Grigson, M A, Rector of Whinburgh, co Norfolk, d 6 Oct 1879, and had issue (with das who d young) 1d to 7d

1d Rev William Shuckforth Grigson, M A (Camb), formerly Scholar Ch Coll, 2nd Cl Trip 1867, Vicar of Pelynt (Pelynt Vicarage, Duloe, S O, Cornwall), b 15 Ap 1845, m 1st, 31 July 1873, Charlotte, da of John Neve of Wolverhampton, d s p 25 Feb 1884, 2ndly, 21 June 1886, Mary, da of Hugh Stott of Lewisham, d s p s 10 Feb 1889, 3rdly, 10 Sept 1890, Mary Beatrice, da of the Rev John Simon Boldero, M A Vicar of Amblecote, and has issue 1e to 7e

1e John William Boldero Grigson, Eastern Telegraph Coy, b 26 Jan 1893
2e Kenneth Walton Grigson, b 29 June 1895
3e Wilfrid Vernon Grigson, b 11 Oct 1896
4e Lionel Henry Shuckforth Grigson, b 25 Jan 1898
5e Claude Vivian Grigson, b 12 Jan 1900
6e Aubrey Herbert Grigson, b 22 Feb 1901
7e Geoffrey Edward Harvey Grigson, b 2 Mar 1905

2d Rev Edward Grigson, B A (Camb), late Rector of Northchurch 1897-1909, &c (West Lodge, Aylsham, Norfolk), b 2 Sept 1846, m 1st, 3 Oct 1872, Eleanor Edith, da of John Sunley of London, d 6 Aug 1904, 2ndly, 16 Jan 1906, Emma Sara Louisa, da of Thomas Abraham Rawlinson of Lincoln's Inn, and has issue 1e to 3e

1e James Edward Grigson, b 25 July 1873, unm
2e Francis Charles William Grigson, b 16 Aug 1875, unm
3e¹ Edith Margaret Grigson, unm

3d Francis Grigson, b 4 Aug 1852, d 25 Sept 1886, m 2 Aug 1881, Anna (Whinburgh, Musgrave Road, Durban, Natal), da of John Edward Alsebrook of Worthing, co Norfolk, and had issue 1e

1e Katharine Marion Grigson, b 1 May 1884

4d Rev Baseley Hales Grigson, B A (Camb), Rector of East Harling (East Harling Hall, Thetford), b 26 Mar 1856, m 5 Oct 1881, Annette Hammond, da and h of Grigson Heyhoe Wigg of Swanton, Morley, co Norfolk, d 15 July 1903, and has issue 1e to 2e

1e Pawlet St John Baseley Grigson, B A (Camb), now of the Bombay and Burma Trading Corporation, b 12 June 1882
2e Olive Vivia Grigson unm

[Nos 95114 to 95412]

460

# of The Blood Royal

5d   Robert John Hales Grigson, b 20 Mar 1858, m 20 July 1897, Dora Anne, da of the Rev John William Hunt of St James', Hull, s p

6d   Barbara Lucy Grigson, m 8 June 1871, Francis Bowman Turner (Westgate-on-Sea), and has issue 1e to 2e

1e   Katharine Mary Turner, unm

2e   Mabel Frances Turner, m 21 June 1902, Laurence Rea, s p

7d   Mary Hales Grigson, b 21 Nov 1849, d 11 June 1905, m as 1st wife, 25 Sept 1878, the Rev George Herbert Jenner, M A (Oxon), Rector of Wenvoe, and had issue

See p 460, Nos 95421-95426.

6c   Mary Anne Hales

2a   Fanny Turner, da and co-h, d 30 Nov 1813, m 28 Dec 1777, Sir Martin Browne ffolkes of Hillington, 1st Bt [G B 26 May 1774], F R S, d 11 Dec 1821, and had issue 1b to 3b

1b   Sir William John Henry Browne ffolkes, 2nd Bt [G B], F R S, b 30 Aug 1786, d 21 Mar 1860, m 21 Ap 1818, Charlotte Philippa, sister of Dominick, 1st Lord Oranmore [I], da of Dominick Geoffrey Brown of Castle MacGarrett, d 23 Dec 1882   and had issue 1c to 5c

1c   Martin William Browne ffolkes, b 16 Jan 1819, d v p 23 July 1849, m 30 Mar 1843, Henrietta Bridget, da of Gen Sir Charles Wale of Shelford, co Camb, K C B, d 14 Nov 1855, and had issue 1d to 3d

1d   Sir William Hovell Browne ffolkes of Hillington, 3rd Bt [G B], K C V O, J P, D L, High Sheriff co Norfolk 1876 and Chairman and Alderman of Norfolk C C, and Chairman Quarter Sessions, Hon Major late 2nd Brigade Eastern Division R A, M P for King's Lynn 1880-1885 (Hillington Hall, Lynn), b 21 Nov 1847, m 6 Ap 1875, Emily Charlotte, da of Robert Elwes of Congham House, co Norfolk, and has issue 1e

1e   Dorothy ffolkes, m 24 July 1902, Capt the Hon John Dawnay, D S O [son and h-app of Hugh Richard, 8th Viscount Downe [I], K C V O, &c, descended from King Henry VII (see Tudor Roll, p 370)] (Wykeham, Yorkshire) and has issue 1f to 3f

1f   Richard Dawnay, b 16 May 1903

2f   George William ffolkes Dawnay, for whom H R H the Prince of Wales was sponsor, b 20 Ap 1909

3f   Ruth Mary Dawnay.

2d   Martin William Browne ffolkes, C E, b 19 July 1849, d 3 Nov 1901, m 28 Jan 1882, Wilhelmine Mary Emily [descended from George, Duke of Clarence, K G (see Clarence Volume, p 417)] (Heacham, Norfolk), da of Col John Davy Brett of Dersingham, co Norfolk   and had issue 1e to 3e

1e   Audrey ffolkes

2e   Barbara ffolkes

3e   Cynthia Mary ffolkes

3d   Etheldreda Isabella ffolkes (Poringland, Norwich), m as 2nd wife, 26 Sept 1871, Henry Birkbeck of Stoke Holy Cross, J P, High Sheriff co Norfolk 1860, b 10 Feb 1821, d 1 Feb 1895, and has issue 1e to 2e

1e   Martin Birkbeck, b 10 Nov 1873

2e   Geoffrey Birkbeck, b 12 Oct 1875, m

2c   Rev Henry Edward ffolkes, heir-presumptive to Baronetcy, M A (Oxon), Rector of Hillington and Rural Dean of Lynn (Hillington Rectory, near Lynn), b 20 Dec 1823, m 24 Ap 1860, Sophia Louisa, da of the Rev Edward Brown Everard, Rector of Burnham Thorpe   and has issue 1d to 9d

1d   William Everard Browne ffolkes, formerly Lieut 4th Batt Suffolk Regt (8 Upton Park, Slough), b 15 Feb 1861, m 21 Ap 1896, Sybil Compton, da of the Rev Richard Compton Maul, and has issue 1e

1e   William Rupert Compton ffolkes, b 7 Aug 1898   [Nos 95443 to 95467.

The Plantagenet Roll

2*d* Edward George Everard ffolkes (*Indian Road, Toronto*), *b* 24 Jan 1862, *m* 4 Aug 1891, Agnes, da of A Strachan of Toronto

3*d* Rev Francis Arthur Stanley ffolkes, M V O, J P, Rector of Wolferton and a Chaplain in Ordinary to H M the King, *formerly* Hon Chaplain to Queen Victoria (*Wolferton Rectory, Norfolk*), *b* 8 Dec 1863, *m* 27 Sept 1893, Isabel Laura Newbery, da of John Newbery Boschetti of Eccles, co Lancaster, and has issue 1*c* to 2*c*

 1*c* Edward John Patrick Boschetti ffolkes, *b* 16 Jan 1899

 2*c* Philippa Frances Boschetti ffolkes, *b* 12 June 1896.

4*d* Robert Walling Everard ffolkes, *b* 1 Feb 1865, *m* 20 July 1884, Ada, da of Col Brierley and has issue 1*c* to 4*c*

 1*c* Mary Emily Margaret ffolkes

 2*c* Ethel Christobel Frances ffolkes

 3*c* Evelyn Maud ffolkes

 4*c* Muriel Everard ffolkes

5*d* Geoffrey Charles Hovell ffolkes, Private Secretary to Hon Joseph Baynes of Natal, C M G (*Hillington, Norfolk*), *b* 3 Aug 1867, *m* 27 Jan 1897, Edith Louisa Pollen, widow of the Rev Charles E Cummings, da of Frederick Haworth.

6*d* Margaret Louisa Everard ffolkes, *m* Jan 1888, the Rev John Erasmus Philipps, M A, Rector of Cockfield and Vicar of Staindrop (*Staindrop Vicarage, Darlington*), and has issue 1*e*

 1*e* Edward James Tracy Philipps, *b* 20 Nov 1888

7*d* Helen Sophia Everard ffolkes

8*d* Charlotte Philippa Everard ffolkes, *m* 25 Oct 1894, Sir Augustus Vere Foster of Glyde, 4th Bt [U K], J P, D L [descended from George, Duke of Clarence, K G, brother of King Edward IV (see Clarence Volume, p 593)], and has issue 1*e* to 3*e*

 1*e* Anthony Vere Foster, *b* 21 Feb 1908

 2*e* Philippa Eugenia Vere Foster

 3*e* Dorothy Elizabeth Charlotte Vere Foster

9*d* Mabel Olive Emily ffolkes

3*c* George Howe Browne ffolkes, M A, J P (*Wolferton Manor House, near Lynn*), *b* 16 Feb 1834

4*c* *Margaret Charlotte ffolkes,* d 23 May 1899, m 8 July 1847, *Francis Hay Gurney of North Runcton, Norfolk, J P, D L [descended from th. Lady Anne, sister to King Edward IV], d 1 Dec* 1891

 See the Exeter Volume, p 684, Nos 57430-57442

5*c* Fanny Louisa ffolkes (*Wolferton Manor House, near Lynn*)

2*b* *Fanny Mary ffolkes,* b 1778, d Ap 1813, bur *at West Wickham,* m 1799, *Gilbert Harvey West of H M Treasury,* b 1780, d 13 Feb 1861, bur *at Corfe,* and had issue (*with* 4 *other sons and* 2 *das who* d s p) 1*c* to 3*c*.

1*c* *Martin John West,* 1st Lieut-Gov of Natal, b 1800, d *at Pietermaritzburg,* 1819, m 1830, *Albina, da of* (—) *Sullivan, and had issue* 1*d* to 3*d*

1*d* Isabel Caroline West, *m* 18 July 1854, Major-Gen Frederick Charles D'Epinay Barclay [2nd son of Sir David William Barclay, 10th Bt [S]], d s p 28 Dec 1890

2*d* *Charlotte Maria West,* d (-), m (—) *Willock, and had issue* 1*e*

 1*e* Isabel Willock, *m* William Wellington Sandeman, Major *late* 78th Highlanders, and has issue 1*f*

  1*f* William Alastair Sandeman

3*d* Albina West, *m* Capt. Robson, and has issue (2 sons and a da)

2*c* *Caroline Elizabeth West,* b 1805, d 1897, m *the Rev Henry Vyvyan Luke, Rector of Thulbear, Stoke St Mary, and Thurloxton,* and had issue 1*d* to 4*d*

[Nos 95468 to 95504

# of The Blood Royal

1d Walter Luke (*Virginia, U S A*), b (—), m (—), da of (—) Pigott, and has issue 1e to 2e

1e Vyvyan Luke, b (—), m (—), da of (—) Douglas

2e Caroline Luke, m Frederick Arthur Berkeley Portman [son of the Rev Henry Fitzharding Berkeley Portman, Rector of Thulbear, Taunton, co Som]

2d Henry Edward Luke (*New Zealand*), b (—) m (—), s p

3d *Emma Fanny Luke*, b 1844, d 1864, m 186-, *the Rev* (—) *Henry Ewen*, and has issue 1e

1e Fanny Ewen

4d *Caroline Harriet Luke*, d 1893, m *Major Burridge*, and had issue (1 son and 2 das)

3c *Maria West*, b 16 *July* 1811, d 17 *Feb* 1892, m 12 *Ap* 1812, *the Rev William Hulme, Rector of Brampton Abbotts, co Hereford*, d 4 *Jan* 1890, *and had issue* (*with a son and da who d unm*) 1d

1d Frances Maria Hulme, m 4 July 1872, Capt Evans Mynde Allen, J P, High Sheriff co Hereford 1910, *late 1st Batt Royal Scots Fusiliers* (*Manor House, Upton Bishop, Ross, Hereford*), and has issue 1e

1e Robert William Allen M A (Oxon), Bar-at-Law I T, and Capt 8th V B T Hussars, b 11 Mar 1873, unm

3b *Lucretia Georgiana ffolkes*, b 1795, d *in childbirth at Bombay* 4 Sept 1828, m 26 *Aug* 1822, *Sir Edward West, Chief Justice of Bombay*, d *there* 18 *Aug* 1828, *and had issue* 1c

1c *Fanny Anna West*, b May 1826, d *at Shelford* 6 May 1869, m *at Hillington as 1st wife*, 1849, *Robert Gregory Wale of Shelford, J P, D L Hon Col. Cambridgeshire Militia, formerly 33rd Regt* [*6th son of the above-mentioned Sir Charles Wale, K C B*], b 11 Aug 1820, d 17 Ap 1892, *and had issue* 1d to 7d

1d *Robert ffolkes Wale of Shelford, Capt 4th Batt Suffolk Regt*, b 17 May 1863, d unm 5 Sept 1891

2d Fanny Lucretia Wale of Shelford, d and co-h (*Little Shelford, Cambridge*), b in Rome, unm

3d Mildred Wale of Shelford, da and co-h, m May 1909, Col Wood, R H A

4d Cecil Henrietta Wale, da and co-h, m 8 Oct 1884, the Rev Harcourt Morley Isaac Powell, Vicar of Wollaston (*Hollaston Vicarage, Northants*), and has issue 1e to 4e

1e Vernon Harcourt de Butts Powell, B A (Keble Coll, Oxon), b 23 Jan 1886

2e Robert Desmond Fitzgerald Powell, b 31 July 1892

3e Edward Blennerhassett Selwyn Powell, b 5 Feb 1897

4e Norah Cecil Wale Powell, b 6 May 1888

5d *Anna Charlotte Wale*, b Oct 1856, d 7 Aug 1891, m *Mar* 1883, *Robert Henry Willis*, and had issue (a da, *Mildred Mary*, b 22 Jan 1884, d *Mar* 1908)

6d Georgiana Isabella Wale, da and co-h, m 10 June 1880, the Rev Arthur Charles Jennings, Rector of King's Stanley [grandson of Adm Sir Edward Hamilton, K C B, R N, descended from James I, King of Scotland, by his Queen, Joan of Beaufort, granddau of John (of Gaunt), Duke of Lancester, K G, in right of which he took his degree as of Founder's Kin at Cambridge] (*King's Stanley Rectory, Gloucester*), and has issue 1e to 3e

1e Arthur Richard Jennings, B A (Jesus Coll, Camb), a Medical Student, b 6 May 1886

2e Richard William Jennings (Jesus Coll, Camb), a Law Student, b 6 Mar 1889

3e Hermione Louisa Farny Jennings

7d Frederica Wale of Shelford, da and co-h (*Little Shelford, Cambridge*) unm

[Nos 95505 to 95523.

463

The Plantagenet Roll

286 Descendants of FRANCIS SAMWELL of Upton (Table XXV), *bapt 15 Sept 1616, d 1657, m. REBECCA, da. of Robert SELSBY of Duston bur 23 May 1708, and had issue (with a son and da d unm.) 1a to 5a*

1a *William Samwell of Gayton, b c 1649, d 25 Feb 1706, m 20 Feb 1684, Agnes, da of Edward Dry of Milton, d 21 Jan 1687, and had issue* [1]

2a *Mary Samwell, bapt 16 May 1651, d (-), m John Goodier of Cransley, Bar-at-Law, and had issue* [1]

3a *Elizabeth Samwell bur 20 Ap 1675, m John Robinson of Great Wymond-ham, co Leic*

4a *Jane Samwell, bapt 24 May 1660, d (-), m W Knight of London*

5a *Frances Samwell, living unm 1682*

287 Descendants of HENRY (NEVILL), 6th Lord ABERGAVENNY [E.] (Table XXVI), *d 10 Feb 1587, m 1st, Lady FRANCES, da of Thomas (MANNERS), 1st Earl of Rutland [E], bur. Sept 1576, and had issue*

See the Exeter Volume, Table XXIV and pp 347-374, Nos 25205-26746, and the Essex Volume Supplement, pp 625-637, Nos 26210 1-393

[Nos 95524 to 97458

288 Descendants of JOHN (GRANVILLE), 1st EARL OF BATH [E 20 Ap 1661] (Table XXVI), *b 29 Aug. 1628, d 22 Aug 1701, m c Oct 1652, JANE, da of Sir Peter WYCHE of London, Comp-troller of the Royal Household, and had issue 1a to 5a*

1a *Charles (Granville), 2nd Earl of Bath [E], 1st Count Granville [H R E 27 Jan 1684], bapt 31 Aug 1661, d 4 Sept 1701, m 2ndly, Feb 1691, Countess Isabella, da of Count Henry of Nassau, Lord of Auverquerque, d 30 Jan 1692, and had issue 1b*

1b *William Henry (Granville), 3rd Earl of Bath [E], &c, b 30 Jan 1692, d unm 17 May 1711*

2a *John (Granville), 1st Baron Granville [E 1703], bapt 12 Ap 1665, d s p 3 Dec 1707*

3a *Lady Jane Granville, da and in her issue (1711) co-h, d 27 Feb 1696, m Sir William Leveson-Gower, 4th Bt [E 1620], M P, d Dec 1691, and had issue 1b to 3b*

1b *John (Leveson-Gower), 1st Baron Gower [E 16 Mar 1703], b 7 Jan 1675, d Sept 1709, m Sept 1692, Lady Catherine, da of John (Manners), 1st Duke of Rutland [E] d 7 Mar 1722, and had issue*
See the Exeter Volume, Table VIII and pp 172-187, Nos 3846-6776

2b *Katherine Leveson-Gower, b c 1670, d 14 Mar 1704, m 16 May (? June) 1687, Sir Edward Wyndham of Orchard Wyndham, 2nd Bt [E 1661], bur 29 June 1695, and had issue 1c*

1c *Sir William Wyndham, 3rd Bt [E], P C, Chancellor of the Exchequer, b 1687, d 17 June 1710, m 1st, 1708, Lady Catherine, d r of Charles (Seymour), 6th Duke of Somerset [E], K G, and had issue*
See the Tudor Roll, Table L and pp 263-292, Nos 24102-25349

3b *Jane Leveson-Gower, d 24 May 1725, m (lic 2 Mar) 1692, Henry (Hyde),*
[Nos 97459 to 101337

---

1 Baker's "Northants," i 225

464

# of The Blood Royal

4th Earl of Clarendon and 2nd Earl of Rochester [E], d 10 Dec 1753, and had issue

See pp 132-133, Nos 15257-15169

4a Lady Catherine Granville, d (-), m Craven Peyton

5a Grace, suo jure 1st Countess Granville [G B 1 Jan 1715], b c 1667, d 18 Oct 1744, m (lic 15 Mar) 1675, George (Carteret), 1st Baron Carteret [E 19 Oct 1681], d 22 Sept 1695, and had issue 1b

1b John (Carteret), 2nd Baron Carteret [E] and (1744) 2nd Earl Granville [G B], K G, Principal Sec of State to George I, b 22 Ap 1690, d 2 Jan 1763, m 1st, 17 Oct 1710, Frances, da of Sir Robert Worsley, 4th Bt [I.], d 20 June 1743, and had issue

See the Tudor Roll, Table XXXII and pp 201-210, Nos 21378-22550

[Nos 101338 to 102723

289. Descendants of BERNARD GRANVILLE, M.P, Gentleman of the Horse and Groom of the Bedchamber to King Charles II (Table XXVI), d 1701, m ANNE, da and h of Cuthbert MORLEY of Hornby, co York, and had issue 1a to 3a

1a Sir Bevil Granville, M P, Major-Gen and Governor of Barbados, d s p 1706

2a George (Granville), 1st Baron Lansdowne [G B], so cr by Anne 1 Jan 1712, and Duke of Albemarle [E], so cr by James III in exile 3 Nov 1721, P C, b 1667, d 30 Jan 1735, m 1711, Lady Mary, widow of Thomas Thynne of Old Windsor, da of Edward (Villiers), 1st Earl of Jersey [E], d 17 Jan 1735, and had issue

See p 377, Nos 62167-62469

3a Bernard Granville of Buckland, co Glos, Lieut-Gov of Hull, M P, d 1723, m Mary, da of Sir Martin Westcombe, 1st Bt [E 1699], and had issue 1b to 4b

1b Bernard (Granville), 2nd Duke of Albemarle [E] as above, d s p 2 July 1776

2b Rev Bevil Granville, d s p in Carolina 1736

3b Mary Granville, so well known for her literary acquirements, b 14 May 1770, d s p 15 Ap 1788, m 1st, 1717, Alexander Pendarves of Roscrow, 2ndly, 1743, the Very Rev Patrick Delany, D D, Dean of Down

4b Anne Granville, da and in her issue (1788) sole h b 1707, d 16 July 1761, m Aug 1740, John D'Ewes of Wellesbourne, co Warwick, d 30 Aug 1780, and had issue 1c to 2c

1c Bernard D'Ewes of Wellesbourne, b 1743, d 1780, m 1777, Anne, da of John Delabere of Cheltenham, d 1780, and had issue 1d to 2d

1d Court D'Ewes, afterwards (1826) Granville of Wellesbourne, b 1779, d 16 July 1848, m 1803, Maria, da of Edward Ferrers of Baddesley Clinton, co Warwick, d 16 Nov 1852, and had issue 1e to 3e

1e Bernard Granville of Wellesbourne, J P, D L, b 4 Feb 1801, d 6 Jan 1869, m 1st, 28 Jan 1828, Mathewana Sarah, da of Capt Mathew Richard Onslow, Coldstream Guards [Bt Coll], d 3 Aug 1829, 2ndly, 27 Oct 1830, Anne Catherine, da of Admiral Sir Hyde Parker [Bt Coll], d 17 Dec 1895, and had issue 1f to 9f

1f Bevil Granville of Wellesbourne, J P, formerly Major Royal Welsh Fusiliers and (1863-1887) one of H M's Hon Corps of Gentlemen-at-Arms, b 20 Jan 1834, d 8 May 1909, m 12 Oct 1865, Alice Jane, da of the Rev Nathaniel Woodhouse, Vicar of Worle and Dulverton [E of Kimberley Coll], by his wife Georgiana [descended from the Lady Anne, sister of King Edward IV (see the Exeter Volume, p 379)], da of Rev the Hon William Capel, d 21 Oct 1901, and had issue 1g to 6g

[Nos 102724 to 103026

The Plantagenet Roll

1g Bernard Granville, Capt 3rd King's Own Hussars (*Wellesbourne Hall, near Warwick*), b 21 July 1873, m 13 Jan 1903, Edith [descended from the Lady Isabel Plantagenet (see the Essex Volume, p 282)], da of the Right Hon Thomas Frederick Halsey of Gaddesden, P C , M P , and has issue 1h to 3h

    1h Bevil Granville, b 26 Dec 1904

    2h Richard St Leger Granville, b 24 Ap 1907

    3h May Granville, b 19 Ap 1910

2g Violet Granville, m 7 May 1889, Walter Henry Maudslay (69 *Cadogan Gardens*, H) s p s

3g May Olive Granville, m Dec 1893, Arthur Hubert Edward Wood of Sudbourne Hall, co Suffolk, J P , D L (*Browhead, Windermere*), and has issue 1h to 4h

    1h Edward Guy Wood, b 30 Oct 1894

    2h Richard Oliver Wood, b 26 Mar 1896

    3h Evelyn Sybil Wood

    4h Alice Ava Wood

4g Muriel Granville, m 14 Feb 1895, Frederick Blomfield (*Netherwylde Farm, St Albans*), and has issue 1h to 4h

    1h Valentine Blomfield, b 1898

    2h Christopher Blomfield, b 1900

    3h Peter Blomfield, b 1903

    4h David Blomfield, b 1908

5g Grace Granville, m 15 Nov 1893, Harold M'Corquodale (*Forest Hall, Ongar*), and has issue 1h to 5h

    1h Kenneth M'Corquodale

    2h Hugh M'Corquodale

    3h Donald M'Corquodale

    4h Angus M'Corquodale

    5h Janet M'Corquodale

6g Morwenna Granville, m 24 Jan 1905, Capt Lionel Halsey, R N [descended from the Lady Isabel Plantagenet (see the Essex Volume, p 282)]

2f George Hyde Granville, H E I C S , b 27 Feb 1837, d 13 Dec 1902, m 18 June 1862, Henrietta, da of Edward Bolton King of Chadshunt, co Warwick, and had issue (with a son d unm) 1g to 2g

    1g Denms Granville, M V O , Chief Constable of Dorsetshire, Capt *late* Royal Warwick Regt (*Shirley House, Dorchester*), b 14 Ap 1863, m 31 July 1895, Margaret Beatrice (see p 536), da of Major-Gen Sir George Henry Waller, 3rd Bt [U K], and has issue 1h

        1h Judith Margaret Granville, b 14 June 1896

    2g Mabel Georgiana Lucy Granville, m 4 Aug 1897, Major Henry Clerk, *late* Queen's Bays (*The Grange, Wellesbourne, Warwick*), and has issue 1h to 4h

        1h Mary Conyers Clerk, b 5 Aug 1898

        2h Valma Clerk, b 11 Oct 1899

        3h Letitia Clerk, b 29 Aug 1904

        4h Georgiana Clerk, b 26 July 1909

3f Frederic John Granville, b 14 Oct 1839, d 15 Feb 1883, m 2 July 1864, Cecilia Anne, da of Robert Hook, d 7 Feb 1877, and had issue 1g to 3g

    1g Charles Delabere Granville, Adm R N , b 21 June 1865, unm

    2g Cecil Horace Plantagenet Granville, settled in Australia, b 2 Jan 1877

    3g Marian Florence Granville, unm

4f Rev Roger Granville, Sub-Dean of Exeter, Rector of Bideford 1878–1896 (*Pilton House, Pinhoe, Exeter*), b 6 Feb 1848, m 20 Sept 1870, Matilda Jane

[Nos 103027 to 103059

466

# of The Blood Royal

[descended from George, Duke of Clarence, K G, brother of King Edward IV (see the Essex Volume Supplement, p 530)], da of Alexander Liebert of Swinton Hall, Lancaster, and has issue 1g to 2g

1g Count Granville, Capt 3rd Batt Devonshire Regt (4 *Cyril Mansions, Battersea Park*), b 6 May 1872, m 11 Aug 1879, Beatrice Mabel [descended from the Lady Isabel Plantagenet (see the Essex Volume, p 205)], da of Major-Gen Henry William Hart Davies Dumaresq, and has issue 1h to 2h

  1h Roger Francis Granville, b 23 June 1909

  2h Barbara Granville, b 25 Ap 1899

2g Eleanor Morwenna Granville, m 2 Aug 1902, Col George Reginald FitzRoy Talbot, R A [descended from George, Duke of Clarence, K G (see Clarence Volume, p 337)] (*Buckerell Lodge, Exeter*), and has issue 1h to 2h

  1h Granville FitzRoy Talbot, b 3 May 1908

  2h Gwendoline Betty Alice Talbot, b 6 June 1905

5/[1] Joan Frederica Mathewana Granville (*Field Place, Horsham*), m as 2nd wife, 10 Aug 1850, the Rev Lord Charles Paulet, Preb of Salisbury [2nd son of Charles, 13th Marquis of Winchester [E]], d 23 July 1870, and has issue 1g

1g Eleanor Mary Paulet, m 1 June 1889, Lieut-Gen Sir Edward Thomas Henry Hutton, K C M G, C B, Col Comdt King's Royal Rifle Corps (*Field Place, Horsham*)

6/[2] *Fanny Granville* (twin), d 1 May 1897, m *as 2nd wife, 22 Ap 1858, the Rev Wellesley Pole Pigott, M A, Rector of Fugglestone-cum-Bemerton and Fovant [1th son of Sir George Pigott, 1st Bt [U K]], d 27 Feb 1890, and had issue 1g to 2g*

1g Wellesley George Pigott, J P, Capt *late Rifle Brigade* (*Blackmore House, Essex*), b 20 Ap 1861, m 7 July 1891, Helen Louise, widow of Capt Frederick W Ind, R A, da of Capt Thomas Donaldson, 3rd Hussars, and has issue 1h

  1h Gerald Wellesley Pigott, b 3 Sept 1896

2g Fanny Ada Pigott (*Greenoaks, Brockenhurst, Hants*), m 25 May 1886, Lieut-Col Charles Berkeley Pigott, C B, D S O [eldest son of Sir Charles Robert Pigott, 3rd and present Bt [U K], J P, D L], d ? p 12 Sept 1897, and has issue 1h to 2h

  1h Berkeley Pigott, b 21 May 1894

  2h Florence Ada Cecile Pigott

7/[2] Louisa Granville (*Moreton, Bideford*), m as 2nd wife, 31 Jan 1872, Sir George Stucley Stucley, 1st Bt [U K], M P, d 13 Mar 1900, and has issue
See p 183, Nos 103415-103418

8/[2] Amy Granville (*Marham House, Downham Market*), m 4 Dec 1861, Capt Henry Bathurst, 23rd Royal Welsh Fusiliers, d 5 Sept 1886, and has issue 1g to 7g

1g Henry Villebois Bathurst of Marham, Lord of the Manor of Old Hall and Westacre (*Marham House, Downham Market*), b 30 Oct 1862

2g Granville Frederick Villebois Bathurst, b 5 Feb 1864

3g Launcelot Villebois Bathurst, b 23 Ap 1870

4g Laurence Charles Villebois Bathurst, M A (Oxon), b 4 June 1871, m

5g Emily Villebois Bathurst

6g Finetta Villebois Bathurst

7g Amy Villebois Bathurst

9/[2] *Harriet Granville*, d 18 Mar 1909, m 28 Dec 1869, *Henry Compton of Minstead Manor House, co Hants, and Mapperton House, co Dorset, J P, D L*, d. 5 July 1877, *and had issue 1g to 5g*

1g Henry Francis Compton of Minstead and Mapperton, J P, D L, *formerly* M P New Forest Div, co Hants (*The Manor House, Minstead, Lyndhurst, Mapperton House, Dorset*), b 16 Jan 1872, m 12 June 1895, Dorothy Ann [herself a
[Nos 103000 to 103086

descendant of King Edward III through Mortimer-Percy], da of Sir Richard Courtenay Musgrave, 11th Bt [E], and has issue

See p 199, Nos 29580-29582

2g George Compton, b 1 Feb 1873

3g Edward Bathurst Compton, Lieut (ret) R N, b 14 Aug 1875, m 23 June 1900, Bertha Alice [descended from the Lady Isabel Plantagenet (see Essex Volume, p 112)], da of the Hon William Sydney Hylton Joliffe [B Hylton Coll], and has issue 1h to 2h

1h Sydney Henry Compton, b 25 Aug 1901

2h Oliver Compton, b 28 Nov 1905

4g Harriet Compton, m 17 Nov 1900, Algernon Charles Wyndham Dunn-Gardner of Chatteris House, co Camb, and Denton Hall, co Suffolk, M A (Oxon) (*Dullingham House, Newmarket*), and has issue 1h

1h [da] Dunn Gardner, b 28 Sept 1904

5g Eleanor Compton, m 8 Ap 1896, Henry Martin Powell of Wilverley, J P [eldest son of Lieut Col William Martin Powell of Brooklands, co Hants, J P] (*Wilverley Park, Lyndhurst, Hants*), and has issue 1h

1h Henry Weyland Martin Powell, b 1902

2c *Rev Granville John Granville, Vicar of Stratford-on-Avon, b 1807, d 26 Ap 1871, m 16 Ap 1839, Marrianne [descended from the Lady Anne, sister of King Edward II] da of Sir Grey Skipwith, 8th Bt [E], d 21 Oct 1878, and had issue*

See the Exeter Volume, p 328, Nos 24139-24151

3c *Mary Granville, d (? s p) 28 Oct 1886, m 1856, Col David Forbes, 91st Regt, d 1885*

2d *Anne Granville, d (-), m 1805, George Frederick Stratton of Great Tew, co Oxon*

2c *Mary D'Ewes, b 22 Feb 1746, d 15 June 1814, m Dec 1770, John Port, previously Sparrow, of Ilam Hall, co Stafford, J P, b 1730, d 9 Aug 1801, and had issue (with 3 sons and a da d s p) 1d to 4d*

1d *John Port of Ilam House, which he sold 1807, b 1773, d 1 Mar 1837, m c 1795/7, Mary, da of Capt Parke, H E I C S, d July 1837, and had issue (with 2 sons and a da d unm) 1e to 4e*

1e *Rev George Richard Port, B A (Oxon), Rector of Oxenton, co Glos, 1838-1855, and of Grafton-Flyford, co Worc, 1855-1875, b 23 Dec 1800, d 28 Dec 1882, m 2ndly, 15 Dec 1859, Frances Elizabeth Ann, da of George Syers of Boughton House, co Chester, b 19 Mar 1824, d 1 Dec 1909, and had issue 1f*

1f *George Brodie MacFarlan Port, b 12 Mar 1863, m 23 Oct 1888, Frances Emma Annie, da of Edward Elliot Chambers of Crow Park and Fosterstown, co Meath, M A (Oxon), Bar-at-Law, and sister of Richard Edward Elliott Chambers of the same, and has issue 1g to 2g*

1g Francis George Richard Port, b 10 Oct 1892

2g Frances Dorothea Mary Port, b 6 Jan 1890

2c *Georgina Port, d (-), m 23 Sept 1830, Charles Penny of Weymouth, J P, d (-), and had issue (with 3 das d unm) 1f*

1f *Charles Brodie Footman Penny, Gen R E, d (-), m. Mary, da of (-) Lord, and had issue (with other sons) 1g to 2g*

1g Arthur Taylor Penny, Capt Hants Regt, b 17 Ap 1871

2g Alice Penny

3c *Louisa Port, d at Versailles 1858, m at Marylebone, 20 Sept 1820, the Rev William Webster, M A, Rector of Church Preen and Easthope, co Salop, formerly Light Dragoons, d 17 Sept 1841, and had issue 1f to 3f*

1f *Frederick Taylor Webster (Huntington House, Holmer, near Hereford), b 10 Ap 1827, m 30 Ap 1853, Mary Ann, da of George Peach Aston of Newton, co Salop, and has issue 1g to 4g* [Nos 103087 to 103116

# of The Blood Royal

1g Frederick Granville Port Webster, b 10 Sept 1863, m 1 Feb 1888, Anne, da of (—) Hargrave of co Warwick, and has issue 1h

1h Frederick Hargrave Webster, b 4 Jan 1889

2g Mary Louisa Webster, m Charles Frederick Deaken (*Canada*), and his issue 1h to 9h

1h Robert Frederick Deaken, *bapt* 20 Nov 1881

2h Charles Keehege Deaken, } *bapt* 21 Nov 1882
3h Guy Barton Deaken, }

4h George Francis Deaken, *bapt* at Buckleton 1 July 1887

5h Bickerton Aston Deaken, *bapt* there July 1889

6h Reginald Grenville Deaken, *bapt* there 1892

7h Mary Wilhelmina Deaken, *bapt* 25 Oct 1884

8h Elsie Winifred Deaken, *bapt* 23 Nov 1885

9h Vera Dorothy Deaken, *bapt* at Buckleton 14 July 1890

3g Emma Elizabeth Webster, *unm*

4g Edith Minna Webster, m

2f Mary Webster, *unm*

3f Edith Webster, m Major Collins, R M , d (—), and has issue (6 children, 4 abroad and 2 in England) 1g to 6g

1g Garnet Wolseley Collins, b 23 May 1883

2g Francis Le Hardi Collins, b 5 Mar 1885

3g Edith Muriel Collins, b 23 Oct 1880

4g Kathleen Maud Wolseley Collins, b 7 Nov 1881

5g Ethel Gwendoline Collins, b 1887

6g (—) Collins

4e *Harriet Port*, d at Brighton after 1876, m Sept 1840, *the Rev Henry Robert Fowler of Felton, co Glos , and had issue 1f*

1f *Augusta Fowler*, da and h , d 15 Mar 1905, m 11 July 1867, *John Ashfordby-Trenchard of Stanton House (Stanton Fitzwarren, near Highworth), and had issue (with 3 sons d young) 1g to 2g*

1g John Henry Mohun Ashfordby-Trenchard, b 4 May 1868

2g Stephen Granville Ashfordby-Trenchard, now (R L 1 Aug 1905) Fowler (*Vista Linda, Torquay*), b 21 July 1872

2d *Georgina Mary Ann Port*, b 16 Sept 1771, d 19 Jan 1850, m 1789, *Benjamin Waddington of Llanover, co Monmouth , and had issue 1e to 3e*

1e *Frances Waddington*, da and co h , b 4 Mar 1791, d at Karlsruhe Mar 1876, m 1 July 1817, *Christian Charles Josias (Bunsen), 1st Baron Bunsen (Freiherr von Bunsen)* [*Prussia*], so cr for life 3 Oct 1857, *for many years Prussian Min Plen to the Court of St James', d at Bonn 29 Nov 1860, and had issue (with a son and 3 das d unm) 1f to 8f*

1f *Rev Henry George de Bunsen, Rector of Donington, naturalised in the United Kingdom 22 Ap 1842, b in Rome 2 Ap 1818, d 19 Mar 1885, m 15 Ap 1847, Mary Louisa, da of Abraham Harford Battersby, formerly Harford, of Stoke House, co Glos , d 20 Ap 1906, and had issue 1g to 2g*

1g Elizabeth Frances de Bunsen, da and co h , m 14 Jan 1880, the Rev William Archibald Sheringham, Rector of Donington (*Donington Rectory, Wolverhampton, co Salop*), and has issue 1h to 2h

1h Charles John de Bunsen Sheringham, b 12 Feb 1883

2h Mary Alsager Sheringham

2g *Louisa Emily de Bunsen, da and co h, b 18 Mar 1749, d 22 Ap 1887, m as 2nd wife, 8 July 1886, Thomas Cheney Garfit of Kenwick Hall, J P , D L , High Sheriff co Linc 1897, formerly Capt Royal North Lincoln Militia (Kenwick Hall, Louth, co Linc , Carlton), and has issue 1h*

1h Henry de Bunsen Cheney Garfit, b 9 Ap 1887 [Nos 103117 to 103144

469
3 o

The Plantagenet Roll

2f *Ernest Christian Louis de Bunsen of Abbey Lodge, Regent's Park*, b 19 Mar 1885, d 13 May 1903, m 5 Aug 1845, *Elizabeth, da of John Gurney of Ham House, co Essex*, d 19 Jan 1903, *and had issue 1g to 3g*

1g Sir Maurice William Ernest de Bunsen, P C, G C V O, K C M G, now H B M's Ambassador to the Court of Madrid (*British Embassy, Madrid*, 2 *Whitehall Court, S W*, *St James', Travellers'*), b 8 Jan 1852, m 2 May 1899, Berta Mary, da of Admin Henry Lowry-Corry [E of Belmore Coll], and has issue 1h to 3h

  1h Hilda Violet Helena de Bunsen, b 3 Ap 1900

  2h Elizabeth Cicely de Bunsen, b 30 Jan 1902

  3h Rosalind Margaret de Bunsen, b 25 July 1903

2g Hilda Elizabeth de Bunsen (8 *Chester Street, Grosvenor Place, S W*, *Bendeleben Castle, Sondershausen*), m 1st, at the Chapel Royal, St James', 17 Ap 1873, Hugo von Krause, Fideicommis-Besitzer of Bendeleben, near Sondershausen, Councillor of the German Embassy, d in London 26 Mar 1874, 2ndly, 20 Sept 1877, Adolph Wilhelm Conrad Rudolph (Deichmann), 1st Baron Deichmann (Freiherr von Deichmann) [Prussia 11 June 1888], d 12 Nov 1907, and has issue 1h to 4h

  1h Wilhelm von Krause, Fideicommis-Besitzer of Bendeleben (*Bendeleben Castle, near Sondershausen*), Diplo Ser, now Councillor German Imperial Legation at Athens, b 10 Feb 1874, *unm*

  2h Baroness Hilda Eveline Marie von Deichmann, m 5 Ap 1905, Karl Bernhard (von Bismarck), 1st Count of Bismarck-Osten (Graf von Bismarck-Osten) [Prussia 19 Dec 1906] (*Schloss Plathe, Pomerania, Prussia*), and has issue 1i to 2i

    1i Karl Ulrich von Bismarck-Osten, b at Rathe 13 July 1908

    2i Ferdinand Otto Bernhard Wilhelm von Bismarck-Osten, b 20 Dec 1909

  3h Baroness Elsa Olga von Deichmann, m 8 June 1910, Baron Walter von Ruxleben (*Schloss Rottleben, Schwarzburg-Sondershausen*)

  4h Baroness Marie Therese von Deichmann, *unm*.

3g Marie de Bunsen (67 *Eaton Terrace, S W*), *unm*

3f *Carl von Bunsen of Mein Genugen, Biebrich, Germany, German Diplo Service*, b 4 Nov 1821, d 12 Mar 1887 m Jan 1856, *Mary Isabel (Castle Townshend, co Cork), da of Thomas Waddington*, *and had issue 1g*

1g Beatrice Margaret von Bunsen, da and h, m 27 Ap 1895, Charles Loftus Uniacke Townshend of Castle Townshend, *late Capt 5th Batt Royal Irish Rifles* (*Castle Townshend, co Cork*, 46 *Lansdowne Road, Dublin*), and has issue 1h to 6h

  1h Charles Richard de Bunsen Loftus Townshend, b 1 Ap 1896

  2h Frederick William Chisholm Loftus Townshend, b 19 Nov 1897

  3h Charles Maurice Waddington Loftus Townshend, b 31 Jan 1899

  4h Edward Arthur Penderell Loftus Townshend, b 20 June 1901

  5h Walter Bevil Granville Loftus Townshend, b 8 Nov 1902

  6h Bernard Hugo Uniacke Loftus Townshend, b 19 Dec 1905

4f *Georg Friedrich von Bunsen, Member of the Imperial German Reichstag*, b 7 Nov 1824, d in London 22 Dec 1896, m 21 Dec 1854, *Emma, sister of Sir Edward Birkbeck, 1st Bt [U K], da of Henry Birkbeck of Keswick Old Hall, co Norfolk*, d 25 July 1899, *and had issue (with an elder son, Carl, d unm) 1g to 7g*

1g Lothar Henry George de Bunsen (*The Abbey, Knaresborough*), b in England 31 Oct 1858, m 1st, 6 Jan 1887, *Mary Anna, da of Sir Alexander Kinloch of Gilmerton, 10th Bt [S], d 22 Feb 1898, 2ndly, 25 June 1901, Victoria Alexandrina [descended from George, Duke of Clarence, K G (see Clarence Volume, p 292)], da of Sir Thomas Fowell Buxton, 3rd Bt [U K], G C M G, by his wife, Lady Victoria, née Noel*, and has issue 1h to 5h

  1h Arnold George de Bunsen, b 15 Dec 1887

  2h Eric Henry de Bunsen, b 24 Sept 1889

  3h Carl de Bunsen, b 13 Oct 1905

  4h Bernard de Bunsen, b 24 July 1907

  5h Ronald Lothar de Bunsen, b 19 Feb 1910

[Nos 103145 to 103169.

# of The Blood Royal

2g Waldemar von Bunsen (*Haus Leppe, Rheinland, Prussia*), b 11 June 1872, m 15 Aug 1903, Marie, da of Geheimer Hofjustizrah Paul Fleischhammer of Berlin, s p

3g Marie von Bunsen, *unm*

4g Else von Bunsen, *unm*

5g Emma von Bunsen, *unm*

6g Hildegard von Bunsen, *unm*

7g Berta von Bunsen, m 3 Aug 1889, Ernest Flagg Henderson, Historian (1 *Mercer Circle, Cambridge, Mass, U S A*), and has issue 1h to 6h

    1h Gerard Henderson, b 13 Aug 1891

    2h George Henderson, b 27 June 1894

    3h Ernest Henderson, b 7 Mar 1897

    4h Hildegard Henderson

    5h Edith Henderson

    6h Frances Henderson

5f Theodore von Bunsen, b (twin) 3 Jan 1832, d *at Heidelberg* 1892, m 1st, c 1876, Norah, da *of Thomas Hill*, and had issue 1g to 2g

    1g Harald von Bunsen, b 1877, m

    2g Moritz von Bunsen, b 1878, m. and his issue

6f Emilia von Bunsen (*Carlsruhe, Germany*), *unm*

7f Mary Charlotte Elizabeth von Bunsen (*Blaise Castle, Henbury, Bristol*), m, 4 Ap 1850, John Battersby Harford of Falcondale, co Cardigan, and Blaise Castle co Glos, M A, J P, D L, High Sheriff co Glos, 1855, d 11 Feb 1875, and has issue 1g to 8g

    1g John Charles Harford of Falcondale and Blaise Castle, Lord of the Manor of Lampeter, J P, D L, High Sheriff co Cardigan 1885 (*Falcondale, Lampeter, South Wales, Blaise Castle, Henbury, Bristol*), b 28 July 1860, m 11 Ap 1893, Blanche Amabel, da of the Right Hon Henry Cecil Raikes of Llwynegrin, co Flint, P C, d 28 Aug 1901, and has issue 1h to 3h

        1h John Henry Harford, b 7 Feb 1896

        2h George Arthur Harford, b 29 Dec 1897

        3h Mary Amabel Harford

    2g Frederic Dundas Harford of Holme Hall, C V O, J P, D L, Councillor of Embassy, Diplo Service (*Holme Hall, E R Yorks, British Legation, Darmstadt*), b 8 Feb 1862, m 29 Sept 1896, Amy Mary Josephine, Lady of the Manor of Holme [descended from George, Duke of Clarence, K G (see Clarence Volume, p 367)], da and co-h of Henry Joseph Stourton of Holme Hall, J P [Baron Stourton [E] Coll], and has issue 1h

        1h Joan Mary Harford

    3g Alice Mary Elizabeth Harford (*Blaise Castle, Henbury, Bristol*)

    4g Constance Emilia Harford (*Hythe House, Staines*), m 23 Ap 1878, John Band of Lochwood, M P, J P, D L, d 8 July 1900 and has issue 1h to 3h

        1h James Alexander Band, b 15 Feb 1879

        2h Jean Edith Band, m 30 Aug 1906, Thomas Algernon Raikes [4th son of the Right Hon Henry Cecil Raikes of Llwynegrin, P C, and a descendant of George, Duke of Clarence, K G (see Clarence Volume, p 407), and has issue 1i to 2i

            1i Thomas Hugh Cecil Raikes, b. 13 Ap 1908

            2i Douglas Charles Gordon Raikes, b. 26 Jan 1910

        3h Margaret Ina Band

    5g Mary Edith Harford (1 *Funchal Villas, Clifton, Bristol*), m 13 July 1878, Alban Gwynne of Monachty, co Cardigan, J P, D L, d 20 Feb 1904, and his issue (a son and 2 das) 1h to 3h

[Nos 103170 to 103199

The Plantagenet Roll

1h Alban Lewis Gwynne, Lieut R N, b 15 Sept 1880

2h Dorothy Mary Gwynne

3h Gladys Evelyn Gwynne

6g Charlotte Louisa Huxford, unm

7g Agnes Clementina Huxford, unm

8g Eleanor Dorothy Huxford, m 23 Ap 1889, John Iltyd Dillwyn Nicholl of Merthyr Mawr J P, D L, High Sheriff co Glam 1899 [descended from the Lady Anne, sister of Kings Edward IV and Richard III (see Exeter Volume, p 651)] (*Merthyr Mawr, Bridgend, Glamorgan*), and has issue 1h to 5h

    1h John William Huxford Nicholl, b 24 Oct 1892

    2h Robert Iltyd Nicholl, b 29 Dec 1896

    3h Gladys Mary Nicholl

    4h Olive Eleanor Nicholl

    5h Rachel Charlotte Nicholl

8f *Theodora Maria Wilhelmine von Bunsen*, b (twin) at Rome 3 Jan 1832, d at Karlsruhe 26 May 1862 m 12 Sept 1855, *August Johann Paul Friedrich, Baron von Ungern Sternberg* [H R E 16 July 1531 and Sweden 27 Oct 1653] d at Karlsruhe 20 Mar 1895, and had issu. (a son and 4 das) 1g to 5g

1g Reinhold Joseph Christian Ernst Jacob, Baron von Ungern-Sternberg [H R E], Major German Imperial Army, Master of the Household and Chamberlain to the Grand Duke of Hesse (*Darmstadt*), b at Heidelberg 25 Sept 1860, m at Darmstadt 21 Sept 1897, Marion Louisa [descended from George, Duke of Clarence, K G, brother of King Edward IV (see Clarence Volume, p 511)], da of Col Emilius Charles Delmé-Radcliffe, and has issue 1h to 2h

    1h Baron Reinhold August Emil Ludwig von Ungern-Sternberg, b 29 May 1909

    2h Baroness Alix Luisa Emilia Marion Hedwig von Ungern-Sternberg, b 7 July 1898

2g Baroness Elisabeth Rosalie Franzisca von Ungern-Sternberg, m at Karlsruhe 29 July 1882, Lieut Col Karl von Reutersward, Swedish Life Hussars, *formerly A D C and a Chamberlain to H M the King of Sweden* (*Stockholm*), and has issue 1h to 4h

    1h Patrick Karl Reinhold von Reutersward, an Attaché in the Swedish Legation at Paris, b 2 Feb 1885

    2h Gösta August Cecil von Reutersward, Lieut Swedish Life Hussars, b 4 Ap 1887

    3h Viktoria Augusta Fedora von Reutersward, unm

    4h Margareta Frances Anna von Reutersward, unm

3g Baroness Theodora Amelie Helen von Ungern-Sternberg, m at Karlsruhe 27 Sept 1878, Gen Friedrich Ludwig Georg von Kloden (*Wiesbaden*), and has issue 1h to 3h

    1h Thilo George Ludwig August von Kloden, Lieut Prussian Army, b at Karlsruhe 21 Ap 1881

    2h Wilhelm von Kloden, Lieut 109th Regt German Army, b at Berlin 22 Sept 1888

    3h Theodora Elisabeth Emelie Franziska Viktoria von Kloden

4g Baroness Marie Hildegard von Ungern-Sternberg (*Potsdam*), m at Karlsruhe 22 Oct 1879, Gen Bernhard von Lippe, A D C to the Emperor, &c, d at Dresden 20 Dec 1896, and has issue 1h to 2h

    1h Albrecht von Lippe, b 24 Ap 1885

    2h Daisy von Lippe

5g Baroness Aga Theodora Luise Emma Franziska von Ungern-Sternberg, m at Herrenalb 11 June 1893, Major Heinrich Wilhelm Friedrich von Bodelschwingh, 20th Regt German Imp Army (*Karlsruhe*), s p   [Nos 103200 to 103226

# of The Blood Royal

2*e* Augusta Waddington, da and co-h, b 21 Nov 1802, d 17 Jan 1896, m 4 Dec 1823, Benjamin (Hall), 1st and only Baron Llanover [U K 27 June 1859], P C, &c, b 8 Nov 1802, d 27 Ap 1867, and had issue (with 2 sons d young) 1*f*

1*f* Hon Augusta Charlotte Elizabeth Hall, d (-), m 12 Nov 1846, John Arthur Edward Jones, afterwards (R L 27 Nov 1848) Herbert, of Llan nth Court, co Mon, J P, D L, d 18 Aug 1895, and had issue

See the Clarence Volume, pp 455-456, Nos 19659-19679

3*e* Emily Waddington, da and co-h, d s p 1817, m as 1st wife, George (Manley), 1st Count de Manley [P S 184-], of Buckland, co Som, Adj-Gen Papal Army

3*d* Louisa Port, b 7 Ap 1778, d 3 July 1817, m 6 Oct 1803, the R v Brownlow Villiers Layard, M A, Rector of Uffington, co Linc, and Chaplain to the Duke of Kent, &c, previously Lieut 7th Fusiliers and A D C to the Duke of Kent, b 19 Jan 1779, d 26 Mar 1861, and had issue (with 2 sons d-p) 1e to 5e

1*e* Brownlow Villiers Layard, Lieut-Col 9th Regt, M P for Carlow, b 14 July 1804, d 7 Dec 1853 m 14 July 1835, Elizabeth da of Capt John Deane Digby, 5th Royal Irish Dragoons and had issue 1*f*

1*f* Brownlow Villiers Layard, F R G S, Lieut-Col formerly Gloucester Regt (Riversdale, Vesuvius Bay, British Columbia), b 3 Jan 1838, m 4 Nov 1882, Clara, da of Robert John Littey, J P, and has issue 1g to 3g

1*g* Brownlow Villiers Layard, Lieut R N, b 24 Aug 1884

2*g* Henry Campville Layard, b 24 Jan 1886

3*g* Arthur Raymond Layard, b 22 Sept 1888

2*e* John Beville Layard, Capt 22nd Madras N I, b 21 Sept 1809, d 12 Feb 1846, m Harriette Cobbe, da of Brig-Gen Thomas Henry Somerset Conway, C B, b 30 Nov 1821, d 12 Ap 1907, and had issue 1*f* to 2*f*

1*f* Beville Brownlow Edward Layard (Para Para, near Pungarehu, Taranaki, New Zealand), b 3 June 1845, m Aug 1881, Ann, da of George Poynter Betts of New Plymouth, Taranaki, and has issue 1g to 2g

1*g* Beville Anthony Layard, b 13 June 1882

2*g* Catherine Louisa Gwladys Layard, m Samuel Russell Feaver, Pharmaceutical Chemist (Opunaki, Taranaki, N Z), and has issue 1*h* to 2*h*

1*h* Mary Catherine Feaver, b 6 Oct 1906

2*h* Helena Jessica Feaver, b Jan 1909

2*f* Harriette Caroline Layard (Para Para, near Pungarehu, Taranaki, New Zealand)

3*e* Bernard Granville Layard, Lieut-Col in the Army, b 10 Mar 1813, d 22 Sept 1872, m 1st, 10 Aug 1841, Mary Anne, widow of (—) Dowker, da of (—) Clarke, d (-), 2ndly, 21 Oct 1847, Anna Maria, da of John Knowles, and had issue 1*f* to 4*f*

1*f* John Granville Layard, b 11 Dec 1851, d (-), m 1 Jan 1879, Gertrude, da of Thomas W Phipson, Q C, and had issue 1g

1*g* Violet Layard

2*f* [1] Mary Ann Elizabeth Layard, b 4 Oct 1842, m Major Frederick George Pym, R M, C B, and has issue 1g to 3g

1*g* Charles Brownlow Pym, b 6 Feb 1864

2*g* John Beville Pym, Capt R M, b 16 Nov 1866, m (—), da of Col Hope

3*g* Marianne Pym

3*f* [2] Maria Louisa Layard (11 Henrietta Street, Bath)

4*f* [2] Georgiana Edith Layard (Harepath Croft, Colyford, Devon)

4*e* Frederick Louis Layard, b 20 July 1815, d (-), m (—), da of (—), and had issue 1*f*

[Nos 103227 to 103265

The Plantagenet Roll

1*f* *Bertie Layard*, b (-), m (—), da of (—), and has issue 1g

1*g* Anna L Layard (*Mitchell Street, Bourke, Australia*)

5*e* *Rev Charles Clement Layard*, b 25 Ap 1817, d 1 Nov 1895, m 3 *June* 1847, Sarah, da of Samuel Somes, d 22 May 1886, *and had issue 1f to 5f*

1*f* *Abel John Layard*, b 20 May 1853, d 17 Aug 1890, m 8 Oct 1884, Catherine (*East Haves House, Bath*), da of the Rev Thomas Hayes, *and had issue 1g to 2g*

   1*g* Ruth Sidney Layard, b 2 Jan 1887

   2*g* Nora Margaret Layard, b 16 Mar 1890

2*f* George Somes Layard, Bar-at-Law, Author and Reviewer (*Bull's Cliff, Felixstowe*), b 4 Feb 1857, m 8 Oct 1885, Eleanor Byng, da of Thomas Gribble, and has issue 1g to 3g

   1*g* John Willoughby Layard, b 28 Nov 1891

   2*g* Peter Clement Layard, b 7 June 1896

   3*g* Nancy Layard, b 8 Sept 1886

3*f* Sarah May Louisa Layard, m 6 Sept 1876, the Rev Henry Robert Whytehead, M A (Camb), Vicar of Warminster (*The Vicarage, Warminster*), and has issue

   See p 314, Nos 12373–12375

4*f* Nina Frances Layard, F L S (*Rookwood, Ipswich*)

5*f* Annie Jane Layard, m 6 Sept 1881, Evelyn Gordon Reeves (*Wiltshire, Matale, Ceylon*), and has issue 1g to 3g

   1*g* Frederick Layard Reeves (*Weharegama, Matale, Ceylon*)

   2*g* Margaret Layard Reeves, m Jan 1908, the Rev Archibald Leslie Keith, B A (Camb), Chaplain of Dimbula Planting Dist (*Talawakella, Ceylon*)

   3*g* Enid Sarah Layard Reeves, *unm*

4*d* Frances Anne Post, b 18 Ap 1783, d 4 Nov 1860, m 11 Aug 1803, Abel John Ram of Clonattin, co Wexford, d v p 3 Nov 1823, *and had issue (with 2 das d unm)* 1*e*

1*e* *Rev Abel John Ram of Clonattin, Hon Canon of Rochester*, b 30 May 1804, d 18 Aug 1883, m 11 Ap 1833, Lady Jane, da of James George (Stopford), 3rd Earl of Courtown [I], K P, d 28 Dec 1873, *and had issue*

   See the Tudor Roll, pp 166, Nos 20048–20068   [Nos 103266 to 103302

---

290. Descendants of Sir EDMUND PRIDEAUX of Netherton, 5th Bt. [E] (Table XXVI), b 13 Nov 1675, d 26 Feb 1729, m. 1st (settl dated 20 21 Feb), 1710, MARY, da of Samuel REYNARDSON, d 12 Aug 1712, 2ndly (lic. dated 6 May), 1714, ANNE, da. of Philip HAWKINS of Pennans, co Cornwall, d. 10 May 1741, and had issue 1*a* to 2*a*

1*a* Mary Prideaux, da and in her issue sole h, d 1758,[1] m James Winstanley of Braunston, High Sheriff co Leic 1718, d Mar 1770, and had issue 1b to 3b

1*b* Clement Winstanley of Braunston, High Sheriff co Leic 1774, d 1808, m Jane, sister of Thomas Boothby, 1st Baron Rancliffe [I], da of Sir Thomas Parkyns, 3rd Bt [E], and had issue 1c to 2c

   1*c* Clement Winstanley of Braunston, J P, D L, d unm 1855

2*c* Rev George Winstanley, Rector of Glenfield, co Leic, d 1846, m Mary Frances, da of the Rev William Birch of Rugby, and had issue 1d to 4d

   1*d* James Beaumont Winstanley of Braunston, d unm 7 July 1862.

---

[1] Fletcher's " Leicestershire Pedigrees and Royal Descents," p 40

# of The Blood Royal

2d Anna Jane Winstanley of Braunston, co Leicester, b c 1825, d 30 Ap 1910, m 18 Oct 1855, Comm Ralph George Pochin, R N , J P [5th son of George Pochin of Barkby Hall, co Leic], d 7 Oct 1897 , and had issue (with 3 sons and a da d unm) 1e to 4e

1e Richard Norman Pochin, now (20 Nov 1905) Winstanley, Lord of the Manor of Braunston and Patron of the Living of Glenfield, Major late E Surrey Regt (Braunston Hall, Leicester), b 19 Ap 1861, m 22 Aug 1907. Kathleen Rachel Dubois, da of (—) Phillips , and has issue 1f

1f Pamela Mary Winstanley, b 25 Jan 1910

2e Francis William Birch Pochin (Duntroon, Oamaru, New Zealand), b 9 Nov 1865 , m Alice Josephine, da of John Borton of Casa Nuova, N Z

3e Edward Carlyon Pochin, M A (Camb), b 1869

4e Emily Georgiana Pochin

3d Mary Elizabeth Winstanley, m Charles James Walker (Newbold Grange, Clarence River, New South Wales)

4d Frances Winstanley

2b Mary Winstanley, b 6 May 1734, d 17 Ap 1818, m 7 Ap 1763, the Rev John Carlyon of Bradwell, co Essex, LL B , Rector of St Mary's, Truro [3rd son of Thomas Carlyon of Tregrehan, co Cornwall], d 21 Sept 1798 , and had issue 1c to 3c

1c Rev Thomas Carlyon, Rector of St Mary's, Truro, and Vicar of Probus, Cornwall, M A , Fellow and Tutor of Pembroke Coll , Camb , b 12 May 1765, bur 5 Feb 1826 , m 22 Jan 1801, Mary, da of William Stackhouse of Trehane, co Cornwall, bur 21 Mar 1843, and had issue 1d to 4d

1d Rev Thomas Stackhouse Carlyon, Rector of St Mary's, Truro, and afterwards of Glenfield, co Leic , M A (Camb), b 15 June 1802 , d 15 Mar 1877 , m 28 Feb 1832, Emily, da of Clement Carlyon, M D , d 23 June 1891, and had issue 1e

1e Charles Alfred Carlyon, B A (Camb), b 5 Sept 1838 , d 26 July 1887 m 3 Nov 1863, Betsey Green, da of Isaac Squires of Woodhouse Eaves, co Leic , and had issue 1f to 3f

1f Thomas Alfred Carlyon (Connemara, Darracott Road, Boscombe Park, Bournemouth), bapt 5 May 1865 , m 17 Ap 1888, Gertrude Elizabeth, da of George William Mitchell [by his wife Eliza Lilian, da of Rear Adm Robert Sharpe, R N], and has issue 1g

1g Thomas Clement Winstanley Carlyon, b 2 Nov 1890

2f Agnes Cassandra Carlyon, m 8 Sept 1886, Philip William Poole Britton, now (R L 29 Ap 1897) Carlyon-Britton, J P , D L , F S A , Lord of the Manor of Hanham Abbots, co Glos, President of the British Numismatic Society, formerly Capt 3rd Batt Royal Inniskilling Fusiliers (Hanham Court, Bitton, Glos , 43 Bedford Square, W C , Junior Carlton) , and has issue 1g to 4g

1g Winstanley Carlyon-Britton, b 25 July 1887

2g Henry Courtenay Carlyon-Britton, Sub-Lieut R N , b 21 June 1891

3g Raymond Carlyon Carlyon Britton, b 16 Sept 1893

4g Ella Carlyon Poole Carlyon-Britton, m and has issue

3f Ellen Gertrude Carlyon, m as 2nd wife, Major Arthur Henry Daniel Britton, formerly Royal Dublin Fusiliers

2d John Carlyon of Truro, M A (Camb), Coroner for Cornwall, b 2 Dec 1804, d 30 Dec 1892, m 8 Dec 1840, Jane, da of Capt Edward Lawrance, R N , d 21 Oct 1890, and had issue 1e

1e Julia Carlyon, b 6 Aug 1842, d (—), m 16 Ap 1863, Robins Foster of Truro , and had issue

3d Rev Edward Carlyon, B A (Oxon), Rector of Dibden, co Hants, b 4 Oct 1808 , d 28 June 1897 , m 1st, 15 Nov 1832, Ann Helen, da of Thomas Harvey of Overross, co Hereford, d 18 Jan 1866 , and had issue 1e to 9e

[Nos 103303 to 103317

475

The Plantagenet Roll

1e Gerald Winstanley Carlyon (*Lyndhurst, Hants*), b 8 Dec 1845, m in Ceylon 27 Ap 1879, Laura Theresa, da of the Rev Llewellyn Lloyd Thomas, Rector of Newport, co Mon , s p

2e Rev Henry Chichele Carlyon, M A (Camb), a Missionary at Delhi, b 6 Oct 1847

3e Anna Stackhouse Carlyon, m 1 June 1865, the Rev Percy Phillipson Izard, B A (Camb), *formerly* Rector of Morstead (*Deepdale, Surrey Road, Bournemouth*) , s p s

4e Augusta Hopton Carlyon, unm

5e Jessie Carlyon, unm

6e Louise Carlyon, unm

7e Mary Evelyn Carlyon, m 6 Nov 1895, the Rev Henry Churton, Vicar of Corkhampton (*Corkhampton Vicarage, Bishop's Waltham*) , s p

8e Helen Brenda Carlyon, m 25 Sept 1878, Charles Frank Lucas, Solicitor (*Glenavon, Carshalton, Surrey*) , s p

9e Caroline Susan Carlyon, unm

4d Charlotte Carlyon (*Lemon Street, Truro*), b 6 Feb 1815 , unm

2c Rev Philip Carlyon, M A (Camb), Rector of St Mawgan in Pydar, co Cornwall, b 15 May 1769, d 21 Mar 1846, m 27 Oct 1808, Mary, da of (—) Phear, d 25 Oct 1854, and had issue 1d to 3d

1d Rev Philip Carlyon of Penmance House, Falmouth, M A (Camb), Rector of Wisbeach 1869-1882 (*Penmance House, Falmouth, Cornwall*), b 30 Dec 1811 , m 31 July 1845, Grace Julia, da of Col Keith Young, 71st Highlanders, d 22 Mar 1895 , and had issue 1e to 6e

1e Philip Carlyon, b 1846

2e Alexander Keith Carlyon of Mount Park, co Midx, J P , D L , and High Sheriff for that co 1906, Bar at-Law (*Mount Park, Harrow-on-the-Hill, Junior Carlton*), b 30 Ap 1848 , m 24 Ap 1873, Julia Ann Augusta, da of Major Thomas Tristram Spry Carlyon of Tregrehan, J P , D L , and has issue 1f to 6f

1f Tristram Carlyon, B A (Oxon), Lieut R F A , b 4 Aug 1877

2f Julia Mary Violet Carlyon

3f Ada Mary Morison Carlyon

4f Dorothy May Carlyon

5f Mabel Young Carlyon

6f Millicent Spry Carlyon

3e Harold Baird Carlyon, M A (Oxon) (*Falmouth*), b 1849 , unm

4e Jessie Morison Carlyon, m 1878, Charles Nicholl, F R C S , d 1881, and has issue

5e Katharine Ogilvie Carlyon, m 1883, the Rev Joseph Chapman, M A , Incumbent of Post Bridge (*Post Bridge, Devon*)

6e Julia Winstanley Carlyon, m 1884, Major Henry MacLeod Young, Inniskilling Fusiliers, d 1899 , and has issue

2d Edmund Carlyon of St Austell, Solicitor, b 1810 , m (—), sister of the Right Hon Sir John Robert Mowbray, 1st Bt [U K], P C , da of Robert Stribbing Cornish

3d Mary Ann Carlyon, m the Rev Michael Turner, Rector of Cotton (*Cotton Rectory, Suffolk*) , and has issue

3c Clement Carlyon, M D , M A , and Fellow of Pembroke Coll , Camb , b 22 Ap 1777 , d 5 Mar 1864 , m 22 Ap 1806, Eliza, da of Thomas Carlyon of St Just and Tregrehan, d 17 Sept 1861 , and had (with other) issue 1d

1d Emily Carlyon, d 23 June 1891, m 28 Feb 1832, the Rev Thomas Stackhouse Carlyon of Glenfield, co Leic, d 15 Mar 1877 , and had issue

See p 475, Nos 103310-103317

3b Anne Winstanley, bapt 4 Mar 1741, d 22 Aug 1814, m 1 Dec 1766,

[Nos 103318 to 103342h

# of The Blood Royal

Leonard Fosbrooke of Shardlow, co Derby, and Ravenstone. co Leic, High Sheriff co Derby, 1764, b 9 *June* 1732, d 8 *Dec* 1801, *and had issue* 1c *to* 2c

1c *Leonard Fosbrooke of Shardlow and Ravenstone,* b 28 *Mar* 1773, d 26 *Mar* 1830, m 8 *June* 1801, *Mary Elizabeth, da of the Rev Philip Story of Lockington Hall,* d 5 *July* 1838, *and had issue* 1d *to* 4d

1d *Leonard Fosbrooke of Ravenstone, J P, D L, Bar at Law,* b 29 *Ap* 1804, d 30 *Dec* 1892, m 3 *Sept* 1859, *Eliza Ann, da of John Lewin of Ravenstone,* d 8 *Ap* 1909, *and had issue* 1e *to* 5e

1e Leonard Fosbrooke of Ravenstone (*Ravenstone, Ashby de-la Zouch*), b 6 June 1860

2e Thomas Henry Fosbrooke (*Rothley, co Leicester*), b 21 Mar 1862, m 17 May 1894, Edith Mary Elizabeth, da of Thomas William Parker of Killamarsh, co Derby, and has issue 1f

1f Mary Cecily Fosbrooke, b 9 Dec 1900

3e Francis Nathaniel Fosbrooke (*Assam, India*), b 5 Mar 1864

4e William Arthur Fosbrooke, served with 57th Coy Imp Yeo in South Africa, b 4 Sept 1870

5e Elizabeth Anne Fosbrooke, m as 2nd wife, 23 Oct 1890, Capt Palmer Kingsmill Smythies, R N, J P, has Zulu Medal and Clasp, and Sudan (1884–1885) Medal and Star (*The Turrets, Colchester, Junior United Service*), and has issue (with a son, Yorick Palmer Fosbrooke, d young) 1f

1f Frances Palmer Smythies, b 20 Ap 1900

2d *Edmund Fosbrooke, Capt 56th Regt,* b 18 *July* 1813, d *at Sorel, Quebec,* 16 *Sept* 1869, m 25 *May* 1841, *Augustine Adele, da of Thomas Penton of Pentonville, Canada,* d 11 *Mar* 1887, *and had issue (with* 2 *sons and a da d s p)* 1e *to* 7e

1e Leonard George James Fosbrooke (*Sorel, Quebec*), b 19 Nov 1850, m Sept 1877, Mary Susan (Minnie), da of (—) Crebassa of Sorel afsd, and has issue 1f to 5f

1f Philip Fosbrooke, b 1878, m

2f Frederick Charles Fosbrooke, b 1883, m

3f [son] Fosbrooke

4f Annie Fosbrooke, b 1881

5f [da] Fosbrooke

2e Henry Fosbrooke, b 17 Dec 1857

3e William Anderson Fosbrooke, b 9 Sept 1861, m Seymour Catharine, da of (—) Irvine of Bootle, and has issue (with 2 elder das) 1f to 2f

1f Henry Fosbrooke

2f Doris Fosbrooke

4e Augustine Adella Fosbrooke, b 15 Jan 1845

5e Frances Fosbrooke, m at Christ Church, Sorel afsd, 9 June 1881, Edward Dudley Montgomery (*Beaumont, near Quebec*), and has issue

6e Sybilla Fosbrooke

7e Ann Fosbrooke, m Norman Massie, and has issue (2 children)

3d *Henry Nathaniel Fosbrooke of Leeds,* b 1 *Ap* 1817, d 15 *Ap* 1880, m 13 *May* 1841, *Sarah, da of Thomas Jacobson of Sleaford, and had issue (with a son and da d unm)* 1e *to* 9e

1e John Henry Fosbrooke, b 19 Feb 1842

2e Philip Laycock Fosbrooke, b 18 Dec 1845, m twice, and d s p in America

3e Charles Edward Fosbrooke, b 25 Jan 1847

4e Leonard Fosbrooke, b 27 Oct 1848, m 21 Mar 1883, Alice Georgiana [da of (—)] Parker of London, and has issue 1f to 4f

1f Herbert Henry Fosbrooke, b 12 Feb 1884

2f Leonard Sidney Fosbrooke, b 20 July 1886

3f Charles Lewis Fosbrooke, b 1890

4f Gladys Mary Fosbrooke

[Nos 103343 to 103371

477

3 P

The Plantagenet Roll

5e Arthur Sydney Fosbrooke of Roundhay Road, Leeds, *b* 15 Nov 1850, *m* 18 Dec 1880, Alice [da of (—)] Parker of Hull, and his issue 1*f* to 4*f*

 1*f* William Henry Fosbrooke, *b* 11 Oct 1881

 2*f* Philip Fosbrooke

 3*f* Frances Lilian Fosbrooke, *b* 21 Mar 1883

 4*f* Ada Mary Fosbrooke, *b* 8 Feb 1885

 6e Sarah Fosbrooke (12 *Grange Terrace, Leeds*)

 7e Sibella Frances Fosbrooke

 8e Annie Mabel Fosbrooke

 9e Jane Diana Fosbrooke

4d *Frances Sarah Fosbrooke*, b 29 *May* 1807, d 11 Nov 1896, m 14 *Jan* 1836, *Thomas Rossell Potter of Wymeswold*, *F R S L*, *the Antiquary, Author of* "*Charnwood Forest,*" &c, b 7 *Jan* 1799, d 19 *Ap* 1873, *and had issue (with 2 sons and 3 das d unm)* 1e to 4e

 1e *Henry Rossell Potter of Lyonsdown, East Barnet, J P*, b 5 *Ap* 1840, d 16 *Sept* 1907, m 16 *Ap* 1879, *Susanna Elizabeth, da of Thomas Higgs of Chipping Barnet, and had issue* 1*f* to 1*f*

  1*f* Charles Fosbrooke Potter, *b* 16 Aug 1883

  2*f* Leonard Fosbrooke Potter, *b* 6 Aug 1885

  3*f* Beryl Rosa Potter, *m* 12 Ap 1909, Arthur E Ware of New Zealand

  4*f* Sybella Frances Potter, *m* 27 Ap 1906, Hermann Tom Schott (*Burna Esperanza, Argentina*)

 2e *Charles Neville Potter, formerly* Assist Accountant Gen H M Customs (*Fernwood, Plaistow Lane, Bromley, Kent*), *b* 24 Nov 1842, *m* 23 Sept 1883, Emma, widow of Albert Dean of Esher, da of William Ward of Belton, co Rutland, and has issue 1*f*

  1*f* Gladys Ward Potter

 3e Rev Herbert Edward Potter, *formerly* Minister of the Bass, Victoria, 1888–1898, &c (*San Remo, Victoria, Australia*), *b* 10 Dec 1846, *m* 1st, Sophia, widow of T Hemsley of Hemmington, da and h of Thomas Eames of Leicester, d 6 Ap 1877. 2ndly, 15 Aug 1881, Mary, da of Thomas Anderson, and his issue 1*f* to 3*f*

  1*f* Thomas Rossell Fosbrooke Potter

  2*f* Frances Sophia Potter

  3*f* Edith Potter

 1e Ada Mary Potter, *b* 29 Mar 1844, *unm*

2c *Frances Fosbrooke*, b 23 *Nov* 1772, d 2 *Jan* 1850, m *John Buckley of Chester*

2a [2] *Anne Prideaux*, d (-), m 1737, *John Pendarves Basset of Tehidy*, b 1713, d 19 *Sept* 1739, *and had issue* [1] 1b

 1b *John Prideaux Basset of Tehidy*, b 22 *May* 1740, d 28 *May* 1756

[Nos 103372 to 103391

291 Descendants of PETER PRIDEAUX (Table XXVI), *d a* 1729, *m* 1st, SUSANNA, widow of RICHARD COFFIN, da of (—) LELLOND, 2ndly (--), and had issue 1*a*

1a *Susanna Prideaux, da and h*, d (-), m *Charles Evelyn of Yarlington, co Som* [*2nd son of Sir John Evelyn, 1st Bt* [*G B*]], b 1708, d *Jan* 1718, *and had issue* 1b

- - - -

[1] The statement in various works that he was the grandfather of Francis Basset of Tehidy, cr Lord de Dunstanville 17 June 1796, is incorrect

# of The Blood Royal

1b *Charles Evelyn,* d 1781, m *Philadelphia, da of Fortunatus Wright of Liverpool, Capt of the "Fane" and "King George" privateers, and had issue 1c to 6c*

1c *Sir John Evelyn,* 4th Bt [G B] b c 1758, d *unm* 14 May 1833

2c *Sir Hugh Evelyn,* 5th Bt [G B], b 31 Jan 1769, d s p 23 Aug 1818

3c *Susanna Evelyn, da and in her issue co-h,* d (-), m *John Ellworthy Fortunatus Wright, Lieut R N, and had issue (2 sons and 4 das)* [1]

4c *Martha Boscawen Evelyn, da and in her issue co-h,* b 1759, d 1794, m *Nicholas Vincent, and had issue 1d to 2d*

1d *Nicholas Vincent,* } *settled in America* [1]
2d *Hugh Vincent,* }

5c *Philippa Evelyn, da and in her issue co-h,* b 1760, d (-), m *1st, Major Daniel Francis Haughton, 69th Regt, 2ndly, Wilbraham Liardet, and had issue* [1] *1d to 6d*

1d *Charles Evelyn Daniel Francis Poplet Haughton,* b 1784

2d *Frederick Hugh Evelyn Haughton*

3d *[son] Liardet*

4d *Philippa Haughton*

5d *[da] Liardet*

6d *[da] Liardet*

6c *Frances Louisa Evelyn, da and in her issue. co-h,* b 1767, d (-), m *the Rev John Griffith of Manchester, and had issue (2 das)* [1]

292 Descendants of Sir JOHN PRIDEAUX, 6th Bt [E] (Table XXVI), b 17 June 1695, *bur* 29 Aug 1766, m 4 Feb 1719, the Hon. ANNE, da of John (VAUGHAN), 1st Viscount Lisburne [I], d 5 Dec 1767, and had issue 1a to 3a

1a *John Prideaux, Brigadier-Gen,* d *(being killed v p at the siege of Niagara)* 19 July 1759, m *Elizabeth, sister of Sir Edward Baynton Rolt, 1st Bt [G B 1762], da of Col Edward Rolt, and had issue 1b to 3b*

1b *Sir John Wilmot Prideaux,* 7th Bt [E], b 13 Feb 1748, d 4 Mar 1826 m *2ndly,* 28 Jan 1791, *Anne Phœbe, da of William Priddle of Farway,* d 2 Sept 1793, *and had issue 1c to 2c*

1c *Sir John Wilmot Prideaux,* 8th Bt [E], b 29 Sept 1792, d *unm* 13 May 1833

2c *Sir Edmund Saunderson Prideaux,* 9th Bt [E], b 23 Jan 1793, d s p s 11 Feb 1875

2b *Edward Baynton Edmund Prideaux,* d (? s p)

3b *Elizabeth Prideaux,* d (? unm)

2a *Elizabeth Prideaux,* d (-) m *Edward Chichester of Northover, co Somerset*

3a *Anne Prideaux,* d (-), m *the Rev William FitzThomas, Rector of Arrow and Beaudesart, co Warwick, and had issue*

293 Descendants, if any, of SUSANNA PRIDEAUX (Table XXVI), d (-), m PHINEAS CHEEK

---

[1] Betham's "Baronetage," m 165 Wheatley's "Diary of John Evelyn," vol 1, folding pedigree

The Plantagenet Roll

294 Descendants of GRACE FORTESCUE (Table XXVI), *bur* 22 Mar. 1694, *m c.* 1671, Sir HALSWELL TYNTE, 1st Bt [E 1673], M P, *bur* 9 Ap 1702, and had issue 1a to 2a

   1a *Sir John Tynte, 2nd Bt* [E], *M P*, bapt 4 Mar 1683, d 5 Mar 1710, m 1704, Jane, da and h of Sir Charles Kemeys, 3rd Bt [E], M P, bur 16 Oct 1747, and had issue

   See p 181, Nos 28352-28372

   2a *Anne or Grace Tynte, d (-), m Arthur Tremayne of Sydenham, co Devon, and had (with possibly other) issue 1b*

   1b *Arthur Tremayne of Sydenham, whose only child d s p Dec 1808*
                         [Nos 103392 to 103412

295 Descendants, if any surviving, of BRIDGET GRANVILLE (Table XXVI), *b* 1620, *d.* 1692, *m* 1st, Sir SIMON LEACH of Cadeleigh, co Devon, 2ndly (he dated 11 Nov), 1661, Sir THOMAS HIGGONS, M P, Diplomatist and Author, *b* 1624, *d* 24 Nov 1691, and had issue 1a to 7a [1]

   1a *Sir Simon Leach of Cadeleigh, K B, d s p July 1708* [2]
   2a *George Higgons*
   3a *Sir Thomas Higgons, Secretary of State to King James III and VIII, in exile Dec 1713 to July 1715* [3]
   4a *Bevil Higgons, Historian and Poet, b 1670, d unm 1 Aug 1735*
   5a *Grace Higgons, m the Rev Sir George Wheeler of Sherfield, co Hants, Preb of Durham 1719, d there 22 Jan 1724, and had issue "many children"* [4] *of whom 1b*
   1b *(—) Wheeler, son and h, d Oct 1716, m (—)*
   6a *Jane Higgons*
   7a *Bridget Higgons*

296 Descendants, if any surviving, of Sir RICHARD GRANVILLE, "the King's General in the West" (Table XXVI), *d* at Ghent soon after 10 May 1659, *m* MARY, widow of the Hon Sir CHARLES HOWARD and *previously* of the Hon THOMAS DARCY and the Hon Sir ALAN PERCY, da and h of Sir John Fitz of Fitzford, near Tavistock, *d* 17 Oct 1671, and had issue 1a

   1a *Elizabeth Granville, living a widow 1664-5, when she petitioned the King for a Privy Purse Pension for herself and her infant son,* [5] *m Capt William Lennard, Capt of the Block Houses at Tilbury and Gravesend 1660, and had issue*

297 Descendants of GERTRUDE DENYS (Table XXVI), *d* 1675, *m.* NICHOLAS GLYNN of Glynn, M P, *d.* 26 Mar 1697, and had issue

   See Supplement

   [1] "D N B," ix 826   [2] Le Neve's "Knights," p 35
   [3] Ruvigny's "Jacobite Peerage," pp 199, 215
   [4] Le Neve's "Knights," p 366
   [5] R Granville's "History of the Granville Family," p 335

# of The Blood Royal

298 Descendants of BRIDGET GRANVILLE (Table XXVI), *bur*. in Bristol Cathedral 14 Feb 1627, *m* 1st [² as 2nd wife¹], Sir CHRISTOPHER HARRIS of Radford, co Devon, M P, *d s p s* 25 Jan 1625, 2ndly, as 1st wife, the Rev JOHN WEEKS, Preb of Bristol

299 Descendants, if any surviving, of MARY GRANVILLE (GREENFIELD) (Table XXVI), *bur* at Lamerton 25 Mar. 1608, *m*. at Kilkhampton 2 June 1586, ARTHUR TREMAYNE of Collacombe, co Devon, *bapt* at Kilkhampton 4 Ap 1553, *bur* at Lamerton 4 Feb. 1635, and had issue (with 3 sons and 3 das known to have *d s p*) 1a to 11a²

1a. *Edmund Tremayne of Collacombe*, bapt at Bideford 17 Oct 1587, bur at Lamerton 25 Sept 1667, m (lic 26 May) 1615, *Bridget, da of Sir John Cooper*, bur at Lamerton 17 Sept 1670, and had issue (with 4 sons and 3 das d s p) 1b

1b *Arthur Tremayne, a Colonel in the Army*, bapt 10 Sept 1627 bur at Lamerton 20 July 1710, m *Bridget, da of Nicholas Hatherleigh of Lamerton*, bur there 12 Oct 1659, and had issue (with 2 sons d s p) 1c

1c *Edmund Tremayne*, bapt 11 Ap 1649, bur at Lamerton 20 Oct 1698, m at Exeter 28 Jan 1674, *Arabella, da and h of Sir Edward Wise of Sydenham, co Devon, K B*, bur 12 Feb 1697, and had (with other children whose issue failed 3 Jan 1809) 1d

1d *Arabella Tremayne*, bapt at Lamerton 27 Ap 1681, d (? s p), m at Maristowe, 18 Dec 1704, *John Harris of Manadon*

2a *Digoric Tremayne*, bapt at Lamerton 22 Jan 1589, bur there 22 Mar 1670, m 1st, 9 Dec 1613, *Mary da of William Addington of Bideford*, bur at Bundstock 23 Oct 1621, and had issue 1b to 2b

1b *Grenfield (Granville) Tremayne*, bapt at Lamerton 2 Oct 1614, ⎫ *living and aged 5 and*

2b *Arthur Tremayne*, b 1617, ⎭ *3 respectively 1620*

3a *Richard Tremayne*, bapt at Lamerton 1 June 1600, *living 1629*

4a *Roger Tremayne*, bur (? unm) at Lamerton 5 Jan 1677

5a *Mary Tremayne*, bapt at Marhamchurch 27 Jan 1591

6a *Ulalia (Eulalia) Tremayne*, bapt at Sydenham Damerell 14 Oct 1593, m (lic 13 Oct) 1613, *Thomas Lower of Trelaske, co Cornwall*, and had issue (with a son and da d unm) 1b to 2b

1b *Thomas Lower of Trelaske*, bur at Lewannick 1687, m (settl 3 May) 1653, *Anne, da of John Roberts of Lanvake*, and had issue 1c to 7c

1c *Thomas Lower of Trelaske, which he sold to John Addis* 22 July 1703

2c *John Lower,* ⎫
3c *Nicholas Lower,* ⎪
4c *George Lower,* ⎬ *all living and mentioned in father's will* 11 Feb 1686
5c *Maurice Lower,* ⎪
6c *Elizabeth Lower,* ⎪
7c *Mary Lower,* ⎭

2b *Mary Lower*, bapt at Lewannick 3 Oct 1616, *living, aged 3,* 1620

---

¹ This marriage is not mentioned in Vivian's "Devonshire Pedigrees," p 418
² Vivian's "Visitations of Devon," p 731   ³ Ibid, p 299

The Plantagenet Roll

7a *Elizabeth Tremayne, living 1659, m at Lamerton 24 Aug 1615, Baldwin Acland of Hawkridge, co Devon, admon 8 Oct 1659, and had issue 1b to 5b*

  1b *Arthur Acland, son and h, aged 4, 1620*

  2b *Mary Acland, bapt at Lamerton 1617*

  3b *Anne Acland*

  4b *Elizabeth Acland, bapt there 9 May 1621*

  5b *Martha Acland, bapt there 29 Sept 1624*

  8a *Mary Tremayne, bapt at Lamerton 4 Sept 1603*

  9a *Margaret Tremayne, bapt there 18 Nov 1604, living 1629, m at Chittle-hampton, 5 Ap 1638, George Slee*

  10a *Catherine Tremayne, m 1st at Lamerton, 26 July 1627, Roger Edgcumbe of Lamerton, co Devon, bapt there 18 May 1595, bur there 28 Oct 1643, 2ndly, at the same place 27 Sept 1651, Humphrey Arundell, and had issue (with 4 das known to have d unm) 1b to 2b*

  1b *Mary Edgcumbe, bapt at Lamerton 25 June 1628, m John Wallis of Tremin, co Cornwall*

  2b *Jane Edgcumbe, bapt there 14 Ap 1638, m John Merrit of Probus, co Cornwall*

  11a *Rebecca Tremayne, m there 21 Jan 1636, John Edgcumbe [younger brother of Roger Edgcumbe, aforesaid]*

300 Descendants, if any surviving, of Sir THOMAS STUCLEY of Affeton, co Devon (Table XXVI), *b* 1620, *d* 20 Sept 1663, *m* ELIZABETH, da of Sir Ralph SYDENHAM of Yolston (who *m* 2ndly, 29 Oct 1677, the Rev. JOHN DODDERIDGE); and had issue (with 2 sons *d s p*)[1] 1a to 4a

  1a *Frances Stucley, da and co h, m the Rev Anthony Gregory*

  2a *Margery Stucley, da and co h*

  3a *Mary Stucley, da and co-h, m 1st, the Rev Thomas Colley, 2ndly, at Braunton, 9 Aug 1685, Michael Arundell*

  4a *Honor Stucley, da and co h*

301 Descendants of LEWIS STUCLEY of Affeton, co Devon, Chaplain to Oliver Cromwell (Table XXVI), *bur* at Worlington 21 July 1687, *m* 1673, SUSANNAH, da of (—) DENNIS, *d* 1692, and had issue 1a

  1a *Sarah Stucley, da and in her issue (29 Dec 1755) sole h, d at Bideford 4 Feb 1742, m 4 May 1697, George Buck, J P, seven times Mayor of Bideford, b there 11 Dec 1671, d 7 Ap 1743, and had issue 1b*

  1b *John Buck of Bideford, M P, three times Mayor of that place, bapt 30 Dec 1703, d 13 Ap 1715, m 1st, 19 Sept 1729, Judith, da and h of William Pawley (or Hawley) of Bideford, d 24 Oct 1739, and had issue 1c*

  1c *George Buck of Affeton, J P, b 7 July 1731, d 26 Jan 1794, m 6 May 1754, Anne, da of Paul Orchard of Hartland Abbey, d 11 Feb 1820, and had issue 1d*

  1d *George Stucley Buck of Affeton, bapt 8 Mar 1755, d 30 Nov 1791, m 8 Ap 1780, Martha, da of th Rev Richard Keats, Master of Tiverton School and Rector of Bideford, &c (who m 2ndly, 1801, Lieut-Col James Kirkman), d 30 Nov 1833, and had issue 1e to 3e*

---

[1] VIVIAN'S "VISITATIONS of Devon," p 722

# of The Blood Royal

1e *Lewis William Buck of Affeton*, M P, b 25 Ap 1784, d 25 Ap 1858, m 18 Ap 1808, Ann, da of *Thomas Robbins of Roundhams, co* Berks, d 12 Ap 1879, and had issue 1f to 2f

1f *Sir George Stucley Stucley* (R L 27 July 1858), *previously Buck, of Affeton*, 1st Bt [U K], so cr 26 Ap 1859, M P, J P, D L, and High Sheriff (1863) co Devon, Col Comdg Devonshire Artillery, b 17 Aug 1812, d 13 Mar 1900, m 1st, 22 Dec 1835, *Lady Elizabeth* (see p 368), da and co-h of William (O Brien), 2nd Marquis of Thomond [I], K P, d 9 May 1870, 2ndly, 31 Jan 1872, *Louisa* (see p 167) (*Moreton, Bideford*), da of Bernard Granville of Wellesbourne Hall, co Warwick, and had issue 1g to 4g

1g Sir (William) Lewis Stucley, 2nd Bt [U K], J P, D L, *late Lieut Col Grenadier Guards* (*Hartland Abbey, Bideford, Affeton Castle, Devonshire, Carlton*), b 27 Aug 1836, m 1st, 15 Ap 1869, Rosamund Head, da of Head Pottinger Best of Donnington Grove, co Berks, d 29 Sept 1877, 2ndly, 5 Feb 1879, Marion Elizabeth, da of Lieut -Col Henry Edward Hamlyn Fane [descended from King Henry VII (see Tudor Roll, p 286)]

2g Edward Arthur George Stucley, Major *late 1st South Australian Regt* (*Thomond, Pitt Park Road, Guildford*), b 12 Feb 1852, m 29 Dec 1892, May, da of the Hon Thomas King, Minister of Education, S Australia

3g Hugh Nicholas Granville Stucley, J P, C A, *late Lieut R N* (*Pillhead, Bidehead*), b 22 June 1873, m 6 Feb 1902, Gladys, da and h of Wynne Albert Bankes of Wolfeton House, Dorchester, and has issue 1h to 2h

1h Dennis Frederick Bankes Stucley, b 1907

2h Elizabeth Florence Stucley

4g Humphrey St Leger Stucley, Capt Grenadier Guards, served at Omdurman and in South Africa 1900-1902, b 7 June 1877, m 22 Oct 1908, Dorothy Beatrice Ross, da and h of Francis Harry Crew of Collipriest, Tiverton

2f *Louisa Buck*, d 11 Ap 1880, m as 2nd wife, 9 June 1840, Samuel Trehawke Kekewich of Peamore, co Devon, M P, J P, D L, d 1 June 1873, and had issue 1g to 4g

1g Sir George William Kekewich, K C B, J P, D C L, M P for Exeter 1906, *formerly Sec Educational Dept, &c* (*St Albans, Feltham, Midx*), b 1 Ap 1841, m 1866, (—), da of (—), and has (with other) issue 1h

1h Winifred Kekewich, m 1900, the Rev Richard Valpy French, LL D, Canon of Llandaff, d (—)

2g Emma Kekewich

3g Louisa Kekewich, m 6 Oct 1874, George John Moore of Appleby, J P, D L [descended from King Henry VII (see the Tudor Roll, p 485)] (*Appleby Hall, near Atherstone, Carlton*), and has issue 1h to 4h

1h Charles Louis George Moore, b 3 Mai 1876

2h Gerald Henry Moore, b 16 May 1877

3h. Arnuld Geoffrey Moore, b Feb 1886

4h Elsie Louise Moore

4g Anna Maude Kekewich

2e *Richard Buck of Bideford*, Capt R N, b 23 Oct 1785, d 7 Aug 1830, m at Algiers and again at Bideford, Angelina, da of Hugh McDonald, Consul General at Algiers, b at Niagara, Canada, 13 Nov 1800, d 11 Dec 1879, and had issue (see Appendix)

3e *Elizabeth Buck*, b 8 May 1787, d 29 Ap 1831, 31 Aug 1816, Col Zachary Clutterbuck Bayley, R A, d 25 Nov 1855   [Nos 103413 to 103128

302 Descendants, if any, of HONOR STUCLEY (Table XXVI), m (—) LUTTRELL

The Plantagenet Roll

303 Descendants of FRANCES STUCLEY (Table XXVI), *d* (-); *m* at Morval 22 Nov 1635, PHILIP MAYOW of Bray, co Cornwall, *d* Oct 1697, and had issue 1*a* to 5*a*.

1*a* *Philip Mayow of Polgover, bapt Jan* 1639, *d* 31 *July* 1710, *m* 1669, *Ursula, da of Alexander Rolle of Parkgate, co Devon, and had issue* 1*b*

1*b* *Ursula Mayow, da and in her issue event* (1786) *sole h*, b 1685, d 14 *July* 1734, *m* 16 *May* 1711, *her cousin John Wynell* (see p 486), *and had issue* 1*c*

1*c* *Philip Wynell, afterwards Wynell-Mayow, of Bray and Polgover, b Jan* 1716, d 1781, *m* 1741, *Betty, da and co h of George Salt of Betley, co Staff*, d 1771, *and had issue* 1*d* to 4*d*

1*d* *John Salt Wynell-Mayow of Bray and Saltash, b* 1717, *d* 1802, *m* 12 *May* 1769, *Mary, da of Robert Doughty of Hanworth, co Norfolk*, d 1820, *and had issue* 1*e* to 4*e*

1*e* *Philip Wynell Mayow of Bray, co Cornwall, and Hanworth Hall, co Norfolk*, b 17 *Mar* 1771, d 28 *Dec* 1844, *m* 22 *July* 1806, *Elizabeth, da of Gen. Charles Deare, H L I C S*, d 10 *Aug* 1844, *and had issue* 1*f* to 3*f*

1*f* *George Wynell-Mayow of Bray, &c*, C B, K L H, *Major-Gen in the Army*, b 31 *Aug* 1808, *d s p* 1 *Jan* 1873

2*f* *Rev Mayow Wynell Mayow of Bray*, M A, *Rector of Southam*, b 8 *July* 1810, d 26 *Feb* 1895, *m* 14 *July* 1846, *Caroline Kate, da of the Rev Alfred Smith of Old Park, Devizes, and had issue* 1*g* to 4*g*

1*g* Mayow Wynell-Mayow of Bray, *Major late* R A (*Bray Manor House, St German's, Cornwall*), b 13 Jan 1850, *unm*

2*g* *Rev Arthur Wynell-Mayow, formerly Vicar of Dunster*, b 23 Dec 1853, d 4 *Aug* 1903, *m* 1 *July* 1890, *Ellen Mary, da of Lieut-Col William Cloves Pamplin of Brighton, and had issue* 1*h* to 3*h*

1*h* Philip Arthur Claude Wynell-Mayow

2*h* Ursula Mary Elaine Wynell-Mayow

3*h* Betty Mabel Courtenay Wynell-Mayow

3*g* Charles Ernest Wynell-Mayow, Capt Border Regt, b 28 Ap 1857.

4*g* Elizabeth Ursula Wynell-Mayow, *m* 14 Jan 1869, the Rev Francis Maundy Gregory, Vicar of St Michael's, Southampton, and has issue 1*h* to 3*h*

1*h* Edward Denys Wynell Gregory

2*h* Arthur John Maundy Gregory

3*h* Stephen Ernest Vincent Gregory, *m* 27 Nov 1906, Dorothy, da. of W. S Bernard Bryan of Southsea, and has issue 1*i* to 2*i*

1*i* Harolde Francis Maundy Gregory

2*i* Cecil Stephen S Bernard Gregory

3*f* *Rev Philip Wynell-Mayow of Shortwood, Wells, co Som*, M A, *Vicar of Easton*, b 16 *May* 1813, d 9 *July* 1890, *m* 10 *July* 1839, *Mary, da of the Rev Benjamin George Heath, Rector of Cresting*, d 22 *Sept* 1892, *and had issue* 1*g* to 7*g*

1*g* Philip Herbert Wynell-Mayow, Capt R N (1 *South Summerlands, Heavitree Road, Exeter*), b 20 Oct 1841

2*g* Rev Herbert Wynell-Mayow, Rector of Plumstead (*The Ark, Plumstead, Hanworth, Norfolk*), b 13 June 1855, *m* 6 Jan 1891, Mary, da of W Dowling of Easton, co Som, and his issue 1*h*

1*h* Philip John Wynell-Mayow, b 13 Aug 1894

3*g* Mary Wynell-Mayow

4*g* Margaret Ursula Wynell-Mayow (*Shortwood, Wells*).

5*g* Fanny Louisa Wynell-Mayow

6*g* Edith Wynell-Mayow

7*g* Emily Wynell-Mayow (*Shortwood, Wells*) [Nos 103429 to 103447

# of The Blood Royal

2e *Rev Robert Wynell-Mayow, b Oct 1777, d Jan 1817, m Oct 1805, Elizabeth, da of William Harding of Liverpool, Merchant (who m 2ndly, the Rev John Marrall, and) d 13 Dec 1862, and had issue (with a son, Robert, d unm) 1f to 2f*

1f *John Harding Wynell-Mayow, Lieut-Col H E I C S, b 20 June 1808, d 5 Nov 1876, m 1st, July 1840, Mary Jane, da of James Willasey of Allerton Hall, near Liverpool, d Jan 1857, 2ndly, 1 June 1859, Theodosia, da of (—) Lee, d (—), and had issue (with a da ly 1st marriage d s p) 1g to 4g*

1g *John Harding Wynell-Mayow of Haputale, Ceylon, Proprietary Tea and Coffee Planter, b 2 Mar 1847, d 26 Ap 1905, m 14 Nov 1874, Helen Mary (Arthur's Seat, Dimbulla, Ceylon), da of William Copeland of Staindrop, co Durham, M D, and had issue (with a son d young) 1h to 11h*

1h John Harding Wynell-Mayow (*New Forest, Galaha, Ceylon*), b 16 Oct 1876, m 22 May 1900, Eliza Marie, da of Shelton Agar, and has issue 1i to 3i

1i Cecil John Shelton Wynell-Mayow, b Ap 1902

2i Mona Betty Shelton Wynell-Mayow, b 8 May 1901

3i Bridget Ida Shelton Wynell-Mayow, b June 1907

2h Edward Wyllasey Wynell-Mayow, b 17 Sept 1879

3h Gerald Wynell Mayow, b 20 Oct 1888

4h Charles Eric Wynell-Mayow, b 12 Ap 1890

5h Kenneth Wynell-Mayow, b 12 Sept 1891

6h Reginald Wynell Mayow, b 4 June 1893

7h Ida Helen Wynell-Mayow, m 15 Oct 1898, Thomas Scovell [son of Col Edward Whitmore Scovell, 96th Regt] (*Morval, Warren Edge Road, Southbourne, Christchurch*), and has issue 1i to 4i

1i Hugh Edward Scovell, b 25 Sept 1901

2i George Francis Scovell, b 9 Jun 1903

3i Grace Helen Scovell, b 25 July 1899

4i Dorothy Gertrude Scovell, b 2 Jan 1904

8h Flora Wynell-Mayow, m 6 Sept 1899, Lionel Charles Maudslay (*Glenholm Sea View, I W*), and has issue 1i to 2i

1i Philip Charles Maudslay, b 4 Aug 1901

2i Gerald Wynell Maudslay, b 8 Dec 1907

9h Constance Wynell-Mayow m 25 Sept 1906, Lawrence Anderson Ewart, and has issue 1i

1i Phyllis Wynell-Mayow Ewart, b 18 Ap 1909

10h Evelyn Wynell-Mayow, *unm*

11h Grace Marian Wynell-Mayow, *unm*

2g ² Robert Sandilands Lawrence Wynell-Mayow, Major *late* North Lancashire Regt (*95 Sydney Place, Bath*), b 7 July 1861

3g ² Edith Vyvyan Wynell-Mayow, *unm*

4g ² Helen Stuart Wynell-Mayow, *unm*

2f *Catherine Anne Wynell-Mayow, b at Lathom, co Lancs, 30 Aug 1815, d 7 Sept 1878, m 1st, at Meerut, 16 Mar (? Ap) 1844, Edward Salusbury Lloyd, Lieut-Col 49th Regt H E I C S [3rd son and in his issue sole h of Richard Hughes Lloyd of Plymog, co Denbigh, Guerclas, co Merioneth, and Bashall Hall, co York], d at Nakodah, India, 21 Jan 1851, 2ndly at Weston, 3 Jan 1860, the Rev Edward Deacon Girdlestone, B A, d 26 Feb 1909, and had issue 1g to 2g*

1g Edward Wynell-Mayow Lloyd, M A (St John's Coll, Camb) (*Hartford House, Winchfield, co Hants*), b 19 Mar 1845, m 31 Dec 1879, Eleanor Elizabeth, da of the Rev John Parsons Hastings, M A, Rector of Mutley, co Worc, and has issue (with a son, Charles Hastings Armitage, R N, b 12 Jan 1887, d 25 July 1902) 1h to 8h

1h Rev John Hastings Lloyd, M A (Queen's Coll, Oxon), b 11 Oct 1881

[Nos 10341S to 10317J

The Plantagenet Roll

2h Arthur Wynell Lloyd (*Rand and Athenaum Clubs, Johannesburg, S A*), b 4 Ap 1883

3h Edward Mayow Hastings Lloyd, C C C (Oxon), b 30 Nov 1889

4h Wynell Hastings Lloyd, b 19 Nov 1904

5h Robert Aubrey Hastings Lloyd, b 26 Oct 1899

6h Catherine Constance Lloyd

7h Eleanor Margaret Lloyd

8h Gladys Mary Lloyd

2g Edward Lloyd, Lieut Col 5th Punjab Cavalry (*Culver House, Bedford*), b 24 Sept 1848, m 31 Dec 1878, Mary Katharine, da of the Rev John Wingfield Harding, M A , Vicar of Cheswardine, co Salop, and has issue (with a 2nd son d young) 1h to 5h

1h Hugh Salusbury Lloyd, Capt R M L I , b 29 Sept 1879 , m 22 Ap 1903, Mary Hilda, da of William Square of Plymouth, M D , and has issue (with a son, Ferrers Tudor Wilmesley Lloyd, b 19 Ap 1901, d 10 Feb 1908) 1i to 2i

1i Patience Hilda Lloyd, b 11 Dec 1905

2i Felicity Mary Lloyd, b 29 Jan 1909

2h Edward Raymond Lloyd, Lieut Roy Inniskilling Fusiliers, b 13 Nov 1882

3h Robin Wynell-Mayow-Lloyd, Lieut R N , b 14 Feb 1884

4h Irene Catherine Lloyd

5h Dorothy Cecilia Lloyd

3e *Mary Wynell-Mayow*, b 1771, d (-), m 19 *Sept* 1799, *the Rev John Richards*

4e *Catherine Anne Wynell Mayow*, b 1780 , d 1823 , m *the Rev John Lukin*

2d *Mayow Wynell-Mayow of Sydenham, co Kent,* b 1753 , d 1807 , m 1776, *Mary, da of Thomas Paulin and had issue* 1e to 3e

1e *Elizabeth Wynell-Mayow,* d (-) , m 1804, *William Dacres Adams of Bowden , and had issue*

2e *Anne Wynell Mayow,* d. Dec 1860 , m 5 Ap 1805, *the Right Hon Thomas Peregrine Courtenay, P C ,M P [E of Devon Coll],* d 7 July 1841 , *and had issue*
See the Exeter Volume, pp 109–110, Nos 1240–1263

3e *Caroline Wynell-Mayow* d (-) , m *the Rev H T Wharton*

3d *Ursula Anne Wynell-Mayow*

4d *Mary Wynell Mayow*

2a *Lewis Mayow*, b 1641

3a *John Mayow of Bath, Physician,* b 1645 , d 1679

4a *Edith Mayow,* b Oct 1637 , d (-), m June 1664, *Nicholas Leigh of Quethiock, co Cornwall, and had issue a da d in infancy* [1]

5a *Francis Mayow,* b Oct 1647 , d 1724, m 4 May 1671, *the Rev Philip Wynell, Rector of Landrake, co Cornwall,* d 1732 , *and had issue* 1b to 8b

1b *John Wynell,* b 1674 , d (-), m 16 Mar 1711, *Ursula, da and event sole h of Philip Mayow of Polgorer,* d 14 July 1734 , *and had issue*
See p 484, Nos 103429–103712

2b *Lewis Wynell,* b 1676

3b *Bassett Wynell,* b 1678

4b *Philip Wynell,* b 1681 , m 1710, *Susanna, da of Philip Mayow of Polgorer, and had a da , Ursula,* b 1714 , d 1786

5b *William Wynell,* b 1684 , d 1723

6b *Frances Wynell,* b 1687

7b *Anne Wynell,* b 1689

8b *Mary Wynell,* b 1694   [Nos 103474 to 103596

---

[1] Vivian's " Visitations of Cornwall "

# of The Blood Royal

304. Descendants, if any, of MARY STUKELEY (Table XXVI), m JOHN COURTENAY of Molland, co Devon [apparently the John Courtenay of Molland, *b* 1630; *d* 24 Ap 1684, who *m* "MARY, da. of (—)",[1] and had issue (with a da, Grace, *bapt* at Molland 8 May 1667, others known to have *d s p*) 1*a*

1*a John Courtenay of Molland,* b 28 *Sept* 1659, d 14 *Sept* 1724, m (*lic* 3 *Oct*) 1681, *the Hon Amy, da of Thomas (Clifford), 1st Baron Clifford [E], bur at Molland 7 Dec 1693, and had issue (with several others who d s p) 1b*

1*b Mary Courtenay, da and (11 Dec 1732) event sole h, b 1 Feb 1687, living 1716, m William Paston of Horton, co Glouc, and had issue 1c*

1*c Anna Maria Paston of Molland, da and h, d (-), m George Throckmorton, afterwards Courtenay-Throckmorton [son and h of Sir Robert Throckmorton, 4th Bt [E 1642], d v p 30 Aug 1767, and had issue]*

305 Descendants, if any surviving, of HUGH STUKELEY (Table XXVI), living 1611; m (lic 17 Aug) 1621, ARMINELLA (see p 488), da of Simon WEEKS of Bideford, and had issue[2]

306 Descendants of LEWIS STUKELEY (Table XXVI), living 1611, m 12 Ap. 1627, MARGERY, da of William COODE of Morval, co. Devon, and had issue 1*a*

1*a Rev Lewis Stukeley or Stucley of Plymouth,* d 22 *Aug* 1693, m at St Andrew's, Plymouth, 5 Feb 1671, Elizabeth, da of (—) Alsopp of Plymouth, d 16 Feb 1702, and had issue (with 3 sons and 3 das d s p) 1b to 3b*

1*b Charles Stucley of Plymouth,* bapt 8 Mar 1677, bur 6 Ap 1720, m at Kingsweare 20 Aug 1709, Anna, da of John Fownes of Whitley, M P, and had issue 1c*

1*c Anne Stucley, da and h, m at Kingsweare 3 Jan 1730, Francis Luttrell of Venn, co Som*

2*b Judith Stucley,* bapt at St Andrew's, Plymouth, 3 July 1673

3*b Elizabeth Stucley*

307 Descendants, if any, of FRANCES STUKELEY (Table XXVI), d (-), m ROBERT DILLON

308 Descendants of MARY STUKELEY (Table XXVI), bur at Bideford 26 Oct 1632, m SIMON WEEKES of Brodhurst Kelley, co Devon, bur 14 Feb 1626, and had issue (with others known to have *d s p*) 1*a* to 8*a*

1*a Francis Weekes,* b *c* 1590, d 28 *Mar* 1637, m 8 *Ap* 1617, Wilmot, da of Richard Coffin of Portlinch, and had issue (with others known to have d s p) 1b to 7b*

1*b Simon Weekes,* bapt 20 *Sept* 1618, m and had issue a son who d s p 1680

2*b John Weekes,* bapt 13 *July* 1623, living 1637

[1] Vivian's "Visitations of Devon," p 251

[2] Vivian's "Visitations of Cornwall," p 722

The Plantagenet Roll

3b Richard Weekes of Hatherleigh, a Gentleman Pensioner of King Charles II, d in the King's Bench Prison 5 Feb 1671, m Dorothy, da of Philip Callyn of Woherston Hall, co Suffolk, and had issue 1c

1c Richard Weekes of Northwyke, bapt 4 Aug 1656, bur 28 Mar 1696, m 11 Ap 1681, Elizabeth, da of John Northmore of Well, in South Tawton, bur 30 Mar 1706, and had issue (with 3 sons d s p) 1d to 3d

1d Elizabeth Weekes, da and event co-h, m 1st (lic Aug) 1705, Tapper Langdon of North Bovey, d s p, 2ndly, George Hunt of North Bovey, and had issue [1]

2d Mary Weekes, da and event co-h, bapt 13 Nov 1638, d (–), m (lic 21 Mar) 1707, Richard Risdon of Spreyton, and had issue [1]

3d Martha Weekes, da and event co-h, bapt 25 Mar 1690, d (–), m Robert Hole of Zeal Monachorum, and had issue [1]

4b William Weekes,
5b Ferdinand Weekes, } living 1637
6b Francis Weekes,

7b Mary Weekes, bapt at Bideford 20 Sept 1619

2a John Weekes
3a Grenvil (Granville) Weekes, living 1637, m 2ndly (lic 17 Sept) 1628, Elizabeth, da (–) of Pomeroy of Exeter, and had issue [2]

4a Simon Weekes
5a Mary Weekes, m (lic 31 Oct) 1621, Thomas Taylor
6a Arimell Weekes, m (lic 17 Aug) 1621 Hugh Stukeley, and had issue (see p 487)

7a Katherine Weekes
8a Arabella Weekes, living 1620

---

509 Descendants of GERTRUDE STUKELEY (Table XXVI), living 20 Feb 1632, m HUMPHREY BURY of Colliton, co Devon (will dated 2 Sept 1631, proved 20 Feb 1632), and had issue (with a son d young) 1a to 2a

1a John Bury of Colliton, b c 1590, living, aged 30, 1620, m Mary, da of Arthur Arscott of Tetcott, co Devon, and had issue 1b to 4b

1b John Bury
2b Humphrey Bury, m and had issue (with an elder son who d s p) 1c to 2c

1c Arthur Bury of Colliton, d (codicil to will 29 Mar 1675 proved 26 Nov) 1675, m Mary, da of (—) Clotworthy, d 1673, and had issue 1d to 2d

1d Humphrey Bury of Colliton, son and h m (lic 13 Dec) 1679, Johanna, da of Thomas Bere of Huntsham, and had issue (with a younger son d s p) 1e

1e Humphrey Bury of Colliton, son and h,[3] m Anne, da of John Cutcliffe

2d John Bury, to have the Barton of Stonegate, in parish of Barnstaple, under father's will

2c Martha Bury, living 1675

3b Mary Bury

4b Gertrude Bury, m the Rev Hugh Shortridge, Rector of Asgreigny, and had issue, named in the will of her nephew John Bury, dated 8 Mar 1667

2a Gertrude Bury

---

[1] Vivian's "Visitations of Devon," p 777   [2] Ibid

[3] Ibid, p 124

# of The Blood Royal

310 Descendants, if any surviving, of Eulalia St Leger (Table
XXVI), *d.* (-), *m* 1st at Lamerton, 26 Sept 1576, Edmund
Tremayne, Cadet of Collacombe, Clerk of the Privy Council
to Elizabeth, *bur* at Lamerton 20 Sept 1582, 2ndly (the
7 Oct) 1583, Tristram Arscott of Annery, co Devon, *d* 7 Ap.
1621, and had issue (with 2 sons by 1st husband, *d* young) 1*a*
to 6*a* [1]

1a *John Arscott, son and h, aged 30 and more 7 Ap 1621, m at Exeter
21 Dec 1605, Alice, da of Thomas Southcot of Borey (who m 2ndly at Islington,
9 Jan 1649, John Pynsent), and had issue (with 2 sons and a da known to have d
young) 1b*

1b *Elizabeth Arscott, bapt at Monkleigh 1611, living and aged 9, 1620*

2a *Tristram Arscott, named in Inq taken on his father's death*

3a *Elizabeth Tremayne, bapt at Lamerton 3 Dec 1577, living 1600*

4a *Philippa Tremayne, b posthumous living 1600*

5a *Mary Arscott, living 20 May 1631, m at Monkleigh 29 Ap 1611 Edward
Trelawny of Menhemot, co Cornwall, will dated 29 Nov 19 Dec 1625, prov
28 May 1631, and had issue (with three other das known to have d s p) [2] 1b to 5b*

1b *Robert Trelawney, son and h, a minor 1621, living 1691*

2b *Anne Trelawney,*

3b *Mary Trelawney, bapt at Pelynt 24 Jan 1620* } *named in father's will
29 Nov 1625, and then
living*

4b *Elizabeth Trelawney, bapt there 29 Feb 1623,*

5b *Dorothy Trelawney,*

6a *Katherine Arscott, m at Monkleigh 17 June 1604, Humphrey Prouse of
Chagford, co Devon, bur there 24 Ap 1648, and had issue (with 4 sons and 1 da
known to have d s p) [3] 1b to 2b*

1b *Elizabeth Prouse, da and co h, m at Chagford 1 Jan 1635, William
Sandford*

2b *Philippa Prouse, da and co-h, m there 6 Jan 1638, Richard Courtenay*

311 Descendants of Sir Francis Coppinger of St. Giles-in-the-Fields
(Table XXVI), *b* 1579, will dated 15 Oct 1626, *m* the
Hon Frances, da and co-h. of Robert (de Burgh), 5th Baron
Burgh of Gainsborough [E], K G , and had issue 1*a* to 2*a*

1a *Nicholas Coppinger of Ratcliff., Stepney, Mariner, d c 1685, m at Stepney
10 Feb 1638, Elizabeth, da of (—) Anderson. and had issue 1b to 5b*

1b *Francis Coppinger of Lincoln's Inn, b 14 Mar 1671, d Dec 1759, m
at St James', Westminster, 28 Ap 1696, Jane, da of the Rev Harvey Garnet Rector
of Kilham, and had issue 1c to 3c*

1c *John Coppinger of Linc In's Inn, b 2 Aug 1697, d s p 9 Nov 1758 m
at Abchurch, Cannon Street, 3 Dec 1724, Katherine, da and co h of Timothy Fysh
of Scarborough, d 16 Ap 1763. and had issue 1d to 8d*

1d *Fysh Coppinger, afterwards (R L 30 Mar 1779) De Burgh, of West
Drayton, co Midx, b 26 Aug 1732, d 1790, m 8 Oct 1765, Easter, da of
Cornelius Burgh of Scarborough, and had issue 1e to 2e*

---

[1] Vivian's "Visitations of Devon," pp 16, 731

[2] Vivian's "Visitations of Cornwall," p 480

[3] Vivian's "Visitations of Devon," p 626

1e *Fysh Coppinger, Capt in the Guards*, unm 23 *Jan* 1793

2e *Catherine Coppinger, da and event sole h*, b 4 *Dec* 1767, d 20 *Sept* 1809, m 22 *May* 1794, *James Godfrey Lill, afterwards* (*R L* 11 *Feb* 1800) *De Burgh, of Gaulstown, co Westmeath*, d 7 *Mar* 1832, *and had issue* 1f *to* 2f

1f *Hubert de Burgh of West Drayton, J P, D L*, b 15 *Nov* 1799, d 1875, m 6 *Sept* 1827, *Marianne* [*descended from King Henry VII* (see the Tudor Roll, p 210)], *da of Adm John Richard Delap Tollemache* [*by his wife Lady Elizabeth, née Stratford*], d 1880, *and had issue* (*with another son and da who d s p*) 1g *to* 3g

1g *Frances de Burgh of West Drayton*, d s p 1874

2g *Edith de Burgh, a co-h to the Barony of Burgh of Gainsborough* [E 1487] (*West Drayton Manor, Uxbridge*), m 2 *Nov* 1867, *Ralfe Oswald Leycester of Toft Hall, co Chester* [*descended from King Henry VII* (see the Tudor Roll, p 209)], d s p 1907

3g *Eva de Burgh, a co-h to the Barony of Burgh of Gainsborough* [E 1487] (*West Drayton Manor, Uxbridge*)

2f *Rev Robert Lill de Burgh*

2d *John Coppinger, Registrar of the Court of Chancery*, b 2 *Oct* 1734, d (*will dated* 4 *Ap* 1800, *p ov June*) 1800, m 31 *Dec* 1764, *Dorothy, da of Joshua Peake, Solicitor in Chancery, and had issue* [1] 1e *to* 8e

1e *Joshua Coppinger*, b 5 *Jan* 1766

2e *John Coppinger*, b 6 *May* 1770

3e *Henry Coppinger*, b 20 *Oct* 1773

4e *Elizabeth Coppinger*, d 26 *July* 1767, m (—) *Brolland*

5e *Easter Coppinger*, b 3 *Nov* 1772, m (—) *Heys*

6e *Dorothy Coppinger*, b 15 *Ap* 1776

7e *Marianna Coppinger*, b 22 *Oct* 1777

8e *Louisa Coppinger*, b 1 *Jan* 1781

3d *William Coppinger*

4d *Nicholas Coppinger*

5d *Henry Coppinger*

6d *Anne Coppinger*

7d *Elizabeth Coppinger*, b 2 *June* 1743, m 3 *Nov* 1767, *Allaston Burgh, of the Pipe Office, London*

8d *Lettice Coppinger*, b 2 *May* 1745

2c *Mary Coppinger*, m *Peter Pierson*

3c *Susanna Coppinger*, m *David Thomas, Pwllywrach, co Glamorgan*

2b *Barnabas Coppinger*

3b *Elizabeth Coppinger*

4b *Mary Coppinger*

5b *Katherine Coppinger*

2a *Lettice Coppinger*, m 1st, *Paul Barnaby, of Greenwich*, 2ndly, *Sir William Hooker, Sheriff of London, knighted* 1 *Feb* 1666   [Nos 103597 to 103599

312 Descendants of the Hon JANE NEVILL (Table XXVI), d. (-); m c 1518, HENRY (POLE), 11th Lord MONTAGU [E], K.G , beheaded on Tower Hill 9 Jan 1539 , and had issue.

See the Clarence Volume, Table II and pp 71–533, Nos 1 to 22807
[Nos 103600 to 126406

[1] History of the Family of Coppinger of Coppinger

313. Descendants of MARY ST. LEGER (Table XXVII.), *d.* (will dated 8 July and proved 13 Dec) 1669, *m* as 3rd wife, 21 Feb 1661, ROBERT (SUTTON), 1st BARON LEXINTON of Aram [E 21 Nov 1645], *d.* 13 Oct. 1668, and had issue 1*a* to 2*a*

1a *Robert (Sutton), 2nd Baron Lexinton [E], Ambassador to Spain for the Treaty of Ryswick,* d 19 *Sept* 1723, m (*luc* 24 *Sept*) 1691, *Margaret, da and h of Sir Giles Hungerford of Coulston, co Wilts,* d *c* 1712, *and had issue* 1b

1b *Hon Bridget Sutton, da and event h,* b 1699, d 16 *June* 1734, m 27 *Aug* 1717, *John (Manners), 3rd Duke of Rutland [E], K G,* d 29 *May* 1779, *and had issue*

See the Exeter Volume, Table VII, pp 159-163, Nos 2471-2912, also Exeter Supplement, 2913-2922, I, and Exeter Volume, 2923-3130

2a *Hon Bridget Sutton,* b 1662.3, *living* 1710, m *the Hon John Darcy [son and h of Conyers, 2nd Earl of Holderness [E], &c], bapt* 5 *Nov* 1659, d v p 6 *Jan* 1689, *and had issue*

See the Clarence Volume, Table LXXVIII and pp 626-637, Nos 28040-28849   [Nos 126407 to 128177

314. Descendants of DUDLEY ST LEGER of St John, Thanet (Table XXVII), *d.* 1642, *m* ANNE, da. of (—) (who *m* 2ndly, 1644, SAMUEL HUSSEY of Ulcombe, co Kent, and) *d* 1646, and had issue (with a son, Warham, *d* young) 1*a* to 3*a*

1a *Anthony St Leger,* b 1637

2a *Dudley St Leger of Maidstone in* 1663 *and Deal* 1694, b 1639, d (-), m 1st, 1663/4, *Winifred [da of* (—)] *Horne of Deal,* 2ndly, 1694, *Mary, widow of* (--) *Weller of Deal, and had issue* 1b to 2b

1b *Edward St Leger of Deal, Surgeon,* b 1665, d 1729, m 1702, *Elizabeth, da of Charles Bargrave of Eastry, and had issue (with 4 other children* d v p) 1c to 2c

1c *Edward St Leger*

2c *Mary St Leger,* m *John Cannon, and was ancestress of* 1d

1d *Edward St Leger Cannon of the Glen, Walmer, Admiral R N, living* 1867 [1]

2b *John St Leger, living* 28 *June* 1711

3a *Anne St Leger,* b 1641, d (-), m 1666, *the Rev Nicholas White, Vicar of St Peter's, Thanet*

315 Descendants of WARHAM ST. LEGER of Heyward's Hill, co Cork (Table XXVII), living Oct 1691, *m* 1677, MARY, da and h of GILES GREGORY of Thurlesbeg, co Tipperary; and had issue 1*a* to 5*a*.

1a *Heyward St Leger of Heyward's Hill,* d 10 *June* 1754, m 1701, *Elizabeth, da of* (—) *Godken, or Gooken, of Courtmasherry, and had issue* 1b to 2b

1b *Warham St Leger of Heyward's Hill,* d 1784, m (*settl* 12 *Feb*) 1742, *Margaret, da and h of Robert Atkins of Waterpark, and had issue* 1c to 8c

1c *Heyward St Leger of Heyward's Hill,* d 1792, m *Anne, da and co-h of Noblett Johnson of Cork, and had issue (with* 1 *other sons* d *unm*) 1d to 2d

1d *Heyward St Leger of Heyward's Hill, J P, D L, Capt Glanmire Cav,* b 1771, d 1847, m 27 *Nov* 1797, *Matilda, da of Noblett Rogers of Lota,* d 1852, *and had issue (with* 2 *younger sons and a da of whom no issue survives)* 1e to 3e

---

[1] *Stemmata St Leodegaria,* by E F St Leger, 1867

The Plantagenet Roll

1c *Anthony Butler St Leger of Heyward's Hill, which he sold* 1852, b 1803, d s p 1866

2c *Heyward John St Leger, of London,* 1867, b 1805, d (-), m 1837, *Sarah* (see below), *da and co-h of Michael Busted Westrop, and had issue (with 2 elder sons d young)* 1f to 3f

    1f *Anthony Marcus St Leger* } (twins), b 1844
    2f *Noble Edward St Leger* }

    3f *Isabella Georgina St Leger*

3c *Cornelia Matilda St Leger*, b 1809, d 1867,[1] m *Edward Galwey of Lota, near Cork, Bar-at-Law [nephew of Vice-Admiral Galwey of Lota[2]], last of the Galweys of Lota, and had issue (with a son, John Edward, b* 1838, d 1840) 1f to 3f[3]

    1f *Matilda Ann Galwey,* m *Edward Murphy of Streamhill, co Cork*

    2f *Isabella Miranda Galwey,* m *H C Herbert, M D, 40th Regt*

    3f *Cornelia Letitia Galwey*

2d *Frances Anne St Leger,* m *R Spread*

2c *Robert St Leger, afterwards Atkins of Waterpark, co Cork,* d 1796, m *Jane da and co-h of Philip Lavallin of Waterstown, co Cork, and had issue (with 3 sons known to have d s p)* 1d to 4d

    1d *Warham Atkins of Waterpark,* b 1780, d 1830, in 1800, *Mary, da of Denis MacCarthy of Macksgrove, co Cork, and had issue (with a da d unm)* 1e

    1e *Robert St Leger Atkins of Waterpark, Major 60th Rifles,* b 6 Mar 1802, d 26 Aug 1858, m 3 Dec 1840, *Sarah Elizabeth, da of James Penrose of Woodhill, co Cork,* d (-), *and had issue* 1f to 4f

        1f *Robert St Leger Atkins of Waterpark,* b 12 Nov 1812

        2f *Louisa Petitot St Leger Atkins,*[4] m *George Moore, R N, M D*

        3f *Mary Elizabeth St Leger Atkins,* m 12 Sept 1874, *Vice-Admiral John Borlase Warren, R N, has Crimean and Chinese Medals [2nd son of Sir John Borlase Warren, 4th Bt [1] (United Service), and has issue* 1g to 3g

        1g *Bessie Geraldine Gundrada Warren,* m 20 Nov 1906, *Sir John Scarlett Walsham, 3rd Bt [U K] [also a descendant of King Edward III through Mortimer-Percy (see p 287)] (Knill Court, Kington, Hereford, Germiston, Transvaal), and has issue* 1h

            1h *Barbara Walsham*

        2g *Mary Dettri St Leger Warren*

        3g *Louisa Ursula St Leger Warren*

        4f *Henrietta Geraldine St Leger Atkins*

    2d *Joseph Atkins*

    3d *Sarah Atkins,* m *Robert Berkeley*

    4d *Jane Atkins,* m *Michael Bustead Westropp [cadet of Westropp, of Attyflin, co Limerick],* b 1779, d (-), *and had issue* 1e to 2e

    1e *Sarah Westropp,* d (-), m 1837, *Heyward St Leger of London, and had issue*

See above, Nos 128178-128180

    2e *Julia Westropp,* m *R Wilkinson*

    3c *Warham St Leger,* d *before* 1847, *probably s p*

    4c *Chichester St Leger,* d *before* 1847.

    5c *Mary St Leger,* b 1746, d 1807, m *Thomas Follett of Lyme Regis, co Dorset, and had issue*   [Nos 128178 to 128190

---

[1] *Stem St Leodegaria*

[2] Burke's "Landed Gentry," 1846, n 1176

[3] "The Galweys of Lota," by C J B Bennett, Dublin 1909, pp 17, 18

[4] Burke's "Landed Gentry," 1886, p 53

# of The Blood Royal

6c *Barbara St Leger,* b 1749, d 21 *Sept (and bur at Clonegal* 24 *Sept)* 1820, m *(lic from St Peter's, Dublin,* 21 *Feb)* as 4th *wife, Ap* 1768, *Alexander Durdin of Shanagarry Castle, co Cork, and Huntington Castle, co Carlow, J P,* b 1712, d 20 *Feb* 1767, *and had issue (with* 3 *sons and* 4 *das who d s p)* 1d *to* 7d

1d *Warham Durdin of Shanagarry Castle, &c,* b 18 *Feb* 1769, d 21 *May* 1823, m 7 *June* 1792, *Anne, da of Thomas Garde of Ballindiness co Cork,* d 9 *Jan* 1817, *and had issue (with* 4 *sons and* 4 *das of whom no issue survives)* 1e *to* 2e

1e *Charles Durdin of Shanagarry Castle,* d 24 *Dec* 1875, m *Anne, da of* (—) *Bowles, and had issue* 1f *to* 5f

1f
2f
3f } *Alive and living in Australia* 1886, *when they shared in the property of their uncle, Warham St Leger Durdin*
4f
5f

2e *Louisa Durdin,* d *in Australia* 1844, m *William Garde of Bilberry, co Cork,* d 5 *Oct* 1895, *and had issue* 1f *to* 2f

1f *William Henry Garde, Lieut-Col, A M S, has Medal and Khedive's Star and Clasp for relief of Khartoum* 1884-1885 *(2 Sidmonton Square, Bray),* b 2 *Mar* 1842, m 25 *June* 1891, *Fanny Nina Hampton, da of Edwin Hampton Downs, and has issue* 1g

1g *Violet Nina Hampton Garde,* b. 1892.

2f *Annie Winifred Garde,* m 11 *Ap* 1871, *St Heber Philip Peard of Cool Abbey, Fermoy (Glenbrook, Lismore, Richmond River, N S W), and has issue* 1g *to* 6g

1g *Ernest St Heber Peard,* b 24 *Dec* 1873

2g *Percy Garde Peard,* b 17 *Jan,* 1880, m 30 *Dec* 1908, *Ada Maude, da of* (—) *Grisdale*

3g *Louisa Alice Peard,* m 28 *June* 1898, *Harold T Carter, and has issue* 1h.

1h *Annie Jean Carter,* b 6 *May* 1903

4g *Mabel Minnie Peard,* m 22 *Dec* 1900, *Edward R J Rohan, and has issue* 1h *to* 2h

1h *Norman Livesey Rohan,* b 19 *Feb* 1905

2h *Dulcie Garde Rohan,* b 7 *Feb* 1903.

5g *Florence Victoria Peard,* m 23 *Dec* 1903, *Charles Sidney Dunlop, and has issue* 1h *to* 3h

1h *Douglas Victor Dunlop,* b 23 *Dec* 1904

2h *Neville Redmond Dunlop,* b 12 *Jan* 1910

3h *Norma Peard Dunlop,* b 14 *May* 1908

6g *Laura Lily Peard, unm*

2d *Alexander Durdin,* b 26 *June* 1772, d 19 *May* 1829, m *Mary, da of Thomas Rhames of co Wicklow [who m 2ndly,* 1840, *William Drury and]* d 21 *Jan* 1875, *and had issue* 1e

1e *Alicia Harriet Durdin,* b 11 *Mar* 1823, d 18 *Ap* 1908, m 1 *Sept* 1840, *William Whitton of Dublin, Solicitor,* d 10 *Aug* 1895, *and had issue* 1f

1f *Mary Alicia Whitton (Glenrar, Howth Road, Dublin),* m 28 *Sept* 1861, *William Blood Smyth of 29 Lower Gardiner Street, Dublin, Solicitor,* d 3 *Ap* 1905, *and has issue (with* 2 *others d young)* 1g *to* 11g

1g *William Smyth,* b 23 *Aug* 1877

2g *John Blood Smyth, Solicitor (29 Lower Gardiner Street, Dublin, Glenrar, Howth Road, Dublin),* b 14 *Oct* 1880

3g *Charles Whitton Smyth,* b 19 *July* 1882

4g *Henry Blood Smyth* } *(twins),* b 21 *May* 1884
5g *FitzGerald Blood Smyth*

6g *Alice Mary Smyth, unm*

[Nos 12819l-128212.

3 R

The Plantagenet Roll

7g Annie Emily Smyth, *unm*

8g Florence Smyth, *m* 8 July 1909, Edward Hartnick Bailey, and has issue 1h

1h Edward Hartnick Bailey, *b* 5 Ap 1910

9g Dora Smyth, *m* 3 Feb 1910, Joseph Watson Connell (*Bank House, Talbot Street, Dublin*)

10g Eleanor Susannah Smyth, *m* 22 Ap 1909, the Rev Matthew Tobias, Chaplain to the Forces at Bulford Camp, Salisbury

11g Irene Mary Smyth, *unm*

3d *Robert Atkins Durdin of Cranmore House, Kildavin, co Carlow, J P*, *b* 16 Oct 1777, *d* 5 Jan 1841, *m* Nov 1809, *Elizabeth da of Thomas Garde of Ballindiness, co Cork, d* 11 Feb 1852, *and had issue (with 2 sons d s p)* 1e to 2e

1e *Rev Thomas Garde Durdin*, *b* 18 Feb 1813, *d* 27 Oct 1902, *m* 28 Feb 1843, *Charlotte, da of Anthony Browne of Rathgar, Dublin, J P, d* 23 Dec 1901, *and had issue (with a da, Mrs Singleton, d s p)* 1f to 2f

1f Robert Charles Garde Durdin, M D (T C D) (*7 Frankford Place, Upper Rathmines, Dublin*), *b* 27 Jan 1850, *unm*

2f Adelaide Durdin, *m* 27 Sept 1888, James Love of Clonkeefy, co Meath, and Kenwick Hall, co Norfolk, *d* 21 Sept 1901

2e *Robert Garde Durdin of Dublin, Solicitor, Lord Mayor of Dublin* 1872, *b* 22 Dec 1817, *d* 19 Oct 1878, *m a* 1847, (*see p 195*), *da of (his uncle) William Leader Durdin of Huntington Castle, d* 17 Oct 1896, *and had issue* 1f

1f Fidelia Barbara Durdin, *m* 17 Ap 1884, William Francis Cooke of Kingstown (5 *Morehampton Road, Dublin*), and has issue 1g

1g Francis William St Leger Durdin Cooke, Trinity College, Dublin, *b* 18 June 1885

4d *William Leader Durdin of Huntington Castle, co Carlow, M D (T C D)*, *b* 10 Dec 1778, *d* 1 Jan 1849, *m* Ap 1820, *Mary Anne, da of William Drury of Ballinderry, co Wicklow, d* 13 Ap 1883, *and had issue* 1e to 2e

1e *Alexander Durdin of Huntington Castle, LL D (T C D), J P cos Carlow and Wicklow*, *b* 6 Mar 1821, *d* 4 Jan 1892, *m* 6 Sept 1851, *Mehan Jones, da of Matthew Hayman of South Abbey, Youghal co Cork, J P, d* 12 Feb 1904, *and had issue* 1f to 4f

1f Helen Alexandrina Mehan Durdin, *m* 1 Jan 1880 (Thomas) Herbert Robertson of Huntington Castle, co Carlow, and 36 Bedford Square, co Mids, J P cos London and Carlow, and High Sheriff for the latter co 1899, M A (Magd Coll, Oxon), and Barrister-at-Law of Lincoln's Inn, *formerly* M P for Hackney (*Huntington Castle, Clonegal, co Carlow, 36 Bedford Square, W C 8 Stone Buildings, Lincoln's Inn Carlton Athenæum*), and has issue 1g to 4g

1g Manning Durdin Robertson, Eton and Magd Coll, Oxon, *b* 29 May 1887

2g Nevill Warham Robertson, Eton and St John's Coll, Oxon, *b* 27 May 1890

3g Magnus Storm Robertson, Eton Coll, *b* 11 Oct 1893

4g Helen Manning Robertson, *unm*

2f Florence Amy Durdin, *m* at St Paul's, Ivy, Virginia, 14 Feb 1893, Alexander Ferrier Beasley of Newstead, co Devon (*Robert's Creek, Vancouver, B C*), and has issue 1g to 2g

1g William Alexander Ferrier Beasley, *b* at Vancouver 13 Oct 1898

2g Winifred St Leger Ferrier Beasley, *b* at Los Angeles, California, 11 May 1891

3f Mehan Lucy Anne Durdin, *b* 17 Feb 1861, *d* 3 Nov 1899, *m* 16 Sept 1886, Walter Henry Benjamin Holloway (*Ivy House, Charlbury, Oxon*), and had issue 1g

1g Mehan Eileen Jane Holloway, *m* 9 Jan 1908, Charles Cheesman, R I C (*The Barracks, Killarney*), and has issue 1h

1h Winifred Mehan Anne Cheesman, *b* 28 Dec 1908

[Nos 128213 to 128232.

494

4f *Harriette Emily Hayman Durdin*, b 7 Dec 1862, d 13 Dec 1894, m 25 Ap 1891, *Richard William Brockfield Irwell* of Clonegan, co Carlow and Charlottesville, Virginia, and had issue 1g to 2g

  1g *Richard Alexander Fraser Irwell*, b at Charlottesville 26 Jan 1894

  2g *Ethel Melvin Irwell*, b at Charlottesville 26 Jan (sic) 1892

2c *Fidelia Durdin*, b 1 May 1823, d 17 Oct 1896, m a 1847, *Robert Garde Durdin* of Dublin, Solicitor, d 19 Oct 1878, and had issue

  See p 494, Nos 128221-128222

5d *Michael Durdin*, b 22 Mar 1782, d after 1840, m *Sarah*, widow of John Harris, da of (--), d 18 Aug 1835, and had issue 1e to 4e

  1e *Michael St Leger Durdin*, living at Port Alma, Canada, 22 Aug 1897

  2e *Alexander Durdin*, bapt 22 Jun 1828,

  3e *Barbara Durdin*,   living in Canada 1882

  4e *Eliza Durdin*,

6d *Sarah Durdin*, b 20 Aug 1773, d (-), m *John Revell* of Ardoyne, co Wicklow, and had issue 1e

  1e *William Revell*, b at Huntington Castle 23 Aug 1805, d in Australia 1882, m *Jane*, da of (--) Ivors of Castle Ivors, co Limerick, and had issue 1f to 2f

    1f *John Revell*, living at or near Brisbane, Queensland

    2f *Eliza Revell*, m *George Harden* of Menai Cottage, Anglesea, and both emigrated to Australia with William Revell and his wife 1862

7d *Barbara Durdin*, b 9 Dec 1785, d (-), m 1824, *Henry Beere* of Black Castle, co Kildare, and had issue 2 das who both apparently d young

7c *Margaret St Leger*, d Feb 1828, m Ap 1768, *William Leader* of Mount Leader co Cork, JP, b 1743, d Ap 1828, and had issue 1d to 4d

  1d *Nicholas Philpot Leader* of Dromagh Castle, co Cork, MP, Kilkenny, d 1836, m *Margaret*, da of Andrew Nash of Nashville, co Cork, d 8 Oct 1858 and had issue 1e to 5e

    1e *Nicholas Philpot Leader* of Dromagh Castle, co Cork, MP, JP, b 1811, d unm 31 Mar 1880

    2e *William Leader* of Rosnalee, formerly Nashville, Bantry, co Cork, JP, d 1860, m 29 June 1817, *Dorothea* (see p 499), da of Richard M Gillicuddy of the Reeks, co Kerry, JP, DL, d 1897, and had issue 1f to 4f

      1f *William Nicholas Leader* of Rosnalee, Dromagh Castle, JP, DL, BA (Camb), formerly Lieut Scots Guards, High Sheriff co Cork 1908 (Dromagh Castle, Bantier, co Cork, Carlton), b 1853, m 21 June 1881, the Hon Eleanor Burke, da of Edmund (Roche), 1st Baron Fermoy [1]

      2f *Francis Henry Mowbray Leader* of Classes, formerly Lieut R A (Classas, Coachford, co Cork), b 1855, m Nov 1879, *Agnes*, da of Thomas Brodrick of Leemount, co Cork, and has issue 1g to 4g

        1g *Francis William Mowbray Leader*, Lieut 2nd Batt Connaught Rangers, b 1881

        2g *Thomas Henry Mowbray Leader*, b 1883

        3g *Mary Gwendoline Leader*, m 3 Feb 1903, *Henry Jellett*, M D [son of the Very Rev Henry Jellett, D D, Dean and Ordinary of St Patrick's Cathedral, Dublin] (34 Merrion Square North, Dublin), and has issue 1h to 2h

          1h *Francis Henry Leader Jellett*, b 28 Feb 1904

          2h *Gwendoline Stella Leader Jellett*

        4g *Aileen Agnes Mowbray Leader*

      3f *Dorothea Margaret Leader*, m 1872, *George Ware* (Woodfort, Mallow, co Cork), and has issue 1g to 5g

        1g *George William Webb Ware*, M B, Capt R A M C, b 9 Sept 1879

        2g *Denis Ware*

        3g. *Ruth Ware*

        4g *Audrey Ware*   [Nos 128233 to 128256.

        5g *Frances Ware*

The Plantagenet Roll

1*f* Margaret Leader, *m* 14 Nov 1883, Henry Bruce Wright-Armstrong of Killylea, co Armagh, J P, D L, High Sheriff co Armagh 1875, and co Longford 1894, &c [descended from the Lady Anne, sister of King Edward IV] (*Killylea Castle, co Armagh; Dean's Hill, Armagh*), and has issue

See the Essex Volume Supplement p 623, Nos 9890 92–99

3e *Henry Leader*, *b* May 1815, *d* 10 *July* 1887, *m* 1st, *June* 1841, *Maria Winifred, da of John Birmingham Miller, Q C, d* 14 *Oct* 1862, *and had issue* (with 3 sons d s p) 1*f* to 3*f*

1*f* Charles Robert Leader, M B (*The Old Hall, Wem, Salop*), *b* at Clonmoyle, co Cork, 5 Sept 1862, *m* 7 Jan 1891, Louisa, da of James Lowe Holmes of Carrigmore, co Cork, and has issue 1g to 2g

1g Stephen Henry Claude Leader, *b* 26 Dec 1896

2g North Lillie Leader, *b* 30 Jan 1895

2*f* *Maria Winifred Leader*, *d* 1885, *m* 2 *June* 1864, *the Rev Edward Lavillan Puxley, Vicar of Steep, formerly Lieut 4th Dragoons, d June* 1909, *and had issue* (with 1 son d unm) 1g to 5g

1g Frank Lavillan Puxley (*Carmarthen*), *b* 6 May 1868, *m* Sept 1903, (—), da of (—), s *p*

2g Greville Lavillan Puxley, *b* 19 Jan 1876, *m* Sept 1907, (—), da of (—); and has issue (1 child, *b* 1908)

3g Frances Kate Puxley   } (*Steep, Petersfield, Hants*), *unm*
4g Winifred Emily Puxley }

5g Florence Lavallin Puxley, *m* (—)

3*f* Ada Henrietta Leader, *m* 19 Aug 1889, Rev Ralph Allan Cumine, M A and Scho (1869) T C D, Vicar of Dunmow (*Little Dunmow Vicarage, Chelmsford, Essex*), and has issue 1g to 4g

1g Ada Isabel Cumine, *b* 4 July 1890

2g Eveleen Maud Eleanor Cumine, *b* 27 Dec 1891

3g Florence Mary Cumine, *b* 3 Mar 1894

4g Cecily Diana Cumine, *b* 10 Dec 1897

4e *Margaret Leader*, *d* 12 *Dec* 1884, *m* *John Newman* [son and h-app of *Adam Newman of Dromore, co Cork*], d v p 13 Aug 1844, *and had issue* 1*f* to 3*f*

1*f* John Adam Richard Newman of Dromore, J P, D L, High Sheriff co Cork 1871, B A (Camb) *b* 5 Aug 1844, *d* 11 *Oct* 1893, *m* 17 *Aug* 1870, *Elizabeth Matilda, da of Lieut Col Robert Bramston Smith of Pencraig, co Anglesey, D L* [by his wife Elizabeth Charlotte, da of Sir Richard John Griffin, 1st Bt], *and had issue* 1g to 3g

1g John Robert Bramston Newman of Newberry (Dromore) Manor, &c, J P, D L, High Sheriff co Cork 1898, B A (Camb), *late* Capt 5th Royal Munster Fusiliers (*Newberry Manor, near Mallow, co Cork, 81 Cadogan Place, S W*), *b* 22 Aug 1871, *m* 1st, 24 Aug 1895, the Hon Olivia Anne, da of the Most Rev William Conyngham (Plunket), 4th Baron Plunket [U K], Archbishop of Dublin, d s *p* 24 Jan 1896, 2ndly, 8 Sept 1898, Geraldine Amelia (see p 497), da of Col William Pretyman

2g Richard Griffith Oliver Newman, Capt 7th Dragoon Guards, *b* 19 Jan. 1876

3g Grace Frances Newman, *m* 20 Aug 1895, Henry Charles Villiers-Stuart of Dromana-within-the-Decies, J P, D L, High Sheriff co Waterford 1898, *formerly* Capt Waterford Art, has S African Medal (*Dromana, Cappoquin, co Waterford*), and has issue 1*h* to 3*h*

1*h* Ian Henry FitzGerald Villiers-Stuart, *b* 23 Nov 1900

2*h* Geraldine Mary Villiers-Stuart, *b* 7 June 1896

3*h* Nesta Mona Villiers-Stuart, *b* 17 Nov 1897

2*f* Frances Dorothea Newman, *m* 22 Feb 1870, Capt Henry E Bridges, *late* 4th Royal Irish Dragoon Guards.   [Nos 128257 to 128285

496

# of The Blood Royal

3f Geraldine Elizabeth Newman, m Ap 1865, Col William Pretyman, *formerly 60th Rifles, b 5 Ap 1822, d 5 Oct 1894, and has issue 1g*

1g Geraldine Amelia Pretyman, m is 2nd wife, 8 Sept 1898, John Robert Bramston Newman of Dromore, D L (see p 496) (*Newberry Manor, Mallow*)

5c *Elizabeth Leader*, d 19 Aug 1903, m 14 Ap 1849, Sir George Richard *Waldie-Griffith, 2nd Bt [U K] D L, b 31 Jan 1820, d 8 May 1889, and had issue 1f to 5f*

1f Sir Richard John Waldie-Griffith, 3rd Bt [U K], J P, D L, Hon Col *formerly Comdg 1st Roxburgh and Selkirk Vol, previously Capt 2nd Dragoon Guards, Chairman Roxburgh Territorial Force Asso, &c (Hendersyde Park, Kelso, Oakfield, Newmarket, co Camb), b 24 Ap 1850, m 11 Ap 1877, May Nina, da. of Col William Irwin of St Catherine's Park, Leixlip*

2f Mary Mona Waldie-Griffith, m 23 Feb 1880, Thomas Taylor of Chipchase Castle and Widdrington, J P, High Sheriff co Northumberland (*Chipchase Castle, Wark-on-Tyne, R S O. The Cottage, Widdrington), and has issue 1g to 4g*

1g Hugh Taylor, B A (Oxon), Lieut Scots Guards, b 24 Dec 1880

2g Thomas George Taylor, Lieut Gordon Highlanders, b 1 Mar 1885

3g Margaret Taylor

4g Violet Mona Taylor

3f May Isabel Gwendoline Waldie-Griffith (*Trefusis, Falmouth*), m 22 July 1886, Thomas Turner Farley of Wartnaby Hall, co Leicester, d 13 Mar 1901, and has issue 1g to 2g

1g Dorothy Gladys Turner-Farley

2g Olivia Anne Turner-Farley

2d *Henry Leader of Mount Leader, co Cork, d 5 Ap 1868, m Aug 1830, Elizabeth Anna, da of the Rev Charles Eustace of Robertstown, claimant to the Viscounty of Baltinglass [I 1512], d 1858, and had issue 1e*

1e *Henry Eustace Leader of Mount Leader, J P, Capt 16th Lancers, b 1833, d 1 June 1876, m 1 Oct 1868, Helen Augusta, da of Lieut-Col Williamson of Carlow Keal, co Cork (who m 2ndly, 1878, Charles Arthur Duncan, Bar at-Law), and had issue 1f to 3f*

1f Henry Williamson Leader of Mount Leader, J P (*Mount Leader, co Cork*), b 18 July 1869, m 28 July 1900, Maud St Leger, da of George Maurice Ievers of Inchera, co Cork, and has issue 1g to 2g

1g Maud Ievers Leader

2g Violet Eustace Leader

2f Lionel Frederic Leader, Capt 8th King's (Liverpool) Regt, b 10 Sept 1870, m 2 Oct 1897, Mabel Campbell, da of E Butler Rowley of Manchester, and has issue 1g to 2g

1g Eustace Lionel Leader, b 1 Oct 1898

2g Marcella Hilda Leader, b 12 Dec 1892

3f Roland William Leader

3d *Eliza Leader, d (-), m 17 July 1800, the Rev Matthew Purcell of Burton Park, co Cork, Rector of Churchtown and Dungourney, d 1845, and had issue (with 3 das who d s p and one whose issue is extinct) 1e to 5e*

1e *John Purcell of Burton Park, D L, b 1801, d 5 Jan 1853, m 14 May 1850, Anna Moore, da of M K Dempsey of Kildare, d 1872, and had issue 1f*

1f Mathew John Purcell of Burton Park, J P (*Burton Park, Churchtown, Buttevant, co Cork*), b 30 Nov 1852, m 29 Aug 1882, Annie Marie, da of Peter Paul Daly of Daly's Grove, co Galway, and has issue 1g to 7g

1g Raymond John Purcell, Lieut 9th Batt Royal Rifle Corps, b 13 May 1885

2g Charles Francis Purcell, b 23 Ap 1891

3g Annie Louisa Purcell

4g Margaret Mary Purcell

5g Elizabeth Mary Purcell

6g Louisa Caroline Purcell

7g Angela Mary Purcell

[Nos 128286 to 128311

497

The Plantagenet Roll

2e *Henrietta Purcell*, d (-), m 1st, 1836, *Richard Labarte of Springfield, co Tipperary* 2ndly, (--) *Townsend*, d s p , *and had issue (2 das)*

3e *Margaret Purcell*, d (-), m 1st, 1832, *William Purcell of Altamira, co Cork*, d *2 Jan 1837* , 2ndly, 1838, *Richard Harris Purcell* (see below), *Bar -at-Law , and had issue 1f to 3f*

1f *Albert Purcell*

2f *Matthew Purcell*

3f *Eliza Augusta Purcell of Highfort, co Cork*, d (-), m *30 Ap 1857, Henry Longfield of Sea Court, co Cork*, b 1828, d *16 Feb 1871, and had issue* 1g to 4g

1g Alfred Purcell Longfield, Major R F A , *b 6 Dec 1862*, m *12 Ap 1898,* Constance Ada, da of Professor James Saunders of Edinburgh , and his issue 1h

1h Ada Kathleen Longfield, b 27 Oct 1899

2g Mountifort Longfield, J P (*Sea Court, Timoleague, co Cork*), b 12 Feb 1866 , m *6 Jan 1891,* Geraldine Spencer (see p 339), da of Henley J Edwards, Ind Navy

3g Mary Longfield, m 1885, Capt Stuart Banks Roupell, R N

4g Kathleen Augusta Longfield, m 1889, Alfred Robinson McMullen

4e *Emily Purcell*, d (-) , m *Francis Sandys Bradshaw of Tipperary , and had issue 1f*

1f Rev Sandys Yuyer Burges Bradshaw , Vicar of Holy Trinity, South Shore, Lancashire, 1882-1905 (*Mossley, Manchester*)

5e *Octavia Purcell*, b 1816 , d *Dec 1836* , m as 1st wife, May 1834, *Richard Gibbings of Gibbings Grove, co Cork*, b 1 Jan 1813 , d 1 Aug *1876, and had issue 1f to 2f*

1f Rev Richard Gibbings of Gibbings Grove, D D , M A (Dublin), Rector of Llanmerewig (*Gibbings Grove, Charleville co Cork , Llanmerewig Rectory, Abermule, co Montgomery*), b 16 Ap 1835, m 11 Jan 1864 Elizabeth Rebecca, da of William Ware, Clerk of the Peace, co Cork , s p

2f *Octavia Mary Emily Purcell Gibbings*, d 7 Ap 1882, m 21 Sept 1859, *James Denis Foley Cronin, M D , Fleet Surgeon, R N* , d 8 Feb 1909 *and had issue (with others who d s p)* 1g

1g John Joseph Cronin, Lieut Col Indian Army, *formerly Muds Regt* , since 26 July 1886 attached to Civil Service, and now Dep Commr , Burma b 25 Sept 1860 , m 1st, Daisy, da of J T Pennefather of Ballylangin Hall, co Tipperary, d 4 Aug 1901 2ndly, Geraldine Frances, da of J E Fottrell of Clonskeagh, co Dublin

4d *Louise Leader*, d 1878 , m 1812, *Richard Harris Purcell of Annabella, near Mallow, and Burnfort Park, co Cork,* d *1849 , and had (with others who d s p) issue* 1e to 9.

1e *Richard Harris Purcell of Annabella and Burnfort Park, Bar -at-Law*, d *3 Sept 1888* . m 1838, Margaret, widow of *William Purcell of Altamira, da of the Rev Mathew Purcell of Burton House, co Cork , and had issue*

See above, Nos 128312-128318

2e *John Harris Purcell of Copeswood, co Cork*, d (-), m *Louisa, da of Thomas Leader of Spring Mount, co Cork , and had issue* 1f to 3f

1f Isabel Purcell, m Charles J Starkey of Woodville, Ballyhooley, co Cork

2f Harriet Purcell

3f Florence Meta Purcell

3e *Pierce Harris Purcell of Shanghai*, b 29 Ap 1830 , d at Cork 29 Ap 1910 , m *Singa Choy of Canton , and had issue (4 sons and 6 das , one of the latter m)* (see Appendix)

4e *Augustus Harris Purcell of Annabella, Windsor, Australia, and Brighton, co Sussex, b* 12 Aug 1833 , m *Emma Elizabeth, da of (—) Hodges of Newton, co Montgomery , and his issue* 1f

1f Ruth Louise Purcell, m Alfred Warre Clarke of Australia

[Nos 128312 to 128332

498

# of The Blood Royal

5e William Charles Harris Purcell (*Bendigo, Victoria*) b 3 Aug 1835, m Annie, da of Angus Cornish of Castlemaine, Victoria, and has issue 1f

    1f Ethel Purcell (*Melbourne*)

6e Thomas Lyndhurst Leader Purcell, b 14 Oct 1836, m s p

7e Elizabeth Anne Harris Purcell, m as 2nd wife, 8 May 1873, Thomas Harriott Fuller of Glashnacree, co Kerry, d (s p by her) 29 Nov 1886

8e Harriet St Leger Purcell (*Rochestownwood, Rochestown, co Cork*), m 18 July 1874, George Roch of Woodbine Hill, co Waterford, and Rochestown, co Cork, J P , D L , d s p 3 July 1894

9e Emily Harris Purcell, m at St John's Church, Buenos Ayres, 5 (—) 1872, Thomas Parsons Riggs Boland [son of Thomas Parsons Boland of Pembroke Passage West, co Cork, J P], d at Ballinahina House 10 Mar 18—

  8c *Dorothea St Leger*, m *James Bennett of Cork, M D , and had issue 1d to 2d*

    1d *(—) Bennett, Recorder of Cork , m and had issue*

    2d *Margaret Bennett*, d 2 Feb 1849, m as 1st wife, *Richard M'Gillicuddy of the Reeks, J P , D L , High Sheriff co Kerry 1823*, b 1 Jan 1790, d 6 June 1866, *and had issue 1e*

      1e *Dorothea M Gillicuddy*, d 1897, m 1st, 29 June 1817, *William Leader of Rosnalie*, d 1860, 2ndly, at St George's, Hanover Square, London, 30 Ap 18—, *the Rev John MacEwan, D D , Rector of Drumtariffe, Procurator of Ardfort and R D , and had issue*
      See p 495, Nos 128243–128265

  2b *Elizabeth St Leger*, m *(—) Archer*

  2a *Thomas St Leger, Barrack Master at Newmarket co Cork*, m 1 Nov 1707, *Gertrude, da of Chichester Fortescue of Dromiskin*

    3a *William St Leger of Kilmurray, co Limerick*, d 1753

    4a *Andrew St Leger of Ballyoholane, murdered 1731*

    5a *Barbara or Elizabeth St Leger*, m 25 Aug 1696, *Richard Roffen*
                          [Nos 128333 to 128361

316 Descendants of JOHN ST LEGER of Cork (Table XXVII), d 1730 , m (—), and had issue (with an elder da d s p.) 1a to 4a

  1a *Elizabeth St Leger, da and co-h*

  2a *Barbara St Leger, da and co-h , m George Lyndon of the Treasury*

  3a *Gertrude St Leger, da and co h , m William O Brien of Aghacross*

  4a *Mary St Leger, da and co h , m John Copley of Springfield, co Limerick*

317 Descendants of MARY ST LEGER (Table XXVII), d 25 Ap 1718 , m 28 June 1679, JOHN GILLMAN of Curraheen, co Cork, bapt 20 Jan 1645 , d 12 Feb 1725 , and had issue 1a to 4a [1]

1a *Heywood Gillman of Curraheen*, d 1753, m 1727, *Hannah, da of the Rev Edward Savers of Doneraile , and had issue 1b to 2b*

1b *St Leger Heywood Gillman of Curraheen*, d 4 Nov 1757, m 1751, *Eliza Anne, da of Harding Parker of Hillbrook, co Cork* [who m 2ndly, 26 Nov 1761, *Sir Henry Martin, 1st Bt* [G B] and] d 6 Mar 1808, *and had issue 1c*

1c *Sir John St Leger Gillman of Curraheen, 1st Bt* [I], so cr 1 Oct 1799, b 21 Nov 1756, d 1815, m 10 June 1790, *Susanna* [descended from George,

---

[1] The statement in Burke's "Landed Gentry," 1871, under O'Callaghan, that there was another da , Ellen who m , 1713, Roger O'Callaghan is incorrect

The Plantagenet Roll

Duke of Clarence, K G (see Clarence Volume, p 507)], da of Sir Thomas Miller, 5th Bt [E], d 30 May 1803, and had issue (with 2 das d unm) 1d to 2d

1d *Hannah Elizabeth Gillman, da and co h*, b 1795, d June 1837, m as 2nd wife, 30 Aug 1853, the Rev John D'Arcy Jarvis Preston of Askham Bryan, J P, M A, d 7 Aug 1867, and had issue 1c

1c Hannah Elizabeth Preston, m 12 Oct 1870, the Rev Edward Barber, Vicar of Carleton 1870-1895 (15 Abbey Terrace, Whitby), and has issue (with a da, Winifred Hough, d unm 29 July 1888) 1f to 3f

1f Charles Edward Gillman Barber, b 12 Oct 1871

2f Frances Mary Barber b 7 Ap 1874

3f Constance Elizabeth Barber, b 18 June 1877

2d *Margaret Emily Gillman, da and co-h*, b Nov 1798, d Aug 1881, m as 2nd wife, 16 June 1832, William Henry Blaauw of Beechland, co Sussex, J P, D L, and High Sheriff (1859), F S A, M A, b 25 May 1793, d 26 Ap 1870, and had issue 1c to 2c

1c *Thomas St Leger Blaauw of Beechland*, J P, b 1 July 1839; d 11 Sept 1893, m 6 June 1867, Fanny Alice, da of Charles John Bigge of Linden, co Northbd, and had issue 1f to 5f

1f Henry Thomas Gillman Blaauw of Beechland (Beechland, Newick, Lewes), b 4 July 1874

2f Bertram William St Leger Blaauw, b 16 May 1876

3f Alice Agneta Emily Mitford Blaauw

4f Frances Catherine Blaauw

5f Margaret Louisa Blaauw

2c Emily Hannah Blaauw (Cissbury, Ascot Heath), m 30 Oct 1860, Capt the Hon Charles Cornwallis Chetwynd [4th son of Richard Walter, 6th Viscount Chetwynd [I]], d 31 Mar 1884, and has issue 1f to 5f

1f Emily Mary Frances Chetwynd

2f Margaret Adelaide Chetwynd, m 5 June 1890, Frank Bousfield Hudson (Oakwood, Roundhay, Leeds), and has issue 1g to 3g

1g Edwin Chetwynd Hudson, b 13 Mar 1892

2g Margaret Elsie Hudson

3g Laura Harland Hudson

3f Louisa Charlotte Chetwynd

4f Julia Alice Chetwynd

5f Katherine Philippa Chetwynd, m 1 Sept 1908, the Rev Knowlton Harold Hampshire, M A (Oxon) (Chiddingfold, Surrey)

2b *Elizabeth Gillman*, m Jasper Lucas of Richfordstown, co Cork, and were probably parents of 1c

1c *Thomas Lucas of Richfordstown*, d (–), m Dorothy, da of (—) Evans, and had issue [1]

2a *Mary Gillman*, m Rowland de la Hide

3a. *Barbara Gillman*

4a *Ursula Gillman*   [Nos 128362 to 128379

318 Descendants, if any surviving, of URSULA ST. LEGER, d 1672, m 1627, the Rev. DANIEL HORSMANDEN, Rector of Ulcombe, d 1655, of KATHERINE ST LEGER, m. 1628, THOMAS CULPEPPER, and of MARY ST LEGER, b 1612; d (–); m. 1632, WILLIAM CODD of Pelicans, Wateringbury (Table XXVII).

[1] Burke's ' Landed Gentry '

# of The Blood Royal

319. Descendants of AGNES or ANNE ST LEGER (Table XXVII), *b* 1555 , *d.* 1636 , *m.* THOMAS DIGGES of Barham and Wooton, co Kent , M P , Mathematician, Muster-Master Gen of the Forces in the Netherlands 1586–1594, *d* in London 24 Aug 1595 , and had issue (with a son and da *d* young) 1*a* to 4*a*

1*a* *Sir Dudley Digges of Chilham Castle, co Kent , M P , Diplomatist and Judge, Master of the Rolls 1636-1639,* b 1583 , *d at Chilham 18 Mar* 1639 , m *Mary, hss of Chilham, da of Sir Thomas Kemp of Ollanleigh, co Kent,* d a 1620 , *and had issue (with 4 sons d v p and one other da* [1]*)* 1*b* to 6*b*

1*b* *Thomas Digges of Chilham Castle,* d 1687, m 17 Nov 1631, *Mary, da of Sir Thomas Abbot, Lord Mayor of London* 1638, *and had issue (with 1 other sons who d s p)* 1*c* to 8*c*

1*c* *Sir Maurice Digges of Chilham Castle, 1st Bt [E. 6 Mar 1666],* b c 1633 , d s p , v p 1672

2*c* *Leonard Digges of Chilham Castle,* b 1651 , m 1717, *Elizabeth, da of Sir John Osborne of Chicksand , and had issue* [1] 1*d* to 3*d*

1*d* *John Digges of Chilham Castle,* d s p 1720

2*d* *Thomas Digges of Chilham Castle, a Col in the Army, sold Chilham, and* d (–), m *Aug* 1721, *the Hon Elizabeth, da of John (West), 6th Baron De La Warr [E], and is said to have had issue* 1*e*

1*e* *West Digges, the Player,* d 10 Nov 1786

3*d* *Elizabeth Digges,* d 1716 , m *Lieut -Gen Adam Williamson, Gov of Gravesend and Tilbury , and had issue* [2] 1*e*

1*e* *Elizabeth Caroline Williamson,* m *Daniel Fox of the Six Clerks Office*

3*c* *Mary Digges,* m 1656, *Sir William Brodnax of Godmersham, co Kent,* d 1673 , *and had issue* 1*d* [3]

1*d* *William Brodnax of Godmersham,* d 1726 , m *2ndly, Mary, da of* (—) *May , and had issue* 1*e* to 2*e*

1*e* *Thomas Brodnax, afterwards (1727) May, and finally (1738) Knight, of Godmersham,* d 1781 , m 11 *July* 1729, *Jane, da and co-h of William Monk of Buckingham, in Shoreham, co Sussex , and had issue 10 children, who were all apparently dead* s p *by* 1794

2*e* *Anne Brodnax,* m *Jacob Sawbridge of Canterbury , and had issue* 1*f* to 2*f*

1*f* *Jacob Sawbridge*

2*f* *Catherine Sawbridge,* m (—) *M'Caulay, M D , and had issue* [1]

4*c* *Margaret Digges* m *the Rev John Castilion, D D , Dean of Rochester and had issue* [1] 1*d*

1*d* *Mary Castilion,* m *Herbert Randolph of Canterbury , and had issue* 1*e*

1*e* *Herbert Randolph of Canterbury, F A S , 1717 , m and had issue* 1*f*

1*f* *Herbert Randolph of C C C , 1765*

5*c* -8*c* 4 *other das*

2*b* *John Digges of Faversham*

3*b* *Dudley Digges, M A (Oxon) and Fellow of All Souls, a Royalist political writer,* b *at Chilham* 1613 , d *at Oxford* 1 Oct 1643

4*b* *Edward Digges of Virginia,* in 1684

5*b* *Anne Digges,* m 1st *at Chilham,* 6 *July* 1633, *William Hammond of St Albans Court, co Kent,* b 1608 , d *at Wilberton, Ely,* 24 Sept. 1661, *2ndly, Sir*

---

[1] Hasted's " Kent," in 130

[2] Burke's " Extinct Baronetcies,' p 160 , Berry's " Kent Genealogies," p 143, &c

[3] Berry's " Kent Genealogies," p 126

[4] *Stemmata Chicheleana,* Table 251   [5] Ibid., Table 261.

The Plantagenet Roll

George Juxon of Canterbury, knighted 1 June 1663, and had issue (with a son and 3 das known to have d unm) 1c to 8c

    1c *William Hammond of St Albans Court*, d 6 May 1685, m 1st, Elizabeth, widow of Stephen Penkhurst of Buxted Place, co Sussex, da of Sir John Marsham, 1st Bt [E], d 1675, and had issue (with 2 other sons s p) 1d to 3d

    1d *William Hammond of St Albans Court*, b 12 Aug 1664, d 1717, m 1st, 1692, Elizabeth, da of John Kingsford, d 1702, and had issue 1e

    1e *Anthony Hammond of St Albans Court*, b 1693, d 1723, m his cousin-german, Catherine, da of (—) Kingsford, d 1722, and had issue 1f

    1f *William Hammond of St Albans Court*, b 19 Ap 1721, d May 1773, m 1745, Charlotte [descended from King Henry VII], da and co-h of the Rev William Egerton LL D [E of Bridgwater Coll], d 1770, and had issue

    See the Tudor Roll, pp 391-397, Nos 29467-29687, and Tudor Supplement, 29570 1-16

    2d *Elizabeth Hammond*, b 1645, d (–), m (lic London dated 6 Aug) 1680, Oliver St John of the Inner Temple [3rd son of Chief Justice Oliver St John, and only son by his 2nd wife, Elizabeth, da of Henry Cromwell], b c 1613, d (–), and had issue [1] 1e

    1e *Oliver St John*

    3d *Anne Hammond*, b 1670, m the Rev William Wotton, D D , Rector of Newport-Pagnell, co Bucks, the Critic, b at Wrentham 13 Aug 1666, d at Buxted 13 Feb 1726, and had issue 1e

    1e *Anne Wotton*, b June 1700, d 11 July 1783, m a 1721, the Rev William Clarke, M A and Fellow of St John's, Camb , Chancellor of Chichester, &c , the Antiquary, d 21 Oct 1771, and had issue (with 2 others d s p) 1f

    1f *Rev Edward Clarke, M A and Fellow of St John's College, Camb* , Rector of Buxted, Traveller and Author, b 16 Mar 1730, d Nov 1786, m 1763, Anne, da of Thomas Grenfield of Guildford, co Surrey, and had issue 1g to 4g

    1g *Rev James Stanier Clarke, LL B , LL D* , Canon of Windsor, Domestic Chaplain and Librarian to the Prince of Wales (George IV), sometime Chaplain R N , &c , Author, b at Minorca 1765, d 4 Oct 1834

    2g *Rev Edward Daniel Clarke, LL D , M A (Camb)* , Traveller, Antiquary, and Mineralogist, b 5 June 1769, d 9 Mar 1822, m 25 Mar 1806, Angelica, da of Sir William Beaumaris Rush, Bt , and had issue (5 sons and 2 das)

    3g *George Clarke, R N* , drowned in the Thames 1805

    1g *Anne Clarke*, m Capt Parkinson, R N , who was with Nelson at Trafalgar

    2c *Dudley Hammond*, m and had issue 1d

    1d *(—) Hammond*, m and had issue 1e

    1e *William Hammond*, living 1719 [2]

    3c *Anthony Hammond of Somersham Place, co Hunts*, b 1641, d 1681, m Amy, da of (–) Browne of co Glos , d 1693, and had issue 1d

    1d *Anthony Hammond of Somersham Place, F R S , M P , Poet and Pamphleteer*, son and h , b Sept 1668, d in the Fleet 1738, m at Tunbridge Wells, 14 Aug 1694, Jane, da of Sir Walter Clarges, 1st Bt [E], M P , and had issue 1e to 3e

    1e *Thomas Hammond of Somersham Place*, d s p [3] c 1758, m 1712, Elizabeth, da of (—) Adams d c 1759

    2e *James Hammond, M P for Truro, the Poet*, b 22 May 1710, d at Stowe 7 June 1742

    3e *Amy Hammond*, d 1754, m 1st, as 2nd wife, 1719, William Dowdeswell of Pull Court, co Hereford, M P , d 1728, 2ndly, 7 May 1730, Noel Broxholme, M D , M I , F R C P , d by his own hand at Hampton, co Midx , 8 July 1748, and had issue 1f to 2f   [Nos 128380 to 128616

---

[1] Noble's " House of Cromwell," ii 29

[2] Ibid, p 95   [3] D N B , viii 1124

# of The Blood Royal

1f Right Hon William Dowdeswell of Pull Court, PC, MP, Chancellor of the Exchequer, d at Nice 6 Feb 1775, m 1747, Bridget, da of Sir William Codrington, 1st Bt [GB], and had issue

See p 79, Nos 9460-9556

2f George Dowdeswell, MP, d (-), m 1760, Elizabeth da of Richard Buckle of Chaceley, and had issue 1g to 4g

    1g William Dowdeswell

    2g Charles Dowdeswell

    3g George Dowdeswell

    4g Frances Dowdeswell

4e Anne Hammond, m Henry Twyman of Canterbury

5e Elizabeth Hammond, m 1st (—) Snow of London, 2ndly, as 2nd wife, John Thomson of Kenfield, b c 1630, d 1712, and had (with possibly other) issue 2 children by 2nd marriage who d young [1]

6e Jane Hammond, m the Rev Isaac Drayton of Little Chart

7e Phabe Hammond, b 1646, d 11 July 1713, m 1st, Thomas Thomson of Chartham [younger brothe of John Thomson ab ve], d 15 Oct 1683, 2ndly the Rev Anthony Middleton, and had issue (with possibly others by 2nd husband) 1d [2]

1d Martha Thomson, b c 1692, d 26 July 1756, m Benjamin Maccaree of Canterbury, and had issue 1e

    1e John Maccaree

8e Margaret Hammond

6b Elizabeth Digges

2a Leonard Digges MA (Oxon), Poet and Translator, b 1588, d at Oxford 7 Ap 1635

3a Margaret Digges, ⎱ *both living 21 Aug 1595, and one of whom m Sir*
4a Ursula Digges, ⎰ *Anthony Palmer, KB, d 1630, to whom Leonard Digges dedicated one of his translations [3]*

[Nos 128617 to 128713]

320 Descendants of THOMAS (LENNARD), 15th BARON DACRE and 1st EARL OF SUSSEX (so cr 5 Oct 1674) [E] (Table XXVIII), *b c* 1653; *d* 30 Oct 1715, *m* 16 May 1674, Lady ANNE PALMER *alias* FITZROY, da of King Charles II by Barbara, Duchess of Cleveland [E], *d* 16 May 1722; and had issue 1a

1a Anne (Lennard), suo jure 16th Baroness Dacre [E] (see p 511), d 26 June 1755, m 1st, 15 July 1716, Richard Barrett-Lennard of Belhouse, co Essex, d v p Dec 1716, 2ndly, as 3rd wife, Mar 1718, Henry (Roper), 8th Baron Teynham [E], d 16 May 1723, and had issue 1b to 3b

1b Thomas (Barrett-Lennard), 17th Baron Dacre [E], b Ap 1717, d s p s l 3 Jan 1786

2b Hon Charles Roper, d v p 1 Feb 1754, m 27 June 1711, Gertrude, da and event co h of John Morley Trevor of Glynde, co Sussex, d 13 July 1780, and has issue

See the Clarence Volume, Tables XLV and LXXVI, and pp 100-101, Nos 15196-15382

3b Rev the Hon Henry Richard Roper, b Nov 1723, d Nov 1810, m 2ndly, 1760, Mary, da of Col Thomas Tenison of Finglass, co Dublin, d 16 Feb 1795, and had issue

See the Clarence Volume, Table XLVI and pp 404-413, Nos 15383-15641

[Nos 128714 to 129159]

---

[1] Berry's "Kent Genealogies," p 16

[2] Ibid, pp 17-95,6

[3] DNB, v 976

321 Descendants, if any surviving, of the Hon HENRY LENNARD
(Table XXVIII), *b* posthumous 1662-3, *d* 1703, *m* MARY,
da of (—) HADDOCK, *d* 1709, and had issue[1] 1*a* to 3*a*

1*a* *Margaret Lennard*, m *Col Lanoye*
2*a* *Catherine Lennard*, m (—) *Jones*
3*a* *Ann Lennard* m *Jerome Tully*

322. Descendants of Lady CHARLOTTE ANTOINETTE MARIE SEPTEMANIE
O'BRIEN (Table XXVIII), *d* at Anteuil, Paris, 4 May 1808,
m 22 Aug 1775, ANTOINE CÉSAR (DE CHOISEUL), 3rd DUKE
OF PRASLIN (DUC DE PRASLIN) [F 1762], K C L H, Deputy
of the Nobility of the Maine to the States General (1789),
Maréchal de Camp (1788), &c, *b* at Paris 6 Ap 1756, *d*
there 28 Jan 1808, and had issue 1*a*

1*a* *Claude Raynauld Laure Felix (de Choiseul), 4th Duke of Praslin (Duc de
Praslin [F], 1st Count of Choiseul [F E 31 Jan 1810], Peer of France (4 June
1814), Chamberlain to the Emperor Napoleon I, O L H, b at Paris 21 Mar 1778,
d there 28 June 1841, m there 12 Ap 1803 Charlotte Laure Olympe, da of Claude
Stanislaus (de Tonnelier), Viscount de Breteuil [F], K M, d there 6 Ap 1861,
and had issue 1b to 6b*

1*b* *Charles Laure Hughes Theobald (d Choiseul), 5th Duke of Praslin (Duc
de Praslin [F], and a Peer (1812), &c, b at Paris 29 June 1805, d there 23 Aug
1817, m there 18 Oct 1824 Fanny Altarice Rosalba, da and h of Horace
François Bastien (Sebastiani), 1st Count Sebastiani della Porta [F E 31 Dec
1809], G C L H, K S L, Marshal of France, d at Paris 17 Aug 1847, and had
issue 1c to 9c*

1*c* Gaston Louis Philippe (de Choiseul), 6th Duke of Praslin (Duc de Praslin)
[F] (Menton, Alpes Maritimes), *b* at Paris 7 Aug 1834, *m* at Geneva, 17 Dec
1871, Marie Elizabeth, da of (—) Forbes of New York, and has issue 1*d* to 7*d*

1*d* Marie Jean Baptiste Gaston de Choiseul, Marquis of Choiseul (Marquis de
Choiseul) (*Rue Bayard 7 (VIII°) Paris*, *Château du Bois-le-Houx, par Fougères
(I et I)*), *b* at Ryde, I W, 15 Nov 1876, *m* at Paris, 18 Dec 1901, Jeanne,
da of Georges Baconnière de Salverte

2*d* Count (Marie César) Gabriel de Choiseul, *b* at Ryde, I W, 20 Sept 1879

3*d* Count (Marie Charles Arnaud Raynald) Gilbert de Choiseul, *styled* Viscount de Choiseul, *b* at Paris 20 May 1882

4*d* Count (Marie Jean Horace) Claude de Choiseul, *b* at Ryde, I W, 20 Oct
1883

5*d* Count (Marie Auguste Eustache) Hughes de Choiseul, *b* at Paris 3 June
1885

6*d* Marie Lætizia de Choiseul

7*d.* (Marie Mathe) Nicolette de Choiseul

2*c* Count (Eugene Antoine) Horace de Choiseul, K L H, Chevalier du Mérite
Agricole, Councillor Gen and Deputy for the Seine et Marne 1869-1871 and 1885
(*Av Montaigne 57 (VIII°) Paris, Viry-Chatillon (S et O)*), *b* at Paris 23 Feb
1837, *m* 22 Oct 1864 the Princess Beatrix Jeanne Marie Josephine, da of Prince
Charles de Beauvau [H R E (1722) Coll], *d* 28 Feb 1895

3*c* Count (François Hector) Raynald de Choiseul, *b* 29 June 1839

4*c* *Marie Laure Isabelle de Choiseul*, *b* at Paris 19 Sept 1826, *d* at Turin,
[Nos 129160 to 129169

---

[1] Nichol's "Topographer and Genealogist," iii 217

504

# of The Blood Royal

28 *Nov* 1878, m 18 *Sept* 1845, *Hermann (de Cordero) Marquess of Roburent and Pamparato*

5c *Charlotte Louise Cécile de Choiseul*, b at *Paris* 15 *May* 1828 d there 11 *Mar* 1902, m 21 *Nov* 1848, *Gen Count Alfred de Gramont, G O L H [3rd son of Antoine, 9th Duke of Gramont [F 1643], G O L H , K S L]*. d 18 *Dec* 1881 , *and had issue* 1d

1d Count Antoine Alfred Arnaud Xavier Louis de Gramont *now* (Decree, 26 June 1901) de Gramont-de-Coigny, Dr ès sciences, Lt de rés d'état-major franc (*Paris*, 179 *rue de L'Université* , *Le Vignal, Pau Basses Pyrénées*), b at *Paris* 21 Ap 1861 , m at Angers, 2 Oct 1886, Anne Marie, da of Paul Emile (Brincard), 1st Baron Brincard [F E 31 Mar 1866], and has issue 1e to 2e

1e Antoine (Louis Marie Arnaud Sanche) de Gramont-de-Coigny b at *Paris* 2 July 1888

2e Diane (Antoinette Constance Anne Marie Louise) de Gramont de Coigny

6c *Fanny Césarine Berthe de Choiseul*, b 18 *Feb* 1830 , d at *Lievy* 1 *Aug* 1897 , m 29 *July* 1852, *Albert (Robert), —th Count of Robersart (Comte de Robersart) [F]*

7c *Alice Jeanne Sianne de Choiseul*, b 22 *Aug* 1831 , d at *Paris* 28 *Feb* 1877 , m *June* 1851, *Count (Antoine Edmond) Eugène de Chabannes [M of Chabannes du Verger [F] Coll]*

8c *Marie Marthe de Choiseul (Massio, Genoa)*, m 13 Sept 1852, Artus Louis Jacques Henri (de Montalembert), 1st Marquis of Montalembert d'Essé (Marquis de Montalembert d'Essé) [F], b 14 July 1824 d 29 Jan 1887 , and had issue 1d to 3d

1d Charles Laurent Godefroy (de Montalembert), 2nd Marquis of Montalembert d'Essé (Marquis de Montalembert d'Essé) [F], b 1854 , m July 1883, Gratienne Constance Agnès, da of (—) Loppin de Montmort

2d Count Raoul de Montalembert d'Essé (*Château de Menilles, Eure*), b (—), m 1 Feb 1888, Alix, da of Marie Joseph Gabriel Xavier (de Choiseul), —th Marquis of Choiseul-Beaupré [F], and has issue 1e to 7e

1e Johan de Montalembert d'Essé, b 20 Jan 1890

2e Jacques de Montalembert d'Essé

3e Xavier de Montalembert d'Essé

4e Alix de Montalembert d'Essé, b 17 Dec 1888

5e Lyna de Montalembert d'Essé

6e Nelly de Montalembert d'Essé

7e Marie Magdalene de Montalembert d'Essé

3d Caroline de Montalembert d'Essé

9c Leontine Laure Augustine de Choiseul, m 22 July 1858, Louis, Marquis d'Adda de Salvaterra (*Inverigo, Como, Italy*)

2b *Count Edgard Laure Charles Gilbert de Choiseul-Praslin*, b 28 *Oct* 1806 , d at *Paris* 5 *Feb* 1887 , m 1852, *Georgina Elizabeth Angelina, da of (—) Schickler*, d 12 *Jan* 1849, *and had issu.* 1c

1c Alix Eugénie Davida de Choiseul, m 21 May 1863, Count Charles Henri François Marie de Mercy-Argenteau [2nd son of Charles François Joseph (d'Argenteau), 3rd Count of Mercy-Argenteau [Netherlands]], and had issue 1d

1d Countess Georgina Davida Adelaide Françoise Marie de Mercy-Argenteau, Lady of the Order of Theresa (D hon de l'O hiv de Therese), m at *Paris* 29 Jan 1885, Duke Claude Emmanuel Henri Marie de Rarécourt de La Vallée de Pimodan, *styled* Count de Pimodan, *formerly* Lieut-Col of Cavalry in the French service [younger brother of Gabriel, 1st Duke of Rarécourt (Herzog von Rarécourt) [Bavaria, 29 Feb 1904], and Duke of Rarécourt de La Vallée de Pimodan (Duca di Rarécourt della Vallée di Pimodan) [PS 31 Oct 1860], —th Marquis of Pimodan (Marquis de Pimodan) [F 18 Aug 1766], 2nd Count of Pimodan (Graf von Pimodan) [Austria, 13 Aug 1852], &c , &c] (*Paris, rue de L'Université*, 98 (*VII*), *Château d'Ochain, par Clavier, Belgium Cercle de L'Union , Jockey Club*), and has issue 1e to 6e [Nos 129170 to 129186

505

The Plantagenet Roll

1c Duke Pierre (Georges Henri Laure Claude) de Ruécourt, *b* at the Château de Bezu, near Vernon, Eure, 3 Oct 1886

2c Duke Henri (Fernand François Gabriel Marie) de Ruécourt, *b* at Amiens 7 Dec 1887

3c Duke Georges (Robert Florimond Claude) de Raécourt, *b* at Paris 7 Dec 1892

4c Duke Louis (Gaston Philippe Marie Isabella) de Ruécourt, *b* at Thouis 10 July 1899

5c Marguerite (Leontine Emma Alix Marie) de Ruécourt, *b* at Abbeville 30 Apr 1889

6c Jeanne (Marie Louise Claude) de Ruécourt, *b* at Boulogne 12 Aug 1895

3b *Cesarine Charlotte Laure Slanie de Choiseul*, b 19 Oct 1807, d 29 Nov 1843, m 30 Nov 1829, *Henri Marie Nicholas Charles, Marquis of Harcourt* (*Marquis d'Harcourt*) [*son and h-app of François Eugene Gabriel, 7th Duke of Harcourt [F 1700], and a Peer, O L H*], b at Paris, 14 Nov 1808, d v p at Mel-sur-Seine 29 Sept 1846, and had issue 1c to 4c

1c *Charles François Marie (d'Harcourt), 8th Duke of Harcourt (Duc d'Harcourt)* [F], *Deputy for the Calvados 1871 and 1876-1881, &c*, b at Paris 21 June 1835, d there 5 Nov 1895, m 27 May 1862, *Countess Marie Ange Thérèse Caroline Al m* (*Paris, 11 rue Laneau*), da of *Charles Joseph François (d'Argenteau), 3rd Count of Mercy-Argenteau* [*Netherlands*], and had issue 1d to 2d

1d *Eugene François Marie Henri (d'Harcourt), 9th Duke of Harcourt (Duc d'Harcourt)* [F], *K L H*, *Capt of Chasseurs-a-pied*, b at Argenteau 15 Aug 1864, d at Paris 17 May 1908, m 2 Sept 1896, *Amelie Françoise Henriette Marie* (*Paris, 47 rue de Varennes, Château d'Harcourt, Calvados*), da of *Marie Charles Gabriel Sosthènes (de La Rochefoucauld) 4th Duke of Doudeauville* [F 1817], and had issue 1e to 3e

1e *François (d'Harcourt) 10th Duke of Harcourt (Duc d'Harcourt)* [F] (*Château d'Harcourt, Calvados, &c*) b 12 July 1902

2e Lydie Françoise Marie d'Harcourt, *b* at Paris 28 Oct 1898

3e Elisabeth Françoise Marie d'Harcourt, *b* at Paris 12 May 1901

2d Count Charles (Felix Marie) d'Harcourt, Capt res du 12e bat de Chass-à-pied (*Paris, 57 Av Montaigne, Château du Champ de Bataille, Neubourg, Eure*), b at Paris 18 Apr 1870, m there 2 Sept 1896, the Princess Henriette Marie Lucie Victurnienne, da of *Marie (de Beauvau), Prince of Beauvau-Craon* [H R E 1722], —th Marquis of Beauvau [F 1664], &c , s p s

2c *Count Louis Marie d'Harcourt, d (? s p)*

3c Count (Charles Marie) Pierre d'Harcourt, ancien capit d'etat-major (*Paris, 11 rue Laneau, Chat au de Grosbois, Cote d'Or*), b at Paris 25 Oct 1842, m there 29 Apr 1874, Alix Adelaide [descended from Kings Henry VII and Edward IV (see the Essex Volume, Tudor Supplement, p 465)], da of Adrien (de Mun), 13th Marquis of Mun [F 1588], and has issue 1d to 1d

1d Count Joseph d'Harcourt (*Paris, 131 rue de Grenelle*), b at Lumigny 20 Dec 1879, m at Paris 1 June 1904, Blanche Anne Marie Josephe, da of Guillaume Charles Joseph Marie (de Melun), 3rd Viscount [F 1819] and Baron [F E 1811] de Melun , and has issue 1e to 3e

1e Bertrand Joseph Marie Pierre d'Harcourt, *b* at Paris 1 Mai 1905

2e Jean Guillaume Marie d'Harcourt, *b* at Paris 6 Sept 1906

3e Guillemette Josephe Marie d'Harcourt, *b* at Brumetz 23 Aug 1908

2d Count Robert d'Harcourt (*Paris, 11 rue de Vaneau*), b at Lumigny 23 Nov 1881

3d Slanie Françoise Marie d'Harcourt, m at Paris 5 Ap 1894, Alexandre Marie Jean Potier de Courcy (Vicomte Potier de Courcy), chef de bat a l'etat-major du IVe corps d'armée t ing (*Le Mans, Paris, 113 rue de Grenelle*), and has issue 1e to 3e [Nos 129187 to 129203

506

# of The Blood Royal

1e Viscount Alfred Pierre Potier de Courcy, b 16 Feb 1895
2e Viscount Xavier René Potier de Courcy, b 18 May 1898
3e Claire Potier de Courcy

4d Adrienne Elisabeth Jeanne Marie d'Harcourt, m at Paris 23 Feb 1899, Maurice Charles Marc René (de Voyer) — Marquis of Argenson (Marquis d Argenson) [F] (Paris, 117 rue Barlet de Jouy, Château des Ormes, Dépt de la Vienne), and has issue 1e

1e Charlotte de Voyer d'Argenson, b 1 Mai 1902

4c Ernestine Jeanne Maria d'Harcourt, b at Paris 25 Mar 1840, d (-), m 15 Ap 1864, Henri, Count de La Tour du Pin-Chambly de la Charce

1b Laure Regine de Choiseul, b at Dieppe 2 Oct 1810, d at Narbonne 11 Feb 1855, m at Paris 12 Feb 1833, Marc Edouard (de Pontevès-Bargème), 1st Duke of Sabran (Duc de Sabran) [F 18 July 1828], d et the Castle du Luc, Arde, 5 Sept 1878, and had issue 1c to 5c

1c Elzéar Charles Antoine (de Pontevès), 2nd Duke of Sabran (Duc de Sabran) [F], K L H, b at Marseilles 19 Ap 1840, d at the Castle of Csicso, Hungary, 6 Ap 1891, m 1st, at Paris, 3 June, Marie Julie, da of Honoré Louis Joseph Marie (d'Albert de Luynes) — Duke of Chevreuse [F 1667] d at the Castle du Lac 15 Nov 1865, and had issue 1d

1d Louise Delphine Marie Valentine de Pontevès, m 1st, at Paris, 10 June 1885, Jules Jean Marie (de Baillardel de Larenty) — Marquis of Tholozan [F], d 25 May 1900, 2ndly, at Hyeres, 1 Dec 1904, Joseph (Horschel) 1st Marquis d'Horschel de Valleford [P S] (Paris)

2c Marie Zosime Edmond (de Pontevès), 3rd Duke of Sabran (Duc de Sabran) [F], b Marseilles 16 Sept 1841, d at the Château de Magnanne 17 Nov 1903, m 1st, at Ménil, Mayenne, 9 Feb 1870, Charlotte Cécile, da of Jules Joseph de la Tullaye, d at Magnanne 19 Dec 1884, and had issue 1d to 3d

1d Hélion Louis Marie Elzéar (de Pontevès), 4th Duke of Sabran (Duc de Sabran) [F] (Château de Magnanne, Mayenne), b there 9 Nov 1873

2d Count Anne (René Louis Marie Elzéar) de Sabran Pontevès, b at Magnanne 13 Sept 1879, m at Paris 27 Nov 1909, Marguerite, da of François Félix Augustin Jubel, Marquis de Limote-Buret

3d Alyette Léonide Elisabeth Regine Marie Delphine de Sabran-Pontevès

3c Delphine Laure Gersinde Eugénie de Sabran-Pontevès (Château de Buisson Rond, Chambéry, Savoy), m at Narbonne 24 June 1852, Ernest Paul Marie (Le Borgne), 3rd Count of Boigne (Conte de Boigne) [Sardinia, 7 June 1816], Member of the Sardinian Parliament, and afterwards Conseiller-general for Savoy b at Chambéry 7 Dec 1829, d at the Castle of Buisson, Savoy, 26 Nov 1895, and has issue (with 2 das d unm) 1d to 6d

1d Benoit (Le Borgne), 4th Count of Boigne (Conte di Boigne) [Sardinia] (Château de Buissonrond, Chambéry, Savoy), b 31 July 1854, m Marie Louise, da of (—) Perquer, d s p 2 Aug 1891

2d Count Elzéard Germain Joseph Le Borgne de Boigne, Officer of Cuirassiers in the French Army, b 12 Feb 1865, d at Alençon 27 Ap 1902, m 18 Nov 1895, Hélène Pauline, da of ( ) de Mandat Grancey, and had issue 1e to 2e

1e François Le Borgno de Boigne
2e Jean Le Borgne de Boigne

3d Edmée Le Borgne de Boigne, m 11 June 1873, Eugène Courtois d'Arcollières (Château de Martorey Morestel, Isère)

4d Marthe Le Borgne de Boigne, m 2 Feb 1884, René, Count de Calonne (Château de Nyon, près St Leger sur-Dheune, Saone et Loire, Château de Paradis, Davaye, Saône et Loire)

5d. Monique Le Borgne de Boigne, } Religieuses
6d Inès-Marie Le Borgne de Boigne, }

[Nos 129204 to 129220

507

The Plantagenet Roll

4c *Anne Marie Inés de Sabran-Ponteves*, b at Marseilles 30 Nov 1836, d at Chambéry 18 Jan 1874, m 1 Aug. 1855, *Charles Felix, Marquis Trédicini de Boffalora*

5c *Marie Victorienne Charlotte de Sabran-Ponteves*, b at Paris 27 Mar 1838, d at the Castle of Roches, Drôme, 18 July 1867, m 25 Oct 1865, *Marie Louis Joseph Alfred de Geoffre de Chabrignac*

5b *Laure Genevière Marie de Choiseul*, b at Dieppe 12 Sept. 1813, d 14 Dec 1873, m 1833, *Charles François Marie Anne Joseph, Marquis of Calvière*

6b *Ilix Laure Marguerite de Choiseul*, b 4 Aug 1820, d at the Castle of Clères 30 Jan 1891, m as 2nd wife, 18 June 1833, Louis Hector (de Galard de Béarn), —th Marquis of Brassac [F], 1st Count of Béarn [F E :1811], a Senator of the Empire (4 Dec 1851) and Min Plen (1853), d 26 Mar 1871, and had issue 1c to 4c

1c *Laure Henri Gaston (de Galard-Béarn)*, —th Marquess of Brassac [F], 2nd Count of Béarn [F E 1811] and (9 July 1868) 1st Prince of Béarn and Viana [Spain], K L H, b at 25 June 1893 m at Paris 10 May 1873, Cécile Charlotte Marie, 13th Princess of Chalais (1450), 9th Marchioness of Excideuil (1713), and 10th Countess of Grignols (1713) [F], 6th Princess of Chalais and Grandee of the 1st Class [Sp 1 Oct 1711], da and h of Count Augustin René Adalbert Paul de Talleyrand-Périgord, and niece and h of Elie Louis Roger (de Talleyrand Périgord), 3rd and last Duke of Périgord [F 26 Dec 1818], 12th Prince of Chalais, &c, d at l'an 11 Dec 1890, and had issue 1d to 6d

1d *Louis Hele Joseph Henri (de Galard-Béarn)* 14th Prince of Chalais (1450), 10th Marquis of Excideuil (1713), and —th Marquis of Brassac (17—) and 11th Count of Grignols (1713) (Prince de Chalais, Marquis d'Excideuil et de Brassac et Comte de Grignols) [F], 3rd Count of Béarn (Comte de Béarn) [F E 1811], 8th Prince of Chalais and Grandee of the 1st Class (1711, confirmed 23 Nov 1904), 2nd Prince of Béarn and Viana (1868) (Prince de Chalais y Grande de España de Primera Clase Prince de Béarn y de Viana) [Spain], &c, styled Prince of Béarn and Chalais (Paris, rue de Commaille, 2 (VIIe), Société Hippique), b at Paris 3 May 1871, m there 23-24 June 1905, Beatrice, da of (—) Wynans of Baltimore, d at St Petersburg 17 Oct 1907, and has issue 1c to 2c

1c Count Gaston (Ross Joseph Henri) de Galard-Béarn, b at St Petersburg 11 Oct 1907

2c (Cecile Nixi Marie) Beatrice de Galard-Béarn, b at St Petersburg 17 Ap 1906

2d Count (Centule Edmond) François de Galard Béarn (Château d'Eslayou, par Lescar, Basse Pyr). b 1875

3d Count Bernard (Etienne Raymond) de Galard-Béarn (Château de Couloutre, par Donzy, Nièvre, Château de Parenchères par Sainte-Foy la-Grand, Gironde), b 1879

4d Count Pierre (Paul Albert Pierre Arnaud) de Galard-Béarn (Châlet Périgord, à Arcachon, Gironde), b 1881

5d Count (Etienne Gabriel) Odon de Galard-Béarn (Chalet Périgord, à Arcachon, Gironde), b 1882

6d Blanche Marie Pauline de Galard-Béarn

2c Count Jean (Césimir Alexandre Gontran) de Galard-Béarn, an Officer in the French Army (Château de Clères, S Inf, Palais Val ry, à Bastia Corse), b 20 Mai 1852, m 24 June 1880, Marie Antoinette, da of Joseph, Count Valéry, a Senator, and has issue 1d to 6d

1d Count Centule de Galard-Béarn, Officier de Cavalerie de Reserve, b 5 Jan 1883

2d Count Hector de Galard-Béarn, Ensigne de vaisseau de 1e classe, b 19 June 1886

3d Count Sancho de Galard-Béarn, b 31 Jan 1888

4d Jeanne de Galard-Béarn

[Nos 129221 to 129233

5d Sabine de Galard-Béarn, m 26 Ap 1910, J. Salomon Koechlin, Capitaine d'Artillerie

6d Pauline de Galard-Béarn

3c Count (Louis Jean Sanche) Arsieu de Galard-Béarn, Attaché d'Ambassade, b 1863

4c Blanche de Galard-Béarn, Religieuse [Nos. 129234 to 129237]

323 Descendants of Lady ELIZABETH BRABAZON (Table XXVIII), d 1725, m 1st, as 2nd wife, Sir PHILIPS COOTE of Mount Coote, co Limerick, bapt. 10 Mar. 1685, d 1715, 2ndly, the Hon PHILIP BERTIE, d s p 1728, and had issue 1a to 3a.

1a Charles Coote of Mount Coote, d 1761, m Catherine, da of Sir Robert Newcomen, 6th Bt [I 1625], and had issue 1b

1b Chidley Coote of Mount Coote, d 24 Jan 1764, m Jane, da of Sir Ralph Gore, 4th Bt [I 1622], M P, and had issue 1c to 2c

1c Charles Coote of Mount Coote, d 17 Sept 1792, m 1775, Elizabeth, da and co-h of Philip Oliver of Altamira, M P, and had issue 1d to 3d

1d Chidley Coote of Mount Coote, b 14 Feb 1776, d 11 July 1843, m 24 July 1797, Ann, da and co-h of the Hon William Williams Hewitt [B Lifford Coll], d 11 Dec 1842, and had issue (with 4 sons d s p) 1e to 3e

1e Charles Eyre Coote, b 5 June 1801, d 12 Mar 1858, m 8 Jan 1828, Catherine Dillon, da of Major Crofton Croker, d 4 Mar 1878 and had issue (with an elder da d s p) 1f to 2f

1f Mary Anne Coote, da and co h, m 5 Feb 1856, William Untack Townsend, d 1888, and has issue

2f Caroline Ahern Coote, da and co-h, m 26 June 1866, Walter James Cummins, and has issue

2e Charles James Coote, Lieut-Col 18th Royal Irish Regt, b 1818, d (-), m Anne, da of Thomas Stewart of Limerick, d 24 May 1853 and had issue (with a son and da d s p) 1f to 3f

1f Charles James Coote of Mount Coote, formerly Capt 18th Royal Irish Regt (Mount Coote, Limerick), b 19 Aug 1837, m 6 June 1867, Emily, da of Very Rev the Hon Henry Pakenham [E of Longford Coll] d s p 23 May 1896

2f Anne Hewitt Coote, m 20 Dec 1866, Henry John Norman of Gildesden, Hayes, Kent, and has issue

3f Ada Coote (Bel Air, Dinard, France), m 17 Nov 1868, the Hon Henry Leslie Pepys [E of Cottenham Coll, &c, descended from the Lady Isabel Plantagenet (see Essex Volume, p 163)], d 18 May 1891, and has issue 1g to 3g

1g Arthur Guy Leslie Pepys, Capt Essex Regt and Adj 5th Batt Royal Warwickshire Regt, b 24 Aug 1875

2g Gerald Leslie Pepys, Capt 57th Wildes Rifles (Indian Frontier Force), b 30 Jan 1879, m 20 June 1907, Charlotte Helen, da of Charles W Lambe Forbes of Auchrannie, co Forfar, and his issue 1h to 2h

1h Charles Donald Leslie Pepys, b 25 Sept 1909

2h Geraldine Mary Leslie Pepys, b 26 Aug 1908

3g Evelyn Pepys, m 3 June 1902, Col John Monteith, C B, formerly 32nd Bombay Lancers (Les Rochers, Dinard, France)

3e Alicia Coote, b in Bath 8 June 1808, d 14 Sept 1855, m as 1st wife, 14 June 1831, John Wingfield King [son of Lieut Gen the Hon Sir Henry King, K C B, 4th son of Robert, 2nd Earl of Kingston [I]], d 19 Sept 1865, and had issue 1f to 8f [Nos 129238 to 129247]

The Plantagenet Roll

1f Henry Edward King, *late* Speaker of the Legislative Assembly, Queensland (*Raymond Terrace, S Brisbane, Queensland*), *b* 9 June 1832, *m* 1 June 1858, Harriette, da of J A Armstrong, and has issue 1g to 8g

    1g Harry Edward Wingfield King, *b* 4 Aug. 1869

    2g John Robert Fitzgerald King, *b* 27 Jan 1871

    3g Wyndham Grey Fitzgerald King, *b* 23 Sept 1872

    4g Gerald Coote King, *b* 9 May 1874

    5g Maurice James King, *b* 31 Jan 1879

    6g Alice Caroline King, *m* 1886, Edward Hubert Waring (*Macknade Mill, Herbert River, N Queensland*), and has issue 1h to 5h

        1h John King Waring, *b* 1888

        2h Hubert Parker Waring, *b* 1889

        3h Frank Jocelyn Waring, *b* 1893

        4h Lavinia Katherine Waring, *b* 1891

        5h Alicia Armstrong Waring, *b* 1898

    7g Katherine Anne King, *m* 1885, William Howe

    8g Ethel Coote King

2f John Robert King, Col R A , *b* 13 Nov 1837, d (–), *m* 26 *Sept* 1872, *Kate Elizabeth, da of Lieut -Gen John Henry Francklyn, R A , C B , and had issue* 1g to 3g

    1g Robert Alen King, *b* 1874

    2g Robert Guy Cecil King, *b* 1877

    3g [da] King, *b* 1880

3f Mary Anne Alicia King, *m* 20 July 1859, the Rev Matthew Kerr, a Presbyterian Minister, and has issue 1g to 3g

    1g John Robert King Kerr, *b* 30 July 1861

    2g Alicia Coote Kerr

    3g Mary King Kerr

4f Caroline King

5f Anne Katherine King

6f Marian Alice King, *m* 1st, 1870, Charles James Buckland, d (–), 2ndly, James Green Davis

7f Isabella King, *m* 12 Nov 1870, William Macdonald Browne , and has issue 1g to 2g

    1g William Coote Browne, *b* 4 Feb 1874

    2g Jessie Alicia Browne

8f Louisa Augusta King

2d *Rev Charles Philips Coote, Rector of Doon, Limerick,* d 1838 , *m Anne, da of Charles Atkinson of Rehins, co Mayo , and had issue (with 2 elder sons known to have d s p)* 1e to 6e

    1e Cholley Oliver Coote

    2e William Philip Oliver Coote

    3e *Mary Coote, m* 1838, *Thomas Lloyd , and had issue*

    4e Eliza Coote, *m* Richard Lloyd

    5e Ann Coote, *m* Capt Stack

    6e Harriet Lucinda Coote, *m.* John Tennant

3d Elizabeth Coote, *m* Major Caleb Barnes

2c *Elizabeth Coote, m James King of Gola*

2a *Cecilia Coote*

3a *Elizabeth Coote*

[Nos 129248 to 129281.

# of The Blood Royal

324 Descendants of Lady CATHERINE BRABAZON (Table XXVIII),
d (-); m ALONZO VERE, and had issue (with 2 sons, Thomas
and William, who d unm[1]) 1a

 1a *Mary Vere*, m (—) *Usher*

325. Descendants of the Hon RICHARD LENNARD, *afterwards* (1644)
Barrett, of Horsford, co Norfolk, and Bellhouse, co Essex
(Table XXVIII), d 1696, m ANNE, da of the Hon Sir
Robert LOFTUS [V Loftus Coll], and had issue 1a to 2a

 1a *Dacre Barrett Lennard of Bellhouse, co Essex, High Sheriff for the co 1706
d 1723, m 1st, Lady Jane, da of Arthur (Chichester), 2nd Earl of Donegal [I],
2ndly, Elizabeth, da and co-h of Thomas Moore of co Monaghan, 3rdly, Sarah,
widow of Richard Saltonstall of Groves, co Essex, da of Sir Capel Luckyn, 2nd Bt
[E 1629], and had issue 1b to 3b*
  1b[1] *Richard Barrett-Lennard, d v p Dec 1716, m 15 July 1716, Anne
(Lennard), suo jure 16th Baroness Dacre [E], d 26 June 1755, and had issue*
  See p 503, Nos 128714–129159

  2b[1] *Dorothy Barrett Lennard, m 1722, Hugh Smith of Weald Hall, co Essex,
and had issue 1c to 2c*
   1c *Dorothy Smith, da and co h, m 1746, the Hon John Barry [E of Barry-
more Coll], and had issue 2 sons who d s p l*
   2c *Lucy Smith d 7 Feb 1759, m 17 Mar 1747, James Stanley, afterwards
Smith-Stanley, Lord Strange [son and h-app of Edward, 11th Earl of Derby [E]],
d v p 1 June 1771, and had issue*
   See the Exeter Volume, Table XLIII and pp 509–513, Nos 44310–44711

  3b *Catherine Barrett-Lennard, m Sir Philip Hall of Upton, co Essex, High
Sheriff for that co 1726, and had issue (with 3 das)[2] 1c*
   1c *Philip Hall*

  2a *Anne Barrett-Lennard d Jan 1718, m Carew Hervey Mildmay of
Marks, co Essex, High Sheriff 1712, b 1658, d 1743, and had issue 1b to 2b*
   1b *Carew Hervey Mildmay of Marks, &c, M P, d s p s 16 Jan 1784*
   2b *Humphrey Hervey Mildmay, b 1692, d 9 July 1761, m 20 Aug 1706,
Letitia, da and h of Halliday Mildmay of Shawford House, co Hants, and Stoke
Newington, d Oct 1749, and had issue*
   See the Exeter Volume, Table XXXI and pp 413–416, Nos 34237–34434
[Nos 129282 to 130327

326 Descendants of the Hon CATHERINE LENNARD (Table XXVIII),
d (-); m CHALONER CHUTE of The Vine, co Hants, and had
issue 1a to 3a

 1a *Edward Chute of the Vine, m and had issue which became extinct 1776*
 2a *Thomas Chute of Pickenham Hall, co Norfolk, after 1700, d (-), m.
Elizabeth, da of (—) Rivett, and had issue which became extinct 25 Sept 1885*
 3a *Elizabeth Chute, m Sir Charles Cotterell, Bt[3] (sic)*

---

 [1] Playfair's "Peerage," iv 207
 [2] Collins, 1779, vi 388
 [3] Burke's "Commoners," i 634

511

The Plantagenet Roll

327 Descendants, if any surviving, of the Hon MARGARET LENNARD (Table XXVIII), m Sir ANNESLEY WILDEGOSS [son of Sir John Wildegoss of Ridgcourt, co Sussex], d s p , and had issue 1a

1a Robert Wildegoss, a student at Leyden, aged 19 in 1634, only son [1]

328 Descendants of GEORGE PARKER of Ratton, co Sussex (Table XXVIII), bapt at Willingdon, June 1620, d 2 July 1673; m MARY, da of Sir Richard NEWDIGATE of Arbury, 1st Bt [E 1677], and had issue 1a to 2a

1a Sir Robert Parker of Ratton, 1st Bt [E 22 May 1674], M P, b c 1655, d 30 Nov 1691, m 5 Feb 1674. Sarah, da of George Chute of Brixton Causeway, d 2 Aug 1708, and had issue 1b to 2b

1b Sir George Parker, 2nd Bt [E], M P, b 1677, d 18 June 1726, m 25 Feb 1692, Mary, da of Sir Walter Bagot, 3rd Bt [E 1627], d 14 May 1727, and had issue 1c to 5c

1c Sir Walter Parker, 3rd Bt [E], b c 1700, d unm 19 Ap 1750
2c Sarah Parker, m Thomas Luxford of Laming, co Sussex
3c Anne Parker
4c Jane Parker
5c Philadelphia Parker, m Nathaniel Trayton of Lewes, and apparently had issue 1d
1d (—) Trayton, m John Lidgiter, and had issue 1e
1e Eleanor Lidgiter who succeeded to the Parker estates, 1750, as heiress of the Traytons, bur at Waldron 7 Feb 1770 m Thomas Fuller [7th son of John Fuller of Brightling, co Sussex, J P], and had issue[2] 1f to 2f
1f John Fuller, m Ann, da of Sir George Elliot
2f Rose Fuller, Merchant
2b Philadelphia Parker, b 1701[3], m Col Piper of Essex [4]

2a Richard Parker of Hedson, co Bucks, m Sarah, da and co-h of Robert Child of Isleworth, co Middx , and had issue 1b to 3b [5]
1b Jeffrey Parker
2b Juliana Parker, m Cecil Bowyer
3b Elizabeth Parker, m William Bowyer

329. Descendants of WILLIAM CAMPION of Combwell Priory, co Kent, and Danny, co Sussex (Table XXVIII), d (—); m. FRANCES, da of Sir John GLYNDE, Sergeant-at-Law to King Charles II. , and had issue 1a to 2a

1a Henry Campion of Danny, co Sussex, and Combwell Priory, co Kent, d (—), m Barbara, da and h of Peter Courthope of Danny aforesaid , and had issue 1b to 2b
1b William Campion of Danny, bapt at Hurstpierpoint 1700, d 1771; m Elizabeth, da of Edward Partenche of Ely, co Camb , d 1768, and had issue 1c to 3c

---

[1] Berry's "Sussex Pedigrees," p 10
[2] Berry's "Sussex Genealogies," p 279
[3] Ibid , p 228
[4] Burke's "Extinct Baronetcies," p 101
[5] Ibid.

# of The Blood Royal

1c *Henry Courthope Campion of Danny*, b 1734, d *July* 1811, m Henrietta, da of Sir John Heathcote, 2nd Bt [G B 1733] M P, d 6 Feb 1771, and had issue 1d

1d *William John Campion of Danny, High Sheriff co Suss* x 1820, b 19 July 1770, d 20 Jan 1855, m 16 Jan 1797, Jane, da of Francis Motley Austen of Kippington, co Kent, d 1857, and had issue 1e to 3e

1e *William John Campion of Danny, J P, D L*, b 16 Nov 1804, d 27 June 1869, m 17 Jan 1829, Harriet, da of Thomas Read Kemp of Kemptown, Brighton, d 3 Jan 1900, and had issue 1f to 5f

1f William Henry Campion of Danny, C B, J P, Hon Col, late Lieut -Col Comdg 2nd Vol Batt Royal Sussex Regt, *formerly Capt 72nd and 53rd Regts* (*Danny, Hurstpierpoint, Sussex*), b 1 Ap 1836, m 2 Sept 1869, the Hon Gertrude [descended from George, Duke of Clarence, K G (see Clarence Volume, p 401)], da of Henry Bouverie William (Brand), 1st Viscount Hampden [U K], and has issue (with a son, Charles, killed in action in South Africa 29 May 1901, and a da d young) 1g to 6g

1g William Robert Campion, b 3 July 1870, m 5 July 1894, Katherine May [descended from the Lady Anne, sister of Edward IV (see Exeter Volume, p 317)], da of Rev the Hon William Byron, and has issue 1h to 4h

1h William Simon Campion, b 1895

2h [son] Campion

3h Dorothy Campion

4h [da] Campion

2g Frederick Henry Campion, b 8 Sept 1872

3g Edward Campion, Lieut Seaforth Highlanders, b 17 Dec 1873

4g Mary Gertrude Campion, *unm*.

5g Alice Campion, m 8 Dec 1908, Charles Augustus Phillimore, M A , and has issue

See p 453, No 95083

6g John Campion, *unm*

2f Charles Walter Campion, B A (Oxon), Bar at-Law of Lincoln's Inn, and Examiner of Standing Orders, House of Commons (*52 Lennox Gardens S W*), b 10 Nov 1839, m 27 May 1879, Charlotte Susan [descended from George, Duke of Clarence, K G (see Clarence Volume, p 128)], da of Hugh Horatio Seymour

3f Caroline Florence Campion (*16 Prince's Gardens, S W*), m 3 Jan 1856, John George (Dodson), 1st Baron Monk-Bretton [U K 4 Nov 1884], P C, Chancellor of the Duchy of Lancaster 1882-1884, Pres of the Local Govt Board 1880-1882, &c, b 18 Oct 1825, d 25 May 1897, and had issue 1g to 3g

1g John William (Dodson), 2nd Baron Monk-Bretton [U K], C B, J P, D L, Capt Sussex Yeo, Private Sec to Sec of State for Colonies (Rt Hon Joseph Chamberlain, M P) 1900-1903, &c (*Conyboro, Lewes, Travellers', Brooks'*), b 22 Sept 1869

2g Hon Ethel Millicent Dodson

3g Hon Mildred Augusta Dodson

4f Frances Campion, m 17 June 1857, John George Blencowe of Bineham, co Sussex, M P, J P, D L, b 28 Feb 1817, d 28 Ap 1900, and has issue 1g to 8g

1g Robert Campion Blencowe of Bineham, &c, J P (*Bineham, Chailey near Lewes, Skippetts House, Basingstoke*), b 16 May 1858, m 28 Oct 1886, Augusta Frederica, da of Frederick Boughton Newton Dickenson of Syston Court, Bath, d s p 13 Ap 1905

2g John Ingham Blencowe, b 14 Dec 1860, m 21 Feb 1889, Mabel, da of James Ingram of Ades, Chailey, co Sussex, and has issue 1h

1h Margaret Blencowe

3g *William Poole Blencowe*, b 6 Feb 1869, d 14 Dec 1900, m 21 June 1900, Muriel, da of Henry Courage of Gravenhurst, Bolney, Sussex, and had issue 1h

1h Deborah Blencowe   [Nos 130328 to 130349

The Plantagenet Roll

4g Florence Charlotte Blencowe, m 25 Feb 1886, Major John William Ainslie Drummond, *formerly* Scots Guards, and has issue (5 children)

5g Harriet Blencowe, m 19 Oct 1892, Col Richard Woodford Deane, Lancashire Fusiliers, and has issue 2 sons and 2 das

6g Frances Isabel Blencowe, *unm*

7g Mary Blencowe, m 29 Ap 1905, W H Edwards, and has issue (1 child)

8g Elizabeth Penelope Blencowe, m 19 Jan 1898, the Rev Arthur Hamilton Boyd, Rector of Slaugham [5th son of Sir John Boyd of Maxpoffle, Lord Provost of Edinburgh] (*Slaugham Rectory, Sussex*), and has issue 1h to 2h

  1h William Arthur Hamilton Boyd b 29 Jan 1901

  2h James Hamilton Boyd, b 18 Jan 1903

  5f *Mary Georgina Campion*, d 26 Nov 1874, m 3 Oct 1861, *the Rev Ferdinand Ernest Tower [cadet of Tower of Huntsmoor Park, co Bucks], b 4 Oct 1820, d 21 Jan 1885, and had issue (with a son d unm*) 1g to 7g

  1g Rev Henry Tower, M V O, M A (Oxon) Rector of Holy Trinity, Windsor, Acting Chaplain to the Forces (*Holy Trinity Rectory, Windsor*), b 15 July 1862, m 4 June 1901, Kate Theresa, widow of S F Gedge, da of the Right Hon H Escombe, Prime Minister of Natal, and has issue 1h to 2h

    1h Ernest Conyers Tower, b 28 Feb 1904

    2h Cicely Tower, b 9 July 1902

  2g Rev Frederick Tower, M A (Oxon), Vicar of Badminton (*Badminton Vicarage, Glos*), b 10 Dec 1863 m 4 Dec 1894, Katrine Amy, da of the Hon G C Hawker of the Briars, Adelaide, S A

  3g William Tower, b 27 Sept 1866

  4g David Eric Tower, b 1 Mar 1870

  5g Walter Ernest Tower (*Old Place, Lindfield, Hayward's Heath, Sussex*), b 9 Mar 1873, m 12 July 1902, Marion Lindsay, da of Æneas Ranald Macdonell, Chief of Glengarry, and has issue 1h to 3h

    1h Anthony Paschal Tower, b 13 Ap 1903

    2h Barbara Tower, b 28 Sept 1905

    3h Cecilia Tower, b 15 May 1909

  6g Agatha Tower, *unm*

  7g May Tower, *unm*

  2e *Rev Charles Heathcote Campion, B A (Oxon), Rector of Westmeston, co Sussex, and Prebendary of Chichester Cathedral, b 11 Feb 1814, d 8 Oct 1888, m 16 May 1842, Cecil Lydia, da of James Henry Sclater of Newick Park, co Sussex, d 26 Dec 1872, and had issue (with 2 sons d s p*) 1f to 4f

  1f Heathcote Francis George Campion, Lieut-Col *late* Connaught Rangers (*Beacon Nursery, Ditchling, Hassock, Sussex*), b 12 Sept 1853, *unm*

  2f Charles Cecil Campion (*Castle Gate, Lodge, Lewes*), b 20 Sept 1848, *unm*

  3f Jane Cecil Campion, m 28 Sept 1892, the Rev Walter Lock, D D, Warden of Keble College (*Keble College, Oxford*), and has issue 1g to 5g

    1g Walter Heathcote Lock, b 5 Dec 1900

    2g Cecil May Lock

    3g Elizabeth Jessie Lock

    4g Lucy Austen Lock

    5g Mildred Susan Lock

  4f Selina Letitia Campion, *unm*

  3e *Frances Henrietta Campion, b 2 Mar 1809, d at San Remo, 15 Feb 1878, m 1 Nov 1843, the Rev Augustus Packe, Rector of Walton, co Leic, d Feb 1861, and had issue* 1f

  1f Georgiana Frances Packe (*Asherne, Dartmouth, Devonshire*), *unm*

  2c *William Campion of Lewes, co Sussex, d there 1818, m 2ndly, 5 Sept 1774, Priscilla, da of John Page of Oporto, and had issue* 1d to 2d

[Nos 130350 to 130378

# of The Blood Royal

1d *Henrietta Campion, da and event co-h*, b at Oporto 16 *July* 1778, d 13 *Mar* 1813, m 20 *Jan* 1820, *the Rev P G Crofts, Rector of St John's, Lewes*

2d *Amelia Campion, da and event co-h*, b 26 *Feb* 1787, d 10 *July* 1849, m 20 *Jan* 1808, *George Courthope of Bedford Square, London, and Whiligh, co Sussex* (see p 517), b Sept. 1767, d 13 *Jan* 1835, *and had issue (with 2 das d unm)* 1e to 4e

    1e *George Campion Courthope of Whiligh, co Sussex, J P, D L, High Sheriff for that co* 1850, b 22 *Feb* 1811, d 7 *Sept* 1895, m 15 *Jan* 1841, *Anna, da of John Deacon of Mabledon, Tonbridge*, d 12 *Dec* 1897, *and had issue (with a son and 2 das d unm)* 1f to 5f

      1f *George John Courthope of Whiligh, co Sussex, and Spivers, co Kent, M A (Oxon), J P, D L, Bar-at-Law, &c (Whiligh, Sussex, St Stephens)*, b 3 Nov 1818, m 21 Sept 1876, Elinor Sarah, da of Lieut Col Edward Loyd of Lillesden Hawkhurst, co Kent, J P, D L, d 25 Dec 1895, and his issue (with 2 sons and a da d young) 1g to 5g

        1g *George Loyd Courthope, M P Rye Div of Sussex* 1906, J P, Bar-at-Law, Capt 5th Batt (Cinque Ports) Royal Sussex Regt *(Fairview, Hawkhurst, Kent, Carlton, Constitutional, &c)*, b 12 June 1877, m 14 June 1899, Hilda Gertrude, da of Major-Gen Henry Pelham Close, B S C, and has issue 1h to 2h

          1h Hilda Beryl Courthope, b 2 Nov 1900

          2h Elinor Daphne Courthope, b 11 Oct 1902

        2g John Edward Courthope, b 28 Jan 1882

        3g Robert Courthope, b 15 Mar 1891

        4g Barbara Frances Courthope

        5g Elinor Joan Courthope

      2f William Francis Courthope, b 2 June 1850

      3f Alexander Courthope, b 20 Jan 1852

      4f Emily Mary Courthope

      5f Frances Albinia Courthope

    2e *Rev William Courthope, Vicar of South Malling, Sussex*, b Jan 1816, d 7 Mar 1849, m 29 Sept 1841, *Caroline Elizabeth, da of John Ryle of Henbury Hall, co. Chester, M P*, d 6 June 1857, and had issue 1f to 3f

      1f *William John Courthope, C B, M A (Oxon), Hon D Lit (Durham), Hon LL D (Edin), Hon Fellow of New College, Oxon, Professor of Poetry, Oxford, 1895-1900, and 1st Civil Service Commissioner 1892-1907, is a Fellow of British Academy of Letters, Editor of Pope's Works and Author of "A History of English Poetry," "The Paradise of Birds," &c (The Lodge, Wadhurst, Athenaeum)*, b 17 July 1842, m 2 Nov 1870, Mary, da of John Scott, Inspector-Gen of Hospitals, Bombay, and has issue 1g to 6g

        1g William George Courthope, b 28 Nov 1871

        2g John Courthope, b 15 Mar 1876

        3g Edward Arthur Courthope, b 28 Nov 1879

        4g Richard Alan Courthope, b 8 Oct 1882

        5g Katherine Courthope, m 1897, the Rev Charles Fiennes Cholmondeley, Rector of Little Sampford [descended from King Henry VII (see Tudor Roll, p 154)] *(Little Sampford Rectory, Essex)*

        6g Emily Mary Dorothea Courthope, *unm*

      2f *Frederic George Courthope, J P (Southover, Lewes)*, b 26 Nov 1845, m 14 Sept 1869, Lucy, da of William Smith Uppleby of Bonby, co Linc, and has issue (with 2 elder sons d young) 1g to 4g

        1g Ronald Frederic Courthope, b 18 Jan 1881

        2g Wilfred Herbert Frederic Courthope, b 28 Oct 1883

        3g Margaret Esther Lucy Courthope

        4g Caroline Hilda Courthope, m 19 Nov 1903, John Grahame Slee *(Oceanside, S California)*

                                                                                  [Nos 130379 to 130402

The Plantagenet Roll

3f *Caroline Susan Courthope* d 22 Mar 1896, m 15 *Sept* 1864, *Vice-Adm George Stanley Bosanquet, R N* (see below) (*Bitchet Wood, Sevenoaks*), *and had issue* 1g *to* 2g

1g William Cecil Bosanquet, M A , M D , F R C P , *late* Fellow of New College, Oxford, b 12 Oct 1866

2g Ethel Bosanquet, m 23 June 1896, the Rev Horace Ricardo Wilkinson, B A , Vicar of Stoke by Nayland [son of Horace Wilkinson of Frankfield, Seal, Chart] (*Stoke by-Nayland Vicarage, Colchester*), d 1908, and has issue 1h *to* 3h

1h Horace Norman Stanley Wilkinson
2h Kathleen Courthope Wilkinson
3h Naomi Wilkinson

3c *Emily Courthope*, d 1 *Jan* 1869, m 4 *Feb* 1830, *Samuel Richard Bosanquet of Dingestow Court, co* Monmouth. *J P , D L , Chairman Quarter Sessions*, b 1 Ap 1800, d 27 Dec 1882, *and had issue (with a son and da d s p)* 1f *to* 10f

1f Samuel Courthope Bosanquet of Dingestow, M A (Oxon), J P , D L , Chairman of Quarter Sessions and High Sheriff (1898) co Monmouth (*Dingestow Court, co Monmouth*), *b* 2 Oct 1832, m 7 Aug 1862, Mary [descended from George, Duke of Clarence, K G (see Clarence Volume, p 111)], da of John Arkwright of Hampton Court, co Hereford , and has issue 1g *to* 3g

1g Samuel Ronald Courthope Bosanquet, LL B (Camb), J P , co Monmouth, b 6 Sept 1868

2g Vivian Henry Courthope Bosanquet, H B M 's Vice-Consul at Moscow, b 13 Ap 1872

3g Maud Bosanquet

2f *Rev Claude Bosanquet, M A (Oxon), Vicar of Christchurch, Folkestone,* b 8 Nov 1833, d 3 *June* 1897, m 22 May 1861, *his cousin-german Amelia Eleanor, da of Vice-Adm Charles John Bosanquet, R N , and had issue (with a son d young)* 1g *to* 4g

1g Rev Claude Charles Courthope Bosanquet, M A (Oxon), Vicar of Linkinhorne (*Linkinhorne Vicarage, Callington, Cornwall*), b 19 Dec 1862, m 9 Feb 1892, Millicent Percy, da of Gen Percy Smith, R E , and has issue 1h *to* 4h

1h Armytage Percy Bosanquet, b 1893
2h Claude Henry Bosanquet, b 1896
3h Lancelot Stephen Bosanquet, b 1903
4h Hilda Mary Bosanquet

2g Charles Richard Bosanquet, b 21 Ap 1865

3g Rev Reginald Albert Bosanquet, M A (Oxon), Chaplain in the Scilly Isles (*The Chaplaincy, Scilly Isles*), b 14 June 1867

4g Eustace Fulcrand Bosanquet, J P co Wilts b 20 Ap 1871, m 6 June 1891, Harriet Maria, da of Frederic W Moore of Buenos Ayres, d 1901, and has issue 1h *to* 2h

1h Nancy Bosanquet
2h Inez Bosanquet

3f George Stanley Bosanquet, Rear-Adm R N (*Bitchet Woods, Sevenoaks*), b 18 Ap 1835, m 15 Sept 1864, Caroline Susan, da of the Rev William Courthope, d 22 Mar 1896, and had issue
See above, Nos 130403–130407

4f Sir Frederick Albert Bosanquet, M A , K C , J P , Common Serjeant for the City of London since 1900, *formerly* Recorder of Wolverhampton 1891 and 1900, and of Worcester 1879–1891, &c (*12 Grenville Place, S W , Cobbe Place, Lewes*), b 8 Feb 1837, m 1st, 22 Aug 1871, Albinia Mary, da of John Curtis Hayward of Quedgeley House, co Gloue , d (–) , 2ndly, 12 Aug 1885, Philippa Frances, da of William Bence Jones of Lisselan, co Cork , and has issue 1g *to* 6g

1g Rev Bernard Hugh Bosanquet, M A (Camb), Vicar of Thames Ditton (*Thames Ditton Vicarage*), b 21 Nov 1872

2g Geoffrey Courthope Bosanquet, b 26 Dec 1876   [Nos 130403 to 130430

516

# of The Blood Royal

3g William Sydney Bence Bosanquet, *b* 9 May 1893.

4g [1] Lilian Bosanquet.

5g [1] Nora Margaret Bosanquet

6g [2] Edith Madeline Bosanquet

5f *Walter Henry Bosanquet of Hope Park, Bromley*, b 10 *Jan* 1839, d 9 Oct 1904, m 5 *Ap* 1866, *Penelope Eliza, da of the Rev Stewart Forster of Southend, Lewisham*, *and had issue* 1g *to* 3g

1g Henry Stewart Bosanquet, *b* 29 Jan 1867

2g Evelyn Mabel Bosanquet, *m* 18 Oct 1900, the Rev William Shuckford Flynn, A K C London Univ (*The Rosary, Heath Road, Hayward's Heath*), and has issue 1h

1h John Henry Flynn, *b* 13 Ap 1903

3g Florence Mary Bosanquet, *m* 23 July 1902, the Rev Bertie Phelips, M A (Oxon), Vicar of Smalley (*Smalley Vicarage, Derby*) [son of Major-Gen Robert Hoskyns Phelips, descended from George, Duke of Clarence, K G (see Clarence Volume, p 112)] (*Church View, Heanor, Derby*) and has issue 1h to 2h

1h Beryl Penelope Phelips }
2h Edith Mary Phelips   } (twins), b 31 Aug 1903

6f *Edmund Fletcher Bosanquet* (*The Court, Wotton-under-Edge*), b 2 Sept 1840, m 20 Jan 1876, Louisa, da of Major Henry Christopher Marriott of Avonbank, co Worc , and has issue (with a son and da d unm) 1g to 3g

1g Edmund Marriott Bosanquet, Lieut R A , *b* 24 Mar 1878

2g Ernest Courthope Bosanquet, Lieut R N , *b* 11 June 1879

3g Catherine Marriott Bosanquet, *m* 28 Jan 1904, Francis Anthony Cedric Wright [son of Philip Wright of Mellington, co Montgomery] (*West Summerland, British Columbia*), and has issue 1h to 3h

1h Noel Nithsdale Wright, *b* 23 Dec 1904

2h Rupert Anthony Wright, *b* 31 Aug 1906

3h Basil Owen Wright, *b* 10 July 1909

7f William David Bosanquet *b* 4 June 1819, *m* 7 Aug 1872, Elinor, da of George Hamilton Verity , and has issue 1g

1g Mabel Bosanquet, *m* Edward Alexander, Ceylon C S

8f *Richard Arthur Bosanquet* (*Bank House, Windsor*), b 25 May 1852 , m 15 Nov 1888, Ruth Rivers, da of Sir Augustus Rivers Thompson, Lieut -Gov of Bengal 1862-1867 , and has issue 1g to 3g

1g Arthur Rivers Bosanquet, *b* 12 July 1890

2g Raymond Francis Bosanquet, *b* 3 Sept 1895

3g Cicely Ruth Bosanquet

9f *Emily Letitia Bosanquet*, d 19 May 1898 , m 3 Oct 1861, the Rev John Lloyd, M A , Rector of Llanvapley, co Mon , and had issue 1g to 2g

1g Emily Mary Edith Lloyd, *m* 26 Aug 1891, Charles John Bosanquet, Electrical Engineer , and has issue 1h to 2h

1h Sydney Courthope Bosanquet, *b* 15 July 1894

2h Leslie Frederick Ives Bosanquet, *b* 17 June 1900

2g Violet Amy Lloyd

10f Fanny Elizabeth Bosanquet, *unm*

4e *Frances Courthope*, d *Jan* 1841 , m *the Rev Henry Watkins*

3c *Frances Barbara Campion*, d (-) , m 1766, *George Courthope of Bedford Square, London, and Whiligh, co Sussex*, d 1828 , *and had issue* 1d to 2d

1d *George Courthope of Bedford Square, London, and Whiligh, co Sussex*, b Sept 1767, d 13 *Jan* 1835, m 20 *Jan* 1808, *Amelia, da of William Campion of Lewes*, d 10 *July* 1819 , *and had issue*

See p 515, Nos 130379–130478

[Nos 130431 to 130538

2d Rev *William Henry Courthope* of *St John's College, Cambridge, Vicar of Whiligh, in Marx, da and co-h of William Peckham of Arches, co Sussex* [1]

2b *Catherine Courthope*, d (-), m 11 *Nov* 1735, *George Courthope of Whiligh, co Sussex, d Ap 1793, and had (with other) issue* 1c

1c *George Courthope of Whiligh, and Bedford Square, London,* b 22 *Nov* 1737, d 1828, m 1766, *Frances Barbara, da of William Campion of Danny Place, and had issue*

2a *Francis Campion,* d (-), m (—) *Clutterbuck of Southampton*

330 Descendants of PHILADELPHIA PARKER (Table XXVIII), d (-); m at Willingdon 1 Feb 1649, SAMUEL BOYS of Hawkhurst, co Kent, b 1617, d 3 June 1688, and had issue [2] 1a to 7a.

1a *William Boys of Hawkhurst,* d 1698, m *Elizabeth, da of Sir Anthony Shirley 1st Bt* [E 1665], *and had issue (with a son and 6 das who all apparently* d s p) 1b *to* 3b

1b *Samuel Boys of Hawkhurst,* d 1753, m *Jane, da of Sir Richard Newdigate, 2nd Bt* [E 1677], *M P, and had issue (with 4 sons and 3 das who all apparently* d s p) 1c

1c *Samuel Boys of Hawkhurst,* d 16 *May* 1772, m *Elizabeth, da and co-h of Thomas Hicks of Mountfield, co Sussex, and had issue (with 2 das d unm)* 1d *to* 3d

1d *Samuel Boys of Hawkhurst, High Sheriff co Kent* 1782, d *at Hawkhurst* 1 *May* 1795, m *Elizabeth, da of Henry Gatland of Cuckfield, co Sussex. and had issue* 1e

1e *Elizabeth Boys, da and h,* b 1 *Feb* 1762, d (-), m 16 *Jan* 1786, *Charles Lamb of Higham, co Sussex, and had issue* 1f

1f *Elizabeth Dorothy Lamb, da and h,* d (-), m *at Salehurst, co Sussex,* 13 *Dec* 1809, *the Rev Thomas Ferris of Hawkhurst, Thackham, and Clothall's, Grinstead, co Sussex [eldest son of the Very Rev Thomas Ferris, Dean of Battle], and had issue (with 3 sons and 2 das who d s p)* 1g *to* 4g

1g *Rev Thomas Boys Ferris, Rector of Guiseley,* b 1 *Nov* 1810, d 2 *Sept* 1878, m 13 *Aug* 1842, *Hannah, da of William Barraclough of Leeds, Manufacturer,* d 22 (?) *Mar* 1902, *and had issue (with 2 sons d unm)* 1h *to* 1h

1h Rev Thomas Boys Barraclough Ferris, M A, and sometime (1868-1870) Fellow of Durham, Rector of Gonalston and Canon of Southwell (*Gonalston Rectory, Notts*), b 1 Ap 1815, m 28 Dec 1870, Maria Teresa, da of William Edward Swaine of York, M D, and has issue (with 2 sons, Arthur Henry and Wilfred, and a da, Mabel Teresa, all d unm) 1i to 10i

1i Rev Thomas Edward Swaine Ferris, M A, Curate of Dunham, Notts, b 2 Oct 1871

2i William Arthur Boys Ferris, Manager and Traveller (*Sherwood, Nottingham*), b 23 Oct 1872, m 18 May 1901, Nellie, da of William Hutchinson Farmer of Nottingham, Lace Manufacturer, and has issue 1j to 2j

1j Joan Farmer Ferris, b 22 Ap 1902

2j Mary Boys Ferris, b 24 July 1906

3i Godfrey Francis Ferris, Assist Sec to Jesuit Fathers' Apostolic Mission House, Washington, U S A, b 13 Dec 1873

4i Cecil Ernest Ferris, Assist Master Southport High School (*Southport, Queensland*), b 9 Mar 1877 [Nos 130539 to 130545]

---

[1] Hasted's "Kent," ii 375

[2] Dallaway's "Sussex," II ii 215, also Berry's "Sussex Genealogies," 1830, p 318

5: Rev Hermann Boys Ferris, L Th Durham Univ, Curate of Holy Trinity, Stockton (1 *Laurence Street, Stockton-on-Tees*), b 6 May 1881

6: Andrew Octavius Ferris, settled in Canada, b 30 Nov 1883

7: Nowell Swaine Ferris, Organist and Choir Master, St Matthew's, Winnipeg, b 21 Dec 1884

8: Ernest Hugh Ferris, Lace Buyer, St Gall, b 22 Sept 1886

9: Dora Christiana Ferris, m 2 July 1907, Cyril Horner Bearder [son of William Corthan Bearder, Lace Manufacturer] (*Nottingham*), and has issue 1*j*

　1*j* Teresa Joyce Ferris Bearder, b 23 Sept 1908

10: Ernestine Emily Ferris, b 12 Mar 1888

2*h* William Godfrey Ferris (*Roseneath, Terrace Road, Dulwich Hill, N S W*), b 16 July 1853, m Emily Eleanor, da of Thomas Chilton, Station Manager, N S W, and his issue (see Appendix)

3*h* Elizabeth Martha Ferris, b 15 Oct 1846, m 4 Nov 1876, the Rev Oscar Dan Watkins, M A (Oxon), Vicar of Holywell, *formerly* Archdeacon of Lucknow (*Holywell Vicarage, Oxford*), and has issue (with 4 other sons, Basil Henry, Clement Reginald, Cuthbert Thomas, and Noel Christopher, who all d young) 1: to 3:

　1: Oscar Ferris Watkins, M A (Oxon), Assist District Commr at Mombasa, British East Africa, b 23 Dec 1877

　2: Laurence Theodore Watkins, B A (Camb), Assist Master, King William's College, Isle of Man, b 6 July 1887

　3: Dorothy Anne Watkins, *unm*

4*h* Cordelia Frances Ferris, m 12 Sept 1883, Herbert Glanville South (62 *Leyham Vale, Streatham*), and has issue 1: to 2:

　1: Algernon Cedric South, b 18 Oct 1885
　2: Bertha Winifred South, b 29 Sept 1887

2*g* *William Ferris, Indigo Merchant,* b 1 Aug 1814, d 23 May 1864, m at Calcutta 10 Jan 1841, Georgina, da of S Robinson of Islington Square, London, d 17 Dec 1873, and had issue (with 2 sons and 2 das d unm) 1*h* to 3*h*

1*h* Georgina Emily Ferris, m 31 Jan 1901, Cyril Ward Perkins [son of the Rev B R Perkins, B C L (Oxon), Vicar of Wotton-under-Edge] (*The Brands, Wotton-under-Edge, Glos*), s p

2*h* Gertrude Cecilia Ferris, m 30 Sept 1879, the Rev William Clarke Leeper, M A (T C D), Rector of Mellis [son of the Rev William Leeper, Rector of All Saints, Lynn] (*Mellis Rectory, Eye, Suffolk*), and has issue 1: to 7:

　1: Leonard Leeper, B E (Royal Univ Irel), A M I C E, Borough Surveyor's Office, Great Yarmouth, b 10 Dec 1880

　2: Rev Clement Leeper, B A, Curate of Retford, Notts, b 9 Feb 1882

　3: Alban Leeper, Prudential Assurance Co, High Holborn, b 25 Jan 1883

　4: Bernard Leeper, National Provincial Bank, Ipswich, b 29 May 1887.

　5: Bertha Mary Leeper, *unm*

　6: Dorothy Leeper, *unm*

　7: Mildred Leeper, *unm*

3*h* Beatrice Alice Ferris, d 27 May 1887, m 6 Ap 1880, *Edward Henry Toulmin* [son of Samuel Toulmin, Bar-at-Law], d 22 Mar 1909, and had issue 1: to 4:

　1: Harold Edward Toulmin, ⎱ settled in New Zealand
　2: Vincent Ferris Toulmin, ⎰

　3: Dora Agnes Toulmin

　4: Edith Alice Toulmin

3*g* *Edward Trott Ferris, Commandant Forces of Nawab of Rampur,* b 20 June 1819, d May 1892, m *Laura*, da of (—) *Evans*, and had issue 1*h* to 2*h*

1*h* Charles Ferris

2*h* Edward Ferris, b 28 Oct 18—, d 23 Aug 1892, m Emma S (12 *Sussex Road, Norwich*), da of (—) *Camplin*, and had issue (a son and 5 das)

　　　　　　　　　　　　　　　　　　　　[Nos 130546 to 130574

The Plantagenet Roll

4g *Godfrey Richard Ferris*, b 8 Jan 1825, d (–), m *Emily* (7 Matlock Road, Torquay), da of (—) Kenny of Halifax, M D , and had issue 1h to 4h

  1h Amy Ferris
  2h Kate Ferris
  3h Susan Ferris
  4h Louisa Ferris

  2d *William Boys*, d (–), m 1777, *Elizabeth*, da and co-h of Richard Harcourt of Wigsall, co Sussex, and had issue (with a son and da d young) 1e

  1e *William Hooper Boys*, d (–), m[1] *Sarah*, da of Sir Barry Collis Meredyth, 7th Bt [I], and had issue[1] 1f to 3f

  1f *William Boys, Consul at Hamburg and (?) Hobartown*, m 1855, Catherine, da of Frederic Roper and had issue

  2f *Corinna Boys*, m 1st, 8 Oct 1851, Ambrose Crawley, H E I C S , d 1849 (sic 1859), 2ndly, 7 Sept 1861, the Chevalier Igham, Prefect of Naples

  3f *Lydia Boys* m 1st, 8 Oct 1851, the Chevalier de Letterstedt , 2ndly, 18 Aug 1864, Paul de Juvenel and had issue 1g

  1g Comte de Letterstedt, m 30 June 1879, Viscount J de Manmorte

  3d *Anne Boys*, living unm 1745

  2b *Anne Boys*, m Benjamin Day of Freehurst , living 1745

  3b *Elizabeth Boys*, m 1st, John Morton , 2ndly, John Sparrow of Beaumaris, co Anglesey

  2a *Grace Boys*
  3a *Cordelia Boys*, m Henry Apsley of Freehurst
  4a *Margaret Boys*, m Richard Banks of Storrington
  5a *Mary Boys* m William Simons of Marden
  6a *Bridget Boys*, m John [son of Walter] Roberts
  7a *Philadelphia Boys*   [Nos 130575 to 130579]

331 Descendants of RACHEL PARKER (Table XXVIII), *bapt* at Wellingdon 13 Oct 1631; *d* 22 Mar 1650; *m* as 1st wife, 20 Jan 1645, WILLIAM GEE of Bishop Burton, co York, *b* 1625, *d* 30 Aug 1678, and had issue[2] 1a

  1a *William Gee of Bishop Burton*, b 1648, bur 15 Oct 1718, m 1st, 23 Feb 1664, *Elizabeth*, da and h of Sir John Hotham, 3rd Bt [E 1661], bur 21 Mar 1684, 2ndly (settlement dated 8 Oct), 1685, *Elizabeth*, widow of John Dicker of Risby, da of Charles Cracroft of Louth, co Lincoln, bur 1 Dec 1726, and had issue (with others known to have d s p) 1b to 5b

  1b *Thomas Gee of Bishop Burton*, bapt 4 Nov 1673, bur 28 July 1750, m 1st, Elizabeth, da of (—), bur at Belfreys 29 June 1730, and had issue 1c to 5c

  1c *William Gee of Bishop Burton*, Col 20th Foot, d v p (being killed at Fontenoy) 30 Ap 1745, m 1st (settlement dated 30 Mar), 1725, *Philippa*, da of Sir Charles Hotham, M P , bur s p s 26 Sept 1728, 2ndly (settlement dated 2 May), 1735, *Elizabeth*, da and event h of Roger Talbot of Woodend, living a widow 1765, and had issue 1d

  1d *Roger Gee of Bishop Burton*, d 9 Dec 1778, m *Caroline* [descended from the Lady Anne, sister of King Edward IV (see the Essex Volume Supplement, p 666)], da and co-h of Sir Warton Pennyman, 5th Bt [E] [who m 2ndly, 29 Nov 1779, Peter Acklam, by whom she also had issue, and] d 24 Mar (Dec) 1811, and had issue 1e to 2e

---

[1] MS additions in Berry's "Kent Genealogies," p 453
[2] Foster's " Yorkshire Pedigrees"

# of The Blood Royal

1e *Sarah Elizabeth Gee, da and co-h*, bapt *at York* 14 *June* 1770, d 28 *Nov* 1832, m 23 *Ap* 1788, *Henry Boldero Barnard of Cave Castle co York*, d 6 *Feb* 1815, *and had issue (with a 2nd son, Charles Lewyns, Capt Scots Greys, killed unm at Waterloo)* 1f *to* 3f

1f *Henry Gee Boldero Barnard of Cave Castle, Capt Scots Greys* b 22 *Feb* 1789, d s p 23 *Ap* 1858

2f *Rev Edward William Barnard of Brantingham Thorpe, Vicar of South Cave,* b 16 *Mar* 1791, d 10 *Jan* 1828, m 25 *Ap* 1821, *Philadelphia Frances Esther [descended from the Lady Anne, sister of King Edward IV (see the Essex Volume Supplement p 676)], da of the Ven Frances Wrangham, Archdeacon of the West Riding, and had issue* 1g *to* 3g

1g *Charles Edward Gee Barnard of Cave Castle, J P*, b 23 *Mar* 1822, d 14 *Aug* 1894, m 5 *June* 1862. *Sophia Letitia, da of the Hon Andrew Godfrey Stuart [E of Castle Stewart [I] Coll], and had issue* 1h

1h *Ursula Mary Florence Boldero Barnard of Cave Castle (Cave Castle, Brough, Yorks),* b 4 *July* 1869, *unm*

2g Rosamond Barnard

3g Caroline Barnard

3f *Sarah Elinor Barnard,* b 11 *Aug* 1810, d 7 *Jan* 1852, m 10 *Oct* 1832, *Joseph [only surviving son of Samuel Delpratt of Jamaica, and had issue (2 sons and 8 das)*

2e *Caroline Gee, da and co-h*, bapt *at Bishop Burton* 19 *Oct* 1774 d 23 *Dec* 1811, m *as 1st wife, Mar* 1792, *Lieut-Col George Hotham [Bt Coll],* d 24 *Dec* 1823, *and had issue*

See the Essex Volume Supplement, pp 666-670, Nos 57622 591-735

2c *Thomas Gee,* bapt 3 *Oct* 1700

3c *Bridget Gee,* bapt 27 *Nov* 1701, d (–), m *1st,* 11 *Oct* 1721, *James Taylor,* bur 28 *Sept* 1754, *2ndly, Ralph Pennyman [youngest son of Sir James Pennyman, 3rd Bt [E]],* b c 1696, d 1762, *and had issue by both husbands*

See the Essex Volume, Exeter Supplement, p 671, for issue by second

4c *Ann Gee,* bapt 31 *Aug* 1703

5c *Catherine Gee,* bapt 23 *Dec* 1707

2b *Matthew Gee,* bapt 17 *Aug* 1675

3b *William Gee,* bapt 11 *Sept* 1676, d a 1717, *when his widow was living*

4b[2] *James Gee of Beverley* bapt 15 *Aug* 1686, d *(will proved* 26 *Nov)* 1751, m 7 *Nov* 1727, *Constance, da. of John Moyser of Beverley, and had issue (with 2 sons d in infancy)* 1c *to* 2c

1c *William Gee,* b 26 *Ap* 1735, *living and then a ward of Richard Burton,* 1751

2c *Rev Richard Gee, Vicar of North Cave and Rector of Leven,* bapt 10 *Feb* 1742, d s p s

5b *Bridget Gee,* bapt 28 *Sept* 1671, d (–), m *at Bishop Burton as 1st wife,* 9 *Sept* 1690, *Sir Charles Hotham, 4th Bt [E 1622], M P for Beverley* 1703, d *Jan* 1723, *and had issue* 1c *to* 4c

1c *Sir Charles Hotham, 5th Bt [E], M P,* d 15 *Jan* 1739, m 1724, *Lady Gertrude, da of Philip (Stanhope), 3rd Earl of Chesterfield [E],* d 12 *Ap* 1775, *and had issue* 1d

1d *Sir Charles Hotham, 6th Bt [E].* d s p *Dec* 1767

2c *Sir Beaumont Hotham, 7th Bt [E],* d 29 *Aug* 1771, m *Frances, da and co-h of Stephen Thompson of Welton, co Yorks,* d 18 *Nov.* 1771, *and had issue* 1d *to* 5d

1d *Sir Charles Hotham, afterwards Hotham-Thompson, 8th Bt [E], K B,* b *May* 1729, d s p. 15 *Jan* 1794   [Nos 130580 to 130727

The Plantagenet Roll

2d *Right Rev Sir John Hotham, 9th Bt* [*E*], *Lord Bishop of Ossory* 1779-1782 *and of Clogher* 1782-1795, b *Feb* 1735, d 3 *Nov* 1795, m 11 *Ap* 1765, *Susan, da of Herbert Mackworth, M P , and had issue* 1e

1e *Sir Charles Hotham, 10th Bt* [*E*], b 24 *May* 1766, d s p 18 *July* 1811

3d *William* (*Hotham*), *1st Baron Hotham* [*I*], *so cr* 7 *Mar* 1797 *with rem to the heirs male of his father, 11th Bt* [*E*], *Admiral of the White*, b 8 *Ap* 1736, d *unm* 2 *May* 1813

4d *Beaumont* (*Hotham*), *2nd Baron Hotham* [*I*] *12th Bt* [*E*], *a Baron of the Exchequer*, b 5 *Aug* 1737, d 4 *Mar* 1814, m 6 *June* 1767, *Susannah, widow of Sir James Norman da of Sir Thomas Hankey*, d 1 *Aug* 1799, *and had issue* 1e *to be*

1e *Beaumont Hotham, Col Coldstream Guards*, b 30 *Ap* 1868, d *Aug* 1799, m 20 *May* 1790, *Philadelphia, da of Sir John Dixon Dyke, 3rd Bt* [*E*], d 20 *May* 1808, *and had issue* 1f *to* 2f

1f *Beaumont* (*Hotham*) *3rd Baron Hotham* [*I*], *13th Bt* [*E*], b 9 *Aug* 1794, d *unm* 12 *Dec* 1870

2f *Hon* (*R H* 1 *Sept* 1835) *George Frederick Hotham, Rear-Adm R N*, b *posthumous* 20 *Oct* 1799, d 19 *Oct* 1856, m 12 *Aug* 1824, *Lady Susan Maria, da and co-h of William* (*O'Brien*), *2nd Marquis of Thomond* [*I*], d 25 *Mar* 1857, *and had issue*

See p 368 Nos 60088-60089

2e *Rev the Hon Frederick Hotham, Prebendary of Rochester*, b 16 *June* 1774, d 10 *Oct* 1854 (?), m 23 *Nov* 1802, *Anne Elizabeth da of Thomas Hallett Hodges of Hemstead Place, co Kent*, d 28 *Jan* 1862, *and had issue* (*with 4 elder sons and 3 das who d s p*) 1f *to* 3f

1f *Rev William Francis Hotham, M A, Rector of Buckland, Surrey*, b 28 *Mar* 1819, d 10 *Sept* 1883, m 31 *Jan* 1855, *Emma, da of John Carbonell*, d 28 *May* 1909, *and had issue* 1g *to* 2g

1g *Frederick William* (*Hotham*), *6th Baron Hotham* [*I*], *16th Bt* [*E*] (*Bereleigh Petersfield Hants, Automobile and Junior Constitutional*), b 19 *Mar* 1863, m 9 *July* 1902, *Benita, da of Thomas Sanders of Sanders Park, Charleville, co Cork, and has issue* 1h *to* 2h

1h *Hon Sylvia Benita Frances Hotham*, b 19 *Sept* 1903

2h *Hon Jocelyne Mary Emma Hotham*, b 18 *Ap* 1908

2g *Frances Emma Hotham*, m 8 *Oct* 1889, the *Very Rev Edward Reid Currie, D D*, Dean of Battle (*The Deanery, Battle, Sussex*)

2f *Louisa Hotham*, b 1807 d 1894, m 12 *May* 1844, *Lieut-Col Patrick Grieve, 75th Regt*, d 11 *Jan* 1853

3f *Frederica Hotham*, d 1 *Sept* 1843, m 12 *Mar* 1840, the *Rev Charles Montagu Doughty of Theberton Hall, co Suffolk*, d 23 *Ap* 1850, *and had issue* 1g *to* 2g

1g *Henry Montagu Doughty of Theberton, co Suffolk, J P, formerly R.N, Bar-at-Law* (*Theberton Hall, near Leiston Suffolk*), b 15 *Mar* 1841, m 21 *Aug* 1860, *Edith Rebecca, da of D Cameron, Chief Justice of Vancouver Island* [and niece of Sir James Douglas, K C B, Governor of Vancouver and British Columbia], d 4 *Sept* 1870, *and his issue* 1h *to* 6h

1h *Charles Hotham Montagu Doughty, now* [*D P* 1904] *Doughty-Wylie, C M G, Maj Royal Welsh Fusiliers* (*Larrock, Grange Road, Eastbourne*), b 23 *July* 1868 m 1904, *Lily, widow of Henry Adams-Wylie, Lieut I M S, da of John Wylie of West Cliffe Hall, Hants*

2h *Henry Montagu Doughty, Capt R N*, b 4 *Sept* 1870

3h *Edith Amelia Mary Doughty*

4h *Katharine Frances Doughty*

5h *Gertrude Millicent Doughty*

6h *Frederica Helen Doughty*

[Nos 130728 to 130740

# of The Blood Royal

2g Charles Montagu Doughty, Hon Litt D (Oxon), b 19 Aug 1843, m 7 Oct. 1886, Caroline Amelia, da of Gen Sir William Montagu Scott McMurdo, G C B, and has issue 1h to 2h

    1h Susan Dorothy Doughty

    2h Frederica Gertrude Doughty

3e *Sir Henry Hotham, G C M G, K C B, Vice Adm of the Red,* b 19 Feb 1777, d *at Malta* 19 Ap 1833, m 6 *July* 1816, *Lady Frances Anne Juliana, da of John (Rous), 1st Earl of Stradbroke [U K],* d *31 Jan* 1859, *and had issue*

    See the Exeter Volume, p 543, Nos 19448-49476

    4e *Frances Hotham,* d 1836, m *Sir John Sutton, K C B*

    5e *Amelia Hotham,* d 1804, m *John Woodcock, and had issue*

    6e *Louisa Hotham,* b 9 *Oct* 1778, d 30 *Aug* 1840 m 1st, as *2nd wife,* 5 *Dec* 1804, *Sir Charles Edmonstone,* 2nd *Bt* [G B 1774], *M P,* b 10 *Oct* 1764, d 1 *Ap* 1821, *2ndly, Jan* 1832, *Charles Woodcock of Park Crescent, Portland Place, London, and had issue by 1st husband (with 3 sons and 1 da d s p)* 1f to 2f

    1f *Sir William Edmonstone, 4th Bt [G B], C B, D L, Adm R N (ret), formerly Naval A D C to Queen Victoria and M P for Stirling,* b 29 *Jan* 1810, d 18 *Feb* 1888, m *July* 1841, *Mary Elizabeth, da of Lieut-Col Parsons, C M G,* d 11 *Aug* 1902, *and had issue* 1g *to* 9g

    1g Sir Archibald Edmonstone, 5th Bt [G B], C V O, D L, a Groom-in-Waiting to H M King Edward VII (*Duntreath Castle, Blanefield, near Glasgow,* 6 *Lancaster Gate Terrace, W, Marlborough*), b 30 *May* 1867, m 30 *Nov* 1895, Ida Agnes, da of George Stewart Forbes [Bt Coll], and has issue 1h to 3h

        1h William George Edmonstone, b 20 Oct 1896

        2h Archibald Charles Edmonstone, b 16 June 1898

        3h Edward St John Edmonstone (for whom H M the King stood sponsor in person), b 3 Nov 1901

    2g Louisa Anne Edmonstone, m 12 Oct 1872, Major-Gen Henry Pipon, R H A (ret), C B (*King's House, Tower of London, E C*) and has issue 1h to 5h

        1h Mary Elizabeth Pipon, m 14 Sept 1899, Capt Cecil Toogood, D S O, Lincolnshire Regt (see Appendix), and has issue 1i to 3i

            1i Alexander Henry Cecil Toogood, b 26 Aug 1900

            2i Harry Reginald George Cecil Toogood, b 29 Feb 1904

            3i Georgiana Natalie Toogood

        2h Emma Philippa Pipon, m 1908, Maurice William Clifford, Lieut Indian Army Reserve, Deputy Examiner of Accounts, P W D, India, and has issue (a da)

        3h Georgina Helen Pipon, m 1901, Herbert Graham Stainforth, Major 4th Indian Cav (see p 570), and has issue 1i to 2i

            1i Graham Henry Stainforth b 3 Oct 1906

            2i Madeleine Susan Stainforth

        4h Evangeline Aimee Pipon

        5h Geraldine Maria Pipon

    3g Charlotte Henrietta Edmonstone (*Carbeile Torpoint, R S O, Cornwall*), m 9 June 1866, the Rev John Francis Kitson, Vicar of Antony, d 1907, and has (with other) issue (see Appendix) 1h to 2h

        1h Antony Buller Kitson, b 1890

        2h Dorothy Euphemia Kitson

    4g Jessie Edmonstone, m 3 June 1884, Edward John Winnington Ingram, Major Royal Warwickshire Regt [Bt Coll], d s p s 5 Aug 1892

    5g Frances Euphemia Edmonstone, m 3 June 1873, Alexander Robert Duncan of Parkhill, co Forfar, Advocate, and has issue (see Appendix) 1h

        1h John Alexander Duncan, b 22 Mar 1878   [Nos 130741 to 130793

The Plantagenet Roll

6g Sophia Edmonstone, m 1 June 1880, James Edward Hope [Bt Coll] (*Belmont, Murrayfield, Midlothian*), b 6 Nov 1852, and has issue 1h to 4h

    1h James Horatio Hope, Lieut Highland L I, b 12 Mar 1881

    2h Reginald John Hope, b 1884

    3h William Douglas Hope, b 1886

    4h Vera Mary Hope

7g Susanna Emily Edmonstone, d 9 May 1886, m 16 Feb 1885, Jonathan Bucknill, d Ap 1898, and had issue 1h.

    1h Susanna Mary Frances Bucknill

8g Mary Clementina Edmonstone, m 1 Oct. 1874, Andrew Graham (Murray), 1st Baron Dunedin [U K], P C , K C V O , Lord Justice-General and President of the Court of Session in Scotland (7 *Rothesay Terrace, Edinburgh , Stenton, Dunkeld, Perthshire*), b 21 Nov 1849, and his issue 1h to 4h

    1h Hon Ronald Thomas Graham Murray, Capt 3rd Batt Black Watch, b 1 Aug 1875 m 19 Feb 1903, Evelyn, da of Sir David Baird, 3rd Bt [U K]

    2h Mary Caroline Murray

    3h Gladys Esme Murray

    4h Marjorie Murray

9g Alice Frederica Edmonstone, m 1 June 1891, Capt the Hon George Keppel, M V O [3rd son of William Coutts, 7th Earl of Albemarle [I] and a descendant of George, Duke of Clarence, K G (see Clarence Volume, p 250)] (30 *Portman Square, W , Marlborough*), and has issue 1h to 2h

    1h Violet Keppel

    2h Sonia Rosemary Keppel

2f Louisa Henrietta Edmonstone, d 14 Mar 1840, m 15 Dec 1829, John Kingston of London , and had issue (1 son and 3 das)

5d George Hotham, General in the Army, b 7 Jan 1741, d 7 Feb 1805, m 16 Dec 1769 Diana, da and co h of Sir Warton Pennyman-Warton, 5th Bt [E], d 17 July 1817 , and had issue

See the Essex Volume, Exeter Supplement, pp 666–671, Nos 57622,591–751

3e Elizabeth Hotham, bapt 10 Jan 1694, d 25 Oct 1737, m Sir Thomas Style, 4th Bt [E 1627] d 11 Jan 1769, and had issue 1d to 2d

    1d Sir Charles Style 5th Bt [E], d 18 Ap 1774, m 7 Mar 1770, the Hon Isabella, da of Richard (Wingfield), 1st Viscount Powerscourt [I], d 24 Sept 1808, and had issue 1e to 2e

    1e Sir Charles Style, 6th Bt [E], d 5 Sept 1804, m 29 Mar 1794, Camilla, da of James Whatman of Vintners, co Kent, d 17 Sept 1829, and had issue (with 2 das d s p) 1f to 2f

    1f Sir Thomas Style, 7th Bt [E], d unm , in Spain, 5 Nov 1813

    2f Sir Thomas Charles Style, 8th Bt [E], J P , D L , M P , b 21 Aug 1797, d s p s 23 July 1879

    2e Dorothy Style, m John Larking

2d Rev Robert Style, Vicar of Wateringbury and Rector of Mereworth, d (–) , m Priscilla, da of the Rev John Davis, d 18 June 1832, and had issue (with 1 son and 1 da d unm) 1e to 6e

    1e Charles Style of Stranorlar, co Donegal, b 1777, d 21 Dec 1853, m Apr 1812, Frances, da of John Cochrane of Edenmore, co Donegal, d 20 Jan 1875 , and had issue (with 2 sons and 3 das d s p) 1f to 3f

    1f Anna Maria Style, d 3 Dec 1902 , m 1838, Lieut -Col John Pitt Kennedy, d 28 June 1879 , and had issue (with a da , Mrs Martin of Cleveragh, who d s p) 1g

    1g Charles Napier Kennedy, b 1852, m 1882, Lucy, da of George Marwood

    2f Elizabeth Style, m 1850, John James Hamilton Humphreys, Bar -at-Law, d 1890, and had issue 1g to 5g

    1g John Bayfield Humphreys, b 1854

    2g Charles Style Humphreys, b 1858   [Nos 130794 to 130972.

# of The Blood Royal

3g Alice Rachel Humphreys, m 1876, Robert Jocelyn Alexander, H M's Inspector of Schools

4g Ethel Humphreys, m 1879, Albert Crease Coxhead

5g Rosamond Humphreys, m 1904, Col William Francis Henry Style Kincaid, C B, R E (United Service)

3f Isabella Style, d Aug 1867, m Sept 1858, John Henry Kincaid of Dublin, d Aug 1867, and had issue 1g to 2g

    1g Charles Style Kincaid

    2g William Henry Kincaid

2c William Style of Bicester House, Oxfordshire, b 12 Ap 1785, d 24 Feb 1868, m 22 Dec 1814, Louisa Charlotte, da of the Hon Jacob Marsham, d 25 Oct 1866, and had issue (with 2 das d s p) 1f to 3f

1f Sir William Henry Marsham Style, 9th Bt [E], J P, D L, High Sheriff co Donegal 1856, M A (Oxon), b 3 Sept 1826, d 31 Jan 1904, m 1st, 18 Dec 1848, the Hon Rosamond Marion, da of Charles (Morgan), 1st Lord Tredegar [U K], d 15 Jan 1883, 2ndly, 2 June 1885, Ellen Catharine (The Firs, Crowborough, Sussex), widow of Henry Hyde Nugent Bankes, and previously of the Rev Charles Henry Barham of Trecwn, da of Edward Taylor Massy of Cottesmore, and had issue 1g to 7g

1g Sir Frederick Montague Style, 10th Bt [E] (Glenmore, Cloghan, co Donegal), b 10 May 1857, m 14 Oct 1886, Caroline, da of Frederick Schultz, and has issue 1h to 2h

    1h William Frederick Style, b 11 July 1887

    2h Louise Violet Style

2g Henry Albert Glenmore Style, b 11 June 1862, m 5 May 1886, Annie Lydia, da of Samuel Fletcher Goldsmith, and has issue 1h to 4h

    1h Glenmore Rodney Style, b 29 June 1887

    2h Rosamond Lydia Style

    3h Brenda Helen Style

    4h Viola Style

3g Rodney Charles Style, Lieut-Col Comdg. 1st Batt Queen's Own, b 4 May 1864

4g Rosamond Louisa Style, d 21 June 1899, m 8 Ap 1872, Henry Price Holford, 10th Hussars, d 21 June 1899, and had issue 1h to 4h

    1h George Holford, b 1872

    2h Arthur Holford, b 1873

    3h Alfred Holford, b 1876

    4h Frederick Holford, b 1881

5g Selma Isabella Style

6g Lydia Frances Style, d 23 June 1900, m 12 Jan 1875, Benjamin Francis Meynell Bloomfield of Castle Caldwell, co Fermanagh, D L, d v p 26 Nov 1886, and had issue 1h to 3h

1h Meynell Caldwell Egerton Rodney Bloomfield of Castle Caldwell (Castle Caldwell, Belleck, co Fermanagh), b 12 Dec 1882

2h Marian Blanche Bloomfield, m 3 June 1903, the Rev Benjamin James du Boe, M A (T C D) Incumbent of Ballintemple (Dundrum, Tipperary), and has issue 1i

    1i Rodney Benjamin du Boe, b 11 Mar 1904

3h Grace Maria Bloomfield, m 6 Dec 1898, Arthur Francis Forster [eldest son of William Stewart Forster of Runwood, Maidstone] (24 Portland Place, W)

7g Mary Louisa Style, m 24 Ap 1884, the Rev Thomas Thornhill Peyton, Rector of St Mary, March, co Cambridge (St Mary's Rectory, March, Ely), b 8 Dec 1856, and has issue 1h

    1h Rosamond Lucy Peyton

[Nos. 130973 to 130997

2f Rev Charles Montague Style, D D, M A (Oxon), *formerly* Fellow of St John's Coll, Oxon, Rector of Warnborough (*South Warnborough Rectory, Winchfield, Hants*), *b* 21 Aug 1830, *m* 24 Sept 1867, Jessie Elizabeth, da of Robert Bullock Marsham, D C L [E Romney Coll], and has issue 1g

1g Richard Charles Montague Style, *b* 20 Sept 1870

3f *Albert Frederick Style*, b 20 *May* 1837, d 28 *Dec* 1895, m 30 *Ap* 1868, *Eliza, da of Henry Tubb of Bicester*, d 30 *Ap* 1898, *and had issue* (*with* 1 *da* d *young*) 1g *to* 4g

1g George Montague Style, B A (Oxon), Capt W. Kent Yeo (*Pickwell Manor, Braunton, N Devon*), *b* 7 Mar 1869, *m* 7 Ap 1896, Eleanora Morrison, da of James Morrison Kirkwood of Yeo Vale Bideford, co Devon, and has issue 1h to 3h

1h Oliver George Style, *b* 1 Feb 1897

2h Priscilla Style

3h Patience Paulina Style

2g Charles Humphrey Style, Major Royal E Kent Yeo (*Crouch House, Boro' Green, Kent*), *b* 8 May 1877, *m* 15 Nov 1899, Annie Maud Harriet, da of Gen Sir Hugh Henry Gough, G C B, V C, and has issue 1h to 5h

1h Charles Richard Style, *b* 13 Ap 1901

2h Humphrey Bloomfield Style, *b* 12 Nov 1902

3h Hubert Anthony Style, *b* 9 Jan 1910

4h Barbara Ann Style

5h Camilla Style

3g Robert Henry Style, Lieut Royal E Kent Yeo (*Boxley House, near Maidstone*), *b* 20 Oct 1881, *m* 15 Feb 1905, Grace Winifred, da of John Bazley-White, and has issue (with 1 son *d* young) 1h to 2h

1h John Peter Style, *b* 1908

2h Betty Winifred Style

4g Florence Louisa Style (*Heathfield House, Bletchington, Oxford*), *m* 22 Nov 1898, Charles Stratton, *d* 1907, and has issue 1h to 3h

1h John Humphrey Stratton, *b* 1900

2h Charles Michael Stratton, *b* 1906

3h Ida Rosemary Stratton

3e *Margaretta Style*, d *Sept* 1863, m *John Johnston*, d *July* 1859, *and had issue*

4e *Henrietta Style*, d (–), m *June* 1808, *John Francis Norris*, d 2 *Nov.* 1851, *and had issue*

5e *Elizabeth Style*, d 4 *Dec* 1851, m *Adm John Drake*, d 6 *Aug* 1864

6e *Clara Style*, d 31 *Dec* 1861, m *July* 1815, *Col Wilson*

4c *Charlotte Hotham*, d 7 *June* 1771, m 31 *Mar* 1725, *Sir Warton Pennyman-Warton, 5th Bt* [*E*], d 14 *Jan* 1770, *and had issue*

See the Essex Volume, Exeter Supplement, p 666, Nos 57622 551–751

[Nos 130998 to 131217

332 Descendants of PHILADELPHIA NUTT (Table XXVIII), *d.* after 1706, *m* c. 1695, Sir THOMAS DYKE of Horeham, 1st Bt. [E 3 Mar 1677] *d* 31 Oct 1706, and had issue 1*a* to 3*a*.

1a *Sir Thomas Dyke, 2nd Bt* [*E*], b c 1700, d 20 *Aug* 1756, m 23 *May* 1728, *Anne, widow of John Bluet of Holcombe Regis, co Devon, da and h of Percival Hart of Lullingstone Castle, co Kent*, d 24 *Nov* 1763, *and had issue* 1*b to* 2*b*

1b *Sir John Dixon Dyke, 3rd Bt* [*E*], b 23 *Nov* 1732, d 6 *Sept* 1810, m

# of The Blood Royal

3 *May* 1756, *Philadelphia Payne, da of George Horne of East Grinstead, co Sussex,* d 31 *Jan* 1781, *and had issue* 1c *to* 2c

    1c *Sir Thomas Dyke, 4th Bt* [E], b 23 *Dec* 1763, d *unm* 22 *Nov* 1831

    2c *Sir Percival Hart Dyke, 5th Bt* [E], *a co-h of the Barony of Braye* [E], *which he successfully claimed,* b 27 *Dec* 1767, d 1 *Aug* 1816, m 26 *July* 1798, Anne, *da of Robert Jenner of Chislehurst, co Kent,* d 27 *Dec* 1847, *and had issue* 1d *to* 6d.

    1d *Sir Percivall Hart Dyke, 6th Bt* [E], b 9 *June* 1799, d 12 *Nov* 1875, m 25 *June* 1835, *Elizabeth da of John Wells of Bickley, co Kent,* d 10 *July* 1888, *and had issue* (*with a son d in the Crimea*) 1e *to* 7e

    1e Right Hon *Sir William Hart Dyke, 7th Bt* [E], P C, J P, D L, co Kent, M A (Oxon), M P for West Kent 1865 1868, for Mid Kent 1868-1885, and for N W Kent 1885 1906, Vice-President of the Committee of Council on Education 1887-1892, Chief Sec to the Lord-Lieutenant of Ireland 1885-1886, and Joint-Sec of the Treasury 1874-1880 (*Lullingstone Castle, Dartford, Kent. Carlton, &c*), b 7 *Aug* 1837, m 30 *May* 1870, Lady Emily Caroline [descended from the Lady Anne, sister of King Edward IV, &c (see the Exeter Volume, p 363)], da of John William (Montagu), 7th Earl of Sandwich [E], and has issue (*with a son d young*) 1f *to* 5f

    1f Percyvall Hart Dyke, J P, B A (Camb), Bar-at-Law (*Lullingstone Castle, Eynsford, Kent. Carlton*), b 27 Oct 1871, m 15 Aug 1908, Edythe, da of W G Harrison, Q C, and has issue 1g

        1g Edythe Frediswide Hart Dyke, b 18 July 1909

    2f Oliver Hamilton Hart Dyke, b 4 Sept 1885

    3f Lina Mary Hart Dyke, m 10 Feb 1902, Alexander John Scott Scott-Gatty [son of Sir Alfred Scott Scott-Gatty, Garter King of Arms] (18 *Buckingham Gate, S W*), and has issue 1g

        1g Edward Comyn Scott-Gatty, b 1903

    4f Hon Mary Hart Dyke, *formerly* Maid-of-Honour to H M Queen Alexandra, m 11 July 1905, Capt Matthew Gerald Edward Bell of Bourne Park, co Kent, 116th (Reserve) Batt (*formerly* 3rd Batt) Rifle Brig (105 *Cadogan Gardens, S W., Bourne Park. Canterbury*), and has issue 1g

        1g Matthew Alexander Henry Bell, b 1909

    5f Sydney Margaret Eleanor Hart Dyke, *unm*

    2e George Augustus Hart Dyke (1 *Grosvenor Place, S W., Wallington*), b 27 Sept 1847

    3e Reginald Charles Hart Dyke (*Dacre Lodge, Cockfosters, New Barnet*), b 1 May 1852, m 1st, 22 Oct 1891, Gunnevere Eva, da of Gen Lord Alfred Paget, C B [descended from the Lady Isabel, aunt of King Edward IV (see Essex Volume, p 107)], d 26 Feb 1894, 2ndly, 10 June 1897, Millicent Ada [descended from George, Duke of Clarence, K G (see Essex Volume Supplement, p 516)], da of Robert Cooper Lee Bevan of Trent Park, co Herts, and Fosbury House, co Wilts, and has issue 1f *to* 2f

    1f[1] Wyndham Douglas Hart Dyke, b 13 Aug 1892

    2f[2] Ashley Francis Hart Dyke, b 16 Oct 1899

    4e Frances Julia Hart Dyke (*Crowbury, Watton, Herts*), m 24 July 1877, Abel Smith of Woodhall Park, Herts, M P [descended from the Lady Isabel Plantagenet (see Essex Volume, p 303)], d 30 May 1898, and has issue 1f

        1f Rachel Caroline Smith

    5e Eleanor Laura Hart Dyke

    6e Sybella Catherine Hart Dyke

    7e Gertrude Hart Dyke, m as 3rd wife, 19 June 1894, the Hon Reynolds Moreton [brother of 3rd Earl of Ducie [U K]] (*St John's, Bishopstoke, Hants*)

    2d *Rev Thomas Hart Dyke, Rector of Long Newton, co Durham, and Lulling-*
[Nos 131218 to 131235

The Plantagenet Roll

stone, co Kent, b 11 Dec 1801, d 25 June 1866, m 4 Feb 1833, *Elizabeth* [*descended from the Lady Anne, sister of King Edward IV*, &c (*see the Exeter Volume, p 536*)]. *da of Thomas Fairfax of Newton Kyme, d 6 Oct 1893, and had issue 1c to 2c*

1c Thomas Dyke of Beaumaris, Clifton, Bristol, M I C E, J P, b 1 Ap 1834 d 6 Aug 1906, m 26 Feb 1863 Georgina Isabella Russell (9 York Crescent Road, Clifton, Bristol), da of Robert Edward Fullerton of Shuthonger Manor, near Teukesbury, and had issue 1f to 4f

1f Perceval Hart Dyke, Capt Indian Army, served in Uganda 1897–1898 (Despatches, Medal with 2 Clasps) and with Zakka Khel Exped 1908 (Despatches, Medal with Clasp), b 24 Aug 1872, m 10 Oct 1900, Louisa Catherine, da of Adm John Halliday Cave, C B, R N and has issue 1g to 3g

1g Trevor Hart Dyke, b 19 Feb 1905

2g Eric Hart Dyke, b 28 July 1906

3g Cicely Hart Dyke

2f Ethel Frances Hart Dyke

3f Winifred Evelyn Hart Dyke

4f Theophania Louisa Hart Dyke

2c Rev Percival Hart Dyke, Hon Canon of Salisbury (*Lullingstone, Wimborne*), b 1 June 1835, m 12 Jan 1864, Margaret Isabella, da of Robert John Peel of Burton-on-Trent, d 10 Ap 1909 and his issue 1f to 3f

1f Robert Percyvall Hart Dyke (*20 Pembridge Mansions, W*), b 3 Nov 1864, m 30 Sept 1908, Mary Harriette Theodora, da of the Rev John Shephard (*formerly Vicar of Eton*), Hon Canon of Christ Church, Oxford, of 39 Princes Square, W and his issue 1g

1g Michael Percyvall Hart Dyke, b 10 Sept 1909

2f Mabel Louisa Hart Dyke m 11 Feb 1892, Harold Gordon (*Meldecombra, Watagoda, Ceylon*)

3f Maud Cecilia Hart Dyke, m 16 Ap 1891, the Rev Walter Basil Broughton, M A Vicar of Brackley, Northants, and has issue 1g to 2g

1g Stephen Percy de Hart Broughton, b 26 Dec 1897

2g Olive Irene Broughton, b 22 June 1892

3d John Dixon Dyke, Lieut -Col H E I C S, b 6 Jan 1803, d 1 Aug 1885, m 10 Feb 1836 Millicent, da of Isaac Minet of Baldwins, co Kent, d 5 Aug 1901, and had issue 1c to 8c

1c Rev John Dixon Dyke, Vicar and Rural Dean of St James' Camberwell (*30 Croxhurst Road, Brixton, S W, Union*), b 31 Oct 1836

2c Edward Hart Dyke, *formerly Col R A*, served in Indian Mutiny (Medal with Clasp) (*Leavers, Hadlow, Tonbridge*). b 11 Nov 1837, m 23 Mar 1893, Elizabeth Grace, da of Col Thomas Stannard MacAdam of Blackwater, co Clare, and his issue 1f to 5f

1f Francis Hart Dyke, b 20 Jan 1898

2f Edward Hart Dyke, b 24 Oct 1899

3f Charles Hart Dyke, b 27 May 1901

4f Percyvall Hart Dyke, b 15 Dec 1902

5f Millicent Grace Hart Dyke

3c Frederick Hotham Dyke, Lieut -Col late 69th Regt, Professor of Military Studies at Camb Univ since 1904, served in Canada 1870 (Medal with Clasp) and in Egypt 1884 (*43 Morshead Mansions, Maida Vale, W, Junior United Service*), b 6 Feb 1840, m 20 Ap 1871, Emily, da of the Rev Charles Faunce Thorndike, and his issue 1f to 2f

1f Agnese Millicent Dyke, m 16 Dec 1893, Richard Thomas Nicholson (M A) (*The Mount, Loughton, Essex*)

2f Winifred Amy Dyke

[Nos 131236 to 131259

4e George Hart Dyke, *formerly* Lieut.-Col Comdg 2nd Batt Northbl Fus, served in Afghan War 1878–1879 (Medal) (*Army and Navy*), b 21 Jan 1847, m 25 July 1895, Edith Louise, da of Thomas William Kinder, Master of Mints of Hong Kong and Japan, and has issue 1f

1f Helen Sandra Millicent Dyke

5c Henry Hart Dyke Adm R N (ret) has Abyssinian Medal (*Sphinx, Banbury, Junior United Service*), b 26 Mar 1848, m 1st, 10 Feb 1886, Louisa, da of William Covey of Lee, Kent, *d s p* 10 Dec 1886 2ndly, 3 July 1900, Mary Blanche, da of the Rev Thomas Prater of Farnborough Banbury, *d s p* 8 June 1905

6c Millicent Dyke }
7c Julia Dyke } (*Camoys Court, Barcombe, near Lewes*)

8e Matilda Dyke (20 *Dartmouth Row, Blackheath, S E*)

4d *Francis Hart Dyke, Queen's Proctor*, b 28 Nov 1803, d 17 *July* 1876, m 1 Dec 1835, *Charlotte Lascelles, da of the Right Hon Sir Herbert Jenner Fust*, P C, d 17 Dec 1899, *and had issue* 1e to 3e

1e Rev Edwin Francis Dyke Rector of Mersham, Kent, Hon Canon of Canterbury and Rural Dean (*Mersham Rectory, Kent*) b 27 Sept 1842, m 22 Nov 1870, Katharine Louisa, da of Sir Frederick Currie, 1st Bt [U K]

2e Evelyn Ellen Dyke

3e Alice Frances Dyke (*Bark Hart, Wokingham, Berks*)

5d *Harriet Jenner Dyke*, d Nov 1883, m 11 June 1835, *the Rev Nicholas Frott, afterwards (R L 4 Oct 1846) Lee, Vicar of Edgware, M A and Fellow of St John's Coll, Camb* (see p 530), d 1858, *and had issue (with a da, Mrs Luard, who d s p)* 1e *to* 3e

1e Edward Dyke Lee of Hartwell, co Bucks, and Totteridge Park, co Herts, J P, Lieut Col and Hon Col 3rd Batt Oxfordshire L I (*Hartwell House, Aylesbury, Totteridge Park, Barnet, Carlton, &c*), b 16 Sept 1844

2e Philadelphia Bruce Lee, m 21 Oct 1876, Liebert Edward Goodill, J P, D L, Major and Hon Lieut.-Col Royal N Gloucester Militia, *formerly* Capt 59th Regt (*Dinton Hall, Aylesbury*)

3e Fanny Charlotte Lee

6d *Laura Dyke*, d 28 Feb 1900, m 9 *Feb* 1847, *the Rev Thomas Prankerd Phelps, M A, Hon Canon of Rochester, Rural Dean and Rector of Ridley* (*Ridley Parsonage, Wrotham, Kent*), *and had issue* 1e *to* 3e

1e Henry George Hart Phelps (*Great Comp, Sevenoaks*), b 17 Nov 1849, m 1886, Joyce, da of J Hassell of Clock House, Darenth, Kent, and has issue 1f to 2f

1f Henry Dampier Phelps, b 1889

2f Vera Laura Phelps

2e Herbert Dampier Phelps, Sub Lieut (ret) R N (*Belle Vue, Fowey, Cornwall*), b 24 July 1851

3e Rev Lancelot Ridley Phelps, M A, Fellow of Oriel Coll, Oxford, and Vice-Principal of St Mary Hall, Oxford, 1889–1893 (*Oriel College, Oxford*), b 3 Nov 1853

2b *Philadelphia Dyke*, b c 1730, d 5 *Mar* 1799, m *at Lullingstone, William Lee of Totteridge, co Herts, M A [son of the Right Hon Sir William Lee, P C , K B, Lord Chief Justice of England 1738 and Chancellor of the Exchequer 1754*], bur 12 *Aug* 1778, *and had issue (with a son, William Lee, afterwards Antoine of Colworth, co Beds, M P , d s p Sept 1825, and 2 das d unm* [1]*)* 1c *to* 3c

1c *Harriet Lee, da and in her issue* (1825) *co h*, d 25 *July* 1794, m 19 *July* 1782, *John Frott of London [5th son of Nicholas Frott of St Helier s, Jersey, Lord of the Lee and Seignory of Melesches] and had issue* [2] *(with a son and 4 das d unm)* 1d *to* 4d

No 131260 to 131276

The Plantagenet Roll

1d *John Frott, afterwards (R L 4 Oct 1816) Lee of Colworth, co Bucks, M A , LL D (Camb), b 28 Ap 1783, d (? s p), m 25 Oct 1833, Cecilia, da of (—) Rutter*

2d *William Edward Frott, Lieut R N , b 28 July 1786, d (? s p)*

3d *Rev Nicholas Frott, afterwards (R L 4 Oct 1816) Lee, M A , Fellow of St John's Coll , Camb , Vicar of Edgware, b 5 June 1794, d 1858, m 11 June 1835, Harriet Jenner, da of Sir Percival Hart Dyke, 5th Bt [E], and had issue*
See p 529, Nos 131269-131271

4d *Philadelphia Frott, b 10 May 1781, d (–), m John Ede of London, Merchant, and had issue* [1]

2e *Louisa Lee, da and either herself or in her issue, if any, co-h, d (–), m Edward Arrowsmith of Totteridge, co Herts*

3e *Sophia Lee*

2a *Philadelphia Dyke, m Lewis Stephens, D D , Rector of Droxford, co Hants, Archdeacon of Barnstaple and Exeter and Canon Residentiary of York and Southwark*

3a *Elizabeth Dyke, d Sept 1739, m as 2nd wife, John Cockman of Kent, M D [brother of (—) Cockman, D D , Master of University College, Oxon]* [2]
[Nos 131277 to 131279

333. Descendants of CATHERINE NUTT (Table XXVIII), b 1662 ; d. 24 June 1708 , m ANTHONY BRAMSTON of Skreens, co Essex, d 26 Jan 1722 , and had issue 1a to 10a

1a *John Bramston of Chigwell, co Essex, b c 1683, d s p 17 Aug 1718, m and had issue 3 das who all d s p*

2a *Thomas Bramston of Skreens, d 1769 , m 2ndly, Elizabeth, da of Richard Berney, Recorder of Norwich, d 1769, and had issue 1b to 2b*

1b *Thomas Berney Bramston of Skreens, M P co Essex, b 7 Dec 1733, d 7 May 1813, m 10 Jan 1764, Mary, da and h of Stephen Gardiner, d 25 Nov 1805 , and had issue 1c to 3c*

1c *Thomas Gardiner Bramston of Skreens, M P co Essex, b 24 July 1770, d 3 Feb 1831, m 1st, 6 Feb 1796, Mary Anne, da of William Bloame of Queen Ann' St, London, d 1 Feb 1821 , and had issue 1d to 4d*

1d *Thomas William Bramston of Skreens, M P , J P , D L , b 30 Oct 1796, d 21 May 1871, m 12 Aug 1830, Eliza [also a descendant of Edward III through Mortimer-Percy], da and co-h of Adm Sir Eliab Harvey of Rolls Park, co Essex, G C B , M P , d 11 Oct 1870 , and had issue 1e to 6e*

1e *Thomas Harvey Bramston of Skreens, J P , D L , formerly Lieut -Col Grenadier Guards (20 Old Burlington Street London, W , Travellers'), b 11 May 1831, m 7 Ap 1864, Honoria Louisa, da of Thomas Thornhill of Fixby Hall, co York , s p*

2e *Sir John Bramston, G C M G , C B D C L , Fellow of All Souls' College, Oxon , Assist Under-Sec of State Colonial Dept 1876-1897 and Registrar Order of St Michael and St George 1892-1907, formerly Attorney-Gen of Hong-Kong and previously of Queensland, &c (18 Berkeley Place, Wimbledon , Travellers'), b 14 Nov 1832, m 14 Dec 1872, Eliza Isabella, da of the Rev Harry Vane Russell, s p*

3e *Rev William Mondeford Bramston, M A , Rector of Willingale Doe with*
[Nos 131280 to 131281.

[1] Lipscomb's " Bucks,' ii 308

[2] In Betham's " Baronetage," iii 4, they are said to have had issue a da , wife of Nicholas Toke, Bar at Law , but the wife of Nicholas Toke, who was of Godington, co Kent, was Eleanor, da and h of John Cockman, M D , by Margaret, his 1st wife, da and h of Sir Felix Wilde, 2nd Bt

# of The Blood Royal

Shellow Bowels, co Essex, b 3 Feb 1835, d 9 Jan 1892, m. 7 July 1868, *Hyacinth Laura, da of the Rev George Chetwode, and had issue 1f to 2f*

    1f Mabel Charlotte Bramston, m 3 Jan 1893, Robert George Baird [Bt of Newbyth [U K 1809] Coll] (*Helmleigh, Granville Road, Sevenoaks*), and has issue 1g to 3g

        1g Robert Douglas Baird, b 19 Dec 1893

        2g George Henry William Baird, b 10 Jan 1903

        3g Elizabeth Mabel Baird

    2f Eleanor Hyacinth Bramston, m 6 Ap 1904, Oswald Francis Massingberd-Mundy [3rd son of Charles Francis Massingberd-Mundy of Ormsby, J P, D L, and a descendant of the Lady Anne, sister of Edward IV (see the Exeter Volume, p 552)] (*Iddesleigh, Granville Road, Sevenoaks*), and has issue 1g to 2g

        1g Francis Massingberd-Mundy, b 1 Sept 1905

        2g John Massingberd-Mundy, b 5 Feb 1907

    4e Georgina Bramston, *unm*

    5e Eliza Harriet Bramston, m 26 Oct 1875, Robert Little (*Hytecliffe, Brisbane, Queensland*), and has issue 1f

    1f Marcus Charles Herbert Little, b 6 June 1881

    6e Emma Alice Bramston m 28 Ap 1864, Major Edward Clerk [5th son of the Right Hon Sir George Clerk, 6th Bt [S], P C, M P] (*Travellers'*), and has issue 1f to 4f

    1f William Henry Clerk, b 19 Sept 1867

    2f Herbert Edward Clerk, b 15 Ap 1871, m 1908, Helen, da of Jules A Heuer

    3f Florence Eliza Clerk

    4f Maud Alice Clerk

    2d *Very Rev John Bramston, Dean of Winchester,* b 12 May 1802, d 13 Nov 1889, m 1st, 1832, *Clarissa Sandford, da of Sir Nicholas Trant,* d Ap 1844, 2ndly, Sept 1846, *Anna, da of Osgood Hanbury of Holfield Grange, co Essex,* d 26 Dec 1897, *and had issue 1e to 1e*

    1e Rev John Trant Bramston, M A (Oxon) (*St Nicholas, St Cross, Winchester*), b 3 Feb 1843, m 29 Dec 1875, June, da of the Ven William Bruce Ady, Archdeacon of Colchester, and has issue 1f

    1f Margaret Clarissa Bramston, m Aug 1904, Robert Douglas Beloe, M A, Assist Master Winchester College (*Kingscote House, Winchester*), and has issue 1g to 3g

        1g Robert Beloe, b 11 May 1905

        2g John Douglas Beloe, b 9 Mar 1907

        3g Isaac William Trant Beloe, b 9 Dec 1909

    2e[1] *Clara Isabella Sandford Bramston,* b Oct 1833, d 28 Mar 1907, m 13 Sept 1860, *the Rev Bixby Garnham Luard, Rector of Birch, Colchester,* d 27 Mar 1907, *and had issue (with a son and da d unm)* 1f to 11f

    1f Frederick Bramston Luard, Capt (ret) West India Regt, b 3 Nov 1861, *unm*

    2f Hugh Bixby Luard, M B (Camb), F R C S, D P H, Capt (ret) Indian Medical Service (*Osmotherly, Yorks*), b 13 Oct 1862, m 13 Ap 1905, Flora Anne Phœbe, da of Colin Alexander McVean of the Isle of Mull, J P, and has issue 1g to 2g

        1g John McVean Luard, b 2 Mar 1906

        2g Mary Clarissa Luard, b 19 Dec 1908

    3f Frank William Luard, Lieut Col R M L I, b 15 Jan 1865, m 1896, Eloine Beatrice, da of Walter Perkins, and has issue 1g to 2g

        1g Betty Frances Clare Luard, b 1897

        2g Joan Anstace de Beauregard Luard, b 1899

    4f Rev Edwin Percy Luard, M A. (Camb), Curate of Birch, b 13 Oct 1869

The Plantagenet Roll

5/ Trant Bramston Luard, Capt R M L I, b 5 Nov 1873
6/ Clara Georgina Luard, b 28 Feb 1866
7/ Annette Jane Luard, b 29 Aug 1868
8/ Helen Lucy Luard, b 17 July 1871, m 1898, M Douglass Round
9/ Kate Evelyn Luard, b 29 June 1872
10/ Rose Mary Luard, b 22 Ap 1876
11/ Margaret Anne Luard, b 10 Mar 1880

3c¹ Mary Eliza Bramston, unm
4c² Anna Rachel Bramston, unm

3d Charlotte Bramston, b 11 Nov 1799, d 1841, m the Rev John Davidson, Rector of East Harptree co Somerset, and had issue (with a da, Elizabeth, who d unm 20 Oct 1909) 1c

1e Anna Davidson (1 Montpelier Terrace, Braddons Hill Road West, Torquay), m 1889, the Rev (—) Wilmot, d s p 1890

4d Elizabeth Bramston, b 25 May 1801, d 6 July 1839, m 1831, Lieut William Hooper R N and had issue 1c to 2c

1c Rev William Hooper, M A, D D (Oxon), Boden Sanskrit Sch 1857, Hon Canon of Lucknow Cath 1906, formerly Vicar of Cressing, co Essex, 1870-1872, Minister of Mt Auckland, N Z, 1889-1891, Principal of St Paul's Div Sch, Allahabad, 1881-1887, author of the Hebrew-Urdu Dict, Greek Hindi Dict, and many other works (Mussoorie, U P, India), b 27 Sept 1837, m 1st, 10 Dec 1862, Charlotte Elizabeth, da of the Rev George Candy, Vicar of South Newington, co Oxon, d 15 Aug 1886, 2ndly, 17 Nov 1891, Mary Priscilla, da of William Robins Matthews of Newport, co Mon, and has issue (with 2 sons d unm) 1f to 6f

1f Joseph Hayward Hooper, Dentist (Feilding, New Zealand), b 10 Ap 1864, m 1892, Flora, da of (—) Sheddan, and has issue 1g to 5g

1g Howard Henry Hooper, b 16 June 1893
2g Victor Candy Hooper, b 2 Mar 1895
3g William Rowlands Hooper, b 22 Ap 1900
4g Ruth Charlotte Hooper, b 26 Oct 1896
5g Flora Mackenzie Hooper, b 8 Sept 1898

2f Richard Henry Hooper, Govt C E (Fernside, Wadestown, Wellington, New Zealand), b 27 Nov 1868 m 1893, Sophia, da of R A Hould of the N Z Justice Dept, and has issue 1g to 3g

1g Richard Kevin Hooper, b 11 May 1908
2g Kate Challis Eccles Hooper, b 25 June 1894
3g Estelle Mary Hooper, b 9 Dec 1900

3f Frederick Kay Hooper (Savu Savu Central, Fiji), b 9 Mar 1871, m 1902, Alice, da of Gideon von Veesey, and has issue (with 2 sons d young) 1g to 2g

1g Basil Frederick Hooper, b 29 June 1905
2g Madeline Christina Anna Bramston, b 6 Nov 1909

1f John Edward Hooper, Schoolmaster (Herbertville, N Z), b 30 Sept 1872, m 30 Mar 1910, Kate, da of (—) Ensor of Wellington, N Z

5f Basil Bramston Hooper, A R I B A (Dunedin, New Zealand), b 17 Ap, 1876, m 29 Ap 1909, Jessie Edith, da of Frederick Henry Seldon of Nelson, N Z, C E, and his issue 1g

1g Aston Seldon Hooper, b 30 June 1910

6f Susan Elizabeth Hooper, Teacher (Nelson, N Z), unm

2c Jane Hooper, m 6 Oct 1864, Capt John Alves Low, R N [brother of Sir Robert Cunliffe Low, G C B](Jerusalem), and has issue (with a da, Augusta Jane, d young) 1f

1f Charlotte Low, m 30 Aug, 1894, Frank T Ellis, Head Master Bishop Gobat Boarding School for Native Boys, C M S, Jerusalem (Jerusalem), s p

2c Rev John Bramston, afterwards Slane of Forest Hall, co Essex, b 21 May 1773, d (—), m 20 June 1801, Mary Elizabeth, da of William Newton, d (—), and had issue (with a son d unm) 1d   [Nos 131310 to 131337b.]

# of The Blood Royal

1d *Maria Elizabeth Bramston Stane*, b 15 June 1802, d 27 July 1890, m 12 Jan 1822, *William Beckford of Hatchford House, co Surrey* [also descended from Edward III], b 23 Mar 1790, d at Rome 21 Jan 1859, and had iss e (with 2 das d unm) 1e to 2e

1e *Francis Bramston Beckford (Witley, Parkstone, Dorset)*, b 2 Feb 1842, m 1st, 8 July 1868, Harriett Lucy, da of Capt Richard Octavius Ward, 10th Hussars, d 19 Ap 1907, 2ndly, 20 Ap 1909, Dorothea Faith, da of Henry Foade of Luscombe, Parkstone, and has issue 1f to 2f

1f *Francis William Beckford (Lypiatt Cottage, Broadstone, Dorset)*, b 1 Feb 1873, m 18 Sept 1907, Maud, da of Charles Fletcher of Bournemouth, s p

2f *Lucy Helen Beckford*, m 30 Ap 1908, Henry John Alexander Kirby [youngest son of T F Kirby, Burser of Winchester Coll] (*Winchester*)

2e *Harriette Marianne Beckford*, unm

3c *Mary Anne Bramston*, b c 1777, d 4 Ap 1865, m 29 July 1797, John Archer Houblon of Hallingbury Place, co Essex, and Welford Park, co Berks, M P, d 1 June 1831, and had issue

See the Exeter Volume, p 344, Nos 25121-25163

2b *Mary Bramston*, d 26 June 1792, m 1758, William Deedes of St Stephens, Canterbury, Chairman East Kent Quarter Sessions, d 16 Nov 1793, and had issue 1c to 3c

1c *William Deedes of Sandling, M P*, b June 1761, d 1834, m 27 Dec 1791, Sophia, da of Sir Brook Bridges 3rd Bt [G B], d 1811, and had issue (with 4 sons who app all d s p, and 2 das d unm) 1d to 9d

1d *William Deed s of Sandling M P, J P, D L*, b 17 Oct 1796, d 30 Nov 1862, m 30 May 1833, Emily Octavia, da of E ward Taylor of Bifrons, co Kent, d 19 Feb 1871, and had issue (with 2 sons and 2 das d young) 1e to 8e

1e *William Deedes of Sandling, M P, J P, D L*, b 11 Oct 1834, d s p 27 May 1887

2e *Herbert George Deedes of Sandling Park and Saltwood Castle, co Kent, J P, Col 60th Rifles and Assist Un ler-Sec of State for War 1878*, b 28 Sept 1836, d 5 May 1891, m 5 Dec 1870, Rose Elinor, da of Maj r-Gen L Barnas, C B, Chief Commr for Oudh, and had issue 1f to 4f

1f *Herbert William Deedes of Saltwood, Lieut 1st Batt 60th Rifles (Saltwood Castle, Hythe, co Kent, 4 Lyall Street, Belgrave Square, W)*, b 27 Oct 1881, unm

2f *Wyndham Henry Deedes, Lieut 3rd Batt 60th Rifles* b 10 Mar 1883

3f *Dorothy Mary Deedes.*

4f *Marjorie Constance Deedes*

3e *Rev Brook Deedes, M A (Oxon), Vicar of Hampstead since 1900 (The Vicarage, Hampstead)*, b Jan 1847, m Feb 1889, Mary Caroline, da of Maxund Brodhurst, I C S

4e *Louisa Deedes*

5e *Mary Deedes*

6e *Margaret Deedes*, m 5 Jan 1871, Halifax Wyatt

7e *Charlotte Deedes*

8e *Jessy Deedes*

2d *Rev Julius De des, Rector of Wittisham co Kent*, bapt 25 May 1798, d 24 Oct 1879, m 11 May 1829, Henrietta Charlotte [descended from the Lady Anne, sister of Edward IV (see the Exeter Volume, p 608)], da of Edward Dering [and grand da of Sir Edward Dering, 7th Bt [E], d 1 Dec 1904, and had iss e (2 sons and 4 das)

3d *Edward Deedes, H E I C C S*, bapt 20 Jan 1802, d at Poona 26 May 1848, m 1846, Emily, da of (—) Cheek of Calcutta, M D, and had issue

4d *Rev Charles De des, Rector of West Carmel, co Somerset*, b 9 Oct 1808,

[Nos 131335 to 131394]

The Plantagenet Roll

d 25 Dec 1875, m 29 Nov 1843, *Letitia Anne* da of the Hon *Philip Pleydell-Bouverie* [E of *Radnor* Coll and a descendant of *George Duke of Clarence K G* (see *Clarence Volume*, p 505)] d 1887 *and had issue*

5d *Rev Isaac Deedes M A Rector of Bramfield* b 13 *Jan* 1811, d *Nov* 1888, m 4 *Oct* 1838 *Elizabeth* da of *George Smith of Selsdon, co Surrey, and had issue*

6d *Edmund Deedes settled in Canada*, b 1812, d (–), m 1846, *Annie*, da of (–) *Kells of Toronto*

7d *Fanny Deedes*, d *Jan* 1869, m *May* 1831, *Charles Andrew* [son of Archdeacon Indrea] d *Jan* 1871, *and had issue*

8d *Israel Deedes*, d 26 *Oct* 1870, m 1 *Aug* 1830 *George Warry of Shapwick co Somerset, J P, Barr-at-Law*, d 29 *May* 1883 *and had issue (with others d s p) 1 to e*

1e *George Deedes Warry of Shapwick, J P, M A, K C, Recorder of Portsmouth & c*, b 7 *June* 1834, d 4 *May* 1904, m 23 *Oct* 1860, *Catherine Emily*, da of *John Castleman Warren of Taunton and had issue (with others d s p) 1f to 3f*

1f *Bertram Arthur Warry of Shapwick, J P, Capt* formerly Essex Regt (*Shapwick House, Bridgwater, United Service*), b 22 *Sept* 1864, *unm*

2f *Ernest Gerald Warry*, b 11 *May* 1871, *unm*

3f *Gertrude Florence Warry unm*

2e *William Taylor Henry, I S O, B A (Oxon)*, b 4 *Dec* 1836, d (–), m *and had issue (see Appendix)*

3e *Georgiana Sophia Warry*, m 23 *Oct* 1866, Capt *Alexander Decimus Toogood*, Bengal Fusiliers, one of H M Corps of Gentlemen-at-Arms, d 4 *Dec* 1874, *and his issue (see Appendix)*]

4e *Anne Marie Warry*

9d *Marianne Deedes*, b 31 *Jan* 1817, d *Feb* 1867, m 26 *Oct* 1842, *the Rev Gordon Frederic Deedes, Lucy of Netherbury, and afterwards (1856–1898) of Haydon*, b 1 *May* 1844, d 9 *Aug* 1898, *and had issue 1e to 5e*

1e *Gordon Frederic Deedes* (*West Coker, Yeovil*), b 1 *Jan* 1848, m 1st, 27 *June* 1878, *Emily Rose*, da of Col *George Augustus Sullivan*, d 18 *Mar* 1881, 2ndly, 3 *July* 1890, *the Hon Alice Fanny Catherine*, da of *Florance George Henry (Irby), 5th Baron Boston [G B] and his issue 1f to 3f*

1f *John Gordon Deedes*, b 22 *May* 1892

2f *Bertram Gordon Deedes* } (twins), b 2 *July* 1899
3f *Percy Gordon Deedes* }

2e *Walter Gordon Deedes* (*Lympstone, Devon*), b 28 *July* 1856, m 24 *Oct* 1895, *Florence*, da of Col *H R Salusbury Trelawny, and has issue 1f*

1f *Phœbe Trelawny Deedes*, b 9 *May* 1899

3e *Rev Arthur Gordon Deedes*, St John the Divine, Kennington, b 4 *Feb* 1861

4e *Agnes Sophia Deedes* }
5e *Isabella May Deedes* } (*Pound Corner, Farnham*)

2c *Rev John Deedes*, b *Dec* 1748, d 2 *July* 1813, m 18 *Sept* 1798, *Sophia*, da of Gen *Gordon Forbes*, d *Feb* 1846, *and had issue*

3c *Mary Deedes*, d 1830, m 1799, *Robert Montague Wilmot, M D , and had issue*

5d *Theodosia Cranston*
4d *Catherine Bramston*
5d *Alice Bramston*, m *Thomas (?) or John Williams (?)*
6d *Mary Bramston*
7d *Elizabeth Bramston*
8d *Grace Bramston*
9d *Sarah Bramston*
10d *Philadelphia Bramston*

[Nos 131394 to 131408

1 Berry's "Essex Genealogies," p 50   2 Burke's "Commoners," ii 432

# of The Blood Royal

334 Descendants of the Hon ANNE LENNARD (Table XXVIII)
d (-), m HERBERT MORLEY of Glynde, co Sussex, d 1641
and had issue 1a to 3a

1a Margaret Morley, da and coh d c 1667, a h[?] p[?] that [?], m Sir
Humphrey Tufton of the Mote and Bobbing Court, co Kent, 1st Bt [E] [b 21 De
1641] [2nd brother of Nicholas 1st Earl of Thanet [E]] d Oct 1659, and had
issue 1b to 2b

1b Sir John Tufton, 2nd Bt [E], b 1663 d s p 11 Oct 1685

2b Olympia Tufton, in her issue sole h, d Sept 1680 m c 1652, Sir William
Wray of Ashby, 1st Bt [E 1660], M P, d 17 Oct 1669 and had issue
See the Clarence Volume, Table LXX and p 551, and the Essex Volume
(Clarence Supplement), pp 571-575, Nos 23486.1-100

2a Anne Morley, da and coh, m (--) Houghton [1]

3a Chrisogan Morley da and coh, m Richard Tufton of Tothill St, West
minster [4th brother of Nicholas, 1st Earl of Thanet [E]] d 4 Oct 1631, and had
issue 1b to 3b

1b John Tufton son and h, d 24 Jan 1649, father of Sir Richard Tufton
who d s p [?]

2b Mary Tufton

3b Christian Tufton, m as 2nd wife Sir Robert Huddleston of Salston, co
Camb, d s p   [Nos 131409 to 131408]

335 Descendants of the Hon MARY LENNARD (Table XXVIII),
d (-), m Sir RALPH BOSVILLE of Bradborne co Kent,
living 1619, and had issue [2] 1a

1a Leonard Bosvill, son and h, m Anne, da of Sir Thomas Ridley, LL D

336 Descendants of KATHERINE WALLER (Table XXIX), d (-),
m as 2nd wife, RICHARD COURTENAY [4th son of Sir William
Courtenay of Powderham, 1st Bt [E], d 1696, and had
issue

See the Essex Volume (Exeter Supplement), p 601, Nos 1618 1-151
[Nos 131409 to 131602]

337 Descendants of THOMAS WALLER of South Lambeth (Table
XXIX), d 1731, m. Anne, da of George Smyth of Beverley,
co York, d 1781, and had issue (with a son, James, who
d s p 1802) 1a to 2a

1a Anne Waller, da and event h, b 1713, d 1801 m 1st, John Allen of
London, d 1760, 2ndly, Jonathan Wathen of East Acton, co Middx, and had
issue 1b

1b Mary Allen, da and h, d (-), m Joshua Phipps of London [2nd son of
Robert Phipps of Walthamstow, co Essex], and had issue 1c to 2c
1c Sir (Jonathan) Wathen Phipps, afterwards (R L 7 May 1814) Waller,

---

[1] Berry's "Sussex Genealogies," 175

[2] Brydges' "Collins," m 440 see also Pocock's "Memorials of the Tuftons,"
1800, p 38 et seq

[3] Berry's "Kent Genealogies," p 481

535

The Plantagenet Roll

1st Bt [U K 30 May 1815], G C H, b 6 Oct 1769, d 1 Jan 1853, m 1st, 23 Feb 1793, Elizabeth, da of Thomas Slack of Braywick Lodge, co Berks, d 20 Jan 1809, and had issue 1d to 4d

1d Sir Thomas Wathen Waller, 2nd Bt [U K], b 24 June 1805, d 29 Jan 1892, m 20 Oct 1836, Catherine da of the Rev Henry Wise of Offchurch, co Warwick, d 24 July 1861 and had issue 1e to 5e

1e Sir George Henry Waller 3rd Bt [U K], Major Gen and Col 7th Fusiliers, b 2 Sept 1837 d 9 Oct 1892, m 21 June 1870, Beatrice Katherine Frances [descended from King Henry VII (see the Tudor Roll, p 384)], da of Christopher John Hume Tower of Huntsmore Park co Bucks J P, D L [by his wife, Lady Sophia Frances, n e Cust] d 7 Dec 1898, and had issue 1f to 4f

1f Sir Francis Ernest Waller, 4th Bt [U K], Capt Special Reserve of Officers, formerly Royal Fusiliers, served in S Africa 1899-1902 (Woodcote, Warwick), b 11 June 1880

2f Wathen Arthur Waller formerly Lieut Northumberland Fusiliers, b 6 Oct 1881, m 1904, Viola, da of Henry Le Suem of La Plaisance, Wynberg, Cape Colony, I S O, J P

3f Margaret Beatrice Waller, m 31 July 1895, Capt Denis Granville, M V O, Chief Constable co Dorsetshire (Shirley House, Dorchester), and has issue

See p 466, No 103050

4f Edith Sophia Waller, unm

2e Rev Adolphus Waller, M A, Vicar of Hunstanton, Norfolk, b 8 Oct 1838, d 16 July 1890 m 19 July 1866 Jamesina (Hunstanton Cottage, King's Lynn), da of Henry L Estrange Styleman Le Strange of Hunstanton, J P, D L, and had issue

See p 412, No 79922

3e Katherine Mary Waller, d 1 May 1884, m as 2nd wife, 10 May 1868, James Sydney Stopford [E of Courtown Coll], d 8 July 1885, and had issue

See the Tudor Roll, p 185, Nos 20925-931

4e Sophia Harriett Waller, m 9 Oct 1866, Arthur Thomas (Liddell). 5th Baron Ravensworth [U K], &c [descended from George, Duke of Clarence, K G (see the Clarence Volume, p 91)] (Ravensworth Castle, Gateshead, Eslington Park, Whittingham S O), and has issue 1f to 5f

1f Hon Gerald Wellesley Liddell (Rooksbury, Weybridge, Surrey, Wellington, &c), b 21 Mar 1869, m 11 Oct 1899, Isolde Blanche [descended from George, Duke of Clarence, K G (see the Clarence Volume, p 516)], da of Charles Glynn Prideaux-Brune of Prideaux Place, and has issue 1g to 3g

1g Robert Arthur Liddell, b 2 Jan 1902

2g Ellen Isolda Liddell, b 5 July 1905

3g Beatrice Sophia Liddell, b 23 Sept 1906

2f Hon Cyril Arthur Liddell, J P (Wellington, Durham County, &c), b 22 June 1872

3f Hon Athol Robert Henry Liddell (30 Elvay St, S W, Garrick), b 2 Feb 1881

4f Hon Emily Agnes Liddell

5f Hon Catherine Anna Liddell

5e Charlotte Louisa Waller (69 Warwick Square, S W)

2d Rev Ernest Adolphus Waller, for whom T R H the Dukes of Cumberland and Cambridge and the Princesses Sophia and Mary stood sponsors, b 11 Dec 1807, d 20 Ap 1845, m 15 Jan 1835, Louisa, da of the Rev Henry Wise of Offchurch, d 22 Oct 1874, and had issue 1e to 3e

1e Rev Ernest Alured Waller M A, Rector of Packington, Hon Canon of Worcester, Proctor in Convocation, and Rural Dean of Kenilworth (Little Packington Rectory, Coventry), b 6 Jan 1836, m 12 Jan 1864, Mary Louisa, da of Henry Burton of Rangemore, co Staff, and has issue (with an eldest son, Ernest Henry, Lieut R Fusiliers, d unm) 1f to 8f
[Nos 131663 to 131686]

536

# of The Blood Royal

1*f* Edmund Waller, *b* 24 Oct 1871 , *m* 14 June 1906, Muriel Grace [descended from King Henry VII (see the Tudor Roll, p 153)], da of the Hon Henry Arden Adderley, J P , D L [B Norton Coll]

2*f* Richard Alured Waller, *b* 1884

3*f* Louisa Jane Marion Waller

4*f* Ella Nutcombe Waller

5*f* Margaretta Waller

6*f* Katherine Louisa Waller, *m* 5 Jan 1899, Henry Arthur Heywood [Bt Coll] (*Christleton Lodge, Chester*) , and has issue 1g to 2g

    1*g* Geoffrey Henry Heywood, *b* 1903

    2*g* Charles Richard Heywood, *b* 1908.

7*f* Beatrice Mary Waller

8*f* Constance Harriett Waller, *m* 1907, Frederick Wyldbore Digby Pinney

2*c* Stamer Waller, C V O , Hon M A (Oxon) Col (ret) R E and a Military Member Oxford Territorial Force Ass , an Hon Equerry to H R H the Duchess of Albany, *formerly* Extra Equerry to Queen Victoria, has Egyptian Medal with Clasp and Bronze Star and 4th Class Midjidie, &c (*28 Bardwell Road, Oxford*), *b* 13 Aug 1844, *m* 23 Ap 1879, Sophia Louisa, da of William Willes of Astrop House, co Northants, *d* 25 June 1893 , and has issue 1*f* to 5*f*

1*f* Stamer Edmund William Waller, *formerly* Lieut Royal Fusiliers, *b* 15 Aug 1881

    2*f* Wathen Ernest Waller, *b* 1886

    3*f* Michael Henry Waller, *b* 1888

    4*f* Louisa Waller

    5*f* Dorothy Waller

3*c* Louisa Mary Waller, *m* 30 Sept 1869, the Rev Daniel Goddard Compton, M A (Oxon), Rector of Barnsley 1874-1901, &c (*The Downs, Clifton Road, West Southbourne, Bournemouth*) , and has issue 1*f* to 4*f*

    1*f* John Henry Compton, *b* 1875

    2*f* William Edmund Compton, *b* 1883

    3*f* Mary Goddard Compton

    4*f* Rose Waller Compton

3*d* Georgiana Waller, *d* 11 Ap 1871, *m* 6 July 1830, the Rev Sainsbury Langford-Sainsbury of Froyle, co Hants, Rector of Beckington cum Standerwick, *d*. 5 Sep 1849 or 1857 , and had (*with a son and da who d s p*) issue 1*e* to 3*e*

1*e* Rev Sainsbury Langford-Sainsbury, Rector of Beckington, *b* 29 June 1831 , *d* 7 July 1892, *m* 3 Aug 1864, Mary [descended from the Lady Anne, sister of King Edward IV , &c (see the Exeter Volume, p 522)], da of John Blandy-Jenkins of Kingston House, co Berks, *d* 5 Nov 1870 , and had issue 1*f* to 4*f*

1*f* Rev Thomas Hugh Langford-Sainsbury, M A (Oxon), Rector of Beckington (*Beckington Rectory, Bath*), *b* 23 Sept 1866 , *m* 2 Dec 1896, Emma Harriot [descended from King Henry VII (see the Tudor Roll, p 350), da of Arthur Harvey Thursby, J P , D L , and has issue 1g to 2g

    1*g* Thomas Audley Langford-Sainsbury, *b* 23 Nov 1897

    2*g* Hugh Waller Langford-Sainsbury, *b* 31 Dec 1902

2*f* Grace Mary Langford-Sainsbury, *m* 17 Ap 1895, the Rev Walter Errington, Rector of Hunsdon (*Hunsdon Rectory, Ware, Herts*) , and has issue 1g to 3g

    1*g* John Errington, *b* Feb 1899

    2*g* George Errington, *b* 1902

    3*g* Mary Errington, *b* 29 Ap 1903

3*f* Katherine Langford Sainsbury, *unm*

4*f* Mary Langford-Sainsbury, *unm*

2*e* Waller Langford Sainsbury, *b* 18 May 1838 , *d* 5 Sept 1898, *m* (—), da of (—) , and had issue 1*f*

1*f* Georgina Langford Sainsbury   [Nos 131687 to 131717]

3c Georgina Catherine Louisa Langford Sunsbury, *unm*

1d *Anna Eliza Waller, d 26 May 1868, m 15 July 1823, John Jarrett of Camerton Court, J P , D L , High Sheriff co Somerset 1810, b 4 July 1802, d 25 Ap 1863 and had issue 1c to 2c*

1c *Anna Mary Jarrett, Lady of the Manor of Camerton, b 25 Jan 1838, d unm 8 Dec 1893*

2c *Emily Elizabeth Jarrett, Lady of the Manor of Camerton (Camerton Court, near Bath), b 4 Dec 1840*

2c *Mary Phipps, d (–), m Thomas Blunt of Chelsea*

2a *Jane Waller, d (–), m Enos Cooper, and had issue[1]*

[Nos 131718 to 131719]

338 Descendants of MARGARET WALLER (Table XXIX), *bur* 9 Jan 1694 , *m c* 1643, Sir WILLIAM COURTENAY of Powderham, 1st Bt [E Feb 1644], *d* 4 Aug 1702 , and had issue

See the Exeter Volume, Table V , pp 102 128, Nos 900 1645, and the Essex Volume (Exeter Supplement), pp 601–606, Nos 1618 1–154

[Nos 131720 to 132619]

339 Descendants of SIMON (HARCOURT), 1st VISCOUNT HARCOURT [G B] P C, Lord High Chancellor of Great Britain 1712-1714 (Table XXIX.). *b.* 1661 , *d* 29 July 1727 , *m* 1st, 18 Oct 1680, REBECCA, da of the Rev Thomas CLARK, M A , *bur* 16 May 1687 , and had issue 1a to 3a

1a *Hon Simon Harcourt, M P , b 1685, d s p 1 July 1720, m Elizabeth, da of John Evelyn of Wotton, co Surrey, and had issue 1b to 2b*

1b *Simon (Harcourt). 2nd Viscount and (21 Dec 1749) 1st Earl of Harcourt [G B]. Viceroy of Ireland b c 1712 d 16 Sep 1777, m 16 Oct 1735, Rebecca, da and h of Charles Sam onne Le Bas of Pipwell Abbey, co Northants, d 16 Jan 1765 , and had issue (with a da), Lady Lee, whose issue failed) 1c to 2c*

1c *George Simon (Harcourt), 2nd Earl of Harcourt [G B], b 1 Aug 1736, d s p 20 Ap 1809*

2c *William (Harcourt), 3rd Earl of Harcourt [G B], Field-Marshal, G C B , b 20 Mar 1743, d s p 18 June 1830*

2b *Martha Harcourt a co-h to the Barony of Fitzalan [E 1295], d 8 Ap 1794, m as 3rd wife, 10 Ap 1844, George (Venables-Vernon), 1st Baron Vernon [G B 1762], d 21 Aug 1780, and had issue 1c to 2c*

1c *Henry (Venables Vernon), 3rd Baron Vernon [G B], b 18 Ap 1747, d 20 Mar 1829, m 1st 14 Feb 1779, Elizabeth Rebecca Anne da of Sir Charles Sedley, 2nd Bt [E 1702] d 16 Aug 1793, 2ndly, 29 Nov 1795, Alice Lucy, da and co-h of Sir John Whitefoord, 3rd Bt [S 1701], d 1 Aug 1827, and had issue 1d to 2d*

1d *George Charles (Venables-Vernon), 4th Baron Vernon [G B], b 4 Dec 1779, d 18 Nov 1835 m 5 Aug 1802, Frances Maria da and h of Adm the Right Hon Sir John Borlase Warren, 1st Bt [G B 1775], d 17 Sept 1837, and had issue*

See the Exeter Volume, pp 90-92, Nos 509-571

2d *Hon Henry Sedley Venables-Vernon, Lieut Col Grenadier Guards, b 1796 d 12 Dec 1845, m 29 Aug 1822 Eliza Grace, da of Edward Coke of Longford Court, co Derby [niece of Thomas William (Coke), 1st Earl of Leicester [U K]], and had issue 1c* [Nos 132620 to 132685]

---

[1] Berry's "Buckinghamshire Genealogies," p 5

# of The Blood Royal

1c *Edward Henry Venables-Vernon, Lieut R N* , b 5 July 1823, d 7 Jan 1856, m 21 Jan 1851, *Louisa Sophia Charlotte, da of th Ven J G de Jour Archdeacon of Mauritius, d* 1895 , *and had issue* 1f

1f *Sir William Henry Venables-Vernon, Bailiff of Jersey, formerly Attorney-Gen for that Island, &c (St Peters House, Jersey, Travellers)*, b 1 Jan 1852, m 18 Dec 1880, *Julia Matilda, da and h of Philip Gossett of Bagot Manor, Jersey*

2c *Right Rev the Hon Edward Venables-Vernon, afterwards (R I. 15 Jan 1831) Harcourt D D , Lord Archbishop of York*, b 10 Oct 1757 , d 5 Nov 1847 , m 5 Feb 1784, *Lady Anne, da of Granville (Leveson-Gower), 1st Marquis of Stafford [G B]*, d 16 Nov 1832 , *and had issue*

See the Tudor Roll, pp 380-383, Nos 28983-29129

2a *Hon Anne Harcourt*, d (-) , m *John Barlow of Alebeak, co Pembroke*

3a *Hon Arabella Harcourt*, d (-) . m *Herbert Aubrey of Clashanger*

[Nos 132686 to 132833

340 Descendants, if any, of ELIZABETH WALLER wife of Sir FRANCIS BARNHAM (*sic*), and of BRIDGET WALLER, wife of Sir THOMAS MORE (Table XXIX)

341 Descendants of the Hon ELIZABETH LENNARD (Table XXVIII.), *d* (-) , *m* 1599, Sir FRANCIS BARNHAM of Boughton Mon-chelsea, co Kent, *d.* 1646 , and had issue (15 children of whom) 1*a* to 11*a*.

1a *Dacres Barnham*, d s p

2a *Sir Robert Barnham 1st Bt [E 1663]* M P , b 1606 d *apparently p in s May or June* 1685 , m 1st, c 1636, *Elizabeth or Anne da of Robert Henley of Henley, co Som* , 2ndly (lic 18 Aug), 1663, *Hannah, widow of* (-) *Lowfield, da of* (-) *Nichols of London*, d 1686 , *and had issue* 1b *to* 5b

1b *Francis Barnham, only son living* 1664, *and then unm*,[1] d s p 1668

2b[1] *Mary Barnham*

3b[1] *Elizabeth Barnham*[2] m *as* 1st *wife, Sir Nathaniel Powell, 2nd Bt* [E], d c 1707, *and had issue (with a son Nicholas, who d s p and d is)* 1c

1c *Barnham Powell* d s p . m *Elizabeth, da of James Clitherow of Boston House, Brentford, co Midx* , *and had issue* 1d *to* 3d

1d *Sir Nathaniel Powell, 3rd Bt* [E], b c 1688 , d *unm* 1708

2d *James Powell, d unm*

---

[1] Visitation of Kent See the " Complete Baronetage,' m 285 In Le Neve's MS " Baronetage " he is said to have m 1st, a lady unnamed , 2ndly, the widow of Lowfield (by whom he is given a dr and h), and 3rdly, Anne, widow of John Shirley The last was the da of Sir Philip Parker, and the licence is dated 12 Sept 1667 In the Waller pedigree (see Table XXIX) Elizabeth (a cousin german of this Francis Barnham) is said to have married a Sir Francis Barnham, and she may perhaps have been the first wife The second is clearly a mistake for his father's second marriage A very confused genealogy is given in Burke's 'Extinct Baronetcies,' and also in Berry's ' Hants Pedigrees ' (p 167) There he is said to have m Anne Shirley, and to have been father of Sir Robert Barnham, 2nd Bt , who d 1728, leaving issue a dau and h , who m Thomas Ryder (see above) As Sir Robert, if he ever existed, cannot have been born before 1668, and as Sir Barnham Ryder (son of the above-named Thomas Ryder and Philadelphia Barnham) was knighted 1711, this descent is impossible

[2] In Berry's ' Hants Pedigrees " (p 167) she is made the daughter of her nephew, Sir Barnham Ryder

The Plantagenet Roll

3d Sir Christopher Powell,[1] 4th Bt [E], M P, b c 1690, d s p 5 July 1742

4b[1] Annie Barnham

5b[2] Philadelphia Barnham, b 1664, m Thomas Rider, and had issue 1c

1c Sir Barnham Rider of Kent, knighted 20 Oct 1711, m 1717, (—), da of Adm Littleton, and had issue 1d

1d Sir Thomas Rider of Boughton Monchelsea, knighted 13/21 Mar 1744

3a Edward Barnham

4a Francis Barnham of Maidstone, will dated 1677, said to have m Margaret (—), and to have had issue (Francis, Robert, Edward, Frances, Grace, and Margaret)

5a William Barnham [1]	6a Dudley Barnham
7a Martin Barnham	8a Margaret Barnham
9a Judith Barnham	10a Elizabeth Barnham
11a Frances Barnham	

342 Descendants, if any surviving, of the Hon FRANCES LENNARD (Table XXVIII), d (–), m Sir ROBERT MORE of Losely, co Surrey, M P, b 21 May 1581, d 2 Feb 1626, and had issue 1a to 4a

1a Sir Poynings More, 1st Bt [E 18 May 1612], M P, b 13 Feb 1606, d 11 Ap 1649, m Elizabeth, widow of Christopher Rous of Henham, co Suffolk, da of Sir John Fytch of Woodham Walter, co Essex, d 13 Sept 1666, and had issue 1b

1b Sir William More 2nd Bt [E], M P, b 1644, d s p 24 July 1684

2a Rev Nicholas More of Loseley, d 22 Dec 1684, m Susan, da of Richard Saunders, and had issue (with Robert, d s p 1689, and Elizabeth, d unm 13 Feb 1692) 1b

1b Margaret More, d 14 Sept 1704, m Sir Thomas Molyneux, and had issue (with a da) 1c

1c Sir More Molyneux of Loseley, d (–), m 1 Mar 1722, Casandra, da and co h of Francis Cornwallis of Abermarles, co Caermarthen, and had issue

3a Robert More, Major in the Army m and had issue 1b

1b Frances More, d s p 1680, m as 1st wife, John Latton of Esher Place, co Surrey, bur 23 Nov 1727

4a Anne More, m John Gresham

343 Descendants of Lady MARY FITZALAN (Table II), b c 1540, d 25 Aug 1557, m as 1st wife, 1556, THOMAS (HOWARD), 4th DUKE OF NORFOLK [E], K G, b 10 Mar 1536, d 2 June 1572, and had issue

See Section 199, p 331, Nos 52611-55152   [Nos 132834 to 133675

344. Descendants of Lady ANNE WENTWORTH (Table XXX), b 8 Oct 1629, bur 8 Jan 1696, m 13 Nov 1654, EDWARD (WATSON), 2nd LORD ROCKINGHAM [E] bapt 30 June 1630, d 22 June 1689, and had issue

See the Exeter Volume, Table XIII and pp 243-261, Nos 8843-9890, and Supp, 9763 1-13   [Nos 133676 to 134736

---

[1] Berry and Burke confuse him with a William Barnham, Mayor of Norwich 1652, and make him marry three times and have numerous descendants. See, however, Henry Woodds' "Family of Woodds," p 18

# of The Blood Royal

345 Descendants of Sir WILLIAM WENTWORTH (Table XXX), d
(–); m. ELIZABETH, da and co-h of Thomas SAVILE of
Hasseldon Hall, co York, and had issue

See the Mortimer-Percy Volume, Part II

346 Descendants of the Hon ANNE HOWARD (Table XXXI), d.
12 Sept 1775, m as 2nd wife, 14 Sept 1729, the Right Hon
Sir WILLIAM YONGE of Colyton, 4th Bt [E 1661], K B, P C,
M P, b c 1693; d 10 Aug 1755, and had issue 1a to 7a

1a. Right Hon Sir George Yonge, 5th Bt [E], K B, P C, M P, Governor of
the Cape, &c, b 1731, d s p 25 Sept 1812

2a Anne Yonge

3a Louisa Yonge, m the Very Rev Charles Howard, D D, Dean of Exeter

4a Charlotte Yonge, m James Stuart Fulk

5a Amelia Yonge, d in or before 1831 m as 2nd wife, 3 July 1774, Sir Edward
Lloyd of Pengwern. co Flint, 1st Bt [G B 29 Aug 1778], d s p 26 May 1795

6a Juliana Yonge, m as 3rd wife, Henry William Sanford of Walford, co
Som (see the Essex Volume, p 335)

7a Sophia Yonge

347 Descendants of GEORGE (VERNON), 2nd BARON VERNON [G B]
(Table XXXI), b 9 May 1735, d 18 June 1813, m 2ndly,
25 May 1786, GEORGIANA, da of William FAUQUIER, d 31 May
1823, and had issue 1a

1a Hon Georgiana Vernon, b 9 Jan 1788, d 13 Sept 1824, m 19 Sept 1809,
Edward (Harbord), 3rd Baron Suffield [G B 1786], d 6 July 1835, and had issue
1b to 2b

1b Edward Vernon (Harbord), 4th Baron Suffield [G B], b 19 June 1813,
d unm 22 Aug 1853.

2b Hon Georgiana Mary Harbord (see p 555), b 23 June 1816, d 13 Nov
1903, m 1st, 2 Oct 1837, George Edward Anson, C B, d 8 Oct 1849, 2ndly,
22 Oct 1855, Charles Edward Boothby, Ranger of Needwood Forest [Bt Coll], and
had issue 1c

1c Mary Anson, m 13 Sept 1877, the Rev Robert Digby Ram, M A, Vicar
of Hampton and Preb of St Paul's [descended from King Henry VII, &c (see the
Tudor Roll, p 166)], and has issue 1d to 3d

1d George Edward Ram, b 1879

2d Frederick Montagu Anson Ram, b 1885

3d Emily Jane Ram, m 1 Oct 1901, Sir John Home-Purves-Hume-Campbell,
8th Bt [S] (Marchmont, Greenlaw, S O), and has issue 1e to 2e

1e Mabel Jane Home-Purves-Hume-Campbell

2e Elsie Barbara Home Purves-Hume Campbell   [Nos 134737 to 134742.

348 Descendants of THOMAS (ANSON), 1st VISCOUNT ANSON [U K
17 Feb. 1806] (Table XXXI), b 14 Feb 1767, d. 31 July
1818, m 15 Sept 1794, Lady ANNE MARGARET, da of Thomas
William (COKE), 1st Earl of Leicester [U.K], d 23 May 1843,
and had issue 1a to 6a

1a Thomas William (Anson), 2nd Viscount Anson and (15 Sept 1831) 1st
Earl of Lichfield [U K] b 20 Oct 1795, d 18 Mar 1854, m 11 Feb 1819,
Louisa Catherine, da of Nathaniel Philips of Slebech Hall, co Pembroke, d 20 Aug
1879, and had issue 1b to 5b

The Plantagenet Roll

1*b* *Thomas George (Anson), 2nd Earl of Lichfield [U K],* b 15 *Aug* 1825, d
7 *Jan* 1892, m 10 *Ap* 1855, *Lady Harriet Georgiana Louisa, da of James
(Hamilton), 1st Duke of Abercorn [I]. K G , P C , and had issue*

See the Tudor Roll, pp 482–483, Nos 33440–33475

2*b* *Lady Louisa Mary Anne Anson,* b 6 *Dec* 1819, d 27 *Aug* 1882, m
26 *Nov* 1838, *Edward King Tenison of Kilronan Castle, co Roscommon, Lt and
Custos Rotulorum and M P for that co , &c ,* b 21 *Jan* 1805, d 19 *June* 1878,
and had issue 1*c* *to* 2*c*

1*c* *Louisa Frances Mary Tenison,* d 9 *Sept* 1868, m *as* 1*st wife,* 14 *June
1866, John Baptiste Joseph (Dormer), 12th Lord Dormer [E],* d 22 *Dec* 1900;
and had issue

See the Exeter Volume, pp 275–276, Nos 10944–10947

2*c* *Florence Margaret Christina Tenison,* d 18 *Oct* 1907, m 23 *Jan* 1872,
Henry Ernest Newcomen (King, afterwards R L 10 Mar 1883, *King-Tenison), 8th
Earl of Kingston [I]* d 13 *Jan* 1896, *and had issue* 1*d* *to* 2*d*

1*d* Henry Edwyn (King-Tenison) 9th Earl of Kingston [I], *late Irish Guards*
(*Kilronan Castle, Keadue , Oakport, Boyle, both co Roscommon , Carlton , Guards,
&c*), b 19 Sept 1874, m 3 Feb 1897, Ethel Lisette, da of Sir Andrew Barclay
Walker, 1st Bt [U K], and has issue 1*e* to 4*e*

1*e* Robert Henry Ethelbert (King-Tenison), Viscount Kingsborough, b 27 Nov
1897

2*e* Lady Sheelah Florence Lizette King-Tenison
3*e* Lady Honor Bridget King-Tenison
4*e* Lady Doreen Kara King-Tenison

2*d* Lady Edith Charlotte Harriet King-Tenison, m 11 Sept 1907, Capt
George Ivor Patrick Poer O'Shee, Prince of Wales' Leinster Regt (see below)
(26 *Hans Crescent, S W*), and has issue 1*e* to 2*e*

1*e* Patrick Ivor Rivallon O'Shee, b 18 Feb 1910.
2*e* Christine O'Shee

3*b* *Lady Anne Frederica Anson,* b 22 *Feb* 1823, d 22 *July* 1896, m *as* 1*st
wife,* 29 *Aug* 1843, *Francis (Wemyss-Charteris-Douglas), 10th Earl of Wemyss and
6th Earl of March [S], 3rd Baron Wemyss [U K] (Gosford, Longniddry , Elcho
Castle, co Perth, &c*), *and had issue*

See the Clarence Volume, pp 253–254, Nos 6095–6116

4*b* *Lady Harriet Frances Maria Anson,* b 26 *Dec* 1827, d 15 *Feb* 1898,
m 7 *June* 1851, *Augustus Henry (Venables Vernon), 6th Baron Vernon [G B],* d
1 *May* 1883, *and had issue*

See the Exeter Volume, pp 90–91, Nos 509–525

5*b* Lady Gwendoline Isabella Anna Maria Anson (*Gardenmorris, Kilmac-
thomas, co Waterford*), m 19 Ap 1865, Nicholas Richard Power O'Shee of Gardenmorris, co Waterford, J P , D L , d 30 Mar 1902, and has issue 1*c* to 5*c*

1*c* Richard Alfred Poer O'Shee of Gardenmorris, &c , Major R E , and Commr
Brito-French Boundary Commission, W Africa, has Benin Exped Medal and Clasp
1897 and West Africa Clasp 1897–1898 (*Gardenmorris, Kill, Piltown , Sheestown,
near Kilkenny*), b 6 Aug 1867

2*c* John Marcus Poer O'Shee, Dep Inspector R I C , b 1869, m 22 Sept
1900, Myrtle Constance, da of Col Ynyr Henry Burges of Parkanaur, co Tyrone,
and has issue 1*d*

1*d* [da] O'Shee, b 19 Ap 1903

3*c* George Ivor Patrick Poer O'Shee, Capt Royal Canadians (Leinster Regt)
and Adj 5th Batt Rifle Brig (26 *Hans Crescent, S W*), b 4 June 1873, m 11 Sept
1907, Lady Edith Charlotte Harriet (see above), da of Henry Ernest Newcomen
(King-Tenison), 8th Earl of Kingston [I], and has issue

See above, Nos 134789–134790

4*c* Gwendolen O'Shee
5*c* Aline Angela O'Shee   [Nos 134743 to 134838.

542

# of The Blood Royal

2a Hon George Anson, Major-Gen and Com-in-Chief in India, b 13 Oct 1797, d in India 27 May 1857, m 30 Nov 1830, the Hon Isabella Elizabeth Annabella [descended from King Henry VII, &c], da of Cecil Weld (Forrester), 1st Baron Forrester [U K], d 29 Dec 1858, and had issue

See the Tudor Roll, p 302, Nos 25625-25654

3a Hon Anne Margaret Anson, b 3 Oct 1796, d 19 Aug 1882, m as 2nd wife, Archibald John (Primrose), 4th Earl of Rosebery [S], 1st Baron Rosebery [U K], K T , P C , d 4 Mar 1868, and had issue 1b

1b Lady Anne Primrose, b 22 Aug 1820, d 17 Sept 1862, m as 3rd wife, 30 May 1848, the Right Hon Henry Tufnell, P C , M P , d 15 June 1854, and had issue 1c

1c Henry Archibald Tufnell, M A (Oxon), b 15 May 1854, d (? s p) 21 Sept 1898

4a Hon Frances Elizabeth Anson, b 9 Jan 1810, d 25 Dec 1899, m 1st, 12 Sept 1835, the Hon Charls John Murray [2nd son of David William, 3rd Earl of Mansfield [G B], K T], d 1 Aug 1851, 2ndly, 10 Sept 1853, Ambrose I sted of Ecton, co Northants, d s p 13 May 1881, and had issue 1b to 2b

1b Charles Archibald Murray of Taymount (Taymount, Stanley Perthshire), b 10 Oct 1836, m 1st, 27 Ap 1865, Lady Adelaide Emily [descended from King Henry VII (see Tudor Roll, p 270)], da of William Basil Percy (Feilding), 7th Earl of Denbigh [E] and Desmond [I], d 24 May 1870, 2ndly, 11 June 1878, Blanche, da of Sir Thomas Moncreiffe, 7th Bt [S] [by his wife Lady Louisa, née Hay], and has issue 1c to 6c

1c Ronald William Murray (Homefield, Fishponds, Bristol) b 10 May 1866, m 16 Feb 1904, Constance Mary Jane [descended from King Henry VII, &c (see Tudor Roll, p 477)], da of Gen Sir Richard Chambre Hayes-Taylor, G C B [M of Headford Coll]

2c Archibald John Percy Murray (Logie House, Methven, Perth), b 16 July 1867, m 9 Ap 1907, Dulcibella, da of Collingwood Lindsay Wood of Freeland, Forgandenny

3c Charles John Murray, Lieut Coldstream Guards and A D C to Gov of British East Africa (Bachelors', Guards, &c), b 1 Dec 1881

4c [1] Margaret Frances Murray, m 10 July 1902, Arthur Holford, late 19th Hussars, and has issue 1d

1d Violet Adelaide Margaret Holford, b July 1905

5c [2] Gertrude Blanche Murray, m 12 June 1907, Alasdair Ronald Macgregor of Macgregor (The Hermitage, Rothesay, Isle of Bute), and has issue 1d to 2d

1d Malcolm Findanus Macgregor, b 2 Mar 1908

2d Dorviegelda Malvina Macgregor, b 5 Ap 1910

6c.[2] Edith Lilian Murray

2b Frederick John George Murray, Col formerly 3rd Dragoon Guards (Dedington, Oxford , Junior United Service , Travellers', &c), b 18 May 1839

5a Hon Frederica Sophia Anson, b 24 Aug 1814, d 11 Oct 1867, m 21 Ap 1838, Lieut -Col the Hon Bouverie Francis Primrose, C B [2nd son of Archibald John, 4th Earl of Rosebery [S], K I], d 20 Mar 1898, and had issue
See the Clarence Volume, p 167 Nos 20762-20779

6a Hon Elizabeth Jane Anson, b 26 Feb 1816, d 15 Sept 1891, m 18 July 1837, Henry Manners (Cavendish), 3rd Baron Waterpark [I], b 8 Nov 1793, d 31 Mar 1863, and had issue 1b to 3b

1b Henry Anson (Cavendish), 4th Lord Waterpark [I] and 5th Bt [G B], J P , D L (Doveridge, Derby), b 14 Ap 1839, m 1873, Emily, da of John Stenning, and has issue 1c to 4c

1c Hon Charles Frederick Cavendish, Lieut R N , b 11 May 1883

2c Hon Mary Cavendish   [Nos 131859 to 131900.

543

The Plantagenet Roll

3c Hon Winifred Cavendish, m 8 Mar 1904, George Ashton Strutt (*Rock House, Cromford, near Matlock*)

4c Hon Norah Lilian Cavendish

2b Hon Eliza Anne Cavendish, m 12 July 1859, Haughton Charles Okeover of Okeover, J P , D L , High Sheriff co Derby 1862 (see p 548) (*Okeover Hall, Ashbourne*), and has issue 1c to 8c

    1c Haughton Eddred Okeover, M V O , Capt 7th Batt King's Royal Rifle Corps, b 10 May 1875

    2c Mabel Alice Okeover

    3c Hon Maude Okeover, *formerly* (1884-1887), Maid of Honour to H M Queen Victoria, m 1st as 2nd wife, 11 Oct 1887, Sir Andrew Barclay Walker of Osmaston, 1st Bt [U K], J P , d 27 Feb 1893, 2ndly, 30 July 1895, John Frederick Lort Phillips of Laurenny, J P [descended from the Lady Anne, sister to King Edward IV (see Exeter Volume, p 115)] (*Laurenny Park, Pembroke*)

        1c Ruth Isabel Okeover, m 3 Nov 1903, Capt Hervey Ronald Bruce, Irish Guards [son and h of Lieut -Col Sir Hervey Juckes Lloyd Bruce, 4th Bt [U K], J P , D L (*Downhill, Coleraine, co Londonderry*)

    5c Edith Mary Okeover, m 11 Aug 1891, Capt the Hon Herbert Tongue Allsopp, J P , *late* 10th Hussars [descended from the Lady Anne, sister of King Edward IV (see Exeter Volume, p 446)] (*Walton Bury, near Stafford*), and has issue 1d

        1d Cynthia Bridget Allsopp

    6c Ethel Blanche Okeover, m 30 May 1899, Sir Peter Carlaw Walker of Osmaston, 2nd Bt [U K], D L , Lieut -Col Comdg Derbyshire Yeo (*Osmaston Manor, Ashburne, Derby , Junior Carlton, &c*), and has issue 1d to 2d

        1d Ian Peter Anthony Monro Walker, b 30 Nov 1902

        2d Enid Walker

    7c Mercy Lilian Okeover, m 20 July 1897, the Hon Assheton Nathaniel Curzon [4th son of Alfred Nathaniel Holden, 4th Baron Scarsdale [G B], and a descendant of the Lady Anne, sister of King Edward IV (see the Exeter Volume, p 455)] (34 *Stanhope Gardens, S W*), and has issue 1d to 4d

        1d Ralph Okeover Nathaniel Curzon, b 24 July 1904

        2d Joan Doreen Curzon, b 13 June 1898

        3d Rhona Lilian Curzon, } twins
        4d Vera Lilian Curzon, }

    8c Victoria Alexandrina Okeover

3b Hon Adelaide Cavendish (10 *Egerton Place, S W*), m as 2nd wife, 3 Dec 1863, Samuel William Clowes of Broughton Hall and Norbury, M P , J P , D L [descended from the Lady Isabel Plantagenet, aunt of King Edward IV], d 31 Dec 1898 , and had issue

See the Essex Volume, p 358, Nos 35369-35378   [Nos 134901 to 134929.

349 Descendants of Sir GEORGE ANSON, G C B , K T S , M P., Gen in the Army and Col 4th Dragoon Guards, Equerry to H R H the Duchess of Kent, Groom of the Bedchamber to H.R H the Prince Consort, and finally Governor of Chelsea Hospital (Table XXXI), b 12 Aug 1769 , d 4 Nov. 1849 , m. 27 May 1800, FRANCES, sister of Sir Frederick Hamilton, 5th Bt. [S 1646], da of Capt John William HAMILTON, d 24 Feb 1834 , and had issue (with 2 elder sons who d s.p.) 1a to 10a

    1a *Frederic Walpole Anson*, Major H E I C S , b 21 May 1806 , d 12 Nov 1818 , m 25 July 1827, Catherine, da of (—) Hanson, b 11 June 1880 , and had issue (with an elder son who d young) 1b to 3b

544

# of The Blood Royal

1*b* Frederick William Norgate Hamilton Anson, *b* (—)

2*b* Thomas Anson, *b* (—), *m* in New Zealand, and has issue

3*b* Frances Anson, d *c* 1846, *m Major Wilkie*

2*a Talavera Vernon Anson, Adm R N, b* 26 Nov 1809, d (-) *m* 1*st*, 13 *June* 1843, *Sarah Anne, da of Richard Potter, M P for Wigan, d* 5 *May* 1846, 2*ndly*, 24 *Aug* 1847, *Caroline Octavia Emma, da of Major-Gen William Staveley, Com -in-Chief of Madras, and had issue (with 2 sons who d s p*) 1*b to* 5*b*

1*b* Charles Vernon Anson, Com R N, *b* 4 Feb 1846, *m* 1 Jan 1871, Louisa Augusta Anne, da of the Hon Robert Hare [E Listowel Coll], *d* 1898, and had issue (Kathleen Louisa Anson, *b* 23 Dec 1874, *d* 26 Feb 1880)

2*b* Edward Harcourt Anson, *b* 7 Feb 1858

3*b* ª Sarah Constance Anson

4*b* ª Charlotte Rose Anson

5*b* ª Adelaide Frances Mary Anson

3*a Octavius Henry St George Anson, Major 9th Lancers, served throughout Indian Mutiny,* b 28 *Sept* 1818, d 14 *Jan* 1859, *m* 1*st*, 20 *Feb* 1845, *Katherine Harriette, da of James Wemyss of Cawnpore, H E I C S* [*E Wemyss Coll*], d 17 *May* 1849, 2*ndly,* 12 *Dec* 1850, *Frances Elizabeth, da of Major-Gen James Manson of London, d* 19 *Feb* 1901, *and had issue* 1*b to* 7*b*

1*b* George Wemyss Anson, J P, Lieut -Col (ret) Indian Army (*Garvock, Kippington, Sevenoaks*), *b* 30 Nov 1848, *m* 28 Nov 1878, his cousin, Katherine Harriette, da of Sir William Muir, K C S I, LL D, and has issue (with a son, Octavius Muir Hamilton Anson, Indian Army, previously Dorset Regt, *b* 13 Nov 1879, *d unm* 29 Aug 1905, and a da *d* young) 1*c* to 4*c*

1*c* George Frank Wemyss Anson, Capt Indian Army, *b* 22 Mar 1881

2*c* Katharine Wemyss Anson

3*c* Mabel Wemyss Anson

4*c* Maud Vernon Anson

2*b* Henry Brooke Anson, Capt R N (48 *St Edward s Road, Southsea*), *b* 7 Dec 1852, *m* 19 Aug 1891, Mary, da of Col Hall, and has issue

3*b* James Okeover Anson, of the Land Survey Dept, New Zealand (*King's Road, Lower Hutt, Wellington*), *b* 7 Ap 1854, *m* 7 Mar 1900, Rebekah Midgley, da of James Naylor of Bradford, co York, and has issue 1*c* to 5*c*

1*c* James Midgley Anson, *b* at Wellington Prov, N Z, 15 Ap 1901

2*c* Victor Hamilton Anson, *b* there 17 Aug 1902

3*c* Robert Alexander Anson, *b* there 30 Sept 1903

4*c* Charles Okeover Anson, *b* there 27 Mar 1905

5*c* Mabel Alice Anson, *b* there 25 May 1908

4*b* Rev Harcourt Suft Anson, Rector of Southover (*Southover Rectory, Lewes*), *b* 24 Oct 1857, *m* 1 July 1886, Edith, da of Edward Thomas Busk, and has issue (with a da *d* young) 1*c* to 6*c*

1*c* Wilfrid Gordon Anson, *b* 14 Sept 1890

2*c* Arthur Harcourt Busk Anson, *b* 28 June 1895

3*c* Cyril Okeover Anson, *b* 29 July 1899

4*c* Dorothy Susan Anson

5*c* Edith Rowena Anson

6*c* Frances Grace Anson

5*b* Octavius Henry St George Anson (*N* 1229 *E Johnson Street, Madison, Wis, U S A*), *b* 8 Ap 1859, *m* at Milwaukee 3 Mar 1902, Charlotte Elizabeth, da of Daniel Andreas Whit Beck

6*b* ¹ Fanny Caroline Anson, *m* 3 July 1866, William Coldstream, H E I C S (69 *West Cromwell Road, S W*), and has issue 1*c* to 6*c*

1*c* William Menzies Coldstream, Maj R E, *b* 19 Feb 1869, *m* 29 July 1897, Adele Margaret Edith, da of Sir John Foster Stevens, and has issue 1*d* to 2*d*

1*d* William John Anson Coldstream, *b* 15 July 1901

2*d* Margaret Anson Coldstream, *b* 24 May 1898   [Nos 134930 to 134960

The Plantagenet Roll

2c George Probyn Coldstream, M B, C M (Edin), b 16 Aug 1870, m 25 Ap 1895, Susan Jane Lilian Mercer, da of Major Mercer Tod, late 43rd Regt, and has issue 1d to 5d

    1d George Anson Probyn Coldstream, b 20 July 1899

    2d William Menzies Coldstream, b 28 Feb 1908

    3d Winifred Mercer Muir Coldstream, b 12 Mar 1896

    4d Enid Lilian Wemyss Coldstream, b 13 Aug 1897

    5d Kathleen Nancy Coldstream, b 5 Aug 1900

3c John Coldstream, I C S, b 23 Dec 1877, unm

4c Margaret Muir Coldstream, m 4 Oct 1890, Thomas Wistar Brown of Philadelphia, and has issue 1d to 6d

    1d Moses Brown, b 6 Nov 1892

    2d William Wistar Brown, b 29 Jan 1896

    3d Margaret Coldstream Brown, b 4 Aug 1891

    4d Frances Mary Brown b 4 Dec 1894

    5d Rhoda Menzies Brown, b 15 Dec 1901

    6d Lydia Wistar Brown, b 16 Ap 1903

5c Katherine Harriette Coldstream, m 25 Ap 1893, Major Ernest Moncrieff Paul, R E, and has issue 1d to 6d

    1d Henry William Moncrieff Paul, b 20 Jan 1894

    2d George Anson Moncrieff Paul, b 31 July 1895

    3d Ernest Kenneth Moncrieff Paul, b 17 July 1897

    4d Cedric Stewart Toller Paul, b 6 Mar 1905

    5d James Stewart Moncrieff Paul, b 22 Feb 1908

    6d Emily Moncrieff Paul, b 8 Aug 1901

6c Elizabeth Huntly Muir Coldstream, m 22 Oct 1901, Reginald Fendale Lowis, Assist Comr Port Blair, and has issue 1d to 4d

    1d John William Anson Lowis, b 27 Sept 1908

    2d Elizabeth Evelyn Lowis, b 30 June 1903

    3d Janet Marion Lowis, b 27 Oct 1904

    4d Mary Hope Wemyss Lowis, b 8 Mar 1907

7b² *Henrietta Constance Anson*, b 5 Nov 1855, d 22 Mar 1886, m 5 July 1877, *Thomas Duncan (183 Portsdown Road, Maida Vale, N W), and has issue 1c to 5c*

    1c Ernest Anson Duncan, a Clerk in the Bank of England, b 22 July 1882

    2c Emmeline Ella Duncan

    3c Frances Christine Duncan

    4c Lilian Mary Duncan

    5c Henrietta Constance Duncan

4a *Rev Thomas Anchitel Anson, M A , Rector of Longford and Rural Dean, b 14 Oct 1818, d 3 Oct 1899, m 5 Aug 1846, Anne Jane [herself descended from Edward III through the Mortimer-Percy marriage], da of Henry Packe of Twyford Hall, co Norfolk, Lieut-Col Grenadier Guards, b 19 Oct 1822, d 1 Sept 1897 , and had issue (with a da , Emily Mary, who d unm 27 Aug 1864) 1b to 8b*

1b Walter Hamilton Anson (*Harkaway, Stanley Avenue, Mosman, N S W), b 19 Aug 1849, m Annie Augusta, da of Robert Wesley Sherlock of Port Luis, Mauritius, and has issue (with a son, Archibald Vernon, d young) 1c to 4c*

    1c Beatrice Kate Hamilton Anson, b 21 Jan 1879

    2c Madeline Anson, b 31 July 1880

    3c Marjorie Doris Anson, b 4 Mar 1892

    4c Olive Audrey Okeover Anson, b 9 June 1894

2b Henry Vernon Anson (*Brookholme, Vanbrugh Park, Blackheath, S E), b 20 Feb 1852, m 10 Mar 1875, Frances Elizabeth, da of John Taylor Gorle, Capt late 40th Regt , and has issue 1c to 7c*

    1c John Anchitel Anson, b 16 May 1876

[Nos 134961 to 134998

2c Henry Percy Richmond Anson, Capt Middlesex Regt, b 20 Oct 1877, m 28 July 1909, Lilian Mary, da of Capt Thomas Daw, Middlesex Regt

3c George Okeover Anson, b 8 Aug 1880

4c Archibald Anson, a Clerk in the London and Westminster Bank, b 8 Mai 1882, m 24 Dec 1907, Mabel, da of Charles Henry Walker Biggs of Glebe Lodge, Champion Hill, S E, and has issue 1d to 2d

    1d Donald Archibald Vernon Anson, b. 5 Ap 1910

    2d Dahlia Anson, b 23 Sept 1908

5c Frances Octavia Anson

6c Mildred Anson

7c Mabel Muriel Gladys Anson

3b Charles George Archibald Anson of the Charties, West Falkland, Falkland Islands, and of Meadow Hurst, Slinfold, co Sussex, a J P for the Falklands (*Meadow Hurst, Slinfold, Sussex*), b 22 Oct 1858, m 7 Ap 1885. Mabel, da of Thomas Kerr, C M G, sometime (1880–1891) Governor and Chief Justice of the Falkland Islands, and has issue (with 2 sons Philip Thomas Archibald, b 23 June 1886 d 26 Oct 1890, and Walter Vernon, b 26 Ap 1890. d 22 Oct following) 1c

    1c Philip Archibald Noel Primrose Anson, b 29 Dec 1903

4b Henrietta Maria Anson (*Bear Wood, Wokingham, Berks*), m 15 Oct 1872, Arthur Fraser Walter of Bear Wood, J P, D L, co Berks, High Steward of Wokingham and one of H M's Lieuts for City of London, d Feb 1910, and has issue 1c to 4c

    1c John Walter, M A (Oxon), Capt and Hon Major 4th Batt Royal Berks Regt, Chairman *The Times* Publishing Coy (*Bear Wood, Wokingham, Berks*), b 8 Aug 1873 m 7 Nov 1903, Charlotte Hilda, da of Col C E Foster, and has issue 1d to 2d

        1d John Walter, b 31 Oct 1908

        2d Pamela Mary Walter, b 24 Ap 1907

    2c Stephen Walter (49 *Cornwall Gardens, S W*), b 16 June 1878, m 16 July 1904, Beatrice Mary, da of James Henry Coleman of Napier N Z, and has issue 1d to 2d

        1d Arthur Ewart Stephen Walter, b 11 May 1905

        2d Eileen Beryl Stephen Walter, b 18 Ap 1908

    3c Dorothy Walter, m 15 Sept 1898, Arthur Edmund Gill (*Chenies, Oakwood Hill, Ockley, Oxford and Cambridge*), and has issue (with a son, Arthur Charles, b 22 July 1899, d Dec 1901) 1d to 1d

        1d Humphrey Clarendon Gill, b 31 July 1903

        2d Geoffrey Walter Gill, b 3 Dec 1905

        3d Edmund Benedict Gill, b 27 June 1907

        4d Margery Gill, b 21 Oct 1901

    4c Olive Walter

5b Constance Louisa Anson

6b Charlotte Isabella Anson, m 16 Aug 1876, the Rev Henry Major Walter, Rector of St Paul's (*St Paul's Rectory, Wokingham*), and has issue 1c to 3c

    1c Elwyn Henry Walter, b 6 Sept 1885

    2c Maud Isabel Walter

    3c Rachel Walter, m 5 Ap 1904, Frederick Thomas Henry Henlé (9 *Radnor Place, Hyde Park, W*), and has issue 1d to 2d

        1d Nevil Frederick Henlé, b 11 Feb 1905

        2d Cordelia Rachel Henlé, b 14 Nov 1907

7b Madeline Anson

8b Ethel Grace Anson, m 30 Sept 1885, the Rev Egerton Corfield, M A (Camb) (*Kirkley, 15 Willis Road, Cambridge*), and has issue 1c to 5c

    1c Egerton Anson Frederick Corfield, b 3 Dec 1887

    2c Bernard Conyngham Corfield, b 22 May 1890   [Nos 134999 to 135032

The Plantagenet Roll

3c Conrad Lawrence Corfield, *b* 15 Aug 1893

4c Hubert Vernon Anchitel Corfield, *b* 21 Dec 1895

5c Ethel Marjorie Corfield, *b* 30 Oct 1891

5a Edward Hamilton Anson, *late* Bengal C S and *formerly* Gentleman Usher to Queen Victoria (57 *Cambridge Terrace, Hyde Park, W*), *b* 2 Dec 1821 , *m* 1st, 4 Jan 1843, Louisa, da of George Bunter Clapcott of Reynstone, co Dorset, *d* 25 Sept 1868 , 2ndly, 5 June 1872, Virginia Arnold, widow of George C Tugwell, da of Major-Gen Mackie, C B , and has issue (with others who *d s p*) 1b to 3b

1b Edward Rosebery Anson, *b* 25 Aug 1855 , *m* and has issue

2b Frank Charles Montresor Anson, *b* 18 Aug 1857 , *m*

3b¹ Grace Etta Anson

6a *Mary Ann Anson*, d 1875 , m 1st, 17 Sept 1823, *the Rev Charles Gregory Okeover of Okeover*, b 11 May 1792 , d 2 Aug 1826 , 2ndly, 11 Feb 1833, *Robert Plumer Ward of Gilston Park, co Herts*, d (–) , *and had issue (with possibly others by 2nd husband)* 1b

1b Haughton Charles Okeover of Okeover, J P , D L , High Sheriff co Derby 1862 (*Okeover Hall, Ashbourne, Derby*), *b* 13 Nov 1825 , *m* 12 July 1859, the Hon Eliza Anne Cavendish [also descended from Edward III through Mortimer-Percy], da of Henry Manners (Cavendish), 3rd Baron Waterpark [I], and has issue

See p 544, Nos 134901–134918

7a *Charlotte Isabella Anson*, d 18 Jan 1842 , m as 1st *wife*, 29 Mar 1828, *Edward Richard Northey of Woodcote, co Surrey, and Box, co Wilts, J P , D L , High Sheriff co Surrey* 1856, *sometime 3rd Guards and 52nd Foot, served in the Peninsular War, Waterloo, &c*, b 8 Feb 1795 , d 2 Dec 1878 , *and had issue (with a son killed in action in South Africa 6 Ap 1879)* 1b to 4b

1b Rev Edward William Northey of Woodcote, M A (Oxon), J P , Lord of the Manors of Cheam, Ewell, and Cuddington, co Surrey, and Joint Lord of the Manor of Box, co Wilts, *formerly* Vicar of Chaddesden, &c (*Woodcote House, Epsom*), *b* 23 Ap 1832 , *m* 22 Aug 1867, Florence Elizabeth [descended from the Lady Anne, sister of King Edward IV , &c], da of Sir John Edward Honywood, 6th Bt [E], and has issue

See the Exeter Volume, p 103, Nos 930–910

2b *George Wilbraham Northey of Ashley Manor, co Wilts, J P , D L , Lieut-Col Cameronians*, b 28 Jan 1835 , d 12 Mar 1906 , m 20 *Sept* 1859, *Louisa, da of Arthur James S Barrow, 23rd and 30th Regts , and had issue* 1c to 12c

1c George Edward Northey of Ashley Manor, J P , Lord of the Manors of Box, Ashley, and Ditteridge, and Patron of one Living, *late* Governor of H M Prison, Manchester (*Ashley Manor, Wilts, Chency Court, Box, Chippenham*), *b* 4 July 1860 , *m* 10 June 1885, Mabel Beatrice Helen, da of Capt F Hunter of Killylung, co Dumfries, and Weston Park, Bath , and has issue 1d to 3d

1d George Evelyn Anson Northey, Lieut 3rd Batt Essex Regt , *b* 10 Nov 1886

2d Armand Hunter Kennedy Northey, *b* 16 Jan 1897

3d Vere Wilbraham Northey, *m* Sept 1910, Austin Gardner

2c *Francis William Northey, Capt 36th Regt* , b 5 *Jan* 1862 , d 9 Aug 1898 , m *Sept* 1888, *Beatrice, da of Capt T Robinson, Indian Army , and had issue* 1d

1d Eileen Northey

3c Herbert Hamilton Northey, Capt Royal Scots Fusiliers, *b* 27 June 1870 , *m* 27 Jan 1903, Elizabeth, da of Neale Thompson of Strathdoon, co Ayr, and has issue 1d

1d Herbert Wilbraham Hamilton Northey, *b* 23 Nov 1906

4c Percy Wilbraham Northey, *b* 31 Jan 1872 , *m* 11 Mar 1896, Rosalie, da of John Roupell, and has issue   [Nos 135033 to 135075

548

# of The Blood Royal

5c Arthur Cecil Northey, Capt. Scottish Rifles, b 11 Nov 1873, m 20 Dec 1905, Madeleine, da of Col Arthur Allen Owen, Royal Bodyguard, late 88th Regt., and has issue 1d

    1d Peter Arthur Owen Northey, b 19 Nov 1906

6c Cyril Brook Northey (Ditteridge House, Wilts), b Oct 1877, m 1 May 1899, Elsa, da of C Thiedemann, and has issue 1d

    1d Rosemary Northey

7c Constance Fanny Northey, m 5 Sept 1888, the Rev Walter Barlow, M A, Rector of St Mary Magdalene, Bridgnorth (St Mary Magdalene's Rectory, Bridgnorth), and has issue 1d to 2d

    1d Walter Northey Cecil Barlow

    2d Percy Arthur Northey Barlow

8c Mary Louisa Northey

9c Alice Northey, m Ap 1883, George Jones Mitton of Mitton, Major 3rd Batt S Staffordshire Regt [descended from King Henry VII (see Tudor Roll, p 319), George Duke of Clarence, K G (see Clarence Volume, p 310), &c] (Mitton Manor, Penkridge, Stafford, Beamish Hall, Allrighton, Salop), and has issue 1d to 4d

    1d George Henwayn Northey Mitton, b 25 Oct 1893.

    2d Gladys Marjorie Alice Mitton

    3d Phyllis May Northey Mitton

    4d Muriel Emil Mitton

10c Mabel Charlotte Northey, m Sept 1902, Reginald Granville, and has issue 1d

    1d Robert Northey Granville

11c Lilian Beatrice Northey, m Oct 1904, Capt Douglas Hunter, R A, and has issue 1d to 2d

    1d Elizabeth Hunter

    2d Pamela Hunter

12c Evelyn Marion Northey, m Ap 1910, Capt Cyril Gepp King's African Rifles

3b Harriet Elizabeth Northey, m 20 Sept 1855, Capt George Ross, R E [son and h of Field Marshal Sir Hew Dalrymple Ross, G C B]

4b Agnes Constance Northey

8a Constantia Anson, d 28 Nov 1842, m 6 Oct 1831, Sir Robert North Collie Hamilton of Silverton, 6th Bt [S], K C B, Member of the Supreme Council of India 1859, who received the thanks of Parliament for his services during the Mutiny, b 7 Ap 1802, d 31 May 1887, and had issue 1b to 5b

1b Sir Frederick Harding Anson Hamilton of Silverton, 7th Bt [S], formerly Major 60th Royal Rifles (Avon Cliffe, Stratford-on-Avon), b 24 Sept 1836, m 28 Sept 1865, Mary Jane, da of H Williams, and has issue 1c to 6c

1c Robert Caradoc Hamilton, Lieut 2nd Batt Norfolk Regt, b 22 Mar 1877, m July 1907 Irene [descended from King Henry VII (see the Tudor Roll, p 154)], da of Sir Osbert L'Estrange Mordaunt 11th Bt [E]

    2c Frank Hamilton b 12 Feb 1878

    3c Constance Ida Hamilton

    4c Mary Louisa Hamilton

    5c Cerise Hamilton, m

6c Ann Eileen Hamilton, m 10 Mar 1906 Edward Cowan [2nd son of Capt Cowan of Alveston]

2b Francis Henry Hamilton, Capt 5th Lancers, b 7 Ap 1840, d 29 Nov 1891, m 12 Ap 1867, Maria Theresa, widow of Major George Ernest Rose, da of Charles Crosbie of Northlands, co Sussex, and had issue 1c to 3c

[Nos 135076 to 135103

1c Francesca Teresa Hamilton, *m* Feb 1894, Capt Victor Bitossi, 2nd Italian Grenadiers, and has issue 1d to 2d

1d Pier Francesco Bitossi, *b* 1895

2d Graziella Bitossi

2c Pyne Hamilton, *m* 18 Aug 1890, Morris Wickersham Cowen of Philadelphia, U S A

3c Ruby Hamilton, *m* 1895, Alfred Wilson Hamilton Barrett (*Pebworth House, Pebworth, Warwickshire*), and has issue 1d

1d Adrian Barrett, *b* 1896

3b Constance Eliza Anne Hamilton (*Tiddington House, Stratford-on-Avon*), *m* 19 Mar 1853, Major-Gen Alexander Ross Eliot Hutchinson, Indian Army, *d* 19 Oct 1908, and has issue 1c to 10·

1c *Alexander John Ross Hamilton Hutchinson, Capt B S C,* b 20 *Sept* 1857, (*2d ∼ p*) 27 *Feb* 1891

2c Rev Robert Hamilton Hutchinson, M A (Oxon), Vicar of St Anselm's, Kennington Cross (*St Anselm's Vicarage Kennington Cross, S E*), *b* 13 Jan 1867, *m* 2 Jan 1895, Alice Amelia, da of William Hornby

3c Anson Vernon Mackenzie Hutchinson (*Robin Ho d, Little River*), *b* 11 Oct 1869, *m* 1896, Helen, da of H Buchanan of Little River, Canterbury, N Z, and has issue 1d to 2d

1d Alexander Anson Hutchinson, *b* 24 Oct 1901

2d William John Buchanan Hutchinson, *b* 24 Feb 1904

4c *James William Hutchinson,* b 21 Feb 1876, d (–)

5c Constance Caroline Hutchinson, *m* 6 Nov 1879, Major Arthur James Lushington, *formerly* Dorsetshire Regt (*Waldo House, Beckenham, Kent*), and has issue 1d to 2d

1d Arthur Edmund Godfrey Hamilton Lushington, *b* 11 Sept 1883

2d Cecil Henry Gosset Lushington, *b* 16 Dec 1884

6c *Louisa Catherine Hutchinson,* d 10 *Ap* 1893, *m* 27 *Jan* 1886, *George William Caldwell Hutchinson,* and had issue 1d to 3d

1d Becher Alexander Colin Hutchinson, *b* 6 Oct 1889

2d Phyllis Irene Constance Hutchinson, *b* 8 Jan 1887

3d Enid Frances Caldwell Hutchinson, *b* 16 Ap 1891

7c Frances Eliza Hutchinson

8c Isabella Harriet Hutchinson, *m* 24 June 1896, Arthur Robert Johnston Dewar, Lieut 5th Batt Warwickshire Regt and Assist Sup of Police, Straits Settlements

9c Georgina Maud Hutchinson, *m* 21 Oct 1903, William Alleyne Paxton Wayte (*Buston Wilts*), and has issue 1d to 3d

1d William Guy Alexander Wayte, *b* 4 Ap 1907

2d Robert Thomas Humphrey Wayte, *b* 28 Dec 1908

3d Cicely Maud Wayte

10c Mildred Irene Hutchinson, *m* 30 Ap 1902, Cornelius Cecil Morley (*St Ann's, Milford Haven*), and has issue 1d to 3d

1d Cornelius William Morley, *b* 22 Feb 1904

2d Dorothy Constance Morley.

3d Violet Irene Morley

4b *Isabella Frances Hamilton,* d (–), *m* 8 *June* 1854, *Capt William Ross Shakespear, Madras Cav,* d 31 *May* 1861, *and had issue* 1c to 2c

1c Robert Henry Shakespear, *b* 17 Mar 1856

2c William Frederick Shakespear, *b* 21 Mar 1861

5b *Louisa Catherine Emma Hamilton* (*2 Hobart Place, S W*), *m* 26 July 1864, Charles Raymond Pelly of Plashet, co Essex [Bt of Upton Coll], *d* 12 June 1879, and has issue 1c to 4c   [Nos 135104 to 135133

# of The Blood Royal

1c Charles Hamilton Raymond Pelly, Major and Hon Lieut-Col R F A (*Aveley, Romford*, *2 Hobart Place, S W*), b 24 Ap 1867, m 1907, Mary Elizabeth, widow of Capt E Trevitt of Haslemere

2c Constance Louisa Pelly, m 1st, 21 Sept 1882, Richard Davis Matthey (who obtained a divorce 1895), 2ndly, 1895, Lloyd Harry Baxendale, J P (*Greenham Lodge, Newbury, Berks*), and has issue 1d to 2d

    1d George Cowper Hugh Matthey, b 1883

    2d Constance Joyce Matthey

3c Ethel Henrietta Pelly, m 21 Aug 1889, Charles Edward Grey Hatherell (*Radford House, near Leamington*, *Bolas Parva, near Wellington, co Salop*, *Charlton King's, Cheltenham*), and has issue 1d to 3d

    1d James Hamilton Grey Hatherell, b 8 May 1891

    2d Rita Constance Ellen Hatherell

    3d Sylvia Adelaide Anna Hatherell

4c Adelaide Pelly (*2 Hobart Place, S W*)

9a Sophia Anson, d 18 Ap 1864, m 11 *June* 1836, *James John Kinloch of Keir, co Kincardine*, d 27 Dec 1877, *and had issue (with 2 other sons and 3 other das* [1]*)* 1b to 6b

1b George Hibbert Anchitel Kinloch, Lieut-Col (ret) *late* Somersetshire L I, b 4 June 1841 m 1st, 7 Ap 1874, Margaret Emma, da of John Thomas White of Cashiobury, co Herts, d 30 July 1881 2ndly, 20 Jan 1886, Frances Jane, widow of Francis Plunket Dunne of Brittas, da of the Rev Robert Hedges Dunne, and has issue 1c to 2c

    1c [1] Victoria Frances Emma Kinloch, m 10 Mar 1897, Henry Arthur Shuckburg Upton of Coolatore, co Westmeath (*Coolatore, Moate, Westmeath*), s p

    2c [2] Grace Theodosia Farquhar Kinloch, *unm*

2b Victoria Charlotte Isabella Kinloch, m 1859, Sir Lesley Charles Probyn, K C V O, Auditor of the Duchy of Cornwall and a Member of Council of H R H the Prince of Wales, Dep-Chairman Great Northern Railway (*79 Onslow Square, S W*)

3b Theodosia Frances Mary Anne Kinloch, m 11 Jan 1859, Gen Charles Raper Stainforth, Ind Army, d 4 Feb 1883, and has issue (see Appendix)

4b Constance Helen Sarah Kinloch, m 26 Aug 1861, Lieut-Col Frederick Morris Alexander, Ind Army, and has issue (see Appendix)

5b *Susan Ferrier Kinloch*, d s p 25 July 1906 m as 2nd wife, 10 Oct 1882, *Chester Workman-Macnaghten, M A*, *Principal Rajkumar Coll*, *Bombay [Bt Coll]*, d s p 1896

6b Julia Catharine Kinloch, m 27 Ap 1878, John Fortune of Bengairn (*Bengairn, Castle Douglas, Kirkcudbrightshire*), and has issue 1c to 5c

    1c Victor Morven Fortune, Lieut Black Watch, b 21 Aug 1883

    2c Lilian Forrester Fortune, m 8 Dec 1898, Major-Gen John Archibald Henry Pollock, C B, Indian Army [Pollock of the Khyber Pass, Bt [U K 1872] Coll] (*East India United Service*), and has issue 1d to 3d

        1d Frederick Arthur Pollock, b 25 Aug 1899

        2d Justina Lilian Pollock

        3d Daphne Victoria Catherine Pollock

    3c Mildred Sophia Fortune m Feb 1902, David Landale (*Shanghai*), and has issue 1d to 2d

        1d David Fortune Landale, b 9 Nov 1905

        2d Margaret Landale

    4c Mary Forrester Fortune, *unm*

    5c Julia Violet Macnaghten Fortune, *unm*

10a *Hon Julia Henrietta Anson, Maid of Honour to Queen Victoria*, d 27 Dec
                                [Nos 135134 to 135159

---

[1] Foster's "Peerage," 1880, p 385

The Plantagenet Roll

1886, m 15 Dec 1841, Sir Arthur Brinsley Brooke of Colebrooke, 2nd Bt [U K], M P b 1797, d 21 Nov 1854 and had issue 1b to 4b

1b Sir Victor Alexander Brooke, 3rd Bt [U K] D L, a Godson of Queen Victoria, b 5 Jan 1843 d 23 Nov 1891 m 28 July 1864, Alice Sophia (Villa Louvence, Pau), da of Sir Alan Edward Bellingham, 3rd Bt [G B], and had issue 1c to 8c

1c Sir Arthur Douglas Brooke 4th Bt [U K], J P, D I, b 7 Oct 1865, d 27 Nov 1907 m 28 July 1887, Gertrude Isabella [descended through three lines from King Henry VII (see Tudor Roll, p 261, &c)] (Colebrooke Park, co Fermanagh), da of Stanlake Ricketts Batson of Horseheath, co Camb, and had issue 1d to 5d

1d Sir Basil Stanlake Brooke, 5th Bt [U K], Lieut Royal Fusiliers (Colebrooke Park, co Fermanagh), b 9 June 1888

2d Victor Mervyn Brooke, b 8 June 1893

3d Arthur Francis Brooke, b 24 Sept 1896

4d Sylvia Henrietta Brooke, b 17 Feb 1890

5d Sheelah Brooke, b 9 Jan 1895

2c Ronald George Brooke, D S O, formerly Major and Brevet Lieut-Col 11th Hussars, served in S Africa as D A A G, &c, 1899-1902, Nile Expedition 1898, &c &c, b 25 Sept 1866, m 6 May 1908, Hallee, da of Orville Howitz of Baltimore

3c Butler Brooke, b 2 May 1870, m 2 June 1910, Mary Viva, da of Cyril Earle Johnston of 4 Boulevard du Midi, Pau

4c Victor Reginald Brooke, D S O, Lieut-Col 9th Lancers and Mil Sec to Viceroy of India (Lord Minto) b 22 Jan 1872

5c Alan Francis Brooke, Lieut R F A, b 23 July 1883

6c Alice Mildred Brooke, m 28 Sept 1896, Lieut-Col James Ramsay Campbell, formerly Shropshire L I [Bt of Succoth Coll] (Ardachie Fort Augustus)

7c Kathleen Mary Brooke

8c Hylda Henrietta Brooke, m 5 July 1899, Capt Frederick Henry Arthur Des Vœux [son and h-app of Sir Charles Champagné Des Vœux, 6th Bt [I]] (31 North Audley Street, W)

2b Harry Vesey Brooke, J P D L, Capt formerly 92nd Highlanders (Fairley, Countesswells, co Aberdeen), b 23 Sept 1845, m 9 Dec 1879, Patricia, da of James Gregory Mon Byres of Tonley, co Aberdeen, and has issue 1c to 6c

1c James Anson Otho Brooke, Lieut 2nd Batt Gordon Highlanders, b 3 Feb 1884

2c Arthur Brooke, Lieut Indian Army, b 13 Feb 1886

3c Henry Brian Brooke, b 9 Dec 1889

4c Patrick Harry Brooke, b May 1895

5c Constance Geraldine Brooke

6c Alice Irene Brooke

3b Arthur Basil Brooke R N, b 1847, d 3 Aug 1884, m 11 Sept 1869, Alice Georgina (33 Egerton Gardens, S W), widow of J Shirley Ball of Abbeylara, co Longford da of the Rev William Norton of Billinglass, and had issue 1c to 4c

1c Harry Brinsley Brooke, 2nd Sec Diplo Ser (British Legation, Berne, Ireland is), b 30 June 1872 m 10 Jan 1907, Hilda Gertrude, da of Henry Tootal Broadhurst

2c Basil Vernon Brooke Comm R N, b 9 Mar 1876

3c Bertram Norman Brooke Capt Grenadier Guards, b 20 July 1880

4c Norah Mary Brooke

4b Constance Henrietta Brooke, m 1st, 3 Oct 1872, Colin John Campbell, younger, of Colgrain, Royal Scots Greys, d v p 6 Aug 1880, 2ndly, 24 Sept 1883,

[Nos 135160 to 135183

# of The Blood Royal

Col. Robert Henry Patrick Doran, *formerly* 1st Queen's Own Royal West Kent Regt. (*Lurganbrac, Brookeborough co Fermanagh*), and has issue 1c

1c Alice Constance Campbell, m 23 Oct 1895, Col. Charles Edward Lefroy *formerly* Comdg 6th Batt Rifle Brig [4th son of Thomas Paul Lefroy of Carriglas, Q C] (*Monkstown House, co Dublin*), and has issue 1d to 4d

  1d Theodore Charles Geoffrey Lefroy, b 25 Jan 1900

  2d Aileen Muriel Lefroy

  3d Constance Elizabeth Lefroy

  4d Gladys Mary Lefroy   [Nos 135784 to 135788

350 Descendants of Gen Sir WILLIAM ANSON, 1st Baronet [U K 1831], K C B (Table XXXI), b 13 Aug 1772, d 13 Jan 1847, m 26 Jan. 1815, LOUISA FRANCES MARY, da and h of John DICKENSON of London [by his wife, Mary, da and h of Lord Archibald Hamilton], d 30 July 1831 and had issue 1a to 5a

1a Sir John William Hamilton Anson, 2nd B* [U K], b 26 Dec 1816, d 2 Aug 1873, m 27 July 1842 Elizabeth Catherine [descented from Lady Isabel Plantagenet], da of Major-Gen Sir Denis Pack, K C B, d 3 July 1903, and had issue

See the Essex Volume, p 159, Nos 19054-19078

2a Sir Archibald Edward Harbord Anson, K C M G, J P Major-Gen (ret) R A, was Lieut-Gov of Penang 1867-1882 and Acting Gov Straits Settlements 1871-1872, 1877, 1879, &c (*Southfield Silverhill, St Leonards on Sea*), b 16 Ap 1826, m 1st, 9 Jan 1851, Elizabeth Mary, da of Richard Bouchier, d 23 Sept 1891, 2ndly, 15 May 1906, Isabella Jane, da of Robert Armitstead of Dunsca, and has issue 1b to 2b

  1b Archibald John George Anson, b 4 Nov 1851

  2b Elizabeth Mary Louisa Anson

3a Mary Louisa Anson, d 15 Nov 1856, m as 2nd wife 8 July 1848 the Rev Matthew Thomas Farrer of Ingleborough, co York, M A, Vicar of Addington and P C of Shirley, co Surrey, b 3 Feb 1816, d 11 July 1889 and had issue 1b to 4b

1b James Anson Farrer of Ingleborough J P, Bar-at-Law, High Sheriff co Yorks 1897 (*Ingleborough, via Lancaster, 50 Ennismore Gardens, Princes Gate, S W*), b 24 July 1849, m 1 Mar 1877, Elizabeth Georgina Anne [descended from the Lady Isabel Plantagenet (see the Essex Volume, p 158)], da of Col Arthur J Reynell Pack, C B, and has issue 1c to 2c

  1c Reginald John Farrer, b 17 Feb 1880

  2c Sydney James Farrer, b 19 Jan 1888

2b Rev William Farrer, M A (Oxon) (*Bisham Vicarage, Marlow*), b 11 Nov 1850 m, 17 July 1879, Edith Sophia da of Frederick Boyd Marson, and his issue 1c

  1c Harold Marson Farrer, b 20 Ap 1882

3b Matthew George Farrer (*The Elms Mortimer, Berks*), b 14 Feb 1852, m 26 Jan 1884 Caroline Rachel [descended from the Lady Isabel Plantagenet (see Essex Volume, p 305)], da of Robert Culling Hanbury of Poles, M P, J P, and has issue (5 sons and 1 da)

4b Mary Charlotte Farrer, m 9 Dec 1890, the Rev Charles Augustus Whittuck, M A (Oxon), Vicar of St Mary's Oxford (*St Mary's Vicarage, Oxford*)

4a Anne Georgiana Frances Anson (*Kingsthorpe Hall, near Northampton*) m 19 Feb 1846, the Rev William Thornton of Kingsthorpe Hall M A [2nd son
[Nos 135189 to 135224

of Thomas Reeve Thornton of Brockhall J P , D L], *b* 22 July 1806 , *d* 20 May 1881 , and has issue 1*b* to 5*b*

1*b* Thomas William Thornton of Brockhall, J P , High Sheriff co Northants 1886, *formerly Capt. Northants and Rutland Militia (Brockhall, near Wedon, Northants)*, *b* 26 July 1850 *m* 6 Sept 1883, Evelyn Margaret, da of Edmund Charles Barton of Daventry , and has issue 1*c* to 5*c*

  1*c* Thomas Anson Thornton, Lieut 7th Hussars, *b* 5 Jan 1887
  2*c* Ronald Edmund Thornton, *b* 13 Ap 1889
  3*c* John Burton Thornton, *b* 19 Nov 1891
  4*c* Rosamond Fremeaux Thornton
  5*c* Violet Eleanor Thornton

2*b* Frances Hugh Thornton, LL B (Camb) . J P , Bar-at-Law (*Kingsthorpe Hall, near Northampton*), *b* 8 Oct 1853 , *m* 19 Aug 1886, Adelaide Ethel, da of W Burchell, *d* 10 May 1903 , and has issue 1*c* to 2*c*

  1*c* Henry Gerard Thornton, *b* 23 Jan 1892
  2*c* Peter Fremeaux Thornton, *b* 23 Ap 1903

3*b* Bertha Anne Thornton, *m* 31 Jan 1884, the Rev Charles Brooke [descended from King Henry VII (see Tudor Roll, p 325)] Vicar of Grendon (*Grendon Vicarage, Northants*)

4*b* Anne Letitia Thornton, *m* 1 Sept 1891, the Rev Edmund Milnes Ellerbeck, *formerly Vicar of Chipperfield, Herts (3 Park Avenue, Bedford)* and has issue 1*c* to 4*c*

  1*c* Ernest Alfred Victor Ellerbeck, *b* 26 June 1897
  2*c* Bertram John James Ellerbeck, *b* 18 July 1899
  3*c* Mabel Mary Ellerbeck
  4*c* Bertha Lilian Ellerbeck

5*b* Mabel Thornton, *m* 1893, James Joseph Maclaren (*Ratho Park, Midlothian*)

5*a* Louisa Frances Maria Anson, *d* 11 *Jan* 1904, *m* 16 *Ap* 1857, *Major Francis Du Cane, R E [younger brother of Sir Charles Du Cane of Braxted, K C M G], d* 4 *Oct* 1889 , *and had issue* 1*b* to 6*b*

  1*b* Francis Charles John Du Cane *b* 7 Jan 1862 , *m* 1891, Gwendolene, da of the Rev Jonathan Harvard Jones
  2*b* Louisa Frances Du Cane
  3*b* Katherine Christabel Du Cane
  4*b* Frances Anne Du Cane
  5*b* Mary Du Cane
  6*b* Caroline Anne Bella Du Cane   [Nos 135225 to 135246]

351 Descendants of Capt EDWARD ANSON (Table XXXI), *b* 28 Ap 1775 , *d*. 18 Mar 1837 , *m* Jan 1808, HARRIOTT, da of James RAMSBOTTOM, *d* 14 Ap 1858 , and had issue 1*a* to 2*a*

1*a* *Charles Anson, b* 20 Oct 1813 , *d* 26 *May* 1851 *m* 22 *Ap* 1844, *Louisa, da of Joseph Collings of Guernsey [re-m 9 Jan 1873, William Tombs Dewé of Coates, co Glouc], and had issue* 1*b* to 3*b*

1*b* William Charles Collings Anson, *b* 18 Ap 1845 , *m* 27 Aug 1878, Eleanor Jane, da of Willoughby Wood of Hollyhurst, co Staff

2*b* Edith Elizabeth Anson, *m* 5 Ap 1865, the Rev Marcus Samuel Cam Rickards of Clifton, M A , F L S , and has issue 1*c* to 3*c*

  1*c* Robert Hilher Traherne Rickards, *b* 20 May 1874
  2*c* Marcus Cecil Anson Rickards, *b* 22 Mar 1878
  3*c* Louisa Caroline Anson Rickards   [Nos 135217 to 135251]

# of The Blood Royal

3*b* Rosalie Harriott Anson, *m* 18 Ap 1878 Capt Edward Maunsell, 13th Hussars

2*a* Harriott Anson, b 19 Aug 1811, d (2 s p), m *as 2nd wife*, 14 Aug 1855, *Capt William Dalgairns, 7th Fusiliers*, d 26 Feb 1869   [No 135252]

352 Descendants of Lieut -Col SAMBROKE ANSON 1st Foot Guards (Table XXXI), *b* 18 Feb 1778, *d* 10 Oct 1846, *m* ELIZABETH [da of (—)] HAWKINS of co Stafford, *d* 22 Mar 1866 ; and had issue 1*a*

1*a* *Elizabeth Grace Anson*, d (2 s p), m 1st 29 Mar 1831, *Thomas King of Alvediston House, co Wilts*, d 23 Dec 1863, 2ndly 22 Nov 1867, *Thomas Jarvis Bennett of Wilton, co Wilts, M D*

353 Descendants of the Rev FREDERICK ANSON, D D, Dean of Chester and Preb of Southwell (Table XXXI), *b* 23 Mar 1779, *d* 8 May 1867, *m*. May 1807, MARY ANNE, da of the Rev Richard LEVETT of Milford, co. Staff, *d* (−), and had issue 1*a* to 6*a*.

1*a* *Frederick Anson, M A , Canon of Windsor, Rector of Sudbury 1846-1876,* b 28 Mar 1811, d 9 Sept 1885, m 7 May 1845, *the Hon Caroline Maria [descended from the Lady Anne sister of King Edward IV], da of George John (Venables Vernon), 5th Baron Vernon [G B], and had issue*

See the Exeter Volume, pp 91-92, Nos 533-565

2*a* *George Edward Anson, C B , Priv. Sec to H R H the Prince Consort and Keeper of the Privy Pur e to Queen Victoria, and Treasurer and Coffer r to King Edward VII when Prince of Wales* b 14 May 1812, d 8 Oct 1849, m 20 Oct 1837, *the Hon Georgiana Mary, da of Edward (Harbord), 3rd Baron Suffield [G B] [re-m 2ndly, 22 Oct 1855, Charles Edward Boothby, Ranger of Needwood Forest [Bt Coll] and]* d 13 Nov 1903, *and had issue*

See p 541, Nos 134737-134742

3*a* *Rev Arthur Henry Anson, Rector of Potter Hanworth and Dean of Chester,* b 10 Aug 1817, d 24 Nov 1859, m 18 Feb 1851, *Augusta Theresa, da of the Right Hon Henry Tuffnell, P C , M P , d (−), and had issue* 1*b* to 5*b*
  1*b* Hugh Anson, *b* 1853
  2*b* Arthur Anson, *b* (posthumous) 20 Jan 1860
  3*b* Anne Anson
  4*b* Alice Anson
  5*b* Lucy Anson

4*a* *Ellen Anne Anson*, d (−), m 24 Aug 1837, *the Rev Temple Hillyard. Canon of Chester and Rector of Oakford, co Devon , and had issue* 1*b* to 6*b*
  1*b* *Frederick Temple Hillyard*, b 18 Aug 1838, d (2 s p) 8 Nov 1877
  2*b* George Anson Hillyard, Capt Rifle Brigade, *b* 7 Nov 1841 m 20 Nov 1878, Grace, da of the Rev Thomas Colville of Rougham
  3*b* Arthur Anson, *b* 16 Jan 1845
  4*b* Henry Anson, *b* 2 Oct 1850
  5*b* *Rev Walter Anson, Incumbent of Doddington* b 6 Ap 1853, d 21 July 1881, m 29 Jan 1879, *Ursula Mary, da of the Right Rev George Edward Lynch Cotton, D D , Lord Bishop of Calcutta [Bt Coll] [re-m 2ndly 1884, the Rev*
          [Nos 135253 to 135299]

The Plantagenet Roll

Arthur Atkinson, Hon Canon of Chester (Highpull, Northop, Flints)], and had issue 1c

    1c George Walter Hillyard, *b* 1880

    6b Ellen Anson

    5a Lucy Frederica Anson

    6a Georgina Frances Anson, *m* 9 Oct 1866, the Rev Adam Charles Gordon, M A, Rector of Dodlestone *d s p*   [Nos 135300 to 135303

354 Descendants of MARY ANSON (Table XXXI), *b* 8 Dec 1763, *d* ( ), *m* 22 Jan 1785, Sir FRANCIS FORD, 1st Bt [G B 1793] M P, a Member of the Council of Barbados, *b* 15 Nov 1758, *d* in Barbados 17 June 1801, and had issue 1*a* to 6*a*

    1a Sir Francis Ford, 2nd Bt [G B], b 15 Feb 1787 d 13 Ap 1839, m 4 Sept 1817, Eliza, da of Henry Brady of Limerick, d 29 May 1875, and had issue 1b to 5b

    1b Sir Francis John Ford, 3rd Bt [G B], b 11 Aug 1818, d 26 Nov 1850, m 31 Oct 1846, Cornelia Maria, da of Gen Sir Ralph Darling, G C B, d 21 May 1896, and had issue 1c

    1c Sir Francis Colville Ford 4th Bt [G B], b 4 June 1850, d 16 Nov 1890, m 25 May 1873, Frances Colvill (see below), da of William Ford, C S I, and had issue 1d to 5d

    1d Sir Francis Charles Rupert Ford, 5th Bt [G B] (30 Bedford Row W C), b 5 Ap 1877

    2d Rev Francis Walter Barton Ford M A (Durham), *formerly* Vicar of Dunton Green (2 Cumberland Gardens, Tunbridge Wells), b (twin) 5 Ap 1877, m 12 Sept 1909, Louisa Ginn, da of Robert McKenzie Nish

    3d Frances Elsie Ford, m 10 Sept 1900, Raymond Carpmael, A M I C E (Beechcroft Shrewsbury)

    4d Helena Blanche Colville Ford ⎫ (Shamrock Cottage, Lymington, Hants)
    5d Cornelia Caroline Ford   ⎭

    2b William Ford, C S I, B C S 1842-1869, had Bar and Medal for services at Delhi during th Mutiny, b 29 Nov 1821, d 18 June 1905, m 27 Oct 1845 Catherine Margaret, da of Major-Gen John Anthony Hodgson, H E I C S, d 23 Oct 1869, and had issue 1c to 4c

    1c Frances Colville Ford (Shamrock Cottage Lymington Hants), m 25 Mar 1873, Sir Francis Colville Ford, 4th Bt [G B], d 16 Nov 1900, and had issue
See above, Nos 135301-135308

    2c Helen Mowbray Ford (Canna Park North Bovey, Moretonhampstead)

    3c Edith May Ford, m 26 Aug 1875, Edward Penrose Arnold-Forster of Catherine J P, D L (Catherine, Burley-in-Wharfedale, Yorks), and has issue 1d to 5d

    1d Forster Delafield Arnold-Forster, Comm R N, b 27 Aug 1876, m 2 Ap 1907, Georgina May, da of Alfred Tucker of Forthampton, Orangia, and has issue 1e

    1e Georgina Margaret Arnold-Forster

    2d William Howard Arnold-Forster, Capt 4th W Riding Howitzer Brig, R F A (Heetwood, Shenston Yorks), b 30 Aug 1882, m 1 July 1909, Angela Mary Wharfedale, da of Henry Wharfedale Tennant Garnett of Wharfeside, Otley, co York, and has issue 1e

    1e Michael Garnett Arnold-Forster, l 28 May 1910   [Nos 135304 to 135320

# of The Blood Royal

3d Edward Trevenen Arnold-Forster (*Wharfedale Farm, Newcastle, Ontario, Canada*), b 16 Sept 1885

4d Francis Anson Arnold-Forster, Lieut 4th W Riding Howitzer Brig , R F A , b 20 Mar 1890

5d Iris Mary Arnold-Forster

4c Kate St Clair Ford (*Canna Park, North Bovey, Moretonhampstead*)

3b St Clair Ford, Capt Bombay S C , b 6 Jan 1830 , d 31 Jan 1896 , m 27 Nov 1862, Eliza Jane (*Zeelugt, Cheltenham*), da of Thomas Smalley Potter of East Court, co Glouc , and had issue 1c to 5c

1c Anson St Clair Ford, b 7 Oct 1864 , m 18 Feb 1903, Isabel Muin Frances, da. of Francis Adams of Llyfnant, Cheltenham , and has issue 1d to 3d

1d Aubrey St Clair Ford, b 29 Feb 1904
2d Peter St Clair Ford, b 25 Nov 1905
3d Drummond St Clair Ford, b 16 Dec 1907

2c Beauchamp St Clair Ford, Major E Yorks Regt , b 7 Ap 1867

3c Leicester St Clair Ford, b 30 July 1879 , m 12 June 1906, Hildred Carlyle, da of Rowland Treehurst of 15 Royal Crescent, Cheltenham

4c Eva St Clair Ford (*Cheltenham*), m 21 July 1898, Henry Cecil Donald, d 27 Oct 1901

5c Ada St Clair Ford, m 29 July 1893, Archibald Hamilton Donald, Solicitor, a Member of H M 's Body Guard for Scotland, *formerly* Major and Hon Lieut - Col (V D) 1st Lanarkshire Vol Rifle Corps (33 *Lynedoch Street, Glasgow*) , and has issue 1d to 3d

1d Colin George Hamilton Donald, b 8 May 1899
2d Eva St Clair Donald
3d Helen Hamilton Donald

4b Eliza Caroline Ford, d (? s p) 5 Jan 1879 , m 1st, 28 Sept 1849, Lieut - Col Christopher Simpson Maling, 68th Regt , d Mar 1860 , 2ndly, 12 Feb 1866, Lieut -Col William Charles Newhouse, late 5th Fusiliers

5b Anna Maria Ford, d 14 Feb 1881 , m as 1st wife, 13 Aug 1851, Gen Sir David Scott Dodgson, K C B , Bengal Army, d 26 May 1898 , and had issue 1c to 5c

1c St Clair Scott Dodgson, b 18 June 1852 , d (? s p)

2c Gerald Colville Dodgson (7 *Court Road, West Norwood*), b 23 May 1855

3c Rev Francis Vivian Dodgson, M A , Vicar of Ellacombe (*Ellacombe Vicarage, Torquay*), b 21 Jan 1859

4c Harcourt Leicester Dodgson. Major 2nd "Queen's Own" Rajput Light Infantry, b 14 July 1864 , d (at *Alipore, India*) 7 May 1904 , m 26 Mar 1889, Agnes Mary (*Gatteridge Manor, Denton, Canterbury*), da of Capt John Millar-Mitchell, R N , and had issue (with a son and dau d young) 1d

1d Alice May Dodgson

5c Ethel Ada Dodgson, m Claud Hamilton (*Galtrim Road, Bray, Wicklow*)

2a George Ford, d (? s p)

3a Rev Charles Ford, M A , Rector of Billingford and Postwick, d 9 May 1863 , m 9 May 1839, Catharine Juliana, da of Henry Stuart of Sidmouth [? niece of Viscount Anson], d 30 Nov 1879 , and had issue 1b to 3b

1b Henry Stuart Ford of Florida, U S A , formerly Lieut R A , b 1 Oct 1843 , d 8 Oct 1895, m 2ndly, 8 Sept 1883, Mary, da of Thomas Wells , and had issue 1c

1c Reginald Severne Ford, b 4 June 1888 , d (–)

2b Rev Charles Primrose Ford, B A (Camb), Rector of St Michael s, Stone (*The Rectory, Stone, Staffs*), b 27 May 1849 , m 2 Sept 1875, Mary Jane, da of the Rev I B Turner, and has issue 1c to 4c

1c Rev Roger Anson Ford, b 5 July 1878
2c Charles Stuart Ford, b 7 Oct 1879

557

[Nos 135321 to 135342

+ B

The Plantagenet Roll

3c Margaret Vernon Ford, m 1 Sept 1904, Reginald Taverner Johnson (*Oaklands, Barlaston, Stafford*)

4c Alice Constance Ford, m 17 July 1907, Cuthbert Bailey (*Godolphin, Wolstanton, Staffs*), and has issue 1d to 2d

1d Helen Mowbray Bailey, b 5 Ap 1909

2d Barbara Vernon Bailey, b 27 June 1910

3b *Catherine Mary Ford*, d s p 27 Oct 1900, m 12 Ap 1864, Henry Prescott Green, d 11 Jan 1892

4a *Mary Ford*, b 1786, d 12 May 1872, m 1st, 24 Feb 1807, Peter Touchet, d (-), 2ndly, 20 July 1816, Capt Henry Elton, R N [*3rd son of Sir Abraham Elton, 5th Bt* [G B], d 10 Nov 1858, *and had issue (with possibly others by 1st marriage, 2 das by 2nd who both d unm*)

5a *Georgina Ford*, d s p Ap 1879, m 4 Mar 1816, I W F Welch of Ebworth Park, co Glouc

6a *Caroline Ford*, d. 24 Sept 1882, m 26 Oct 1822, John Hyde of Ardwick, co Lancaster, d 25 Mar 1848, and had issue 1b

1b *Francis Colville Hyde of Syndale, Ospringe, co Kent, J P, Capt East Kent Yeo*, b 24 July 1826, d 9 Mar 1892, m 19 June 1850, Charlotte Amelia (*Wilderton, Branksome Park, Bournemouth), da of Gen Sir Ralph Darling, G C H, and had issue (with others who d s p*) 1c to 8c

1c John Colville Hyde, b 11 Mar 1853, *unm*

2c Francis Frederick Musgrave Hyde, *late Lieut East Surrey Regt*, b 16 June 1861, m 26 Jan 1907, Mary Jane, widow of Capt Frederick Bults, *late 77th Regt*, da of the Rev James Briggs, s p

3c Bertram Charles Anson Hyde, b 2 June 1863, *unm*

4c Arthur Colville Hyde, *late Major York and Lancaster Regts*, b 9 Sept 1866, m 1901, Lilian Amelia, da of (—) Todd, and has issue 1d

1d Arthur Frederick Colville Hyde, b 24 Dec 1901

5c Isabel Anne Hyde, *unm*

6c Evelyn Elizabeth Hyde, m 18 Oct 1893, the Rev Cyril Eden Fawcett, d 29 Aug 1894

7c Emily Mabel Hyde, m 1 Aug 1894, the Rev William Jacob, and has issue 1d to 4d

1d Isabel Frances Jacob, b 28 May 1895

2d Evelyn Mary Jacob, b 14 Nov 1897

3d Constance Kathleen Jacob, b 6 Oct 1900

4d Lois Amelia Jacob, b 27 Nov 1901

8c Dorothy Frances Hyde, *unm*   [Nos 135343 to 135359

355 Descendants of ANNE ANSON (Table XXXI), b 22 Feb 1768, d 25 May 1822, m. 20 Dec. 1792, BELL LLOYD [Baronet [G B 1778] Coll, 2nd son of Bell Lloyd of Bodfach, co Montgomery, brother of Edward Pryce (Lloyd), 1st Baron Mostyn [U K]], d. July 1845, and had issue 1a to 2a

1a *Edward Bell Lloyd, Lieut 16th Lancers*, b 3 May 1794, d 8 May 1864, m 1819, Lowry, da of Robert Morris, d 14 Feb 1878, and had issue 1b to 2b

1b *William Lloyd, of the General Post Office for 37 years*, b 7 Jan 1824, d 28 Nov 1878, m 21 Mar 1854, Anne, da of Charles Stuck, b 31 Dec 1837, d in America 11 Sept 1908, and had issue (with other sons and a da, Mrs Davy, of whom no issue survives) 1c to 2c

1c *William Anson Lloyd*, b 27 Ap 1859, d 1890, m 5 Sept 1881, Elizabeth, da of George Wheeler, and had issue 1d to 2d

1d Ernest William Lloyd

2d Violet Anson Lloyd   [Nos 135360 to 135361.

558

# of The Blood Royal

2c Edward Bell Lloyd (47 *Ravensdale Road, Stamford Hill, W*), b 22 Dec 1862, m May 1888, Alice Maud Mary, da of George Aubrey, and had issue 1d to 3d

    1d Alice Anson Lloyd

    2d Beatrice Alice Lloyd

    3d Clarice Audrey Lloyd

3c Thomas Mostyn Lloyd, b 1865

4c Frederick Victor Lloyd, b 14 Feb 1867, m Oct 1901, Dorothy, da of (—) Omagh, and has issue 1d to 2d

    1d James Mostyn Lloyd, b 1906

    2d Gladys Anson Lloyd, b 1903

5c Constantine Cynric Lloyd, b 1874

6c Constance Ellen Lloyd, m 27 Sept 1887, the Rev James Silvester, M A (Oxon), Vicar of Great Clacton (*Great Clacton Vicarage, Clacton-on-Sea*), and has issue 1d to 2d

    1d Anson Lloyd Silvester, b 11 Dec 1888

    2d James Mostyn Silvester, b 20 Feb 1891

7c Laura Letitia Lloyd

8c Eleanor Arabella Lloyd

2b Anne Anson Lloyd, *unm*

2a *Ven William Henry Cynric Lloyd, M A (Oxon), Archdeacon of Durban,* b 13 *Jan* 1802, d 3 *Jan* 1882, m 1st, 3 *July* 1832, *Lucy Anne [descended from George, Duke of Clarence, K G (see Essex* Volume Supplement, p 574)], *da of the Rev John Jeffreys,* d 14 *Feb* 1843, 2ndly, 23 *May* 1844, *Ellen, da of the Rev Henry Norman, and had issue* 1b *to* 12b

1b William Henry Anson Lloyd, b 26 Feb 1848

2b Albert Charles George Lloyd, b 5 June 1851, m 1882, Eleanor (divorced 1901), da of Swainston Harrison

3b Alfred Norman Mostyn Lloyd (430 *Burger Street, Pietermaritzburg*), b 28 Sept 1868, m 29 Ap 1895, Harriet, da of the Rev Canon Crompton, d 28 Feb 1904, and has issue 1c to 2c

    1c Theodora Cynric Lloyd, b 21 Mar 1901

    2c Gwynedd Lloyd, b 18 July 1899

4b[1] Frances Anne Lloyd (*Knesebeck-strasse 9, Charlottenburg, Berlin*)

5b[1] Lucy Catherine Lloyd

6b[1] Jemima Charlotte Lloyd, m at Cape Town, 22 Nov 1862, Dr Wilhelm Heinrich Emmanuel Bleek, Librarian Grey's Library, Cape Town, and has issue 1c to 4c

    1c Edith Mabel Bleek

    2c Mabel Augusta Lucy Bleek, m 4 May 1899, Karl Albert Jaeger, and has issue 1d to 2d

        1d Wilhelm Heinrich Immanuel Friedrich Jaeger, b 21 May 1903

        2d Johanna Maryanthe May Jaeger

    3c Dorothea Frances Bleek

    4c Wilhelmine Henriette Anna Bleek

7b[1] *Julia Elizabeth Lloyd,* d (*unm*) 1 *Jan* 1909

8b[2] Ellen Lloyd,

9b[2] Henrietta Lloyd,   } *unm*

10b[2] Victoria Hope Natalia Lloyd,

11b[2] *Adelaide Octavia Susan Lloyd,* d 22 *May* 1908, m *Feb* 1883, *Robert Trelss Nimmo of Durban, and has issue*

12b[2] Isabella Lloyd, *unm*   [Nos 135362 to 135394

The Plantagenet Roll

356 Descendants of COLUMBUS INGILBY of Clapdale Hall and Aust-
wick, co York, *afterwards* of Lawkland Hall (Table XXXII),
bapt 28 Sept 1642 , *bur* at Clapham 15 May 1716 , *m* at
Leeds Parish Church, 9 Dec 1676, ANNE, sister of Joseph
Proctor of Leeds, Clothworker, da. of (—) PROCTOR, *bur* at
Clapham 25 May 1737 ; and had issue 1*a* to 6*a*

1*a* *John Ingilby of Lawkland,* bapt 25 *Mar* 1679 , d 1746, *leaving issue
which became extinct before 1800*

2*a* *Thomas Ingilby of Austwick, co York,* bapt *at Clapham* 21 *Dec* 1685 ,
bur there 17 *Oct* 1765 , m (*bond dated at Lancaster* 19 *June* 1723), *Agnes, da of
Thomas Foster of Austwick and Clapham,* bur *at Clapham* 28 *July* 1766 , *and had
issue* 1*b*

1*b* *Columbus Ingilby of Clapdale Hall and afterwards of Lawkland,* bapt
5 *Dec* 1724 , bur 19 *Nov* 1801 , m *Ellen, da and co-h of Thomas Abbotson of
Kilnsey Hall, co York,* bur 12 *Ap* 1795 , *and had issue* 1*c*

1*c* *John Abbotson Ingilby of Lawkland, Lord of the Manor of Lawkland,* bapt
16 *Jan* 1764 , d 21 *Oct* 1831 m *at Thornton* 19 *June* 1787, *Margaret, da of
Richard Hodgson of West House, Thornton-in-Lonsdale,* d 26 *Mar* 1824 , *and had
issue* 1*d to* 3*d*

1*d* *Thomas Ingilby of Lawkland, J P ,* bapt 8 *Ap* 1788 , d 6 *Dec* 1846 , m
1 *June* 1813, *Margaret, da of Christopher Brown of Stainforth, co York,* d 26 *Feb*
1852 , *and had issue (with* 2 *sons and* 3 *das d s p)* 1*e to* 3*e*

1*e* *Christopher Ingilby of Lawkland, J P , b* 17 *Mar* 1824 , d 1 *Nov* 1889 ,
m 4 *Dec* 1849, *Anne, da of Thomas Watters of Kendal, co Westmorland,* d 13 *Ap*
1891 , *and had issue* 1*f*

1*f* Rev Arthur Ingilby of Lawkland Hall, co York, J P , B A (Camb), *formerly* Rector of St Johns Episcopal Church at Oban (*Harden, Austwick, Yorks*),
b 9 *Dec* 1852 , m 7 *Sept* 1880, Constance Alice Ynyr, da of the Rev Edward
Cadogan, Rector of Wicken , and has issue 1*g*

1*g* Alice Ynyr Christobel Ingilby, *b* 6 Aug 1881

2*e* *Elizabeth Ingilby,* b 12 *July* 1815 , d 20 *Sept* 1878 , m 28 *Ap* 1841,
Thomas Bairstow of Royd Hall, near Kildwick, co York, b 7 *Ap* 1808 , d 2 *Dec*
1867 , *and had issue (with* 3 *sons and* 3 *das d young)* 1*f to* 2*f*

1*f* Walter Bairstow, J P , High Sheriff co Northants 1908 (*The Lodge, Towcester*), *b* 2 Sept 1857 , m 13 Sept 1882, Marion, da of Alfred Sharp of Bingley,
and has issue (with a da d young) 1*g to* 4*g*

1*g* Geoffrey Walter Ingilby Bairstow, *b* 1 Aug 1891.

2*g* Cyril Thomas Alfred Bairstow, *b* 2 July 1903 ,

3*g* Agnes Irene Bairstow, *m* 20 Feb 1908, Harold Edward Cherry (*Geary
House, Bretty, Burton-on-Trent*)

4*g* Marjorie Victoria Bairstow

2*f* Ellen Bairstow, *m* 1 June 1881, Joshua Robert Jennings (*Ormonderley
Close, Ripon*) , and has issue (with a son d young) 1*g to* 2*g*

1*g* Rev Robert Ingilby Jennings, *b* 12 June 1882

2*g* Agnes Ellen Jennings

3*e* *Anne Ingilby,* b 20 *Feb* 1823 , d 10 *Jan* 1910, m 16 *June* 1842, *John
William Foster of Clapham and Horton-in-Ribblesdale, co York, D L, b* 16 *July*
1812 , d 18 *Oct* 1879 , *and had issue* 1*f to* 6*f*

1*f* *Thomas Foster, Lieut* 63*rd Regt, b* 9 *Ap* 1843 , d *in Canada* 10 *Ap*
1880 , m 21 *Nov* 1866, *Leila [da of* (—)] *Nowell of London,* d 15 *May* 1885 ,
and had issue 1*g to* 5*g*

1*g* Bryan Nowell Foster (*Cross Roads, Upper Skwiache, Nova Scotia*), b
[Nos 135395 to 135405

# of The Blood Royal

27 Jan 1870, m 1 May 1894, Elizabeth, da of David Johnson of Upper Skwiache and had issue 1h to 3h

    1h Francis Ingleby Foster, b in Canada 6 Dec 1897

    2h Thomas Hesleden Foster, b in Canada 6 Dec 1899

    3h Hilda Jane Foster, b in Canada 28 Feb 1903

  2g Herbert Ingleby Foster (*Silchester, near Reading*), b 20 Feb 1874, *unm*

  3g Thomas William Foster (*Johannesburg*), b 5 Dec 1879, *unm*

  4g Jessie Maud Foster, m 10 Mar. 1892, Walter Vavasour Hemingway (*Poplar Grove, Wapella, Canada*), and has issue 1h to 2h

    1h Dorothy Hemingway

    2h Mabel Hemingway

  5g Alice Blanche Foster, m 1 Oct 1894, John Godfrey Beedie (*Parkin, Assa, Canada*), and has issue 1h to 4h.

    1h Reginald Beedie, b 17 Jan 1898

    2h Violet Beedie, b 7 Sept 1897

    3h Doris Marion Beedie, b 30 Dec 1901

    4h Margaret Anne Beedie, b 15 July 1906

  2f *Bryan Hesleden Foster, Major 44th Regt*, b 1 *Aug* 1845, d 20 *Mar* 1889, m 8 *Sept* 1875, *Isabel, da of Henry Robinson of The Cliff, Wensleydale, and had issue* 1g *to* 3g

    1g John Foster (*Burnside, Horton-in-Ribblesdale*), b 11 Nov 1877, *unm*

    2g Alice Foster, m 20 Aug 1901, Mark Feetham [son and h of John Feetham of Whinfield, J P] (*Whinfield, Darlington, Durham*), and has issue 1h

      1h Margaret Isabel Feetham

    3g Mabel Foster, m 15 Sept 1909, Arthur Feetham [5th son of John Feetham aforesaid]

  3f John Foster (*Douk Ghyll, Horton in Ribblesdal., Settle*), b 22 Aug 1849, m 4 Sept 1876, Ethel Anne, da of the Rev Thomas James Clark of Horncastle, co Linc, M A, *s p*

  4f William Foster (*Beechwood, Iffley, Oxon*), b 19 Aug 1851, m 2 Dec 1874, Martha Rebecca Margaret, da of William Lister Marriner of Keighley, co York, and has issue 1g to 8g

    1g Charles Alban Foster, Lieut Worcestershire Regt, b 14 May 1883

    2g William Gerald Marriner Foster, b 22 Feb 1885

    3g Margaret Rebecca Foster

    4g Aveline Ingleby Foster

    5g Alice Joan Foster

    6g Ruth Anne Lister Foster

    7g Rhoda Mary Foster

    8g Maud Mael Foster

  5f Alice Foster, m 9 May 1876, Thomas Theophilus Secundus Metcalfe, Capt 2nd West York Mil (*Claydon House, Lechlade, co Gloucester*), and has issue 1g

    1g Geoffrey Bryan Theophilus Metcalfe, *formerly* Lieut 8th Hussars, b 23 May 1878, m 26 Sept 1907, Agnes Maletta, da of Charles O'Keeffe, *formerly* of Marble Hill, co Cork

  6f Florence Foster, m 13 June 1882, William Herbert Lister Marriner, M B (Lond) [son and h of William Lister Marriner of Keighley, co York] (*Craig Vacn, Poole Road, Bournemouth*), and has issue (with a da d young) 1g to 3g

    1g Bryan Lister Marriner, Lieut R A, b 22 Ap 1888

    2g Humphrey Ingilby Marriner, b 12 Aug 1892

    3g Alice Audrey Marriner

  2d *Arthur Ingilby (or Ingleby) of Lancaster Lieut 1st Dragoons*, bapt 18 *Mar*.

[Nos 135406 to 135438

The Plantagenet Roll

1794, d 10 Ap 1824 m *Jan* 1813, *Bessy, da of James Proctor of Lancaster, d 18 Jan 1857 and had issue 1e to 4e*

1c *William Ingleby of Douglas, Isle of Man, sometime 11th Hussars,* b 7 July 1817, d 21 Nov 1883, m *at Nottingham,* 31 *Jan 1852, Margaret Gilbert, da of Gabriel Brittain of Butterley Park, co Derby,* d 26 July 1885, *and had issue (with 2 das d young)* 1f to 3f

1f *Arthur Ingleby, Shore Superintendent, Liverpool (6 Spellow Lane, Kirkdale, Liverpool, N),* b 21 Jan 1854, m 1st, 17 May 1876, Elizabeth Jane, da of Richard Wilkinson of Liverpool, d 15 July 1888, 2ndly, 19 July 1890, Sophia Amelia, younger da of the said Richard Wilkinson, and has issue 1g to 7g

2g[1] Arthur Gilbert Ingleby (440 *Stanley Road, Bootle, Liverpool, W),* b 11 Oct 1878, m 30 July 1901, Agnes, da of George Taylor of Liverpool

2g[1] Richard Henry Ingleby, b 20 Aug 1885

3g[2] John Ingleby, b 22 Ap 1900

1g[1] Elizabeth Ann Ingleby, b 15 Ap 1877

5g[2] Emily Ada Ingleby, b 11 Feb 1891

6g[2] Eleanor Ingleby, b 11 Oct 1892

7g[2] Florence Ingleby, b 22 Sept 1896

2f *Fred Holland Ingleby, in Garrison Artillery,* b 15 Sept 1868, *unm*

3f Charles Ingleby, b 1 Nov 1857, m 24 Mar 1881, Annie, da of Philip Draper of Liverpool, d 24 Dec 1892 and has issue 1g to 3g

1g Philip Draper Ingleby, b 26 Ap 1886

2g Annie Ingleby, b 13 Ap 1884

3g Lizzie Ingleby, b Oct 1890

2c *Bessie Ingleby,* b 23 Dec 1815, d 5 *July* 1882, m *at Lancaster,* 14 Feb 1834, *Edward Cox of Lancaster,* b 10 Dec 1799, d 30 Mar 1849, *and had issue*

3c *Agnes Ingleby,* b 18 May 1822, d 4 Nov 1859, m 1st, 4 June 1842, *John Miller of Lancaster,* d Feb 1852, *2ndly, Sept 1855, George Reginald Kemp of Lancaster, and had issue (by 1st husband)*

4c *Margaret Ingleby,* b 5 Feb 1812, d 17 May 1886, m *at Barnes, co Surrey,* 23 Feb 1854, *John Palmer of Liverpool,* b 15 Feb 1817, d (–) *and had issue*

3d *Robert Ingleby of Austwick, co York,* bapt 29 Ap 1795, d 24 Ap 1863, m 13 Sept 1826, Mary, da of William King of Austwick Hall, d 21 June 1897, *and had issue* 1e to 2e

1e *John Ingleby of Austwick, Major North Craven Rifles (Austwick, Clapham, co York),* b 22 Sept 1829, *unm*

2e *Margaret Ingleby (Standard House, Northallerton),* m *at Clapham, Yorks,* 23 Nov 1852, William Thrush Jefferson of Northallerton, co York, Solicitor, b 30 Mar 1820, d 13 Ap 1891, and had issue 1f to 10f

1f John Ingleby Jefferson of Messrs W T Jefferson & Son of Northallerton, Solicitors (*Standard House, Northallerton*) b 1 Sept 1853

2f William Dixon Jefferson (*North House, Ripon*) b 30 May 1855, m 23 Feb 1892, Mary Stuart, da of the Rev Samuel Gray and had issue 1g to 2g

1g Ingleby Stuart Jefferson, b 7 Jan 1893

2g Julian Jefferson, b 10 July 1899

3f Robert Ingleby Jefferson, Manager Skipton Branch Bank of Liverpool (*Skirton, Skipton*), b 13 Feb 1857, m 30 Aug 1899, Arabella Florence, da of the Rev John Meire Ward, M A , Rector of Clapham, s p

4f *Arthur Jefferson,* b 2 Sept 1859, d 15 Ap 1892, m 15 Dec 1886, *Georgina, da of William Penreth,* d 3 Ap 1891, *and had issue* 1g

1g Dorothy Margaret Lennox Jefferson (*Campsie, Stirling*), b 4 Aug 1888, m 7 Oct 1909, Edmund Gilling Hallewell of Schenectady, N Y , and has issue 1h

1h John Lennox Hallewell, b 15 Aug 1910   [Nos 135439 to 135460

562

5*f* Charles Wilkin Jefferson (*Schenectady, U S A*), *b* 8 July 1863, *m* 7 Nov 1889, Margaret A, da of Charles Dyer, *d* 16 May 1906, and has issue (with an elder son, Jack, *d* 18 Jan 1891) 1g to 2g

   1g Charles Wilson Jefferson, *b* 15 Jan 1895

   2g Margaret Elizabeth Jefferson, *b* 26 Jan 1892

6*f* Mary Jefferson, *m* as 2nd wife, 28 Jan 1886, Sylvester Richmond, M D [descended from the Lady Isabel Plantagenet (see the Essex Volume, p 130)] (*Greenhithe, Kent*), and has issue 1g to 2g

   1g Arnold Ingleby Richmond, *b* 3 Aug 1887

   2g Sylvia Richmond, *b* 19 Mar 1892

7*f* Annie Jefferson, *m* 23 Jan 1890, Arthur Dewhurst (*Sunnybank, Otley Road, Skipton*), and has issue 1g to 3g

   1g Godfrey Jefferson Dewhurst, *b* 2 Mar 1894

   2g Joan Ingleby Dewhurst, *b* 7 Nov 1890

   3g Nancy Stevenson Dewhurst, *b* 16 May 1900

8*f* Cicely Jefferson, *m* 2 June 1892, George James Ernest Gardner (*South Parade, Northallerton*), and has issue 1g to 2g

   1g George Dudley Gardner, *b* 29 July 1896

   2g Grace Ingleby Gardner, *b* 27 Aug 1893

9*f* Margaret Elizabeth Jefferson, *m* 5 Jan 1897, Harry Yeoman (*The Green, Brompton, near Northallerton*), and has issue (with a son, Henry Dixon, *d* in infancy) 1g to 3g

   1g Philip Yeoman, *b* 10 Feb 1901

   2g Antony Yeoman, *b* 8 Mar 1907

   3g Ruth Yeoman, *b* 29 Oct 1897

10*f* Florence Jefferson, *m* 12 Ap 1898, the Rev Stewart Dalrymple Crawford, B A (*Masham, Yorks*), and has issue 1g to 2g

   1g Frazer Stewart Crawford, *b* 13 Sept 1901

   2g David Stewart Crawford, *b* 24 Feb 1904

   3a *Mary Ingilby*, bapt 8 Nov 1677

   4a *Margery Ingilby*, bapt 29 May 1681

   5a *Margaret Ingilby*, bapt 5 Aug 1683, m 27 Oct 1705, *Christopher Procter*

   6a *Elizabeth Ingilby*, bapt 19 Ap 1689   [Nos 135461 to 135480

357 Descendants of Sir CHARLES INGILBY of Austwick Hall, co York, one of the Barons of the Exchequer [E](Table XXXII), *bapt* at Clapham, co York, 20 Feb 1644, *bur* there 6 Aug 1719, *m* ALATHEA, da of Richard Eyston of East Hendred, co Berks, *bur* at Clapham 19 Sept 1715, and had issue (with a da , Anne, *d* unm at Liége) 1a to 4a

1a *Thomas Ingilby of Austwick Hall, Sergeant-at-Law*, bapt at Clapham 15 May 1684, bur there 13 Feb 1729, m at Bentham 11 Aug 1717, *Elizabeth*, da of William Husband of Bentham Hall, co York, and had issue (with a son and da d s p) 1b to 1h

1b *Charles Ingilby of Austwick Hall*, bapt at Clapham 22 Aug 1724, bur there 14 Sept 1773, m there 11 Aug 1756, *Agnes, widow of (—) Armistead, da of George Jackson of Far End, Austwick*, bur 15 Feb 1806, and had issue which became extinct 14 Ap 1844

2b *Elizabeth Ingilby*, bapt at Clapham 4 Mar 1718, bur at Halifax 1755, m Jan 1747, *James Carr of Giggleswick, a Solicitor in Halifax and afterwards in Preston*, bapt 14 Ap 1715, d 1794, and had issue 1c

1c *William Carr of Preston, Solicitor*, b 3 July 1747, d 1799, m *Fidelia, da of John Bulcock of Langroyd, near Colne*, d 1819, and had issue (with 3 sons and 3 das who d s p) 1d to 2d

The Plantagenet Roll

1*d* *George Thomas Carr*, b 1791, d 17 *Jan* 1828, m *Sarah, da of William Midgley of Colne, co Lanc*, d 9 *Ap* 1848, *and had issue (with a son, George Thomas, d unm* 29 *Nov* 1908) 1*e to* 2*c*

1*c William James Carr of Langroyd, Solicitor*, b 1823, d 24 *May* 1882, m *Martha Joanna da of Henry Binns of Rippouden, co Yorks*, d 14 *July* 1898, *and had issue* 1*f to* 5*f*

1*f James Carr of Colne, Solicitor, Registrar of Colne and Nelson County Court (Thornton House, Thornton-in Craven, Yorks)*, b 5 Oct 1850, m 29 *Ap* 1882, *Mary Ellen, da of James Spencer*, *and has issue* 1*g to* 5*g*

    1*g* William James Carr, *b* 30 *Jan* 1883

    2*g* Muriel Carr, *b* 29 *May* 1884

    3*g* Winifred Carr, *b* 16 June 1887

    4*g* Elsie Mary Carr, *b* 23 Aug 1890

    5*g* Doris Noel Carr, *b* 25 Dec 1893

2*f* Rev William Henry Carr, M A (Oxon), Vicar of St Peter's, Westleigh (*Westleigh Vicarage, Lancashire*), b 1 Feb 1854, *unm*

3*f* Edward Carr, J P (*Langroyd, Colne*), b 11 Aug 1867, m 14 June 1900, Ann Mabel, da of Joseph Henry Threlfall of Moorlands, Foulridge, *and has issue* 1*g to* 3*g*

    1*g* Edward Rulehrilgh Carr, *b* 27 Ap 1907

    2*g* Evelyn Carr, *b* 5 Oct 1902

    3*g* Joan Carr, *b* 29 Oct 1905

4*f* Mary Ada Carr, *unm*

5*f Helen Carr*, d 5 Oct 1899, m 1st, 4 Oct 1883, *Francis Benjamin Brodribb of Colne, Surgeon*, d 17 Nov 1893, 2ndly, 1897, *William Lyons Lovett of the same, Surgeon*, *and had issue* 1*g to* 5*g*

    1*g* William Carr Brodribb, *b* 22 June 1886

    2*g* Francis George Brodribb, *b* 8 Sept 1890

    3*g* Frederick Lyons Lovett, *b* 3 Mar 1898

    4*g* Helen Margaret Brodribb, *b* 4 May 1885

    5*g* Edith Mary Brodribb, *b* 6 Oct 1888

2*c Mary Carr (Colne, Lanc)*, b 30 *Ap* 1821 m 16 *July* 1844, John Joseph Ayre of Colne, *and has issue (with a son d s p)* 1*f to* 2*f*

    1*f* Eleanor Eames Ayre

    2*f* Georgina Birdsworth Ayre

2*d Elizabeth Carr*, d (–), m *John Birdsworth of Preston*, d 1816, *and had issue* 2 *sons who d unm*

3*b Dorothy Ingilby*, bapt *at Clapham, co York*, 19 Feb 1722, bur *there* 29 *May* 1765, m *at Lancaster* 28 *Ap* 1712, Thomas Armistead of Austwick, *and had issue*

4*b Mary Ingilby*, bapt 12 *July* 1723, *living a widow* 14 May 1755, m *James Bond of Stainforth, co York, and Bury St Edmunds, a non-juror [grandson of Thomas Bond by his wife the Hon Henrietta, da and co-h of Thomas (Jermyn), 2nd Baron Jermyn [E]]*, b 1721, d (–), *and had issue*

2*a Dorothea Ingilby*, bapt *at Clapham, co York*, 27 *Ap* 1681

3*a Mary Ingilby*, bapt *at Clapham, co York*, 25 *Ap* 1683, d (–), m *William Estcourt of Bremellham and Cowich, co Wilts, of which latter he was life tenant under the terms of his marriage settlement [son of Sir Thomas Estcourt of Pinkney Park, co Wilts]*, bur *at Clapham* 29 Aug 1727, *and had issue (with 2 sons and 2 das d young, and bur at Clapham)* 1*b to* 6*b*

1*b William Estcourt*, b *at Lawkland Hall and* bapt *at Clapham* 21 *Jan* 1709

2*b Mary Estcourt*, bapt *at Clapham* 5 *Jan* 1711

3*b Elizabeth Estcourt of Austwick*, bapt *at Clapham* 7 Feb 1716, m (*lic York dated Feb*) 1746, *Charles Harrison of Ripon*, d (–), *and had issue* 1*c*

# of The Blood Royal

1c Charles Harrison of Newbridge, Nidderdale, co York, Lawyer, bapt in Ripon Cathedral 6 June 1758, d 8 Dec 1823, m 1st, (—), da of (—), 2ndly, Isabella, da of Charles Charnock of Leeds d 15 June 1864, and had issue 1d to 4d

1d [1] Charles Harrison, afterwards (R L 10 May 1822) Harrison-Batley, M P for Beverley 1821-1830, Recorder of Ripon 1816-1833, b c 1786 d 1 Aug 1835, m May 1822, Anna, widow of John Lodge Batley of Masham, co Yorks, da of (—), and had issue (1 son and 1 da)

2d [2] Rev William Estcourt Harrison, Vicar of Sturton, co Notts, b 13 Ap 1809, d 17 Oct 1887, m 6 July 1859, Margaret (1 St Peter's Grove, York), da of William Battye of Skelton Hall co York, and had issue 1e to 3e

1e Arthur Estcourt Harrison, Major Royal Artillery (Chargrove House, Shurdington, near Cheltenham), b 21 Jan 1865, m 7 Oct 1897, Mabel, da of George Clark of Sunderland, and has issue 1f to 2f

1f Margaret Estcourt Harrison
2f Rachel Estcourt Harrison

2e Richard Scholefield Estcourt Harrison (Canada), b 19 June 1867 unm
3e Margaret Gertrude Estcourt Harrison, unm

3d [2] Charnock Ingleby Harrison Capt 65th Regt, H E I C S, bapt 25 Aug 1810, d 6 Nov 1848, m 10 Mar 1838, Mary Ann, da of Capt John Tritton, 24th Light Dragoons, d 10 Sept 1872, and had issue 1e to 2e

1e Charles William Ingleby Harrison, Col R E, late Chief Engineer of the United Provinces and Oude, and Sec to the Govt of India, presented with a Sword of Honour at Addiscombe 1858 (Court Royal, Dehra, Dun, India), b 28 June 1839

2e Marion Ellen Harrison, now (D P 1909) Oswald (2 Park Avenue, Dover), m 20 Dec 1862, Col James Williamson, formerly Oswald, 26th Punjaub Infantry [son of James Oswald of Shieldhall, M P, who had three lines of descent from King Edward III], d 16 June 1877, and had issue (with a son, Charnock Ingleby Harrison, Lieut 26th Punjaub Infantry, b 13 Nov 1864, d unm 14 Jan 1892) 1f to 4f

1f Oswald Charles Williamson, now (D P 8 Mar 1910) Williamson-Oswald, F R G S, Major R A, served in Burma 1887-1889 (Medal and 2 Clasps) Waziristan Exp 1894-1895 (Clasp), Chitral with relief force 1895, Tochi Field Force, N W Frontier 1897-1898 (Medal with Clasp), and South Africa 1901 (Medal with 4 Clasps), J P, b 20 Sept 1863, m 9 Oct 1908, Margaret Malcolm, da of William Carson of Carnalea House, co Down, and has issue 1g

1g Praxeda Estcourt Isabella Emily Williamson Oswald

2f Noel Williamson, now (D P 1 Oct 1910) Williamson Oswald, F R G S, Assist Political Officer at Sadiya, Assam, formerly Lieut 4th Batt West York Regt, b 27 Oct 1868

3f Theodora Williamson, m 29 Sept 1898, Major Kenneth Combe, R H A (Ryston Lodge, Newbridge, co Kildare)

4f Agnes (Nancy) Williamson, M B (Lond), who has now (D P 18 Jan 1909) with her mother reverted to the name of Oswald

4d [2] John James Harrison, Chaplain R N, b 15 Feb 1818, d 17 Mar 1888, m 3 Oct 1866, Louisa Edith (Barn Park, Boscastle, Cornwall), da of the Rev Frederick William Darwall of Sholden, and had issue 1e to 8e

1e John Frederick Harrison b 26 Jan 1868, d 11 Aug 1901, m 1 Aug 1901, Ruth (52 Goldstone Villa, Hove), da of the Rev Frederick King of South Molton, and had issue 1f

1f Richard Ingleby Harrison, b 14 Aug 1903

2e Charles Ingleby Harrison, b 2 Jan 1876, unm
3e James Ingleby Harrison, Lieut R N, b 3 June 1881, unm
4e Francis Ingleby Harrison, b 27 Ap 1883, unm
5e Janet Frances Harrison
6e Isabella Louisa Harrison
7e Mary Ingleby Harrison
8e Margaret Anne Ingleby Harrison

[Nos 135501 to 135520

4 C

4*b* *Katherine Estcourt*, bapt *at Clapham, co Yorks*, 18 *Nov* 1720

5*b* *Dorothy Estcourt*, bapt *at Clapham* 4 *Dec* 1725, *confirmed in Lawkland Hall Chapel* 14 *May* 1755 *by the Right Rev Francis Petre, Lord Bishop of Amorium*

6*b*. *Anne Estcourt*, b *at Lawkland Hall, and* bapt *at Clapham* 26 *Dec* 1721

4*a* *Alethea Ingleby*, bapt *at Clapham* 23 *Feb* 1685, bur *at Giggleswick* 17 *July* 1770 , m (—) *Fell of London, Apothecary*

358. Descendants of ISABEL INGILBY (Table XXXII), *d* 16 Ap. 1793 , *m* RICHARD SHERBURN of Stonyhurst, co Lancaster , and had issue

See the Mortimer-Percy Volume, Part II

APPENDIX

PAGE 37 —Though it is probable that descendants of Lady Elizabeth Woodroffe may still exist, they have not up till now been satisfactorily traced Burke ("Peerage," *sub* Northumberland) says that her "descendant and sole heiress *m*, 1719, Aaron Scales of Ranskill, co Notts, and is now represented by Edward Peacock of Bottisford By this "descendant and sole heiress" is presumably meant the "Elizabeth, sister and h of Samuel Woodroffe, the last male heir of the Woodroffes of Ranskill, a branch of the Woodroffes of Wolley, co York," who in the Peacock pedigree, printed in "English Church Furniture" (edited by the above-named Edward Peacock, 1866, p 78), is there stated to have married Aaron Scales of Ranskill One of their [? daughters and] co-heirs, Mary [? Scales], is further stated to have *m* Robert Shaw of Bawtry, and to have had issue, a da and co-h, Martha, who *m* at Coopersall Church, co Essex, 3 Ap 1790, Thomas Peacock (*b* at Northorpe, 21 Nov 1766, *d* 1 June 1824), grandfather of the said Edward Peacock A further descent would also appear to be indicated, since the father of Thomas Peacock, another Thomas Peacock (*b* at Scotter, 10 Mar 1738, *bur* at Northorpe, 27 Ap 1782), *m* Abigail (*bur* at Northorpe, 24 Feb 1772, aged forty), da and co h (with her sister Keturah, *bur* at Northorpe, 10 Ap 1808, aged seventy-eight), of an Aaron Scales of Ranskill, though it is not stated whether the last-named Aaron Scales was identical with the first, or if he were, whether the mother of Abigail and Keturah was the said Elizabeth Woodroffe Inasmuch, however, as the Woodroffes of Ranskill, though they may have been a branch of the Wolley family, were certainly not descended from the above Richard Woodroffe of Wolley, no descent from, or representation of, Lady Elizabeth can be vested in the Scales or Peacock families

Of Maximilian Woodroffe, the eldest son, Banks (*Baronia Anglica Concentrata*, i 369) says that he went to Virginia, where his cousin, the Hon George Percy, had previously gone, and that in a MS entitled "Indigested Chronology" among the Stirling papers in the Historical Library at New York, he is said to have planted Virginia and to have discovered Powhattan, now called James, River, that he *d* 1652, having *m* Mabel, da and h of Arthur Paver of Wetherby, and had issue a son and h, Maximilian, who *d v p* 1644, leaving by his wife Eleanor, da of William Paver of Braham Hall, an only child Milliana, who *m* John Paver of St Nicholas House, York, and was ancestress of Percy Woodroffe Paver, *b* 1829, living 1843 This descent, which was printed in *Notes and Queries*, 6th S vii 29, wants proof, which the Editor has been unable to obtain

Page 86 —The children of Georgina Fanny, *née* Bourchier, and her husband, Edward Raven Priest, are as follows, viz. 1g to 4g

    1g Edward Raven Priest, Electrician, *b* 12 June 1880, *m* May, da of (—) Chapman of Brisbane

    2g Ella Constance Priest, *b* 5 Jan 1869, *unm*

    3g Jessie Beatrice Priest, *b* 29 Sept 1872, *m* Richard Cheriton of Waul, West Australia, Farmer

    4g Janet Mary Priest, *b* 10 Mar 1875, *m* Arthur O'Connor of Perth, West Australia, Journalist

Page 156, line 26 3c *d* 6 Ap 1910

Page 319, line 1 2i (Malcolm Orton) has two younger children, viz —

    7j Constance Orton,

    8j Nattie Charlotte Orton, *b* 20 Nov 1907.

Appendir

4ı (Allan Orton) has issue 1ı to 3ı

1ı Allan Orton, *b* 9 Sept 1906

2ı Reginald Bruce Orton, *b* 6 May 1908

3ı Elizabeth Jean Orton, *b* 19 May 1910

5ı (Mrs Mee) has two younger children, viz —

3ı Caroline Jeannie Mee, *b* 21 Nov 1898

4ı Bowery Bradley Mee, *b* 1 July 1900

8ı (Mrs Whittaker) has issue 1ı

1ı Orton Whittaker, *b* 6 Dec 1906

10ı (Mrs Nixon) has issue 1ı to 2ı

1ı Jack Orton Nixon, *b* 24 Jan 1907

2ı Reginald Orton Nixon, *b* 8 May 1908

11ı (Mrs Hintz) has issue 1ı

1ı Orton Sutherland Hintz, *b* 15 Nov 1907

Page 326 4*d* (Mrs Smallpiece, *née* Frances Molineux) had issue (with 3 other sons and 2 das who *d s p*) 1*c* to 2*e*

1*c* *George Molineux Smallpiece*, b 21 *Ap* 1841, d (–), m 12 *Oct* 1869, *Beatrice Mary, da of 1 Savory of Potters Park, Chertsey, and had issue* 1*f to* 2*f*

1*f* George Albert Molineux Smallpiece, *b* 12 Feb 1872

2*f* Frances Molineux Smallpiece, *m* Capt Frank Arthur Horridge, *late* Duke of Cornwall's Light Infantry, *s p*

2*c* Robinson Smallpiece (*Merry Hills, Loxwood, Billingshurst*), *b* 29 Aug 1850, *m* 1st, Annie Rachel, da of Adolphus Marx of Nottingham, 2ndly, Sarah Rose, da of Samuel Muggeridge of London, *s p*

3*c* Cordelia Molineux Smallpiece, *unm*

Page 370, line 25 (Mrs Fuhrhop, *née* Hoare) has issue 1*f* to 3*f*

1*f* Otto Fritz Fuhrhop, *b* 1 Ap 1907

2*f* Helen Mary Fuhrhop, *b* 4 Dec 1902

3*f* Daisy Wilhelmina Fuhrhop, *b* 1 Jan 1908

Page 483 2*c* (Richard Buck of Bideford) had issue 1*f* to 3*f*

1*f* *Rev Richard Hugh Keats Buck, B A (Camb), Rector of St Dominick, co Cornwall, and Hon Canon of Truro Cathedral,* b 4 *Mar* 1815, d 15 *Dec* 1893, m 29 *Jan* 1852, *Mary, da of the Rev Joseph Bradshaw,* d 19 *Jan.* 1893, *and had issue* 1*g to* 2*g*

1*g* Rev Richard Eustace Stukeley Buck, Rector of St Alban's (*St Alban's Rectory, Cornwall*), *b* 4 Nov 1853, *m* 7 Jan 1891, Mary Constance, da of John Richards Paull of Bosvigs, Truro, and has issue 1*h* to 4*h*

1*h* Richard Vivian Stukeley Buck, *b* 14 Oct 1891

2*h* Constance Angelina Mary Buck

3*h* Veronica Charlotte McDonald Buck

4*h* Ida Alexandra Amelia Buck

2*g* Ida Frances Harriet Buck, *m* in Rome, Oct 1902, Capt Luigi Falchetti, *s p*

2*f* Lewis William Buck, Major-Gen M C S (3 *Cavendish Place, Bath*), *b* 13 Jan 1824, *m* at Wattaer, East Indies, 19 May 1854, Henrietta Jane, da of Col David Archer, and his issue (with 2 sons *d* unm) 1*g* to 6*g*

1*g* Lewis Archer Buck, F R C S, *b* 1855, *unm*

2*g* William Tennant Buck, Major (ret) Durham L I, *b* 23 May 1862, m in Bombay Cathedral 1898, Beatrice de la Poer, da of Charles de la Poer Beresford, and has issue 1h to 4h

1h William Stuckley de la Poer Beresford Buck, b 1 Feb 1903
2h Reginald Claude de la Poer Beresford Buck, b 31 Mar 1905
3h Grace Eileen Joly de la Poer Beresford Buck, b 30 Jan 1899
4h Kathleen Manners de la Poer Beresford Buck, b 22 June 1900

3g Walter Keats Buck, m s p
4g Harriette Grace Buck, m 1880, Col George Godfrey, Madras S C, d s p 1890
5g Annie Mary Buck
6g Ethel Maude Buck (3 *Cavendish Place, Bath*)

3f *Martha Buck*, d (—), m *Major Oliver D'Arcy, 18th Regt*, d 3 Feb 1880

Page 498, line 50 The issue of 3e (Pierce Harris Purcell) is as follows, viz 1f to 10f

1f George Harris Purcell
2f William Harris Purcell
3f Charles Harris Purcell
4f Richard Harris Purcell
5f Henrietta Harris Purcell
6f Rosina Harris Purcell, m Arnold Kohler (*Walsrode, Hanover*)
7f Louisa St Leger Harris Purcell
8f Eva St Leger Harris Purcell
9f Minnie Harris Purcell
10f Amy Harris Purcell

Page 519, line 11 2h (W G Ferris) has issue (besides a da, Olive May, d young) 1i to 5i

1i William Thomas Chilton Ferris, b 29 May 1890
2i Arthur Guiseley Ferris, b 11 June 1891
3i Ronald Boys Ferris, b 29 Jan 1899
4i Eric Charles Ferris, b 15 May 1900
5i Leslie Francis Ferris, b 15 Jan 1907

Page 523, line 45 3g (Mrs Kitson) has issue 1h to 9h

1h William Edmonstone Kitson, b (—), m Muriel Lindsay, da of Collingwood Lindsay Wood of Freeland, co Perth, J P, D L
2h Rev John Archibald Kitson, Rector of Brechin (*The Rectory, Brechin*), b (—), m Mary Catherine (see below), da of Alexander Robert Duncan of Parkhill, and has issue 1i to 3i
1i John Duncan Kitson
2i Alexander Frederick Kitson
3i Joan Frances Kitson

3h Charles Kitson, b (—)
4h Robert Kitson, b (—)
5h Frederick Kitson, b (—)
6h Antony Buller Kitson, b (—)
7h Geraldine Kitson, m the Rev Lewis Evans, Vicar of Eton (*Eton Vicarage, Windsor*), s p
8h Rosamond Kitson, unm
9h Dorothy Euphemia Kitson

Appendix

Line 52 (Mrs Duncan) has issue 1h to 4h

1h John Alexander Duncan, b 22 Mar 1878, m Dorothy, da of (—) Weston, and has issue (a da)

2h Basil W Duncan, b (—), unm

3h William E Duncan b (—), unm

4h Mary Catherine Duncan, m the Rev John Archibald Kitson (*Brechin*), and has issue

See above

Page 534, line 20 2e (William Taylor Warry) had issue 1f to 2f

1f Richard Arthur Warry, b 6 Aug 1886

2f Muriel Joan Warry, b 4 Jan 1888

3e (Mrs Toogood) has issue 1f to 4f

1f Cecil Toogood, D S O , Capt Lincolnshire Regt, b 31 Mar 1870, m 14 Sept 1899, Mary Elizabeth (see p 523), da of Major-Gen Henry Pipon , and has issue

See p 523, Nos 130779–130781

2f Elba Georgina Toogood

3f Dora Isabel Toogood

4f Evelyn Maud Toogood

Page 551, line 30 3b (Mrs Stainforth) has issue 1c to 4c

1c Lesley Charles Stainforth, Col Indian Army, b 23 June 1860, m Helen, da of (—) Bell

2c Herbert Graham Stainforth, Major 4th Indian Cavalry, b 18 May 1865, m 1901, Georgina Helen (see p 523), da of Major-Gen Henry Pipon , and has issue 1d to 2d

1d Graham Henry Stainforth, b 3 Oct 1906

2d Madeline Susan Stainforth, b 26 July 1902

3c Douglas Anson Stainforth, R N , b 12 Aug 1874

4c Edith Vernon Stainforth, m 9 Oct 1890, Charles Frederick Cross (53 *Chepstow Place, W*), and has issue 1d to 3d

1d Charles Ralli Cross b 30 Sept 1893

2d Lionel Lesley Cross, b 7 June 1899

3d Daisy Marion Cross, b 4 Sept 1891

Page 551, line 32 4b (Mrs Alexander) has issue 1d to 2d

1d Ernest Vernon Alexander, b 13 Sept 1863 , m 1883, Ina, da of (—) Giles, and has issue 1c to 2c

1c Lelia Constance Alexander

2c Mary Helen Alexander

2d Eva Constance Alexander, m 12 Sept 1895, the Rev Frederick Ball, M A (Oxon), Chaplain Royal Navy (7 *Naval Terrace, Sheerness*), and has issue 1e to 2e

1e Vernon Frederick Ball, b 19 Oct 1899

2e David Herbert Alexander Ball, b 5 Mar 1903

INDEX OF NAMES

Index

Index

574

Inder

Index

579

Index

p 561, 135425, Charlotte P E Lady, p 462, 95481, D E C V, p 462 95484, F I, p 561 135106, H I p 561 135109 H J, p 561, 135108, J, p 561 135419 J p 561 135423 M M p 561, 135432 M R, p 561, 135427, P E V p 462 95483 R A L, p 561, 135430, R M, p 561 135431, T H, p 561 135107 T W p 561 135110 W p 561, 135421, W G M, p 561 135426
Fothergill, C T, p 200, 29610 E G I, p 446, 94691, F H G p 446, 94689 H M B, p 446, 94690, M H S, p 200, 29611, P G L, p 416 91688, R, p 200, 29609, M W S p 200 29608
Fowell, Mrs E L F, p 165, 17543
Fowler, Capt C W H, p 50, 306 C W, p 50 308, F B p 50, 307, F M, p 118, 10745 10767, G S, p 118 10744, 10766 M p 118 10746, S G, p 169, 103140
Fox, A I, p 238, 36915, A S, p 329 41211, B E, p 238 36916, C D p 238, 36913, C D p 238 36914, D p 329 43212, K, p 238 36917, Hon Mrs S C p 329, 43210 Mrs S K, p 415, 79996
Francis V C, p 165 17524, Mrs E C p 165, 17527, H p 165 17532, H V p 165, 17529 Mrs S G, p 65, 737
Frankland, B C, p 300, 40158 K M C p 300 40156, M A M, p 321, 42625 Mrs M V p 321, 42624, Mrs M J p 300, 40153 M O L p 300, 40159, Lieut R C C p 300 40154, R L S p 321, 42626, Lieut T H C p 300 40155
Fraser F p 230, 46520
Freeman, Mrs C, p 146, 16545 79884, E S, p 146, 16548, 79886, H A, p 146 16516, 79884, K M, p 146, 16547, 79885
French A J P, p 149, 16616, A M, p 149, 16622, A S, p 316, 42484, A S p 433, 85809, Mrs C E G, p 433 85807 D p 149, 16613, D M, p 348, 59567, E B, p 316, 42491 E F p 316, 42492, F C, p 149, 16611, H N p 316, 42485 H O'D, p 149, 16620 Mrs

H S, p 149, 16619, I H, p 149, 16615, L S p 149 11621, M A, p 316, 42488, M D p 149, 16618, M M p 316 42494, Mrs R, p 318 59566, R L, p 316, 42486 R M p 316 42487, R S p 149 16612, R W, p 149 16617, S O'M, p 149 16619, T F p 149 16614, Mrs W p 483 104420
Fuell E M p 495 128234, R A T p 495, 128234]
Fry D H p 127 11627, Rev C L M p 127 11626 Mrs I I, p 127, 11625
Fulahop D W, p 568 (App), Mrs L M p 570 60136 61440, H M, p 568 (App), O I, p 568 (App)
Fuller Mrs A I p 407, 79711 Mrs L A H p 499 128436, C R, p 361 59931
Fulton Mrs A G, p 103, 10225, 10401, B S p 212 30043, E A, p 212, 30045, E M W, p 212, 30037, F, p 211 30019, F R, p 211, 30026, G, p 211, 30022, G S p 211, 30028, G M W, p 211 30027, H, p 211, 30024, H A, p 212, 30044, Major H T, p 212, 30042, J O, p 211, 30021, L H W, p 212, 30038, N, p 211 30025, O H C p 212, 30041, P J, p 212, 30039, Col R, p 211, 30020, R R p 389 71810, S A W p 212 30036, S W, p 212, 30035, W M, p 212 30040, W W, p 211, 30023
Furley, Mrs R M, p 149, 16631
Furlonge, A, p 417, 80050, Mrs A, p 413 79951, A S, p 417, 80052 C W p 417, 80046, C G H de L, p 417, 80047, Lieut C le S, p 413, 79953 80058, E A, p 417, 80053, C R, p 417 80054, Lieut G H S, p 413, 79952, 80057, G Le S, p 417, 80048, Col G W p 417 80056, I A R, p 417, 80055, L E A p 417, 80049, M E p 417 80051
GAGE, 5th Vct p 38 1, B E F p 39 16, C W p 40 56, L F F, p 39, 17, Maj E M B p 38 12, F, p 40 57, G E, p 38, 11, 51 G E, p 49, 21, 55 Hon H R p 38 2 Hon I A, p 38, 3, J S D, p 39 14, Maj M F, p 39, 15,

Hon V B, p 38, 4, W H St Q, p 38, 40 50, Hon Y R p 38, 5
de Galard Béarn B, p 509, 129237, Ct B E R p 508 129225, B M P p 508, 129228 Ct C p 508, 129230 Ct C I T p 508 129224, C N M R p 508 129223, Ct E G O p 508 129227, Ct G E I H p 508 129222, Ct H p 508 129231 J p 508 129233, Ct J C A p 508 129229, Ct L I S A p 509, 129236, P p 509 129235, Ct P P A P A, p 508 129226, Ct S p 508 129232
Gallwey Fanny C Lady, p 225, 36891
Garbett, L M p 177, 27212, Rev C F p 177 27211 C S, p 177 27213 L M K, p 177, 27215, L C p 177 27214, Mrs S C, p 177 27210
Garde V N H p 493, 128192, Lieut Col W D p 493 128191
Gardener, B A, p 214, 30111 Mrs L W p 214, 30112, V A, p 214, 30113
Gardner Mrs C, p 563, 135471, D F p 418, 80080, Mrs F N, p 418 80077 G E p 563, 135472, G I p 563 135473, G M, p 418, 80081 N P E, p 418, 80079, R L, p 418 80078 Mrs V W, p 418 135071
Garfit A p 268 38301, H de B C p 469 103114, M p 268, 38303, M L, p 268, 38304, S F, p 268, 38302, Capt W, p 268, 38298
Garrow Winthy Mrs H E, p 448, 94726, H O, p 448, 94727
Garth A D p 109, 10452, 41628, C, p 110 10457, 41633 G D, p 109, 10451 41627, H p 109, 10453, 41629, M p 109 10454, 41630, P, p 109, 10455 41631, R p 109, 10450, 41626, W, p 110, 10456, 41632
Gattiker, A M, p 81, 9710, C F, p 81, 9716, C J, p 81, 9722, D M p 81, 9721 Lieut F A, p 81, 9727, G G O p 81, 9715, G W F, p 81 9724, J K, p 81 9729, M E G p 81, 9712, M L, p 81, 9717, M I, p 81, 9718, M L p 81 9719, M L S p 81 9710, M W, p 81, 9700, R H W, p 81,

9713 R M G, p 81, 9714, V L de M, p 81 9711, W R, p 81 9723
Gayer, Rev A C S, p 150, 16637, C M A, p 150 16638, D M, p 150, 16639, F M, p 150 16641, E H F, p 150, 16635, Mrs E M, p 148 16580, E P, p 150, 16636, Rev E R, p 149, 16633, L H, p 150, 16610, Capt H W, p 150 16634
Geach G C, p 81, 9780, Mrs J, p 81 9779
Geddes A J W, p 215, 30127, D C p 215, 30136, Capt E D E, p 215, 30125, E L L, p 215, 30128, Mrs E J p 215, 30124, G O, p 215, 30138, Capt M H R, p 215 30126
Gepp Mrs E M p 549, 135094 M H p 115, 80000 Mrs M N, p 415, 79999
de Gex R C, p 105, 10270 41452
Gibbings, Rev R, p 498, 128420
Gifford, C M E, p 310, 41942 41453, E F p 310 41943 43136, J p 310, 41944, 43137, Hon Mrs M p 310, 41941 43131, V M, p 310 41945, 43138
Gilbert Cooper A p 165, 17523 17806, A E, p 164, 17518, 17801 Mrs C L, p 164 17517, 17800 M F, p 164 17520, 17803, W N R, p 164, 17519, 17802
Gilbertson Mrs I de W, p 280 38837, M D F p 280 38838
Gill B F p 105, 10279, 41455, Mrs D, p 547, 135016, E B, p 547, 135019, F E, p 105, 10277, 41453, G W, p 547, 135018, H C, p 547, 135017, Mrs p 547 135020, O T E, p 105 10278 41451
Gilbert Lieut C R, p 366, 59962 Mrs L M, p 193, 28940, 29217, Hon Mrs L M C p 366 59960, G M, p 366, 59965 G M G p 366, 59963, H A, p 366, 59961, S E, p 366, 59964
Gilles Smith, A C, p 289 39047, C B, p 289, 39046, M, p 289, 39045
Girdlestone C p 417, 80064 Mrs C W p 417, 80059, F C, p 417, 80063, H, p 417, 80065, H B, p 417, 80062, L F p 417 80061, N S, p 417, 80060, p 417 80066, V p 417, 80067
Gladstone, 1st Vct, p 44,

582

Index

Index

585

Index

Index

Index

Index

590

Index

Index

Index

Index

597

4 G

Index

598

599

Index

Index

601

247, 37473 ; N. G., p. 247, 37474 ; O., p. 247, 37472 ; Mrs. V., p. 65, 740 ; V. I., p. 248, 37489 ; Capt. W. M., p. 247, 37471

Thomson, Mrs. M. A., p. 353, 59675

Thorley, Mrs. M. U., p. 117, 10727

Thornburgh-Cropper, E. D., p. 169, 17692

Thorne, Hon. Mrs. M., p. 44, 161

Thornhill, Mrs. A. M., p. 353, 59679 ; C., p. 353, 59680 ; Mrs. F. A., p. 288, 39018 ; H., p. 288, 39019 ; K., p. 288, 39020 ; P., p. 288, 39021 ; S., p. 288, 39022

Thornton, A. F., p. 396, 72285 ; Mrs. A. G. F., p. 554, 135224 ; A. N., p. 396, 72290 ; A. R., p. 396, 72295 ; B. G., p. 396 ; 72284 ; C. A. M., p. 396, 72281 ; Rev. C. C., p. 395, 72266 ; Rev. C. C., p. 396, 72279 ; C. Du P., p. 396, 72280 ; C. E. C., p. 405, 79665 ; C. M., p. 396, 72291 ; C. S., p. 397, 72305 ; D. M., p. 396, 72293 ; E. C., p. 396, 72289 ; E. L. R., p. 396, 72292 ; E. M., p. 396, 72286 ; E. M., p. 397, 72306 ; F. H., p. 554, 135231 ; F. R., p. 397, 72298 ; G. H., p. 395, 72262 ; Rev. G. R., p. 397, 72297 ; Capt. G. St. L., p. 396, 72268 ; H. E., p. 395, 72263 ; H. G., p. 395, 72264 ; H. G., p. 554, 135232 ; J. B., p. 554, 135228 ; Rev. J. G., p. 396. 72269 ; K. E. C., p. 396. 72287 ; Rev. L. S., p. 396, 72283; Mrs. M. D., p. 405, 79664; M. L. R., p. 397, 72300 ; M. R., p. 396, 72296 ; P. C., p. 396, 72267 ; P. F., p. 554, 135233 ; P. S., p. 395, 72265 ; R. C., p. 396, 72282 ; R. E., p. 554, 135227 ; R. F., p. 554, 135229 ; R. H., p. 396, 72270 ; S. R., p. 396, 72294 ; Lieut. T. A., p. 554, 135226 ; Capt. T. W., p. 554, 135225 ; V. E., p. 554, 135230 ; W. M., p. 396, 72288

Thornewill, A. B., p. 60, 564 ; E. N., p. 60, 562 ; H. M., p. 60, 565 ; H. P., p. 60, 563

Thorold, E. M., p. 310, 41946, 43139 ; F. H., p. 157, 16827 ; Sir J. H., 12th Bt., p. 310, 41933, 43126 ; M. G., p. 310, 41940, 43133

Threlfell, C. R. M., p. 355, 59716 ; Mrs. M. A., p. 355, 59715

Thumann, Mrs. J., p. 294, 39479

Thwaites, Mrs. M., p. 424, 80220, 80364

Timberlake, Mrs. F. S., p. 208, 29899 ; W. B., p. 208, 29900

Tinne, Mrs. L. B., p. 203, 29706

Tisdall, Mrs. B. T., p. 195, 29024, 29105, 29295

Titchfield, M. of, p. 226, 36411

Tobias, Mrs. E. S., p. 494, 128217

Todd, Mrs. C., p. 63, 665 ; D. A., p. 63, 666

Tollemache, A. H. W., p. 223, 36362 ; E. L. C., p. 223, 36363 ; H. E. A., p. 223, 36364 ; Mrs. S. E., p. 223, 36361

Tomlin, Mrs. H., p. 249, 37533 ; H. G., p. 249, 37534 ; L. J., p. 249, 37535

Toogood, A. H. C., p. 523, 130779 ; Capt. C., p. 570 (App.) ; D. I., p. 570 (App.) ; E. G., p. 570 (App.) ; E. M. p. 570 (App.) ; G. N., p. 523, 130781 ; Mrs. G. S., p. 534, 131398 ; H. R. G. C., p. 523, 130780 ; Mrs. M. E., p. 523, 130778

Torck van Pallandt, 8th B., p. 378, 64085, 64098

Torkington, A., p. 85, 9796, 9980 ; Capt. C., p. 85, 9790, 9974 ; C., p. 85, 9805, 9989 ; C. C., p. 85, 9792, 9976 ; C. R., p. 85, 9804, 9988 ; D. M., p. 85, 9794, 9978 ; E., p. 85, 9803, 9987 ; G., p. 85, 9806, 9990 ; G. S., p. 85, 9791, 9975 ; Lieut.-Col. H., p. 85, 9799, 9983 ; I., p. 85, 9797, 9981 ; J. E. B., p. 85, 9793, 9977 ; M. C., p. 85, 9802, 9986 ; M. D., p. 85, 9795, 9979 ; Capt. O. M., p. 85, 9801, 9985 ; R. H., p. 85, 9800, 9984

Torry, J. S. A., p. 373, 60211, 64415

Tottenham, C. L., p. 195, 29033, 29114, 29304 ; E. L., p. 195, 29039, 29120, 29310 ; F. L., p. 195, 29035, 29116, 29306 ; G. M., p. 195, 29040, 29121, 29311 ; P. M., p. 195, 29034, 29115, 29305

Toulmin, P. M., p. 205, 29739, 29998 ; D. A., p. 519, 130572 ; E. A., p. 519, 130573 ; Mrs. E. L., p. 204, 29723, 29982 ; Mrs. E. V., p. 415, 80001 ; G. M., p. 205, 29740, 29999 ; H. E., p. 519, 130570 ; H. W., p. 204, 29724, 29983 ; I. M., p. 205, 29741, 30000 ; L., p. 204, 29738, 29997 ; P. M., p. 204, 29725, 29984 ; V. F., p. 519, 130571

Tower, A., p. 514, 130367; A. P., p. 514, 130364 ;

B., p. 514, 130365 ; C., p. 514, 130359 ; C., p. 514, 130366 ; D. E., p. 514, 130362 ; E. C., p. 514, 130358 ; Rev. F., p. 514, 130360 ; Rev. H., p. 514, 130357; M., p. 514, 130368 ; W., p. 514, 130361 ; W. E., p. 514, 130363

Towler, C. J., p. 327, 43190 ; E. W., p. 327, 43189 ; Mrs. L. M., p. 327, 43188

Townley, Mrs. A. R. M., p. 426, 80283, 80427 ; C. E., p. 426, 80284, 80428 ; G. M., p. 426, 80285, 80429 ; R. C., p. 426, 80286, 80430 ; S. G., p. 426, 80287, 80431

Townsend, Mrs. M. A., p. 509, 129238

Townshend, B. H. U. L., p. 470, 103163 ; Mrs. B. M., p. 470, 103157; C. M. W. L., p. 470, 103160 ; C. R. de B. L., p. 470,103158 ; E. A. P. L., p. 470, 103161 ; F. W. C. L., p. 470, 103159 ; Capt. H. de B. F., p. 365, 59953 ; M. F. S., p. 365, 59952 ; W. B. G. L., p. 470, 103162

Traill, C. J., p. 136, 16054 ; J. M., p. 136, 16057 ; J. W., p. 136, 16053 ; M. H., p. 136, 16058 ; Rev. R. R. W., p. 136, 16056 ; S. G., p. 136, 16055

Trappes, Mrs. F. L., p. 372, 60175, 64379

Treherne, Mrs. B., p. 282, 38887

Trench, S. G. B., p. 130, 12210, 72012, 81043 ; T. C., p. 130, 12211, 72013, 81044 ;

Trenow, Mrs. S. H. L., p. 65, 731

Trevor, Mrs. A. R., p. 127, 11608 ; Mrs. H., p. 370, 60131, 64335 ; R. S. R., p. 127, 11609

Trew, Mrs. A. M., p. 327, 43185 ; B. M., p. 327, 43187 ; J. M'C., p. 327, 43186 ; M., p. 327, 43191

Tritton, C., p. 444, 94596 ; L., p. 444, 94595 ; O., p. 444, 94594

Trollope, Rev. C. H. B., p. 401, 77850, 79359 ; C. W. A., p. 401, 77853, 79362 ; C. Z., p. 400, 77827, 79336 ; D. M. A., p. 401, 77856, 79365 ; E. M., p. 401, 77851, 79360 ; F. W., p. 401, 77852, 79361 ; G. H. A., p. 401, 77854, 79363 ; H. L., p. 400, 77848, 79357 ; L. E. A., p. 401, 77855, 79364 ; M. E. A., p. 400, 77826, 79335

Troyte-Bullock, A. C., p. 49, 283 ; Capt. C. J., p. 49, 280 ; C. V., p. 49, 277 ; Lieut.-Col. E. G., p. 49, 273 ; E. G., p. 49, 275 ; E. M., p. 49, 282 ; G. V., p. 49, 274 ; H. A., p. 49, 278 ; M., p. 49, 279 ; M. C., p. 49, 281 ; M. W., p. 49, 276

Troyte - Chafyn - Grove, Mrs. A., p. 49, 272

Truell, C. E., p. 189, 28854 ; Lady C. S., p. 189, 28839 ; E. G. S., p. 189, 28841 ; G. M., p. 189, 28853 ; K. A., p. 189, 28852 ; L. A., p. 107, 10316 41492 ; R. H. S., p. 189, 28840 ; W. H. S., p. 189, 28842

Tryon, J., p. 152, 16671, 72483 ; M., p. 151, 16669, 72481 ; S., p. 152, 16670, 72482

Tuckey, Mrs. A. K. R., p. 125, 11568 ; Mrs. F. J., p. 361, 59833 ; R. E. O., p. 125, 11569

Tudor, Mrs. B., p. 196, 29058, 29139, 29329

Tufnell, F. E. S., p. 224, 36382 ; Mrs. G. A., p. 224, 36380 ; R. E., p. 224, 36381

Tugwell, Rev. G., p. 94, 10032 ; H. W., p. 94, 10033

Tullibardine, Capt. the M. of, p. 66, 750, 57169

Tupper, Sir (C.) L., p. 348, 59563 ; F. G., p. 348, 59565 ; G., p. 348, 59564 ; Capt. R. G. O., p. 348, 59568

Turnbull, A. E., p. 253, 37862 ; Col. C. F. A., p. 178, 27227 ; D. R., p. 178, 27228 ; Mrs. M. H., p. 253, 37861 ; M. H., p. 253, 37863 ; M. R., p. 253, 37864 ; S. N. E., p. 178, 27229

Turner, Mrs. B. L., p. 461, 95444 ; Mrs. E. I., p. 211, 30018 ; J. E. U. P., p. 371, 60160, 64364 K. M., p. 461, 95445 ; Mrs. M. A., p. 476, 103342

Turner-Farley, D. G., p. 497, 128295 ; Mrs. M. I. G., p. 497, 128294 ; O. A., p. 497, 128296

Turnor, A., p. 130, 12183, 71985, 81016 ; A. B., p. 130, 12187, 71989, 81020 ; B., p. 130, 12194, 71996, 81027 ; B. K., p. 130, 12209, 72011, 81042 ; C., p. 392, 72015 ; C. H., p. 130, 12182, 71984, 81015 ; C. R., p. 130, 12185, 71987, 81018 ; C. O., p. 130, 12193, 71995, 81026 ; C. Y., p. 130, 12192, 71994, 81025 ; E., p. 130, 12190, 71992, 81023 ; E., p. 130, 12195, 71997, 81028 ; E. C., p. 130, 12191, 71993, 81024 ; G. A., p. 130, 12189, 71991, 81022 ; H. B., p. 130, 12184, 71986, 81017 ; J., p. 392, 72017 ; C. J., p. 130, 12186, 71988, 81019 ; R., p. 393, 72016 ; Maj.

Index

Index

604

Index

INDEX OF NUMBERS IN THE TUDOR, CLARENCE, EXETER, AND ESSEX VOLUMES WHICH REPEAT IN THE PRESENT

OWING to the very great number, it has been found impossible to include in the Index to the present volume the names of those persons descended from Edward III through the Lady Elizabeth Percy, *née* Mortimer, who at the same time have a senior descent from her brother, the Earl of March, which has been set out fully in one of the four preceding volumes. In order, however, that any person whose name appears in any of these preceding volumes may at once be able to discover whether he or she is also descended through the Mortimer-Percy line, an index to those numbers in the Tudor, Clarence, Exeter, and Essex Volumes is here given, with their equivalent number in the present book.

In order to make this quite clear, the following example may be given. If the name of Lieutenant Alexander Hood is referred to in the index to the Tudor Volume, it will be seen that his descent is through the families of Percy (Smithson), Seymour, Thynne, Finch, Seymour, Gray, Brandon, and Tudor, to Edward IV, and so to Edward III, his number being 21015. Glancing down the following index of numbers, it will be found that this number (21015) = Nos 834, 16244, 55253, and 88156, which shows that he has, besides the descent through the Tudor line (and any other descent which can be found in the Clarence, Exeter, and Essex Volumes), four other lines of descent from Edward III through the Mortimer-Percy marriage. These other four lines of descent can be traced by referring to the numbers in the present volume.

No 834 occurs on page 68, and by following the line there given back to pages 68 and 67 and Table III, it will be found that the two lines merge by the marriage in 1715 of Algernon, 7th Duke of Somerset (a descendant of Edward III through Mortimer-Percy), with Frances Thynne, a descendant of Edward III through the Tudor line (see the Tudor Roll, Table XXIV, &c)

No 16244 occurs on page 143, where the paternal descent of the said Lieutenant Alexander Hood from Edward III through Mortimer-Percy is given, the two preceding descents being through his mother, *née* Percy, the three now merging in his person.

No 55253 occurs on page 231, and to follow this up it will be necessary to refer to the Clarence and Exeter Volumes, the said Lieutenant Hood being also descended from Edward III through both George, Duke of Clarence, and his sister, the Duchess of Exeter, and by following the same plan it will be found that the descents are traced out until they all finally unite in the Tudor line before mentioned.

No 88156 occurs on page 455, where the descent is traced, through the Mortimer-Percy marriage, to Thomas (Thynne), 1st Viscount Weymouth (died 1714), who married Lady Frances Finch, a Tudor descendant (see Tudor Volume, Table XXIV).

This may sound complicated, but it is inevitable when one is dealing with thousands of persons, many of whom have a great many lines of descent. A little trouble, however, will enable any who find their names in one of the previous volumes, followed by a number which repeats below, to trace it once their line or lines of descent through the Mortimer-Percy marriage.

Index of Numbers

TUDOR ROLL

TUDOR SUPPLEMENT (ESSEX VOLUME)

Index of Numbers

CLARENCE VOLUME

CLARENCE SUPPLEMENT (ESSEX VOLUME)

Index of Numbers

EXETER VOLUME

Index of Numbers

Index of Numbers

ESSEX SUPPLEMENT (MORTIMER-PERCY VOLUME— PART I)

The Exeter Volume

SUPPLEMENT

41

SUPPLEMENTARY TABLE OF EXETER AND ESSEX
DESCENTS CONTAINED IN SUPPLEMENT

Lady Anne Mortimer. = Richard (Plantagenet),
See Table I. p. 1 of | Earl of Cambridge,
this Volume. | *c.* 1375 + 1415.

a. 1424
Richard, 3rd Duke of = Lady Cecily Nevill.
York, K.G., declared
heir to throne of
England, 1412 + 1460.

Lady Isabel Plan- = Henry, 2nd Count of
tagenet, | Eu, 1st Earl of Essex,
+ 1484. | 1406 + 1483.

Edward IV., = Lady
King of | Elizabeth
England, | Wydville.
1441 + 1483.

a. 1447
Lady = (1) Henry, Duke
Anne Plan- | of Exeter,
tagenet, 1473 1430 + 1473, *s.p.s.*
1439 + 1476. = (2) Sir Thomas St.
Leger, K.B.

William, (1) = Lady
Viscount | Anne
Bourchier | Wydville,
+ *v.p.* 1471 | + 1489.

Lady Anne St. Leger, = Sir George Manners,
da. and h., | 12th Lord Ros,
1474 + 1526. | + 1513.

Hon. Cicely (1) = John, 8th Lord Ferrers,
Bourchier. | of Chartley,
| + 1501.

Thomas, 1st Earl of = (2) Eleanor Paston,
Rutland, K.G., | + 1551.
+ 1543.

Walter, 1st Viscount = (1) Lady Mary Grey.
Hereford, K.G., | + 1534.
c. 1491 + 1558.

1536
Henry, 2nd Earl of = (1) Lady Margaret Nevill.
Rutland, K.G., | *See Mortimer-Percy Vol.,*
+ 1563. | *Table XXV.*

Hon. Sir William = Jane Scudamore.
Devereux.

1573
Lady Elizabeth (1) = Sir William Courtenay,
Manners. | of Powderham,
| 1553 + 1638.

Margaret Devereux, = Sir Edward Littleton,
yr. da. and co.-h. | of Pillaton, M.P.

Francis Courtenay, (1) = (2) Elizabeth Seymour,
of Powderham, | + 1658.
1576 + 1638.

Annie Littleton. = Humphrey Salwey,
| of Stanford,
| *c.* 1575 + 1652.

Sir William Courtenay, = (2) Margaret Waller.
1st Bt., | *See Mortimer-Percy*
1628 + 1702. | *Vol., Table XXIX.*

Edward Salwey, Lord = [——].
Chief Baron of the
Exchequer.

1670
Francis Courtenay, = Mary Bovey.
M.P.,
1651 + *v.p.* 1699.

Elizabeth Salwey, (2) = Sir Francis Winnington,
yr. da. and co-h. | M.P.,
| + 1700.

1704
Sir William Courtenay. = Lady Ann Bertie.
2nd Bt., | + 1718.
1676 + 1735.

1689
Mary Winnington, = Felix Calvert, of
1673 + 1729. | Albury, M.P.,
| 1663 + 1736.

1734
Eleanor Courtenay. = Francis Basset, of
1711 + 1764. | Heanton,
| 1714 + 1757.

Felix Calvert, of = Mary Calvert,
Albury, M.P., | 1703 + 1757.
1692 + 1755.

1762
Elizabeth = John Hooke Campbell-
Eustacia | Hooke, Lord Lyon
Basset, | King of Arms,
da. and co-h. | + 1795.

1763
Eleanora, = John Davie,
da. and co-h., | of Orleigh,
1741 + | co. Devon.

1755
Anne = Christopher
Calvert, | Anstey, the
1732 + 1812. | Poet,
| 1724 + 1805.

(41)   (41*a*)   (201)

614

THE EXETER VOLUME

SUPPLEMENT

Pages 110-112   Delete Section 41 and in place thereof read—

41 Descendants of ELIZABETH EUSTACIA BASSET (Supplementary Table), d (-), m 31 July or 1 Aug 1762, JOHN HOOKE CAMPBELL, *afterwards* CAMPBELL-HOOKE, of Bangeston, co Pembroke, Lord Lyon King of Arms 1754-1795 [E of Argyll Coll and uncle of John, 1st Lord Cawdor [G.B]], d 1 Sept. 1795; and had issue (with 2 sons and a da. who *d.s p*) 1*a* to 2*a*

1*a Charlotte Campbell-Hooke, da and co-h*, b c 1768, d 8 *Jan* 1819, m as 2*nd wife*, 22 *Sept.* 1796, *Sir Thomas Gage of Hengrave, 6th Bt* [*E*], d 1 *Dec* 1798, *and had issue* 1*b to* 2*b*

1*b Lucy Gage*

2*b Emma Gage*, d 17 *June* 1845, m 31 *July* 1826, *John Collett, M P* [*son of Ebenezer John Collett of Locker's House, Hemel Hempstead*], *and had issue* 1*c*

1*c* Charlotte Eustacia Collett

2*a Louisa Caroline Hooke Campbell, da and co-h*, b 18 *Sept* 1773, d *at Manchester* 31 *Mar* 1863, m 25 *Aug* 1798, *Henry Hulton, Lieut.-Col Comdg Blackburne Mil* [*3rd son of William Hulton of Hulton Park, co Lanc*], b 27 *Nov* 1765, d *Sept* 1831, *and had issue (with 3 sons and 3 das d s p)* 1*b to* 4*b*

1*b William Adam Hulton of Hurst Grange, Preston, J P , D L , Bar at-Law, Judge of County Courts*, b 18 *Oct* 1802, d 3 *Mar* 1887, m 15 *Sept* 1832, *Dorothy Anne, da of Edward Gorst of Preston*, d 1 *May* 1886, *and had issue* 1*c to* 5*c*

1*c* Rev Henry Edward Hulton, M A (Oxon), Rural Dean of Chelmsford (1886) and Hon Canon of St Albans (1900), *formerly* Vicar of Great Waltham 1876-1906 (*Bercham Manor, Chelmsford*), b 21 June 1839, *unm*

2*c* Frederick Campbell Hulton, Clerk of the Peace, co Lancaster, b 23 June 1841

3*c* George Eustace Hulton, b 14 July 1842

1*c* Alyne Louisa Elizabeth Hulton (*Catisfield Lodge, Fareham*), m 6 Aug 1871, James Mathias [son of Lewis Mathias of Lamphey Court, Pembrokeshire], d 3 June 1886 and has issue 1*d* to 4*d*

2. 1*d* William Delamotte Mathias, b 29 May 1877

3. 2*d* James Herbert Mathias, b 8 Sept 1881

4. 3*d* Maria Frederica Mathias

5. 4*d* Dorothy Alyne Louisa Mathias

5*c* Mary Caroline Hulton

2*b Rev Campbell Bassett Arthur Grey Hulton, Hulme Exr , Oxford, Ellerton*
[Nos 12637 to 12639

615

The Plantagenet Roll

Prize, 2nd Class, Rector of Emberton, co Bucks, 1860–1878, b 3 *May* 1813, d 30 *Ap* 1878, m 27 *Mar* 1845, *Sarah Stokes, da of Samuel Fletcher of Manchester,* d 4 *July* 1876, *and had issue* 1c *to* 13c

1c Campbell Arthur Grey Hulton of Manchester, Merchant (*Hotel Metropole, London*), b 16 Mar 1846, m 21 Ap 1875, Florence, da of James Burton of Tyldesley, d 12 Ap 1898, and has issue 1d to 3d

   1d Rev Campbell Blethyn Hulton, Rector of Turvey (*Turvey Rectory, Beds*), b 30 May 1877, m 5 Aug 1903, Dorothy, da of John Heelis of Manchester, s p

   2d Roger Adam Hulton, b 29 July 1878

   3d John Meredith Hulton, Lieut Royal Sussex Regt, b 8 Jan 1882

2c Jessop Henry Fletcher Hulton, of Messrs Fullager, Hulton, Bailey & Co of Bolton, Solicitors (*Astley House, Bolton*), b 17 Oct. 1848, m 1st, 16 Aug 1875, Eleanor Brada, da of the Rev Samuel Simpson of Lancaster, d 4 Feb 1887, 2ndly, 2 July 1895, Blanche, da of Simon Martin, B C S, and has issue 1d to 3d

   1d Jessop Arthur Hulton, served in South African War as Lieut Railway Staff Corps, b 3 Aug 1878, m Anabel, da of (—) Jones of Birmingham

   2d Charles Edward Hulton, Solicitor, b 26 Ap 1881

   3d¹ Brada Hulton, m 15 Aug 1901, Spencer Hogg, Bar-at-Law (*Orchard House, Altrincham*), and has issue 1e to 2e

      1e Jessop Martin Spencer Hogg, b 3 Dec 1903

      2e Brada Elizabeth Spencer Hogg

3c William Stokes Hulton, Artist (6383 *Calle della Testa, SS Giovanni e Paolo, Venice*), b 23 Oct 1852, m 1886, Constanza Maria Orsola, da of Vincenzo Mazini, and has issue 1d to 2d

   1d Gioconda Hulton, b 5 Oct 1887

   2d Edith Teresa Hulton, b 6 Aug 1890

4c *Henry Hulton, of the Fiji Islands, Planter,* b 5 *Feb* 1854, d *unm* 9 *Dec.* 1883

5c Reginald Edward Hulton, Engineer (*Brynhir, Tenby*), b 10 June 1857, m 16 Sept 1886, Sydney Alice, da of the Rev E Cadogan, and has issue 1d to 2d

   1d Edward Campbell Hulton, b 19 Sept 1898

   2d Mary Hulton

6c Charles Copley Hulton, b 12 Jan 1860, *unm*

7c Samuel Fletcher Hulton, Bar-at-Law, Author of *Rixæ Oxonienses, &c* (10 *King's Bench Walk, Temple, E C*), b 20 Feb 1862, *unm*

8c Frederick Courtenay Longuet Hulton, Major 1st King's Dragoon Guards, b 14 Mar 1864, m 16 June 1895, Nelly, da of (—) Darvel, and has issue 1d

   1d Rowena Hulton

9c Mary Louisa Hulton (40 *Cadogan Place, S W*), m 14 Ap 1869, William Clarence Watson, Ottoman Vice-Consul in London, d 7 Feb 1906, and has issue 1d to 9d

   1d William Donald Paul Watson, b 19 Ap 1872

   2d Hugh Gordon Watson, b 13 Ap. 1874

   3d Edith Campbell Watson

   4d Margaret Louisa Watson

   5d Evelyn Mary Watson

   6d Sylvia Maud Watson

   7d Helen Lilias Watson

   8d Cicely Cunninghame Watson

   9d Violet Watson

10c Sarah Beatrice Hulton, m 9 Jan 1878, the Rev George Frederick Sams, M A (Camb), Rector of Emberton (*Emberton Rectory, Newport-Pagnell, Bucks*), and has issue 1d to 7d   [Nos. 1263/11 to 1263/41.

# of The Blood Royal

1*d* Frederick Edward Barwick Hulton Sams, *b* 22 Nov. 1881.

2*d* Cecil Henry Hulton Sams, *b* 9 May 1883

3*d* Kenneth Assheton Hulton Sams, *b* 26 Oct 1884

4*d* Mona Beatrix Hulton Sams, *m* 11 Ap 1909, Henry Johnston Carson (*Belvedere, Upper Drive, Hove*)

5*f* Elsie Campbell Hulton Sams

6*d* Florence Marjorie Hulton Sams, *m* 16 Sept 1908, Sir William George Eden Wiseman, 10th Bt [E] [see Exeter Volume, p 397] (*Holyport, Berks*)

7*d* Sidney Alyne Hulton Sams

11*c* Harriet Alyne Hulton, *m* 7 Aug 1879, Richard Fred Austin, of Messrs Austin & Austin of 3 and 4 Clements Inn, London, Solicitors (*on Hyde Park Mansions, Marylebone Road, N W*), *s p*

12*c* Gertrude Jane Hulton, *m* 5 June 1888, the Rev Reginald Illingworth Woodhouse, Rector of Merstham (*Merstham Rectory, Surrey*), and has issue 1*d* to 3*d*

    1*d* Reginald Courtenay Hulton Woodhouse

    2*d* Gertrude Helen Hulton Woodhouse

    3*d* Rosamund Hulton Woodhouse

13*c* Edith Helen Hulton, *m* 10 July 1889, Edward Grant of Lichborough, M A (Oxon), J P, D L, High Sheriff of Northants 1893, Alderman of the County Council and Lord of the Manor and Patron of Maidford (*Lichborough Hall, Weedon*) and has issue 1*d* to 3*d*

    1*d* Edith Muriel Grant, *b* 21 Aug 1890

    2*d* Violet Helen Grant, *b* 11 Aug 1891

    3*d* Frances Enid Grant, *b* 20 May 1898

3*b* *Louisa Caroline Mary Anne Hulton*, b *at Pembroke* 9 *Aug* 1799, d *at Preston* 15 *Aug* 1825, m *there* 21 *June* 1823, *John Addison of Preston, Bar-at-Law, Recorder of Clitheroe and a County Court Judge,* b 21 *Ap* 1794, d *at Preston* 14 *July* 1859, *and had issue* 1*c*

1*c* *Anne Agnes Addison, da and h*, b 1 *Aug* 1821, d *at* 29 *Sussex Gardens, London,* 14 *Feb* 1900, m *at Preston* 15 *Oct* 1845, *Gen John ffolliot Crofton, Col* 6*th Reg* [*Bt of Mohill* [*U K*] *Coll*], b 9 *Oct* 1802, d *at* 29 *Sussex Gardens afsd* 17 *July* 1885, *and had issue* 1*d* to 4*d*

    1*d* *Rev Addison Crofton, M A* (Oxon), b 13 *July* 1846, d *at Genoa* 12 *Jan* 1904, m 7 *Aug* 1873, *Mary Pilkington, da of John Hall of Baddingstone,* d 7 *May* 1903, *and had issue* 1*e* to 2*e*

        1*e* Annie Crofton

        2*e* Sydney d'Abzac Crofton } (*Linton Court, Settle, Yorkshire*)

    2*d* Henry Thomas Crofton, Solicitor (*Oldfield, Maidenhead*), *b* 23 July 1848, *m* 7 Sept 1871, Martha Pilling, da of Joseph M'Keand, and has issue 1*e* to 4*e*

        1*e* John ffolliott Frederick Crofton, Solicitor, *late* Capt 3rd Vol Batt Cheshire Regt, *b* 1 Jan 1877

        2*e* *Josephine Christie Crofton,* d 20 *May* 1906, m 7 *Sept* 1897, *Herman Barker-Hahlo* (*Foxlease Park, Lyndhurst*), *and had issue* 1*f* to 3*f*

            1*f* John Francis Crofton Barker-Hahlo, *b* 2 Oct 1901

            2*f* Alice Christine Barker-Hahlo

            3*f* Frances Natalie Barker-Hahlo

        3*e* Alice Addison Crofton

        4*e* Gladys Noelle Crofton

    3*d* Rev William d'Abzac Crofton, M A (Oxon), Vicar of Codicote (*Codicote Vicarage, Welwyn, Herts*), *b* 3 June 1854, *unm*

    4*d* *Caroline Anne Agnes Crofton*, b *at* 29 *Sussex Gardens, London,* 27 *Jan* 1852, d *at Liverpool* 2 *Jan* 1880, m *at St James', Paddington,* 21 *Jan* 1879, *Ralph Crine Clayton of Liverpool,* d *in Jermyn Street, London,* 13 *Sept* 1904, *and had issue* 1*e*

[Nos 1263 42 to 1263,67

The Plantagenet Roll

1*c* Gerald Edward Came Clayton M A (Oxon), Bar-at-Law (*Pen-ar-wel, Llanbedrog, Wales*), b at Liverpool 27 Dec 1879, m at St James', Spanish Place, London, 28 Ap 1908, Violet Alice Ione, da of Baron Oscar de Satgé de Thoren, and has issue 1*f*

1*f* Ralph Dominic de Satgé Clayton, b 18 Feb 1909

4*b* Anne Beatrice Hulton, b 1 Sept 1801, d at Manchester 19 Sept 1866, m at Moreton-in-Marsh 21 Ap 1840, the Rev Samuel Farmer Sadler, d at Blackpool 31 Oct 1862, and had issue 1*c*

1*c* Samuel Campbell Hulton Sadler, Deputy-Clerk of the Peace for co Lancaster, b 14 Nov 1842, d at Southport 5 Aug 1904, m in London 30 Nov 1867, Annie, da of Nelson Cain, d 22 Dec 1887, and had issue 1*d* to 8*d*

1*d* Telfourd Hayes Sadler (*Bronx, New York, U S A*), b 23 Sept 1868, unm

2*d* Reginald Cobham Sadler (*Mabel Lake, Lumby, British Columbia*), b 2 Ap 1874, m 24 June 1906, Mary, da of (—) Hanson

3*d* Catherine Annie Sadler, m at Southport 3 Ap 1902, Herbert Foyster, of Messrs Foyster, Waddington & Foyster of Manchester, Solicitors (*Bramcote, Parkfield Road, Didsbury*), and has issue 1*e*

1*e* Eileen Selma Foyster

4*d* Gertrude Muriel Sadler, m 15 Feb 1908, Charles Henry Marriot Wharton, Bar-at-Law (3 *Wellington Street East, Broughton, Manchester*), s p

5*d* Edith Beatrix Sadler, m 10 July 1902, Charles Henry Gardner, Banker (244 *Upper Chorlton Road, Manchester*)

6*d* Eleanor Louisa Sadler, unm

7*d* Mabel Cecilia Sadler, m 8 Oct 1903, the Rev Edward William Whitley, B A, Rector of Framilode (*Framilode Rectory, Stonehouse, Glos*), and has issue 1*e*

1*e* Edward Campbell Rodbard Whitley

8*d* Florence Winifred Sadler, unm   [Nos 1263 68 to 1263/79

41*a*. Descendants of ELEANORA BASSET (Supplementary Table), b at Heanton Punchardon 9 June 1741, d (–), m at Atherington 18 Aug 1763, JOHN DAVIE of Orleigh, Buckland Brewer, co Devon, d (–), and had issue (with 3 other sons and 2 das who d unm) 1*a* to 9*a*

1*a* Joseph Davie, afterwards (1803) Basset, of Watermouth and Umberleigh, b 18 May 1764, d 10 Dec 1846, m 1799, Mary, da of Christopher Irwin of Barnstaple, d 21 Ap 1862, and had issue 1*b* to 4*b*

1*b* Arthur Davie Basset of Watermouth, b 14 May 1801, d 8 Dec 1870, m 4 Dec 1828, Harriet Sarah, da of Thomas Smith Crawfurth, b 14 July 1806, d 18 Dec 1863, and had issue 1*c* to 2*c*

1*c* Rev Arthur Crawfurth Davie Basset of Watermouth, M A, b 11 Aug 1830, d unm 23 Ap 1880

2*c* Harriet Mary Basset of Umberleigh and Watermouth (*Watermouth Castle, Ilfracombe, Umberleigh, Atherington, &c*), m 7 Jan 1858, Charles Henry Williams, now (R L 11 Oct 1880) Basset, J P, D L, Major N Devon Hussars [son of Sir William Williams, 1st Bt [U K]], d 1 Feb 1908, and has issue 1*d* to 2*d*

1*d* Walter Basset, Lieut R N, b 20 Sept 1863, d 27 May 1907, m 18 Nov 1890, Ellen Caroline Charlotte, da of Adm Sir William Montague Dowell, G C B

2*d* Edith Basset Basset, m 18 Oct 1882, Capt Ernest Charles Penn Curzon [E Howe Coll], late 18th Hussars and has issue 1*e* to 2*e*

1*e* Charles Ernest Basset Lothian Curzon, b 10 May 1885

2*e* Lorna Katherine Curzon, m 27 Oct 1908, Capt Quintin Dick

2*b* Rev Francis William Davie Basset, Rector of Heanton Punchardon, Devon, m Mary, da of William Cartwright of Teignmouth   [Nos 1263/80 to 1263/81

618

# of The Blood Royal

3b *Augusta Mary Basset*, d (-), m 17 *Ap* 1827, *the Rev William Bickford Coham of Coham and Dunsland, LL B*, bapt 6 *Ap* 1792, d 2 *July* 1843, *and had issue* 1c *to* 2c

1c *William Holland Bickford Coham of Coham and Dunsland, J P , D L*, b 28 *July* 1828, d 22 *Sept* 1880, m 3 *Sept* 1857, *Dora Elizabeth Louisa* (see p 620), *da of Gen Sir Hopton Stratford Scott, K C B , and had issue* 1d

1d *Elinor Mary Bickford Coham of Coham, m* 5 *June* 1883, John Blyth Fleming, now (R L 1883) Coham Fleming, J P , D L , High Sheriff co Devon 1887 (*Coham, co Devon , Upcot Iven d, Sheepwash, co Devon*), and *has issue* 1e

1e *Blyth Bickford Coham-Fleming, b* 5 Sept 1884

2c *Augusta Christiana Davie Coham of Dunsland and Arscott*, d 13 *July* 1901 , m 29 *Ap* 1858, *Major Harvey George Dickinson*, d *Nov* 1866 , *and had issue* 1d *to* 3d

1d *Arscott William Harvey Dickinson*, M A (Oxon), J P , Bar-at-Law (*Dunsland, Brandis-Corner, N Devon , The Tower, Compton Gifford, S Devon*), b 23 *Ap* 1859 , m 11 Jan 1893, Mary, da of the Rev Sabine Baring Gould of Lew Trenchard , and has issue 1e to 3e

1e *Arscott Sabine Harvey Dickinson, b.* 28 *Nov* 1893

2e *Edward Dabernon Dickinson, b* 27 June 1895

3e *Bickford Holland Coham Dickinson, b* 16 July 1900

2d *Augusta Frances Courtenay Dickinson*, d 14 *Oct* 1892 , m 3 *Nov* 1883, *Henry Morton Tudor Tudor, Rear-Adm R N , and had issue* 1e *to* 2e

1e *Douglas Courtenay Tudor, b* 9 *July* 1891

2e *Alice Irene Tudor, m* 12 *Dec* 1906, Lieut John Evelyn Bray, R N

3d *Elinor Mary Coham Dickinson, m* 14 *Ap* 1884, Capt William M'Coy FitzGerald Castle, R N , and has issue 1e to 2e

1e *Basil Langford Harvey Castle, b* 13 Sept 1892

2e *Violet Eleanor M'Coy Castle, b* 22 Sept 1888

4b *Mary Davie Basset*, d (-), m. 1826 *Gen Sir Hopton Stratford Scott of Woodville, Lucan, co Dublin, K C B , and had issue* (*with a da , Augusta, who d unm*) 1c *to* 7c

1c. *Hopton Basset Scott, Lieut-Col , formerly* 19th *Regt* (*Locksley, Shankill, co Dublin*), b 22 *Mar* 1829 , m 15 *Dec* 1865, Alice Jane Blaine, da of Henry Blaine , and has issue (with 3 sons (Hopton Arthur, b 1868 , d 1907, Herbert Courtenay, b 1871 , d 1899, Raynold Woodville, b 1877 , d 1896) and a da (Agnes Gertrude, d 1877), who all d unm) 1d to 8d

1d. Edward Baliol Scott, b 1872

2d Gerald Basset Scott, b 1875

3d George Ernest Blaine Scott, b 1883

4d John Davie Scott, b 1883

5d Alice Mary Scott

6d Edith Margaret Scott

7d Dora Cecil Scott

8d Marjorie Ruth Scott

2c Courtenay Harvey Saltren Scott, Col *formerly* 71st H L I (*Pennant Hall, Abermule, R S O , co Montgomery*), b 24 June 1833 , m 11 Feb 1862, Margaret Julia, da of James Colquhoun , and has issue (with a son who d young) 1d to 2d

1d Eleanor Margaret Scott, m as 2nd wife, 10 Feb 1891, Sir Edward Arthur Barry, 2nd Bt [U K], J P , Major Berks Yeo (*Ockwells Manor, Bray, Berks , Hill Head House, Hants , Cavalry*), and has issue 1e to 4e

1e Edward Courtenay Tress Barry, b 23 Jan 1895

2e Cicely Eleanor Barry

3e Margaret Colquhoun Barry

4e Rosamond Barry

[Nos 1263 85 to 1263 110

The Plantagenet Roll

2*d* Adelaide Louisa Scott, *m* James Gray Flowerdew-Lowson, and has issue 1*e* to 3*e*.

    1*e* Courtenay Patrick Flowerdew-Lowson, *b* 1 Ap 1897

    2*e* Denis Colquhoun Flowerdew-Lowson, *b* 20 Jan 1906

    3*e* Eleanor Margaret Flowerdew-Lowson, *b* 9 Ap 1892

3*c* Osmund Walter Scott (*Smytham House, Torrington, Devon*), *b* 11 Jan 1837, *m* 31 May 1864, Julia Georgina, da of Samuel Brown of Clifton, and has issue 1*d* to 4*d*

    1*d* Hopton Stratford Scott, *b* 20 June 1867

    2*d* Evelyn Mary Scott, *b* 23 Mar 1866

    3*d* Julia Augusta Scott, *b* 22 May 1870

    4*d* Florence Adelaide Scott, *b* 26 Jan 1873

4*c* George Townsend Scott, 52nd Regt, *d* 21 Feb 1879, *m* Charlotte, da of (—) Pearse, *d* 22 Sept 1900, and had issue 1*d* to 2*d*

    1*d* Violet Ethel Scott, *m* 17 July 1905, Edward Gordon Stewart McClellan [2nd son of Col McClellan, 3rd Dragoon Guards] (*East Brook, Wokingham, Berks*), and has issue 1*e* to 2*e*

        1*e* Greville Aleck Stewart McClellan, *b* 17 Oct 1906

        2*e* Dora Violet McClellan, *b* 8 Feb 1908

    2*d* Kathleen Mary Scott, *m* 17 Jan 1903, Capt Ferdinand Ewing M'Clellan, Somersetshire L I [eldest son of Col McClellan afsd] (*St Margaret's, Shortlands, Kent*), s *p*

5*c* Adelaide Harriet Scott (4 *Markwich Terrace, St Leonards-on-Sea*), *m* 1870, Capt Edward John Thomas Montrésor, 55th Regt [son of Gen Sir Henry Montrésor of Denne Hill, co Kent], *d* 1907, and has issue (with 4 sons and a da who *d unm*) 1*d* to 4*d*

    1*d* Edward Henry Hopton Montrésor, Lieut-Col *late* Bengal Lancers, *b* 8 May 1851, *m* Bertha, da of Gen Hennessy, and has issue 1*e* to 2*e*

        1*e* Charles Egerton Montrésor, *b* 22 Dec 1892

        2*e* Marion Montresor, *b* 21 Jan 1880

    2*d* Henry Scott Montrésor, *b* 18 June 1859, *unm*

    3*d* Louis Bassett Montrésor, Capt R F A, *b* 17 Feb 1874, *unm*

    4*d* Constance Mary Montrésor, *m* 8 Oct 1889, Walter William Gordon Beatson [son of Major-Gen Beatson, R E] *d* 7 May 1897, and has issue (with a son who *d unm*) 1*e* to 3*e*

        1*e* Roger Stewart Montrésor Beatson, *b* 20 July 1890

        2*e* Claude Gordon Beatson, *b* 13 Jan 1894

        3*e* Walter William Gordon Beatson, *b* 5 Aug 1897.

6*c* Dora Elizabeth Louisa Scott, *m* 3 Sept 1857, William Holland Bickford Coham of Coham and Dunsland, J P, D L (see p 619), *d* 22 Sept 1880, and has issue

See p 619, Nos 1263,85–1263/86

7*c* Susan Agnes Scott (*Suncote, Austen Way, Gerrard's Cross, Bucks*), *m* 20 Oct 1864, Major Augustus Leacock Marsh, 55th Regt, *d* 8 Mar 1876 and has issue 1*d* to 6*d*

    1*d* Hopton Elliot Marsh, Major R G A, *b* 6 Nov 1865, *m* 30 Dec 1896, Ethel, da of Col Morton Taylor, R A, and has issue 1*e*

        1*e* Kathleen Marsh, *b* 26 Sept 1897

    2*d* Francis Courtenay Marsh, Capt 2nd Border Regt, *b* 27 Ap 1867

    3*d* Frederick William Marsh, *b* 20 Nov 1868

    4*d* Edward Augustus Marsh, *b* 29 Jan 1870

    5*d* Julia Augusta Marsh, *m* 25 Jan 1894, Frederick Feist, and has issue 1*e*.

        1*e* Doris Evelyn Feist

    6*d* Ada Caroline Mary Marsh, *m* 17 May 1896, Stanislas Sigismund Zaleski

        [Nos 1263/111 to 1263/145

# of The Blood Royal

2a Rev Charles Davie, Rector of Heanton Punchardon, Devon, b 15/18 Aug 1765, d 1836, m 1801 Bridget, da of (—) Boyfield of Lee, co Kent, and has issue 1b to 2b

1b Charles Christopher Davie, Capt 67th Regt, b 1803, d 1874, m 1840, Eliza Frances, da of Capt (—) White of Barnstaple, d 1905, and has issue (with others d s p) 1c

1c George Christopher Davie, b 1841, m 1868, Annie Smith, da of Thomas Dickson of Harley Street, London, and has issue (with 2 das d unm) 1d to 3d

1d Charles Christopher Davie (21 Selborne Road, Hove), b 18 Aug 1869, m 28 Nov 1900, Beatrice Paulina Mabel, da of Henry (Walrond), 9th Marquis of Vallado and a Grandee of the 1st Class [Spain], Lieut-Col and Hon Col late 4th Batt Devon Regt, and has issue

See Mortimer-Percy Volume, Part I p 78, Nos 9453–9454

2d Bertie George Davie (24 Eccleston Square, S W), b 16 Nov 1874, m 29 Aug 1903, Flora Helen Frances [descended from the Lady Anne, sister to King Edward IV, &c (see Essex Volume Supp, p 622)], da of Major Michael M Creagh Thornhill of Stanton-in-Peak, co Derby, J P, D L, and has issue 1e

1e Humphrey Bache Christopher Davie, b 1904

3f Annie Frances Davie

2b Mary Jane Davie, b 1802, d s p 19 Aug 1857/8, m 1st, 1877, Capt John May of Broadoak, near Barnstaple, J P, D L, d (–), 2ndly, 6 Aug 1857, Frederick Lee

3a John Davie, Post Capt R N , in command of the Conqueror at St Helena, during the imprisonment of the Emperor Napoleon there, b 1770, d (–), m Jemima, da of (—) Tapper, and had issue which became extinct 4 May 1900

4a Peregrine Davie, H E I C S , d (–), m (—), da of (—), a Gen in the French Service, d (–), and had issue (with a son, Calmar, who d unm in India) 1b to 2b

1b Peregrine Davie

2b Eleanora Juliana Davie, b 1811, d 11 Oct 1884, m 10 Sept 1828, Capt John Wynch, Madras Horse Artillery, commanded Artillery with Gen Lang's Force 1818 [2nd son of George Wynch, Madras C S (by his wife Mary, widow of (—) Smyth, and da of John Secker, youngest brother of Thomas, Archbishop of Canterbury 1758-68), who was 5th son of Alexander Wynch, Governor of Madras, 2 Feb. 1772-Dec 1775, see p 236], b at Dindigub 5 June 1796, d 11 Jan 1880, and had issue (with a son, George Peregrine, and a da, Eleanor Jane, who both d unm) 1c to 7c

1c Henry St Maur Wynch, Col formerly H E I C S , b 23 Dec 1833, m 1st, at Greenwich 18 Aug 1892, Laura Edith, da of Henry Habbijam, d 7 Dec 1894, 2ndly, (—)

2c Rev John William Wynch, Assist Chaplain, Madras Ecclesiastical Estab, 14 Jan 1861-14 Jan 1886 (36 The Park, Ealing), b at St Thomas' Mount, Madras, 23 Dec 1835, m 6 Sept 1860, Mary Jane, da of Lieut-Col Frederick Minchin, H E I C S , and has issue (with 2 das who d young) 1d to 3d

1d Frederick John Wynch, Lieut-Col Comdg 41st Dogras since 19 Oct 1907, b 28 Aug 1862, m 1 Mar 1892, (—), da of (—) Jones, and has issue 1e to 4e

1e Wilfred Alexander Davie Wynch, b 29 Ap 1899

2e Avice Wynch, b 19 Dec 1892

3e Phyllis Loveday Wynch, b 3 Feb 1895

4e Audrey Wynch, b 24 Mar 1897

2d Eleanora Mary Davie Wynch, m 1 Mar 1881, Capt Charles Brenton Wickham, R A , and has issue 1e to 2e

1e John Charles Wickham, Lieut R E , b 23 June 1886

2e Evelyn Wickham

3d Lilian Gordon Wynch, unm   [Nos 1263,146 to 1263/163

4 A

3c Alexander Wynch, Lieut.-Col (ret.) Madras Artillery (105 *Park Street, Grosvenor Square, W*), b 1 Aug 1838, m 1st, 26 Oct 1865, Mary Jane, da of Lieut.-Col Balmain, Royal Madras Artillery, d 19 Dec 1867, 2ndly, 20 Dec 1876, Mary, da of James Hole and has issue (with a son, Alexander Balmain, b 21 Sept 1866, d unm 20 July 1888) 1d to 2d

1d¹ Mary Balmain Wynch, m 4 Sept 1890, William Reid Lewis (*Philadelphia*), and has issue (with a da, Denys de Budt, who d young) 1e to 2e

1e Eleanor Lewis, b 14 Aug 1891

2e Marguerita Balmain Lewis, b 3 Nov 1891

2d² Ethel Alexandra Wynch, m 20 Dec 1905, Edward John Urwick, and has issue 1e to 2e

1e Edward Hilary Urwick, b 4 Oct 1906

2e Maurice Alexis Urwick, b 30 Mar 1909

4c *Edward James Wynch, Major Madras Army,* b 23 Oct 1840, d s p 7 Sept 1882

5c Mary Jane Wynch, m 1st, 24 Dec 1872, Arthur Leared, M D, F R C P, d 16 Oct 1879, 2ndly, 16 Sept 1893, Edmund Philip Carleton, Consular Agent at Alcazar, Morocco (*Tangiers*), s p

6c Florentia Sole Wynch, m 18 June 1874, Robert Edward Master, Madras C S (*Hillingdon Furze, Uxbridge*), and has issue 1d

1d Eleanora Frances Master, m 11 Dec 1901, Walter S Curtis, Bar.-at-Law (4 *Norfolk Crescent, W*), and has issue 1e to 3e

1e Lilias Marion Curtis, b 13 Oct 1902

2e Rosemary Curtis, b 8 Oct 1905

3e Adelaide Gabrielle Curtis, b 31 July 1909

7c Julia Charlotte Secker Wynch, b 26 Dec 1850, unm

5a *Eleanora Dane,* d 1840, m 22 *Sept* 1802, *the Rev Lewis Lewis of Gwynfe, J P, D L, Rector of Clovelly,* d 1826, *and had issue* 1b to 3b

1b Lewis Lewis of Gwynfe, J P, D L, b 23 Dec 1805, d 8/9 Jan 1859, m 9 Mar 1830, Sarah Simmons, *da of William Colbourne of Colbourne,* d 19 Feb 1890, *and had issue* 1c to 8c

1c Charles Bassel Lewis of Gwynfe, J P, D L, Major late 44th and 25th Regts, &c, b 13 Dec 1831, d 15 Oct 1903, m 29 Jan 1863, Sarah Amelia, da of Samuel Brown of Clifton, and had issue 1d

1d Eleanora Constance Lewis, m 9 Feb 1898, Col James Henry Worthington Pedder (*Gwynfé House, near Llangadock, co Carmarthen, Hillside Hatherley, Cheltenham*), and has issue 1e

1e Eleanor Barbara Pedder, b 27 Nov 1905

2c Lewis Gwyn Lewis, Lieut Indian Navy, b 21 Sept 1834, m 30 Oct 1872, Blanche Mary, da of (—) Fitzmaurice, and has issue 1d to 2d

1d Christine Eola Lewis, m 6 Jan 1900, Joseph M Davey, s p

2d Olive Eleanora Lewis, m 12 Sept 1899, Harold Ashton Tonge, s p

3c Edward Studley Lewis (*New Zealand*), m and has issue (2 das)

4c Frank Davie Lewis (*Australia*), b 31 May 1838, m (—), and has (with possibly other) issue 1d

1d Albert Thomas Lewis

5c George Septimus Lewis, b 21 Sept 1848, m twice, and has issue 1d to 2d

1d¹ Studley Lewis, Lieut 5th Fusiliers

2d¹ George Lewis

6c Eleanora Jane Lewis, unm

7c Eustatia Harriette Lewis, m 1875, the Rev Henry Sylvester Alison (*Barming Heath, Maidstone*), and has issue 1d to 5d

1d Henry Lewis Guthrie Alison, b 1882   [Nos 1263/164 to 1263/191

2d Constance Annie Alison, m 1897, Edward Browne, and has issue 1e to 4e

    1e Helen Mary Browne, b 1898

    2e Constance Margaret Browne, b 1901

    3e Catherine Alison Browne, b 1905

    4e Elinor Laura Browne, b 1908

3d Clare Alison

4d Winifred Bell Alison

5d Eustatia Violet Alison

    8c *Augusta Blanche Lewis*, d s p 31 Oct 1890, m 1p 1890, James Maddan

2b *Thomas Lewis*, d (—), m 19 Ap 1836, *Victoire Maria*, da of the Hon Andrew Houston of Grenada, W I , and had issue 1c to 6c

    1c *Andrew Courtenay Lewis*, b 31 Jan 1837, d (—)

    2c Charles Houston Lewis, b 17 Feb 1844

    3c *Arthur Whalley Lewis*, b 16 July 1847, d (—)

    4c Alexander Goldwyre Lewis, b 28 Feb 1849

    5c William Studley Lewis, b 30 Mar 1851

    6c Eleanora Harriette Lewis, b 13 Jan 1838 *unm*

3b *Eleanora Elizabeth Lewis*, b 19 Oct 1803, d 13 Ap 1866, m 3 Oct 1827, *Charles Bishop of Dôlgarreg, co Carmarthen*, b 12 Aug 1799, d 7 June 1886, and had issue (with a da , *Frances Gwenllian*, who d unm 1904) 1c to 11c

    1c John Bishop, Bar -at-Law and a County Court Judge (*Dôl-y-garreg, Llandovery, S Wales*), b 19 Nov 1828, m 1884, Caroline Florentia Affleck, da of Morgan Pryse Lloyd of Glansevin, and has issue (with a son, John Ivor Pryse, who d aged 7, 1892) 1d

    1d Frances Gwenllian Enid Bishop

    2c Charles Bishop (*Cwmrhuddan, co Carmarthen*), b 18 Sept 1832, m 29 Ap 1868, Helen Lexey, da of John Carnegie of Redhill, co Kincardine, and his issue (with 2 das Alice Caroline Ayliffe, b 22 Aug 1872, d 2 Nov 1893, and Christine Harriet Sybil, b 17 Sept 1880, d 8 Ap 1905, who both d unm) 1d to 2d

    1d Lexey Eleanora Edith Bishop, m 30 June 1892, George Maximilian Lindner , and has issue 1e to 6e

        1e George Austin Carnegie Lindner, b 13 June 1893

        2e Charles Frederick Harold Lindner, b 8 June 1901

        3e Courtenay Peter Lloyd Lindner, b 20 Aug 1904

        4e Doris Lexey Margaret Lindner, b 8 July 1896

        5e Charlotte Eleanora Rosamond Lindner, b 20 May 1898

        6e Helen Nancy Beryl Lindner, b 25 Mar 1907

    2d Helen Frances Amy Bishop, *unm*

    3c Arthur Bishop, b 27 Jan 1837

    4c Edward Bishop, Com (ret) R I M (*Bath*), b 7 May 1840, m 15 Feb 1877, Isabella Jane Eleanor, da of A Wilkins, R I M , and has issue 1e to 5e

        1e Charles Arthur Bishop, Capt R M A, b 22 Feb 1879, m 1 June 1905, C M, da of (—) Betham, s p

        2e Alfred Edward Bishop, Capt Mounted Police, b 8 Jan 1883, *unm*

        3e Isabel Gwen Bishop, *unm*

        4e Frances Amy Bishop, m 9 July 1897, M H Reynolds, Indian P W D , s p

        5e Violet Caroline Bishop, *unm*

    5c Lewis Bishop (*Brincithen, Llandilo, Carmarthen*), b 10 Jan 1842, m 27 Ap 1871, Ramona Jannette, da of William Poor Neville, and has issue 1d to 3d

    1d John Walton Bishop, b 1 Dec 1880, m 27 June 1906, Dorothy Isabel, da of Malcolm de Saumarez Edye   [Nos 1263/192 to 1263/223

2d Ramona Isabel Joan Bishop, *m* 9 Sept 1903, Capt Thomas Charles Bedford Holland, Devonshire Regt (*Hove, Brighton*)

3d Marguerite Muriel Gardner Bishop, *m* 30 July 1896, Major Alexander John Henry Swiney, R E , and has issue 1e to 2e

1e George Alexander Neville Swiney, *b* 10 June 1897

2e Henry Richard Terence Swiney, *b* 30 Mar 1901

6c Richard Henry Bishop, *b* 17 May 1843

7c Rev Rhys Bishop, Rector of Letton and Willersley (*Letton Rectory, co Hereford*), *b* 15 July 1841 , *m* 13 Aug 1884, Amy, da of James Crighton Nelson of London , and has issue 1d to 2d

1d Rev Lewis Cornewall Bishop, Curate of St Philip's, Lambeth, *b* 23 June 1885 , *unm*

2d Stella Eleanora Bishop, *unm*

8c Juliana Elizabeth Bishop, *b* 10 Oct 1830 , *m* Oct 1855, the Rev James Copner of Hartland, co Devon , and has (with 2 younger sons who *d unm*) issue 1d to 4d

1d Charles James Copner (*Laston, Ilfracombe*), *b* 28 July 1856 , *m* 19 Ap 1883, Hebe Constance, da of Charles John Down , and has issue 1e to 1e

1e Charles John Pomeroy Copner, *b* 19 Mar 1891

2e Mary Constance Copner, *b* 10 Feb 1885

3e Hebe Gwenllian Copner, *b* 31 Dec 1887

4e Alice Marjorie Copner, *b* 13 July 1889

2d *Arthur Lewis Copner,* b 28 Feb 1858 , *d 31 May 1894,* m 29 Oct 1890, *Margaret Helen, da of John Michael Blagg , and had issue 1c to 2e*

1e Arthur Bruce Copner, *b* 21 July 1892

2e Eric Cecil Lewis Copner, *b* 10 Aug 1894.

3d Francis John Copner (*Cranmore, Headcorn*), *b* 30 Ap 1865 , *m* 30 Dec 1893, Beatrice Sylvester, da of William Gill , and has issue 1e to 2e

1e James William Francis Copner, *b* 4 Ap 1902

2e Eleanora Aimée Vye Copner, *b* 6 July 1896

4d Florence Katherine Copner, *m* 20 July 1892, Francis Edward Blagg [son of John Michael Blagg of Cheadle, co Staff] (*Westmark, Petersfield*) , and has issue 1e to 3e

1e Francis Osmond Blagg, *b* 27 Nov 1893

2e Claude Edmund Langley Blagg, *b* 27 Jan 1895

3e Raymond Courtenay Blagg, *b* 29 Ap 1900

9c Caroline Eleanora Bishop, *unm*

10c Harriett Susan Bishop, *m* 17 Ap 1883, the Right Rev John Lloyd, D D , Lord Bishop of Swansea and Suffragan for the Diocese of St David's (*Cantref Rectory, Brecon*) , and has issue 1d to 4d

1d Charles Geoffrey Lloyd, Lieut Essex Regt, *b* 12 Mar 1884

2d Constance Mary Ethel Lloyd

3d Eleanor Kathleen Myfanwy Lloyd

4d Olwen Isabel Lloyd

11c Mary Augusta Bishop, *m* 21 July 1875, Thomas Noon Talfourd Strick (*Llanfair, West Cross, R S O , Glamorgan*) , and has issue 1d to 4d

1d Edward Talfourd Strick, *b* 13 Jan 1883

2d Courtenay Charles Strick, *b* 24 May 1886

3d Gladys Eleanora Rachael Strick, *m* 1 Jan 1907, Bertram Lloyd Meek , and has issue 1e

1e Richard Ombler Meek, *b* Oct 1908

4d Eileen Mary Strick   [Nos 1263/224 to 1263/258

# of The Blood Royal

6a *Julia Davie*, d (–), m *the Rev John Beadon of Christian Malford*

7a *Eustatia Davie*, d 11 Nov 1843, m *at Herinton Punchendon Aug 1797, Major William Shairp of Kirkton, 29th Regt , J P , D L , co Linlithgow [cad t of Houston, being eldest son of Major William Shairp by his wife Ann Bromley Mordaunt, grandda of Sir John Mordaunt of Tangiers, K B , and grandson of Alexander Shairp, for 31 years a Director of the Bank of Scotland, and Treasurer of the City of Edinburgh 1738–39* (b 25 May 1686 , d 20 Feb 1775), *2nd son of Thomas Shairp, Baron of Houston, M P*], b 20 June 1775 , d in Jersey 1840 , *and had issue (with 4 other sons and 4 das who d unm)* 1b to 3b

1b *William Joseph Shairp, a Clerk in the Colonial Office, Sydney,* b 1798 , d *at Sydney, N S W , Nov 1847,* m *there 3 Oct 1827, Sophia, da of James Milson of North Shore, Sydney,* d 1877 , *and had issue (with a son and da d young)* 1c to 5c

   1c William Milson Shairp, b 14 May 1829 , *unm*

   2c Alexander Davie Shairp, b 23 Oct 1846 , *unm*

   3c Eustatia Elizabeth Shairp, b 7 Aug 1830 , *unm*

   4c Sophia Frances Shairp, b 15 Feb 1832 , d 9 Mar 1881

   5c Elizabeth Milson Shairp, b 9 Jan 1843 , m 17 July 1861 , Henry Hocken Bligh, b at Bodmin, Cornwall, 19 Oct 1826 , d at Sydney 30 July 1904 , and had issue (with a son and da d young) 1d to 6d

      1d Henry Albury Gaden Bligh, b 22 Sept 1862 , *unm*

      2d William Milson Bligh, b 16 Aug 1867 , m 1898 , Lilian Mabel, da of (—) Day

      3d Ernest Mordaunt Bligh, b 11 June 1879 , *unm*

      4d Rose Eustatia Lowry Bligh, b 23 Ap 1864 , *unm*

      5d Caroline Ernestine Bligh, b 3 Mar 1866 , m 1898, Charles Thomson and has issue 1e to 2e

         1e Carl Thomson

         2e Jean Thomson

      6d Florence Mary Bligh, b 27 May 1872

2b *Alexander Mordaunt Shairp, Lieut R N ,* d *(being killed at sea)* 4 June 1848 , m 18 Jan 1834, *his cousin Emily, da of Major Alexander Shairp of Stonehouse, Plymouth,* d Sept 1895 *and ha! issue (with 2 sons who d s p)* 1c

   1c Francis Mordaunt Shairp, Lieut-Col (ret) R M *(The Bungalow Hedge End, Botley, Hants),* b 5 June 1842 , m 14 Nov 1877, Elise Mary, da of Edward La Trobe Budd, and has issue 1d

      1d Mordaunt Douglas Shairp, b 29 Aug 1878

3b *Stephen Francis Shairp of St Maur, St Leonards,* b 29 Jan 1806 , d *at Southsea* 24 Nov 1886 , m 26 Aug 1844, *Caroline, da of Charles Michelmore of Highfield House, Totnes,* d 29 Feb 1884 , *and had issue (with 2 other sons and 2 das who d s p)* 1c to 8c

   1c Stuart Courtenay Shairp (1 *Marlborough Gate, Hyde Park, W*), b 1 May 1851 , m 4 Aug 1885, Marie, da of Henry Charles Warre Ekins [son of the Rev Robert Ekins, Vicar of Godalming, by his wife Eliza, a da of Sir Charles Warre Malet, 1st Bt [G B], F R S], and has issue (with a da , Evelyn Mary, who was b 6 and d 23 July 1889) 1d to 2d

      1d Alexander Mordaunt Shairp, b 13 Mar 1887

      2d Stephen Francis Shairp, b 22 June 1892

   2c Eustatia Emily Shairp (2 *Mansfield Place, Richmond Surrey),* m 23 July 1884, Charles George Herring, d 7 June 1882 , and has issue (with a son, Charles Eustace, who d *unm*) 1d to 7d

      1d Sydney Herring, b 14 Sept 1868 , m 25 Feb 1908, May, da of (—) Powall

      2d Arthur Grendon Herring, b 23 Oct 1869 , m 15 June 1891, Maude, da of (—) Ridley , and has issue 1e

         1e Maude Ridley Herring

                                            [Nos 1263/259 to 1263 279

The Plantagenet Roll

3d Stephen Francis Herring, *b* 1877, *unm*

1d George Norman Herring, *b* 19 Ap 1882, *m* Feb 1905, Winifred, da of (—) Smith, and has issue *1e*

 1e Charles Norman Herring, *b* Oct 1905

5d Florence Gertrude Herring, *m* 26 Mar 1890, Thomson Chiene Shepherd (*Gleghornie, North Berwick*), and has issue *1c* to *3c*

 1c Thomson Shepherd, *b* 14 June 1894

 2c Emily Elizabeth Shepherd

 3c Florence Gertrude Shepherd

6d Lilian Mary Herring, *m* 7 Sept 1894, James Francis Shepherd, and has issue *1e* to *1e*

 1e James Chiene Shepherd

 2e George Edward Shepherd

 3e Eileen Shepherd   ⎱ (twins)
 4e Kathleen Shepherd ⎰

7d Lucy Mignon Herring, *m* 30 Ap 1903, Douglas Frederick Charrington [son of John Douglas Charrington, by his wife Mary, *née* Herring] (2 *Mansfield Place, Richmond, Surrey*), and has issue *1e*

 1e Norman Douglas Charrington, *b* 9 Aug 1909

3c Caroline Lucy Shairp, *unm*

4c Fanny Gertrude Shairp, *unm*

5c Annie Shairp, *m* as 2nd wife, 1886, Col Henry Vansittart Riddell [Riddell of Riddell, Bt [S 1628] Coll]. *d s p* by her 1888

6c Eleanora Beatrice Shairp, *m* 22 Sept 1893, Major Philip Sykes Murphy Burlton, I S C, and has issue *1d*

 1d Henry Lionel Granville Burlton, *b* 13 June 1896

7c Edith Shairp, *m* 18 Sept 1883, Henry Glennie Reid [son of Lieut.-Gen C S Reid, R A], and has issue (with a da, Nora, who *d* in infancy) *1d* to *3d*

 1d Charles Henry Stuart Reid, *b* 27 July 1884

 2d Hugh Courtenay Reid

 3d Edith Ivy Reid

8c Emma Rosalie Pender Shairp, *m* 30 Nov 1882, Col Granville William Vernon, lately Comdg 2nd Batt Bedfordshire Regt, and West India Dept, Jamaica [4th son of John Edward Venables Vernon of Clontarf Castle, co Dublin, J P, D L] (23 *Onslow Square, S W*), and has issue (with a younger son who *d* in infancy) *1d*

 1d Charles Edward Granville Vernon, *b* 29 Sept 1883

8a *Charlotte Davie, d 1847, m 1802, Gen Jasper de Brisay, 4th Dragoons. d 22 Nov 1818, and had issue 1b*

1b *John Theophilus de Brisay, b 24 Jan 1804, d 25 Sept 1846, m 1828, Harriette, da of Capt Lestock Wilson, Indian Marine, d 12 Nov 1855, and had issue (with a son, George, d s p) 1c*

1c Rev Henry Delacour de Brisay, M A, *formerly Vicar of Gettenhall, co Stafford* (11 *Bradmore Road, Oxford*), *b* 5 Dec 1831, *m* 11 July 1854, Jane Amelia, da of Philip Marett, *d* 21 Mar 1904, and had issue (with a da, Mrs Baker, who *d s p* 1893) *1d* to *3d*

 1d Rev Henry Lestock Delacour de Brisay, M A, Rector of Northill (*Northill Rectory, co Bedford*), *b* 16 Mar 1860, *m* 15 Oct 1891, Emily, da of the Very Rev Robert Forrest, D D, Dean of Worcester, and has issue *1e* to *2e*

  1e Aubrey Cust Delacour de Brisay, *b* 5 Nov 1896

  2e Robert Lestock de Brisay, *b* 27 Nov 1897

 2d Jane Marguerite de Brisay, *unm*

 3d Beatrice Mary de Brisay, *m* 3 Dec. 1896, William Priestley Barber, *d s p* 2 Aug 1908   [Nos 1263/280 to 1263/310

# of The Blood Royal

9a *Mary Davie*, d 15 *June* 1859, m 1st, 11 *Feb* 1811, *John Alexander Lumsden*, *Lieut* 80*th Regt*, d 1812, 2*ndly*. *Capt Michael Jones of Lisgoole Abbey*, co *Fermanagh*, d 20 *Aug* 1864, and had issue 1b to 3b

1b *Alexander John Henry Lumsden*, b 24 *Mar* 1812, d 9 *Oct* 1891, m in *Bermuda c* 1840, *Emma Jane, da of Capt N Skinner of Bermuda, R N*, and had issue 1c to 4c

1c *Charles Arthur Lumsden (Ashprington, Totnes, Devon)*, b 24 Sept 1811, m. 3 July 1886 Frances Elizabeth, da of the Rev C Penny, and has issue 1d

   1d Alexander Louis Courtenay Lumsden, b 18 July 1891

   2c Richard Francis Hopton Lumsden, b 14 Jan 1847 *unm*

   3c Mary Elizabeth Lumsden, *unm*

   4c Emily Augusta Gordon Lumsden, *unm*

2b *William Christopher Jones*, b 30 Mar 1815, d c 1860(?), m 9 *Jan* 1858, *Isabella, da of (—) Denham of Fairwool Park, co Fermanagh*, and had issue 1c

   1c Michael Obins Jones, b 16 Mar 1839

3b *Michael Obins Seely Jones*, b 4 *Sept* 1818, d v p 5 *Ap* 1860, m 19 *Feb* 1846, *Kate, da of Travers Homan of Colga, co Sligo*, d 18 *Jan* 1847, and had issue 1c

   1c *Kate Mary Barrett Jones (Rosslare, Sligo)*, m 24 Aug 1871, Edward Willoughby Fowler of Cleaghmore, co Galway, J P [grandson of the Right Rev Robert Fowler, Lord Bishop of Ossory and Ferns, by his wife the Hon Louisa *née* Gardner, and great-grandson of the Most Rev and Right Hon Robert Fowler, Archbishop of Dublin, D D, K P, P C], b 6 Aug 1831, d 17 Jan 1900, and has issue 1d to 5d

   1d Willoughby Jones Fowler, Capt R G A, b 25 Feb 1873, m 20 July 1905, Gwendolen Ada, da of Col William Burton Wade, C B, and has issue 1e

      1e Kathleen Muriel Fowler, b 10 Jan 1908

   2d Cecil Arthur Fowler, b 6 Feb 1876

   3d Edward Gardiner Fowler, Lieut R G A, b 2 Dec 1879

   4d Charles Knox Fowler, b 28 Ap 1882

   5d Elizabeth Katherine Fowler   [Nos 1263/311 to 1263 323

INDEX OF NAMES

SUPPLEMENT TO THE EXETER VOLUME

628

The Essex Volume

SUPPLEMENT

ANNE, *née* CALVERT, WIFE OF CHRISTOPHER ANSTEY, Esq,

A DESCENDANT OF KING EDWARD III., AND THE COMMON ANCESTRESS OF ALL THOSE
WHOSE NAMES APPEAR IN THE ESSEX SUPPLEMENT.

From an Oil Painting in possession of the Corporation of Bath, by William Hoare, R.A.

THE ESSEX VOLUME

SUPPLEMENT

Page 306 Delete lines 23 to 36, and in place thereof read—

201 Descendants of ANNE CALVERT (Supplementary Table, p 614), *b*
7 May 1732, *d.* 31 Jan 1812; *m* 20 Dec 1755,[1] CHRISTOPHER
ANSTEY of Trumpington, co Camb., the Poet, Author of the
" New Bath Guide," &c, *b* 1724, *d* 3 Aug 1805, M I. in
Walcot Church, Bath, Monument in Westminster Abbey, and
had issue 1*a* to 11*a*

> 1*a* *Rev Christopher Anstey, Vicar of Stockton-on-Tees to 1782, and Norton, co Durham, M A (Camb)*, b 1756, d ~ p 19 Dec 1827, m 8 [*not* 21] *June* 1783, *Elizabeth, da of William Grey of London*, d 23 Nov 1821, 2n*dly*, 1825, *Elizabeth, da of John Grey of Norton*, d 20 Sept 1876

> 2*a* *Robert Anstey, Capt 21st Light Dragoons, Pensioner of St Johns* 7 July 1799, d 12 Ap 1818 [*will dated* 18 *Dec* 1817, *pr P C C* 20 *July* 1818], m 1st, 21 Ap 1791, *Lucretia, a Lady of the Holy Roman Empire, widow of William Light, H E I C S, da of Theodore von Luders, a Hereditary Knight [H R E ,* 1763]. *Charg d'Affaires and Councillor of the Russian Embassy in London*, d Ap 1794, 2ndly, (—), and had issue 1b

> > 1*b* *Diana Matilda Anne Anstey*, m *before* 1817, *the Rev John Peregrine Lascelles Fenwick*

> 3*a* *John Anstey, M A (Camb), Bar-at-Law and Secretary of the Audit Office, and a Commissioner for Auditing Public Accounts, appointed Special Commissioner to investigate claims of American Loyalists, Author of the " Pleader's Guide," &c*, d 25 Nov 1819, m [2] *Helen, da of Ascanius William Senior of Pilewell, co Hants, and Cannon Hill House, co Berks, a Master in Chancery, by 1st wife*, b 18 Oct 1763, d 3 Mar 1837, and had issue 1b to 7b

> > 1*b* *Christopher John Anstey of Trumpington* d *unm*

> > 2*b* *William Jekyll Anstey, Postmaster General of Jamaica, and formerly in the Audit Office*, d (—), m *Balbina, da of* (—), *and had issue* 1c *to* 9c [3]

> > > 1*c* *William Anstey*
> > > 2*c* *Frederick Anstey*
> > > 3*c* *Herbert Anstey*
> > > 4*c* *Frank Anstey*
> > > 5*c* *Emma Anstey*
> > > 6*c* *Sofie Anstey*, m *Castle Smith*
> > > 7*c* *Louisa Anstey*
> > > 8*c* *Fanny Anstey*
> > > 9*c* *Laura Anstey*

---

[1] *Gentleman's Magazine*, 1756, p 126 *Notes and Queries* (22 Oct 1881) gives 20 Jan 1756

[2] In *Notes and Queries*, 6th Series, iv p 324, he is is incorrectly said to have m in 1794 the da of Francis Pierson of Mowthorpe Grange, co York

[3] Most, if not all, of the sons emigrated to Canada and U S A, and the daughters are now (1909) all dead

The Plantagenet Roll

3b John Thomas Anstey *of Bath, H E I C S ,* b 28 *Ap* 1795 , d 1 *Oct* 1885 , m 1823, *Charlotte, sister of Sir Edmund Filmer, 8th Bt* [*E*], *da of Capt Edmund Filmer,* d 10 *Dec* 1865 , *and had issue* 1*c to* 5*c*

1*c* Rev John Filmer Anstey, M A (*2 St James' Terrace, Regent's Park, N W*), b 13 Aug 1824 m 1st, 25 June 1851, Caroline, da of the Rev E A Daubeny, *d s p* 11 *Ap* 1864 , 2ndly, 17 Nov 1867, her sister, Annie Daubeny, by whom he has issue 1*d*

1*d* Caroline Mary Anstey, m is 2nd wife, 27 Oct 1904, Major Frederick Samborne-Palmer (*2 St James' Terrace, Regent's Park, N W*)

2*c* Edmund Francis Anstey, Capt *20th Regt .* b 1825 , d *at Brighton,* 12 *Dec* 1869 , m *at Weston, near Bath,* 2 *Jan* 1861, *Charlotte Maria, da of the Rev Henry Hodges Mogg of Newbridge Hill House, near Bath , and had issue (with an elder da , Mrs Samborne-Palmer,* d s p) 1*d*

1*d* Frances Charlotte Anstey, b 14 *Jan* 1862 , d. 17 *Oct* 1907, m 7 *June* 1888, *Sidney Whitman, F R G S , Political Writer and Author, represented the* New York Herald *during Armenian Conspiracy Aug* 1896, *during Greek War* 1897, *and with Turkish Mission through Kurdistan, &c ,* 1897–1898 (*6 Russell Road, Kensington, W . Junior Athenæum), and had issue* 1*e to* 3*e*

1*e* Herbert Francis Anstey Whitman, b 15 Jan 1892

2*e* Sidney Athol Anstey Whitman, b 20 Jan 1903

3*e* Eleanor (Elsa) Mary Anstey Whitman, b 21 Sept 1889

3*c* Charlotte Anstey, b 12 *July* 1827 , d 7 *Dec* 1891 , m 8 *Oct* 1848, *Thomas Bennett of Castle Roe,* d v p 15 *Oct* 1856 , *and had issue (with a son* d *unm)* 1*d to* 2*d*

1*d* Rev Edmund Thomas Anstey Bennett of Castle Roe, *formerly* Vicar of Littleton, co Hants, M A (Oxon) (*Castle Roe, Coleraine, co Londonderry ,* 43 *Stanhope Gardens, S W*), b 9 Aug 1849 , m 24 Sept 1872, Laura Maria, da of Lieut - Col Thomas Edmonds Holmes, Oxfordshire L I , and has issue 1*e to* 3*e*

1*e* Lionel Edmund Anstey Bennett, *late* Oxfordshire L I , served in South Africa, was severely wounded 1901, Medal with 3 Clasps (*Arthur's*), b 18 *Ap* 1875 , m 19 *Ap* 1898, Anna Constance Georgina, da and h of Gen the Hon Charles Dawson Plunkett [son of 11th Lord Louth] , and has issue 1*f*

1*f* Constance Evelyn Bennett, b 10 Feb 1899

2*e* Eveline Anstey Bennett, m 26 Feb 1895, Francis Edward Drummond-Hay, M V O , Consul for Norway [son of Sir Francis Ringler Drummond-Hay, E of Kinnoull Coll] (*British Consulate, Christiania) , and has issue* 1*f to* 2*f*

1*f* Claude Francis Drummond-Hay, b 31 July 1898

2*f* Donald Drummond Hay, b 28 Oct 1906

3*e* Muriel Grace Charlotte Anstey Bennett, m 6 July 1908, Thomas Erskine Lambert, *late* 13th Hussars [eldest son of Cowley Lambert of Little Langley, Guildford]

2*d* Rev Thomas John Filmer Bennett, M A (Camb), *formerly* Incumbent of Curzon Chapel, Mayfair, b 26 July 1854 , m 1877, Alice Sarah, da of Charles Marsh of 34 Grosvenor, Bath , and has issue 1*e to* 3*e*

1*e* Maurice Filmer Bennett, Capt. R M L I , b 2 July 1878 , m 11 Sept 1906, Bianca Rosalie Russell, da of the Rev S Russell Stephens, Vicar and Patron of St Stephen's, Lewisham

2*e* Harold Filmer Bennett.

3*e* Alice Filmer Bennett, *unm*

4*c* Ellen Anstey, b 28 *Nov* 1829 , d 9 *Mar* 1902 m 28 *May* 1850, *Lieut - Col* John Marcon *of Wallington Hall, co Norfolk, J P , formerly* 12th *Regt ,* d 3 *July* 1883 . *and had issue* 1*d to* 8*d*

1*d* John Marcon, Lord of the Manor of Edgefield, co Norfolk, and Patron of the Living, J P , b 14 Ap 1853

2*d* Edith Ellen Marcon (*Burgh Heath Lodge, Surrey),* m 14 Ap 1880, the

[Nos 32817/1 to 32817/18

# of The Blood Royal

Rev Charles Greenwood Floyd, M A , Rector of Holme and Runcton [4th son of Major-Gen Sir Henry Floyd, 2nd Bt [U K]], d 26 Feb 1903, and has issue 1e to 3e

1e John Marcon Floyd, b 25 May 1882

2e Arthur Bowen Floyd, b 21 Jan 1888

3e Helena Margaret Floyd, m 11 July 1906, Cecil James Shuttleworth Holden [descended from King Henry VII, &c (see Tudor Roll, p 485)] (*Park Lodge, Ingatestone, Essex*), and has issue 1f

1f Richard Arthur Shuttleworth Holden, b 10 Ap 1909

3d Annie Marcon (*Gunthorpe Hall, Brimingham, R S O , Norfolk 6b Eaton Square, S W*), m 4 July 1872, Edward Bowyer Sparke of Gunthorpe, J P , D L , High Sheriff co Norfolk 1877 [descended from King Edward III through Mortimer-Percy], d 1 June 1910, and his issue

See the Mortimer-Percy Volume, p 423, Nos 80200–80203

4d Charlotte Amelia Marcon, m 6 July 1876, Capt Ernest de Montesquieu Lacon, Chairman of E Lacon & Co, Ltd , Mayor of Great Yarmouth 1897, *late* Duke of Cornwall's L I [4th son of Sir Edmund Henry Knowles Lacon, 3rd Bt [U K]] (*2 Wilton Terrace, S W*), and his issue (with a son d young) 1e

1e Dorothy Mortlock Lacon, m 30 Ap 1908, Herbert Kevill Davies, *late* 7th Hussars (*Croft Castle, Herefordshire*), and has issue 1f

1f Geoffrey Somerset Ernest Kevill-Davies, b 20 Oct 1909

5d Florence Marcon (6 *Ovington Square, S W*).

6d Blanche Marcon }
7d Eleanor Marcon } (*Eaton Mansions, S W*)

8d Eveline Marcon

5c *Caroline Anstey, d s p 9 Mar 1879 , m as 2nd wife, 12 Aug 1871, Col Charles St Lo Malet [2nd son of Sir Charles Warre Malet, 1st Bt [G B]*

4b *Charles Alleyne Anstey, M A (Trin Coll , Oxon), for many years (1819–1864) a Master at Rugby School and afterwards Rector of Cathorpe, near Rugby, and Vicar of Coggs, near Witney,* b 25 *May* 1797 , d 19 *Aug* 1881 , m 1821, *Ann, da of Thomas Townsend of Rugby,* b 1803 , d 1861 , *and had issue (with 3 das d s p)* 1c *to* 8c

1c *Charles Christopher Anstey, M A (Camb), Rector of St Levan, Cornwall,* b 10 *Jan* 1826 , d 13 *Oct* 1877 , m 16 *Aug* 1855, *Frances Mary* (34 *Edith Road, West Kensington, W), da of Harry Scott Gibb of London, J P , formerly R A , and had issue* 1d *to* 4d

1d Rev Harry Christopher Scott Anstey, Chaplain Indian Ecclesiastical Establishment, b 25 Jan 1864 , m Nov 1887, Bertha Amelia, da of Theodore Paul of Thwaite St Mary, Norfolk , s p

2d Bessie Couper Anstey, m 10 Jan 1887, Zuitzen Houkes (*Tarrigindi Road, Annesley, Queensland*) , and has issue 1e to 3e

1e Zuitzen Houkes

2e Frances Maud Houkes, b 1888

3e Ada Houkes

3d Maud Lisle Anstey, *unm*

4d Amy Townsend Anstey, *unm*

2c Rev Henry Anstey, M A (Oxon), *formerly* Rector of Leighton Buzzard, *previously* Vice-Principal of St Mary's Hall, Oxford, Author of *Epistolæ Academicæ, Munimenta Academica, &c* (*St Levan, Downfield Road, Clifton, Bristol*), b 23 Sept 1827 , m 1st, 13 July 1851, Anna Maria, da of Capt John Woodford Chase [by his wife Louisa Millicent, *née* Thomas, of Ripple Hall, co Wore , and Epsom], d 13 Dec 1857 , and has issue (with a da d unm) 1d to 2d

1d John Walter Benjamin Anstey of Swanfels (*Swanfels, Yangan, Queensland*),
[Nos 32817,10 to 32817,13

b 25 Nov 1857, *m* in Australia, (—), da of Joseph Rigby of Dingle, Yangan, and has (with possibly other) issue 1*c* to 2*e*

    1*c* Henry Anstey, *b* c 1896

    2*c* Eleanor Parkhurst Anstey, *b* Aug 1894

2*d* *Alice Mary Anstey*, b at Oxford 18 *July* 1856, d 12 *Dec* 1895, m *at Slapton*, 8 *July* 1885, *Henry Cookson of Cot-field, Surgeon-Major Indian Army, F R C S* (*Cotefield, Leighton Buzzard, co Bedford*), *and had issue* 1*c* to 2*e*

    1*c* Henry Anstey Cookson, *b* 1 July 1886

    2*c* John Power Hicks Cookson, *b* 5 Feb 1888

3*c* Francis Senior Anstey (*Kamloops, British Columbia*), *b* 16 Aug 1830, *m* at Detroit, Mich , U S A , 22 Ap 1856, Ann, da of James Doherty, Collector of Customs, Ammersville, Ontario, and has issue (with a son, Walter Herbert, *d* young) 1*d*

    1*d* *Charles Townsend Anstey*, b 2 *Feb* 1857, d (—) (*having left on a prospecting expedition in 1893, and his not since been heard of*), m *at Portland, Ore , U S A , Georgina Dunno* (*Box 124, Seattle, Wash*), *da of Theophilus Thayer of Boston, Mass , and had issue* 1*c* to 3*c*

        1*c* Charles Alleyne Anstey, *b* 7 Oct 1880, *m* at San Francisco, Winifred Mary, da of Frank Treanor of Sacramento, Cal

        2*c* James Dunno Anstey, *b* at Oakland, Cal , 22 June 1883 , *m* Lily Bertine, da of L M Larson of Seattle , and has issue 1*f*

            1*f* Georgina Julia Anstey, *b* at Los Angeles, Cal , 7 Oct 1909

        3*c* George Roy Anstey, U S Civil Service (*Seattle, U S A*), *b* at Oakland afsd 25 Feb 1885

4*c* Elizabeth Anstey (*South Leigh, Oxon*), *m* 3 July 1855, the Rev Gerard Moultrie, M A (Oxon), Rector of South Leigh, *d* 1885 , and has issue 1*d* to 8*d*

    1*d* Rev Bernard Moultrie, B A (Keble Coll , Oxon), Rector of Christ Church, St Leonard's (*Christ Church Rectory, St Leonards-on-Sea*), *b* 10 Jan 1859 , *unm*

    2*d* Rev John Moultrie, B A (Oxon), in Holy Orders of the Catholic Church, *b* 3 Feb 1860

    3*d* Rev Laurence Gerard Moultrie, Rector of Valley (*Valley Rectory, N Dakota, U S A*), *b* 10 Aug 1866 , *m* at Janesville, Min , 23 Oct 1895, Carrie Isabella, d of Brewster Dane of Minnesota, U S A , and has issue 1*e*.

        1*e* Gerard Earle Moultrie, *b* 25 Mar 1898

    4*d* Rev Austin Moultrie, B A (Keble Coll , Oxon), Rector of Matatile, Kaffraria, *formerly* Vicar of St Saviour's, Leeds (*Matatile Rectory, Kaffraria*), *b* 4 Dec 1867 , *m* at Port St Johns, Kaffraria, 1901, Blanche, da of (—) Shaw of Cape Colony and has issue (with a da , Mary, *d* young) 1*e* to 2*e*

        1*e* John Austin Moultrie, *b* 22 Oct 1902

        2*e* Elizabeth Anstey Moultrie, *b* 31 July 1906

    5*d* Eleanor May Moultrie, *m* 11 Aug 1880, the Rev Walter Edward Wallace, *d* 9 July 1891 , and has issue (with a son *d* young) 1*e* to 4*e*

        1*e* Alexander Moultrie Wallace, *b* 8 May 1881

        2*e* Gerard Percy Wallace, *b* 29 Mar 1885

        3*e* Cyril Walter Wallace, *b* 1 Oct 1890

        4*e* Margaret Wallace, *b* 16 June 1887

    6*d* Adela Moultrie, *unm*

    7*d* Mary Moultrie, *m* 13 Ap 1887, the Rev Arthur East, B A (Camb), Rector of South Leigh (*South Leigh Rectory, Witney, Oxon*), and his issue 1*e* to 3*e*

        1*e* Arthur Gerard East, *b* 16 March 1889

        2*e* Michael Edmund East, Cadet R N , *b* 22 Mar 1893

        3*e* Rupert Moultrie East, *b* 18 Aug 1898

    8*d* Agatha Moultrie, *unm*   [Nos 32817,44 to 32817/71

# of The Blood Royal

5c Emily Caroline Anstey, m 21 July 1852, Frederick Thomas Haggard, Author of numerous pamphlets on economic subjects, especially Tariff Reform (*Broadwater Down, Tunbridge Wells*), and has issue 1d to 7d

1d Frederick Charles Debonnaire Haggard (*Tomlyns, Hutton, near Brentwood, Essex*), b 8 Oct 1857, m 26 June 1890, Grace, da of Thomas Fairbank of Windsor, M D, and has issue 1e

1e Victor Ernest Debonnaire Haggard, for whom H H the Princess Victoria of Schleswig-Holstein was Sponsor, b 9 May 1908

2d Reginald Anstey Haggard, b 13 Feb 1862, m 3 Sept 1888, Alice, da of Alexander James Gibb, and has issue 1e

1e Ruth Elsie Haggard, b 11 July 1889

3d Emily Annie Haggard, m 21 June 1894, William Wolfran Gardner Cornwall, *formerly* Indian Civil Service (*Burford Lodge, Elstead, Surrey*), s p

4d *Edith Isabella Ellis Haggard*, b 1855, d 23 Nov 1901, m 1889, *Alfred Baker*, and had issue 1e

1e Kenneth Baker, b 21 Ap 1890

5d Eleanor Haggard, m 20 Dec 1894, John Edward Ivor Yale [eldest son of Edward Yale-Jones-Parry of Plas-y-Yale, Denbighshire, and Madryn Castle, co Carnarvon, J P, D L], d 1896, and has issue 1e

1e Ivor Eleanor Yale

6d Mabel Sarah Haggard, m 18 Sept 1906, the Rev Henry James Clayton (*Hillcrest, Mulgrave Road, Croydon*), and has issue 1e

1e Henry Richard Michael Clayton, b 11 Aug 1907

7d Mildred Haggard, *unm*

6c Mary Louisa Anstey (16 *Talbot Square, Hyde Park, W*), m 11 Oct 1866, Lieut Col Edward Law, Royal Dublin Fusiliers, d s p 10 June 1883, 2ndly, 1 Oct 1889, m Surg-Gen Robert Cockburn, Indian Medical Service, d s p 30 Ap 1899

7c *Isabella Jane Anstey*, b 5 Sept 1836, d 28 July 1903, m 1st, *at Rugby*, 27 Dec 1859, *the Rev Raymond Brewster Smythies, M A (Emmanuel Coll, Camb)* [*descended from King Edward III through Mortimer-Percy* (see that Volume, p 126)], d 19 Jan 1861, 2ndly, *at Calcutta*, 1868, *Major-Gen Robert Yeld Chambers and had issue 1d to 3d*

1d Raymond Henry Raymond Smythies, Major (ret) P W V South Lancashire Regt, author of "Historical Records of the 40th Regt" [descended from King Edward III through Mortimer Percy (see that Volume)] (*Army and Navy Club*), b at Rugby 19 Nov 1860, *unm*

2d Robert Anstey Chambers, *formerly* Lieut Northumberland Fusiliers (23 *Fitz George Avenue, W*) b at Barrackpore, India, 5 Sept 1869, m 4 Aug 1902, Maud Grace, da of Patrick Neil Barry of Boston, U S A, and has issue 1e to 3e

1e Robert Vyvian Raymond Chambers, b 16 Mar 1905

2e Vernon Stewart Chambers, b 7 May 1910

3e Isabella Dorothy Anne Chambers, b 20 May 1903

3d David Macdonald Chambers (23 *St Mary's Mansions, W*), b at Dinapore, India, 29 Aug 1876, m 30 Oct 1900, Elizabeth Adelaide, da of Adam William Black of Edinburgh, and 44 Hyde Park Square, London, and has issue 1e to 2e

1e Elizabeth Isabella Macdonald Chambers, b 20 Nov 1901

2e Margaret Adelaide Irene Chambers, b 24 Ap 1905

8c Lucy Amelia Anstey (*Wyverstone Rectory, near Stowmarket*), m 1865, Maj Justinian Armitage Nutt, 109th and 27th Regts, d (-), and has issue 1d to 2d

1d Ida Cecilia Nutt, m Nov 1896, the Rev Ernest Arthur Milne, M A (Oxon), Rector of Wyverstone (*Wyverstone Rectory, near Stowmarket, Suffolk*), s p

2d *Eva Mary Nutt*, b 4 Jan 1874, d 11 Ap 1902, m *at Plymouth*, 2 June 1896, *Capt*, now *Lieut-Col, Reginald Seward Ruston, the Devonshire Regt (St Columba's, Killiney, co Dublin, Army and Navy*), and had issue 1e to 2e

[Nos 32817/72 to 32817/93

635

The Plantagenet Roll

1e Sylvia Mary Ruston, b 1 June 1897.

2e Margaret Joan Ruston, b 29 July 1900

5b *George Anstey, in the Audit Office, d (? unm).*

6b *Helen Anstey, d (? unm) 1880*

7b *Caroline Anstey, d 1879 , unm*

4a *Thomas Anstey, went to India, d (? s p) in Bath*

5a *Arthur Anstey, afterwards Anstey-Calvert, executor to will of brother,* 20 July 1818

6a *William Anstey, 6th son, bur with father in Walcot Church*

7a *William Thomas Anstey, 7th son, bur with father in Walcot Church.*

8a *[da] Anstey*

9a *[da] Anstey*

10a *Caroline Anstey, d (-) , m 1790, Henry Bosanquet of Clanville, co Hants, High Sheriff for that co 1815, d 29 Jan 1817 , and had issue (with a da d unm) 1b*

1b *Henry Bosanquet of Clanville Lodge, b. 29 Dec 1793, d 31 Jan 1861 , m 6 June 1827, Mary, da of William Richards of Clatford, co Hants, and had issue 1c*

1c Henry Anstey Bosanquet of Clanville, M A , J P , Bar-at-Law (*Clanville Lodge, Hants*), b 25 Mar 1828 , m 4 Sept 1861, Mary Anne, da of Lieut-Col Francis Luttrell of Kilve Court, co Som , and has issue 1d to 3d

1d Mary Bosanquet, m 4 Dec 1890, Robert Shafto Adam, B A (Oxon), Bar-at-Law [2nd son of Sir Hugh Edward Adam, 3rd Bt [U K], M P] (*9 Lower Berkeley Street, W*), and has issue 1e to 2e

1e Allan Henry Shafto Adam, b 3 Nov 1897

2e. Camilla Mary Shafto Adam, b 24 May 1895

2d Edith Caroline Bosanquet, *unm*

3d Amy Louisa Bosanquet, m 23 Oct 1900, the Rev James Phlips, Vicar of Yeovil and Prebendary of Wells (*Yeovil Vicarage, Somerset*) , and has issue

11a *Sarah Anstey, 4th da , bur with father in Walcot Church , m as 1st wife, Rear-Adm Thomas Sotheby* [see Mortimer Percy Volume, p 346], *and had issue (with a son and da who d in infancy) 1b to 2b*

1b *Sarah Sotheby, d s p . m the Rev Armytage Gaussen*

2b *Elizabeth Sotheby, d 1859, m as 2nd wife, 1829, Capt Charles Thomas Thruston of Pennal Tower, co Merioneth, R N , d 1858 , and had issue 1c*

1c *Clement Arthur Thruston of Pennal Tower, Bar-at-Law, High Sheriff co Merioneth 1870, b 12 June 1837 , d 9 June 1883, m 2 Oct 1861, Constance Sophia Margaret, da of Gen Lechmere Coore Russell of Ashford Hall, co Salop, C B , and had issue (with a son killed in Uganda, unm) 1d to 3d*

1d Edmund Heathcote Thruston of Pennal Tower, J P , D L , *late Capt 3rd Batt Royal Welsh Fusiliers, previously Mid R N (25 Cambridge Road, Hove, Brighton , Pennal Tower, Machynlleth*), b 10 Dec 1863 , m 8 May 1896, Lucy [descended from King Henry VII (see Tudor Roll, p 509)], da of Sir Wilfrid Lawson, 2nd Bt [U K], M P , and has issue 1e to 4e

1e Edmund Wybergh Thruston, b 6 Dec 1903

2e John Wilfrid Russell Thruston, b 30 Oct 1910

3e Margaret Thruston, b 1 Aug 1897

4e Horma Thruston, b 23 Jan 1901

2d Marion Janet Thruston

3d Olwen Millicent Thruston   [Nos 32817/91 to 32817/108

636

INDEX OF NAMES

SUPPLEMENT TO THE ESSEX VOLUME

Printed by BALLANTYNE, HANSON & Co
Edinburgh & London

' This great compilation is well worthy of an extended commentary It must become a necessity for every one studying the history, and especially the local history of the last four centuries — *Notes and Queries*

THE BLOOD ROYAL OF BRITAIN
(TUDOR ROLL)

BEING A COMPLETE TABLE OF ALL THE DESCENDANTS NOW LIVING
OF EDWARD IV AND HENRY VII, KINGS OF ENGLAND, AND
JAMES III, KING OF SCOTLAND, AND OF ALL THE
SUBSEQUENT SOVEREIGNS OF THESE REALMS

Containing 134 Genealogical Tables and the names of some 11,723 living Descendants of the above named Kings, with over 36,000 lines of descent, with an Illuminated Frontispiece of the Missal containing the only record of the Birth of Henry VII, Five Photogravures, and Fourteen other Portraits

In One Volume, folio, Cloth, about 650 pages, £4, 4s net (limited to 500 copies)
Fifty copies on Japanese Vellum, £10, 10s net
A small number of both editions are still to be had

THE PLANTAGENET ROLL OF THE BLOOD ROYAL

BEING A TABLE OF ALL THE LIVING DESCENDANTS OF EDWARD III,
KING OF ENGLAND

1 **The Clarence Volume**, containing the descendants of George, Duke of Clarence, K G, brother to King Edward IV With a series of Portraits *In One Volume, folio, Cloth, about 730 pages, £4, 4s net A few remain (limited to 500 copies)*

' The compiler has put into the present sumptuous volume the same deep and widespread and diligent research which marked the Tudor volume that preceded it ' —*Pall Mall Gazette*

2 **The Exeter Volume**, containing the descendants of Anne, Duchess of Exeter, sister to King Edward IV and the Duke of Clarence With a series of Portraits *In One Volume, folio, Cloth, about 730 pages, £4, 4s net A few remain (limited to 500 copies)*

' The Marquis de Ruvigny displays once more in the third or Anne of Exeter volume of ' The Plantagenet Roll of the Blood Royal, that patent industry which has now won for him general recognition of the real value of his work —*Athenæum* (26th Jan 1907)

' The attempt which is now being made to construct a table of the living descendants of Edward III proceeds on the right lines, and is a very great advance upon any previously published works on the subject —*The Genealogist* (April 1907)

3 **The Essex Volume**, containing the descendants of Isabel, Countess of Essex, aunt of King Edward IV and the Duke of Clarence *In One Volume, with a Supplement to the three preceding works, folio, Cloth, about 700 pages, £4, 4s net A few remain (limited to 500 copies)*

' The Marquis de Ruvigny is producing a series of works which are not only of great interest in themselves but will be of inestimable value to the genealogist '—*The Guardian* (27th Sept 1907)

' The ' Isabel of Essex ' volume has appeared Like its predecessors, it is a splendid and portly volume, finely printed and artistically clothed, and is a marvel of completeness and interest —*Army and Navy Gazette* (28th Dec 1909)

5 **The Mortimer-Percy Volume** *Part II in preparation Uniform with the preceding volumes, and at same price (10s to Subscribers, £3, 3s net)*

THE JACOBITE PEERAGE

BARONETAGE, KNIGHTAGE, AND GRANTS OF HONOUR

Extracted from the Warrant Books of James II and VII and James III and VIII among the Stuart Papers at Windsor Castle and other Sources And supplemented by Biographical and Genealogical Notes

The work is issued in a handsome volume small folio, bound in canvas, with gilt top, at TWO GUINEAS NET (limited to 250 copies)

" Up to the highest standard of modern research —*Notes and Queries*

THE NOBILITIES OF EUROPE

AN ANNUAL INTERNATIONAL PEERAGE, CONTAINING ARTICLES
ON THE NOBILITY IN EACH COUNTRY, WITH LISTS OF
THE EXISTING TITULAR NOBLES IN EACH

EDITED BY THE MARQUIS DE RUVIGNY

Illustrated   Cloth price One Guinea

The 1909 Edition (307 pages), of which only a few copies remain, treated specially of those titles of nobility conferred abroad on British subjects or descendants, or of which the holders have been naturalised or are resident in the United Kingdom, and of certain foreign orders borne by Britons

The 1910 Edition (456 pages) contained short articles by well-known writers on the nobility in each country, treating of the laws and customs relating to the creation and descent of dignities therein, with complete lists of the extant titular nobility of Great Britain and Ireland, the Austro German Empires, Spain, Hungary, Denmark, Sweden, Norway, Finland, Malta, Portugal, and Belgium, and tentative lists of those of France, Russia, Italy, and the Papal States

The 1911 Edition will contain genealogical accounts of the Royal Houses, and will commence one of the noble houses, and will contain special articles on and lists of the Nobility of France, the Holy Roman Empire, Russia, &c

" To those who have constantly to turn up details of this kind the work should prove a positive boon, particularly as the information it contains is not readily available in any other record "— *The Daily News* (13th April 1909)

"A mass of detailed information accompanies each subject' *The Times* (1st April 1909)

"Will be found of great and increasing value for historical as well as ordinary reference purposes "— *The Scotsman* (22nd March 1909)

"In 'The Nobilities of Europe' the Marquis de Ruvigny breaks fresh historical and genealogical ground So far as we are aware, there is nothing in English literature beyond scattered and fragmentary matter dealing with the subject of his extremely interesting and valuable book   The volume is clearly destined to become a standard work of reference "— *The Guardian* (29th September 1909)

"' The Nobilities of Europe' is one of those books of which we cannot have too many   This volume is assured of a place alongside standard books on the Peerage and Knightage "— *The Dundee Advertiser* (30th April 1909)

" It is obvious that a work of this description is needed "— *The Western Mail* (1st May 1909)

"Both interesting and useful   the volume will be found a valuable companion to Debrett and Burke, while it will serve as an interesting commentary on the reading of history '— *The Western Morning News* (30th April 1909)

" For international, historical, and social reasons is destined to take an important place amongst works of reference "— *The Glasgow Herald* (10th May 1909)

THE ANCESTORS OF KING EDWARD III.
AND QUEEN PHILIPPA OF HAINAULT

BY THE MARQUIS DE RUVIGNY

A large folding Table mounted on canvas and bound in cloth, uniform with the Plantagenet Roll, shows their descent from Alfred the Great, William the Conqueror, Charlemagne, St Louis, the Emperor Frederick Barbarossa and between three and four hundred other Sovereigns—the lower half of the sheet being left blank, so that any one can write or have printed his or her own descent downwards from King Edward on it

One Guinea net

LONDON   MELVILLE & COMPANY, 12 BUCKINGHAM STREET, STRAND, W C

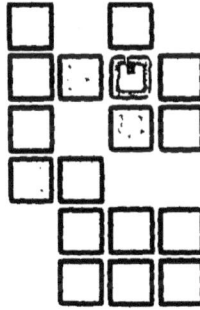

Milton Keynes UK
Ingram Content Group UK Ltd.
UKHW012218020224
437193UK00004B/108